Contemporary Literary Criticism

Contemporary Literary Criticism

Excerpts from Criticism
of the Works of Today's
Novelists, Poets, Playwrights,
and Other Creative Writers

Dedria Bryfonski
Phyllis Carmel Mendelson
Editors

Gale Research Company
Book Tower
Detroit, Michigan 48226

STAFF

Dedria Bryfonski, Phyllis Carmel Mendelson, *Editors*

Sharon K. Hall, *Associate Editor*
Laurie Lanzen Harris, Robert Navarre, *Assistant Editors*

Sharon R. Cillette, *Production Editor*

Linda M. Pugliese, *Manuscript Coordinator*
Jeanne A. Gough, *Permissions Coordinator*
Judith Fischer Rutkowski, *Research Coordinator*
Laura A. Buch, Thomas E. Gunton, Jacqueline Sharp,
Carol A. Sherman, David J. Szymanski, *Editorial Assistants*

Special acknowledgment to Gerard J. Senick, *Editor, Children's Literature Review*

Preface

Literary criticism is indispensable to the layman or scholar attempting to evaluate and understand creative writing—whether his subject is one poem, one writer, one idea, one school, or a general trend in contemporary writing. Literary criticism itself is a collective term for several kinds of critical writing: criticism may be normative, descriptive, interpretive, textual, appreciative, genetic. Conscientious students must consult numerous sources in order to become familiar with the criticism pertinent to their subjects.

Until now, there has been nothing resembling an ongoing encyclopedia of current literary criticism, bringing together in one series criticism of all the various kinds from widely diverse sources. *Contemporary Literary Criticism* is intended to be such a comprehensive reference work.

The Plan of the Work

Contemporary Literary Criticism presents significant passages from the published criticism of work by well-known creative writers—novelists and short story writers, poets and playwrights. Some creative writers, like James Baldwin and Paul Goodman, are probably better known for their expository work than for their fiction, and so discussion of their nonfiction is included.

Contemporary Literary Criticism is not limited to material concerning long-established authors like Eliot, Faulkner, Hemingway, and Auden, although these and other writers of similar stature are included. Attention is also given to two other groups of writers—writers of considerable public interest—about whose work criticism is hard to locate. These are the newest writers (like Robert M. Pirsig, Erica Jong, and William Kotzwinkle) and the contributors to the well-loved but unscholarly genres of mystery and science fiction (like Georges Simenon, Agatha Christie, Robert Heinlein, and Arthur C. Clarke).

The definition of contemporary is necessarily arbitrary. For purposes of selection for *CLC,* contemporary writers are those who are either now living or who have died since January 1, 1960. Contemporary criticism is more loosely defined as that written any time during the past twenty-five years or so and currently relevant to the evaluation of the writer under discussion.

References Given to Bio-Bibliographical Material

Notes in many entries directing the user to consult *Contemporary Authors* for detailed biographical and bibliographical information refer to a series of biographical reference books published by the Gale Research Company since 1962, which now includes detailed biographical sketches of about 50,000 authors who have been active during the past decade, many of whose careers began during the post-World War II period, or earlier.

Each volume of *CLC* lists about 175 authors, with an average of about five excerpts from critical articles or reviews being given for the works of each author. Altogether, there are about 1100 individual excerpts in each volume taken from about 250 books and several hundred issues of some one hundred general magazines, literary reviews, and scholarly journals. Each excerpt is fully identified for the convenience of readers who may wish to consult the entire chapter, article, or review excerpted.

Each volume covers writers not previously included and also provides significant new criticism pertaining to authors included in earlier volumes.

A Note on Page Citations

Beginning with *CLC-5,* the method for referring to page numbers in the original sources has been standardized. Page numbers appear after each fragment (unless the entire essay was contained on one page). Page numbers appear in citations as well only when the editors wish to indicate, with an essay or chapter title and its *inclusive* page numbers, the scope of the original treatment.

No Single Volume Can be Exhaustive

A final word: Since *Contemporary Literary Criticism* is a multivolume work of indefinite but considerable size, neither this volume nor any other single volume should be judged apart from the concept that a single volume is but a part of a larger and more comprehensive whole.

If readers wish to suggest authors they are particularly anxious to have covered in coming volumes, or if they have other suggestions or comments, they are cordially invited to write the editors.

A

ABE, Kōbō 1924-

Abe is currently the Japanese novelist most frequently translated into English. Attention was drawn to his work when it became widely known that the classic film *Woman in the Dunes* was based on an Abe novel. Since then Abe has written a number of provocative novels and short stories which bear the influence of trends in Western literature and philosophy, particularly existentialism. Abe also has a growing reputation in this country as a science fiction writer. (See also *Contemporary Authors*, Vols. 65-68.)

With *Suna no Onna* (The Woman in the Dunes) Abe has written a novel of exceptional force. It is the story of a man obliged by strange circumstances to live with a young woman in a pit of sand. They live in a house at the bottom of the pit, and shovel the sand every day so they will not be buried by it. The atmosphere is intense and nightmarish: the sand falls constantly and everywhere. The two are obliged to live together in anguish and moral torment, though the hope of escape always dawns. All of this—the life in the sand pit, the authentiticy and meticulous attention to detail—gives an extraordinary and haunting strength to the unusual theme. Minute precision and abundance of detail, the indifference to physical suffering, and the refined cruelty are all in the line of Japanese tradition. It is a well-balanced novel with excellent construction and skilful building of suspense. Circumscribing itself by dealing with only one subject and one scene, extreme concentration is attained which accounts for its extraordinary haunting intensity. Bitter and dry satire against man and society is the main reason for this apparently perverse nightmare.

In Abe's short story *Akai Mayu* (The Red Cocoon), a man changes into a cocoon; in *Bo* (The Stick), a man changes into a stick. There is a barren coldness, a frightening loneliness, and also literary artificiality in these stories. Probably no one else has used the technique of Kafka in such a modern, personal way, but what is lacking here is the deep, rich Kafka symbolism. (pp. 208-09)

Abe has found a new literary dimension for expressing the awesome loneliness of the individual lost in a monstrous city like Tokyo. He cannot find human ground in which to plant his roots; he cannot cultivate ties with other men strong enough to satisfy his yearning for friendship and human solidarity. In his recent novel *Moetsukita Chizu* (The Ruined Map), Abe treats the theme of man lost in a huge labyrinth—the modern city—by writing of a private detective who searches for a lost man named Nemuro. The information he gathers from various sources is too complicated and too intermingled. People in the huge city are only superficially connected to one another. Thus, a man can never be found in this monstrous riddle in which individual existence and life itself lose all meaning. (pp. 209-10)

Kōbō Abe, more successful as a novelist, has also written plays. The best known is *Yurei wa Koko ni Iru* (Here Is a Ghost), a satirical comedy of a young man who finds a fortune in the idea of convincing people that many ghosts live among them. . . . The play flows rather slowly in an amusing tone with songs inserted here and there in the way that Brecht made famous.

A rather original theme is developed in *Tomodachi* (Friends), the fantastic story of a family that invades the home of a bachelor. A family with five children and a grandmother come with their suitcases to sleep and stay. They pretend to feel a great affection for the tenant of the house (who does not pay his rent on time). The eldest daughter tries to seduce the bachelor, although it is her sister who is in love with him. Finally, the family succeeds in putting the bachelor into a cage. There he dies, and the family goes away. The bizarre tale has a dry humour and social satire hidden in its strangeness. (pp. 225-26)

> *Armando Martins Janiera, in his* Japanese and Western Literature *(© 1970 by Charles E. Tuttle Co., Inc.), Tuttle, 1970.*

The action of ["The Box Man"] seems to take place inside [a cardboard] box, which has become a kind of labyrinth for the box man, a porous, breathing skin. "The more you struggle, the more new passages you make in the labyrinth, the more the box is like another layer of outer skin that grows from the body, and the inner arrangement is made more and more complex."

The sad truth of the box man's existence is that the "waterproof room" he wears on his back hasn't satisfied his quest to be without an identity. Scribbling on the inside walls of the box, he invents a past, present and future that crash together in his brain. With an irony that turns in upon itself, he becomes a creature of multiple identities. . . .

"The Box Man" becomes a book in search of a narrator. Arguing with one of his possible selves, the box man speculates: "Perhaps it is I who am going on writing as I imagine you who are writing as you imagine me."

At times the novel reads like a curious amalgam of Robbe-Grillet and Beckett, but without the precision of "Le Voyeur" or the crisp, beautiful tones of "Molloy" (this, in part, can be blamed on the creakiness of any translated text). Yet "The Box Man" is an invention with its own crazy pull. It is a difficult troubling book that undermines our secret wishes, our fantasies of becoming box men (and box women), our urge to walk away from a permanent address and manufacture landscapes from a vinyl curtain or some other filtering device.

Abe's book is a stunning addition to the literature of eccentricity, those bitter, crying voices of Melville's Bartleby the scrivener and Dostoevsky's underground man. It gnaws at the reader, forces him to question his values, his Shibboleths and his ritualistic props, and shoots an energetic poison into his ear. "The Box Man" is funny, sad and destructive, an ontological "thriller" that bumps into and contradicts its own clues. . . .

"The Box Man" is a much more daring creation [than his earlier "The Woman in the Dunes"]. Rougher, less controlled perhaps, it is a more frightening book. (p. 6)

> *Jerome Charyn, in* The New York Times
> Book Review (© *1974 by The New York*
> *Times Company; reprinted by permission),*
> *December 8, 1974.*

In range, depth and style, the works of Abe Kōbō represent a considerable departure from the writing of almost all the Japanese novelists and dramatists who preceded him. From his earliest novels, short stories and plays, Abe has been concerned with an artistic expression of the break between man and his world—a common phenomenon today in the East as well as the West. He has written novels that explore problems of existence in narratives of almost mythic simplicity, most of them touching in one way or another on the problem of human alienation. Some of Abe's themes which illustrate this general problem of alienation are: the individual's search for the "roots of existence" that will serve to ground his identity; the difficulty people have in communicating with one another; and the discrepancy between the mind and the external world, or between inner and outer reality.

Another important theme in Abe's fiction is the conflict between the two kinds of *kokyo,* or "homeland". There is the place where one was born, and there is the place or ground or foundation for living in such and such a way. The first meaning represents to Abe the everyday, the routine, the inauthentic life which one leads as part of the impersonal crowd of people that make up any community. It is this *kokyo* that one must reject in order to find the other *kokyo:* the true "home" of one's existence.

In presenting these themes, Abe uses settings and characters which are themselves metaphors of human alienation. He uses strong, universal metaphors in such a way that they become a basis for his narrative art. By using metaphors, Abe expresses complex ideas not by analysis, nor by making an abstract statement, but by a sudden perception of an objective relation. This relation is expressed in one commanding image.

Abe's narratives, which are built around a single metaphor, are developed with a kind of dream literalism. He maintains a rather consistent adherence to a tone of realism carried through a series of episodes which taken collectively are thoroughly unrealistic and irrational. Abe shows a meticulous care for concrete detail worthy of the most confirmed naturalist or realist. His precision and concreteness give the impression of reality to the dream or nightmare. In this regard, Abe, who is sometimes considered thoroughly Western in his approach to literature, is solidly in the Japanese tradition with his emphasis on the concrete and the particular. Abe builds up the impression of reality, even in improbable situations, through the accumulation of realistic details.

The unity that Abe achieves in his fiction is, in general, a unity of image rather than of action. Perhaps this makes his works less satisfactory to someone who prefers a traditional narrative with a beginning, middle and end, but Abe's works depend for their effectiveness on an intensity of the image that is built up through the narrative.

Abe's themes and literary methods are very well illustrated in the novel which is probably his best work to date, *Suna no Onna (The Woman in the Dunes).* It is an extended narrative centering around a man named Niki Jumpei, a schoolteacher and insect collector who disappears one August afternoon and seven years later is officially declared missing. A gripping story on the surface level, it is, however, more than that: the novel presents a probing study of a person's search for a new self in a cruel and challenging world of sand. Sand is the novel's central metaphor, standing for the shifting reality in which the hero must come to terms with himself and his surroundings, find roots for his existence and discover who he really is.

The first page of the novel strikes a theme that recurs throughout the book and in many other works of Abe's fiction: escape. At the end of a paragraph discussing the high number of persons reported missing every year, and the small proportion of those found again, there is the matter-of-fact statement: "Many disappearances, for example, may be described as simple escape". . . . (pp. 1-2)

Abe includes in [the] opening scene of the novel a rather lengthy discourse on the nature and properties of sand, set down as a result of the hero's investigations into the substance, which had come to intrigue him so much. Some of the conclusions about sand serve to build up, at an early stage in the narrative, the complexity and weight of the central metaphor, which comes to bear much of the burden of unifying and amplifying the story as it unfolds. Sand, for instance, is omnipresent, always being renewed, never-resting, and destructive. . . . (p. 3)

[Sand] comes to represent in the novel a kind of mythic force, endowed with superhuman powers and vaguely hostile to human life: "The barrenness of sand . . . apparently was due to the ceaseless movement that made it inhospitable to all living things." . . . It is no wonder that this powerful, awesome, and vital "being" should appeal so strongly to the imagination of the withdrawn, ineffectual schoolteacher whose uneventful life was a monotonous succession of boring, routine days. . . .

In the opening pages of the book, Abe has told us just enough about the central character to make him appear as a very real person, a trifle dull and pedantic, but an ordinary, average man. Niki Jumpei's speculations about sand have already projected him into the role of a contemporary Everyman, stuck in a dehumanized routine and, perhaps unconsciously, looking for a way to excape, expecting the perpetual movement of the sand to help him somehow.

From the very beginning of the novel the main character and the central image of the book are closely woven together, and in this way the dream character of the narrative begins to take shape: "While he mused on the effect of the flowing sands, he was seized from time to time by hallucinations in which he himself began to move with the flow." . . .

Abe has successfully brought off a very difficult accomplishment in this early section of the book: while presenting many of the central character's reflections in the third-person narrative, he has maintained a certain mystery and ambiguity about the hero's feelings, motivations and goals. (p. 4)

Part Two comprises the bulk of the novel, extending up to the last four chapters which make up the third part. The theme of escape is strong in this second part, as Niki Jumpei tries to devise various schemes for getting out of the sandpit. Related to the escape theme is the theme of *kokyō*. The hero's reflections on the world that he left, with its "glum and gray" colleagues, make it clear that this was not the sort of "home" in which he could easily live a full life as a free human person, sure of his own identity. Therefore what would "escape" mean for the hero if it did not mean returning to his former life? Abe skillfully keeps the question in the air, never actually articulating it.

Parallel to these two themes is the theme of human loneliness, which is closely related to them, and is heightened in the novel by the device of having the woman in the dunes serve as a kind of double for the man: in her loneliness, alienation, and the absurdity of her life, he comes to see his own loneliness, alienation, and the absurdity of his own life "in the world".

The characters are developed with considerable care throughout the second part, but Abe tells us no more about them than is necessary for the plot to unfold and the various themes to develop. There is always a certain ambiguity and elusiveness to the characters which is crucial for maintaining the dream atmosphere and the necessarily ambiguous ending. . . .

The contrast between the world outside and the small world at the bottom of the sandpit is effectively used by Abe to show that inauthentic life above the ground, in civilized society, is not very different from inauthentic life in the dunes. This contrast and similarity is illustrated, for example, when the man and the woman are discussing her lack of freedom. (p. 8)

The relativity of what different people call "freedom" is an idea that is never far from the surface of Abe's narrative. Here too the central image of sand colors the interpretation: shifting, moving, lacking in continuity. . . .

It is not until towards the middle of the book, however, that the sand metaphor becomes explicit. The hero recalls a conversation he had had with one of his colleagues:

> ". . . The reason I brought up the example of sand was because in the final analysis I rather think the world is like sand. The fundamental nature of sand is very difficult to grasp when you think of it in its stationary state. Sand not only flows, but this very flow is the sand. I'm sorry I can't express it better."
>
> "But I understand what you mean. Because

in practical education you can't avoid getting involved in relativism, can you?"

> "No, that's not it. You yourself become sand. You see with the eyes of sand. . . ."
>
> (p. 9)

While in flight, Niki Jumpei passes the other sandholes in the village where other people are carrying on the same deadly existence he has just escaped from. . . . The enumeration and repetition of objects is a device that Abe uses to good advantage to illustrate dullness, monotony and routine. (p. 11)

Suna no Onna, as written, stands as a remarkably unified work of fiction in which a contemporary alienated Everyman comes to grips with modern everyday reality in the form of the all-encompassing sand, the novel's central metaphor. (p. 16)

Everything in the novel is built around the central metaphor of sand: plot, characters, themes and imagery. The plot is relatively simple and straightforward, as is appropriate for a narrative in which the author is inviting us to look beneath the surface of events and consider metaphysical problems. Abe takes less liberties with time and place and the ordinary conventions of realistic fiction than he usually does. And yet for all the attention to concrete detail, this is not a realistic novel, but a narrative developed as a dream might unfold, dramatizing the inner life of the central character in his efforts to escape unreality and come to terms with himself and the world around him.

The plot seems to be determined by Abe's central concern: to develop the metaphor of sand around which the novel takes shape. Thus the plot cycle, involving the hero's alternating acts of rebellion and periods of resignation, reinforces the images of sand: discontinuous, unpredictable, moving constantly and imperceptibly. The discontinuity of sand is likewise related to the crucial event with which the plot begins: the hero's decision to escape his everyday routine and possibly build a new future for himself. Sand too is related to Niki Jumpei's creative act on which the plot hinges at the end of the novel. For Abe the desert is "the idea of creation". In this case it is matter for human ingenuity to experiment with, a source of possibilities and avenues of investigation for the creative mind. In *Suna no Onna* the sand is crucial for Niki Jumpei's discovery, and thus it is literally in the sand that he comes to find his own identity.

The character of Niki Jumpei is very carefully and interestingly drawn. There is a great deal that we know about him and yet a great deal that we do not know. Ordinary, mediocre, decent at the beginning of the book, he becomes frighteningly animal-like and inhuman in his treatment of the woman as the book progresses. Abe controls the information we have about the hero so that our gradual understanding of him develops with the process of self-realization he himself pursues. The total picture we get is of a very immature person, self-centered and insecure. His rational, analytical approach to life is a defense against becoming too closely involved with reality. His relationship with the woman remains problematic throughout the novel. Although at times compassionate and understanding, he treats her for the most part as a mere appendage to his own needs and plans. There are hints that this attitude is changing as the novel ends, but nothing is made really clear.

Part of Abe's success in this novel lies in the effective veil of mystery he keeps over the character of the woman. First of all, there is no clear physical description given of her, and no name. She is always "the woman". We see her mostly through the eyes of the hero, and our perceptions are always somewhat clouded. This enables Abe to set her up as a mirror for the man, in whom Niki Jumpei comes to see himself, thus growing in self-knowledge. If there seems to be a slight inconsistency in the characterization of the woman (a fluctuation between pity and hardheartedness, a mixture of innocence and seductiveness) this can partly be ascribed to the mirror function fulfilled by her character in the novel, and partly to the subordination of character to the central metaphor. Inconsistency is appropriate to illustrate the flow of sand, with no continuity between yesterday, today and tomorrow.

The various themes in the novel also serve to reinforce the principal metaphor of sand. The theme of disappearance establishes the freedom for the hero to move with the shifting sand, not tied down to his former identity or profession or responsibilities. The connected themes of flight and search for a homeland are closely related to the sand image, since the wilderness is the place to which one escapes to erase the past and seek to create a new future. The theme of creativity points to the central image again, with sand as a vast resource offering matter for man's ingenuity, and thus the possibility of escape from alienation. Also connected with sand is the theme of loneliness: the man's and the woman's as they are trapped in their sandy prison and isolated from one another; the vast stretches of uninhabited dunes; the isolated homes at the bottom of the sandpits that make up the village.

Besides the sand imagery, Abe makes considerable use of insect imagery in the novel. This is appropriate enough, since the hero is an insect-collector, and the story is set in a place where insects are likely to be plentiful. People are frequently compared with insects, and vice versa, illustrating the level to which persons are reduced in the condition of alienation. The wall imagery for which Abe was noted in his earlier stories is present here in the walls of sand imprisoning the hero at the bottom of the pit. But sand is the principal image, theme, main character and plot.

Throughout the entire novel, Abe consistently faces real human situations at a deep level and expresses his vision of reality with imagination and art. Abe's vision of man and his world is a nightmare vision, and the conscientious attention he gives to realistic detail emphasizes the dreamlike quality of his narrative. Like Kafka and Beckett, whose works Abe's fiction resembles in some respects, Abe has created an image of alienated man which is disturbing and disquieting. But also like those two writers, Abe has shown a skill and depth in this novel which has made it a universal myth for our time. (pp. 16-18)

> *William Currie, "Abe Kōbō's Nightmare World of Sand," in* Approaches to the Modern Japanese Novel, *edited by Kinya Tsurutu and Thomas E. Swann (copyright, 1976, by Monumenta Nipponica), Sophia University, 1976, pp. 1-18.*

* * *

ADLER, Renata   1938-

American critic, short story writer, and novelist, Renata Adler is best known for her contributions to *The New Yorker*. *Speedboat* is her first novel. (See also *Contemporary Authors*, Vols. 49-52.)

"Speedboat" makes no concession to any craving—vulgar or sophisticated—for an engrossing narrative. Furthermore, though concerned fleetingly with motivations, "Speedboat" avoids the sustained psychological rendering of character as rigorously as the novels of Robbe-Grillet, but without attempting their quasi-musical purity as linguistic constructs. The book does have an emotional impact—a strong one—but one that derives more from a painfully exact transcription of the life many of us lead than from the creation of a powerfully imagined fictional world. From almost any approach one chooses to take, "Speedboat" is a non-novel.

Yet it is a very good book: elegantly written, often funny, vivid in its presentation of the absurdities, the small and great horrors, the booby-traps with which our daily existence is strewn. Essentially it is a collage, an assemblage of tiny anecdotes, vignettes, overheard conversations, aphorisms and reflections. . . .

The book's compelling interest comes from the way the narrator reports and reflects upon the phenomena that fall within the range of her edgy and perplexed sensibility. . . .

"Speedboat" is a quintessentially "New York" book with its radical-chic parties, conversations with analysts, late-hour excursions to Elaine's, its encounters with rats, cab-drivers, early-morning stealers of the neighbor's Sunday Times, dubious loiterers, doorstep winos, glibly illiterate City University students. . . .

The fragments of which "Speedboat" is constructed are seldom longer than a paragraph, though a few run to two or three pages. Repetitions, even sequences occur, though there is no real progression or resolution. The episodes and overheard conversations are believable, if bizarre. . . . Though Miss Adler is a realist in miniature, the cumulative effect of her book is dizzyingly surrealistic—and to my mind the impact is far greater than the deliberate, though perfunctory, surrealism to which so many contemporary "serious" novelists resort. In the presentation and analysis of her specimens Renata Adler is an exquisite craftsman. Her style is luminously exact, subtle in its rhythms, capable of both concrete immediacy and arresting generalizations. (p. 6)

Unlike the products of the French New Novelists—or what Gore Vidal has recently called the "plastic fiction" of their American disciples—"Speedboat" is neither boring nor dehumanized. Though paragraph by paragraph the book is entertaining and often brilliant, it can, because of its density and lack of narrative propulsion, have a clogging effect if subjected to too sustained a reading. (pp. 6-7)

> *Robert Towers, in* The New York Times Book Review (© *1976 by The New York Times Company; reprinted by permission), September 26, 1976.*

It's only incidental praise of Renata Adler to say that she has written one of the best books I know of about contemporary New York with her first novel, *Speedboat*. . . . But it could hardly have sprouted from any soil besides Manhattan concrete. (p. 112)

Calling it a novel perhaps stretches a point. It is a gathering of stories, most of which have been published over the last couple of years in *The New Yorker*. . . . And the stories themselves are assemblages of small moments that lack the coherence of plot but nevertheless overlap and iridesce like the scales of a fish.

Although there are dozens of amusing walk-on figures, character in this book resides wholly in the voice of its faceless narrator. We learn that the voice belongs to a woman of about thirty-five, unmarried, a journalist, educated at an eastern private school for women, nicely connected, and addicted to observation. But what we learn of the circumstances of her life is more or less inconsequential: this is a novel of sensibility—it is *all* sensibility, and the only patterns of the book are the tracks a mind leaves in trying to come to terms with its surroundings.

The surroundings are the modern urban world, for which New York is the richest symbol, and the condition that Renata Adler addresses can be described in all sorts of sociological and artistic clichés. Anomie. Alienation. Absurdity. But the sensibility itself is not so easily categorized. It begins in wit. (pp. 112-13)

If Renata Adler—not to make the mistake of assuming that she and her heroine are the same, though obviously they share some qualities—has a single, simple virtue, it's that she trusts her own eyes. She doesn't fail to see the pieces that don't fit into the puzzle. ("The problem is this. Hardly anyone about whom I deeply care at all resembles anyone else I have ever met, or heard of, or read about in the literature.") Her world is full of defeated expectations, stories without endings, crossed wires and missed connections; it is an epidemic of inappropriate response and loss of affect.

But for all its attention to modern woes, *Speedboat* is free of stock response. No lamentations of vulgarity. No intimations of systemic evil. No love of madness, no chic despair. It is the work of someone who simply won't relinquish the right to say . . . "how strange." Every page in this book is touched by humor, but beneath the mirth lies a sort of ferocity. . . .

Renata Adler is a spare, self-possessed writer who can do more in an aphoristic aside than many novelists can do with a chapter. Her book now and then luxuriates unfairly in its own formlessness, but at its center it is disciplined and clear-headed. (p. 114)

Richard Todd, in The Atlantic Monthly *(copyright © 1976 by The Atlantic Monthly Company, Boston, Mass.; reprinted with permission), October, 1976.*

Renata Adler seems deliberately to have written the kind of novel she least admires. *Speedboat* has no plot, no tears, no characters flat or round, no conflict of great ideas, no deep scheme. You do not merely note the absence of such things; you miss them actively because the author has made you miss them. She has created a world precisely opposed to one we would prefer, has done so down to the form of her presentation which, as an argument against itself is effective on those grounds alone. But there is more to this book than cleverness.

The narrator (without a narrative) is a woman journalist whose "mind is a tenement," she says. The novel, then, is a form of slumming: half-baked reports on times and places —not hers alone, and in no special order—as if she were keeping a scrapbook of passages used in her articles, or perhaps discarded. To call her tone dispassionate would suggest that passion is sensed in abeyance, but that isn't it. If anything the tone is surprised, sometimes falsified for a laugh, sometimes genuine: one brilliant survivor peering with chatoyant eyes at the life which threatens her to the point of amusement.

Speedboat is concerned with the speed of that life. Our journalist has a mind of the ancients that naturally pulls back and away, which is the source of her ironies. She can write one sentence, for example, that moves in two directions, forcing a standstill: "His children own the town these days, for what it's worth." Everything else in the novel is going forward in spurts and plunges, too fast even for the celebrants who wish to move with the machines, so that the giddy lady who insists on riding in a brand new speedboat breaks her back from her own excited bouncing. Fractures in other passages are less severe, but in their battles with passengers the planes and boats and trains are clearly winning. Every chapter after the first begins with a ride. . . .

[The] feeling one takes from *Speedboat* is in fact not the intellectual condemnation of a speed-bound world, but how wasteful it is for this woman to live in such a place. The senseless races she observes seem made for singles, people with feather-weight luggage who run better unencumbered by family and other ties. In a swift aside she dryly mocks the memorable lines of her college education, citing "only connect" from Forster's *Howards End,* the one phrase all English professors seem born with. But the mockery turns on her who unwillingly has mastered the life of no connections to the point where the novel ends, and she hesitates to tell her lover that she is pregnant.

She feels only connected to her words. She seems not so much a journalist by profession as a journalist by birth, as if implying that in a life of no events (the novel begins: "Nobody died that year. Nobody prospered") everyone is a journalist. Personality becomes the event. The investigative reporter is not an investigator of experience, but an investigator of self as it succumbs to experience. The crime or folly exposed sends someone to jail or to the corner, yet its main public value is cathartic. The people know pity and terror thanks to the journalist who has found a way of becoming a pity or terror by entering the story he writes. A way of life, of giving life to a dead thing. (p. 32)

Nothing in *Speedboat* is supposed to hurt you, but it does, which is probably what Adler is saying about the speed machines as well. The novel closes on the phrase "you can't miss it," meaning "you're never going to find it." The phrase has all the goodwill in the world. (pp. 32-3)

Roger Rosenblatt, in The New Republic *(reprinted by permission of* The New Republic; © 1976 by The New Republic, Inc.), *October 16, 1976.*

Renata Adler's novel *Speedboat* gave me a glimpse of what happened to those who grew up in the '50s. *Speedboat*'s title derived from a one-page anecdote about a young woman who, through overenthusiastic response to a ride in a new speedboat, breaks her back: ". . . she exaggerated every happy bounce. Until she broke her back. . . . Martin said How too like life all afternoon." So now I know that the '50s people are still around, as brittle as ever, trying to slouch, so they don't break their backs.

Neither Adler nor her protagonist Miss Fain are in any danger from overenthusiasm. Miss Fain suffers from exquisiteness of sensibility. She has few passionate interests, other than precision in language. Her drugs are Valium and Scotch and martinis. She seems to be an accidental spectator at the events of her own life. Even where it is clear she has made choices, there is a numbness, a passivity. (p. 469)

Much of the material in *Speedboat* was published as separate units in *The New Yorker.* . . . Each unit consists of a collection of anecdotes and fragments ranging from two lines to several pages. The order of presentation of fragments in any given unit, and in the book itself, sometimes seems to matter, sometimes does not. Because Adler's subject is fragmentation, because she tries to build, as John Hollander puts it in a dust jacket comment, "a world of anecdotes in which any kind of Whole Story would appear to be a well-intentioned lie," she runs into difficult formal problems.

To give credit, Adler is a brilliant stylist. Her use of irony is assured and often delicate; her sense of humor is finely honed. She does try to weave a slight narrative thread into *Speedboat,* while keeping her fragmented method. But a novel consisting of fragments, to be successful formally, must be woven carefully. There must be composition, as in music or painting. Otherwise, if one's meaning is about the randomness of experience, and Adler's meaning seems to be this, one falls flat into the imitative fallacy. . . .

When I first began to read *Speedboat,* it seemed to me that the book had a chance to be stunning, authentic. In the first three chapters there is a tension in their careful ordering, a silk cord being wound tighter and tighter. In these chapters Adler quietly builds momentum with her seeming randomness, her dispassion, her precision. When I got to the end of Chapter 2, where she says

> Suppose we blow up the whole thing. Everything. Everybody. Me. Buildings. No room. Blast. All dead. No survivors. And then I would say, Let's just have it a little quiet around here.

I found I had ridden thirty blocks past my bus stop. To have created a degree of tension where the simple repetition of a phrase, "and then I would say, and then I say . . ." can convey such pain, such intensity, takes extraordinary technical virtuosity. At that point I thought this talented book had a chance to be a great one. If she could pull that silk cord for another 150 pages, I would be happy to ride the bus all day.

The next chapter was "Brownstone," a somewhat different arrangement of which won the O. Henry Award in 1974. "Brownstone" in either version, comes close to being a perfect piece of writing. The structure of "Brownstone" is arhythmic, jarring. The bones of a self-contained narrative show through in a way that demonstrates, reinforces, the sense of dislocation, terror, absurdity that haunts the tenants of the brownstone Fain lives in. . . .

"Brownstone" seemed a perfect piece of writing and so I got off the bus. There's something I call a "bouncer" in fiction. It's a piece, an episode that bounces the reader right out of a book. A piece that is complete in itself, inserted into a novel, is a bouncer. It cannot be woven into the fabric without making a big lump. I am not talking about an independent episode, though an independent episode, if woven badly, can certainly make lumpy fiction. I'm talking about something formally complete, self-contained, musical, the images and rhythms finished. "Brownstone" is like that. It blows the linear tension in *Speedboat,* and it bounced me right off the bus.

After "Brownstone" the structure of *Speedboat* disintegrates. Selective randomness becomes sloppy randomness. Insight becomes pretension. Precision becomes hair-splitting. What has been moving becomes simply mannered.

I got irritated, I sulked over *Speedboat.* Adler's stylistic brilliance is almost overwhelming. I told myself she is too obviously intelligent to think she can make a virtue of the imitative fallacy. Or is she? . . .

I think Adler knew she lost control of her book formally. Otherwise she would not have taken so many wild shots in the last third of the book; she would not have left all these pithy, meaningful clues; she would not have dropped so many keys that don't quite fit. And she would have been able to think of an ending that made sense. (p. 470)

> *Blanche M. Boyd, "A Mannered Slouch,"*
> *in* The Nation *(copyright 1976 by the Nation*
> *Associates, Inc.), November 6, 1976, pp.*
> *469-70.*

In the reviews of Renata Adler's *Speedboat,* a work of unusual interest, many critics asked whether this "novel" was really a novel. The book is, in its parts, fastidiously lucid, neatly and openly composed. It is the linear as opposed to the circular construction that leads to the withholding of consent for the enterprise, at least on the part of some readers.

The narrator—a word not entirely apt—is a young woman, a sensibility formed in the 1950s and '60s, a lucky eye gazing out from a center of complicated privilege, looking with the cool that transforms itself into style and also into meaning. (p. 3)

For the girl, the past has not set limits and the future is one of wide, restless, interesting "leaps." Not the leaps of lovers (she has lovers, but this is a chaste book), not leaps of divorces, liberations, but a sense of the way experience seizes and lets go, leaving incongruities, gaps that remain alive as conversation—the end result of experience. (pp. 3-4)

To be *interesting,* each page, each paragraph—that is the burden of fiction which is made up of random events and happenings in sequence. *Speedboat* is very clear about the measure of events and anecdotes, and it does meet the demand for the interesting in a nervous, rapid, remarkably gifted manner. A precocious alertness to incongruity: this one would have to say is the odd, dominating trait of the character of the narrator, the only *character* in the book. Perception, then, does the work of feeling and is also the main action. It stands there alone, displacing even temperament.

For the reader of *Speedboat,* certain things may be lacking, particularly a suggestion of turbulence and of disorder more savage than incongruity can bear. But even if feeling is not solicited, randomness itself is a carrier of disturbing emotions. In the end, a flow is more painful than a circle, which at least encloses the self in its resolutions, retributions, and decisions. . . .

In *Speedboat,* the girl, perhaps worried that her autonomy is out of line, like a much-used expense account, announces that she is going to bear a child. In this way she chooses the impediments of nature to act as a brake on the rushing, restless ego. (p. 4)

What is honorable in "so it goes" and in the mournful shimmer . . . in *Speedboat* is the intelligence that questions the shape of life and wonders what we can really act upon. It is important to concede the honor, the nerve, the ambition. . . . (p. 6)

> *Elizabeth Hardwick, "Sense of the Pres-*

ent," in The New York Review of Books
(*reprinted with permission from* The New
York Review of Books; *copyright* © *1976
NYREV, Inc.), November 25, 1976, pp. 3-4,
6.*

[In] Renata Adler's *Speedboat* [the central figure] . . .
hardly exists at all except as style. *Speedboat* is prodi-
giously witty, learned in every department of American
foolishness just now, and definitely fun. It is a marvellously
attentive essay in the cultural pretentiousness of everything
over-valued and over-priced, not forgetting our dreams. . . .
Some of the best pages in it deal with the misuse and misap-
propriation of language, with cultural dry-rot, with cultural
faking. The book's great achievement is that Renata Adler
has remained a tourist in the most familiar places. No one
understands better the mystique necessary to devaluation.
Or as another tourist, Gertrude Stein, put it: "Remarks are
not literature."

But witty and necessary as *Speedboat* is, I fail to understand in what sense it is a work of fiction. The "heroine,"
or the style, significantly moves from profession to profession, from one example to another of the fact that the emperor is still passing by without a stitch to his name. The
movement from incongruity to total mystification is irresistible! But nowhere in the book did I see plain the anxiety
that makes it necessary for the narrator to move on so fast.
(pp. 23-4)

Alfred Kazin, in The New Republic *(reprinted by permission of* The New Republic;
© *1976 by* The New Republic, Inc.*), November 27, 1976.*

The narrator of Renata Adler's first novel is called Jen
Fain; significantly, it took a good deal of searching to remind myself of this. For I suspect Adler feels the same way
about a name as one of her characters does about a suntan:
When you have one, what have you got? In this cerebral
book names, like all the other usual narrative devices—
plot, character, dialogue—are too fashionably unfashiona-
ble to be bothered with, and one wonders why the narrator
is christened at all. Everyone else is merely dismissed: a
"polo-playing Argentine existential psychiatrist," an
"Indo-Chinese lesbian restaurant owner."

Such is the wit of *Speedboat*, with its bluejeaned young
men and women who wear granny glasses over their contact lenses, its radicals in analysis, its nine-year-old who
wears a "silver electric chair on her charm bracelet," its
bartender who mixes a Last Mango in Paris. If you are
amused, fine; if not, you may feel, as I did, that Jen Fain
speaks for Renata Adler when she says, "It is no accident
that boredom and cruelty are great preoccupations in our
time."

Speedboat is the perfect title for Adler's world, through
which journalist Jen Fain rushes and reports, trying to
cope, managing to laugh. Vignette piles upon vignette here,
with all the random chaos that has made the 20th century a
cliché before its time. Jen Fain is always at the center,
though, and our response to her largely determines our response to the novel.

What I find least attractive about Adler's narrator is her
fleshlessness. We get inside her head as she takes her reporter's notes on the '70s, but we also find her becoming
pregnant without ever getting a strong sense that she slept
with anyone. Jen tells us we are all "fighting for our lives,"

yet Adler's narrative choices allow us to share that fight
only from the most intellectual distance. *Well of course!*
many literary critics would counter. Other eras, however,
asked more from fiction; future eras may ask more again.

What I admire about Jen Fain is that she (like Adler) realizes this: The crisis in contemporary fiction is one she embraces. . . . "There are only so many plots," she writes.
"There are insights, prose flights, rhythms, felicities. But
only so many plots. At a slower pace, in a statelier world,
the equations are statelier."

These, then, are the criteria Adler offers us to measure her
work by: insights, prose flights, rhythms, felicities. *Speedboat* does not even have what many readers would still call
a "story" (though things happen, things change); we are
asked to look elsewhere for our pleasure.

And so we return to the chaos at the book's core, to the
international-set anecdotes that structure it, and to the
struggles of Jen Fain, who would fain laugh in the city as
escape to the country. (p. 19)

I find something ultimately disturbing about *Speedboat*.
Sanity, we are told, is "the most profound moral option of
our time." What is meant by sanity is suggested by the
novel's ending: "It could be the sort of sentence one wants
right here is the kind that runs, and laughs, and slides, and
stops right on a dime."

In other words, dealing with future shock, keeping sane in
the city, making do. Is this the sentence we need, and, in
fact, always compose ourselves (as the major character in
our own lives)? Or is *Speedboat* symptomatic of another
kind of sentence entirely, one imposed by a fashionable intellectual climate? Is Jen Fain, with her witty coping, admirable? Or rather, to quote from Norman O. Brown's *Love's
Body*, is her "resisting madness . . . the maddest way of
being mad"? (pp. 19-20)

Charles Deemer, "A Fleshless Comedy," in
The New Leader (© *1976 by the American
Labor Conference on International Affairs,
Inc.), December 20, 1976, pp. 19-20.*

There is [a detached and abstracting] intelligence in Renata
Adler's *Speedboat*, labeled a novel by her publishers but
much less persuasive as narrative fiction than as a blending
of autobiographical fragments with reportage. A valuable
satirist, Adler is as incisive as Mary McCarthy on the pretensions of academics, intellectuals, and financially comfortable culture-vultures. (p. 587)

But one way of crystalizing Adler's limitations, one way of
acknowledging the relative modesty of her claims as a novelist, is to observe that [her] witty and telling lines also represent the author in one of her warmest, most sympathizing
humors. . . . In most of the crisply written, discontinuous
anecdotes that comprise *Speedboat*, Adler's narrator remains just as distant from her topics, and also frequently
speaks in gloomier accents, alluding self-consciously to
Yeats's overworked prophecy of our slouch toward apocalypse. . . . Except for a few significant sentences in the final
pages, this world-weary narrator describes her anxious urban life, her journalistic tours through territories of pain
and folly, even her own sexual experiences, with the neutral dispassion of an archeologist sifting alien fragments.
Her disembodiment is so severe, confessions of bafflement
and disconnection rush so easily from her lips, that her authority as a witness to outer events is radically enfeebled,
and *Speedboat* comes to seem the authentic register of a

malaise that resides not in the world but in the narrator herself. . . . [The] alienation and emotional numbness projected by Adler's narrator-double must seem familiar to anyone acquainted even superficially with the now attenuated conventions of literary modernism. *Speedboat* is genuinely persuasive as an autobiographical document, as a self-judging exposé of the easy posturing, the essentially derivative and *literary* nihilism, to which intelligence and sensibility are peculiarly vulnerable in these muddled times. Adler herself understands this, or comes to understand it during the course of her writing, for she ends her book with a paragraph that opens itself to vital energies that have been largely absent from the text until now, energies of sympathy and imagination that are inaccessible to mere wit or to satire even at its most ambitious. The paragraph begins with a surprising description of the narrator's lover: "Jim has in his mind, I think, one erratically ringing alarm clock, one manacled dervish, one dormouse, replete with truisms, and one jurist with a clarity of such an order that I tend to love his verdict in most things." Nothing in the book has quite prepared us for this affection and playfulness, which constitute an unmistakable judgment upon the self-protecting disengagement to which the narrator has been captive. Intelligence and accurate perception retain their centrality in her scheme of things, but are deepened measurably by her willingness to risk closeness and honest feeling. Her temperament has not reversed or radically transformed itself, but it has begun to open and to enlarge. "It could be," she says in her final sentence, as if to signal her rejection of the styles of avant-garde irony that had earlier defined her as a writer and as a woman, "It could be that the sort of sentence one wants right here is the kind that runs, and laughs, and slides, and stops right on a dime." (pp. 587-88)

David Thorburn, in The Yale Review *(© 1977 by Yale University; reprinted by permission of the editors), Summer, 1977.*

*   *   *

AGNON, S(hmuel) Y(osef)   1888-1970

Born Shmuel Yosef Tchatsky in Buczacz, Galicia (formerly Austria-Hungary; now Poland), Agnon settled in Palestine (later Israel) in 1924 and remained there until his death. Agnon found the material for his fiction, which possesses an ironic, lyrical quality, in ancient Hebrew folklore. He was the recipient of the Nobel Prize for Literature in 1966, the first Israeli and the first author writing in Hebrew to receive this award. (See also *CLC*, Vol. 4, and *Contemporary Authors*, Vols. 17-18; obituary, Vols. 25-28, rev. ed.; *Contemporary Authors Permanent Series*, Vol. 2.)

[The title of Agnon's story,] "The Face and the Image," is a metaphorical translation of the Hebrew *Ha-panim la-panim,* which literally translates into "The Face to the Face.". . . Presumably the reference exists to establish an ironic contrast: the proverb [from which this phrase is taken] asserts that man comforts man, but the narrator of the Agnon story is an isolated individual. As is characteristic of many titles, the title ["Ha-panim la-panim"] provides crucial guidance to the central meaning of the story. But we do not realize the full nature of this guidance unless we recognize that this phrase not only appears in Proverbs; more crucially, it appears in a variant form—*panim el panim*, "face to face"—in Genesis and in Exodus. In Genesis 32:30, after his famous wrestling match where he has been renamed Israel, Jacob says, "I have seen God face to face, and my life is preserved." And in Exodus 33:11 it is writ-

ten, "And Jehovah spoke unto Moses face to face, as a man speaketh unto his friend." These are well-known passages: *panim el panim* is as famous a phrase to a Hebrew speaker with a minimum knowledge of Jewish culture as, say, "Home of the Brave" would be to the average American. Therefore, part of the content of the Agnon title is in its echo of *panim el-panim:* that is, in the contrast between the face confronted by its mirror-image and with "God."

The central plot situation in the story is the narrator's failure to be able to visit his ill—dying or perhaps already dead —mother as a result of a series of awkward mishaps set up by the narrator himself. "The Face and the Image" is from the collection *The Book of Deeds,* and the characteristic story there is non-realistic. . . . [The] mixture of realism and surrealism in "The Face and the Image" encourages a symbolic interpretation of this story in which the mother emerges as, say, the "old faith," certainly as its representative. . . . Thus the narrator at the end of the story is not sitting face to face with his mother, the representative of the old faith, but rather in strange surroundings. He is surprised by a mirror-image of himself "reflecting back every movement of the hand and quiver of the lips, like all polished mirrors, which show you whatever you show them, without partiality or deceit." Significantly, the "image rose" when he is trying to avoid recognizing the consequences of his not being by his mother's side. In the final line of the story, the "I" says that "it, namely, the revelation of the thing, surprised me more than the thing itself, perhaps more than it had surprised me in my childhood, perhaps more than it had ever surprised me before." Presumably what is revealed to him is his isolation, his folly, his impotence.

Instead of wrestling with God or speaking to Him face to face, the narrator at the end is speaking with himself and wrestling with his own self-image: man in his folly, his self-confusion and isolation, in his impotence, and perhaps in his vanity as well, cannot return to the old faith—some such statement emerges as the central theme of this story, a meaning that is anticipated by the title *Ha-panim la-panim,* and by its echo of the more famous *panim el panim.* (pp. 184-85)

Bernard Knieger, "Shmuel Yosef Agnon's 'The Face and the Image'," in Studies in Short Fiction *(copyright 1975 by Newberry College), Spring, 1975, pp. 184-85.*

Agnon, in his private life, was a religious, observant Jew, and his profession of faith is, indeed, apparent in his writings. However, there is no doubt that he was a modern writer, experiencing and expressing the basic problems of the modern Jew. His manner of presentation can mislead the reader to assume that Agnon is a writer of the old school, for he developed his own style by adopting some classical forms of Mishnaic Hebrew along with a style that had flourished in Hasidic writings. His themes, too, may mislead the reader to consider Agnon as representing the traditional life of the past. While this may be true with regard to *Bilvav Yamim* (In the Heart of the Seas) and *Hakhnasat Kalah* (The Bridal Canopy), in *Ore'ah Natah Lalun* (A Guest for the Night) the quest for one's identity and for the meaning of the past is already subtly introduced. Indeed, one may find nostalgia in Agnon, but one also finds nightmare. This is especially true in many of his short stories in *Sefer Hama'asim* (The Book of Deeds). Indeed, it is this ambiguity of religiosity and secularism that is most characteristic of some of Agnon's writings. (p. 456)

Judaism, to Agnon, can never be attained in a secularistic context. Jewish nationalism, too, as may be seen from his point-of-view, is part and parcel of traditional, normative Judaism. . . . In order for the Jew to maintain his Jewish identity, he must remain within the framework of traditional Judaism. However, Agnon was sensitive enough to know that the modern, atraditional Jew desires very much to retain his Jewish identity, but has difficulties finding his satisfaction within the norms of traditional Judaism. (p. 459)

Moshe Pelli, in Judaism *(copyright © 1976 by the American Jewish Congress), Vol. 25, No. 4, Fall, 1976.*

The Day of Atonement (*Yom Kippur*) is the most sacred of Jewish Holidays and, not surprisingly, a recurring theme in modern Hebrew literature. (p. 37)

A son and a grandson of Jewish scholars and community leaders, Agnon personifies the religious consciousness of modern Hebrew letters. Agnon is also strongly nationalistic, and Zionism and its ideals are closely knit with his religious tenacity. [The] ghetto becomes in Agnon's hands a viable community, distinguished by its cultural uniqueness and moral excellence.

In spite of Agnon's profound admiration for the pietistic way of life, he is aware of the dissonances within it and of the forces of disintegration slowly but steadily washing away its foundations. In his writings, therefore, strains of nostalgia clash with visions of a nightmare; idyllic lyricism, which suffuses the evocations of the past, is countered by macabre surrealism when Agnon turns his attention to the realities of the present. (pp. 37-8)

Yom Kippur serves Agnon as a setting for the portrayal of both the harmonious state of man at peace with God and his soul and for the state of chaos and disorientation when man has lost his way to God and to himself. The contrast between two such Days of Atonement is brought out in a story "Pi Shnayim" ["Twice as Much"], told by the protagonist in the first person. His childhood memory of the Day reflects an ideal belief and a beauteous harmony; the experience of the present adulthood conveys loss of way in the Dantesque sense . . . and a resulting chaos.

[The] ideal *Yom Kippur* as retrieved from the treasury of the childhood memories . . . [is described as a] lyrical evocation . . . imbued with muted tenderness and gently modulated strains of awe. The images and figures of speech are closely bound with the sense of smell and with visual pictures. It is the smells of hay, wax, and honey which lend the memory its earthly roots, but it is light that infuses it with a spiritual significance. . . . The source of light is not in the burning candles but in the hallowed figure of the father which is interchangeable with that of Moses. It radiates the light which the candles only reflect. The spirit in its perfect purity emanates a sanctity which settles on the material world and illuminates it. This Day of Atonement shows man at peace with the Almighty, and the Almighty bound by loving kindness to His people.

In contrast to the idyll retained from childhood memories, the Day of Atonement experienced through the consciousness of the adult narrator is a demonic distortion of the dream, coming in fragmented episodes. First, there is a sinister occurrence in the synagogue on the eve of the solemn day: . . . "I noticed that they were unrolling the *Torah* for the Day of Awe, and that they were unrolling it upside down, the written part down and the empty one up. I was

grieved that the *Torah* was treated with such irreverence, but I kept silent because I was a guest.". . . This uncanny event is followed by an open outrage—people feasting on the day of fasting, the son of the rabbinical judge (dayan) among them. . . . This gluttonous eating is described not only as a religious outrage but even more so as a repugnant spectacle of excess, its dehumanizing effects reminiscent of Pieter Bruegel's "The Land of Cockayne." This scene is followed by another, surrealistic and even macabre. . . . [A] mysterious figure which takes the narrator's place in the synagogue might have been death itself, or perhaps the narrator's *alter ego.* But whatever its identity, there is no doubt about the impact of the entire image of *Yom Kippur* in this sequence. It is chaotic, confused, haunted by an unspecified fear and sinister fantasies—a far cry from the harmony and sanctity of the child's memory of the Day. Man has lost his wholeness and his harmonious relationship with God.

The story "Pi Shnayim" is part of *The Book of Deeds,* a collection of some of Agnon's most concentrated attempt to translate into modern idiom the peculiarly Jewish consciousness of the contemporary universal malaise. What Kafka did in German, Joyce and Beckett in English, and the existentialists and avant-garde writers in French, Agnon did in modern Hebrew. The haunting fear, the sense of sin and guilt which pursue modern man's consciousness, and the lingering feeling of a gradual dissolution of the whole web of familiar culture, typify the stories of *The Book of Deeds.*

Agnon drew on the wealth of popular themes and motifs in Jewish legend and religious thought thus creating a literary medium with which he evokes an atmosphere of alienation and bewilderment. The macabre touches of death, shrouds, spectres and grotesque desecration, are part of the popular *aggadah* inherited from the strange messianism of the Lurianic *Kabbalah.* This demonology of the *beit-hamidrash* (house of prayer and study) is artistically manoevered by Agnon to bring out the modern feeling of spiritual rootlessness. Thus he expresses the plight of secularized Jewish awareness in authentic Jewish concepts. The dislocation of faith experienced in the sanctuary of religion reveals particularly vividly the anguish of the disinherited mind.

Agnon's great achievement is to have forged a vehicle for conveying this plight in a fictional form. Motifs charged with a significance peculiar to a distinct culture have been recharged by him with new vitality and made into symbols of universal human value. The modern preoccupation with nihilism and with the absurd has found a means of expression in those archetypal forms.

Agnon's style in *The Book of Deeds* is Kafkaesque. Dream and reality merge and mingle, "until the things of dream were like the things of wakefulness". . . . Particular objects and experiences lose their distinctiveness and fade off into a mass of disjointed memories and shreds of impressions. Time plays mischievous tricks on the protagonist and creates a surrealistic mood. The Days of Atonement, which serve as a pivot for the Jewish consciousness and a reliable starting point for measuring the cyclic rhythm of time, merge and collapse one upon the other. . . . The image of the perfect *Yom Kippur,* again conveyed as a harmonious memory from childhood, is described in Agnon's Introduction to a new edition of *The Days of Awe.* . . . As in "Pi Shnayim," this scene is an apotheosis of an ideal as seen through a child's eyes. But there is an additional element in this picture: for the child all the people are one. The child discovers a concrete manifestation of the idea of a true community of spirit on this solemn occasion. The sanctity of the House of Prayer and the intensity of the moment reveal to the child an ideal which he conceives as absolute and eternal. . . . [The] infinite and the immortal seem to be included in this vision which has neither a beginning nor an end: "It did not occur to me that one can stop it." The assurance of continuity which the scene conveys to the child is the longed-for mode of existence of the adult. (pp. 38-40)

In one of Agnon's major novels, *A Guest for the Night,* the narrator is the guest who comes back to his native town to reestablish his old ties with it and with the tradition for which it stands. But it is a belated return. The town is in ruins, the tradition in shambles, and the narrator, instead of drawing on the old sources to invigorate his own spirit, finds that the roles have to be reversed, and that it is he who must rekindle the dying embers of life. His arrival coincides with the eve of the Day of Atonement. (pp. 40-1)

The Day of Atonement is identified with radiance, and the dreariness of the present augments by contrast the radiance of the past. The contrast between the present and the past is further emphasized by scenes connected with the river Stripa. In his memories the river acquires a sanctity which emanates from the holy day. . . .

> The water comes and the water goes; as it comes, so it goes, and an odor of purity rises from it. It seems as if nothing has changed since the day I stood here with Father, of blessed memory, and nothing will change here until the end of all the generations. . . .

The narrator tries to recapture a mode of feeling by going through the motions which he knows by heart. The reminiscences in which the father figure is the focus, and the setting which connects the present with the past—the bridge, the flowing water—all blend into the holiness of the day and are raised into a picture of sanctity and Divine Grace. The passage is a poetical evocation of an elegiac mood. The repetition of "comes" and "goes," the never ending renewal of the flow of water, elevate the river to a symbol of continuity and accentuate the narrator's yearning for the past. A melancholy nostalgia for what was and is no more is exquisitely presented in this nocturnal scene.

With the nostalgia goes a feeling of trust in the absoluteness of the old values. To convey this conviction Agnon uses a subtle technique. When he writes "The water comes and the water goes; as it comes, so it goes," he introduces the cadence of *Ecclesiastes* ("The sun also ariseth, and the sun goeth down," ". . . unto the place from where the rivers come, thither they return again"; Eccl. 1:5 and 7). But whereas in the biblical text the cadence is used to emphasize "vanity of vanities," the futility of it all, Agnon for once is not ironic, but sees in this rhythm cosmic stability and absolute values. (p. 41)

On this Day of Awe, when God judges his creatures, decreeing life or death, forgiveness or damnation, Agnon sees fit to judge the Judge. Agnon's criticism is implicit. He does not directly point an accusing finger at the Almighty. He does not even turn his attention to the most obvious injustice—the suffering of his people. Instead, he dwells on the flaws in the religious service which, of course, are due to the deprivation and suffering of the people, which, in turn, are implied to be the Almighty's responsibility. (p. 42)

The Day of Atonement serves as a means for Agnon to criticise God and express his anguish about the disintegration of the *stetl.* As befits the solemn occasion of *Yom Kippur,* the narrator ostensibly pays tribute to the Almighty, but in truth it is a mock tribute: "See how humble is the King who is the King of Kings, the Holy One, blessed be He, who said, 'Mine is the silver and mine is the gold,' but has not left Himself even an ounce of silver to adorn his Torah.". . . The sarcasm is doubly blasphemous, because the words which are used for expressing a pious reverence are here twisted into a parody of God's insufficiency; and because the occasion, which normally calls for contrition and self-effacement, is turned into a denunciation of the Judge.

Nonetheless, the accusation of God, the doubts of His omnipotence, or benevolence, are not meant to express a total despair of God or unequivocal rejection of belief. Agnon's sardonic tone remains within the bounds of religion. For, ultimately, Agnon does not want to reject God. He clings to Him, for he wants to escape modern man's loneliness and the existential fear of cosmic indifference. It is the fundamental clinging to God that explains Agnon's argument with Him, as is the case with Agnon's biblical precursor, Job. (p. 43)

> *Miriam Roshwald, in* The International Fiction Review (© *copyright International Fiction Association), January, 1977.*

* * *

AMIS, Kingsley   1922-

A distinguished English novelist, short story writer, poet, editor, and essayist, Amis won critical acclaim in 1954 with the publication of his first novel, *Lucky Jim.* His prose is characterized by its comic texture, and his subject, in his own words, is the "relations between people." Amis's interest in science fiction has been sustained throughout his career: he was coeditor of the *Spectrum* science fiction anthologies and was the author of the first English full-length critical survey of the genre in *New Maps of Hell.* He has also written under the pseudonym Robert Markham. (See also *CLC,* Vols, 1, 2, 3, 5, and *Contemporary Authors,* Vols. 9-12, rev. ed.)

Kingsley Amis is not the first writer to demonstrate that old age is material for a kind of harrowing comedy. Muriel Spark, for one, did it in her first and best novel "Memento Mori." But [in "Ending Up"] Amis avoids her cautionary moral, her note of *dies irae,* just as he avoids the more popular airs of gloating sentimentality and gratuitous ferocity. He neither sniggers, nor swaggers, nor waxes indignant. The hard and polished surface of this novel offers no purchase for the grip of any attitude or thesis or moral. "Ending Up" is funny and upsetting, but not tendentious.

The five septuagenarian protagonists are funny because they keep tripping over the gaps between their intentions and their abilities. They are upsetting for the same reason. . . .

Behind the stiffening bodies, thickening voices and wooden gestures, Amis's characters remain all-too-human. . . .

[Even] the sudden, maybe too sudden, nastiness of the ending does not point to a generalization. We gather not that old age is like this, but that old age is like this for people like this: for people whose bad luck or temperament made them unable to invest in other people when they were flush with youth. Even that, however, sounds too much like the moral this novel is too businesslike to have.

"Ending Up" is remarkable, among other things, for its rounded concision and self-sufficiency. Its formal virtues are the kind we usually think of as classical, the virtues, as William York Tindall put it, of making the most out of self-imposed limitations. My rough estimate is that of his 11 novels, only in "Lucky Jim" and in "The Green Man" did Amis make as much out of his virtues and limitations. (p. 5)

> *George Stade, in* The New York Times Book Review (© *1974 by The New York Times Company; reprinted by permission), October 20, 1974.*

[Kingsley Amis] can make his characters stand up on the page like brilliant cut-outs springing to life as one opens the book. Everybody has a funny voice and a distinctive, usually remarkably ghastly, suit of clothes. If you look closely, you can see the jagged cardboard edges, but Amis gets them into action so fast that only a very sour critic indeed would complain of their coarse colours and rather hasty scissorwork. His new novel, *Ending Up,* is one of the best he's ever done: a brutal comedy which is not so much about old age as about the problem of why people ever bother to get born at all. (p. 87)

In the hands of anyone else, *Ending Up* should have been an unbearably bleak book. But Amis sets in on his old people with the relish of Billy Bunter at a dorm feast. He turns weakness and pretension into good copy, and, oddly in a novel which affects such weariness at the vanity of human life, infects us so thoroughly with his enjoyment that the whole thing becomes a long whoop of delight. One feels that, unlike Larkin, whose poem "The Old Fools" shares a lot of surface features with *Ending Up,* Amis does not really mean what he says. His pessimism, finally, doesn't stand a chance against the overweening force of his good humour. (p. 88)

> *Jonathan Raban, in* Encounter (© *1974 by Encounter Ltd.), November, 1974.*

[One] expects from Kingsley Amis more than a rehash of familiar material [as presented in *Rudyard Kipling and His World*]. Precisely because of the author's sparkling talents as a novelist and essayist, he disappoints the reader who looks for the customary touches of wit, elegance and verve. Intermittently Amis writes with genial good humor, but his general style is subdued, sometimes flat. . . . (p. 101)

Amis's relaxed, tolerantly amused manner is more appropriate to *Lucky Jim* or *Take a Girl Like You* than to a serious study of Kipling. Yet is he serious when he writes that "Kipling produced among others the most harrowing poem in our language"—by which he means "Danny Deever"? Does Amis really believe that Kipling is "clearly our best writer of short stories"? For the discriminating reader, Amis's judgments, sometimes provocative but mostly irritating, fail to do their subject justice. (p. 102)

> *Leslie B. Mittleman, in* World Literature Today *(copyright 1977 by the University of Oklahoma Press), Vol. 51, No. 3, Winter, 1977.*

Science fiction—for which Amis [in "The Alteration"] proposes two alternative terms, Time Romance and Counterfeit World—tends lamentably toward description, explication and stasis, and these must be offset by simple characters and a melodramatic plot to animate didacticism. Amis provides them. His protagonist is another in the lengthening list of precocious children in our current literary culture. To Edwin Mullhouse, Jeffrey Cartwright, Billy Twillig and J. R. Vansant we now add Hubert Anvil, the precocious 10-year-old possessor of a beautiful soprano voice. Of course the Church covets it, wants Hubert to preserve that voice and repay God's favor to him by cultivating his talent. This will require castration. "I know it's glorious to have God's favour and I'm as grateful for it as I can be," Hubert says, "but I can't prevent myself from wishing it had taken another form."

With only a few weeks in which to submit or escape (coincidence is the secret rocket-fuel of this and most S.F.), Hubert becomes the nexus of a struggle among diverse interest groups in and out of the Church. Unfortunately the central issue—roughly, life vs. art—is not much to the point. (For which see "Ode on a Grecian Urn" or, more appropriately, E. B. Browning's "Musical Instrument.") In addition, the only alternative world is an Edenic America but also a puritanical religious tyranny, though milder—they impose apartheid upon the Indians and they also castrate, but only for social reasons, not esthetic ones—and Amis's moral issue is based on simplistic and rhetorical notions. For instance, he suggests that "there might be some sort of natural case against mutilating a child for the greater glory of music or God or His Church or anything else whatever." Nature—so often red in tooth and claw—is a shaky foundation for kindly ethics; so is Amis's backup basis, truth. A superficial Jesuit is made to say: "I feel nothing but wonder and gratitude when I look on so many centuries of patience, hope, content, trust, constancy, restraint and certitude, so much art, letters, music, learning, all founded upon one great lie." We are meant to shudder, but only those who have found a satisfactory truth will do so. The rest of us will recognize those shudderers as dangerous, and by Amis's own criterion, since no one firmly convinced of an ultimate truth, a truth without any countertruths and complements, can rightly tolerate dissent from it.

A plot must have an outcome; and here, as in almost any work in which particular characters and events are manipulated to demonstrate general meanings, the working out is disappointing if not absurd. Amis's strength expresses itself as always not in thought but in the tangential humor. His Pope is a delight before the plot transmogrifies him; a dull-witted Yorkshireman, he observes that "if there's one thing we can't abide at any price it's sin. We think we can safely say that. . . . Yes, we think we can safely say that." His motto, wonderfully, is "no time like the present." Amis also has great fun with altered titles; we hear of "St. Lemuel's Travels," for instance, "The Wind in the Cloisters" and "Lord of the Chalices." He also nobly reminds his readers of Anthony Burgess's "The Wanting Seed," a better novel than his own, though less showy. But one shouldn't carp: this is heavenly S.F., by God. . . . Perhaps that might have been worded better. (pp. 4, 27)

> *J. D. O'Hara, in* The New York Times Book Review (© *1977 by The New York Times Company; reprinted by permission), January 30, 1977.*

It always puzzled me to see Kingsley Amis numbered among the rest of those young English writers of the Fifties. Remember them bundled together under a banner that now has no more than nostalgia value—the Angry Young Men? He didn't belong in that crowd. He didn't seem, well, angry enough. Was John Osborne angry? You bet. Alan Sillitoe? Furious. But Amis, essentially a comic novelist, seemed merely to be miffed at the social inequities that sent the others into hooting, howling frenzies. He just joked about them.

Yet all that is about 20 years in the past. And if today John Osborne seems to have lapsed into silence (temporarily, one hopes) and Alan Sillitoe has grown almost jolly, then you should also know that Kingsley Amis is no longer the pink-cheeked jester who used to amuse the Establishment far more than he irritated it. He has, as they say in *Rolling Stone,* gone through some pretty heavy changes. . . .

Beginning with *The Anti-Death League* (1966), he has produced a number of very dark novels, among them the mysterious "ghost story" *The Green Man* and that pernicious comedy *Girl, 20,* surely the bleakest funny book ever written. In these and other books his concern has been increasingly metaphysical, even theological. He has dealt so deftly with the big eschatological questions he raises, making such appealing use of his distinctive blend of elegant wit and plain foolishness, that practically nobody seems to have noticed what he is up to.

His latest novel, *The Alteration,* though quite different from anything he has written previously, fits neatly into this established pattern. It is, in fact, the most overtly and specifically theological of all his books, for it deals with a practice that, until the nineteenth century, was not only permitted but encouraged by the Roman Catholic Church; that is, the castration of gifted boy sopranos so that they might continue to sing on into manhood in the same high voices. . . .

Has Kingsley Amis, then, written an eighteenth-century historical romance? No, he has done something far more subversive than that. *The Alteration* belongs to a fairly rare sub-genre of science fiction, the so-called counterfeit- or alternative-world novel. . . .

Just what is the counterfeit-world sub-genre and what relation does it have to science fiction? Amis himself defines it as "a class of tale set more or less at the present date, but portraying the results of some momentous change in historical fact." It is, in other words, social science fiction in which the what-if factor has been drawn from past events. . . . (p. 28)

The Alteration . . . is only intermittently and superficially funny. The novel's humor is the one thing that appeals to me least about it. Most of it seems to have been added as an afterthought, simply because Amis thinks it is still expected of him.

Granted the basic *idea* of the book is funny—the present imagined as a direct extension of the medieval past—but Amis has not taken any more from his imaginary history of Europe than is absolutely necessary for the purposes of the plot. Here and there along the way he has tried to toss in some laughs, most of them using the device of introducing historical personages into his counterfeit world in altered roles. . . .

Fundamentally, *The Alteration* is another of Kingsley Amis's angry screeds against the Catholic faith and the Catholic idea of God. And it is not just what Amis sees as the life-hating, sex-hating aspect of High Christianity—something that made possible such monstrous phenomena as the castrati—that concerns him here. . . .

But Kingsley Amis is castigating much more than that. Speaking through one of the more daring clergymen in *The Alteration,* he reflects on how much has been "founded

upon one great lie. . . . At first a lie nobody had the smallest need for, since become the sole necessity." And the lie he is talking about is, for Amis, Christianity itself. At the end of *The Anti-Death League,* his oddest and most extreme book and in some ways his best, Amis allows some talk of reconciliation, of forgiving God the wrongs He has done humanity. But there is none of that in *The Alteration.* It is an almost bitter book by a man grown angry in middle age. (p. 29)

Bruce Cook, in Saturday Review (© *1977 by Saturday Review Magazine Corp.; reprinted with permission), February 5, 1977.*

In *The Alteration* Kingsley Amis considers the plight of a gifted child in [an alternative] world. . . . Amis plays [the] game more wittily than most writers about "alternative worlds" would do, and it's a nice touch that his world knows of ours, quite inaccurately, only from the science fiction stories schoolboys read on the sly. And I'm glad to find a usually opinionated writer allowing the relative value of his world and ours to seem an open question. . . .

The main character of *The Alteration* is Hubert Anvil, a marvelous boy soprano whom the Vatican musical authorities propose to castrate for the greater glory of God and His art. . . .

Amis isn't famous for his compassion, but here he affectingly catches and respects a child's puzzlement about the threatened loss of something he knows about only from descriptions, trying to care because other people seem to. . . . [Knowing] so little, he finally accepts his alteration without strong regret. This is sad for us but not really for him, Amis seems to suggest, like his altered world itself, which we don't like to imagine but would probably live in more or less contentedly if we had to. Whatever is, is—if not right—at least tolerable and probably no worse than anything else. If no Beethoven, then more Mozart.

In the light of our own recent history, this seems to me an intolerable moral, though not, coming from Amis, a surprising one. He has lately been negotiating between "serious" fiction and humbler kinds like thrillers, and fantasy stories. . . . But if the democratizing of high art is a healthy enterprise, Amis's way of doing it exposes the major premise of the kinds of popular fiction he's concerned with: the stimulating variety of detail in a story of crime or imagined worlds leads finally back to an idea of human nature as immutably fixed and gravely flawed. To appropriate the title of his critical study of science fiction, we can draw "new maps of hell," but the territory represented remains the old, known one that was ours—was *us*—all along.

Such an outlook can encourage a saving contempt for all forms of "authority" and for the self-deceptions that encourage us to assume or obey it—*The Alteration* is alive to the extent that it reminds us of Amis's wonderful *Lucky Jim.* But its major mood is that of a tired, anti-ideological quietism which insists that secular choices are futile. The best I can say for that message is that it is conveyed in a surprisingly subdued and often affecting way. (p. 31)

Thomas R. Edwards, in The New York Review of Books (*reprinted with permission from* The New York Review of Books; *copyright © 1977 NYREV, Inc.), March 3, 1977.*

AMMONS, A(rchie) R(andolph) 1926-

An American poet in the romantic tradition of Emerson and Whitman, Ammons won the National Book Award in 1973 for *Collected Poems*. Originally from rural North Carolina, Ammons in his best poetry examines the relationship between nature and humanity. (See also *CLC*, Vols. 2, 3, 5, and *Contemporary Authors*, Vols. 9-12, rev. ed.)

"When Whitman said 'O Pioneers'"—observed F. Scott Fitzgerald—"he said all." With Fitzgerald the cry had already become a groan, but the American urge to "sing possible / changes / that might redeem," in A. R. Ammons's words, proves stubborn, and our writers' wagons can still be heard heading out of town, creaking for joy. If not toward a greater America then toward "eternal being," or "heterocosm joyous," they make their dauntless way. The Romantic dream of returning at dawn "wet / to the hips with meetings" is quite dead in England, but our own Ammons and W. S. Merwin, among others, are out without their long boots. Like the more troubled Pound, Stevens and Williams before them, like Emerson, Thoreau, Melville, Whitman, they are poets of a possibly redeeming change, a change sought in what Emerson called "an original relation to the universe."

At the start, Ammons and Merwin were like brothers out in the same field, and when Ammons began his "Hymn" with "I know if I find you I will have to leave the earth / and go on . . . into the unseasonal undifferentiated empty stark," the words, the very style, might have come from either poet. But Ammons was always, as it were, the older brother—more moderate, hanging behind, less eager for "far resolutions." And while Merwin has run on toward "the decimal of being," Ammons has turned back. Once oblique, prophetic, isolate, cloud-browsed, he has become almost folksy. "Redemptions despise the reality," he observes, disapprovingly, and says: "I expect to promote good will and difficult / clarities: I'm tired of bumfuzzlement and bafflement."

Ammons's new "good will" is Romantic, but so democratic, so accepting, so rationalized, that it is almost casual: he is in no haste at all to hitch his wagon to a star. He now seeks "the good of all in the good of each." As for his "difficult" clarity, it is chiefly the "unmendably integral" connection of everything to everything else in the universe. "Touch the universe anywhere and you touch it / everywhere." What survives of his pared Romanticism is the seed-choked belief that "nothing is separate.". . . Ammons has gone on to develop . . . explicitly, laboriously, abstractly, the concept of reality as a great fugue, a holy unity. This concept is, as he says, the "mysticism" of modern science, the radiance glimpsed in the cooperative lives of a cell as well as in the long reach of the galaxies (which are directly accountable, observes this science, for the inertia of matter—for such calm as there is—in all the other galaxies). Nothing is separate. Nothing is even different, at the core: there the universal unit, the "nervous atom," "spins and shines unsmirched." Still, "having / been chastened to the irreducible," Ammons says, "I have found the / irreducible bountiful." There are "many rafts to ride and the tides make a place to go."

In colonizing for poetry the structural models of science, Ammons has become an intellectual's Whitman, afoot with a laboratory vision that, for all its abstract vocabulary, and however palely, he lectures and tweaks into poetry. Between the hieratic Romanticism of Pound, Stevens and Merwin and the "nude" Romanticism of Whitman, he takes a place near W. C. Williams, his language more textbooky but his procedures more open. Because his "idealism's as thin as the sprinkled / sky and nearly as expansive," one can move about freely in his sensibility; it is neither frost nor frolic. The appeal of this new, pulled-up Romanticism is its levelness, including the way it constantly levels with the reader. The cold hand of science has taken the fever out of this prophet's brow: he just chats intelligently, on and on, happy with the scheme of things, wanting you to be happy, too.

With his "most open suasion," his desire for an "open form" that offers "room enough for everything to find / its running self-concisions and expansions, its way," Ammons has created a new poetic structure: the poem as democratic continuum. Where Whitman's numbered sections are new breaths, new embraces, Ammons's are artificial overlays on a non-stop monologue that keeps pace with the "progressing / motions" of the universe. Random, flexible, this "Form of a Motion" will turn in mid-line from, say, the "plenitude of nothingness" among galaxies to the "neck-nicking walk" of pheasants, or the United Nations, or a visit with the poet Philip Booth—turn as amiably and unanxiously as the universe itself includes the microbe and the Milky Way, being an intermediary to all. With its "full freightages of recalcitrance," "Sphere" means to be a vision "gravid" with reality, a vision of the contrarieties and reconciliations of the very motions of being.

One of those modern poems that pose in front of a mirror, "Sphere" talks repeatedly about itself, betraying hopes that it fails to fulfill. It tells us we may "dip in anywhere," which is true, but also that "the poem reaches a stillness which is its form," which is true indeed of most poems, but not of poems that let you "dip in anywhere." The "mutual magnetisms" between the manifold elements of the poems are as weak as Ammons's idealism—weak as a direct consequence of the theoretical securities, the abstractness, of that idealism. The "harmony" . . . simply fails to appear. There is only the continuity of Ammons's language, its "flexible path," and the telling and retelling of his intellectual beads: *motion, multeity, diversity, form, nothingness, stayings, changes, radiality,* etc. And how could it be otherwise in a poet, so given to ratiocination, to explicit "suasion"? (p. 2)

Having sacrificed the dramatic, having dieted and professed his Romanticism, having drained off all but a wetting of the implicit, Ammons has left almost everything to his intelligence, the crispness of his language, the geniality of his tone, and the greatness of his subject, his *reasonable* approach to Romantic "spirituality." If the result is the "open" American counterpart of the closed Augustan verse essay—equally an *essay*—still in this reader's palm, at first weighing, it feels major. Though it has nothing of the feat about it it has scope, is original and blandly imposing. And to his linear discourse Ammons gives just enough "jangling dance" to shock "us to attend the moods of lips." Although almost nothing in the poem moves or ravishes, almost everything interests and holds—holds not least because it tests, and find thin, the spiritual satisfactions available in being a conscious part of a universe afloat in nothingness. The talk is not desperate but, by and large, is just talk. The subject is not really in Ammons as the kind of happiness that threatens to swell into a yelp or surf onto silence. But Romanticism has always been in trouble; dissatisfaction is its nature; Ammons is doing what he can. (p. 3)

Calvin Bedient, in The New York Times
Book Review *(© 1974 by The New York
Times Company; reprinted by permission),
December 22, 1974.*

Diversifications . . . gracefully extends [Ammons']ongoing
achievement. There are no new departures here, but there
are poems that join all but the heights of previous Ammons.
Consistently an Emersonian, Ammons writes in a ceaseless
dialectic of ethos or Fate struggling with pathos or Power,
and is triumphant in the sparse but wonderful syntheses of
Freedom that emerge in new poems like "Narrows," "Ballad," "The Unmirroring Peak," and most clearly in "Pray
Without Ceasing," the longer, incantatory poem that ends
the book with a chilled but assured comfort: "pray without
ceasing: / we found hailstones in the grass / and ate them to
cool: / spurred stones / with interior milkwhite halos, / an
arrested spangling: / the high hard water / melted / aching
our tongues." (pp. 24-5)

Harold Bloom, in The New Republic *(reprinted by permission of* The New Republic;
© 1975 by The New Republic, Inc.), November 29, 1975.*

In the poetry of A. R. Ammons water is thicker than blood.
He can devote a poem to the sinuous, sinewy course of a
stream, he conveys the various musical qualities of snow
melting from the roof and raindrops after a storm breaking
out "at a thousand quiet / points." Water, like spirit, can
stand for the real speech of nature, the expression the poet
wants to catch in his poetry. This fluidity resembles the
fluency of Ammons' best work: it flows, quick and slippery, or it meanders with broad sweeps till it moves to a
majestic estuary, joining with the limitless ocean.

The language of the poems floats the reader through Ammons' experiences though he is careful to suggest that
words are only traps and nets. Things are merely themselves. . . . But beyond the words is spirit, essence, the
sound of words, that music which "by the motion of / its
motion / resembles / what, moving, is." And motion announces life, the stretch and tension in and between things,
the polarities: "the poet, too, moving and / saying through
the scary opposites to death."

These references to water, motion and the relation of poetry to them are all brought into play at the end of his gossipy aesthetic credo, "Essay on Poetics," where Ammons
quotes a section from a scientific article on the life of an
estuary which emphasizes a kind of border region between
salt and fresh water: the creatures are subject to the dangers of changes upsetting the balance between salt and
fresh. Ammons sees that seething amphibious life with the
imminence of sudden catastrophe as beautiful. . . . (p. 92)

Such an approach to poetry certainly has its own risks and
possibilities. To look at all the diversities within nature, to
generalize a philosophy to embrace the one and the many,
to abstract thought from an observing eye that focusses
haphazardly, such a poetry can lose itself in mere reportage
of the wonders of nature or bog down in wordy philosophic
discussion. Yet Ammons can take a limitless focus (and his
poems, though they are finished, nearly always suggest an
openness, as if the poetic spirit could continue to fix on
other aspects of the subject he is writing about), indulge in
digression, simply because all the multeity of existence has
some place within his scheme of looking: "I think what I
see: the designs are there. I use / words to draw them out."
So there is an urge towards inclusiveness within a big po-

etic form in his poetry and, in a sense, to read through the
Collected Poems is to immerse oneself in one long rambling
discursive poem. Everything opens out—the book becomes
a large form in which the mind can travel around, and just
as a small creek changes, is diverted, flows fast and slow,
widens to reach out to the sea, so the impulse behind
Ammons' work is a continuing motion. For him, this urge
in his poetry is to establish a central radiance (one of his
favourite words) that shines at the centre beyond all this
fiddle with words and detail: "the progression is from
sound and motion to silence and / rest."

Such a poetic mission leads into all kinds of paradoxes: a
piling up of detail may simply offer detail and nothing else,
or it may lead to large abstractions, and it is difficult for the
poet to define what is central or irrelevant if the poetry tries
to include a mass of detail to stress diversity. It requires the
reader to allow himself to be taken into the poet's confidence, as he presents the designs he sees. . . . The poetry
becomes a mutual process of evolving from the poet's vision transformed into words that go two ways: defining and
"sailing over." That accounts for the unique tone of Ammons' language—the large abstractions side by side with
meticulous exactness of detail, the sudden lurches into colloquialisms to buttonhole the reader, and his conversations
with living things in nature. He speaks directly to trees and
mountains, to himself and to the reader. All is an ongoing
flux, a method that found its way into his first book-length
poem *Tape for the Turn of the Year,* in which Ammons
found an almost perfect method to allow his notion of organic form to function. . . . *Tape* is just such a poem; the
poet involved with his own life transfers that involvement
to the adding maching tape he has threaded into his typewriter, a tape he will continue to write on until it is finished.
So he transcribes his life, his ideas, his domesticities, his
chagrin at the unwritten life of the tape lying rolled and
untouched, cheating a little here and there, trying to find his
muse on dead days, reporting directly, until the reader is
caught within the process. . . . The *lived* poem will continue, so the mutual lives of poet and reader move on within
the poem and outside the poem. Ammons in this poem succeeds splendidly, and the fundamental image of time around
which the tape twines itself is a particularly effective one:
the turn of the year, the new evolving from the old as the
tape turns in the machine to unravel itself into a new poem.

No such wedding of form and content occurs in Ammons'
latest long poem, *Sphere: The Form of a Motion.* The
looseness that Ammons believes in derives here from the
use of a form the poet has tried before. . . . [It is] written in
three- or four-line stanzas, sometimes split into sections
containing three or four stanzas, though there seems to be
nothing definite about such paragraphing, running on as
they do indiscriminately, often with no periods. Breathing
space is provided by commas and colons only. Such a form
fits snugly into Ammons' concern with flux and motion,
and yet somehow the form seems too arbitrary. . . . Ammons has imposed a form but tried to free it from too rigorous a fixity, so that his usual digressions, his direct colloquialisms, his sudden switches into the common details of
his domestic life find a place within this form, stitched
within his generalizations about the one:many problem that
is at the root of his ideas. But this form does not have the
implicit rightness of *Tape;* its very looseness militates
against the idea of a kind of order within diversity that the
poem attempts to express. It does not give the sense of
being an inherent part of the idea itself, whereas in *Tape*
the form arises naturally within the process of the poem.

Right at the beginning of the poem Ammons sounds the theme of the cycles of creation, with death providing life for others, so that the polarities are an integral part of the process of living. (pp. 92-5)

Obviously such themes as energy and motion need the kind of open form Ammons has always attempted to find, but this one tends to straggle on, crossing over the boundaries of the stanzas, though no real unity comes across by means of the stanzaic pattern. But for the most part another structure manages to zipper the parts together. In each long ten- to twenty-stanza section, three items are repeated, so that a kind of parallelism operates.

Firstly, each section devotes itself to an idea which Ammons introduces by generalization or scientific precept. Secondly, he works the idea through by example. (pp. 95-6)

Each large section of the poem . . . coheres around some specific detail, and these, for me, are the memorable parts of the poem. . . .

By such a method does Ammons move the separate portions of the poem to unity, for each large section of the poem veers into these specifics from a main generalization or abstract thought. Besides these two parallelisms, a third reference crops up in each section, a reference to the question of poetry's place in the cosmic motion. (p. 96)

Obviously, all these parallels and interconnections make for an interesting poem, though those abstractions and the stanzaic sloppiness constantly distract the reader from this vision of an energetic and expansive universe mirrored in the poem itself. *Sphere* will not replace *Tape* as the definitive long Ammons poem, but then Ammons has no interest in being definitive. As a poet he will continue to risk as many of his own poetic possibilities as are inherent in the motions of poetry itself, and I, for one, will look forward to his next volume, watching him "lean in or with or against the ongoing." (p. 97)

> *Peter Stevens, "Risks and Possibilities: The Poetry of A. R. Ammons," in* The Ontario Review *(copyright © 1975 by* The Ontario Review*), Fall-Winter 1975-76, pp. 92-7.*

Two things appear to be gaining ground in poetry. One of these is a fascination with the use of ritual. The other attempts what Paul Léataud calls in his journals "writing well by writing badly". Both turn up together in the later sections of *Sphere*.

The two are opposed in many ways. Treated as techniques, one is a controlling device, the other (if it represents more than a paradox, and I think it does) is a way of moving away from control at least temporarily. (p. 352)

In the early sections of *Sphere* Ammons uses rituals that are close to domestic habits, the familiar work patterns of the writer, and what goes on about him. . . . In the later sections the movement of the poem follows the "jangling dance" by which "Enlil became a god and ruled / the sky . . .". The rituals are part of a ceremony with cosmic significance carried out on the earth floor among ruins: "I want my ruins sanctioned into the artifice of ruins . . .".

A ritual dance is nothing if not formally structured, but close to the section I have quoted Ammons takes up the second theme:

> . . . I don't know about you,
> but I'm sick of good poems, all those little rondures
> splendidly brought off, painted gourds on a shelf: give me
> the dumb, debilitated, nasty, and massive, if that's the
> alternative. . . .

In a certain mood of impatience I can imagine almost any reader saying "yes" to that. But, in the first place the statement begs an almighty question—what is this "good poem" we agree to damn (Ammons hardly gives us an identikit portrait of one). In the second place, we are being forced into an either/or situation that is neither good sense nor good rhetoric ("Do you want your meat burnt or raw?"—I can think immediately of better choices). (pp. 352-53)

The attempt to include everything and to write on through bad and good regardless until you "write right", brings up at once the question of form. The search for a kind of "formless form" that gives a setting for experience, ideas, etc., without displaying them as *nature morte*— . . . has been an obsession in almost all the arts in the past seventy years. It is the subject of several poems in Ammons's *Collected Poems: Summer Session . . . , Poetics, Essay on Poetics,* and, most subtly and effectively, *Corsons Inlet*.

But there is nothing hidden or disguised about the form in *Sphere,* and the rigidity makes for difficulties over and over again. . . .

There is another difficulty and that is the division of voices. Well over half the poem is written in the relaxed and casual voice of the poet as our familiar who ruminates over many things, most of them close to home. The ruminating is nothing if not low key. (p. 353)

Even the radical changes in *Collected Poems*—from high flying voice to lingo/vocative/colloquial, back to high flying voice again—do not prepare us for the voice of the *poeta-vate* who emerges in the later sections of *Sphere*. The Whitmanesque overtones are acknowledged and they result in passages that would be memorable in isolation—the complaint against the readers, the invitation to everyone to write poetry—but there are very obvious signs of strain and the transition from one voice to another is unnatural.

Problems of form and voice tend to emphasize something I find more disappointing than either, something I have touched on already. Certainly it is not the long, discursive, and philosophizing poem as such that I am judging, but the quality of thought in this particular poem. . . . Some of the longer poems in Ammons's *Collected Poems* are paradoxically fuller, as well as better realized, than *Sphere*. (p. 354)

> *Michael Mott, in* Poetry *(© 1976 by The Modern Poetry Association; reprinted by permission of the Editor of* Poetry*), March, 1976.*

[There is a] kind of nature poetry, rooted in times when most towns were small and many highly intellectual poets were rusticated for one reason or another, that has returned during this century in often rather baffling, footloose guise. Its shaping ritual is the walk, the climb, the trip, and the voyage, actions lending themselves all too easily to a vaporous abstraction.

A. R. Ammons began his career as the latter sort in full eclectic spate. The plot of his best poems of the Fifties and early Sixties before he started teaching at Cornell was largely a swift, sometimes brilliantly executed play of disjointed perceptions fleshing out a very private psychodrama. Charming and appealing digressions there were, to which I'll return. But the dominant voice seemed to have been sired on *The Duino Elegies* by an Emerson, a Dickinson transsexed, a Hopkins, Dylan Thomas, or Roethke— all the intoxicated solipsists of an age that requires such minds to fabricate their own plots, to expect little aid from tradition. Recently, though, with admirable recklessness and uneven results, he has been remaking himself closer to the Frost or Hardy model. Joining the academy just when its boom times were passing, assuming its by now well known and often dramatized responsibilities, he gave his existence a new visibility not unlike Frost's out there "north of Boston," a life gently freighted with old solemnities, not too far and not too near.

So much for the gains. Now the difficulties. Readers of his newest long poems, "Extremes and Moderations," "Essay on Poetics," "Hibernaculum," and especially *Sphere: The Form of a Motion*—a rambling, confiding, button-holing poem of 155 12-line sections—will know what they are. In *Sphere* Mr. Ammons makes a grand broken field run and a curious performance it is. To dodge about and reach a point not already plotted for him by one or more of the imposing exegetes lured to his earlier work by its obvious need for exegesis required some fancy footwork. You can think of Ammons as a sort of country-and-southern Prometheus nailed down on Cayuga Heights (above Ithaca!) by the Zeus of respectability, tormented by the eagle of higher criticism in the shape of Harold Bloom. Or, what seems more likely, you can detect in all his recent work clear notes of irreverence mixed with affection and amusement toward the gaudier theories of his friends. (pp. 49-50)

Ammons is cooler, more reflective, absorptive, and self-contained than [James] Dickey ever was and in him the Southeast may be making one last convulsive effort to put its message across; namely, that throughout its now expiring century of gothic, baroque, and neoclassical flamboyance it was secretly nurturing a middleness, an ordinary absolute center-cut Americanness, second to none. Faulkner's Ratliff and Horace Benbow suggested as much, so did the Faulknerian humor; but the message was ambiguous. *Sphere,* however, is not; it's an amiable but firm rejection of any highstrung ideologue's project for Ammons' apotheosis either as a sainted solitary or as a panurgic prophet of spiritual democracy. One must salute him for braving the pitfalls of such an operation—occasional forcings of tone, unwitting smugness, sententiousness, cuteness, *blague.* Denis Donoghue thinks he has isolated the problem by conceiving it to be formal, by accusing the poet of surrendering to an American mania for mere size, for imagining that a few dozen short poems strung end to end might make a qualitative leap into grandeur. But the fact that Ammons is keenly aware of such objections, has worked them into the poem, seems to indicate that he had no choice. The American atmosphere forced him into the optative mood— maybe these topics and digressions *would* make the orbicular leap, maybe if the poet's heart were pure enough a trip around his head *would* emerge as a mystic sphere. No choice in any case but to try.

Let me suppose for the rest of this review that a kind of intractable confusion may be the real entelechy, the formal and final end, of Dickey and Ammons who began so suavely and self-assured. And that we should make of it what we can and not waste time advising them to return and seek their lost innocence. Harold Bloom, always generous when his feelings are stirred, is prepared to call Am-

mons "great" but at the price of sternly reproving him for swerving from the path of Whitmanlike prophecy that his Emersonian instincts, again according to Bloom, fatally marked out for him. "Ammons has got to learn to be a different kind of poet than he was, and he is still in the process of learning that this different kind will return him to origins again, though with a more exacting music than he set out to bring into being." And why should he do this? Because he had early discovered a way to be transcendental and modern at the same time, by identifying the true American Sublime as the Void, by projecting the lyric pain of this discovery in a new species of Counter-Sublime. Like a man always seen going beautifully downhill. Which, Bloom finds, is quite in keeping with the "disastrous" times and makes Ammons the very latest of his cherished late-comers. The poems he chooses as the most telling expression of such counter-prophecy—"Corson's Inlet," "Saliences," "Gravelly Run," "Guide," "Bridge," "Peak," and the lovely passage in "Hibernaculum" that begins ". . . to lean belief the lean word comes, / each scope adjusted to the plausible:"—are the right poems for his thesis.

Still, one must pause to ask if in his zeal to consecrate only this high-tragical, philosophical Ammons Bloom may not be reserving too much drama to himself and making it too neat. There are facetious or whimsical notes in all but a very few poems that set us on our guard. Also many fine poems that don't cast so much as a glance at these elevations. Maybe Bloom should ask himself whether, if Emerson is the fountainhad of our poetry, we ought not to read as Emersonically as the sage's descendants write, with the same hospitality toward wide swings of mood and purpose, with the same dexterity in matching tone to technique, form to theme. (In formal variety Emerson's own poetry is as "romantically" unstable as Byron's. Sometimes he sounds like Plotinus arranged for a German village band, sometimes, as in the beautiful "Threnody" on the death of his son, like a pure-bred Metaphysical.)

My guess would be that it is neither Emerson nor Whitman (certainly not Whitman) that Ammons is currently undermining but a too portentous Idol of the Tribe called Poetry which, in some of its current academic investitures—subtlety piled on subtlety like the shawls of an Eastern princess —has become a real spook. Bloom is a great potentate who having been given an eloquent nightingale sends it out to be gilded and fitted with a clock-work larynx.

As a matter of act, Ammons' poems had already begun to group themselves into thematic clusters a good while before he began writing long poems in earnest. To my mind it's the interplay between these clusters that gives Ammons his chief vitality. (pp. 50-2)

Even Bloom acknowledges that this poet was never a naive visionary. Rather, a rueful, sportive, lyrical civil engineer, a musical geo-physician. Who would want to scuttle his prose sense of this transmogrifier of our prosiest disciplines, when he offers so novel a mixture of the contemplative and the suburban-saturnine, makes of "Extremes and Moderations" a pungent ecological fable, turns aside to tell us how to drain a swamp or dig a well, how to pick pears so the branches won't jerk the best ones out of reach, who above all is one of the most accomplished celebrators of the seasonal backyard drama since the great Alfred Lawn Tennyson himself? Rarely dropping his role as *homme moyen américain* Ammons can flourish a vocabulary of "saliences" and "suasions," motions, forces, and forms in mountain, wind, brook, and tree, with no missionary intent to substitute his vocabulary for ours. If he shaped his normally elegant style from examples of Williams, Marianne Moore, Dickinson, Cummings, Dickey, Roethke, or Merwin, he also aspires to their modesty.

Transplanted from the relative solitude of North Carolina to the goldfish prominence of Cornell, he issued a lowbrow poetics to balance the high, a Leopold Bloom to enliven the Harold. (pp. 53-4)

Diversifications features 65 new poems, most quite short, and two showpieces, "Three Travelogues" and the 19-page "Pray Without Ceasing." Its general effect is of the usual charm, of compactness, assurance, good-humored summary and mild second thoughts. Most of the poems seem thrown off in the intervals of harder work.... "Three Travelogues" is another handsome syncretic exercise in auto-intoxication out in the boondocks, pregnant with phrases like "a white-sailed cloud's blue hull of rain.".... It's too early to say much about "Pray Without Ceasing," a phantasmagoria or verbal happening wherein passages of characteristic eloquence or quiet elegance are answered by tormented newsreel episodes from the Vietnam war, with frantic doodling, demented witticisms, and grim premonitions. My shaky opinion is that he had very little new to say about the poem's ostensible subject, or else put thought aside and ruffed like a grouse, spread like a peacock or cobra. The time of mutation is not yet, not for him, not for us. (pp. 55-6)

> *R. W. Flint, "The Natural Man," in* Parnassus: Poetry in Review *(copyright © by Parnassus: Poetry in Review), Spring/Summer, 1976, pp. 49-56.*

Those who first became acquainted with the work of A. R. Ammons by reading his more recent poetry have probably been surprised by looking back to the early poems reprinted in his *Collected Poems: 1951-71*. A large number of the poems dated between the years 1951 and 1955 ... do not seem to be characteristic of his mature work. Ammons has set these poems in a grim, at times overtly Gothic, world of death, shame, grief, and unexplained loss, and he has centered them around gestures of mysterious impotence or failure. (p. 67)

The landscape that haunts these early poems is less Ammons' native rural South than it is the ancient Near East. It is the landscape of Sumerian mythology, to which these poems abound in reference. Its God is unapproachable, and its earth is one of dust, sand, wind, and desert. One feels that the landscape is burdened with a timelessness that is stifling to the creatures of time; in it, apocalyptic transformation, though yearned for, is inconceivable.... Ammons' early poems abound in examples of failed heroes and seers.

Ammons' lyric voice in his early poetry is that of a seer who has no social or individual characteristics but is instead a presence of more than ordinary awareness and longing. The seer, moreover, is one who has lost or never securely had a saving message or special revelation; one could say that he is the creation of a Christian sensibility which had lost its faith in the "good news" of the New Testament and had delved back into the eschatological pessimism of the older Jews and Sumerians. The poems begin as the seer enters their largely mythic landscapes, unlocated in place and historical time. They begin with statements that have biblical and visionary overtones, such as "I went out to the sun," "Turning from the waterhole I said Oh," "I came in a dark woods upon / an ineffaceable difference," or "I

came upon a plateau." The seer then moves through the mysteriously, often whimsically, often ominously changing landscape into encounters with gods or phantasmagora that are intentionally and suggestively indefinite. Though magically capable of extraordinary movement ("So I left and walked up into the air"), the seer is curiously unfree, damned to failure in an indeterminate quest ("How shall I / coming from these fields / water the fields of the earth / and I said Oh, / and fell down in the dust"), or to protracted wanderings, or to a quest for failure that ends without attainment of self-annihilation.... (pp. 68-9)

Ammons' early work ... seems to lie far afield from the poetry that leads immediately up to "Corson's Inlet" and then into his major long poems; it seems to have little to do with Ammons' reputation as an Emersonian "nature poet." Though the distance between the absoluteness of the early poems and the speculative liveliness of the later work is great, the change is by no means arbitrary. Ammons' achievement has been to relativize and multiply the absolute for the sake of imaginative survival and the promise of a nearly unlimited intellectual growth. He abandons the seer of the early poems for an astonishing variety of inventions of voices and personae, the variety of which becomes clear only as one surveys a large number of poems. Ammons humanizes the seer and gives him specific identities. Though Ammons compromises thereby the absoluteness of his visionary quest, though he absorbs more of the imperfect properties and knowledges of time, he is imaginatively freer within these limitations. He has consciously humbled himself to accept an object, imperfect earthly nature, for his now controlled but always resurgent longings.

In doing this, Ammons begins to expand his work in two directions. He brings it closer to the American commonplace, and he opens it to a broad eclecticism of knowledge and wisdom. He enters, in short, the mainstream of American visionary poetry. The poetry after *Ommateum* gradually reveals the extent of and the principal sources for Ammons' spiritual eclecticism. Behind the bulk of it (the only major exception being perhaps *Tape for the Turn of the Year*) lies a varied use of Greek thought, the Ionian nature philosophy that is the point of origin of Western science, and a personalized use of ideas and terminology that comes from Eastern thought, ultimately Laotse, named by Ammons as his "philosophical source in its most complete version." Most of Ammons' mature writings—in idea and strategy—are made up of his interweaving of these separate sources, and their union is like the union of compensatory opposites. Ammons' juxtaposition of intellectual speculations with his references to emptiness or the void, his virtuosic capacity to give precise though fluid form to idea and perception coupled with his repeated attainment, within the rapid flow of his verse, of moments of stillness or serenity reveal how he has united his two very different sources. (p. 70)

Most immediately striking in the poetry dated in the *Collected Poems* between 1956 and 1966 is the great variety of voices and lyric selves that Ammons has created. Sly or serious inquirer, chanter, celebrant, country skeptic, diarist, observer, reasoner: the speakers range in utterance from the formal, hortatory, or celebrative Whitmanian chanter of songs to the wry, ironic doubter of prophecy. Ammons often addresses the reader directly, rupturing the absoluteness of the early lyrics. Sometimes, he will address the reader's soul with Whitmanian urgency, and sometimes he will appeal to the reader's interests and sympathies in a breezily chatty manner. (p. 71)

Ammons' main interest, as it emerges from the variety of his middle poems, is in the realm of the changing in nature and its accessibility to the mind. Ammons discovers two complementary approaches to this theme. The most familiar is Ammons' remarkable ability to rationalize process into flowing order and to make it intelligible by means of the Ionian concepts of the one and the many. This is a realm of intellection at which Ammons is an unparalleled master. Ammons presents his "one" as ungraspable, not to be fully thought or experienced; he sees experience of it as a destruction of self. The world short of the one is the human realm. In it, Ammons exercises the full play of his mind; he brings the world of multiplicity into changing orders by means of an intellectual resourcefulness which is as fluid and undogmatic as natural process. It is not logical reasoning, but an underlying motion in the mind which parallels, precariously, the motions of things. (p. 72)

The less familiar strain in Ammons' poetry is a mode that is not of motion and the mind, but of an underlying receptivity in both the cosmos and man. Ammons sees this receptivity as something prior to identity or self; it is his version of Taoist emptiness or void. In the cosmos, the void contains process, and, in the person, the void is a cultivation of inner stillness and receptivity. . . . Ammons argues that the poem, as well as the self and cosmos, has an inner stillness and vacancy. It is a wholeness accessible even where the mind in motion fails to attain the one, rebuffed by the provisionality of its orders. It is the stillness against which the provisionality of motion has meaning and form. Ammons makes explicit the fact that these two modes coexist as parallels in his imagination in his poem "Two Motions."

The justifiably well-known poem "Corson's Inlet" integrates rather than juxtaposes, as does "Two Motions," these modes of imagination. The poet's active mind is no longer animated into motion by an external wind, but is completely in his possession, and it is fused with the full acceptance that "Overall is beyond me," an acceptance that, fully realized, yields "serenity." The poem is a walk and thus a mixture of the active and the passive, not a voyage or a nonvoyage, the opposing terms of "Two Motions." The fact that it is a casual walk, yet a walk for meditative discovery, locates it somewhere between the uniqueness and goal-directedness of a quest and a passive vacancy of receptivity to its surroundings. In a walk, one loiters and absorbs as much as one attempts to get anywhere; in a repeated, daily walk, this passive absorbtiveness is emphasized. Ammons' controlling idea in the poem is active. It is the mind's ever recrudescent and expanding capacity to "fasten into order enlarging grasps of disorder," to combat increasing entropy. (pp. 72-4)

The "freedom" of "Corson's Inlet" is the unfinished quality of nature and of vision. The poem balances subtlety in order with a maximum of possibility, and this balance of order and possiblity allows the experience of freedom. (pp. 74-5)

In *Tape for the Turn of the Year,* Ammons takes the wisdom of "Corson's Inlet" as far into the American commonplace as one could wish. A long, skinny poem, written on an adding machine tape that Ammons found at a home and garden supply store, it extends through several hundred pages and a five-week period of time his achievement of freedom within time, his precarious balance of continuum and surprise.

Ammons bases his *Tape* upon an affectionate parody of the *Odyssey.* He relocates the epic story to a diary-like account of his passage through a little over a month's time, and he breaks the voyage of Odysseus up into a series of internal and external side-trips or forays and encounters with daily eventualities or accidents. Like Odysseus, Ammons has a destination, a home he seeks; this is one of the main themes of the poem. With wonderfully disguised slyness, Ammons seeks another Ithaca, as he is waiting to hear about a job offer from Cornell University, Ithaca, New York. The theme of homecoming itself is, however, far more complex. The opening sections of the poem announce it as a story of "how / a man comes home / from haunted / lands and transformations" to an "acceptance of his place / and time." The poem thus becomes, in theme and in overall form, the attainment of a way of "going along with this / world as it is." Ammons' resources are those of "Corson's Inlet," active intellection and receptive wisdom; the goal of his quest can also be put in the terms of "Corson's Inlet" as the continuing and ever unfinished attainment of a partial humanization of nature and naturalization of the imagination. (p. 75)

The *Tape* is . . . set in the mid-world of "Corson's Inlet," a world whose visibility and clarity of form is rooted in the active knowledge of Greek philosophy and receptive wisdom of Taoism. Something that is specific to the *Tape,* however, is an expansion of Ammons' religious and philosophical eclecticism. More than in any other poem, save perhaps the most recent long poem, *Sphere,* Ammons suspends this mid-world in darkness, a darkness out of which the clarity of fact emerges with the same attained sweetness as invests the "natural light" attained at the end of the atypical poem "Bridge." (pp. 76-7)

The *Tape* is Ammons' essential poem of America. Whereas some of the poems prior to "Corson's Inlet" echo Whitman's mode directly and with remarkable success, the *Tape* is both highly personalized and rich in indirect echoes. Ammons writes it as a song of myself, a self, however, empiricized and provincialized. Though the poet remains the representative man and the poem is a poem of America, the poet and poem attain this status through their provinciality and smallness or homeliness of delineation. (p. 79)

Ammons' long poems since *Tape for the Turn of the Year* —the major ones are "Essay on Poetics," "Extremes and Moderations," "Hibernaculum," and the book-length poem *Sphere: The Form of a Motion* and a comparatively minor, but sheerly delightful one is "Summer Session"— make use of the continuous form of the *Tape,* but alter its import and effect in a number of ways. (p. 80)

Ammons' change in mode signifies an important development away from the *Tape;* it is a slight push away from his former attempt to naturalize the imagination and toward an attempt to assert the autonomous freedom of the imagination. Ammons explicitly avoids a complete liberation from nature, however; the distinction is an important and subtle one. At one point, early in the poem, Ammons writes "what this is about," the "'gathering / in the sky' so to speak, the trove of mind, tested / experience, the only place to stay . . . the holy bundle of / the elements of civilization, the Sumerians said." This "gathering in the sky" is akin to the Heavenly City and the ungrasped Overall of Ammons' earlier poems, though it is now no longer a destruction. It is "impossibly difficult"; it is an ideal that guides human action, inaccessible, nonexistent in a literal sense, but nevertheless an ideal to be striven for. (pp. 80-1)

[In "Essay on Poetics"] Ammons builds a model of the ideal poem which serves as the "symbolical representation of the ideal organization, whether / the cell, the body politic, the business, the religious / group, the university, computer, or whatever." "Ideal" means a level of abstraction from nature and not what constitutes nature; as an ideal, it is something nonexistent but which guides human striving.

To understand just how poetry forms a model for the ideal organization necessitates some reference to the controlling image for the "Essay," an image that comes from the field of cybernetics. Ammons' new form of conceptualization and thus partial humanization of nature involves transforming nature into information bits: this transformation means first an act of abstraction and second a kinetic act of relation of the parts. Ammons reworks the model of order and entropy he used in "Corson's Inlet" into the model of cybernetics. It is a cooler and a higher-speed model, and this determines a change in the tone of the verse. Interpreting physical processes now in terms of conceptual processes, rather than in terms of "laws of nature" which are prior to and perhaps antagonistic to those that govern mental processes, Ammons has made a subtle change in both the mode and the vision of his poetry. His abstraction of reality into information-bits is precarious, and "language must / not violate the bit, event, percept, / fact—the concrete—otherwise the separation that means / the death of language shows"; how precarious this is, and how impotent we are to control the processes consciously, is illustrated by Ammons' meditation on the word "true." The word "true," related etymologically to "tree" and therefore the elm tree of the essay, itself physically composed of more "bits" than the mind can handle, is shown to contain greater resonance and rootage of meaning than a logical mind can comprehend. Not in logic then, but only in poetry, a medium capable of dealing with greater complexity in motion, is abstraction possible. To accomplish this end, poetry has, for one thing, the capacity for illusion, as it can heighten "by dismissing reality." Once the bits are abstracted, they are immediately, as a part of that abstraction, brought into relational motion: both speed in motion and intellectual virtuosity are essential, as one can see from Ammons' stunning printout of variations on William Carlos Williams' "no ideas but in things." If Ammons should stop on any word, "language gives way; / melting through, and reality's cold murky waters / accept the failure." Just as computers in action retain information by rapid electronic circulation of it, so Ammons' verse retains its meaning in its mobility. (pp. 82-3)

The ideal is a maximum of unity without distortion or suppression of any of the bits. Poetry is the highest model: it has resources beyond those of computers. (p. 83)

We are back again in Greece and China in the long poems in *Collected Poems,* the themes of which are intellection and the quieting or giving up that represents wisdom. A familiar technique of the "Essay" and of the later poems generally is something that echoes classic American silent films. Ammons will multiply information, pour more into the poem than a rational analysis is capable of, will then, if an explosion of nonsense is not the result, recover himself with a gesture of giving up that returns the mind, suddenly, to integration. After multiplying the considerations that make it impossible to ever determine the location of the elm in his backyard, let alone say anything about its inner structure, Ammons falls back into a wonderful self-recovery that also recovers the wholeness of the elm:

I am just going to take it for granted
that the tree is in my backyard:
it's necessary to be quiet in the hands of the marvelous:
(pp. 83-4)

Frederick Buell, "'To Be Quiet in the Hands of the Marvelous': The Poetry of A. R. Ammons," in The Iowa Review *(copyright © 1977, by The University of Iowa), Winter, 1977, pp. 67-84.*

* * *

ANDRIĆ, Ivo   1892-1975

A Serbian novelist, short story writer, and poet, Andrić is usually described as an epic novelist whose principal themes are fear and human isolation. A skilled craftsman and excellent storyteller, he writes in a lyrical, poetic style about his native region, endowing it with universal significance. In a world where the individual is dominated by historical forces, Andrić sees the enduring beauty of art as man's sole consolation. He was awarded the Nobel Prize for Literature in 1961. (See also Contemporary Authors, **obituary, Vols. 57-60.)**

While the subject of all three [novels in the Bosnian trilogy] are the people of Bosnia, *Bosnian Chronicle* delves deepest into those elements of the turbulent Bosnian heritage which give it its unique ethnic and spiritual flavor. This is the territory—roughly the size of West Virginia—which has been the contending ground of Eastern and Western cultures for almost two thousand years. . . .

This, then, is the tortured, flamboyant tapestry of Andrić's stories—stories in which Bosnian men and women live their perilous and extraordinary lives amid oppression and cruelty, ever haunted by visions of freedom and human dignity which history has dangled before them but has been painfully slow to deliver. (p. v)

The main themes of Ivo Andrić's writing—causative interplay of guilt and human suffering, the individual versus tyranny, the warping of men's destinies through historic circumstance—which are explored singly in some of his stories, are woven in *Bosnian Chronicle* into a harmonious whole. The elegiac mood of his early poetry, the preoccupation with personal sin as an agent of general evil, which marks his longer stories written between the wars, are transmuted here into a relentless, many-leveled scrutiny of the character, psychology, and moral sap of a whole people. What is the truth behind the harshness of Bosnian life and its tormented heritage, how real is that audible and visible melancholy which the Austrian Colonel von Mitterer, in *Bosnian Chronicle,* speciously calls *Urjammer*—ancient misery? Why, as a discerning Yugoslav critic has asked, is "everything weighed down by some heavy and sinister burden, as if paying back who knows what kind of ancient and eternal debt"?

For his answer Andrić turns to the past, and his quest is absorbing and illuminating. The act is neither escapism nor a deliberate turning back on the modern world, but a clear-eyed, unsentimental pursuit of durable values and pertinent atavistic wisdom. It is the method of a compassionate researcher who knows that much of the truth of an individual and his group lies locked in his antecedents and must be dredged up for the sake of the total truth. So his answers are neither pat nor necessarily flattering to his subject.

The past, like the present, is ridden with guilt and evil, individual as well as communal, but it also yields a residue of good. Long centuries of oppression have forced the Bosnian character to grow like a stubborn plant in one of the country's mountain passes, close to the ground and bending with the wind. But there is also a hard core of patrimony that shows through, a hardy perennial undergrowth which no wars, tyranny, or brutalities could trample out of existence. In that patrimony, heroism, nobility, and greatness of heart exist side by side with moral turpitude and coarseness. Enduring values are handed down through generations and become a distinctive heritage. And all of it together, in Andrić's special amalgam of storytelling and large-scale canvas, makes for powerful, often shocking, but always fascinating and engrossing reading. (pp. vii–viii)

> *Joseph Hitrec, "Translator's Note," in* Bosnian Chronicle *by Ivo Andrić (copyright © 1963 by Alfred A. Knopf; reprinted by permission of Alfred A. Knopf, Inc.), Knopf, 1963, pp. v–viii.*

[The] main theme in all three novels [of Andrić's 'Bosnian Trilogy'] is human isolation. For Andrić man, set against the vast panorama of history, is insignificant—fearful of external disaster and inwardly aware of his own insecurity in a world where everything is ephemeral, however much he may long for constancy. The particular history of old Turkish Bosnia, with its despotism and violence, thus portrays the broader theme of man's tragic struggle against the oncoming darkness of change and death. Against this Andrić sets man's creativity, as in the Muslim view of the symbolic meaning of that bridge on the Drina, which sees it as a work of lasting beauty, bridging the gulf of change. And it is because she resolutely suppresses love, creativity and spiritual awareness in her relentless pursuit of purely material wealth that Raika, the woman from Sarajevo who lived in lonely isolation in Belgrade, is such a tragic figure. (p. 69)

> *Konstantin Bazarov, in* Books and Bookmen *(© copyright Konstantin Bazarov 1974), November, 1974.*

Before assessing the extent to which the description of *Travnik Chronicle* as a clash of two cultures from opposed worlds in a world which is alien to them both may be considered justifiable, it is necessary to state the ambiguity contained in this description of the novel. In the first place, the 'two cultures from opposed worlds' may be interpreted as the cultures of France and Austria, drawn into opposition through their conflicting national aspirations which eventually lead them into political, military, and diplomatic conflict and the clash recreated in the novel by the public antagonism between the [French and Austrian] consulates. . . . It is evident that there are two clashes from opposed worlds in *Travnik Chronicle*, one within the 'West', the other between the 'West' and the 'East'. These two clashes, however, should not be viewed as conflicting features of the novel since they are fundamentally associated by virtue of the fact that together they recreate the historical circumstances in which the novel is set. As such, these clashes may be considered to be historically mutually complementary. It is not necessary to argue for or against either of these clashes in order to determine which clash is the more adequate description of the novel, for they represent the two halves of an historical whole: that is, the two major aspects of the historical condition of Bosnia in the first two decades of the nineteenth century. Rather, it will be more rewarding to determine the extent to which a description of *Travnik Chronicle* purely in terms of historical circum-

stances may be considered justifiable; that is, whether *Travnik Chronicle* may be reasonably described as the re-creation of these clashes, as an historical novel in which the author lays the major emphasis upon conformity of plot and character to historical condition. Owing to the assumption, perhaps because of the novel's title, that Andrić's intention is purely the recreation of Bosnia's historical condition in the early nineteenth century, the novel has been evaluated almost entirely in terms of how accurately and truthfully Andrić has depicted this condition. . . . [Evaluations] of Andrić's purpose and his ability as a novelist, 'the historical novelist', are insensitive and unjust, for the recreation of historical circumstances, of the opposed worlds, and the depiction of Bosnia are not ends in themselves but the means whereby Andrić treats of more fundamental prescriptive and philosophical questions. (pp. 830–31)

The clash between the French and Austrian consulates, drawn into conflict by the interests of the governments they represent, forms a framework within which much of the subject matter of the novel is concentrated. The struggle between the consuls, Daville on the one hand and von Mitterer and eventually his successor von Paulich on the other, to win the attentions and favours of the resident vizier, their conflicting exultations at the successes of their national armies and their battle to win the support or at least the neutrality of the hostile natives of Travnik, are clashes which are waged throughout the novel. (p. 831)

'In fact, it was only the aims of their official work which differed; everything else was identical or similar'. Thus, underlying the clash from opposed worlds which determines the public conflict between the consuls, there is the level of the individual, private world in which the similarities of the two men's plights far outweigh their ostensible differences. It is evident that there is not only a clash between the public opposed worlds, but also that there is a clash between the public image and the individual world of the two consuls. Andrić shows at length how the conflict in the public world prevents a realization of the similarities which exist in the private world. These, then, are the two faces of reality in *Travnik Chronicle*. At the consuls' very first meeting, where their official status represents the 'two cultures from opposed worlds', Andrić exposes the dualism which will exist throughout the novel. When they meet '. . . only the lingering sense of duty and propriety kept them from patting each other on the shoulder, as any two sensible men might have done in their common plight'. . . . The public world, or historical circumstance, over which men have no control is seen clearly to condition the frustration of the individual world and no matter how pronounced the parallels in the individual world, the public image, conditioned itself by historical circumstance, will finally override them. For Andrić, the consuls are 'predestined to be rivals' (or opponents—*suparnici*), a fact which is all the more tragic since the reader is shown a whole array of areas in which the two men might have grown in understanding of each other. The clash between the French and Austrian consulates is, therefore, an indispensable aspect of the novel for it provides a public image to which the individual, private world may be contrasted. (p. 832)

The dichotomy between the public and the private worlds permeates much of the experience of characters in the novel who find that their public face, their official duty, is concerned with the clash of the opposed worlds of France and Austria. That Andrić is in this respect making a philosophical point about the way in which he perceives life may be illustrated by the way in which he expresses this dualism of the human world. It is no coincidence that such expressions are most frequently found in the early stages of the novel, for in this way Andrić hopes to preclude any interpretation of the novel purely in terms of the public and historical world. . . . Clearly Andrić sees the private personal world of men as the only means of evaluating their lives. . . . [The] most significant personal conflict is that between Daville and des Fossés. The lack of communication between these two Frenchmen is a particular but outstanding feature of the novel. . . . Daville and des Fossés have fundamentally different perceptions of the public world. . . . Des Fossés perceives the public world which, in the context of the novel, means the clash between France and Austria, as essentially futile. . . . Daville believes that the public world is of significance, yet as he grows older and wearier, a gradual disillusionment sets in. . . . Here, then, is another clash within the novel, between, in Andrić's words, the 'two different worlds of Daville and des Fossés'. The des Fossés world of the new generation, which chose to 'live life' and was not interested in 'Daville's world of ideas', and the Daville world of romanticism and idealism. Like the clashes in the public world, these in the private world are also created ironically by Andrić, for despite the differences between them, Daville and des Fossés have much in common. (pp. 832-33)

Like the clash between the French and Austrian consulates, the clash between West and East provides the basic framework within which much of the subject matter of the novel is treated. This clash, however, leads the reader to an understanding of the frustrations of the native population of Bosnia, whereas the former clash leads the reader to an understanding of the conflicts and parallels between the 'foreigners' in Bosnia. The clash between West and East, between Christian and Moslem, is expressed most philosophically by the inhabitants of Travnik, who have been subjected to the battle between the Christian and the Moslem worlds since the fourteenth century. Thus, it is Cologna, 'who dresses in a weird assortment of Turkish and European garments', symbolizing Bosnia crucified between East and West, who tells des Fossés of the meaning and significance of the historical conflict between the East and the West for Bosnia. . . . Cologna is a man who perceives the damage and the futility of the clash of opposed worlds, the man who 'amazes' des Fossés and who, by the end of the next chapter (Sixteen), is dead. . . . In the narrative we can see the brilliance of Andrić's use of circumstantial irony: the man who is best equipped to heal the split between West and East (symbolized by his conversation with des Fossés and by his clothing and willingness to change faiths in order to protect human life) and between the French and the Austrians (symbolized by Daville's use of him to convey the letter which will bring the consulates back into communication with each other) has his own life cut short by the public, historical opposition of worlds. (p. 834)

Andrić presents the major character of Mehmed Pasha's entourage, Tahir Beg, to form yet another parallel between the Residency and the consulates. Tahir Beg is 'the brains' of the Residency, just as in many respects d'Avenat and de Rotta are in a sense 'the brains' of the French and Austrian consulates respectively. Furthermore, Tahir Beg suffers from a permanent wound on his left side 'which closed and re-opened several times a year', and it is known that de Rotta is hunchbacked. All three men, Tahir Beg, d'Avenat, and de Rotta have obscure or questionable origins. There

are, thus, parallels between the West and the East in the individual world established by Andrić's symbolic use of physical degeneration to indicate mental decay. The climax of the author's use of physical abnormalities to convey mental perversion is reached at an official, public meeting of the vizier with the two consuls and the Begs when 'a great heap of severed human ears and noses began to grow on the mat—an indescribable heap of wretched human flesh, salted and blackened by its own dried blood'. . . . Andrić uses this scene also to convey the split between the public and the private worlds. (pp. 835-36)

Andrić's emphasis lies with the consequences of the clashes caused by historical circumstances rather than with historical facts proper. Through a consideration of the way in which the opposed worlds and historical circumstances condition *all* men's lives, Andrić makes philosophical suggestions about all humanity within a framework which is necessarily realistic, set at a specific time in history. Philosophical and prescriptive arguments in scientific dissertations make only philosophical and prescriptive points, but philosophical suggestions within a realistic context, showing how these points are arrived at in human terms, make pointers for the whole of humanity. This is the basis of Andrić's talent. . . . [Although] insufficient as a description of the novel, 'the clash of cultures from opposed worlds' and historical circumstances is an indispensable aspect of *Travnik Chronicle,* for without it, Andrić has no realistic context and thus no grounds for argument. We may not agree with Andrić's opinion that men have little control over their public lives and the circumstances which condition their activity, but in *Travnik Chronicle* Andrić is consistent in every intricate detail which stems from such a belief. It is this fact which makes the novel frighteningly convincing, as the implications concern all humanity, East or West, French or Austrian. That all we truly have, 'the final tally of good and evil in our existence' stems from our own isolated individual and personal world is made crystal clear throughout the narrative. (p. 836)

Von Mitterer, the Austrian consul, is replaced by the younger von Paulich. The characterization of this man provides a useful clue to Andrić's attitude towards the public world, and thus towards the novel itself. Von Paulich's voice is dry and factual. He functions like a disinterested higher spirit or like unfeeling Nature herself. 'That whole, unusually handsome man moved and lived as though in some cold armour, behind which all trace of personal life or human weaknesses and needs was lost'. . . . He is representative of the automaton, utilized to work in the official capacity of Austrian consul. Implicitly von Paulich has no personal life, no individual or private world; he is utterly without emotion. He is, for this reason, the man best equipped to cope with the public world and the author senses that by creating such a character he is in no danger of the reader sympathizing with his character and thus indirectly with the public historical world which is the root of the frustration in human life, the barrier which prevents human beings from coming to an understanding of each other.

At the opposite extreme, Andrić portrays a man who has no significant public life, a monk who is characterized entirely in terms of his 'private, individual world', Fra Luka. . . . Fra Luka is, however, a pitiful eccentric who wastes time chasing mice and spends his whole life in the adventures of self-will. He is also the only character in the novel who could be called 'happy' in all senses of the word.

Andrić's implication is that in order to discover real happiness, humanity has to cut itself off from the public world over which it has no control. (p. 837)

No matter whether East or West, French, Austrian, or Turkish, all the 'roads' for Andrić are essentially the same. From this, implications for all humanity can be drawn, as Daville attempts to do in the latter states of the novel. His words are not about 'opposed worlds' or 'alien lands', they are about the 'common course of all humanity'; its fundamental similarities rather than its superficial differences.

> And playing over this humble, mechanical chore was a vague but obstinate thought, like a recurring tune: that somewhere out there the 'right road', the one he had sought all his life in vain, must nevertheless exist. And not only did it exist, but sooner or later someone was bound to stumble on it and throw it open to all men. He himself had no idea how, when or where, but it was sure to be found sometime, perhaps in his children's time, or by his children's children, or by a generation yet to come. . . .

This then is our consolation, for Daville 'the soundless inward melody that lightens his work'. (p. 838)

> *Alan Ferguson, "Public and Private Worlds in 'Travnik Chronicle'," in* Modern Language Review, *October, 1975, pp. 830-38.*

*   *   *

ANOUILH, Jean   1910-

A leading French dramatist, Anouilh has also written screenplays and worked as an editor and translator. He has divided his plays into several categories: the *pièces noires* ("black plays"), presenting evil as the triumphant force in life, and the *pièces roses* ("rosy plays"), presenting the triumph of good, are two of these categories. To Anouilh, the *pièces noires* and *pièces roses* correspond to the genres of tragedy and comedy. Two other categories used by Anouilh to describe his plays are the *pièces brillantes* ("brilliant plays") and the *pièces grinçantes* ("annoying plays"). Drawing from historical sources, including Greek, French, and English, Anouilh has created for the modern theatre, in a modern idiom, works such as *Antigone*, *L'Allouette* (a drama based on the life of Joan of Arc), and *Beckett*, which have become masterpieces of the modern theatre. (See also *CLC*, Vols. 1, 3, and *Contemporary Authors*, Vols. 17-20, rev. ed.)

Anouilh is a psychological dramatist, although not in the modern pseudoscientific sense; he is also the chief contemporary exponent of tragedy in the drama. Most of his tragedies are based on classic themes; they are simultaneously a modern expression of the Aristotelean tragic principle and a sensitive approach to the portrayal of psychological processes.

To Anouilh humanity is made up of two kinds of people: the anonymous mass of normal and rational nonentities who accept the banality of daily existence, and the heroes. The first group is motivated chiefly by a desire for happiness, not the ecstasy of the saint but the *petit bonheur* of the unambitious. This is the race which populates the earth and performs the daily drudgery which is the price of human existence. . . . (p. 331)

The second group rejects this banality. Where the ordinary man realizes the imperfection of the human lot but nevertheless grasps at the petty happiness that is offered him, the hero has the courage to say "no." It is this second race which supplies the world with saints, martyrs, Caesars, artists, assassins, prophets, and above all with tragic heroes; for the man who refuses to say "yes" to life thereby condemns himself to a tragic end. These are "those you imagine stretched out, pale, a red hole in the forehead, a moment triumphant with a guard of honor, or between two gendarmes. . . ." It is not that the hero deliberately chooses this path; he is condemned to it by the nature of his personality. He can no more escape tragedy than the ordinary man can escape banality. The ordinary man and the hero belong to different species, and they are condemned to perpetual misunderstanding, suspicion, and enmity; human existence is an eternal struggle between heroism and happiness. Out of this antithesis Anouilh fashions his dramatic conflict. It is significant that he includes all his Greek plays in the two collections he entitles "pièces noires"; to him classic mythology is indissolubly linked with tragedy and death.

In Anouilh's first *pièce noire, Eurydice* (1941), it is Orpheus who assumes the role of nay-sayer and chooses death for himself and Eurydice rather than compromise with banality. This is not the ordinary classic interpretation of the myth, nor is it the interpretation put upon it by most modern dramatists; yet it preserves the essence of the classic myth: a man and a woman are separated by death, the man defies Death itself to win her back, but loses her when he cannot resist the temptation to gaze straight into her soul. (pp. 331-32)

[Orpheus] prefers no life at all to a life which demands compromise as its price. . . .

Antigone (1942) treats the same basic theme, but utilizes a different technique. Like most other modern Antigone plays, it is based on Sophocles; the period and décor remain that of classic Greece. But there is an anachronistic, modern element which serves to give the action an aura of timelessness. The drama is played in modern dress; Creon wears evening clothes, and the palace guards wear battle-jackets and carry automatic rifles. Such incidental anachronisms aside, the plot roughly follows Sophocles. (p. 333)

Like *Antigone, Médée* (1946) is laid in an ostensibly classic setting modified with modern details and vernacular. The story follows Euripides' *Medea;* the major change in plot is that Anouilh's Medea dies at the end of the play to provide a more spectacular climax. Some of Anouilh's anachronisms are startling: Medea is converted to something like a gypsy who travels about in a ramshackle caravan and is forbidden entrance to the local village. . . . The celebration which marks the betrothal of Jason and Creusa is a good deal more like a Bastille Day than a pagan orgy; there are street dances, music, fried-food stalls, free wine, and a fireworks display as a climax. Medea's nurse is converted into a garrulous old French peasant, with a rough peasant craft and a healthy zest for living. . . . Thus Anouilh reclothes his characters for the modern audience: the sorceress of Colchis becomes a pseudo-gypsy and her nurse a rustic gossip out of Balzac.

But Anouilh's Medea, like Orpheus and Antigone, is a heroic personality who moves in a realm apart from the rest of mankind. Her dominating passion is her love for Jason; for him she stole from her father and killed her brother, for him she committed all the other bloody crimes for which she is now treated as a pariah. To Medea this love is an absolute passion; it admits of no limits, and no other considerations have the slightest influence on her actions. When this love is betrayed there is no resignation in her heart to fill the vacuum, and she can think only of blood, revenge, and death. After thus establishing Medea as a Dionysian, virtually psychotic character, Anouilh then creates Apollonian foils to throw the character Medea into relief. Jason and his father-in-law Creon, and to some extent the nurse, are reasonable beings who have accepted the imperfections of existence; they have said "yes" to life where Medea has said no. (p. 334)

The essence of tragedy as it was understood by the ancients was that a noble hero came to his downfall through an inherent fault in his character; usually this flaw consisted of an excessive fervor or self-confidence. When the classic tragedy demonstrates that *hybris* brings its inevitable *nemesis,* it is merely reiterating that the Dionysian personality carries within itself the seeds of its own catastrophe. This is precisely the nature of the catastrophe which arrives to the heroes of Jean Anouilh: fanatic idealists who will accept no compromise, they come to destruction because they are born into a world in which compromise is the price of existence. Most of the other tragic heroes of modern drama are not tragic in this sense; they are destroyed only because they could not achieve their ends. Anouilh passes beyond this modern pseudo-tragedy to arrive at the essence of the tragic situation, and his technique proves itself in the unmistakable emotion of *katharsis* the spectator feels at his plays.

Anouilh himself distinguishes between true tragedy and catastrophic melodrama in a curious passage he inserts into the middle of Antigone. While Creon muses over the mysterious burial of Polynices, the chorus comes forward and analyses the situation with a remarkable scholarly detachment. "It's nice, the tragedy. It's calm, restful. In the melodrama, with those traitors, those desperate villains, that persecuted innocence, those avengers, those Saint Bernards, those glimmers of hope, it's horrible to die, almost by accident as it were. You might have escaped, the good young man might have arrived in time with the gendarmes. In the tragedy you can relax. In the first place, you're at home—after all, everyone's innocent! It isn't that there is someone who kills and someone who is killed. It's just a question of arrangement. And then, most of all, the tragedy is calm because you know there's no hope, no dirty hope; you're caught, you're caught after all like a rat, it's all on your shoulders, and all you can do is cry out—not groan, no, not complain—to bawl at the top of your voice what you have to say."

Tragedy should speak to us, as it spoke to the Greeks, as a living and contemporary human drama; the action should appear to involve persons like ourselves who are seen in predicaments we can understand. If this feeling of timelessness is not present, if we feel we are viewing a "historical" drama, we cannot believe the tragedy is our tragedy, and the drama degenerates into mere spectacle. Anouilh's dramas, written in modern vernacular and filled with the objects and figures of our own daily life, achieve a universality in time which would be impossible in a mere sterile imitation of the external apparatus of classicism. (pp. 334-35)

> *Donald Heiney, "Jean Anouilh: The Revival of Tragedy," in* College English *(copyright © 1955 by the National Council of Teachers of English; reprinted by permis-*
> *sion of the National Council of Teachers of English), Vol. 16, No. 6, March, 1955, pp. 331-35.*

[Of] all the playwrights . . . in our modern times, Anouilh has the surest sense of the stage. His skill is breathtaking, and one cannot withhold admiration. Within the bounds of the genre—fantastic comedy—I know of nothing more accomplished in range and dramatic skill than the first act of *Léocadia (Time Remembered);* and that skill is evidenced even in the difference which exists between the reading and the stage effect of the play. Owing to the fact that the old Duchess, a key character in the play, has to unfold at the beginning the elements of the plot which make the play plausible, the reading might be a trifle slow, but with the characters on the stage this first act becomes a bewildering display of moods in the course of which the audience is tossed about between fantasy, amazement, wild laughter and sheer pathos at the extravagant love of the old Duchess for her nephew or at the plight of young Amanda having landed in what undeniably looks like a mad-house.

Of course, Anouilh's theatrical skill is widely recognized, and people fall back for denigration on questions of ethics and generally end in describing him as a nihilist, a pessimist, or, even worse, an amoralist. These strictures may have some validity if his characters are judged not from the auditorium but from the study or the drawing-room. It is true indeed that Antigone is a thorough nihilist, a little girl obsessed with the idea of death. . . . [However, the] nihilism of Antigone or of Eurydice is more symbolic than realistic; it is more the expression of a belief or an attitude towards life than an attempt at projecting life objectively on the stage. Besides that, Antigone has an element of topicality or of historical truth which cannot be dissociated from the characters and the actions of the play. But for the rest, for amoralism and promiscuity, these things exist, and our problem is surely not to condemn them as aspects of behaviour which we regret in life but as elements which are part of a dramatic picture meant to produce, through acceptance or rejection of what happens on the stage, a rewarding aesthetic experience. (pp. 170-71)

There are plays, and they are not the best or the greatest, in which the didactic or the moralizing elements are explicit; they illustrate beliefs or ideas passionately held. As far as one can see, Anouilh holds no religious or philosophical belief which he tries to put forward in his theatre. His plays are not, like Sartre's, above all a means to illustrate certain beliefs; they are rather the direct projection of his amused, detached or aggrieved observation of the comic or sad human saraband which is life. The morality is part of the aesthetic experience. (p. 174)

Anouilh does not opt for non-being, since he starts from being in the world, but it is obvious that the purity of which he dreams is not of this world and that death and silence are the only possible aims of anybody longing for ideals so opposed to life. Death, of course, becomes for him not another aspect of Being, but non-being or a kind of ideal Platonic world in which only purity exists and in which the particulars, categories or universals regain the transcendence and immutable fixity of ideas. (p. 175)

One might feel that by now Anouilh has overstated or is labouring his theme; yet it is obvious that there is at the very core of his dramatic work a real experience of soiled idealism and of absurd cruelty imposed by life on purity, and it is that experience which confers imaginative truth upon his attractive or repulsive characters. . . . By now the dream of disillusionment threatens to become a stifling nightmare, the mocking wit, the brilliant satire of the early plays seem to be tapering off into sheer savagery, as in *Ardèle, Colombe* or *La Valse des Toréadors,* and one might at times feel inclined to repress a polite yawn or a sigh of impatience at the prolonged family resemblance of his characters; yet one could never say that he has lost his humanity or that his dramatic skill has degenerated into mechanicalness. Admittedly, the machinery is at times slightly shrill, as in *Colombe* or *La Valse des Toréadors,* yet in spite of that, the old General's plight and his desperate attempts to find a way out of his limitations remain very real, and so does the broken happiness of the two lovers in *Colombe.* (pp. 175-76)

The pessimism of Anouilh is . . . the revolt of a sensitive being appalled and wounded by the cruelty of life and expressing man's despair at never being able to know his true self or to meet another self in a state of purity. . . . His heroes and heroines are alone, and when they hope to escape from their loneliness through another they generally realize that there is no escape, that life soils everything and that unless they choose to live a lie, death is the only solution—or failing death, the acceptance of suffering as a refining fire which will consume the dross into the ashes of a life devoted to an ideal. (pp. 176-77)

The degradation of being without money and of being compelled to reckon all aspects of human life and above all of human happiness in terms of money is what seems to haunt Anouilh's early dramatic career and is the theme of his early plays. (p. 177)

It is obvious that Anouilh can blend fantasy and realism with perfect skill and can easily transport us into realms where anything can happen. . . . He lacks [, however,] the depth of vision and the imagination to realize that the tragic character, the hero or the being who embodies myth, is something essentialized and something which cannot be entangled in a trivial form of petty, homely realism which must not be confused with tragic irony or the grotesque element. . . . (p. 192)

Anouilh excels in fantastic comedy, a genre which enables him to give free rein to his inventiveness. He is never hampered by realism, which he uses skilfully in order to build up character. Whenever necessary, as in *Le Voyageur sans Bagage* or *La Valse des Toréadors,* he brings about an ending merely to fit the characters, in the same way as Molière did at the end of *Tartuffe* when he brought in the king's power. He is keenly aware that the theatre is not a photograph of life or a place to display pedestrian realism, but a place where, behind the footlights, conventions preside and acting is what counts. His characters, his main ones at least, are both real and unreal, sophisticated *personae* or masks standing for certain human traits and miserable wretches plagued with all the weaknesses of men. The blend of reality and fantasy enables him to convey, midst laughter or a frozen grin, the most startling ideas and the strangest freaks of human behaviour. Although he is not strictly speaking a poet, there are in his plays beautiful moments expressed in true poetic language which rises beyond character into a world of its own. His language, less poetical, less rich, less precious, has a greater range than that of Giraudoux, and is certainly a subtler and more pointed instrument in satire and biting comments against vulgarity or social weaknesses. . . . It is the human reality and not systems or concepts which Anouilh is after, and

that is why his characters, full of human contradictions, are emotionally alive. It is in fact not what they think, but above all what they feel which is the main factor and the link between a family of characters all involved in similar problems. (pp. 202-04)

> *Joseph Chiari, in his* The Contemporary French Theatre: The Flight from Naturalism *(© 1958 by Joseph Chiari), Rockliff, 1958 (and reprinted by Gordian Press, 1970).*

Anouilh puts ["The Waltz of the Toreadors"] into the category of what he calls 'grinçante', literally 'grating' or 'grinding' of teeth or possibly more affectionately 'gnashing' them. (p. 43)

[This] is one of Anouilh's plays in which the finer feelings come into view far more prominently than in the more cut-and-dried, 'black' or 'rose' works. Teeth-gnashing implies some kind of torment, and there is genuine torment—or there should be—in the scenes . . . of the military ball of Savnur. . . .

It is in [the] depth of morality that Anouilh shows with St Pé that puts him alongside other heroes of the absurd—the rational absurd of Camus as opposed to the other, so called 'absurd' writers like Ionesco and Adamov. . . . Although between Sartre and Camus, the more weighty, serious moralists, and Anouilh, some would say the epitome of froth, there is held to be little in common, there are many affinities. What is fate, what is soul, what is identity, what is real, what is truth: all these questions keep, or should keep, jumping out at us between the sleights of hand, the ingenious stage-craft. (p. 44)

> *Garry O'Connor, in* Plays and Players *(© copyright Garry O'Connor 1974; reprinted with permission), April, 1974.*

Anouilh's characters have always suffered from anguish; they have always engaged in the game of illusion, contemplating themselves before a mirror and thus introducing themselves to their other personalities; they have always fallen within the tradition of the marionette theatre of the old Italian commedia dell'arte. When writing such plays as *Le bal des voleurs* (1932), *Le rendez-vous de Senlis* (1937) or *Léocadia* (1939) Anouilh stressed the role of pure fancy and frolic in the creation of fantastic situations; he showed his creatures how to "escape" reality on flights of courage or folly. His dramas were a fascinating mixture of parody, comedy of manners and of character, psychological portraiture, fantasy, detective stories, with touches of vaudeville every so often. His theatre was sensitive, original and deeply moving.

The same cannot be said of *L'arrestation.* Anouilh uses the same techniques he has used for the past forty years—with felicity in the early plays, but not so with the latest ones. No new dimension has been added in *L'arrestation.* . . . The repetitious nature of the platitudinous plot is sad. The interminable flashbacks as the characters live out the various stages of their lives add to the chaos, confusion and general boredom of the play.

Unlike Rimbaud and Genet, who retired from writing after creating their masterpieces, Anouilh just keeps grinding out one play after another. Unless he lives a *new* experience, unless he digs deeply into himself, I doubt very much that another masterpiece will be forthcoming. He should feel elated since he has given the world some very great plays. (p. 829)

Bettina L. Knapp, in Books Abroad *(copyright 1976 by the University of Oklahoma Press), Vol. 50, No. 4, Autumn, 1976.*

* * *

ASTURIAS, Miguel Ángel   1899-1974

Nobel Prize-winning Guatemalan novelist Asturias was, until his death, the dean of Central American writers. The themes of his most important novels, *The President* and the three books that comprise his "Banana Republic" trilogy, reflect his ardent anti-imperialism along with his deep concern for his countrymen. His blending of myth and surrealism and his forays into automatic writing have given Asturias the reputation of being a difficult writer. (See also *CLC*, Vol. 3, and *Contemporary Authors*, Vols. 25-28; obituary, Vols. 49-52; *Contemporary Authors Permanent Series*, Vol. 2.)

[Far] too taken with existence, his own existence, to actively and sympathetically become engrossed with Europe's post-war hassles [in the mid-1920s], Miguel Ángel promptly disrobed reality of her austere dress and affectionately arrayed her in the sensual, colorful, transparent silks of his mind's fancy. The first artistic expression of this spiralling kaleidoscopic perspectivism of reality, vignettes or literary sketches created solely for journalistic consumption, was not long in coming. . . .

To the delight of [its] readers, the title ["In the Country of Modern Art"] proved to be deceptive. Instead of an impersonal running commentary on the contemporary artistic movements in Paris, they found before then an intimate letter describing perfume's sensual allurement and enchantment over man's senses, signed by Miguel Ángel and addressed to a lady friend at home. (p. 86)

[Just] as the reader prepares to savor his incursion into the private life of the foreign correspondent, the author in one short, humorous step shatters his relished illusions. (p. 87)

After the devilishly ambrosial aura of "In the Country of Modern Art," there sprang from Miguel Ángel's pen a continuous string of comic, humorous, ironic articles. Knowing no boundaries, his kaleidoscopic mind pricked with equal zeal the dark haunts of theosophy, the festive world of dance, the codes of social mores, and the depthless secrets of capillary philosophy. . . . [Those pieces that best illustrate this literary vein may be divided] into the following categories: theological, biological and social.

The theological set consists of two radically disparate, but equally entertaining, works: "Krishnamurti and His Hallucinating Devotees" and "June Cherries.". . . (pp. 88-9)

The . . . dichotomy between what ought to be and what actually is constitutes the comic axis of "Krishnamurti and His Hallucinating Devotees." Starting with the title and continuing on through to the last sentence, Miguel Ángel constantly forces his reader to fix his attention on those aspects which cannot help but shatter the lofty ideals of this spiritual body. Religion, not politics, here makes for a strange bedfellow. (p. 89)

The comic exaltation of crass materialism over the consecrated ethereal aspirations of the soul, however, does not stop here. As the reader has undoubtedly surmised, [the characters of "Krishnamurti and His Hallucinating Devotees" are] inelastic beings, automatons rigidly trudging through the waters of life's stream, incapable of adapting themselves to the ever-changing course of the sun's light. In and by itself this is quite amusing, but what makes it outlandishly funny is the author's ability to substitute self-awareness, spiritual and moral attributes for mangled gestures that spastically span the surface of a spineless shell in human disguise. (p. 90)

The phrase "Life is a bowl of cherries" may very well be an English saying, but its message recognizes no language barrier. "June Cherries" is curiously refreshing, as refreshing as the meat of the fruit consumed by Miguel Ángel while he composes his work. The article is written spontaneously, at least this is the impression the author wishes to convey to his readers. . . . If we now couple the above rambling style with the unexpected juxtaposition of three seemingly disparate, unrelated items—cherries, signs of punctuation and God—we will have the basic ingredients which give the article its humorous effect.

Of the three, the cherries form the central core around which everything else in "June Cherries" revolves. The article starts out simply enough with a declaration by Miguel Ángel that he intends to converse only about cherries: "Between cherry and cherry, we shall chat about cherries. . . ." But then, as he muses over the fact that he must, at least momentarily, freeze his words every time he prepares to spit out a pit, his mind abstracts the formal qualities of the pit and immediately associates them to, of all things, signs of punctuation. And what can be inferred from such a startling identification? Well, if nothing else, that the rhythm of his sentences will not be determined by mental constructs, but by base appetite: ". . . that, after all, our conversation will be cut short upon spitting out the pits, that is, the signs of punctuation: a period, when after spitting out a pit we continue to chew on the meat of the cherry; by a period and new paragraph, when the pit is thrown out at the very end; and by a colon, when the fruit itself has two pits." At this point both his desire to talk about "cherries" and his interest in the relationship cherries-punctuation signs disappear, leaving the reader with the common denominator "Between cherry and cherry" which is now suddenly pegged to God. Miguel Ángel's curiosity has again abruptly shifted, this time to God's meditations on Eve. In good standing with God, he is privileged to hear His discourse, as God, imitating our journalist, pops a cherry in His mouth. How amusing that God should find thought in human food (and in such a nonnutritional element as the cherry!), that (thanks to the pits) He contribute unconsciously to the punctuation of Miguel Ángel's article, and that stroking His beard, made of flax no less, He be perplexed by problems like any other mortal being, instead of resolving them with lightning speed:

> And just like us, between one cherry and another, "with His hand stroking his beard of flax," Jehovah said to himself: "From an ear? She will be curious. From the forehead? She will be proud. From one of the eyes? She will be a coquette. From the nose? She will be sensual. From the mouth? She will be a liar. From the palate? She will have a sweet tooth. From the feet? She will be a streetwalker. From the heart? She will be jealous. From the gut? She will be lascivious. . . ."   (pp. 91-2)

From theology we pass to biology and indirectly, in all three instances to be analyzed, back to God again. Two of the three works that comprise this category deal with reviews of lectures given at the Sorbonne by the eminent Indian botanist Sir Jagadis Chandra Bose (1858-1937) and the famed archaeologist Salomon Reinach (1858-1932): "A Hindu Sage at the Sorbonne" "Capilarología" ["Capillariology"], respectively; the other, "God Save You, Future Humanity," reflects on the predictions levelled by a reputed although unnamed French doctor on the future baldness of women. (pp. 92-3)

The humorous effect of ["A Hindu Sage at the Sorbonne"] depends not on one but on a number of cleverly combined devices. Miguel Ángel erases values by identifying science, a respectable branch of knowledge, with charlatanry (we must not forget that Reinach considered his theory of "capillariology" scientific and that it was an outcome of profound, prolonged and careful deliberation on the scholar's part). (p. 94)

[Perhaps] the most complex of Miguel Ángel's work in this vein is "God Save You, Future Humanity," the last of the articles to be analyzed in the biological set. The comments and images in this sketch run wild after Miguel Ángel briefly presents the source of his reflections, namely, the prediction of a famed, but curiously anonymous, French physician, that in the future women will walk the streets bald. As in "June Cherries," the piece impresses the reader as being written spontaneously ("I am going mad and I had better put an end to this . . ."), but differs from it in the greater logic of its incoherency. . . . [It] has some resemblance to "Krishnamurti and His Hallucinating Devotees," without, however, any of the latter's caustic didactic undercurrent. (pp. 94-5)

More than any of the other pieces analyzed up to this point (with the exception of "Krishnamurti and His Hallucinating Devotees"), "God Save You, Future Humanity" resembles a play, more specifically, a marionette production. This effect is obtained by applying diminutives (in this instance, a first step toward the grotesque) to its general characters—"papacitos-mamacitas" ["papas-mamas"]— which reduce them to puppet-like size, and by lachrymose speech: "Children of my heart, one should say to all those now growing up, my son yet unborn, your mother will be bald, horribly bald, and . . . will be in constant search of cosmetic preparations and home remedies to combat that grave malady." Moreover, it introduces the grotesque, absent in the other works, exaggerating the appearance of women to the point of completely destroying their graceful qualities. (p. 95)

We have . . . noted his careful, calculated handling of the linguistic elements which, as we shall now see, rescues "God Save You, Future Humanity" from turning into a satanic horror canvas in the decadent tradition of Baudelaire. No signs of spleen, of disgusting boredom, of a nauseous disillusionment with life find echo in this work. When all is said and done, the *billete* is written in a frolicsome, merry and witty mood. (p. 96)

[Irony and the common element also appear in "God Save You, Future Humanity."] The author's self-awareness throughout the article, which we have already noted in detail, is one such instance of irony. Another is found in the title which must be discussed with the ending if we are to grasp its subtle implication. The title, describing as it does humanity's sad fate and its ultimate salvation in God—He apparently is the only force capable of reversing the tides and fortunes of time—contradicts Miguel Ángel's final plea that women actively assist life along its inevitable, downward course. Understandably, this greatly curtails the powers of Jehovah. He no longer is the master, but rather a slave who must patiently and reluctantly abide by the rules and regulations of His own creation. As for the comic element in words, we shall add two more examples to those already discussed: Miguel Ángel's fondness for punning and his delightful grammatical inversion of phrases which, due to the general mocking-lugubrious tone of the article, essentially fail to change the significance of the text. . . . I am going mad and I had better put an end to this, urging my women readers to cut their hair to alleviate the task for both death and baldness which, come to think of it, is almost the same thing. Bald today, dead tomorrow. Dead today, bald afterwards. (pp. 96-7)

Overwhelmingly concerned with humanity's shallow capers, Miguel Ángel will employ humor and the comic as social correctives, criticizing those who, for example, worship death in life; pay homage to material wealth; respond theatrically; mindlessly or automatically to life's everchanging moments; consciously perpetuate a feeling of shame for the naked body, permit vanity to conquer the mind; and those who lose sight of reality by incongruously becoming impassioned over words. But fixing one's spyglass so close to the ground is, lamentably, an act fraught with danger. In general we can say that Miguel Ángel bows to reality's demands and sacrifices art to reason and to anecdote: once their prosaic grapnel has hooked fast into fancy, they will pull her down from the heights and rake her tirelessly across earth's zero surface. (pp. 97-8)

Exceptions to the above remarks are "Bananas-slide" and "Nude Women." Of the two, "Bananas-slide"—the title refers to a supposedly popular dance of American origin in vogue in the late nineteen-twenties—cleaves most to terra firma. Not that "Nude Women" ascends to the celestial spheres (the piece treads upon fertile human circumstance), but whereas its treatment of reality is light and sportive throughout, that of the extensive opening passage of "Bananas-slide" is acridly corrosive. Structurally speaking, the bitter socio-political tirade, uttered before our author joins a soirée pulsating with bacchanalian intensity, is at variance with the core's artistic rendition of simultaneous action—through skillful use of montage, Miguel Ángel successively sweeps across the ballroom and registers various moments which, captured in medias res, recreate a synchronous vision of life—and with the fantasy of the closing scene where Miguel Ángel's transoceanic reader is suddenly transported to Paris and converted into a fictional character with whom the author interrelates. In short, the unconcealed passion and venom of the introductory segment destroy the organic unity of "Bananas-slide" and, lamentably, also render static an otherwise dynamic and highly entertaining work.

But if the work fails structurally, it does, however, show a degree of coherency in its rich exploitation of the comic. (pp. 99-100)

["Nude Woman," a literary sketch,] derives its jocular tone from the author's persistent manipulation of the absurd and his constant use of the hyperbole to express his views. The first example of the absurd occurs at the very outset of the informally written essay as Miguel Ángel introduces the endearing figure of the XVI century mystic Saint Theresa on the heels of the unadorned, albeit provocative, title "Nude Women": "Saint Theresa states for good reasons that one's imagination is diabolical." Amusing as Miguel Ángel's devilishly twisted synthesis of Saint Theresa's idea on the nature of man's imagination may strike us, the real thrust of the author's humor here lies in his having related apparently incompatible elements. For the juxtaposition of a devout, sublime soul devoted exclusively to God with fleshy erotic beings—surely also faithful followers of Pan—indubitably creates a diabolical atmosphere of mirth. (pp. 101-02)

But where the use of the absurd triumphs completely is in the Guatemalan revealing scrutiny of the extreme measures taken by the Parisian society to garnish the natural state of human nakedness. Admitting that the act of disguising oneself is intrinsically humorous, when such an act becomes an eccentric mannerism to the point where it is envisioned as normal behavior, then man's masquerade from nature, his flight from life and reality, is hilariously linked to the world of the absurd. (pp. 102-03)

The comic element in words, in turn, manifests itself on many levels. It destroys the codes of human decency by making man deeply aware of the 'nastiness' of his corporeal shell through the colloquial expressions "en cueros" ["in one's naked skin"] and "en pelo" ["stark naked"]; it promotes contrary feelings and ideas other than those literally expressed. . . . (p. 103)

[Miguel Ángel's] works as rule are deeply rooted in reality and rarely, as in "June Cherries," do they spring from pure fantasy. He learned to describe his vision and criticism in highly articulate, playful, and aesthetic terms. Within the realm of the comic, no form escaped his attention. He was equally versatile and at home in developing the comic in character, the comic element in forms, in movements, in situations, and in words. He was a skillful master of the art of the disguise, of the grotesque . . . , of the art of exaggeration leading to caricature, and of rendering man as a mechanical object or as a puppet devoid of human vitality. His use of language, for which Miguel Ángel clearly stands out in Spanish American literature, seen through his sensitivity to verbal nuances, the plasticity of his style, his inclination toward parody and irony are here fully developed for the first time. (p. 104)

> *Jack Himmelblau, "Miguel Ángel Asturias' Dawn of Creativity (1920-1930): The Minstrel of Merriment," in* Latin American Literary Review *(copyright © 1973 by the Department of Modern Languages, Carnegie-Mellon University), Fall-Winter, 1973, pp. 85-104.*

The Eyes of the Interred is the culminating novel of his 'banana-plantation' trilogy, the first two of the sequence being *The Cyclone* and *The Green Pope*. . . .

Asturias converts the tropical foliage into verbiage. His passion for his country and people expends itself in the lush jungle bred by random poetic association. The same rhetorical emphasis is brought to the description of a tree as is brought to the miseries of the serfs. A neutral aesthetic eye moves from a description of the varying tones of the light filtering through the banana groves to the human beings who are cutting and loading the fruit.

Nearly all Latin American writing has the quality of being a virtuoso performance. The reader is trapped inside the writer's head. Occasionally, this may be diverting and even clever. . . . [*The Eyes of the Interred* illustrates] this tendency to literary acrobatics. But the fact is that surreal divagations and electronic adumbrations are not enough. (p. 300)

> *Shiva Naipaul, in* New Statesman *(© 1974*
> *The Statesman & Nation Publishing Co. Ltd.), March 1, 1974.*

The Eyes Of The Interred is couched in a rhetoric that is more Latin than American, and the book suffers from an excess of historical somnolence.

It is almost exhilarating to read the first two or three hundred pages, since the language has a surface sheen which reflects the world in its own image. The ostensible heroes of the book, the poor and the oppressed, are invaded by its presence as though it were an incantation and the purlieus of aestheticism have never seemed more heroic. . . .

In other words, this is not a novel consumed by 'social realism.' Asturias's language is too grandiose to encompass the range and tactility of ordinary reality, and it quickly becomes inflated and romantic: "he took care of the fans at the Granada, dirty with old wind that had become dust on the sadness of cold metal." When you fuel so much sound and fury into the dust, ordinary human life must scream to be heard. Unfortunately, Asturias's language of revolution is flat and peripheral, it becomes nothing more than the lifeless mouthing of slogans: "You said it Malena! Real love takes part in the future conquest of the world." The Malena in question is a schoolmistress who, as you can see, believes in mixing business with pleasure.

Asturias maintains the momentum of his writing only with the considerable use of cliché and lyrical abreaction. I am not sure how much this is the invasion of translator's demotic, but I am assured that the English is faithful to the point of idolatry. Here is a passage which suggests the flesh and spirit of the book:

> The sound of the bells was followed by a hailstorm, as if all around the silence of the night had broken into pieces. A rain of almonds with dark corneas and clear pupils that bathed it in looks. And another, another wave of hail, as if suddenly billions of tears had solidified over the nearby graveyard, beat him with its seed of naked eyes, watery, congealed.

The images glissade into each other to create a rhetoric rather than a sense; the lyrical slackness promotes a confusion of thought and an imprecision of feeling, and we are left with the sour and bankrupt manipulation of stock reaction. Any substantial, human reality is, of course, exiled from this *finesse* and Asturias becomes a Stylist and an enormous bore. Since everything resides on the surface, there can be very little complexity or development within the novel. The romance between revolutionary and schoolmistress, for example, remains at the level of perspex and the transformation of Malena into a revolutionary simpleton is handled heavily and clumsily. There is a story but no plot, speeches but no characters.

Novels that depend upon rhetoric must also depend upon images, metaphors and allegories rather than upon motive and character. . . . The imaginative substance of the novel is taken from images of death and putrefaction, or what Asturias calls a "dead man's tone," and the novel takes on a grotesque swerve. . . .

A lover of language is no lover of people, and Asturias shows very little instinctive sympathy for the helpless masses under the iron control of his style. They remain the brute stuff of his dreams, the residue of his fantasies.

Peter Ackroyd, "Manner from Heaven," in The Spectator (© *1974 by* The Spectator; *reprinted by permission of* The Spectator), *March 9, 1974, p. 296.*

Politics is the great literary theme of Latin America, as individualism is of North America. One of the foremost explorers of that theme was . . . Miguel Angel Asturias. . . .

Asturias . . . is best known for novels that examine political and economic issues with anger and satire. *The President* is his penetrating study of the prototypical Latin American dictator. The novels *Strong Wind, The Green Pope* and *The Eyes of the Interred,* which make up his trilogy on the U.S. banana companies, depict the exploitation and corruption which Asturias saw as central to their operations in tropical America. . . .

In *Men of Maize,* . . . Asturias starts with the fundamental Latin American political issue, the control of the land. But this novel reveals an Asturias less concerned with the politics of the capital city than with magical Mayan traditions.

The novel takes place in the highlands of Guatemala, where the ancient Indian culture has survived alongside the western-oriented society introduced by the Spanish conquest. Despite 400 years of contact, the Indians and the Spanish-speaking *ladinos* look at the world through different eyes.

Maize, or corn, is the basic food in the highlands. Since it is so central to the diet, the Indians believe that man is quite literally made of corn. Therefore it is sacred, as sacred as human flesh.

This respect for corn, and for the earth which produces it, is violated by the capitalist *ladinos* [who clear the land for farming]. . . . But the destruction of the land is no worse a crime than selling the corn for profit. To the Indians, it is as if a man were to sell his children. . . .

At one level the story . . . may be read as symbolic of the Spanish conquest itself. The social and economic order violently introduced by the Spanish four and a half centuries ago is still tenuous, not only in the highlands of Guatemala, but throughout the Andes of South America as well.

No one is quite what he seems in this world where magic is matter of fact. Nicho Aquino, the faithful postman who links the highlands and the capital, one day changes into a coyote to follow a wizard who may explain his wife's absence. And the postal system, the connection with the outside world, simply disappears with him.

Nicho is only one of the characters who suddenly change form. A rider and his horse are turned into a star. The army colonel . . . is shrunk into a tiny toy soldier. It is a surrealistic world—not the surrealism of France where Asturias lived in the 20s and 30s—but rather a surrealism which springs from the world view of the Indians of Central America. Asturias, who did graduate study into the ancient cultures and religions of the region, sought in his writing to continue their great narrative tradition. In *Men of Maize,* that tradition comes to life in a magical tale.

Patrick Breslin, "Alien Corn," in Book World—The Washington Post (© The Washington Post), *August 17, 1975, p. 3.*

*   *   *

ATWOOD, Margaret   1939-

Canadian poet, novelist, and critic, Atwood utilizes a highly

developed introspective technique in her exploration of self and country. (See also *CLC,* Vols. 2, 3, 4, and *Contemporary Authors,* Vols. 49-52.)

What is remarkable about [*Power Politics*] is not so much [its] highly distilled acid nastiness, nor even Atwood's controlled progress from relatively narrow personal bitterness to a broad and mythic view at the end which shows the lovers as part of a vast geological and then amphibian mass, but their humor in the face of it. The book is a *tour de force,* though that isn't all. To change metaphors as abruptly as Atwood, it is a murderously sharp weapon, cauterizing, not self-serving, and there is pleasure in the hefting of it. For one thing, she, the speaker, is a writer. Take that literally, take it metaphorically, what she seems to be saying is that it is not so much the deadly clinches that hurt as the distances: the irony, the incessant creation and revision of their images of each other, their attempts at control, their subtle, posturing self-victimization, its literary satisfaction. Killing him, no matter how deserving of murder he may be, she gives her performance self-consciously, and so despises herself as well. . . . [Those] moments in which she floats away from herself, decomposing, turning to water, or crystallizing at a grotesque distance from herself, will be familiar to anyone who has read Atwood before. . . . She has even made a novel, *Surfacing,* almost entirely out of [a] mythology of earth-air-water (now much fire in her, except that, as reader, you burn: she is at home in stone and coldness, not in heat). . . . (pp. 149-51)

I find it remarkable that Atwood has been able to take those images, which must by now be comfortable to her, nearly domesticated by familiarity, and make them live so fiercely. It is the dynamic structure of the book that does it, the near-plot of the drama of dissolution, the illusion of specificity, done with mirrors (though he asks for the "One forbidden thing: love without mirrors"). In the end she has convinced us that

> In the room we will find nothing
> In the room we will find each other

which may sound like Merwin but comes out of a universe of killers and near-suicides much more dramatic, less metaphysical, than his. (pp. 151-52)

No man could take offense at the knives Atwood has so skillfully wielded (thrown?) in *Power Politics.* She may go for his private parts (which are not necessarily or solely sexual) with the blade of this book, but those mirrors she uses do not distort. Her poems are terribly fleshless, bony, as vulnerable as they are cutting. They show her naked and impaled, fiercely alone. The blood belongs to both of them, man and woman, and, by her hard and deadly skill, to anyone who touches it. (p. 152)

Rosellen Brown, in Parnassus: Poetry in Review (copyright © *by* Parnassus: Poetry in Review), *Spring/Summer, 1974.*

Quite simply, I cannot trust these poems [in *You Are Happy*], nor are they trustworthy in an exciting way. Poetry, after all, is a serious and dangerous game, playing with words, thoughts, feelings. I, for one, don't have much else. But the elements of Atwood's poetry and of her own predicament are carelessly squandered, and the reader is little convinced of the importance of caring when the poet clearly does not. . . . One's expectations are laughed at, one's imagination turned into fancy. Atwood plays cheap tricks, tricks with more than mirrors. . . .

Atwood uses a wilful obscurity to pretend to profundity; her fashionably arcane invitations do not function as initiations; and the imperatives which she histrionically declares are facile—childish whimpers, adolescent moans, social anguish. (pp. 129-30)

J. E. Chamberlin, in The Hudson Review *(copyright © 1975 by The Hudson Review, Inc.; reprinted by permission), Vol. XXVIII, No. 1, Spring, 1975.*

Margaret Atwood continues to construct her guided missiles which have a deadly force of their own, poems so neat and silent that they move in space like an invisible invasion, descend, pierce the mind and leave a wound. And yet in spite of her sense of life as mostly wounds given and received (expressed in [*"You Are Happy"*] in a long series of Circe poems, no small boldness in the act of taking a myth so sacrosanct and doing it anew), Atwood attempts here both a new indifference and a new humility in her chronicle of the relations between man and woman (the chronicle as spiky and lethal in "Power Politics," her last book). . . . We recall that Stevens wanted to write a fourth section of his "Notes Toward a Supreme Fiction," to be called "It Must Be Human," and could not. To be human, Atwood daringly reminds us in the quotation from the gospel of the taunt addressed to Jesus by the mockers at the crucifixion, is to be "incapable of saving" oneself. I must not leave this volume, which has virtues on every page, without mentioning Atwood's comic sense, beautifully visible in the poem from the Circe sequence, "Siren Song," where we learn the secret of

> the one song everyone
> would like to learn: the song
> that is irresistible:
>
> the song that forces men
> to leap overboard in squadrons
> even though they see the
>   bleached skulls.
>
> The siren continues, luring the
> man closer and closer:
> Come closer. This song
>
> is a cry for help: Help me!
> Only you, only you can,
> you are unique
>
> at last. Alas
> it is a boring song
> but it works every time.

This light side (with its own tight-lipped truth behind it) engenders the various songs of transformations of the men-turned-to-animals in the Circe sequence, which, though they have good lines, seem more often the work of the fancy than of the imagination, and are occasionally willed into being. Nonetheless, Atwood lets very little dross into her volumes, and she always repays rereading. (pp. 33-4)

Helen Vendler, in The New York Times Book Review *(© 1975 by The New York Times Company; reprinted by permission), April 6, 1975.*

[*You Are Happy*] is an affirmative book . . . , and I was surprised to see Toronto reviewers going on as usual about Atwood's bleak, relentless, morbid vision as if this were only *Power Politics* revisited. Even the first section, in which the protagonist expresses grief, regret and remorse

(as well as anger) over the failure of a past relationship, is warmer and more sympathetic than any of Atwood's earlier icy (and often accurate) analyses of the wicked ways of men, women and modern urban societies. My favourites among her earlier books, *Surfacing* and *The Journals of Susanna Moodie,* perhaps foreshadowed the development that is found here. Her new poems are earthier in the best and most positive sense. (p. 87)

The book's second section, "Songs of the Transformed," contains marvellously imaginative poems spoken by humans who have been changed into animals. From this perspective "there are no angels / but the angels of hunger"; these poems get down to the basic realities of hunger and death. All life is predatory, and all of us are transformed to corpses in the end. In the third section, "Circe/Mud Poems," the problem of the sexual relationship is re-explored in terms of the story of Circe and Ulysses; again, this is a highly imaginative treatment in which Circe's enchanted island is recognizably a Canadian rural setting. The section concludes with the suggestion that perhaps the lovers are not after all trapped in that unhappy story. In the fourth section, "There is only one of everything," a man and a woman appear to move, at first tentatively and then with joyous confidence, toward the new kind of relationship described above. The cruelty of myth has been left behind; the sacrifice and offering are voluntary, and in this there is freedom. In earlier Atwood collections one felt that even the body was regarded as a prison, but here it is singled out for praise.

The book seems, then, to be a turning point in the poet's development. Technically, too, it is an advance over *Power Politics*. Many individual poems from that book tend to lose their force when removed from the context of the whole sequence; moreover, some of the shock-tactics and surreal effects seem to me inadequate to the psychological processes they are attempting to represent. Here there is more technical variety than in the past, manifesting itself partly in an effective use of the prose poem; one feels that most poems are autonomous and interesting in and for themselves, as is each of the four sections, and yet all contribute to a coherent whole—a human statement, a journey. I think we may be grateful to Margaret Atwood for facing up to the most difficult facts of our existence and for putting the case for joy so minimally and so well. (p. 88)

Tom Marshall, in The Ontario Review *(copyright © 1975 by* The Ontario Review*), Spring-Summer, 1975.*

Margaret Atwood is all things to all people. If you want, she's a nationalist. If you want, she's essentially a feminist or a psychologist or a comedian. She's a maker and breaker of myths or she's a gothic writer. She's all these things, but finally she's unaccountably Other. Her writing has the discipline of a social purpose but it remains elusive, complex, passionate. It has all the intensity of an act of exorcism. . . .

Selected Poems has the coherence of a grand design. By the end of the book you can't help seeing that there's a consistent goal underlying all Atwood's poetic adventures. She has a poem, "Tricks with Mirrors," where the mirror is addressing a narcissistic lover: I like to read it as a parable about her art.

> Don't assume it is passive
> or easy, this clarity

with which I give you yourself.
Consider what restraint it

takes: breath withheld, no anger
or joy disturbing the surface . . .

It is not a trick either,
it is a craft:

mirrors are crafty. . . .

Metaphors aside, this craft is easy for mirrors and hard for poets. It's especially hard if you're trying to reflect a country which has no image of itself, and this is the premise of *The Circle Game*. On the surface, it's a conventional book, a parable of the mid-1960s, featuring an exodus from the city to the wilderness in search of the real Canada. But if you look closely, it's the story of someone who is trying to enter the cycles of nature by becoming part of the "warm rotting / of vegetable flesh.". . .

The Animals in That Country (1968) introduces that now-famous brand of Atwoodian irony, and it's Atwood's most overtly political book. Industrial expansion, for her, means that the machine takes over mind and body, making people into lethal robots: "I reach out in love, my hands are guns." This is the germ of *Power Politics,* where the lover will become the imperial aggressor, and the love affair an imitation of guerrilla warfare. Irony, of course, is the weapon of a civilized mind. For the duration of the book, Atwood reinstates the mind which was renounced in *The Circle Game* and will again be abdicated in *The Journals of Susanna Moodie* (1970). . . .

I have a special fondness for Atwood in her ironical aspect, but *Susanna Moodie,* in its way, is a perfect book. *Procedures for Underground* appeared in the same year. Poetically, it's a pale reflection of *Susanna Moodie* and it's the only one of Atwood's books that doesn't break new ground. (p. 59)

Power Politics is vintage Atwood, it's a mirror where every vampire/victim finds his/her own face. And it's her best known book because it strikes a nerve in the collective tooth. . . .

Atwood's affinities . . . are with an earlier form of society, closer to nature than ours. It could be that she sees clearly because she's outside, watching the war: Reason and Progress in one camp, Innocence and Fate in the opposite camp. Or it could be that she knows how seductive false gods are. At any rate, violence and war hover on the edge of the lovers' magic circle—mankind is present on the island in the section called "Songs of the Transformed," where those of us who have surrendered our humanity have a chance to speak.

The bestiary is perhaps Atwood's most brilliantly conceived series of poems. The domestic animals are bitterly resentful, the wild animals are sorrowful. They sing about good and evil, and about a society which cannot distinguish between good and evil. They are sometimes comic and always deadly serious. Mirrors, as Atwood says, are crafty. Mirrors also have the disgusting habit of revealing what we would rather forget. But let the corpse have the last word, because the corpse knows what kind of mirror Atwood's poems are. . . . (p. 60)

> *Linda Sandler, "The Exorcisms of Atwood," in* Saturday Night *(copyright © 1976 by* Saturday Night*), July/August, 1976, pp. 59-60.*

As a literary genre, growing-up-female-in-the-1950s is as threadbare as a pair of bleached denims, but *Lady Oracle* is utterly unlike any feminist novel I know. For one thing, Atwood has a sense of humour. For another, she's working with "common woman." Joan [the protagonist] doesn't belong to any neurotic élite, and when she encounters the species she finds it puzzling and inconsistent. It wants multiple orgasms, but it also wants help with the dishes. "The Scarlet Pimpernel," she says to herself, "does not have time for meaningful in-depth relationships.". . .

Margaret Atwood's *Lady Oracle* . . . is an exquisite parody of an obsolete generation. So far, it's been privileged information that Atwood's a brilliant comedian. I vote we make it public, because one or two critics should know. (p. 59)

> *Linda Sandler, in* Saturday Night *(copyright © 1976 by* Saturday Night*), September, 1976.*

Margaret Atwood . . . writes novels whose pervading theme is—yes—beginning again: old material but freshly and deftly arranged, which is what matters. The protagonist of her first novel, *The Edible Woman,* consumes her past in the form of a cake, thus freeing herself from it, at least symbolically. In her second, *Surfacing,* the literal surfacing of the protagonist from the waters of the lake in which her father had drowned represents her rising from death (the past) to life.

Eating and drowning are Miss Atwood's favored modes of escape. The protagonist of *Lady Oracle* [Joan Foster] . . . casts off the shambles of her complicated past by faking her own drowning in the foul waters of Lake Ontario. . . .

In this novel, as in life, true escape from the detritus of the past is as impossible as the notion is sometimes tantalizing. Joan Foster is a compulsive examiner of shards as well as a compulsive dreamer; the two are as irreconcilable and inextricable as Joan and Louisa. Her problem is that they must be reconciled. . . . Joan/Louisa may no more escape the past, real and imagined, or evade the future than Hamlet his death, but by journeying into the ruins she may, possibly, rise above them. . . .

Words are Miss Atwood's medium, and she uses them well. To lay out the seemingly bizarre skeletons of her novels may do them a disservice, particularly *Lady Oracle.* It is, in fact, a very funny novel, lightly told with wry detachment and considerable art. Disbelief is willingly suspended. Its plot is complicated but the novel is never confusing and if, in the end, it remains only tentatively resolved, so does life, except in the end.

> *William McPherson, "New Lives for Old," in* Book World—The Washington Post *(© The Washington Post), September 26, 1976, p. 1.*

Joan Foster has an identity crisis with a difference: she knows who she is all right, but there are too many of her. As Joan, she is the colorless wife of Arthur, a pompous graduate student who spends most of his time flitting from one tiny leftist movement to another. As Louisa K. Delacourt, she is an enthusiastic writer of the sort of quickie Gothics that are sold in the dime stores she claims to work at when she's really at the library doing costume research. Joan chose her nom de plume in honor of her Aunt Lou, the only person who cared about her when she was a miserable, fat teen-ager, and this past is another secret: Arthur must never find out that her stories of high-school popularity and cheerleading are lies. It's a hard act to keep up. When Joan produces "Lady Oracle," a book of automatic writing described by her publishers as halfway between Rod McKuen and Kahlil Gibran, her new status as the toast of Toronto brings her little pleasure. . . .

In spite of many funny moments, "Lady Oracle" moves too slowly and is basically too serious to distract us from its clumsy contrivances. And so the zany narrative, perhaps intended to spice a familiar tale of feminist woe, points all the more plainly to a deeper unanswered question: who are these people, anyway? (p. 7)

Like her heroine, Margaret Atwood seems to have two literary selves. The first, upon which her considerable reputation is based, writes spare, tense poems full of images drawn from the bleak landscape of her native Canada and suffused with a quasi-mystical animism. This self has also written an extraordinary novel, "Surfacing," in which the sick relations between the sexes are explored as part of a larger sickness in the relations between man and nature. In both "Surfacing" and the poetry a powerful sense of place compensates for a large vagueness where human beings are concerned. The other Atwood is the author of "Lady Oracle" and an earlier "The Edible Woman," a comic novel about a young woman who escapes a conventional marriage by raising her consciousness in the nick of time. Both these books lack the metaphoric and mythic force of the other work while sharing with it a limited interest in individual character. Instead of archetypes and myths, they offer us the stock figures and pat insights of a certain kind of popular feminist-oriented fiction. It may be that the genre is not congenial to Atwood's real gifts: perhaps the very confusion of "Lady Oracle" is a measure of her discomfort. Her best work is so original, so energetic, that one is tempted to guess that "Lady Oracle" is for Atwood what Gothics were for Joan: a flight from the demands of her truest, most thoughtful self. (pp. 7-8)

> *Katha Pollitt, in* The New York Times Book Review *(© 1976 by The New York Times Company; reprinted by permission), September 26, 1976.*

[*Surfacing*] synthesizes a number of motifs that have dominated [Atwood's] consciousness since her earliest poems: the elusiveness and variety of "language" in its several senses; the continuum between human and animal, human being and nature; the significance of one's heritage, including not only personal ancestors but the gods and totemic figures of primitive cultures; the search for a location (in both time and place); the brutalizations and victimizations of love; drowning and surviving. (pp. 387-88)

The "search for the father" and the sense of a symbolic journey underline the novel's mythical implications from the outset. . . . Told from the first person point of view in a flat, emotionless tone, the narrative echoes what the protagonist gradually discovers and reveals about herself: a total spiritual numbness which dates back, as one learns through flashbacks, not only to her dead marriage and the abortion but to the break from her parents and the confused values of her childhood. (p. 388)

The mixture of anticipation and reticence, promise and danger, attending such a journey is one of Atwood's poetic preoccupations, articulated most directly in the title poem in the volume, *Procedures for Underground*. . . . Though the narrator of *Surfacing* expects that she must pass through the proverbial hell and purgatory before reaching her destination, the reader gradually learns that the hell is, in fact, behind her; not new suffering but assimilation and acceptance of her previous suffering is the path towards wholeness.

That the journey has a sacred dimension becomes even clearer through the course of the narrative, as Atwood explores the confusing religious values that have become paralyzing rather than redemptive for her narrator. (pp. 389-90)

Drowning or submersion is . . . one of the most persistent images in Atwood's writing, appearing not only as the central metaphor in *Surfacing* but in numerous poems. . . . In her study of Canadian literature [*Survival*], Atwood explains the ubiquitous metaphor, observing "The Canadian author's two favourite 'natural' methods for dispatching his victims are drowning and freezing, drowning being preferred by poets—probably because it can be used as a metaphor for a descent into the unconscious . . .". (pp. 392-93)

Using the symmetry of drowning by water/drowning by air, and death of the parent/death of the child in *Surfacing,* Atwood . . . imaginatively condenses the implications of the contemporary schism between flesh and spirit, secular and sacred, conscious and unconscious; the destroyed fetus is the anomalous buried half of these necessarily complementary pairs. The frequent references to mutilation, amputation, anaesthesia, and the robot-like, mechanized or wooden reality of the narrator's own immediate past are now seen as the consequences of her abortion. In removing life, "they had planted death in me like a seed. . . . Since then I'd carried that death around inside me, layering it over, a cyst, a tumor, black pearl . . .". . . . To interpret this image simply as a political statement against abortion would be to misunderstood the significance of the fetus as Atwood's metaphor for the self-destructive diseases of contemporary life, and the incomplete development of the self.

Moreover, the narrator's spiritual malaise is revealed as a product of her separation not only from the future (the unborn child) but the past (her dead parents). Her descent into her deeper self discloses the poverty of the conventional religious values she had only partly assimilated; the reality of her father's death (the death of her childhood "god") is the catalyzing shock which forces her guilt to surface. At the same time, however, she realizes that her father's legacy was not negation but affirmation: his rejection of Christianity was actually a liberation from dogma, and his gift to her is the map to a genuine sacred place where each person confronts his or her own personal truth. "These gods, here on the shore or in the water, unacknowledged or forgotten, were the only ones who had ever given me anything I needed; and freely". . . . Atwood's poem, "Dream: Bluejay or Archeopteryx," powerfully adumbrates this same cluster of archaic and contemporary images:

> in the water
> under my shadow
> there was an outline, man
> surfacing, his body sheathed
> in feathers, his teeth
> glinting like nails, fierce god
> head crested with blue flame.

Whereas language has been a key to unlocking her past self thus far, the narrator realizes that she must now transcend it in order to complete her quest, for "language divides us into fragments, I wanted to be whole". . . . Through her protagonist's journey, Atwood suggests the broader paradox of the poet, who must use language to signal what is ineffable. At this point the narrative shifts to increasingly mythic images (suggesting the collective unconscious and its archetypal motifs as proposed by Jung). The narrator, in gratitude for her revelation at the bottom of the lake, leaves an item of clothing to propitiate the gods; at the same time, she is beginning to strip away the layers of civilization, and feeling begins to seep back into her numbed being. Accepting the message from her father's gods—the knowledge from the head, or how to see—she now seeks out the lesson she knows must be waiting for her from her mother—a knowledge from the heart, or how to feel. Again, she returns to her parents' cabin for further clues and again finds them in visual rather than verbal form.

The picture she recognizes as her mother's legacy is actually a drawing that she herself had made as a child:

> On the left was a women with a round moon stomach: the baby was sitting up inside her gazing out. Opposite her was a man with horns on his head like cow horns and a barbed tail.

> The picture was mine, I had made it. The baby was myself before I was born, the man was God, I'd drawn him when my brother learned in the winter about the Devil and God: if the Devil was allowed a tail and horns, God needed them also, they were advantages. . . .

Of the images in *Surfacing,* either verbal or visual, this pictograph most poetically and economically synthesizes the motifs that Atwood has so meticulously developed. The typical childhood schematic resembles the primitive rock drawings that the narrator's father had recorded, besides repeating the link between ontogeny and phylogeny suggested throughout the novel. Moreover, it anticipates not only the narrator's later career as an artist, but also reflects the fact that the truth she seeks is already within herself— and is a non-verbal one. The subject of the picture is her own past: herself in the fetal state in her mother's womb, and the collective representation of the feminine principle expressed through maternity—which she had aborted. The male figure "opposite" in the drawing represents the complementary aspects of these elements: it is simultaneously her father, the masculine principle, a god (who, with his horns and tail, mends the Christian rift between God and Devil, good and evil), and, specifically, the nature deity of the rock paintings whose sacred place discloses the truth. In order to become whole, the narrator must "translate" the pictograph—immersing herself in its metaphoric language by living out all of its implications.

Significantly, just as she finds the drawing, her companions announce to her that the body of her father has been found on the lake bottom. But the confirmation of her own earlier discovery is not cause for grief. Denying the limiting reality of such facts, she exults, from the perspective of her newly found vision, that "nothing has died, everything is alive, everything is waiting to become alive". . . . (pp. 394-96)

The knowledge of the meaning of death revealed at the bottom of the lake corresponds to her unconscious half, now joined with her conscious self to form a whole. She vows to bear the symbolic child—who is both the released guilt of her past and the potentiality of the future—by herself, animal-like, alone, rather than strapped into the death machine that civilization provides. (p. 396)

[The] narrator finds taboos and directives everywhere; she exists in a state of primitive consciousness in which each object in the outer world is invested with sacred and personal significance. Everything remotely associated with human civilization is forbidden, even food and shelter. She eats roots and builds an animal-like lair. By reducing herself as much as possible to a kind of animal state that is symbolically both pre-human and pre-birth, she hopes to recover the archaic language necessary to communicate with the spirits of her parents. (Several of Atwood's poems focus on the transformation into and out of an animal state, including "Eventual Proteus" in *The Circle Game;* "Arctic syndrome: dream fox" in *The Animals in That Country;* "Departure from the Bush" and "Looking in a Mirror" in *The Journals of Susanna Moodie*.) Feeling herself pregnant with what may be a "fur god with tail and horns" . . .—an emblem of the godhead recently conceived within her—she is rewarded for her purifying sacrifices by momentary visions of each of her parents.

These visions crystallize the parallel themes which Atwood has consistently developed throughout *Surfacing*. On the metaphysical level, the narrator returns to the primeval time before the Fall and the knowledge of good and evil, when man was undifferentiated from the godhead, unconscious of his separate (and divided) self. Having incorporated the redemptive values of the nature deities embodied by her parents' spirits in place of the earlier confusions of distorted Christianity, she has forgiven herself for her sins against the human condition, thus reaffirming the sacred ties between generations and between man and nature. On the psychological level, she has relived her guilt-ridden personal past as well as the collective past—regressing through the abortion, her dead marriage (which she had experienced as the state of continual falling, "going down, waiting for the smash at the bottom" . . .), and her own pre-human vestiges. In establishing identification with both the feminine (maternal, generative) and masculine (knowledge, wisdom) principles, she generates her own creative potentiality through rejoining the severed halves of her being.

As the visionary reality recedes "back to the past, inside the skull, it is the same place" . . ., she re-enters her "own time". . . . She has recovered not so much the images of her actual parents as their symbolic reality and significance for her; their spirits can only provide one kind of truth. From them she has learned that salvation and redemption are never total, never complete; they must be constantly renewed in the present. As her parents shrink to what they really were, mere human beings and not gods, she accepts their imperfection, including the one fact that she had resisted for so long—their mortality. To accept that is to accept death itself, which, she has learned, is simply to accept life. But she also realizes that she can refuse to be a victim or to play word games that in their falsification of reality are (like her brother's arbitrary categories of good and evil) a form of death.

Like the hero of the mythological quest, she must bring the boon of knowledge back to the level of mundane reality, must translate it back into the language of sanity. In keeping with this realization, she "surfaces," choosing to return to Joe. Though he is only half-formed (and not a particularly positive character, as developed earlier in the novel), he represents a kind of animal purity and dogged devotion to her. Moreover, having recovered the capacity for love and faith, she has no one else with whom she can live out her new self-discoveries. Such a muted affirmation to conclude the novel may ring false, in view of the wholeness of vision finally achieved by the narrator. But it is consistent with Atwood's observation that

> in Canadian literature, a character who does much more than survive stands out almost as an anomaly.... [Still], having bleak ground under your feet is better than having no ground at all. . . .
>
> (pp. 397-98)

Mapping the symbolic journey into both the private and collective heart of darkness, Atwood has thus created a powerful account of modern civilization and its diseases. Elsewhere she has noted that paranoid schizophrenia—the split personality—is "the national mental illness" of Canada. However, the problem of self-division that she diagnoses in *Surfacing* resonates on a number of other levels; the illness is a metaphor of the human condition itself. The only cure is the journey of self-discovery: down and through the darkness of the divided self to the undifferentiated wholeness of archaic consciousness—and back.... *Surfacing* renders not only the archetypal journey into the self but Atwood's own personal journey back through the stages of her evolution as a poet. The novel both reveals and imaginatively extends the unity of theme and image of her previous work, expressing her ability to work within traditional frameworks to achieve an original vision. In the poem entitled "The Journey to the Interior," the narrator—like the protagonist of *Surfacing*—realizes

> that travel is not the easy going
> from point to point, a dotted
> line on a map, location
> plotted on a square surface
> but that I move surrounded by a tangle
> of branches, a net of air and alternate
> light and dark, at all times;
> that there are no destinations
> apart from this.
>
> (pp. 398-99)

> *Roberta Rubenstein, "'Surfacing': Margaret Atwood's Journey to the Interior," in* Modern Fiction Studies *(copyright © 1976, by Purdue Research Foundation, West Lafayette, Indiana, U.S.A.), Autumn, 1976, pp. 387-99.*

Margaret Atwood's new novel [*Lady Oracle*] is a compound of domestic comedy, Jungian psychology and social satire, stirred with wit and flavoured with the occult. (p. 84)

Atwood means to give her heroine [Joan] a quality of helpless vulnerability, but endows her with an ironic sensibility so keen as to make her seem the strongest character in the book, a cool and amused observer rather than the chief sufferer. This is a minor failing, however, and it is a relief to turn from the humourless intensity of *Surfacing* to the urbane comedy of *Lady Oracle*. In the former novel, the heroine's grim entry into a primeval world and her determined rejection of human contact conveyed a kind of superior contempt for the equivocations and compromises of everyday life, as well as a feminist hostility to a society which reduces women to the level of sex objects. In some respects the pattern is repeated in *Lady Oracle*: the heroine, trapped in an identity she detests, searches for some meaning in her life; shedding men along the way, she undergoes a ritual death and rebirth, flirts with dark powers in

her psyche, and emerges to a new awareness of self. Also reminiscent of *Surfacing* is the book's attack on the crassly materialistic concerns of North American life, on the vulgarity of a society dedicated to show. Yet in *Lady Oracle* these themes become largely a source of satiric humour; there is none of the morose self-righteousness which marks the tone of the earlier novel. Atwood has not lost her seriousness of purpose, but her vision has broadened, and she has developed a maturer sense of the possibilities inherent in any given situation. (pp. 84-5)

The heroine's search for emotional fulfilment and psychic integration gives coherence and direction to a plot that might otherwise seem rather creaky and disjointed. As is often the case with fiction cast in autobiographical form, the narrative follows an episodic line, and parts of the action are sometimes very tenuously connected.... Still, such weaknesses seem slight beside the deftness in Joan's career and introduces so many unusual and interesting characters. She has, too, an admirable control of style; her ability to insert the telling phrase and her eclecticism of reference give her writing a liveliness and polish that are unusual in Canadian fiction. (pp. 86-7)

> *Herbert Rosengarten, "Urbane Comedy," in* Canadian Literature, *Spring, 1977, pp. 84-7.*

Lady Oracle is proof that when it comes to fiction, the whole is sometimes not equal to, let alone more than, its parts. Many of the parts of Atwood's finally unsatisfying third novel are witty, excellent, insightful. . . .

Lady Oracle is . . . an uneasy mixture of Gothic parody and a comedy of manners. The parody of the Gothic shows us still another side of Atwood.... Her main character's Costume Gothics reveal what might be a scholarly knowledge of the field as well as an uncanny feel for the psychology behind them. Likewise, much of the comedy of manners, the social comedy, strikes precisely the right note. . . .

But these various aspects never emotionally connect or mesh into a unity: in fact, the parodic and satiric parts detract from the most interesting and moving material—the evocation of the heroine's childhood. . . . [The] vision of fatness—its causes, trial and results—is the finest aspect of the novel. (p. 283)

What is perhaps most disturbing about *Lady Oracle*—and a clue to its ultimate failure—is its strange closeness and yet distance from *Surfacing*, Atwood's last novel. Many of the same themes and images pervade both works. In both first-person novels we have heroines interested in magical transformation, exploration of the past, especially in relationship to parents, death and the disappearance of a body, mystical religion, an examination of the sources and uses of art. But where magical transformation involved a genuine quest in *Surfacing*, here it is automatic writing and false drowning. Where mystical religion meant trying urgently to contact the local nature-spirits in *Surfacing*, here it is an easy world of aged spiritualists. Where the growth in *Surfacing* involved abandoning commercial art and seeking deeper roots in childhood drawings and Indian pictographs, here the art is Gothic novels rejected in the end—in favor of science fiction. On one level, *Lady Oracle* seems almost a parody or weird distortion of Atwood's most serious themes.

In essence, *Surfacing* is an exploration, a quest novel; *Lady Oracle* is an entertainment, an escape novel—in both senses of the word. The resolution of *Surfacing* is aesthetically and emotionally satisfying, entailing as it does a genuine metamorphosis, a psychological transformation. The resolution of *Lady Oracle* is witty, emblematic and contrived—a comic gesture. This is unsatisfying because the novel is basically serious, unlike Atwood's first novel *The Edible Woman,* which has the same sort of conclusion. (pp. 283-84)

[Finally,] when we hear the mysterious footsteps down the hall approaching our heroine, we no longer care if she is "saved" or "got"—we and, I suspect, her creator, can't quite believe, let alone feel for her. (p. 284)

> *Bonnie Lyons, in* The New Orleans Review *(© 1977 by Loyola University), Vol. 5, No. 3.*

* * *

AYCKBOURN, Alan   1939-

A British playwright, actor, director, and producer, Ayckbourn is best known for *Absurd Person Singular* and *Time and Time Again.* (See also *CLC,* Vol. 5, and *Contemporary Authors,* Vols. 21-24, rev. ed.)

The best kind of comedy, we know, has an underpainting of darkness; the comic mask resembles nothing so much as a grinning death's-head. Alan Ayckbourn's *Absurd Person Singular* is well aware of this: a witty and resourceful comedy that imperceptibly darkens into a dance—not of death, but of death-in-life. It is, then, the best kind of comedy, yet fairly far from the best specimen of its kind. Still, as commercial theater goes (and it goes farther than some highbrows and avant-gardists would have it), this British comedy is not inconsiderable; with more such plays around, the theater would be undergoing not exactly a renaissance, but a good prodding into action. (p. 108)

> *John Simon, in* New York Magazine *(© 1974 by NYM Corp.; reprinted by permission of* New York Magazine *and John Simon), October 28, 1974.*

[*Absent Friends*] centres round a tea party, though the phrase 'absent friends' is more usually coupled in English domestic ritual with the raised glass. (p. 26)

[The tea party] may have some emblematic significance as a national institution in Mr. Ayckbourn's mind. But wouldn't almost anybody you can think of surely break out the light ale, if not the champagne-style sparkling wine, to cheer up a long-time-not-seen chum whose fiancée has recently drowned? The aim is apparently a kind of muted, genteel *Walpurgisnacht* à la Albee. And, in theory, it could be more ghastly and touching to summon up the ghosts of the selves that might have been amid cream and cakes, with the pram in the hall, than with alcohol and horseplay, and a barman in a white coat. In practice, as a play in performance, these incongruities give the production the air of a charade played for laughs which are only half-intended.

This said, I must add that I respect the author's determination at the peak of his success as the British Neil Simon . . . to show us that what is funny to the audience can be tragic to the characters, and that there is no lump in the throat to equal a swallowed laugh which turns sour. And I admire his decision to forego obvious alarms and excursions, open breaches and unforgiveable wounds, . . . all the more disturbing and real for being never quite out of control. . . .

Absent Friends is a serious, almost clinical, presentation of the nature of marriage where the most painful moments occur, not when the participants recognise its weaknesses, but when the outsider mistakes them for strengths. . . .

Mr Ayckbourn's one flaw seems to me that in his concern to avoid facile sensationalism, and through his pity for his people, he has allowed them to carry on taking the pills. By tranquillising them, he has let us off the hook. What was needed at the end was the knife. Both we and they could take it. (p. 27)

> *Alan Brien, in* Plays and Players *(© copyright Alan Brien 1975; reprinted with permission), September, 1975.*

The audacious Alan Ayckbourn has written a farce that in sheer, dogged length surpasses "Parsifal" and that tinkers with time and space in a fashion intricate enough to give an Einstein pause. And for what? Why, to tell us a story that could almost certainly be inscribed in longhand on the head of a ha'penny. If I forgive Ayckbourn for the outrageous disproportion between the grand scale of his handiwork and the meagreness of its content, I do so on the best and simplest grounds in the world—that he is a very entertaining writer, and that his farce, which consists of three full-length plays . . . , is likely to make you laugh far more often than it is likely to make you look at your watch. The over-all title of the work is "The Norman Conquests," and the Norman in question is an assistant librarian in a small English town. His conquests, unlike those of the warrior race to whom he presumably owes his name, are amorous rather than military; for this Norman, 1066 hints not of history but of the number of a bedroom in some seedy Sussex hotel. . . .

Norman, who protests that his only goal in life is to make people happy, is Priapus incarnate. He woos women as other men breathe, and, alas, wins them. His victims are eager to believe the grossest flatteries on their way to his bed; however base his calculations, they invariably prove successful. This is indirectly to observe that Mr. Ayckbourn's merry comedies depict a misery seemingly ineradicable; as anyone familiar with his earlier "Absurd Person Singular" is aware, he regards human relationships in general and the marriage relationship in particular as little more than a pailful of cozily hissing snakes. Of the six characters that compose the dramatis personae of "The Norman Conquests," only one is capable in maturity of giving and receiving ordinary human affection, and it is a clue to our playwright's view of life that this person is the one for whom the worst deprivations of love and self-fulfillment are reserved. Well! It is surely late in the day to manifest astonishment over the pessimism that gives energy to our writers of comedy; what *is* astonishing is that we all go on laughing so cheerfully as the gifted Mr. Ayckbourn scourges us to the gallows. What is it that we are laughing at? (p. 60)

> *Brendan Gill, in* The New Yorker *(© 1975 by The New Yorker Magazine, Inc.), December 22, 1975.*

In a note appended to the program of *The Norman Conquests,* Alan Ayckbourn describes his trilogy as a set of plays relating its events from three different viewpoints, which can be seen in any order ("like a three-ended ball of string"). . . . I've never seen, nor would I rather see than be, a three-ended ball of string; and Mr. Ayckbourn's statement makes more sense than his set of plays only by virtue of its greater brevity.

The Norman Conquests is not much of three plays, and even less of three plays in one. It is, in fact, one play in three. . . .

If you were to shuffle all three plays together, arranging all twelve scenes in proper time sequence, you would end up with one hell of a boring six-hour rewrite of your basic British weekend comedy (*pace* Noël Coward's *Hay Fever*). Then, armed with a large box of blue pencils, you could cut out the endless reiterations, the vampings-till-ready, the extensions via obvious and gratuitous slapstick, and end up with one moderately respectable comedy of manners. In all likelihood, your result would closely resemble Mr. Ayckbourn's first play, *Table Manners,* to which the two others have been appended as marginalia. You would also end up with the most polished work of the three, the one with the most consistent shape and the least reliance on brute force for its overall effect. You would not, however, have nearly as interesting a work as Mr. Ayckbourn's *Absurd Person Singular.*

The real deficiency in *Norman* is its lack of true comedy. *Singular* furnishes that in full measure and in wide range, and *Norman* is, by contrast, a gag show pure and simpleminded. In its full, protracted length, it further becomes an exercise in draping three sets of gags across the same skeletal plot, an exercise possibly valid in playwriting courses, but hardly stageworthy. Furthermore, Mr. Ayckbourn has an annoying way of rubbing our noses in even some of his most genial inventions. Perhaps inspired by *Punch* cartoon captions from around 1880, he often pads out his best gags with one line too many. Example: Annie to Sarah: "He (Norman) seduced me on the rug." Sarah: "*Which* rug?" Annie: "It doesn't matter which rug." In the theater, or even in print, the joke plays itself out with Sarah's response; Annie's added line pricks the comic balloon. Or again: Norman (sardonically, looking at an underfilled dinner plate): "Is this lettuce leaf all for me? I cannot believe my good fortune." Sentence number two is a redundancy; here, too, less would have been more.

Alan Rich, "Absurd Persons Triplicate," in New York Magazine *(© 1975 by NYM Corp.; reprinted by permission of* New York Magazine *and Alan Rich), December 22, 1975, p. 75.*

Alan Ayckbourn [is] a master hand at turning the bitter apathy, the stale absurdity which most English playwrights now find characteristic of Britain's lower-middle-class existence into hilarious comedy. He does this so well and so often . . . that perhaps only the English, in tune with the material, can sense the sorry state of moral flatulence that underlies the . . . laughter. (p. 700)

Harold Clurman, in The Nation *(copyright 1975 by the Nation Associates, Inc.), December 27, 1975.*

B

BAINBRIDGE, Beryl   1933-

An English novelist whose fabric is working-class life in Liverpool, Bainbridge is noted for her telling portrayals of family life among the have-nots. A masterful delineator of character, she is said by Katha Pollit to be "never less than sharply and savagely ironic." (See also *CLC***, Vols. 4, 5, and** *Contemporary Authors***, Vols. 21-24, rev. ed.)**

The Bottle Factory Outing . . . is one of those fictions which depend for their success on balancing comedy and horror, and on adjusting every movement to maintain the delicate weighting which contains the outbreak of tragedy within the nervous, cheerful frame. When the trick works, as it does here, the double-vision effect is unsettling and gnawing, disturbing. Miss Bainbridge by now must be reckoned a thoroughly original, even formidable, writer with a great skill for suggesting acres of complicated matter within a few paragraphs; but despite her undeniable talent, this book seems to me disappointingly thin. . . .

[The] odd inconsequence of this book seems to me to derive from a lack of emotional urgency—required, in a book of this sort, to give point to the jumpy fun. (p. 627)

> *Peter Straub, in* New Statesman (© *1974 The Statesman & Nation Publishing Co. Ltd.), November 1, 1974.*

Miss Bainbridge is bearing up very well; she sets her face resolutely towards the sad and the seedy, the squalid and the sloppy, and yet she never aspires to cheap sentiment. . . .

Miss Bainbridge writes a dry and uncomplicated prose which spares her characters nothing; other people's aspirations are always comic, and Miss Bainbridge [in *The Bottle Factory Outing*] is so much the outsider as to be almost omniscient. Italians are very passionate and cannot help but be amusing, too, what with the "Aye, aye, aye" and "No, no, no," the broken syntax and the rolling eyeballs. All good comedy, of course, eventually breaks its own spell and there is a sour and haunted strain through the book. . . . The removal of the ultra-heroine disturbs the narrative somewhat, and . . . the prose becomes a little damper and a little more forced; the final sequences of the book are devoted to a who-didn't-do-it line which finally runs dry when the comedy turns into a fable. Freda's death

is the final incongruity, and when she is all over there is nowhere else for the book to go. (p. 573)

> *Peter Ackroyd, in* The Spectator (© *1974 by* The Spectator; *reprinted by permission of* The Spectator*), November 2, 1974.*

Miss Bainbridge keeps her sense of comedy throughout ["The Bottle Factory Outing"]. Comedy concerns itself with knowing how to live and makes its jokes out of people who don't know how. She is curious to see how her characters, all sensible and all full of good will, can botch their best efforts with such consistency. One reason is that each is blinded by a private and mistaken view of everybody else. Amenities perfected by the Late Stone Age, such as eating, defecation, conversation and sex, are all insurmountable problems in this novel. And when the rhythms of industry can better accommodate the ritual of burial than any rhythm available to Miss Bainbridge's characters, we have a complete picture of people from whom every advantage has escaped, leaving them to reinvent a culture, and to wring their hands.

Loss of culture is comic; loss of civilization is tragic. Miss Bainbridge has her comic eye on cultural confusion. She makes us see that it goes deeper than we think and touches more widely than we had imagined. The most appalling muddles can still be laughed at, and laughter is a kind of understanding. (p. 7)

> *Guy Davenport, in* The New York Times Book Review (© *1975 by The New York Times Company; reprinted by permission), June 8, 1975.*

[*The Bottle Factory Outing* is an] absorbing social comedy, if also an implacably grim one. Miss Bainbridge . . . is a masterful plotter of schemes in which lust, avarice, and cruelty win the day every time over the nobler impulses of humankind. Her talent is for grounding these schemes in entirely credible characters, a talent notably evident in this tale of two female misfits whose emotional lives revolve entirely around their fellow employees in a bottle factory. . . . For the most part, . . . and this is a factor typical of the novel's strengths, the men and women behave strictly according to the social rules of their tradition, ethnic codes for whose details Miss Bainbridge has a keen eye. The denouement is a monstrous act in which all the characters have a share of responsibility. Kindly as they all are, each one sees his part through. That they do is a final judgment on them and one altogether typical of the merciless vision that rules this novel. (p. 30)

Dorothy Rabinowitz, in Saturday Review *(© 1975 by Saturday Review/World, Inc.; reprinted with permission), July 26, 1975.*

[In Beryl Bainbridge's world] all is solipsism, a world which may or may not exist, characters who may be invented by other characters, even feelings which succeed other feelings so rapidly as to cause the reader to doubt that they were ever felt at all. Ann, a single girl living in Hampstead, is the only reality in *Sweet William*. (p. 70)

Sweet William is more subdued and less bizarre than *The Bottle Factory Outing,* but the same slightly loony sensibility is at work, and there is a similar atmosphere. It's a world of twilight, peopled by indistinct figures who don't quite connect, communicating in words which can't be taken at face value. Ann's feelings are always on the surface; she is volatile, emotionally unstable, lacking a cultural framework, without a history. She is an instinctive existentialist: everything has to be invented and experienced for the first time. Words often fail her; language and syntax are imprecise; the big Truth isn't there. But the little truths sometimes slip through. . . . (p. 71)

James Price, in Encounter *(© 1976 by Encounter Ltd.), February, 1976.*

[Bainbridge's talent] is an odd and in a muted way fantastic talent, as is perhaps necessary in modern English writers who manage to escape the rather stifling conditions of normal contemporary competence. Her book that best demonstrates it is *The Dressmaker,* in which an illiterate GI is murdered by a dedicatedly deprived old lady in a small Liverpool house; she stabbed him in the neck with her scissors, ''she was that annoyed.'' But the pathetic slaughter with which Bainbridge likes to end her stories is little more than the gesture with which the disgust heaped up in the course of accumulating lacerating details, the pain of all the accurately depressing dialogue, is swept off the page. Though they are sometimes funny, and often very compassionate, Bainbridge's novels cannot really bear themselves.

Deprived and exploited women are probably her main interest, their minds and bodies drained, like their environments, of value. . . .

The Dressmaker has a horrible accuracy of place and period—Liverpool, 1944—that authenticates its fable, and gives it a central place in Bainbridge's rapidly developing *oeuvre. The Bottle Factory Outing* is wilder and funnier. The hopeless aspiration to love and a brilliant future is more cruelly put down, and this time it is the game, deprived heroine herself who has to be disposed of, her corpse huddled away so that, representing anyway only a lack, she would not on removal be missed. The latest novel, *Sweet William,* though very effective, is a shade less impressive than the earlier work, partly because the mess is still there at the end. . . .

Nostalgia would not be the right word for Bainbridge's attachment to the past; she is always looking back at something from which it was imperative to escape. But our lives are distorted like the feet of Chinese women, forever, and all Bainbridge's women are evidence of whatever it was that ruined England and made it absurdly small. (p. 42)

Frank Kermode, in The New York Review of Books *(reprinted with permission from The New York Review of Books; copyright © 1976 NYREV, Inc.), July 15, 1976.*

Although Beryl Bainbridge has emerged in recent years as one of the most interesting and dependable of contemporary British writers, her work has not really caught on over here. . . . (p. 1020)

Certainly, [she] works in a somewhat minor mode. Her fictional world is a grey, dank, and closed place. Her characters, usually discontented, lonely, and discarded working-class women, are rather limited beings, seemingly incapable of growth or change. Yet because of the care and control Miss Bainbridge exercises over her material, and because of the originality of her approach, she often seems to transcend that material. Though she develops her dark, claustrophobic little stories slowly and softly, the atmosphere she creates is unsettling, often threatening. She is to a large extent a realist, and her characters tend to be rather prosaic, but still there is something slightly off-center and crazy about her particular world. We frequently find ourselves laughing in the dark.

Sweet William, her latest novel, is certainly the least dark and bizarre of her books, far brighter and more open than either *Harriet Said* or *The Secret Glass.* In fact, with each new book Miss Bainbridge appears to be moving further away from her shadowy realm. One notices a change in her style as well. Her delivery has become increasingly precise and concise. Her pace has quickened. She now treats her pathetic women in a much more overtly comic manner. Miss Bainbridge has been most successful in *The Bottle Factory Outing,* in which she retained the dark qualities of her earlier books but managed to relate her story more crisply and comically than ever before. We find that same crispness and wit in *Sweet William,* but the characteristic menace is gone, and we do miss it. (pp. 1020-21)

Still and all, Miss Bainbridge relates her tale with such spirit and includes so many nice little comic touches and observations along the way that she succeeds in holding our interest and entertaining us as well. . . .

Sweet William is a delightfully written book, and when it concludes we find we are affected by it more than we had anticipated. Yet it is perhaps too easy at times and too inconsequential, lacking that unsettling vision of Miss Bainbridge's earlier books. Though her ease is to be admired, one hopes that in her next book she will couple it with a return to the shadows. (p. 1021)

Ronald De Feo, "Out from the Shadows," in National Review *(© National Review, Inc., 1976; 150 East 35th St., New York, N.Y. 10016), September 17, 1976, pp. 1020-21.*

A Quiet Life might equally well have been named with another phrase which occurs near the end of the novel: 'A Close Family'. The family concerned—and if the surname is ever mentioned, I missed it—is indeed close: stiflingly, murderously close. Their house is effectively reduced to its kitchen by a combination of poverty (the cost of heating) and the mother's compulsive cleanliness. (p. 22)

Though at first glance *A Quiet Life* seems as uneventful as the title suggests, there is tremendous subterranean life. With surgical delicacy and saintly humour, Beryl Bainbridge exposes the web of repression in which this family is caught. It would be impossible here to give an account of the complex power relations among the four protagonists; but in the last analysis, all of them—even 'free' Madge—are victims rather than manipulators. . . .

This is a subtle, moving, witty book. Its only real fault is that it reaches a dramatic climax, a convulsion of the web under extreme tension, which seems superfluous within the logic of the novel. It's the old problem of the ending: the classic pattern of crescendo and brief diminuendo is inappropriate to a lot of contemporary work, but still devilishly hard to avoid. The rest of the book is perhaps more accurate as an adolescent's perception: many overlapping rhythms, with unpredictable concentrations and relaxations, the larger pattern of events visible only in hints and glimpses. In its deft and unemphatic way, *A Quiet Life* is a tragic, comic, study of what has been called 'the psychosocial interior of the family'. (pp. 22-3)

> *Nick Totton, in* The Spectator (© *1976 by* The Spectator; *reprinted by permission of* The Spectator), *October 9, 1976.*

*   *   *

BAKER, Elliott   1922-

Baker is an American novelist, short story writer, and playwright. His first novel, *A Fine Madness,* is considered his best. A rebellious farce, it shares certain characteristics with the novels of Heller and Kesey. Baker has subsequently written other novels, but none has received the critical acclaim of the first novel. (See also *Contemporary Authors,* Vols. 45-48.)

Elliott Baker's first novel, *A Fine Madness* (1964), is a good example of the failure of much post-World War II American fiction to achieve artistic success. Whether or not this novel belongs to the category of black humor (if that is indeed a category) is of no real importance. But it does reflect the recent interest in the picaresque anti-hero whose misadventures in various aspects of American life are intended as a comment on that life and on the possibilities of a genuinely human existence in our time. . . .

In the first sentence of the novel, the beginning of a poem appears in [the protagonist's] mind—a poem which is completed finally on the last page. During the novel, Samson accumulates the parts of this poem in bits and pieces. So the central action concerns Samson's recovery of his creative imagination in the face of all obstacles, including himself. (p. 71)

The examples of [Samson's] irresponsibility, his amorality, his cruelty, and his failures could be [expounded at length], but the point is clear: Samson is a representative of one of the mythic poetic types of the last hundred or so years—the literary bohemian who lives only in the holiness of the imagination. So his madness, if it is a madness, is a fine madness, as the title indicates. And the value for which Samson stands is the measure of all other values and people in the book.

The only counterpoise of any significance to Samson is Dr. Oliver Wren, a psychoanalyst. . . . [Dr. Wren] is committed to his own field as Samson is committed to poetry. For him the psychiatrist as scientist is the true pioneer, as for Samson the poet serves this function. Oliver is interested in particular in the study of genius and of evil, and he thinks that the psychiatrist may "hold the only possible existing key to genius and evil." . . .

Baker's choice of a psychoanalyst as Samson's main antag-

onist is more than accidental. As far as Samson is concerned, of course, all of society, from his former wife to literary critics, is out to destroy his poetic talent. But for him psychiatrists embody in a very concrete way the extent to which society seeks to probe and compel the mind of all those who violate its conventions. . . . [The] choice of psychiatry as embodied in Oliver is doubly appropriate: it is something that Samson dislikes, and it stands not only for science but for rationalistic humanism as well. (p. 73)

Samson draws the line of battle in terms of long familiar opposites: thought against feeling, reason against imagination, science against poetry, the real against the ideal. These pairs are, of course, some of the standard terms in a cultural debate at least as old as the Romantic movement of late eighteenth-century Europe. And it is a debate which . . . is still very much alive. . . .

Baker has established a conflict of great potential interest. These two men, each personally complex, each representative of a view of life at war with the other, could provide a lively and illuminating conflict. (p. 74)

But Baker is either unwilling or unable to sustain this beginning. Probably he never intended to attempt anything other than what he has done. Unfortunately, what he does turns potential originality into the rather ordinary story of the rebellious poet against a hostile, anti-poetic world, the whole spiced with enough wit to sustain interest. The tone of the book definitely favors Samson. And to say that most of what he does is destructive either to himself or to others is to miss the point that this destructive quality is of the essence of the truly creative process. Were Samson of such a mind, he thinks, he could destroy much of society with the simple force of his creative energy. . . . (p. 75)

Thus, when Samson seduces someone's wife, buys a camera without money to pay for it and gives a false address, lies to his boss, and causes a riot at the ladies club meeting, we are to understand that these and other deliberate floutings of any conventional moral sense are the inevitable (and hence genuinely moral) results of the contact between Samson's disruptive creative genius and society. And when Oliver proves finally unable to equal Samson; when Samson seduces Oliver's conveniently bored wife, Lydia; and when, with the connivance of Oliver, Samson is turned over to Dr. Massey to have a lobotomy, we are clearly to understand that Samson has won over Oliver. But he has won without a contest. For the farcical events of Samson's admission to Para Park (a sanitarium in Connecticut), his seduction of Oliver's wife, and the moral capitulation of Oliver to the opportunity for revenge on Samson, are not really a development of the conflict between Samson and Oliver. No conflict has occurred. It has been abandoned for the sake, apparently, of giving Samson an unearned victory. And once Oliver capitulates, there is no one left but a gallery of caricatures: Dr. Kropotkin, the easily seduced female psychiatrist at Para Park; Dr. Voegler, a lecherous oldtime orthodox Freudian, whose pet interest is what he calls the *phallus thaumaturgist;* Dr. Massey, the psychosurgeon who wants desperately to prove that schizophrenia is tractable to lobotomy; and X. O. Waterfall, the fastidious and pedantic poet-critic from Princeton who pronounces Samson no poet at all, not even a minor one. Samson emerges battered and bruised from the combined assault of all these and other enemies. But he is unbowed, and his personality and imagination, unaffected by the surgery, remain apparently beyond the reach of an evil society.

Such a conclusion should, presumably, be comforting. For the novel tells us that the most creatively vital part of a chosen few will always remain beyond culture, even if this chosen few necessarily despises its less fortunate contemporaries. But an important question remains: not a question of the rightness or appropriateness of Samson's victory, but of the imaginative realization of that victory. Baker has achieved neither the potential complexity in the character and conflict of Samson and Oliver nor a genuine social setting in which character and conflict can develop. We have instead simply moral Samson and immoral society—or rather, poetic Samson and unpoetic society. We are told that Samson is a great poetic spirit but not really shown why. We are told that the society he opposes is corrupt and uncreative, but we see only a group of caricatures as proof. We are asked to believe that Samson's creative energy can defeat all obstacles, but we are not allowed to witness the struggle between Samson and Oliver in a way which does imaginative justice to both sides. (pp. 75-6)

[The] view of life embodied in Samson is not only Baker's but also that of a whole literary generation, from the early 1950's to the present. It is a view which affirms the value of the spontaneous, the instinctual, the anti-intellectual, and the imaginative against the destructive and coercive forces of society. From this point of view, Baker's novel becomes almost a literary cliché or a thinly disguised sermon which indicts society and shows the only way to salvation in the person of Samson. Again, what is wrong is not the indictment or the way to salvation but the failure to earn either through an imaginatively adequate conflict. (p. 77)

A Fine Madness demonstrates the limitations of the novel of personal formula quite clearly: a withdrawal of imaginative sympathy from the reality of those persons and institutions which fall outside the sympathy of the author. The result is a resolution by manipulation and trickery, not by the natural interaction of the characters on each other. With its own brand of romantic primitivism, indeed, *A Fine Madness* reveals the incapacity of such a view of human conflict in the novel to represent adequately the moral ambiguity of that conflict and to avoid such trickery. But it also shows the existence of good fictional material, which a novelist of Baker's obvious talent should be able to turn to good account. (p. 78)

> *Richard W. Noland, "Lunacy and Poetry: Elliott Baker's 'A Fine Madness',"* in Critique: Studies in Modern Fiction *(copyright © by the Bollingbroke Society, Inc. 1966), Vol. VIII, No. 3, 1966, pp. 71-80.*

When it comes to American authors writing about nervy, basically serious adolescent boys, the line, as they say, forms on the right. J. D. Salinger, Philip Roth, Charles Webb; a host of lesser names would swell the list. Now Elliott Baker brings us his version of troubled youngmanhood—1939 version—in the shape of Tyler Bishop [in *The Penny Wars*]. To be fair to Mr. Baker, who often writes extremely well and never less than adequately, any close comparisons between Tyler and Holden Caulfield et al. would be fruitless; in that respect, he has borrowed nothing. The way in which the novel is organized, however, is undeniably familiar: a serious base (the discovery that the world is not such a nice place, that life is not so easy) with a somewhat farcical topping (making use of adolescent confusions, cumbersome virginity and so on).

The book is episodic, a technique which provides Mr.

Baker with an opportunity to create incidents that stick in the mind like a good anecdote: the pompous Dr. Axelrod, for example, loathed by Tyler but favoured by Tyler's recently widowed mother, berates an audience in a rundown cinema for laughing at a caricature of life in Nazi Germany; "What about Leibniz?" he bellows, "What about Goethe?" Cameos like this are most often used to get laughs—Tyler's attempt at seduction is a successful instance—but Mr. Baker can use the method to other ends with equal success, and the book ends on a note of violence which is all the more effective for being unexpected. (p. 39)

> The Times Literary Supplement (© *Times Newspapers Ltd., 1970; reproduced from* The Times Literary Supplement *by permission), January 8, 1970.*

["Pocock & Pitt"] is dangerously funny, whatever else it may not be. . . .

The actual narrative line twists and doubles back on itself—with enough surprises and reversals to dazzle the most jaded reader.

Despite these surprises and reversals—and despite the presence of Super-Agents—do not think this is a detective story or spy thriller. Not at all. No Agatha Christie or Georges Simenon or S. S. Van Dyne or even Graham Greene (Greene's "entertainments" being, as everybody is aware, nothing but very fine detective stories) could have written such a book as "Pocock & Pitt." To do what Baker has done here requires a highly refined sense of the ludicrous, the blackest kind of insight into what makes man the comic and tragic creature he is, a mind that often hovers between reality and fantasy, and the willingness (one wants to say courage) to follow where fantasy takes him. The readers of Baker's first two books ("A Fine Madness" and "The Penny Wars") know that if he is to be compared to other writers, he must be put into the demented, brilliant company of such men as J. P. Donleavy and Joseph Heller.

Now, after all those roses, may I throw a gentle brick? If I could, I'd like to ask Mr. Baker why he felt it necessary to bring in all the spy stuff. Yes, yes, I know its funny. I know it provides the opportunity for that intricate and exceedingly clever plot line. I know that it is high farce and satire on the whole Secret Agent thing. But I also know that what makes this book memorable is Wendell Pocock, alias Winston Pitt. No spies enter the book for the first 85 pages. For all of Part I, Wendell has it by himself. And God knows he's enough.

We see him dying in America. We see his terrible wife, his terrible children, his failed dreams of education and making something useful of his life. He is a wonder. He is excruciatingly alive. Then the opportunity comes to desert, to leave America, to quit his awful job, to do some of what is in him to do. He takes the opportunity and we participate in his rejuvenation. When he finds freedom, his heart grows stronger. When he gets the chance to do something useful, it gives him the strength to act and to live again.

What I'm getting at is that Wendell Pocock holds this book together. He *is* the book. And the business of the spies and the complicated plot only serve to weaken his hold on our hearts. I was genuinely moved by him and his plight, and I was just sorry as hell that he had to haul around all that extra "entertainment."

Even so, I feel that Wendell Pocock will remain in my memory as long as, say, Major Scobie or Hazel Motes or Miss Lonelyhearts. And that's saying something.

Harry Crews, "For Elliott Baker, Roses and One Brick," in The New York Times Book Review (© *1971 by The New York Times Company; reprinted by permission), September 26, 1971, p. 2.*

It is not easy to describe what happens in *Pocock & Pitt* because the action is so involute, the turnings so strange and surprising. Yet all of the incidents have been prepared for in some way, are made to seem almost logical, leading like crooked corridors into other crooked corridors. One has the impression of a structured novel about the unstructured, disheveled, unreasonable world with which Pocock attempts to cope. ... *Pocock & Pitt,* which assimilates a combination of elements as unlikely as Henry James's *The Ambassadors* and Evelyn Waugh's *The Loved One,* is essentially a cultural fairy tale, raising the question Can man survive as a *human* entity in an antihuman world he himself has created?

The best passages in *Pocock & Pitt* are those where reality lurches toward nightmare—moments when the reader is shocked into a recognition of the grotesque underside of reality. Yet, despite a gift for seeing life as a fine madness, Baker has not written a perfect novel. Too much of it depends on facility—on surprising twists of plot and a kind of farce that seems too easy to do. The central figure, Wendell Pocock, is treated as a foil, and the minor characters are all manipulated for whatever bit of tragic farce can be squeezed from them. The elaborate business of the espionage agents who leave a rose or (in the case of the American) a Tootsie Roll, as calling cards on the broken bodies of their victims is amusing, perhaps, as a burlesque of Ian Fleming; but in the meantime Baker's serious theme has evaporated. Baker seems unsure of what kind of novel he is writing. His vision of contemporary bleakness is conveyed with authority only intermittently in *Pocock & Pitt;* the rest of the book is devoted to a facile giddiness. (pp. 62, 69)

Emmet Long, in Saturday Review (© *1971 by Saturday Review, Inc.; reprinted with permission), October 16, 1971.*

Mr. Baker's rue-laden stories [in *Unrequited Loves*] draw heavily on the memoirist in him. ... If Mr. Baker has a trouble it is in the peculiar nature of his authority, an ironic intrusiveness that persists throughout the style here, and usually not to the advantage of the narrative. Still, it is a fault born of confidence, and on the whole that confidence is justified, for Mr. Baker is, in addition to being something of a didact, an inordinately witty writer. Two tensely wrought stories, "Celia" and "The Portrait of Diana Prochnik," are, each in its chilling way, emblems of the author's capacity for rendering the simultaneous nature of human experience. It is a sensibility capable of recording the seaminess, the pleasure, the embarrassment of any given moment and of appearing to do so, moreover, all at the same time. It is no small capacity, and Mr. Baker's collection of stories is no small achievement. ... (p. 28)

Dorothy Rabinowitz, in Saturday Review/World (© *1974 by Saturday Review/World, Inc.; reprinted with permission), February 23, 1974.*

*   *   *

BALDWIN, James   1924-

Baldwin is a black American essayist, novelist, short story writer, and playwright. His work consistently reflects a moral

purpose: to make art reflect a sense of reality and clarity, rather than the falsehood of illusion. (See also *CLC,* Vols. 1, 2, 3, 4, 5, and *Contemporary Authors,* Vols. 1-4, rev. ed.)

Of the fiction produced by American Blacks after the Hughes-Wright-Himes generation, James Baldwin's ... *Going to Meet the Man* (1965) seems to me the most important single short story collection and its controversial title piece the most powerful story by a recent American Black writer. Out of such stock characters as a Southern sheriff, his sexually unexciting wife, and his brutally mistreated black victims, Baldwin has created another hideous parable of the sixties (a story still so shocking in its impact as to evoke more than one cry of protest when I included it in an anthology designed for university students three or four years ago). As in his essays and other works of nonfiction, "Going to Meet the Man" brings more forcefully to mind than any news stories or telecasts what it must mean to be black in a white man's world, a world in which the sheriff Jesse can say with all sincerity that he was a "good man, a God-fearing man ... who had tried to do his duty all his life" and this after recollecting the events of the day and the young black he has almost beaten to death. The whole terrible paradox of irreconcilable forces and immovable objects is suggested. ... (p. 235)

William Peden, in Studies in Short Fiction (*copyright 1975 by Newberry College), Summer, 1975.*

A decade ago, as an undergraduate, my colleagues and I spent hours poring over the works of James Baldwin. He seemed so sure-footed, then, so certain in his vision of this country, that his lacerating words were like balm to the black students who were on a whirligig in search of their identities. Because he existed we felt that the racial miasma that swirled around us would not consume us, and it is not too much to say that this man saved our lives, or at least, gave us the necessary ammunition to face what we knew would continue to be a hostile and condescending world. ...

Now Baldwin has published a long essay, "The Devil Finds Work," the 17th book bearing his name, but the event does not call for rejoicing. In fact it brings forth not a little pain, for this work teems with a passion that is all reflex, and an anger that is unfocused and almost cynical. It is as if Baldwin were wound up and then let loose to attack the hypocritical core of this nation. And to what avail? None that I can see, for although the book purports to be an examination of the way American films distort reality, its eclecticism is so pervasive, that all we are left with are peregrinations of the mind and ideas that jump around and contradict each other. And this from a man who was, for my money, the best essayist in this country—a man whose power has always been in his reasoned, biting sarcasm; his insistence on removing layer by layer, the hardened skin with which Americans shield themselves from their country. (p. 6)

Baldwin has said all [that he says in this work] before. And better. And one must be dismayed, finally, by the style of this book, which seems to be a rococo parody of his own work. ...

Well, what has happened to the finely honed delivery, the sense of assurance, the rootedness of this writer? I think that Baldwin, in love and at war with his society, suffers from the distance that he has put between himself and his beloved. And because a man who loves or fights as in-

tensely as he does must constantly be replenished by contact with the object of his imagination, I wonder about the
pleasures of his exile. For they seem to be, at best, quixotic, since America rides Baldwin and will not let him go.
And so, "The Devil Finds Work" is disappointing because
the author must repeat, from a distance, what he has been
telling us for a long time, and what he knows we know that
he knows. The possible force, then, is scattered, willy-nilly,
to the winds, and all that vision and moral weight that fortified a generation, become as disturbing as the memory of a
hurricane on a placid summer's afternoon. (p. 7)

> *Orde Coombs, in* The New York Times
> Book Review (© *1976 by The New York
> Times Company; reprinted by permission),
> May 2, 1976.*

Roughly halfway through [*The Devil Finds Work*]—a long
essay that indicts American films for distorting or evading
reality—James Baldwin writes: "I think it was T. S. Eliot
who observed that the people cannot bear very much reality. This may be true enough, as far as it goes, so much
depending on what the word 'people' brings to mind: I
think that we bear a little more reality than we might wish."
One is surprised by the digression; it appears to rebut the
spirit of his own argument against Hollywood.

It also seems to contradict the charge of refusing to confront reality that Baldwin has consistently brought against
white Americans. Throughout his career as a moral essayist
and social critic—one of the more distinguished such careers in our language—a principal point has been that most
whites shun things as they are, especially relating to blacks,
by taking refuge behind safe and comfortable illusions and
by falsifying whatever they are not quite able to sidestep.
He has tried to pursue these Americans, to corner them
with what he holds to be the truths of their country and
their inner lives. Does his mild dissent from Eliot suggest
that he has had a measure of success? . . .

[The] heart of his case against Hollywood is a critique of
the invalid terms in which movies re-create the world, and
of the "inadmissible fantasies" in which they too often
deal. Whether or not the film industry and its millions of
uncritical subscribers will be impressed is open to argument, but Baldwin's formulation will find support among
more thoughtful moviegoers and certainly among those, like
blacks, who hunger in vain for valid celluloid representations of their lives.

In *The Devil Finds Work,* Baldwin takes a sometimes tortured retrospective look at a number of the films he has
seen since his boyhood in the 1930s. (p. 18)

Baldwin misses in movies what he found initially in the
church and later in the legitimate theater. In both, he explains, "a current flowed back between the audience and
the actor: flesh and blood corroborating flesh and blood—as
we say, testifying." Compared to the exchanges and valida-
tion of truth and experience occasions of that kind allow,
the cinema is inherently false: "The camera sees what you
want it to see. The language of the camera is the language
of dreams."

Nevertheless, some time ago Baldwin allowed himself to be
talked into going to Hollywood to write a screenplay based
on *The Autobiography of Malcolm X.* What, beyond the
stipends, could he have dreamed would satisfy him? And
why, as soon as he realized what would inevitably happen,
did he not turn right around and go back home?

After allowing himself to fall into the further trap of accepting a "technical" assistant, who set about translating virtually every scene Baldwin wrote to fit the perceptions of
the studio, he finally realized that the film was being produced "in the interest of entertainment values." Baldwin
walked out at that point, "but the adventure remained very
painfully in my mind, and indeed, was to shed a certain
light for me on the adventure occurring through the American looking glass."

That is an astonishing conclusion from a man who has just
spent the greater part of his book leading us to believe he
was quite hip to everything taking place in the American
looking glass. And it is only one reason why, despite Baldwin's largely effective case against Hollywood, I found
myself curiously dissatisfied and disappointed with *The
Devil Finds Work.*

Other baffling moments of inconsistency also fray the
thread of Baldwin's argument. The book lacks, too, the
natural and sustained fluency that marks his better efforts
and enables us to recognize the urgency and validity of his
passions. Parts of this essay are labored, as if it were an
uphill task he had grittily committed himself to complete—
or, thinking now of his title, a little work he had found for
his idle hands.

In addition, his constant digressions from the main theme,
to report on everything that floats into his mind, repeat far
too much of what he has said a number of times before.
One of the things he says about *In the Heat of the Night*
could be said of *The Devil Finds Work*—that there is in it
"something strangling, alive, struggling to get out."

A final disappointment is perhaps not Baldwin's fault: He
has succeeded in raising expectations so high that scrutiny
of his work and demands on his excellence grow more rigorous and merciless with each new book he writes. Our
expectations, though, may be as unrealistic as they are unfair, and certainly on the basis of his past work Baldwin has
earned from us a number of things, not the least of which is
our patience. Still, he would further justify that patience by
bringing us fresh news—about himself and ourselves—and
not going over familiar territory. (pp. 18-19)

> *Jervis Anderson in* The New Leader (©
> *1976 by the American Labor Conference on
> International Affairs, Inc.), May 24, 1976.*

I have always seen two James Baldwins: an opportunist
who took on subjects and opponents as fashion dictated,
and a first-rate novelist and essayist who told us things
about ourselves that most Americans needed to know but
mostly refused to accept. I never quite trusted his early attacks against *Native Son,* but I thought his own *Go Tell It
on the Mountain* was—and still is—one of our finer novels.
The Devil Finds Work has left me with a slightly different
picture. I see in it an older and wiser man who need no
longer look for the opening to get himself listened to, but
who at the same time has stuck with his old topics in spite
of great changes in his audience. Moreover, this book falls
far below his earlier works like *Notes of a Native Son* and
The Fire Next Time. Yet, it has given me an affection for
its author that I have never had before.

Baldwin's professed subject in *The Devil Finds Work* is the
white American film, and his thesis is that white American
film makers have, from *Birth of a Nation* to *Guess Who's
Coming to Dinner,* falsified the American racial experience
in a most obvious and destructive way. This is not a very

new thesis or a very hard one to defend. It *is* hard to make it sound compelling and important when the social protest that it embodies has generally begun to dissolve. (p. 25)

The Devil Finds Work is not simply a rehash of *The Fire Next Time*. Nor is it revolutionary in the 1963 sense. There is something, in fact, a little decadent about it, autumnal, like a fruit that has ripened just a little past the proper time for picking. It is on the down side of growth, without the crisp firmness of its earlier stages. In a way, this essay closes out a vital period, and is therefore occasion for sadness. Not only does it mark the disappearance of many conditions that made Baldwin's earlier work so exciting but it suggests that Baldwin's powers really have declined. Yet, contradictorily, what I want to write about is the depth and wisdom of this book, which comes from a man of letters whose life has been twisted and strained in multiple ways but who has kept his eyes open and his mind sharp. Baldwin uses the movies here as a pot for mixing a number of ingredients, principally his own spiritual and intellectual evolution and white America's assiduous clinging to its self-delusory dreams of reality. (pp. 25-6)

This is not, in other words, a book on conventional film criticism. But we wouldn't expect it to be. Baldwin has never worked that way. He has always taken the personal route. In examining his own emotions and reactions, it is as if he is examining those of the nation. This has been his importance to us all. In his excursions into his psyche, delineating with Dostoevskian shamelessness the details of his hurting bruises and wounds, he has often spoken for all of us, has offered himself as a metaphor of our self-inflicted national injury. Thus, in *The Devil Finds Work,* the main character is Baldwin himself, and the movie we watch unfold is about Baldwin's increasing understanding of himself and the American film industry, and through it, America itself. (p. 26)

Something has happened to Baldwin's style here, and to his ability—or willingness—to develop a point clearly and coherently. His sentences are jerky, convoluted, full of suspended phrases and interminable modifications. His discussions seem to be going somewhere, then terminate in a dead end, like an unfinished freeway or stairs that lead to a blank wall. His prose and his ideas *struggle*. Why? This is what every reviewer will be asking. What has happened to one of our master essayists? And every reviewer will have his own theory. . . .

[This is] mine. Baldwin has changed like the rest of us. But unlike the rest of us, he has not developed a new emphasis. He has taken the old subject of race and made it even more personal. In doing so he has seen new complexities amidst the old themes, and a social system whose contradictions are ever more obviously more conflicting than contrasting. In probing perhaps more deeply than ever before into American racial practices he has turned up a conclusion that no white will be comfortable with: that prejudice, to put it simply, is so much a part of the culture that to eradicate it means to replace the culture with something else. He does not state this with the younger confidence of thirteen years ago, or warn us of an Armageddon—"the fire next time!" He is, indeed, almost inarticulate. . . . But old warrior that he is now becoming, he knows the truth with a sadness that goes beyond bitterness and despair. Who can express such knowledge easily?

I am disappointed in this essay. I think it fails as a coherent piece. But that is almost like saying that the aging bear has

failed, caught finally in a trap it always knew was there, contemplating its wound and, in extraordinary patience, waiting for its fate. (p. 27)

Jerry H. Bryant, "American Dream Language," in The Nation *(copyright 1976 by the Nation Associates, Inc.), July 3, 1976, pp. 25-7.*

When James Baldwin goes wrong (as he has taken to doing lately), it usually seems less a failure of talent than of policy. Of all our writers he is one of the most calculating. Living his life on several borderlines, he has learned to watch his step: driven at the same time by an urge to please and a mission to scold.

In his early days, the twin urges came together to make very good policy indeed. White liberals craved a spanking and they got a good one. But then too many amateurs joined in the fun, all the Raps and Stokelys and Seales, until even liberal guilt gave out. And now the times seems to call for something a little different. *The Devil Finds Work* . . . shows Baldwin groping for it—not just because he's a hustler, at least as writers go, but because he has a genuine quasi-religious vocation. In the last pages he richly describes a church ceremony he went through as a boy, akin to attaining the last mansions of mysticism: and you have to do *something* after that. Your work, even your atheism, will always taste of religion.

And this is the first problem we come across in the new book. Because the subject is movies, and most movies simply do not accommodate such religious passion. So his tone sounds false. He may or may not feel that strongly about movies (it's hard to believe), but sincerity isn't the issue. A preacher doesn't have to feel what he says every Sunday: rhetoric is an art, and Baldwin practices it very professionally. But the sermon's subject must be at least in the same ball-park as the style, or you get bathos, the sermon that fails to rise.

Since Baldwin is too intelligent not to notice this, we get an uneasy compromise between old habits and new possibilities. The folks pays him to preach (to use his own self-mocking language), so he turns it on mechanically, almost absent-mindedly, lapsing at times into incoherence, as if he's fallen asleep at the microphone. But since getting mad at the movies is only one step removed from getting mad at the funnies, he escapes periodically in two directions, one bad and one good.

The bad one is to change the subject outrageously in order to raise the emotional ante: thus there are several references to how white people like to burn babies that totally stumped me. A prophet should disturb all levels of opinion and must therefore be something of a precisionist. But this stuff passes harmlessly overhead. Blacks have been known to kill babies too, in Biafra and elsewhere, but nobody said they like it. People apt to be reading Baldwin at all have long since graduated from this level of rant. He may write for the masses, but he is read by the intelligentsia.

But his second escape at times almost makes up for the first: which is simply to talk about movies according to their kind, with amusement, irony and his own quirky insights. More writers should do this: we were raised as much in the movie house as the library, and it's pretentious to go on blaming it all on Joyce. In Baldwin's case a movie case-history is doubly valuable because his angle is so solitary, shaped by no gang and deflected by no interpretation, and shared only with a white woman teacher, herself a solitary. Nobody ever saw these movies quite the way he did, or ever will.

Unfortunately the childhood section is tantalizingly short, and the adult's voice horns in too often, but some fine things come through: in particular the way the young Baldwin had to convert certain white actors into blacks, even as white basketball fans reverse the process today, in order to identify. Thus, Henry Fonda's walk made him black, and Joan Crawford's resemblance to a woman in the local grocery store made her black, while Bette Davis' popping eyes made her not only black but practically Jimmy himself.

This is vintage Baldwin: and if he lacks confidence in his softer notes he shouldn't (his sentimental notes are another matter). He does not automatically *have* to lecture us on every topic he writes about. In this more urbane mode, his racial intrusions often make good sense. (pp. 404-05)

He talks at one point of the seismographic shudder Americans experience at the word homosexual, but he handles it pretty much like a hot potato himself: talking around and around it without quite landing on it. Again this is policy (the word homosexual does go off like a fire alarm, reminding us to put up our dukes) but in this case, I think, too much policy. When Baldwin holds back something it distorts his whole manner. The attempt to seduce is too slick. And this, just as much as his compulsion to preach when there's nothing to preach about, diverts him from his real lover, truth. He is not seeing those movies as an average black man, but as a unique exile, and the pose is beginning to wear thin.

So, the tension remains. He has been away a long time and I'm sure he has a story to tell about that, perhaps his best one yet. It is hard to believe that in Paris and Istanbul his mind was really on American movies: but they might have been something in the attic that he wanted to get rid of. And the attempt is worthwhile if only for the sake of some sprightly lines . . . and random bangs and flashes. He even talks several times of *human* weakness (as opposed to white weakness)—including his own: which suggests that the hanging judge may be ready to come down from his perch and mix it with us.

But for now he remains up there wagging his finger sternly at the converted and the bored. And with so many clergymen, he too often deduces Reality solely by intelligence in this book, and while he has more than enough of that quality, it tends to fly off in bootless directions unless anchored by touch. He is right to love the stage. His art needs real bodies. But anyone who sees reality as clearly as Baldwin does must be tempted at times to run like the wind; and perhaps, for just a little while, he's done that. After all, that's what movies are for—even for those preachers who denounce them the loudest. (pp. 406-07)

> *Wilfred Sheed, "The Twin Urges of James Baldwin," in* Commonweal *(copyright © 1977 Commonweal Publishing Co., Inc.; reprinted by permission of Commonweal Publishing Co., Inc.), June 24, 1977, pp. 404-07.*

* * *

BARKER, George   1913-

Baker is an English poet, novelist, essayist, and playwright. Although his best poetry is among the finest written in the English language, much of his work is uneven in quality. The antithesis of the detached academic poet, Barker in his writing has been described as Dionysiac, verbally extravagant, esoteric, and self-indulgent. (See also *Contemporary Authors*, Vols. 9-12, rev. ed.)

Throughout Barker's poetry, the fulfillment of a need for union with a divine and a human presence is threatened by his alienation from both, by his compulsion to struggle against the beloved woman or brother of God, even as he seeks their nurture. In depicting the perennial contest, Barker often combines the role of prophet inspired by a vision of potential salvation and his adversary, ever tempted by self-love, the will to destruction, and death itself. . . .

Barker uses classical myth in his poetry to suggest that the infection of love by violence and death, the hell implicit in the promise of eternity, and the conflict ever present in the world around him spring ultimately from the same warring powers in the universe. These exist within God himself, who is described as part of the poet's own nature, or as a beneficent yet threatening figure with whom he merges. . . .

> *Lillian Feder, in her* Ancient Myth in Modern Poetry *(copyright © 1971 by Princeton University Press; reprinted by permission of Princeton University Press), Princeton University Press, 1971, pp. 378-79.*

Literature is not a competition. Yet poets will invariably be compared with their contemporaries and with their predecessors. Barker's verse is not so perfect as Dylan Thomas's, nor is his vision so intense. Yet his range is wider; his feeling not deeper but more general. For this reason his achievement may not be so obvious, it may not be so completely attained. But if the daisies and the buttercups are plentiful and perfect, a rose is not the less a rose for having a thorn where the petals should be. What really makes a man a real poet except the size of his soul, it is very difficult to say. But it is as equally difficult to fail to realize it, when a writer turns out to be one. George Barker is. . . . (pp. 12-13)

Unlike any other poet of his generation whose work is at all mentionable in the same sentence as his, George Barker's prose is not of any great stature. It is only fair however not only to Barker, but to any readers this may have, to point out that Edwin Muir's opinion of his prose is quite the opposite. But for one of his readers at least he must stand by his verse alone. The quantity of this is considerable. He wrote what is perhaps the worst book ever to have been written by a real artist, in which it is stated throughout that sex is filthy and she whom you do it with dirty. The name of the book, *The Dead Seagull*. One can never forgive Barker for writing that sort of nonsense, but one can forgive oneself for not being able to forgive him. . . .

Barker is a Byron who hasn't got a Greece. He is a knight errant without a sword, or to be fairer, the sword is there all right but his hand is paralysed by the trouble in his heart. By this it must not be understood that he is unaware of what has taken place during the years which have contained the first half of his writing life. (p. 14)

Barker, who has a considerable talent for humanity, has been left somewhat in the air, not ignoring [causes], but not being able either to cope with them or to assimilate them into his work. He was too much of an artist to offer us easy slogans. Because his feelings were deeper, because simply he was more of a poet, he didn't jump on to political platforms during the thirties like those poets of the literary generation that immediately preceded his. (pp. 14-15)

Barker is almost as completely unpolitical as it is possible for a contemporary to be. Yet, like Byron, he goes far beyond the conventional poetic subjects for his material. . . . The things that worry a politically-concerned person often trouble him. Yet the trouble does not lead to revolt, much less to a desire for power. He wants to understand, sometimes to escape, never to win. He identifies himself with such varied forerunners of St John the Divine and François Villon. He is capable of spoiling a good poem by a noisy line, but never of trying to make one out of any emotion that is not an integral part of his own deep feeling. (p. 17)

The world of George Barker is a place for sinners. It is not a street of barricades, nor is it a house where one prays. Yet the nature of the poetry in him is the plentifulness of forgiveness. He is original without being unique. He is very much of this world, in so far as it is a vale of tears, without being seduced by worldliness. His technique is in advance of his maturity. He is married to poetry, he is not just having an affair with words. But he is still waiting for the cock to crow whereas, according to the calendar of his achievements, he should be getting ready for the gift of tongues. . . . Whatever verse, however, his muse may have in reserve for him, and he for the steadily increasing number of his readers, that poetry which he has already written, punctuating as it does his unplanned and wandering journey, proves beyond mere praise that he has embarrassed this language and these years with 'The tremendous gentleness of a poet's kiss'. (p. 18)

> *Paul Potts, "Many Happy Returns," in* Homage to George Barker on His Sixtieth Birthday, *edited by John Heath-Stubbs and Martin Green (© Martin Brian & O'Keefe Ltd. 1973), Martin Brian & O'Keefe, 1973, pp. 11-20.*

'J'ai cultivé mon hysterie avec jouissance et terreur.' This remark by Baudelaire might well have come from Barker. It relates closely to his view of the character of the poet, which is mantic, Sybilline, Dionysian, in fact mad—in character lunatic, but distinguished from the merely insane by a quality of moral dedication: 'one could, with some truth, call a lunatic a poet without intentions, and a poet a lunatic with intentions.'

In the poet lives, in schizoid unease, on the one hand the natural man (lunatic), and on the other the moral maniac with a vision of innocence, but the poet himself is not simply one or other of these. Nevertheless, it is the moral element that transforms the otherwise merely mad into the responsible. (p. 59)

The play *In the Shade of the Old Apple Tree* places him so close to the orthodox Catholic view of good and evil, that he may as well be called a 'Catholic' poet. (p. 60)

Barker's view of the Evil one, 'the downward demon pull', suffers a gradual refinement of definition over the twenty-five years covered by the collected poems.

There is not however any clear vision of the nature of beatitude and no notion of redemption, that one could seriously believe in, emerges.

What becomes clearer and more constantly present, explicitly and in underlying feeling, is the vision of

> That desert of human loves
> Individual loneliness

In this play there is the inevitability of sin and betrayal, and the dreadful consciousness of this inevitability.

The question of Original Sin is clearly at the heart of Barker's vision. And we are not far away from the world of Charles Baudelaire here. The world of *Les Fleurs du Mal*, and perhaps more of the diaries and the criticism. There is the same view of sin, and this is related to a view of the sexes as divided by their ethical position; man living in relation to an absolute, cursed by a sense of the ideal, woman living entirely in a world of relationships.

The position of pride and of ego, the 'satanic I am', the recognition that prayer occupies a higher category than the poem, the view of poetry as what Jacques Rivière has called a 'raid on the absolute and its results a revelation,' all are common to Barker and Baudelaire.

There is also Baudelaire's famous concern with correspondences and his view of the character of true intelligence in this respect. For Barker the correspondences constitute the key to poetic profundity, that is, the poem is profound in terms of what it conceals, for the multiplicity of faces behind the mask which it apparently consists of.

The image is for him the discovered fact of the imagination.

> What Michelangelo saw hidden in a piece
> of dirt . . . what Jehovah forbids made of
> himself because when the image has been
> given to a thing or an idea then the thing or
> idea has been subjugated. The image is made
> up of words, words are made up of the al-
> phabet, and the alphabet is the twenty-six
> stations of the cross to the Logos.
> The poem is what happens to the image.

In experiencing 'the multiplicities or correspondences that the image conceals' he discovers that 'the poetry is the correspondent'. Thus the poem is the special agent whose function is to 'arrogate the unknowable'. It is the instrument of the imagination which seeks to honour and acknowledge the absolute. The poem will always conceal more than it discloses. To rule out the numinous would be totally to degrade the role of the poem and of the poet. (pp. 61-2)

[There] is [an] overriding character of all poetry, that it affirms, glorifies, praises.

It is in the light of this fact that the morality of Barker's poetry must be viewed, for few poets have shown a clearer and more constant awareness of this central aspect of the activity than he has. (p. 62)

One is involved in obscure matters when one raises the position of human uncertainty, human despair even, in the scale of great moral certainties that constitute the poem. But this very concern has been conspicuously Barker's. (p. 63)

Two things run through the work of Barker which demonstrate his relationship to Baudelaire: his vision of evil and his sense of the Void.

These things are analogous but not identical. Baudelaire's *Le Gouffre* is a profound and universal fact of all our psychology, and Barker's gibbering void is another manifestation of it. But with the characteristic difference that he has discarded the devious satanic approach. Their common ground may well be simply Augustinian Christianity. (p. 64)

It will not be surprising if reflection on the work of a poet who believes that . . . 'the image exercises its profundity in proportion to the number of strata or masks it wears to conceal, and at the same time to characterize, the profundities in which it exists' . . . reveals that the Mask plays a role of some importance both in his imagery and in his attitudes.

By the Mask I do not mean merely that which hides its essential character or origins in an appearance that is somehow contrary to its true nature. I do not mean merely perversity. There is that too, but also there is the ritual, the personal rite. And there is this as an instrument for excavation in territory too terrifying for direct vision, for direct statement. (p. 67)

Thus the mask is what allows a man to penetrate in deep regions of the mind and soul and yet survive, not to disappear forever.

If it were possible to penetrate into the ultimate regions where the poem has its most profound existence then he who so penetrated would do precisely this, disappear. This is how I interpret Barker's introductory lines to his collected poems:

> 'And what, said the Emperor, does this poem
> describe?'
>   'It describes,' said the Poet, 'the Cave of the
> Never-Never.
> Would you like to see what's inside?' He offered his
> arm.
>   They stepped into the poem and disappeared
> forever.

These verses should have forewarned those reviewers of Barker's poems who approached the task armed with the principles of the anti-romanticism of the early part of this century. We are still overshadowed by the prodigious task performed by Pound and Eliot, the strictures and prejudices arising from it have been invoked in derogation of Barker. For such criticisms his work presents an easy enough target. Nevertheless, it is best to leave these objections behind when we enter the world of Barker's consciousness. For here in a region of religious pressure, where the wounded eros cries out for liberation from the mesh of a guilt-ridden subconscious, a region of old eschatological thought and even older instincts towards immolation, these objections lose much of their usefulness. For the rhetoric is not the vague dressing up of unimportant doubtful attitudes to look like poetic experience, it is the result of attempting to speak of the unspeakable. (pp. 67-8)

The use of the terms 'Poet' and 'Emperor' and the 'Cave of the Never-Never' and the gentle air of allegory and fable introduces us to one aspect of the mask the Barkerian vision wears. There is the characteristic lightness of touch, which although abandoned on necessary occasions is never wholly beyond his command, but which does not disguise the serious fact that Barker writes always as Poet, dedicated and possessed, trapped certainly in the biological cage, but speaking from that far world of ultimate mysteries.

Here then is one Mask. Unexpectedly that of THE POET. The poem then becomes a formal rite, and in keeping with this we find a severe and at times maniacal attention to form. A love of the riddle, the pun, the inversion. I do not feel that this requires demonstration. . . . A superficial reading of the verse leaves us still at the level of this Mask

and not yet hearing the strange undertones of the anguished human. (pp. 68-9)

The Mask hides the personal suffering.

The raw material of the poems, the occasions of moral distress, the minutiae of defeat and humiliation are not made known. These have been apotheosised into the poem and are contained in it. To such an extent that certain poems of Barker's, that wear the mask of simple poetic invocations, can be read as biographic detail, given the key. The key is not given, we discover it occasionally and by accident, but the poetry in its innate character bears no relation to the confession. (p. 69)

I doubt if it is possible to discuss Barker's work at all seriously without penetrating to some extent into the world of religious belief. He himself asserts the supreme importance of religion. For him poetry cannot usurp the responsibilities of religion. The poet cannot operate without the sanction of the religious man, whereas the religious man can pray without reference to the poet. The category of prayer being of a higher order than that of the poem. (p. 71)

Viewed in the light of the Mask many of the difficulties presented by Barker's rhetoric disappear.

What appears to be verbalism has meaning. Provided we remember the relationship to reality postulated by Barker's concept of THE POET.

In the first place the heightened language represents the real or actual world of event and fact as it is apotheosised into the poem. It is at the same time a description of event and a transposition of event onto a higher moral plane. In this way the religious man in Barker is satisfied by the poet in him, and the suffering human is also expressed. The mask of the poet contains the reality of the human and the reality of the religious man. Its meaning proceeds in deepening layers, the key to which lies in the moral needs of the reader. Just as its origin lies in the moral needs of the poet.

Barker's poems, although they wear a formal, ritual, and rhetorical dress for the most part, are in fact as full of things as an old lumber room. (pp. 73-4)

His poems do not contain lies in that they are true to the conditions of their own existence. This existence is not conditioned by the idea of communication, or instruction, or social usefulness. For Barker, the only possible vehicle of communication is love, not words, and 'if a little love gets through/Then we are luckier than most'. But in fact he offers no anodyne to the truth that we are each one irrevocably doomed to aloneness; and art for him is, as Samuel Beckett has it, the apotheosis of solitude. (p. 74)

In the work of Barker I see a deeply religious nature break silence in anguish. And the anguish has its roots in the internecine embrace of eros and the spiritual man in the person of the poet. (p. 75)

> *Pat Swift, "Prolegomenon to George Barker," in* Homage to George Barker on His Sixtieth Birthday, *edited by John Heath-Stubbs and Martin Green (© Martin Brian & O'Keefe Ltd. 1973), Martin Brian & O'Keefe, 1973, pp. 57-75.*

Barker is an emotional spendthrift over-ready to risk the slip-shod and second-rate in the cause of pulling off an impressive effect. At its worst this emerges as a sort of aimless emotional lunging, a flowing, rhapsodic imprecision which betrays abstraction in the act of enforcing intensity. . . . (p. 72)

There's some radical lack of mediation throughout [*In Memory of David Archer*] between the discursive and the visionary, so that the first slackens into looseness and the second softens into mere vagueness. Even so, the authenticity of the emotional impulse is impressive, even when the verbal textures are laid on too thickly; Barker is willing to reveal himself . . ., and while the unstaunched flow of that confessionalism leaves a good many ragged edges, it also conveys the sense of an individual voice rather than of an anonymous ('timeless') Nature-poet. (p. 73)

> *Terry Eagleton, in* Stand *(copyright © by* Stand*), Vol. 15, No. 4 (1974).*

[Both George Barker and Ted Hughes], in Barker's phrase, are 'victims of crashed astrology', discovering that 'God is dead, but his death can wrestle.' *Calamiterror* begins at an impasse,

> None till his spirit like the thermometer
> climbs
> Out of his own abdominal abysms . . .

and ends by having to accept the terms of that impasse: 'No secret move/Disturbing blood but to god transfuses.' It is the first convolution of what becomes, throughout Barker's poetry, 'the serpent continually swallowing itself'. He seeks an escape, in the final section of *Calamiterror,* into political commitment, but for Barker this is very much a temporary expedient. . . . (p. 83)

Poetry has only two subjects, Barker argues, Sex and Death, and through most of his work they are intricately at war. Sex, that brings him repeatedly to the little death, is the life urge. From this Manichean double armlock he is never able, and ultimately refuses, to escape: 'Siamese monster of Christ and the Devil/I coil my sins in ecstasy around me'. There is a contrast here with C. H. Sisson, another poet whose sexuality and Christianity are in conflict. In Sisson the self-hatred thus engendered comes close to forming a life-hatred. In Barker this never happens, or almost never. It is the difference between an Anglican and a Roman Catholic sensibility. Whereas the Puritan strain has made Anglican piety an astringent, individual tradition, the Catholic Church is so overwhelming an institution, its hold so ineluctable, that Barker can, virtually has to, both celebrate and rebel. He can inveigh against God the Heavy Father in his 'Sacred Elegies' and still appeal to 'The Five Faces of Pity'. Barker's quality as a religious poet is that he is an impenitent, as most of us are. The poems hold in tension the conflicts basic to any relationship, spiritual or personal: the recognition of need, for instance, and the reaction of defiance that immediately follows. (p. 84)

The 'Four Cycles of Love Poems' . . . mark the pivotal point of Barker's *Collected Poems 1930-1965*. The First Cycle is an extraordinary achievement, a sequence of homosexual love poems as elaborate as they are passionate. Nemesis follows in the Second Cycle, the estrangement of wife and child. The Third and Fourth Cycles struggle with the loss, attempting to shape comfortable words out of what seems a cry wrung from the heart of self-knowledge:

> The ache at the break of the heart
>   Is nothing: a pearl knows this.
> What remains eternally intolerable is always
>   The justice, the justice.

Sadly, it is as much a turning point for the work as for the life. It means that since his early 'thirties Barker's poetry has had to deal almost entirely in the material of recollection and regret. . . . Barker's talent needs to be combative, to be struggling with that coil of good and evil: now the coil has snapped. Once the Faustian debt is paid (and paid handsomely) in the latter half of *Collected Poems,* there is nothing left to him but shadow-boxing. Theories of poetry now rise from their proper, subliminal station to become the material of the verse itself. As the abstraction increases, so the rhetoric inflates: 'O pinnacles where the elected princes die/With their dogstar boots on and a truth in hand'. Marooned at these heights, Barker floats over the late 'fifties like a left-over barrage balloon.

Edwin Muir greeted *Calamiterror* as the work of a major poet, 'still at the unformed stage'. Twenty years later, in the *Penguin Book of Contemporary Verse,* Kenneth Allott felt bound to point out that Barker was *still* at the unformed stage. The problem is that Barker's style reflects the circularity of his themes. Not only does he fall victim . . . to the monotomy of high intensity, but his own credo, that poetry is the acceptance, not the criticism, of life, tends to preclude any development. The impulses of celebrant and rebel are so balanced that they cancel each other out, from the upward/downward antithesis of *Calamiterror* to the tables turned turtle of 'Goodman Jacksin and the Angel'. This circularity dizzies poet as well as reader, with the result that critics have generally turned for the paradigm of Barker's style to his shorter works. (pp. 84-5)

I cannot help feeling, though, that to concentrate on the shorter poems, as though Barker were merely a stylist *manqué,* is to miss the point. It is not just that the energy of the long poems subsumes individual blunders. It is that their genetic process, by which images fuse and divide and fuse again, to propagate like cells, bodies forth Barker's real theme, which is the making and marring of his own soul. The unease of recent critics with Barker's work springs partly, one suspects, from an unease with this sort of undertaking. The *Collected Poems* begin as a modern Divine Comedy, with the circles of Heaven, Purgatory and Hell tangled together like the bands of a harem ring. They end with the spiralling descent, as Barker says, of a proud mind into its self-made abyss. In this sense . . . the *Collected Poems* form a Faustian testament. A partial, flawed testament, certainly. But at least a testament of some kind.

Thus the *Collected Poems 1930-1965* stand on their own, a single volume: one hopes that future printings will allow this to remain so. It is a pity that *The True Confession of George Barker,* . . . which should have formed the comic counter-mask, is so infected with the weaknesses of Barker's middle period. . . . The collections of Barker's middle period are so much shadow-play because intensity has been replaced by wearied obsession. Old tricks and familiar images are repeated time and again, not because they have come freshly to mind, but because they are all the poet seems to know.

The recovery does not come until Barker finds in the short-line patterns of *Poems of Places & People* . . . a way of breaking up his old verse habits. Even here appearances can be deceptive: often the old verse movement is merely chopped up differently. At its best, though, the new style seems to reawaken Barker's interest in shaping the verse, in achieving suggestion rather than statement. More significantly still, the old Siamese monster reawakes, that ambivalence of Sex v Death out of which Barker writes best. In

'Venusberg' this gives him his first truly sustained sequence since the *Collected Poems*. (pp. 85-6)

Dialogues etc may well mark another phase of his work, in that it suggests a new kind of energy, a more detached, free-ranging vitality. The ironies are tighter, at once more incisive and more human. The wit of 'On the Beach at Forte Dei Marmi' or 'Miranda' is a subtle, forgiving wit, a far remove from the gusto of Barker's earlier comic style. . . . God and Magog, who conduct the eight Dialogues, are each given a touch of character, so that the Dialogues work as something of a double-act. They are well-timed, too, in another sense, being spaced through the book to chime with other themes. All in all, it is an adroit collection. The key quality, perhaps, is the restraint in handling pathos, which produces the plangency of 'Even Venus Turns Over' or 'Dialogue III'. Barker has always been a haunted poet. Here, for the first time, he shows a lightness of touch that is itself haunting. . . . (p. 86)

> Roger Garfitt, "Ballooning," in London Magazine (© London Magazine *1976*), August-September, 1976, pp. 83-6.

* * *

BARNES, Djuna 1892-

American novelist, short story writer, and dramatist, Barnes has earned wide acclaim for her remarkable novel *Nightwood*. The characters of her fiction are haunted and obsessed, existing in a nightmarish setting. In his introduction to *Nightwood*, T. S. Eliot notes the novel's "great achievement of style, the beauty of phrasing, the brilliance of wit and characterization, and a quality of horror and doom very nearly related to that of Elizabethan tragedy." Barnes has also written under the pseudonym of Lydia Steptoe. (See also *CLC*, Vols. 3, 4, and *Contemporary Authors*, Vols. 9-12, rev. ed.)

Of the fantastical quality of her imagination; of the gift for imagery . . .; of the epigrammatic incisiveness of her phrasing and her penchant, . . . akin to the Elizabethans, for dealing with the more scabrous manifestations of human fallibility—of all these there is evidence in *Ryder*, Miss Barnes's first novel. But all this might well have resulted only in a momentary flare-up of capricious brilliance, whose radiance would have been as dazzling as it was insubstantial. *Ryder*, it must be confessed, is an anomalous creation from any point of view. Although Miss Barnes's unusual qualities gradually emerge from its kaleidoscope of moods and styles, these qualities are still, so to speak, held in solution or at best placed in the service of a literary *jeu d'esprit*. Only in *Nightwood* do they finally crystallize into a definitive and comprehensible pattern. (p. 26)

While the structural principle of *Nightwood* is the same as of *Ulysses* and *A la recherche du temps perdu*—spatial form, obtained by means of reflexive reference—there are marked differences in technique that will be obvious to every reader. (p. 27)

Proust and Joyce accept the naturalistic principle, presenting their characters in terms of those commonplace details, those descriptions of circumstance and environment, that we have come to regard as verisimilar. Their experiments with the novel form, it is true, were inspired by a desire to conform more closely to the experience of consciousness; but while the principle of verisimilitude was shifted from the external to the internal, it was far from being abandoned. At the same time, these writers intended to control the abundance of verisimilar detail reflected through consciousness by the unity of spatial apprehension. But in *Nightwood* . . . the naturalistic principle has lost its dominance. We are asked only to accept the work of art as an autonomous structure giving us an individual vision of reality; and the question of the relation of this vision to an extra-artistic "objective" world has ceased to have any fundamental importance. (p. 28)

Ordinary novels, as T. S. Eliot justly observes, "obtain what reality they have largely from an accurate rendering of the noises that human beings currently make in their daily simple needs of communication; and what part of a novel is not composed of these noises consists of a prose which is no more alive than that of a competent newspaper writer or government official." Miss Barnes abandons any pretensions to this kind of verisimilitude, just as modern painters have abandoned any attempt at naturalistic representation; and the result is a world as strange to the reader, at first sight, as the world of Cubism was to its first spectators. Since the selection of detail in *Nightwood* is governed not by the logic of verisimilitude but by the demands of the décor necessary to enhance the symbolic significance of the characters, the novel has baffled even its most fascinated admirers. (p. 31)

Since *Nightwood* lacks a narrative structure in the ordinary sense, it cannot be reduced to any sequence of action for purposes of explanation. One can, if one chooses, follow the narrator in Proust through the various stages of his social career; one can, with some difficulty, follow Leopold Bloom's epic journey through Dublin; but no such reduction is possible in *Nightwood*. As Dr. O'Connor remarks to Nora Flood, with his desperate gaiety: "I have a narrative, but you will be put to it to find it." Strictly speaking, the doctor is wrong—he has a static situation, not a narrative, and no matter how hard the reader looks he will find only the various facets of this situation explored from different angles. The eight chapters of *Nightwood* are like searchlights, probing the darkness each from a different direction yet ultimately illuminating the same entanglement of the human spirit. . . .

[The first four] chapters are knit together, not by the progress of any action—either narrative action or, as in a stream-of-consciousness novel, the flow of experience—but by the continual reference and cross reference of images and symbols that must be referred to each other spatially throughout the time-act of reading. (pp. 31-2)

[Chapters five through seven] are completely dominated by the doctor, "Dr. Matthew-Mighty-grain-of-salt-Dane-O'Connor," whose dialogues with Felix and Nora—or rather his monologues, prompted by their questions—make up the bulk of these pages. (p. 43)

[To] find anything approaching [these dialogues'] combination of ironic wit and religious humility, their emotional subtlety and profound human simplicity, their pathos, their terror, and their sophisticated self-consciousness, one has to go back to the religious sonnets of John Donne. It is these monologues that prove the main attraction of the novel at first reading, and their magnetic power has, no doubt, contributed to the misconception that *Nightwood* is only a collection of magnificent fragments. Moreover, since the doctor always speaks about himself *sub specie aeternitatis*, it is difficult at first to grasp the relations between his monologues and the central theme of the novel. (pp. 43-4)

[The] book cannot be understood unless the doctor is seen as part of the whole pattern, rather than as an overwhelming individual creation who throws the others into the background by the magnitude of his understanding and the depth of his insight.... It is this attitude that, in the end, dominates the book and gives it a final focus.

"Man," the doctor tells Felix, "was born damned and innocent from the start, and wretchedly—as he must—on those two themes—whistles his tune." Robin ... was described as both child and desperado, that is, both damned and innocent; and since the doctor generalizes her spiritual predicament, we can infer that he views the condition of the other characters—and of himself—as in essentials no different. (p. 44)

Because of his knowledge of man's nature, the doctor realizes that he himself, and the other people in the novel, differ from Robin only in degree; they are all involved to some extent in her desperate dualism, and in the end their doom is equally inescapable. (p. 45)

Nightwood does have a pattern—a pattern arising from the spatial interweaving of images and phrases independently of any time-sequence of narrative action.... [The] reader is simply bewildered if he assumes that, because language proceeds in time, *Nightwood* must be perceived as a narrative structure. We can now understand why T. S. Eliot wrote [in his preface to *Nightwood*] that "*Nightwood* will appeal primarily to readers of poetry," and that "it is so good a novel that only sensibilities trained on poetry can wholly appreciate it." Since the unit of meaning in *Nightwood* is usually a phrase or sequence of phrases—at most a long paragraph—it carries the evolution of spatial form in the novel forward to a point where it is practically indistinguishable from modern poetry. (p. 49)

> *Joseph Frank, in* Sewanee Review *(reprinted by permission of the editor,* © *1945 by The University of the South), Summer, 1945 (and reprinted as "Djuna Barnes: Nightwood," in* The Widening Gyre, *Indiana University Press, 1963, pp. 25-48).*

Djuna Barnes in "The Antiphon" has invented a language which would flabbergast an ordinary, cultivated reader, give pause to a brave lexicographer; it so hallucinates the day as to leap into another century (backward or forward as you may think). It is this extraordinary poetic language by which she will be known. The plot of her play, concerning the dire results of Mormon polygamy in the relations of a cast-off wife with her daughter and sons, loses no chance, in a decrepit house, to hide in the art-irradiated artificial talk. If it could be acted, the action would not be notable; the actors are puppets on which to hang ideas and diatribes, but the interwoven characterization of mother and daughter is notable. It is better as a poem, a verse play for reading, than as a verse play for production. Nevertheless, I should think H. James would have enjoyed it, been startled by it. Sin and incest are shown as irremediable. (pp. 619-20)

Djuna Barnes is a creeper into worm-holes, the worm-holes of frustration, incest, and death. But from her dung heap, what a startling bloom of language! (p. 620)

[I wish] that Djuna Barnes had written a less esoteric play, one more for acting than for reading. (p. 623)

> *Richard Eberhart, in* Virginia Quarterly Review *(copyright, 1958, by the* Virginia Quarterly Review, The University of Virginia), *Vol. 34, No. 4 (Autumn, 1958).*

The black humor of *Nightwood* is ... particularly illus-

trated in the grotesque, violent characters, the detached attitude toward the descriptions of outrageous clothes and houses, and the parody of the novelist's role.

These comic elements are part of Barnes' larger thematic concern with modern man's separation from a more primitive animal nature—at first glance, hardly the theme for a humorous novel.... In *Nightwood,* humanity, day, and present contrast with beast, night, and past. Thus Robin is introduced as an "infected carrier of the past" and as having "the eyes of wild beasts." Her various love affairs with Felix, Nora, and Jenny illustrate a search for someone to tell her that she is innocent, for, as Barnes suggests, awareness of innocence leads to consciousness of moral values and, in turn, to humanity. Robin's three principal lovers, however, are unable to help her achieve the human state. Caught up in their own senses of alienation, and goaded by selfish love of Robin, they become animal-like themselves in their desperation to appropriate the bestial woman.

The numerous love affairs are destructive, painfully pursued, and selfishly concluded, for each character searches for a lover who might alleviate his sense of incompleteness. The longed-for reunion between animal and human states never takes place, and the characters are left with an impossible choice: to be primarily human, which means the painful awareness of alienation; or to be primarily animal, which means the longing for moral consciousness. Barnes suggests that the scale has tipped too far on the side of humanity, and she would probably agree with Dr. O'Connor's advice to Nora: "Be humble like the dust, as God intended, and crawl".... (p. 46)

Happily, however, Barnes has not written a novel of unrelenting gloom. Her sense of humor is evident from the beginning, and her use of funny elements with a depressing theme reflects the perplexing mixture so vital to black humor. Because Barnes reserves many of her comic touches for description rather than action, analysis is difficult.... Recognition of the comedy ... depends upon the individual reader, for Barnes maintains total authorial detachment. (pp. 46-7)

None of these people can be called [a character] in the conventional sense. They do not "live," nor are they "round," and the reader is never encouraged to identify with them. Like the characters in many contemporary black humor fictions, Barnes' people are static and subordinated to theme. *Nightwood* provides insight into the disordered human condition by conveying generalizations about love, bestiality, and religion, and it avoids the reader's expectations of verisimilitude and character development. (pp. 49-50)

In addition to the already recognized work of Djuna Barnes' contemporary, Nathanael West, *Nightwood* remains the most successful early example of the American black humor novel. Published nearly twenty-five years before the critical acceptance of this new comic fiction, it illustrates the major principles of black humor, particularly the extreme detachment of the author, the comic treatment of ugliness and violence, and the disruption of the conventional forms of the novel. Closer to the fiction of Hawkes or Pynchon than to the work of Hemingway or Dos Passos, *Nightwood* stands out among post-World War I American novels as one of the first notable experiments with a type of comedy that makes the reader want "to lean forward and laugh with terror." (p. 53)

> *Donald J. Greiner, "Djuna Barnes' 'Nightwood' and the American Origins of Black*

Humor," in Critique: Studies in Modern Fiction (*copyright © by James Dean Young 1975), Vol. XVII, No. 1, 1975, pp. 41-54.*

[Djuna Barnes'] compounding of the unlike in juxtaposition, objects of essential dissimilarity compelled into adjacency, is fully in accord with surrealistic techniques. It may frequently remind us of the compulsions of Giorgio di Chirico. Eliot's contention that her work will appeal primarily to readers of poetry is upheld, of course; but the commitment of the poetry may be far other than Eliot was willing to recognize. This much is certain: Whoever studies the French affinities of American artists after the First World War will be obliged to take Djuna Barnes into serious account. (p. 181)

> *James Baird, "Djuna Barnes and Surrealism: 'Backward Grief,'" in Individual and Community: Variations on a Theme in American Fiction, edited by Kenneth H. Baldwin and David K. Kirby (reprinted by permission of the Publisher; copyright 1975 by Duke University Press, Durham, North Carolina), Duke University Press, 1975, pp. 160-81.*

*   *   *

BARONDESS, Sue Kaufman
  See KAUFMAN, Sue

*   *   *

BARTHELME, Donald   1931-

American novelist and short story writer, Barthelme has been dubbed by Peter Ackroyd "the P. G. Wodehouse of surrealism" for his experimental fiction. Most critics agree that the lack of organization in his prose reflects his doubt of any fundamental structure in society. (See also *CLC*, Vols. 1, 2, 3, 5, 6, and *Contemporary Authors*, Vols. 21-24, rev. ed.)

Barthelme is a shrewd writer if ultimately a trivial one, and it is clever of him to choose a relatively peripheral historical conflict [in *Snow White*] in order to show how all sides are interchangeable, each having its own spurious myths . . . and its own clichés. . . . Equally characteristic of the new American writing is the way this total disillusionment with the supposed "complexities" of history turns directly into verbal clowning: two opposed alternatives of participation in a Mexican revolution suddenly switch into a farcical tangent, expressed in mock-serious language, about the lack of "personally-owned horses" and how it has afflicted "U.S. youth." The technique ostentatiously destroys distinctions between what is central and what is peripheral in human experience. The course of history itself is seen not as a weighty, momentous development in experienced time, but as an abstract scheme of contentless dates, perhaps a diagram in a notebook, "the bottom half of the 20th century" from which the speaker peers up at the mechanically interchangeable figures of Pershing and Pancho Villa somewhere near the top. Such a sense of history as symmetrically indifferent pointlessness is shared by others of the new American novelists, but Barthelme may well infer the most consistent artistic consequence of this sense by openly withdrawing from the serious representation of men and women caught in the web of history to a mimicry of verbal and cultural gestures, the fiction devised chiefly as a collage of linguistic waste products, a study of what the author himself calls "the trash phenomenon" in language.

> *Robert Alter, "The New American Novel"*

(*reprinted from Commentary by permission; copyright © 1975 by the American Jewish Committee), in Commentary, November, 1975, p. 47.*

[*The Dead Father*] is full of delights, even if not all of them attach themselves to one another.

There is a way of talking about Barthelme that allies him with a distinguished modernist movement—disciple of Borges, exemplar of the ideas of Roland Barthes, and so on—but this overlooks the distinctive pleasures of his work, his gift for parody and social satire. He has an ear as deadly as a black belt's hand. He speaks dozens of the specialized dialects that make up our language, and he mocks their pretension and the pretentious surety of those who use them. If he addresses himself mainly to sufferers of contemporary spiritual malaise, he is particularly merciless on the language that is used to describe that illness. He sometimes indulges in low college humor. He cuts up, is cute. But at his best, he achieves a lunatic poise; he provides a way of listening to the cacophony around us; he gives comfort. . . .

The Dead Father becomes a symbol of some plasticity. He is God first of all. God as a father. And father as God. After that he's what you will: The Novel, Western Culture, Truth, Duty, Honor, Country. He is the order that we seek, and the control we seek to escape. A symbol with multiple possibilities—but still a heavy symbol, and it isn't at all clear at the start that Barthelme can bear up under the load. But he inventively does. (pp. 112-13)

Sentiment earns a larger place for itself in this novel than in anything Barthelme has written before. It resides, mostly, in The Dead Father himself. . . . The Dead Father has died only "in a sense." He is "dead but still with us, still with us, but dead." He has lost his clout. He knows he's bound for the grave. But he speaks. He occasionally breaks away from his cable and accomplishes some mayhem. (pp. 113-14)

We are sorry to see The Dead Father go, when the bulldozers appear and begin to fill his grave. He reminds us of whatever it is that we imagine to have existed in a more coherent world. Not to put too fine a point on this, but if Barthelme continues in this direction, he might become a disturbing novelist. (p. 114)

> *Richard Todd, in The Atlantic Monthly (copyright © 1975 by The Atlantic Monthly Company, Boston, Mass.; reprinted with permission), December, 1975.*

Donald Barthelme's first book [was] *Come Back, Dr. Caligari*, and in 1964 it was surprising and delightful to find serious literary intentions being pursued with indifference to the distinction between "high" and "popular" culture.

But the radical quality of Barthelme's early stories was often blunted by the nature of his materials and his audience. If he was writing studies in a dying culture, they were also —like *The New Yorker*, where most of his work appeared —meant to seem amusing and unthreatening to the creatures of that culture, living or at least imagining cosmopolitan lives while keeping up with the charming vulgarity outside. . . . [His] Last-Days-of-Pompeii implications are covered over with Perelman-like whimsy, . . . [and] the governing mood remains unshakably chic.

That mood was shaken in *Unspeakable Practices, Unnatural Acts* (1968). These stories consider with surprising directness the pressure of political and social turmoil upon the static, ahistorical world that the culture of affluence represents as life. Barthelme's collages begin to include strong images of ethnic vengeance ("The Indian Uprising"), crisis politics ("Robert Kennedy Saved From Drowning," "The President"), the law-and-order mentality ("The Police Band"), the purposeless technology of modern war ("Report," "Game"). But this overtly political mood moves into more generalized forms of anxiety in *City Life* (1970), as if Barthelme had answered no to the question he posed in "Kierkegaard Unfair to Schlegel": "Do you think your irony could be useful in changing the government?"...

[In *Sadness* (1972) an] occasional image of Vietnam, busing, or racial violence intrudes, but these now seem scarcely more menacing than the appearance of King Kong at a party—he turns out to be an adjunct professor of art history at Rutgers who's as easily subdued by pleasure as anyone else.... (p. 54)

No condemnation is intended here. For all its alertness to realities beyond the media, *Unspeakable Practices, Unnatural Acts* seems to me (except for *Snow White*, a tedious countercultural soap opera) Barthelme's thinnest book, just as *Come Back, Dr. Caligari* and *Sadness*, which in their different ways are the least concerned with social and political matters, are probably his best. The terms of Barthelme's art don't easily accommodate the most difficult terms of life, and a distant and grave sense of absurdity, not feeling close-up, is what he has to give us.

But even in the subdued moods of his recent work something recalcitrant remains alive.... *The Dead Father* is stripped down ... and its economy of means seems to suit our recent discovery that material possibilities which used to seem limitless are terribly small after all.

The Dead Father is described by its publishers as "a novel," and although that's not quite right, still it is a more connected work of fiction than anything Barthelme has yet written. The connections are admittedly rudimentary: a recurring set of characters with ordinary names like Thomas, Julie, and Emma, who embark on a quest, broad comedy alternating with pathos, intimations of "larger" significances that are decently obscured by some attention to what's human and social. There is even, in the best eighteenth-century practice, a digressive book-within-a-book as well as continuing exchanges of anecdotes and personal histories. The methods, that is, are ones that Fielding or Dickens would be easy with.

They would have been less easy with the substance of Barthelme's book. The Dead Father ("dead only in a sense"), in one of his aspects a colossal Gulliverian figure, has always *been* the reality of his children.... He is God, machine technology, civil and economic law, an idea of the world as ordered, equitable, and perhaps benign, an embodiment of collective selfhood and its history like Joyce's Finn or Blake's Albion.

He is also, dead or not, the Father, the terrible possessor of the power that was here before we were, the continual reminder of how little power and freedom we can negotiate for ourselves. (pp. 54-5)

The idea of "fatherhood as a substructure of the war of all against all" happily doesn't completely overwhelm the novelist's playful interest in his characters—the Dead Father can sometimes seem a lovable old rascal or a pa-

thetic figure beset by rather priggish young enemies, and the book is unexpectedly sad, as if much of the fun had gone out of watching centers fail to hold. But they do fail, they are failing all around us, and in reading this new book I was struck by this sophisticated writer's attaching to conventions of fictional order disintegrative devices that are more suggestive of Beckett than of Perelman. There are long passages of intricately contrapuntal dialogue in which "character" almost, but not quite, disappears into the random retrieval of cultural data.... [Such] passages, in a book built out of the wreckage of a great literary form, seem to me to convey more affectingly than Barthelme's earlier, more glossy work the mysterious power of language to perpetuate itself, if nothing else, even with the bleakest material. *The Dead Father* does not always succeed, but it suggests a hopeful future for a writer whose talent may not yet have found its most hospitable form of expression. (p. 55)

> *Thomas R. Edwards, "Barthelme the Scrivener," in* The New York Review of Books *(reprinted with permission from* The New York Review of Books; *copyright © 1975 NYREV, Inc.), December 11, 1975. pp. 54-5.*

The Dead Father [is a] cold short narrative ... written at an extreme distance from life, out of literary models and the author's idea of a defunct avant-garde. *The Dead Father* is God, we are told at one point, but the tyrannic authority of the past will do. It seems clear only that Barthelme finds clarity simplistic and is enchanted with the attenuated jokes of modernity. Here may be found his Lucky speech, his *Watt* palaver, his Joycean flourishes, his Kafkaesque dream, etc. It's all very cynical and chic, like Woody Allen's posture of the twirp taking on the big guys once again.... Real freedom, if that is what Barthelme is seeking in laying the image of the father to rest, will come in a release of his comic talent from the merely fashionable. He is ingenious in dealing with the madness of sophisticated urban life but he is not yet angry enough to dig out from under the clods of pastiche that muffle his own voice. (pp. 408-09)

> *Maureen Howard, in* The Yale Review *(© 1976 by Yale University; reprinted by permission of the editors), Spring, 1976.*

One of the reasons—I think it is the principal reason—for the basic antagonism that obtains between aestheticism and fatherhood is the relation in which aestheticism stands to nature. Simply stated, aestheticism sets itself *against* nature, toward which it adopts an attitude of irony and condescension. Aestheticism opposes the authority of all biological imperatives. By extension, moreover, it casts doubt on all principles of continuity and necessity based on or implied by the laws of nature, for which it is eager to substitute the disjunctions and self-inventions of cultural artifice. Toward language, as toward life, it holds an essentially "plastic" view. Finding the *données* of nature an intolerable imposition on the freedom of the mind to impose its will on experience, aestheticism seeks a radical redress of its grievances in the realm of culture. Oscar Wilde's famous quip about life imitating art was always, perhaps, more amusing than true, but there is this to be said for it: it does, without question, apply to the life of culture even if it does not apply to the life of nature, and it is usually culture that the aesthete has in mind when he speaks of "life."...

One way of understanding Freud's whole psychological edifice is to see it as a challenge to and criticism of the aesthetic dissembling that characterized the European culture of his day, which, though bourgeois and eminently respectable, was completely in thrall to the conventions of decorative euphemism on which aestheticism depends. Between Beardsley, say, and Freud there is a curious symmetry of vision, with Beardsley choosing to celebrate all those dislocations of the psyche that Freud set out to repair. (p. 56)

[In *The Dead Father*] the ghosts of the aesthetic movement meet the phantom fears of the Freudian family romance. Fatherhood is caustically enthroned as ogrehood, and all familial relations reduced to offenses of taste—the only offenses that can any longer be taken seriously from the aesthetic point of view. Yet something has happened to the feigned detachment and hauteur that once characterized the aesthetic attitude. No longer secure in its distance from the world, it has adopted the tactics of a more militant and polemical irony—the tactics of Dada. In *The Dead Father*, the assault on fatherhood and the aggrandizement of art— twin aspects of a single struggle—are accomplished by means of a style in which all emotions but the aesthetic are shown to be ridiculous and destructive. At the same time, since the assault on fatherhood is inevitably an assault on childhood, the virtues of aestheticism are identified with the freedom and fetishism of childhood. Which is, indeed, to return to the aesthetic assumptions of Dada—a name which, in this context, acquires yet another irony.

Taking his cue from the triumphant revival of Dada in the visual arts, from which he has borrowed actual visual devices in some of his earlier works, Mr. Barthelme has fashioned a fictional style, at once deadpan and disjunctive, mocking and digressive, that is the literary equivalent of the Dada collage. The aim is, apparently, to write a kind of "children's book" for adults—a genre that permits the author to address knowing readers with a wink as he distends his narrative with vivid and amusing irrelevancies that, like the details of a crowded collage, can be counted on to lend a sense of mystery and complexity and a certain decorative appeal to what, in the case of *The Dead Father*, is actually a rather simple fantasy of filial revenge.

The story itself, such as it is, has the quality of a fairy tale or folk tale that has been scissored, Dada-style, into shreds, and then reassembled with derisory and disproportionate embellishments. The fun is in the embellishments, and the moral is in the tale—there, and in the ["Manual for Sons"] of moral instruction that Mr. Barthelme inserts into the narrative lest we mistake his already obvious purpose. For Mr. Barthelme is, with all his waggishness, a very didactic writer, and *The Dead Father* is, despite its facetious tone, a very moralistic book—but moralistic, to be sure, in the new fashion, which yearns for life to be free of all condition and contingency and which, as a consequence, despises all evidence of growth, attachment, and maturation as an obstacle to its cherished ontological freedom. Or, as Julie, the foolish "heroine" of *The Dead Father*, explains to its eponymous victim: "They are [fifty-year-old] boys because they don't want to be old farts. . . . The old fart is not cherished in this society."

The Dead Father—he is given no other name in the book— is the dreaded and archetypal "old fart" incarnate, and *The Dead Father* itself is a mock-epic account of the journey to his own burial he endures at the hands of his son, Thomas, who is aided by a retinue of disreputable revelers. The Dead Father is, in this surrealist odyssey, an immense and

horrific figure, at once a corpse being dragged by gigantic cables overland to his monumental grave in a distant place and a talkative, demanding, imperious, terrible-tempered tyrant, very much alive in asserting his terrifying and irrational appetites and prerogatives—a figure straight out of *Ubu Roi,* only magnified in size and fury and silliness, and redrawn to the lineaments of Freudian fatherhood. But this Father is also the state, if not indeed society itself—symbol of all authority and order, which, in Mr. Barthelme's social cosmos, is always and inevitably an insane authority and a malevolent order. (pp. 56-7)

[Every chapter] offers a variation or illumination of the themes sounded in the prologue—the dreaded omnipotence of the Dead Father, and Thomas's wish to see him really dead and buried. The progress of the narrative is the fulfillment of that wish as the Dead Father, despite all his railing and resistance, is slowly, painfully stripped of his authority and placed in his grave.

There is almost no action to speak of in this narrative, but a lot of talk in which there are references to action. . . . [Mainly], they all talk to or about the Dead Father himself, or watch his progressively enfeebled antics. Even in his decline—and this, I take it, is Mr. Barthelme's point—it is still the Dead Father who is in control, who cannot be exorcised even in death.

It is for the Dead Father that all vitality is reserved, which, given the terms of Mr. Barthelme's style, means that he gets the best lines and the most vivid images. (pp. 57-8)

What momentum *The Dead Father* attains, however, is to be found in the campaign against fatherhood itself. There are two sides to this campaign—one devoted to delivering the Dead Father to his grave, the other (the source of greater anguish for Thomas) devoted to resisting the terrible fate of replacing him, of relinquishing boyhood for fatherhood itself. Early on in the novel, the conflict between fatherhood and aestheticism is made quite explicit. (p. 58)

Compounded of nonsense and primitive fear, the ["Manual for Sons"] spells out the case against fatherhood in all its aspects, from the aesthetic to the social to the sexual, and concludes by denying the son any hope of recompense for what he has suffered at the hands of fatherhood, even the hope of patricide. . . . "We have seen that the key idea, in fatherhood, is 'responsibility.'" Mr. Barthelme tells us in this "Manual for Sons," and it is responsibility, above all, that must be abjured.

The Dead Father . . . is Mr. Barthelme's most explicit statement of the view that has governed all of his work—a view that holds life itself in contempt, and seeks a redress of its grievances in the kind of literary artifice that shuts out all reference to the normal course of human feeling. Art, in the scenario of this style, is a weapon in the war against nature, and nature, paradoxically, the enemy of innocence. His, I think, is the most sophisticated, because the most calculated and refined, expression of that hatred of the family that was a hallmark of the ideology of the counter-culture of the 60's, and distinguished from other such expressions by allying itself with art, rather than with nature, in its search for innocence and escape. Perhaps it is that alliance—so distant from the vulgarities of the counterculture itself—that has won Mr. Barthelme his great following among critics and professors and literary editors, if not among the readers of fiction. For what he offers that specialized public is the illusion that salvation lies in the inner sanctum of their own profession. (pp. 58-9)

Hilton Kramer, "Barthelme's Comedy of Patricide" (reprinted from Commentary *by permission; copyright © 1976 by Hilton Kramer), in* Commentary, *August, 1976, pp. 56-9.*

There are many Barthelmes. . . . There is, of course, Barthelme the stylist, who has raised the deadpan style to heights barely dreamed of by the florid. And there is Barthelme the surrealist, a mind more puissant in this mode than any this side of Jorge Luis Borges. There are also Barthelme the wit, the storyteller, the psychologist. [But *Amateurs* presents] an opportunity to examine yet another avatar: Barthelme the social critic.

There are 20 stories in *Amateurs,* and all of them might be construed as social criticism in one way or another: critiques of the family (with subthemes of isolation and escape), of class structures, of peer-group pressures and collective decision-making; studies in the modes of leadership: charismatic, permissive, bumbling, scared; biopsies of social symbol and ritual, of role-playing and hierarchies; critiques of the small societies that are formed everywhere by two people. In perhaps 75 per cent of the stories, the intent of social criticism seems deliberate, even predominant; in a few, it is obvious, though it can be obvious in slightly devious ways.

It is obvious in "The Sergeant," a nightmare about a middle-aged man inducted into the army by mistake and strangled in red tape. It is obvious in the story of social manipulation that begins, "So I bought a little city (it was Galveston, Texas) and told everybody that nobody had to move, we were going to do it just gradually, very relaxed, no big changes overnight." But you may have to look twice to notice the ways in which this story is an analogue of the Vietnam experience. It is less obvious in "The Great Hug," which can be read simply as a tale of yin and yang but also contains buried observations on the relation of the artist to society. . . .

[In] most of Barthelme's stories, the main action is something that (we tell ourselves) could never actually happen as described; the stories go beyond mere accuracy of detail to present a basic concept, a metaphor of social relations which is truer and more sharply focused in its overtones, its implications, precisely because it cannot be read satisfactorily on the level of mere "what happened next" narrative. The special power of these images is based on the fact that they *are* mixed metaphors; we are able to see a particular aspect of our society more clearly because it is seen through a distorting lens. Barthelme, like the modern composers who have found strange new beauties in dissonance, has taken a technique that the manuals solemnly warn against and made it, with incredible brilliance, the basis of a whole system for writing fiction.

Joseph McLellan, "How Real is Real," in Book World—The Washington Post *(© The Washington Post), November 28, 1976, p. H3.*

Barthelme's greatest debts are not to the art world or to camp but to Gogol and Kafka and especially Borges. His true American ancestor is S. J. Perelman, his predecessor at "The New Yorker," where most of Barthelme's stories first appear. But Perelman would never write such fiction. . . . Perelman's antic haymakers spring from the irrepressible green id, the old Adam (Groucho Marx) who screams "hands off!" to mass culture. Barthelme, forty

years and three wars later, has no such angry all-American optimism. For Barthelme we're all trapped in culture, top to bottom, inside and out, highbrow and low, mired in the Oedipus complex, chattering clichés, isolated, alienated prattling consciousnesses—no green leaf of freedom within, no exit in sight. "Oh there's brain damage in the east, and brain damage in the west . . . and in my lady's parlor—brain damage," he writes.

In this he seems a New York cousin to Samuel Beckett. But Beckett is always the bleak modernist, the "stoic comedian," full of serious stuff, high art, even the jokes in earnest, absurd always spelled with a capital A. Barthelme is funnier, even silly, a veritable squirrel of wit, collecting bits of verbal trash and customized consumer culture junk from the blather and bump of New York city life. It's as if Beckett's ashcans had been rounded up to serve as ornamental vases or cocktail party favors.

Barthelme's stories are assemblages: fragments of conversations, monologues, historical and literary snapshots, glimpses of domestic strife, the burdens and groans of urban child-raising and sexual activity. Many have little nervous bursts of violent action—slaps, cuts, gashes, a quick flash—that interrupt the deadpan descriptions and lists of artifacts and urban totems, the samples of technical jargon and intellectual nattering. At his best—in the two story collections "Unspeakable Practices, Unnatural Acts" and "City Life" and in the section "A Manual for Sons" in his novel "The Dead Father"—Barthelme's collages have a poignant, ruminative undertone that gives the flickering juxtapositions a kind of nihilistic sheen that is beautiful and moving. He can be extraordinarily intelligent and poised—a Pierrot on skates. And yet he sometimes seems content to coast along, relying on his perfect pitch and fine collector's eye. He can sound a lot like such on again, off again New York poets of the 60's as Frank O'Hara or Kenneth Koch, as in his story "You Are as Brave as Vincent van Gogh" in this new book, "Amateurs". . . . (p. 17)

[His] surprises can turn nasty or go flat. The famous style then becomes a mannerism, self-duplicating, an automatic reflex not an act of local intelligence. The collage becomes a pastiche. The absurdities become as routine as the clichés that convey them: the japes become jokes, the satire a lampoon.

"The idea is to *use* dreck, not write about it," said William H. Gass. "Barthelme is often guilty of opportunism of subject (the war, street riots, launching pads, etc.) and to be opportune is to succumb to dreck. . . . cleverness is also dreck. The cheap joke is dreck. The topical, too, is dreck. Who knows this better than Barthelme, who has the art to make a treasure out of trash, to see *out* from inside it. . . . A seriousness about his subject is sometimes wanting. When this obtains, the result is grim, and grimly overwhelming."

Unhappily, ["Amateurs"] is, for Barthelme, relatively weak. It would delight, astonish and perplex if it had come from any other writer. (pp. 17-18)

Some of these [stories] are funny, some amusing, some flat, some nasty. Almost every one contains a flawless sentence or two. But there's much less variety and kaleidoscopic color in these stories, fewer voices, fewer threads combining, than in Barthelme's best work. And there are times when Barthelme resorts to violent fantasy to keep things lively, as if the language weren't enough. After the elegance of the passage ending "little specks of white had started to appear in the crisp, carefully justified black prose," he abruptly goes to "I picked up the hammer and said into the telephone, 'Well, if he comes around here he's going to get a face full of hammer. A four-pound hammer can mess up a boy's face pretty bad. A four-pound hammer can make a bloody rubbish of a boy's face.'" It's not just the content but the need for such an easy shock that is crass here.

Which raises the question of all pop art, of all cool avoidance of narrative, all pure, ironic, amoral literary construction. If the modern urban world is dreck, garbage, sound and fury signifying nothing, how moving, instructive, important can pop art be? If such stories operate on less than full esthetic power—if the language goes slack, the invention mechanical, the jokes too much like college humor, the contrasts too crude and hostile—then they're in danger of becoming not a foil or a transcendence of their material but a contributor to the mess, an accomplice after the fact, part of the problem.

Narrow peepholes show partial truths; a single tone is not a melody, no matter how pure it may be. A style is not a body of work. Nabokov and Pynchon are so much larger, so various, so historical. In several of his earlier books Barthelme commanded a great range of voices and allusions; he seemed to blend history, personal life, the comedy of manners and verbal detritus into a comic 60's wasteland. It's disheartening to see him here often coasting on his style, for a style can become a habit, a nervous tic, no longer responsive to experience, but self-generating, self-fulfilling, self-reflexive, a closed circuit. White noise. (p. 18)

> *Richard Locke, in* The New York Times Book Review *(© 1976 by The New York Times Company; reprinted by permission), December 19, 1976.*

Donald Barthelme's fiction now stands as the central exhibit of what we have come to call, for lack of anything more resonant or memorable, the "post-modernist" imagination. Widely imitated yet inimitable, he invests his fables, collages and word games with such style that they stand as touchstones for narrative art of the last two decades.... Still, privately if not in print, more than a few of the admirers of his first three collections, especially the brilliant *City Life,* have felt a measure of disappointment in his latest work. The perils in his method have surely been as obvious to him as to his readers from the start, the fey preciosity that threatens to turn the fictions into stand-up monologues done by a collector of middle-high camp, and the extraordinary facility which threatens to make some of his pieces seem astonishing, and yet forgettable, exercises. Happily, all questions of the direction of Barthelme's recent work are irrelevant to his latest collection, *Amateurs.* It is a gathering of previously uncollected stories, many from the early 1970s. There are no visual tricks, no old engravings, only words. (p. 119)

It is ... a rich, diverse collection, an index not of where Barthelme wishes to move next but of where he has been, when his talent has been most virtuoso and sure of itself.

The collection, by placing itself as it does over the past six years of Barthelme's career, rather than at its leading edge, invites some kind of assessment. I suggest two ways into the question of what Barthelme, in his richest and most inventive period, has amounted to. "'The world is everything that was formerly the case,' the group leader said, 'and now it is time to get back on the bus.'" So begins the

last paragraph of "The Educational Experience." What that sentence does—never mind the context—is to bring together Wittgenstein known, digested, exhausted, and inverted and to couple the Wittgenstein echo with a kind of wit that is quintessentially American, flip, tough, and facile, the kind of wit that we all recognize in its purest form in S. J. Perelman or Woody Allen. The absurdist or nihilist vision in its official European forms has never been particularly congenial to American readers, not that we cannot share its assumptions—most of us in some sense do. It's that other cultures' absurd visions either are funny in ways we cannot respond to or are not funny at all. Even the comedy of Beckett strikes most American readers as being rather strained, forced, stylized out of all human recognition, and not very funny, which is why Beckett is much admired in this country but little read. The special power that Heller, Pynchon and Barth, for example, have brought to the nihilist vision is an American comedy, full of bad taste, wisecracks, ethnic jibes, allusions to Pop culture, pratfalls, stand-up routines, and the kind of inspired ingenuity that takes us, in a sentence, from an inverted Wittgenstein quote, processed through the mind of a tour guide, to the loading of the bus itself. Nobody else does this like Barthelme, who has read everything, whose inventiveness is inexhaustible, and whose wit is both intricate and very funny.

Secondly, Barthelme has made a set of social and emotional responses for the people in his fictions that refract, in some uncanny way, the contours of our sensibility. People in Barthelme cope with technology, the myths of technology, the interruption of technological flow, useless inventions. People in Barthelme cope with media barrages, ideas, spokesmen, official announcements, encyclopedias, short courses, messages. They cope with social names, famous names, improbable names, historical names, product names, codes. They try to eat well—beer and sauerkraut, Colonel Sanders's Kentucky Fried Chicken, herb tea with sour cream, steak and eggs, chicken livers *flambé.* They try to remember, pay attention, start over, figure what to do next. Somehow that rhythm which Barthelme handles so well, of crisis and coping, carries, partly because it is stylized into myth, a potent sense of the callousness and courage, the knowingness and the poor mute innocence with which we meet our own strange world of experience. (p. 120)

> *Philip Stevick, in* The Nation *(copyright 1977 by the Nation Associates, Inc.), January 29, 1977.*

[*Come Back, Dr. Caligari*], and the books which followed in the next few years, caused several critics to speak of [Barthelme] as a writer of great promise, who would carry American fiction forward in avant-garde, experimental directions. But increasingly the promise failed of fulfilment as each new Barthelme volume appeared. There seemed to be no gain in design, but a perceptible gain in glossiness and whimsicality. . . .

[In] Barthelme there is a true uncertainty about the narrative subject. Usually the narrative-like sequence is urged forward by its own means of expression rather than by what it expresses.

Barthelme's dissipated promise, his situation of having a great future behind him, had more to do with the genre, that of experimental fiction, in which the critics located his writing. His career raises the question: does experimental fiction work as a literary category? More precisely, does it have a principle of growth, a developmental biology, so to speak, such as orthodox naturalistic fiction has so conspicuously possessed? . . .

The Dead Father has more of an air of fulfilling literary destiny than any other of Barthelme's recent books. The scale matches the content; this is a single, continuous work (Barthelme's first since 1967) and not a miscellany of bagatelles from *The New Yorker*. The presiding image of the Dead Father . . . is complicated but coherent. The Dead Father represents *pater familias,* deity, *ancien régime* aristocrat, the law, moral rectitude, and even our picture of reality.

The disparate ''aspects'' of this figure make the discontinuities and contradictions of the narrative appropriate. There is also a level of our experience at which these aspects fit together. Blake and Freud, for instance, were interested in this level; indeed Barthelme's Dead Father must be the twin brother of Blake's Nobodaddy. Barthelme's interest in classical mythology is also reminiscent of Freud: the book is, roughly, a retelling of the myth of the Golden Fleece, and he mentions certain other clasical legends (though it would be too much to say that any of these are interpreted in Freud's sense).

To think in a Freudian way, and to bring myth and magic into fiction, can sound like good tactics for an authentically modern writer to adopt as long as we forget what the old, orthodox novel was really like. But the developmental biology of the old novel was always keyed as much to the utterance of fantasies as to the depiction of the world. Thus Dickens's Mr Dombey, an unreal figure and a comprehensive expression of authority, is not so far removed from Barthelme's Dead Father. More particularly, there has long been a tradition of unorthodox fiction in which paternity is a central interest. *Tristram Shandy, Ulysses,* and *Molloy* are its major texts. Indeed to set the last of these—while thinking also of Beckett's Pozzo—beside *The Dead Father* is to see that Barthelme is not advancing experimental fiction one jot (and to remind oneself what the sense of inevitability and sureness of purpose in an innovative literary text is like).

Stylistically, also, Barthelme is indebted to Sterne, Joyce, and Beckett. He likes pastiche, lists, ribaldry, inserted visual elements, puns, and many kinds of incongruity of tone.

> *Michael Mason, ''Paternity Pursuit,'' in* The Times Literary Supplement *(© Times Newspapers Ltd., 1977; reproduced from* The Times Literary Supplement *by permission), June 17, 1977, p. 721.*

*　　*　　*

BEATTIE, Ann 1947-

American novelist and short story writer, Beattie is a frequent contributor to *The New Yorker*. Her stories and her novel, *Chilly Scenes of Winter*, are concerned primarily with the fortunes of the Woodstock generation in the spiritless seventies.

If the non sequitur were an art form, then Ann Beattie, author of [*Chilly Scenes of Winter,* a] novel and [*Distortions,* a] collection of short stories, would be its matron saint. ''Matron'' seems apt, whatever Beattie's age, and no matter that both books are firsts, since her style effectively girdles any youthful awkwardness, bulging hy-

perboles, and the passion that might redeem both.

Her taste for the non sequitur, with its lack of logical causation, lends itself to the creation of characters whose behavior is not conventionally or even recognizably motivated. . . .

The characters in both the novel and stories are fleshed out (or, rather, painted by number) in a collection of disjointed details, so that, although they are sometimes intriguingly eccentric, they lack an emotional core. Childhood histories, kinship patterns, recipes, and tastes in pop music do not necessarily add up to anyone we care about or remember.

Chapters and stories seem equally fragmented. We get glimpses of odd, painful, or potentially humorous patterns. But instead of mining her own offbeat sensibility, the author scurries off to a safer ground of more facts.

Beattie's most successful stories are those that deal with the directly bizarre: . . . these stories have an emotional resonance and a sense of direction and completion that the other, more episodic stories lack.

Beattie has an instinct for the grotesque that verges on the edge of real wit and pain. She is obviously a first-rate craftswoman with an eye for idiosyncratic detail. I only hope that in her future work she will not keep her instincts and characters so much under glass. (p. 37)

> *Susan Horowitz, in* Saturday Review *(© 1976 by Saturday Review/World, Inc.; reprinted with permission), August 7, 1976.*

As gratified readers of ''The New Yorker'' know, Ann Beattie is the best new writer to come down that particular pike since Donald Barthelme. . . .

She combines a remarkable array of technical skills with material of wide popular appeal. Her characters inhabit our drab contemporary worlds and brood like us about their lovers, families, politicians and lives. They range from barely mobile children to the barely mobile elderly; bright and limited, educated and not, male and female, stoned and straight, exuberant and dogged, they compose a wide-screen panorama of Life in These United States.

Traditionally the novel has relied on action spun out and woven into a plot, complete with beginning and end. Little in our own lives corresponds to this orderliness, and our own sensibilities are seldom so goal-oriented, except in supermarkets. Beattie understands and dramatizes our formlessness. She is especially the artist of situations, not plots, and her novel [''Chilly Scenes of Winter''] is an excellent example of this predilection. . . . (p. 14)

Beattie renews for us the commonplaces of the lonesome lover and the life of quiet desperation. . . . The novel's major theme . . . is not waiting for an answer or Laura or love, but waiting itself, wistful anticipation, life unfulfilled and yearning. Immersing us in specificity, Beattie makes us feel these generalities on our pulse.

But ''Chilly Scenes'' is also the funniest novel of unhappy yearning that one could imagine. Funnier. It is continually, inventively and perceptively humorous, both in what it reports and in the quietly elegant shape of its reporting. . . . (pp. 14, 18)

[There are] moments, with their texture of sadness and comedy, [that] evoke our own lives directly, with none of the fashionable evasions of symbolism; they imply that life signifies, perhaps, but only in the sense that ''there's a divinity that shapes our ends, rough-hew them how we will.'' (p. 18)

J. D. O'Hara, in The New York Times Book Review *(© 1976 by The New York Times Company; reprinted by permission), August 15, 1976.*

After a slow start Anne Beattie's novel, *Chilly Scenes of Winter,* warms up to give us a serious portrait of the generation just entering its thirties, the group left aimless and despondent by the fizzling out of the flaming causes of the '60s. . . . Beattie's novel allows us to see them in depth and with sympathy.

Beattie deftly allows Charles [the protagonist] and his companions to grow into the full humanity they share with the rest of us, and even leads Charles to a surprisingly happy ending. He deserves it, we feel, just as we deserve more novels by Annie Beattie.

By contrast, *Distortions,* Beattie's collection of stories, is disappointing. The word ''scenes'' would perhaps be more apt here than in the title of her novel, since that is all we are given—a series of static scenes, humorless still-lifes of people who do not have any meaningful connections to humanity and who do not move, feel or grow.

The stylistic excellence of her writing is undeniable, but Beattie is unable to make us feel any empathy for most of the characters in *Distortions*—perhaps because they are too self-absorbed to feel any for each other. Unattached to the past, looking forward to no future, they live only in the present (in which tense most of the stories are written), captured like creatures in amber and clearly going nowhere. The distortions Beattie presents as characters . . . have no meaningful relationships with other people, and no resemblance to any people most of us have known. There is, therefore, no reason for us to want to establish a relationship with them.

The best story in the collection, ''Hale Hardy and the Amazing Animal Woman,'' may be taken as a metaphor for the bleak message of all the rest. Young Hale Hardy is obsessed with visiting the Grand Canyon—but not alone. He must have a female companion. Significantly, any female will do. The cruelty he exhibits (and does not feel) in tricking his Amazing Animal Woman into accompanying him is felt by us, for she is not the animal he perceives her to be, but a very human woman indeed. And once Hardy reaches his goal and stares into it, the abyss of the canyon is a precise mirror-image of the vast emptiness inside him—and inside too many of the other people in Beattie's stories.

Kristin Hunter, ''Where Have All the Passions Gone?'' in Book World—The Washington Post *(© The Washington Post), October 3, 1976, p. F5.*

Ann Beattie's first novel, ''Chilly Scenes of Winter'' . . . thaws quite beautifully; our first impression, of a pale blank prose wherein events ramify with the random precision of snow-ferns on a winter window, yields, in the second half, to a keen warmth of identification with the hero, Charles, and an ardent admiration of the author's cool powers. Miss Beattie, as readers of her short stories know, works at an unforced pace. Her details—which include the lyrics of the songs her characters overhear on the radio and the recipes of the rather junky food they eat—calmly accrue; her dialogue trails down the pages with an uncanny fidelity to the low-level heartbreaks behind the banal; her resolutely un-

metaphorical style builds around us a maze of familiar truths that nevertheless has something airy, eerie, and in the end lovely about it. Her America is like the America one pieces together from the *National Enquirers* that her characters read—a land of pathetic monstrosities, of pain clothed in clichés, of extraterrestrial trivia. Things happen ''out there,'' and their vibes haunt the dreary ''here'' we all inhabit. . . .

[All characters] . . . are exquisitely modulated studies in vacancy, and grow on the reader like moss. At first, Miss Beattie's unblinking sentences, simple declarative in form and present in tense, remind one of Richard Estes' neo-realist street scenes, which render with a Flemish fineness the crassest dreck of our commercial avenues, omitting no detail save pedestrians. After some pages, her tableaux seem more like Segal's plaster-bandage sculptures, their literal lifelikeness magically muffled in utter whiteness. But then color steals into the cheeks of her personae, a timid Wyeth sort of color at first, the first flush of our caring, and this color deepens, so that her portraits at last appear as alive, as likely to make us laugh and cry, as any being composed in these thin-blooded times. (p. 164)

If the moral limbo of this book has an angel in it, it is Joplin; the characters' tenebrous values point backward to her, to the time of violent feeling and communal ecstasy. The novel's literary patron saint, though, is all fifties: J. D. Salinger. . . .

Miss Beattie seems to feel sorry for this whole decade. Her range of empathy is broad and even lusty. . . . And she succeeds in showing love from the male point of view, not in its well-publicized sexual dimension but in the pastel spectrum of nostalgia, daydream, and sentimental longing. The accretion of plain lived moments, Miss Beattie has discovered, like Virginia Woolf and Nathalie Sarraute before her, is sentiment's very method; grain by grain the hours and days of fictional lives invest themselves with weight. (p. 166)

John Updike, in The New Yorker *(© 1976 by The New Yorker Magazine, Inc.), November 29, 1976.*

It's been a popular notion that those white, middle-class males who came of age in the late 1960s would have a hard time finding a witty, sympathetic fictional prototype for the same reason they've produced so few good stand-up comics: they took themselves and their generation far too seriously and they preferred ''vibes'' to words. (How do you make literary pungence from the worship of Jerry Garcia and Hermann Hesse?) And, as anguished as they were by the Vietnam draft, their mantle of Suffered Irony was turned around by the Women's Movement. So how do you convey these young men's romantic confusion and cuckoldry without an implicit ''Aha! He deserved it!'' (p. 45)

I was waiting for [someone] to write what it was *really* like to graduate from college and find only clerk and salesmen jobs available; for these young men to love women too busy with other missions to love them back; and to wistfully replay 10-year-old Dylan cuts the way generations of disillusioned ex-frat boys before had reveled in old football victories.

Then I read *Chilly Scenes of Winter* and found that a 28-year-old woman, Ann Beattie, had assumed the task of locating this turn-of-the-decade hero and had performed it with sublime wit and humanity. (pp. 45-6)

Beattie's wit keeps . . . obvious symbols from being mere "things-were-so-much-better-then" clichés. And her ability to put compassion and intelligence in the most offhand, shrugging dialogue keeps [Charles, her protagonist,] from becoming just one more New Lost Generation melancholic.

Rather, through Charles's dignified vulnerability, his equal measures of earnestness and cynicism, and his tender friendship with Sam, Beattie has written a very sophisticated valentine to those young men who happened upon adulthood at a time when Love was all over postage stamps and placards and rock stations but was just about to be withdrawn by the culture, the economy, and the women they had innocently come to take for granted.

In *Distortions,* a collection of 19 of Beattie's short stories . . . , we meet the supporting players in Charles's America. Like ensemble actors in a blackout revue, different characters often wear the same names from story to story. And, diverse as they are, they all echo the same bewilderment at having a complaint without a clear reason or target.

Beattie understands that members of the Baby Boom/Youth Culture Generation have had the dubious privilege of being able to carry their childhoods on their backs. As young adults, her characters are still playing Cowboys and Indians and yearning for a simpler, sterner era without so many oppressive choices. (pp. 46-7)

Ann Beattie knows that while automation and conformity were the banes of a previous age, freedom and self-expression—the next age's remedies—have proved to be no less paralyzing. Satirically, sadly, and truthfully, she writes of familiar fights against the damning arbitrariness of our charmed post-industrial lives. (p. 47)

> Sheila Weller, "*A Valentine to the Guys Who Grew Up In the '60s,*" in Ms. (© 1976 Ms. Magazine Corp.), December, 1976, pp. 45-7.

[Ann Beattie's] subject matter is a certain shiftlessness and lack of self-apprehension besetting people in their twenties and thirties. . . . She conveys the drabness of these lives by her tone and by an almost hallucinatory particularity of detail. We are taken on that round of grocery shopping, walking the dog, getting the worthless car fixed, which Auden had in mind when he said that "in headaches and in worry, / Vaguely life leaks away." But Beattie's writing is not tedious; there is, instead, something graceful and painstaking about her fidelity to the ordinary. (pp. 62-3)

[In "Imagined Scenes," from *Distortions,* we] guess at the "real facts" of the woman's life because we care about her, her sadness has been made significant. It follows that the author has cared about her in the making. But then it is more astonishing to perceive that the woman cares so little, so indistinctly, for herself. She is not suspicious, she has no imagination; the mark of Beattie's respect for this creation is not to have slipped her some healthy suspicion, as it were, under the counter. In this forbearance the writer resembles some impossible ideal of a loving parent who succeeds in not interfering in her children's lives. To love one's characters—Tolstoy is the presiding genius here—is to allow them to be who they are.

A risk of a particular kind attends this achievement and Beattie is not immune to it. The style of much "serious fiction" in recent years has tended to be cool, to attend scrupulously to the surface of events, with a language pruned and polished in respect of its own surface. Now Beattie's writing has something in common with this style: her sentences are often plain, flat, their grammar exposed like the lighting fixtures in avant-garde furniture boutiques, and the effect is at first wearying. Only later does the sympathetic center of her work betray itself. We may feel misled by the outward reserve, but, again, her willingness to distort when necessary, her passion for the particular, is ultimately an index of her concern for the integrity of things and people in themselves.

Many of the people in [*Distortions* and *Chilly Scenes of Winter*] verge on the grotesque. . . . Here, too, Beattie risks a convergence with her slicker contemporaries, whose fascination with the grotesque is full of smugness about what is "normal." (Beattie herself invokes the photographs of Diane Arbus in several places, but I for one have never quite decided what Arbus's relation to her subjects really was.) There is a dog in *Chilly Scenes of Winter* who is a good example of Beattie's success with the grotesque. The dog is purchased to replace an entirely admirable dog who has died of old age, much mourned. But the new dog is ugly—part dachshund, part cocker spaniel—as well as hapless and insomniac. And yet, the people around him feel the dog must be fed and must not be compared to his predecessor; at night, his audible perambulations must be endured. Because, "terrible genetic mistake" that he is, the dog, named "Dog," is real and undeniable. He is part of that world of fact that Beattie honors almost compulsively, whatever its unwelcomeness or distortion.

The central figure of the novel, *Chilly Scenes of Winter,* is a young man named Charles, whose quality of self-ignorance is Beattie's fullest, most intelligent image. He does not know that he is smart, and apparently does not wish to know it, because he has chosen to work in a government office where his abilities are irrelevant. He does not know that he is kind: his many services to others are unmarked by signs of sympathy, generosity, concern, or liking; he is made dizzy by his sister's assertion that he is good. His knowledge that he is unhappy is merely circumstantial. Approaching thirty, he has come to terms with none of the absurd relationships that comprise his life. . . . Charles's only workable relationship is with his friend Sam, his constant companion, who is present on nearly every page. It is significant that Sam as portrayed by Beattie is dull, shapeless, unrealized. His friendship with Charles is at once blank and affectionate. Its very existence is capable of surprising them, when they must notice it. . . . (pp. 63-4)

Charles and Sam know nothing, in fact, about the causes of their loneliness except the details of the pleasureless routine it imposes upon them. Charles is forever gazing hungrily into a cupboard bare of anything except Tuna Stretcher and a jar of pickles, forever wondering at the existential courage of people who do all their shopping on one day for the week ahead. . . . Charles's eye for detail reflects the paradox of Beattie's own: a passive accuracy of observation masks an active, unsettling distrust of what one sees.

[There is] one aspect of Ann Beattie's writing that seems to me regrettable. Charles's mother's baths, his own baths, his sister's showers; Sam's car, Pete's car; dogs and cats; medical references, doctors, disease—all these constitute what used to be called "motifs" or images. Details drifting from person to person, thing to thing, they bend too steadily and purposefully toward significance, betraying an obtrusive self-consciousness about craft which is rather rare in Beattie's work. This seems to me directly at odds with the vitality of her talent, her capacity to conjure the independence and actuality of things.

Given her particular subject matter, it hardly seems necessary to underline Beattie's pertinence to the present cultural-political pass. In *Chilly Scenes of Winter,* in the story "Fancy Flights" [from *Distortions*], and elsewhere, our attention is called to a contemporary pathos whose effects few have yet begun to gauge: the sadness over the passing of the 60's. It is by no means necessary to feel this nostalgia in order to ponder its importance. Let me say at once that Beattie herself does not seem sad. Some reviewers have referred to the image in "Fancy Flights" of an ex-hippie locked in his bathroom, smoking dope and talking to his daughter's bunny rabbit. . . .

But the reviewers have failed to remark that this is one of Beattie's only *un*sympathetic portraits, the only one of her protagonists she doesn't like.

Charles's lament for the passing of the 60's, which is more to the point, occurs in abrupt, anxious seizures of lostness and bewilderment. "Elvis Presley is forty," he says. "Jim Morrison's *widow* is dead." The tone is that same tone in which he laments the waning quality of Hydrox cookies: "What happened to them? They used to be so good. Sugar. No doubt they're leaving out sugar." It is witty of Beattie to confine the sociological import of her novel to such trivial remarks. She conveys adroitly the sensibility of After-the-Fall, without making fictive claims for the heights from which we fell. The Golden Age mythology and its attendant rhetoric will inevitably attach, for a while, to talk about the 60's. This represents, of course, a historical distortion, matched in its badness of fit only by the myth that the New Left was the Antichrist. Beattie's presentation of Charles's nostalgia for the 60's suggests that such longing has the limits of an elegy to lost innocence, and the advantages, too. It distorts, but it also provides, however disingenuously, the idea that things can be better than they are, because they have been better before now. As usual, the prospects for hope seem to depend upon some degree of mystification. (p. 64)

> *John Romano, "Ann Beattie & the 60's"*
> *(reprinted from* Commentary *by permission;*
> *copyright © 1977 by the American Jewish*
> *Committee), in* Commentary, *February,*
> *1977, pp. 62-4.*

[An] attentiveness to ordinary human encounters distinguishes Ann Beattie's *Chilly Scenes of Winter,* a fine first novel which records the reluctant passage into adulthood of a twenty-seven-year-old survivor of the Woodstock generation. The novel incorporates characters and situations Beattie had treated earlier in her *New Yorker* stories, nineteen of which have been gathered under the title *Distortions* and released as a companion to the novel. But the novel is a more interesting and significant performance, richer in psychological nuance and in documentary power. Though there are many isolated passages in *Distortions* that exhibit Beattie's descriptive care and her talent for truthful dialogue, only one of the stories, "Snake's Shoes," has the sustained authority of the novel. One reason for the novel's superiority is that it is less tendentious than the stories, less confined by neo-absurdist attitudes toward contemporary experience. The novel is thus less somber than the stories and registers on every page a lively, generous alertness to the antic or comic in human relations. The characters in *Chilly Scenes* are respected more consistently than their

counterparts in the stories, and although their vivid idiosyncrasies are always comically before us, what is odd or distinctive in their behavior belongs to their personalities, is rooted in Beattie's powers of observation and dramatic representation. Too often in the stories, in contrast, one feels the pressure of a surrealist program, the influence of Barthelme and Pynchon, behind the author's choice of details or in the often schematic resolution of her plots.

Chilly Scenes is written in the present tense and relies heavily on dialogue and on a purified declarative prose not unlike good Hemingway, but much funnier. This disciplined young novelist takes care to differentiate even her minor characters, and one of her most memorable cameo players declares herself only as a voice through the telephone—a nervous, guilty mother trying to trace her wayfaring daughter in two brief conversations that momentarily distract the protagonist during this final winter of his prolonged adolescence. The hero himself is wonderfully alive: a gentle bewildered man, extravagantly loyal to old friends and to the songs of the 'sixties, drifting through a final nostalgia for the mythologies of adversary selfhood he absorbed in college and toward an embarrassed recognition of his hunger for such ordinary adventures as marriage and fatherhood. The unillusioned tenderness that informs Beattie's portrait of her central character is a rare act of intelligence and mimetic art. (pp. 585-86)

> *David Thorburn, in* The Yale Review *(©*
> *1977 by Yale University; reprinted by permission of the editors), Summer, 1977.*

*   *   *

BEAUVOIR, Simone de   1908-

French novelist, essayist, playwright, autobiographer, and proponent of the existentialist philosophy, Beauvoir is a long-time associate of Jean-Paul Sartre. In her novels Beauvoir is concerned with explicating her philosophy, as in, for example, *The Mandarins,* **which explores the problem of commitment and action among French intellectuals following the Second World War. She is the author of the immensely influential** *The Second Sex.* **(See also** *CLC,* **Vols. 1, 2, 4, and** *Contemporary Authors,* **Vols. 9-12, rev. ed.)**

When she is 75 or 80, will Simone de Beauvoir provide us with still another installment of her life? For those of us who have become addicted to the series, that would not be unwelcome. On the other hand, it is difficult to imagine what more she can really add besides an accumulation of further ventures which do not substantially alter her basic views and values. One does not expect her to renounce her socialism, her humanism, her feminism or her atheism in her remaining years. . . . Her experiences of still another decade may prove of historical interest but—in view of her current volume of memoirs of the past decade—would reveal little more of this rational, self-contained, voluble woman than we already know.

One direction in which she might go is that of more intimate introspection and analysis, like Anaïs Nin: but she deplores Nin's "narcissism," and despite her frankness about herself in so many areas, she has a Puritanical reticence about her personal emotional life, particularly with Sartre, for which in these let-it-all-hang-out times we should be grateful. Another way she might go, in carrying her anti-militarism and her disillusionment with existing Socialist states to a logical conclusion, would be to question the efficacy of military force even in violent revolutions. But that is an unlikely development at this stage of her life. Though she abhors violence personally, she affirms in many ways and at many junctures her belief in the necessity of "counter-violence" by oppressed peoples in response to the violence, overt or latent, of oppressive groups or governments. This struggle is the implicit theme of the . . . second half [of *All Said and Done*], which includes her travels in Japan, the USSR and other East European countries, Egypt and Israel, and her participation in the Russell War Crimes Tribunal, in the 1968 student uprisings in France and finally in the women's movement.

The struggles of the oppressed are partly what this volume of Beauvoir's memoirs are about, but not exclusively. The first half of the book is a more personal reassessment of her life and that of her friends, catching us up on people we met in earlier volumes. It is as if she were responding to an overwhelming correspondence, the way some people duplicate accounts of their yearly family adventures at Christmas and send them to friends with whom they've been out of touch and to whom they don't have time to write. . . . She writes of how her childish perceptions have changed, her conception of time, her increasing awareness of her finity. The void of death she no longer finds overwhelming—"but still I do not get used to it."

Emerging from these introspections after some 40 pages, Beauvoir becomes her more extroverted self. (p. 732)

I felt some disappointment in reading this volume of Beauvoir's memoirs. While I did not expect the unity that she herself remarks as distinguishing her first volume, *Memoirs of a Dutiful Daughter*, from subsequent ones, I found this one her most disjointed. Many of its eight sections are interesting in themselves, but some of the accounts read like *Memoirs of a Dutiful Daughter, Part II,* with every lap of her journeys, every historic site described as a schoolmistress might describe it for her pupils. Sometimes she tells the reader too much, and one feels slightly insulted; at other times her references are too cursory or oversimplified. The personalities and issues involved in the Russell Tribunal are examples: when one is personally acquainted with some of the people and events she writes about, her descriptions seem inadequate, even misleading. Still, it is impossible not to be enlightened by some aspect of her accounts, whether historical, geographical, political or aesthetic. (pp. 733-34)

> *Ann Morrissett Davidon, "A Life Well Lived for All That," in* The Nation *(copyright 1975 by the Nation Associates, Inc.), June 14, 1975, pp. 732-34.*

Numerous times throughout her voluminous work Beauvoir asserts that one of the goals she has pursued most obstinately (the word is hers) has been to strip away the hypocrisies, prejudices, lies, and mystifications that obstruct our perception of reality and prevent us from seeing the truth. (p. 2)

An even more basic impulse in her work is an irresistible urge to communicate her own experience, to re-create her own life. Aware of the fact that she does not possess the kind of inventive imagination that characterizes the very greatest creators of fiction, Beauvoir, who nevertheless has written several important novels, maintains that the creation of a fictional world has never been her intention. In 1972 at the age of sixty-four she looked back on the many books she had written and declared that her mission as a writer was not to create an *oeuvre d'art,* but rather to communicate as directly as possible the feel of her own life. (p. 3)

Begun before the outbreak of the war, *L'Invitée* [(*She Came to Stay*)] opens with an epigraph by Hegel: "Each consciousness seeks the death of the other." Even though Beauvoir did not come upon Hegel's statement until she had already done considerable work on her novel, it neatly expresses the book's underlying metaphysical theme. The novel's strength is precisely the manner in which Beauvoir manages to give this abstract theme sensuous form and to incarnate it in the lives of her three principal protagonists.

In addition to illustrating one of the metaphysical themes that runs through existentialist thought, *L'Invitée* is, in the best tradition of the French psychological novel, a study of the devastating effects of love and jealousy. (p. 30)

One of the curious features of Beauvoir's work as a whole is that the dogmatic and sometimes oversimplified assertions in her sociological or polemical studies are often contradicted by her novels. In the former she establishes theoretical positions and, marshaling her considerable intellectual powers, defends them forcefully. In the latter she evokes, to use her phrase, the opaqueness of contingency, that is to say, the ambiguities of life as experienced emotionally.

Thus, the kind of love that is called authentic in *Le Deuxième Sexe* [(*The Second Sex*)]—a love which somewhat resembles the "generous friendship (*amitié généreuse*) that characterizes the love of Cornelian heroes—is a freely chosen partnership of two autonomous beings who share a common goal and hold each other in the highest esteem. In *L'Invitée,* however, this type of love is shown as being illusory for two basic reasons: seeing the relationship between people as one of hostility, Beauvoir illustrates the existentialist view that each consciousness affirms its autonomy and liberty by active opposition to every other consciousness (the metaphysical motif of the novel), thus making of Françoise's and Pierre's supposed oneness a momentary illusion; secondly, although existentialism, in theory at least, tends to adopt the Cartesian separation of mind and body and so assures autonomy for the consciousness, Beauvoir's novels tend to show characters—especially female characters—who react emotionally, at times even hysterically, when confronted with personal problems and dilemmas (the psychological aspect of the novel). (pp. 32-3)

In her famous and combative analysis of "the second sex," Beauvoir fails to come to grips with this feminine need (it is she in her novels who depicts it as such) to cling to a man and to have one or more passionate love affairs—a need that is central to her own life and to that of her heroines. (p. 34)

[*L'Invitée*] has a decidedly claustrophobic atmosphere. Most of it consists of long and inconclusive conversations among the three protagonists (either together or in couples). . . . (p. 35)

Pierre . . . is something of a question mark. Beauvoir herself notes that in general she had greater success with her female characters than with her male characters. In the case of Pierre, she explains, she did not wish to pattern him too directly after Sartre. Seen essentially through the admiring eyes of Françoise, he has Sartre's creative energy, generosity, and strong personality, but he remains rather abstract and seems more like a caricature than a real person.

Beauvoir's refusal to present authorial analyses of her protagonists and her reliance on dialogue to reveal the psychological motivation of her characters are a result of her concept of the novel, which in turn has its roots in her philosophical position concerning appearance and reality. Like Sartre, she rejects the traditional view, particularly strong in thinkers of Neoplatonic persuasion, that there is a difference between appearance and innermost reality, between the exterior world and our inner life, between our words, our glances, our acts, and our secret being. Supporting her argument by references to Hegel, Beauvoir affirms that the real must never be conceived as an interiority hidden behind external appearances. The exterior hides nothing; rather it expresses.

But since appearances are subject to endless interpretations, it follows that reality is never fixed. It is ambiguous and multiple. Contrary to her philosophical works which set forth opinions clearly, the novels express ambiguities, doubts, and hesitations. Technically this is achieved by telling the story from different points of view. (pp. 36-7)

[Beauvoir's] dialogue, which is finely articulated and neatly phrased, tends to be highly stylized. Noting that she wished to imitate and not copy the kind of speech she heard around her, Beauvoir says that a good novelist never reproduces the stammerings of a real conversation. The dialogue in *L'Invitée* is in harmony with the overall stylization of the novel.

The theme of the novel is made explicit—probably too explicit—in a conversation between Pierre and Françoise. "You're the only person I know," says Pierre, "who bursts into tears on discovering in someone else a consciousness similar to your own. Everyone experiences his own consciousness as an absolute. How can several absolutes be compatible? The problem is as great a mystery as life or death. What surprised me is that you should be affected in such a concrete way by a metaphysical situation." (p. 39)

Throughout all her work, Beauvoir tends to view the self as inescapably locked in conflict with others. In *L'Invitée* this enmity is shown as being derived from the very nature of consciousness itself. . . . Beauvoir has always tended to divide mankind into two opposing camps: "adversaries and allies" the two fundamental categories through which she seems to grasp experience. She has remarked that "we always work for certain people against others." The adversaries and the allies differ from book to book, but the two categories remain constant, giving her world its basic order. (p. 40)

It is . . . probably a mistake to read Beauvoir's novels as if they were principally novels of ideas, containing a philosophical content which, like a lode of ore, must be extracted even at the expense of ruining the surface texture. At their best, they are evocations of a concrete, living reality. Concerned with the dense and shifting texture of existence, Beauvoir dramatizes in *L'Invitée* the difficulty of living and the walled-in or claustrophobic quality of human experience. . . . Occasionally verbose, often delicately ironic and densely poetic, *L'Invitée* is one of Beauvoir's best books. (pp. 41-2)

There are novels which, because of an intricate design or an extensive and radical use of ellipses, must be read twice to be fully comprehended. Few novels require a second reading as urgently as *Le Sang des autres, 1945 (The Blood of Others)*. The difficulty lies not in the narrative line,

which is basically simple, but in the manner in which Beauvoir constructs the novel. Impressed by Dos Passos, Faulkner, and other American writers, she wished to experiment with form in an attempt to evoke the dense, shifting, ambiguous texture of life. To achieve this end she tells her story from different points of view. The unheralded shifts from one point of view to another mean that a reader does not know at first who is speaking, to whom the personal pronouns refer, and whether the narrative is being related by the author or through the consciousness of a particular character.

Gradually, however, the voices become recognizable. Characters emerge, and the reader becomes aware of the fact that the confusion and indeterminateness which he felt in the opening pages is the calculated effect of a skillful writer who wishes to express the complexity of existence. (pp. 49-50)

Beauvoir evoked her somber mood during the war years far more convincingly in *Le Sang des autres* than in her pompous and simplistic comments written some thirty-odd years later. (p. 56)

Beauvoir's success in *Le Sang des autres,* as in *L'Invitée,* is not essentially in illustrating an abstract idea (which she does) but in evoking the increasing heaviness, density, and solidification of existence through an ever more complicated network of relationships among a limited number of protagonists. In her second novel as in her first, the dilemma of interpersonal relationships is revealed in its starkest, most tragic form in love. (pp. 56-7)

Despite Beauvoir's didactic zeal in *Le Sang des autres,* the notions of commitment, of solidarity, of guilt and responsibility are ultimately shown as being as profoundly ambiguous as the notion of art. [The central character's] commitment to the cause of the working classes reinforces rather than diminishes his spiritual isolation because he realizes that there is an unbridgeable gulf between himself—the bourgeois intellectual who pretends to be a proletarian—and a genuine proletarian. (p. 62)

Numerous themes from *Le Sang des autres* are treated, albeit in a somewhat different register, in [Beauvoir's only play, *Les Bouches inutiles*]. Once again the basic idea is the inevitability of making choices and the subsequent moral accountability for the choices made. (p. 63)

Although caught up in a momentous personal and public crisis, the characters seem lifeless. Beauvoir's failure here, as elsewhere in her fictional work, is due to a certain lack of imaginative intensity. Furthermore, she tends to reduce the characters to ethical attitudes. Moral lessons, instead of being worked out imaginatively and dramatically through the characters, are condensed into aphorisms that, taken together, constitute a breviary not only of existentialist thought but of Beauvoir's curious and ambiguous kind of feminism as well.

In Beauvoir's fictional world, the female characters, who are usually endowed with their creator's sensibilities, strive essentially for happiness, whereas her male characters seek to justify their lives by struggling for a cause, by participating in some kind of *oeuvre,* either a work of art or a political enterprise. Curiously, Beauvoir, who in *Le Deuxième Sexe* denies that there are peculiarly female characteristics, is less dogmatic in her fiction and joins Colette, whom she resembles but little, and Rebecca West, to whom she is somewhat closer, in discerning in women a distinctly feminine aptitude for happiness, a will-to-live that is specifically female. However, unlike the characters of Colette or West, Beauvoir's female characters seem unable to realize their happiness unless they team up with a man whose aspirations they espouse and whose projects they make their own. In other words, her women cannot get along without men, whereas her men could, it seems, get along admirably well without women. (pp. 64-5)

Sexual love is valorized in Beauvoir's world only when it is sublimated into comradeship. Such sublimation usually occurs when the interests of the community are threatened —in moments of social or political upheaval, in a climate of urgency and crisis. Love that does not assume the form of a fraternal struggle against the evils that stalk the world is considered individualistic, a word which for Beauvoir evokes the bourgeois mentality. It is characterized by the sorrows of sex. Since only her female characters are victims of this dolorous kind of love, which is endured rather than created, it is associated with woman's subservience— often willingly accepted, Beauvoir admits—in a man-governed world. (pp. 65-6)

[*Tous les hommes sont mortels (All Men Are Mortal)*] is an ambitious work, a book in which one can see Beauvoir reaching out for a broad, all-inclusive subject. However, its cargo of ideas is borne aloft by a cast of characters so wooden and unconvincing that the novel never really comes to life, and must in the final analysis be called a relative failure. Still, it marks an important step in Beauvoir's evolution; here she meditates leisurely not only on death and time but also on the history of humanity and on the vanity as well as the validity of political action. Beauvoir later described the book accurately when she called it "an organized digression whose themes are not theses but points of departure toward unpredictable meanderings." (pp. 68-9)

Sight is the primary sense in Beauvoir's world. In her autobiography she declares that she can conceive of living without any one of the senses except sight. Her fundamental enterprise is to *see* reality, to unmask the truth (*dévoiler* is one of her favorite words), and then to expose it to the eyes of others. (p. 69)

Closely associated with Beauvoir's concern for appearances and her use of a vocabulary that suggests the theater is her frequent mention of mirrors. A rich symbol, the mirror is often used in her work to suggest not only narcissism but also a character's search for his own identity. Significantly, it is Beauvoir's heroines rather than her heroes who peer into a mirror in a vain attempt to define themselves and to give meaning to their lives. . . . From the existentialist perspective, meaning can come only from acts, from a project, and the fact that so many of Beauvoir's heroines identify with the image of themselves that is reflected in a mirror, in the eyes of a lover or . . . in the eyes of an applauding public, is a comment on the inauthenticity and passivity that is their lot.

Narcissistic posturing before a mirror suggests a solipsistic attitude, an entrapment in the circle of self, a denial of transcendence toward the future or of intentionality, to use the word existentialists borrowed from Husserl. It thus suggests a rejection of life itself. Indeed, in Beauvoir's work, especially in *Tous les hommes sont mortels*, reflections in mirrors, in eyes, or in water often evoke the presence of emptiness or of death. (p. 70)

Closed upon themselves, the young women who populate Beauvoir's fiction no doubt represent a revolt against all those forces, societal or biological, which tend to push them into preordained roles in life. However, viewed not as incarnations of an idea but as fictional characters endowed with a psychological makeup, they are narrow-minded, petulant, and singularly unpleasant. Beauvoir has repeatedly displayed her considerable talent for creating disagreeable young heroines. (pp. 71-2)

All of Beauvoir's novels, but especially *Tous les hommes sont mortels,* are punctuated with joyous celebrations. Her autobiography, too, is marked by *fêtes* commemorating victories both small and great. The most elaborately described and intensely felt *fête* in her work is the liberation of Paris in 1944, recounted both in the autobiography and in *Les Mandarins* [*(The Mandarins)*]. (p. 76)

As a study of womankind, *Le Deuxième Sexe* clearly belongs to anthropological sociology. But while analyzing the situation of women in general, Beauvoir was preparing the way for a study of a particular woman—herself. Seen in this light *Le Deuxième Sexe* is a long preamble to the four volumes of the autobiography she would later write. (p. 94)

[Each] of Beauvoir's books is an account of an education. In the novels it is the fictional characters who gradually perceive reality; in her nonfiction it is Beauvoir herself who writes her books to mark the various stages on her way toward truth.

Le Deuxième Sexe is a mammoth edifice that rests on two slender postulates: first, that man, conceiving of himself as the essential being, the subject, has made woman into the unessential being, the object, the Other; second, that there is no such thing as feminine nature and that all notions of feminity are therefore artificial. Both postulates are enunciated in the introduction and are derived from concepts elaborated by Sartre in *L'Être et le néant* [*(Being and Nothingness)*], a book to which Beauvoir frequently refers as if to a sacred text whose validity and authority no right thinking person could question. "The perspective I am adopting," she announces at the end of the introduction, "is that of existentialist ethics."

Borrowing directly from Sartre, Beauvoir declares that the category of otherness is inherent in consciousness itself. "Otherness is a fundamental category of human thought. No group ever conceives of itself as the One without immediately setting up the Other in opposition to itself." Furthermore, awareness of otherness arouses a feeling of hostility. The dialectics of aggression is one of the most characteristic features of Beauvoir's work. Not for a moment does she imagine that opposites can sustain and complement each other. In order to assert itself, each consciousness must strive for the destruction, the annihilation of the other. This, in fact, was the theme of *L'Invitée,* written before existentialism had yet been codified into a philosophical or ideological doctrine. (p. 95)

Beauvoir's second postulate—that there is no feminine nature—is derived from one of the most fundamental of existentialist principles, namely that there is no human nature, the word nature being understood here as essence. Sartre expressed this notion in his famous formula, existence precedes essence, by which he meant basically that man need not conform to any archetype, that only in the very process of living does he create his own values, his being, his essence. If there is no archetypal human nature, there obviously can be no feminine or masculine nature. As Beauvoir expresses it in one of the most telling aphorisms in *Le Deuxième Sexe:* "One is not born a woman; rather one becomes a woman." (p. 96)

Beauvoir's basic argument in [the last section of volume 1] is that for a boy there is no distinction between his vocation as a human being and his vocation as a male. "Humanity is male," she asserts in another of those aphorisms which reveal her fondness for the trenchant, incisive utterance that overstates and distorts the argument and that has provoked the ire of a number of readers. For a girl, however, there is a profound divorce between her condition as a human being and her vocation as a female. If adolescence is so difficult for girls, Beauvoir argues, it is because they must abandon the childhood image they have had of themselves as autonomous beings, as individuals, and accept the role of dependence and relative submission that society demands of them. They must pass from being essential to being unessential. (p. 103)

It is easy enough to criticize *Le Deuxième Sexe* for this or that supposed flaw. Beauvoir no doubt fails to come to grips with maternity and family life. She no doubt advocates a kind of "virile independence" that is better suited to a woman who is unmarried, childless, exceptionally intelligent, violently ambitious, and relatively well-off (in short, like Beauvoir) than to the majority of women.

Furthermore, the existentialist suppositions on which the study rests are debatable. Beauvoir herself wrote in 1963 that if she had to rewrite the book she would give far greater importance to economic matters and far less to philosophical speculation about the nature of consciousness. More specifically, she says that she would base the notion of the Other, together with the Manicheism it entails, not on an idealistic, *a priori* struggle pitting each consciousness against every other consciousness, but on the economic reality of supply and demand. Although Beauvoir does not explain why she would build her study on a somewhat different foundation if she had it to do over again, any faithful reader of Sartre knows why. The reason is simply that in 1960 Sartre published *Critique de la raison dialectique* (Critique of Dialectical Reason), a mammoth philosophical and political treatise in which he argues that all human history has been a history of scarcity and a bitter struggle against shortage. In brief, Beauvoir would rewrite *Le Deuxième Sexe* to bring it in line with Sartre's revised philosophical and political theories. The most faithful of disciples, she clearly (and admittedly) takes her cue from Sartre in all matters relating to existentialist doctrine.

It is perfectly true that *Le Deuxième Sexe* suffers from a certain repetitiveness. Rather like a prosecuting attorney who brings in every scrap of evidence, Beauvoir builds up her case deliberately and without haste. Her strategy . . . is to accumulate evidence, to heap up data until the reader is overwhelmed ("discouraged" and "petrified" are Suzanne Lilar's words) by the mass of information. Only rarely does Beauvoir display her superb talent for satire; the pages in which she discusses certain male writers who have spoken arrogantly of women, notably Claude Mauriac and Montherlant, are written with marvelous verve and gusto. On the whole, however, the tone is earnest, humorless, and a bit pedantic.

Despite all the criticisms that have been leveled at *Le Deuxième Sexe,* the fact remains that it is the most important, the most forceful vindication of women's rights to have appeared in the twentieth century. In this book more than in any of her others, Beauvoir has realized her wish to leave a mark on the world. Not that she deluded herself into thinking that she could transform the condition of women. No significant change can come about, she insists, without the overthrow of capitalism. But she adds with excessive modesty, for her book has probably provoked more changes in individual lives than she can know of, that at least she has helped her female contemporaries to become conscious of themselves and of their situation. (pp. 105-07)

The underlying theme of [*Les Mandarins*] is . . . descent from enthusiasm, intoxicating triumph, and rapture into the murky, unheroic business of daily existence, characterized by *taedium vitae,* by broken dreams, and by the specter of boredom.

This theme was a favorite of the romantics and again illustrates how broadly and pervasively Beauvoir's work, like that of many important twentieth-century writers, is colored by romanticism. Her despair, usually expressed as fear of old age and death, the histrionic aspect of this despair as well as the equally theatrical nature of her joy and exultation, her reforming zeal and desire to act, her insatiable thrust for experience, her earnest but also self-indulgent sincerity, her didacticism, her desire to be modern and to seize the real, her refusal to separate literature or art from life, her often repeated view that man strives for the impossible, for being, and falls back into the relative, into existence—all these are part of the enormously rich, romantic heritage that has determined so many of our attitudes in the twentieth century and that has sustained much of our literature and art. (p. 109)

In order to evoke the density, complexity, and opaqueness of reality, Beauvoir uses in *Les Mandarins* a technique she had used earlier. She alternates third-person narrative chapters in which the central figure tends to be Henri Perron . . . with chapters narrated in the first person by Anne Dubreuilh. . . . Events are thus seen from different perspectives. Character is revealed, not through authorial explanations, but through the highly subjective appraisals that the various protagonists make of a situation. (p. 110)

Les Mandarins has a breadth of historical perspective, a density, and a richness of texture that make it wholly worthy of the Prix Goncourt it won in 1954. Writing in the early sixties, Beauvoir declared that most of the fiction published during the fifties, especially the *nouveau roman,* completely ignored the momentous events that shaped postwar Europe. "So many things," she said, "have happened since 1945, and fiction has scarcely expressed any of them. Future generations that might want to learn about us will have to consult works on sociology, statistics, or simply read our newspapers." They would also have to read *Les Mandarins,* but not just because it is a fine chronicle. Beauvoir insists that an imaginative projection of experience, as distinguished from a mere chronicle of events, conveys the "significance" of experience. That is precisely what *Les Mandarins* does. It recaptures the human significance of ethical and political problems that were intensely personal and emotional concerns for Beauvoir, Sartre, and their friends among the non-Communist Left during the years immediately following the war.

Beauvoir's seriousness of purpose in *Les Mandarins* is wholly admirable. If the novel falls short of being great, it is once again because Beauvoir lacks the imaginative intensity that characterizes supreme creators of fiction. Her vision is simply not powerful enough to enable her to formulate in fictional characters the schemes of redemption and enlightment that effect an expansion of the reader's own moral vision or awareness.

Furthermore, the novel provides the reader with few pleasures of style. Indeed, the prose is by and large colorless and graceless, marked by colloquialisms and occasional vulgarity. It will not do to say, as several critics have, that the author of *Les Mandarins* simply does not write well. Beauvoir's shift toward a style that strikes many readers as leaden and undistinguished is probably one consequence of her postwar loss of faith in literature as something sacred.

French critic Serge Julienne-Caffié has suggested that the dialogue in *Les Mandarins* is the linguistic equivalent of the socialist and democratic state which the characters in the novel (they all speak quite similarly) wish to see established in France. It is certainly true that in *Les Mandarins* and in most of her subsequent books Beauvoir contemptuously rejects any belletristic attitude toward literature, an attitude she proclaims to be eminently bourgeois.

There may be yet another explanation for Beauvoir's inclination to write prose that often seems deliberately pedestrian, consciously limited to the spoken language. Despite their vitality and their incessant activity, Beauvoir's mandarins are ultimately shown as living not in the world of action but in what Nietzsche called "the prison house of language." Momentous social and political forces are at work shaping the world around them while they, infatuated with their own words, talk on and on, only dimly aware of the fact that no one is really listening. (pp. 119-20)

Still, beneath the surface texture of language that is at times perversely charmless, a reader of *Les Mandarins* can discern—particularly in the pages that are dominated by the female characters—the peculiar current of emotionalism, tenderness, and lyricism, intense yet discreet, that runs stealthily through all of Beauvoir's works and that combines with the author's intellectual toughness to create a literary voice unmistakably her own. Flawed though it may be, *Les Mandarins* must surely be counted among the most significant French novels published since World War II. (p. 121)

Beauvoir's post-1950 tendency to subordinate ethical to political concerns was clearly evident in *Les Mandarins*. It would continue to mark much of her later work. In fact, one of the most distressing features of the third volume of the autobiography is Beauvoir's inclination to view as an enemy anyone who does not share her political convictions. Such an attitude is hardly the perfect stance for a writer who presents long portions of her autobiography—especially the section dealing with the decade of the fifties—as a faithful chronicle of events. Beauvoir seldom if ever declares that her dislike, often hatred, for this or that person is simply the result of opposing political views. Instead, she nearly always denigrates individuals who disagree with her by cataloging their supposed moral flaws, their alleged weaknesses of character. (pp. 126-27)

"The most important, the most irreparable thing that has happened to me since 1944," noted Beauvoir in the early 1960s, "is that I have grown old." Indeed, the theme of old age and the closely related theme of death had always been present in Beauvoir's work, but they had remained in the background, much like a menacing cloud on the horizon. During the 1950s, when Beauvoir was in her forties, her disenchantment with the political scene in Europe was exacerbated (or perhaps partly provoked) by her realization that she was growing old. The ten or so books she wrote from 1950 to 1972 are all, with the exception of *La Longue Marche* [(*The Long March*)], marked by a deepening awareness of old age. (pp. 130-31)

Une Mort très douce, 1964 (*A Very Easy Death*), which Beauvoir called a *récit*, is one of her shortest books. Sartre has called it her best. On one level, it is an almost clinical, at times harrowingly dispassionate, account of an old woman [Beauvoir's mother] dying of cancer in a modern hospital. The contrast between the messiness of life (the tears, the cries of pain, the pus, the unpleasant body odors, the soiled sheets, the vomiting) and the cool efficiency of modern medical technology (the various machines attached to her mother's body, the doctors themselves, well groomed, well paid, and condescending) is all the more striking because it is understated. Beauvoir's language can be as sharp, as clean, as impersonal as a scalpel. With remarkable skill, she paces her account of her mother's decline in such a way that when death comes the reader experiences, as in a good tragedy, relief from the intolerable anguish that has steadily mounted.

The anguish, however, is essentially Beauvoir's own and not her mother's. On another level, then, *Une Mort très douce* is an epilogue to *La Force des choses* [(*The Force of Circumstance*)]. It is part of Beauvoir's autobiography.

Watching her mother die, Beauvoir feels compassion for the old woman's ravished and anguished body. She cannot forget, however, that her mother is a member of the hated French bourgeoisie. "I was saddened," Beauvoir writes, "by the contrast between the reality of her suffering body and the nonsense with which her head was stuffed." Beauvoir's portrait of her dying mother is thus composed of two contrasting tones: compassion for the suffering body and ironic contempt for the old woman herself, for the life she led, and for the values she professed.

When Mme de Beauvoir remarked that she was glad to be in Hospital C. because she had heard that it was so much better than Hospital G., Beauvoir, by the very way she tells the incident, turns the trivial comment into yet another example of the fatuous vanity of the bourgeoisie. Since Mme de Beauvoir was not told that she was dying of cancer, Beauvoir weaves the theme of deceit into her account of her mother's death. Cunningly she equates the atmosphere of hypocrisy which surrounds the dying woman with the atmosphere of falsehood that characterized (in Beauvoir's view at least) the bourgeois milieu in which her mother had lived. The two kinds of falsehoods (if indeed they are falsehoods) are of a totally different order. By deliberately blurring the distinction between them, Beauvoir indulges in a kind of sophistry that mars not a few pages of her work. (pp. 134-35)

Beauvoir's inability to see her mother except through ideological lenses is chilling. Although elsewhere she has written eloquently about the difficulty of communicating with others and about the opaqueness of the Other, she seems to believe that her mother was perfectly transparent, so shallow (or bourgeois) was she. The cavalier way in which she passes judgment on her mother borders on arrogance. There is scarcely a page in *Une Mort très douce* that is not informed by the author's ironic glance. (p. 136)

The grief in *Une Mort très douce* is genuine, but it is not grief at her mother's death. In the final analysis, the book is an elegy in which Beauvoir laments the dissolution of her own being. (p. 137)

The obvious danger in writing a novel [like *Les Belles Images*] composed largely of platitudinous dialogue is that the reader, instead of shuddering at the emptiness and vacuity of the bourgeois way of life—which he is clearly meant to do—might well find the book dull and unrewarding. Smart tittle-tattle about stereo sets, vacations in Bermuda, and ultra-modern architecture palls very quickly.

The principal character, Laurence, is married to an up-and-coming architect, has two daughters, and works for an advertising agency where she has been very successful designing advertisements for things like tomato sauce. The title of the novel is an ironic reference to the "lovely images" she creates.

Each of the characters in the novel is minutely intent on keeping up appearances and on projecting an acceptable image of himself—an image as slick, as artfully deceptive as those created by Laurence. Unlike the other characters, who seem to have no reality beneath the glib image they project, Laurence senses dimly that her life is somehow out of joint. As the result of three incidents, her vague malaise becomes a full-scale existential crisis which is accompanied by nausea (a rather worn image, coming nearly thirty years after Sartre's *La Nausée* [*(Nausea)*]. (p. 138)

Les Belles Images contains many of Beauvoir's usual themes. However, they are here expressed in images that are facile, pat, and rather too obvious. Eager to jolt the reader into contempt for the bourgeoisie, Beauvoir has indulged her taste for didacticism at the expense of imaginative insight. (p. 141)

Each of the three female voices that emerge from *La Femme rompue* [*(The Woman Destroyed)*] tells a tale of disintegration, prodigious bad faith, and, above all, overweening egotism. They are the hysterical voices of women who are too monstrously selfish, too lacking in perception to be entirely credible as fictional characters. Furthermore, Beauvoir's vulgar and pedestrian prose—a prose that ultimately strikes the reader as an unpleasant affectation—is leaden and oppressive, adding to the generally sodden effect of the book. In the final analysis, both *Les Belles Images* and *La Femme rompue,* skillfully constructed as they may be, are decidedly inferior to Beauvoir's best fictional work. (pp. 142-43)

[In] none of Beauvoir's books is the everyday hum of life, the trivia of daily existence, more pervasively present than in *Tout compte fait* [*(All Said and Done)*]. From her leisurely enumerations of weekends spent in the country, museums visited, books read, films seen and music heard, there clearly emerges the unmistakable voice of the author who is intent on defining the meaning of her private experience.

It is a voice that is as steady as ever but somewhat more subdued, less abrasive—a voice tinged, certainly not with sadness or fatigue, but with a sense of inevitable conclusion. "I have a keen awareness of my finitude," Beauvoir says simply. "Even if my creative work will encompass two or three more volumes, it will remain what it is." (pp. 146-47)

On the last page of *Tout compte fait* Beauvoir, with a remarkable sense of plenitude, notes that she has written the very books she had hoped to write when she was twelve years old. Having rejected the notion of writing for posterity, she always wished to write for her contemporaries. Looking back on her many books, she concludes her autobiography with remarks that are both a summing up and a succinct statement of the distinctive nature of her literary opus:

> I have not been a virtuoso of writing. I have

not, like Virginia Woolf, Proust, or Joyce, resuscitated the shimmer of sensations nor caught in words the external world. But such was not my intention. I wished to make myself exist for other people by communicating to them, in the most direct way, the flavor of my own life. I have pretty well succeeded. I have made adamant enemies, but I have also made many friends among my readers. That is all I wanted.   (p. 148)

> *Robert D. Cottrell, in* Simone de Beauvoir *(copyright © 1975 by Frederick Ungar Publishing Co., Inc.), Ungar, 1975.*

*   *   *

BEHAN, Brendan   1923-1964

Behan was an Irish dramatist and novelist. His total literary output is not large and his reputation will most likely rest solely on his two full-length plays, *The Quare Fellow* and *The Hostage,* and one autobiographical work, *Borstal Boy.* *Borstal Boy* was written after Behan's involvement with the I.R.A. led to his arrest and confinement in the reformatory at Borstal. He died of complications resulting from excessive drinking. (See also *CLC,* Vol. 1.)

Brendan Behan is a primitive author in the best sense—instinctive, untutored, uninfluenced. The two plays by which he is known—*The Quare Fellow* and *The Hostage*—both show this primitivism even in their published forms, which have been considerably reworked by Joan Littlewood. Brendan Behan, it should be noted, is emphatically not a member of the New English Dramatists movement. His first play, *The Quare Fellow* (1945), was written well before Osborne's breakthrough with *Look Back in Anger,* and his second, *The Hostage* (1957), is related neither in theme nor in style to the angry-young-man syndrome. For Brendan Behan is most definitely not an angry young man, though he has far more reason to be one than any of the writers dubbed with that title by the critics. . . . The main thing that strikes one about Behan's work is the compassion and understanding that he has for both sides of any conflict—for jailed and jailers in *The Quare Fellow,* for English and Irish in *The Hostage.* The only type of person that Behan cannot stomach is the person who tries to impose his authority and swell his dignity in the name of some abstract ideal, which, Behan implies, is not really sincerely held but manufactured to justify the person's behavior. Behan's villains are thus the mealy-mouthed, hypocritical prison visitor Holy Healey in *The Quare Fellow* and the puritanical, self-important I.R.A. leader, whose behavior ironically apes that of the British upper-class officers, in *The Hostage.* (pp. 303-04)

> *George Wellwarth, "Brendan Behan: The Irish Primitive," in his* The Theater of Protest and Paradox: Developments in the Avant-Garde Drama *(reprinted by permission of New York University Press; copyright © 1964, 1971 by New York University), revised edition, New York University Press, 1971, pp. 303-06.*

For all its faults, *The Hostage* is *alive,* and my reading of the play inclines me to believe it is even more alive than I found it to be in the production. The life of the work emanates from the assorted characters and cartoons (and it is not at all certain that the latter are less vital on the stage than the former), and from the author's personal buoyancy as manifested in dialogue, song, and a blithe scorn for self-inflationary idealism. His very irreverence is a form of piety, a regard for the preciousness of life. A considerable compassion, secured against sentimentality by Behan's ebullient writing, wells up from the cross-currents of the wayward action when young life is put in jeopardy by ideological righteousness. If *The Hostage* is, so to speak, "antiplay" it is fortunately also anticant. One could develop considerable affection and a rather amused respect for its author. And one could feel honestly indebted to him for being almost the only Irish writer since Joyce and the young O'Casey to spare us Celtic mist and windy heroics while treating the subject of nationalist conflict. Yet it must be admitted that Behan's success in engaging a "big" theme lay mainly in ignoring his plot and dissolving his theme. And in this respect so highly individual a writer as the author of *The Hostage* appears to have much in common with other contemporary writers whose commendable success in picturing life is associated with a reprehensible success in reducing it to insignificance. (p. 497)

> *John Gassner, in his* Dramatic Soundings: Evaluations and Retractions Culled from 30 Years of Dramatic Criticism, *introduction and posthumous editing by Glenn Loney (© 1968 by Mollie Gassner; used by permission of Crown Publishers, Inc.), Crown, 1968.*

[Of all Behan's works, only] his two plays, *The Quare Fellow* and *The Hostage*, and the autobiographical *Borstal Boy* . . . demonstrate his talent. These works, appearing between 1954 and 1958, brought Behan critical acclaim and public success. Unfortunately, although he desired and deserved such recognition, he had not the self-assurance and self-discipline to take it in stride. (pp. 3-4)

Behan had a very limited knowledge of stagecraft and lacked the artistic discipline to sit down and mold his work into a finished form. These shortcomings were real, but they should not obscure the fact that Behan wrote, in *The Quare Fellow,* entertaining and effective drama. The play is loose and rambling in structure, lacks the unifying focus of a central character, and is weak in plot and climax, but it still succeeds. And it does so because of the language and the perceptive and moving vision of that glorious and benighted creature, man, that Brendan Behan put into it. (p. 20)

Although there is a great deal said about hanging and although the play is strongly opposed to legalized execution, *The Quare Fellow* is not merely a diatribe against capital punishment. It is a study of human nature which irreverently but compassionately confronts man with a reflection of himself, his society, and the facile distinctions he makes about his own behavior and that of his fellow creatures. Not only are the penal system and government-sanctioned executions subjected to close scrutiny, but so are public attitudes toward such matters as sex, politics, and religion.

Although it deals with a number of serious themes, *The Quare Fellow* is filled with humor, much of it hilarious. However, within almost every humorous line and scene there is a bite. Spontaneously one laughs at the deftly delivered witticisms, only to sense, in the midst of laughing, the presence of pain. This occurs time after time, and the viewer, while enjoying the gaiety of the proceedings, sees his prejudices, pretensions, and preconceptions, and those of his society, exposed for what they are. Viewing the play is

a bittersweet experience out of which emerges an energetic affirmation of life. (p. 21)

Opposed to the senseless destruction of human life, *The Hostage* has been described variously as tragicomedy, music hall comedy, and theatre of the absurd. Whatever the label, there is no doubt the play succeeds with audiences, that it is good theatre. However, as drama, it is not up to the standard of *The Quare Fellow*, which is itself a flawed work. *The Hostage* is lacking in characterization, form, and structure, and many of the comic lines and sequences have no relation to the characters, events, and themes. The play succeeds by virtue of its robust vitality and the candor and compassion of its vision of human nature. The combination of these particular strengths and weaknesses is characteristic of all Behan's works; what varies from work to work is the degree to which the positive factors overshadow and outweigh the negative. (p. 39)

> *Raymond J. Porter, in his* Brendan Behan *(Columbia Essays on Modern Writers Pamphlet No. 66; copyright © 1973 Columbia University Press; reprinted by permission of the publisher), Columbia University Press, 1973.*

*   *   *

BELL, Marvin   1937-

An American poet and editor, Bell divides his time among writing, teaching, and editing. He has edited *The North American Review* and has been coeditor of *Midland II*. (See also *Contemporary Authors*, Vols. 21-24, rev. ed.)

[Bell] often deploys barrages of surrealistic humor, somewhat in the manner of Mark Strand or James Tate. . . .

[Any] use of humor in an essentially serious poem requires a kind of intelligence which is rare among poets, though poets often praise it: . . . Bell not only [sees himself and his] surroundings clearly but [renders] them without overinflation. [He has] the ability to make sense, rather than gratuitous use, of more or less subjective imagery. . . .

Bell's range—the variety of themes, tones and line lengths which he has mastered—is quite wide. The inclusion of the sixteen earlier poems [in *A Probable Volume of Dreams*] shows how far Bell has extended his range since they first appeared. His voice is sometimes evasive, often idiosyncratic, so that the reader is simultaneously engaged and kept, for a time, at a distance. This effect is sometimes achieved by means of a device which Strand and Tate also use; I mean the use of an addressed "you" who is more like a translated "I". (p. 122)

The style of those poems is lean, with short lines and sentences which carry an economy of emotion which would constrict if it were not for Bell's control over the placement of ironies. . . .

The conscientious wit which keeps the earlier poems from going flat has also directed the development of Bell's style toward the more discursive poems which are collected for the first time in this book. The economy remains, but the range of emotion and the depth of exploration are increased; the resulting poems are characterized by longer lines and a more inclusive vision. Even the surrealistic humor has been extended to include such verbal exuberance as [a poem] . . . spoken by a poet who is "locked in / the English Department". . . .

Bell's poems move out from a great variety of departure points; in this limited space, I cannot give a fair indication of his versatility. He is concerned with war, love and the kinds of mental life in which a poet and teacher is caught up. He approaches these subjects as a man remembering, thinking and believing. If his music is low key, it is almost always appropriate to his themes.

"Toward Certain Divorce," which is among the best poems in the volume, is a narrative meditation spoken by a visitor in the home of a man and a woman who are planning to separate. The last few lines are typical of the later, more discursive style; they show that a poet, if he is strong enough, can handle the problem of sentimentality, not by avoiding it but by facing it squarely and earning his use of it. (p. 123)

> *Henry Taylor, in* The Nation *(copyright 1970 by the Nation Associates, Inc.), February 2, 1970.*

What is immediately impressive about *A Probable Volume of Dreams*—the title is taken from one of the poems, 'Tree-tops', and the word 'dream' occurs frequently—is its variety and versatility. The quality of the poetry is uneven, but the range of subject-matter, emotion and tone is extraordinary. Bell writes about things personal and public, about love, marriage, divorce, children, politics, war, Jews, America, about dreams and nightmares and realities. His technical range is just as extensive. He varies from the simplicity and directness of poems like 'The Affair' to the complexity and allusiveness of poems like 'Poverty in Athens, Ohio'. He can write compact, intense imagistic poems like 'My Hate', which is based on a single conceit. He can also write more relaxed and open-textured, though no less powerful, poems like 'The Perfection of Dentistry', arguably the best poem in the book. Occasionally he even employs a quasi-allegorical idiom, as in 'Wanting to Help' and 'Time We Took to Travel'. He can be elegaic, as in the moving but unsentimental 'An Afterword to my Father'; wryly comic, as in 'A Poor Jew'; and hilariously funny, as in 'The Delicate Bird who is Flying up our Asses'. At times he is serious to the point of sombreness, as in one of his best poems, 'The Extermination of the Jews'; but he can also be *almost* gaily lighthearted, as in 'The Danger at Funny Junction'—*almost,* because Bell's pervasive humour usually has dark, even sinister, undertones. The surface lightness and verbal playfulness of some poems is deceptive. A smile can mask an anguished grimace; a joke, a cri de coeur. In 'World War III', for example, Bell puns on 'the American right wing'—the context is of military aircraft—and ends in an almost offhand way with grim, low-key humour:

> You decide against shelter.
> Instead, you stand on your porch.
>
> In the sun,
> that old fireball,
>
> you stand on your porch with your family.
> You tell them not to worry.
>
> It's a nice day, you say,
> such warmth on your skin.

This ironic understatement, almost comically euphemistic, is far more effective in articulating the horror felt at the prospect of nuclear warfare than the ponderous banalities usually found in treatments of this well-worn theme.

It is therefore clear that Bell's poetry exhibits the inclusiveness, the determination to confront and encompass the totality of human experience, that has characterized much of the best American poetry since Whitman and that helps to explain why so many American poets of this century, especially major ones, have attempted large-scale, even epic, structures. . . . Indeed Bell is distinctively American in other ways, particularly in his handling of words and rhythms. Donald Justice's claim that Bell has been 'redefining the language, not the words only, but the very grammar of it' may be an exaggeration; but for a non-American, reading Bell is like reading a foreign language you think you know but suddenly find you do not know all that well after all, especially when it comes to nuances and connotations.

Bell's poetry undoubtedly has its roots in American speech, and the speaking voice can be heard very clearly at times. . . . Yet if his poetry is colloquial, it never descends to chattiness, the great danger with Bell's kind of poetry and one of the prevailing vices of contemporary poetry. On the contrary, Bell's writing can modulate from the colloquial to the eloquent, even to the rhetorical, without any sense of strain, as it does at the end of 'The Students':

> And it is almost enough, and it is almost a
>   book,
> just to do what's next, up the stairs,
> into the picture, into your marriage, into the
>   dark,
> writhing into the goals, O pleasure!

This degree of discipline, entirely appropriate in this case to prevent hysteria or mawkishness, is unusual in Bell, but he is too good a poet to try to do without control, even though he is capable of a freewheeling, 'stream of consciousness' style. . . . Bell steers an individual course between formalism and formlessness, and avoids both academicism and the self-indulgent meandering that has been an unfortunate though necessary part of the revolt against academicism in America during the last fifteen years.

Bell's poetry is not a poetry of statement or of ideology but of exploration. He maps out emotional territory. He is a geographer of the psyche. In 'The Perfection of Dentistry' he writes, 'we have words for the cabinets of our emotions', and in his poetry Bell is intent on unlocking those cabinets. Many of his poems are voyages of discovery, attempts to articulate something felt or experienced but not fully understood, it would seem, until the writing of the poem. His work is, in Eliot's words, 'a raid on the inarticulate', but his equipment is neither shabby nor deteriorating. He gropes towards the truth, towards a definition of reality, and this tentativeness is sometimes enacted in the writing. . . . (pp. 35-7)

A poem by Bell is therefore very difficult to paraphrase. As Archibald MacLeish might say, a Bell poem is. He seldom sets out to express a point of view, to expound an idea, or to preach. There are few certainties in his work, and traces of polemicism are rare, even in his poems about war and politics, but on occasion he can be blunt, as in 'What Songs the Soldiers Sang':

> The songs, too, about their singing, are lies.
> The truth is that some songs were obscene
> and that there were no words for others.

Satire is by no means excluded from Bell's work, but he is essentially an ironist, not a satirist. 'The Perfection of Dentistry', in which he investigates the impact on a North

American sensibility of the alien way of life and values of Mexico, could easily have become satirical, but Bell achieves a richer and deeper effect by recording the human contradictions and complex ironies of the situation without attempting to pass judgment, 'without any irritable reaching after fact and reason', to quote Keats on Negative Capability.

An important feature of Bell's poetry is fantasy, a genuinely surreal fantasy that never degenerates into whimsy even though it is frequently linked with comedy. Because his work resists labels and pigeonholing, Bell cannot be described as a surrealist or an expressionist, but such descriptions are at least partly valid. Since the real world of the twentieth century that Bell confronts is so bizarre and irrational as to be almost a fantasy world or bad dream, fantasy is often superior to 'realism' as a way of illuminating reality and approaching the truth. Kafka and Beckett are much better 'realists' than Arnold Bennett and John Osborne. Bell's handling of fantasy is extremely varied and flexible. In some poems, such as 'The Delicate Bird who is Flying up our Asses' and 'The Hole in the Sea', he sustains the fantasy throughout. In others he counterpoints fantasy against reality, often with comic and ironic results, as in 'On Returning to Teach'. In 'The Israeli Navy' fantasy approximates to comic extravaganza, whereas in 'The War Piece' he employs a bird and insect fantasy to convey a horrific vision of nuclear war. (p. 37)

Perhaps the most irritating aspect of Bell's poetry is his fondness for puns and word-play. One poem, for example, is called 'Verses *versus* Verses'. Of course there is nothing intrinsically wrong with his verbal ingenuity. It depends on how he uses it, and it can be effective, as 'black, widow cloud' is, with its marvellously appropriate pun on the deadly black-widow spider. . . .

But in 'The Affair', a serious poem about New England Puritanism faced with the demon of sex, 'the seeds of awful pleasures', with the ambiguity of 'awful', the implied pun on 'lawful pleasures', and 'seeds' used both literally (semen) and metaphorically, sticks out like an ill-timed erection or an unwanted pregnancy. There is a similar incongruity later in the poem—'making the fair game tremble', with its complex play on 'fair sex', 'game bird' and 'fair game'. Other poems exhibit the same tendency. 'A Picture of Soldiers', an otherwise rather good poem about the First World War, is marred by puns on 'rank', 'batteries' and 'arms'. (p. 38)

For all the diversity of *A Probable Volume of Dreams,* an individual and immediately recognizable voice can be heard throughout. Some poems may recall the work of other poets—'Her Dream House' is reminiscent of Berryman's 'Desires of Men and Women' in some ways—but there is no evidence of pastiche. Influences have been digested and absorbed. Much of what has been said about *A Probable Volume of Dreams* is also true of *The Escape into You,* although this sequence represents an advance on the earlier book in certain respects. There is a greater intensity and urgency in much of the writing, a swirling linguistic energy that initially takes one's critical breath away. The poetic textures are frequently richer and the imagery denser. . . . Many of the poems give the impression of having been written under considerable emotional pressure, sometimes approaching the fever-pitch of Sylvia Plath's last poems, as in 'On Utilitarianism':

> We turn rubber into trees, flowers,
> make a cow of loose leather, a sow's ear
> of a ruined purse, we change wine to blood,
> bread into flesh, as if there were no tomorrow
> we change men into women, alter the course
> of the stars, we try to beat the odds.

The note of desperation here is partly produced by the absence of heavy punctuation and by the way in which the lines strain against the stanza form as if they were attempting to break through its rigidity. Even the syntax is compressed—'as if there were no tomorrow' can refer to both the previous and the following words. At times Bell's desire for concentration results in an extremely terse, clipped idiom, as in the verbal staccato of 'The Embrace':

> Clip the tender parts
> together, they said. Joined. Holy
> because married.

On other occasions the poetry flows more smoothly, but the emotional and referential shifts are so rapid that Bell is using a kind of poetic shorthand or telegrammese. . . . (pp. 38-9)

Furthermore a number of poems, such as 'A Biography', 'You, Heavenly' and 'The Drifting', begin abruptly and dramatically. Bell frequently plunges into an experience heart-first and with nerves exposed, dragging his half-comprehending reader with him.

Among the fruits of this highly-charged style are epigrammatic phrases that linger in the memory, such as the final, paradoxical line of 'American Poets'—'We multiplied, but we didn't reproduce'. . . . (p. 39)

Bell also succeeds brilliantly in reviving some of the most conventional metaphors of love poetry, such as the likening of the lover to a ship in a storm ('Rescue, Rescue') and the comparison of the growth of love to that of a tree ('Song: The Organic Years'). But if there are gains, there are also losses, and the losses are inseparable from the gains. In general the poems in *The Escape into You* are much more personal than those in *A Probable Volume of Dreams,* and much more difficult—difficult to the point of obscurity in several cases. In *A Probable Volume of Dreams* Bell seems more distanced from what he is writing about, so that even in the more personal poems he is capable of viewing himself with a considerable degree of objectivity. In 'The Perfection of Dentistry', for example, he achieves a delicate balance between involvement and detachment, and the emotional honesty of the poem depends to a large extent on the delicacy of this balance. In *The Escape into You* this balance is upset in favour of the personal. The increase in poetic vitality is offset by the decrease in comprehensibility. Sometimes the imagery and associations remain intractably private. What, for example, do the final lines of 'Virtuoso of the X' mean, and what precisely is the significance of the allusion to the genocide of the Jews in Nazi concentration camps? (pp. 39-40)

[Bell] does make very considerable, at times excessive, demands on his readers. His poetry may communicate before it is understood, but he fails in a number of poems to objectify a personal experience sufficiently to make it meaningful to his readers.

Some of the difficulties are inherent in the nature of the sequence, a sequence without narrative or logical continuity, 'a diary without dates, fragments of a story without any names, part of a life' as Donald Justice describes it. In a way the sequence *is* 'The Pornographic but Serious History' of Marvin Bell, a non-stop emotional and spiritual striptease. The sequence is divided into six sections, and certain groups of poems concentrate on one main theme—a love affair, a marital crisis, Jews—but the links between poems are often omitted. The obvious comparison is with John Berryman's much longer sequence, *His Toy, His Dream, His Rest,* especially as Bell uses what may be called Berryman form, a poem of three six-lined stanzas, in all but two cases ('The Children' and 'The Willing'), and these involve only minor variations. It is only through this self-imposed discipline that Bell achieves as much objectivity as he does and is able to shape his personal experience into poetry without becoming incoherent. Nevertheless Bell is not imitating Berryman. It would be more accurate to say that he is taking on Berryman on Berryman's own terms. Like Berryman, Bell is aiming at a large-scale but loosely constructed poem that is inclusive and flexible enough to contain a complex American consciousness (Jewish-American in Bell's case) in all its moods. The sequence encompasses tragedy and comedy, anguish and laughter, the holocaust of the Jews and bawdy love poems. In other words *The Escape into You* is tremendously ambitious. It is therefore not surprising that its success if only partial. But what is certain is that Bell possesses a powerful, original and mature poetic voice. Donald Justice has said that 'if there were a Jewish school of poets, as of novelists, Marvin Bell could be the whole school himself'. As yet Bell is not of the stature of Saul Bellow or Bernard Malamud; but if he continues to develop he could be, and might then become an important influence on American poetry in the coming decades. (p. 40)

Peter Elfed Lewis, "The Poetry of Marvin Bell," in Stand *(copyright © by* Stand*), Vol. 13, No. 4 (1972), p. 34-40.*

What can be said about a poet who complains like David Ignatow, sings like John Berryman, and sees like Theodore Roethke? That Marvin Bell has talent and is one of our most important poets. At their best, Bell's new poems snap with the wit and depth of Yiddish proverbs. "Residue of Song," Bell's third book of poems, is a kind of personal history. Like the history of the Jewish religion, the figures of father and son dominate. . . . "Residue of Song" is a book about origins, the poet telling us that "The proper study of man is where he came from!" Despite the logic and wit of the poet's complicated personal grammar, the finest poems move quickly, dropping the rationally conceived verbal pretensions for a greater associative content —poems such as "The Present," "To the Sky," "Song of the Immediacy of Death," and the graceful concluding poem, "The Hurt Trees." If there is a weakness to Bell's new book, it is his tendency to give in to an excess of word play, particularly in the third and fourth sections. Nevertheless, Marvin Bell's new book, by way of the poet's own imperfect personality, successfully woos the reader. (p. lvi)

Virginia Quarterly Review *(copyright, 1975, by the* Virginia Quarterly Review, *The University of Virginia), Vol. 51, No. 2 (Spring, 1975).*

To the ten poems from his giddy pamphlet *Woo Havoc,* first published in 1971, the same year as his "sequence" *The Escape into You,* Marvin Bell has added, to make up this book, a vaudeville of his undertakings and achievements thereafter and given it a peculiarly apt title [*Residue of Song*]. In law, a *residue* is that part of an estate remaining after the satisfaction of all debts and previous devices. Now I should not care to say that Bell had satisfied *all* previous devices, for there were so many of them to be satisfied, but I think he has given enough satisfaction to have a considerable estate on his hands, or within his reach.

It is no accident, to coin a phrase, that the poems from the pamphlet are dedicated to the poet's sons and that so many of the poems subsequent—particularly a series of thirteen called "You Would Know"—are devoted to the poet's father: this chain-of-generations is what has always bound Bell closest to his gift, the links in the family romance he finds so indissoluble, from the first poem in the book:

> The universe, remember, is a ribbon
> where we follow back to the beginning
> and so meet that one of whom you were thinking
> when you mistook being here for being there

to the penultimate *& Son,* in which Bell accommodates himself to the fact "that one is where one doesn't want to be"—that is, one is either with "the dead, where we live", or preparing oneself to become a monster daddy to the future. This tremendous sequentiality of Bell's admits of very few gaps, lacunae, let-ups: when they occur, the world appears to stop, everything falls apart. And that is the moment one writes poems, of course—one writes poems to keep things together, to get the world going again: "my way of trying propriety", as Bell says.

Admirable, the way this poet's wit is won over to his task as witness; as he ransacks the world for evidence ("Suddenly, we were responsible for discourse, whereas,/years earlier, we had been held only by the moon."), even the change of seasons is no more or no less than an inflection of the generations, a page from the great Oedipal chronicle which abides, the one thing we can count on: "Leaf-taking has turned to winter." There is a guarantee—in the goofiest, the most guarded of these poems, as in the most pietistic ones—that anything noticed, anything thought of or recurred to will be brought into the tradition, the handing-down, even when it appears to be no more than a betrayal:

> But to go from here to there, swervingly,
> to miss the edges, is hard but what you have to do,
> though it's not yet on your minds to send back word.

To send back word. One hadn't realized one was far enough ahead to send word *back,* and suddenly, there is that dead father, there is all this consequent life around one, here are these sons:

> And the maniac's me. The manic's panic's
> mine. It's been that or a headstone.

This last quotation reveals, I think, the reach of Bell's desperation, as of his delight in a sort of hand-to-microphone diction, the variety-show of talking which will keep things in hand, as I have said, until we reach the hospital or heaven or maybe just the next hideout, the escape into you. . . . [There] are "conventional" success like *From a Distance,* a poem which strikes me as Bell's most beautiful achievement, his most finely realized inheritance of man's estate. But that's not what he's after, that's not what he *takes after,* as we might say of the heir, the convulsive infant coming into his own. Whatever concessions have been made—gratifyingly—made to my sense of decorum, they do not signify here so much as what is not conceded; Bell is in search of those psychosomatic dangers not yet registered by poetry, even by his own; and the search does him honor, if there's little comfort, and a great deal of menace, in it:

Did I forget what's closest to my heart?
Ache, peril, fissure, clot and blast.

(pp. 346-47)

Richard Howard, in Poetry *(© 1975 by The Modern Poetry Association; reprinted by permission of the Editor of* Poetry*), September, 1975.*

* * *

BELLOW, Saul   1915-

Canadian-born Jewish-American novelist, short story writer, essayist, and playwright, Bellow was the 1976 recipient of the Nobel Prize for Literature. His strongly felt belief in the possibility of maintaining selfhood in a world that levels individualism is a major theme throughout his work. His heroes, who personify his optimism, are some of the most memorable in contemporary fiction. Bellow has also been the recipient of the National Book Award and the 1976 Pulitzer Prize for Fiction. (See also *CLC*, Vols. 1, 2, 3, 6, and *Contemporary Authors*, Vols. 5-8, rev. ed.)

Herzog's final self-acceptance has been attacked, and vehemently, as a "fatty sigh of middle-class intellectual contentment." The resolution of the book has been assailed, even by friendly critics, as offering either too little or too much.... And in fact the general critical tendency has been to find fault with its ability to resolve at all: "Herzog is finally as arrogantly complacent in his new-found affirmative position . . . as Bellow dares to allow him to be."

From the standpoint of schlemiel-literature, this criticism is entirely beside the point. Insofar as the schlemiel is a comic hero, he is promised a "happy ending," if not in the normal sense, then at least in his own self-appraisal.... In every conceivable empirical test the schlemiel may fail, but he never fails in his final self-acceptance; otherwise the whole premise of the loser-as-victor would be destroyed.

Then, too, criticism of Herzog's complacency does not seem to take into account the degree to which Herzog is an ironic hero, still in the schlemiel tradition. The ironic smugness is present in the very first sentence, for the man who says "If I'm out of my mind, it's all right with me" already appears to be "pretty well satisfied to be just as it is willed." On the other hand, Herzog can go further in self-criticism than even the severest of his critics, and he is usually more unsparing, as well as wittier, in pointing up his own flaws.... Herzog is under no prolonged illusion about his Christlike goodness. He recognizes that his sympathy is socially meaningless and morally fattening, and he mocks it. So too his multifaceted importance to the human race.... If Herzog does ultimately accept himself, he does so in the spirit of compromise.

The ending is also typical of schlemiel conclusions in that the character's salvation, not his benevolence, is its exclusive concern. The saint is concerned for others and is canonized for his ability to affect attitudinal or substantive change. While he too, like our hero, risks being thought a fool, his glory is invariably recognized, perhaps post-humously, but without equivocation. Salvation for the schlemiel, to the contrary, is always partial and personal. He does not affirm the objective presence of goodness, but merely the right and the need to believe in it as one component of the human personality. Herzog is always being exposed to social evils, yet always, by his own admission, as a spectator whose concerns are his own feelings and his own conscience. It may be, as Norman Mailer has com-

plained, that with *Herzog* the reality of the novel has coagulated into mere moral earnestness. This is the limitation of all schlemiel works, a seemingly inevitable quality of the genre. What once appeared in the novel as the individual's interaction with his society has now narrowed to a study of the individual's reaction to society. (pp. 92-5)

As observer in the courtroom, Herzog becomes a witness to horrors far greater than any in his own experience, and more deeply personalized than those of history or the daily news. He is exposed to life-size barbarians, his neighbors, in a brutal challenge to his apple-cheeked humanism. (p. 95)

It is hardly accidental that the murder dramatized for Herzog is just the sort of murder from which no shred of meaning can be extracted, one which like Auschwitz stands outside the scope of rational thought. Herzog "experienced nothing but his own *human feelings,* in which he found nothing of use." The only resolution he draws—and that irrationally—is to protect his own child.

The courtroom drama is a "play within a play," exploring the subject's relation to what is basest in the modern world. These are horrors that cannot qualify as economic or social problems. Nothing *can* be gained for the murdered boy, no symbolic assurance that the world will be better for his death, no religious murmurings, no personal revelations. Nothing is learned from the murder of this child or from the murders of millions of such children. Now Herzog is a kind, thoughtful humanist, and what is he to do with the anguish dumped on his doorstep? His response is not effective, merely affective. When his life touches the uncomfortable, he struggles to understand it. He does not, however, give up his life to it. The irony merely intensifies, as Herzog continues to worry about his soul (*his* soul!) on a trip through Hades. Herzog knows this is petty (petit) and knows also it is necessary because that is his function as a human being. "The strength of a man's virtue or spiritual capacity measured by his ordinary life."

Elsewhere Bellow has written: "We make what we can of our condition with the means available. We must accept the mixture as we find it—the impurity of it, the tragedy of it, the hope of it." It is just this emphasis on *mixture* that distinguishes Herzog and other Jewish schlemiels from the meek Christians like Melville's Billy Budd or Faulkner's fabled corporal. Schlemiels are not creatures of the Manichean imagination: even Charlie Chaplin's *The Great Dictator* divides the alternatives of civilization too sharply between innocence and guilt to be an authentic part of the genre. Though the moral dilemma must always be presented as a confrontation between opposites, its tone is determined by the implied purity of each faction. Herzog and his comic forebears are themselves a little tainted; never having known the primal innocence of Eden, they do not pull up their skirts in outrage at the appearance of villainy, and having no ascetic inclinations, their own chances of "staying clean" are slight. The otherworldly purity of the saints, products of the Christian literary imagination, is best suggested by their silence or stuttering: holiness beyond speech. The stained humanity of the schlemiel pours out in obsessive verbosity. Yet to say that the polarization between good and evil is less extreme is not to imply that the moral concern is any the less acute. In an article written concurrently with the last parts of *Herzog*, Bellow puts the proposition as follows:

either we want life to continue or we do not. If we don't want to continue, why write books? The wish for death is powerful and silent. It respects actions; it has no need of words.

But if we answer yes, we do want it to continue, we are liable to be asked how. In what form shall life be justified? That is the essence of the moral question. We call a writer moral to the degree that his imagination indicates to us how we may answer naturally, without strained arguments, with a spontaneous, mysterious proof that has no need to argue with despair.

Herzog is such an attempt at proof. (pp. 95-7)

Is the fool escaping his adult responsibilities, or is he alone fulfilling them? If the only alternatives are the Ayn Rand objectivists and Herzogian innocents, may the progress of civilization not indeed depend upon him?

Not the author or reader, but the character himself raises these questions. (p. 97)

Herzog's internalization of irony sets him apart from Bloom, from whose saga his name alone is lifted: in *Ulysses,* Joyce has placed in apposition "the persuasive surfaces of personalities as they see themselves, and these characters as they are," even when he seems to be offering a stream of consciousness. The very form of the mock epic imposes the shadow of his heroic predecessor over a dwarfed Bloom. Joyce called his work *Ulysses,* but Herzog casts his own little light. In *Herzog,* the protagonist is endowed with the complexity of mind and ironic vision that in *Ulysses* remains the prerogative of the author. The result is not an ironic exposure of life, but rather an ironic life, exposed.

Herzog is finally the character who lives according to a twofold perception of himself in relation to the world, both giant and dwarf, alien and center of the universe, failure and success, cuckold and great lover, intellectual and schlemiel. The single reality of the naturalists is for him insufficient. . . . Herzog addresses himself seriously, if not earnestly, to his and, as he sees it, the world's situation: "We must get it out of our heads that this is a doomed time, that we are waiting for the end, and the rest of it, mere junk from fashionable magazines." The intellectual rejection of pessimism is ultimately coupled with a psychological readiness to accept, even bless, the future. The ironic life accepts itself. "Anyway, can I pretend that I have much choice?"

Because Herzog's irony is internalized, there is less than the usual ironic distance between author and character. This opens the book to charges of sentimentality, since modern literature and literary criticism are very much concerned with distances and masks, and we are frankly unaccustomed to committing our disbelief to the hands of a reliable narrator. In this work, the author's position or point of view is not noticeably different from the protagonist's. Herzog steers his pumping heart between the Scylla of Madeleine ("Feel? Don't give me that line of platitudes about feelings") and the Charybdis of Valentine, the false commercialized whirlpool of a heart. He controls the novel even when he is not yet in control of himself. Bellow has written a humanist novel, presenting one individual's life— a life by all standards a near-failure—which in its intelli-

gence and energy commands our attention and affection. *Herzog,* a study of irony as a modern form of moral vision, is the more *engagé* because of Saul Bellow's minimal irony about his subject. (pp. 99-100)

> *Ruth R. Wisse, "The Schlemiel as Liberal Humanist," in her* The Schlemiel as Modern Hero *(© 1971 by University of Chicago Press), University of Chicago Press, 1971 (and reprinted in* Saul Bellow, *edited by Earl Rovit, Prentice-Hall, 1975, pp. 90-100).*

On the first page of [Bellow's] first novel, *Dangling Man,* his protagonist denounces the Hemingwayesque "code of the athlete, of the tough boy. . . . If you have difficulties, grapple with them silently, goes one of their commandments. To hell with that! I intend to talk about mine, and if I had as many mouths as Siva has arms and kept them going all the time, I still could not do myself justice." The exorcism, however, was not to be so easily accomplished, and it was not until 13 years later that Bellow made the more extended and successful effort in *Henderson, the Rain King.* Though its protagonist is not Jewish, it is the parody of Hemingway that all right-thinking American-Jewish writers had unconsciously been awaiting. The title character, who shares Hemingway's initials, is a middle-aged American millionaire who fails to find happiness or peace by trying to raise pigs or cope with his family. He flees to Africa, rejects the safari approach to seek out the natives, becomes a kind of local deity through no talent of his own except brute strength and sheer stupidity, discovers that one is akin to the kind of animal one identifies with, has his vision, and then flies safely out of Africa and back, presumably, to connubial bliss and domestic tranquility—an ending whose very hopefulness, especially cast in such a form, mocks those achieved by Hemingway's protagonists, and of course by Hemingway himself. (p. 49)

Bellow's early protagonists are young seekers somewhat akin to Salinger's. (Augie March, for instance, says, "I have always tried to become what I am. But it's a frightening thing. Because what if what I am by nature isn't good enough?") His later and more interesting ones are middle-aged ex-athletes rebelling against a kind of male menopause that seems to threaten them with an eternity of their present condition unless they break immediately and violently out of their inertia through the conquest of untamed jungle (as in *Henderson, the Rain King*), or of women (in *Herzog*), or of self (in *The Last Analysis*). At the beginning of their works it appears that they have already been wherever it is they are going to get, are too blind to know this, and so in a frenzied, picaresque manner strive to attain or recapture a world and a way irrevocably gone. Yet they end, oddly enough, like Malamud's characters and like *Portnoy's Complaint,* at a beginning, or at least a stasis, a still point in the turning world where, if anywhere, beginnings are still possible. (pp. 52-3)

> *Alan Warren Friedman, in* The Southern Review *(copyright, 1972, by Alan Warren Friedman), Vol. VIII, No. I, Winter, 1972.*

[Reading] Bellow is like taking a crash course in Great Ideas (Some Flaky) of Western Man. Dostoevsky, Rilke, Horace Mann, Walpole, Jung, Valery, Balzac, Houdini, Proust, Marx, Darwin and a dozen or more others get sentences or paragraphs [in *Humboldt's Gift*]. . . .

Bellow's novel does have a plot, but it barely supports the ups and downs, lateral wanderings and intellectual cold sweats of Humboldt and Charlie. It's so fragile at any moment it threatens to collapse under their weight. The delicate tedium sent me to watering the plants, sharpening pencils, and lying down to drain the head. *Humboldt's Gift* is a funny, sad, brilliantly written boring novel. Along with a scheme for publishing all the world's new ideas in a magazine called The Ark, Charlie plans to issue a major statement on the disease of boredom. He passes the infection on to Bellow. (p. 1)

I don't think *Humboldt's Gift* is Saul Bellow at his best. His people all talk like one another. He falls victim to the sound of his mind working. Humboldt's gift of hope born out of absurdity is verbal manipulation. Renata's behavior comes from whim, not motive. By the time the talking is over Bellow himself seems to have grown tired and run out of ideas.

But even a low-key Saul Bellow is more powerful than most of our contemporary novelists. A master need not create masterpieces to assert his art. As Degas once said to Camille Pissarro, "It would be such a treat if you could produce some very careful outlines of cabbages." (p. 4)

> *Webster Schott, "A Muted Bellow," in* Book World—The Washington Post (© The Washington Post), *August 24, 1975, pp. 1, 4.*

The great novelist is one who is willing to take intellectual risks, daring to impose his own uniquely wrought order on the offerings of imagination and memory without being rigid or sentimental. What has given such redoubtable weight to the work of Saul Bellow . . . has been this risk in the celebration of mind as passion.

Bellow, more than any other contemporary writer, is the exuberant novelist of ideas, pursuing his difficult, hard-earned vision amid the oppressively distracting and comic turbulence of urban Jewish life in the United States. Even his least intellectual hero, the picaresque Augie March, is intoxicated with the cerebral elixir of first principles, immutable as the tides, that convert the racketing chaos of America into constraining notions about destiny, character and fate.

To understand these troublesome words is, for Bellow, to be that much less at the mercy of capricious experience. His heroes are constantly asking not who they are—they know who they are, identity is never their crisis—but what they are metaphysically part of. Augie describes this as "a feeling about the axial lines of life, with respect to which you must be straight or else your existence is merely clownery, hiding tragedy." Tommy Wilhelm, in *Seize the Day,* weeping uncontrollably in the rubble of his hope, continues to yearn for "a promise that mankind might . . . comprehend why it lives! Why life, why death." And Artur Sammler, the oldest of Bellow's representative men, spent and weary, with only a short time remaining to his long and parched survival of Hitler's Europe, feels obliged to ask, in the end, whether he has met the terms of his contract; he knows he must never allow himself to forget why he has been put here—"to do what was required of him."

Indeed, all of Bellow's heroes, from Joseph in *Dangling Man* through the jaded but intractable Sammler, have been unequivocally certain about their personal assessment of an extraordinarily complex range of issues and events, and this outspokenness, this absolute lack of ambivalence, has been among the major delights of Bellow's fictional achievement. I can think of no other 20th-century American author

whose work, drawn entirely and inexhaustibly from his life and his exploration of the perilous landscape of philosophic and cultural ideas, has so fully and clearly reflected his own opinions and judgments. He is always the writer who takes himself as a sample of one in dealing with the world.

The powerful moral conviction contained in each of Bellow's novels, however, becomes a form of torment to Charlie Citrine, the questing narrator of *Humboldt's Gift,* who has not yet made his way through a recently sighted metaphysical maze. "I had neither vivid actuality nor symbolic clarity," he admits, "and for the time being I was utterly nowhere." Sammler's brutally earned assurance is still far beyond Citrine's grasp.

To be sure, Citrine is another of Bellow's obsessively speculative and much-put-upon protagonists. (pp. 19-20)

Bellow is the only novelist equal to the task of creating memorable caricatures that match those of Dickens, and in his brilliant gallery of eccentrics and grotesques . . . Humboldt is an instant classic. . . . When Charlie ultimately comes into Humboldt's legacy—a letter written in the fresh air of sanity not long before he died—the clear voice of the master talker affirms Citrine's faith in his theosophical efforts ("Remember: we are not natural beings but supernatural beings"). . . .

Unfortunately, somewhere around the moment Charlie opens Humboldt's letter from the grave, the novel itself goes askew, spinning out of control with erratic implausibility, creaking with bizarre and mechanical improvisations that seem either astonishingly sentimental and out of character for Bellow, or desperately inventive. What makes the book particularly puzzling is that for the first time one cannot hear the voice of a principal Bellow character asserting the confident moral and intellectual opinions of the novelist himself. At the age of 60, a writer of ideas should be more than ready to make his richly earned statement about the "axial lines" of life and death, but in *Humboldt's Gift* Bellow is curiously detached, reluctant to be completely candid about Charlie's embrace of Steiner's "spiritual science" and mystical arithmetic.

Nothing in Bellow's earlier work—or, for that matter, in brilliant parts of *Humboldt's Gift*—begins to persuade me that his skeptical intelligence can be in agreement with Steiner's pompous elaborations of the invisible. Bellow's eye and ear for the human comedy of pretentious significance have always been too acute, too reasonable, to let me equate Citrine's "mission" with that of the author. What I miss here is the persuasive resonance of conviction that has always been an essential part of Bellow's vigorously sardonic genius. And what comes through by the end is that—depending on the part of *Humboldt's Gift* one is reading—this is Saul Bellow's best and also least satisfactory novel. (p. 20)

> *Pearl K. Bell, "Bellow's Best and Worst," in* The New Leader (© 1975 by the American Labor Conference on International Affairs, Inc.), *September 1, 1975, pp. 19-20.*

Charlie Citrine, the narrator of Saul Bellow's fine new novel, seems closer to its author than any of his heroes hitherto. Sensitive, tough, witty, dapper, deeply Jewish and in several senses metaphysical, he was raised in Chicago and studied at Wisconsin before hitting New York. . . .

The plot of *Humboldt's Gift* is as neatly scaffolded as a legacy tale by Dickens, with suspense, scares, false trails, surprises, jokes and pratfalls. Yet, as in Dickens, few but the literal-minded would read it for that alone. What stand out most are the characters—Charlie himself and Humboldt, but equally the opulent Renata, Charlie's mistress, less sensual than she seems and privately wittier, two-timing Charlie, besotting him, and answering to something more in his nature than panicky, middle-aged lechery. Protean and deeply private, with her nice little nuisance of a boy and her appalling mother, she seems at times like a fleshly version of David Copperfield's Dora, maddening, unknowable, the huge, warm trap of a desperately unsuitable mate. (p. 484)

[The] theme is typically Chicago: and the city is a further major character in the novel. There are others. . . . But the windy city dwarfs its windier citizens. 'In Chicago you become a connoisseur of the near-nothing.' 'I knew that what you needed in a big American city was a deep no-affect belt, a critical mass of indifference. . . .' (pp. 484-85)

Manoeuvring his large cast, Saul Bellow sometimes seems [a lightning conductor]. But like other writers, only more so, he has the strange power of attracting and concentrating whatever may be in the air. . . .

Mortality is very present in *Humboldt's Gift;* and Saul Bellow's sense of being a shaman for forces no one understands is expressed more openly than some readers may expect. . . . But while Bellow's and Charlie's vision remains rooted in actuality—noting, for instance, 'the false smile that swept the country about 15 years ago . . . you drew your upper lip away from the teeth, while looking at your interlocutor with charm'—the here and now is not allowed to be a tyrant. . . . *Humboldt's Gift* is as much a summa as anything Bellow has written yet. (p. 485)

> *Richard Mayne, "A Long Cool Summa," in* The Listener (© *British Broadcasting Corp. 1975; reprinted by permission of Richard Mayne), October 9, 1975, pp. 484-85.*

Free style and fixed categories, will and idea, mental geography and urban reality, *odi et amo,* the heart's reasons and the mind's imperatives, carnal compulsion and theoretical need, *member virilis* versus *mens cogitans*—these are only a few of the antitheses, some the author's, some my own distillations, that come to mind when one thinks back upon the books that Saul Bellow has written during the last three decades. *Dangling Man,* the title of his first novel, could serve as a collective description of his heroes: the Hendersons, Herzogs, Wilhelms, Sammlers, all swinging on delicate threads of reason between opposing truths and immiscible realities. The contradictions close in, the string is cut, and the novels become arenas of desperate struggle, filled with events that, like feral predators, stalk Bellow's characters in their times of vulnerability, refusing to be disciplined by thought or tamed by affection, capricious, cruel, and comic appetites whetted only further by efforts to understand them.

When, some years ago, I wrote that Bellow's novels "do not so much end as wear themselves out," I was describing his formal handling of these conflicts, the novelistic method of qualification, speculation, and cultural gloss with which he, through his characters, battles the rambunctious events of his narrative and tries to effect between the gritty details of naturalism and the generalities of an imaginative intelligence some sort of stylistic agreement. I intended this description of exhaustion both as an observation that Bellow often seemed not to trust the conventions of fiction and as

an appreciation of what he was able to achieve by refusing the temptation of neat narrative resolutions. He, his characters, and the readers struggled on to the very end, grappling with ironies and complexities that spilled well over the boundaries of his fiction. And if such struggles often made for a ragged, disjointed aesthetic experience, they also infused Bellow's novels with a vitality and intelligence that were unique in American fiction. (p. 74)

Sammler admits there is a covenant involved in human existence and a knowledge of the manner in which it must be kept. His labors are bent upon justifying the covenant's terms and the pain they cause, on making the bargain acceptable to mortal feelings. Thought and theory are not then voyages of discovery, but rather attempts at compassionate demonstrations of the necessary justice in the intuited imperatives of life. By admitting such knowledge, Sammler affirms and ennobles the attempts of the Herzogs and Hendersons to reconcile this awareness of human purpose with the errant, disconnected data of their personal lives.

Mr. Sammler's Planet is a refined tribute to the struggle between human consciousness and the accidental life of passion, between the philosopher's need to justify and the novelist's duty to depict. With *Humboldt's Gift,* Bellow still affects the zest and seriousness of these old combats, but his arena has become much smaller, his spectacles more contrived, and his adversaries affected with a commonplace exhaustion before their contests even begin. I am told that there is a good deal of autobiography in this novel and this may explain Bellow's reluctance to give the protagonist of *Humboldt's Gift* any of the intellectual strength and interesting human virtue that offset the frequent tone of self-pity and social petulance in his earlier central characters. But the fact that Humboldt is modeled after the poet Delmore Schwartz or that Bellow's involvement in the founding of *The Noble Savage* had circumstances in common with the attempts of his narrator-hero, Charles Citrine, to start a magazine called *The Ark,* is extraneous to criticism. Whether Bellow has been harsh on himself or on the materials of pure imagination, he has written a book that tries to bully and bustle the reader into a point of view about the artist and society that is a mixture of antic exaggeration and simplistic *parti pris. Humboldt's Gift* is a sad, shallow book, a statement of intellectual and artistic surrender that has as its only interesting quality that crude sense of humor a writer can sometimes wring out of the wilful abasement of his characters. (pp. 74, 76)

> *Jack Richardson, "A Burnt-Out Case" (reprinted from* Commentary *by permission; copyright © 1975 by the American Jewish Committee), in* Commentary, *November, 1975, pp. 74, 76-8.*

Critics may dispute vigorously the comparative meanings and values of [Bellow's] world, but there seems to be a relatively satisfied consensus as to what it consists of.

It is dominantly urban in setting, Jewish middle-class intellectual in texture, gently or savagely ironic in tone. Its time span moves from a remembrance of immigrant communities shortly after World War I, through the years of the Depression and World War II, and up to the present. (Although the Holocaust is only infrequently referred to directly, its shadow hovers over the whole time period in foreboding or reminder.) This city-centered world shifts between Chicago and New York, and although there are sporadic interludes in the countryside and trips to Mexico, Europe, Africa, and Israel, Bellow's narrative seems most at home with subways rumbling underfoot and skyscrapers looming in the polluted air. Yet, for all the people who throng its streets, Bellow's world is a lonely one. His typical protagonists live their daily routines of work, play, and crisis so exclusively and introspectively that when they do meet a friend or stranger, the encounter tends to be charged with a passion that the meeting hardly merits. Preeminently, it is an explosively comic world—frequently grotesque, sometimes poignant, occasionally maudlin or bitter. Bellow consistently aims his ridicule at both the absurdly deficient culture within which his protagonist strives to live a meaningful life, and the pathetic illusions and self-deceptions that his protagonist brings to this desperate struggle. In a statement that might serve as a thematic emblem of much of his work, Bellow once wrote: "It is obvious that modern comedy has to do with the disintegrating outline of the worthy and humane Self, the bourgeois hero of an earlier age." Bellow has tried to guard against the varied temptations that this statement implies. He has tried to resist a sentimental nostalgia for the unrecoverable values of that earlier age; he has insisted intently that the new is not necessarily good just because it is new, nor is it even inevitably better than what may be left of the old. His is fundamentally an uncomfortable middle-of-the-road position, the tense stance of the rationalist who despairs of rational solutions to human frustration but who is constrained to accept no guide superior to rationality—crippled, incomplete, and irresolute as it may be.

I think that it is the inherent ambivalence of this posture—indelibly manifest in his style and in the structures and thematic concerns of his fiction—that has made Bellow vulnerable to attack from the two extremes on either side of him. To the traditionalists, he appears to be surrendering too much to the assaults of history and change; through their eyes, he may seem fashionably cynical, pessimistic, or irresponsible. From the opposite camp, he has been subject to harsher charges: naïveté, sentimentality, and, ultimately, compromising his ideals: being willing to accept the tepid principle of "making do" rather than daring to leap beyond rationality. . . . The characterizations of Moses Herzog and Artur Sammler were often fused and confused with the person of Bellow himself, and the understandable but unjust demand that the artist find solutions that his society could not was laid upon him and his works as a measure of their fatal deficiency. This particular furor appears to have abated, at least temporarily, and Bellow is now on the verge of being regarded as an elder statesman of American letters—a position of eminence subject to even greater dangers, I believe, than the political exacerbations of the late '60s. (pp. 2-3)

> *Earl Rovit, in his introduction to* Saul Bellow, *edited by Earl Rovit (© 1975 by Prentice-Hall, Inc.; reprinted by permission of Prentice-Hall, Inc., Englewood Cliffs, New Jersey), Prentice-Hall, 1975, pp. 1-4.*

"Cutting back and forth between the various levels of action" in time-present enabled Flaubert . . . to present movement within scene with a kind of simultaneity that approximates Pound's concept of an "intellectual and emotional complex in an instant of time."

Bellow performs a similar feat in *Seize the Day.* Tommy Wilhelm moves through time, from his prebreakfast appearance outside his hotel room to his attendance at the funeral of a stranger in midafternoon; but the narration renders this successive movement in a series of eight stills, or scenes. Instead of cutting back and forth between levels of action in time-present, as Flaubert does, Bellow's omniscient narration most often cuts back and forth between time-present and time-past in the mind of Tommy Wilhelm. The setting and time-present form the frame that contains Wilhelm's reflections on time-past and its effect on his current situation. Because Wilhelm's mind is the integrating agent of time and place—and also of action—his mood is the primary device for establishing the limits of individual scene. Juxtaposing time-past and time-present within the context of setting and through the mind of the protagonist has the effect of, if not actually arresting time, at least rendering it in slow motion, so that "spatial form" is achieved and the focus falls on the intrareferential relation among the parts that make up scene (language, action, character, mood, and so forth) and, finally, that contribute cumulatively to the total image that is the book. Slow motion is appropriate to *Seize the Day* because it suggests the movements of a man under water. (p. 56)

[The last scene] is Wilhelm's death by drowning, and every scene in the book has pointed toward this culminating moment. The salt water of his tears is the medium of his suffocation. Wilhelm cries for the failure that he has been, for the death-in-life that he has experienced. He cries for the pretender soul, now put to rest, whose misplaced values caused him to be married to suffering in all aspects of his existence. He cries for the time he has wasted and the mistakes he has made. His tears are tears of grief.

He cries also, however, for mankind, for those millions—like himself—who have howled like wolves in anguish and loneliness from city windows at night. He cries for all men who must suffer and die; he cries for what Virgil called the *lacrimae rerum,* the tears of things.

Because he is able to transcend his personal grief, Wilhelm's tears are also tears of joy. In destroying the pretender soul, Wilhelm prepares for the coming of the true soul. . . . Where there has been alienation, there is now the possibility of communion. Wilhelm's drowning, then, is also a baptism, a rebirth. It is clearly a sea change, demonstrating that, as St. John of the Cross stated, the way down is also the way up.

The unity of effect achieved in *Seize the Day* results from the skillful blending of all the elements of fiction in tightly constructed scenic units functioning very much like poetic images built around a controlling metaphor. Each scene extends the central image of Wilhelm's drowning by embodying a particular aspect of his life that has contributed to the pressure that finally overwhelms him in literal failure and symbolic death and rebirth. Unity is enhanced further by cross references between scenes. . . . "Spatial form" in a larger sense is achieved, then, both within and between scenes. (pp. 70-1)

> *M. Gilbert Porter, "The Scene as Image: A Reading of* Seize the Day," *in* Saul Bellow, *edited by Earl Rovit (copyright © 1975 by M. Gilbert Porter; reprinted by permission of M. Gilbert Porter), Prentice-Hall, 1975, pp. 52-71.*

If Henderson is a descendant of the *miles gloriosus,* the braggart soldier of classical comedy, or the *alazon,* the imposter and intruder, he is also a descendant of Sophocles' Ajax—who, deceived and humiliated by the gods when they turned him from a heroic warrior into a clownish butcher, remained a hero. And if *Henderson, the Rain King* wavers between the mock-heroic and the heroic, Bellow weights the balance toward the latter. The underlying epic formality of Henderson's speech and the archetypal pattern of his quest withstand the incongruous colloquialism and the mocking parody. Henderson's innocence, his conscience, his sense of responsibility, his capacity for feeling and acting, as well as his pride, his impulsiveness, and his vengefulness—all of his character traits—are extraordinary, beyond conventional measure, and certainly beyond moderation. Also beyond conventional measure is his awareness and acceptance of an absurd situation. (p. 73)

Henderson's exuberance, the sheer quantity of all he reaches for and internalizes, and the catholicity of his taste, as well as the openness of his style and the rhetorical patterns of his speech that encompass the colloquial and the mundane, lead us to think of the epic persona of "Song of Myself." Yet there is a signal difference in the ways Henderson and Whitman encounter the contradictions of their worlds. Whitman embraces reality and merges with it. He breathes in fragrances that are fair and foul. . . . He becomes each object that he looks upon, and that object becomes a part of him. But Whitman's embrace ultimately denies the singularity and separateness of others. Despite his celebration of multiplicity, his long catalogs undermine uniqueness and translate quality into quantity. Despite his enthusiasm for contradiction, his parallel phrases and coordinate clauses tend to level out differences. Despite his call for the individual reader to travel his own road, the only individual who emerges from "Song of Myself" is that of the persona. Indeed, Whitman's embrace is implicitly acquisitive and self-aggrandizing. (pp. 73-4)

Henderson also embraces reality. . . . Yet his embrace is more aggressive than Whitman's. And it is only part of the response of this "soldierly temperament" to a world he both loves and hates, accepts and rejects. (p. 74)

Henderson's aggressive response to the world, unlike Whitman's embrace, is an affirmation—and evocation—of separateness, uniqueness, and vital reciprocity. Indeed, Henderson's posture might owe less to Whitman than it does to Melville. For Ahab's assault, far more than Whitman's embrace, affirms the contradictory nature of reality and the uniqueness of others. Ahab responds to the senseless violence and injustice of a world that is also splendid and enriching. His obsessive assault on the white whale may turn him into a lonely monomaniac, and he may turn himself and his crew into destructive and self-destroying instruments, but in the process Ahab grows in humaneness and in his capacity to love. In the end, he fully recognizes the separateness and the unique value of [different] persons. . . . In the end, that is, Ahab's assault is less possessive than Whitman's embrace, and comparison leads us to a clearer evaluation of Henderson's "soldierly temperament" and to a sharper description of his posture. Henderson's aggressive response to the world, like Ahab's, is an assault on reality. But it is an ambiguous assault, for, unlike Ahab's, it contains an element of tenderness. Indeed, it contains the Whitmanesque embrace. (p. 75)

That Herzog's letters remain unsent and even unfinished may lead us to describe Herzog as an alienated intellectual, inert and solipsistic. His ultimate posture—lying in a hammock on his dilapidated Ludeyville estate while chronicling his failures—might confirm such a conclusion. But the power of the novel and the palpable drive of its energy

should prompt us to look further. And if we do, we find that Herzog's letters are his assault on reality. Herzog attempts to seize reality as Henderson seized the huge wooden goddess—but with language—and the agon is just as strenuous, and just as ambiguous. . . . (pp. 75-6)

Herzog's attempt to "keep tight the tensions" while attacking injustice and irrationality is, like Henderson's assault on reality, an affirmation and evocation of pluralism—the separateness and the diverse energies of others.

Even though Henderson's assault leads to comic and calamitous failures, his action does effect change. Herzog's letter writing, on the contrary, makes no difference in the course of his life or in the course of history. Moreover, as Henderson's story ends he is running in circles around his homebound plane on the frozen runways of Newfoundland; the ending is joyous and open and the energy level is high. Herzog, on the other hand, comes full circle at the end, for he has never actually left his hammock in Ludeyville. He has come to terms with his failures, but his energy is drained. He is satisfied to "remain in occupancy," with "no messages for anyone. . . . Not a single word," and we experience a feeling of inertia and entropy. The difference between these successive novels may be explained by the fuller and more consistently comic conception of Henderson, but even more by Bellow's shift from a hyperbolic, mythic, and oblique approach to one that deals with modern life more directly and personally. That is, though Herzog remains in a heroic mold and retains something of Henderson's "soldierly temperament," his decisions are more like those of a real person—Bellow himself—living in the modern world. (pp. 76-7)

Herzog derives much of its power, suspense, and direction from a linear dynamic of inevitable and impelling forward motion. The linear dynamic peaks in the melodramatic sequence. But it begins to build its momentum early in the novel, as Herzog's taxi presses through the traffic toward Grand Central Station. And, as the train hurtles toward Woods Hole, it impels Herzog's furious letter writing; indeed, it forms an ironic or contrapuntal contrast to the discontinuity and random direction of Herzog's letters. . . . (pp. 77-8)

The linear dynamic of inevitable and impelling forward motion does not, however, dominate the novel as a whole, any more than it does the sequence on the train. Rather, our total experience of *Herzog* arises from the conflict between the linear dynamic and the random dynamic of Herzog's letters and reminiscences. Inasmuch as Herzog assaults reality with language, let me describe this conflict—or Herzog's ambiguous assault—as a conflict of traditional grammar with a grammar of energy. For it is with traditional grammar that Herzog, the rational humanist, tries to harness the random social, political, and psychological energies of the past and present. And it is with a grammar of energy that Herzog, the man of passionate feeling, perceives the world and its history.

In the traditional grammar, the Ludeyville frame of the novel is Herzog's present tense—the "now" from which he reflects on the action line that has led to his present "occupancy." The action line is Herzog's past tense—beginning with his decision to flee New York and Ramona, and leading through his abrupt departure from Martha's Vineyard, his evening with Ramona, his visit to the New York City courtroom, and the melodramatic sequence—the final scene of which drives Herzog to Ludeyville. But the past-tense line of action is continually broken by Herzog's jumbled and disconnected recollections of events that took place even earlier. The event line, which no matter how jumbled or disconnected is easily and inevitably reconstructed by the reader, is Herzog's past perfect. (p. 78)

Although the narrative is driven by its traditional grammar, there is a counterdynamic that can only be described by a grammar of energy or forces. Herzog's letters are like vectors, spinning off the past-tense line of action, aiming in various directions but, due to all the countervailing forces in the field, never completely toward the past or present. Due to their high energy level, the obliqueness of their directions, and their incompleteness, they have the effect of fracturing the novel's traditional grammar. (p. 79)

We are impelled by the forward motion of the novel's dynamic. We are anxious to find out what happens to Herzog. . . . But at the same time, we are driven centrifugally in the random-directions of his unsent letters and his disconnected reminiscences.

Henderson assaults reality physically. Bellow's remarkable achievement in *Henderson, the Rain King* is to create an ambiguous hero, sensitive and blustering, intelligent and buffoonish, reflective and impulsive, in touch intellectually with the main currents of modern life and pugnaciously anti-intellectual. Furthermore, it is to bring Henderson's complex agon with the modern and primitive worlds almost entirely into the physical realm. In *Herzog,* Bellow's achievement is almost the reverse: it is to endow the mental agon of an intellectual buffoon with physical energy. Through what I have tried to describe as a conflict of grammar, Bellow evokes uniquely and palpably the heroic agon of a man who would change reality into language, who struggles to "keep tight the tensions without which human beings can no longer be called human."

Herzog assaults reality with language. He attempts to harness the random political, social, and psychological energies of the past and present with sentences, paragraphs, and letters that proceed logically from salutation to signature. The ambiguity of Herzog's assault derives from an agon between consciousness and grammar—between reality as it is perceived phenomenologically and the order required for making sentences. This is the same order that is required in making a traditional novel; and Saul Bellow is engaged in an agon very much like that of his protagonist. Herzog, despite his personal experiences of failure and despair, and despite his awareness that history is driven irrationally by the violent clashing of egos, continually affirms his faith in rational humanism. Bellow, despite his restless experimentation in narrative forms, and despite his lessons from Joyce in subjectivity and discontinuity, continually affirms his faith in the traditional novel. He continually affirms the heroic potential of character, the rational order of plot, the possibility of attaining wisdom through an understanding of cause and effect. Bellow's faith in the traditional novel leads him to impose a linear and causal pattern on an experience that seems to undermine linearity and causality. However, the linear impulse in *Herzog* cannot, with any authenticity, be progressive or evolutionary. Nor does Bellow succumb to the deterministic regression of naturalism—the domino effect of an inescapable causality that, with increasing momentum, strips a character of his humanity. Hence, the narrative line in *Herzog* follows the path of entropy: Herzog moves to a state of maximum consciousness, which is also a state of inertia, and the novel comes full circle to a point where all its energy is spent, not

because this is Bellow's comment on the modern condition but because of his allegiance to the traditional novel.

Still, the narrative line is only one component of *Herzog's* structure. And the conflict between the novel's linear impulse and its irrational energies expresses the heroic agon of a bold and honest writer as he ambiguously assaults the contradictions of Western history, the human psyche, and the modern experience. (pp. 79-80)

> *Richard Pearce, "The Ambiguous Assault of Henderson and Herzog," in* Saul Bellow, *edited by Earl Rovit (copyright © 1975 by Richard Pearce; reprinted by permission of Richard Pearce), Prentice-Hall, 1975, pp. 72-80.*

Bellow's most important cultural essays—"The Thinking Man's Wasteland" (1965), his talk to the PEN Conference in 1966 (as it later appeared in *The New York Times Book Review*), and, in 1971, "Culture Now: Some Animadversions, Some Laughs"—address themselves directly, and with often startling crudity of mind, to the cultural issues which came to dominate his fiction after *Seize the Day.* In particular, *Herzog* in 1964 and *Mr. Sammler's Planet* in 1968 are efforts to test out, to substantiate, to vitalize, and ultimately to propagate a kind of cultural conservatism which he shares with the two aggrieved heroes of these novels, and to imagine that they are victims of the cultural debasements, as Bellow sees it, of the sixties.

The fact that some of his best work—*The Victim, Dangling Man,* and *Seize the Day*—are generally regarded as distinguished contributions to the literature of the Waste Land tradition would not in itself invalidate his disparagements of that tradition or of the academic promotion of it. Other writers, including Mailer, have managed to live within some such complex of attitudes to their own and to our profit. The difference in Mailer's case is that he has a confidently zestful appetite for, and an assurance in his capacities to cope with, the cultural obscenities which might otherwise force him into those feelings of self-righteous victimization so crippling to Bellow's work. Without knowing it, Bellow is far more alienated than Mailer. It shows in his writing; or rather in the evidence that the act of writing, and the promise of cultural mastery which might be engendered by it, is not in his case sufficient to save him from the feelings of victimization visited on his heroes. And yet he likes continually to imagine that it is. Thus when he speaks out in the PEN address against "the disaffected, subversive, radical clique," he doesn't seem to recognize there, anymore than in his novels, that he is exposing his own "disaffection," poorly disguised by bad jokes. . . . (p. 81)

Bellow's problem in the sixties is that the imagined forces of dissolution are not, in [that address] or elsewhere in his writing during the period, substantially enough evoked, are indeed too trivially evoked, to teach him, in Empson's phrase, "a style from a despair."

Despite some surface differences, the style of *Herzog* and of *Mr. Sammler's Planet* projects the same authorial presence: of a man nursing imagined betrayals, a man who chooses to retaliate by historical pontifications which, given his own sense of the wastes of history, are intellectually barren, and who nonetheless tries to validate what he says by a species of comic evasion. The comedy, that is, is a way of convincing us that because he himself presumably knows he's being rhetorically banal, the banality must therefore illustrate not the deprivations of his imagination but the bankruptcy of contemporary culture. No one who does not hopelessly confuse culture with literature and both of these with the limits set by the accomplishments of Saul Bellow is apt to be convinced by this procedure.

The test is all in the "doing," as James said long ago, and it is peculiar that those who share Bellow's cultural conservatism have failed to ask themselves whether or not his performance as a writer, as distinct from his opinions as a would-be thinker, contribute to the vitalization either of literary culture or the language. On any close inspection, Bellow's rhetorical ambitions are seen to be disjointed from those aspects of his later fiction which are most compelling —the brilliance of detailed, especially of grotesque, portraiture, and a genius for the rendering of Yiddish-American speech. In *Herzog* in particular, his writing is most alive when he writes as a kind of local colorist. And yet, in the language of analysis and Big Thinking with which he endows his hero, and it is, again, of a piece with the canting style of Bellow's essays, he wants to be taken as a novelist of civilization, especially the civilization of cultural degeneracy as it affects the urban-centered Jew in the American sixties.

That he tries to localize these immense concerns within essentially Jewish material is not the problem. After all, the Jewish writer in the American city is potentially as well situated within the tensions of a great cultural conflict as was Faulkner in the Mississippi of the Snopses, the Faulkner of the middle period when he was writing out of what a similarly beleaguered writer—Yeats in Ireland—called his "ill luck." Bellow feels threatened in his role as public defender of two distinct yet historically harmonious cultural inheritances: of the Jew as poor immigrant, the outsider whose native resources save him from the bitterness of alienation, and of the Jew as successful *arriviste* in American society, enriched and burdened all at once by traditions of high culture. Now a kind of insider looking out, he yearns for those cultural supports which, since World War II, have been commercialized by the society at large if not submerged entirely under the tidal waves of mass produced taste. All differences allowed, a similar combination of inheritances is precisely what fired the genius of Faulkner and Lawrence and Yeats, all of whom were also at the crossroads where high and what might be called native culture find themselves both threatened and courted by the commercialized culture of the middle. (pp. 82-3)

In the writings of this century where there is a disposition about the state of the culture similar to Bellow's, there is also a kind of stylistic and formal complication generally missing from his work. This complication is not "academic" or faddish or willful. Instead it reflects a confirmed sense of the enormous effort required both to include, with any kind of human generosity, and then to correct, by the powers of style, the preponderant influences of pop culture and of a ruined education system. Some of the consequences to Bellow's work of the essential timidity of his effort—like all timidity it tends to be both self-pitying and vindictive—have been noticed by Morris Dickstein and Richard Locke and by a few of the reviewers of *Mr. Sammler's Planet*. But *Herzog*, while being universally praised, was nonetheless equally flawed, an indication of what was later to become more evidently the matter. (p. 83)

Bellow is in the novel whenever he wants to be simply by becoming Herzog, the confusions at many points between the narrative "I" and "he" being a blunt and even attractive admission of this. But the identification of hero and author is apparent in other, ultimately more insidious ways. Thus Herzog is allowed to characterize himself in a manner usually reserved to the objectivity of the author: the letters he writes, and never mails, to the living who betrayed his love, to the dead thinkers who betray his thinking, to the living great who betray him politically are, he says, "ridiculous." (He does not himself betray the book by also admitting that the letters, for all the parroted praise the reviews have given them, are frequently uninventive and tiresome.) (p. 84)

Allowing no version of the alleged betrayals other than Herzog's, Bellow still must protect his hero's claims to guiltlessness by a process all the more ultimately effective for being paradoxical: he lets Herzog's suffering issue forth less as accusations against others than as self-contempt for his having been cozened by them. There could be no more effective way to disarm the reader's scepticism about the confessions of such a hero within so protective a narrative form. Bellow can thus operate snugly (and smugly) within the enclosure of his hero's recollections, assured, at least to his own satisfaction, that he has anticipated and therefore forestalled antagonistic intrusions from outside. He really does want Herzog's mind to be the whole world, and the hero's ironies at his own expense are only his cleverest ruse in the arrangement. No wonder, then, that Herzog's talk about himself and about ideas is, in passages that carry great weight, indistinguishable from the generalized Bellovian rhetoric by which here, as in Bellow's other novels, "victims" become "modern man," their situation the World's: "He saw his perplexed, furious eyes and he gave an audible cry. *My God! Who is this creature? It considers itself human. But what is it? Not human in itself. But it has the longing to be human.*"

The recurrence of such passages in Bellow's work is only one indication of how straight we are to take them, of how much he tends to summarize himself in the pseudo-philosophical or sociological or historical expansions of the otherwise parochial situations of his heroes. Perhaps the most lamentable result of Bellow's complicity at such points is that he loses his customary ear for banality of expression or for the fatuity of the sentiments. I don't know another writer equally talented who surrenders so willingly to what are by now platitudes about his own creations. Seldom in Faulkner, even less in Joyce, and far less frequently in Lawrence than people who can't listen to his prose like to believe, do we find what the literary ragpickers call key passages. Where such passages obtrude in writing that asks us to be discriminating about style, as they do in Fitzgerald and Hemingway as well as in Bellow, there is always a lack of assurance in what Bellow has himself called "the sole source of order in art": the "power of imagination." And he distinguished this from "the order that ideas have." "Critics need to be reminded of this," he remarks in "Distractions of a Fiction Writer." (p. 85)

Between his evident intellectual ambitions and the fictional materials he thinks congenial to them there is in *Herzog*, as in *Henderson, the Rain King* and in *The Adventures of Augie March*, a gap across which these novels never successfully move. Sections of the present book read like a lesser *Middlemarch*, the longest of the "ridiculous" letters offering pretty much what Bellow-Herzog want to say about "modern" life. Herzog's interest in romanticism is itself an expression of a familiar concern of Bellow: the effort to preserve individuality during a period of economic and scientific acceleration with which it is supposedly impossible for the human consciousness to keep pace. Henry Adams, among others, gave us the vocabulary; George Eliot predicted the condition; Bellow the novelist is victimized by it. What I call the gap in his novels between their intellectual and historical pretensions, on one side, and the stuff of life as he renders it, on the other, prevents me from believing that he is himself convinced by his snappy contempt for "the commonplaces of the Waste Land outlook, the cheap mental stimulants of Alienation." Quoted from a letter of Herzog's these are obviously identical with Bellow's own attitudes. My objection isn't merely that Bellow would replace the "commonplaces" of alienation with even more obvious commonplaces about "the longing to be human." I mean that his works, the truest and surest direction of their energy, suggest to me that imaginatively Bellow does not himself find a source of order in these commonplaces.

Lawrence, who would have found Bellow interesting, was right: "Never trust the artist. Trust the tale. The proper function of the critic is to save the tale from the artist who created it." (pp. 85-6)

Though Bellow is among the most intelligent of contemporary American writers, I can't find in [his protagonist's] glib presumption to Thought any difference between his and Herzog's presence. Distinction of intellect is of course not necessary to fiction; but what is most bothersome . . . is Bellow's failure to acknowledge the comic preposterousness of [Herzog's] kind of mental activity . . . , a pretension that might itself characterize the hero were he not . . . indistinguishable from the author. Nothing but nothing in Herzog's career . . . suggests that his self-hood or self-development has been "this great bone-breaking burden." Such terms describe nothing in the book. They refer instead to a literary historical commonplace about the self to which Bellow wants his book attached. . . . [The] vocabulary continues to mythologize a life that has been shown to be at most pitiably insipid. Typically, even the effort at inflation gets blamed on the times: Herzog abuses himself for thinking in a way so "up-to-date and almost conventional.". . . . Not every hero in modern literature is allowed uncritically to try on for size so many distinguished roles and then to say not that they don't fit but that they are too much in season. . . . What is missing is any indication that Bellow is aware of the *essential* irrelevance, the *essential* pretension and shabbiness of the self-aggrandizing mind at work in, and for, the hero.

To a considerable degree the novel does work as a rather conventional drama of alienation, though this is precisely what Bellow doesn't want it to be. It is about the failure of all available terms for interpretation and summary, about the intellectual junk heap of language by which Herzog-Bellow propose dignities to the hero's life and then as quickly watch these proposals dissolve into cliché. A similar process goes on in *Augie*, against the competition of an anxious and often phony exuberance, and it was there that Bellow began to fashion a comic prose which could bear the simultaneous weight of cultural, historical, mythological evocations and also sustain the exposure of their irrelevance. His comedy always has in it the penultimate question before the final one, faced in *Seize the Day*, of life or death —the question of what can be taken seriously and how seriously it can possibly be taken. The result, however, is a kind of stalemate achieved simply by not looking beyond the play of humor into its constituents, at the person from whom it issues, at the psychological implications both of

anyone's asking such questions and of the *way* in which he asks them.

It seems to me that Bellow cannot break the stalemate with alienation implicit in his comedy without surrendering to the Waste Land outlook and foregoing the mostly unconvincing rhetoric which he offers as an alternative. That is why his comic style in *Herzog*, even more than in *Henderson* or *Augie*, is less like Nathanael West's than like that of West's brother-in-law, S. J. Perelman. Both Perelman and Bellow raise the question of "seriousness" by piling up trivial detail, by their mock submission to the cheery hope of redemption that people find in the ownership of certain "things," in certain styles, in certain totemic phrases, . . . and for an equivalent to Perelman's high "theatric" mode see Madeleine's bitch performance when she makes her switches "into the slightly British diction [Herzog] had learned to recognize as a sure sign of trouble."

Bellow has greatly increased the range of such comedy, from the clutter of "things," a post-Depression comedy, to the clutter of ideas and culture, a comedy after affluence. But he is still anxious to stay within that comedy. He doesn't dare ask any questions about it or about the characters from whom it emerges. That's why the comparison to Perelman is an apt one. And I mean no criticism of Perelman, whose intentions are not those of a novelist, particularly of novelist-as-thinker. I mean to say that Bellow's failure to ask tough questions about where he *himself* wants to be taken seriously, a failure of his ruined recent play, *The Last Analysis*, doesn't allow me to take him seriously when he chooses to talk about Herzog's struggle for self-development or when, after the scene in court, he allows reference to "the unbearable intensity of these ideas." In question are such ideas as: "If the old God exists he must be a murderer. But the one true God is death." Sophomoric tag-lines don't deserve the status of "ideas." Whatever they are they're really as comfortable as old shoes, especially when you can so believe in their "unbearable intensity" that you can lie down. And it is from that position that the story is told. (pp. 87-9)

Richard Poirier, "Herzog, or, Bellow in Trouble" (originally published in a slightly different version in Partisan Review, *Spring, 1965), in* Saul Bellow, *edited by Earl Rovit (reprinted by permission of Richard Poirier), Prentice-Hall, 1975, pp. 81-9.*

Saul Bellow is not a sexist. The women in his novels are like the men, a sad, crazy, mixed-up lot. They fall into two basic categories: the victims and the victimizers, the latter tending to be more colorful. If they appear less three-dimensional than the men, and if they are certainly less sensitive than Doris Lessing's heroines, this is the natural consequence of novels in which the protagonist tends to be a middle-aged Jewish male with a world view to match his ethnic bias. Women are very important to him, but he often finds them strange, illogical, and disturbing. They represent one more pressure on his already overburdened psyche. . . . Because the narrative method is one that filters women through his consciousness, women possess reality only as they act upon him. However, even such a limitation in point of view does not usually produce the Henry Miller type of distortion or Philip Roth fantasy figures, because the Bellow protagonist recognizes, at the least, that women are complex. He does not underestimate his antagonists in the battle of the sexes.

Misery is the common state of the Bellow "hero"; some, such as the comic rain king Henderson, struggle against this, and others, such as Tommy Wilhelm, just give up. But however down and out the "hero" is, there is still, somewhere, a willing female who ministers to his needs. And he has many needs: he is vain; he fears aging; he has difficulty maintaining his pride in a hostile environment; even his clothes don't suit him. Because he is decidedly heterosexual, he must also worry about his appeal to women. To make life still more difficult, there is a counterpart to the willing female: the castrating wife. This woman feeds on human flesh, preferably her husband's. She is either a hysteric or a cold fish, sometimes both. The hero's journey through life is shaped to a great extent by his encounters with these various females. Like Odysseus, he attempts to subdue the wily Circes; unlike Odysseus, he rarely succeeds.

Despite their easy categorization into two basic types—the destructive ones who victimize the hero, and the nurturers who tend to be his victims—Bellow's women are not merely sex objects. Each is an individual with a full range of idiosyncracies. They all have souls and they all suffer. Because their only roles in the novels are those they play in the protagonist's life, they are all girl friends, wives, or mothers. They have no other role, such as friend, colleague, doctor, or lawyer. Certainly, their sexual attractiveness is among their most salient features, or, as in the case of ex-wives, their lack of attractiveness. For some reason, almost all Bellow ex-wives wear bangs and have cold eyes and cold voices; maybe this is the essence of ex-wives. (pp. 101-02)

The Jewish penchant for noisy suffering reaches its zenith in Moses Herzog, who drags his battered ego across Europe, into the Berkshires, out to Chicago and back, and on a brief and ludicrous trip to Martha's Vineyard. Always there are women to tend to him, sweet creatures of the flesh who seek to heal the wounds inflicted by life in general but also by the virulent Madeleine, Herzog's second wife. (p. 102)

Madeleine keeps him wallowing in bathos, and this is her secret power: she recognizes his need to suffer, and she feeds it. Meanwhile, poor Ramona, with her endless patience, must sit and listen to Herzog's monologues about the malevolent Madeleine. . . . Totally involved in compiling [a] meticulous, resentful catalogue of her mannerisms, Herzog is insensitive to the needs and feelings of the woman he is with, Ramona.

This is perhaps the essential trait of the self-involved Moses Herzog type: insensitivity toward others. . . . His self-absorption leaves him capable of infatuation or obsession, but hardly of love. Thus, for Herzog, women necessarily fall into the category of either victim or victimizer; he can have no other relationship with a woman, for sympathetic women don't understand his need to be kicked in the groin, and the Madeleines who do kick him are cold, blue-eyed bitches. Of course, he refuses to see the logic of his life pattern, and can therefore be free to indulge himself in great bouts of self-pity. . . . The problem [for the protagonists of both *Herzog* and *The Bell Jar*] is similar: a paranoid anxiety that the world is designed to make one miserable, and only fast footwork and constant vigilance can prevent one from being exploited endlessly in sexual combat. Esther and Herzog share an ironic world view; they are not without humor in their characterizations of others, but their own insecurities lead them to place people

in boxes too narrow to be just. They become convinced that they are the only truly sensitive souls. With such an attitude, members of the opposite sex become part of the general conspiracy. (pp. 104-05)

Perhaps the most obviously successful Bellow "hero" is Eugene Henderson, the mad, gargantuan African rain king. Despite the failure of his first marriage and the shakiness of his second, he is a comic man. He is also a chaotic man, and of course he is a great sufferer even though he is not a Jew. What he seeks is some sort of meaning in life, and for this he runs away to Africa. Like Herzog, he is pursued by his own internal demons. He is also pursued by women. What is it that makes these Bellow men irresistible to women? In Henderson's case it is a genuine mystery, even to himself. (pp. 107-08)

What makes Henderson special among Bellow protagonists becomes clear in the course of the novel: his ego is not based on sexual conquest, and he is thus saved from the energy-draining need to brave the bedroom battle continuously. (p. 109)

Does [Saul Bellow] know that one of his specialties is setting up confrontations that are ultimately dissatisfying to both men and women? Is he aware that the very concept of a battle between the sexes is self-defeating, for in that war there are no winners, only greater or lesser losers? Of course, he does not use the war metaphor specifically, as Norman Mailer does, but the male-female dialectic in his fiction clearly involves a power struggle. Marriage is his usual field of battle, and bad marriages are the norm. Women are generally perceived, either consciously or unconsciously, as "the enemy" by the protagonist, or at least as the opponent in a rather deadly sporting event. (pp. 111-12)

Considered as a group, the novels *Seize the Day, Herzog,* and *Henderson, the Rain King* exhibit certain perceptions and concerns that recur in Bellow's fiction. Male-female relations are an area of life that causes much pain. They tend to be spiritually debilitating. There are almost no instances of successful couples. (p. 112)

Again and again, these three novels make clear that women cause pain. Men may cause pain too, but we are left to infer this from the action for we are never allowed a subjective view of the woman's experience. Women are characters in the movie that flashes through the protagonist's head. Bellow does not attempt to penetrate their skulls; they have no monologues. The only self that they reveal is that which the protagonist perceives. . . . Because the common denominator of the three male protagonists is their ability to suffer, it is clear that the women who leave the greatest marks on their lives are those who produce the most suffering. The patient types are lost by the wayside, and only the truly insidious females are allowed to feed on the hero's entrails like tapeworms. Henderson breaks free of this syndrome by running away to Africa and wrestling with real, live demons instead of those that lurk within, making a man seek pain instead of pleasure. Of course, Lily never fit into the super-bitch category that Madeleine and Margaret fill with such style, but Henderson was managing to turn her into a very unsatisfying wife all the same. What becomes clear is that if a man is neurotic enough, he can kill any relationship, and if he is really eager to mess up his life, he invariably chooses a woman who is happy to cooperate in this project.

Whether Bellow creates such patterns because he believes

they are the only ones possible or because he is engaged in charting a modern American phenomenon is difficult to determine. These relationships are consistently neurotic, but they are not aberrations. According to Rollo May, the lack of the ability to love is a major characteristic of modern life; he suggests that contemporary man separates sex and love to his own detriment. . . . Herzog may be the archetypal twentieth-century product: the intellectual who can analyze any situation with devastating precision and irony, but who is incapable of almost all simple pleasures—acutely aware and acutely unhappy simultaneously. Is he Saul Bellow in a thin disguise? I do not know. He certainly has much in common with the middle-class, middle-aged American Jewish male intellectual as artist—the Philip Roths, Norman Mailers, Leslie Fiedlers, and others. (pp. 112-13)

If Bellow takes sides in the battle of the sexes, he is only making the natural alliance with his sex that one would expect. He is not very hopeful about satisfaction. His talent lies in his precision in chronicling frustration and pain. He can locate the wound; he cannot cure it. Clearly, his sympathies lie with his protagonists, a not unusual situation in the history of the novel. First-person narratives (and Bellow's are all more or less of this variety) are always likely to suffer from bias; in this case, it is not a bias that mitigates truth. (p. 114)

> *Victoria Sullivan, "The Battle of the Sexes in Three Bellow Novels," in* Saul Bellow, *edited by Earl Rovit (copyright © 1975 by Victoria Sullivan; reprinted by permission of Victoria Sullivan), Prentice-Hall, 1975, pp. 101-14.*

Saul Bellow has come closer than any other novelist during the past two decades to transmuting into fiction those forces that isolate the sensitive American from his peers. He has done so in each of his novels, including . . . *Mr. Sammler's Planet,* in which he probes and dramatizes at length the frenzied rejection by the young and dissident of the computerized social bureaucracy in which they find themselves. He sympathizes with their concerns, but he scorns their behavior and their reluctance even to attempt viable solutions. Negation for its own sake, he makes clear, offers society or the individual few meaningful values.

Some reviewers have professed surprise and dismay at this novel; they find in it a "new Bellow," an aging ideologue exhibiting a new, irrational fear of the young, the radical, and the black. No longer their beloved King Saul—literary innovator, trend-setter, and articulate champion of the rebellious young—Bellow is, in their eyes now, merely one more dated establishment littérateur. As evidence, they point out that Artur Sammler is both European and elderly; both elements, they insist, are firsts for a Bellow hero: never before has Bellow identified with a foreign protagonist, much less one several decades older than himself. Such strictures, admittedly, make good reading, but they are mostly irrelevant and essentially untrue; nor is the surprise and consternation these critics display valid.

For Bellow has managed, in *Mr. Sammler's Planet,* to shift his angle of vision without altering any of the views he has expressed repeatedly in fiction and forum. His primary concern, as always, is at the loss of moral and intellectual authority in America by the rational, the disciplined, the humane. Contributing heavily to the erosion of national thought and art are the pressures and distractions of American city life, the social excesses of history, culture, and news that assault and tire the mind. . . . This cultural surplus is confronted daily by artists and writers—and by every Bellow hero, from the dangling Joseph to the beleaguered Artur Sammler. Each is, like Moses Herzog, a displaced, intellectual victim whose survival depends on his rejecting these exploitative forces. Each tries to wrench from urban disorder a measure of moral coherence. (pp. 124-25)

Every Bellow wanderer is caught up in this "urban clutter" of noise, dirt, and smell, and each is forced to recognize that all dreams of escape—geographic or spatial—are sentimental nonsense. Spring season or pastoral life, Africa or Mexico, moon or ocean bottom—not one guarantees relief from inner demons or outer pressures. Man must struggle at home for his emotional life, Bellow insists, and in an age that is complex, hostile, and increasingly proud of being revolutionary. But for Bellow, the times are "more disheveled than revolutionary." (p. 125)

Artur Sammler's reactions to people and events are totally consistent with those expressed by Saul Bellow in fiction and essay, lecture and interview. A decade ago, in "The Writer as Moralist," Bellow noted a "struggle going on . . . between Cleans and Dirties. The Cleans want to celebrate the bourgeois virtues . . . steadiness, restraint, a sense of duty. The Dirties are latter-day Romantics and celebrate impulsiveness, lawless tendencies, the wisdom of the heart." Neither side has a monopoly on virtue, he argued, and each is vulnerable to irrational behavior. (p. 126)

Artur Sammler . . . speaks for Bellow—and does so despite his advanced age and foreign birth. Too much, in fact, has been made of Sammler's age, for Bellow's heroes have generally been growing older. . . . More significantly, perhaps, Bellow presented in his first novels lonely young heroes beset by older opportunists—or "reality instructors" —who sought to dominate or cheat them. These young fellows were themselves overwrought romantics often fearful of their own sanity and excessive natures—whereas their antagonists were "dry, controlled little guys" who could take life and others in stride.

With Artur Sammler, Bellow admittedly varies this pattern. From Joseph to Herzog, his protagonists are loners who, though surviving their varied encounters, end up on tentative terms with society. Sammler too is a loner, but his circumstances are reversed: he defends the social verities and traditions. And whereas earlier the older, secondary figures . . . presented those ideas meant to be eccentric, amusing, unreliable, here the elderly hero voices the serious views. (pp. 126-27)

Sammler (whose name echoes "Uncle Sam," and in Yiddish *zammler* or "collector," and in German "storage battery") stands as a fixed point—a firm observer of the American scene and an exponent of old-style humanism. From that double vantage point he rejects the decade's proliferating lunacies: the immoral politics (of right and left), the hip life styles, and the obsession with originality. "Is our species crazy?" he asks. "Plenty of evidence." (p. 127)

[The] *principles* old Sammler admires are those Bellow has advocated since his first novel. *Dangling Man* ends with the youthful Joseph, exhausted by directionless freedom, proclaiming the joys of "regular hours," "supervision of the spirit," and "regimentation." In Bellow's next novel, *The Victim,* Marcus Schlossberg (like Sammler, an elderly Jewish journalist) insists that man can choose between being "lousy and cheap" or having "greatness and beauty." Which should he choose? "Choose dignity," declares the old man. "Nobody knows enough to turn it down."

Sammler shares both views. Yet he recognizes better than most the soul's individuality. What he deplores is not each man's need to be unique, but the current mass obsession with an originality that rejects tested cultural models for the grotesque and bizarre. For if he is past passion, he is hardly dispassionate as he muses on the connections between human madness and death. The holocaust and his own escape from the grave are the experiences by which Sammler measures all events. These have strengthened his belief in limits, reason, tradition.... He does not agree with the young dissidents he encounters that man can survive without rules, dignity, order....

Clearly, intellect and knowledge, Sammler has learned, are not enough: without a conscience, man is merely an intellectual animal. (p. 128)

[Harsh] comments on the young and their culture have stirred anguished cries of "sellout" from former Bellow admirers. His novel, they declare, attacks modernism only to champion tradition and convention to the point of reaction.... Several are annoyed by his failure to mention the Vietnam War; others find most painful the incident in which Sammler, invited to lecture at Columbia University, is shouted down by his ragtag, longhaired audience. One youth yells that the old journalist can have nothing valid to say because at his age he cannot achieve orgasm. Sammler leaves, pondering the new critical standards. "How extraordinary! Youth? Together with the idea of sexual potency? All this confused sex-excrement-militancy, explosiveness, abusiveness, tooth-showing, Barbary ape howling." ... [Most reviewers have] missed—or chosen to miss —Bellow's point. Rather than "put down the new cultural dissidents," Bellow, as Robert Alter rightly insists, "views them with a compassionate sadness."

Nor does Bellow attack modernism and radicalism, but only their misuse: the abuse or distortion, in any form, of human knowledge, language, and experience is what angers him. (pp. 129-30)

Bellow hardly champions, as some have claimed, either humanism unqualified or thought without action. (p. 131)

The strangest misreading of Bellow has been by those who see [Bellow's use of the black] pickpocket not merely as an expression of "Jewish outrage at the state of the nation" but of the novelist's "hostility" to black skin. This "racist" view requires the reader not only to ignore the impressive black figures in *Henderson, the Rain King* but also to scan *Mr. Sammler's Planet* with one eye closed. For Sammler, the graceful, catlike thief resembles a masterful African princeling, and his fall makes clear that neither Sammler nor Bellow approaches the law's moral complexities as a rigid constructionist. Indeed, when Sammler sees the pickpocket choking—almost deservedly—his young friend Lionel Feffer (near the Lincoln Center, no less), he feels responsible.... Ironically, Sammler, who in the Zamosht Forest killed a German soldier with deliberate pleasure, is now appalled by Eisen's ferocity [in attacking the pickpocket]. "This is much worse," he tells himself. "This is the worst thing yet." ... Near murder is for the old humanist too high a price even for law and order.

Bellow cannot resist a laconic comment on Sammler's

moral confusion: he has Eisen (also a death-camp survivor) reject the older man's hairsplitting. "You can't hit a man like this just once," Eisen stutters. "When you hit him you must really hit him. Otherwise he'll kill you. You know. We both fought in the war.... If in—in. No? If out—out. Yes? No? So answer." ... Sammler lacks an adequate response. He can only recall that he had himself committed murder, and the action had taught him "that reality was a terrible thing, and the final truth about mankind overwhelming and crushing." Trying to reject so "vulgar and cowardly" a conclusion, he has been reminded repeatedly that extreme moments are met only by moral extremes— with philosophic niceties proving absurdly inadequate. One recent description of the humanist-as-hero seems apt here. "Standing next to the existential man," Harold Simonson writes, "the traditional humanist as a fictional character can only be described with ridicule and hollow laughter. His cultivated taste and learning show him sadly inadequate to confront his real condition."

Bellow clearly agrees.... (pp. 131-33)

As he does in each of his novels, Bellow here shows his readers man at his worst and best, reminds them again that, regardless of circumstances, the individual can do more than lament his fate; if nothing else, he can give thought to his conscience and responsibility to others. (p. 134)

> *Ben Siegel, "Saul Bellow and Mr. Sammler: Absurd Seekers of High Qualities," in* Saul Bellow, *edited by Earl Rovit (copyright © 1975 by Ben Siegel; reprinted by permission of Ben Siegel), Prentice-Hall, 1975, pp. 122-34.*

The best living American novelist is also a man of brains. Veteran reader, seasoned talker, Saul Bellow handles ideas with the same juggling ease that he tells stories. Over the years he has shown a gift for the bravado of polemic, also an endearing weakness for the heart-catching phrase. All this represents a notable change from that tradition of 20th-century American writers—intuitive artists, redskin magicians of literature—who behaved as if intellectual work were a sin against the creative spirit.

Visiting Israel for several months in 1975, Bellow kept an account of his experiences and impressions. It grew into an impassioned and thoughtful book, sometimes an exasperating one....

Through quick sketches and vignettes, Bellow evokes places, ideas, people, reaching a sharp if patched-together picture of contemporary Israel. Writers are often drawn to this loose form, since it allows them to dazzle and flee, shift tones at will, evade the labor of transitions. Yet a reader may find it frustrating, if only because one expects from a writer like Bellow more sustained argument, deeper probing. We don't get it.

What we do get is often wonderful. Steeped in the skepticisms of Chicago but still responsive to the war-cries of ideology, Bellow proves a keen listener. Like every other visitor to Israel, he soon tumbles into "a gale of conversation." He loves it: it makes him feel at home....

Simply as a travel book, "To Jerusalem and Back" is spotty. There are a few remarkable descriptions, such as one in which Bellow finds "the melting air" of Jerusalem pressing upon him "with an almost human weight. Something intelligible, something metaphysical is communicated" by the earthlike colors of this most beautiful of cities.

"Elsewhere you die and disintegrate. Here you die and mingle." But notice that even here Bellow quickly shifts from place to human response. (p. 1)

The impression that overwhelms Bellow repeatedly is that living in Israel must be as exhausting as it is exciting: a murderous barrage on the nerves. Israel, he writes, "is both a garrison state and a cultivated society, both Spartan and Athenian. It tries to do everything, to understand everything, to make provisions for everything. All resources, all faculties are strained. Unremitting thought about the world situation parallels the defense effort. These people are actively, individually involved in universal history. I don't see how they can bear it."

As against the fineness of such a passage, Bellow succumbs a few times to moods of apocalypse, bemoaning American "innocence" before the evil forces of the world. We are "lightly chloroformed" by our naïve good will and refuse to see that the world is caught up in a struggle to the death. . . .

We have echoes here of Solzhenitsyn's jeremiads and, much less impressively, of those lugubrious essays in magazines so different as "Commentary" and "The National Review" foreseeing the end of civilization because Western liberals have "gone soft." But isn't this sort of thing just as abstract and ideological, just as out of touch with the complicated realities of politics, as the vulgar-marxism of Jean-Paul Sartre which Bellow rightly attacks? . . .

Bellow's voice in this new book is mellower than in the past; he has found his way back, after "Sammler" and "Humboldt," to the world's charms. (p. 2)

Irving Howe, in The New York Times Book Review *(© 1976 by The New York Times Company; reprinted by permission), October 17, 1976.*

Bellow has not often published anything other than novels and stories; but he has occasionally written short pieces of reporting and reflection combined—such as a magazine essay fifteen years ago on Khrushchev, which still stands up tolerably today. *To Jerusalem and Back,* while recognizably Bellow's work, is something of a departure. [Written in the form of a diary, it] handles the stuff of the daily headlines without the tools of metaphor, and it is obviously meant, among other things, to affect, directly and quickly, what is called public opinion. From one aspect, *To Jerusalem and Back* is in the tradition of political pamphlets, which have their ground in the moment they are written, and which act to educate and rally sentiment, the sooner the better. From another angle, this book should be read as a continuation of Bellow's life-long meditation on the themes of good-heartedness and private longing in an age of commercial, cultural, and political racketeering. (p. 80)

[Continually] in *To Jerusalem and Back* Bellow . . . enacts the role of one of those reality instructors who hold forth in his novels, about whom he evidently has mixed feelings. Here the object of the teaching is at once the reader and Bellow himself. There is no pretense that Bellow is about to pick up something new about human nature at his age, but he can learn how it has revealed itself in arrangements and crimes, and in the particulars of the look and history of a region—the Middle East—with which he was previously not very familiar.

Like his other books, this is bookish and down to earth. . . .

To Jerusalem and Back is certainly not an optimistic book; however, it is not despairing, either. So far as Bellow undermines the conventional wisdom for himself and for a far larger audience than his authorities can command, his book has a liberating effect. (pp. 80, 82)

Bellow is incorrigible. Disappointed, educated, he remains a humanist, a liberal. If he acts the reality instructor, demanding of readers that they forswear illusion, it is not so he can give them the lowdown, and rub their noses in that other lie, which holds that humans today are universally mean and worthless. Nor does Bellow, in contrast with the colorful gallery of steam-bath philosophers who inhabit his novels, appear to relish the task he has taken on. To inform himself and think about the "butcher problems"—the Sixth Fleet, the terrorist bomb that explodes in a restaurant in Jaffa Road—is unpleasant. He would rather be enjoying literature, or sitting in one of Jerusalem's quiet places, being moved mystically. . . .

What is real, the "consummate mildness" of personal, poetic experience, or the "butcher problems"? Which one prevails? Bellow's debate with himself on this throughout *To Jerusalem and Back,* continuing when he is home again in Chicago, provides the book with a dimension beyond polemic. (p. 83)

Edward Grossman, "Unsentimental Journey" (reprinted from Commentary *by permission; copyright © 1976 by the American Jewish Committee), in* Commentary, *November, 1976, pp. 80-3.*

[In *Humboldt's Gift*] Citrine compares his past life to that of a somnambulist—hopelessly immersed in his own vastly entertaining intellectual dream world while all around him the world was caught up in a demonic frenzy which the conventional "head culture" could not even recognize, let alone explain. . . . At the book's close there is just a slight chance that Citrine will finally wake up and that he will penetrate, somehow, to the heart of a reality that has so far eluded him.

In *To Jerusalem and Back* Bellow begins where *Humboldt's Gift* leaves off. Like Citrine, he no longer believes that the ideals of freedom, dignity and enlightenment can command automatic assent. . . .

To Bellow, Israel's anguish and triumph is exceptional in the extreme. The fact that so many Israelis have lived through so much ought to qualify them, "to enter deeper realms of thought than most people have the opportunity to enter."

By and large, though, Bellow is disappointed. In conversations with Israeli intellectuals he hears little more than the platitudes and banalities that, like Charlie Citrine, he has come to despise. (p. 16).

Bellow is not a systematic political thinker, and the arguments he presents are more in the nature of moods, intuitions and attitudes than carefully thought out positions. . . .

To Jerusalem and Back remains an important and most engaging work. . . . Saul Bellow is . . . bent on a major enterprise: he intends to awaken us out of our educated complacency, to enlarge our moral imagination by forcing us to come to grips with the awesome reality of Auschwitz, and with the other horrors of our century. Trying to tear his own mind away from "civilized" appearances and convictions, he is willing to entertain opinions that seem to depart, at times, from rationality itself. Even to dare such a task requires extraordinary courage. Nor does the ultimate success or failure of Bellow's undertaking really matter. Only the effort counts. (p. 17)

> *Joseph Shattan, "Saul Bellow's Journey,"*
> in Congress Monthly, *November, 1976, pp.*
> *16-17.*

One of Bellow's greatest gifts is his flair for extraordinary characterization. Think of Tommy Wilhelm or Henderson or Herzog or Mr. Sammler. Charlie Citrine [narrator of *Humboldt's Gift*] has something in common with them all. He is profligate, lustful, extraordinarily learned, talented, and, in his present circumstances, greatly disorganized and all but helpless in the face of his own indolence.... [The] existential sickness, the big malaise, is closing in on him. To follow Citrine through his days, to be told his thoughts and to hear his talk, is a liberal education. He has read everybody; he remembers every line that he ever read and he is prepared with a quotation, a phrase or a page, on any subject.

The novel gains much of its force from the richness of its contrasts: between past and present, Citrine and Humboldt, youth and age, honesty and deception, but most of all—in the overwhelming irony of the human state—between the concrete annoyances that rob us of our joy and the larger questions that nag at our common consciousness. (p. 124)

Humboldt's real gift is a deliverance of the spirit.... One thinks immediately of old truisms: that we must give to receive, lose to gain, escape through fear into courage. All of this is inherent in Bellow's wild story, in Citrine's alternately profound and comic dialogue, in the sexual adventures and incidents of violence, in all the movement and noise that pervade Citrine's world. There is no escaping life so one must live it, and it is in portraying the living of it that Bellow is at his best. He succeeds because he can do what is increasingly rare in our time: he can give us a sense of a world, of a society, of ourselves and the way we live now. His range is one of his greatest assets. Chicago appears to be his love, but the world is his stage, and all sorts and conditions of men are his personae. He knows their faces, their voices, their inmost longings. In telling about them, he discovers much about us all. (p. 125)

> *Walter Sullivan, in* Sewanee Review *(re-*
> *printed by permission of the editor; © 1977*
> *by The University of the South), Winter,*
> *1977.*

To Jerusalem and Back ... , Saul Bellow's report of his trip to Israel, is subtitled "a personal account." As such, it cannot be faulted for no doubt it reflects his perceptions. But some serious questions arise when these perceptions are alleged to relate to the social and historical reality. Bellow speaks of his "American even-handedness" and "objectivity," which so irritate his Israeli hosts. In fact, however, he is a propagandist's delight. He has produced a catalog of What Every Good American Should Believe, as compiled by the Israeli Information Ministry....

Like any volley of random shots, some of Bellow's comments hit near the mark, but there is no internal evidence to determine which. Argument and evidence are not really his business. In their place we find snippets from Proust and Baudelaire and Ruskin on Thucydides in a display of world-weary wisdom.

Bellow asserts without qualification that "the root of the problem is simply this—that the Arabs will not agree to the existence of Israel." But matters are not quite that simple....

Like many other Western intellectuals, Bellow seems to overlook the fact that Jewish experts may not be the best source of evidence on Arab sentiments.... *To Jerusalem and Back* contains extensive accounts of conversations with Israelis and pro-Israeli commentators, including government officials, professors, and Jewish experts on Arab affairs. One Arab voice (granted a single paragraph) is also included. On this evidence, Bellow reports the attitudes and beliefs of the Arabs under Israeli control, informing us that they are prospering and generally content. (p. 29)

The one Arab whose remarks Bellow reports is the editor of a Jerusalem newspaper. With a bit more enterprise, Bellow could have discovered what the Arab press reports. (p. 30)

Bellow reports that "the Jordanians built a road over Jewish graves," one of the many Arab atrocities. He fails to mention that the ancient Arab cemetery of Mamillah, where companions of the Prophet are buried, "has been swept away, a rubble of earth, tombs and the bones of their occupants, by Israeli municipal bulldozers," to create "a garden, a parking lot and a public lavatory" (British correspondent David Hirst). Nor does he report that cemeteries (along with homes, wells, etc.) are routinely destroyed as Arab areas are cleared for Jewish settlement—facts easily documented from the Israeli press.

Bellow is outraged that the Egyptian army distributed a booklet calling on soldiers to kill the treacherous Jews, even prisoners. He is right to be outraged. He cites this as evidence that "the West does not understand the Arab world; neither does Israel." Actually, Israel should have no difficulty in understanding. The Israeli Army Chaplaincy distributed a no less appalling booklet explaining the duty of killing non-Jews, even civilians, according to Rabbinic law. It was withdrawn only after exposure in the left-wing press in 1975. But of this, we hear nothing. The fact is that religious fanaticism—no small problem in theocratic states—is rampant and threatening on both sides of the border. (p. 31)

An ad for *To Jerusalem and Back* cites Philip Toynbee praising Bellow as "among the most intelligent and imaginative of living Americans." The book, he says, will remind the reader who knows Israel "of all that he found so lovable about it." That Bellow is imaginative in his reconstruction of history and social fact is no doubt correct. But it is Toynbee's second statement that captures the thrust of the book most accurately. Applied to any country, the term "lovable" is outlandish. But when intellectuals speak of countries in this way, we are on familiar turf.

Bellow has an engaging ability to skim the surface of ideas. He also has a craftsman's talent for capturing a chance encounter or an odd circumstance. Beyond that, his account of what he has seen and heard is a disaster, and the critical acclaim it has received reveals much about the state of American intellectual life. (p. 32)

> *Noam Chomsky, "Bellow's Israel," in* New
> York Arts Journal *(copyright © 1977 by*
> *Richard W. Burgin), Spring, 1977, pp. 29-*
> *32.*

Debilitated, disconnected, [*Humboldt's Gift* was] a twisted shadow of what it might have been. . . . [*To Jerusalem and Back*], for all its brevity . . . and random reminiscing, is one of the best stories Bellow has ever produced. It is the hub, actually, of the various roads Bellow had to travel in his most recent game with himself, which we might call "Going to Jerusalem." The open road of life, "the plain man's pathway to heaven," the Avenue of the Stars, the research-paper route . . . and so on.

The book shows, in striking fashion, just what it is about Bellow that makes him such a rare (literary) bird. For example: (a) his sense of presence without egotism; (b) his eagerness to relate intelligently to people on all levels (particularly now that his reputation is secure beyond challenge —*To Jerusalem* antedates his Nobel laureateship, incidentally); (c) his essential vitality (he was a youthful ever-ready sixty, with a new wife in tow when he made the trip); (d) his deeply committed, research-library brand of intellectuality; (e) the omnivorous curiosity of the born writer-observer. Particularly this factor: his whole is greater than the sum of its parts. Which is not to say that he is an exemplary person or an exceedingly kind and fairminded individual, necessarily. He seems, for example, to have treated Meyer Levin rather shabbily years ago precisely because of Levin's commitment to *a kind* of Zionist support, which some might now read into the present book. But the point is, Bellow has regained much of his earlier verve, and it is as if he is wearing bells on his fingers and bells on his toes, and hence shall have music wherever he goes. Except in the occasional sad or despairing passages in *To Jerusalem* . . . music wherever he goes. (pp. 202-03)

Bellow shows us how he continually assimilates the outside world to his own ever growing mind. Very much like Walt Whitman, he "is large, he contains multitudes." With this book we are able to see what an up-to-date *Leaves of Grass* approach to writing would be like. (pp. 204-05)

[By] chance (I would like to believe), the book—*unlike his novels*—ends on an uncharacteristic *down* note: "The eagerness to kill for political ends—or to justify killing by such ends—is as keen now as it ever was." Those who have read Bellow well, who know his academic association with the University of Chicago's Committee on Social Thought, his anthropological studies, his ultimate "gamecock of the wilderness" crow of triumph or hope, may prefer to take a wait-and-see attitude. Perhaps the old Bellow will reassert itself. He has had music—of a sort—wherever he went. There is a good deal of it in *To Jerusalem and Back*. And, whatever his concluding remarks here, he is still in the middle of his many-layered story of life, just as Israel is, despite momentary outward appearances and temporary moods. (p. 205)

> *Samuel Irving Bellman, "Rambling Scenario of Life," in* Southwest Review (© *1977 by Southern Methodist University Press), Spring, 1977, pp. 202-05.*

* * *

BENCHLEY, Peter   1940-

An American novelist and children's writer, Benchley is the author of *Jaws* and *The Deep*. (See also *CLC*, Vol. 4, and *Contemporary Authors*, Vols 17-20, rev. ed.)

[Is] "The Deep" as exciting as "Jaws"? Well, no, of course it's not. For primitive thrills, a man-eating shark gobbling bathers off the summer beaches of Long Island beats sunken Bermudian treasure six ways to Sunday.

"Jaws" was a once-in-a-career inspiration like Ira Levin's "Rosemary's Baby." But "The Deep" is a neat adventure novel. Benchley clearly loves underwater exploration. He conveys its alarms and beauty with joyous physical enthusiasm. He has come up with odd information about the oceanic transmutation of long-lost treasure, the verifications necessary to establish its authenticity and the power struggles among those who hoist it to the surface.

The human heavies in this novel—a sinister black revolutionary and a traitor concealed among the good guys—are a conventional lot, whose machinations pale beside the menace of slow-cruising sharks that laze overhead during the divers' ocean-floor maneuvers and the needle-toothed moray eels darting suddenly from the reef cavities in which the treasure rests. There is sufficient expertise and underwater chill in "The Deep" to make it satisfying beach-bag cargo. (p. 111)

> *Walter Clemons, "Chilly Waters," in* Newsweek (*copyright 1976 by Newsweek, Inc.; all rights reserved; reprinted by permission), May 10, 1976, pp. 109, 111.*

If David and Gail Sanders were real people, rather than the protagonists of Peter Benchley's "The Deep," the odds are that they would buy the book, read it with a pleasure mitigated only by the degree to which they thought the purpose of reading novels to be moral or intellectual self-improvement, and then stand in line a year or so from now to see the movie. Author Benchley, whose first novel "Jaws" converted bathers in the relatively domesticated precincts of the Long Island seashore into wilderness adventurers and provoked shark sightings in Nebraska, may have done it again. While no one could predict a repeat of the remarkable commercial success of "Jaws," Benchley's novel shows that besides being a very competent writer of fictional entertainments he is what they call one shrewd cookie. (p. 8)

What one gets from Benchley, and this, I think, is the essence of his commercial genius, is *escape*. Instead of wallowing among the commonplaces of our culture's self-doubt, Sanders is lucky enough to have An Adventure. But for the mundane accidents of fate it might have been you or me. (pp. 8, 10)

With the exception of some minor motivational absurdities that one expects in this kind of novel, Benchley's plot is tightly constructed and yields the maximum in suspense. His style is for the most part unaffected and clear: it offends less often than it pleases. Many readers will feel improved by the constant flow of sheer information the book contains on such pertinent topics as the history, sociology and climate of Bermuda, the flora and fauna of the sea, skin diving, treasure hunting and underwater salvage. Benchley obviously knows what he is talking about and incorporates it smoothly into his story. Some Quality Lit fans are going to be annoyed by a minor rash of sententious dialogue about what it all means that occurs toward the end. Other readers will find some of the violence gratuitous; and still others will be made uneasy by the blackness of all the bad guys and the whiteness of the good ones except Treece. But as the book makes little of it so perhaps should we. Without going so far as to say that "The Deep" will amuse everyone equally well, one may confidently predict that the only readers who will not read it through to the end would never dream of picking it up at all. (p. 10)

> *Gene Lyons, in* The New York Times Book

Review (© 1976 by The New York Times Company; reprinted by permission), May 16, 1976.

* * *

BERGER, Thomas 1924-

American novelist, playwright, editor, and short story writer, Berger has had a steady output of novels since the publication of *Crazy in Berlin* in 1958. *Little Big Man*, a mock-heroic parody of the Old West and probably his best known novel, was made into a successful motion picture. In recent fiction, notably *Regiment of Women* and *Who Is Teddy Villanova?*, Berger has continued to write in the comic-satiric vein that is gaining him increasing recognition. The latter is an excellent burlesque of the conventional detective novel. (See also *CLC*, Vols. 3, 5, and *Contemporary Authors*, Vols. 1-4, rev. ed.)

[Surely Thomas Berger] should sign his novels Tom Berger by this time, if only as a hint to the reviewers, who can't make head or tail of him, that he really is a good guy. Berger's trouble with the critics is that he cannot keep a straight face, no matter what he's writing about. He has insulted history (*Crazy in Berlin*), all of Cincinnati (*Reinhart in Love*), and Custer's Last Stand (*Little Big Man*). [In *Killing Time*] he goes for what has always had its share of the licks in his novels, The American Mind, an organism that Mr. Berger can isolate, apparently by powers miraculous, and see with unbefuddled gaze.... The American mind is lonely, unintegrated, antisocial, other-directed, is poor in group-motivated direction, *vocaliter nauseolissimo*. It needs, of course, well, you know, it needs ... but never mind.

Gentlemen, meet Lee Harvey Oswald. Meet a thoroughly lethal idealistic cry baby, spawn of America. He is, when he is upper-middle-class, straight and clean, and named Whitman, the very pride of America. A bit down the social scale, and named Speck, he is still 100 per cent American.... [He] is a sweet, gentle Mama's boy, and it's worth the price of the novel to meet Mama, as goofy a woman as ever George Price drew or showed you the secret of a whiter wash on TV.... A jury of middle-aged American mothers would probably find him their ideal of a son: he is so pure he wishes he were sexless (dear boy!); his heart is tender toward the lame and blind and helpless. He is, in short, that inexplicable *schmuck*, The American Murderer. (pp. 1282-83)

This is not a *roman à clef* but a *roman à crochet*: practically any key will fit. The police, lawyers, families of the deceased: all are examples of the drifting mind Mr. Berger has undertaken to study....

[Mr. Berger] is ... the best satirist in the United States, the most learned scientist of the vulgar, the futile, and the lost, and the most accurate mimic in the trade. Behind the very prose in which he has cast this novel one can detect the wad of gum and the tabloid reporter's prurient glint of depraved genius for the sickening, satisfying detail that sells newspapers. None of Mr. Berger's other novels is written in such lunch-counter prose; he has invented it for *Killing Time* alone....

But one must not imagine that Mr. Berger is merely a diligent camera. Detweiler is one of the most complex characters in modern fiction, the first outrageously impenetrable character in a gallery of outrageous characters.... Some graduate student with half a mind will soon write him up for the English journals as a Christ Figure. He smells of Dos-

toyevsky and Mary Baker Eddy. He is part Quaker, part Rasputin. The eeriest thing about him is that he is wholly believable, which is to say, of course, that Thomas Berger is a magnificent novelist. (p. 1283)

Guy Davenport, in National Review *(© National Review, Inc., 1967; 150 East 35th St., New York, N.Y. 10016), November 14, 1967.*

Sneaky People ... is a novel laid in small-town Midwestern America in the mid-1930s. Yet it is written with the altered sensibilities and in the style of the mid-Seventies, a style which permits a degree of license on the printed page that would have been inconceivable in a novel written about the mid-Thirties *in* the mid-Thirties. Thus, despite the attention lavished on period details—brand names, radio shows, and vanished mores alike—the net effect is *une plastique*, an imposture rather than a convincing reproduction of the life of the time. Counterfeits need to be even more carefully contrived than the real thing. (p. 1127)

The whole of *Sneaky People*, in fact, reads as *Our Town* might have, had it been written by Henry Miller. But as Thornton Wilder or even John O'Hara knew, to name two extremes among contemporary chroniclers, in the genuine novels of the Thirties, sex was only one of the things people had on their minds.

Mr. Berger's talents and style are exceptionally well-suited to reflect current life. When used to reproduce the features of an age so remote in standards from the present, however, they result in grotesque caricatures rather than penetrating portraiture. Since some of us need all the help we can get in fathoming our own times, let us hope Mr. Berger's next novel is set in the Seventies. (pp. 1127-28)

Rene Kuhn Bryant, "Berger's Plastic Nostalgia," in National Review *(© National Review, Inc., 1975; 150 East 35th St., New York, N.Y. 10016), October 10, 1975, pp. 1127-28.*

"Who Is Teddy Villanova?" is a black comic parody of tough-guy detective fiction out of Hammett and Chandler. Despite its seedy urban setting and wildly violent, hypertrophied plot, it is written in Berger's arch, allusive and rhetorically exhibitionistic style: loquacious, periphrastic, euphuistic—as if spoken by a demented William F. Buckley. By hitching his narrative to the detective novel, Berger has been forced to keep the plot moving, no matter how baroque his style becomes. As usual, his chief emotion is Swiftian contempt for the mindless, unlettered, sordid spectacle of modern life—in this case here in New York City. Yet there is also a manic glee in his endless vituperation. His comic verbal excess is the opposite of Joan Didion's terse, implosive style [in "A Book of Common Prayer"]. And if her temptation is bathos, Berger's is a kind of garrulous masturbatory cultural snobbery. His book is a cartoon; hers a novel. (p. 53)

Richard Locke, in The New York Times Book Review *(© 1977 by The New York Times Company; reprinted by permission), April 17, 1977.*

Who is Teddy Villanova? The question that confounds and torments Russell Wren, the unlicensed private investigator who narrates Thomas Berger's latest novel, is not likely to keep many readers tossing at night. For in this takeoff on the private-eye novel, the arbitrary complexities of plot defy sustained attention. Which is as it must be: Berger's tribute to Hammett, Chandler and Macdonald is mainly a series of gags at the expense of those worthies, their intricate tales peopled by bizarre characters, and the whole concocted spirit of their enterprise. Is Berger, then, paying them deference or merely making mock of them? In either case, he has produced a work that is in many ways superior to its models.

Russell Wren does have one thing in common with Sam Spade and Philip Marlowe and Lew Archer—he is honest. Without the incorruptible integrity of the protagonist, the center of any detective story, even a spoof, could not hold. But there the resemblance ends. Private eyes are tough guys who know how to deliver a kidney punch. Although Russell Wren, our battered eye, receives as many beatings per chapter as any detective hero in the literature, he wouldn't hurt a fly. He is less capable of self-defense than the small singing bird whose name he bears. (Or is he named for the celebrated 17th-18th century English architect who built so many churches, including St. Paul's? The derivation of names is of no small moment in a novel where the policemen are called Hus, Zwingli, Knox, and Calvin. Or are they policemen?)

Fiction's private eyes are usually shrewd analysts of humankind, experienced in the workings of life. When Wren sets himself to making deductions from the peculiar events that keep happening all around him, the reader can be certain of only two things: First, he will be entirely rational; and second, he will be entirely wrong. He is a victim of forces that do not submit to reason. . . .

One of Wren's problems is that he is more at home with the magic of words than with events. . . .

Actually, the whole book is a game of words; the very names in the lobby directory of Wren's dilapidated building keep reshaping themselves. And when it comes to puns, Berger has no mercy.

"'Excuse me for what might appear an impertinence,' I said to Washburn. 'But does your wife happen to be Teutonic?'

"'Too *tonic*?' he replied in what seemed genuine bewilderment.'". . .

The temptation to quote from *Teddy Villanova* is irresistible; it is a series of skits that display, with great humor, Berger's special joy in juggling the language. A conversation between Wren and one of the detectives who keep popping up (is he really a detective?) becomes a contest in erudition:

"And what about Big Jake the Wop?" asks Wren, seeking clarification on a small point.

The detective replies: "No, Jake the Wop *or* Big Jake. To combine them is superfetation."

"Damn him," thinks Wren. "I had never heard that word in speech, and never read it but in the text of T. S. Eliot." (p. 12)

To rate a writer's works tends to be a fatuous enterprise, so I shall refrain from hazarding an opinion as to whether this novel is better than Berger's notable *Little Big Man*. What it is has in common with that otherwise quite different book is that it takes its inspiration from human quirkiness, bafflement at the world and irrepressible strivings. It is carried off with zest and a special sort of style that kids itself with

exemplary earnestness. And, in case I haven't yet gotten the news across, it is very funny. (p. 13)

Walter Goodman, "The Shamus as Schlemiel," in The New Leader (© *1977 by the American Labor Conference on International Affairs, Inc.), May 23, 1977, pp. 12-13.*

Who Is Teddy Villanova? is first person and extravagant, not so much a parody of Hammett and Chandler as a confident, exceedingly literary adaptation of the form. Seventies cool rather than Forties bite. . . . This may be likable, but it is hard to imagine anyone liking a whole book of it. Chandler's style was often ornate and self-conscious. To make that style only words calling attention to themselves seems more an occupation for a late-night competition among friends than for a novelist.

Some sections are tedious. . . . But . . . late in the novel, I was unexpectedly enjoying myself, because the story is good enough to keep Berger himself interested in what he is doing. If you enjoy private-eye novels presumably you do so because you like the mode, but what distinguishes a good from a bad one is the way the story reveals materials that in some way are being savored rather than simply used. Berger's story is nonsense. Cops and fake cops, dead bodies that reappear but were never dead, alliances that shift so frequently that at some moment everyone except the hero is or seems to be an ally or enemy of everyone else, and, governing all, Teddy Villanova, who may commit murders, or counterfeit money, or run brothels for fetishists, or sell office buildings, or deal in obscene art objects on classical themes—or, most likely, not exist at all, in which case the problem is who invented him.

What the story manages to express, however, far better than the comments on the subject made by Berger's hero, is a view of New York. When a cop says "Did you cause that man to shuffle off his mortal coil?" I feel embarrassed, as much by its inanity as coming from New York's police as by the limpness of the joke. But when the swirling tale leads the private eye from being saved from arrest by the Gay Assault Team, to sleeping all night in a Barca-Lounger left on a sidewalk in front of a brownstone, to a gunning down in Union Square, to a high-rise where a stewardess who may be a Treasury agent lives, then the motion itself expresses a decadent, improbable, fascinating wilderness that is familiar enough to be plausible and distinctive, too. The hero is beyond conspiracy theories about the city, despite the countless possible conspiracies against him, because nothing, and no one, surely, could have thought up New York. (pp. 39-40)

In this novel the first person seems fully justified. Everything the hero sees is simply out there, existing not to be understood but to be encountered, and, if possible, accepted, and everything the hero is can be said in mannered prose since he is a figure without inwardness or complexity. At the end the hero is as he was at the beginning, but given what has happened, this is an accomplishment. . . . *Who Is Teddy Villanova?* is a good, accomplished minor novel; in these puffed up times I hope one can still offer such a judgment as genuine praise. (p. 40)

Roger Sale, in The New York Review of Books (*reprinted with permission from* The New York Review of Books; *copyright* © *1977 NYREV, Inc.), May 26, 1977.*

BERRY, Wendell 1934-

Berry is an American poet, novelist, and essayist. Although primarily known as a poet, his reputation as a novelist has been growing steadily. Berry writes in a clear, conventional prose style about the people and the region of his native Kentucky. (See also *CLC*, Vols. 4, 6.)

One of the major uses of the novel is to define modes of life; we value Turgenev for his understanding rather than for his narrative skill. He is, as the Europeans use the word, "a poet," and Mr. Berry elicits the same appreciation. *A Place on Earth* is one of the most beautiful records ever made of a particular shape of American life. Its form is musical, and though it contains many brilliant passages of narrative—two of them involving that vulgarest of monsters to be bred from the American mind, the automobile—it is not essentially a narrative but a long elegy. Mr. Berry's prose is an essayist's; he touches his subject with an inquisitive hand. He has no talent for objectivity or satire or any degree of coldness. He is thoroughly Kentuckian in beguiling us into a kinship with his characters. And he has written a novel the goodness of which is deep down in its wisdom, for it neither asks nor answers questions, nor fidgets with ideas; it projects whole and articulately a picture of a world.

If the novelist understands his world as well as Wendell Berry, he cannot trim it to satisfy existing literary forms. The pace of his novel is that of Kentucky itself, and the plot is nicely natural and wild, as devious and unstopping as a Kentucky river. At a time when novels vie with one another for notoriety, so warm and humane a book distinguishes itself with its intelligent and wholesome difference, and is all the more welcome for that. (p. 1282)

> *Guy Davenport, in* National Review (© *National Review, Inc., 1967; 150 East 35th St., New York, N.Y. 10016), November 14, 1967.*

[*Findings*] is comprised of two sequences, *The House* and *The Handing Down*, and a coda of three brief elegiac poems. The book reads slowly and gains cumulative force through its unvarnished, honest dealing with the basic grounds of human life. Berry may find himself suddenly popular among the emerging crowd of ecology enthusiasts, for ecology is preeminently his theme. It is not just that he writes in a rural setting out of a reverence for nature and a fear of its being despoiled; his poems are an attempt at *placing* man in his environment, at rediscovering the roots of community, family and locale that preserve men from alienation. *The Handing Down* is most successful in developing these concerns: it has for its hero an old man who is "in the habit of the world", who yet, remembering steamboats, can say, "'I've lived in two countries / in my life / and never moved.'" Berry's voice is not modulated enough, perhaps, to carry off sequences as long as these with entire success—sometimes a passage which you might, in a more patient mood, accept as unaffected simplicity, can seem flatfootedly commonplace. I think the poems could have been pruned a bit to their advantage, but they still show Berry to be a valuable poet. Without raising his voice he commands respect. (pp. 112-13)

> *Robert B. Shaw, in* Poetry (© *1970 by The Modern Poetry Association; reprinted by permission of the Editor of* Poetry), *November, 1970.*

Farming: A Hand Book brought to mind eighteenth-century instructive poems like Dyer's *The Fleece* or Grainger's *The Sugar Cane*, also Samuel Johnson's dismissal of the former by insisting that "The subject, Sir, cannot be made poetical. How can a man write poetically of serges and druggets?" Here is Wendell Berry in the garden:

> the early garden: potatoes, onions,
> peas, lettuce, spinach, cabbage, carrots,
> radishes, marking their straight rows
> with green, before the trees are leafed;
>
> raspberries ripe and heavy amid their foliage,
> currants shining red in clusters amid their foliage,
> strawberries red ripe with the white
> flowers still on the vines . . .

Everybody loves marvelous vegetables and fruits, though it is hard to see what they're doing there in the poetic line. "Johnson said, that Dr. Grainger was an agreeable man; a man who would do any good that was in his power . . . but 'The Sugar-Cane, a Poem' did not please him; for, he exclaimed 'What could he make of a sugar-cane? One might as well write "The Parsley-bed, a Poem"; or, "The Cabbage-garden, a Poem".'" The title of Wendell Berry's poem, of which a few lines were just quoted, is *The Satisfactions of the Mad Farmer* yet there is no madness, no strangeness in the verse; rather there are endless tributes to "the work of feeding and clothing and housing, / done with more than enough knowledge / and with more than enough love, / by men. . . ." Eventually one feels smothered in goodness and sincere human response to The Land. Things do not noticeably liven up in a short play called *The Bringer of Water* that has timeless characters named Mat and Hannah and Little Margaret, and an eighty-four-year-old wonder called "Old Jack Beechum" who begins a poetic line with "Piss on them!" In general, everything is so designedly moving and humble and always wise, wise that I could only feel depressed. It would all be forgivable if the poems sang in your head; but to my ears they sounded no more musical than Guthrie's, and just about as morally complex. (p. 163)

> *William H. Pritchard, in* Poetry (© *1971 by The Modern Poetry Association; reprinted by permission of the Editor of* Poetry), *December, 1971.*

[*The Memory of Old Jack*] takes for its subject the thoughts of a 92-year-old Kentucky farmer, Jack Beechum, on the last day of his life. It is 1952. Beechum's mind sets off on a journey that draws him back to the last days of the Civil War. Then forward, as he learns to work and to put himself in touch with his land. He moves through successes and failures, a friendship, enemies, courtship, a loveless marriage, a romance. Occasionally the present interrupts Beechum's thoughts for a meal or a greeting as Berry effortlessly shifts the reader 50 years in mid-paragraph.

It is not a story that trades in nostalgia; nor even, until the last 30 pages, in any facile celebration of pastoralism or "lost values." Up to those final scenes, which deal with the events following Beechum's death (corrupt city relatives give Old Jack an obscene funeral and ride roughshod over those who learned from and took care of him), there is not a false note in the book.

Jack Beechum is senile. He experiences the present as a man going blind. The past is supernaturally clear, the way a long-dead friend turned a phrase or moved an arm can organize 20 years of Old Jack's life. Like a field worked every spring for half a century, everything in Jack Beechum's life that he refuses to surrender, or that refuses to surrender to him, has been gone over again and again, until it has given up its last kernel of meaning or mystery. His life exists at once in his mind and outside of himself, as if it were both predestined and a conscious creation, a work of art—a life that can simultaneously be reexperienced and judged for its worth.

The book at first seems to be a celebration of Jack Beechum's character, but its genius is in Berry's voice, a tone that harmonizes Beechum's adventures into the past with his last hours in the present. The book is not *about* the past, or the way in which the past is a prelude to the present, but rather about the way in which the past can be made congruent with the present, made part of it. Following Old Jack's thoughts, one feels a strange lucidity. When one understands that Berry intends this senility as an expression of Jack Beechum's will, the book turns into poetry:

> Having no longer the immediate demands
> of his place and work to occupy his mind, he
> began to go into the past. His place and his
> life lay in his mind like a book and what is
> written in it, and he became its scholar.

Only a few works in recent years have insisted that one man or woman's life, lived in rhythms of its own, can make more sense out of the American past, and connect us to it more surely, than a chronicle of great events or biographies of the Men Who Made History. One can think of the TV version of *The Autobiography of Miss Jane Pittman,* the Band's second album, Theodore Rosengarten's *All God's Dangers. The Memory of Old Jack* is of a piece with them. And that Wendell Berry loses his hold on the book once Jack Beechum is dead is perhaps as it should be. Berry invented a character, found its rhythm, and then let that rhythm play itself out. That done, there was nothing more that needed to be said.

> *Griel Marcus, "Old Jack: The Harvest Has Surely Come," in* Rolling Stone *(© 1975 by Rolling Stone Magazine; all rights reserved; reprinted by permission), December 4, 1975, p. 89.*

* * *

BERRYMAN, John   1914-1972

American poet, short story writer, and critic, Berryman is probably best remembered for his *The Dream Songs* which, according to M. L. Rosenthal, entered Berryman into "the post-war current of confessional poetry." A much-honored poet who ended his own life, Berryman received the Pulitzer Prize and National Book Award for *The Dream Songs.* (See also *CLC,* Vols. 1, 2, 3, 4, 6, and *Contemporary Authors,* Vols. 13-16, rev. ed.; obituary, Vols. 33-36.)

The ambitiousness of [*Homage to Mistress Bradstreet*] resides not so much in its length—it runs to only 458 lines—as in its material and style. This is no middle flight. Despite the discrepancy in scale, the manifest intention of the poet inevitably recalls that of Hart Crane in *The Bridge:* to relate himself to the American past through the discovery of a viable myth, and to create for his vehicle a grand and exalted language, a language of transfiguration. If Berryman has been less fortunate than his predecessor in his search for a theme and a language, his failure nevertheless, like Crane's, is worth more than most successes. (p. 213)

As the first woman to write verse in English in America . . . [Anne Bradstreet] survives in the annals of our literature, companioned always by her florid title [*The Tenth Muse, Lately Sprung up in America*]. To imagine her as the symbolic mother-muse of American poetry is, however, to stretch the point, as Berryman himself is well aware, for the mediocrity of her performance is too blatant. . . . It is the life, the spirit, rather than the work, to which Berryman pays his homage. . . . Obviously, in a consideration of the American heritage, Anne Bradstreet is not to be dismissed lightly; but just as obviously she cannot easily be cast in an heroic mold. Part of the imaginative sweat of Berryman's poem is produced by his wrestle with his subject. (p. 214)

Berryman's poem seethes with an almost terrifying activity. . . . Time and time again the medium comes powerfully alive, packed with original metaphor and galvanic with nouns and verbs that seem interchangeably charged with inventive excitement. At his best, in his moments of superlative force and concentration, Berryman writes with dramatic brilliance: "I am a closet of secrets dying," or again, ". . . they starch their minds./Folkmoots, & blether, blether. John Cotton rakes/to the synod of Cambridge." *Homage to Mistress Bradstreet,* I began by saying, is a failure, for reasons I must proceed to demonstrate, but it succeeds in convincing me that Berryman is now entitled to rank among our most gifted poets.

After at least half-a-dozen readings, in which many of the difficulties of the text and the form have been resolved, I still retain my first impression that the scaffolding of the poem is too frail to bear the weight imposed upon it. To put it in other terms, the substance of the poem as a whole lacks inherent imaginative grandeur: whatever effect of magnitude it achieves has been beaten into it. The display of so much exacerbated sensibility, psychic torment, religious ecstasy seems to be intermittently in excess of what the secular occasion requires; the feelings persist in belonging to the poet instead of becoming the property of the poem. (p. 215)

In particular, the love-duet in the central section tends to collapse into a bathos somewhat reminiscent of Crashaw's extravagant compounding of religion and sex. . . . [The] poet interrupts Mistress Bradstreet's flights with protestations of devotion that strike me as being curiously incongruous: "I miss you, Anne.". . . "I have earned the right to be alone with you," etc., to which she at length replies, "I know. / I want to take you for my lover." It is presumptuous to be arbitrary about matters of taste and tone, but I cannot gainsay that I find such lapses damaging. The explanation for them is not that the poet suffers from emotional compulsions—these are the very fountainhead of art—but that he has been unable to canalize them totally into the creative process, with the result that they appear as extraneous to his fiction instead of subsuming it. (p. 216)

Berryman has evolved, for his language of rapture and of the "delirium of the grand depths," a dense and involuted style which in its very compression and distortion is best adapted for the production of extraordinary, not ordinary, effects. There is much that is extraordinary in his poem, often as a consequence of the magnificent conversion of the ordinary, but it is in the nature of the long poem that it must sweep into its embrace certain phenomena whose virtue is to be what they are, to resist transubstantiation—and here Berryman is tempted to inflate what he cannot subjugate. "Without the commonplace," remarked Hölderlin, "nobility cannot be represented, and so I shall always say to myself, when I come up against something common in the world: You need this as urgently as a potter needs clay, and for that reason always take it in, and do not reject it, and do not take fright at it.''

A portion of Berryman's vocabulary and most of the idiosyncrasies of his technique can be traced back to Hopkins, witness such lines as these, spoken by Anne in the crisis of childbirth:

> Monster you are killing me Be sure
> I'll have you later Women do endure
> I can *can* no longer
> and it passes the wretched trap whelming and I am me
>
> drencht & powerful, I did it with my body!

But Hopkins, to be sure, would have known better than to let the last phrase get by. (Hysteria is not an intensity of tone, but a laxness, a giving in. By the time Anne has pressed out her child—we are spared few of the physiological details—we must be prepared to accede to the premise that never has there been such an excruciating, such a miraculous birth, and we boggle at the superfluity of the assault on our disbelief.)

In his uncompromising election of a language of artifice Berryman, like Hopkins, does not hesitate, for the sake of the emphasis and tension he aims at, to wrench his syntax, invert his word-order. The rewards of his daring are not to be minimized. The opening stanza, for example, seems to me to move with beautiful ease and dignity; the tone, the pressures, delicately controlled; the details small and particular, but the air charged with momentousness.... But when the dislocations have nothing to recommend them beyond their mechanical violence, the ear recoils.... [Hopkins], however radical his deflections from the linguistic norm, keeps mindful of the natural flow and rhythms of speech, which serves him as his contrapuntal ground.

Throughout his poem Berryman handles his varied eight-line stanza, derived perhaps from *The Wreck of the Deutschland* and composed in a system of functional stressing adapted from Hopkins's sprung rhythm, with admirable assurance. Few modern poets, I think, can even approximate his command of the stanzaic structure. The alterations of pace through his juxtaposition of short and long lines are beautifully controlled; and the narrative-lyrical functions are kept in fluid relation, with the action riding through the stanza, which nevertheless preserves intact the music suspended within it.

Homage to Mistress Bradstreet can bear the kind of scrutiny that an important poem exacts. The flaws are real for me, but the work remains impressive in its ambition and virtuosity. (pp. 217-19)

> *Stanley Kunitz, "No Middle Flight" (originally published in* Poetry, *July, 1957), in his* A Kind of Order, A Kind of Folly (© *1935, 1937, 1938, 1941, 1942, 1947, 1949, 1957, 1963, 1964, 1965, 1966, 1967, 1970, 1971, 1972, 1973, 1974, 1975 by Stanley Kunitz; reprinted by permission of Little, Brown and Co. in association with the Atlantic Monthly Press), Atlantic-Little, Brown, 1975, pp. 213-19.*

It cannot be denied that at some point in mid-career Berryman momentously shifted his stance toward his art and the experience that his art fed upon, just as Lowell did with his

"Life Studies" (1959). And the shift seems to have to do, not surprisingly, with that inescapable figure in every American poet's heritage, Walt Whitman. Berryman's 1957 essay on Whitman, . . . printed for the first time [in "Freedom of the Poet"] and deliberately placed by him so as to introduce all his pieces on modern poetry, is thus a document of capital importance. On the other hand, if Berryman thus belatedly weds himself to the Whitmanesque strain in the American tradition, this doesn't in the least mean—as it too frequently does in what passes for informed discussion on these matters—a rejection of the European, or of "formalism." Berryman remained a poet to whom it came naturally, as late as 1965, to talk of "problems of decorum," and as late as 1968 to go for a title—"His Toy, His Dream, His Rest"—to Giles Farnaby in the 16th-century Fitzwilliam Virginal Book.

My own guess is that the significance of "Song of Myself" for the later Berryman isn't to be charted in terms of poetic theory, however generously interpreted, but has to do with two aspects of the Whitmanesque poet that have often been remarked on—first, his egalitarianism (his "democracy"), and second, his shamelessness. In that case, the pathos and the distinction of Berryman's career reside first in his having a haughtiness which Whitmanesque democracy was permitted to chastise (in 1947 in Cambridge, England, the lordly urbanity of Berryman of Clare Hall was vividly remembered); and second in his having a natural shamefastness which Whitmanesque openness was permitted, with the help of alcohol, to outrage.

As a young American in England, nearly 40 years ago, Berryman appears to have hopped aboard the Dylan Thomas bandwagon, then vociferously rolling. And it is tempting to date from that experience, not from the encounter with Whitman 15 years later, Berryman's conversion to some vulgarly debased notion of the poet as society's sacrificial scapegoat. Biographical documentation yet to come may establish that indeed the Dylanesque life style did have its attractions for Berryman. But in the present state of our knowledge it is prudent, as well as charitable, to suppose that [to] the young American . . . Dylan represented a Celtic, an indigenously Welsh, imaginative tradition challenging the received and authenticated English establishment. . . .

Another piece now printed for the first time, dating from about 1960, is an essay on "Don Quixote," which I suspect is even more important than the Whitman essay for getting our bearings on the late Berryman. It is extremely scholarly; the learning, though it is worn lightly and deployed only to be serviceable, is very impressive. It is also a profoundly Christian piece of writing, which insists, if I read it right (for it's written with admirable clarity, yet needs to be much pondered), that Cervantes's comic masterpiece comes into focus only if we read it as a work of fervent though disenchanted piety. This is important, because the notion is abroad that Berryman in his last two collections wobbled or wavered into an unconsidered sort of Christian salvationism. On the contrary his Christian allegiance dates from much farther back in his life. And remembering how the astonishingly sustained six-line stanzas of "The Dream Songs" (1969) make up a minstrel show colloquy between "Henry" and "Mr. Bones," how can we fail to make the connection with Quixote and his interlocutor Sancho Panza? Berryman's suicide was "quixotic"; just so—and we owe it to him to learn what he thought the quixotic figure signified. (One thing it signified was "humility," as one thing the Whitmanesque figure signified was "humiliation";

and one way to regard all Berryman's poems of the 1960's is as one long potential exercise in self-humiliation.)

As for "death wishes"—yes, they do crop up, quite insistently. . . . But "death wish" sounds too glib, too clinically dismissive. If that is anywhere near the right diagnosis of Berryman's trouble, we can be sure he arrived at it himself long before we did. In any case the possibility doesn't in the least qualify my sense that the man behind this book was not only one of the most gifted and intelligent Americans of his time, but also one of the most honorable and responsible. (p. 4)

> *Donald Davie, in* The New York Times
> Book Review (© *1976 by The New York
> Times Company; reprinted by permission*),
> *April 25, 1976.*

The patterned movement of *The Dream Songs* is its dancing; its fiery mass Berryman's life of chaotic circumstance and his powerful imagining. Ultimately one cannot divorce dance from dancer, the overall flow of *The Dream Songs* from John Berryman. I mean more than just the impossibility of *wholly* distinguishing Berryman from the singer of the Songs, Henry—though that too. *The Dream Songs* is open-ended: open to Berryman's life and ended by an act of his will and, irrevocably, by his death. One could say the poem stops rather than ends: thus in contrast to long poems which complete some narrative or logical design. Although patterning is everywhere in the poem, it is everywhere local. There is the structured movement within Songs and the grouping of Songs; but there is no actual or implied overall pattern by which all the groups are ordered, the whole finished and sealed. Thus the poem combines shape and flow, patterning and openness.

Pattern is tightest in the individual Songs with their surface arrangement of triple sestets (there are about twenty exceptions, most of which consist of an added line), the sestets following only casually a stress order of 5-5-3-5-5-3. Just as important is Berryman's shaping of Song content. Before leaving for Ireland to assemble the last four Books of *The Dream Songs* he told Jonathan Sisson that, besides unpublished Songs whose fate he would decide, he was taking with him "a large body of manuscript which is fragmentary, dealing with beginnings and ends and some middles." Remarkably the Songs—with their beginnings, middles, and ends—are not formally monotonous. (pp. 146-47)

Berryman's experimentation sometimes leaves one at a loss for a descriptive label. For example, consider the arrangement of Song 66. The powerful and clear spiritual stance of a fourth-century Desert Father, humorously conveyed "over the telephone," ironically contrasts with the lunatic medley of the world and Henry circa early June 1963, the Father's words woven through the whole Song yet, appropriately, parenthetically isolated from it. The weaving keeps the form from being a simply juxtaposed presentation of one thing, then another; the isolation keeps it from being an interaction. Perhaps such structuring should be called "thematic counterpoint." Whatever the label, both strands have their identifiable beginning, middle, and end. Despite the consistency of such structuring, the Songs' several modes—logical, narrative, lyric, dramatic, and other—give them a greater formal variety than, say, the lyric meditations in a sonnet sequence—be it Shakespeare's or Berryman's own.

Besides creating patterned movement within the Songs, Berryman arranged many of them into clusters of varying

cohesion. . . . Berryman observed that "Some of the Songs are in alphabetical order; but, mostly, they just belong to areas of hope and fear that Henry is going through at a given time." In fact, alphabetical order is not very extensive in the poem; what little of it there is could be accounted for by chance, so it does not seem an ordering principle at all. But Berryman's mention of alphabetical order suggests that for some Songs a search for immediate thematic context will prove fruitless. Immediate context is worth checking, however, for as Berryman also maintained, it clarifies certain Songs: "you don't need to follow the specific details if you hear the tone of the Song in relation to the Songs around it." (pp. 147-48)

Berryman considered the themes of the first three Books to be loss, death, and terror (and partial recovery), and he already planned the fourth Book to consist of posthumous Songs. In a loose sense, the first three Books do comprise variations on such thematic groupings. . . .

[However,] Berryman's method in these first three Books seems to have been not so much writing Songs to fit a preconceived theme as writing Songs and then selecting among them and figuring out some plan by which to organize them. . . . In writing the Songs of Book 4, on the other hand, Berryman seems to have taken the reverse tack, first deciding to have a Book of Songs set in the grave and then writing them. (p. 150)

The last Book is the only one to parallel a circumscribed period in Berryman's life and to suggest chronological order. (p. 151)

The different principles of organization which govern the other Books of *The Dream Songs* do not lead one to expect chronological order in them, nor do they provide it. (p. 152)

This does not mean the whole poem is without plot, but the plot is of casual rather than necessary order—variations on the personality of Henry as he lives, remembers, and dreams at various times over a decade. Any *ulterior* overall structure Berryman emphatically denied. . . . Describing the poem's plot Berryman said: "[It's] the personality of Henry as he moves on in the world. Henry gains ten years.". . . I don't think Berryman meant one traces the gain in some linear way: . . . aside from Book 7 one cannot maintain even a fiction of *chronological* order. Neither can one become involved with Henry's mental, moral, or emotional "growth" or "decline" because the poem does not chart such growth or decline. That "Henry gains ten years" is an indication of the poem's scale rather than its linearity.

What holds *The Dream Songs* together, given that it is formally tightest on local levels and loosest overall, is the strong cohesive power of all the Songs being Henry's. Reading from Song to Song one becomes involved with Henry's character: things opaque in one Song often are illuminated by others. It is not just that Henry's personality acts to string together the individual Songs, which are "admittedly more independent than parts usually are" and which generally are more rigidly structured than the whole poem. Because they are all expressions of Henry's character the Songs take on a new cast. It is as if by intussuception *The Dream Songs* turned its Songs more fully into itself, making a dramatic monologue on an epic scale. At the same time, the Songs retain their various modes. . . . An extra dimension is added to anecdote, love lyric, and eschatological meditation because all, by context, establish and manifest Henry's character.

The whole poem's "ultimate structure" is the ongoing and epic enterprise of probing and expressing that character—without, at the same time, developing some narrative action with a grand finale. Not even the materials of the last Book, which continue themes found throughout the poem, are drawn together into a final resolution; as Henry says, its design is "not cliffhangers or old serials / but according to his nature" (Song 293). The rest of the Song in which he says this exemplifies that the poem was not written according to some preconceived design, for Henry "sings" about a daughter not born when it began. Certain critics, moved by Henry's evident love for that daughter in the last Song, have made the excessive claim that the whole poem ends on a grand harmony. Henry talks of scolding his daughter in the last Song, and I take it that his loving scolding is related to her growing older ("heavier"). His feeling seems to be that as one grows older one's life becomes more disharmonious: one thinks of Henry's first Song memories of a golden childhood, disastrously altered, and his meditation in Song 270 on womb return. . . . It makes little difference whether one thinks of the last Song in the context of its composition—Berryman in imagined rebuke of his daughter as infant or perhaps fetus—or in its context at the end of Book 7's partly fictional year—Henry scolding a now four- or five-year-old daughter (in Song 303 Martha is "aged four"). In either case, growing "heavier" means moving away from the golden world of womb or childhood and, like a Thanksgiving turkey, toward the disaster of maturity and death. Henry's desire that his daughter *not* grow "heavier" contrasts with his hope, expressed in Song 293, that she *will* grow into a stable adult. It is interesting that critics who have stressed Henry's great love for his daughter in the last Song have not mentioned its psychologically retrogressive aspect. (pp. 154-56)

Berryman considered *The Dream Songs* a victory because Henry still survives at the poem's "end." He did not consider it a victory because Henry has resolved all or even any of his problems. . . . (pp. 156-57)

The open-ended form of *The Dream Songs* seems to imply that Henry is free to turn into the mature and integrated personality described by certain critics. Free, that is, in the sense that there are no artistic obstacles to such development. The only obstacle is the insurmountable one of John Berryman's death, for if anyone else were to write an eighth Book of Songs it would not be an eighth Book of Berryman's poem. One can pay homage to a poet by imitating his voice, but imitations of Berryman's Songs are not Berryman's Songs. In the years after *The Dream Songs* was published John Berryman did try radically to reform his life. He also began to imagine and write about a character, Alan Severance, who would succeed in coming to terms with his various problems, chief among them alcoholism, and who would achieve self-integration. There are at least two unattached Songs in which Henry undergoes trials of alcoholic reformation similar to those of Berryman and Severance. . . . Had Berryman not committed suicide and had he decided to add more Books to *The Dream Songs* they very likely would have paralleled the experience of Alan Severance.

But a *Dream Songs* of eight or nine or ten Books could itself be open to possible subsequent Books on Henry's relapse. I suggest that any critic who proceeds by analysis of the metaphysical stance of poems cannot significantly discuss a poem such as *The Dream Songs.* Different Songs provide different stances, and it is questionable whether the whole poem's openness can be said, itself, to imply a stance. Also, it may be that even the openness is open to the development of closure. It would take a bolder critic of form than this writer to deny the possibility. . . . Could he have developed new terms, in subsequent Books, which *would* have resulted in an end to his story? I do not raise this question because I believe strong closure necessarily makes a better poem (in his essay, "Dr Williams' Position," Ezra Pound suggested there is a lot of great world literature in which major form is remarkable for its absence). I raise the question to face more fully what it means for a poem to be open-ended. (p. 157)

In these matters we do well to take into account, when possible, *how a poem came to be as it is* in our theorizing about *what it is* we ultimately have. Such *historical* study of a poet's evolving intention sharpens our evaluation, also, of the formal *theories* about what we have which are advanced by others. I have observed that in individual Songs Berryman fashioned tightly structured units, while overall, *The Dream Songs* is an open-ended process. Edward Mendelson's "How to Read Berryman's *Dream Songs*" seems to make these same points [see *CLC*, Vol. 4]. Mendelson says that Berryman's Songs, unlike Pound's Cantos, have a recognizable beginning, middle, and end; he says that the "essential form" taken on by the whole poem is "survival" and "moving-on"; he concludes that "at the same moment that it closes, the poem thrusts itself out of its frame into the undefined future." It seems to me astonishing, therefore, that in the same essay he theorizes that all poems have closure. . . . I repeat: it is not "the *closure* of art" which ends *The Dream Songs;* unlike its Songs the whole poem does not have an Aristotelian beginning and middle and end; if anything *seals* the poem, it is not some larger closed structure—actual or implied—but Berryman's death. (p. 158)

Tradition is itself a human construct, a way of understanding the abundance of human creation by grouping works according to abstract commonalities. Trying to discern traditions or, rather, constructing traditions, can be useful as long as the effort does not distract one from the important differences among literary works. . . . (p. 160)

Henry's chaotic self and his great suffering are often contrasted, in *The Dream Songs,* with the fixed and timeless perfection of stone art. Certain rare lives, of course, can fascinate us as being, like stone monuments, paradigms of eternity. . . . Just as there are lives which can imitate artistic perfection, there is art which can reflect, in its form as well as in its subject matter, human temporality and ambivalence. *The Dream Songs,* often fixed and perfect on the level of Song form, is in its subject and "major form" such art. It grew and changed with the life of the poet who wrote it, and it did not truly end until he did. . . . The metaphor for *The Dream Songs* cannot be a stone temple garden, or the carved capital on a cathedral pillar, or sculptured figures which do not doubt or suffer, gain or lose. Rather than something fixed and perfect, the metaphor must be something flashing and bursting. . . . Better still, it should be something organic. One reads in Song 75 that "Henry put forth a book." (pp. 160-61)

Jack Vincent Barbera, "Shape and Flow in 'The Dream Songs'," in Twentieth Century Literature *(copyright 1976, Hofstra University Press), May, 1976, pp. 146-62.*

In Berryman's poetry, from the Alexandrinism of his *Son-*

nets to the putative heroics of his Dream Songs, the major subject is literature itself, or, more precisely, life's insufficiency, when contrasted with literature, where we can seemingly control the outcome of things. In place of Malraux's museum without walls, we have in Berryman's work an anthology without bindings, a gathering together of figures, motifs, icons, and legends from great writers of the past. In the Dream Songs, for example, the last half of the work becomes increasingly obsessed with the act of writing, in fact with the act of writing the Dream Songs. It is as if, after the exhaustion of the first hundred and fifty or so, the Dream Songs revealed their true subject: their author's attempt to establish his literary talent for the sake of posterity. The later Songs, when dealing with the trip to Ireland and the various details of the author's fame, including a feature in *Life* magazine (that ultimate triumph of "image" over word), often settle for a prosaic syntax. These later poems lack the whipsaw irony of the earlier efforts, as Berryman's syntax gradually unknots itself. He abandons puns and dialects and crazy rhymes, and we arrive at the affective center of his world, a desire to be enrolled among the "immortals," like Yeats, even if it means neglect and deprivation in his current life, as it did with Delmore Schwartz, Berryman's friend and symbol of the intellectual poet with a burdensome sensitivity further encumbered by vast learning. Near the end of his life Berryman was capable of beginning his talk with college audiences by saying, "Well, why don't you go ahead and ask me how it feels to be famous?" (pp. 168-69)

The confessional poet wants in some sense to be his own muse, to do for himself what Rodin did for Balzac, to make of the individual artist a type of genius, the grand culmination of an epoch, an artistic style, and a vision of life. Only then can the poet take his place with the immortals, only then will the rules of discourse be recast and the audience be made up of the dead and the not-yet-born.

In the ironic balance between display and evasion, Berryman's Henry appears a master. Here, in a late Dream Song, he talks to himself about himself, an occupation the confessional poet is often at pains, though unsuccessfully, to avoid:

> —Oh, I suffer from a strike
> & a strike and three balls: I stand up for much,
> Wordsworth and that sort of thing.
> The pitcher dreamed. He threw a hazy curve,
> I took it in my stride & out I struck,
> lonesome Henry.
>
> These Songs are not meant to be understood, you
>   understand
> They are only meant to terrify and comfort.
> Lilac was found in his hand.

Here Berryman is simultaneously Casey at bat and the Poet Laureate, self-parody and self-glorification jostling each other with knowing wit. The offhanded irony of "and that sort of thing" occurs often in the Dream Songs and is the extension of the mixing of modes that becomes the work's characteristic signature. The inversion of "out I struck" allows Berryman to have the anticlimax, by a syntactical punning (the major artistic breakthrough of the Songs), become a triumphant announcement of new heroic ventures. The not-quite-sentimental reference to "lonesome Henry" is followed by a direct and fairly unironic "message" to the reader, like those moments when the comedian cuts into his own patter to say "seriously, folks." So Ber-

ryman lets us know he wants to be identified with the mainstream of literary fame ("Wordsworth and that sort of thing") and yet doesn't want to lose the common touch, as the baseball figure makes clear, especially if he can play with the literary and mock-dramatic elements in the national "pastime." The suffering and loneliness suggest the terrifying purpose of the Songs, while the poet's ability to take fate's hazy curve balls in his stride suggests he can also be comforted by his art. Adrienne Rich has suggested that only two men in this age know what the American language is, in all its fullness and impurity, and they are Bob Dylan and John Berryman. I would amend that to say that both men have been very successful at creating a private language out of the cultural confusion of the age and in finding an audience (though Dylan's is obviously so much wider the comparison is rather strained) of true believers who are willing, almost before the fact and despite the repetitiousness of the art, to see in the mock-casual defiance of respectability an artist who belongs at the top of the list, an artist who merits his fame by flaunting it. Unlike Dylan, however, Berryman ends with a limited audience, smaller than that of baseball, and smaller too than that of Wordsworth, since it must be made up of those who "follow" both with a disinterested, yet animated, curiosity. (pp. 170-71)

Charles Molesworth, in Twentieth Century Literature *(copyright 1976, Hofstra University Press), May, 1976.*

As a critic Berryman was always likely to say anything as long as he thought it true. . . .

Such a voice is unlikely to be subject to the intimidation of current fashions; and throughout [*The Freedom of the Poet*] Berryman practices comparison and analysis with great skill and inventiveness, as when he finds, in the words of his title, Shakespeare's freedom (in *Macbeth*) to lie in a freedom of language. (p. 23)

As far as I can detect, Berryman's own critical procedures are analogously free. He admits to having been influenced by Eliot, Pound, Blackmur and Empson, all of course inimitable in their extravagant brilliances, but is slave to nobody —to the extent that no large axes are ground, no ideology of politics or literary doctrine provides a base from which spring the essays, Berryman comes as close as one can (there are disagreements about how close one can come) to being his own man, interested in literature as literature, reading—like Dr. Johnson—solely to be instructed through pleasure. . . . But the finest stretch of writing comes in three back-to-back essays on American prose writers: Dreiser, Fitzgerald and Ring Lardner. Grouped under the rubric "Enslavement: Three American Cases," they add up to 30 pages as humanly penetrating and sympathetic as they are critically severe and sound. (pp. 23-4)

William H. Pritchard, in The New Republic *(reprinted by permission of* The New Republic; © 1976 by The New Republic, Inc.), June 5, 1976.*

Full credentials as a poet (and John Berryman certainly had those) do not necessarily mean that one will also be able to write an interesting literary essay. The essayist needs to be a poet of a particular kind: a Matthew Arnold rather than a Shelley, a T. S. Eliot rather than a William Carlos Williams or an E. E. Cummings. The poet who writes essays worth preserving in book form must see himself as part of a living tradition, and a good part of his poetry (not all, or *that* would be unreadable) is likely to be based on secondary experience.

It is mildly surprising, then, to find such a fat and readable book of literary essays [*The Freedom of the Poet*] by a poet who is taxonomized with Roethke, Plath, Wright (and even, I suppose, Jong) in something called the "Confessional School." Richard Wilbur, perhaps; but Berryman?

Could there be such a genre as the confessional literary essay? Indeed there could. Explore, for instance, the essays of Eliot on the Elizabethan dramatists, the metaphysical poets, Baudelaire and Laforgue, and it is not hard to find passages where the author seems to be writing about himself (as a poetic sensibility, not as the hero of an autobiography) and so it is with Berryman. "Prufrock's Dilemma" in this collection could by no means be relabeled "Berryman's Dilemma"; it is a very professional, almost textbook-style analysis of one of the cornerstones of modern poetry, yet it does yield a nuance of generalized autobiography. . . .

If [Berryman] had not joined the growing line of poets who have followed Hart Crane to self-destruction (Berryman, Sexton and Plath within recent memory), he might have less notoriety, but he would be no whit less a poet. It is the central fact about him and the fact that emerges with greatest impact from these thoughtful, well-written, thoroughly professional essays. He may be a member of a particular school, but he stands apart from and somewhat above most of its other members (perhaps even Lowell and Roethke, though they are splendid poets) in the objectivity of his vision.

The difference can be grasped most clearly, perhaps, by comparing his "Beethoven Triumphant" (from *Delusions, Etc.*) with Adrienne Rich's "The Ninth Symphony of Beethoven Understood at Last as a Sexual Message" (from *Diving into the Wreck*). Berryman's Beethoven is a richly realized figure who produced a series of masterpieces (several named and evaluated in the poem), had trouble with his landlord, relatives and patrons, differed notably from Mozart in his working methods, left coffee and candle drippings on his *Odyssey* and lived largely out of phase with his times. In Rich's poem, Beethoven is clearly a projection of the poet. . . . Rich's poem has energy; Berryman's has depth; it is the poem of a man who could write three dozen literary essays worth preserving and reading for what they tell us of the subject, not the author.

Still, Berryman's personality peeps through. . . .

Ultimately, these essays may help to dislodge Berryman from the cramped pigeonhole assigned him by those who manufacture and affix literary labels. If he is, in fact, a member of a "confessional school," he enlarges that school beyond the limits of its name, and a special kindergarten or remedial category is needed to distinguish him from some others in the school. He stands out from a swarm of navel-observers by the clarity, the breadth, the objectivity of his vision. We turn from these essays (and the handful of short stories, also clearly observed and finely detached, which fill out the volume) to reexamine the poetry; and we note in a new light that his first big success was a poem not about John Berryman but about Anne Bradstreet—really about Bradstreet, not as a symbol or a projection but as a person. And that his most durable sequence of poems (or single, large, segmented poem if you prefer) deals not with Berryman but with a character named Henry, who is sometimes, in some aspects, Berryman (perhaps) but who is

also, always, someone else, viewable with detachment, irony, wholeness. . . .

What [the essays] offer is a profile of a mind, slightly different from but congruent with the mind that lives in the poems: bright, active, endlessly curious, troubled at times, intricately concerned with the verbal arts, detached, humorous—an excellent sort of mind for a poet and one which Berryman applied to his chosen tasks with consummate skill. (p. H4)

> *Joseph McLellan, in* Book World—The Washington Post *(© The Washington Post), June 6, 1976.*

Throughout [Berryman's] Columbia and Cambridge University years (1932-1938) and into the middle 1940's the young poet wrote the lyrics that were later collected in *Short Poems* (1967). With a few notable exceptions this work has no voice, or, rather, it has too many voices, with Van Doren, Yeats, Auden, and Ransom as the most audible echoes—Yeats saved Berryman from the then-crushing domination of Eliot and Pound. Ominous, flat, social, indistinctly allusive, and exhausted, most of these poems, invariably organized in prudent stanzas with carefully plotted rhyme schemes, seem to have been written by a well-programmed computer with Weltschmerz. There are references to heartbreak, fear, sorrow, and hatred, but it is clear that the poet, keeping his most intimate feelings in harness, was far more conscious of civic woe than of his own. It is hard to believe that the public voice of this work would modulate into that of Mr. Bones, of *The Dream Songs*, a man to whom nothing in the world is more important, or, in an odd way, universal, than his own private sorrows. The poetry of *The Dispossessed* (1948) shows a slight movement in the direction of the later work, particularly in a marvelous sequence of "Nervous Songs" that anticipate, both in form and content, the dream songs. For the most part, however, the apprentice work is very much a product of its time.

The two sequences written during his thirties show Berryman escaping the domination of Auden and company to invent a language peculiarly his own. His *Sonnets*, written in 1948 (but not published until 1967), are the record of a knock-down-and-drag-out adulterous love affair. Couched in the most conventional of forms, they nevertheless bristle with the pain, euphoria, jealousy, and wrenching despair that are so clearly missing in the impersonal earlier lyrics. Only a theme that appealed to his deepest needs could have brought this poet to the necessity of "crumpling a syntax," could have transformed an empty monk of the Yeatsian order into love's "utraquist," one who speaks or writes two languages, such as Latin and the vernacular. It is primarily the experiments with colloquial language, slangy, often inelegant, hot off the heart, that give this book of conventional structures its unconventional power and importance. (p. 3)

Homage to Mistress Bradstreet dramatically moved its creator, then thirty-nine, into the front rank of living poets. . . . Its fifty-seven stanzas (the model is Yeats' "In Memory of Major Robert Gregory") are characterized by a soaring lyricism, by intensely compressed discords, jagged, Hopkinesque rhythms, unexpected allusions, puns, repeated harmonies, scrupulously crafted image patterns, haunting cadences. There is nothing like the language of this sequence in Berryman's earlier work, and certainly nothing quite like the poem in American literature. Had he written nothing else Berryman's position as a significant poet would be assured.

He went on, however, to create his "Song of Myself," his *Cantos,* his *Paterson.* The 385 *Dream Songs,* composed over a period of more than ten years, record the life in progress of an imaginary character, named, among other things, Henry House, who bears a striking resemblance to the poet himself. Again adopting a fairly rigid form (eighteen lines made up of three six-line stanzas), the songs reveal, in a fashion alternately disturbing and hilarious, Henry's griefs, lusts, joys, terrors, and hopes, his preoccupation with his dead father, and his quest for his lost Father. The sequence represents Berryman's attempts to get his guilt and fear out in the open as a means of exorcizing them. The vitality, grave comedy, and outright buffoonery of much of the work vitiate against an uncritical acceptance of the nightmares the songs contain, the wit and high spirits warding off much of the horror. It is, however, because the nightmares are recounted, the terrors revealed, the guilt expressed, that the poet can go on dreaming and muddling through.... Some of the songs are baffling and others are remarkably self-indulgent. On the whole, however, the sequence is an eccentric masterpiece, a triumph of technical virtuosity, invention, and imagination. Berryman created for this work a luxuriant language, one made up of archaic and Latinate constructions, crumpled syntax, odd diction, idiomatic conversation, blues and nursery rhyme rhythms, minstrel show dialect, and a number of other things as well. It is a language that has been praised, damned, imitated, explicated, annotated, and thoroughly misunderstood. (pp. 4-5)

When Berryman completed this massive sequence he thought of himself as an epic poet and had no expectation of writing any more short poems. One day, however, he composed a line, "I fell in love with a girl," and, liking its factuality, continued in the same vein. The subject was entirely new, he felt, "solely and simply myself . . . the subject on which I am a real authority, so I wiped out all the disguises and went to work.". . . In 1970 *Love & Fame,* containing something to offend nearly everyone, was published, and in 1972 a revised version, with some of the more tasteless poems deleted, came out.

In this book Berryman leaves behind both his persona, Henry, and the baroque intricacies of the songs—the poems are written in a direct, unadorned style often resembling prose. The work, which appears at first glance to be a series of uncensored personal revelations, some fairly startling, took a drubbing from many reviewers. The unprecedented exhibitionism of the first two sections in particular caused unsympathetic critics to overlook the later poems, which quietly undercut the hubris of the earlier parts. In the 7000 lines of the *Songs* Berryman is able to say the most intimate and outrageous things. Since he is speaking through Henry, however, a reader, even if he makes little distinction between poet and speaker, can attribute any especially shocking excesses to the "imaginary" character. It is one thing for Henry Pussycat to lust after every young woman he sees, quite another for John Berryman, sans mask, to announce, in the first stanza of a book, that he fell in love with a "gash" and that he has fathered a bastard. And isn't it, after all, *regressive* for a distinguished poet and chair-holding professor to carry on about adolescent fondlings, student council elections, penis lengths, college grades, and the number of women (79) he bedded as a young man?

If these things were all the book contained it would, indeed, be appropriate to dismiss *Love & Fame* as a tasteless mistake. The work, however, is more complex and more serious than the bawdiness of the opening sections might suggest. In a foreward to the second edition, Berryman, after characteristically attacking those who misread the book, suggests that each of the four movements (he means, I think, each of the last three) criticizes backward the preceding one. My own sense is that the book can most helpfully be analyzed in terms of its two halves, the second representing a total repudiation of the values inherent in the two sections that make up the first. The title helps explain this movement. At the end of Keats' sonnet "When I Have Fears That I May Cease To Be" the speaker announces, "then on the shore / Of the wide world I stand alone and think / Till Love and Fame to nothingness do sink." In the second half of Berryman's book this notion of declining to nothingness is fully examined: love and fame, postulated in the first parts as lust and Public Relations, yield to "Husbandship and crafting." The book, thus, takes a dramatic turn at the beginning of section three, progressing from the poet's randy and confident young manhood into his depressed present, from ribald skirt-chasing and self-promotion to a humble series of prayers to God, who judges a man's merit not by his verses but by his virtue. (pp. 5-6)

[The] Berryman of the last books is, more than anything else, a religious poet, a man seeking desperately to recover the faith of his childhood, a son engaged in a struggle with a Father who is simultaneously his antagonist and the only possible source of hope. "I believe," he seems to say throughout these prayers, "help thou my unbelief."

Composed in the four line stanza . . . that makes up the whole of the book, the prayers, though at times tediously predictable . . . are moving petitions from a self-effacing suppliant, "severely damaged, but functioning." They resolve the themes introduced in the earlier sections: "I fell in love with a girl" gives way to "I fell in love with you, Father," and the preoccupation with the sort of fame associated with *Time* is replaced by the assertion that "the only true literary critic is Christ.". . . The book's final line reveals how far the poet has travelled from his obsession with public approbation: "I pray I may be ready with my witness." (p. 7)

Love & Fame [does not] represent one of the poet's major achievements. It is neither so brilliant nor so interestingly eccentric as either *Mistress Bradstreet* or the *Songs.* There is, nevertheless, after the complexities of these sequences, much that can be said for a work that strives for direct, unambiguous communication, and that more often than not achieves its goal. The Berryman canon, missing this vulnerable book, would be noticeably slighter.

Delusions, Etc., though it contains a handful of poems that are superior to anything in *Love & Fame,* stands, by contrast, as an honorable failure. Why is this so? Largely, I think, because the work, lacking the internal development of the earlier book, is a miscellaneous collection of often incoherent utterances from a soul in a state of intense agitation, a state that precludes, more often than not, the kind of control required if desperate emotion is to be translated into formal art. The first and final sections reveal the poet's anguished quest for faith.... These "holy" poems, unlike those in *Love & Fame,* tend to be disputatious, as if the poet, protesting too much, were now trying to convince himself and his God of his faith. (p. 8)

Though the book as a whole is inferior to *Love & Fame* it does contain several poems that are finer than anything in that work and I include here "He Resigns," the two dream songs, and "Beethoven Triumphant." Berryman's friend William Meredith has said of the latter that it has "the force and complexity of a late quartet." (p. 9)

Made up of twenty-seven stanzas ranging from four to eleven lines each, "Beethoven Triumphant" reveals Berryman as historian, as music critic, and as eulogist. The poem bears a striking resemblance to *Homage to Mistress Bradstreet,* borrowing from that work a mode of intense compression ("tensing your vision into an alarm / of gravid measures, sequent to demure"), inclusion of little-known biographical facts ("When brother Johann signed 'Real Estate Owner,' you: 'Brain Owner'"), movement from objective narrative to direct address ("Koussevitzky will make it, Master; lie back down"), emphasis on physical decay ("your body-filth flowed to the middle of the floor"), and introduction of contemporary detail ("I called our chief prose-writer / at home a thousand miles off"). As in his earlier poem Berryman conjures up the spirit of a long dead artist, analyzes, lovingly if somewhat pedantically, the basic qualities of this artist's nature, and provides a valedictory coda. Where the Bradstreet sequence closes on a note of quiet affection, however, the Beethoven tribute ends with a powerful crescendo: "You march and chant around here! I hear your thighs." The final phrase, which sounds so odd out of context, actually works, resolving an image introduced in the opening stanza.

Berryman clearly empathizes with the composer, whom he shows to be misunderstood, physically disabled, a troubled sleeper, eccentric, churlish, absent-minded, vain. In lines that echo the "Ode on a Grecian Urn" (and that suggest his own desire for oblivion) he rejoices that the man died during his prime, thus spared the burdens of old age: "Ah but the indignities you flew free from, / your self-abasements even would increase." And he attempts to approximate, through his language, the glories of "the B Flat major," "the Diabelli varia," and "the 4th Piano Concerto" as a way of documenting this sense of identification. His poem, with its irregular stanzas, is not meant to suggest a concerto, or a sonata, or a symphony, but its richly musical individual lines clearly do attempt to suggest Beethoven's powerful rhythms and ecstatic tonalities. Nowhere in Berryman is the language purer. The opening lines, for example, melodious, even cello-like, are representative: "Dooms menace from tumults. Who's immune / among our mightier of headed men?" In addition to the obvious assonance of Doom-tumults-who-immune, there are secondary harmonies provided by from-along-of, and by menace-headed-men. The slant rhyme and the numerous "m" sounds add to the consonance, as does the insistent percussive beat. "One chord thrusts, as it must / find allies, foes, resolve, in subdued crescendo," the poet writes later, the sound, once again, underscoring the sense of the words. (pp. 10-11)

> *Joel Conarroe, "After Mr. Bones: John Berryman's Last Poems," in* The Hollins Critic *(copyright 1976 by Hollins College), October, 1976, pp. 1-12.*

["Henry's Fate"] presents . . . the problem of untangling from the eccentric manner and the abnormal desolation what is profoundly compelling in Berryman's poetry.

The flat term "normal" seems, oddly, to help. The unmis-

takable, catchy, melancholic manner of the Dream Songs— the gags and ampersands, the jumble of baby-talk, minstrel-talk, slang, high eloquence and quotation, the cubist pretzels of syntax, the dimestore, frail mask of "Henry"— has been adored, imitated, even made into a cult; it has become the "Berrymanishness" of Berryman. But the manner is, I think, more of a cost or exorbitant means than an achievement; it served Berryman as an awkward, huge set of quotation marks, bracketing-off what was petty, disordered, stupid or torn in his life. The manner was an inefficient, spuriously charming machine that could be presented as clearly not-himself: not the deeply literary, high-minded man who had to share his life with a threatened, low, drunken robot of a body. The Dream Songs try to punctuate the difference between the life he seemed to have to live and what he knew was profound and normal within him.

What his best poems give us, then, is himself: a bravely reasonable man of average stature working at the controls of a grotesque machine, which is also himself. When the poem works, this situation lends itself to a range of tones. It can be comic in a rakish, humane way, . . . or it can meditate, gravely and plainly, upon terrible facts. . . . (p. 15)

"Henry's Fate" consists of 45 Dream Songs, a section of about a dozen other poems, a section of unfinished poems and fragments, and a final section of poems about hospitalization, therapy, alcoholism and suicide. The fragments, as the editor explains, are included for what they show about Berryman's working habits and writing plans; except for a few parts of "Washington in Love," they are bad, so very bad in the case of a jocular, mock-epic "The Children: Proemio" to an unwritten long poem, that publication may have been a mistake.

The other poems in this volume cannot be so dismissed; they are not mere sweepings. Rather, there is the characteristic, difficult range of the apish . . . and the nearly angelic. As with earlier work, it takes time and alertness to sort out the posturing from the genuine penetration. This is true because the poems offer so very much of the rhetorical baloney Berryman could not resist—or, perhaps, could not do without—and so very much, too, of his large and compelling mind. Several of the poems start or flare up brilliantly to end lamely. . . .

And again, the lines and poems that are most plain-spoken and the least "like Berryman" often seem to be the deepest, the most realized. The best lines in the title poem of "Henry's Fate" are like that. And also as before the best poems are "confessional"—not always in the current sense of sensational gossip about oneself, but in the older sense of confiding a personal faith or conviction. His faith was in the idea of a form that might seem to embrace his pettiness and exaltation, and make them cohere. . . .

John Berryman's poetic gift was his power to make his whole mind known to his reader: what we feel in his poems is his "awful center." He loved fame, and made us know him. Shelley wrote that "the love of fame is frequently no more than a desire that the feelings of others should confirm, illustrate, and sympathize with our own." In communicating that desire, Berryman was not one of the generous poets, those poets—like, say, Elizabeth Bishop—who create the world for us, generating its forms from what they feel. Berryman was not generous, but expansive, and what he unselfishly gives us is the world of his own soul. (p. 41)

> *Robert Pinsky, "45 Posthumous Dream*

Songs," *in* The New York Times Book Review (© *1977 by The New York Times Company; reprinted by permission), April 3, 1977, pp. 15, 41.*

*   *   *

BIOY CASARES, Adolfo   1914-

Bioy Casares is an Argentinian novelist, short story writer, essayist, and screenwriter. He is an inventive, imaginative writer whose name is frequently linked with Jorge Luis Borges. The two have, in fact, collaborated on film scripts, and like his fellow Argentinian, Bioy Casares is preoccupied with labyrinths and metaphysical puzzles. He has also published under the pseudonyms Martin Sacastru and Javier Miranda, and has collaborated with Borges under the joint pseudonyms H(onorio) Bustos Domecq and B. Suarez Lynch. (See also *CLC*, Vol. 4, and *Contemporary Authors*, Vols. 29-32, rev. ed.)

Borges greatly influenced Adolfo Bioy Casares . . . and collaborated with him on a number of books, including the well-known *Antologia de la literatura fantástica* (1940), a landmark in Spanish American magic realism, to which [Bioy Casares' wife] Silvina Ocampo also contributed. . . . In his collaborations with Borges [Bioy Casares] employs footnotes to create the impression of a pseudo essay and to lend credence to the fantastic events they narrate. Like Borges he uses dreams, doubles, and time reversal. (pp. 221-22)

Bioy's themes include not only magic and temporal fusion but also man-woman relationships, quite often narrated in ironical and satirical fashion. His most famous novel, in whose prologue Borges rejects Ortega's lament about the impossibility of new fictional themes, is *La invención de Morel* (1940), about a scientific machine that projects reproduced reality on space and time, including touch, smell, and sound to give an illusion of everlasting life to the creations of the lonely scientist. (p. 222)

> *Kessel Schwartz, in his* A New History of Spanish American Fiction, *Volume II (copyright © 1971 by University of Miami Press), University of Miami Press, 1971.*

In contemporary Latin American fiction the characters always fail even to communicate with one another. Thus in the novels of Bioy Casares each character is presented as a wholly separate *island*. Sheer conversation between one character and another is like an adventure across a stormy channel, a risky crossing between islands. Standing on one's own island, one can moreover only perceive a fragment of the other island's coastline. Who knows, maybe it is concealing an entire continent? The *other* is ultimately an inscrutable mystery.

Bioy Casares extracts a great deal of fun out of his characters' failure to communicate. His novels and short stories are fundamentally comic, the comedy being based on the vast gap that separates what a character imagines his interlocutor to be from the fact of what he really is. Thus in stories like 'El don supremo' and 'Confidencias de un lobo' the heroes are convinced they have achieved a spectacular success with the girls they respectively encounter only to discover that their motives were notoriously less flattering than they imagined them to be. Even more hair-raising is the dilemma of the narrator of *La invención de Morel* (1940), who falls in love with a woman without suspecting that she is living on a different plane of reality from him al-

together: she turns out to be a sort of holographic image, a three-dimensional, living photograph of her now long-deceased original self. (p. 91)

> *D. P. Gallagher, in his* Modern Latin American Literature *(copyright © 1973 by Oxford University Press; reprinted by permission), Oxford University Press, 1973.*

Since Bustos Domecq does not exist, Argentine Authors Jorge Luis Borges and Adolfo Bioy-Casares had to invent him [for their *Chronicles of Bustos Domecq*]. Why? Because Domecq is the pure incarnation of the middleman between a world gone culturally haywire and the uncomprehending mass of mankind. His function: telling people why they should admire nonsense. This inept critic is a figure of Chaplinesque pathos: a tastemaker totally lacking in taste, a perpetual target of the avant-garde's custard pies.

As this collection of mock essays about mock artists amply demonstrates, no aesthetic theory is too lunatic for Domecq to explain and applaud. . . .

Borges' gnomic stories have, of course, earned him a worldwide following, and he and Bioy-Casares (a longtime friend and disciple) are up to something a bit more ambitious than a parody of a hapless critic. The real target of their often uproarious gibes is modernism—or the part of it that zealously pursues theories of "pure" form into Cloud-Cuckoo-Land. The result, which Domecq never perceives, is invariably monstrous: novels and poems that cannot be read, art that cannot be seen, architecture—freed from the "demands of inhabitability"—that cannot be used.

> *Paul Gray, "Bloodless Coup," in* Time *(reprinted by permission from* Time, *The Weekly Newsmagazine; copyright Time Inc. 1976), March 29, 1976, p. 74.*

*   *   *

BORGES, Jorge Luis   1899-

Argentinian essayist, poet, and short story writer, Borges is considered a master of twentieth-century letters. A measure of his unique genius is the coining of the word "Borgesian" to describe his creations, many of which are characterized by the hallucinatory and fantastic. Borges has collaborated with Adolfo Bioy Casares under the pseudonyms of H(onorio) Bustos Domecq and B. Suarez Lynch. (See also *CLC*, Vols. 1, 2, 3, 4, 6, and *Contemporary Authors*, Vols. 21-24, rev. ed.)

Borges [is] the archetypal writer of the Literature of Exhaustion. . . . (p. 11)

The first proposition of the Literature of Exhaustion [is] that authors can no longer write original literature and perhaps cannot write any literature.

This hypothesis about literature . . . provides the key to Borges's writing. . . .

A critic can most quickly clarify Borges's work, and simultaneously explain the basic features of the Literature of Exhaustion, by describing the Chinese box arrangements in some of his works. (p. 12)

Each box in one of his systems represents either a real or imaginary state of being. The plot of the fiction makes clear the place of each box by showing which boxes it encloses and which boxes enclose it. In "Tlön, Uqbar, Orbis Tertius" the largest, outermost box is Borges, the maker of the whole arrangement. The story itself is the next box, as one looks inside, and in it lies the border between reality and imagination, as one commonly understands these terms. This box is real because it exists in print, imaginary because Borges created it. Next comes the box of the secret society, although the reported inclusion of real people like Berkeley in the society gives it an aura of reality. The society creates the next two boxes: Uqbar, an imaginary land, and Tlön, another imaginary land that supposedly exists in Uqbar's literature. To understand the crucial Tlön layer one must make this visual representation more elaborate by imagining paths leading from this box. One path leads further inward to another box, Orbis Tertius, one more imaginary world. Another leads to the philosophical systems of Tlön. Another leads to the hrönir, an annex of the Tlön box built on the side toward the realistic section of the system. Because human minds create them the hrönir are imaginary, but because of their substantiality they are real. The fourth path from the Tlön box, representing the cone and compass, leads all the way back to the real world, where these objects intrude.

The differences among these four alternatives show what literary exhaustion means. The cone and compass are immediately exhausted—in other words, they cannot be used anymore for literary purposes—because they are material objects and appear in the real world, which cannot be extended in any significant sense. The hrönir and the philosophical systems, being imaginary, can each generate one more layer, but then they are exhausted and do not make possible another box. These three paths represent "exhaustion" in one sense of the word: a condition in which all possibilities have been used up. Orbis Tertius represents exhaustion in the other sense: the method that was used to create it can be used to create an infinite number of possibilities. That is, one can imagine worlds inside it ad infinitum.

Thus, Borges has written a story that belongs to the Literature of Exhaustion because he has based it on a belief that literary possibilities—symbolized by objects in the story—are used up, and he has employed this hypothesis to produce another work of fiction and to imply that the imagination can create endless and inexhaustible possibilities. This story makes another point about the imagination in addition to proclaiming its infinity, and also resolves the apparent contradiction at the base of this kind of literature, by implying that the realms of reality and imagination are less distinct than most people believe. That is, finally the imagination is inexhaustible because it spills over into "reality." The Chinese box system of this story reveals this attribute of imagination: one layer is both real and imaginary; other layers belong to one of these categories but also seem to belong to the other. By looking as naively as possible at this sophisticated arrangement one can pop it into focus, just as a quick second viewing often makes clear the meaning of a visual puzzle. This second glance should reveal that everything in the story as story (rather than as print on a page) is imaginary because Borges created it. Because a reader almost certainly will forget this obvious fact as he tries to sort out the real and imaginary elements in the story and then will realize it again suddenly, Borges dramatically makes his point that these realms cannot be separated at all. He sets this almost inescapable trap for the reader because, as a writer, he believes that the imagination is superior to reality. (pp. 13-15)

In "The Zahir" Borges makes a Chinese box arrangement by using the familiar device of the story within a story, but these stories relate to each other and to some themes in a typically Borgesian way. The frame story's narrator is writing a fantasy that strikingly revivifies the tradition of metaphors that begins with the Anglo-Saxon kennings. These powerful tropes have recently fascinated Borges so much that he has begun to study the language in which they are constructed. Within the frame story, which is brightly ornamented with these metaphors, lies an account of the narrator's discovery of a Zahir, an object that recapitulates, and eventually can replace, the whole universe. Almost at the end of the story appears a reference to the Sufis doggedly reciting names till they become meaningless. These three main elements in the story—the kennings, the Zahir, and the Sufis' repetition of words—all show that language and therefore literature can replace life. (pp. 15-16)

A similar but less sophisticated device appears in Borges's work not as a way to put together a story but as a recurring idea, a thematic equivalent of the Chinese boxes. This is the *regressus in infinitum,* an infinite series. . . . (pp. 16-17)

Borges's dependence on aesthetic subjects and techniques like the Chinese boxes and *regressus in infinitum* may make his work seem a bit limited and precious. Limited it is, but deliberately so, because he sees no value in many possible realistic topics which he deems inappropriate to literature. One should not call his work precious in a pejorative sense. He may work on a small canvas but he works on it exquisitely. The painter of miniatures does not necessarily have less skill than the titanic artist who covers entire walls. It may be useful to enumerate the kinds of subject matter Borges does not use and to explain his reasons for rejecting them or turning them to his own purposes. Then the area he has concerned himself with will stand out in sharper outline.

The topics he has avoided include nearly all the subject matter of realism. . . . He quarrels with realism primarily because it fails to recognize that, because words do not correspond exactly to the real world, a writer cannot connect with that world, so he would do better to pull in his borders and create a coherent, self-contained aesthetic artifact. (pp. 17-18)

Borges also rejects the realistic material that lies closest to a writer's hand: his own life. Some of his early poems do not conform to this generalization, but even they use autobiographical material in a peculiar way. Borges himself does not appear very often in them but he imbues them with his love of Buenos Aires—he called an early volume *Fervor of Buenos Aires*—and of Argentina. . . .

According to Borges, a writer should eschew autobiography because it is part of realism (which for him is prima facie evidence) and because during the act of writing the personality of the writer vanishes and a disembodied spirit replaces it. (p. 19)

[*Realistic*] writers merely reproduce themselves rather than creating something new. He does not say that all literature ultimately is autobiographical, but that realistic literature is futile. Very possibly he also means that a writer has no face —no personality—except his work.

The sociopolitical world does not interest Borges either. (p. 20)

[He] almost completely [avoids] psychological themes and psychological analyses of his characters. Borges's characters perform peculiar, even outrageous, actions but rarely for any discernible motive. Extreme things happen to them.

Reading a Borges story, one feels like a baffled child watching lunatics; one does not empathize with the characters. Rather he watches Borges move them around as he would watch a Grand Master marshal the pieces on a chessboard.

Finally in regard to the subjects he avoids, Borges seems to have little interest in writing historical fiction. This does not mean that his work has no historical ingredients, only that in it he transforms history into an aesthetic construct. That is, according to him "it may be that universal history is the history of a handful of metaphors.". . . He bases *The Book of Imaginary Beings,* seemingly a *jeu d'esprit,* on this view of history as well as on some of the other major principles of his work. A compendium, it presents an ahistorical survey of both Western and Eastern culture that endlessly elaborates a few metaphors. Like his bias against autobiographical literature, his bias against historical literature appears under the surface of "Pierre Menard, Author of the *Quixote.*" This fiction implies that if a man living in a later century can exactly reproduce *Don Quixote,* the original version cannot have been linked in any way with its historical era. He attempts to discredit historical literature because he has a more pervasive antipathy: to time, the material of history.

After he dismisses all of these subjects, Borges has left little except aesthetic themes; his literature basically is about literature, a quality that links him with the Symbolists. Writers of this kind of literature build an artificial construct, rather than rendering in artistic form meaningful details from a meaning-laden world. . . . "The Library of Babel" contains Borges's most vivid exposition of the reason why he creates artificial literature primarily about literature. The library described in the story oppresses a viewer because of its regularity: made of hexagonal cubicles, and having five shelves on each wall, thirty-two books on each shelf, 410 pages in each book, forty lines on each page, eight letters in each line. . . . In this story the universe is a library, and the books, both individually and collectively, mean nothing substantive. The only meaning in the universe derives from its relentless order or, in other words, its artifice.

For example, Borges makes literature from literature by frequently modeling one work on another work. He considers acceptable this strategy and the use of allusions because they repeat earlier literature, whereas he considers memory harmful to writers because it repeats reality. (pp. 20-2)

Borges has also in other ways made literature from literature and from literary theory. In addition to his stories that use Chinese boxes, most of his fictions, and even more clearly his essays, belong in this category. . . . This obvious point need not be belabored, but some of the more interesting examples of it should be cited. He has an unusual trick of writing reviews of imaginary books, which he does, for example, in "The Approach to Al-Mu'tasim". . . . This tactic suggests that the "real" aspect of books, their physical presence, does not matter. (p. 23)

His work develops the theme of literature so extensively and in so many ways that the world begins to evaporate before a reader of his work and a book takes its place. This replacement, another of his favorite motifs, appears, for example, in "Fastitocalon" in *The Book of Imaginary Beings.*

Borges has been interested in myth nearly as long as he has been interested in its kinsman, literature. . . . He . . . equates myth and the world of the imagination, of literature, not the world of archetypes or whatever. *The Book of*

Imaginary Beings contains myth in this special sense, because Borges composed it from bits of earlier literature. However, it is not a handbook of mythology in the usual sense. Misinterpreting Borges's use of "myth" opens the door for fundamental misreading of his work. (p. 24)

Borges understands the arguments against creating a highly aestheticized literature, of divorcing himself as completely as possible from the mundane world in order to try to make pure form. But he deems the dangers far less weighty than the rewards. And even though he occasionally watches and evaluates himself at work, checking his premises, he has for a long time rigorously adhered to his principles. A reader must meet him on these aesthetic grounds, not on the grounds of myth in the usual sense or on any nonliterary grounds like sociology.

In spite of his carefully limited subject matter, Borges does interesting things with genre, especially when he uses a reader's preconceptions about whether or not a certain genre usually is realistic. He does this to make the boundary between reality and imagination seem arbitrary, if not meaningless.

To be specific, in "Tlön, Uqbar, Orbis Tertius" he raises the problem of genre by imitating a genre. Although this is a work of fiction, references to Borges himself and Bioy Casares and the presence of apparent facts make it seem like an essay. An imaginary encyclopedia article, another genre, also plays an important part in the narrative. This imitation serves two purposes. First, it illustrates one sense of exhaustion by implying that the possibilities for original fiction have dried up so that a writer has no choice but to imitate other forms. Second, it tricks the reader by playing on his past reading experience. He expects the truth or at least the writer's version of it from an essay, and even more so from an encyclopedia. But a reader accustomed to opening his *Britannica* or a book of essays when he wants a fact will enter a phantasmagorical world when he opens the pages of "Tlön, Uqbar, Orbis Tertius." Most likely he will immediately wonder whether classifying works into genres will lead to real distinctions, and perhaps he will begin to doubt the reality of other categories. (p. 26)

This genre [fiction] well suits a writer interested primarily in philosophical themes. Among his themes, one of the most important, both to his work and to the Literature of Exhaustion in general, is time. Borges has said, "I think that the central riddle, the central problem of metaphysics —let us call it thinking—is time." In novels the appearance of this theme, even in exotic forms, surprises no one, since it traditionally has been one of the handful of dominant themes in that genre. Borges has never written a novel, but he retains his fascination for this topic. His interest in time does not contradict his antipathy toward realism because his treatment of this theme differs radically from most realists'. Realistic novelists usually consider time to be one of their most useful building blocks since it is a vital constituent of the real world they try to describe, but Borges, an antirealist, argues against the existence of time. He vigorously attacks time, confident that the more he can discredit it, the more discredited will be reality and realism. (pp. 28-9)

Borges does not go unarmed into battle with time. He has read widely in philosophy, though he has chosen his reading to give himself not a conventional training in the history of philosophy but ideas for his writing. He believes that there is a clear-cut argument about this issue. His allies, the idealists, hold an anti-time position, whereas most other philosophers believe that time exists. (p. 29)

Disliking time, Borges almost inevitably dislikes its store-house, memory. Both evils afflict the title character in ''Funes the Memorious,'' which shows how they work in combination. Funes always knows the time precisely without consulting a watch, but his remarkable ability does not please him: he tells others the time in a shrill, mocking voice. Nor does anything else please him. He feels oppressed and he lives like a prisoner, restrained physically by an injury and restrained mentally by his constant awareness of time. His other peculiarity, an unerring and all-encompassing memory, burdens him even more. Remembrances pile up in his mind until they leave no room for thought. He continually recalls things, shuffles them by converting numbers into things, catalogues his memories. Despite the illusion of newness that these projects afford, he merely repeats old things. This futility indicates memory's flaw; rather than getting on with the task of creating infinite new possibilities, it repeats old ones. At last Funes fills with memories so that he dies, appropriately of congestion. The manner of his death states a warning about the unendurable pressure of memory. (p. 33)

Borges much less frequently disparages the other main constituent of the real world, space. He does, however, attack it in ''The Zahir,'' using a clever two-part strategy. First, he reduces the world to a single thing. Then he obliterates that thing, thereby completely destroying the real world. (p. 34)

Borges distinguishes among kinds of patterns, some valuable and others valueless. He approves of purely aesthetic patterns clearly presented as such. For example, he favors a patterned prose style, and he certainly does not write chaotically and slovenly. He meticulously composes his burnished works. He also carefully orders the body of his work by discreetly using repetition to create patterns of thematic resonances. Borges makes his own patterns, but other writers mistakenly find patterns either in the world or in literary conventions. The realists sometimes see patterns that do not exist; for example, psychological writers presume to display the etiology of their characters' personalities. Traditionalists also err by selling themselves into bondage to literary conventions.

Borges's objection to patterns becomes clearer if one analyzes his references to a specific kind of pattern, symmetry. He disapproves of symmetry, first, because it is an important attribute of reality. (pp. 35-6)

Symmetry oppresses none of Borges's characters more than Erik Lönnrot in ''Death and the Compass,'' who begins by worshipping it. This bookish detective sees a symmetrical pattern developing in a series of murders. Because the person who kills a delegate to a Talmudic conference leaves a note saying ''the first letter of the Name has been uttered,'' Lönnrot anticipates three more murders to fill out the ''name.'' He works out one symmetry by plotting the first three murders on a map and then adding the appropriate fourth point to the equilateral triangle. He deduces the day of the last murder by realizing that each of the first three happened on the third day of a month. When his vectors of space and time converge and he goes to apprehend the criminal, he confirms his reasoning based on symmetries: ''the house of the villa of Triste-le-Roy abounded in pointless symmetries''.... But the scenario of this drama of symmetries turns into an elaborate trap laid by his ene-

mies. Basing their plans on Lönnrot's obsession with symmetry, they have brought him to their lair to kill him. (pp. 36-7)

Borges often signals his disapproval of people who believe in these negative themes. Such characters simply die. The villains kill Lönnrot, and Dahlmann in ''The South'' is about to die as the story ends because he has allowed himself to be drawn into a knife fight that he has no chance of winning. Borges's sturdy and persistent opposition to the limited and realistic themes of time, memory, space, and symmetry suggests that he just as strongly favors infinite and idealistic themes. (p. 37)

His many-pronged attack on realism and reality proceeds slowly against an implacable enemy. Sometimes he makes imaginative creations seem real, and reality seem imaginative. As an idealist, he feels justified in doing this. He told L. S. Dembo, ''I wonder why a dream or an idea should be less real than this table for example''.... Besides the obvious source, Berkeley, the influence of Schopenhauer, especially his belief that the will produced the world, led Borges to this belief. A writer who accepts idealism gains primarily an increased number of possibilities for subject matter, since the imagination can create an infinity of objects.... Thus, the impossibility of distinguishing between the real and the imagined frees a writer from the realists' compunction to describe the world accurately, so he can write in any way he likes about anything. (pp. 38-9)

In his fictions various kinds of imaginary constructs replace the world or part of the world. For instance, the lottery of Babylon starts on a small scale, but it gradually grows until it is the only reality in Babylon, or until Babylon has no reality. The citizens of Babylon are disturbed that this lottery has replaced their previous lives. They can neither escape nor control this seemingly omnipresent lottery that denies them all freedom of choice. Borges objects on simpler grounds: the lottery is not an aesthetic construct but a real one and therefore inherently unsatisfying. He also presents characters who act in a certain way because they are analogues of other literary characters. These cases appeal to Borges because they are literary. In these examples works of literature actually determine action that appears to be freely performed. Also in these examples the real world, according to the norms of the fictions, gives way to the imaginary world. (pp. 39-40)

Borges frequently notes, always positively, the conjunction of dream and literature, which makes possible the replacement of reality by literature....

Dream and world will almost inevitably resemble each other in some ways, however, because the world, as well as literature, is a dream. (p. 42)

In the most famous of Borges's dream fictions, ''The Circular Ruins,'' a hero goes to a ruined temple and begins slowly, meticulously to dream a man. When he succeeds, the man he has dreamed apparently becomes a part of reality, but soon the dreamer realizes that that is a dubious honor because he himself has been dreamed by another person. This story offers more than a shrewd preparation for a trick ending. The circularity of the ruins, undoubtedly important because Borges mentions it in the title, provides a hint as to this fiction's basic meaning. Like the fearful sphere in its circularity and its status as the only obviously real thing in the universe, this ruin represents infinity. The plot of this fiction represents the same thing because the dreamer dreaming a dreamer begins an infinite regress.

Thus, these devices demonstrate a now familiar point: literature dependent on dreams has more possibilities than literature dependent on reality, and perhaps its possibilities are unlimited. This meaning in turn suggests the premise on which Borges bases his development of the topic of dreams: dream, world, and literature ultimately merge into one entity.

This premise typifies idealism, a philosophy that has been hinted at by Borges's development of some of the themes already discussed. His debts to Berkeley, Bradley, Schopenhauer, and other thinkers in this tradition should also be clear by now. (p. 43)

The other main ideas that Borges approves have less, or no, connection with idealism. One of the most peculiar notions he toys with is that only one man exists in the world, and he is all men. He states this succinctly in "The Immortal": "one single immortal man is all men".... In his catalogues of various men who have held ideas in common Borges hints at the similarity of several men, a less extreme version of this idea. These catalogues also apply this idea to the realm in which it becomes meaningful for Borges, literature.... He uses this idea, too, against realism, for a world populated by only one man hardly suits the concept of identity, which is important to the realists' world-view. The belief that there is only one author contradicts another premise of realism, that persons with definite identities living in definite times and places wrote each work of literature.

Borges aims secretly at realism as he develops his theme of the relation between language and reality. Realism partly depends on the belief that language can mirror reality, but he will not accept this belief. At least he disputes it in regard to the language of men. The narrator of "The God's Script" considers that "in the language of a god every word would enunciate that infinite concatenation of facts".... But man falls far short of this ideal; he cannot capture the concatenation of the universe in many words, much less in one. Man sometimes finds instead that his words have only the barest purchase on things, or no purchase at all. (pp. 44-5)

Words can also be too powerful for the realist, altering reality instead of reporting on it. In "The God's Script" Borges mentions a combination of fourteen words that make whoever utters them omnipotent. Words can further confound realists by adding to reality. A combination of letters created one of the imaginary beings, the Golem.... In "The Library of Babel" Borges describes the utmost power of words. Here words have completely taken over the universe. These attributes of language frustrate the realist but delight the idealist, because, like many of the other ideas Borges favors, they create a myriad of possibilities.

These last few themes help make Borges's fictional world insubstantial and Protean. He usually subordinates the theme of metamorphosis to other themes like idealism or dreams, but once in a while it appears independently. (pp. 45-6)

Borges considers the world to be in a constant flux rather than fixed for eternity. This notion would meet with little argument, but his process theory of art is more controversial. On this matter he seems Romantic, emphasizing the process of creating art, rather than the completed product, in order to glorify the mind that created art. Process intrigued the Romantics because of their adulation of inspiration, but Borges has more complicated reasons for empha-

sizing process, as this examination of his themes should indicate. His world constantly changes because the unreality of the "real" world forces him continually to create his own world of art. The alternative emphasis on product, a Classical position, binds writers to traditional rules of composition and forces them carefully to imitate "real" objects. Both rules and imitation repel Borges. His position on these questions appears in "The Secret Miracle." As long as Hladik continues to tinker with his play, to keep writing it, he remains alive. When a product issues from the process he dies.

Although Borges sometimes presents his ideas discursively, even in his fictions, he also frequently develops them by means of images. Besides varying his presentation, this imagistic method, especially in the case of his major images, gives him another way to achieve repetition and thereby attack time.... The labyrinth, the mirror, and the circle are his most important images and also the most closely related to the Literature of Exhaustion.

The labyrinth's complexity results partly from its inherent nature and partly from the frequency with which this image occurs. This complexity makes it necessary to examine it in a large number of contexts. By understanding the labyrinth one can understand much of Borges's art. Appropriately, something that has a hidden answer itself reveals the hidden answer to his work, this condition being a Borgesian *regressus in infinitum*. Most critics have been unable to operate convincingly in the face of these difficulties; they see only one facet of this many-faceted image. Most of them focus on the negative aspects of the labyrinth. (pp. 46-7)

For one thing, their comments are limited to the labyrinth's role as a symbol of the world's chaos. If it meant only this, it would be a banal image, its banality multiplied by each appearance. Typically, Borges also adds an aesthetic dimension to this image's meaning. Realism's invalidity follows as a corollary from the theorem that the world is labyrinthine. (p. 47)

But the labyrinth also has a positive side because of its connection with the Literature of Exhaustion. One's guide to this aspect of it must be John Barth, since he seems to be the only critic who has recognized it. He understands this image more fully than other critics because he places it in its proper context instead of looking at it in isolation. He sees, as no one else does, that a person in a labyrinth must exhaust all possibilities of choice (of direction) before he can reach its center.... In other words, one response to the depletion of literature, though still not the best, is to write so as to exhaust all the possibilities presented to one. In this light, the labyrinth appears positive, because successfully dealing with it symbolizes a valuable literary goal. This feature makes up for some of the frustration in store for everyone who tries to work his way through the labyrinth of the world. (p. 48)

The center of the labyrinth, the goal for which the hero endures the almost endless wrong turns, represents a better way to create literature. Critics who discuss only the labyrinth's negative aspect have not seen this goal. Sheer luck cannot be depended upon to find the center, and the exhaustion of possibilities constitutes only a holding action till a better way is found. No, one should expect the labyrinth to have a secret key. The ubiquity of this secret key theme in Borges's work contributes another vital clue to the meaning of the labyrinth, and again most of the critics have missed it. (pp. 48-9)

It is much easier to write about the necessity of finding one's way through the labyrinth without actually making the trip. This abstruse idea becomes clearer if one remembers that the Literature of Exhaustion produces fresh work by pretending that literature is depleted and by using this situation as material, rather than facing the depletion directly. More specifically, Barth points out that Borges need not actually write the encyclopedia of Tlön; he merely has to state the idea. The hidden key, then, is to make labyrinths instead of trying to solve them. (pp. 49-50)

In Borges's work the mirror contrasts with the labyrinth. If the latter represents the Literature of Exhaustion, the former represents realism. The mirror naturally symbolizes realism since it imitates existing objects, as eighteenth century literary theory indicates. Borges states the contrast between mirrors and labyrinths (in this case, a labyrinthine book) in the first sentence of "Tlön, Uqbar, Orbis Tertius," which also is the first sentence of both *Ficciones* and *Labyrinths:* "I owe the discovery of Uqbar to the conjunction of a mirror and an encyclopedia." (pp. 50-1)

To Borges, even when he was a child, mirrors meant the same thing they mean to him now, and they caused the same fear, as he told Richard Burgin. . . . In a disconcerting essay, "The Draped Mirrors," he confirms this: "as a child, I felt before large mirrors that same horror of a spectral duplication or multiplication of reality". . . . Perhaps the young Borges also spurned the mirroring of reality in the realistic works in his father's fine English library. It also would be interesting to know how he would have reacted as a child to a fairytale-like story about mirrors, "Fauna of Mirrors," that he tells in *The Book of Imaginary Beings*. In it the mirror-people are banished to their mirrors and forced to repeat the actions of men because of their invasions of the human kingdom, with which they had previously lived in harmony despite their differences. The storyteller predicts that the Fish will be the first of the mirror-people to give up this mimetic function. If so, they will become like writers of the Literature of Exhaustion.

The complications of Borges's circle imagery arise chiefly because he uses it both to attack the realists and to defend his own kind of literature. That is, like his labyrinths, his circles sometimes are positive, sometimes negative. Two discordant properties of circles cause this ambiguity when he relates them to literature. A circle shares with the kind of art he favors its virtue of self-containment. But if one imagines either the circle moving or someone moving around it, the starting point will eventually be reached again, making it repetitious and finite, like realism and other depleted types of literature.

The essay on the Uroboros in *The Book of Imaginary Beings* lists objects whose circularity represents infinity: the Greek conception of the ocean, the world-circling serpent, etc. Borges uses a circle in "The God's Script" to describe a mystical union with the divinity. The wheel that appears during that union is everywhere at once and infinite and contains opposites. A third positive use of the circle image occurs in "The Circular Ruins," where Borges connects it with idealism because the main character goes to a circular ruin to dream a man. This last example refers to a self-enclosed dream world that the real world cannot touch. In Borges's work infinity, timelessness and dreamlikeness are all qualities of the same type of art. In "The Circular Ruins" Borges adds a variation to his circle imagery. When the dreamer learns that he, too, is dreamed, one can picture

the situation as a circle within a circle, perhaps ad infinitum.

This last phenomenon, oddly, appears also in one of the negative uses of the circle image. The outer circle in "The Secret Miracle" is Hladik's circular delirium; the inner circle is his play. The play's repetition makes it negative. The seven gongs of the clock, the light from the setting sun, the Hungarian music and the words that open the play are repeated at its end. Thus, the error of Hladik that leads to his death, finishing the play, like so many of the details in Borges's fiction, can be put meaningfully into an aesthetic context. Hladik's error shows that art must not be circular or otherwise finite. (pp. 51-3)

Some of Borges's themes and the limitations he imposes on his subject matter help shape his characters. His lack of interest in psychology, it will be recalled, makes most of his characters two-dimensional. He says, with some accuracy, "I'm afraid there are no characters in my work. I'm afraid *I'm* the only character." His interest in philosophical topics accounts for the large number of intellectuals in his work, and his aesthetic interests call for many readers and writers. (pp. 53-4)

Among his most significant characters are the doubles. The essay on the double in *The Book of Imaginary Beings* sketches in the background of these characters and gives many examples, both legendary and literary. Among the inspirations he mentions for the concept is one of his own favorite images, the mirror. His own doubles, however, differ from most other doubles in literature because he creates them to make a metaphysical, and ultimately an aesthetic, point rather than a moral point. That is, he uses doubles to refute the belief that people have clearly defined identities, a major premise of realism. His three most important doubles are composed of a murderer and a victim. . . .

Erik Lönnrot, the detective, and Red Scharlach, the criminal, in "Death and the Compass" clearly are, respectively, victim and murderer, but only their names indicate that they are doubles. Because *scharlach* is German for "scarlet," *rot* is German for "red" and *Erik* almost invariably suggests "the Red," their names become Red Red and Red Red. (p. 54)

Borges is the quintessential writer of the Literature of Exhaustion. Barth and Nabokov have always been interested in a staple theme of realistic fiction, love, and this has tempered their literary experiments and kept a door open for their return to a more realistic mode. Borges has, however, shown little interest in this theme. (p. 59)

Attempts to discredit [Borges] can be answered quite well. He writes mainly about literary matters, but Henry James's dictum that we must grant a writer his donnée should justify that attribute. The other serious charge, that he repeats himself, has a good deal of truth to it. But his philosophical reason for being repetitious probably justifies it. . . .

His poetry seems quite undistinguished. His early contribution to Ultraism may have been important in the history of Spanish literature, but considered from an international viewpoint, Ultraism differs only slightly from the earlier experiments of the Imagists. . . .

His essays are more impressive, because of their grace, originality and wit. The philosophical ones may be too idiosyncratic, because of the ideas they defend and the thinkers they revere, to hold up as philosophy. They do not belong to this category, however, for Borges writes about the ideas and thinkers who have the greatest literary possibilities for him, not those who are the most impressive philosophically. (p. 60)

The crown of his works is his fiction. Judged in almost any way, it qualifies for the first rank in contemporary literature. The originality of his forms and ideas is indeed impressive. He carefully polishes these works, using a magisterial technique and deftly combining the elements of fiction. And they rank high in a category often ignored by critics: they delight a reader, both because they entertain him and because they provide for him a vicarious experience of a subtle mind at work on fascinating matters.

Besides his work's intrinsic value, it also has heuristic value, since he has inspired many other contemporary writers. He seems to have founded the Literature of Exhaustion, identifying its opponent to be realism and working out its basic themes and techniques. A reader who can thoroughly understand "Tlön, Uqbar, Orbis Tertius" will have a good grasp of this whole movement. (pp. 60-1)

> *John Stark, "Jorge Luis Borges," in his* The Literature of Exhaustion *(reprinted by permission of the Publisher; copyright 1974 by Duke University Press, Durham, North Carolina), Duke University Press, 1974, pp. 11-61.*

[Borges'] driest paragraph is somehow compelling. His fables are written from a height of intelligence less rare in philosophy and physics than in fiction. Furthermore, he is, at least for anyone whose taste runs to puzzles or pure speculation, delightfully entertaining. The question is, I think, whether or not Borges' lifework, arriving in a lump now (he was born in 1899 and since his youth has been an active and honored figure in Argentine literature), can serve, in its gravely considered oddity, as any kind of clue to the way out of the dead-end narcissism and downright trashiness of present American fiction. . . .

Borges' narrative innovations spring from a clear sense of technical crisis. For all his modesty and reasonableness of tone, he proposes some sort of essential revision in literature itself. The concision of his style and the comprehensiveness of his career . . . produce a strangely terminal impression: he seems to be the man for whom literature has no future. . . .

A constant bookishness gives Borges' varied production an unusual consistency. His stories have the close texture of argument; his critical articles have the suspense and tension of fiction. The criticism collected in *Other Inquisitions, 1937-1952* almost all takes the form of detection, of uncovering what was secret. He looks for, and locates, the hidden pivots of history: the moment (in Iceland in 1225) when a chronicler first pays tribute to an enemy the very line (in Chaucer in 1382) when allegory yields to naturalism. His interest gravitates toward the obscure, the forgotten: John Wilkins, the 17th-century inventor *ab nihilo* of an analytical language; J. W. Dunne, the 20th-century proponent of a grotesque theory of time; Layamon, the 13th-century poet isolated between the death of Saxon culture and the birth of the English language. Where an arcane quality does not already exist, Borges injects it. (pp. 170-71)

Implacably, Borges reduces everything to a condition of mystery. His gnomic style and encyclopedic supply of allusions generate a kind of inverse illumination, a Gothic atmosphere in which the most lucid and famous authors loom somewhat menacingly. (p. 171)

The tracing of hidden resemblances, of philosophical genealogies, is Borges' favorite mental exercise. Out of his vast reading he distills a few related images, whose parallelism, tersely presented, has the force of a fresh thought. "Perhaps universal history is the history of a few metaphors. I should like to sketch one chapter of that history," he writes in "Pascal's Sphere," and goes on to compile, in less than four pages, twenty-odd instances of the image of a sphere "whose center is everywhere and whose circumference nowhere." These references are arranged like a plot, beginning with Xenophanes, who joyously substituted for the anthropomorphic gods of Greece a divine and eternal Sphere, and ending with Pascal, who, in describing nature as "an infinite sphere" had first written and then rejected the word *"effroyable"*—"a frightful sphere." Many of Borges' genealogies trace a degeneration: he detects a similar "magnification to nothingness" in the evolutions of theology and of Shakespeare's reputation; he watches an Indian legend succumb, through its successive versions, to the bloating of unreality. He follows in the works of Léon Bloy the increasingly desperate interpretations of a single phrase in St. Paul—*"per speculum in aenigmate"* ("through a glass darkly"). (p. 172)

Borges is not an antiseptic pathologist of the irrational; he is himself susceptible to infection. His connoisseurship has in it a touch of madness. In his "Kafka and His Precursors," he discovers, in certain parables and anecdotes by Zeno, Han Yü, Kierkegaard, Browning, Bloy, and Lord Dunsany, a prefiguration of Kafka's tone. He concludes that each writer creates his own precursors. . . .

As a literary critic, Borges demonstrates much sensitivity and sense. The American reader of [*Other Inquisitions, 1937-1952*] will be gratified by the generous amount of space devoted to writers of the English language. Borges, from within the Spanish literary tradition of "dictionaries and rhetoric," is attracted by the oneiric and hallucinatory quality he finds in North American, German, and English writing. He values Hawthorne and Whitman for their intense unreality, and bestows special fondness upon the English writers he read in his boyhood. The *fin-de-siècle* and Edwardian giants, whose reputations are generally etiolated, excite Borges afresh each time he rereads them. . . . (p. 173)

[Of] this generation none is dearer to Borges than Chesterton, in whom he finds, beneath the surface of dogmatic optimism, a disposition like Kafka's. . . . Much in Borges' fiction that suggests Kafka in fact derives from Chesterton. As critic and artist both, Borges mediates between the postmodern present and the colorful, prolific, and neglected pre-moderns.

Of the moderns themselves, of Yeats, Eliot, and Rilke, of Proust and Joyce, he has, at least in *Other Inquisitions,* little to say. Pound and Eliot, he asserts in passing, practice "the deliberate manipulation of Anachronisms to produce an appearance of eternity" (which seems, if true at all, rather incidentally so), and he admires Valéry less for his work than for his personality, "the symbol of a man who is infinitely sensitive to every fact." The essays abound in insights delivered parenthetically—"God must not theologize"; "to fall in love is to create a religion that has a fallible god"—but their texts as a whole do not open outward into enlightenment. Whereas, say, Eliot's relatively tentative considerations offer to renew a continuing tradition of literary criticism. Borges' tight arrangements seem a bizarre specialization of the tradition. His essays have a quality I can only call *sealed*. They are structured like mazes and, like mirrors, they reflect back and forth on one another. There is frequent repetition of the adjectives and phrases that denote Borges' favorite notions of mystery, of secrecy, of "intimate ignorance." From his immense reading he has distilled a fervent narrowness. The same parables, the same quotations recur; one lengthy passage from Chesterton is reproduced three times. (pp. 174-75)

Turning from Borges' criticism to his fiction, one senses the liberation he must have felt upon entering "the paradise of the tale." For there is something disturbing as well as fascinating, something distorted and strained about his literary essays. His ideas border on delusions; the dark hints—of a cult of books, of a cabalistic unity hidden in history—that he so studiously develops are special to the corrupt light of libraries and might vanish outdoors. It is uncertain how seriously he intends his textual diagrams, which seem ciphers for concealed emotions. Borges crowds into the margins of others' books passion enough to fill blank pages; his essays all tend to open inward, disclosing an obsessed imagination and a proud, Stoic, almost cruelly masculine personality.

Dreamtigers, a collection of paragraphs, sketches, poems, and apocryphal quotations titled in Spanish *El Hacedor (The Maker),* succeeds in time the creative period of narrative fiction his essays foreshadow. It is frankly the miscellany of an aging man. (pp. 175-76)

One feels in *Dreamtigers* a calm, an intimation of truce, a tranquil fragility. Like so many last or near-last works—like *The Tempest, The Millionairess,* or "Investigations of a Dog"—*Dreamtigers* preserves the author's life-long concerns, but drained of urgency; horror has yielded to a resigned humorousness. These sketches can be read for their grace and wit but scarcely for narrative excitement; the most exciting of them, "Ragnarök," embodies Borges' most terrible vision, of an imbecilic God or body of gods. But it occurs within a dream, and ends easily: "We drew our heavy revolvers—all at once there were revolvers in the dream—and joyously put the Gods to death."

The second half of this slim volume consists of poems, late and early. Poetry was where Borges' ramifying literary career originally took root. The translations, by Harold Morland, into roughly four-beat and intermittently rhymed lines, seem sturdy and clear, and occasional stanzas must approximate very closely the felicity of the original. . . . (p. 178)

Together, the prose and poetry of *Dreamtigers* afford some glimpses into Borges' major obscurities—his religious concerns and his affective life. Physical love, when it appears at all in his work, figures as something remote, like an ancient religion. . . . Though *Dreamtigers* contains two fine poems addressed to women—Susana Soca and Elvira de Alvear—they are eulogies couched in a tone of heroic affection not different from the affection with which he writes elsewhere of male friends like Alfonso Reyes and Macedonio Fernández. This is at the opposite pole from homosexuality; femaleness, far from being identified with, is felt as a local estrangement that blends with man's cosmic estrangement. There are two prose sketches that, by another writer, might have shown some erotic warmth, some surrender to femininity. In one, he writes of Julia, a "sombre girl" with "an unbending body," in whom he sensed "an intensity that was altogether foreign to the erotic." In their

walks together, he must have talked about mirrors, for now (in 1931) he has learned that she is insane and has draped her mirrors because she imagines that his reflection has replaced her own. In the other, he writes of Delia Elena San Marco, from whom he parted one day beside "a river of vehicles and people." They did not meet again, and in a year she was dead. From the casualness of their unwitting farewell, he concludes, tentatively, that we are immortal. "For if souls do not die, it is right that we should not make much of saying goodbye."

It would be wrong to think that Borges dogmatically writes as an atheist. God is often invoked by him, not always in an ironical or pantheistic way. . . . While Christianity is not dead in Borges, it *sleeps* in him, and its dreams are fitful. His ethical allegiance is to pre-Christian heroism, to Stoicism, to "the doctrines of Zeno's Porch and . . . the sagas," to the harsh gaucho ethos celebrated in the Argentine folk poem of Martín Fierro. Borges is a pre-Christian whom the memory of Christianity suffuses with premonitions and dread. He is European in everything except the detachment with which he views European civilization, as something intrinsically strange—a heap of relics, a universe of books without a central clue. (pp. 180-81)

Perhaps Latin America, which has already given us the absolute skepticism of Machado de Assis, is destined to reënact the intellectual patterns of ancient Greece. Borges' voracious and vaguely idle learning, his ecumenic and problematical and unconsoling theology, his willingness to reconsider the most primitive philosophical questions, his tolerance of superstition in both himself and others, his gingerly and regretful acknowledgment of women and his disinterest in the psychological and social worlds that women dominate, his almost Oriental modesty, his final solitude, his serene pride—this constellation of Stoic attributes, mirrored in the southern hemisphere, appears inverted and frightful. (p. 182)

The great achievement of his art is his short stories. (p. 183)

"The Library of Babel," which appears in *Ficciones,* is wholly fantastic, yet refers to the librarian's experience of books. Anyone who has been in the stacks of a great library will recognize the emotional aura, the wearying impression of an inexhaustible and mechanically ordered chaos, that suffuses Borges' mythical universe, "composed of an indefinite, perhaps an infinite, number of hexagonal galleries, with enormous ventilation shafts in the middle, encircled by very low railings." Each hexagon contains twenty shelves, each shelf thirty-two books, each book four hundred and ten pages, each page forty lines, each line eighty letters. The arrangement of these letters is almost uniformly chaotic and formless. The nameless narrator of "The Library of Babel" sets forward, pedantically, the history of philosophical speculation by the human beings who inhabit this inflexible and inscrutable cosmos, which is equipped, apparently for their convenience, with spiral stairs, mirrors, toilets, and lamps ("The light they emit is insufficient, incessant").

This monstrous and comic model of the universe contains a full range of philosophical schools—idealism, mysticism, nihilism. . . . (p. 185)

Though the Library appears to be eternal, the men within it are not, and they have a history punctuated by certain discoveries and certain deductions now considered axiomatic. Five hundred years ago, in an upper hexagon, two pages of homogeneous lines were discovered that within a century were identified as "a Samoyed-Lithuanian dialect of

Guaraní, with classical Arabic inflections" and translated. The contents of these two pages—"notions of combinational analysis"—led to the deduction that the Library is total; that is, its shelves contain all possible combinations of the orthographic symbols. . . . (p. 186)

The Library of Babel . . . has an adamant solidity. Built of mathematics and science, it will certainly survive the weary voice describing it, and outlast all its librarians, already decimated, we learn in a footnote, by "suicide and pulmonary diseases." We move, with Borges, beyond psychology, beyond the human, and confront, in his work, the world atomized and vacant. Perhaps not since Lucretius has a poet so definitely felt men as incidents in space.

What are we to make of him? The economy of his prose, the tact of his imagery, the courage of his thought are there to be admired and emulated. In resounding the note of the marvellous last struck in English by Wells and Chesterton, in permitting infinity to enter and distort his imagination, he has lifted fiction away from the flat earth where most of our novels and short stories still take place. Yet discouragingly large areas of truth seem excluded from his vision. Though the population of the Library somehow replenishes itself, and "fecal necessities" are provided for, neither food nor fornication is mentioned—and in truth they are not generally seen in libraries. I feel in Borges a curious implication: the unrealities of physical science and the senseless repetitions of history have made the world outside the library an uninhabitable vacuum. Literature—that European empire augmented with translations from remote kingdoms—is now the only world capable of housing and sustaining new literature. Is this too curious? Did not Eliot recommend forty years ago, in reviewing *Ulysses,* that new novels be retellings of old myths? Is not the greatest of modern novels, *Remembrance of Things Past,* about its own inspiration? Have not many books already been written from within Homer and the Bible? Did not Cervantes write from within Ariosto and Shakespeare from within Holinshed? Borges, by predilection and by program, carries these inklings toward a logical extreme: the view of books as, in sum, an alternate creation, vast, accessible, highly colored, rich in arcana, possibly sacred. Just as physical man, in his cities, has manufactured an environment whose scope and challenge and hostility eclipse that of the natural world, so literate man has heaped up a counterfeit universe capable of supporting life. Certainly the traditional novel as a transparent imitation of human circumstance has "a distracted or tired air." Ironic and blasphemous as Borges' hidden message may seem, the texture and method of his creations, though strictly inimitable, answer to a deep need in contemporary fiction—the need to confess the fact of artifice. (pp. 187-88)

> *John Updike, in his* Picked-Up Pieces *(copyright © 1975 by John Updike; reprinted by permission of Alfred A. Knopf, Inc.), Knopf, 1975, pp. 169-88.*

Suddenly, and without logical and convincing reasons, a culture produces in a few years a series of creators who spiritually fertilize each other, who emulate and challenge and surpass each other until, also suddenly, there enters a period of drying up or of mere prolongation through imitators and inferior successors.

That chance seems to have manifested itself in modest but clearly perceptible proportions in the cultural zone of the River Plate in a period that runs approximately from 1920 to the present. There, without too many premonitory signs,

the dimension of the fantastic bursts forth in the principal works of Jorge Luis Borges. It erupts in Borges with a force so compelling that, seen from outside of the River Plate, it appears to concentrate itself almost exclusively in his works. We in Argentina, however, situate Borges's narrative within a context which contains important precursorial and contemporary figures . . .; even before Borges the fantastic was already a familiar and important genre in our midst. (pp. 527-28)

In Jorge Luis Borges, the leading figure of our fantastic literature, misunderstandings accumulate, usually to his great delight. I will limit myself here to pointing out that what some literary critics admire above all in Borges is a genius of geometrical invention, a maker of literary crystals whose condensation responds to exact mathematical laws of logic. Borges has been the first to insist on that rigorous construction of things which tend to appear, on the surface, as absurd and aleatory. The fantastic, as it appears in Borges's stories, makes one think of a relentless geometrical theorem—a theorem perfectly capable of demonstrating that the sum of the square of the angles of a triangle equals the execution of Madame DuBarry. Stories such as "The Circular Ruins," "The Garden of Forking Paths" and "The Library of Babel" reflect this type of theorem construction, which would seem to hide a secret dread not only of what Lugones called strange forces, but also of the imagination's own powers, powers which in Borges are subjected immediately to a rigorous intellectual conditioning.

Nonetheless, others of us feel that despite this rational rejection of the fantastic in its most irreducible and incoherent manifestations, Borges's intuition and sensitivity attest to its presence in a good portion of his stories, where the intellectual superstructure does not manage to, nor does it probably want to, deny that presence. When Borges entitles a collection of stories *Ficciones* or *Artifices,* he is misleading us at the same time that he winks a conspiratorial eye at us; he is playing with that old ideal of every writer, the ideal of having at least some readers capable of suspecting a second version of each text. I will limit myself, of necessity, to one example which hits close to home. In his story "The Secret Miracle" Borges plays with the idea that in certain circumstances a man can enter into another dimension of time and live a year or a century during what other men live as a second or an hour. There is already a story based on this idea in a medieval Spanish text, *El Conde Lucanor,* and Borges himself uses as an epigraph to his story a fragment from the Koran which reflects the same concept. The theme is also dealt with in the psychology of oneiric life, which shows that certain dreams encompass multiple episodes that would demand considerable time to be carried out consecutively, and that, nonetheless, the complex plot of such dreams can end, for example, with a shot from a gun which abruptly awakens us and makes us realize that someone just knocked at the door. It is clear that the dream has been integrally constructed in order to lead to that supposed shot from a revolver, a fact which obliges one to admit that the dream's fulfillment has been almost instantaneous while the fact of dreaming it seemed to transpire over a long period of time. In other words, one could say that on certain occasions we slip into a different time, and those occasions can be, as is always the case with the fantastic, trivial and even absurd.

But Borges does not want things to be trivial and absurd, at least not in his stories, and "The Secret Miracle" is based once again on the rational and erudite crystallization of something which others grasp only in its unrefined state. The story relates that Jaromir Hladik, a Jewish writer condemned to death by the Nazis, awaits with anguish the day of his execution by firing squad. This man has written philosophical texts in which the notion of time is examined and discussed, and he has begun a play whose ending suggests that the work is circular, that it repeats itself interminably. On the eve of his execution Hladik asks God to grant him one more year of life in order to finish this play, which will justify his existence and assure his immortality. During the night he dreams that the time has been given to him, but the next morning he realizes that it was only a dream, since the soldiers come and take him to the firing squad. In the moment that the rifles take aim at his chest Hladik continues to think about one of the characters in his play; and in that same moment the physical universe becomes immobile, the soldiers do not shoot, and the smoke of Hladik's last cigarette forms a small petrified cloud in the air. Only Hladik can know that the miracle has been fulfilled and that, without moving from his place, thinking it instead of writing it, he has been granted the year he had asked for to complete his play. During the course of this year Hladik creates and re-creates scenes, he changes the characters, he eliminates and adds on. Finally, he needs to find only one word, an epithet. He finds it, and the soldiers shoot. For them only an instant has passed.

This theme, which we also find in Ambrose Bierce's admirable story "An Occurrence at Owl Creek," is not, as Borges's story might pretend, simply a literary artifice. I have already noted the frequent presence of this theme in literature and in dreams, and I have even included it in a passage of my own story, "The Pursuer"; in my case, however, I have no reason to obscure the authenticity of my personal experience and to create of it an ingenious superstructure of fiction. In my story what happens is exactly the same as what has happened to me various times in analogous circumstances. (pp. 528-30)

I think that at this point you have an idea of our way of living and writing the fantastic in the River Plate area. . . . (p. 530)

> *Julio Cortázar, "The Present State of Fiction in Latin America," translated by Margery A. Safir, in* Books Abroad *(copyright 1976 by the University of Oklahoma Press), Vol. 50, No. 3, Summer, 1976, pp. 533-40.*

In Praise of Darkness . . . is the work of a man facing the dark of blindness. . . . [The] mood is that of late life, but the tone is relaxed, the manner below declamation but above speech, and the texture a kind of lyric conversation. Even an ability to follow no more than the sounds of Spanish will reveal in the parallel (and definitive) Spanish text, the long vowels which bear a gravity sometimes missed in the English.

Borges, as ever, is openly and winningly elusive. In his preface he writes:

> Time has led me to the use of certain devices: . . . to feign slight uncertainties, for, although reality is exact, memory is not; to narrate events (this I got from Kipling and the Icelandic sagas) as if I did not wholly understand them; to bear in mind that the rules I have just set down need not always be followed and that in time they will have to be changed.

The cool confession of craft and the acceptance of such pragmatism give Borges the authority of a conjuror. He is a poet who builds on his knowledge of what is to happen and the reader's dependence upon him through ignorance of the outcome. In "The Gauchos" he offers eighteen statements defining a composite view of the precise nature of their way of life. Seemingly the bold distinctions and the removing of misunderstandings are there to clarify our picture of these men. Then, the penultimate line reveals that the whole procedure has not been to establish a case but to deceive us into building an acceptable factual picture which Borges tugs from under our grasp:

> They lived out their lives as in a dream,
>   without knowing
>   who they were or what they were.

Smartly, Borges leaves his poem by the back door of teasingly irrelevant wisdom: "Maybe the case is the same for us all."

Throughout the collection a wry sense of paradox feeds uncertainty into the systems of thought. . . . (pp. 74-5)

The ironies make a habitable place for uncertainty: the Knight in a second poem on Dürer's engraving is "aloof", "unshaken", "eternal", but he is also "unreal": the poet, following a different, shorter way than he, has lived where nothing is firm but everything is real. His security lies in flux, in the knowledge of particularity. Unobtrusively Borges opens up and looks at the loss which all life's celebrators must face. (p. 75)

> *Desmond Graham, in* Stand *(copyright © by* Stand*), Vol. 17, No. 4 (1976).*

*   *   *

BOURJAILY, Vance   1922-

Bourjaily is an American novelist and editor. The Second World War and its effect on the life of a generation of Americans is a central concern throughout his work. He was co-founder of *discovery*, a literary magazine which he edited from 1953 to 1955. (See also *Contemporary Authors*, Vols. 1-4, rev. ed.)

"Now Playing at Canterbury" comes from the same source as most of Bourjaily's other fiction, his life. There's no other source for most novelists. That's why so many become repetitious. In Bourjaily's case the life has led to some startling fiction, beginning with his first novel, "The End of My Life" (1947). It came from his experience as an American Field Service ambulance driver in World War II. . . . It got him into John W. Aldridge's "After the Lost Generation" club in the early 1950's with Norman Mailer, Gore Vidal, Truman Capote and others now famous, forgotten or self-destroyed.

If the promise was great, the glory never really came. Literary New York sent Bourjaily roses at the start and frequently weeds later on. . . .

"Now Playing at Canterbury" is the novel Vance Bourjaily's career has promised us. It hears America hurting and crying. It also hears America singing, feels it changing, sees it swinging and going on and on through fields of Iowa corn, down the Buck Rogers freeways, up over our concrete pueblos spearing the sky. "Now Playing at Canterbury" is Vance Bourjaily at 54 and discovering Breughel populating America.

Bourjaily believes life is good. Perhaps so much literary fiction is depressive because it's written by young consciences yet to be tried. You have to pass 40 to know what not to hope for. Bourjaily celebrates life, incants it right from the start. (p. 3)

Chaucer's Canterbury was a holy place, tomb of Saint Thomas à Becket. Bourjaily's Canterbury equivalent is the cultural center. Art is holy in State City. Whether it will be entombed there, Bourjaily doesn't say. Instead, he shows us how Americans do their work, play with one another, think about art, satisfy lust, fight authority, suffer abominations and otherwise carry on their lives in the years of nihilism and atrocity, the early 1960's to the mid-1970's. . . .

Problems of structure and motivation, questions of attitude, issues of focus intrude on the bawdy and lyrical melodies of "Now Playing at Canterbury." Sex and love seldom find one another. I wonder whether the family may not be at the foundation of the United States as primary authority rather than political combinations. Families don't exist in "Canterbury." Bourjaily's comic-strip dialogue and imitation Chaucerian verse smile from his pages mindlessly. Bourjaily is a crafty entertainer. But . . . he needs control. "Canterbury" gets windy, even gassy. Yet how Bourjaily can write!

America, Vance Bourjaily has found you. His novel works. It's literature in the service of life, Bourjaily's 12 year vision of the good and the bad in recent United States history, human beings as strong and weak as the social weights that crush them and the animal drives that get them up again. "Now Playing at Canterbury" will be argued. It will be deflated. It will be read and remembered. (p. 4)

> *Webster Schott, in* The New York Times Book Review (© *1976 by The New York Times Company; reprinted by permission), September 12, 1976.*

[*Now Playing at Canterbury*'s] considerable heft and the titular allusion to Chaucer are signs that High Seriousness is about to be committed. . . .

The Chaucer of *The Canterbury Tales* appears only in the author's purloined formula: toss some interesting strangers together and stir. . . .

Bourjaily does not always sense when his powers of invention are flagging. Some of the interpolated tales are simply dull. Others are tricked out with bad mannerisms. One limps along in rhymed couplets. Another makes extensive —and pointless—use of comic-strip balloons filled with dialogue. A young black performer talks and thinks in a free-associating patois lifted and badly fumbled from *Finnegans Wake*.

Fortunately, Bourjaily has chosen a framework loose and capacious enough to absorb the bad with the good. And his virtues have never been on better display. He can capture American speech and cage it on the page without loss of vitality. His sympathies are generous; his descriptions of the nation's heartland landscapes throb with passion. Because its parts are greater than the sum of its whole, *Now Playing at Canterbury* will disappoint those who are still searching for that Loc Ness monster of the literary swim, the Great American Novel. No matter. It should be accepted gratefully for what it is: a minor piece, flawed but undeniably alive.

> *Paul Gray, "American Whoppers," in* Time *(reprinted by permission from* Time, The

Weekly Newsmagazine; *copyright Time Inc. 1976), September 13, 1976, p. 75.*

Legend has it that Hemingway, broken in mind and about to die, spoke well of Vance Bourjaily's talent. . . . Fifteen years and three novels later, Bourjaily still hovers in that penumbra where able writers try and fail to write a book of real importance. His new novel, twelve years in the writing, is not that book, not the book Bourjaily meant it to be: the Big American Novel that would let him bask finally in the glare of a major literary reputation.

[*Now Playing at Canterbury* is] a big book, all right, and the talent that Hemingway observed glitters fitfully among its many pages, but as a novel it's a mess—pretentious, shallow, complacent and mannered often to the point of self-indulgence. (p. 81)

To stress the Chaucer connection, Bourjaily includes an animal story and another in lame iambic couplets. But Chaucer had the wit to keep the frame for his tales unobtrusive; Bourjaily has not. His characters, drawn so thin as to be translucent, scratch at each other and constantly change beds; most speak only in the author's tone of voice, so, when everyone changes beds once more at the end, it seems that Bourjaily is straining for confusion, for self-parody.

The idea for the novel that Bourjaily has not written is sound. One could, from such a framework, write stories that illustrate some truths about America. But the novel that Bourjaily *has* written is not about American truths, but about fantasies: the orgy fantasy, the pot-bust fantasy, the student-power fantasy, the Vietnam-war-resistance fantasy. I do not mean that what Bourjaily writes about is untrue, but that his treatment of what is true, or is a good myth, is false, that he gives us America at the same remove from reality that television gives it to us. His stories offer no narrative or moral perspective that is new or freshly observed, no information about students or blacks or bombings or drugs that could not have been researched from TV news or TV situation dramas. His characters, strong and weak guys all, at their best resemble characters from old movies that we see on late night television. (pp. 81-81A)

Bourjaily has traded in the author's omniscience, as Tolstoy and Hardy understood it, for a smug knowingness. "Billy Hoffman, in he shuffles," is not just a bad sentence, it is corrupt because the author is clearly pleased with it, has worked to make it just as awful as it is. This sort of writing, combined with a plot that is not developed, but simply extended by the yard, results in a book that few caring readers should want to finish. . . . (p. 81A)

> *Peter S. Prescott, "The Chaucer Connection," in* Newsweek (*copyright 1976 by Newsweek, Inc.; all rights reserved; reprinted by permission), September 13, 1976, pp. 81, 81A.*

[Vance Bourjaily] has just published his seventh novel, *Now Playing at Canterbury* . . ., which is set in "State City" (a midwestern university town). In a way, it's a comic meditation on what happens when art marries into the academic family.

The novel revolves about the production of an opera, composed and written by university people, with a cast of students and faculty members, enacted at the university's opulent theater. The opera is awful—at least judging by its libretto—but no matter, the singers all have other things on their minds. Much of the book consists of long digressions, memories told in the voice of one or another of the troupe. The design belongs to the *Canterbury Tales*, hence the title. . . .

Bourjaily has always been a life-embracing novelist, and he successfully populates this novel with a set of characters meant to remind you of the world's variety. (p. 111)

Its cleverness and high spirits carried me much of the way through this overlong . . . book, but before the close another emotion seemed to be creeping into the text, a furtive sadness. The feeling can be located not so much in the book's characters as in the institution that subsumes them, the university with its big-as-all-outdoors generosity toward its artists. . . . Not that the living is bad: the living is good, as this novel testifies. Money and time, fellowships and fellowship farms on the edge of town, dinner parties featuring home-raised baron of lamb. The living is good, but it causes a bit of free-floating malaise, a feeling of unnaturalness. What all Bourjaily's characters seem to share is a hunger for authenticity, and a sense that real life, however rocky or sordid, lies behind them, or perhaps ahead of them; lies somewhere where they are not.

Bourjaily gazes on this plight with amusement, tolerance, and affection. One truth he wants to remind us of is that mediocrity and genius spring from similar impulses, and that those impulses live in all people. . . . But there's a wistfulness to this book, a muted-longing for grandness, the emotion of one who wonders what Fitzgerald would think if he came to one's seminar on Fitzgerald. (p. 112)

> *Richard Todd, in* The Atlantic Monthly *(copyright © 1976 by The Atlantic Monthly Company, Boston, Mass.; reprinted with permission), October, 1976.*

*   *   *

BRUNNER, John   1934-

Brunner is a British author of science fiction novels, short stories, and poems. A prominent and prolific author, he began writing science fiction of the futuristic variety, but in recent years has been writing fiction of the near-future. His extrapolations of present sociological trends, such as ecological problems, overpopulation, and invasions of privacy, have made him the most important science fiction author writing in this vein. He has also written under the pseudonym of Keith Woodcott. (See also *Contemporary Authors*, Vols. 1-4, rev. ed.)

[Like] Kipling, Brunner is fascinated with the machineries and dynamics of empire. Both born in advantaged circumstances, they perceived from childhood the structure of corporate civilizations and are fascinated with the spectrum of psychological types in a society of classes. Kipling found the aristocracy stupid from snobbery; Brunner finds the power elite stupid from greed. Kipling found the lower class without an identity; Brunner finds mass man hysterical with the dangerous complexity of his civilization.

Both seem preoccupied with the progress of England's two greatest colonies. India pervaded Kipling's writing, and he found America wonderful and unimaginably powerful. America is Brunner's India. It is the setting for three of his most serious novels—as well as many others. He has seen America's power and its unwitting threat to the survival of the planet. (pp. 64-5)

Standing on the shoulders of such as Kipling, Brunner is

perhaps well described as metapolitical, in pursuit of the sort of total understanding of civilization that can finally liberate man from all coercive myths—national and otherwise. The men differ in their propositions for the survival and prosperity of humanity, but both desire happiness for every individual human being. (p. 65)

Brunner chooses the speculative mood because it is an optimum medium for proselytizing the popular imagination. It is parabolic and homiletic. The catch is that effective parables for modern civilizations require enormous scientific and humanistic knowledge. . . . What, after all, would you really need to know to secure an empire? Kipling tried to know it. Brunner has tried to know it. But now there is more to know. And Brunner wants to secure a planet, at least. Accordingly, the information displayed in his most recent writing is encyclopedic. At the heart of *SOZ, TJO,* and *TSLU* [*Stand on Zanzibar, The Jagged Orbit,* and *The Sheep Look Up*] is the computer, enabling and potentially controlling the information explosion. . . .

Brunner's speculative writing is . . . essentially expository fiction. This is the hallmark of speculative writing and not especially remarkable. What is remarkable is Brunner's consistent grace and intelligibility in explaining and abstracting civilization just beyond the threshold of the present. . . . He is facile in miming dialect and convincing in the transformation of his British-English ear to an American-English one—necessary for American scenarios. He does this so well that his slips become exceptions. . . . He is a master of the pun, that encounter with the word which on one level yields amusement, . . . while on another level it yields terror by its very possibility because when the meaning captured in a word can be seen to bifurcate, the word itself is no longer trustworthy. (p. 66)

With few exceptions, such as the short story "Fair" (1956), that interpolates a section of the narrative with counterpointing commercial rap lines, or *Threshold of Eternity* (1959), which includes a "paragraph" composed of alternating lines from two separate paragraphs, distinguishable by means of one set of lines in italics, his writing is uncomplex in plot and structure, imaginative in setting, and peopled with characters that answer the folk imagination's need for heroes and various shades of villain. In style it employs a discourse that serves excellently to present story and exposition without getting in the way of suspense and a good read. At the same time it often provides samples of the social critique that will become the main intention of *SOZ, TJO,* and *TSLU.* Examples include *The Atlantic Abomination* (1960), presenting one of the most truly hateable aliens in science fiction by the simple device of having it spend a lot of time insisting that humans were sentient excrement and almost unworthy to serve it. It makes mental slaves of men. Some readers have seen the alien as an analogue for the fascist state. In *The Whole Man* (1964) Gerald Howson is a sympathetic hero whose growth from ugly cripple to parapsychological superman is one of the best examples in all science fiction wish-fulfillment romps of this sort. *The Squares of the City* (1965) employs a chess game actually played by masters as the organizing metaphor in a narrative tour de force. The result is a story that dramatizes the vicious manipulative process of a power elite in a colonized country. One feature of the work is the inclusion at the end of the text of an index of the chess pieces and their story-character equivalents. The effect is a "dramatis personae" directory. To this is added an annotation of "pieces taken," functioning as an obituary. Brunner utilized these narrative features in *SOZ, TJO,* and *TSLU.* (pp. 67-8)

[The title character of *The Traveler in Black*] is an undoer of myths, theologies, and sciences, all of which process in fact as "magics," political and epistemological vested interests, that operate to frustrate an ultimately coherent understanding of the universe which courageous and selfless reason might otherwise achieve. Variations upon this theme appear in *SOZ, TJO,* and *TSLU.* In fact, language and conventionally paced narrative, themselves indictable as solipsisms, are submitted to an ordeal in these three works. The "traveler" might have written them. (p. 68)

[*SOZ, TJO,* and *TSLU*] are built of many dozens of vignette-like sections which ultimately organize into montage effects. . . . Each commences with a series of sections which are imagistic and friezelike, catching characters and civilization like runners in mid-stride. . . . Succeeding sections catch the runners in new postures, lending the effect of a stop-action sequence of several characters' adventures interspersed with clips of a particular stage of the world, especially as supplied by news media, to suggest the significance of the adventures. The "caught" postures engender a subliminal suspense, incompleteness, or sense of balance precariously maintained, if not on the verge of being altogether lost. This suits the books' themes that warn of gravely unbalanced modern civilization. The opening sections of *TJO* provide a good example:

> ONE   PUT YOURSELF IN MY PLACE
> I-
> TWO   CHAPTER ONE CONTINUED
> -solationism.

The "I" as presented is a pun and a participant in oxymoron, the nature of pun being symbol with unresolved references; oxymoron provides references as contradictory but newly intelligible only in relation to each other. "-solationism" completes "I" and simultaneously contradicts the resolution in the context of an at once revivified cliché, "PUT YOURSELF IN MY PLACE." Here the very fabric of language registers instability—a frequent Brunner tactic.

Balder pictures symbolizing civilization caught at the threshold of catastrophe open *SOZ* and *TSLU.* "Context (1)" in *SOZ* presents a slice of the stock opening script for a television news program (it might be called "jive as cliché"). About five hundred words deliver time, weather, and inescapable commercials. Then, nothing. The actual news is unimportant; perhaps less truthful than the commercial rap. . . . The effect upon the first-time reader is that of a person the rhythm of whose breathing has been interrupted. (pp. 69-70)

For the three works the principle setting is the United States, no more remote in the future than sixty years in *TJO* and a decade or less away in *TSLU. SOZ* lies somewhere in between. The "realism" of *TSLU* is more appalling than that of *TJO* because *TSLU* takes place more nearly in the present. All the works present worlds that might be generalized as polluted. *SOZ* features the population explosion, pollution with people. *TJO* presents a vision of the information explosion, pollution with data. *TSLU* may be the last word in "realistic" stories of a polluted planetary envelope. Brunner is successful in conveying the impression of a pea-soup-thick, toxic atmosphere layering most of North America. Each novel dramatizes the replication, multiplication, and exponential proliferation of commodities manufactured in a "progressing" civilization: data, people, and garbage. . . . [In] each story the computer

is a power-controlling implement employed by the captains of government and industry to manipulate mass man and direct world economy to their personal aggrandizement. In such a world psychological survival for the average man becomes precarious. He is paranoid in the "jungle" of civilization as his ancestors were paranoid in the natural jungle. However, faithful to the myth of progress, society's response to paranoid behavior, finding prisons and penal codes at least indelicate, is to replace incarceration with "commitment". . . to a sanitarium.

In each work there is the threat of being declared insane and sent to an asylum waiting for those who would disturb civil "order." The sanitarium is a major setting in *TJO.* (pp. 70-1)

Brunner is well aware that characters in the expository fable of speculative writing are rarely more than stereotypes or emblems. He sketches them well in this mode and has great fun in the storyteller's game of naming the characters according to their character. (p. 72)

Brunner also includes what might be construed as an oracle character in each novel. . . . They may be shades of Henry James's "central intelligence" characters. All are socially conscious, visionary intellectuals, fugitive from earlier academic associations, socio-anthropology, psychology, and ecological biochemistry. As such, quotations from their "writings" or dialogue are made to speak explicit diagnoses of the problems of population explosion, cultural mental health, and planetary ecology with which the works are concerned. By using them Brunner avoids the dated "Dear reader, now I shall explain" convention. They are ubiquitous in the respective stories as soothsayers, frustrated messiahs, and general markers of the message that is to be taken seriously amidst a snowstorm of "messages" broadcast by the also ubiquitous "media" of the stories. One might, of course, question the reliability of the revelations of these oracle characters. They do, after all, speak in words—whose meaning is pervertible. Even so, their moods are wholesome and constructive. They are good men thinking about chaotic civilization. In this role they do not participate in personally intimate relationships with any of the other sympathetic characters. They are rather teachers in search of learners. They appear celibate, seasoned in existential ordeal, and "ordained." Across the works they are one voice, three ways named. . . .

[Brunner] is an excellent poet, writes fine, tight short stories, and is a first-rate essayist. Moreover, he demonstrates a willingness to utilize "voices" of every genre from poem through senate record to grocery list. . . . Much science fiction is flat because it employs a monotonously homogeneous voice for all its characters. (p. 73)

For Brunner's purposes, Brunner is master of hundreds of voices. The effect of his writing is that it cannot be said to have a characteristic style; it has rather a trans-typical style, without which no speculative writing can be intellectually and aesthetically estimable. . . . This is so because, whether the speculative vision is of the parallel present, the past, or the future, alternative, retrospective, or extrapolated voices and styles are required to present it with fidelity and authenticity. (pp. 73-4)

It is generally Brunner's principle to modify or invent a word as an efficient symbol for a condition, practice, device, social type, etc., for which otherwise a number of words must be employed. The intent is to make a complex phenomenon simple by facilitating the naming of it—especially a phenomenon for which it has not been politically popular to have an easy name. On balance this seems a good device to aid the encounter with the technological and psychopathological chaos of Brunner's "Americas." Alternately, he takes a common word like "lead" and defines it socio-physically, causing surprise and consequently new understanding in the reader. "Lead" is verbally relocated from safe to dangerous associations, as it has been physically relocated by a nature-poisoning civilization.

Brunner's mastery of styles further serves his intent that the novels be seen as well as read. Persons, places, things, and their gestalts are to be visualized objectively—even empirically—diminished as little as possible by subjective authorial associations. He is the antithesis of the "automatic" or "navel-contemplating" writer. With very little modification *SOZ, TJO,* and *TSLU* would be film scripts. . . . The titles *Stand on Zanzibar* and *The Jagged Orbit* compress sharp, if somewhat bizarre, images. *The Sheep Look Up* is more abstract but plays upon spectacle with the word "look." The McLuhanesque composition of the novels plays to the visually conditioned reader. (pp. 74-5)

Finally, Brunner is a satirist. Indeed, if we entertain seriously the thesis of Kingsley Amis's *New Maps of Hell,* that speculative writing must yield a form of satire, Brunner may represent a modern epitome. The speculative writer and the satirist may be the same: both employ exaggeration, caricature, magnification, and extrapolation, all elements of classic reductio ad absurdum. Out of control the speculative and the satirical visions dissolve into nonsense. . . . Brunner's control is excellent. Appropriately, *SOZ*'s millions multiply; its media are saturated and it is media-saturated; its citizens live in a dope fog. The facile collapsing diction of the narrative personifies a cultural psyche at an advanced stage of becoming nondiscursive, precedent to becoming nonverbal, precedent to becoming nonsentient. The narrative of *TJO* is more conventional, sketching a dystopian nightmare in which the masses participate in a dream-myth, a pervasive televised pabulum strained and assembled by computers—a comment on the innocuous fare of present-day media. . . . The systematic exaggeration that *TSLU* exhibits may be a principal factor for disapproval of it by a few obstinate reviewers. The novel is gloomy, scenically so. But the speculative satirist must insist that if you emulsify your atmosphere with the stupidly proliferated garbage of your civilization, you will have murk—gloom. Brunner is most clever in *TSLU* with impositions such as the baby cooked in its mother's womb by an unshielded micro-wave appliance, or the polluted rainwater which reacts with hair-set lotion to discolor or dissolve hair.

Traditional notions of satire suggest obligations to comic effect. Strategic exaggeration often yields ludicrous absurdity, even when the underlying theme is tragic. Joseph Heller and Kurt Vonnegut, who share a sensibility with Brunner, can put readers in hysterics. Read in short sittings, Heller's *Catch-22* . . . is funny, though the novel's point is that war is painful and vicious. Vonnegut's "Harrison Bergeron" makes comedy. . . . The story's message, of course, is appalling. Brunner, too, is richly equipped to create comic effect. . . . In the relentless horror of *TSLU* comic effect is appropriately stunted. When it appears, it often works as surprise by bitter vulgarity. . . . Or it is macrocosmically grotesque. . . . (pp. 75-7)

In any case, the laughter evoked by Brunner's work is not as committed as for Heller's and Vonnegut's. I can merely suggest some explanations. Exaggeration of the crucial produces distortion that is tragic. The focus of *Catch-22*'s exaggeration and caricature is upon the niggling events and procedures of World War II military experience. They are historically real and familiar—even domestic. Taken individually, a typical incident should not threaten the balance of civilization. The reader can laugh at it. Vonnegut's settings are futuristic and sociologically sweeping. But they often disarm the reader with their apparent whimsy. Events and furniture seem thrown together in a maverick allegory that does not compel us to referents in a real future. The reader can laugh at them. On the other hand, Brunner's comic effect, while it participates in these modes, outstrips itself. The laugh cannot last because Brunner's future events and furniture have the suggestion of authenticity. And for precisely this reason they do not strike many readers as immediately familiar. Even domestic detail has become strange, just when Brunner's careful extrapolation has convinced the reader that the detail, "the satch filter in the comweb slot" (future technology's answer to junk mail) is perfectly predictable. Understanding a Brunner exaggeration frequently makes it too late to laugh. (p. 77)

> *John R. Pfeiffer, "Brunner's Novels: A Posterity for Kipling," in* The Happening Worlds of John Brunner, *edited by Joe De Bolt (copyright © 1975 by Kennikat Press Corp.; reprinted by permission of Kennikat Press Corp.), Kennikat, 1975, pp. 63-77.*

[In his poems, novels, and novellas, as well as in his short stories, John Brunner] generally conforms to the accepted conventions for successful writing. His style, tone, imagery, sense of plot, and conflict are consistent throughout the whole of his work. The quality of his work varies, of course, but that is the case with most writers. . . .

Brunner's stories fall into two categories by point of view used. Seldom does he tell a story from a minor character's point of view; his stories are, then, either first-person stories or stories told from the omniscient point of view. The latter type predominates. (p. 78)

The omniscient point of view gives Brunner the freedom to make up all the rules of the game himself. He can make decisions freely concerning time and space. He can bring old characters to a new setting, as in "Judas," or he can bring new characters to an old reality, as in "Fifth Commandment." He can take the reader forward in time to create a new arena entirely for the story, as in "Singleminded" or "A Better Mousetrap." In short, Brunner writes most of his short stories from the omniscient point of view —and takes full advantage of that technique.

When Brunner does use the first-person point of view, as in "Fairy Tale," it can be a stunning success. In that epistolary story Brunner faces a basic problem. For plot reasons, the protagonist, Barnaby Gregg, must be alone at the story's end. The story, moreover, depends on the distillation or refraction of circumstances within Gregg's mind, its basic meaning being inextricably bound to Gregg's understanding of the chain of events leading to his decision to write the letter. Here Brunner could have opted for the omniscient point of view. But it is important for us to be inside the protagonist's mind *only,* to perceive the others through his eyes, for the others—and indeed the problem of time lapse itself—are the vehicle of the story. Gregg's story is fantastic; therefore it is necessary that only he understand the events he relates. First-person point of view becomes a necessity. (p. 79)

[In "Orpheus' Brother"] Brunner is able to detail the calmness and deliberation with which the narrator goes about his horrible deed, to suggest the real horror of the story, precisely because he uses first person.

One reason why any writer uses first-person point of view is to facilitate vicarious participation for the reader. Perhaps Brunner's most successful use of first person for that reason is in "The Totally Rich," a story told by a man who is capable of perceiving all the nuances of the action. . . . The plot calls for intimate scenes between the narrator and the woman who is the subject of the story. Because the woman is the subject, Brunner could not have used an omniscient point of view; that is to say, it is important for the reader *not* to see the inside of her mind. The gradual revelation of what motivates her, as seen by the narrator, is what constitutes the story itself. . . .

Brunner is frequently playful, is often serious and somber, is predictably cynical. He is seldom, if ever, intimate. He controls the tone of his stories carefully, although occasionally he surprises even himself. (p. 81)

By far the most frequent tone in Brunner's short stories is that of cynicism. Time and again men fall into the traps which they naively lay for themselves. One wonders where Brunner stands to gain such an aesthetic perspective/distance. As individuals, men emerge as fools—uxorious or otherwise. Brunner's prefaces are especially illustrative: "Human beings have been defined as 'the only animals lazy enough to work hard at saving themselves trouble'". . . . "If the dolphins are in fact intelligent, let's for God's sake hope they are too intelligent to want any part of this human lunacy. . . ." Brunner is equally cynical about the systems under which men operate and by which men are ultimately judged. "The trouble seems to lie in the fact that perfect inhabitants of a perfect society would need to be the children of perfect parents". . . . (p. 83)

Repeatedly Brunner writes stories about foolish men dealing with foolish, impotent systems. But the point of all this cynicism is this: we (Brunner and the reader) are *excluded,* except as *we* choose to involve ourselves in any way but intellectually with the madness that Brunner sees as rife in our world. The very nature of the cynic puts him somehow outside what is going on, gives him esoteric insights into the folly of men and circumstances. Brunner generously allows us to stand outside with him, to share his point of view, to laugh, however darkly, at the foibles of his fictional creatures.

As stated earlier, all of these varieties of tone and mood are controlled, are carefully built in. They show us that we are dealing not with a mere teller of stories, but with an acute observer of the human condition—one who can make us share his attitudes toward us for a time, even though we are dimly aware that we are somehow being manipulated.

The human condition that Brunner observes, and allows us to observe with him, covers an astonishing range of time, space, and imagination. Some of his stories are historical in conception, as are "Fair Warning" and "The Nail in the Middle of the Hand." Some, such as "The Totally Rich," are basically contemporary in setting. By far the bulk of Brunner's stories, however, are futuristic in orientation. But the settings themselves are mere window dressing; *the human condition varies little, if at all, throughout the whole of Brunner's short fiction.* It has often been said that there are no new stories, and that the true test of a storyteller is how well he can retell an old story. (p. 84)

Brunner's short fiction is more often than not set in the future. His stories, however, are peopled by characters understandable and credible in terms of what we know about man and his foibles *now.* This should not be interpreted as a weakness in Brunner's writing; on the contrary, it is a basic strength. Brunner himself is something of a historian; that shows very clearly. And it is reasonable to surmise that Brunner is of the "history repeats itself" school.

His stories are predicated on the basic condition of mankind as it has always been and, as Brunner projects, it always will be. The characters in Brunner's stories are governed by the basic needs, just as characters throughout history have been. They make *human* choices in the face of their predicaments, and that is what gives the reader such a high degree of catharsis, of pleasure through vicarious identification. Were Brunner to project a new breed of men into a new set of circumstances, the results would be disastrous.

The moral principles upon which Brunner's plot resolutions hang are traditional as well. Typically, Brunner's stories feature a moment of epiphany for the hero that occurs at the moment of climax. The hero realizes suddenly, inspirationally, what all the preceding action *means,* and that meaning changes his life—or his view of life. (p. 91)

Moreover, the moment of revelation is realized in forms of traditional moral values. Typically, the good earn their reward, the stupid and corrupt get what is coming to them. . . . Note that the morality of the stories is the morality that we were all brought up on. New morality does not go with new settings; rather, the readers' morality stays with the readers. This is a shrewd tactic on Brunner's part. . . .

[His] humor might be characterized in two ways: a kind of playful attitude on Brunner's part, as mentioned earlier, and a kind of deeply black humor which can only come after the genuine despair of understanding some aspect of the human condition. (p. 92)

In his preface to *Time-Jump* Brunner discusses the nature of his humor. His perception of what he considers funny is particularly illuminating . . . :

> The Germans have a term which English
> lacks, and it neatly spans the area where
> science fiction and comedy meet. They say
> *Galgenhumor:* gallows humor.
>   Right.
>   This is the humor of someone standing on
> the scaffold with the noose around his neck,
> distracting the executioner and the crowd
> with wisecracks in the hope that the cloud of
> dust on the horizon may—just by the
> slimmest of chances *may*—portend the
> arrival of a royal reprieve.

That description is particularly apt, as Brunner's brand of humor is just that: a holding action. His formula is simple: take a trend observed to be happening in society and project its logical conclusion. That conclusion is something we can laugh at *now;* we may not laugh at all if/when it really happens. (p. 93)

The weakest of Brunner's humor can be found in the "Galactic Consumer Reports." . . . The basic device in these stories is to substitute consumer goods from some far-future time for the kinds of products being analyzed in these magazines now. There are two reasons why these stories do not succeed. First, the structure to which Brunner commits himself is too restrictive; he cannot move about as freely as he does in his other stories. A second reason, dependent upon the first, is that Brunner is forced by the structure of the story to make the products analyzed so futuristic as to be incredible. (p. 94)

Brunner does not allow the structure of his stories to dominate at any time. Rather, he cloaks his conflicts in a wealth of detail, futuristic and otherwise. His characters, no matter how far removed in time or space from our present situation, are completely credible; they function on the basis of the same values as do Brunner's readers. Over and over he takes our present value systems and tests them in situations where they have never been tested before. They hold up well, for the most part. Through this kind of value-testing Brunner shows us that some of the periphery of our value systems is indeed superfluous. Does it matter much if, as in "Eye of the Beholder," the artist himself appears grotesque to the human eye with its built-in set of expectations? Of course not; the concepts of art, beauty, creativity and expression all remain valid. And, in terms of the human condition as we understand it, why shouldn't they? (pp. 94-5)

> *Stephen C. Holder, "John Brunner's Short Fiction: The More Things Change . . . ," in* The Happening Worlds of John Brunner, *edited by Joe De Bolt (copyright © 1975 by Kennikat Press Corp.; reprinted by permission of Kennikat Press Corp.), Kennikat, 1975, pp. 78-95.*

John Brunner's poetry is about poetry—what it is (and what it isn't), what it has been in the Western tradition, and what it can be to help man either survive in this world or build new ones. While his poetry is often satire or explicit social protest, his primary subject is the poem itself as liberating music. Each poem is a further statement and embodiment of an aesthetic which he describes pointedly in the title of his first volume, *Life in an Explosive Forming Press.* . . . (p. 96)

Poetry [according to Brunner] is a sculpting of words in time and space, as they appear on a page, as they sound to an audience, as they are breathed by a reader. Poetic "statement" explodes into packed images of poem as sculpture.

"Life in an Explosive Forming Press" represents, as much as it states, his aesthetic. In a subtitle he calls the work "A Modern Sonnet" in order to manipulate the reader's expectations about conventional form. Before they are even in tune, the reader's presuppositions are immediately violated by a first line that begins with "and." A settled sensibility expecting suspenseful build-up in the form of the sonnet is repeatedly dislodged by middle-of-the-sentence syntax. . . . (p. 97)

Though Brunner unifies "Wordsharp" in part through the use of a dramatic frame, he also embeds his images in what Charles Olson has called "composition by field, as opposed to inherited line, stanza, over-all form, what is the 'old' base of the non-projective." Brunner's use of "projective verse" means that he often sets up a poem on the page structurally so that it will most closely approximate its rhythms as it is read aloud. Each image works also according to what Pound and the Imagists called the "language of common speech," which itself creates "new rhythms." Brunner's images most resemble what Pound described as "hard and clear, never blurred nor indefinite."

And his style further demonstrates the conventional Imagist belief that "concentration is of the very essence of poetry."

Often Brunner speaks through an observer-narrator who blends self-reflective commentary with dramatic incident and dialogue. The result is generally images tightly packed in a particular spatio-temporal context. (p. 98)

Brunner's propensity to create layers of interlocking yet conflicting tones contributes significantly to the complexity his speakers manage to sustain [in "Multiple Choice"]. As a fade-out, "Multiple Choice" surfaces inner conflicts faced by the surgeon-poet who now cuts loose his creation for analysis by the critic trained in "paper chromatography." Curiously, although the poem concludes his first volume, Brunner generally introduces his poetry readings with it. The tone is learned, pompous, even smug, and ever-threatening, beckoning the audience (with Brunner—as distinct from his speaker—presiding) to explore and to enjoy exploiting the poetic resources of "the subtlest language ever evolved on earth." (p. 100)

Brunner as theorist . . . sounds like Wordsworth or perhaps any practicing poet who works by "projecting the mores and emotional responses of realistic human beings in a realistically different environment". . . . (p. 102)

Patterns of humor from light puns to invective . . . orchestrate Brunner's musical rhythms and provide the clearest link between poems embodying his aesthetic and his satire or poems of social comment. (p. 104)

The extent to which Brunner "applied a film technique to prose fiction" . . . underscores obvious similarities between his science fiction at "the forward interface of now" and the social satire in his own poetry.

Brunner's poetic satire is equally effective, though less immediately jarring than his poems on poetry. His pack of images deals contrasts, paradoxes; exploding sounds turn back upon themselves to create at once self-conscious irony that is personal with consciously limited perspective, and direct commentary which itself carries less force but which serves to counterpoint other "wordsharp" images. Brunner's satiric poems are generally about using people, things, and destructive technology in ways that are out of tune with the basic life processes. Opposition between the "simple" and the "perilous," "freedom" and "repression," images of mind cut off from body, of napalm destruction and the corruption of money are of course stock subjects for the satirist. Less obvious are his images of urban society, officials co-opting "movements," and the hypocrisy of the white liberal.

As poetic sculptor, Brunner has his satirical persona surgically cut and reshape his perceptions in three basic patterns. Above all else, his speakers emphasize a deterioration in modern man's inability to see life whole as an ongoing process. And measured against this standard of an integrated "felt" existence, his satiric vision sharply attacks the perversions and distortions of mechanized society and man's interiorizing of its wrenched, dualistic values. Finally, as corollaries to this general state of the life force run amuck, the speakers probe the dissonance of violence, greed, and hypocrisy in the Present Interface of Now.

"Balance" is itself a key term in Brunner's world of explosion and disequilibrium. In "On Balance" he suggests that *using* people, things, and human reason itself perversely merely to escape momentary difficulty produces destructive technology. Child abuse, slavery, and official execution are products of ''the pure white light of reason'' gone out of balance. Similarly, in ''He Was Such a Nice Chap—Why Did He Do It?'' Brunner portrays the impotence of the disintegrated psyche that doesn't understand ''the art of letting go,'' a picture of modern man whose mind is ''cut off from his body.'' Emerging from the dualism of man's fragmented perceptions and values is a sense of hopelessness that finds expression in . . . overt self-destruction. (pp. 104-05)

As poet, Brunner starts with the twofold assumption that words create and define the worlds we know and that the process of creating through words is important *and* fun. He therefore develops an aesthetic in the poems themselves, an aesthetic of ''the best words'' sculpted into ''their right order'' to create humor that can be subtly disarming or supercharged, and social commentary that can be witty satire or explicit protest or both. Brunner and his speakers thus self-consciously observe themselves in action. Following the influence of *Tristram Shandy*, Brunner the poet writes poems about poems, theories about theory, and satirizes satire—all of which help create the sense of distance that pervades his works on the whole. Commenting on the almost absolute fusion of theme and structure he is seeking in his poetry, Brunner acknowledges that he wants ''to be able to discipline in formal pattern . . . things which ordinarily are too terrible, too disgusting, too repulsive to be accepted—except with a shock and a shudder''. . . . (pp. 107-08)

> *Ronald Primeau, '''It Goes Bang': Structures of Rhythms in the Poetry of John Brunner,'' in* The Happening Worlds of John Brunner, *edited by Joe De Bolt (copyright © 1975 by Kennikat Press Corp.; reprinted by permission of Kennikat Press Corp.), Kennikat, 1975, pp. 96-109.*

Given the computer's significance, it is understandable that much of today's science fiction deals with this machine. Unfortunately, science fiction . . . has its share of technophiles (those who see human survival as mainly dependent upon further technological development) and technophobes (those who see further technological development as the major threat to human survival); such simple-minded approaches are neither realistic nor useful. Yet, in the hands of a superior practitioner, the speculative and extrapolative nature of science fiction makes it an unparalleled tool for exploring the fundamental questions raised by the man-computer relationship and its societal consequences. John Brunner, whose works deal extensively with computers and their human effects, is especially well suited to be the focus of such an analysis. Few authors draw such complete and informed pictures of the computer in our future. . . .

Brunner accepts the basic principle that social relationships determine specific technological design and applications; technology is not self-creating. The capabilities and assigned tasks of his major fictional computers certainly reflect the values and interests of their owners and operators. . . .

Most familiar computer uses exist in Brunner's works and provide insights into the man-computer relationship. (p. 168)

Many problems of internal unrest and imbalance in modern industrial societies, so graphically depicted in Brunner's major works, may be due to the absence of internal control systems of adequate scope, speed, and reliability. The computer can meet these needs. Brunner recognized this in a very early novel, *The Threshold of Eternity*. In grandiose space-opera tradition an interstellar war between man and aliens rages through space and time. Human resources have been totally mobilized for the war effort and dispersed defensively throughout the solar system. The narrow margin for victory tolerates no inefficiency. Yet it is not an oppressive society, for mankind is joined in mutual dedication to the common good. People laugh and love, as well as fight. The heart of this system is a computer, the only possible means for the coordination of such a complex and far-flung assemblage.

Brunner perfects this image in a recent story, ''Bloodstream.'' The city has become a living organism, the next major stage of human sociocultural evolution; the socially patterned acts of individuals in business, communication, transportation, and so forth, constitute the internal structures which function to keep this superorganism ''alive.'' In effect, the entire city is a self-regulating biological machine. The disruptive person is analogous to a disease germ, the police to antibodies.

Technology does not automatically solve human problems; it does increase our alternatives. . . . Brunner appreciates this; he is certainly no believer in the inevitability of effective action through technological advance.

This is humorously illustrated in *TJO* [*The Jagged Orbit*] by the ''desketary,'' a computerized secretary and information storage and retrieval system used by psychiatrists at a mental hospital. It is a very useful machine, keeping patient records, recording therapy sessions, giving access to banked data, and capable of visual data display, statistical analysis, and language translations. But it breaks down whenever it ''hears'' blue language: ''What in the world was the good of letting the contract for the Ginsberg Hospital's computing system to a firm which was currently hiring as many neo-puritans as was IBM? When at least eighty percent of the patients he was trying to cope with were suffering from sexual hangups, it was a constant source of irritation to have these censor-circuits expressing reflexive mechanical Grundyism all the time''. . . . Thus do human choices structure technology.

The treatment of mental illness provides a more serious example. Doctors at the Ginsberg compute patient personality profiles which are compared with ideal ''healthy'' parameters. Hospital chief Elias Mogshack, himself mentally disturbed, expounds a psychiatric theory based on extreme individualism, a doctrine so alienating that patients are rendered increasingly unable to function in society. Yet this theory is the basis for defining the ''healthy'' parameters. As one character observes, ''It sounds more as though they sew a straitjacket and trim the poor devils to fit''. . . .

Likewise, the development of accurate data by the computer is not a substitute for value decisions. When Thomas Grey, insurance actuary in *TSLU* [*The Sheep Look Up*], discovers that life expectancy in the United States has been going down for the past three years, his only action is to order a hike in life insurance premiums. (pp. 169-70)

Finally, the greater range of alternative actions made possible by technological advance means little if people are not aware of them. . . . Science fiction's solution is computerized ''teaching machines.'' Presumably, Brunner utilized such devices to [teach information and, in some works, values]. (p. 171)

The computer as worker is a . . . major area of Brunner's fictional concern. This includes computer-assisted automation and its two subtypes, robots and androids. . . . Given the overpopulated and high-consumption worlds typical of his major works, Brunner obviously has extrapolated the continued development of automation. These societies could not exist at all without such systems. Unfortunately, abundance for so many coupled with conspicuous consumption . . . produce intolerable strains on the environment and world resources. Under such conditions living standards will fall, as *TSLU* demonstrates. This problem is rooted in the economic and political systems depicted by Brunner, with computer technology treated as neither cause nor savior; Shalmaneser and Robert Gottschalk are ethically neutral entities, and neither can act outside their programs.

Brunner creates a very advanced system of automation in "Thou Good and Faithful," a story which symbolically sums up his view of the relationship between technology and man. A military expedition from Earth is scouting for planets suitable for future colonization. They discover a park-like world apparently inhabited by gentle, yet independent, robots [which are under the direction of massive, master computers]. . . . A master computer explains to the Earthmen that their creators were once much like the humans, preferring quantitative expansion over qualitative growth. But the creation of an ultimate system of automation proved to be the tool needed to turn the vanished species toward transcendent concerns. Eventually the machines helped their creators "evolve" beyond the old material world, which was given to the computers as a gift. Now these machines were offering themselves, and potential transcendence, to mankind. They are, and can only be, good and faithful servants. (pp. 171-72)

Brunner provides an excellent example of an advance in computer technology likely to add new industries, jobs, and products to the economy. A "full range of contemporary domestic autonomic services" is introduced in "You'll Take the High Road." These are specialized, miniature robots, apparently the product of a technological breakthrough equivalent to the development of fractional horsepower motors which gave us home power tools, kitchen appliances, and many specialized industrial tools. A whole new world of consumer goods appears, including the "chess autonome," "cerebresponsive chronological autonome" (a clock keyed to a specific person's brain), "liquor autonome" (in this case, the mixologist is shaped like a St. Bernard), the "Jackson-POLAC computer" (paints wall murals), "Cordon Bleu autonome" (a cook), and "General Purpose autonome" (your own man Friday). (pp. 172-73)

Although the "autonome" represents an important development, Brunner's treatment is tongue-in-cheek. He recognizes the tendency for abundance to trickle off into decadence and waste. His "autonomes" are snobs, nagging their owners to buy more of them and making invidious comparisons with nonowners. Thorstein Veblen's leisure class is alive and well in science fiction.

The development of sophisticated robots in human form, androids, eventually leads to questions of android rights and human-android relations. Brunner's *Into the Slave Nebula* is set in an affluent, leisure-oriented society based on android labor. The androids are made of organic material and are human in capacity, response, and appearance, except for their blue skin. They feel joy and pain, yet they have no rights. They are bought and sold, worked and

harmed at will by their owners. The analogy with human slavery is clear, and this is Brunner's intention.

But from the standpoint of computer development another point can be made. The line between man and machine eventually disappears. This is the ultimate step, far beyond today's master-slave relationship between computer and man and even beyond the symbiotic relationship in Brunner's "Wasted on the Young," where human brains are used as control units in automated systems. In evolutionary terms, technology is equivalent to an extension or modification of man's basic organic equipment. The computer extends man's mind in the same sense that the telescope extends his eye. Perhaps man is already a cyborg, an entity part man and part machine which functions as a whole. Stripped of all his technology, man could no more survive than if he were deprived of any other vital organ. . . .

Forecasting is a third major area of computer applications found in many of Brunner's stories. . . . (p. 173)

Unfortunately, Brunner makes computer forecasting look very easy. . . . Computer capability cannot substitute for the lack of basic social, cultural, and psychological knowledge of how social systems function. This is frequently overlooked by physical scientists, professional futurists, and science fiction authors. Yet many anticipated developments in forecasting will not occur without growth in the social and behavioral sciences commensurate with computer developments. . . . It is no coincidence that those characters acting as problem solvers in many of Brunner's works include sociologists, anthropologists, and ecologists. This contrasts sharply with traditional science fiction heroes, who tend to have engineering or physical science backgrounds. (p. 174)

Brunner's balanced insight provides a useful guide; the computer is simply a tool man uses to achieve his ends. Once created, a machine may generate unintended consequences or be put to evil uses, but basically it will perform as man designed it. Blaming the machine for this equates to condemning the hammer for missing the nail but not the thumb. Humanity remains the problem and the solution. (p. 175)

> *Edward L. Lamie and Joe De Bolt, "The Computer and Man: The Human Use of Non-Human Beings in the Works of John Brunner," in* The Happening Worlds of John Brunner, *edited by Joe De Bolt (copyright © 1975 by Kennikat Press Corp.; reprinted by permission of Kennikat Press Corp.), Kennikat, 1975, pp. 167-76.*

*   *   *

BURGESS, Anthony   1917-

Burgess is an English novelist, editor, translator, essayist, composer, and critic whose inventive use of language and unique wit are displayed in such works as *A Clockwork Orange*. **Admittedly influenced by James Joyce, Burgess has endeavored to explicate his genius in** *Here Comes Everybody: An Introduction to James Joyce for the Ordinary Reader*. **He was born John Anthony Burgess Wilson and has published under the pseudonym of Joseph Kell. (See also** *CLC*, **Vols. 1, 2, 4, 5, and** *Contemporary Authors*, **Vols. 1-4, rev. ed.)**

Anchored to asexuality by stepmother fantasies and an excretion fetish, committed poet and vulnerable recluse, Enderby, the corpulent, flatulent, likeable anti-hero, was a major character created by Anthony Burgess in that year of writing five novels, 1959, which doctors said would be his last. *Inside Mr Enderby* appeared in 1963 and the sequel, *Enderby Outside,* in 1968. Now the trilogy is completed with a book in which Enderby, though nominally relegated to the subtitle, fights what seems to be Burgess's biggest ever battle on the last day of his, Enderby's life. For since we left Enderby in Tangiers, Burgess's *A Clockwork Orange* has been made into a film by Stanley Kubrick and subsequent real-life alleged imitations of the activities of Alex and his droogs have been labelled Artist Answerable and laid at Burgess's door. In a newspaper interview at the time, he promised that his new book would reply.

It has. *The Clockwork Testament* is a brilliant and very funny book. In it Burgess has sustained that novelistic ability to which he referred generally in *The Novel Now* 'to create what the French call an *oeuvre,* to present fragments of an individual vision in book after book, to build, if not a *War and Peace* or *Ulysses,* at least a shelf' as well as 'fusing the comic and tragic in a fresh image of man'. The wider issue of the artist's responsibility has prompted him to cook a virtuoso cadenza, allusively presenting ingredients from the opus larder as Artist's Credentials—taste and judge. Enderby has written a filmscript based on Gerald Manley Hopkins's poem *The Wreck of the Deutschland,* the film company have had re-write men lace it with flashbacks and up the tempo, and now the media are asking Enderby what he intends to do about a case of nun-slaughter in Ashton-under-Lyme where they are banning Hopkins from the bookshops. 'Me? I'm not going to do anything. Ask the buggers who made the film. They'll say what I say —that once you start admitting that a work of art can cause people to start committing crimes, then you're lost. Nothing's safe. Not even Shakespeare. Not even the Bible.' And to the television company inviting him for the chat-show: 'I see. I see. Always blame art, eh? Not original sin but art.'

Burgess has cooked with original sin before but, then as now, cannily. He does not believe in doctrinaire novels: in *The Novel Now* he has said that the deeper issues in his books 'are not my concern; they are strictly for the commentators.' In the same work he warns of the danger of moving the novel 'too far out of the sphere of enjoyment: any work of art must be compromise between what the writer can give and what the reader can take'.

It is difficult to say whether Burgess has been limited by his credo: he has been helped by what he calls the comic propensity which he cannot overcome, and by a technique with character, situation and even language which echoes cartoonist Gerald Scarfe's approach to a subject, taking each physical feature and pushing it as far as it will go. Burgess meets our need 'to be reminded of human insufficiency, to be told stories of anti-heroes' with creations like Enderby, guarding against mere exaggeration of anti-heroic fantasy by never overstepping the mark of credibility in his projections of contemporary society. Enderby, on the strength of his film-script and his 'not-unknown' poems, takes up a post as Visiting Professor of Creative Writing at the University of Manhattan and becomes the vehicle of Burgess's concern about original sin, liberalism, violence, literacy, the confluence of cultures, television, hypocrisy, social anaesthesia, separately massive issues which also grow out of each other's heads. . . .

In talking about his 1962 novel *The Wanting Seed,* Burgess referred to the essential process of 'the finding of a set of

symbols for the problem we're all facing . . . and of the kind of myths, the kind of social patterns which must emerge from this'. What better set of symbols to start with in *The Clockwork Testament* than those of Hopkins's poem, which Robert Bridges only read once before forming his opinion of it, and which sets the trial of life firmly in a context of the Fall of Man and the Passion of Christ, to show that each man and all the world must be prepared to succeed by failure and ask, in Hopkins's words:

> . . . is the shipwreck then a harvest,
>   does tempest carry the grain for thee?   (p. 88)

The Clockwork Testament throws out leads from the Burgess philosophy in every direction important to him. It acknowledges his debt to Joyce as an example of what Burgess, citing *Ulysses,* has called 'parody of the literature of action'. It reiterates his fear of a world locked in a relentless alternating cycle between liberalism and totalitarianism. It alludes, in the person of Enderby, to Huxley's Savage in *Brave New World,* who 'rejects the new sinless . . . order' and 'thinks that man ceases to be man when he is incapable of squalor, shame, guilt and suffering'. Burgess presents Enderby as unable to tolerate Negro protest because Enderby has not evaluated protest in context, at the same time as contrasting 'ethnic agony' with the world agony of Hopkins's poem. Yet he avoids laying down the law, opting here, as in *A Clockwork Orange,* to follow Isherwood's example of drawing a powerful picture 'on the margin of entertainment'. With Isherwood it was the decay of bourgeois German society; with Burgess it is violence.

But whatever the issue—and Burgess has made violence his particular issue in order to point the futility of what Enderby calls the attempt to 'educate people out of aggression, great liberal fallacy that'—it is set here in the wider arena of the artist's duty. Perhaps one should look, for a final clue, not to minor Enderby but to major Shakespeare. In his fictional biography *Nothing Like the Sun,* published two years after *A Clockwork Orange,* Burgess gives to the Earl of Southampton and to WS two key observations on the difference between violence in art and in life. First the Earl, goading WS for not wanting to witness Tyburn executions, says: 'He who makes Tarquin leap on Lucrece and everything the filthy world could dream of happen in *Titus.* Well, you cannot separate so your dreaming from your waking. If you would indulge the one, you must suffer the other.' WS replies: 'I will not look.' And then WS, later: he is thinking about getting audiences to sustain the theatre: 'It is the drawing-in that is needed, blood and murder (well, it is there, it is the world, I would be what the world itself would be).'

This is the same dilemma which has occupied Burgess throughout his work: the dilemma of withdrawing from life in order the better to confront it and yet having a human obligation fully to participate. *The Clockwork Testament* is an important and exceptional book because it shows how the apparent hopelessness of the dilemma reinforces the crucial role of the artist in society and proves that he is bound to reply, to cries of Artist Answerable, that the fault is and always has been in Man. (p. 89)

Graham Fawcett, "The Grain in the Tempest," in Books and Bookmen *(© copyright Graham Fawcett 1974; reprinted with permission), August, 1974, pp. 88-9.*

[The] novels of Anthony Burgess . . . imitate life fairly straightforwardly in their way, but are also recklessly untidy and very much aware of themselves as fiction. Ender-by, for example, in *The Clockwork Testament,* is writing a long poem about Augustine and Pelagius and is teaching in New York while Burgess, as we know if we read the news-papers, was teaching in New York and writing a long poem about Moses. This suggests a leakage from life into fiction, which is quite different from a confession or the creation of a roman à clef, and which can be felt in the books, I think, even apart from any information one may collect about Burgess's career. It is this leakage, along with Burgess's very attractive combination of frivolity and intelligence, that gives his novels . . . energy and complication. . . .

Beard's Roman Women is not an evasion of life, it is an apparent exorcism of a piece of past life, clearly successful for Beard, and perhaps useful for Burgess. The novel is based, the blurb says, on "an autobiographical episode," but that seems to be putting it rather mildly. The death of a woman you have been married to for twenty-six years is hardly an episode, and the subject of the novel is widower's guilt, the haunting of a man by his dead, sick wife, as he tries to start again with fresher, firmer female bodies, and to balance the loss of a marriage that he thinks of as a civil-ization, a system of delicate signs and meanings, by the gain of healthy sex and a sense that he is not as old as he thought he was.

The other subject of the book is the conquest of death by anticipation, and this again echoes an "autobiographical episode"—Burgess's twenty-year-long postponement of a death diagnosed as early and certain. (p. 41)

[Ghosts] turn all of Beard's relations with women into ver-sions of his selfishness and cowardice, and it is a virtue of the book that this point of view is put with some authority. "Time's been good to you," Beard says to his old girlfriend at the airport. She, thinking of her cancer and her ampu-tated breast, says "How do you know?" Again, Beard, referring to his wife, trying to express sympathy for the girlfriend, says, "Cirrhosis isn't too bad a thing to die of," and the girlfriend, speaking for the double class of women and the dying, says, bitterly, "Have you ever died of it?"

But then, once the accusations are out, Burgess helps to let Beard off the hook by making him such a likable, disorgan-ized, drunken clown. There is some sense in this, even some moral sense: why beat your breast if you're beyond improvement? And it is true that Burgess's heroes are al-ways at their best when their lives are completely out of control. But there is also a reluctance to face the questions the novel itself throws up. There is only guilt, and the re-cord of guilt's more dramatic manifestations, and scarcely any inspection of possible grounds for guilt. *Beard's Ro-man Women* is a lively book but it is a shallow one, and we are likely to remember its gags—"His dentist had once told him that he was one of the lucky few whose teeth would outlive him. He would have preferred his work to, but you could not have everything"—and its language—"such thoughts panted thought his mind"; "the regular sort of cremation regularly ignited by the local funeral directors"—when we have forgotten its ghosts and the neglected brief they almost brought against Beard-Burgess.

This is perhaps as Burgess would wish, since in a note on his *Moses* he suggests that "our salvation lies in under-standing ourselves" and that "such understanding depends on a concern with language." I hope our salvation doesn't depend on *Moses,* a rambling, amiable epic in loose verse, which Burgess used as the basis of his script for a television

film starring Burt Lancaster. It is far closer to DeMille's *Ten Commandments* than it is to the Book of Exodus, and although it reiterates some of Burgess's favorite themes—the heavy burden of free will, the need to respect and yet to order the multiplicity of the given world—it is finally too much of a lumbering anachronism to be anything other than a curiosity. Its language sometimes catches an interesting rhythm and flow, and a man who can incorporate *verbatim* whole stretches of the King James version of the Bible without breaking his stride or his diction is clearly some sort of master of pastiche, but the verse of *Moses* is too often just sad doggerel. (p. 42)

Michael Wood, in The New York Review of Books *(reprinted with permission from* The New York Review of Books; *copyright ©* *1976 NYREV, Inc.), September 30, 1976.*

In modern literature dying seems the last frontier. I don't mean this as an Irish bull or a Sam Goldwynism; rather that as a subject matter for artistic treatment it's the only one left veiled and mysterious enough to solicit the over-in-formed modern imagination. . . .

Anthony Burgess took up novel-writing when a doctor in Brunei told him he had only a year to live. The several ti-tles he produced that year were intended as an estate for his wife. The diagnosis was mistaken and Burgess has contin-ued with his writing, astonishing us all with his productivity and originality. By a sad irony, his first wife passed away in the mid-1960's. To describe his new novel, "Beard's Ro-man Women," as a death trip is not to hint that it is full of autobiographical *cris du coeur,* but to suggest he knows more about his subject than can be gained through library research. . . .

"Beard's Roman Women" has a surprise ending which I would not give away even if I fully understood it. Burgess is full of literary sleight-of-hand like his use of the demotic Trastevere poet Belli as a leitmotif and the framing of the book's last scene in a musical setting of Dryden's "Ode for St. Cecilia's Day":

> The dead shall live, the living die
> And music shall untune the sky.

Now there is confidence! But whether the reader can be confident that Burgess in this book has unknotted the enigma of dying, I am not so sure. (p. 8)

Julian Moynahan, in The New York Times Book Review *(© 1976 by The New York Times Company; reprinted by permission), October 10, 1976.*

* * *

BUTOR, Michel 1926-

A French novelist, essayist, and poet, Butor is an exponent of the "new novel." His work was influenced in both form and content by Proust and Joyce. His dedication to the renovation and development of the novel encompasses experimentation with the concepts of time and space. (See also *CLC,* **Vols. 1, 3, and** *Contemporary Authors,* **Vols. 9-12, rev. ed.)**

[When] Butor in his fascinating but solemn *La Modification* (1957) works a dozen different journeys simultaneously into one man's stream of consciousness, we are conscious of both device and evocation: he is manipulating things to make a point, and encouraging us to re-live similar experi-ences of our own—all of this within the novel. But when

Butor in *L'Emploi du temps* (1956) superimposes two temporal sequences and justifies the superimposition as 'quite natural since in real life one's mental analysis of past events takes place while other events are accumulating', he is both right and wrong. Right to evoke everyone's experience; wrong to justify *art* and *device* as 'natural'. Art is not natural. (pp. 204-05)

Paul West, in his The Modern Novel, *Volume I* (© *Paul West 1963*), *Hutchinson University Library, 1963.*

There is hardly a literary genre that Michel Butor has left untouched. He has gained world-wide reputation primarily as a novelist. . . . It would, however, be a mistake either to ignore his essays and his poetry or to divide the remainder of his books too neatly into separate categories. (p. 3)

Poetry can be sought either by emphasizing framework—as Valéry did—or by opening the doors to lyricism. Butor has confessed to having been overwhelmed by Shelly's "Ode to the West Wind" when he was fourteen. His lyricism seems instinctive, but if, so far, he has not completely forsaken it, his main interest has been in the architectural approach. To him the framework of a work of art is not only that which distinguishes it from commonplace objects and appearances; it is also the means through which thought reflects upon itself and "reality in its totality becomes conscious of itself before it criticizes and transforms itself." To put this in terms of author-reader relationship, poetry is the means the author uses to impose upon the reader an awareness of himself, of his relationships with others, and of his situation —such an awareness being the necessary prelude to a desire to modify his existence.

Passage de Milan, Butor's first novel, is a fascinating book. Although not exemplifying his art in its most accomplished form, it reveals his aesthetic structures and ethical concerns. The title is characteristic in its ambiguity: in French, "Milan" is both an Italian city and a bird of prey (the kite), while "passage" refers to a small city street (mews or alley) as well as to the act of passing by, or over. The rich associations that are evoked by the city of Milan— its material and artistic wealth, and its history of proud independence—are heightened by the repeated passing of what Butor has called a hieratic bird—also thought to be a cruel and bloodthirsty scavenger.

The initial sentence of *Passage de Milan,* unlike those of later novels, is short, impersonal, and banal, and it can be translated without loss: "Father Ralon leaned out of the window." It is much like the beginning of any number of earlier twentieth-century novels that for the sake of realism attempt to plunge the reader *in medias res* without artificial preparation. With the next few sentences, however, the particular tone that is Butor's slowly emerges out of the commonplace. What the priest sees as he looks out is a scene of Paris at dusk—a city enclosed by a wall of smog the color of iodine, chestnuts, and old wine. He looks out on a vacant lot featuring two scraggy trees and a pile of junk; the latter seems unchanging, but careful observation reveals that each day some objects are removed and others added, according to the needs of an unknown and mysterious owner—just as mysterious as the people who move into the lot by night, lighting small fires to keep themselves warm. Contrasting with the junk heap, but resembling it in several ways, masses of roofs, gutters, walls, balconies, and windows rise beyond it and reflect briefly the setting sun. Above it all, a kite is soaring; it is early spring. The

sentences that render that scene are relatively long and complex; restrictive adverbs and clauses translate the difficulty there is in any attempt to apprehend reality, while several qualifiers, partners in the same attempt, surround the important nouns. The priest enjoys watching the scene at this particular hour of the evening. When daylight wanes he shuts the window, and sitting at his desk, watches the panes gradually cease being transparent and become reflective. As the story unfolds, and the novelist reveals the darker recesses of his being, the novel too, presumably, becomes less like an open window and more like a mirror. (pp. 8-9)

It soon becomes apparent that the novel will deal primarily, not with any of the characters who are being introduced one by one and almost, it seems, ad infinitum, but with the life of the apartment building as a whole. At this point, the significance of what Father Ralon has seen from his window at the outset becomes clear: a microcosm of society, the building, with its numerous floors, inhabitants, and visitors, is analogous to the city; it is also analogous and reducible to the junk pile on the neighboring lot. One need not proceed very far before suspecting that the plot, closely circumscribed in space, will also not extend over any great length of time. Indeed, *Passage de Milan* begins at seven on a Friday evening and ends, twelve chapters later, at exactly seven the following morning. The framework of the novel is thus provided by time, and time is hieratic: throughout the night, bells of a nearby convent toll the hours; a priest opens the novel, and another priest closes it. As priests of other religions relied on birds to foretell the future, birds are linked to the Ralons; the kite, bird of prey, casts a shadow of death on the house when Father Ralon looks out. (pp. 10-11)

Life is regulated by a complex series of rituals that inhibit communication. Some activity takes place via the back stairs, but this hardly gives the building any sense of unity. The novel, on the contrary, does have unity: this is provided by the tight limiting of time, and somewhat ironically, by ritual—that of the main party given on the fifth floor, supplemented by smaller parties given elsewhere. The entire building is fully conscious of, and affected by, the Vertigues' party. With the exception of the sponsors, however, the occupants of the building are affected as if by the presence of an exterior object; the participants themselves do not merge into the party: they merely contribute their own private worlds of ambition, hate, or desire. The ritual that provides aesthetic unity becomes the mirror that reveals the extent to which rituals can also produce disunity and isolation.

Butor's handling of this situation in *Passage de Milan,* pointing to weaknesses as well as to strengths, foreshadows an evolution that is shown in his two subsequent novels. Whenever he attempts a certain distance from his characters, he loses his grip on the reader. At one point, in presenting the Mogne dinner party, he attempts to describe the rites involved, rites that result in the complete mechanization of a reunion that should have brought warmth and joy to the participants. He succeeds to the extent that those pages become cold and mechanical; but he fails to the extent that the reader tends to become as bored as the participants. Obviously, Butor does not possess Flaubert's talent for destructive irony. When, on the other hand, he enters into a character's consciousness and uses his gifts for sympathy and empathy, the reader, too, is carried along. The more promising part of the novel begins with chapter VI, during the midnight pause at the Vertigues' party, when a buffet supper is served and the solitary consciousness of each individual adds its melody to a counterpoint of interior monologues that nevertheless make some of the characters aware of the groups to which they belong elsewhere.

If *Passage de Milan* has plot (and subplots) and individualized characters, these necessary ingredients of fiction play only secondary roles. Structure—that is, the manner in which such ingredients and other materials are combined into the framework—is of primary importance. Here, all the ingredients are overwhelmingly oriented in the direction of failure, which, through the reflective process, acts as a warning; symbolic elements, such as have been pointed out earlier, serve to extend that warning to our society as a whole. Rituals that should bind actually separate. . . . (pp. 11-12)

Several years later, *L'Emploi du temps,* a most superior novel, fulfilled the promise implicit in *Passage de Milan.* In this novel, poetry lies as much in the lyricism of the sentences as in the architecture; a spell-casting tone, intermittently noticeable in the earlier work, is maintained throughout, partly as a result of a first-person narrative technique; the very first words, Proustian in their evocative power, are like the opening chords of a symphony, setting the mood and penetrating into the reader's unconscious mind: "Les lueurs se sont multipliées." Not lights, but glimmers of lights, and quite possibly glimmers of understanding as well. The sentence, vague, harmonious, and tantalizing, stands out as a separate paragraph.

The second paragraph, consisting of a single ten-line sentence, introduces a physical setting from which precise topical references have been omitted. The event described is so commonplace, however, that such omissions facilitate the identification of reader with narrator and enable Butor to concentrate on the structure that will give the action uncommon significance. Seven months previous to his telling the story, the narrator has arrived by train, at night, in a strange city whose faint lights, seen through the windowpanes, are those mentioned in the initial sentence. Alone in his compartment, his head numb from the noise of the train, he has been dozing; as the noise abates, his full consciousness returns, and he looks out; it has been raining. At this point, something happens that recalls the beginning of *Passage de Milan:* the windows are black and covered with droplets of rain—mirrors reflecting small fragments of the weak ceiling light inside the train.

Travel, darkness, solitude—the evocation of these three leads one to suspect that the novel will deal with a quest, and the reflecting raindrops point to an inner quest. (pp. 13-14)

The weak ceiling light in the train matches [the] inner weakness [of the narrator, Jacques Revel], which is thrown back at him by the events he is involved in, like the reflections in the raindrops. (p. 14)

Butor's conjuring up an imaginary city [Bleston] rather than setting his story in Manchester, where he spent two years between 1951 and 1953 (Revel's diary dates coincide with those of the year 1951-52), was probably intended to heighten symbolic values; by inventing monuments and names he has been able to bring in mythical elements that underline his purpose. The arbitrary but plausible span of one year, which allows for no individual future or past, restricting the novel to those events that have taken place within that time, could well stand for the whole of a man's

life. That it may also allude to the Christian myth of man is suggested by Revel's early fall in a muddy street, a fall caused by a woman, which indirectly and unconsciously leads Revel to feel responsible for the attempt on the life of one George Burton, who has three personalities and has written mystery stories, for one of which he has adopted the pseudonymic initials J. C. Allusions to classical myths abound: their presence is adumbrated by the novel's division into five parts, reminiscent of the five acts of French neoclassical tragedy, which drew so many of its themes, suitably distorted and assimilated, from Greek and Roman antiquity—and Butor, of course, will provide his own purposeful distortions. These divisions, also corresponding to the five months during which Revel actually writes his journal, are superimposed on the twelve months of his stay and the twelve sections of the city. Each part, in turn, is divided into five chapters, one for each week or portion of week in a month; since he does not write during weekends, each week also have five days. The architecture of the novel thus clarifies its title: an "emploi du temps" is a schedule, but it can also refer to the function of time or to the use that is made of time. (pp. 14-15)

[A] clerk in a stationery store [sells Revel] maps of the city; one of these included an outline of the city bus routes that looked like a mass of tangled thread—the thread that will guide him through the city of Bleston. In that occurrence we have an example of Butor's technique of gradually introducing mythical allusions: a few pages later, reference is made to the labyrinth that was built in one of the city parks, and we must wait another twenty pages before encountering the name of Theseus. Thus a partial analogy is established, buttressed by many other subsequent overt references, between Revel and Theseus, Ann [the clerk] and Ariadne, Ann's sister Rose and Phaedra, Bleston and the Labyrinth, and so forth. There is no real identification, however, nor is *L'Emploi du temps* a retelling of that or any other myth. Butor's starting point may well lie in the habit, not uncommon in schools and colleges, of tagging classmates and teachers with literary or historical names; in *Passage de Milan* he used the device fleetingly, and in a situation close to its source, when he had one of the Mogne boys, in an interior monologue, think of his eldest brother first as the Prince of Wales, next as Aeneas, and then as Esau. Whatever the source, the literary value of this was most probably brought home to Butor by his study of the language of alchemy, where "symbols are variable terms, and their grouping clarifies their meaning." The process seems as much related to a poet's belief in the suggestive power of words as it is to a storyteller's delight in myths. . . . In *L'Emploi du temps,* Revel constantly seems to shuttle between at least two respondents: at one moment he is a mole burrowing in the darkness of the city, and a migrating bird looking down at the same city from above; he is a virus in a tissue, and a man observing it through a microscope; he is Theseus, he is Cain, and he is also Oedipus.

Like Oedipus, he is a man looking for a murderer. That aspect of the plot is, at the end of part I, imposed upon the reader through the juxtaposition, within a few pages, of a newspaper headline concerning a murder in Bleston, of Revel's purchasing the thriller by George Burton entitled *The Murder of Bleston,* and of a stained-glass window depicting Abel's murder by Cain. Revel, somewhat in spite of himself, assumes the part of a detective, whose role, precisely according to the author of the mystery story he has read, is "to unveil and to unmask."

Butor is concerned with Bleston not as a city contrasted to the country or the sea, but as a city among cities, as a microcosm of civilization, like Paris in *Passage de Milan*. The enmity of Bleston toward Revel—and the dangers it harbors—stems from its lulling, numbing, blinding powers. He is threatened with passively going through the comfortable motions of civilized life, just as characters in the previous novel went through the empty motions of their rituals. When he fights Bleston, Revel is undoubtedly a hero. He commits many errors, however, and the question that implicitly dominates the background of the narrative is what to accept and to reject and how to express this rejection of the contemporary world. Consciousness of himself and awareness of what, in the past, has molded his environment and himself will assist him, he hopes, in answering those questions. Like Butor, he writes in order to give meaning to his life; his effort results in partial failure, not because he chose the wrong means but because he must preserve the freedom of the reader in order to allow him, too, to seek a meaning for his own life. The hero fails so that the novel may succeed.

La Modification, Butor's third novel, published one year after *L'Emploi du temps*, may well have been written to give expression to problems that were originally intended for development in that novel but had to be eliminated for aesthetic reasons. The kind of Joycean symbolism so characteristic of the first two novels is almost completely absent from the third; instead, we focus on the single action of one individual, clearly circumscribed in time and space, actually and symbolically.

The framework is provided by the long train trip from Paris to Rome: the book opens as the main character [Leon Delmont] enters his compartment in Paris and closes as he leaves it in Rome. (pp. 17-19)

Basically, this novel is about bad faith (in the Sartrian sense). Delmont's attitude is related to Revel's. . . . Actually, Delmont is a Revel who fails to respond to the challenge of his situation—through the first part of the novel at least. He is, apparently, a cultured individual, who upon accepting the agency for an Italian typewriter firm in Paris, first expressed a desire not to be contaminated by his job. . . . Very soon, however, he became exactly like the men he associated with, and his entire life was changed. That is one of the "modifications" that precede the one that constitutes the main subject of the book. As the word implies, it is only a superficial change, for Delmont's expressed intention not to be contaminated by his situation was merely a gesture in bad faith. His true project entailed the acceptance of the job and everything that went with it. . . . The affair he later initiated in Rome was a similar type of modification: it constituted neither an authentic rapport between human beings, nor the true rejuvenation and liberation it might have been. (pp. 19-20)

The handling of myth in *La Modification* is much what it was in the previous novels. Like the plot, it is also less complex; essentially, it is limited to two recurring allusions. First, the careful reader is led to suspect what will happen because of a number of references to Julian the Apostate. Like Julian, Delmont hates the Christian church (here, of course, more specifically the Catholic Church), and like him, he lives in Paris as the representative of a Roman power. The fact that this power, the typewriter firm, is but a perversion and a caricature of the Roman Empire is obviously a commentary on Delmont's life. . . . Second, and beginning about the middle of the book, allusions to the

legend of the Master of the Hunt—"le Grand Veneur," who, clad in black, roamed the Fontainebleau forest on horseback—emphasize Delmont's guilt and desperation. Like the voice of conscience, the fabled huntsman's cries—"Do you hear me?" or "Are you expecting me?"—reverberate throughout the forest.

The impact of *La Modification* is enhanced by the adoption of a most effective device: the second-person narrative. . . . What its generalized use does here is to emphasize the accusatory quality present in all of Butor's novels. As a result, this novel reads somewhat as though it were spoken by a detective or a prosecuting attorney showly building up an airtight case against a suspect—who, indeed, is finally proved unworthy of his mistress's love. The second person also allows for an ambiguous author-reader-character relationship, with the reader oscillating between identification with the prosecuting author, or with the guilty character. (pp. 21-2)

In *L'Emploi du temps*, the effectiveness of Bleston as a symbol is due in no small part to the mysterious life the city exudes from its streets, stones, parks, rivers, monuments, and soot-laden atmosphere. In *La Modification*, the city of Rome casts a spell on Delmont's extramarital affair, helping to transform it into a myth, even undermining the reality of the city of Paris. (p. 22)

Places—and with Butor places are almost invariably cities —are, to use his own metaphors, sources from which to drink and foreign texts from which selections are to be translated into his native language. Details, seemingly numerous, are chosen either in order to light a spark of recognition within the reader's mind, or for their direct contribution to the structure of the work. An object may be "like an emblem or a caption, none the less explanatory or enigmatic because it is a thing." Objects as explanatory captions have filled the nineteenth-century novel; objects as enigmatic emblems are more characteristic of the contemporary one, and Butor suffuses them with what Aragon, in his surrealist period, called *le merveilleux quotidien*.

The publication of *Le Génie du lieu* . . . signals a turning point. The fact that Butor wrote those poetic essays indicates that he was no longer satisfied that everything could be made to fit into the architecture of a novel. In 1958, he probably reached the end of what might be termed a syncretic period. Since 1958, in addition to critical essays, he has written more and more imaginative works other than novels. He has not only consented to the publication of older poems but has written new ones as well.

Degrés (1960) is a masterpiece. This novel could be viewed as a sort of enlargement of the previous ones in that it strikes more chords which reverberate more deeply within the reader; it also evidences a stylistic refinement, in that the lyricism of his language so noticeable in *L'Emploi du temps* has been toned down considerably. Most definitely present is what probably must be considered a permanent element of Butor's aesthetics—especially when his critical statements are taken into consideration—the emphasis on a strong architecture.

The initial impetus to the narrative lies in an attempt to recapture the meaning and consciousness of a given hour in the life of a contemporary French lycée, its teachers, and its students, at the beginning of the school year. . . . A teacher, Pierre Vernier, decides to write the account of that school period for the benefit of his nephew, Pierre Eller, who happens to be a student in his class. (pp. 23-4)

The narrative, told in the first person, is set in motion in solemn, ritualistic fashion: "I walk into the classroom, and I step up onto the platform." Restrained and often matter of fact, the tone, with few exceptions, does not perceptibly change as the story proceeds. The syntax, however, becoming increasingly complex, like that of *L'Emploi du temps* and *La Modification,* expresses the multiple interrelationships at hand.... Quite possibly, the train of thoughts described in the longer sentences of the book flash by within the same period of time described by the initial sentence. This, of course, is narrator's time and bears little relation to reader's time; but it does lead us to one of the many important themes of *Degrés*—the relationship between author's truth and reader's truth. The writer is deceitful, in order to permit the reader to reach authenticity. (pp. 24-5)

Degrés is, in part, the account of a sacrifice: that of Vernier, who accepts death so that Eller might live a better life. Vernier is writing a document for Eller to read later on, when he is better able to understand what happened, and also when he has forgotten what happened. But he is writing for others, too, for anyone who might have been a student in a lycée, or anyone who might even have come into contact with such a person. While this has often been the purpose of the artist in general—to preserve for posterity the memory and the meaning of events that would otherwise be forgotten—two considerations qualify Butor's purpose.

The first reflects ironically on the so-called universality of a work of art. Malraux has remarked that painters imitate not nature but other painters, and that their works are judged in turn through a confrontation with other paintings. The same is true of literature, and Butor acknowledges that books are written for people who have had what we would call a "liberal" education—a rather restricted universality. Hence, the hopeful glance cast in the direction of those who might have dealings with the privileged group.

The second consideration is related to the first and derives from the very nature of the events being recorded. What Vernier is transmitting to a hypothetical posterity is the description of the process by which Western man acquires knowledge and consciousness of the past. In other words, he is providing a description of the transmission and showing how faulty it is. Furthermore, his account is pointedly oriented toward recapturing the spirit of a particular period of the past, the Renaissance. The day that constitutes the focal point of the narrative is October 12, Columbus Day, and what Vernier calls his pivotal lesson deals with the discovery and conquest of America. Among the many texts that are read in his and other classes are a number of passages from Rabelais, beginning with those pertaining to reform in education—and there again the narrative reflects upon itself. As a result, description is once more transformed into accusation; what stands indicted is not only an educational system, for the lycée has a symbolic status similar to that of Bleston, but a whole aspect of Western culture. Implicit in the indictment is a challenge and a hope that we will react against our past as the Renaissance reacted against the Middle Ages, and then proceed beyond those changes that were instituted during the sixteenth century. The reaction that is called for is in many ways similar to that illustrated by Jacques Revel and Leon Delmont; but in *Degrés* illustration makes way for a kind of exhortation.

Never does Butor expressly exhort, preach, or condemn. It is the reader who, through the juxtaposing of events, descriptions, and quotations, is forced to make certain judgments. The devices used are common enough, but the confrontation of two common devices can produce forceful results. (pp. 26-7)

The architecture of *Degrés* is one aspect of the novel of which most readers are not aware, and this in itself is an indication of how successfully it has been integrated into the work as a whole.... [The] division into three parts does more than distinguish the supposed narratives given by members of a related family group—two uncles and a nephew; for within the school there are many other such triangles, where the relationships are not so close as in the first, decreasing with each successive group, until the relationships become, so to speak, negative (a colored student, the physical education teacher, and the Catholic chaplain). The three parts are thus divided into seven sections, new characters being introduced in each section: three per section in the first part (including all eleven teachers), two in the second part, and one in the third, for a total of forty-two. The blood relationships of part I become neighborhood relationships in part II, solitudes in part III—mirroring the deterioration of relationships in the main group. As the bonds between characters break up, however, the unity and meaning of the novel become more evident; as accidental connections fade into the distance, *Degrés* affirms a truer human link among individuals. The breakups that occur are reminiscent of those noticed earlier in *Passage de Milan,* but they point toward a transcending of the failing relationships, a striving for the universal brotherhood of man. At the conclusion of *Passage de Milan* one of the characters escapes from Europe. In a loose but significant parallel to such an implied rejection of European values, *Degrés,* explicitly stressing the merits of non-European civilizations, derides "this exclusivity of civilization which it [Europe] continues to arrogate to itself, despite all the proofs which it has unearthed, and which it continues to seek and produce, nourishing this contradiction, this great fissure, this great lie which saps and undermines it." The antagonism between Europe and the world recalls, on a grander scale, the one between Revel and Bleston. (pp. 28-9)

Histoire extraordinaire is an essay based on a dream of Baudelaire, which the poet told to his friend Asselineau.... What needs to be noted here is, first, the importance given to dreams, a lesson Butor may have learned from the surrealists as much as from Freud; and, second, the similarity there is between the basic patterns of *Histoire extraordinaire* and of the novels like *L'Emploi du temps* and *Degrés,* with their constant interaction between past and present, dream (or fantasy) and reality. Whatever its merits as a critical essay on Baudelaire, this volume may serve to illustrate one of Butor's basic approaches toward an understanding of the interaction between consciousness and events. (p. 29)

Mobile cannot really be forced into any of the conventional categories of novel, essay, or poem, although the last term, remembering how much poetry the novel has absorbed, comes closest to defining it. But instead of imposing a label upon such a work, it might be better simply to keep the rather indefinite description of the subtitle, and call it a "study," so long as one bears in mind the full artistic and musical connotations of the French word *étude.* A certain amount of virtuosity is implied, and that is surely present in *Mobile.* (Like the architecture of *Degrés,* however, it is unostentatious to the point where several critics have accused Butor of being too facile.) The primary component of that architecture is supplied by the many cities and towns of the same name in the United States. . . . In each state, analogues are thus introduced, provided by such names as exist in other states that are either geographical neighbors or alphabetically contiguous. (p. 30)

The visits [to the various states] are anything but realistic. The chapter on New York is built around the five cities of Salem, Clayton, Franklin, Manchester, and Canton—Salem providing a link with New York's alphabetical predecessor, New Mexico, and the four others echoing the names of cities in a number of other states. In addition, each of those cities provides a shift of locale and a side trip to a nearby state: three to New Jersey, three to Pennsylvania, two to Connecticut, and so on. Conversely, while "in" Vermont or Massachusetts, the reader also makes several sorties into New York. The representation of each state, made up from the total of such visits and side trips, unmistakably achieves poetic truth: for the importance of any state is less a consequence of its geographical size, or any other single characteristic, than of its role and influence in the life of all the other states. (pp. 31-2)

The important thing about *Mobile* . . . from the standpoint of its potential effect on the reader is the manner in which the components have been assembled in order to produce the picture, or "representation." Discontinuous accounts of the 1692 Salem trials and of writings by Franklin and Jefferson, newspaper extracts, advertisements, signs, brief statements, names of people, cities, counties, and states form a strange mosaic or, as the text suggests at one point, a patchwork quilt. Naturally, the juxtaposition is not haphazard; as with the states themselves, the basic order is alphabetical (almond through vanilla for ice cream, B. P. through Texaco for gasoline, among others), and a number of complicated modifications are subsequently introduced in order to achieve maximum effect from various confrontations: the procedure is a generalization of the one already noted for *Degrés,* one that is not unrelated to the surrealist image. (p. 33)

The devices used in *Mobile* are meant to disturb the reader's complacency, just as they were intended to do in *Degrés.* They occasionally do more than that and produce something that had been missing in the previous works: humor. Its absence from, say, *L'Emploi du temps* is perhaps no more disturbing than its lack in Greek tragedy; on the other hand, humor might have relieved the monotony of a few pages from *Passage de Milan.* Whether Butor has managed to introduce it in *Mobile* because he does not quite feel so closely involved in his subject or because of greater artistic maturity is a question for which only his future works can provide the answer. (pp. 35-6)

With *Réseau aérien* (1962) Butor begins experimenting beyond the printed page. This work . . . is a kind of playlet in multiple-dialogue form involving passengers of airliners all over the globe. Two couples leave Paris for New Caledonia; one flies east, the other west, and both reach their goal more or less at the same time. Dialogues among other passengers, none of whom makes the complete trip, alternate with those of the two main couples until they get off at various intermediate points. . . . The total impression is one of a choral song of mankind in which unidentified individuals blend their common preoccupations about different things and countries into elemental melodies of love and hate. Trivial concerns, expressed in prosaic fashion, dominate in the early dialogues. Later, as distance, imagination, and dreams affect each traveler, the themes become more basically human; the language waxes lyrical, discursive logic makes way for instinctive association, and ordinary talk is metamorphosed into poetry. (pp. 37-8)

There is much in *Description de San Marco* (1963) to remind one of *Mobile.* But where *Mobile* gave only one of a number of possible modulations based on the same series of states, objects, and texts, and was not intended as an account of actual travels in the fifty states, *San Marco,* evolving out of a detailed visit to St. Mark's in Venice, stays very close to its subject. On one level, the book mirrors its title perfectly. . . . Mere description, however, does not satisfy Butor; detailed as this one is, it is obviously not exhaustive, and the nature of the selections and the quality of the commentaries serve to orient the work. (p. 38)

Through their confrontation and out of the wealth of descriptive praise, the ever-present element of denial, so characteristic of Butor, is impressed upon the reader: quite early, he is reminded that the church owes its very existence to a theft (that of the evangelist's body), and in the last pages that butchers' stalls and wooden outhouses once confronted the Byzantine magnificence of the square.

If it is not easy to appreciate or fully evaluate works like *Réseau aérien* or *Description de San Marco* from a reading of the text alone, the task becomes nearly impossible where something like *Votre Faust* (serial publication begun in 1962) is involved. Subtitled "Fantaisie variable genre opéra," it was written in collaboration with the musician Henri Pousseur, at the latter's suggestion. . . . Fascinated by some of the aesthetic ideas he found in Butor's critical essays, [Pousseur] suggested that the two of them collaborate on a "mobile opera," using the Faust theme as a point of departure. The result, a transposition of the legend to a contemporary setting, pictures the artist—in this instance a composer—as Faust, while Mephistopheles appears in the guise of a producer.

With characteristic ambiguity, Butor conveys the impression that the producer is also directing the very performance we are witnessing. As in Goethe's version, the curtain rises on a "Prologue in the Theater"; for theatrical atmosphere, however, this prologue is closer to the opening scenes of Claudel's *Le Soulier de satin.* A calculated informality—a discussion of the show that is about to be put on—aims at a closer communion between actors and audience, stage and house, and (in *Votre Faust* much more than in *Le Soulier de satin*) forces the action to become a commentary upon itself. With the "Prologue in Heaven" irony creeps in: we are in almost total darkness, and the sound is produced not by the music of the spheres but by a small orchestra on stage playing a traditional canon. (pp. 39-40)

By now it would seem that two familiar themes of Butor's writings have been stated again. The main character [Faust] is trying to compose a work, and even though we already surmise that he will fail in his endeavor, it turns out to be the very one we are watching. Also, the temptation that faces him is that of complacency and inactivity: the conditions of his contract are such as to banish from his mind both care and conscience. Beyond the plot outline, however, and in a fashion that can only be alluded to here, the techniques used in the novels and more obviously in *Mobile* play a major role. Literary quotations and allusions are supplemented by musical ones, projection screens are added to traditional lighting effects, and liberal use is made of recorded tapes, along with instruments and voices singing or speaking in five different languages. All are viewed as basic units in the work, like words in a poem, and a number of modulations are effected that bring them in contact with one another to produce a series of neo-surrealist metaphors.

The conclusion of part one also marks, for the spectator, the end of the fixed portion of the operatic fantasy. Butor and Pousseur will not proceed on their own but, through the producer-director, request instructions from the audience. This is the most striking feature of *Votre Faust:* the word "variable" in the subtitle means that a number of versions are available.... Preposterous as the procedure might seem it simply brings out into the open the necessary, tacit collaboration between author and reader or spectator, of which suspension of disbelief is but the indispensable premise. More than that, though, the device serves to emphasize human freedom and responsibility. The manipulation of freedom by an author is a complex and contradictory process, and no matter how well the reader's freedom has been preserved, no matter what illusions one may harbor concerning that of the characters, their fate has necessarily been sealed once the book has been written. Here, the solution to a seemingly insoluble quandary is sought by playing upon the instinctive identification of the audience with the hero and, through that audience, by helping to restore his freedom of choice. (pp. 41-2)

With *Votre Faust* Butor has perhaps come to the close of a second stage in his creative activities. If his first period was somewhat syncretic and found its expression almost exclusively through the novel, the second one can truly be termed explosive. (p. 44)

A sign of a writer's stature is his power of assimilation. When first reading Butor, one is not tempted to say, This is like Faulkner, or like Joyce, or like Proust. The critic, after some pondering, will begin to see analogies, and scholars will set themselves the task of unraveling threads of the elusive phenomenon known as literary influence. Plots, themes, and techniques will eventually be traced to their sources. On such raw materials, however, Michel Butor has indelibly stamped the seal of his unique art. (p. 46)

Leon S. Roudiez, in his Michel Butor *(copyright © 1965 Columbia University Press; reprinted by permission of the publisher),* Columbia University Press, 1965.

Among the best of the postwar novelists, Michel Butor occupies a high place. He is one of those novelists who, by reason of his remarkably controlled language and the seriousness of his literary theory, refuses to allow literature to be considered a diversion. He believes that the authentic work of fiction manifests a new way of being, and this is revealed by the form of the novel. New fictional forms may reveal new things in the world, and new relationships between things and people. In speaking of *Finnegans Wake,* Butor points out that for each reader such a work becomes an instrument of intimate self-knowledge.

The subject matter of Butor's *La Modification* (1957) would be suitable for a conventional psychological novel. A man in Paris takes a train for Rome in order to see his mistress and bring her back with him to Paris. During the trip he changes his mind; his project is no longer valid when he reaches Rome. He has been changed by the places he sees from the train, by his compartment in the train, by Rome,

where he is going and which occupies his thoughts. All of these matters physical and mental become the real characters of the novel which force Léon to alter his decision. The reasons for his change of heart are complex, and no reader can be sure of the real reason. This is one of the points of *La Modification,* and indeed of the *neuveau roman:* it is impossible to reach any specific unalterable truth.

Butor's characters are revealed to us by the places where they live, by those places that oppress them. The hero is quite typically a prisoner. In *L'Emploi du temps* (1956), Jacques is a prisoner in the town of Bleston for 365 days. In *La Modification,* Léon is a prisoner for twenty hours in the Paris-Rome express. In Butor's first novel, *Passage de Milan* (1954), all the inhabitants of an apartment house are imprisoned there from seven in the evening until seven o'-clock in the morning.

La Jalousie and *La Modification* differ widely in style and manner, but in common they have traits associated today with the *nouveau roman.* The type of hero who was endowed with a civic status and a biography has disappeared from this new type of novel. Subject matter based upon a continuous narrative and anecdotes and episodes has given way to the description of a world where nothing is stable or certain, and where characters, as we know them in the traditional novel, do not exist. The principal character in the *nouveau roman* is no one in particular, but he is a figure whose fantasies become a world in themselves, far more real than the world he is looking at.

Thus the art of . . . Butor shows an emptiness, a hollowness at the heart of reality. The new structure of these novels demonstrates this experience of emptiness and absence. We are never told, for example, that the husband in *La Jalousie* is jealous, but we may feel this by watching him watch his wife standing beside a man. The function of the *vous* used by Butor in *La Modification* is a form of call or challenge to the reader by which we realize that the language of the novel is that of an inquisition, and the reader is being assumed into the stream of consciousness. (pp. 299-300)

Wallace Fowlie, "Michel Butor," in his French Literature: Its History and Its Meaning *(© 1973 by Prentice-Hall, Inc.; reprinted by permission of Prentice-Hall, Inc., Englewood Cliffs, New Jersey),* Prentice-Hall, 1973, pp. 299-300.

The almost simultaneous appearance of the first works of Robbe-Grillet and those of Michel Butor created the impression of a new *school,* rather than of innovative individuals. But it is becoming increasingly difficult to link these two writers together. Moreover, Butor has taken a theoretical stand very different from Robbe-Grillet's. Rather than trying to find a new definition of limited scope for the novel, Butor has pursued a wide-ranging, ambitious quest extending to the whole of literature. (The French word "recherche," which Butor used to describe his literary program, means "research" in the sense of searching anew, of quest.)

Butor's quest is based less on a feeling that the old forms of expression are worn out than on a feeling that these forms are too narrow and too restricted to express a world that had become extraordinarily enlarged. The writer is thus forced to forge new means of expression. "The quest for new forms of the novel with greater power of integration thus plays the triple role of denunciation, exploration, and adaptation, in relation to our awareness of reality,'' he wrote in *The Novel as Research*. Butor's denunciation was not only literary; the old forms, repeated out of laziness, which were blind or untruthful, went hand in hand with a conservative social order. But Butor's main stress was on adaptation; reality, which for Robbe-Grillet was—in an ambiguous way—to be annulled and then used, and for Nathalie Sarraute was to be pursued in the form of authenticity, was for Butor the subject of an optimistic, wonderstruck exploration. He is like Claudel, but with a dry, brittle lyricism. And it is worth noting the importance for both Claudel and Butor of the myth of a "new world," without which the universe is incomplete.

But Butor, the most realistic of the new novelists, has also been the one most interested in form, the one whose language is the most complex and the freest in relation to its subject. Butor's first works were not nearly so radical as Robbe-Grillet's, because Butor was much less interested in breaking with the traditional framework of the novel than with dealing with specific subjects while still preserving a great deal of that framework. (pp. 97-8)

[While] he retained the traditional framework of the novel, Butor's aim in these works was to find an order (frequently symbolized by some kind of schedule) in a reality that seems to reject order in both time and space. Thus, the quest for order acknowledged the lack of order. The past resuscitated in the present is added to the past, or modifies it; the movement of consciousness and of the writing reacts on the object described; the event has to be described from multiple and contradictory viewpoints.

The novel as a quest, a re-search, for order could not end in anything other than failure, and the story of that failure is told in all these novels, in *Degrees* in particular. But Butor renounced the novel rather than the quest, and he who began by accepting what Robbe-Grillet rejected from the start was to contest far more. Indeed, one cannot use the term "novel" to describe Butor's more recent works, such as *Mobile* (1962, Mobile) and *Réseau aérien* (1962, Aerial Network), in both of which he superimposed images and assembled and dismantled linguistic structures. (pp. 98-9)

The audience Butor addresses his works to has become more and more an audience of listeners (we hear tones and dissonant or harmonious voices) or of viewers (we see striking typographical arrangements) than of readers following the thread of a text by an abstract effort of the imagination. He has moved away not only from the novel but from literature, toward a synthesis hinted at in the composer Luciano Berio's *Omaggio a Joyce,* for example.

Butor has tried to make his style escape from any set pattern. It is almost impossible to speak of a characteristic Butor sentence structure. His sentences are either protracted or succinct, flowing or syncopated, as required by the subject and the psychological time response; they are less comparable to written communication than they are to parts of a musical score or a typographical construction. Butor, like the others, has ultimately given us structures to play with, and we are even invited to make our own choices, to use the elements provided—the scenario to be enacted or the happening to be pursued—to give our own performance. But Butor's game is quite different in spirit from that of the other new novelists because, in the arid landscape of contemporary questioning, his work has something of the "modernist" exaltation of the 1920s. His game is not so much a compensation—what remains in spite of all

—as it is a gift of happy discovery in a world that is inexhaustible and continually renewed. (p. 100)

Gaëtan Picon, in his Contemporary French Literature: 1945 and After *(copyright © 1974 by Frederick Ungar Publishing Co., Inc.), Ungar, 1974.*

In his latest book [*Matière derêves* Butor] for the first time uses highly personal materials—dreams, memories—to create the five stories of the work. Each has a title and a recognizable story line, but the action is interrupted and diffused by a host of substructures. Many of these often minute subsections begin with the name of a city . . . visited by the narrator. Another device used by the narrator is to enclose a slide in a letter, a slide that may evoke associations or a name in literature, such as Chateaubriand, Balzac, Stendhal, Constant, Kafka or Zola. The text is studded with the words or names of members of the author's family that constantly arise in his mind and let him express his love for them or make him call out for their help when he is in anguish. Also used are such techniques of the new novel as repetition, regression and intertextuality. The whole kaleidoscopic view is imbued with mystery and rapidly changing images that defy rational explanation and startle the narrator as well as the reader because they are truly "such stuff as dreams are made on."

The narrator, who calls himself Michel Butor most of the time, seems to be asking the same unanswerable questions that appeared in his earlier *A Change of Heart:* "Who are you? Where are you going?" With anguish he "watches the screen" where his life story is shown. Simultaneously viewer and person viewed, he experiences rational and irrational forces from the most secret recesses of his mind. As the film progresses, he tries to describe and comment on what he sees. Speaking of "feverish, contaminated or agitated texts," he still strives to interpret what he sees. But unconscious, irrational behavior usually represses critical thinking. (pp. 53-4)

Although in *A Change of Heart* Butor has already used a dream in which the narrator wanders through a forest that keeps closing up behind him, nothing he has ever written equals the horror of [some of the scenes of] nightmares. Nowhere has he bared his non-rational side and libidinal drives so fully. In fact, he has always endeavored to avoid confrontation with the irrational, unconscious side of life.

Understandably, Butor dedicates *Matière de rêves* to "the psychoanalysts, among others," where "others" should be taken to refer to the large audience of all those interested in "seeing" what happens on levels of insight revealed only in dreams as described by a lucid man who possesses the words both to convey the experience and the courage to render it in powerful images. (p. 54)

Anna Otten, in World Literature Today *(copyright 1977 by the University of Oklahoma Press), Vol. 51, No. 3, Winter, 1977.*

In some instances Butor sees the writer in the role of a detective ferreting out an overt or a covert crime such as fratricide. On other occasions he bestows on him the part of a psychologist unearthing original sins and repressed complexes. At all times, however, in his Hermetic fiction, Butor projects in his writer-protagonist the role of an anthropologist engaged in the process of probing beyond the limits of the individual consciousness into the set up of the family, the clan, the age group, the generations and their gaps, the entire nation with its history and ramifications reaching into the buried primordial past common to all humanity. . . .

As varied as his novels may be, whether they feature only one hero or anti-hero such as Delmont or Revel, the Revealer, or a group such as the adolescents in *Degrés,* or the families in *Passage de Milan,* they display one common theme: a crisis of identity followed by a partially successful or aborted epiphany. In whichever milieu the plot is set and however the ultimate outcome may be resolved, the main question which arises in each and every one of his works of fiction is how to trace identities. An individual Self is related to ever-broadening circles of relationships in an effort to abolish the feeling of isolation and alienation which surrounds modern man beset by a tendency to ignore or forget his roots.

Butor makes it perfectly clear that his protagonists represent a totality of human experience and are by no means unique. In *La Modification* the narrator Léon Delmont uses the second person to involve the reader in his ordeal. He is an average traveling salesman at life's crossroads and comes to realize who he is, by some inner Eleusynian experience. Not only is he everyman, but in every child, man or woman he encounters, he sees his own children, wife or acquaintances at some various stage of life. Stripped of the myths he had projected upon them, all women are interchangeable, as he realizes their resemblances and similar gestures on parallel occasions. (p. 32)

Consciousness can be acquired on a personal level as well as on a collective one. Most people live by myths which must be demystified if we are to understand ourselves and others and stop projecting our fears, hates, and prejudices upon them. Butor's goal is to let the reader acquire more awareness by realizing that his common humanity reaches beyond family, clan, nation, religion, or race. He always sympathizes with the Promethean or accursed man who revolts against the subjection of son to father, pupil to teacher, colored to white, present to past. Slavery is archaic, so are conventions, social sham and pious cover up of lies. The disease must be exposed lest it fester in us and explode. Man must face the past and view it dispassionately, as historical fact cannot lie buried without reasserting itself. We cannot even afford to ignore prehistory for in it we will find roots common to all men. . . . By realizing the tenuous bond between ourselves and the vanishing natural world which is our habitat, we may acquire a better understanding of ourselves and of our milieu, and stand less alienated in the Diaspora of modern cities. We can grow richer and wiser by reversing the trend of distrust and hostility which we project toward our brother whom too often we treat as the "Other." (p. 36)

Adèle Bloch, "Michel Butor and the Social Structure," in The International Fiction Review *(© copyright International Fiction Association), January, 1977, pp. 32-6.*

C

CALDWELL, Erskine 1903-

A novelist and short story writer of the Deep South, Caldwell is best known for his novels *Tobacco Road* and *God's Little Acre*. Caldwell blends comic pathos and broad humor, often suggesting serious themes in a seemingly naïve manner. The family, race relations, and traditional moral values are confronted by ideological and social conflicts in many of Caldwell's finest works. (See also *CLC*, Vol. 1, and *Contemporary Authors*, Vols. 1-4, rev. ed.)

Mr. Caldwell has allowed himself to be claimed by the group which insists that social criticism is the be-all and end-all of the drama. He has himself been associated with various efforts to draw public attention to conditions among the economically depressed class in the South, and his novels deal ostensibly with life as it is lived by members of this same class. It would, however, be difficult to find any works whose tone or effect is less that of the simple sociological preachment than these novels and the plays which have been made from them. Instead of earnestness one discovers a brilliant but grotesque imagination and a strange humor which ranges from the Rabelaisian to the macabre. (p. 121)

[Of] Mr. Caldwell one may say that the rank flavor of his work is as nearly unique as anything in contemporary literature. One may, to be sure, assign him his special place in a rather vague tradition. He is, let us grant, as "hard-boiled" as Hemingway and as brutal as Faulkner. Like the latter he loves to contemplate the crimes and perversions of degenerate rustics; like both, his peculiar effects are made possible only by the assumption of an exaggerated detachment from all the ordinary prejudices of either morality or taste and a consequent tendency to present the most violent and repulsive scenes with the elaborate casualness of a careful pseudo-naïveté. Yet Mr. Caldwell is not, for all that, really like either Hemingway or Faulkner. Hemingway has something of the dogged, repetitious gravity of one of his own drunks; the second sometimes suggests the imbecile earnestness of his favorite half-wits; but when Caldwell is being most characteristically himself the mood which dominates his writing is the mood of a grotesque and horrible humor. The element of which he is most aware and that which he seems most determined to make us perceive is the element of an almost pure macabre. His starveling remnant of the Georgia poor-white trash is not only beyond all mo-

rality and all sense of dignity or shame, it is almost beyond all hope and fear as well. As ramshackle and as decayed as the moldy cabins in which it lives, it is scarcely more than a parody on humanity, and when some hidden spark of anger flashes briefly forth, or when lust—the most nearly inextinguishable of human impulses—motivates a casual and public seduction or rape, one is bound to regard these crimes almost as one regards the deeds of that traditional embodiment of moral imbecility, Mr. Punch. Perhaps it is difficult to believe that a play which centers about the determination of an old man to return a twelve-year-old child to her husband, which involves the almost continuous presence of a rutting female monstrosity with a hare lip, and which ends with the death of an old woman beneath the wheels of an automobile, can be funny. Yet funny it was, to me at least, and funny—though perhaps ambiguously so—it was also, I believe, intended to be.

That the material would fall most easily into a tragic or quasi-tragic pattern is obvious enough. Mr. Caldwell does violence to all our expectations when he treats it as comedy, but he succeeds because he manages to prevent us from feeling at any moment any real kinship with the nominally human creatures of the play. All comedy of whatever sort has as a necessary condition the fact that the spectator maintains his sense of separateness from the personages involved, that he is not inside and feeling with them but outside and judging by standards different from theirs. . . . Mr. Caldwell puts this law to its severest test by endeavoring to maintain a comic detachment in the face of characters so depraved that mere revulsion, if nothing else, would seem to make detachment impossible. It would be interesting to inquire how one may account for the fact that this detachment is, to a considerable extent, maintained, and one obvious answer would be that the characters themselves are represented as creatures so nearly sub-human that their actions are almost without human meaning and that one does not feel with them because they themselves obviously feel so little. (pp. 122-24)

Even if it be judged by the broad standards of the present moment [*Journeyman*] is a violent and bawdy piece which makes no apologies, either sentimental or otherwise, for its violence and bawdiness. Anyone who denounced it as lewd and perverted would be taking a position understandable enough if not necessarily justified. But to treat the [theatrical adaptation of the novel] as it was treated, to speak as if it were the mere meanderings of an illiterate, is to exhibit a blindness difficult to comprehend in view of the fact that its imaginative force is the one thing which no one, it would seem, could possibly miss.

Mr. Caldwell . . . is said to think of himself as a realist with a sociological message to deliver. If that message exists it would be even more difficult to find in *Journeyman* than it was in *Tobacco Road* and one might maintain in addition that the chief characters, far from being realistic portraits of real human beings, are absolute monsters. But there is no use discussing what a work of art means or whether or not it is "true to life" unless one is convinced that the work "exists"—that it has the power to attract and hold attention, to create either that belief or that suspension of disbelief without which its "message" cannot be heard and without which the question of its factual truth is of no importance. And to me the one incontrovertible fact is that both Mr. Caldwell's novels and the plays made from them do in this sense "exist" with uncommon solidity, that his race of curiously depraved and yet curiously juicy human grotesques are alive in his plays whether they, or things like them, were ever alive anywhere else or not. And if they seem, when abstractly considered, highly improbable, that only strengthens the tribute one is, in simple fairness, bound to pay to the imagaination of a man who can make them credible. Perhaps this imagination is corrupt and perverted. Perhaps—though I don't think this is true—the world would be better off without Mr. Caldwell's vision of its corruption. But that is not the point. The point is that his imagination is creative in the most direct sense of the term. His creatures live, and no attempts at analysis can deprive them of their life. (pp. 125-26)

> *Joseph Wood Krutch, in his* The American Drama Since 1918: An Informal History *(copyright © 1939 by Random House, Inc.; reprinted by permission of the Trustees of Columbia University in the City of New York), Random House, 1939.*

A learned man of letters has complained that Erskine Caldwell's characters are grotesques. He missed the prophecy. What was grotesque to him has become truth for us. Caldwell is a writer rich in the humor of everyday living, sympathetic, and yet without illusions. Chekhov's sweetened, tough humor has this quality. Caldwell is a simple teller of earthy tales with a style as simple as Hemingway's, with Hemingway's talent of rubbing out the metaphysical while leaving in its resonance. . . .

Erskine Caldwell excels in depicting the underlying horror of the quest for daily bread. "Saturday Afternoon" is a short story that belongs with the best of American fiction. Few have equaled its hands-off style. The characters are on the page as life has made them.

> *Morris Renek, "Rediscovering Erskine Caldwell," in* The Nation *(copyright 1975 by The Nation Associates, Inc.), June 21, 1975, p. 758.*

In the manner of Jack London, Caldwell has been a writer taken more seriously abroad than in America. Here, too, he was a power in paperback, however, a king when that form of publication was new. . . . Like Henry Miller, Caldwell had discovered early on a use for eroticism that was unmistakably his own, although, like Hemingway, his effort was always to simplify as much as possible whatever he saw. He wrote about poor people, rural people, who lived for mealtimes, girlfriends, jalopy rides, and his method of sim-

plifying by repetition was not merely an imitation of Hemingway. Caldwell's short stories because of their efficiency, like Hemingway's, hold up better than his novels do when reread now. But Caldwell's way of writing in what amounts to "panels," like a comic strip, and yet of conveying sexual longing and the hard misery and stupefaction of country poverty experienced by people who can't read or write, was original with him. (p. 3)

He was aloof. He lived, for example, in San Francisco through the period when the Beat Generation writers flocked there, a better writer than the other older writers who played to the crowd and at whose feet they sat—and really more germane to the best purposes of the Beats, it seemed to me.

The trouble with Caldwell seems to have been that he was finally lackadaisical. The eye that could distill so narrowly, the decent heart that roamed Tobacco Road, first alone and later with the photographer Margaret Bourke-White ("You Have Seen Their Faces"), rather soon stopped looking for new insights. Hoping that a change of geography might renew him, he went to Maine, but wrote about it as if it were Georgia again. The recent work of Dahlberg, Farrell or Miller—even when they fail—keeps pushing, pushing with intellectual tension, technical experimentation and passionate avowals; but "Afternoons in Mid-America," Erskine Caldwell's tour of the states between the Mississippi and the Rockies, is embarrassingly insipid. Not only clumsy and stylistically anemic, it lacks ambition. I doubt whether it could have been published under a pseudonym. Years ago an interviewer quoted Caldwell as saying that he seldom read, because for a writer to read the work of other writers would be like a doctor swallowing another doctor's prescriptions. In the vogue of anti-intellectualism, other people are saying somewhat the same thing, but, from Hemingway on down, they never *believed* it. One has the feeling Caldwell did, and consequently vegetated. (pp. 3, 72)

Like John O'Hara in his late stories, [in "Afternoons in Mid-America"] Caldwell is dipping back through 50 or 60 years of memories, but whereas in O'Hara it was a pleasure to sense the range of recollection at the writer's disposal, here there is no bite or discipline, no old-pro's vigor of craftsmanship. Even his way with dialogue, once the equal of O'Hara's, has fallen off to casual indifference. . . .

Still, this offspring of his frailty is not without some pretty passages. . . .

Bourke-White evoked the wordless silences with which Caldwell communed with a dirt farmer in 1936, listening, leaning on the fence, not imposing himself, as the man haltingly explained how things were. And, now 74, he kept me burning the midnight oil the other night with "Tobacco Road" all over again. (p. 72)

> *Edward Hoagland, in* The New York Times Book Review *(© 1976 by The New York Times Company; reprinted by permission), November 14, 1976.*

Caldwell's literary reputation did not follow the usual pattern of gradual rise, gradual decline and fall, and subsequent critical "rediscovery." According to his own account, no editor would consider publishing his work for seven years, but when his luck turned in the early 1930's he could scarcely miss. The reviewers, and there were many of them, found the stories in his first two books, published in 1930 and 1931, brutal and distasteful but "stunningly imaginative," and when *Tobacco Road* appeared in 1932, the critics were confused, as if they had never seen a book such as this before, as if conventional criticism could not apply to it. Three widely discussed books in two years is an auspicious beginning for a young writer, and the fact is that Caldwell was the first well-recognized Southern novelist of this century to remain in and write about his region. The influence of *his* South on the rest of the country and indeed the world was enormous, much more significant initially than the South of Faulkner, Wolfe or Warren. (p. 729)

[Erskine Caldwell's characters] are neither honorable nor dishonorable, moral nor immoral, and [their] lives give us neither cause for hope nor justification for suffering. Caldwell's novels make no attempt to create metaphors which explain the shadow on the wall, much less the source of the light, and what finally emerges against the backdrop of depression and Reconstruction literature is that Caldwell is not a *Southern* novelist at all but is, instead, a Southern *journalist,* in the same sense Sherwood Anderson was a journalist. We've been trying to read Caldwell in the same way we read other Southern novelists—as myth makers—instead of accepting and admiring him for his keen eye and ability to make certain kinds of facts come alive.

That is not to say that Caldwell cannot tell stories as well as anyone else in Georgia or Mississippi, nor that his books are less accomplished, but that he has no interest in sustaining honor as The Code; Caldwell's books are not and have never pretended to explain the pillars of Southern society: religion, history, place, and responsibility. They are like a camera whose lens will produce only a sharp and unmistakeningly realistic photograph, and it is our own failing as readers that we wish to take his portraits as representations of something larger, of all Southerners. The pictures seem, in fact, almost more real than their subjects, but it is only through such super-realism that Caldwell makes any statement at all. There is little difference between his novels and the four books of photographs with commentary which he and his wife produced together, and perhaps all of his novels should have carried the same title as his much praised book of photographs, *You Have Seen Their Faces.*

When Americans began reading Southern literature in the 1930s they sensed only that somewhere on the other side of the cultural wall was a land whose violence might help them put their own upheaval to rest. Not until Caldwell came along as a portrait painter were there clear models of the Southerner, or one type of Southerner, and Caldwell's books became primers, if not prerequisites, for all the other Southern novels read in subsequent years. If ever an audience was primed for a writer, it was the sensitive American reader of the dust bowl 1930s, and Caldwell limned his portraits so stunningly that he could not be ignored; for at least a decade Caldwell's characters become synonymous with the Southerner, and readers outside the region believed he alone could instruct them in the Southerner's obscure psyche. Caldwell's books provided a clear, precise beginning, and it might be speculated that Caldwell hastened our ability to comprehend Faulkner and the others by presenting us with the setting out of which the Snopes's emotional complexities could arise. Sadly, it has been to Caldwell's detriment that he does his journalism so effectively, and so realistically that we believed he was making the sort of myths and metaphors Hemingway had with his journalistic fiction. But such was not the case, and we emerge from Caldwell's novels with no sense that violence has meaning or structure.

Having performed the vital service of unlocking fundamental mysteries of the South, Caldwell's photographs became not only unnecessary but annoying. Yes, yes, we said to Caldwell, you've shown us the ugliness and we know too well how it looks. Show us something else. Make the ugliness into something worthwhile which will alleviate our fears. But Caldwell refused, and he outgrew his usefulness, making a nuisance of himself by continuing to show us the obvious, and refusing to create myths which would help set things right again.

Caldwell's characters are incapable of redemption, not because they are evil but because they are not given that option by their creator. We reject them for it and for their emptiness, and in our rejection we affirm our belief in honor. Caldwell does not imbue his personae with enough perception to be either honorable or dishonorable; they do not know enough to know that they want to change. Unlike the depraved characters in other Southern novels, his possess no emotional consciousness and so, as men of conscience, we do not wish to identify with or care about them for very long. And so it is likely that Caldwell will be the least favored of Southern writers until the code of honor and spirit of redemption which the South gave to the nation falls into disfavor. (pp. 730-31)

> *Walton Beacham, "Against the Grain," in* The Nation (*copyright 1977 by The Nation Associates, Inc.*), *June 11, 1977, pp. 729-31.*

* * *

CALISHER, Hortense   1911-

American novelist, short story writer, and essayist, Calisher has a refined Proustian insight into the psyche of her characters and a keen sense of language. These are best displayed in her chronicles *False Entry* and *The New Yorkers*. (See also *CLC*, Vols. 2, 4, and *Contemporary Authors*, Vols. 1-4, rev. ed.)

The purest of entertainers, and novelistic in the old-fashioned sense, Miss Calisher is, in addition, among the most literate practitioners of modern American fiction, a stylist wholly committed to the exploitation of language. It is nothing short of wonderful to follow a Calisher sentence as it moves from low to middle to high flight, to watch it gather force and then stop just short of ripeness—as it can invariably be depended upon to do. The stories themselves [in *The Collected Stories of Hortense Calisher*] are a remarkably varied lot, for Miss Calisher knows the pitch and flavor of a great many voices, both of the upper- and lower-middle-class sort. Caste and class is her subject, and one nowhere more compellingly grounded than in her sketches of childhood, in which the society of the classroom and the schoolyard is portrayed in all its biting and complex reality. Small ups and downs aside, virtually all of the 36 stories here have that consistent life, that strong sense of abundance, characteristic of a genuine literary power. In sum, a notable achievement. (pp. 17-18)

> *Dorothy Rabinowitz, in* Saturday Review (© *1975 by Saturday Review/World, Inc.; reprinted with permission*), *October 18, 1975.*

Hortense Calisher has her own way with the story form. Her stories make a somewhat slow, decorous and stately progress, in the direction she destines for them, stopped only to be enriched in texture by complex, decorative words and phrases. They move on, ending so that we are struck each time by the inevitableness of her steps, by the exact rightness of her coda.

Curiously enough, it is from our realization of their *difference* from "real life" that we derive our satisfaction. In life we are told the history of a man or a place to whose conclusion the teller has only rarely been a witness. We receive the story along the implacable, flat and incomplete lines of chronology—this happens and then that. Calisher's accomplishment is that she lifts the tale out of the commonplace, carrying it away from the harness of hard fact by her fine verbal textures. Seen through her eyes the real world is not prosaic. Placed in lyrical, poetic spaces, it is thick and rich with implication.

She has never been much for plot. What happens in her stories is what she has defined as "an apocalypse, served in a very small cup." Sudden awarenesses, epiphanies of character are her métier, which perhaps explains why, to my mind, her stories seem more impressive than her novels. Prophetic revelation does not extend well; the tea cup is the proper vessel for sudden, small visions into the spirit. In a blaze of light, as startling as Paul's Damascan vision, we see, not a string of events, but a tableau, frozen, static, inevitable—and instructive.

But if nothing happens in the traditional sense, there is another more solid kind of knowledge we acquire of the life and nature of her characters. She catches likeness with eerie accuracy ("calls up" might be more accurate: I have the image of a fakir, cross-legged, drawing upon his pipe, as characters slowly materialize out of smoke) and this may be the result of her choices. Almost a third of [her stories in "The Collected Stories of Hortense Calisher"] are about her family. . . . She is best, I think, with them because she allows herself to wander among them, an awkward, under-valued, sensitive child among proud, attractive, transplanted, late Victorian Southerners, living out their well-to-do "comfortable" lives in New York. No resentment ever clouds these firm portraits. . . . She remembers their oddities and their essential differences with accepting love. These stories are literally the core of the book, having been moved here from other locations and order in other books. Now they form a chronological hub from which her perceptions on other subjects radiate so that, with very little further imaginative stretch, one can feel a novel forming.

But she is very good, too, with the people she knew and knows about in New York, the city people and those transplanted to the city—the chic and the lonely, the proud and the dispossessed. . . . (p. 3)

It is perhaps old-fashioned of her, in the light of modern explicitness, but Calisher can evoke with one word the completion of sexual satisfaction more successfully than lesser and more graphic writers achieve in several pages. . . .

One looks about for writers of the short story to "place" her among. Language: one thinks of John Updike. Economical evocation of place: perhaps Graham Greene or, in some ways, the Joyce of "Dubliners." Subdued passion: once or twice, Flannery O'Connor. Even if we acknowledge her apprenticeship to Henry James (she would seem to belong among that happy few he marked off as those upon whom nothing is lost) she has her own quality. It is hard to relate her to others in the New York school, because her New York, after all, is an interior landscape, seen very individually.

What do her stories actually *do*? They take us into the private depths of lives about which we know almost nothing until the moment at which she chooses to begin her story. In "Point of Departure" we are not told the names of the two characters, or anything about how they look or their private histories, nothing except the important thing: their intersecting fates and the moment at which they meet. We enter her world willingly, because she has shown us life, or the ashes of it, in her very small cup. (p. 4)

> *Doris Grumbach, in* The New York Times Book Review *(© 1975 by The New York Times Company; reprinted by permission), October 19, 1975.*

[*The Collected Stories of Hortense Calisher*] reminds us that Miss Calisher, the author of several novels and a recently published memoir, deals in commodities we rarely find any longer. She believes in firm structures and plots. Her stories are filled with the detail that establishes mood and place. Her prose is leisurely, cadenced, sparked with images from a poet's flint.

To be sure, not all of Miss Calisher's stories are equally successful. "In Greenwich There Are Many Gravelled Walks," the opener of the collection, is perhaps too carefully machined—its gears well-meshed, but exposed. "The Scream on 57th Street," however, is a multi-layered tale of psychic terror that Henry James would have envied; details deftly shift and join to form conflicting patterns.

The Elkin stories are among Miss Calisher's richest achievements. They are to New York what Joyce's *Dubliners* is to Dublin, the subtlest social observation wrapped in rue. In them, the city's old West Side comes to life once again, the rambling apartments with their twisting halls, high-ceilinged rooms, carved cupboards, and dark, over-stuffed furniture; the servants, meek, tyrannical or harassed; the smells of the kitchens; the propriety and fuss of clothes, meals, routines, manners.

These autobiographical pieces about the Elkin family have much to say about families everywhere. . . . They tell of the wounds inevitably inflicted in the most loving households, wounds that ache and shape events for generations.

These stories also sound a theme that resonates through all Miss Calisher's work: the isolation we cannot avoid and cannot face. . . .

It is obvious that for Miss Calisher the human drama is the main one going. Her stories, symmetrical, conclusive, polished to the glint, are classics of their kind. (p. 19)

> *Eugenie Bolger, "Endangered Species," in* The New Leader *(© 1976 by the American Labor Conference on International Affairs, Inc.), January 19, 1976, pp. 18-19.*

The title of one of Hortense Calisher's earlier collections, *Extreme Magic*, is an apt description of her legerdemain with the short story genre. The *Collected Stories* should regain readers for the author, readers who have found it difficult to keep the faith after experiencing her recent novels. . . . What *The Collected Stories* makes clear is that Hortense Calisher not only is best at writing short stories, she is one of *the* best. (pp. 317-18)

Of all the things to praise, plot is not one. Her story lines often are fragile, if not non-existent. This is because in her fiction incident is subordinate to insight. The landscape of her stories is more often than not a psychescape of the protagonist. It is impossible to overpraise the psychological acumen which the author brings to each story. . . .

One must also praise the beauty of Ms. Calisher's language. Not since Elizabeth Bowen has such gorgeous prose been employed to spin a tale (and Bowen, like Calisher, seems to have studied the figures in Henry James's carpet). . . . (p. 318)

Ultimately one must praise Ms. Calisher's range. She writes of the urban and the suburban, the adult and the adolescent, the male and the female, the historical past and the hysterical present. Her most persistent theme is failure—of love, of marriage, of communication, of identity. One of her singular abilities is to link or relate the individual defeats of her protagonists to the defeat of traditional social and moral values in the world at large, a world which has either progressed or regressed to the point of ignoring or defeating former standards of behavior or excellence. (pp. 318-19)

> *Robert Phillips, in* Commonweal *(copyright © 1976 Commonweal Publishing Co., Inc.; reprinted by permission of Commonweal Publishing Co., Inc.), May 7, 1976.*

*   *   *

CALVINO, Italo   1923-

Italian novelist and short story writer, Calvino was a member of the Italian resistance during World War II; the events of this time recur in his work. His fiction blends reality and fantasy in both realistic description and surrealistic expression. (See also *CLC,* **Vol. 5.)**

What Italo Calvino has done [in *Il castello dei destini incrociati*] is to take two different packs of Tarot cards, a fifteenth-century one from Renaissance Italy, and a much more plebeian one from eighteenth-century Marseilles, and to dispose the individual cards as systematically as he found possible as the supports of brief narratives. His use of the cards, in fact, is very precisely the use of them once made by fortune-tellers. But his methods are more complicated. As the title suggests, the stories he makes up from the sequences of adjoining cards must be made to intersect. . . .

The stories in [the first] half are adapted to the origins and opulence of the particular Tarot cards they were written to accompany: they are courtly, gallant, formal, and eventually introduce characters and episodes from the *Orlando Furioso,* in a perfectly appropriate anachronism.

Because [the] second pack of Tarot cards had a quite different and less glossy origin than the first one, Calvino has also tried to induce a different kind of story from it, exploiting his yen for apocalypses: in the Tavern the narratives readily become disorderly and overstep the civilized bounds imposed on the earlier set. In particular, there are constant prophecies of how nature may take its revenge on mankind and eventually reassume full occupation of the inhabited world.

This, if you like, is a desperate reminder that the author himself is in trouble, that the cards are proving recalcitrant to his highly contrived schemes. And one of the charms of the *Castello dei destini incrociati* is the stealthy way in which Calvino so often dramatizes the very activity he is engaged on, so that such inescapable themes as the Grail quest merge pleasantly with the very cerebral endeavours of the progressive novelist.

The book is a limpid and elegant essay in the semiotics of narrative, as much a critical as a creative work. Its chief lesson is of the possibly inexhaustible resources of each image as an element in a story.

> *"Card Play," in* The Times Literary Supplement *(© Times Newspapers, Ltd., 1973; reproduced from* The Times Literary Supplement *by permission), December 14, 1973, p. 1529.*

Calvino's seventh novel [*Invisible Cities*] is a sensuous delight, a sophisticated literary puzzle. Within the imperial gardens, Kublai Khan and Marco Polo rest in their hammocks, smoke their pipes and create reality. Polo describes the cities outside the garden walls which are "invisible" to the Khan. "But are they real?" Kublai wonders, with good reason. Calvino has deployed 55 sketches of imaginary cities, fictive constructs reminiscent of utopias or Dante's *Inferno,* or Borges' "Tlön, Uqbar, Orbis Tertius." The short sketches, from 300 to 700 words each, are enigmas, like Zen *koans,* intended for the reader's meditation:

> If you choose to believe me, good. Now I will tell how Octavia, the spider-web city, is made. Between two mountains, a suspended net supports a city. . . .

Calvino plays with images, spatial jokes, associations by form. Besides these refined games, there is usually a philosophical problem: "Suspended over the abyss, the life of Octavia's inhabitants is less uncertain than in other cities. They know the net will last only so long."

The sketches are arranged in formidable symmetry with at least three ordering principles. First there is the frame tale, as in *The Arabian Nights,* or in Calvino's own tradition, *The Decameron.* (Oddly enough the lives of Boccaccio and Polo probably overlapped a decade.) Within the frame, Polo's tales edify and entertain the emperor. The sketches are further ordered by one group of 10, seven groups of five, and a final group of 10. These are numbered in a bizarre fashion, which we find to be a countdown: 1;2, 1;3, 2, 1, so that each of the nine sections self-destructs (with the exception of the last, which somehow reconstitutes itself in symmetry with the first). These groupings are esthetic games of abstract design.

The third order leads us from abstraction into the themes of the book. There are 11 categories of cities (such as thin cities, trading cities, cities and the dead) that repeat in an elaborate, additive pattern, as if these basic patterns could organize (or create) the known world. The repetition of these categories invites the reader to make comparisons, to find recurring ornaments and meanings. As Polo says, "Everything I see and do assumes meaning in a mental space."

History and geography become mental spaces; all reality is thought. Aggressively he explores the Cartesian dualism of mind and matter, giving primacy to the mind, promoting solipsism, making life a chess board. The poor Khan ponders his own chess board, struggling to keep up with Polo's dazzling fluency: "By disembodying his conquests to reduce them to the essential, Kublai had arrived at the extreme operation: the definitive conquest, of which the empire's multiform treasures were only illusory envelopes. It was reduced to a square of planed wood: nothingness. . . ." Such frightening purity is worthy of Mallarmé. (pp. 30-1)

This is not a book for a general reader seeking linear plots, clear morals, social realism. *Invisible Cities* is a volume for lovers of hypothesis, mannerism, conundrum and fantasy. (p. 31)

> *Albert H. Carter, III, in* The New Republic *(reprinted by permission of* The New Republic; © *1974 by The New Republic, Inc.),* December 28, 1974.

[Calvino's] fictional and critical work is solidly placed at the crossroads of the major issues in contemporary social, cultural, and literary theory—Marxism and structuralism, anthropology and semiotics, popular culture and antinarrative. Under the guise of telling us tongue-in-cheek sophisticated fairy tales or self-conscious modern epics, he forces us to rethink through notions such as form and content, language and style, literary imagination, creative discourse, the role of science, the purpose of literature, the artist's participation in society. His achievement, however, has not yet been fully understood. (p. 414)

It is often said that Calvino's writings oscillate between two extremes, one being sociopolitical involvement resulting in a style that may be called "neorealist," and the other the fantastic or escapist literature of works like *Le cosmicomiche* or the recent *Le città invisibili* (1972). This polarity is believed to be caused by divided impulses or irreconcilable interests in the author. I would like to argue that, on the contrary, Calvino's works remain constantly focused on a basic vision of human activity as both praxis and poiesis, and that, if thematic polarity does exist in his narrative, it is not a contradictory impasse but rather a dialectic process reflecting his awareness of the very nature of culture as the highest and unique form of human "doing." I believe that Calvino's message can be best understood in the light of certain basic concepts that are central to his work and to the recent formulations of semiotic literary theory: the notions of langue and parole as defined by Saussure, narrative and discourse structures as defined by Propp, Greimas, and Todorov, the poetic function of language as defined by Roman Jakobson, the unconscious or symbolic function as defined by Lévi-Strauss, desire as redefined by Lacan, and the notion of *écriture* (writing, script) discussed by Barthes and Derrida. (pp. 414-15)

[It] is the conceptual basis of structuralism and semiotics that intrigues and affects Calvino the writer, giving a new slant to motifs and concerns already apparent in his earlier works and suggesting new modes of expression, new stylistic solutions.

Looking at the whole of Calvino's fiction, one is surprised to find, under a wealth of invention and an extraordinary stylistic variety, a remarkable constancy in what structural analysis would call (a) semantic content and (b) thematic investment, that is to say, the actantial or character oppositions and plot development that sustain the movement of each narrative (a), and the thematic elements that convey its first or most immediate meaning (b). For example, most of the tales of *Cosmicomics* and *t zero* are based on the binary actantial opposition of Subject-Opponent and Subject-Object. . . .

In other words, the functional sequence of events making up the plot of Calvino's tales is constant and very simple, often consisting of only a few essential functions among the thirty-one that Propp showed to constitute the fairy-tale archetype. Likewise, the themes invested in this simple structure are the very elementary contents of human experience: desire, rivalry, guilt, the impulse to express and to

communicate, the need for self-affirmation but also for belonging, the necessity to make ethical and existential choices. His longer tales usually show the journey of discovery or quest pattern, which is particularly evident in his first novel, *The Path to the Nest of Spiders,* and which is significant in view of Calvino's ideological and stylistic use of myth and folktale as his chosen narrative form. (p. 415)

Discourse may be defined as the particular way in which the semantic elements are organized by means of constructional and stylistic devices such as narration and point of view, spatial and temporal patterns, imagery, language, special subcodes, etc. In contrast to the stability of thematic and semantic structures, narrative discourse in Calvino is directly responsible for the extraordinary originality of his ever-changing formal solutions, from his first "neorealist" novel and short stories to the allegorical tales of *I nostri antenati* (1963), the cosmogonic and mathematical fiction of *Cosmicomiche* and *Ti con zero,* the philosophical and political vignettes of *Marcovaldo* and *La giornata di uno scrutatore,* the "oneirigrams" of *Le città invisibili,* and the combinatory games of his latest *Il Castello dei destini incrociati* (1973). (pp. 415-16)

Calvino's discourse evolves, not in the sense of a perfectible movement or progress, but diachronically, inasmuch as it is linked to the historical time of Calvino the writer. The narrative persona, screen of the historical and biographical person, which had been embodied in the naturalistic child-hero Pin, and in Qfwfq, spirit of the natural and technological evolution, or of scientific and mathematical thought, is further metamorphosed [in *Invisible Cities*] into the pure voice of a discourse totally rarefied, lyrical, oneiric, beyond the threshold of antinarrative. . . .

[All] his writings bear witness to a precise ideological intent, an unambiguous poetics. (p. 417)

Both lexicon and syntax are subject to a deformation consisting mainly in the juxtaposition of the common "spoken language" usage and a highly specialized, scientific or literary language. . . . The numerous examples of *enumeración caótica* have their syntactical counterpart in the stream-of-consciousness passages such as the beautiful last paragraph of "All at One Point" or the whole of "Il sangue, il mare" ("Blood, Sea" in *t zero*) whose very title reflects the purposeful lack of syntactical organization.

Graphic symbols, different print types, and unusual spelling are also used to supply a strong visual perception (e.g., the signs hanging from the galaxies in "The Light-Years") or to indicate that a different temporal mode is used (i.e., the synchronic vs. the diachronic in Pt. II of "The Spiral"). Particularly original to Calvino are the purely graphic signifiers like the names of the characters of *Cosmicomics,* which are totally impossible to articulate as sounds, but visually suggest the qualities of their referents: the symmetrical, orderly molecular structure of Qfwfq, the unimaginative and gossipy narrow-mindedness of Mr. $Pber^tpber^d$, archetypal Fellinesque sexuality in Mrs. $Ph(i)Nk_0$, introverted visionary complexity in the sister $G'd(w)^n$, or the terrestrial longleggedness of L11. In some of them a phonic suggestion is included: the uncivilized "immigrants" Z'zu, Mr. Hnw ("who later became a horse"), and De XuaeauX, the lover of Mrs. $Ph(i)Nk_0$, who simply has to be a Frenchman. . . . Finally, the formulas of "t zero," used for individual and diachronic characterization . . . as well as for the synchronic system of interrelated characters and events in each of the possible time universes of the story . . . reveal the purely functional nature of narrative characters as roles or actants, and correspond to the more and more abstract narrators of their respective works. Even when, after *t zero*, Calvino no longer uses formulas as characters, but rather mythical or folklore figures, he represents them in the iconic fixity of the figures of a deck of cards (*Il Castello dei destini incrociati*). (pp. 417-18)

[The] specific and unique feature of Calvino's imagery is that it is based on the reversal of the semantic code, or on shifts from one code to another and, therefore, in addition to any or all of the . . . terms [usually applied, such as sur-realistic, comic, plastic, and technological,] it is always ironic, self-conscious, self-reflexive. (p. 419)

All attempts to imagine or to describe analogically not only a difficult abstract notion like the curve of space, but any aspect of the world, are the product of the human capacity for formal organization and symbolic representation which Lévi-Strauss has identified as the symbolic function, stand-ing at the origin of human society and culture. Such capaci-ty, Calvino maintains, is able to produce infinite forms, and not limited, as claimed by the opponents of structuralism, to carrying out a single program inherent in the structure itself. Within the framework of the langue, the parole is capable of infinite variety, because the forms produced are the result of a dialectic interaction between the structuring capacity of the mind and the reality with which, at any given time, we must come to terms. Of literature in particu-lar he says:

> Readings and lived experience are not two universes, but one. To be interpreted, every experience of life recalls certain readings and becomes fused with them. That books are always born of other books is a truth only seemingly contradictory to this other truth: that books are born of practical day-to-day life, and of the relationships among men.

Thus the shifts in codes observed in Calvino's imagery are not there to denounce the absurdity of the world, but, on the contrary, to prove its certainty. (p. 420)

The awareness on the part of the writer of performing an act of writing, the questioning of one's motivations, pur-pose, responsibilities in writing, and of the very meaning of writing is reflected by a hyperconscious, willful manipula-tion of the code(s). Although this poetic and esthetic prob-lem is also central to the work of other writers as different as, for instance, Borges, Barth, and Sollers, the formal and ideological solutions given remain as distinct as the (natu-ral) languages in which they write. In Calvino, metalinguis-tic and metanarrative references have the main function of exposing, or even exploding, the code so that a new one may be created. No code or system is given once and for all, no matter how established or accepted by tradition.

Language, the primary and oldest code, is questioned. . . . [The] whole of "A Sign in Space" is about the nature of the linguistic sign, arbitrary and unmotivated, the result of the human need to express and symbolize. The social nature of the institution of language, for which communication is a circuit, as Saussure described it, is reflected in the frus-trated isolation of Qfwfq whose signs of self-defense cannot be read or answered for billions of years. . . . The chivalric code of medieval legends and romances, Charlemagne's paladins, the Crusades, the Knights of the Holy Grail, and Ariosto's readaptation of that code, itself in turn becoming

the code of Renaissance epic and heroic literature, are uti-lized again in another system which incorporates elements and values of the modern industrial society, of Freudian psychology and Marxist economic theory, in *The Nonexist-ent Knight*. Countless and continuous references to other fictional works are mingled with references to literary, mythical, and historical figures and events. . . . In fact, there are so many that only a cross-reference index could list them properly. (p. 421)

[*Il Castello dei destini incrociati (The Castle of Crossed Destinies)*] consists of two parts, two sets of tales told by different narrators in the manner of Boccaccio or Chaucer, the respective "frames" being a Castle and a tavern (Calvi-no's capitalization) surrounded by a forest, in an indefinite time and location. The essential formal innovation is that, the narrators having magically lost the ability to speak (i.e., to use the linguistic code), the tales are told by means of a substitute code or system, namely, the tarot deck. . . . Here language, imagery, and metalinguistic references are all dic-tated by the particular narrative code (the tarot) that the author imposes, as a strictly constraining grill, on his mate-rial.

That the book can sustain our interest, and in fact increase it as we read on, is indeed, on Calvino's part, a feat of in-ventiveness and stylistic mastery. But more important, it is a proof of the infinite resources of the human imagination, of the boundless freedom of the parole which exists and defines itself against the constricting rules of a closed inter-nally coherent system, the langue. . . . If the opposition between langue and parole, as given unconscious structure and individual unique expression, is resolved by poetic jus-tice in favor of the parole, it is because Calvino stresses the presence of the langue (of the code) which in his work ap-pears in the guise of the fairy tale, myth, the epic-heroic code, the city as a system of social, architectonic, econom-ic, visual, and emotional relations.

But the writer's parole is written and, once written, it be-comes itself a system. The book, which is meant to be one vision of reality, must not be allowed to become the only view of what is. Thus the system-book must in turn be ex-posed and exploded, and for this purpose Calvino builds into the system the seeds of its destruction, the self-con-scious metalinguistic irony. (Once the cards are all on the table, and the guests have told their stories, the deck is re-shuffled and the telling begins anew. . . .) Each of Calvino's fictions proposes new forms, new combinations of elements within the narrative structure as if, in order to escape from the closure of writing, which inevitably selects and fixates the undifferentiated flux of living memory and awareness, the writer must constantly seek to recover the images left out, the possibilities not realized, the elements latent in the system and not utilized, in a continuing effort to construct new models of possible universes, of invisible cities, of sys-tems closed but constantly and dialectically reopened.

What I have called the evolution of Calvino's discourse from the neorealism of his early tales to metarealism, myth-ical discourse, and antinarrative is both the sign of an ex-traordinary literary awareness and a perfectly consistent statement of his poetic and ideological vision: human activ-ity is at once "doing" and "saying," praxis and poiesis. (pp. 422-23)

Teresa De Lauretis, "Narrative Discourse in Calvino: Praxis or Poiesis?" in PMLA, *90 (copyright © 1975 by the Modern Lan-*

guage Association of America; reprinted by permission of the Modern Language Association of America), May, 1975, pp. 414-23.

The reader needed evidence that Calvino was capable of thought, and he was to find it in "The Watcher." There were no games in this story. It presented the thoughts of a leftist assigned as observer to a polling place in a Catholic hospital for freaks: the crippled, the ugly, the mentally retarded, the deeply and permanently disturbed. Few of these men and women have known any life outside the hospital—which is to say, outside the caring and shaping arms of the Church. For him the Church has always stood immovably against any change that will bring Italy closer to human decency, but now he must admit that it has been silently caring for people he had not wanted to admit existed. He must cope with the revulsion he feels at having to look at these people, and he must ask himself seriously when someone shall be recognized as human and allowed to participate in decisions being made about his future. The watcher suffers no blinding conversions, makes no sudden retreat to his own slogans. He—and the reader—experience a slow-motion epiphany that brings back to their minds the reality hidden behind those necessarily simplistic slogans we use as battle flags. This story proved to the reader that Calvino is in fact a deeply thoughtful man.

Perhaps Calvino has one of those brains that turn to verbal play only when they become weary. I do not think so. *Cosmicomics* and *t zero* and *Invisible Cities* leave afterimages, and those afterimages persist in the mind with the stubbornness shown by those odd facts, proverbs, formulas, and paradigms that one fastens on in the stupid conviction that some day they will be useful. Not knowing when, not knowing how, but knowing with certainty that they will eventually be used. (p. 215)

The Path to the Nest of Spiders is a story about the Italian resistance movement in the closing days of the 1939-45 war as it would have appeared to a child. Calvino is answering postwar Italian critics of the movement by showing that Italy owed even the most selfish, incompetent, and disagreeable of those fighters a debt of honor. . . . The novel is in the neo-realistic mode reminiscent of films like *Bicycle Thief* and *Shoeshine*. . . . (pp. 215-16)

Would I have guessed in 1947 that the writer of *The Path to the Nest of Spiders* would later write *Invisible Cities* and *t zero*? Not for an instant. Yet the Calvino we know today is shadowily present in that younger man. . . .

The Path to the Nest of Spiders is a thoughtful answer to postwar backlash against the [resistance] movement, and the argument has a certain elegance. The unit Calvino invents for [the child] Pin to join includes individual fighters so disoriented that they would have fought with equal passion in the uniforms of its enemy. Nevertheless—as he points out through his spokesman, Kim—their blind energies do contribute to the goals of the movement. The movement did have a noble purpose, even if they did not.

It was Kipling's Kim who played the Great Game of espionage in British India, and it is the minor character bearing his name who will most interest the reader of *The Path to the Nest of Spiders* in 1977. Kim perceives reality and questions himself in the manner of the Calvino we know: "But, after all, is this only a struggle between symbols? Must a man, to kill a German, think not of that German but of something else, with a substitution which is enough to turn his brain? Must everything and everybody become a

Chinese shadowplay, a myth?" One could write a long, unnecessary book on Calvino's mind with this passage as epigraph.

What we readers come to suspect, of course, is that just as Pin looks with only vague comprehension at the machinations of the violent, sex-driven adults in his alley and at the maneuvers and killing of the resistance fighters—so we who read the later works have only a dim comprehension of what is ultimately at stake: what is to be gained or lost by Calvino's risking. The nests in the title of this first novel are spider nests Pin has found for himself—cunning little tunnels with doors and traps that no one else knows about—and it is this labyrinth whose secret he will share with the person who finally proves a true friend. I shall resist the impulse to draw the analogy between Pin and Calvino, the true friend and the reader, the spiders' nests and the labyrinths of the writer's later work.

Beneath Calvino's cleverness, there is a fine, honest mind in fullest possession of itself in those later stories we awkwardly call fantasies (which I *have* now finished and am rereading). *The Path to the Nest of Spiders* does not have the power of these fantasies, but it is a novel anyone can enjoy: it has a special importance to those of us who have already taken an interest in one of the really good minds in Europe today. (p. 216)

Thomas J. Roberts, "Calvino Before the Fantasies," in The Nation *(copyright 1977 by the Nation Associates, Inc.), February 19, 1977, pp. 214-16.*

Although not yet as well known as he deserves to be, Italo Calvino is one of the world's best living fabulists, a writer in a class with Kobo Abé, Jorge Luis Borges and Gabriel García Márquez. He is most famous for his dazzling, astonishingly intelligent fantasies—"The Nonexistent Knight," "The Cloven Viscount," "Invisible Cities," "The Baron in the Trees"—but his mastery is equally evident in what might be called, loosely, his whimsical science fictions on the history of the universe—"Cosmicomics" and "t zero"—and in his more-or-less realistic fictions, for instance "The Watcher and Other Stories." In the realistic stories and in "The Baron in the Trees," Calvino creates substantial, moving characters and fully elaborated, thoroughly convincing fictional worlds. In all his books, but especially in "Invisible Cities," he has moments where the prose turns into pure, firm lyric poetry. In the science fictions he brilliantly translates modern scientific and mathematical theory into fictional emotion; and everywhere his final pursuit is metaphysical. His strange new production, "The Castle of Crossed Destinies," uses all these talents, rises directly from the world view he has been developing all these years, yet is like nothing Calvino has done before.

The book is, in a way, a collection of tales. The framing story concerns a group of pilgrims who, after traveling separately through an enchanted forest, come together at a castle or, perhaps, a cavern (no one is sure) and, trying to tell each other their stories, discover that have they lost their ability to speak. The tales are worth hearing, we know in advance. The hair of all the pilgrims, both young and old, has been turned white by their adventures. One of the pilgrims hits on the idea of telling his tale by means of tarot cards. He selects the cards which best represent himself, he thinks, then adds a line of other cards, and, with the aid of grimaces and gestures, tells his tale.

His actual story may or may not have much to do with the

tale we are reading since we get only the narrator's interpretation, and the narrator is by no means sure of himself—an annoying, unsatisfying business, the narrator will readily admit. But the cards are all the pilgrims have, and they decide to do their best with them. Another pilgrim chooses his cards and tells his tale; then other pilgrims follow, compressing their narrative lines with those of other pilgrims when they need to make use of some card already played. By the time all the cards are on the table, the interlinking of tales—or the narrator's interpretation of the cards laid down—is incredibly complex and subtle: a history of all human consciousness through the myths of Oedipus, Parsifal, Faust, Hamlet and so on, and a history of Calvino's career as a novelist, since the pilgrims' tales repeatedly allude to Calvino's earlier fiction.

"The Castle of Crossed Destinies" is an ambitious, "difficult" book, though short, and one's first inclination may be to make top-of-the-head judgments: "overly ambitious," "annoyingly complex," "lacking in sentiment." Like Kafka—or Chaucer—Calvino makes plodding comedy of our scholastic need to explain things. Like those writers, he uses a squinty, insecure narrator who's forever searching out answers, mostly getting wrong ones, or raising intellectual obstacles in his own path. Such comedy inevitably slows the pace. Again, one may feel that Calvino's review of his own career as a writer is a touch self-regarding, even coy. . . . Or, thinking of the emotional power of books like "The Baron in the Trees," one may complain "The Castle of Crossed Destinies" is lacking in warmth.

Those objections—and others—may have at least some validity, but to register them, even in the timid way I've done, is to feel oneself squeaking like a mouse. Cranky, self-conscious, confusing and confused, "The Castle of Crossed Destinies" is a shamelessly original work of art. Not a huge work, but elegant, beautiful in the way mathematic proofs can be beautiful, and beautiful in the sense that it is the careful statement of an artist we have learned to trust.

All Calvino's philosophy is here, subtly reassessed: the idea of existence as an act of will confirmed by love ("The Nonexistent Knight"), the tragicomic mutual dependence of reason and sensation ("The Watcher"), Calvino's usual fascination with chance, probability and will and his theory of value (mainly worked out in "The Cloven Viscount," "Cosmicomics" and "t zero". What comes through most movingly, perhaps, is Calvino's love for the chance universe we are stuck with. (pp. 15, 29)

Calvino's celebration of things as they are comes through . . . in the central allegorical images, the tales and the structure of the whole. The place where the pilgrims meet—our world—is perhaps a castle fallen on hard times, becoming a mere inn, perhaps a tavern doing splendidly, becoming a castle. The meeting of minds and hearts we all hunger for, as pilgrims, is impeded by difficulties—language and interpretation, our differences of background (adventures in the woods), and the infuriating fact that no pilgrim's story is entirely unique: we need each other's cards, yet the cards never carry exactly the same meaning twice. ("Each of us," Calvino remarks elsewhere, "is a billion-to-one shot.") But despite the problems, the pilgrims tell their tales, each mixing his destiny with the other's destiny and thus helping to evolve (as the universe evolved in Calvino's science fictions) a total providence, so to speak—an enveloping work of art.

Art is a central theme here. Like the universe, it is partly

brute substances in random combination. Studying the cards on the table, wishing to tell his own story, dear to him simply because it is his own, the narrator complains that he has lost his story in the stories of others. Thinking toward despair, he remarks: "Perhaps the moment has come to admit that only tarot No. 1 honestly depicts what I have succeeded in being: a juggler, a conjurer, who arranges on a stand at a fair a certain number of objects and, shifting them, connecting them, interchanging them, achieves a certain number of effects." But through a fiction he learns that his deterministic philosophy is wrong. The tale of St. George and the Dragon shows him that "the dragon is not only the enemy, the outsider, the other, but is us, a part of ourselves that we must judge." Art cannot preserve our passing moments, make us live forever, but it can help us to live well.

Calvino has made his narrator both writer and reader (interpreter of the cards), both creator and victim of creation. In the metaphor of the cards he has exactly described the process of art as concrete philosophy, how we search the world for clues as a gypsy searches the cards, interpreting by means of our own stories and a few unsure conventions. Finally, he claims the search is moral and potentially tragic. Despite the permutations, tale by tale, we always learn the same tale of man: we celebrate and cleanse or we die, destroyed by our betters. . . .

Like a true work of art, Calvino's "The Castle of Crossed Destinies" takes great risks—artificiality, eclecticism, self-absorption, ponderousness, triviality . . . and, despite its risks, wins hands down. (p. 29)

> *John Gardner, "The Pilgrims' Hair Turned White," in* The New York Times Book Review (© *1977 by The New York Times Company; reprinted by permission), April 10, 1977, pp. 15, 29.*

In the effort to keep fiction magical, modern authors have resorted to alchemically elaborate trickery. . . . Italo Calvino, than whom no living author is more ingenious, tells the mingled tales of "The Castle of Crossed Destinies" . . . by means of tarot cards. The frame device is simple: travellers meet in a castle—or, in the second section, a tavern—where their powers of speech are magically taken from them, and a tarot deck is placed at their disposal. (p. 149)

The cards are depicted in the margin as they are laid down, so the act of narration is double and cunningly merges, in the voiced uncertainties and multiple possibilities of interpretation, with the act of listening, of understanding. "Invisible Cities," Calvino's previous work (his books can no longer be called novels; they are displays of mental elegance, bound illuminations), contained the idea of wordless speech. . . . The cardplay of Calvino's present exercise all but dissolves the reality of the tale itself. The writer reads as he writes; we read with him; the plane of narrative becomes a beaded curtain through which reader and writer loom to each other as one giant character seen in a speckled mirror. The price paid for this illusion is a certain tedium, short as "The Castle of Crossed Destinies" is. The chimerical "invisible cities" were, though fantastical, oddly solid and fascinatingly inventive. The personal histories related by tarot symbols—and the rules of the game call for many —flicker into sameness, blurred reshufflings of old romances and medieval themes, and eventually show themselves as the mere stories, thin and worn, of Parsifal and Faust, Hamlet and Oedipus, Lear and Lady Macbeth.

"The world does not exist," Calvino imagines Faust to be saying through the cards. "There is a finite number of elements whose combinations are multiplied to billions of billions, and only a few of these find a form and a meaning and make their presence felt amid a meaningless, shapeless dust cloud; like the seventy-eight cards of the tarot deck in whose juxtapositions sequences of stories appear and are then immediately undone." So much for the magic of fiction. The tale-teller's prestidigitation and significance-seeking swirl around an empty center; the "bald circumference of the *Ace of Coins*" is read to mean that "every journey through forests, battles, treasures, banquets, bedchambers, brings us back here, to the center of an empty horizon." Calvino contemplates the death not of that notorious old moribund the Novel but of the Story, of the hopeful impulse that makes beginnings and seeks outcomes and imagines adventures in the middle. A collection of stories may not be the best means of illustrating this theme. For all his inventiveness and affectionate regard for the traditional fables he transmutes, they (with some exceptions; the tales told by women take on life) seem in the telling scantly sketched, too quick for the eye, too remote for the heart, professedly arbitrary. (pp. 149-50)

There are two decks used, and two sections: the "Castle" of the overall title and a second, not quite symmetrical half, entitled "The Tavern of Crossed Destinies." The castle sequence is more rigorously organized than the tavern sequence. (p. 150)

[As] we wander in the unmannerly inn of this second section, through tale after tale, we feel something is wrong. The same cards recur too often; the apocalyptic and erotic notes are struck too effortlessly, chiming with Calvino's usual cosmic and metropolitan preoccupations; there is an unchecked fluency. The nub of the problem can be located by those who, like this assiduous reviewer, trouble to trace with colored crayons a few specimen narrative sequences on the full spread of cards reproduced on page 98: *the cards have been used in no special order.* Calvino in his afterword confesses his breakdown of procedure. . . . (pp. 153-54)

Now, this most amiable of avant-gardists cannot resist a tour de force. Having written a novel about a viscount who, being cut in half, doubly thrives, he must follow it with one about a baron who lives a long, full life entirely in trees, and that with one about a knight who is, behind his armor, nonexistent. Within his absurd premises he remains rigorous. Here, having played the cards one way, he picks them up again but, instead of overtopping his previous trick, finds himself overwhelmed. The effect is disturbing, like a sonnet in which the poet fails to rhyme the sestet, having perfectly rhymed the octave. Why, if the cards are to be used so freely, use cards at all? If the first set of tales seemed at intervals mechanical, this second set feels a touch copious and pompous; the narrative sprouts historical and philosophical asides and self-conscious declamations: "But will I not have been too pontifical? I reread. Shall I tear it all up? Let us see." The afterword less gnomically describes Calvino's struggles with the second section, the maddening complications he conceived and discarded, his awaking in the night "to note a decisive correction," his abandonment of the project for a year, his decision to abandon "ironclad rules," break out of "this maniacal obsession," and "publish this book to be free of it."

The magician has been bewitched. The cards, his tools, have rebelled. Our aesthetic unease goes deeper than the analogy with rhyme suggests. "The Waste Land," its couplets so cavalierly slashed by Pound, and "Prufrock" before it, showed the effectiveness of rhyme that comes and goes, like a ghost behind the arras, as Eliot said of metre, "to advance menacingly as we doze, and withdraw as we rouse." Formal correctness has so long ceased to be required of poets that those who adhere to it are viewed as eccentrics—who for a time published their own magazine, *Counter/Measures.* But cards possess a more ancient and intimate connection with order and disorder than poetic prosody. A deck of cards is a type of machine not easy to construct, a machine for producing random order. As such it admits, in its suspension of material causality, the possibility of divine pronouncement. It is the essence of cards, once shuffled and dealt, to constitute a given, whether the given is a bridge hand or a human fortune. As long as Calvino, having made his initial arrangement, took it as a given and read stories into it every which way, the infinite plasticity of the narrative art was demonstrated, and the infinite pluralism and final empty monotony of human experience were forcefully implied. But when, in the second set, he reads the cards selectively, the presiding narrator suffers a sharp demotion in magical capacity, and nothing is proved, however much is asserted in the style of "we have seen these greasy pieces of cardboard become a museum of old masters, a theatre of tragedy, a library of poems and novels." Calvino's array of medieval legend, Shakespearean melodrama, and twentieth-century woolgathering seems messily synoptic, a gaudy mulch. The book is published "to be free of it," in disarray. By breaking the rules of his own game, and breaking faith with his own splendid cleverness, Calvino has lost the definitive fatalism of the cards. (pp. 154-55)

> *John Updike, "Card Tricks," in* The New Yorker (© *1977 by The New Yorker Magazine, Inc.), April 18, 1977, pp. 149-56.*

Language for Calvino is a kind of plague, something like the smog, or the swarm of ants, which appear in his earlier stories. It is what we live in and long to get out of. But since Calvino doesn't want to give up communication, or even to break the linear clarity of his elegant prose, he must use language to point us toward other possibilities of expression: the comic strip (as in *Cosmicomics*), Marco Polo's objects and pantomimes, and, in *The Castle of Crossed Destinies,* the tarot pack. . . .

[The] tarot pack is not only a machine for constructing stories, as Calvino modestly says, it is a labyrinth where all the world's stories can be found. But they have to be *found,* and finding them, it seems, does not interfere with the inexhaustible mystery of the labyrinth itself, which is organized, Calvino says, around "the chaotic heart of things, the center of the square of the cards and of the world, the point of intersection of all possible orders." . . .

This new work as a whole doesn't have the grace and tenderness of *Invisible Cities*—there is something too dogged, too methodical about Calvino's application of his imagination to the tarots—but it has the discreet pathos which is never far from the surface in any of Calvino's work. "When you kill, you always kill the wrong man," Calvino says in a gloss on the story of Hamlet. And Calvino's fiction, with its allusions to the denser speech of the visible world and indeed of life itself, is a monument to one of literature's most important half-truths: When you write, you always write the wrong book. (p. 36)

Michael Wood, in The New York Review of Books *(reprinted with permission from* The New York Review of Books; *copyright ©* 1977 NYREV, Inc.), May 12, 1977.

The Tarot, a gaudy set of cards generally used for prophecy, is . . . complicated. One look at the eerie figures of the pack—the Popess, the Page of Coins, the Hanged Man—is enough to make it clear that these emblems are so embellished and so abstracted that they have become religious figures of unusual power. But the cards also represent early forms of narrative—the story of the past as well as of the future—and it is in this sense that Italo Calvino has used them in his latest book [*The Castle of Crossed Destinies*]. (p. 22)

Calvino believes in his writing, not in the stories; as a consequence his prose has a peculiarly weightless quality which the translator, William Weaver, has beautifully evoked. Calvino just concerns himself with the various orders and sequences which he has so assiduously and so obsessively created out of the cards. But by establishing such a distinctive set of relations, by forming circles and squares and double axes, the threat of disorder is—to use the old phrase—always on the cards. . . . (pp. 22-3)

[It] is as if the necromancer and the clairvoyant, by using the Tarot, can achieve what the novelist always fails to: '. . . our elderly neighbour, now that he finds a deck of tarot in his hands, wants to compose again an equivalent of the Great Work, arranging the cards in a square in which, from top to bottom, from left to right and vice versa, all stories can be read, his own included.' But the Great Work slips away so easily, since the cards themselves are signs to be read only in relation to each other. They are, literally, 'about' nothing: 'The kernel of the world is empty, the beginning of what moves in the universe is the space of nothingness. . . .'

Some of the stories in the book culled from this knowledge are very elegant, and Calvino's fables seem to be perched precariously beyond the confines of ordinary narrative. In his previous book, *Invisible Cities,* a traveller returns with stories of eerie and enormous cities which bear some relation to those we know but somehow exist outside ordinary time and space. And so it is in this book: the fables which Calvino has rescued from the ultimate chaos of Tarot-playing are strange mixtures of the ancient and the modern, of solemn mythical personages and Calvino himself, pictured as the King of Clubs and clutching a gigantic pencil. The intervention of this card into the game allows Calvino to enter his main theme, which is the fortune of writing. . . .

The Castle of Crossed Destinies is elegant, tightly constructed and totally self-enclosed. The only thing to do is to pack up the cards, leave the castle which may or may not represent the novel, throw out the Tarot pack which is pretty but in the end stale and pointless, forget about religion and all of its pagan substitutes, and begin another book. And this, I imagine, is what Calvino is now doing: '. . . to begin writing again as if I had never written anything before.' (p. 23)

Peter Ackroyd, "Sharp Cards," in The Spectator *(© 1977 by* The Spectator; *reprinted by permission of* The Spectator), May 14, 1977, pp. 22-3.

CAPOTE, Truman 1924-

An American novelist, short story writer, playwright, and essayist, Capote came to literary fame as a young man, and he has remained a literary celebrity ever since. His early writings focused on the Deep South, where he was born, but his later works have varied tremendously in locale and style. His best known work, *In Cold Blood,* **was in the vanguard of the formation of a new genre, the nonfiction novel. Capote is currently at work on** *Answered Prayers,* **portions of which have appeared in** *Esquire.* **The thinly veiled portraits of many of Capote's friends that appeared in these excerpts created a minor sensation in literary and social circles and have made the book notorious even before its publication. (See also** *CLC,* **Vols. 1, 3, and** *Contemporary Authors,* **Vols. 5-8, rev. ed.)**

Truman Capote has been the most talented and enduring of our writers of precocious sensibility. He is a master stylist and craftsman; he writes the prose sentence at least as well as any of his contemporaries. His first and best novel, *Other Voices, Other Rooms* (1948), published at twenty-three, is a brilliant and original work. Yet when one looks behind the flashing soft-colored lights of the prose, what is the novel really about? Its ageless child-hero's loss of innocence? The boy's search for a father? His initiation into homosexuality? The narrative deals with these concerns, and to that extent they are what the novel is about. But Capote's magical stagelike world, in which Joel performs his nightmarish rite of passage, is not to be believed. It is the stuff that literary children's dreams are made of. Despite its waxwork of horrors—the paralyzed father, the girl whose throat has been cut, the lovesick dwarf, the female men, and the masculine women—there is no evil in Capote's bittersweet paradise; there is wickedness, or rather naughtiness, but that is another matter—or no matter at all. Can a novel be about anything when there is nothing real at stake? Joel doesn't fall; he is prefallen. In accepting Cousin Randolph as his father-mother-lover, he is merely fulfilling the predefined pattern of his fantasies. By the same token, the corrupt Randolph is also innocent, as are all the perversities of Capote's inverted Eden. Decadence is innocence. All is innocence. No one in the novel is held responsible for his acts, and by and large each act is as good, indifferent, and inevitable as another. The problem is not that Capote's world is immoral but that among innocents morality is beside the point. Without morality, however, the rest, the titillating horrors of sensibility, are beside the point. (pp. 7-8)

Jonathan Baumbach, in his introduction to The Landscape of Nightmare: Studies in the Contemporary American Novel *(reprinted by permission of New York University Press; copyright © 1965 by New York University),* New York University Press, 1965, pp. 7-8.

[*The Dogs Bark: Public People and Private Places*], containing most of [Capote's] non-fiction work apart from *In Cold Blood,* is unlikely to add much to his artistic reputation, and some younger readers unacquainted with his fiction might wonder what all the fuss has been about. Without doubt the two best pieces here are the best-known: *The Muses Are Heard* and the Marlon Brando interview, *The Duke in His Domain* (1956). They were both written for the *New Yorker,* and embarked upon as stylistic exercises to warm up for the full-scale 'non-fiction novel' *In Cold Blood,* his bid for glory. They are good precisely because they got Capote out of himself, providing him in each case with substantial subject matter at a time when his material was getting perilously thin. There is a firm narrative line in *Muses,* and Capote's real strength lies in his story-telling ability rather than in analysis, speculation or argument. In the classic Brando piece he has worked within the standard *New Yorker* profile formula—the detached superior author, the sporadic injection of facts and other people's opinions, the subject drawn out by bland civility, and so on—to produce a portrait that is not only more revealing than the sitter supposes but more complex than the artist intends. . . .

Little of the rest is particularly memorable, and some is hardly worth collecting. The early travel pieces, composed between 1944 and 1950 and published in a private edition as *Local Color,* are thin and over-written, rhetorical in the sense that Yeats meant when he said that 'rhetoric is the will trying to do the work of the imagination'. . . . [There is] a bitchy, camp, affected style and tone of voice by no means confined to the juvenilia but return whenever Capote doesn't have much to focus on outside himself.

Except when he slips in the occasional good anecdote, his later vignettes of people are not much more engaging than those of places, less thumb-nail portraits than palm-tickled miniatures. In them he puffs his friends, drops names, and invites us to accept him as the Boswell of the jet set.

> *Philip French, "Watch It, Jockey!" in* New Statesman (© *1974 The Statesman & Nation Publishing Co. Ltd.), June 28, 1974, p. 929.*

The world of Truman Capote has always seemed oddly independent of Time. A frozen interior . . . like the decorative heart of one of Colette's French crystal paperweights.

In fact, it is just over a quarter of a century now since this vaguely malevolent, gnomish sprite, Will-o'-the-wisp with sting, springing from the swamps, decaying mansions and decadent families of the Deep South, flitted across the bestseller horizon with his Gothic dream sequence, *Other Voices, Other Rooms,* and before you could say freak, or fluke, had consolidated his fey, fairy-tale success with *The Grass Harp.*

Recovering their breath, blinking a little, the bandwagoneers, the serious critics too, promptly set to on their feverish analyses, yielding naïvely to the easy temptation of the penny-plain label. Clearly influenced by Faulkner. Indisputably, the Welty-McCullers neo-Faulknerian School. More waspishly: one of the Effete Dandies or Homosexual Decadents derived, of course, from Faulkner.

Shrill squeak of protest. No, says Capote, no. Understandable but untrue. The real progenitor was none other than 'my difficult subterranean self'.

The Faulkner-Welty-McCullers resemblance apparently derives from geographical accident. (pp. 84-5)

Hanging up his Southern harp, Truman Streckfus Persons —to accord him his baptismal identity—embarked upon the first of his continuing literary metamorphoses. . . .

Capote (no stick in the mud, he, writing the same book over and over again) has been applying the needle point of his pen—or should it be obsessively sharpened pencil?—to descriptive journalism. Finely-wrought miniatures of private places and public faces. [*The Dogs Bark*] contains many splendid examples of these new direction pieces.

Verbal petit point, worked into the prettiest pictures, silken threads deep-dipped in vividest local colour. Exterior monologues.

Then . . . the capsule bursts. The greatest change of all. Chameleon Capote capers off to the Kansas Badlands. Prospecting reality—for real. The Gothic dream becomes a Gothic nightmare. Close focus on a multi-murder in cold blood.

In Cold Blood, 1966. A new literary form trumpeted the advance publicists. The 'non-fiction novel'. The pre-publication claims were, like the orgasms of overpraise with which publication was in due season ecstatically greeted, grossly exaggerated. Poe, and many another, had done it all before. The book was competent (let us not be niggardly, *highly* competent) journalism. Most admirably suited to its original milieu—*The New Yorker.* There was the blood reek of reality in its pages . . . and yet . . . practised artist that he is, Capote could not resist retouching reality. The old ingrained narcissism would not be denied. Capote thought himself so deeply into the characters of the killers, evilly retarded children, that he, and we, the readers, end up in the unreal world of their dreams. After the great flirtation with reality we find ourselves back in the glass bed.

Of course, it may turn out that those paperweights are neither glass nor isinglass, but simply simulacra fashioned of translucent ice. There *is* a coldness in Capote's blood. A little warmth could melt out those isolate interior worlds.

Perhaps, even now, he is planning to write in lukewarm blood.

There are signs, hopeful signs, and echoes above the barking of the dogs. . . . (p. 85)

> *Richard Whittington-Egan, "Needle-Pointed Penman," in* Books and Bookmen (© *copyright Richard Whittington-Egan 1974; reprinted with permission), August, 1974, pp. 84-5.*

"Whoever gossips *to* you will gossip *of* you," goes the old Spanish proverb, and this one came home to roost for the International Set's *crème de la crème* with the publication in the November *Esquire* of Capote's "La Côte Basque 1965"—the "tail" of the long-awaited "kite" called *Answered Prayers* that is the writer's next major work of fiction. (p. 44)

"La Côte Basque 1965" is a 13,000-word story about a luncheon between "Lady Ina Coolbirth," a fortyish multiple divorcee on the rebound from an affair with a Rothschild, and the innocent narrator, "Jonesy," at Henri Soulé's exclusive Manhattan restaurant. While drinking champagne and eating a soufflé Furstenberg, "Lady Ina" gossips about the International Set, telling one "no-no" after another on one and all, including herself. Capote has peopled his story with real persons, using their real names, as well as with a number of other real persons, using fake names. (p. 45)

For years Capote has been society's adored and adorable resident intellect and court jester. In a world where parties are still often "given against someone" . . . where bitchery, snobbery, and hauteur are still prized right along with poise, manners, and money . . . where the merits of plastic surgeons are argued in the same way the religious used to argue theology—*gossip* has always been the great staple, the glue holding beleaguered life-styles and sinking social values together. But it's one thing to tell the nastiest story in the world to all your 50 best friends; it's another to see it set down in cold Century Expanded type. (p. 49)

Dotson Rader [said of this story]: "Marvelous, beautiful writing. It's unimportant whether it's true or not, since it is presented as fiction. Truman was always treated by these people as a kind of curiosity, expected to do his act. That was humiliation coming from people who had no qualifications other than being rich and social. Everybody in the world has been telling Truman their deepest confidences for years and he never said he wouldn't use them." . . . Geraldine Stutz, a woman of fastidious opinions: "It's only a scandal to a small insular world; most people won't know, and couldn't care less about who might be who. What counts is that it is a wonderful piece of writing and an extraordinary re-creation of the tone and texture of those days in that world." . . . [Joel Schumacher said]: . . . This same world thinks it supports art and artists, but never understands that all a writer has is his experience. . . ." (pp. 50, 52)

[Capote told Liz Smith:] "Why did I do it? *Why?* I have lived a life of observation. I've been working on this book for years, collecting. Anybody who mixes with a certain kind of writer ought to realize they're in danger. [Chuckle.] I don't feel I betrayed anybody. This is a mere nothing, a drop in the bucket. To think what I *could* have done in that chapter. My whole point was to prove gossip can be literature. I've been seriously writing this for three and a half years. I told everybody what I was doing. I discussed it on TV. Why has it come as such a great big surprise?" . . . "Look, I'm not using Proust as a model because what I'm doing is in the latter half of the twentieth century as an American. But if someone like Proust were here now and an American, he'd be writing about this world. People say the language is filthy. I think that's the way people talk and think now—exactly. I think it's beautifully written. . . ." (pp. 52, 55)

He turns serious: "Look, my life has been dominated by my own levels of taste in art, especially the art of narrative prose writing, wherein my particular art lies. I have never compromised that. . . ." (p. 56)

> *Liz Smith, "Truman Capote in Hot Water,"* in New York Magazine (© *1976 by NYM Corp.; reprinted by permission of* New York Magazine *and Liz Smith), February 9, 1976, pp. 44-56.*

* * *

CARPENTIER, Alejo 1904-

Carpentier is a Cuban novelist, short story writer, poet, musicologist, and scriptwriter. A versatile writer whose novels reveal the wide range of his interests, he has been both a pioneer and a continuing advocate of the "new novel" in Latin America. Even though Carpentier has been accused by critics of indulging in stylistic complexities and occasional pretentiousness, he is still considered to be an important writer. After having lived in Paris for many years, Carpentier returned to his native Cuba where he has resided since the revolution. (See also *Contemporary Authors,* **Vols. 65-68.)**

Getting into the minds of the chieftains of totalitarian power, understanding megalomania from inside the megalomaniac, is a task fiction rarely sets itself. The Hitlers and Goebbelses themselves tend, of course, to abandon any early aesthetic plots for other scenarios, leaving their victims, the Kafkas, to write the novels. And it clearly takes a peculiarly set imagination to press convincingly beyond the victim's view or the mere externalia—the stuff that

launches a thousand biographies and histories per decade—actually to inquire what it's like right inside the padded-cell of the dictator's head. . . . Alejo Carpentier, in an extraordinarily arresting, richly brewed and complexly ordered new novel [*Reasons of State*] (his first for 12 years), puts up the exuberantly baroque Head of State of a minor Latin American country. . . .

All this might, of course, amount to just another leery look at messy South American politickings in the familiar way of novels from Conrad to Greene. But, noticeably, it's European characteristics and dilemmas that are being scrutinised in Head of State's country: it is a Spanish clime (whose proud rosters of virgins fill pages), its leaders love French and Italian arts and fight on Roman or German models. In Paris, 'over there' means South America, but in the Americas 'over there' means France. And the novel bonds South America and France inextricably together, so eventually it's European reaction that the novel is calling in question. This awareness, however, comes only gradually home to the reader, and summary mustn't imply that these analytically dry bones are all. On the contrary, the writing makes a continually intoxicating bravura, giddying with imaginative inventiveness (who else since Dickens, for instance, would have soldiers vengefully machine-gunning the wax shop-window mannequins during a shopkeepers' strike?), strong on social history, slyly jibing about Catholicism and conservative politics, continuously—page after page after page—enticing. (p. 722)

> *Valentine Cunningham, in* New Statesman (© *1976 The Statesman & Nation Publishing Co. Ltd.), May 28, 1976.*

Some writers run against cliché and correct or destroy it; Carpentier surprises because he builds on the stereotype. His book is a fiction about the fiction Europeans and Yankees have created out of Hispanic America. But it is no easy parody of coca-colinization; it is an elaborate entertainment about cultural impositions that are themselves parodic. . . .

Of his several novels, *The Lost Steps* (1956, published in English in 1967) is considered his masterpiece. *Reasons of State,* a rather old-fashioned "modernist" novel, suffers from a certain staginess and overcontrivance. . . . Carpentier's unnamed Head of State—his main character—is a poster figure, motivated mainly by a pragmatic sense of the rough game he plays, and virtually all the other characters are faceless subordinates. Nevertheless, the book is good enough to make me want to read the works that have earned Carpentier his considerable reputation abroad. (p. 15)

With the enumeration of [Parisian] pleasures we are introduced to the first of many long catalogs of smells, tastes, sounds, colors, brand names, literary tags, music, and details of *fin de siècle* painting and sculpture. Not since Balzac, who is himself mentioned more than once, has a novel been so oppressively furnished. . . .

Carpentier risks the fallacy of imitative form with these tallies of real and imaginary trivia. As Diderot observed, the actor playing a drunken comedian must not himself be drunk. Fortunately, the lists do not get out of control; they are seen, in all their profusion, as the colonizers of Latin America, the agents of distortion and deformity. (p. 16)

> *Ruth Mathewson, "A Brute of a Life," in* The New Leader (© *1976 by the American*

Labor Conference on International Affairs, Inc.), July 5, 1976, pp. 15-16.

While American novel-writing suffers from loss of markets and intellectual decay, the "boom" in South American fiction continues to astound readers the world over with the freshness, energy, and sweep of its products. Out of a dozen or so major authors (Borges and García Márquez are the best-known here), Alejo Carpentier remains the one least recognized in these parts.... Some readers may be put off by Carpentier's displays of learning, an encyclopedism that ranges over anthropology, history, geography, botany, zoology, music, folk and classical, the arts, visual and culinary, and countless forgotten novels and verse—in all an erudition easily rivaling that of Borges....

Carpentier's fiction regularly depicts individuals swept—often against their wishes—into the larger social struggle; they thereby become participants in history and embody the conflicts of their times. *Reasons of State,* Carpentier's latest work, shows a similar pattern—the protagonist, an unnamed military Dictator, makes history in the 1910s, only to be undone by a new history in the 1920s. Snuggled in his Paris mansion, indulging a slavish love of *belle époque* France, the Head of State chronically absents himself from his native Nueva Córdoba (a kind of composite of all Latin American nations), leading a life of sex, booze, and "culture," and hobnobbing with puffy aristocrats; an effete monarchist Academician, third-rate opera hacks, Gabriele D'Annunzio, and even (why not?) characters from Proust. Periodically called home to quash (with United Fruit aid) barracks rebellions and an elusive Professor's anarchist crusade, the Dictator always sets sail again for France, where his would-be friends mock his origins—and indeed ditch him when his political massacres, becoming hot news, make him a liability in their salons....

Reasons of State is not a psychological study in tyranny à la O'Neill or Pushkin. Carpentier rather places the Dictator (who is actually something of a cultural-historical caricature) within a broader global process, shows how the petty brutalities of South American politics ultimately interlock with European and, later, U.S. interests, demonstrates how these mustachioed military despots serve as the regional link in a vast world system, one whose specific local manifestations are economic dependency, false prosperity from overseas wars, a servile regard for things foreign (what Mexicans call *malinchismo*), and of course U.S. military invasions (approximately seventy-five of them in Latin America since 1800). This is no drama of the individual soul, but an imaginative evocation of the material and cultural forces of history.

Unlike Carpentier's previous books, which were a bit on the solemn side, *Reasons of State* exhibits a new lightness of touch, a wry and rollicking humor—notably in the character sketches. (p. 15)

Reasons of State is something of an uneven book, and therefore not Carpentier at his very best.... Unlike the Dictator's adventures in Paris, the impersonal account of postwar disruptions in Nueva Cordoba reads too much like abstract reportage; whereas France and Francophilia vividly become flesh in a handful of characters, no one figure sufficiently incarnates the economic crisis or the invading Yanks.... (pp. 15-16)

Though lesser Carpentier still comes off a great deal better than most of our novel-writing today, *Reasons of State* will probably carry little impact here. It treats areas of experience—flowery oratory, slavish Europhilia, foreign military occupation, and one-man rule—profoundly alien to our own political world, which is more one of pious homilies, lofty cultural insularity, invading foreign lands rather than being invaded, and a smoothly-functioning machinery of 100-man rule. Precisely because of these national differences, however, Carpentier's novel (like those of Fuentes or García Márquez) can furnish already-interested Americans more insight into the social dislocations of the Southern continent then many a Yankee Poli Sci professor could. (p. 16)

Gene H. Bell, "Cuba's Alejo Carpentier," in New Boston Review *(copyright © 1976 by Boston Critic, Inc.), Fall, 1976, pp. 15-16.*

*   *   *

CHARYN, Jerome   1937-

American novelist, short story writer, playwright, and editor, Charyn, who typically writes in a surrealistic, comic style, is a versatile, talented writer who so far has failed to write a major novel. He writes well about the emotional misfits and the dispossesed living in urban ghettos. (See also *CLC,* **Vol. 5, and** *Contemporary Authors,* **Vols. 5-8, rev. ed.)**

Marilyn the Wild is flawed by its own rampaging vitality. A Charyn character cannot simply put on a coat: Esther Rose's "fist burrowed into her sleeve like the skull of a groundhog." Too many adversaries shrill in the same vituperative key. Even lovers snarl their sweet nothings, as if they were pouring poison into each other's ears. Yet the author endows his most grotesque characters with a certain beauty. His kinkiest people—an albino Negro pyromaniac, a senile, one-eyed dishwasher—are the imaginings of a major talent. (p. 96)

LeAnne Schreiber, "A Terrible Beauty," in Time *(reprinted by permission from* Time, The Weekly Newsmagazine; *copyright Time Inc. 1976), April 19, 1976, pp. 94, 96.*

What's to be done with this foolish thing, the father? Let him circle himself to zero, as Joseph Heller does Bob Slocum in "Something Happened." Drag him mumbling and dead to a far part of the land, as Donald Barthelme does in "The Dead Father." Orbit him out into transcendent space with Saul Bellow's Charlie Citrine of "Humboldt's Gift."

Or set him up for a double fall—a stumble as man, a bumble as myth—as Jerome Charyn does in his exciting and deceptive new novel "Marilyn the Wild." Our father is half a myth for conceiving us. We trip him so he can see he has fallen on us. "Marilyn the Wild" examines the damage with compassionate precision.

Charyn's man-myth is Isaac Sidel, a Manhattan police inspector who presided over Charyn's last novel, "Blue Eyes." Sidel is the "Moses of Clinton and Delancey," a gray knight known as "Isaac the Pure" and "Isaac the Just." He "sleeps with his notebook" and gouges the eyes of the unjust. Sidel daily battles alien crime combines, checks would-be supercops, tolerates ineffectual F.B.I. agents and confronts sleazy journalists.

It is not easy being an idea of order on the East Side, but the domestic entanglements of the mythic cop most interest Charyn and the reader.... Charyn's game is more than just revealing the official hero's private weaknesses. He shows how Sidel's absorption in his own paternal myth both causes the novel's plot and prevents Sidel from solving it equitably. . . . (p. 54)

The plot—as it should be—is pure convention; plenty of risks, coincidences, melodrama and ritualized scenes. This conventionality satisfies the detective reader's expectations and makes for a first-rate entertainment. More important, it reflects the mythic rules Sidel lives within. Travesty would have been easy. Instead Charyn artfully half-turns the detective from against itself to examine the paradoxes of fatherhood and authority, mythology and manhood.

"Marilyn the Wild" continues the pleasures of "Blue Eyes"—social and religious multiplicity, eccentric street people, close attention to gesture and voice, and colloquial energy. . . . The characters are wild; they close upon one another, bartering, demanding, consuming, berating, gouging. Myth's penetration of the everyday creates an atmosphere of force and danger. (pp. 54, 56)

After "Marilyn the Wild" sells a lot of copies, I hope the movies buy it. I'd like to see Charyn slow down (nine books in 12 years) and consolidate his considerable strengths into a major work. At present he threatens to be the American Anthony Burgess, who wrote too many partial books too quickly early in his career. Like Burgess, Charyn's novels have often exploited an eccentric subject or have been written to a convention. "Marilyn the Wild" uses its formula expertly and sensitively. Now maybe Charyn won't need it any longer. (p. 56)

> *Thomas LeClair, in* The New York Times Book Review *(© 1976 by The New York Times Company; reprinted by permission), May 2, 1976.*

"The Education of Patrick Silver" concludes Jerome Charyn's trilogy of novels ("Blue Eyes" and "Marilyn the Wild" are the first two) about New York cops and marginal crooks and killers who suggest an animated cartoon by a Chagall of the Ashcan School. The novels stress, among other things, a fluidity of affiliations between its cops and crooks: Patrick Silver, an ex-policeman too addicted to Guinness stout to remain useful to the force, has switched sides. He is now employed by the Guzmanns, a family of criminals headquartered in the Bronx, as bodyguard to the feebleminded 44-year-old Guzmann "baby," Jerónimo. (p. 5)

It is not clear why the novel is named for Patrick. He isn't especially central to the book. In fact it is the author—rather than any of his characters, rather than his story—who dominates. His novel is a vigorous performance, but more kinetic than dynamic, its notably fluent language a kind of novelistic blarney, lavish with hyperbolic verbs, with a nearly surreal physicality. . . . After a while, the color of the details starts to run. The book—the whole trilogy—has a lilt to it, but the lilt ends up cavorting solo.

This effect must be accountable in part to the smallness of the story the book has to tell; the linguistic bravura exists as if to buck up a weak plot—essentially a lot of cops and robbers running around Greenwich Village and the Bronx, Guzmanns hiding or fleeing, Sidel and his men sniffing, tailing, tackling. The story has mobility but little body.

Charyn's ripe language also reflects his book's load of exoticism. To a point, it is a strength of the novel and the trilogy that its cast of characters is so colorful—Jewish cops, a cop from Harvard, Patrick Silver an Irish Jew, the Guzmann Marranos, Spanish or Portuguese Jews originally, passing as Christians. (pp. 5, 17)

Though the stew is too spicy, and ultimately heavy, it speaks for Charyn's sophisticated sense of New York. He apparently has investigated the city's entire body, within and without, and he has written it up in Charynese. The exoticism weakens to the extent that the novel's characters are "characters." The local color, for all the authenticity one knows to be its basis, is often too pointedly garish to be convincing, and actually helps to drain the book of impact. . . . "The Education of Patrick Silver" is not sadism. It is certainly talented. But it is mostly plumage. (p. 17)

> *Richard P. Brickner, in* The New York Times Book Review *(© 1976 by The New York Times Company; reprinted by permission), September 5, 1976.*

* * *

CHEEVER, John   1912-

American short story writer and novelist, Cheever draws successfully from his middle-class suburban experience to produce a fiction that paints a disturbing picture of what is wrong with upwardly-mobile America. His major thesis is the difficulty in establishing and upholding a moral identity in a society where family life and the community are disintegrating. Cheever was awarded the National Book Award in 1958 for *The Wapshot Chronicle*. (See also *CLC*, Vols. 3, 7, and *Contemporary Authors*, Vols. 5-8, rev. ed.)

Ezekiel Farragut, the hero of . . . *Falconer*, inhabits a religious and social topography roughly bounded by the contours of his name. Voices of Old Testament prophets reverberate down the corridors of his psyche, while, outwardly, he displays both the polish and the paranoia we have come to expect from Cheever's heroes. . . .

As the novel opens, the state is in the act of appending something new to Farragut's name—the number 734-508-32. He is being incarcerated in Falconer Prison for a crime of which he feels himself to be innocent, the murder of his brother. With this fact Cheever takes his largest risk, for aside from the sheer *implausibility* of it, two other problems arise out of [this] Cheever novel. . . . Readers are liable to expect from it either a social document, a protest of some kind over the horrors of our penal system, or, more typically, a Cheever portrait of an alienated upper-middle-class American simply translated behind bars. Both elements are in fact present, but it would be a pity to come away from this book having got no more from it than that. Those who suspend their disbelief will find that, in *Falconer*, John Cheever has written a stunning meditation on all the forms of confinement and liberation that can be visited upon the human spirit. . . .

[Cheever] has incorporated into the novel a symbolic richness usually associated with densely imaged poetry or the best crafted short story. In this and in his willy-nilly coupling of the sacred and profane he is reminiscent of John Donne. (p. 374)

To say that the novel proceeds in symbolic or metaphysical terms is not to deny that the flesh is involved; it is, and often in the grossest way. At Falconer the flesh is always being aroused or abused, subdued or gratified, either in reality or in recollection. Terrible scenes of cruelty, degradation and lust take place. However, when we look at these fleshly encounters of Farragut's and those of his fellow inmates, Cuckold, Jody, Chicken Number Two and the rest, the quality that distinguishes the greater portion of them is, curiously, purity. . . . The determined air of normalcy, of heterosexuality, in all of the attitudes displayed in [many] passages accounts for much of their appeal, and explains why they are to so large a degree successful in breaking down the reader's own prejudices. (pp. 374-75)

Neither the possibility that these encounters are mere lonely substitutes for heterosexual love, nor the sense in which they manifest themselves as brotherly—or, at least on some level—familial feeling is allowed to obscure their darker components of narcissism and, even, necrophilia.

The theology . . . throughout the novel is interesting and sophisticated. Sin is interpreted as a radical failure of love and a consequent enthrallment (a kind of imprisonment) to fear. Love casts out fear, as the evangelist tells us, and one of the processes Farragut is undergoing in the Falconer "Correctional Facility" is nothing less than the rehabilitation of his ability to love. More than anything else, this accounts for the softening light that washes over so many of the prison scenes.

One particular measure taken by Cheever bears remarking in this matter of the book's strange and winning purity: it represents, I believe, both an instance of legitimate poetic license and a profound theological principle on Cheever's part. Though most readers will not consciously notice that it is missing—there is more than enough obscene and scatological language to produce convincing replicas of prison argot—*Falconer* contains not a single instance of blasphemy. Farragut, a methadone addict, is once heard to cry out, in the midst of a withdrawal agony, for someone to "Get me my fix, for Jesus Christ's sake!" But no man who describes himself in a letter to his bishop as "a croyant" can be supposed at that moment to be taking the name of the Lord in vain.

Cheever says nothing directly that would explain his decision to delete this prominent feature of the vernacular. One can only suppose that he considers swearing unsavory, and that he knows—as he tells us that Farragut doesn't—"what importance to give unsavory matters. They existed, they were invincible, but the light they threw was, he thought, unequal to their prominence." Cheever, as narrator, goes on to note that what is unsavory "only seemed to reinforce Farragut's ignorance, suspiciousness and his capacity for despair." By daring to eschew that kind of unsavory matter here, Cheever may actually be striving for the opposite—a salutary effect upon all of us. (p. 375)

[It] will be apparent from what has been said so far that this is no ordinary novel. Better say it is a new version of an old story form, a parable. . . . His final word to us is an admonition to "Rejoice." *Falconer* is truly a parable for our times. (p. 376)

> *Janet Groth, "Cheers for Cheever," in* Commonweal *(copyright © 1977 Commonweal Publishing Co., Inc.; reprinted by permission of Commonweal Publishing Co., Inc.), January 10, 1977, pp. 374-76.*

[Exile] and estrangement [have] always been present in Cheever's fiction, from the early stories on. But in the beginning Cheever characters appeared to be exiled merely by their own errors or passions or foolishness. . . . They yearned always after some abstraction symbolized by the word "home," after "tenderness," after "gentleness," after remembered houses where the fires were laid and the silver was polished and everything could be "decent" and "radiant" and "clear."

Such houses were hard to find in prime condition. To approach one was to hear the quarreling inside. To reach another was to find it boarded up, obscene with graffiti, lost for taxes. There was some gap between what these Cheever people searching for home had been led to expect and what they got, some error in expectations, and it became increasingly clear that Cheever did not locate the error entirely in the hearts of the searchers.

For a while he appeared to be locating this error in the "modern world," and he did in fact make extravagant ironic use of the fractures peculiar to postwar America. The demented verities and sweet wilds of the family farm had been tamed into suburbs: Shady Hill, Bullet Park, Proxmire Manor, where jobs and children got lost. Discharged housekeepers and abandoned secretaries reappeared as avenging angels. Your neighbor might take the collection at early communion on Sunday, but he might also take a billfold from your bedroom on Saturday night. So might you. Your child might be beautiful and fragrant, but one morning that child might be too sad to get up. So might you. Guns kept at home tended to get fired. Planes going home tended to crash. (pp. 1, 22)

I suspect that [a] secret wish to read novels in which the protagonist is an improved version of the reader—a kind of point man in history's upward spiral and someone you might want for dinner—is far from dead in fancy circles. These readers see through Cheever's beautiful shams and glossy tricks, past his summer lawns and inherited pearls, and what they see is this: a writer who seems to them to be working out, quite stubbornly and obsessively, allegorical variations on a single and profoundly unacceptable theme, that of "nostalgia," or the particular melancholia induced by long absence from one's country or home.

"Nostalgia" is in our time a pejorative word, and the emotion it represents is widely perceived as retrograde, sentimental and even "false." Yet Cheever has persisted throughout his career in telling us a story in which nostalgia is "real," and every time he tells this story he refines it more, gets closer to the bone, elides another summer lawn and pulls the rug from under another of his own successful performances. He is like a magician who insists on revealing how every trick was done. Every time he goes on stage he sets for himself more severe limits, as if finally he might want to engrave the act on the head of a pin. "The time for banal irony, the voice-over, is long gone," reflects Ezekiel Farragut, the entirely sentient protagonist of Cheever's new novel, "Falconer." "Give me the unchanging profundity of nostalgia, love and death." In this sense of obsessive compression and abandoned artifice "Falconer" is a better book than the "Wapshot" novels, a better book even than "Bullet Park," for in "Falconer" those summer lawns are gone altogether, and the main narrative line is only a memory. (p. 22)

Cheever has a famous ear, but he is up to something more in "Falconer" than a comedy of prison manners. Events are peculiar. . . . On its surface "Falconer" seems at first to be a conventional novel of crime and punishment and redemption— a story about a man who kills his brother, goes to prison for it and escapes, changed for the better— and yet the "crime" in this novel bears no more relation to the "punishment" than the punishment bears to the redemption. The surface here glitters and deceives. Causes and effects run deeper. . . .

Of all those Cheever characters who have suffered nostalgia, Farragut is perhaps the first to apprehend that the home from which he has been gone too long is not necessarily on the map. He seems to be undergoing a Dark Night of the Soul, a purification, a period of suffering in order to re-enter the ceremonies of innocence, and in this context the question of when he will be "clean" has considerable poignance. As a matter of fact it is this question that Cheever has been asking all along—*when will I be clean* was the question on every summer lawn—but he has never before asked it outright, and with such transcendent arrogance of style. . . . In this way "Falconer" is a kind of contemplation in shorthand, a meditation on the abstraction Cheever has always called "home" but has never before located so explicitly in the life of the spirit. (p. 24)

> *Joan Didion, in* The New York Times Book Review *(© 1977 by The New York Times Company; reprinted by permission), March 6, 1977.*

Falconer is a surprising book, far stranger even than *Bullet Park*, which was, in its juxtapositions and denouement, unsettling enough. . . . [Cheever] has succeeded in writing a story in which the grossly tangible details of prison life interact with a series of vividly narrated but often wildly improbable events to create what seems to be the author's private version of hell. . . .

Except for one brief episode dealing with the escape of another prisoner, the novel concentrates exhaustively upon Farragut's present and past experiences, both as he himself perceives them and as they are unflaggingly elucidated for us by the author. We are led to contemplate as well as share the outrage of a sensitive, cultivated, and wounded man who, believing himself to be essentially innocent, is subjected to the stupefying routine and progressive degradation of this new environment. . . .

Though the raw material for social protest abounds here, *Falconer* is a novel with other intentions. I doubt that prison reform occupies a very high place on Cheever's list of social priorities. Even the uprising at Attica (called "Amana" in the novel), which takes place during Farragut's confinement, serves chiefly to show the fearfulness and demoralization of the guards at Falconer. Cheever's focus is upon behavior, idiosyncrasy, sudden acts of kindness, bizarre happenings, the aesthetic and other adaptive responses to a world of automatically flushing toilets, blaring radios, and diminished egos. . . .

It is the tonality, even more than the subject matter, that distinguishes *Falconer* from Cheever's previous fiction. The prevailing atmosphere is one of extreme sordidness, relieved only momentarily by the old Cheever whimsicality, tenderness, and insouciance. Cheever's stylistic sprightliness is undiminished, but the intrusion of a coarsened vocabulary often produces grotesque effects. . . .

Yet the continuities with the earlier fiction are almost as striking as the obvious departures from it. From the beginning Cheever's short stories and novels have been concerned with the precariousness of life, with the trap doors in the polished flooring of Sutton Place apartments, with the criminal possibilities of Shady Hill and Bullet Park. The gracefulness of Cheever's manner, his trickiness, the snobbish appurtenances, his lyrical and descriptive powers have all to some degree disguised—or at least made amusing—the role played by hateful and murderous impulse in the lives of his characters. (p. 3)

The homosexual emphasis in *Falconer* will perhaps startle some Cheever readers accustomed to his frequent and often lyrical celebrations of heterosexual sportiveness. But a close look at his fiction during the last decade reveals numerous occurrences of homosexual material—occurrences to which the straight characters invariably respond with fear or distaste. . . . A dramatic shift in expressed affect has taken place—a shift that simultaneously links *Falconer* with the earlier books and distinguishes it from them.

Despite the differences in subject matter and tone, Cheever's approach to narration remains much the same. He continues to manipulate his characters highhandedly, while commenting brightly upon their milieu, motives, and behavior. At its best, this distancing achieves the effect of inspired gossip. The surface is always lively and interesting, full of arresting detail, full of surprises. The commentary is usually intelligent and entertaining enough to compensate for its intrusiveness. But the Cheever manner, so often brilliantly successful in his short stories, entails disadvantages in his longer fiction. In the two Wapshot books, surfeit results from the existence of too many cleverly narrated episodes—a tedium not uncommon in the reading of long, semi-picaresque novels. In *Bullet Park* and especially in *Falconer,* both shorter and more tightly organized books, there is, I think, an unresolved conflict between the explosive potential of the material and the very "brightness" of its manipulation.

Cheever quite arbitrarily makes Farragut a professor and then provides nothing to make such an occupation credible. While Farragut's response to drug-deprivation is unforgettably vivid, the fact that he is an addict in the first place strains belief; certainly it is lent no support by the shallow psychologizing of the commentary or the claim that "His generation [Farragut is forty-eight] was the generation of addiction." Even Farragut's ingenious escape supplies not so much an ending to the novel as a nimble cop-out, for Farragut's future—to say nothing of his continued freedom—is quite simply unimaginable in view of what has been established about him. Cheever seems perfectly aware of this frivolity and half mocks it.

I am not suggesting that Cheever should struggle into a straitjacket of psychological realism, but I do wish to convey my strong sense that he has not yet discovered a fictional mode that can contain the powerful stuff with which he is now dealing. Still, whatever its shortcomings as fully achieved literary art, *Falconer* compels attention as the darkened realization of much that has been implicit in Cheever's fiction all along. It is an engrossing short novel, a notable addition to his now extensive *oeuvre*. (pp. 3-4)

> *Robert Towers, in* The New York Review of Books *(reprinted with permission from* The New York Review of Books; *copyright © 1977 NYREV, Inc.), March 17, 1977.*

[*Falconer*] defies literal interpretation. It is a story in the classic Cheever mold, both bizarre and touchingly real, absurdly beautiful.

Prison is a familiar metaphor for hell, and in *Falconer* Cheever toys skillfully with Christian symbolism. But the novel's most dramatic appeal arises from more potent stuff than intellectual gamesmanship. Loss of freedom is a nightmare that haunts us all, springing from some incalculable subconscious sense of guilt. Cheever confronts the nightmare and artfully lays it to rest. (p. 91)

Amanda Heller, in The Atlantic Monthly *(copyright © 1977 by The Atlantic Monthly Company, Boston, Mass.; reprinted with permission), April, 1977.*

A John Cheever character has wandered into the wrong novel and doesn't know how to get out. Where am I? Here, Céline's hospital; there, Kafka's penal colony; yonder, some William Burroughs; back aways, the Bible, with God in a bad mood and the sun-crazed desert prophets explaining why. Whatever happened to suburbia?

Certainly Ezekiel Farragut *is* a Cheever character—an upper-middle-class Wasp with marital problems. . . .

Cheever people are often punished for not having wanted more boldly. Still: "Almost everyone I love has called me crazy." And that's typical, too. Cheever people care with such passion for the ordinary—"the chords, the deep rivers, the unchanging profundity of nostalgia"—that they seem wacky, wrong for this world, waiting for an accident.

From previous experience with Cheever . . . one expects that Ezekiel's luck, or charm, will run out. Gusts of chance —in Cheever country, chance is a sort of secular substitute for evil—will unmoor him. He will consult himself, like a compass: surely inside this mess of memories and desires there is a moral pole toward which the knowing needle swings and points. Something will be required of him: an extravagance, a surprise, a rhapsody, a proof.

But hold on. Ezekiel is also a heroin addict. Ezekiel murders his own brother with a fire iron. Ezekiel is sent to prison, gets beaten up, has a homosexual love affair, and busts out. Wow. . . . [The] Falconer Correctional Facility [is] a long way from Shady Hill, St. Botolphs, and Bullet Park. It is as if our Chekhov—and some of us believe Cheever to be our Chekhov—had ducked into a telephone booth and reappeared wearing the cape and leotard of Dostoevsky's Underground Man. Modernism, the literature of fire alarms, has caught up with him.

It's not that violence and death have been missing from Cheever in the past. (p. 88)

But always in the past these have seemed to be accidents, arranged so as to throw into relief the fragility of all that Cheever holds most dear: the sanctuaries of love. . . . He seemed to be reminding us of how foolish we were in our tacit claim "that there had been no past, no war—that there was no danger or trouble in the world."

He did his reminding in a prose at once evocative and dreamy. (Does it still need saying that the English language is lucky John Cheever writes in it?) The accidents could be thought of as dreams, to which the dreamer responded as if "to a memory that I had not experienced." . . .

Not so inside the walls of *Falconer.* The violence and death are real. (pp. 88-9)

Outside the walls, the sweet prose is still at work. Cheever hasn't forgotten how. There are flashbacks—flares, really, or grenades—by whose bright brief light we see something of Ezekiel's soulscape. . . .

And there are swatches of that surpassing tenderness, that respect for the intimacy and the mystery of men and women together, that Cheever alone among male American writers seems capable of producing: Ezekiel's letter to his girlfriend, "exalted by the diagnostics of love"; his safari for fox grapes in the hoarfrost to prepare his wife's favorite jelly; notations on the loneliness of single men in Chinese restaurants; the irony of Christmas; rain dripping from gun towers. . . .

Cheever has left Shady Hill in a black van through the twilight zone and into hell. (He has, in fact, taught at Sing Sing.) Inside Falconer, Ezekiel is unknowingly cured of his addiction, subdues the past and, with the help of a miracle, escapes—just as, with the help of an earlier miracle, his lover Jody had escaped. This strikes me as being at least one miracle too many, especially as it comes on top of several improbabilities. . . . But what was implicit in *Bullet Park*—the imagery of a kind of muscular Episcopalianism— runs rampant in *Falconer.* Ezekiel's durance vile is full of miracles and prophets, mechanical and plastic Holy Ghosts, ciboriums and chalices, the Eucharist, and "fallen men" in "the white light" beyond redemption. And Ezekiel himself is almost literally resurrected from the dead, bloody but unbowed.

Is this symbolism necessary? I'm not sure. It sent me to the Bible to read up on Ezekiel (which in Hebrew means "God strengthens"), and God *was* in a bad mood in that book, wrathing at the mouth, tossing around the twelve tribes, rattling dry bones. It also sent me to William Butler Yeats to read up on falcons: "Turning and turning in the widening gyre . . . the centre cannot hold. . . . Mere anarchy is loosed upon the world." I'm still not sure. And yet a certain anarchy is proposed.

Into what does Ezekiel escape? Into, apparently, an idea of love not as a sanctuary but as a relinquishing. Sanctuaries are prisons. . . . Out of extremity, Cheever seems to be saying, emerges an irreducible and persevering *me,* and a laissez-faire economy of the emotions. . . .

Sentence by sentence, scene by scene, *Falconer* absorbs and often haunts. As a whole, it confounds. Shady Hill has been reversed, turned inside out like a glove or one of those stars that ends up, under pressure of gravity, a black hole in space: the cell. And like a black hole, it transmits mysterious signals. It seems more asserted than felt, more willed than imagined, and an odd valedictory tone predominates, as if everything must be left behind in order for the self to forage for a new connection. . . . It is sad . . . that one of the few novelists who knows how to write about the dialectic between men and women (and their children) with a gentle seriousness, a palpable joy, should have made himself a stranger. (p. 89)

John Leonard, "Crying in the Wilderness," in Harper's *(copyright © 1977 by Harper's Magazine; all rights reserved; reprinted from the April, 1977 issue by special permission), April, 1977, pp. 88-9.*

Though pocked with obscenities, Cheever's language [in "Falconer"] tends to be well-behaved, even dull; there are lamenting, generalizing, run-on sentences, but little of the plangent sorrowing grace that was so affecting when Cheever was back home on the darkening green, far from this sensational material. "Falconer" is forceful in its deliberately sordid way; but it is finally unpersuasive. It is rare for a writer to take such risks, to try to reach for more than he grasps, and Cheever is a serious, honorable artist; but the universal praise his novel has received is wishful thinking: the book feels forced. (pp. 3, 52)

Richard Locke, in The New York Times Book Review (© 1977 by The New York

Times Company; reprinted by permission), April 17, 1977.

Falconer is in another country altogether, yet its story is told by our own nonchalant, witty Cheever. As only he could, he drops small, perfect tales drawn from his hero's and the other prisoners' memories. . . .

Since Cheever clearly did not intend his Falconer to be realistic, perhaps he was using the prison walls to make us feel fully what it is to be free. In one scene Farragut peers down from his cell window at the two steps leading out of the prison and marvels at the unmindful way visitors emerge into the open. . . .

Cheever goes further: Without freedom, life is still infinitely precious. The dying Chicken II, totally friendless, about to leave the emptiest existence on earth, says that it has been "like a party, even in stir—even franks and beans taste good when you're hungry, even an iron bar feels good to touch, it feels good to sleep . . .".

The life Cheever is celebrating—make no mistake about this—is a life strictly without women. Confinement may, in fact, be a sort of wish-fulfillment. Only in prison can a man be safe from that baneful figure in so many Cheever stories, the vixen wife. Gifted with a talent for inventive, capricious, emasculative cruelty, she has somehow gained a hold over her husband from which he cannot free himself.

The message was not immediately apparent in Cheever's earlier work, partly because it fitted into what was thought to be the *New Yorker* formula: First dig your pit, then push your character into it. Marriage was so universal a state that its unhappiness could be taken as a metaphor for the sadness of the human condition. Now, though, there are "alternative life styles." Cheever, in his own sly way, may be offering one. (p. 15)

Hope Hale Davis, in The New Leader (© *1977 by the American Labor Conference on International Affairs, Inc.), April 25, 1977.*

Falconer is a book about prison life, always lively but in places a little sloppy, sometimes comic and occasionally rather contrivedly horrific. Mr Cheever is the quintessential *New Yorker* writer, with lashings of style and a good deal of fancy, but not very much awareness of how most people actually live and behave. . . .

The approach to prison experience is realistic, in the sense that food and cell conditions are described, the other prisoners are credible characters, homosexual relations develop. There is no pretence at realism, however, in the depiction of Farragut or in several of the incidents described, and the contrast between manner and material cannot be other than jarring. We would like to believe what we are told, but Mr Cheever does not encourage us to do so. . . .

Falconer teaches again the endlessly unlearned lesson that to mix realism and fantasy is almost always not only dangerous but damaging. Almost all the prison scenes are extremely vivid, whether they concern a slaughter of the prison cats, Farragut's homosexual experiences, or the excitement roused by a prison revolt nearby. They have a power, and a depth of feeling, that is rare in Mr Cheever's work. On the other hand the flashbacks are generally unconvincing, and the book depends on them to show the origins and nature of Farragut. They are also marred by occasional verbal excesses of a highly literary kind.

Julian Symons, "Soul behind Bars," in The

Times Literary Supplement (© *Times Newspapers Ltd., 1977; reproduced from* The Times Literary Supplement *by permission), July 8, 1977, p. 821.*

* * *

CHRISTIE, Agatha   1890?-1976

An English novelist, short story writer, dramatist, poet, and essayist, Christie is celebrated as one of this century's foremost mystery writers. She has written over 100 novels, firmly establishing her character Hercule Poirot as the antithesis of Sherlock Holmes in the annals of English detective literature. Jane Marple is another of her memorable creations. Christie has also written under the pseudonyms of Mary Westmacott and A. C. Mallowan. (See also *CLC*, Vols. 1, 6, and *Contemporary Authors*, Vols. 17-20, rev. ed.)

It would be nice if one could say that ["Curtain," the] final adventure of the most engagingly preposterous detective of the Golden Age were the best, but unhappily that isn't so. The very best Christies are like a magician's tricks, not only in the breathtaking sleights of phrase that deceive us but also in the way that, looking back afterward, we find the tricks to have been handled so that our deceit is partly self-induced. . . . ["The Murder of Roger Ackroyd"] was a technically outrageous book, one that shocked detectival purists like S. S. Van Dine, who said that she had cheated. "Curtain" has all of "Roger Ackroyd's" outrageousness, but only a fraction of its cunning. In the end one has a distinct sense of contrivance.

This need not much affect our appreciation of Poirot, or his creator. Poirot was originally conceived as a detective who should be, in style and appearance, totally unlike Sherlock Holmes. He certainly cannot be called more than two-dimensional. . . . [However,] in the best stories, by some . . . miracle, Poirot is a more convincing reasoner than any other fictional detective of his period. His vocabulary may be odd, and some of his recent cases are peopled by decidedly old-fashioned or out-of-date characters—like Colonel Luttrell and Major Allerton in "Curtain"—but Poirot himself is in some strange way believable.

Now that she has killed off her most famous character, it seems right to say something about Agatha Christie's own achievement. She is one of the much-diminished band of classical detective-story writers, for whom the detective and the puzzle are the thing. In recent years she has made some formal concessions to modernity, but none to the way life is actually lived. There are no more butlers and housemaids in her books, but nobody is seen doing any work. People may be labeled doctor, lawyer, secretary, accountant, but what they really are is suspects in a murder puzzle. They live in a world remote from the muggings of the 87th Precinct, the sexual or financial secrets of Simenon's provincial France or the seedy violence of Raymond Chandler's California. Like her contemporaries Dorothy Sayers and Margery Allingham, Agatha Christie was not only a lady but also ladylike, and she did not care to write about such things. Her books, like those of her sisters in crime, say something about manners but nothing about life. Yet within her chosen and unstrained limits, this serpent of old Thames has given all detective-story addicts immense enjoyment, and she has been the champion deceiver of our time.

Julian Symons, "Hercule Poirot, il est mort," in The New York Times Book Review (© 1975 by The New York Times Company; reprinted by permission), October 12, 1975, p. 3.

[Christie's] characters are neither interesting in themselves nor particularly indicative of any class or country, but the parade of the suspects can leave someone not paying much attention to believe that the carefully timed appearances of each is a sign of carefully ordered lives, lived, in spite of the overwhelming evidence, better than their own.

What animates Christie's tireless completion of her appointed rounds is her imperious innocence. Not only is someone "guilty," but in order for people to be suspects at all they must have done something to be guilty about. But these motives are only squiggles, passions for which Christie only knows the words. The murderer, when exposed and if male, may say "damn," but otherwise no one is distinguishable from anyone else. All suspects get equal time, and seem guilty of nothing more than being dull. In this way Christie does what is called playing fair. Readers of mysteries want a book that stays resolutely a book, walled off from life, and there may not be so much as a whimper of humanity in all eighty-five books.

What in other writers or in life one might call sexism, snobbery, or racism is in Christie only a passion for keeping the squiggles in place. What in other writers might be an image of hell, paradise, or both—an isolated group on a train or a boat, in a country house or a village—is in Christie only a backdrop for the dance of words. At some moments in some of the books one suspects she is being shrewd or observant about a character. Perhaps she is, too, but soon that potentially interesting character, or situation, is ordered back into the lockstep of the dance, because we must get on with it. (pp. 37-8)

> *Roger Sale, in* The New York Review of Books *(reprinted with permission from* The New York Review of Books; *copyright © 1976 NYREV, Inc.), April 29, 1976.*

It was a glorious moment in Conan Doyle's *The Final Problem* when Sherlock Holmes and the arch-villain Moriarty tumbled to their deaths at Reichenbach Falls, their bodies locked together in a wrestling embrace. It had all the elements of an inevitable end, the great detective concluding his life work by destroying his own mirror image. . . .

The death of Hercule Poirot in Agatha Christie's *Curtain* has similar elements. Like Holmes, Poirot is facing the arch-antagonist of his career, a villain who sits at the center of a web of seemingly unconnected murders, who will strike again, but who cannot be caught because there is no proof of crime. Like Holmes, Poirot faces a criminal whose powers are a twisted version of his own. . . . And like Holmes too, Poirot goes down with his enemy, leaving behind a letter that will explain the final events to a bewildered assistant.

But here the similarities end. Poirot's death is much less dramatic. The aged, arthritic Belgian detective and his older but no wiser Watson, Captain Hastings, return to Styles, the country estate of Christie's first book which introduced the pair fifty-six years ago. . . . The setting can hardly match Switzerland's rapids, Poirot is but a dim reflection of Holmes, and his antagonist is nowhere near so terrifying as the evil professor. For all the earnest straining after legend here, it does not quite work. (p. 80)

Curtain is not a triumph. Though written many years ago, it

is already permeated by that weariness and solemnity which would become more evident in Christie's works as she grew older. One of her earlier virtues was a refusal to take herself too seriously. She enjoyed the game—laying out the false clues, the countless motives, the innumerable threads of coincidence and threats of murder, in a seemingly hopeless tangle, wasting no time on unnecessary description or character development except as these might serve as clues for the detective or red herrings for the reader. These early books claim no motive other than entertainment—some even had "Casts of Characters" in front which read like advertisements for the movies they might go on to become. . . . But *Curtain,* though written at a time when Christie could still turn out an engaging story, has little of this lightness and playfulness. Already there are hints of that bombastic and moralizing side of Agatha Christie—the one given to railing at the "younger generation" and such things—which would become more and more apparent as she aged.

In *Curtain* there is little respite from Christie's earnestness and "insights"; the book is all but buried under them. Worst of all, the puzzle and its solution—usually the centerpiece of Christie's mysteries and the part she executed best—simply do not come off. Her most memorable books . . . are memorable chiefly for that final unraveling when, most often, the suspects are gathered together to witness the unveiling of the murderer. The reader too witnesses an almost magical transformation of the events of the book through a paradigmatic act of understanding. But in *Curtain* this transformation fails to occur because the design of the book violates the rules of the genre. For one thing, the puzzle itself is a fraud, involving as it does a partial deception by Poirot of both Hastings and the reader. Secondly, the criminal's methods are absurd, even in the permissive context of mystery fiction. Thirdly, and most important, the criminal acts themselves are performed out of motives which are irrational and hence inaccessible to the reader. In mystery stories the introduction of unpredictable, irrational elements is inexcusable—one cannot play chess when one's opponent overturns the board. (pp. 80, 82)

Christie's crimes have a curious regularity to them. . . . These . . . are "class" murders, crimes which arise out of demanding another's place and not knowing one's own, or out of a desire to preserve an illusion hitherto sustained by deceit. The setting and the characters are usually British and sufficiently affluent to warrant the presence of a "butler." Poirot, on the other hand, is an outsider to the system, and thus in a perfect position to rectify the misdeeds of the criminal—another outsider, but one who is disguised. The denouement of these stories always involves the restoration of order, the return of things and people to their proper places in the hierarchy via a ritual exorcising of the disguised criminal.

Beyond the comforting, indeed the primal, regularity of these stories, however, there is something which also recalls the earlier, religious meaning of the word mystery: "truth that man can know by revelation alone," as Webster puts it. The unmasking of the deceiver . . . must come as a complete surprise, as revelation; the traitor may be anyone, but he is never what he seems, and he must be subtle, crafty, and clever, a diabolical opponent. The detective for his part has the conviction of the prophet doing God's will on earth. As the criminal works from below, so does the detective work from above; he sees through the masks of men's souls and finds the one among them who is dissembling virtue. With the purging of the criminal from the community, the random collection of former suspects is bound together for a moment and transfigured into a society bearing witness to revealed truth. Like the religious rites of ancient times, the solution of the mystery imparts "enduring bliss to the initiate." Poirot departs, leaving behind a better world; the victim, having played his necessary part in the drama, is all but forgotten.

Stretching a point perhaps, one could say that the skeleton of Christie's plots is in fact similar to that of the mystery-passion plays of the Middle Ages, with their ritualized tale of vengeance upon evil and the triumphant reversal of Christ's death. In this similarity, perhaps, lies one reason for the persistence in the contemporary detective novel (almost alone among literary genres) of overt prejudice against Jews and other outsiders. (pp. 83-4)

Curtain attempts to universalize the myth of the dark outsider by moving the criminal into every individual and thereby, so to speak, internalizing the Levantine. But the attempt is simply beyond the author's reach; *Curtain* is a mere gesture, a slight wave of an arthritic hand. Still, it will serve as a finish to Poirot. His death is no great loss. "I have a bourgeois attitude toward murder," he once remarked. "I disapprove of it." But though Poirot destroyed many villains before his own demise, he did not destroy the fear of these villains—the foreigners, traitors, climbers, and imposters, hiding among us, and plotting against us. It was this fear that was at the heart of Agatha Christie's darkness, and possibly of her popularity as well. (p. 84)

> *Edward Rothstein (reprinted from* Commentary *by permission; copyright © 1976 by the American Jewish Committee), in* Commentary, *June, 1976.*

In a fifty-five year period a writer's style is bound to change, but although Christie's language has altered from using Victorian terms like "hark" for "listen" and "tantalus" for "bottle" in her books of the twenties, and even though her plots have evolved in line with the world's intrigues and wars, her basic genius of palming the ace in the best tradition of legerdemain has never varied.

Certainly her best mysteries include *Murder on the Orient Express, The ABC Murders, And Then There Were None,* and, of course, *The Murder of Roger Ackroyd,* but I have two favorites of my own that I would like to mention: *Towards Zero,* while Poirot-less, has Superintendent Battle of Scotland Yard who uses cool British logic to solve the crime in much the same way that Poirot uses Gallic reasoning. This complex mystery is built on an unsuspected murder committed by a child who has grown into a guilt-ridden, psychopathic adult. Another favorite is *Death Comes as the End,* one of the mystery novels that comes from Christie's experiences on archaeological digs. . . . This mystery takes place in ancient Egypt, where human nature and motivation are shown to be strikingly similar to today's.

Through the years I have continued to check out the latest Christie thriller at the library, and I enjoyed every one. I did, however, consider that enjoyment as a sort of throwback to childhood—like a taste for Crackerjack. It wasn't until I was packing for a year's stay in Central Africa that I realized that my logic had been arguing with my taste. I could take just so many pounds of books with me, and since there was no other kind of entertainment where I was going, I had to consider what sort of fiction I wanted to have with me for pure relaxation and enjoyment. There was

no question about what I wanted to read by a kerosene lamp; Agatha Christie mysteries won by a landslide. (pp. 184-85)

> *Betty Jochmans, "A Note Written on the Day that Agatha Christie's Death Was Announced," in* Prairie Schooner *(© 1976 by University of Nebraska Press; reprinted by permission from* Prairie Schooner*), Summer, 1976, pp. 183-85.*

The writing in "Sleeping Murder" is flat but heavily influenced by psychiatry, with many references to childhood traumas, guilt complexes, persecution manias.

Christie's working people—servants, gardeners, nurses—are usual caricatures, and her "romantic" newlywed couple as usual live up to their names, in this case Gwenda and Giles. Her technique of making innocent people look momentarily guilty and sinister ones appear suddenly innocent is rigid and mechanical, and the puzzle itself conforms to Raymond Chandler's classic description of the formula British puzzle story about "how somebody stabbed Mrs. Pottington Postlethwaite III with the solid platinum poniard just as she flatted on the top note of the Bell Song from Lakmé in the presence of fifteen ill-assorted guests."

And yet, for all her adherence to formula, Christie in one way transcends it. "Sleeping Murder" is not among her most skillful works, but it displays her personal sense of what she calls "evil," of murder as an affront and a violation and an act of unique cruelty. She was not an imaginative or original enough writer to explore this, but when Marple tells us here that "it was real evil that was in the air last night," Christie makes us feel her curious primitive shiver. It is certainly the most interesting aspect of her personality and probably accounts for her extraordinary success. (p. 1)

> *Gavin Lambert, in* The New York Times Book Review *(© 1976 by The New York Times Company; reprinted by permission), September 19, 1976.*

* * *

CLARKE, Austin C(hesterfield) 1934-

Barbadian novelist and short story writer, Clarke has written a trilogy about the problems that West Indian immigrants encounter when they attempt to assimilate into a predominantly white culture. Clarke, whose preoccupation is with black awareness, is presently the major West Indian novelist of his generation. (See also *Contemporary Authors,* **Vols. 25-28, rev. ed.)**

Austin Clarke's . . . *Storm of Fortune* is the second volume of a trilogy begun with the 1967 publication of *The Meeting Point.* It picks up from the mid-crisis ending of the first book to develop further the intertwined stories of the group of West Indian friends coping with immigrant life of Toronto in the Sixties. Much of the novel's focus is still on Bernice Leach, middle-aged live-in maid at the wealthy Forest Hill home of the Burrmanns. It dwells further on Bernice's uptight relationship with her erratic mistress, and with the loneliness and insulation of the Barbadian woman's three years in this "savage" place with its riches, its snow, and its decided coolness to black people. . . . In both these novels it is as if the flat characters of a Dickensian world have come into their own at last, playing their tragicomic roles in a manner which owes much to Clarke's extraordinary facility with the Barbadian dialect his characters speak and think in. . . . (pp. 106-07)

Austin Clarke is not writing specifically racial novels as such, but he is bound to explore the impact of racist situations and he has chosen a rich variety of ways to dramatize them. . . .

The narrative line is no more complete than it was in *The Meeting Point,* and even if it should be rounded out in subsequent work, story sequence per se seems to matter less than that this novelist should continue to create his Brueghel-like canvasses with their rich and contrasting detail and mood. (p. 108)

> *Diane Bessai, in* Canadian Literature, *Summer, 1974.*

["The Bigger Light"] is the third book in Austin Clarke's trilogy about black Barbadians in Toronto. It finds his hero, Boysie Cumberbatch, grappling with a problem that has haunted immigrant novels since Abraham Cahan's "The Rise of David Levinsky"—the price of success. At 49, Cumberbatch has a thriving office-cleaning business, solid investments in real estate and a deepening identity crisis.

Mr. Clarke, a novelist of exceptional gifts, traces his hero's attempts to get a coherent view of a life that is broken up into compartments. One fragment consists of his old, West Indian associations, now abandoned. Another is his increasingly alienated relationship with his wife Dots, who spins in her own separate orbit. And a third is his new "image," that of a man of property, respected by his banker, yet somehow dissatisfied with himself. Mr. Clarke's novel slides easily between introspection and observation. Having arrived, his hero is now without goals. He can't go home again, as a letter from an old down-home friend assures him. His everyday world is corroded by frustrations, real and imaginary. His search for a total picture of himself, "the bigger light," is rich in subtle perceptions. (p. 12)

> *Martin Levin, in* The New York Times Book Review *(© 1975 by The New York Times Company; reprinted by permission), February 16, 1975.*

In ["The Bigger Light"], the final novel of a trilogy, Mr. Clarke's naturalistic saga about the black West Indians of Toronto has been pared down to just two main characters—Boysie Cumberbatch and his wife, Dots. . . . [Boysie's] problems aren't very interesting to read about at first, for they exist largely as targets for Mr. Clarke's amusement, and, as in the previous novels, the reader can easily feel trapped in the drabness of the characters' lives. It would be wrong to give up on this novel, though, for Mr. Clarke has one very great gift: he sees unerringly into his characters' hearts. Without forcing them into a crisis (although they make a few hesitant fresh starts), he allows richer and richer expression of their vague, stifled hungers—for love, for purpose, for magic, for vitality, for "the bigger light." The universal longings of ordinary human beings are depicted with a simplicity and power that make us grateful for all three volumes of this long and honest record. (p. 140)

> The New Yorker *(© 1975 by The New Yorker Magazine, Inc.), February 24, 1975.*

West Indian writers like Clarke, . . . George Lamming, and Harold Sonny Ladoo depict their little island societies as centres of violence, extreme poverty, and cultural parochialism. . . .

Most of this gloomy background, out of which Boysie [the protagonist] emerges, appears in Clarke's first two novels about Barbados, *Survivors of the Crossing* (1964) and an excellent boyhood novel, *Amongst Thistles and Thorns* (1965). The sense of defeat among the poor islanders is enlivened by the humour of the characters and their glowing fantasies about the presumed wealth of relatives and friends who make it big in the fatlands of the United States or Canada. . . .

In his immigrant trilogy, Clarke follows the West Indians out to the promised land. A migrant pattern is set. The women go to Canada to work as domestics, save what little money they can, then send for their husbands or lovers who themselves eventually settle in as menial labourers, cleaners, and taxi-cab drivers. They suffer inevitable race prejudice but gain some small prosperity, ever glad to be free of Barbados. . . .

In *The Bigger Light,* Clarke explores the inevitable alienation of Boysie as the most successful of his group of friends. He has risen from humiliating unemployment to running his own . . . prosperous office-cleaning company. Reflecting Boysie's own stability and complacency, *The Bigger Light* is less frenetic and nearly empty of the incidents and wild dialogue of the first two novels. (p. 71)

The tragedy of Boysie is that he has been expected to do and understand too much beyond his powers to achieve. In this way he is no different from many men of his age group, regardless of background. What makes his story, or any other of the mid-life genre, so fascinating is that while Boysie should be warming up to one last struggle with himself and the world, he is already standing in the ruins of his life.

Like Clarke's other novels, *The Bigger Light* is engagingly written; the characters are so real you could reach out and touch them. It's hard to fault Clarke on anything except, perhaps, stretching too little material over too long a novel. But I shouldn't quibble. Good novels like this are rare. (p. 72)

> *John Ayre, in* Saturday Night *(copyright © 1975 by Saturday Night), June, 1975.*

The Bigger Light's real theme is the predicament of those who leave a stagnant homeland for a nation where they will never feel at ease. (p. 440)

When the book opens, [the marriage of the two central figures, Boysie and Dots,] has already frozen into mutual hatred. They no longer know each other, and Boysie feels that they never did. He spends his morning gazing out the window, waiting for a woman who each day emerges from the subway, crosses the street, and disappears. Dots, who is childless, thinks continually of adopting a little invalid, a white girl suffering from brittle bones whose story she read in the newspaper. Neither Boysie nor Dots ever makes contact with these fantasy figures, which only express their loneliness.

Throughout the novel, Boysie is "thinking." Since he has little education, his thoughts do not really take him anywhere. He circles aimlessly around his own isolation. Though unhappy in Canada, he cannot return to Barbados. Money-making does not satisfy him, but the black community center repels him by its shabbiness and air of militancy. He can never become assimilated in his new home, nor is he comfortable with other West Indians. In one sense, he is a classic case of newly rich anomie. Yet his plight is also that of the Canadians themselves. The Toronto we see in *The Bigger Light* is a barren, chilly place. From Boysie's apartment window, we watch its abandoned old people as they walk cautiously through the snow to buy liquor, returning with their brown paper bags. The goal of money-making, as Clarke presents it, is the only one white North America offers. And embracing this goal, Boysie discovers it to be dead. He also discovers the sterility behind Canada's smug, cozy exterior. Yet he cannot go home, for "home" is a place of venal politicians and profiteering U.S. businessmen.

The Bigger Light is a painful book to read. Though Boysie's thoughts, his letters to the newspapers, his obsessively repeated listening to Judy Collins's *Both Sides Now* give a slight sense of movement to the novel, basically it is static —a story of two people with many things to say and no one to say them to, who hate themselves and bitterly resent the society around them. At the end of the book, Boysie leaves for the United States. It is hard to imagine that he will find here what he lacked in Toronto. Certain African novelists have also dealt with the isolation of self-made blacks, but none with Clarke's bleak intensity—perhaps because Clarke's black hero is also living in the middle of a white world. In reading *The Bigger Light*, we are forced to look hard both at the dead-end life of black immigrants and at the inhuman machinery that surrounds and destroys them. (p. 441)

> David Rosenthal, "In the Snows of Canada," in The Nation *(copyright 1975 by the Nation Associates, Inc.), November 1, 1975, pp. 440-41.*

*   *   *

COCTEAU, Jean   1889-1963

Cocteau is a French poet, novelist, playwright, essayist, and film-maker. His concern with myth and mythological themes is expressed in such works as his drama *Orphée.* **One of his most arresting works is the haunting novel** *Les Enfants Terribles,* **a horrifying view of French bourgeois life.** *Les Enfants Terribles,* *Orphée,* **and other of his works were made into films under Cocteau's direction. (See also** *CLC,* **Vol. 1, and** *Contemporary Authors,* **Vols. 25-28;** *Contemporary Authors Permanent Series,* **Vol. 2.)**

With regard to *Antigone* [Cocteau] says: "I have tried to give a bird's eye view of *Antigone,* so great beauties disappear, others are brought out; perhaps my experiment is one way to bring to life the old masterpieces." Or again, about *Roméo et Juliette:* "I wanted to operate upon a drama of Shakespeare in order to discover the bones under the adornments; I have therefore chosen the most adorned, the most beribboned." There is no need to stress the lack of foundation of such assertions; they merely show Cocteau's inability to appreciate the poetry of Sophocles or that of Shakespeare. The final result is that his *Antigone* is a public square conversation-piece deprived of any atmosphere or pathos; as for his *Roméo et Juliette,* one must read it in order to realize how Cocteau, "in search of the bone", has reduced the most moving poetry to an ossuary.... What Cocteau clearly means [in the expression "poésie de théâtre"] is that the kind of poetry he is after is not poetry contained in words, but poetry created by all kinds of devices, some of them admittedly apt and purposefully used in the theatre. Later on, in the same preface, he says: "Thanks to Diaghilev and others, we witness in France the birth of a genre which is neither ballet nor opera, and it is in that direction that the future lies." At least, that was the

future as Cocteau saw it. The production of his plays and other forms of entertainment, in the course of which he brought together famous painters, musicians, choreographers and dancers, shows the kind of synthesis he had in mind. His ideal—very Wagnerian indeed—was that a play ought to be written, staged, dressed and provided with musical accompaniment by one single man; but he added, "that perfect athlete does not exist". One must concede that as a film producer, with all modern scientific apparatus at his disposal, Cocteau has certainly done his best to achieve that ideal.... (pp. 103-04)

In my view, his "poetry of the theatre" is an aesthetic emotion of varying intensity, but it is not poetry. A certain atmosphere or a climate created by all sorts of devices, ranging from chiaroscuro lighting to fantastic supernatural shapes, may or may not create an emotional state conducive to poetry, but it is certainly not poetry. The whole thing is likely to remain in a kind of inchoate state in which feelings, shapes and thoughts are different from what they normally are; but unless these things coalesce into form or, to be precise, into words, there is no poetry. Cocteau himself seems to me to be the prototype of the writer who gets into such states of exhilaration in the course of which the human being hovers half-way between the real and the unreal, in a world where all sorts of unco-ordinated ideas and feelings float swiftly across the mind, yet lacking the vision which discriminates and fuses together these elements of chaos into the consistency and coherence of organic life. All men are filled with poetic possibilities, but the lightning force which fuses all these possibilities into existence and timelessness is very rare. Cocteau has at times felt that force, though it never lasted long enough to enable him to write a full poetic drama. More often than not he has taken the shadow for the substance, and he has failed to see that no amount of staging, acting or other devices can produce poetry, unless there is poetry in the words. Surprise, for instance upon which Cocteau relies so much, is, true enough, an element of poetry; a poem must be something new; the words, the images, the rhythm used must have that vitality which makes of each poem a new experience; but surprise is only a means to an end, and by itself it is no more poetry than a poetic theme is poetry. This phrase— "the poetry of the theatre"—which has achieved such fame, is a confusing phrase, which seems to me to be typical of many of Cocteau's unfounded claims. (pp. 104-05)

In *La Machine infernale,* Cocteau has taken the myth of Oedipus, not as Sophocles did, at the point when, after many years of married life, Oedipus is about to be hurled headlong into well-nigh unbearable suffering, but when he reaches Thebes with hopes stretching wide before him. Cocteau concentrates chiefly on the meeting with the sphynx, life in the palace, the marriage and the bridal night. The undoing of Oedipus only occupies approximately a tenth of the play; coming after some very amusing chit-chat, it is divested of its emotional context, and is a kind of Parisian drawing-room comedy which makes us expect at any moment the ring of a telephone bell calling away Tiresias to his patients, or the horn of a motor-car waiting at the door to whisk away Oedipus, with Antigone at the wheel. (p. 106)

[We] have a sample of Cocteau's resourcefulness, in his display of all the well-known tricks of comedy ... so that we find ourselves right in the middle of a typical *comédie bourgeoise.* What this has got to do with poetry, or, for that matter, with the myth of Oedipus, is a question which need not be asked, for poetry has certainly no place here—unless one might be tempted to find something poetical in the more than obvious use of the incident of the scarf and the brooch as omens of what is going to follow seventeen years later, or in the very transparent symbolism of the dream.... This play shows Cocteau's inventiveness and gifts as a producer and film-director, but if it were described as poetic drama, then anything could be poetic drama—the flying trapeze, the girl who jumps through the hoop, or the dancing horse: all are feats which have that important element of surprise advocated by Cocteau. (pp. 107-08)

Orphée is Cocteau's most successful handling of a myth, and his nearest approach to poetic drama. Although the play takes place in a modern setting and with all the stage skill that Cocteau can muster (and that skill is great indeed), the atmosphere of the ancient myth is on the whole preserved.... Cocteau also has humanized the myth, which therefore loses much of its tragic mystery and also takes on the romanticized colours of the death-wish and the belief that only in the absolute, in the beautiful world of death, can one reach complete happiness. So Death is a beautifully dressed woman, with fascinating eyes, who comes to anaesthetize pain and to bring bliss to men. Who could resist her? Very few indeed; and nobody can be surprised at Orpheus' peevishness towards his wife and his longing to return to such a beautiful mistress. The great journey through Hell, which is part of the original myth, the suffering endured in order to know what cannot be known in the shape of man, the divine song which can rouse stones and trees to dance and women to madness, all that is whittled away and replaced by a horsy muse, a poetry committee of jealous volatile women and a typically French police station. The technical skill of Cocteau is once more impressive; but the elementary wisdom of the horse which, as Jocasta remarked to Tiresias, requires faith to be believed, the symbolism of the reflected mirrors where one can read one's fate, the handling of the supernatural, doves, Death and her attendants, are neither very original nor poetic.... One cannot deny the effectiveness of all these assets deployed in *Orphée,* or its novelty and influence since it was first produced in 1925, yet we are bound to say once again that this play, although remarkable theatre, and although it is the nearest approach to it, does not come anywhere close enough to poetic drama as exemplified by the works of poets like T. S. Eliot or Claudel, to mention only contemporaries. In recent years Cocteau has turned *Orphée* into an excellent film; it is perhaps as a film-director that he can make full use of his versatility, his inventiveness and his technical skill. (pp. 109-10)

> *Joseph Chiari, in his* The Contemporary French Theatre: The Flight from Naturalism *(© 1958 by Joseph Chiari), Rockliff, 1958 (and reprinted by Gordian Press, 1970).*

Cocteau sensed that his creative talents were not of the first magnitude. Even at the height of his success he was insecure, often doubted his abilities, and pursued the friendship of the great with obsessive zeal. But he also recognized and encouraged budding genius in others, and frequently aligned his own work with current innovations. Jean Cocteau's output is staggering in quantity and diversity, encompassing novels, plays, poems, films, essays, autobiographical writings, journalism, painting, and a voluminous correspondence. Much of this *oeuvre* is minor and some is frankly bad, but enough of it is outstanding, either intrinsically or as pure invention....

While Cocteau left his strongest mark on the theater, it is by no means the limit of his importance. *The Children of the Game* is a haunting novel of youth, classic in form yet highly original in its portrayal of a brother and sister living in a bizarre world of their own. As a film-maker, too, Cocteau achieved distinction. His first venture in movies, at a time when he knew nothing about the medium, was that remarkable attempt to depict the functioning of the poetic imagination, *Blood of a Poet* (1930), a milestone in cinema history.... Subsequently he learned the métier and made a number of films, including the charming fairy tale *Beauty and the Beast* (1945) and the movie version of *Orphée* (1949).

Much of Jean Cocteau's work is weak, derivative, inconsequential. But his failures do not diminish his major accomplishments, and hardly justify some of the harsher criticism aimed at him. Doesn't an artist have the right to be judged by the best of his work? (p. 32)

> *Tom Bishop in* Saturday Review *(© 1970 by Saturday Review Inc.; reprinted with permission), September 19, 1970.*

Poetry is a collection of sixty-three poems in which Cocteau introduces a whole new set of topics, themes, and motifs: the clown, the circus, the sailor, water, the dancer, the angel, the flag, the handkerchief, the elevator, travel, love, the horrors of war, and the athlete. Though some of these images and subjects appeared in Cocteau's earlier works, they are used in a different manner in *Poetry*. The athlete, for example, to whom Cocteau had always been attracted, now becomes a symbol for the poet. Impressed by the strength of the man who controls every aspect of his body, whose muscles are forever trim, whose strength increases with exercise, he feels that the poet, in a similar fashion, must also keep active, must take time out for training in order to reassess his worth. A simple style with fewer ellipses, devoid of accoutrements, more classical perhaps in design and demonstrating at the same time greater depth and force, mark *Poetry* with quite striking aspects.

In the poem "Spain" ("Espagne"), for example, Cocteau takes a series of popular images, those usually associated with this country, plays with them in such a way as to very nearly construct a vast canvas in words. A fan, gold, velvet, ebony, bulls, a *corrida*, a man singing to the accompaniment of a guitar—all these pictures appear in various sections of the poem, lending drama and color to it. What Picasso, Braque, Léger, Delaunay, de Chirico had done on canvas, Cocteau was now accomplishing in poetry, though he was not the first to try. This technique consisted of breaking up concrete objects as one conceives of them rationally, representing them in their variegated roles, and destroying the intellectual concepts of time and space, thereby achieving simultanity and actuality. (pp. 50-1)

Death, a theme which grows in importance as Cocteau's work evolves, is not always looked upon as evil or as the harbinger of pain. It can be beneficent, when considered symbolically, as a withdrawal from life, as a sinking into self, resulting in a surge of new ideas, feelings, and sensations, "Which dies when it must in order to be more fully alive." It was this kind of death which enabled Cocteau to write his classically metered "Plain-Chant." Rejecting his former frenetic life, he burrowed within and reached new depths of cognition, with beauty of form and classical restraint. (p. 54)

In *The Professional Secret* [a critical essay], Cocteau ...

expands upon what he had merely touched upon in *The Discourse of the Great Sleep* and which will become an important principle in his art: *angelism*. The image of the angel in no way resembles the child's conception of this figure: a good and kind being who watches over man. Actually, Cocteau's angel is a projection of himself, a composite of opposites that pull and tug at each other, creating the tension that results in the work of art. (p. 55)

Cocteau in no way attempted to abolish reality *as he saw it*. Indeed, he refused to "attenuate" or "arrange" the "ridiculous" elements he encountered in life. On the contrary, he accentuated those very aspects, striving to portray a world which was "more truly real than the truth," as Ionesco would do years later. Cocteau insisted, rather, on a reality in depth. The two narrators in *The Wedding on the Eiffel Tower,* were brought out into the open, their thoughts and attitudes were aired. Nothing remained hidden. "I illuminate everything. I underline everything," Cocteau wrote. Man's inner world with all of its hideous and beautiful aspects must be laid bare.

A play for Cocteau must form a cohesive whole. It must be simple and orderly, direct and to the point. Ideally, it should be created by one individual, "a universal athlete," as he called him, who would be capable of writing, directing, decorating, costuming, and even acting and dancing the production. Since such a goal is almost impossible to realize, Cocteau felt that this "universal athlete" should be replaced by a "friendly group" [: musicians, poets, and painters]. (p. 60)

Cocteau's style is replete with images, humor, exoticism, metaphors, and similes. The images he uses are important in that they reveal certain aspects of his protagonists' personalities. Images such as glass, windowpanes, and mirrors have certain common qualities: they reflect, are brittle and hard, transparent to a certain degree, and thin. And like these objects Cocteau's creatures are continually looking about, gazing at each other directly or indirectly (a reflection of themselves), as though trapped in a Hall of Mirrors, unstable; their ceaseless activity leads them into a state of total confusion, rendering them incapable of finding any meaning in their lives. (pp. 62-3)

In *Thomas the Impostor* the war is seen as a treacherous, selfishly motivated, ghastly joke. The confusion and disorganization brought on by war, for example, which is an outward manifestation of man's inner chaotic world, is described simply as "The war began in the greatest disorder. This disorder never ceased, from one end to the other." (p. 65)

Metaphors and similes add to the dynamism of the novel. The development of the war, for example, is likened to the ripening of a fruit which falls from a tree. The satiric overtones of such an image are many; the triviality of the falling apple can have devastating effects, for example, as witnessed by the biblical story. Certain images are humorous because of their extravagant and outlandish nature. Mme Bormes' [immoral] life is compared to the artistry of a piano virtuoso who "can draw all the effects possible which musicians draw from mediocre as well as beautiful compositions. Her duty was pleasure." There are images of an unpleasant nature which are presented in a flippant manner, and underline thereby the horror of various situations. A wounded soldier, for example, who could no longer be operated upon, is described in the following manner: "They had to let gangrene invade him as ivy does a statue." (pp. 67-8)

In this postwar novel, Cocteau dramatizes the incompatibility between the inwardly focused life of the poet whose reality lies in his imagination, and the rational and prosaic life of the man who lives in the workaday world. If Guillaume [the novel's main character], the charming, naïve poet is to survive at all in the world, he must be allowed to relate in his own way to the outside world which, in turn, must respond to him on his terms. (p. 68)

[Cocteau's] novels are veritable lessons in classical simplicity and clarity; his poetry is sensitive and studded with images, possessed of a plastic beauty rare in modern literature; his theatrical enterprises are examples in fervor, dynamism, and fantasy. (p. 69)

Opéra is the poetic transportation of the many nuances of feeling he experienced when bereft of his love [after the death of Raymond Radiguet]. Certain verses are detailed depictions of his opium fantasies, and these lend a haunting and almost frightening quality to the entire work. Other poems, relating the pain he felt in his most lucid moments, are replete with images drawn with the precision and surety of a Phidias or a Praxiteles. Cocteau's poetic credo, as revealed in *Opéra,* is still one of detachment, which he takes to be a prerequisite for creative art.

The poems devoted to Cocteau's opium fantasies ("By Himself" and "I fly in dream") are chiseled in incisive strokes. The feelings of lightness and giddiness are conveyed in harmonious tonalities, a blend of sharp consonants and free-flowing vowels, very nearly concretizing his drug-induced euphoria. During these periods he seemed to attain a kind of second sight that enabled him to discern the invisible from the visible, the inhuman from the human, and to express these visions in dramatic and poignant terms.

In "Mutilated Prayer" ("Prière mutilée") angels, glaciers, stars, and transfigurations of strange, haunting shapes all come into focus. In this poem the author seeks to do away with the realm of matter, in the platonic sense, which he finds so constricting and stultifying. He opts for the heavenly realm of the spirit, God's domain. . . . In "Mutilated Prayer," the poet confronts the mysterious cosmic forces, watches the angels as they climb the mountains, and within him, he feels a divine presence. He demands to be charmed, loved, and cared for by God, refusing voyages, theater, and all the artifices of life on earth. (pp. 73-4)

In other poems, Cocteau uses whole series of images (glass, quartz, ice) to express the shallowness and pain of existence. These hard and cutting images convey to the reader a real feeling of physical suffering. At other instances, like De Quincey and Baudelaire, Cocteau describes a series of visions which seem to have emerged directly and intact from his childhood: snow statues melting before the viewer's eyes, sleeping forms which reveal themselves to the dreamer, an array of strange relationships. (pp. 74-5)

"The Angel Heurtebise" ("L'Ange Heurtebise") is the most important and complex poem of the series. Cocteau again takes up the question of *angelism*, which he had defined in terms of an artistic formula in *Professional Secret,* that is, the poet must be self-sufficient; he must be emotionally and intellectually detached from the world. (p. 75)

In *Opéra,* Cocteau uses both Christian and pagan symbolism, drawing from each that which he needs. His finely chiseled verses with their assonances and repetitions, take on an almost three-dimensional aura; though the images are abstract, they become palpable, acting entities, are of and yet removed from the land of the living. Like the poet in "Angel Heurtebise," Cocteau navigates free between inner and outer reality, emerging intact, with keener sight and sensibilities which, in turn, permit him to penetrate more deeply into ever greater mysteries. (p. 76)

[The] Greek tale [of Orpheus] became a humorous, yet disturbing drama, centering not about a heavenly couple, but rather on an "infernal ménage." The play, replete with puns and witticisms, introduced viewers into a magical and mysterious world of cleverly manipulated symbolism and imagery. (p. 78)

Cocteau dramatizes three themes in Orpheus: the conflict between the Male and the Female principles in the universe, the source of poetic inspiration, and an explanation of Death. (p. 79)

Clearly, the Orpheus legend also serves to explain Cocteau's feelings concerning death. For the ancients, Death was an initiation which each person must experience before passing into another realm of existence . . . to rebirth. The Orpheus myth, a Hellenization of the Osiris cycle, taught the necessity of purifying the soul through expiation and religious consecration.

Cocteau retains certain of these ancient beliefs. For this reason, despite the humor and the irony in the play, there is always the element of mystery and a sense of the supernatural. Cocteau considers life a temporary state; a passage way toward another realm. (pp. 81-2)

Theatrically speaking, *Orpheus* is an exciting work. Objects become ritualistic symbols, virtual protagonists. Divested of their customary functions, these objects (doors, mirrors, gloves, glass) acquire new and startling meanings. Gloves are not merely used to keep hands warm or for reasons of fashion; they become mysterious entities. . . . Cocteau's mirror, like Alice's looking glass, becomes a door that leads to the other world—life's counterpart. It is a mysterious and magical instrument.

Endowed with new functions and powers, objects created a feeling of uneasiness among the spectators. "Even familiar objects," Cocteau wrote in his preface, "have something suspicious about them." (pp. 82-3)

Cocteau introduces another interesting technique to his drama: he purposefully breaks the audience-actor empathy. For example, after Orpheus has died and his head remains on stage, the audience is not only shocked but disconcerted when the head reveals his identity; it declares itself to be Jean Cocteau and gives his address. Strangely enough, the destruction of the theatrical illusion serves to reinforce it still further. The audience's identification goes beyond the play's characters, to the author himself; the spectators have become the dramatist's accomplices and are permitted to share in his secrets and his jokes. They are participating members of an arcane club. (p. 83)

[Les Enfants Terribles] is Cocteau's great work: a novel possessing the force, the tension, poetry, and religious flavor of an authentic Greek tragedy. The characters in this novel, however, are quite different from their ancient forebears. Cocteau's protagonists, unlike their ancestors, are endowed with modern marionette-like qualities, and they react to the strings jiggled by destiny in a brittle, seemingly unfeeling manner.

From the very outset of the novel, Cocteau plunges his

readers into a double world, at once actual and mythical. The work, therefore, has a metaphysical quality with a strong sense of the ominous and the occult. Juxtaposed to this other worldly atmosphere, over which no one seems to have any control, is the everyday functional world in which the protagonists live. The intertwining of both of these worlds creates a work which is unique in French literature. (p. 88)

Children of the Game is an allegory which expresses, through its symbolism, the tragedy of human destiny. As in Greek drama, an outside event or force is needed to set the dramatic mechanism in motion, so in Cocteau's novel, the white snowball which [the bully] Dargelos hurls at [the fragile] Paul acts as the catalyst. This act symbolizes destiny, irrevocable and all-powerful. The throwing of the snowball also represents an intrusion from the outside into the inner world of the innocent dreamers. At the end of the novel, a similar event occurs: Fate (Dargelos) sends the poison to Paul.

Fate's role in the story, the symbolism of the events reported, and the enigmatic and "mysterious" nature of the protagonists, combine to give *Children of the Game* a religious quality. Like a liturgical drama it has its gods and goddesses, its hierarchy, rituals, incantations—all played out by five children: Dargelos, Elisabeth, Paul, Agathe, and Gérard. (p. 91)

One of the outstanding features of the *Children of the Game* is the manner in which Cocteau catches and describes with such accuracy the protagonists' innermost thoughts and sensations. . . . The frequent omissions of rational plot sequences, the starkly drawn portraits of the children, the flavor of mystery and excitement which comes with the introduction of the unknown . . ., and the march of Fate . . . lend an enduring haunting quality to the book. (p. 94)

The Life of a Poet (La Vie d'un poète) was a visual transposition of Cocteau's own unconscious. It contained those images that had always been meaningful to him: mirrors, mobile and talking statues, guardian angels, a chimney, cards, a hermaphrodite, and the like. These objects, startlingly photographed owing to Cocteau's rich imagination, immersed viewers in a totally new visual experience. (p. 95)

The Infernal Machine is Cocteau's most original and important dramatic work. (p. 96)

Cocteau, like the Surrealists in this respect, is forever interested in disclosing the mysterious and hidden realm of the unconscious world, discovering its motivations and revealing these in all of their brute force. (pp. 97-8)

The Oedipus legend had always held enormous fascination for Cocteau. First he had adapted Sophocles' *Antigone* (1922), then came a free translation of *Oedipus Rex* (1925), now an original four-act play *The Infernal Machine* (1932) on the same subject. (pp. 98-9)

Cocteau underlined the already intense conflict present in the Oedipus story by achieving time simultaneity, permitting the characters to live in a double world (past and present) at the same time. He succeeded in bringing about such a feat by scenic manipulation. "A scene within a scene" was constructed right on the proscenium. The characters, who lived in the contemporary world, performed on a brightly lit daislike structure placed in the center of the stage; the rest of the area, symbolizing the ancient mythological, inexorable aspect of existence, was clothed in darkness.

To deepen audience identification, Cocteau put into practice his old credo: the theater should not be removed from, or be a substitute for, reality, but should be immersed in it. The modern scene, therefore, is reproduced with force and vigor. The soldiers in *The Infernal Machine* are contemporary figures who speak in present-day slang, jazz music blares forth from night clubs, and talk of revolution and war continues throughout. This realism makes disturbingly actual the plight of the entire family—a whole society—which is at the mercy of an inescapable fate.

Though the sense of awe present in the dramas of Aeschylus and Sophocles has been erased by Cocteau to a great extent, the supernatural elements still abound. Images and objects such as statues, columns, a scarf, and broaches take on the meaning and stature of human beings. They seem to actively act and talk on stage and so become vital to the drama itself, while dreams, miracles, ghosts, and a series of coincidences add terror to the already palpable presence of mysterious forces over which man has no control.

For Cocteau, man is fate's toy and is doomed to suffering. Whatever joys he experiences are merely traps set by the gods to make his eventual agony of defeat that much more acute: "For the gods to be royally entertained their victim has to fall from very high. The universe is a giant unmerciful machine bent upon the total annihilation of the human being." (pp. 99-100)

It can be said that Cocteau's dialogue was never—until [*The Infernal Machine*] so nervous, so direct and filled with such a sense of anguish. (p. 103)

The Infernal Machine is a work which will last not only because of its intrinsic verve and poetry and exciting theatrical qualities, but because it has transformed a profoundly stirring story into modern terms able to move the spectator through laughter . . . to tears . . . through shock . . . to anguish. . . . Furthermore, the introduction of objects used in the platonic sense as living *essences* and harbingers of events, and which are expertly interwoven in the drama, makes the play's impact that much more forceful and terrorizing. (pp. 103-04)

To try to evaluate Cocteau's contribution to the arts, one must divide his works into five principal categories: the theater, the novel, poetry, art criticism, and motion pictures.

In the theater, Cocteau rejected the popular well-made play characteristic of the naturalist school, with its flesh-and-blood characters and, its real-life props. This is not to say that he fled from realism into the arcane world of fantasy. On the contrary, Cocteau never tried to "arrange" reality nor to "attenuate" it; but rather to introduce a new vision of reality, by accentuating it. . . . Nothing could be more true-to-life, as Cocteau saw it, than the reality of *Parade, The Do-Nothing Bar,* or *The Wedding on the Eiffel Tower,* where the impossible becomes possible.

Under Picasso's and Apollinaire's influence, Cocteau brought the arts into the theater: dance, music, painting, and poetry. He achieved a unity of the arts in *Parade,* with his symbolic argument, Picasso's *décor* and costumes, and Erik Satie's music. (p. 158)

Cocteau, . . . dehumanized his characters, rendering his theater non-psychological and as objective as possible. His creatures never existed on a personal level; they were types, functions, symbols, instincts, or inanimate objects. . . . In *The Wedding on the Eiffel Tower,* there was a complete rejection of individualism. Two photographs representing the modern age became the chief protagonists. They deployed all their attributes to crush all personal characteristics. Even the bride and the groom (and the guests), as each uttered platitude upon platitude, came to represent not one wedding couple, but millions. (p. 159)

Aside from Cocteau's novels and his plays, he contributed greatly to the film industry. Here he was able to combine his literary and visual talents, those he could neither fulfill in his poetry or in his drawings. *The Blood of a Poet* has all the hallmarks of a masterpiece, uniqueness of vision, and impeccable execution. *Orpheus, Beauty and the Beast, The Eagle with Two Heads,* and *Intimate Relations* are also unusual films, from both a photographic and literary point of view. Cocteau's use of closeups, the focused and restrained emotions, the extreme simplicity of gestures, the sparseness and objectivity of dialogue, and the deliberate and effective timing of sequences all contribute to memorable hours in the movie theater. (p. 163)

> *Bettina Liebowitz Knapp, in her* Jean Cocteau *(copyright 1970 by Twayne Publishers, Inc.; reprinted with the permission of Twayne Publishers, A Division of G. K. Hall & Co., Boston), Twayne, 1970.*

One of the accusations most frequently leveled against Jean Cocteau is that there is no continuity in his work, that he created merely for the sake of effect without having any real goal in mind. Yet, if the evidence is fairly examined, it becomes clear that this is not the case, at least in his conception of stage performance. One of his earliest esthetic formulations is an article entitled "Le Numéro Barbette" which appeared in the July 1926 issue of the *Nouvelle Revue Française,* and his last play, *L'Impromptu du Palais Royal,* produced and published in 1962, is a theatrical presentation of his theories of theater. The latter is in fact a refinement, a sophisticated version of the former. However dissimilar Cocteau's plays may appear, they are linked by the same high ideal of the craft of theater: if their likenesses have been obscured, it is because they are united not by a theme or a message but rather by a conception of the art of the stage, of what theater as spectacle means. Cocteau was never interested in a play *qua* text; instead, he strove to create a certain art-object/spectator relationship based on illusion and enchantment. That this essential aim never changed in the course of his career becomes evident through a comparison of "Le Numéro Barbette" and *L'-Impromptu du Palais Royal.*

"Barbette" (the stage name of Vander Clyde) was one of the most highly respected trapeze artists and female impersonators of the 1920s and 30s. . . . [The] subject matter of "Le Numéro Barbette" is ultimately theoretical and oriented around questions of perception and illusion. From the transvestite's performance emerges one of the basic structures of Cocteau's theater. (pp. 79-80)

The two aspects of Barbette's act that distinguish it from all others resembling it . . . are its premise of total illusion or deception and its impeccable craftsmanship. These are precisely the two subjects that form the core of Cocteau's article:

> Don't forget that we are in the theater's magic light, in this 'malice-box' where truth is of no value, where what is natural is worthless, where short people become tall

and tall ones short, where only card tricks
and sleights of hand whose difficulty the
public doesn't even suspect can manage to
hold firm. . . .

It is clear that for Cocteau entering an auditorium is tantamount to participating in a reality completely removed from that of everyday. Different rules apply and, most important, the nature of perception changes completely. If the theater has a "magic light" that distorts ordinary objects, then whatever is presented on the stage must first be altered: it must be transposed just as music is transposed from key to key. In most cases, actors realize such a transformation through their make-up or costumes. Yet, they usually retain elements of who they really are, whereas Barbette succeeded in altering who he was as completely as possible.

The basic assumption underlying Cocteau's conception of theater as presented in "Le Numéro Barbette," then, is his tenet that the art of the stage presupposes deception. Acting is a game whose success is measured by the degree to which the audience accepts the game as reality. While modifications of such a position are not uncommon in the history of the theater, Cocteau's stand is radical in that it contains such great emphasis on shifting from one type of reality to another. . . . For there to be theater . . . the simple convention of illusion that underlies most acting is not enough: there must be a double order of illusion, a double step from commonplace reality. (p. 81)

In a play on the word *trompe-l'oeil,* Cocteau summarizes Barbette's performance as "this machine of witchcraft, of emotions, of *trompe-l'âme* [the soul] and of *trompe-les-sens* [the senses]." . . . One of the key words in his description is evidently, the word "deceive": at every moment, the spectators find themselves surrounded by a web of untruth which they believe, which in the atmosphere of a theater they accept as reality. More interesting, however, and ultimately more important for an understanding of Cocteau's work as a whole is the word "machine," because it underscores the deliberateness and precision that characterize every facet of a production. From Death's mechanized ritual in *Orphée* to Oedipus' calculated destruction in *La Machine infernale,* machines and mechanical devices form one of the constants in Cocteau's theater. However random the action on stage may seem, it is nevertheless controlled by an unalterable order. Nothing Barbette does is left to chance: what appears to be carried out with ease or nonchalance has in fact been planned with attention to the smallest detail. Barbette's act is an example of machine-like perfection, it epitomizes a mechanism that is designed to trick and that is, hence, a metaphor for theater. Therefore, flawless craftmanship emerges as perhaps the primary criterion for judging a work of art. (p. 82)

While *L'Impromptu du Palais Royal* seems more complex because it is in the form of a play with dialogue, it is nevertheless—with the exception of a discussion on the nature of time—little more than a statement of the concepts that can be deduced from "Le Numéro Barbette." As its title indicates, it falls into the category of plays like Molière's *Impromptu de Versailles* and *La Critique de L'École des femmes* or Giraudoux's *Impromptu de Paris* in which the subject of the work is theater. Both Molière and Giraudoux wrote scripts in which the characters consisted of a troupe of actors supposedly at ease and speaking informally. Obviously, such a device is a convention but it is one that intrigued Cocteau because of its essential ambi-

guity: in an impromptu actors appear not to be acting. They are therefore playing the role of actors and, hence, the action merely seems to be unpracticed. Therefore, such a form was an ideal vehicle for the expression of ideas on illusion, tricks and machine-like perfection. (p. 83)

By unmasking dramatic conventions, Cocteau destroys the myth of spontaneity and allows his spectators to glimpse the secrets of dramatic art. However, he does so in such a charming, indirect fashion that the *Impromptu* is probably one of his greatest triumphs in sleight of hand. (p. 84)

However many years may separate Barbette's act from *L'Impromptu du Palais Royal,* the formal continuity between the two works is nevertheless unmistakable. To qualify as theater, a performance must surpass the old truism of "realistic representation." A stage is not "the real" as it is defined in daily life. It is another sort of reality that has as its very basis the concept of trickery—and not merely a shoddy make-believe, but a game so convincingly and skillfully formed as to be accepted. The world of the stage should charm the spectator, captivate him so that he falls under its spell. Representation is not sufficient: what is presented must be perceived without question as what it is supposed to be.

The "secret" behind achieving such a goal appears to be a well-constructed machine, in Cocteau's vocabulary. No detail is left to chance. Even in the *Impromptu* whose characters blatantly inform the spectator at every turn that he is being deceived, the cleverness of the dialogue creates an impression of improvisation. The structure of the replies is such that the two planes of game interact in quick ricochets which evoke carefree play. Paradoxically, making a series of actions look unplanned requires the utmost in preparation. Each component of the whole must be properly timed, properly arranged. Therefore, just as in the contrast between Nijinsky on and off stage, appearance and reality have little in common. Underlying every successful work for the stage, Cocteau would argue, whether on the level of choreography, performance, or text, is a guiding mechanism that denies the premise of chance in art. Therefore, perfection in craftsmanship must be the criterion for judging the quality of an artisan. (pp. 85-6)

It appears that the universe to Cocteau was nothing more than a trick mechanism which deceives humanity by hiding the truth. Therefore, the plot of *La Machine infernale* is a game of the gods that Oedipus and Jocasta do not understand until they have been destroyed by it. Barbette is a woman until the audience finally sees him as a man. The structural elements of *Renaud et Armide, Les Parents terribles* and *L'Aigle à deux têtes* resemble components that mechanically, inevitably produce a result that could have been predicted if the forces at work had been known. What is important is that the forces are never evident, that the characters in the play occupy the same position in regard to their world as the spectators do in regard to what is happening on the stage; in each case, so many factors are hidden that the observer can grasp the truth only partially. He is, hence, a victim of illusion. In this light, *L'Impromptu du Palais Royal* emerges indeed as an appropriate summary of Cocteau's work for the theater, because the production appears completely superficial and frivolous. . . . Each word, like each object, presents a sort of "warning," a kind of indicator that things are not what they seem. The complexity of the whole becomes evident only when the mask (in whatever form it may take) is removed:

a masculine Barbette, the triumphant gods, and smiling actors all preclude the simple.

A definition of theater suitable for Cocteau must necessarily contain the idea of stage presentation, it must include much more than a text. Without performance, there are no games, no trick, no interlocking networks of reality and illusion which form the essence of theater. Reading the dialogue of *L'Impromptu du Palais Royal* or an outline of Barbette's act immediately gives the secret away, and secrecy is obviously one of the premises which guide Cocteau. Only in a performance of utmost skill can the sleight of hand succeed and the guiding mechanisms remain hidden. Continuity in Cocteau's theater . . . is to be found in structure rather than in content. Whatever the subject matter of the play may be, whether the tone is light or dark, the work is nevertheless constructed in the dualistic fashion that was prefigured by *le numéro Barbette* and that has become Cocteau's trademark. (pp. 86-7)

> *Lydia Crowson, "Cocteau and 'Le Numéro Barbette'," in* Modern Drama *(copyright © 1975, University of Toronto, Graduate Centre for Study of Drama; with the permission of* Modern Drama*), March, 1976, pp. 79-87.*

*   *   *

CONDON, Richard   1915-

An American novelist and playwright, Condon is probably best known for *The Manchurian Candidate*. Concerned with paranoia in contemporary society, Condon writes in a style that is cynical, hard-boiled, and often funny. Condon is, according to L. J. Davis, "an ingenious and original [writer] with a genuine gift for dialogue and characterization." (See also *CLC*, Vols. 4, 6, and *Contemporary Authors*, Vols. 1-4, rev. ed.)

You would expect Richard Condon to start in a galloping rush, and you would not expect him to stop. He doesn't. *Money is Love* is joyous, manic, and very hard to take. You feel you have to keep smiling to humour the Jolly Giant Funster who comes bulging out of the prose, cornucopically unloading his fantasticated blather on to your poor old head. The story purports to be about money, and its over-intimate connection with morality. . . . [One] of the first casualties of time-slip and overkill is the money/morality tie-up; no earthbound satirical purpose can flourish where there is virtually unlimited narrative freedom. What does survive, despite frequent collisions with low-flying Olympian farceurs, is a sense of head-shaking wonderment at the omnicompetence of the truly ambitious and acquisitive female. . . . Some private tribute may be intended here; but the general reader is unlikely to be roused from his moral recumbence. In fact, I don't know of a recent novel more likely to pin him to the horizontal. (p. 285)

> *Russell Davies, in* New Statesman *(© 1975 The Statesman & Nation Publishing Co. Ltd.), September 5, 1975.*

Condon is James M. Cain minus the rawness that makes Cain occasionally powerful. He is Thomas Pynchon without style or imagination; his wit takes the form of "There were Californian, Italian and French movie queens—all three female." (p. 4)

In a piece he wrote last year for "The New York Times Magazine" Condon says that he discovered he could be a novelist when he knew he was paranoiac, and that the classic symptom of paranoia is "retrospective falsification," which is also "what storytelling is." And "technically, novels are nothing more than opinionated views of emotion and consequence expressed in character and action." A real writer might be able to get away with such casualness but for a writer whose sense of either emotion or consequence is something derived from a textbook, Condon is just giving it all away. At the center of "The Whisper of the Axe" is Agatha Teel, the master revolutionary; about her emotions Condon has the opinion that a smart and clever black woman must finally want to punish Americans by killing enough of them so the ones remaining will overthrow the Government and begin to reorder life properly. Not that that is so very smart or clever a thought. Condon knows, however, that everyone has had such a thought for a few fleeting seconds at one time or another, and he is willing to make something he calls "character and action" out of diagrams made from such simple impulses. Then he will assure us Agatha Teel must be smart and clever because she ends up with the $237,000 worth of stolen diamonds and the gross receipts of $409 billion in 1975. If this is paranoia, it is paranoia turned statistical and bureaucratic. (pp. 4-5)

> *Roger Sale, in* The New York Times Book Review *(© 1976 by The New York Times Company; reprinted by permission), May 23, 1976.*

Along with the narrative power of *The Whisper Of The Axe*, Condon's greatest single achievement is to keep the reader baffled as to his real motives. Is he dead serious? Is this a glorious spoof of every pop cultural fantasy he can think of? Is it completely satire?

You never quite know. After a while you cease to care as *The Whisper Of the Axe* skitters back and forth in time, dredges up themes from earlier Condon novels (*Winter Kills* and *Arigato* as well as *The Manchurian Candidate*), invents brilliant new devices and roars to its climax which will not be revealed here.

The thriller, as literature, is having a considerable revival. One recent critic suggested that thrillers are or shortly will be the truest medium for the expression of contemporary America (a judgment that depends on your view of contemporary America). Be that as it may or may not be, the contemporary masters of the thriller understand their primary obligations: to tell a good story and to reflect the fears and fantasies of their time.

Condon is one of the living masters of the genre. Whether he ultimately means *The Whisper Of The Axe* as spoof or he is writing with a completely straight face, he knows the rules. It is one hell of a story. Condon now lives in Ireland but his new novel is a brilliant reflection of American fears and fantasies—a part of the way we live now. (p. F8)

> *Roderick MacLeish, in* Book World—The Washington Post *(© The Washington Post), May 30, 1976.*

"The Abandoned Woman" is a chic combination of cynical, hard-boiled satire and cruel, off-color humor. . . .

As is often the case with Mr. Condon's work, the prose becomes most animated and persuasive precisely when it is spiked with images of physical revulsion. During lengthy stretches of this "historical novel," however, Mr. Condon eschews imagery altogether in favor of what Gore Vidal calls "plastic fiction": names, documents, places, dates, genealogies and pared-down fragments of history pile up unremittingly and arbitrarily. The clipped syntax and pseudo-documentary narration in the present tense only increase the oppressive nuts-and-bolts ennui of a novel that substitutes an accretion of factual and concocted data for atmosphere and subtlety. Even the "ribald" sex scenes promised by the dust jacket are buried under name-dropping and history lessons. (p. 17)

Other than the cruelty jokes, which are at least told with a certain conviction, the attempts at humor are similarly disorienting and wearisome. Sometimes the humor takes the form of affected breeziness, as when the narrator describes Caroline and George as "the hardly happy-go-lucky young couple"; at other times it tries to emerge in embarrassingly off-key dialect, as when Queen Charlotte Sophia insists upon putting a chaperon in the carriage with the newly married Princess Charlotte and Prince Leopold because "'It iss zo improber dat dey drive off, t'igh to t'igh, alone.'" Mr. Condon's touch is about as light as the "globes, globules, and chunks of sagging fat" of Prince George's endlessly described "super-stomach."

Because the mixture of 19th and 20th century idioms is careless and haphazard, the funniest lines often seem unintentional. One moment the dialogue sounds like psychiatric jargon . . . , the next moment like poorly paraphrased T. S. Eliot . . . , the next like the more ornate language that we at least vaguely expect of 19th-century royalty.

It is possible, I suppose, to assume charitably that Mr. Condon is improvising some farfetched species of collage or parody. . . . But since the narrator is continually writing careless sentences, one might assume that he is indulging as well. (pp. 17, 30)

> *Jack Sullivan, "Caroline Wronged Again,"*
> *in* The New York Times Book Review (©
> *1977 by The New York Times Company;*
> *reprinted by permission), June 5, 1977, pp.*
> *17, 30.*

*   *   *

CREELEY, Robert   1926-

American poet, novelist, short story writer, and editor, Creeley was one of the founders of the "Black Mountain movement" in poetry. His verse, in method, is a concise development of communication, while, in subject matter, it often deals with the lack of it. He has had an important effect on contemporary American poetry. (See also *CLC*, Vols. 1, 2, 4, and *Contemporary Authors*, Vols. 1-4, rev. ed.)

[*For Love: Poems 1950-1960* shows] Creeley moving toward the gradual definition of his own original style, his own range of emotion, his own pattern of imagining. Creeley has a subtle, almost feminine sensibility, and the best of his poems are those dealing with the intricacies that exist between men and women. The poems move back and forth between the mood of loneliness on the one hand and on the other the repeated exhortation, "Be natural." The poems fulfill this plea in their plaintiveness, their refusal to oversimplify, in their aloneness, even in their mannerisms. They evade the bold statement, luxuriate in the inconclusive, and often strike perfectly the note of the dying fall.

Creeley's poems are as delicately patterned as a butterfly's wing, particularly in his later work. Since he prefers moods of perplexity, of quiet currents below the surface, of bittersweet lack, his poetic techniques are curiously suitable and

often highly effective. Again and again you will come across one of his poems containing a subtle rhythm which winds back on itself, involute as a seashell, and in which the rhythm itself casts the illumination. For instance, in "The Rain," the poem begins in shadow and ends in light, all controlled by rhythm, moving from evasion to certainty. . . . His occasional pure lyrics also depend on [his] simplicity, not to say naïveté, of language.

I doubt, however, whether it is pedantic to suggest that Creeley's grammar and punctuation are often very uncertain indeed, to the extent of confusing the meaning of his poems, and sometimes of making them downright ridiculous. . . . He is very foolish . . . not to use question marks in place of periods when they are needed. These may seem like small matters, but in elusive poems like Creeley's, it takes only a very slight shift of weight to upset the balance. (pp. 85-6)

> *Peter Davison, in* The Atlantic Monthly
> *(copyright © 1962 by The Atlantic Monthly*
> *Company, Boston, Mass.; reprinted with*
> *permission), November, 1962.*

Creeley has not always proposed pleasure for his immediate poetic object. *For Love,* even *Words* (a really notable book for all its faults), raise too many questions about ideas and sincerity. *Pieces* is another matter altogether, the perfection of what Creeley aimed at in *Words.* Gone are those seductive angels. Creeley does not test himself against his poetry, he masters it. . . . *Pieces* is a very wise and very beautiful book of verse. It enacts the piecemeal achievement of a vision to scrupulous and catholic that what by method is merely muscular and aesthetic becomes in the end profoundly moral. (pp. 200-01)

> *Jerome McGann, in* Poetry (© *1970 by The*
> *Modern Poetry Association; reprinted by*
> *permission of the Editor of* Poetry), Decem-
> *ber, 1970.*

Love, relationship, and the attendant emotions are more than recurring concerns for Robert Creeley; they are almost trademarks of his work. Even when he is writing about the difficulties of language (a common theme), he is ultimately concerned with the loss of communication between people—a roadblock to relationship. Similarly, his verse rhythms potentially express emotion even when the subject is neutral; a tight-throated, short line is especially evident at readings. Why, then, does Creeley's poetry and fiction represent sexual love as the epitome of human fulfillment, yet love constantly fails? Unlike the poems, his short stories, *The Gold Diggers* (1965), and novel, *The Island* (1963), constrain him to dramatize his themes in specific contexts, so we may more easily look to Creeley's fiction for the answer. The failure of love seems to be rooted in the delusive sexual imagination of his protagonists, particularly the men. Their inability to cope with social reality leads them to create their own world—usually an expression of sexual fears which foredoom any genuine sexual involvement. While such solipsism is preferable for some of Creeley's characters, for most it becomes a trap that is difficult to escape. Their conflicting subjective experience is the focus of Creeley's often surreal narratives.

The sexual imagination of Creeley's characters is often indistinguishable from their outer circumstances; a person or situation may be an objective correlative or psychological "projection" of the protagonist's subjective feelings. (p. 59)

Although Creeley writes about the subject of love, the point of view is almost always that of the unloved speaker in his solitude. That the psychology of the would-be lover rather than the image of his love is the subject of Creeley's love lyrics might explain why women so often have multiple, interchangeable identities in the poems; the poet's *idea* or imagined possibility of woman takes the place of any particular woman. (p. 61)

The force of the masculine imagination is, then, very powerful in Creeley's writing. The failure of love, like a self-fulfilling prophecy, is primarily spun out of that imagination; the protagonist creates impossible situations for the survival of love (the helpless jealousy in "Mr. Blue," and the dream in "The Seance"). . . . When a relationship fails, solipsism appears to be the only alternative. The highly developed private world amounts to a compensation for an abandoned public one—yet the private world is clearly unacceptable. (p. 62)

One senses an incompleteness in [his] stories, perhaps because Creeley directs his energies to the articulation of his characters' disturbed sexual imaginations, showing little interest in exploring just what has gone wrong in their public world. Creeley seems to draw on the interiorized consciousness as his greatest creative resource. It is his vantage point as well as his subject. Creeley is concerned with the horror of the isolated self, the dehumanization of life without community. In his poetry, isolation is often traced to weak bridges between people that our minds and language provide, part a problem of perception and expression too rooted in the self. . . . Creeley suggests in his poems that the way out of solipsism, the extreme condition of isolation, is love. Experience must be shared to be enriched, a seeming impossibility.

Since Creeley's themes are isolation and loneliness, many of his stories involve people who try to break out of such condition and, in this sense, are about quests, journeys of the mind and body which eventually fail. (pp. 63-4)

Ultimately, Creeley seems to disbelieve in the love his characters can never quite obtain. His more positive stories suggest that loneliness is man's natural condition and that one must accept the fact before one can accept oneself. (p. 64)

The themes of isolation, the destructive sexual imagination, and the need to escape the self are more extensively and satisfyingly developed in Creeley's novel, *The Island*. The principal theme of the novel, the stories, and much of the poetry is the necessity of human relationship, however difficult to maintain. One of the strengths of the novel is that Creeley portrays destructive isolation in various forms and is careful to avoid slick solutions or alternatives; he does not oversimplify human experience. (p. 66)

His short stories suggest that the failure of love is due to a fear of sexuality and a preference for the self-created reality over the unacceptable real world. *The Island* extends the possibilities of isolation by rendering a marriage as lonely as an individual. The fear of sexuality is also a fear of any vital communication with the world. (pp. 68-9)

Perhaps Creeley has fashioned in his characters models of the artist as a reluctant solipsist who tries to compensate in his imagination for an unattainable contact with reality. The failure to communicate is a social as well as an artistic poverty, yet Creeley's expression of his characters' private worlds is rich in understanding and feeling. (p. 69)

John G. Hammond, "Solipsism and the Sexual Imagination in Robert Creeley's Fiction," in Critique: Studies in Modern Fiction *(copyright © James Dean Young 1975), Vol. XVI, No. 3, pp. 59-69.*

No one has more successfully practiced the hard, dry, anti-poetic style that represents a significant strain in modern writing than Robert Creeley. It is the kind of verse that illiterates claim not to be literature, since it lacks the sentimental effusiveness that is popularly associated with poetry. What is one to make of a poet who is prepared to expose his most trivial domestic complaints?

> Let me say (in anger) that since
>   the day we married
> we have never had a towel
> where anyone could find it,
> the fact.

I recognize, though my own system of documentation is different from his, that "the fact" is terribly important to Creeley, as it is to me, and that he is relentless in his determination to record it as strictly, as sparely as he can. He is chary even of metaphor, as though it were a form of decoration. This purism breeds a cold and narrow strength. His aesthetic is related to that of several painters of his generation—Jasper Johns is the most familiar name—who insisted on presenting, in explicit detail, the American flag as American flag (a composition of stripes and stars) or a slice of blueberry pie as a slice of blueberry pie, stripped of all background, connotation, or symbolic aura, as if to say, "Here is the thing-in-itself: take it for what it is, and take it now." One could argue that the reality of "the fact," given the findings of modern physics, is a supreme fiction, but this objection has not inhibited a strong tendency in the modern arts that can be called actualism. Creeley, it seems to me, is the most persuasive of the actualist poets, all of whom derive in varying degrees from W. C. Williams. In the best of his collections, *For Love*, Creeley is emotionally freer than he has been before, without rejecting his minimalist technique. . . . (pp. 259-60)

More recently Creeley's work, which has always shown a predilection for word-play, has moved in the direction of conceptual art. The increasing dryness, impersonality, and abstraction of his new poems would seem to betoken a temporary exhaustion or numbness of feeling rather than the hardening of an aesthetic credo. (p. 260)

Stanley Kunitz, in his A Kind of Order, A Kind of Folly *(© 1935, 1937, 1938, 1941, 1942, 1947, 1949, 1957, 1963, 1964, 1965, 1966, 1967, 1970, 1971, 1972, 1973, 1974, 1975 by Stanley Kunitz; reprinted by permission of Little, Brown and Co. in association with the Atlantic Monthly Press), Atlantic-Little, Brown, 1975.*

From the very first, with the publication of *For Love: Poems 1950-1960*, Robert Creeley declared himself an experimenter: his interest has not been primarily in either ideas or in things, but in allowing what is *there* to be expressed in words, in sounds and rhythms that communicate states of mind that are not quite emotions, and not quite concepts. For Creeley, rhythmic modality is the very essence of poetry; he has never been interested in subordinating his art to statements of a social or political nature, nor has he been interested in developing form *per se*. He follows William Carlos Williams: "The poet thinks with his poem. In that lies his thought, and that in itself is the profundity." Had Creeley not gone on to become a quite substantial poet he would have achieved a sort of minor celebrity in poetry circles by having stated a truth there to be expressed, so far as contemporary poets are concerned: "Form is never more than an extension of content." (p. 26)

He has been called a Minimalist, and while the term is ambiguous enough it can perhaps be justified, if by Minimalist we mean an artist who rather ascetically eliminates a great deal from his imagined landscape in order to focus upon the essential (which must always be a state of mind, a *response,* rather than an attempt to present the stimulus). The poems as we have them sometimes seem the after-effects of poetic moments, emotion not recollected—or reconstructed—but transformed into its equivalent in terms of consciousness. The event, the experience, is completed; the emotion has run its course; what remains is the description of the emotion's passage, for whatever it is worth. . . .

Admittedly there are dangers in so laconic and spare an art, for if one does not grant Creeley the premises of his poetry, if one objects to the stumbling, stuttering, ostensibly accidental nature of the finished product, it cannot be argued that there are peripheral matters of closely observed detail, rich and provocative language, wit, or wisdom, or even venom, to compensate for the deliberate modesty of revelation. Yet Creeley has stated that he doesn't want to write "what is only an idea, particularly my own"; if the world can't be evoked, "flooding all the terms of my thought and experience, then it's not enough, either for me or, equally, for anyone else." The difficulty with Creeley's poetry, particularly with assessing it, is that the *idea* of the poem often seems somewhat more interesting than the poem itself. (p. 27)

Selected Poems consists of work from *For Love, The Charm, Pieces, A Day Book,* and *Words,* as well as 16 more recent poems. *A Day Book* contains a kind of poetic journal, a record of Creeley's experiences in London and elsewhere, addressed at times to certain friends (Bly, Jim Dine, Marisol), at other times meant to be a dialogue with himself, an unsystematic collection of brief notes. "Wish I were home at this precise moment—the sun coming in those windows. The sounds of the house, birds too." And again: "Wish Joan Baez was here / singing "Tears of Rage" in my ear. / Wish I was Bob Dylan—/ he's got a subtle mind.")

It was fashionable for a while in the '60s to refuse to revise, so that one retained the spontaneous flow of the mind, its blunders as well as its successes, but after the passage of even a brief space of time such experimentation appears to have been merely self-indulgent—as when Creeley wonders aloud how to spell "MacCluhan" (sic) or wishes that a book on Tolstoi were reprinted when in fact it has been in paperback for some years (as he later notes, parenthetically). Such formless, directionless work undercuts the effect of the more disciplined poetry that surrounds it. Too often the reader is an unwilling and unimpressed witness to the poet's interior life, and to his insistence upon his own *ordinariness.* Since Williams, the elevation of the presumably trivial into art has become fairly commonplace, and there is the danger that a once-revolutionary concept can become, in a generation or less, another poetic convention.

But *A Day Book* is not representative of Creeley's art at its best. For that we must go to such powerful, succinct poems as "The Innocence," "Wait For Me," "The Door," "The

Rhythm," and "Kore"; and to the long, groping, painful elegy "For My Mother". . . . At such times Creeley is absolutely mesmerizing in his ability to suspend and to define the passage of thought, the process of experience in all its ironic, inexorable sadness. No poetic theories are required to support such art: it achieves its own permanence by relating at once to our own groping, semi-articulate wonder. (pp. 27-8)

> *Joyce Carol Oates, in* The New Republic *(reprinted by permission of* The New Republic; © *1976 by The New Republic, Inc.), December 18, 1976.*

[Among] all the poets who have followed the line of William Carlos Williams and Charles Olsen—Projectionists, Black Mountaineers—Creeley is most the romanticist; even, as he has unabashedly said, the sentimentalist. It isn't simply the romanticism of Shelley either, but on back through Lovelace and Herrick, the troubadours, Catullus, to the ancient Arcadians; and forward too into our own time. Odds are that when Creeley was young he read the poems of Elinor Wylie, not without appreciation.

He placed himself, at any rate, squarely in the Western tradition to which most of us who write poetry belong, the secular lovers. He eroticized thought and experience totally, and his religion (since all poets are religious) was joy in self and world. But then, like all romanticists, he fell prey to uncertainties. What is self, this bundle of unconscious, conscious self-consciousness? And what is world? If Eros is its pervading spirit, what happens when man is cast out of nature into solitariness, our so well-known modern condition of alienation?

Williams said: "No ideas but in things." Yet he said it, inevitably, in words, and if words are more than palpable sound, if they mean anything, then they *are* ideas, they are abstract. So Creeley fights his battle of self and not-self, his obsession, in language forever straining to escape abstraction, and forever failing. (p. 58)

Well, in the beginning he wrote what we expected, love poems, wrote them beautifully, using Williams's formal notions to realign the traditional stanzaic lyric, keeping his language hard, direct, unadorned. He was, and is, our finest verse technician. (pp. 58-9)

History, the outside, otherness, these torture him, more and more in recent poems. Momentary song is not satisfactory. It strikes me that his whole later work is a poetry of *dis*satisfaction, and that the irritation of it gets into his words and forms, making them snippy and acute. More and more he has turned to unplayful word games and wise conundrums.

> What
> by being not
> is—is not
> by being.

He has turned away, as real poets all must, from what his talent does most easily. Let rhyming go, what we need is truth, and he has pushed himself relentlessly toward harder formulations. What has it done to his poetry? It has changed it, but beyond that I cannot say, and I distrust anyone who thinks he can. Hardy and Hopkins were fools in their time. Seventy-five years from now we—someone—will know what Creeley has done.

Meanwhile the "Selected Poems" is a necessary book for

anyone still unacquainted with his work. Creeley is one of our most interesting poets certainly, and I think perhaps our purest, however the word is taken. (p. 59)

Hayden Carruth, "A Secular Lover," in The New York Times Book Review (© 1977 by The New York Times Company; reprinted by permission), May 1, 1977, pp. 58-9.

*   *   *

CUMMINGS, E(dward) E(stlin) 1894-1962

Cummings, an American poet, playwright, essayist, and novelist, was one of the most innovative poets of his time. Avoiding highly intellectual concerns, Cummings's poems were often deliberately simplistic. A sensual poet, Cummings experimented with grammar, punctuation, and typography in order to better present his attempts to fully realize himself through his senses. Some of Cummings's best known works are *The Enormous Room, The Balloon Man,* and *Fifty Poems.* (See also *CLC,* Vols. 1, 3.)

Mr. Cummings' poems depend entirely upon what they create in process, only incidentally upon what their preliminary materials or intentions may have been. Thus, above all, there is a prevalent quality of uncertainty, of uncompleted possibility, both in the items and in the fusion of the items which make up the poems; but there is also the persistent elementary eloquence of intension—of things struggling, as one says crying, to be together, and to make something of their togetherness which they could never exhibit separately or in mere series. The words, the meanings in the words, and also the nebula of meaning and sound and pun around the words, are all put into an enlivening relation to each other. There is, to employ a word which appealed to Hart Crane in similar contexts, a sense of synergy in all the successful poems of Mr. Cummings: synergy is the condition of working together with an emphasis on the notion of energy in the working, and energy in the positive sense, so that one might say here that Mr. Cummings' words were energetic. The poems are, therefore, eminently beyond paraphrase, not because they have no logical content—for they do, usually very simple—but because so much of the activity is apart from that of logical relationships, is indeed in associations free of, though not alien to, logical associations. In short, they create their objects. (p. 75)

There is, for the poet, no discipline like the justified reservations of his admirers, and this should be especially the case with a poet so deliberately idiosyncratic as Mr. Cummings. I have been one of his admirers for twenty-one years since I first saw his poetry in the *Dial;* and it may be that my admiration has gone up and down so many hills that it is a little fagged and comes up to judgment with entirely too many reservations. Yet I must make them, and hope only that the admiration comes through.

First, there is the big reservation that, contrary to the general belief and contrary to what apparently he thinks himself, Mr. Cummings is not—in his meters, in the shapes of his lines, in the typographical cast of his poems on the page —an experimental poet at all. In his "peculiar" poetry he does one of two things. He either reports a speech rhythm and the fragments of meaning punctuated by the rhythm so as to heighten and make it permanent in the reader's ear— as famously in "Buffalo Bill" . . . , but just as accurately elsewhere as, for example, in poem 27 [in *50 POEMS*] or in

trying to do so he makes such a hash of it that the reader's ear is left conclusively deaf to the poem. I assume he is attempting to heighten sound in the failures as well as the successes; if he is not, if he is trying to write a poetry in symbols which have no audible equivalents—a mere eye poetry—then he is committing the sin against the Holy Ghost. My belief is that the high percentage of failures comes from his lack of a standard from which to conduct experiments, and without which experiment in any true sense is impossible; so that in fact many of his oddities are merely the oddities of spontaneous play, nonsense of the casual, self-defeating order, not nonsense of the rash, intensive order. There is no reason he should not play, but it is too bad that he should print the products, for print sheds a serenity of value, or at least of "authority" upon the most miserable productions which are very deceptive to the innocent.

It should be emphasized in connection with this that Mr. Cummings is an abler experimenter than most poets with rhythm and cadence and epithet; and that these experiments come off best when he is not engaged in false experiments with meter—when he is writing either heightened prose as in "Buffalo Bill," or when he is writing straight-way meter of four or five iambic feet. Which is what one would expect.

My second reservation . . . has to do with his vocabulary, which seems to me at many crucial points so vastly over-generalized as to prevent any effective mastery over the connotations they are meant to set up as the substance of his poems. I do not mean it is just hard to say, which is of little importance, but that it is hard to *know,* which is very important, where you are at in poems which juggle fifty to a hundred words so many times and oft together that they lose all their edges, corners, and boundary lines till they cannot lie otherwise than in a heap. But this reservation . . . applies to no more than half the new poems; for Mr. Cummings' practice has improved with his increasing interest, as it seems, in persuading his readers of the accuracy of the relationships which his words divulge.

My third reservation is minor, and has to do with the small boy writing privy inscriptions on the wall. . . . My complaint is meant to be technical; most of the dirt is not well enough managed to reach the level of either gesture or disgust, but remains, let us say, coprophiliac which is not a technical quality. (pp. 76-7)

Special attention should be called to the development of fresh conventions in the use of prepositions, pronouns, and the auxiliary verbs in the guise of substances, and in general the rich use of words ordinarily rhetorical—mere connectives or means of transition in their ordinary usage— for the things of actual experience. There are questions which may be asked of which the answers will only come later when the familiarity of a generation or so will have put the data in an intimately understandable order. How much of the richness depends on mere novelty of usage, the gag-line quality? How much depends on the close relationship to the everyday vernacular, the tongue in which Who and Why and How and No and Yes and Am, for example, are of supreme resort, and are capable of infinite diversity of shading? How much depends perhaps on Mr. Cummings' sense of the directional nubs, and the nubs of agency and of being, in his chosen words; a sense that resembles, say, the dative and ablative inflections in Latin? How much, finally, depends on the infinite proliferating multiplicity of available meanings in his absolute commonplaces made suddenly to do precise work? The questions would not be worth asking did not each furnish a possible suggestion as to the capacity for meaning and flavor of his usage; nor would they be worth asking if there were not a major residue of his verse, as standard as death, which his oddities only illuminate without damaging. (pp. 77-8)

> *R. P. Blackmur, "Review of '50 POEMS'," in* The Southern Review *(copyright, 1941 by Louisiana State University Press), Vol. 7, No. 3, Summer, 1941 (and reprinted in* E. E. Cummings: A Collection of Critical Essays, *edited by Norman Friedman, Prentice-Hall, Inc., 1972, pp. 75-8).*

A lifelong addict of the circus, vaudeville, and burlesque, Cummings loves to puncture words so that he can fling their stale rhetoric like straw all over the floor of his circus tent, to take a pompous stance that collapses under him, to come out with an ad-lib that seems positively to stagger him. But the very point of all this is that it occurs within a vocabulary that is essentially abstract and romantic, and that the performance is by a man who remains always aloof, whose invocation of love, spring, roses, balloons, and the free human heart stems from a permanent mistrust of any audience.

This duality of the traditionalist and the clown, of the self-consciously arrogant individualist and the slapstick artist, makes up Cummings' world, and it is this that gives special interest to the autobiographical sections of [*i: Six Non-lectures,*] a book that otherwise, though as delightful as anything he has ever written, tends to lapse into defensive quotations from his own writings and opinions. For in coming to Harvard he came back to his own—to the town he was born in, to the university whose intellectual inheritance he so particularly represents, to the memory of his father, a Boston minister and onetime Harvard instructor, whose influence is so dominant in his best work. The remarkably exalted memories Cummings gives us of his Cambridge boyhood . . . is the background of his familiar opposition between the idyllic past and the New York world in which he has to live. Cummings is not merely a traditionalist in the mold of so many American poets, a mold that recalls those other American inventors and originals, such as Ford and Edison and Lindbergh, who are forever trying to reclaim the past their own feats have changed; he is the personification of the old transcendentalist passion for abstract ideals. In his knowingness with words, in his passion for Greek and Latin, he takes one back to Emerson and Thoreau, who were perpetually pulling words apart to illustrate their lost spiritual meaning. Underneath the slapstick and the typographical squiggles, Cummings likes to play with words so that he can show the ideals they once referred to —and this always with the same admonitory, didactic intent and much of Thoreau's shrewd emphasis on his own singularity.

It is these old traits that give such delightfulness, and occasionally something of his hoped-for disagreeableness, to Cummings' "egocentricity," which he pretends in these lectures to apologize for yet which is actually, of course, not a subjective or narcissistic quality at all but the very heart of his Protestant and fiercely individualistic tradition. (pp. 169-70)

In the new American scriptures, fathers don't count. But Cummings' cult of his father is, precisely because it will strike many Americans as wholly unreal, the clue to all that makes Cummings so elusive and uncharacteristic a figure today. For just as the occasional frivolousness of his poetry is irritating because it is *not* gay, because it is snobbish and querulous and self-consciously forlorn in its distance from the great urban mob he dislikes, so the nobility and elevation of his poetry—which has become steadily more solid, more experimental and moving—is unreal to many people because of the positive way in which he flings the *true* tradition in our faces with an air that betrays his confidence that he will not be understood.

Cummings' wit always starts from the same tone in which Thoreau said that "I should not talk so much about myself if there were anybody else whom I knew as well." It is both a conscious insulation of his "eccentricity" and an exploitation of his role. But Emerson and Thoreau, even in the rosy haze of transcendentalism, were resolute thinkers, provokers of disorder, revolutionaries who were always working on the minds of their contemporaries; Cummings' recourse is not to the present, to the opportunities of the age, but to the past. And that past has now become so ideal, and the mildly bawdy satires he used to write against the Cambridge ladies of yesteryear have yielded to such an ecstasy of provincial self-approval, that we find him in these lectures openly pitying his audience because it did not have the good sense to be born in his father's house. (pp. 170-71)

Cummings' poetry has ripened amazingly of recent years, but it has not grown. And charming and touching as he is in this little autobiography, he remains incurably sentimental. This sentimentality, I hasten to add, is not in his values, in his dislike of collectivism, in his rousing sense of human freedom; it is in his failure to clothe the abstractions of his fathers with the flesh of actuality, with love for the living. The greatness of the New England transcendentalists was their ability to reclaim, from the commonsensical despairs of a dying religion, faith in the visionary powers of the mind. More and more, in Cummings' recent books, one sees how this belief in imagination, this ability to see life from within, has enabled him to develop, out of the provocative mannerisms of his early work, a verse that is like lyric shorthand—extraordinarily elastic, light, fresh, and resonant of feeling. At a time when a good deal of "advanced" poetry has begun to wear under its convention of anxiety, Cummings' verse has seemed particularly felt, astringent, and musical. But it is precisely because Cummings is a poet one always encounters with excitement and delight, precisely because it is his gift to make the world seem more joyful, that one reads a book like this with disappointment at hearing so many familiar jokes told over again, while the poet escapes into a fairyland of his fathers and points with a shudder to all who are not, equally with him, his father's son. (p. 171)

> *Alfred Kazin, "E. E. Cummings and His Fathers," in* The New Yorker *(© 1954 by The New Yorker Magazine, Inc.), January 2, 1954 (and reprinted in* E. E. Cummings: A Collection of Critical Essays, *edited by Norman Friedman, Prentice-Hall, Inc., 1972, pp. 168-71).*

[Cummings] has used language with no concession to conventional recognition; he has always wanted his reader to drop all the accoutrements of the grammarian and the rhetorician that he may be wearing as protective clothing and to approach his poems, as it were, naked and unafraid. The reader should be free of preconceptions about English poetry, unafraid to "reconsider his standards of acceptance."

This is not to say, however, that Cummings does not know rules and tradition. He is instead a prime example of the old adage that an artist must know all the rules before he can break them. Cummings is no primitive, though he sometimes uses words as a child does; he is no Walt Whitman with a barbaric yawp, no untutored child of the prairie working in what is essentially an alien medium. . . . His first book of poems, *Tulips and Chimneys* (1923), revealed the fact that he had had a classical education, although the poems in it that looked forward to his later writing were much more noteworthy than those which were traditionalist. And although he continues to work in the sonnet—perhaps his most memorable poetry is in this form—he long ago abandoned the language of Rossetti and Keats for one which fits his highly personal insight into experience. At its most highly developed state, in his later books, Cummings' language becomes almost a foreign one, usually possible to figure out for a reader who knows English, it is true; but he will get its full meaning only if he has read a great deal of Cummings and if he "knows the language."

It is unfortunate that most of the critical appraisals of Cummings' poetry were made early, shortly after his first books were published. Since those days—the twenties—were full of literary and artistic ferment, and a new poetic talent was to many people at least as exciting as a new baseball player, it is natural that he should have received a great deal of attention then; it is perhaps also natural that as the first shock caused by his poetry died down into acceptance of what seemed a fixed technique of an established poet, the critics should have turned their eyes elsewhere. Cummings, too, was somewhat out of the mainstream in the thirties. He was not popular with the New Critics because he was too personal and unintellectual; he did not think or write in their groove. Nor was he popular with the critics of the left who demanded their own variety of social consciousness in a writer. His "immorality" was too blunt for the Humanists, and his verse was too uncommunicative for the attackers of the cult of unintelligibility. When his last three volumes of verse came out, no one took the trouble to give Cummings the reappraisal that his poetry needed and deserved; very few people noticed the fundamental change of attitude which manifested itself in his growing reverence and dedication to lasting love; even fewer noted the development in his use of language. Thus in 1955 an essay, "Notes on E. E. Cummings' Language," by Richard P. Blackmur, written in 1930, remains the only extensive treatment of the subject; and too many people think of his language, as they think of the subject matter of his poetry, as if it were all of a piece, which it most emphatically is not. (pp. 80-2)

Many of the things that Mr. Blackmur said are still accurate descriptions of some of the phenomena of Cummings' language; the trouble is that his remarks are incomplete. They do not consider Cummings' later practices of using one part of speech as another, of leaving out words so that the resulting condensation is so dense as to be almost impenetrable, of thoroughly scrambling English word order with the same effect. Mr. Blackmur was instead occupied with such things as Cummings' tough-guy attitude and his romantic egoism, with his overuse of certain favorite words to which he seemed to assign private meanings, and with the question of whether such diction did not make his poetry impenetrable. Mr. Blackmur concluded unequivocally that it did; and, if in 1952 he saw no need for modification of his note [in his *Language As Gesture*], one assumes that he still thinks so. (pp. 82-3)

Although his language, especially in the later books, is intricate and difficult, what [Cummings] asks of his reader is, as always, the frank approach of a child; and it is this attitude which he himself takes to his mother tongue and to its tenets and rules. Of course, such an approach is consistent with that most salient feature of his viewpoint, his glorification of the child (or the "maturely childish" adult); he is, when he fashions language as a child would, merely practicing what he preaches. It is doubtful whether he ever said to himself, "I shall form and use words as if I have not completely mastered the idiom of the English language, although I know its rules"; but this is precisely what, in his first ventures into unusual language, he began to do. He divested himself of the literate adult's prejudices against such things as double negatives, redundant superlatives and comparatives, and non-dictionary words. (p. 83)

[In] *Tulips and Chimneys,* although the greater part of his language is conventional and sometimes even banally "poetic," one finds such unusual usages as *unstrength, purpled, Just-spring, eddieandbill, puddle-wonderful, almostness, greentwittering, quiveringgold, flowerterrible, starlessness, fearruining, timeshaped, sayingly.* Except for *sayingly* and *almostness,* which are among the first examples of his changing one part of speech into another, and *unstrength,* there is nothing very startling about most of these words. The mere printing of two words together, as in *greentwittering,* might be considered more a typographical technique than a linguistic one, although it is apparent that when Cummings combines two words to form one adjective he usually creates a new concept by the juxtaposition of two unlike descriptives: *flowerterrible, timeshaped.* (It is such language as this that Mr. Blackmur objects to; he would say that it is impossible to determine the exact meaning of such words as *flowerterrible* and *timeshaped,* and undoubtedly he is right.) *Tulips and Chimneys* abounds with such words and with phrases that are made up of conventional words in unconventional juxtapositions. . . .

These phrases that (one must agree with Mr. Blackmur) convey a thrill but not a precise impression swarm through the book but are not able to occupy it exclusively. In contrast to them are many images which depend for their power upon the unexpected but which manage to convey an accurate reproduction of the poet's thought, which show, indeed, that the poet *had* a thought and not merely a rush of words. (p. 86)

The language of *Tulips and Chimneys,* . . . like the imagery, the verse forms, the subject matter, and the thought, is sometimes good, sometimes bad. But the book is so obviously the work of a talented young man who is striking off in new directions, groping for original and yet precise expression, experimenting in public, that it seems uncharitable to dwell too long on its shortcomings. (p. 88)

Cummings' linguistic usages in *Tulips and Chimneys* and in the two books which soon followed it & [*AND*] and *XLI POEMS* [are similar]. These books were published within three years and are fairly much alike (although the typographical distortions that reach extremes in & [*AND*] were barely hinted at in the first book); in style and in subject matter the three books are the work of the same youthful poet. (p. 89)

Although . . . the early books are punctuated with favorite words (*thrilling, flowers, utter, skillful, groping, crisp, keen, actual, stars,* etc.) almost as copiously as another author would use commas, an awareness of these words is not unrewarding if one wishes to understand Cummings. The words *flower* and *stars* are, as he uses them, not mere substantives representing a thing in nature but are metaphorical shorthand for concepts which Cummings finds admirable: the flowers, for example, representing growth, being, aliveness; the stars standing for the steadfastness of beauty in nature.

Such adjectives as he continually uses . . . , though they are admittedly overworked in the early books to the point of tiresomeness, are nevertheless indicative of his viewpoint: he admires phenomena that can be described as crisp, keen, actual, gay, young, strong, or strenuous, and dislikes the groping, the dim, the slow, the dull. In reading the early poetry, it is often necessary to know which of Cummings' words are, in Hayakawa's terms, "purr words" and which are "snarl words" in order to get any meaning from the poem. As Cummings progressed, he outgrew his penchant for such expressions as "thy whitest feet crisply are straying" . . . and grew into his mature style, which is something infinitely more precise, often more concrete, and which relies more on such straight-forward words as nouns and verbs than on piled-up adjectives for its effects.

To refer, however, to Cummings' words as nouns and verbs is to make things sound much simpler than they are, for the one outstanding characteristic of his mature style is his disrespect for the part of speech. It would be more accurate instead to say that he *uses* words as nouns, for instance, which are not normally so; it would be hard to find any one of his later poems which does not utilize a word in a sense other than its usual one. *Yes* is used as a noun to represent all that is positive and therefore admirable, *if* to stand for all that is hesitating, uncertain, incomplete. The style thus becomes spare; the later books contain many poems written in extremely short lines, lines which, utilizing the simplest words, say a great deal. (pp. 89-90)

[By] accepting the fact that the poet may be saying something worthwhile and may be seriously trying to convey both truth and beauty as he sees it, one will try to look through the poet's eyes. To understand Cummings fully, more so than in understanding most other poets, it is necessary for one to have read much of Cummings. To a reader familiar with his techniques such a statement as "yes is a pleasant country" is as penetrable as a deep, clear pool; it might, however, seem more opaque to one reading him for the first time. Such words as *yes* and *if* take on a historical meaning within the body of his poetry, a meaning not divorced from their traditional ones but infinitely larger: *yes*, for instance, conventionally is used in a particular situation; as Cummings uses it, *yes* represents the sum of all the situations in which it might be used. And such a technique as "who younger than / begin / are" is not too complicated to be used by some practitioners of the art of writing for mass consumption, as witness the first line of a very popular song from *South Pacific:* "Younger than springtime, you are." (pp. 90-1)

Babette Deutsch has described Cummings' use of these words as follows [see *CLC,* Vol. 3]:

> His later poems make words as abstract as "am," "if," "because," do duty for seemingly more solid nouns. By this very process, however, he restores life to dying concepts. "Am" implies being at its most responsive, "if" generally means the creeping timidity that kills responsiveness,

and "because" the logic of the categorizing mind that destroys what it dissects. Here is a new vocabulary, a kind of imageless metaphor.

Why, Miss Deutsch might further have explained, generally means to Cummings a state of uncertainty, a searching for direction from sources outside oneself, an unspontaneous demanding of reasons and causes in the face of life. A person who is a *why* is generally a subject for ridicule, being, like an *if,* a timid creature who thinks, fears, denies, follows, unlike an all-alive *is.* (p. 92)

Right though she is in assigning meanings to Cummings' *am's, if's,* and *because's,* Miss Deutsch does not get to the root of the technique used in these words when she describes them as examples of "imageless metaphor." Metaphor has as its base the use of comparison and analogy, of the verisimilitude within dissimilitude that exists between two images, actions, or concepts. Actually, a closer insight into the real nature of these words is found in Mr. Blackmur's study, though, in contrast to Miss Deutsch's commitment to the technique, his definition of the process comes within a general attack on Cummings' language. He says at the end of his essay that all of Cummings' "thought" (the quotes are Mr. Blackmur's) is metonymy, and that the substance of the metonymy is never assigned to anything. "In the end," he concludes, "we have only the thrill of substance." Metonymy is based on reduction rather than comparison: an object associated with a thing is substituted for the thing itself (as *crown* for *king*), or a corporeal object is used to represent an abstract concept or idea (as *heavy thumb* for *dishonesty*). When Mr. Blackmur says that Cummings' metonymy contains only the "thrill of substance," he means that in the case of such a word as *flower,* one of Cummings' favorite metonymical vehicles, the substance—flower—is there but the idea of which it is a reduction is neither present nor ascertainable. If the reader receives a "thrill" from such a word as *flower,* well and good; but Mr. Blackmur asserts that a thrill is all he will receive.

It must be remembered that Mr. Blackmur's essay was written after only the earliest of Cummings' books had appeared; none of them exemplify his mature style—in those days *flower* and *star* were about as far as he had gone in the direction of metonymy. In his use of *why,* however, he has extended not only the uses to which a particular word can be put but also the accepted limits of metonymy: he has taken an abstract word and made it stand for a host of ideas, the negative characteristics mentioned above. Mr. Blackmur's "thrill of substance" is therefore not applicable to Cummings' present use of metonymy, for such words as *why* do not represent a substance and certainly, if they are isolated, convey no thrill. That it is possible for *why* to induce a thrill is seen in the lines quoted above, but the thrill comes not from the "substance" of *why* but from the uniqueness of its use; perhaps also there is a thrill of comprehension which comes when the implication of the metonymy strikes the reader.

Again, if one accepts Mr. Blackmur's argument it is unanswerable; he would say that to derive an implication from a metonymical concept is not enough, that the idea or object which the "substance" represents must be precisely known. However, there must perhaps have been a day when *heavy thumb* was not a universally accepted reduction for dishonesty; the person who created this particular metonymy must have been doing a rather original thing, and his created expression must have had to go through a process of recognition into acceptance before it came to be unquestioned. That Cummings' metonymical usages are unlikely to go through this particular process is immaterial; such metonymies as *why* and *yes* are a little too subtle, too closely based on a poet's private convictions, to find a place in ordinary language. It should not be concluded, however, that their meaning cannot be understood. . . . (pp. 92-3)

To understand a Cummings metonymy, one can bring his plain common sense to bear first, and, in the case of such expressions as "who younger than / begin / are" or "and should some why completely weep," common sense is often enough to establish a correct meaning. (p. 93)

[His] technique in creating new uses for such words as *if, why, because, which, how, must, same, have,* and *they* on the one hand and *now, am, yes, is, we, give,* and *here* on the other is to accumulate meanings for each of them that total up to the same kind of positive and negative oppositions that are set against each other throughout his work. . . . (pp. 94-5)

[He] makes each of these words self-subsistent in terms of the context in which they appear, and, by varying the meanings in each usage, makes the words metonymical reductions for a whole set of concepts. In a way he is creating an easy cipher of meaning, penetrable but not completely so at first sight. And is this not also the case of any author who utilizes a few dominant symbols in order to express his special insight into experience, who must make each use of a symbol function in its context and yet adds to its meaning with each repeated use? (Hawthorne's repeated use of light and shadow in his works might be cited as an example of this method.) The success of a metonymous or symbolic system of this sort depends partly upon the degree to which the poet objectifies and clarifies his conception of the world, partly upon the effects of freshness and vitality his language produces; when one comes across such lines as the following there can be no doubt that Cummings is successful in both respects:

> she laughed his joy she cried his grief
> bird by snow and stir by still
> anyone's any was all to her

Using a traditional rhetorical pattern in the second line (*little by little* serves as a model for it), he superimposes a metonymous structure: *bird* and *snow* are reductions of summer and winter; *stir* and *still,* of all manner of activities. The net result of such a line is a new and delightful sense of linguistic invention, precise and vigorous.

To say that Cummings is successful in objectifying his conception of the world and in achieving a freshness and vitality of language is not to diminish the difficulty of many of his poems. Nor is it meant to say that his metonymical usages are not overworked, just as were his favorite adjectives in *Tulips and Chimneys.* What was originally a fresh idea, and what still has great power if used with discrimination—his utilizing abstract words to be the "substance" of a metonymy—can become boring, tiresome, and even meaningless if called upon constantly to carry the whole weight of a poem. Just as the word *flower,* which obviously was a symbol for something, when used in every poem became a mere word, to be accepted and passed over, so a constant succession of *which's* and *who's* and *why's* and *they's* begins to roll off the tongue too quickly for the mind to make the transference from the "sub-

stance" to the idea for which it stands; and the force of the metonymy is lost. A poem written almost exclusively in these words loses, too, its beauty and grace; one-syllable abstract words are not particularly melodious, and a poem in which they are not frequently interspersed with words which are more interesting in themselves, or more concrete, is likely to plod along (like Pope's "And ten low words oft creep in one dull line"), one metonymy after another, never skipping or dancing or singing.

However, at the same time that Cummings developed the metonymy to its ultimate use he was growing in another direction: many of his poems became much more, not less, musical than his earlier ones. In the earlier books he had placed his dependence upon the sonnet form, often upon a grand manner, and sometimes upon free verse; but he very seldom wrote a poem which cried out to be sung, which could be read only with a joyous, pronounced rhythm. Such poems as these occur frequently in the last three books. Cummings has given up being grand and derivative and become simple and himself. If he utilizes old verse forms, they are more likely to be of the nursery rhyme than of the Spenserian stanza. His lines, as has been mentioned, are often short; his meter is usually iambic; his words—when they are not metonymies—are colloquial. As a result, one can read these poems with a sense of the child's pure delight in poetry; Cummings himself has become more maturely childish as he has grown.

The rhythmical poems do utilize the typical abstract word metonymies—it is a rare poem in his later books which does not; even his satires make use of them to some extent —but the metonymies are likely to be placed in the context of concrete words and lively happenings. (pp. 95-6)

[A] progression from the external to the personal, from the outer world of "mostpeople" to the inner world of "us," finds its expression, sometimes quietly, sometimes with childish innocence, sometimes with a dauntless courage, in poem after poem in the volume *1 x 1.* . . . And, as he begins one of the most beautiful of his sonnets: "one's not half two. It's two are halves of one:". . . . This whole conception of i-you-we (or my-your-our) becomes one of Cummings' most frequently used metonymies. Its impact, to anyone who knows that "two are halves of one," is immediate. . . . In the i-you-we metonymy the whole is greater than the sum of its parts, and the metonymy itself becomes a prime example of Cummings' ability to use the simplest words as a shorthand for concepts which represent his own convictions. It is fitting that his most musical poems should be the ones . . . in celebration of i-you-we; for to Cummings love is still the most joyous of all things. Mature love to him becomes not more sober and settled but more intensely lyrical, less tortured, more a thing for singing and dancing and child-like delight. *We* takes its place along with *yes* and *now* and *is* as the metonymies for all that is best in this "really unreal world." (pp. 98-9)

Robert E. Maurer, "Latter-Day Notes on E. E. Cummings' Language," in The Bucknell Review (© 1955 by The Bucknell Review), May, 1955 (and reprinted in E. E. Cummings: A Collection of Critical Essays, edited by Norman Friedman, Prentice-Hall, Inc., 1972, pp. 79-99).*

E. E. Cummings probably used Bunyan's *Pilgrim Progress* as an organizing principle of *The Enormous Room* because he suspected that for most people in his generation its spiritual power and moral lessons were either forgotten or misunderstood. *The Enormous Room* is surely an intentional *Pilgrim's Progress....* (p. 121)

A retrospective reading of the contemporary notices dramatizes the general response of reviewers that *The Enormous Room* was pretty strong meat. Readers felt compelled to take sides on the crucial issue of the book's "gratuitous filthiness." Yet it was not apart from its crudities, we feel today, that the book was "quite worthwhile," but because of them. Like a number of his younger contemporaries, Cummings had intuitively divined the efficiency of filth as metaphor, and like Swift before him, succeeded in conveying an excremental vision of life with unmistakable power. In addition, by ringing changes upon the allegorical structure of conventional pilgrimages, he evolved a Paradise within an Inferno, a Celestial City upon the ruins of the City of Destruction. In short, if Christian could no longer journey to the Delectable Mountains, Cummings would bring the Delectable Mountains to Christian....

The parallel journey is spiritual, not literal, yet the identification of the narrator with Christian is illuminated at crucial instances in such a way as to reflect a fundamental dependence upon the earlier allegory. (p. 122)

The Enormous Room manipulates the images of the erotic, urinary, and excremental to symbolize the most precious mysteries of Christian brotherhood. In not perceiving Cummings' extraordinary use of the "excremental," earlier critics of *The Enormous Room* have misunderstood its intention.

Cleanliness is next to ungodliness in Cummings' ludicrously inverted scheme of things. The only physically clean beings are the non-prisoners. The "very definite fiend," Apollyon, who is the director of the prison, is an impeccable dresser, a terrifying little monster whose most disgusting feature is his inhuman fetish for personal cleanliness.... It is a perfectly obvious irony that, behind his puppetlike façade of cleanliness, Apollyon is responsible for the filthiest of prisons. (pp. 124-25)

The theme is at once revolting and transcendent: human excrement, normally the object of universal disgust, symbolizes human brotherhood and, eventually, Christian Salvation. The most prominent feature of The Enormous Room is its odor.... (p. 125)

Cummings' violent dismissal of the ordinary forms of things does not imply that he has rejected the ultimate spiritual meanings which the forms should symbolize. Civilization itself is unspeakably corrupt; it is reflected in the injustices of governments, the ironies of power-struggles between nations, and the horrors of a chaotic and meaningless war. In the microcosm of The Enormous Room it is represented by *Le Directeur,* by the Black Holster (brutal chief of the *plantons*), and by the "Three Wise Men" and their Inquisition. Above all, civilization's least satisfactory product is the unthinking and insensitive American, the incommunicative, middle-class, self-satisfied average-man, represented here as "Mr. A."... Cummings' "war-time" Mr. A.—section-chief of an Ambulance Service subsidized with Morgan money—reappears in the post-war poems in civilian clothes as the prototype unthinking-American immortalized, in all of his fastidiousness, in the cynically-portrayed subject of "POEM, OR BEAUTY HURTS MR. VINAL," defecating (with a hun-dred-mil-lion-oth-ers) on a "sternly allotted sandpile," emitting a "tiny violetfla-vored nuisance: Odor?/ono." (pp. 126-27)

What most disturbed Cummings in the immediate post-war years was a mass insensitivity to the distressing and, relevantly, stinking conditions of war (and, by extension, of civilization). Those who refused to use their noses except to avoid the actual smell of life became, like the Cambridge ladies of the sonnet, possessed of furnished souls and comfortable minds merely; their daughters, like their lives, were "unscented" and "shapeless."... *The Enormous Room* was addressed to this unscented majority in the hope that it would be not merely shocked but would somehow sense ... that Christian brotherhood existed among human odors, not beyond them. (p. 127)

In choosing for his prototype fool an overcivilized, anal American with a supersensitive nose, Cummings discovered an essential symbol. Inevitably, therefore, his own pilgrim would need to be able to smell his fellow-human beings in order to progress with them toward the Delectable Mountains. In contrast, the impostor Count Bragard, who cannot tolerate the stink of his fellow-prisoners, is clearly identifiable with the worst excesses of modern civilization: he prostitutes his art; his real god is not Cezanne, but Vanderbilt. (pp. 127-28)

"In the course of the next ten thousand years," wrote Cummings after his return to New York, "it may be possible to find Delectable Mountains without going to prison."... While he was in captivity, however, he found that communication was only possible with those "common scum" who had not been hopelessly indoctrinated by civilization. Bunyan's Worldly Wise-men, for Cummings, constituted the majority of the "monster manunkind."... "The Great American Public," he wrote, had a "handicap which my friends at La Ferté did not as a rule have—education ...." Communication, then, in The Enormous Room, if it were to exist among the prisoners at all, had to be established upon some deeper principle than spoken language. The principle was that of a communion of the Elect. Words were inadequate.... Cummings is careful to make the point that The Zulu spoke no conventionally communicable language, and yet "I have never in my life so perfectly understood (even to the most exquisite nuances) whatever idea another human being desired at any moment to communicate to me, as I have in the case of The Zulu." (pp. 128-29)

The emphasis, as in any rite of passage, is upon what the initiate has learned from his journey. In this instance, the maimed hero can never again regard the outer world (i.e., "civilization") without irony. But the spiritual lesson he learned from his sojourn with a community of brothers will be repeated in his subsequent writings both as an ironical dismissal of the values of his contemporary world, and as a sensitive, almost mystical celebration of the quality of Christian love.

Even if we admit the ingenuity of Cummings' device in *The Enormous Room,* we may still ask if the enormity of the conceit, developed so fully as it is, succeeds. Until one returns directly to Bunyan's allegory, he may forget just how scummy the Slough of Despond actually was. Bunyan implies that a virtually inescapable condition of man's spiritual salvation is that he "wallow for a time," and become "grievously bedaubed."... [The Slough of Despond] is a necessary part of the journey. Similarly, Cummings implies that The Enormous Room is "necessary," although he hopes that "In the course of the next ten thousand years it may be possible to find the Delectable Mountains without going to prison." (pp. 130-31)

There remains the question of obscenity in *The Enormous Room*. Could Cummings have succeeded, as reviewer D. K. Lamb put it, "without being so gratuitously filthy"? Had William Thackeray lived to read *The Enormous Room,* he would unquestionably have called it "filthy in word, filthy in thought, furious, raging, obscene," as he described *Gulliver's Travels* to a group of nineteenth-century ladies. But happily, such a view of "filthiness" has been demonstrated to be superficial, and despite the persistence of a few critics in reading Swift as personal history, . . . [we have learned] that to regard *Travels into Several Remote Nations of the World* as evidence of coprophilia in Swift is itself madness. Thus, while it is important to comprehend the meaning of the excrement in Houyhnhnmland, it is trivial to be offended by its odor.

Without insisting upon the parallel between the pilgrimages of Bunyan's Christian and Swift's ironic Gulliver [although this point has been critically discussed], I would nevertheless agree with [Samuel Holt Monk], who sees a "grim joke" in Gulliver himself being "the supreme instance of a creature smitten with pride."

The significance of such a view for readers of Cummings is this: Gulliver, in his rationalistic pride, is no longer able to smell his fellow human beings without experiencing a wave of nauseating disgust. Having lived in the super-rational "civilization" of the horses, he finds the odor of human beings altogether repugnant. Cummings' twentieth-century pilgrim provides us with an alternative. In a world of rationalistic, super-scientific, deodorized, Nujolneeding Gullivers, he found it necessary for his salvation to escape into a community of odorous human beings. He discovered them by being imprisoned among them in The Enormous Room. (pp. 131-32)

> *David E. Smith, "'The Enormous Room' and 'The Pilgrim's Progress',"* in *Twentieth Century Literature (© 1965 by IHC Press), July, 1965 (and reprinted in* E. E. Cumming: A Collection of Critical Essays, *edited by Norman Friedman, Prentice-Hall, Inc., 1972, pp. 121-32).*

Although he is not generally accorded any attention as a religious poet, E. E. Cummings did, on occasion, produce poems which can only be classified as "divine." Most of these poems were published during the last decade of his career when, according to Norman Friedman [in *e. e. cummings: The Growth of a Writer*], "the image of the actual world faded in favor of the visionary core." Although the poems which may be termed religious without qualification are not numerous, it seems inevitable that a poet who devotes so much of his career to depicting the transcendence of the mundane by human lovers should in time turn to transcendence with the active assistance of a loving God. . . .

Cummings's approach to God is of a tentive nature, in keeping with his view that anything or anyone either measurable or completely definable is of little value. This approach is evident in a number of Cummings's poems, such as "no time ago," "to start, to hesitate; to stop," Number 42 of *95 Poems,* and Numbers 51, 53, and 55 of *73 Poems.*

The sonnet "when you are silent, shining host by guest" serves as a celebration of the love of an essentially unknowable God for the individual, for "every" man and for nature. (p. 70)

[For] all its heartfelt humility and tentativeness, this sonnet presents an essentially optimistic celebration of God's love and its effects in the awakening of the one, of the "every," and of nature. In the all-inclusiveness of the transcendence it depicts, the poem mounts a cogent counterargument to the view enunciated by [some critics] that Cummings is capable of finding joy only in the self. (p. 75)

> *G. J. Weinberger, "E. E. Cummings' Benevolent God: A Reading of 'when you are silent, shining host by guest',"* in Papers on Language and Literature *(copyright © 1974 by the Board of Trustees, Southern Illinois University at Edwardsville), Winter, 1974, pp. 70-5.*

As cummings makes clear, there are apparently two plays in [*him*]. One is a markedly personal play and another, seemingly less personal, consists of a series of vaudevillesque skits embodying the environment or moral climate in which the writer (the central character) dwells. This person may be taken to be cummings himself in painful dismay amid the jungle of our civilization, especially as it manifested itself during the 1920s. He was inspired by feelings of utmost tenderness and tormented by the horrendous tumult and fatuity of the time. If his "hero" talks crazy, with a touch of the adolescent and certain intimations of Pirandello it is pretty much as the inebriate cummings himself talked, as if he were trying to thread his way through the impediments of inner disturbance and overstrained nerves without descending to platitude.

This emotional confusion leads to both stylistic and structural discrepancies. The play begins (and in large part continues) as a series of feverish images of a girl undergoing anaesthesia during an abortion. She is "me," who thinks of her lover as "him": they have no other names in the play. But the play constantly shifts its focus; many of the scenes are inconceivable as emanations of "me's" spirit.

The play's purest element is contained in duos of love. They are the most sensitive and touching in American playwriting. Their intimacy and passion, conveyed in an odd exquisiteness of writing, are implied rather than declared. We realize that no matter how much "him" wishes to express his closeness to "me," he is frustrated not only by the fullness of his feeling but by his inability to credit his emotion in a world as obscenely chaotic as the one in which he is lost.

That world is fantastically reflected in comic spiels of commercial publicity in the second and longest act of the "other play." There is, too, an extraordinarily grotesque travesty of Americans in Gay Paree, the paradise of tourists in the 1920s. In another scene, Fascist bombast is lampooned; in still another, evangelical hot air as a solace to the impoverished and hungry—the depression was just around the corner—is scathingly mocked.

But in the end we return to the "unfinished" play which "him" is trying so desperately to write, the play with heartbreak at its core, in which "him" proclaims, "I am an Artist, I am a Man, I am a Failure." In this manner, the play's dichotomy achieves unity. Just so, the play, disjointed and flawed, still breathes with imagination and lyric life. (pp. 604-05)

> *Harold Clurman, in* The Nation *(copyright 1974 by the Nation Associates, Inc.), May 11, 1974.*

Cummings' early poetry and art [bore] affinities with that of the Decadents: sensuality abounded, often gratuitously, and the will to shock the complacency of bourgeois arts and letters went hand in hand with an art-for-art's-sake undercurrent. But as the self-conscious lushness of his early poems dropped away, a new firmness took its place: the impulse towards economy replaced the temptation towards prolixity. It is no accident that long poems disappeared from his later volumes. Neither is it an accident that as Cummings progressed he became more representational in his painting and drawing. The immediacy of the outer world impinged more and more upon the inner fantasies; satire replaced luxurious sensuality, and the artist who began with the interests of a Beardsley drew closer to the viewpoints of a Daumier.

Yet throughout this period of growth and development there remain constant similarities between poems and drawings. In each, he is seeking to convey the delight and humor which his own quick wit found in the world around him. And in each, he is seeking the most economical means to convey ideas and feelings about ideas. In each, too, he is seeking precision. At times that precision comes (as in sonnets and early drawings) from a synthesis that incorporates rhyme and meter or weighs each stroke of the pencil and calculates its effect on the whole. At other times the precision is more intuitive—the quick accurate sketch of a walking man or seated girl, or the swift description of a character aided by an arrangement of words that is less reasoned than felt. Above all, in both poetry and drawing, he seeks movement and life. His word of supreme praise—applied, for example, to Eliot's poetry and Lachaise's art—is "alive." Perhaps his own early work in *The Dial* is best summarized by a comment he made on the work of the latter man: it is "the absolutely authentic expression of a man very strangely alive." (p. 504)

Rushworth M. Kidder, "'Author of Pictures': A Study of Cummings' Line Drawings in 'The Dial'," in Contemporary Literature (© 1976 by the Board of Regents of the University of Wisconsin System), Vol. 17, No. 4, Autumn, 1976, pp. 470-505.

D

DAVIE, Donald   1922-

Davie is a British poet and critic. Concerned as he is with style and grace, he is in many respects a neo-Augustan poet. His poetry, cerebral and technically complex, has often been criticized as deficient in humanity. Most critics, however, recognize and applaud the recent direction in Davie's poetry towards the personal. (See also *CLC*, Vol. 5, and *Contemporary Authors*, Vols. 1-4, rev. ed.)

I first encountered Donald Davie through the challenging and inventive criticism found in the pages of his *Purity of Diction in English Verse* and *Articulate Energy*. Davie's imaginative selection and juxtapositions of poems were woven into continuous arguments that never disposed of those poems by wrapping them up in interpretative tinfoil ("well, now that's done and I'm glad it's over!") but helped them instead to open out and open up to the reader. The books were exhilarating stimulants to one's own critical practice; they provided a standard of loving care directed at the art of poetry which the critic never presumed was less than indispensable. In . . . *Thomas Hardy and English Poetry*, . . . the belief is still that the poet "is what society cannot dispense with", and Davie practices on Hardy and some modern and contemporary poets who are indebted to him, the kind of scrupulous, unfailingly lively attention we now expect from him as our right. It was probably because of my high regard for this criticism that, becoming aware of Davie as also a poet who had then published two volumes (*Brides of Reason*, 1955; *A Winter Talent*, 1957) I took the "also" literally and considered the poetry a pastime out of which had come some delightful, slight efforts, very much subordinate to his larger labors as a critic.

The publication of Davie's collected poems has made me reconsider my priorities to the extent of realizing that a body of work of this magnitude can't be taken as "also" to anything else, no matter how good the something else may be. Although it is perhaps rash to quote from a notebook entry Davie himself describes as a "vulnerable" piece of writing, I believe it has enough interest to figure as a more general musing about his poetic career taken whole:

> It is true that I am not a poet by nature, only
> by inclination; for my mind moves most eas-
> ily and happily among abstractions, it relates
> ideas far more readily than it relates experi-
> ences. I have little appetite, only profound

admiration, for sensuous fullness and imme-diacy; I have not the poet's need for concreteness. . . .

He goes on to say that most of the poems he had written thus far (it was 1957) were not "natural" since their thought could have been expressed in a non-poetic way; and that while these poems weren't shams he had determined in the future to write only poems "which are, if not *naturally*, at all events *truly* poems throughout". . . . We might think then of the often-anthologized *Remembering the Thirties* with its dialectical and sprightly consideration of the virtues and limitations of "nowadays" preferring "a neutral tone". One understands the sense in which this witty poem is not "natural"—it can be firmly taken in hand once you work it out, though I doubt that its "thought" expressed in a non-poetic way could have stayed with me the way it has, because impressed on my ear through stanzas, rhyme, and the pointed intelligence of verse. But by 1957 Davie had also written *The Mushroom Gatherers* which sounded not at all like *Remembering the Thirties*. . . . (pp. 289-90)

[It] would be misleading to claim that Davie began to write "true poems" by suppressing his ego, by refusing to get the jump too quickly or thoroughly on his subject, or, relatedly, by insisting piously that the non-human, stone, what won't be turned into a symbol or translated, is what we should really admire instead of our messy psyches, reeking of the human (to appropriate one of his own coinages). Anyone who protests as much as Davie has in his poems that we should "Never care so much / For leaves or people, but you care for stone / A little more" is bound to protest too much. Charles Tomlinson can write about stone, stonily; Davie by contrast has to worry the notion within the poem, and is worried by it. . . . It is not that over the course of the years from *Brides of Reason* to *Essex Poems* and beyond Davie's "I" has turned into a real person . . ., but that the "I" has become more strange as his experience, with age, has authentically widened. (p. 291)

William H. Pritchard, "Donald Davie's Poetry," in Poetry (© *1973 by The Modern Poetry Association; reprinted by permission of the Editor of* Poetry), *August, 1973, pp. 289-93.*

In his best work [Davie's] sparsity is inseparable from an animating elegance; but there is little elegant about the language of *The Shires*. What there is, rather, is a kind of resonant blankness both of form and content—a blankness which embodies the absence of any living relationship to the culture he writes of. Taking the English counties one by one may seem at first glance a kind of courteous ritual of re-engagement, but it emerges more as a mechanical setpiece, a literary sport, akin in some ways to the *Epistles to Eva Hesse*. It's difficult to repress the suspicion that Davie no longer has anything to write about—or at least that he won't have until he addresses himself with more candour and complexity than this book reveals to the 'unfinished business' (his phrase) of his fraught relation to English culture.

Charles Tomlinson is one of the English poets Donald Davie admires, and it isn't difficult to see why: both men are committed to an unusually intimate correlation between certain problems of aesthetic technique—of poise, control, clarity, perception—and the character of certain moral values by which they seek to live. In their equableness, moderation and scepticism, those values are firmly rooted in English social democratic ideology; part of Davie's problem, however, is that they also stand askew to the concrete social embodiments of that ideology in their high-toned preoccupation with style, privacy and excellence. Defending social democracy against 'extremism' while lambasting its philistinism, assailing the imaginative torpor of empiricist England while clinging to sophisticated versions of common sense: the contradictions within which Davie's work moves concern the relation of the liberal intellectual to an advanced stage of bourgeois society with which he can neither identify nor disengage. (pp. 75-6)

> *Terry Eagleton, in* Stand *(copyright © by* Stand*), Vol. 16, No. 3 (1975).*

Davie's poetry is more rich in human interest than any of his English contemporary's excepting Larkin's. It is worth recalling that in the debate with A. Alvarez published in *The Review* in 1962 ("The New Aestheticism"), it was Davie who insisted that "A good poem is necessarily a response to a human situation."

His most recent book, *The Shires*, was leapt on rather gleefully by most English reviewers when it appeared: how silly he was to think he could get away with this, try for a modern *Poly-olbion*, one poem for each shire. If good poems are necessarily responses to human situations, in justice one would have to admit that the air in *The Shires* is something pretty thin, the "situations" gasping to be put in quotation marks. . . . Some of the shires fail, as it were, to jog Davie into rich enough reverie or rhetoric. Yet, and even though it's right in general to suspect appeals to the volume "as a whole" (thus redeeming individual poems from failure), this one is special enough, with its forty shire-poems in alphabetical order, Bedfordshire to Yorkshire, to disarm a too scrupulous worry over whether an individual poem really succeeds or not. They *do* help each other out.

Aside from the subject-matter, which as a geographically ill-informed and curious American fascinates me, one's pleasure is less in the experience of particular poems than in the tour (or tour de force) director's voice: polite, urbane, witty, speculative, resigned, sinking from high to low, from elevated sentiment to private mumbling, formal to unbuttoned. And it is through the variety and range of this voice that the "human situation" of the whole book emerges: that of somebody who lived there once—more or less intensely, depending on the shire—who chooses now to

focus on a bit of imaginative territory by looking at its trees or its traffic patterns, its castles or cathedrals, its historical figures or remembered relatives. . . . Since, as Eliot reminds us, we can't say where "technique" begins or ends, I find that a humanly touching thing has been made out of trivial occurrence. Not deeply moving, but humanly touching; there is someone talking to me, exploring through performance his doubts and uncertainties, his momentary clarities. . . . And if, on occasion in this volume, the voice sounds too privately allusive, bluffingly cryptic rather than truly complex, it is also human to be these things. The poems to come from Donald Davie will, I suspect, extend the scrutiny of self, England, history, which is what *The Shires* is about. But they will also continue to charm and puzzle, tease and even annoy by their human presence; he couldn't get rid of his urbanity if he tried, and for the urbanity I am grateful. (pp. 231-34)

> *William H. Pritchard, in* Parnassus: Poetry in Review *(copyright © by* Parnassus: Poetry in Review*), Spring/Summer, 1976.*

Donald Davie is still thought of as a 'Movement' poet, that is, one who made his name in the 1950s, publishing his poems in the same places as other university-based poets such as John Wain and Kingsley Amis. . . .

[The] reasoning quality of Davie's first poems, like those of fellow 'Movement' poets, was ascribed to the influence of critics like Empson and Leavis. There certainly was, and still is, cross-fertilisation between his work as critic and teacher of literature and his work as poet. (p. 15)

In [his] second book [of poetry, *A Winter Talent*], the tendency to obscurity of utterance, which may derive from Empson's influence, has disappeared, what ambiguousness there may be in the style working now only to the poetry's advantage.

The significant changes in Davie's work do not appear, however, until *after* the publication of *A Winter Talent*. . . . The later poetry, from *The Forests of Lithuania* (1959) on, may be seen as aiming at a way of knowing the world we are in, as turned away from the extreme self-consciousness of the 'Movement' in favour of commitment to the world beyond the self, absorption in experience of the world shared with others. (pp. 16-17)

[Eliot and Yeats] admonish, they exhort, they curse, they pray, but they rarely work in the modest fashion of Davie's poetry. The difference is not accidental; it is a difference of stance. Davie is among us, living with us; his predecessors were in important ways outside the society for which they wrote. They saw themselves as prophet or priest; his role is that of a man speaking of men, a man speaking to men. (p. 19)

In Davie we have to do with a poet who has applied himself just as much as Eliot or Yeats ever did to the problems of modern society, one who has fashioned a style and found a subject-matter appropriate to that society in much their way. Only he has rejected their stance, their removal in spirit from their own society. (When Davie writes about Eliot and Yeats—and he has done so at length about the former—he tends to underplay the prophetic role in Eliot, and to overplay it in Yeats.) The poet in the modern tradition whom Davie finds most congenial is Ezra Pound, about whom he has written two books; perhaps the reason is that Pound's wanderings . . . gave him a perspective on life, an attentiveness to things in themselves and to the idiosyncracies of place and custom, and even a modesty, which are all lacking in his rivals but which must commend themselves to such a poet of man-on-the-move as Davie.... Pound's modesty, Pound's heightened sense of human mobility (the protagonist of *The Cantos* is, in one light, Ulysses, the supreme wanderer of the western world), Pound's restatements of the most ancient human values ('What thou lovest well remains . . .'), all these are qualities held in common with Davie.

Add one more: Pound's awareness of *voice* as the medium of poetry, and his consequent opposition to what he termed 'the rhythm of the metronome'. In Pound's poetry this led to the adoption of free verse, a refusal to be content with the current notions of the rhythms permissible in English verse. 'I believe,' he said, 'in an absolute rhythm, a rhythm, that is, in poetry which corresponds exactly to the emotion or shade of emotion to be expressed'. Such exactitude seemed to demand, often, the 'freedom' of free verse.

Davie uses free verse—unrhymed, with no regular distribution of stress, with no established length of line—occasionally. He does not appeal to Pound's practice consistently, except in so far as it embodies Pound's principle: 'to compose in the sequence of the musical phrase, not in sequence of a metronome'. Sticking to that principle means attending very carefully to the potentialities of the human instrument, the voice. Davie has been helped in this not only by the example of Pound, but also by that of the Russian poet Boris Pasternak, who far excels Pound in richness of sound and rhythm.

His work has been of the greatest importance for Davie. Pasternak's *Poems 1955-59,* published with a good translation into English by Michael Harari (1960), radically changed the nature of Davie's poetry, revealing gifts hitherto unsuspected, allowing Davie to speak in his own voice by one of those fruitful exchanges between one culture and another of which Eliot's transmutation of French models gives us another example. *Events and Wisdoms* (1964) is the book in which this influence is first felt; it is also, and not by accident, that in which the idea of poetry as a way of knowing the world we are in finds its most complete expression. (pp. 20-1)

Davie has always favoured traditional poetic forms. Rhyme and metre are important to him. (p. 22)

[The attention to sound and rhythm, the variety of tone,] the flexibility of a line subdued to 'the rhythm of a metronome'—these are all qualities of the poetry of our own century deployed by Davie on behalf of a view of what our unsettled, our mobile society needs, the stability of judiciousness and fair-mindedness. It is our very rootlessness that makes such placeless, timeless little dramas as are the matter of 'Vying' [a post-Pasternak poem] important for us: our certainties have to be these, of personal pieties and honesties, and we would wish to possess them as completely as this poet, poised yet quick to each nuance of feeling, does here. Among his contemporaries Davie has one equal only in the evocation of such human assurances— Philip Larkin. (pp. 23-4)

Davie's kind of 'strength' is associated with the use of a plain diction, drawing as much on the traditions of prose as on those of poetry. This . . . he derives from the eighteenth century, and it may be seen at work in 'Tunstall Forest', where it is a kind of leaven to the more poetical lines like 'But quiet is a lovely essence'. That is a poem of the 'sixties; Davie's first two books recall far more often, and it

would seem intentionally, the formality, the accuracy, the prosaic strength of poets like Johnson, Goldsmith and Cowper. (p. 26)

[Generalisation] was congenial to Davie in his beginnings— 'my mind moves most easily and happily among abstractions, it relates ideas far more readily than it relates experience,' he noted of himself in those days. And his fondness for it was strengthened by his admiration for poets like Cowper or Goldsmith. To my mind, though, it is [the] generalising mode [of 'The Garden Party'] that makes it, polished and elegant as it is, a minor thing. Such generalisation belongs to the eighteenth century; it is confident of values which are shared, of a community of feeling which in our time cannot be assumed, has to be won, as the obliquity of '"Abbeyforde"' or 'Tunstall Forest' does it.....

The openness to experience and to the reader which we find in the later poems is not to be found [in the earlier poems]: and yet such openness, such assurance of basic human qualities as are manifest, and with such wit and tenderness, in 'Vying', are the very qualities that our unsettledness requires.

Davie, then, is a poet who has changed and grown with the passing of time, yet without abandoning what was truly of value in his early work, its 'strength', the poetic use of a prosaic diction. The distinctions between words made in 'Tunstall Forest' are not of the same order as that contained in the line in 'The Garden Party' 'I shook absurdly as I shook her hand', but they are built upon that order. In 'Tunstall Forest' the poet's voice and stance are quite different. 'The Garden Party' does demand a certain kind of voice to complete its meaning: 'There is that sort of equalizing rule'—the tone is one of enforced reasonableness, a resigned detachment. But in 'Tunstall Forest', where the sentence uncoils at length, flexed against the regular alternation of line-length, we are close to a *developing* utterance, one whose responsive poise changes from one moment to another as perception itself shifts, sees further—we are, in short, close to those 'knots of intonation which carry the voice without pause from one line to the next' that [has been] admired in Pasternak. (pp. 27-8)

To invoke [Wordsworth's] name is at once to see the qualities which are absent in Davie. His poetry, it seems to me, lacks a sense of the religious; and though he is not averse to thinking in his poetry there is no *stretch* of thought we could compare, say, with 'Tintern Abbey'. And though Wordsworth is famous for his egotism and Davie populates his poems with his family and his friends, it is Wordsworth who strikes one as seeing more deeply into the individual nature. There is, too, enough of the prophet in Wordsworth to allow us to see the necessary short-comings of fairmindedness. The positive Wordsworthian aspect of Davie lies in his subject-matter and in his manner of being dramatically lyrical. (p. 30)

In so far as Davie is concerned with 'elemental sanctity and natural piety' in a landscape where 'all the sanctuaries have been violated' (we can imagine what 'Abbeyforde' looks like), he is extending a central Wordsworthian theme in a natural fashion. The author of '"Abbeyforde"' is, then, Wordsworthian, and the same Wordsworthian light shines around such a poem as 'Middlesex' . . . from *The Shires* (1974)—a book pretty generally misunderstood ..., but whose intention is very fully glossed by the passage just quoted.... (p. 31)

Pound; Pasternak; the English eighteenth century; Wordsworth. The real poets take their place with their masters, true both to their own day and to a tradition. Donald Davie is one of them. (p. 32)

Martin Dodsworth, "Donald Davie," in Agenda, *Summer, 1976, pp. 15-32.*

'In the Stopping Train' may prove as crucial a poem in Davie's development as 'With the Grain' and 'England', though it is more satisfyingly complete as a poem than 'England' and rhythmically more compelling than 'With the Grain'. Intellectually it is less obscure and emotionally more probing than either. The earlier poems were symptoms of formal and ethical changes in the poet, while 'In the Stopping Train', engaging as it does, albeit gingerly, profoundly personal issues along with wider social issues, is a consolidation, a fusion of Davie's public and private voices in a puzzling but resonant parable. In it meaning and medium are so fused that the reader is not tempted to paraphrase. If he were, the poem would not submit to it. Here Davie is triumphantly, to re-apply his own words about 'With the Grain', 'a poet by nature', not 'only by inclination'. If abstractions occur, the incidents and images give rise to them and provide them with substance. The immediacy, if not 'sensuous', is fully dramatic in rhythmic modulation and in the episodic presentation. Davie's resolution of his earlier problem with abstraction has not been, finally, his conscious attempts at particularity—in the long historical poems especially—nor in his fine satirical writing, but in the allusive spoken verse of *Essex Poems*, in *The Shires*, and now supremely in 'In the Stopping Train'.

This poem is part and parcel with *The Shires* because they, too, if not always so compelling, occupy that region between the subjective and the communal experience—of landscape, history, and culture—and attempt to integrate the particular experience and response, the tissue of the I's experience, with that of the You's he has addressed, latently or patently, in many of his earlier poems. *The Shires* is not travelogue, nor is it autobiography, though it has elements of the latter. In it Davie attempts to do with literal particulars what more fashionable poets have attempted with legend, myth, or easy rhetoric, projecting their vision without examining—as a responsbile artist will—the nature and quality of the projector. In *The Shires* and 'In the Stopping Train' Davie is engaged in just this: examining the voice and the experiences that make it speak as it does.

The Shires are poems of dissent and celebration—dissent against elements in his own past, our common past, and the contemporary realities of England, and the apparently wilful neglect of our most precious common possession: language. In 'Essex', more disturbingly than ever before, Davie works his dominant 'language theme', not satirically as often in the past, but with his intense personal perplexity at his own experiences at Essex University. Language—and our culture, our traditions of order and community, all come into his considerations. This and other poems in *The Shires* evoke the empty forms and the broken or corrupted forms—social ('Sussex'), intellectual and imaginative ('Cornwall'), and communal ('Devonshire'). Hollow habit, ignorant ceremony, naive conservatism, ahistorical radicalism, are aspects of England he, revisting, dissents from, with a measured passion in some respects like Yeats's fury against materialism among the Irish petit bourgeois, though without Yeats's flamboyance, with more of a sense that he, too, is implicated.

His celebrations are equally measured and potent. They

can be historical, but most interesting is his celebration of a beloved who becomes representative of a larger object and a particularly passionate identity with place and nation. She, like most of the women in the sequence, has common sense, fidelity, and intelligence which reflect on him. He does not idealise—he seldom does—but celebrates, even if he must satirise himself in the celebration ('Worcestershire', 'Hampshire'). Implicit, too, in the *terms* of the expression, these poems—like the *Six Epistles to Eva Hesse* —suggest the values, the history (personal and cultural) and the attitudes which prompt dissent. The language, the complex of traditions and historical accidents which impell the poet to speak in the way he does and to subject himself to criticism, are better—one must use the word *morally* better —than the individual who speaks. They provide a context where things fall into perspective. The speaker becomes one among those 'things'. This is something very different from impersonality of voice. It is more like the eighteenth century voice Davie now seldom directly imitates. He may be speaker, but he is always squaring himself with the outer world, he is one among many subjects. His response is to situation, not to self. The little dramas of his own past he enacts not to re-present and grandify the Young Davie but to present the experience which is the point of relevance, the only point of communication. He shares this approach with Hardy, showing himself unwilling to falsify particulars. That is why his 'I' is not distracting and we follow it and watch, not what it is but what it says and does, those empirical events which may contain meaning for us. This anti-subjectivism in a sequence so full of autobiography is one of *The Shires* most perplexing qualities. 'In the Stopping Train', tending towards parable, heightens this particular paradox and is—perhaps *therefore*—more penetrating. In it, not incidents of a literal past but essentially mental experiences are realised. There are few empirical facts to be squared; the entire spare structure of images (especially that of the reflecting pane) and ideas, which another poet might make confessional, Davie makes resonant with political and moral overtones, without limiting the poem to one meaning. Stripped of literal autobiography, the poem can be taken as *typical*. This he does, in part, by identifying a 'he' beside the 'I' and contemplating that curious third person. Between them, finally, there is 'you', 'dear reader'. Davie calls us in as mediators between the 'I' and 'he'. He would cause us to judge, and yet we would be judging, I imagine, our own case as much as his. Where, previously, he has addressed us, here he implicates us.

Davie's predicament—rare enough at this time—is that he is a poet with public meanings, well aware of the romantic element in any espousal of Augustan values in an age such as this, devoid of consensus, community, standards of truth —*in fine,* moral and cultural constants. But he is not a *public poet,* cajoling us from the rostrum. What enriches his most recent poetry—and worries his readers a little, too—is the spirit in which he has recourse to autobiography, the tendency in some of *The Shires* poems to be over-referential and obscure. Earlier obscurities in his work could be resolved by the reader's patient study; the new allusiveness seems occasionally remote, impenetrable. (pp. 33-6)

Davie's work, all of it, is beamed towards England. . . . His exile has intensified his commitments, not dulled or altered them.

Davie's exile seems to me to have been an inevitable product of his Englishness, an attempt to preserve intact cultural roots, values, his very language, challenged by force, not argument, in various ways in England; while at the same time maintaining his dual vocation as poet and teacher. There is a sense in which Davie, among our poets, is the arch-Parliamentarian, as Sisson is the arch-Monarchist. (p. 36)

Exile has of course changed his poetry. The transition, the shock of it, was registered in *Essex Poems* most accurately, where he doubted his motives, and where his technical resources grew. *The Shires* are interesting because, now the shock has worn off, and now England has changed further, he returns as a once-insider to register survivals and changes. He brings his own experiences of England, his beliefs about what has happened here since his departure, and squares them with the reality he finds. (p. 37)

Davie's peculiar relationship with his own and our common past, and his explorations of it, are often like Hardy's. While a poet such as Tennyson idealises the past, Hardy again and again—in poems and novels—shows it as unrealised. A wrong turn, an oversight, blight a life permanently. If this is true of the individual, some of Davie's poems suggest obliquely how true it may also be of a community or a whole society. 'Devonshire' in *The Shires* is an obvious example. So too are 'Staffordshire', 'Sussex', etc. . . . What is left undone, lost, forgotten, despised, what is ill-done or destroyed, despoils the future. The area affected might be a place, an institution, our language. Hardy's pessimism is essentially psychological. Davie's seems to me social. Without uttering prophesies, the poems subtly warn, presenting the evidence. The present is contrasted with a past—not necessarily pre-Industrial—in which culture and ethics, in the Arnoldian sense, were complementary aspects of a single truth, in which the artist was socially as responsible for the ideas he promulgated as the teacher, clergyman or politician, and in which ideas had consequences, and the poet who spoke falsehood spoke at his peril, for he addressed men of common sense. (pp. 38-9)

A comparison between 'Gloucestershire' and 'Devonshire' —complementary poems—shows the two sides of Davie's concern, the dissent and the celebration. The 'native gift for townscape' of the 'pre-industrial English' contrasts with the evocation of Plymouth, re-destroyed after the Blitz by what Betjeman has called the 'Plansters'.

'In the Stopping Train' complements and extends *The Shires* because it helps to define a speaker. If there are analogues for the poem, one might be Yeats's 'Hic et Ille'. For Davie identifies a 'he', while continuing to speak as 'I'. The 'he' is not, mercifully, shrouded in incense and mystery like Yeats's Africanus. . . . The 'he' is 'the man going mad inside me'; not 'me', rather, a might have been or still to be 'me', a haunting presence, not an identity. It is a 'he' whom experience reduces, does not mature. That 'he' is 'the bastard', the Edmund *in* the Edgar figure (there is more than a slight touch of dementia—Kafkaesque if not Shakespearean—in the speaker's rhythms and syntax). The 'he' is punished by being compelled to inaction, on a slow train, deprived of distraction, forced back upon himself. The 'train'—offering only time, jolts, stops and starts, is a 'train of thought' as much as anything else. Its ultimate destination, in the most unsettling part of the poem, is self-knowledge and the action that can follow it. . . . (pp. 39-40)

There may be an excess of cuteness in the writing . . ., the stage directions, the 'rising' panic forced back by 'Sit down!', the pun, and the clever line endings. My feeling is that the rhythm is sufficiently strong to force these dis-

tracting effects into service and make them part of the thought process of the 'he' undergoing the punishment. (p. 41)

The journey reveals the nature of 'his' hatreds (human), and loves (artistic). Implicit in the poem, in the 'I' as it were, is a rejection of the wilful, subjective *use* of reality; a rejection of an art not responsible to its subject matter, and a language used restrictively, of perhaps—and this is why the poem is so interesting in the context of Davie's oeuvre —an exclusive diction which reflects an excluding attitude of mind, a choice to reflect in a work of art not wholeness but preference, a partisanship which has no commerce with truth. But of course, beyond the moral issues the poem raises, are the psychological issues. 'I' and 'he' are aspects of one character wrestling with itself. (pp. 41-2)

The poem seems to me crucial to an understanding of Davie's recent work. 'I' and 'he' occupy one carriage in the train, and in Davie. Despite the wit of the language, there is an element in the rhythms and the abrupt enjambments of uncontrolled, or at least indeterminate, tone—almost wry, yet somehow manic. As a poem, it seems 'a gift', as though it came as a surprise to the poet, as to us; and it suggests almost a new *source* of poetry that Davie has seldom tapped before. It is a matter of rhythm and the organisation this rhythm finds in the matter. Basically three-stress, like much of Davie's recent work, the lines distribute their stresses not prosaically, as in the weaker of *The Shires* poems, nor with the emphasis of thought, but with a haunting apparent regularity, like the running of a train over sleepers, altering pace, but constant—though we could not scan them. Also, even those sections which do not rhyme *seem* to rhyme, a curious authority I have found only in one other modern poet.

Unfamiliar, new, it may stand as a model for Davie of the *intensity* of poem he will court in future, though it is absurd of me to suggest that such poems can be willed into being. But certainly the 'Medallions', two short poems published in *Poetry Nation V*, give reason to believe that Davie, whose evolution from the 'pasticheur of late-Augustan styles' has already been momentous, is going further. The obscurities are no longer literary, obscurities of references, but more often darknesses, resonant without the ear-trumpet of a footnote. His 'self-consciousness' is becoming, not a consciousness of style or persona, but of *self*.

I like to think that, were Davie putting together *The Shires* this year rather than last, he would include more than he did in that book. Even if 'In the Stopping Train' was written in France, and about an experience there, and other poems in California, and others somewhere between, they belong together, as his *Collected Poems* did. There he had the audacity to give us everything he could find. His next book should include *The Shires* enriched—and clarified— by the work around them. (pp. 43-4)

> *Michael Schmidt, "'Time and Again': The Recent Poetry of Donald Davie," in* Agenda, *Summer, 1976, pp. 33-44.*

The title of [Davie's] most recent book is *The Shires,* and it suggests something of the nostalgia and, yes, old-fashioned inclusiveness of design in this expatriate's attempt to gather up the whole of his well-remembered England in one sequence of short poems. However, *The Shires* only manifests unmistakably certain qualities which have always been present in his poetry and which make it as intrinsically English as that of any post-war writer. (p. 45)

[A] combination of poise and directness distinguishes much of Davie's later poetry, and even when we disagree with his values it can often be . . . extremely powerful and moving. But the cost in personal and artistic terms has also to be reckoned . . .: for Davie there never has been an easy and sympathetic commerce with the everyday urbanized England, sordid elements and all, of Larkin's poetry. Though Davie has always insisted, rightly, that his poetry is concerned with 'the relationship of man with man', the men and women he has in mind are not Titch Thomas nor Mr Bleaney nor the unforgettable suburban housewives of 'Afternoons'. Among Davie's more personal and accessible lyrics are many beautiful love poems and portraits of friends, but his love poems are to his wife and his friends are exceptional people; the people loved and portrayed are not not-English but neither are they representative as Larkin's characters (himself included) usually are. (p. 47)

Davie's poetry of England has historical geographical and 'high-cultural' dimensions which are all but missing from Larkin's—which are, indeed, uncharacteristic of the poetry written by Englishmen of their generation. [Although their differences are significant, it is important to keep in mind] Davie's close early association with the poets—Kingsley Amis, Thom Gunn and Larkin among them—who appeared with him in *New Lines* and together constituted the nearest thing to a collective reform movement in English poetry that has surfaced in a long time.

I do not wish to exaggerate the cohesiveness, much less the supposed grey uniformity, of 'the Movement', nor do I mean entirely to deny that it was, among other things, a publicity gimmick. But the published statements of Davie, Amis, Robert Conquest and D. J. Enright at that time leave no room for doubt that they were consciously working along similar lines and in reaction to the excesses, real and supposed, of the British poets of the preceding generation and the early Anglo-American modernists. Certainly they shared similar social class origins, educational experiences and professional aims. In these respects (and in some few of their poems) they also resembled the brilliant American 'Reactionary Generation' of Yvor Winters, Louise Bogan, the Fugitives and—admittedly a special case—Hart Crane. The parallel may remind us, among other things, how far even a very wayward genius must normally carve with the grain of his generation if he is to make anything at once authentic and new, but also, because there are now several mature (but not strictly national) literatures in one language, how extremely difficult it might be to identify one's true brethren and ancestors. . . . [A] transitional poem, 'North Dublin', . . . is characteristic of the Movement in important respects but is peculiarly Davie's own in others and points ahead to his more experimental pieces of the Sixties. Though apparently slight, it is a sturdy and elegant poem. . . . (pp. 47-8)

'North Dublin' exemplifies many of the central virtues—and limitations—of Movement poetry. Above all it is lucid and rational, syntactical and (though 'irregular' by Movement standards) traditionally measured. While implicitly acknowledging the power and impressiveness of radical ideologies and the rhetoric they employ, the author goes in fear of fanaticism and all appeals to the irrational. To say that his poetics are Apollonian rather than Dionysian would be broadly accurate but would still imply larger claims for poetry than, at that time, Davie and the other Movement poets cared to make. If such poetry strikes us as 'verse' rather than 'Poetry', it does so partly because of its modest

themes and tone but also, especially, because of its poverty of metaphor. In the last stanza of 'North Dublin' the only metaphor—'By their lights'—is so shopworn that we hardly recognize it as such. But that of course is the point: we have lost touch with the origins of this metaphor for enlightenment, in the Inner Light of the Puritans, and it is Davie's object to draw attention to the cultural power these 'dead' metaphors of dead creeds still have to control our living processes of thought and feeling. In doing so he is following his own prescription, in *Purity of Diction in English Verse,* for

> the poetry which attempts, in Mr. Eliot's phrase, to 'purify the language of the tribe'. For if the poet who coins new metaphors *enlarges* the language, the poet who enlivens dead metaphors can be said to *purify* the language.

Though they might choose other means to do the job, probably all of the Movement poets could have agreed to a common aim to 'purify the language of the tribe'. They aimed, all of them, to write poetry which at least had the virtues of good prose. (p. 51)

Purity of Diction and still more *Articulate Energy* (1955) betrayed more familiarity and even sympathy with Pound's writings than was considered good for an Englishman and poet during the early Fifties, and Davie went so far as to maintain provocatively that the American poet had influenced him 'more deeply and constantly than any other poet of the present century'. I am not sure that this was quite true in 1955, but it was rapidly becoming true and often the influence was most significant when least apparent. For the most Poundian aspects of Davie's career during the past two decades have been those which required a departure from the particular practices not merely of his English contemporaries but of Pound as well. 'North Dublin' is a case in point. Aside from its American Offshot, eighteenth-century British civilization was only marginally interesting to Pound, but Davie is nowhere closer to him and further from the Movement than in the many poems in which he has sought to recover that civilization (especially during its intenser moments of interaction with foreign cultures) for the modern literary imagination. And it may well be that these 'history poems', the chief of which is the quite recent 'Trevenen', will turn out to be Davie's richest gift to his countrymen. Another Poundian aspect of Davie's career has been his openness to many poetic influences from many literatures—so that, particularly during the middle and late Sixties, his ways of seeing and writing probably were influenced as much by Pasternak as by Pound. Often, of course, Davie's 'imitations' of Pound have been of his methods as well as his spirit, and any comprehensive account would have to include instances of indebtedness ranging from the Poundian 'homage' of *The Forests of Lithuania* (1959) to the ideogrammic medley of 'England' (1969). (pp. 52-3)

'Dorset', from *The Shires,* may be taken to represent, in many respects, Davie's happiest adaptations of Poundian method to the norms of English poetry. . . . [While] 'Dorset' is written in fairly regular blank verse and correct English syntax, the organizing principles of the poem are chiefly those of the Pisan Cantos. The procedure is essentially that of reverie, with sudden and apparently wayward shifts of perspective and with multiple allusions to learned or autobiographical matters. In Pound's case this procedure often bewilders readers at the outset and turns them away without a crumb of meaning, but in Davie's less radical variant enough is immediately communicated to encourage a further and closer reading, supported perhaps by reference to the most obvious and available glosses. (pp. 53-4)

['Dorset'] closes with a hint of improvisation, confirming our sense that here and in many other post-Movement poems Davie has learned from Hardy but rejected his formal symmetries in favour of a more fluid, though still carefully channeled, movement of sound and image.

'Dorset' then is not the sort of poem that once led Charles Tomlinson to speculate that 'what fertilized Davie's talent was, I think, the example of . . . that excellent poet, Yvor Winters . . . like Mr. Winters', Davie's poetry can be "laurel, archaic, Rude," without being unduly self-conscious'. For in turning his back on the Gothic symmetries of Hardy, Davie was also moving away from the neoclassical symmetries of his late, great predecessor at Stanford, and also, as in 'Dorset', sometimes venturing to employ the cryptic allusions, abrupt transitions and associative structures which Winters condemned in the poetry of Pound and Eliot a full generation earlier than the Movement. So much for the example of Winters? Well, we have to recall that Winters and the Movement had their differences, too, and that even in an exceptionally 'Poundian' poem like 'Dorset' Davie's poetry retains enough of the virtues of good prose (and the virtues of an accentual-syllabic measure) to exclude it from the camp of American open-form poetry. His is not quite Winters' way of conserving the traditional strength of English poetry whilst at the same time capitalizing on the technical and perceptual gains of the French *symboliste* and American modernist masters, but, as Tomlinson contends, Winters' example was probably crucial for Davie's development beyond as well as within the Movement. For whatever the differences between Davie and Winters and Pound —and they are sometimes major and irreconcilable differences—Davie shares with the two Americans a similar internationalist perspective on the art of poetry and an equally proud, candid estimate of the poet's high, learned calling. His fellowship with these transatlantic shades is a living kinship as well as with the mighty dead of his own native tradition. (p. 56)

> *George Dekker, "Donald Davie: New and Divergent Lines in English Poetry," in* Agenda, *Summer, 1976, pp. 45-56.*

** * **

DELANY, Samuel R. 1942-

An American science fiction novelist and short story writer, Delany is an experimental writer who calls his works "speculative." He has been awarded science fiction's Nebula Award four times.

[Delany is], of course, deeply concerned with myth; no doubt, any science fiction writer must be so concerned, since the writing of science fiction is, at its best, a myth-making process. However, Delaney . . . [does] not concern [himself] with any particular myth so much as [he concerns himself] with the rationale behind all myths; that is, [he explores] the reason why men need and create myths. . . . [Delany is] essentially concerned, not with ideas, but men; [he allows his] characters to create mythos out of other characters, and then proceed to show the human truth that is masked by the mythic façade. (pp. 37-8)

Samuel R. Delaney chooses to explore the rationale of human myth-making. His heroes are very often poets, musicians, singers—figures who may be termed "prophets" or

"seers." In *The Einstein Intersection,* for example, he postulates a universe in which the figures of imagination and myth are real; and the artist-hero, Lo Lobey, assumes responsibility for confronting and dominating a variety of mythical creatures, including dragons, minotaurs, and, ultimately, "Kid Death."

In his novel *Nova,* Delaney again includes an artist among his major characters; in this case, Mouse, a Greek-Turkish Gypsy jack-of-all-trades who, finding vocal expression difficult because of a congenital defect of the larynx, expresses himself through sound and color by means of a technologically sophisticated instrument called a "sensory syrinx." Although Mouse is not precisely the "hero" of *Nova,* it is he who ultimately becomes the most important figure, as I shall try to demonstrate.

The nominal hero of the novel, Lorq Von Ray, can indeed be typified as a "Frontier hero," a gigantic figure who reaches into the unknown depths of space to bring back wealth and power in the form of Illyrion, a powerful element formed in the explosion of a star (that is, a nova). (p. 38)

Because of the damage done to his nervous system, Von Ray, while successful, is unable to tell of his success. It is, therefore, the role of Mouse, who had been among Von Ray's crew on this voyage, to tell the tale for him; to portray, in sound and color on the "sensory syrinx," the myth of Von Ray's quest. We can see in this novel that, while heroes exist and fill certain roles, the hero is nothing without the singer, or myth-maker, to carry the tale to the people, and interpret it for them. Ultimately, the singer or myth-maker is the true hero of his own myth.

It can be deduced from such examples as the works of . . . Delaney that, while science fiction is, indeed, literature of ideas and essentially concerned with myth, we cannot isolate any single myth or cluster of myths that science fiction is concerned with. Moreover, it must be seen that, in those novels which are concerned with the myth-making process, individuated characters are not . . . inconsequential. It is true that, in the "myth" which the singer-hero finally produces, individuated character may be lost, and replaced by a personification of some idea; but, if we are to study the myth-making process, as [Delany does], we must see very clearly the individual and action upon which the myth is based, if only to better understand the new creatures who exist only in the myth. (pp. 38-9)

> *Ronald M. Jacobs, "Some Notes on 'Science Fiction and the American Dream'," in* The CEA Critic *(copyright © 1974 by The College English Association, Inc.), March, 1974, pp. 37-9.*

["Dhalgren's"] form is unmistakably circular. The first words in the book—"to wound the autumnal city."—seem to be the end of a sentence, and the last words of the book —"I have come to"—seem to be the beginning of the same sentence. This obvious echo of "Finnegans Wake" is both daring and defensible. It is Delany's way of flagging his intent, of proclaiming the standards he wishes to be judged by. (p. 27)

One thing is certain: "Dhalgren" is not a conventional novel, whether considered in terms of S.F. or the mainstream. But since a great deal of science fiction falls into the sub-category of "space opera"—callow adventure stories that use outer space and the far future as convenient backdrops—perhaps "Dhalgren" can best be classified as a "space-time opera." If the book can be said to be *about* anything, it is about nothing less than the nature of reality. (pp. 27-8)

As in Joyce's "Ulysses," mythological allusions abound. However, the most important fact about Delany's novel—in terms of contemporary science fiction, at least—is that nothing in it is clear. Nothing is *meant* to be clear. (p. 28)

The dissolving landscape, the ambiguous characters, the freakish events are all presented as having a reality (of some kind) outside the author's mind. Bellona [the "autumnal city"] may be a nightmare, but it is, to paraphrase Joyce, a nightmare of history. . . .

In "Dhalgren," the premonitions of subatomic physics and cosmology are given flesh. The universe, as experienced by an ordinary person from day to day, no longer follows the old rules. Presumably, there are some rules, but they are not understood yet, and there is no assurance that men can ever know them.

To thrust the reader into this universe (instead of merely telling him about it, as in "The Einstein Intersection") Delany has found a style to match his theme: the texture of "Dhalgren" is dense and intricate, totally unlike anything else in recent science fiction. (p. 30)

I am afraid that "Dhalgren" is precisely the kind of book that most people turn to S.F. to get away from. Its virtues are apparent; but it is a chore to read. In fact, a book like "Dhalgren"—genuine S.F. conceived and executed on this level of sophistication—would have been unimaginable 10 years ago. Only in the last decade has the Academic Critical Apparatus taken serious note of science fiction. "Dhalgren" may be the first S.F. novel written with at least one eye on this new S.F. audience—the students and professors of literature who are always seeking grist for their mills of exegesis. (p. 31)

> *Gerald Jonas, in* The New York Times Book Review *(© 1975 by The New York Times Company; reprinted by permission), February 16, 1975.*

Samuel R. Delany is the most interesting author of science fiction writing in English today. No one else has managed to put the space-defying, time-denying adventure story to such high purpose—in novels like "Empire Star" (1966) and "The Einstein Intersection" (1967)—without sacrificing the narrative drive that made such stories appealing in the first place. His writing has always been experimental in the best sense: he poses a problem, embeds it in a familiar sf context and then bombards it with high-energy language to see what particles of insight he can dislodge. By the very nature of this technique, Delany is bound to be more successful in some books than others. In last year's "Dhalgren," the high purpose was more evident than the narrative drive. ["Triton"] is his most controlled, and therefore his most successful, experiment to date. . . .

First and foremost, "Triton" is a novel of manners—those of a rich and complex society in which the avowed highest good is the free expression of each individual's personality. (p. 30)

[The] problem that Delany poses is this: given virtually unlimited freedom for self-expression, what happens to a person who cannot decide what to express?

Delany has written about seriously disturbed characters

before. The premise of several of his earlier novels was that only gifted madmen are fit to live in a galactic civilization where literally any human fantasy can be realized on one planet or another. The scope in "Triton" is much smaller, which only makes [the protagonist's] disturbance more poignant. . . . By the end of the book [the protagonist's] despair has reached almost Kierkegaardian proportions. While mercilessly anatomizing that despair, Delany also manages to suggest the ecstasies of fulfillment that await those who overcome their fear of freedom. (p. 31)

> *Gerald Jonas, in* The New York Times Book Review *(© 1976 by The New York Times Company; reprinted by permission), March 28, 1976.*

*   *   *

DELIBES, Miguel   1920-

Delibes is one of Spain's leading authors; his publications to date have included two Spanish language texts familiar to many American students. Delibes's novels have maintained a consistently high quality. Having begun as a realist, he has most recently written symbolic parables that have been likened to the novels of Franz Kafka. (See also *Contemporary Authors,* **Vols. 45-48.)**

Miguel Delibes paces [the story of the characters in *Smoke on the Ground*] as deliberately as nature's movements, and populates his tragic idyl with memorable ragtail characters whose exuberance, meanness, and distress he lets us feel with no touch of strain or sentimentality. (p. 497)

> The Antioch Review *(copyright © 1973 by The Antioch Review, Inc.; reprinted by permission of the editors), Vol. XXXII, No. 3, 1973.*

[A] new stylistic approach, beginning late in 1967, definitely *Contraola* (or, "counterwave"), was barely perceptible in the works of several young, new and exciting Spanish novelists. Not until 1969 did this neo-Baroque, highly intellectual, objectivist style, somewhat imitative of the French *nouveau roman*, reach its culmination in Spain (possibly thereby forecasting its own decline or decadence). What is especially surprising to the Spanish public is that Miguel Delibes, a mature and widely renowned Spanish novelist, embraced the *Contraola*, seizing the "new" techniques created by younger, less well-known writers and using them in his latest novel, *Parábola del náufrago* [(*Parable of a Drowning Man*)]. (p. 245)

[In] *Cinco horas con Mario (Five Hours with Mario)*, . . . Delibes began to embrace the interior monologue and other techniques of the behaviorist novels. . . . (p. 247)

Delibes has been always considered a major novelist whose career is constantly developing, growing in quantity and quality, and becoming more prestigious because of his consistent use of Realism and his attachment to rural themes, which display a variety of character types. Delibes is also known as a conscientious practitioner of his craft, always seeking some new theme and new means of novelistic expression. . . . Critics acknowledge his skepticism, pessimism, reactionary vision of nature, his love for the man of instinct, of nature in contrast to a "civilized" product, in short, his negative view of progress and "civilization," his black humor and cold intellectualism. (pp. 248-49)

[Delibes'] true artistry lies in the works that retain Castillian settings and themes. Delibes is a sharp observer of daily life, with refined sensibilities and an enormous capacity to capture within his writings the essences of nature by means of his starkly Realist style. When he first began his writing career, his works appeared unconvincing and the reading public were unreceptive; however, his novels gained in veracity over the years because of a progressively purer or refined style.... In [his latest novels] he combines humor, tenderness, nature and tragedy in a harmonious manner, reviving the theme of nature as a literary element indispensable to the human condition and portraying this harmony through his extremely personal style. (p. 249)

Cinco horas con Mario marks the decisive turning point in Delibes' writing career, as it stylistically departs from everything written before it, demonstrating the revelation (through its three hundred pages of interior monologue) of story and characters in a Proustian or Joycean manner, whose psychic meanderings break all ties with chronological time and physical space (as we know them) in fiction. (p. 250)

When asked about his own novels, Delibes said, "for me, the essential thing in a novel is the characters. That they be living or lifeless depends upon the quality of the work. A well-developed character can make the most absurd of stories convincing...." (p. 251)

[*Parable of a Drowning Man*] is one of the best novels to come from the New Wave (or Counter-Wave), properly crowning the 1960's with its fresh experimental design within a genre becoming stale through reliance upon outmoded intellectual models, stereotyped plots and imitation of other literary schools. That the New Wave has been sustained and reinvigorated by a writer not really placed in its generation is both alarming and gratifying at the same time. (p. 255)

[Unlike] its predecessor, *Volverás a Región,* Delibes' novel is accessible, decidedly not labyrinthine, overly intellectually demanding, or hermetic. It does not suffer from the faults of *Volverás* but rather, through its unique style and simple plot, projects an equally harrowing but far more intelligent, humorous (*black* humor, that is) and devastating probe into man's degeneration and ruin.

Delibes' point of view, however, may no longer be that of the Spaniard but of Everyman. In fact, there are few (if any) intellectual or geographical ties in the novel where the reader might conclude the "mythical" country or enterprise Delibes describes is really Spain or any Spanish-speaking country. Delibes has raised his sights to the universal human condition. (p. 256)

[The] novel ... consists of a witty barrage of verbal and stylistic pyrotechnics that left this reader both amazed, delighted and dazzled. On page one, Delibes begins with a series of conventions replacing normal punctuation (as we know it) which is indeed, revolutionary for the reader. For example, he transcribes phonetically the signs of punctuation: "Behind the fence comma was the little house of Genaro open parenthesis who was now called Gen colon Here, Gen! close parenthesis comma ...."....

Parable is not divided into chapters like all of his previous works, nor is there any progressive continuity of the narrative thread along traditional Delibean lines. The novel is written mostly in the third person but there are sections (usually in italics) when Jacinto's conscience speaks (as he looks into a mirror or sees his image reflected elsewhere) which are narrated in the second person singular in the

form of an interior monologue. Within these monologues and general texts, there are elliptical thoughts, changes of time, interpolations of different themes, onomatopoeia, repetition, details deliberately selected to reinforce thought patterns, an extended use of syllabification and capital letters, apocopated words in Spanish used to form the new language of "the contract.".... Delibes' novel is a refreshing exercise in the intelligent use of the aforementioned stylistic techniques, which help to evoke the philosophy, parody, satire, black humor and grotesqueness inherent in Delibes' principal thematic concerns. (p. 257)

If we dare to perceive any "structure" as such in the novel, we might say it exists on two separate levels where different tenses are utilized: on the first, Delibes uses the present tense, narrating Jacinto's adventure in the cabin, gradually being overtaken by [a] hydra, giving us the actual sensation of life as the events occur; on the second, he employs the past tenses (imperfects and preterites), which relate the causes of Jacinto's illness, facts about his work, home, the city in which he lives, themes handled such that the impression is given that something has already occurred and something belongs to the past. Apart from the notion of structure or style, Delibes develops his characters and themes in extraordinary fashion, embracing or escaping the totally crushing philosophies which appear to us in the realm of impersonal and sometimes cryptic, ironic and paradoxical slogans.... Most amusing is Delibes' playfulness with the Spanish language (using a lack of punctuation and then a super-abundance of it) to achieve within his characters (and readers) their mental confusion, so that we may feel the confused and disoriented sensations of Jacinto. (pp. 258-59)

There are certain hilarious episodes that are etched in Delibes' uncanny "black" humor. (p. 259)

Perhaps the most moving section of the novel occurs near its conclusion when Jacinto realizes he is a prisoner of the hydra and vainly tries to send messages for help but to no avail. In one of his interior monologues, Jacinto discusses the meaning of reality: "The world neither sees, nor hears, nor understands, because the blind do not see and the deaf do not hear and no one can understand what one does not see nor hear".... Jacinto has been reduced to the most elemental level of communication in his struggle for survival, a struggle he eventually loses. Delibes presents the reasons for Jacinto's downfall early in the novel in a capsulized biography: "In May, 1966, he has shown an unhealthy curiosity about the reasons behind his work.... He mistrusts words ... and trusts only in man and in his goodness. (Under observation by the State)".... When Jacinto the man becomes *jacinto* the metamorphosized ram, Delibes even reflects these changes in the spelling of his name. (p. 260)

One cannot help wondering about Delibes' reasons for completely breaking stylistically and thematically with his former literary production (his neo-realism in favor of extreme subjectivism), unless he finds *Parábola* will have greater historical and literary relevance for him and his fellow Spaniards.... Although there is nothing so terribly new in the thematic or stylistic realms of Delibes, if we consider his novels in comparison to international literature, we nevertheless find that unlike many such similar practical works by his contemporaries (or predecessors), *Parable* is a novel that deserves to be read and bears re-reading. For it is a novel to mull over, not only for its thought content, but for its style. As one critic put it, "*Par-*

able is a plethora of intellectual content, whose technique is overshadowed by its theme.'' It is a book one cannot forget and one that is basic to the development of the novel genre in Spain as well as a key work in understanding the revolutionary turnabout in thinking and artistic accomplishments of Miguel Delibes himself. It may very well be the pace-setter for the ''New'' New Wave of the 1970's. (p. 261)

Ronald Schwartz, "Delibes and 'Parábola del náufrago'," in his Spain's New Wave Novelists: 1950-1974 *(copyright © 1976 by Ronald Schwartz), Scarecrow Press, 1976, pp. 245-64.*

* * *

DeLILLO, Don   1936-

DeLillo is an American novelist. In 1971 he made an auspicious debut with *Americana*, followed the next year by *End Zone*, a book ostensibly about football but in reality concerned with the growing corruption of language and life in America. Now, several novels later, DeLillo is gaining recognition as the serious, often brilliant writer promised by his first two novels.

It's pretty clear from the outset [of *End Zone*] that Don DeLillo's college football players are something more than your run-of-the-mill, helmeted and padded Neanderthals with talent for little more than running into each other at full tilt. American football is a confusing business, it's true, but the players in *End Zone* make claims for the game which extend way beyond bewildering numerical chants:

> ''Our uniforms are green and white'', he said. ''The field itself is green and white—grass and chalk markings. We melt into our environment. We are doubled in the primitive mirror.''

Each of the men in the Lagos College team (anyone who cares to seek for significance in the name is welcome to do so) appears to be suffering some sort of identity crisis: not the least among them being Gary Harkness, whose view of football as a microcosm of the holocaust dominates the novel. Not that Mr. DeLillo restricts the analogies to matters of violence, logistics and partisan pride; the real comparison, it seems, lies in the abstruse terminologies: what Gary refers to as ''elegant gibberish''. . . .

All in all, the parallels seem self-defeatingly tenuous, with the attempts to mythologize the game sounding like an academic's apologia for leaving the library (''The spectator's pleasure, when not derived from the action itself, evolves from a notion of the game's unique organic nature''). The author's insistence on characterizing the rest of the cast as an odd lot does little to support the analogies he draws from their on-field activites. One of the players, Anatole Bloomberg, tells how he is oppressed by his name—''It was my name that caused the trouble, the Europeaness of my name. Its Europicity. And there was another thing. Some names possess a smell. I didn't like the way my name smelled. It was like a hallway in a tenement where lots of Bulgarians live''—and, paradoxically, the more we hear the less believable Bloomberg becomes. The voice is not his; he is a numeral in the author's tactical play.

It is significant, perhaps, that the book is most successful and most enjoyable when the narrative is forced to be straight about football and characters alike. . . . (p. 1045)

The Times Literary Supplement (© *Times Newspapers Ltd., 1973; reproduced from* The Times Literary Supplement *by permission), September 14, 1973.*

Once it was thought fashionable, particularly among writers of the Bloomsbury persuasion, to condescend to American literature. How vigorous it is, and yet inelegant. How magnificent its country energy, yet its language lacks breeding. . . . Now all has changed: among serious writers of American fiction mandarin is the most admired style. The reader is confronted with cleverness, skittering symbols, pockets of amiable pedantry, a language so musical that he can almost sing the paragraphs. Plots have been jettisoned for a theme-and-variations effect—a story that extends but does not progress. Characters have been dumped with the result that all the voices in the story echo but one voice—the author's.

The trouble with mandarin writing is not that it hasn't produced good fiction—it has produced some of our best—but that it is by definition an elite line of work, as difficult to perform well as it is tempting to imitate. Our very best mandarins are stalked by talented disciples: Donald Barthelme by Robert Coover, Thomas Pynchon by Don DeLillo. I have no doubt at all that if we hadn't had ''V'' and ''Gravity's Rainbow'' we would not now have ''Ratner's Star.'' (p. 90)

To be really disappointing a novel cannot be really bad. What's needed is a developing tension between the author's talent and reader's hopes on the one hand and the author's performance and reader's frustration on the other. ''Ratner's Star'' provides such exquisite tension in large measure. DeLillo knows how to write brilliantly, even movingly, but he doesn't know when he's writing dully, doesn't know when his book has started to die in his typewriter. ''Ratner's Star'' is twice too long; as its terminal signs (failing inspiration, metastasis of exhausted ideas and dialogue) progress in the second half it becomes virtually unbearable. There are too many cartoon characters, too many familiar situations and too much talk without insight, without any real *vision* at all.

Part of this failing may come from running too closely in Pynchon's tracks (the story even has a mysterious recurring symbol, a boomerang, embarrassingly like Pynchon's V's and rockets), part from the difficulties of writing satire in an ambiguous age. What's gone wrong with much of our recent satire is that it hasn't changed at all in the past fifteen years, and our society has—or at least the way we think about society has changed. We need to rethink what's actually grotesque in our society and to that end I propose a temporary moratorium on such stock figures as life-denying scientists, mad generals, obsessive Jews with New York accents, evil psychoanalysts, sane lunatics, lecherous ministers. We can revive them in a few decades with their energy restored from lying fallow. (pp. 90, 93)

Peter S. Prescott, "Mandarin's Apprentice," in Newsweek *(copyright 1976 by Newsweek, Inc.; all rights reserved; reprinted by permission), June 7, 1976, pp. 90, 93.*

There is no easy way to describe *Ratner's Star*, a cheerfully apocalyptic novel. Imagine *Alice in Wonderland* set at the Princeton Institute for Advanced Studies. . . .

DeLillo has an ear for specialized language, and the satirical possibilities therein, that most novelists should be willing to kill for. . . .

DeLillo parodies brilliantly and ruthlessly the cult of science, its heartlessness, its private languages, its barren self-love. . . . The book is, in the end, as elegantly meaningless as a mathematical abstraction, though it is considerably more unnerving and far more entertaining. (p. 86)

> *Amanda Heller, in* The Atlantic Monthly *(copyright © 1976 by The Atlantic Monthly Company, Boston, Mass.; reprinted with permission), August, 1976.*

With each day's new terrorist event—in Entebbe or Wall Street or mid-town Manhattan—it becomes more natural that terrorists start showing up as prototypical figures in novels; but in novels they have their uses. They replace the car crash as a means of violent and sudden death, replace psychiatrists and holymen as spokesmen of authority. Like the fools in Shakespeare they are satirical; like clowns, with their air of comic befuddlement, they call attention to the significance of things whose significance we had missed. Until their comeback, some of their powers—for instance, the power to effect retributive justice—had been lost to authors. Perhaps they are the only moral agents anyone can believe in now.

Still, nobody thanks a moralist, as Don DeLillo must know. His brilliant earlier books have been much praised but not so much read, perhaps because they deal with deeply shocking things about America that people would rather not face. "End Zone" (1972) connects football and nuclear warfare; "Ratner's Star" (1976) plays with science and science fiction; and "Great Jones Street" (1973) looks at rock music, nihilism and urban decay.

In "Players" . . . DeLillo wittily deploys terrorists to explore all the secret places in contemporary sensibility. In the prologue, passengers standing in the piano bar of an airplane in flight are watching a film of hippie marauders shooting and hacking to death a band of golfers. . . . The passengers laugh, cheer, clap. It is the terrorists whom they applaud. "To the glamour of revolutionary violence," remarks the author, "to the secret longing it evokes in the most docile soul, the piano's shiny tinkle brings an irony too apt to be ignored." This elegant, highly finished novel does not shrink from suggesting the complicity of Americans with the terrorists they deplore.

Though they give themselves timely airs, novels have never been very good at looking at what's going on in the world; the workbags of novelists are weighted with tricks for avoiding it. (p. 1)

[Nostalgia], one of DeLillo's many targets, is an implicit comment on the present, but the present gets lost in a welter of antimacassars. A sense of the present also gets lost in novels in the fashionable confessional mode, which, by funneling life through the mesh of private sensibility, do succeed in reducing it to manageable literary proportions but sacrifice any authentic social vision to idiosyncrasy and richness of characterization. . . . Not that novels are obliged to look grandly at the whole state of things, but it is significant how few try. It is a measure of DeLillo's bravura that he tries, and a measure of his art that, for all his deceptive simplicity, even plainness, he succeeds.

"Players" is about two Everymen, Pammy and Lyle Wynant, a fun New York professional couple. Since Freud, we've been used to the way novelists normally present a character: looks normal, is secretly strange and individual. In the first of the many inversions of appearance and reality

that structure the book, Pammy and Lyle look interesting and seem to do interesting things, but do not interest themselves. The richness is only superficial. Put another way, the novel is not a romantic one about how they don't get along in society, but how they are *of* society and their normality is what we hate to recognize. The tone is comic; the style is Candid Camera. Their smallest gestures are closely observed: "Lyle checked his pockets for change, keys, wallet, cigarettes, pen and memo pad. He did this six or seven times a day, absently, his hand merely skimming over trousers and jacket." We hear not their impassioned but their odd bits of conversation, the ones they actually transact life with: "Goody, cheddar." "What's these?" "Brandy snaps." "Triffic." "Look out." "No you push me, you." Their voices are just distinguishable: Lyle is elaborate, ironic; Pammy credulous. (pp. 1, 16)

DeLillo abandons the ordinary assumption of fiction that action is caused by character and character by experience, some of which, at least, it's the author's duty to suggest. Pammy and Lyle have no history; they are without pasts, were never children, come from nowhere. . . . You experience the existence of Pammy and Lyle as though they were the subjects of a photo-realist painting, without curiosity or quarrel, the way the world of others is always experienced by the self. Pammy and Lyle: What made them like this? They *are* like this. Society disrupts the cherished relation of cause and effect dominated in fiction by the family; DeLillo suggests that the Zeitgeist may count for more than mother love. . . .

What's clear in DeLillo's view is that repression is what people (Lyle and Pammy) seek. It's not that the structures of existing society are not repressive, but that these structures are not felt. Society is perceived as a void, an unmanageable chaos in which people must make their own order. . . .

Few recent novels have found so admirably congruent a form for their subject. The tight, carefully balanced structure, recapitulating the book's idea of people's appetite for boundaries, might have seemed too rigid to contain the unruly, even violent, strangely comic events. Instead, it suggests the ruthless tendency of people to establish order over chaos. . . . DeLillo's attention to detail is masterful. He suggests that though freedom is what people ostensibly want, too naïve a definition of it brings a reaction as frightening as chaos. This is not a fashionable idea, but DeLillo convinces you that it is true. The discoveries of artists do not always—perhaps seldom—corroborate political fashions. But the wit, elegance and economy of Don DeLillo's art are equal to the bitter clarity of his perceptions. (p. 16)

> *Diane Johnson, "Beyond Radical Chic," in* The New York Times Book Review *(© 1977 by The New York Times Company; reprinted by permission), September 4, 1977, pp. 1, 16.*

*   *   *

DENNIS, Nigel 1912-

Dennis, a British novelist, playwright, poet, and essayist, is probably the best satirist to emerge in Britain since Wyndham Lewis. In America his fame rests largely upon one novel, *Cards of Identity*, a satirical fable that has been cited as a minor classic. (See also *Contemporary Authors*, Vols. 25-28, rev. ed.)

Cards of Identity is an ambitious satire, partly allegorical, which is weakened in the end by the purely negative values underlying it. The Identity Club has its yearly conference at a large country mansion and, using modern techniques of psychological persuasion, the members of the Identity Club persuade the owners of the mansion and the local doctor to accept the roles of old family servants. Papers are delivered, anecdotes about identity-changing or the assumption of fantasy identities are told, and the performance of a mock-Elizabethan play leads eventually to the murder of the Club President and his suppression by a younger and more ruthless rival. The satire is ambivalent; it is partly satire on modern means of mass persuasion, and on the uneasiness which many people feel today unless they can adapt themselves to a stereotyped role. But the cruel and frivolous members of the Identity Club seem to be regarded by Mr. Dennis with a certain Nietzschean complicity, and the ruthlessness of the whole scheme is in the end distasteful. Mr. Dennis lacks that basic sympathy with the human weaknesses which make up human nature.... [His first novel, *Boys and Girls Come Out to Play*,] remains a disagreeable and rather over-elaborated but powerful and sourly amusing book. (p. 172)

> *G. S. Fraser, in his* The Modern Writer and His World *(copyright © 1953, 1964 by G. S. Fraser), Andre Deutsch, 1964.*

["A House in Order," a] novella (if parable isn't a better word), comes at a time that is hardly momentous for the literature of captivity and breakaway, a time when all the false uniforms have been moth-eaten into dust. The odds are that now-it-can-be-told no longer finds ears flapping to hear it. Nigel Dennis has written an escape story that is not topical on those terms. On which other terms he intended it to be judged is far from clear.

His pivotal character is an army cartographer ["X"], an unbelievably craven P.O.W., who betrays no one, reveals nothing of value to the enemy, and yet stays alive and unharmed through efforts that ultimately approach the heroic. It is a strange little story....

If the author's object was to prove that they also serve who only shiver and wait, that an accidental valor can be spawned by extreme cowardice, then why the queer, unworldly menace of the formative chapters? The occupational intriguing of the Colonel, the Commandant, and the Deputy Commissioner of Prisoners of War, is presumably relevant to the character of their captive, but it is hard to see how. Indeed the coexistence of the first two officers on the same site—for so long—needs some explaining. Apprehensive though he is, the prisoner himself appears to be wondering who is in charge around here. If he were a theatergoer, he might suspect that it was Ionesco....

In readability and general competence the book is up to the standard Mr. Dennis set with his memorable "Cards of Identity." But if we are to take a clarity measurement—temp. approx. 50 degrees.

> *Frank Littler, "The Ordeal of X," in* The New York Times Book Review *(© 1966 by The New York Times Company; reprinted by permission), October 30, 1966, p. 73.*

In its comic, inventive and somewhat heartless fashion, *Cards of Identity* probes at contemporary dilemmas: its satirical examination of the way in which the traditional symbols of English identity are losing their validity is an important part of its meaning. Nigel Dennis is one of the most

accomplished and idiosyncratic of living English novelists, and in his most recent novel, *A House in Order,* he continues to dwell on the question of identity in a way that is at once more personal and less culturally specific than in *Cards of Identity,* though it is an equally distinguished work. (p. 74)

> *Bernard Bergonzi, in his* The Situation of the Novel *(reprinted by permission of the University of Pittsburgh Press; © 1970 by Bernard Bergonzi), University of Pittsburgh Press, 1970.*

*   *   *

DIDION, Joan   1934-

American novelist and essayist, Didion, an excellent journalist, has assumed the role of chronicler of the moral wasteland of Southern California. She is probably best known for *Play It As It Lays*. (See also *CLC*, Vols. 1, 3, and *Contemporary Authors*, Vols. 5-8, rev. ed.)

Hollywood as metaphor for everything that is tawdry, artificial, and superficial about America has become a cliche in contemporary fiction. Those novels about Hollywood which are still read—West's *The Day of the Locust,* Mailer's *The Deer Park,* Fitzgerald's *The Last Tycoon,* Schulberg's *What Makes Sammy Run?*—succeed by transcending the limitations of their subject matter. Countless other ones have faded as quickly as the sunset in the West they describe because their voyeuristic concern was with Hollywood as Hollywood, their fascination with tinsel as tinsel.

Joan Didion's *Play It As It Lays* (1970) belongs to that former group of novels which enlarges upon the limited nature of its material. Although its setting is Hollywood, its heroine is an actress, and movie making figures prominently in its action, the novel is as much "about" Hollywood as *Heart of Darkness* is "about" Africa or *The Stranger* is "about" Algeria. Like those novels, *Play It As It Lays* depends upon an intimate connection between setting and theme; but also like them, its overriding thematic concern is man's relationship with himself and with existence in general. Didion's novel is neither primarily a sociological commentary on the values of contemporary American society nor a psychological case study of its heroine. It is, rather, a picture of personal dread and anxiety, of alienation and absurdity lurking within and without. For although Hollywood is her setting, nothingness is Didion's theme. (pp. 64-5)

What saves *Play It As It Lays* from degenerating into banality is Didion's control over her material, her skill in focusing attention not on the events in Maria's life so much as on her cumulative response to them. The real action of the novel takes place in the mind and heart of Maria as she is forced to deal with her experiences. Viewed from a medical point of view, she might well be classified as a near schizoid personality whose experiences have precipitated a severe emotional crisis resulting in the loss of an integrated personality. In a more profound sense, however, her sickness is neither emotional nor psychological; it is ontological. She is suffering not from a nervous breakdown, but from the breakdown of a world around her which threatens to engulf her whole being with nothingness. (p. 65)

Maria says she answers "Nothing applies" to the battery of psychological tests put before her.... Maria displays impatience at the obtuseness of others because she has "been out there where nothing is".... Her confinement in the sanitarium is not to be viewed as a solipsistic retreat but as a temporary withdrawal from the world in preparation for a future re-emergence, wounded but wiser, with a wisdom born of pain.

In this way, *Play It As It Lays* is closer in spirit and theme to the works of Camus and Sartre than to those of Nathanael West.... *Play It As It Lays* testifies on every page to [what Camus calls the] eloquence of the void as Didion relentlessly explores the emotional shock of the encounter with absurdity. The refrain "Maria said nothing" is repeated with increasing persistence throughout the novel until it takes on the characteristics of a ritual chant. In its silence, the statement itself becomes eloquent, illuminating the almost palpable nature of Maria's dread.... She has heard the silence of the void, has encountered that absurdity Camus describes, and has learned the truth of Beckett's observation that there is nothing more real than nothing.

For the title to her collection of essays, *Slouching Towards Bethlehem*, Joan Didion chose the final line of Yeats' "The Second Coming." Her overriding concern in those essays and in her two published novels—the first was *Run River* (1963)—is with the broken center, with things falling apart, with "anarchy loosed upon the world." However, where the emphasis in the essays is primarily on the sociological impact of such fragmentation (the title essay, for example, deals with hippie life styles in San Francisco), *Play It As It Lays* focuses on a highly personal and private version of the broken center. (pp. 65-7)

What distinguishes Maria's experience from that of most heroes of existential novels is that hers is uniquely feminine, not that Didion has written a blatantly feminist tract, nor that Maria's encounter with nothingness is ultimately qualitatively different from a man's. However, one must understand her experiences as a woman to appreciate fully the nature of her crisis.... Just as Ellison's hero is shaped by the particular nature of his experiences as a black man in America, Maria is shaped by experiences uniquely feminine. Just as the Invisible Man could say, "Who knows but that, on the lower frequencies, I speak for you," Maria can speak for many who are neither women, nor actresses, nor residents of Hollywood. (pp. 68-9)

Maria may well be compared with Esther Greenwood, the heroine of Sylvia Plath's *The Bell Jar*.... Didion, [unlike Plath], however, is purposely vague about the exact details of Maria's breakdown because she is more interested in the metaphysical rather than the psychological implications of her illness. (p. 70)

Play It As It Lays is not a nihilistic novel. Although Maria encounters nothingness, she survives. (p. 72)

Didion's narrative technique recalls Eliot's line from *The Waste Land*, "A heap of broken images," images of alienation and desolation, fragments of banal conversations, the minutiae of everyday life joined in a mosaic of nothingness. Instead of a flowing narrative, a broken and disordered pattern is brought about by frequent juxtaposition of past and present, important and trivial scenes, and first and third person narration. What emerges through Didion's careful selection and rendering is a bleak and haunting picture of nothingness. Since so many chapters are short, some only a few lines long, the reader is struck most profoundly by the empty spaces, the blankness on the pages of the book. These silences between the chapters become as disturbing and eloquent as the emptiness of the void itself, as significant as the refrain of "Maria said nothing" in communicating vacuity. (pp. 75-6)

Above all, Didion's laconic prose style communicates Maria's situation both powerfully and movingly. Her style is reminiscent of Hemingway's in its surface simplicity, its concreteness, its avoidance of abstractions and artificiality. Like Hemingway, Didion understands that less is frequently more, that understatement can often communicate more emotion than overstatement. (p. 77)

With relentless attention to telling detail, a perceptive eye for sharply-etched characters, an unerring ear for the absurdities and non sequiturs that pass for daily conversation, and a diamond-hard unsentimental style, Joan Didion has fashioned a remarkable novel which never misses in its portrayal of a modern woman caught in a mid-twentieth-century crisis. She has cast anew, in her unique idiom, one of the prevailing concerns of modern literature: confrontation with the void. Despite its preoccupation with death, suffering, boredom, and despair, *Play It As It Lays* is always fresh and alive. (p. 78)

> *David J. Geherin, "Nothingness and Beyond: Joan Didion's 'Play It As It Lays',"* in Critique: Studies in Modern Fiction *(copyright © by* Critique, *1974), Vol. XVI, No. 1, 1974, pp. 64-78.*

It is true, of course, that in [Didion's] novels ... the central figures are both female and undone. Inchoate half-mad women adrift in the world, they can in no way be taken to exemplify the resilience and strength of woman. Her women are ruined creatures—destroyed not by man or society but by their lack of character. Didion is one of the few extant novelists who still proclaims that character is destiny. She knows that her protagonists have been damned because they do not practice self-denial, sacrifice, and self-discipline.

At their root, Didion's novels are prophetic novels. Stripped of their contemporary sophistication, they denounce self-delusion, indulgence, and vanity, and include auguries of the abyss.

The apocalyptic strain is especially evident in Didion's new novel, *A Book of Common Prayer*, a novel which rises from the ashes of the recent past. It is written out of the disorders of that period in the early 1970s when, for a time, ... the old tablets of the laws of social behavior lay smashed and abandoned. It is no wonder that Didion (a conservative moralist in the best sense of the term) felt herself to be in the heart of darkness.

A Book of Common Prayer is the story of what happens to Charlotte Douglas, the last American dream girl, the last American innocent, after she is informed by the FBI that her sweet and well-loved daughter, Marin, has set off a pipe bomb, hijacked a plane, and disappeared, sending back a tape of babbling revolutionary rhetoric. But the novel is not so much a story as it is a metaphor for America's fall from grace. *A Book of Common Prayer* begins at the Order for the Burial of the Dead.

The trouble with *A Book of Common Prayer*, in terms of its impact on us, lies in Didion's misreading of the actual state of the union. We are not dead souls, the edge of the abyss was not even close, and we Americans have fallen from grace and lost our innocence so many times that by now the supply of both seems inexhaustible.

Let me say that I think Joan Didion is one of our very best writers. I read over her collection of essays, *Slouching Towards Bethlehem* (1968), with the same delight I take in listening to old Billie Holiday records. Didion writes more movingly of time and loss than any other writer of my generation. In her essays. Not in the novels. She has the capacity, I think, to be the Chekhov of our time, but her novels do not come alive because they are insufficiently distanced from her own anxiety—too relentlessly ironic in tone, too emotionally controlled, as if the form itself were the bars of a cell built to contain the madman in the attic.

There is, however, one section of *A Book of Common Prayer* in which Joan Didion evokes the real terror and sadness of the human condition as well as any writer can. Here, Charlotte Douglas, after the first revelation of her daughter's terrorist identity, struggles desperately to deny what has happened, to reclaim from the immutable present her daughter of lost possibility. Then, as in that moment when we come upon a newspaper photograph of a parent bent over his dead child's body, we respond viscerally out of our common knowledge of the anguish of irretrievable loss. (pp. 63-4)

> *Margot Hentoff, "Slouching towards Babel," in* The Village Voice *(reprinted by permission of* The Village Voice; *copyright © by The Village Voice, Inc., 1977), February 28, 1977, pp. 63-4.*

Joan Didion will be remembered by readers of *Play It as It Lays* as an original and witty novelist whose voice once heard is not easily forgotten, and by those lucky enough to have come upon her book of essays, *Slouching Towards Bethlehem,* as a critical writer of power and perception. I think [*A Book of Common Prayer*], for all its difficulties and tangles, is her best so far; it is proof of her talent and of an intellect at play in the fields of fiction.

The "tangles" mentioned above are plot intricacies.... One of the difficulties lies in the disappearing voice of the narrator whom Didion takes great care to set up: a 60-year-old American anthropologist, Grace Strasser-Mendana.... (p. E1)

The thread of this textured negation of a static plot ... is Didion's prose. It is simple, direct, repetitious, as though the repetition of a noun from one sentence to the next, or a part of speech repeated again and again in subsequent sentences, provides a continuity, or a sense of it, to the otherwise jumbled plot-elements. The dialogue is full of wit, and when it is not witty it is terse, pointed, accurate. These purposive repetitions might represent Grace's careful scientific observations, unliterary and accurate, the kind of prose we might expect from an anthropologist giving witness, writing her report on a culture full of civilized cruelty, revolutions, violent destructive change, lost wealthy drifters, and drunken, doped deluded upper-class specimens.

Or perhaps her rhetoric is the language of religious litany, as the title indicates to us, liturgic petition from a lost people to an absent god. *A Book of Common Prayer* has many such levels, tied together by supple, original prose. We touch its texture more than engage in its events.... (p. E3)

> *Doris Grumbach, "Pray It as It Lays," in* Book World—The Washington Post *(© The Washington Post), March 3, 1977, pp. E1, E3.*

Didion writes with a cool, cynical irony which suggests that to expend energy is vulgar, or at any rate pointless. She creates characters who are neither likable nor admirable and pits them against each other in situations which she

warns us in advance will end badly for them all. Chilly ingredients for a novel. Yet Joan Didion's patented brand of intelligence, craftsmanship, and caustic wit makes *A Book of Common Prayer* an absorbing story and a touching one. (p. 91)

> *Amanda Heller, in* The Atlantic Monthly *(copyright © by The Atlantic Monthly Company, Boston, Mass.; reprinted with permission), April, 1977.*

In the title essay of her superb collection, "Slouching Towards Bethlehem" (1968), Joan Didion draws back briefly from her painful study of the Haight-Ashbury dropouts to comment on the possible meaning of the "social hemorrhaging" she has been observing at close range. The drifting, inarticulate children of the 1960's, drug-besotted and prematurely aged, take on for Didion an almost allegorical significance. They are the pitiful casualties of an immense and perhaps inexplicable social change—an "atomization" prophesied by ... Yeats ... in "The Second Coming".... ["A Book of Common Prayer"] investigates the consequences of this breakdown over the past two decades, particularly on parents and children. (p. 1)

Joan Didion is not, of course, alone in her passionate investigation of the atomization of contemporary society. But she is one of the very few writers of our time who approaches her terrible subject with absolute seriousness, with fear and humility and awe. Her powerful irony is often sorrowful rather than clever; the language of "A Book of Common Prayer," like that of "Play It as It Lays," is spare, sardonic, elliptical, understated. Melodrama is the nature of Didion's world, but very little emotion is expressed, perhaps because emotion itself has become atrophied. (p. 34)

Has the novel any significant flaws? I would have wished it longer, fuller: I would have liked to know more about the daughter, for instance. But Joan Didion's art has always been one of understatement and indirection, of emotion withheld. Like her narrator, she has been an articulate witness to the most stubborn and intractable truths of our time, a memorable voice, partly eulogistic, partly despairing; always in control. (p. 35)

> *Joyce Carol Oates, "A Taut Novel of Disorder," in* The New York Times Book Review *(© 1977 by The New York Times Company; reprinted by permission), April 3, 1977, pp. 1, 34-5.*

Joan Didion's "A Book of Common Prayer" is ... accomplished and intelligent; despite its odd title, it doesn't peddle Christian virtue or the easy nihilism that marred her last novel, "Play It as It Lays." More technically elaborate and thematically richer than Didion's other works, "A Book of Common Prayer" is distinguished by uncommonly vivid social details, voices and landscapes and the clenched intensity of its prose.... [It] is full of extraordinary vignettes of the 1960's and early 1970's. (p. 52)

"A Book of Common Prayer" has much that is sour to say about political fashions in both the United States and underdeveloped countries. The cultural politics of its sharp-eyed realism is profoundly conservative. The chic depravity of the many characters' sexual and intellectual lives is energetically and remorselessly portrayed. But the almost monomaniacal control, the solemn, utterly sardonic voice, is troubling. There is unwavering, humorless contempt behind so much of the brilliant writing. Yet even more disturbing is the grand guignol, the melodramatic violence, that sometimes seems to overwhelm the writer and cause the hard-boiled style, like Hemingway's, to become sentimental, self-indulgent. "A Book of Common Prayer" is admirable, but V. S. Naipaul's "Guerrillas," which dealt with similar material, is far more impressive. (pp. 52-3)

> *Richard Locke, in* The New York Times Book Review *(© 1977 by The New York Times Company; reprinted by permission), April 17, 1977.*

Didion's descriptions [in *A Book of Common Prayer*] are a marvel. But it is rather a case where one might say, "I see the clothes, now where is the emperor?" We never get to know or understand Charlotte Douglas [the novel's central character] at all.

Partly at fault is the overbearing objectivity of the supercool Sra. Grace, who functions in the narrative like a kind of Intourist guide, rebuffing attempts at penetration while providing an official version of the events which unfold before you as in a movie. And you feel for her the same antagonism. You are constantly wanting to slip away from her and find out what Charlotte is thinking; hoping that, if you can just slip away from Sra. Grace, you will luckily meet up with Joan Didion, a penetrating and brilliant understander and explainer of things (*Slouching Towards Bethlehem*) as well as a brilliant describer of them. . . .

As it is, one can invent the meaning for oneself (one reviewer believes it to be a story of maternal constancy). Probably the meaning is meaninglessness, or delusion, as Sra. Grace says. Didion seems to write under the rubric of Robbe-Grillet's dictum that the genuine writer has nothing to say, but has only a way of speaking. . . .

For a century or more, art has been trying to clear its skirts of didacticism and exist for its own sake. . . .

The utility, for writers, of fiction that eludes meaning is evident. Things that mean something are thought to have messages, and the composing of messages, like child care, seems to be a duty which, in most societies, no one really wants. . . .

[It] is not surprising that Didion has tried to avoid the intensely subjective mode that seems to predominate in recent fiction by women and has tried to make herself vanish with the Tarnhelm of Art—or the rainbow cloak of Manner. (p. 6)

Should novels have a message? And the other great unresolved question in modern fiction has to do with character. No objections have yet been raised to the presence of characters in novels, of course; the worry is over whether it is allowed for us to like and care about them. Over whether it is necessary at least to identify with them in order for a fiction to "work." (pp. 6, 8)

[Didion invents] characters who are altogether real (who indeed will seem, to some, to have been drawn from recent history). They have pasts, minutely particularized; their peculiarities are their own, elaborately studied, consistent, unique; they even have real addresses and real labels—always good labels—in their clothes.

But Didion does not wish to intrude on what the French call the *mouvements intérieurs* of these characters, a phrase which suggests, to the English speaker, the queasiness with which matters below the surface are viewed. No polite

person should wish to intrude upon a *mouvement intérieur.* Yet the transaction between reader and character, whatever it is, seems to involve the character's confidences about his emotions. Without them, Didion's book is like a serious, exciting, but strangely silent film; the motives, anxieties, passions, and delusions are all presented in pantomime.

It's hard not to be of two minds about this. On the one hand one feels it's appropriate enough for an age when meaning, like value, has abrogated its claim anyway and only surfaces remain. On the other is the undeniable fact that this starved, lean prose is like a high-protein diet. Didion's writing is high protein, but leaves the reader a little hungry for the starchy pleasures of the inner life. . . .

Female power. Didion's woman narrator, by controlling a trust, controls the republic of Boca Grande, even though it's ostensibly run by her male relations, whose childlike *machismo* she does not take seriously. Charlotte takes neither of her husbands seriously. Her daughter is a successful hijacker while it is her male companion who is apprehended and hangs himself. Both Charlotte and her daughter exist in the vivid yet dreamlike world of romance, where women are accountable to no one; they have in fact replaced the men. Despite the formalism of Didion's presentation, hers is the world of Conrad and Graham Greene, but now it is women who have obscure crises of spirit in seedy hotel rooms and die forlorn and solitary deaths in warm climates.

It makes a change from the fictional world (or the real one) where husbands do not understand you, wives are not fulfilled, children are tiresome, and that includes all the other details of female despair which, without surrendering their authentic claim to our attention, are not such good reading either. (p. 8)

> *Diane Johnson, in* The New York Review of Books *(reprinted with permission from* The New York Review of Books; *copyright © 1977 NYREV, Inc.), April 28, 1977.*

[Some novels] suffer not from neglect, but from the wrong kind of attention. They are discussed too quickly for their bearing on contemporary issues, read too hastily as investigations of the modern condition. This is the case, I think, with Joan Didion's *A Book of Common Prayer*, . . . a book whose generally favorable yet somewhat confused reception may unfairly doom it to the status of period piece. The New York *Times,* for example, has recommended it is a "novel that searches the wreckage of the 1960s."

It is that, but it is also much more: a witty and oddly moving work that requires a slow reading, a kind of "shaking down" to be appreciated. True, it deliberately risks consignment to the category of the merely topical through its extraordinary specificity. . . .

In the brilliant journalism collected in *Slouching Towards Bethlehem* [this specificity] seemed to enable [Didion] to control her sense that "the world as I had understood it no longer exists." At the same time, "naming" intensified the terror in some of her reportage. . . . In Didion's Hollywood novel, *Play It as It Lays*, details become compulsive: the heroine's precarious—and unsuccessful—defense against breakdown.

One of the many advances of *A Book of Common Prayer* over Didion's early fiction is in the subtle use of precision of language to establish (and limit) the authority of an intelligent, skeptical, non-obsessional narrator. (p. 16)

[Didion] has written in an essay that her own generation, born in the '30s, was "the last to bear the burdens of home, to find in family life the source of all tension and drama." Charlotte [the protagonist] shares this burden. . . .

To think about family dramas is to find new implications in the book's title, taken of course from the liturgy composed by Bishop Cramner for the Church of England in 1552. There are few religious references in this "profane" novel. . . . The section of the eloquent old prayer book the author probably had in mind is that devoted to various family rituals—matrimony, baptism, the "churching" or Thanksgiving of women after childbirth, the order for the burial of a child. . . .

[Associations] with rituals that recognize suffering seem to me to enrich and "warm" the novel. There is, however, a quite different set of connotations that tends to chill it, one that might be called not religious, but superstitious. This is the *True Confessions*-style exploitation of lost or disfigured children. . . .

I think I understand why some readers find Didion's work unfeeling. It is not, as they say, because she "writes too well," but because they are defending themselves against this *Rosemary's Baby* dread she sometimes generates. Still, in *A Book of Common Prayer* she shows that she knows the difference between anxiety and emotion. One hopes that this superior namer will continue to identify real fears and earned guilts. (p. 17)

> *Ruth Mathewson, "Family Dramas," in* The New Leader *(© 1977 by the American Labor Conference on International Affairs, Inc.), May 9, 1977, pp. 16-17.*

There is a certain segment of the American population for whom each day is an exercise in futility bound together only by certain rituals—shopping at exclusive stores, recalling elegant childhoods, peering into the pointless, limpid pools of water that gather outside $120-a-day hotel rooms. No one has ever succeeded in portraying these people as well as Joan Didion.

In her first novel, *Run River,* Miss Didion illustrated at great length the life of a rancher's daughter from California who, under pressure that would be small by most standards, goes insane. In *Play It as It Lays,* the heroine is a former model who, also for no clear reason, simply loses the ability to function and, after throwing aside family, career, and conventional behavior, narrates her story from a mental hospital. Now comes *A Book of Common Prayer,* a lineal descendant of those two stories about life at the breaking-point. This too is a story of a despoiled, broken human being playing out a life which signifies not quite nothing, but close enough. . . .

Like all Joan Didion heroines, [Charlotte of *A Book of Common Prayer*] becomes, as we watch, the living dead, with no goals, hopes, or ambitions, no faith in anything, no capacity for deep feeling, a virtual automaton, capable primarily of bringing harm to those around her. Like all Joan Didion heroines, she can do nothing with nothing; and she does not even try. She tries only to establish a new routine and, heartbreakingly, fails even at that.

And yet, like *Run River* and *Play It as It Lays, A Book of Common Prayer* is an exquisite, magnificent, breathtaking piece of fiction. It is written in a spare style reeking of the poetry and exoticism of the tropics. I cannot think of a living writer whose prose matches Miss Didion's level of simple elegance, or the tremendous lyricism of passages such as the ones describing life for Charlotte Douglas in the Caribe Hotel in Boca Grande. But it is now clear that Miss Didion's medium is not her only message. In her splendid book of essays, *Slouching towards Bethlehem,* something comes out which is the key to why her novels interest a wider audience than psychiatrists and New Critics: in those essays, there is a uniform sense that life is not much more than a series of rituals. They may be the rituals of the rich or of the poor, of dentists in San Bernardino or of John Wayne on location, but they are still rituals, and, to Joan Didion, they are what life is made of.

More than that, rituals tell what kind of people we are. As Miss Didion wrote in the essay "On Self-Respect" (in *Slouching towards Bethlehem*), ". . . to give formal dinners in the rain forest would be pointless did not the candlelight flickering on the liana call forth deeper, stronger disciplines, values instilled long before." In Miss Didion's three novels, and especially in *A Book of Common Prayer,* we see what happens to people who vainly summon these deeper, stronger disciplines. They are people one step beyond the stage where rituals can reform life, but, for them, ritualism is still synonymous with living. Once the rituals cease, life stops—either through incarceration or through literal death. When Charlotte Bogart Douglas exhausts routine, she gets killed. Why not? There is nothing else for her to do.

What Miss Didion is exploring, here as throughout her works, is ritual as a means of survival. Through her descriptions of the rich shopping-bag ladies of California, she makes us see that those mundane habits we have grown accustomed to regarding as deadening can in fact be that which makes life possible. It is an inadequate defense for Miss Didion's pitiful heroines, but a rite, a ritual, a common prayer is worth having. In *A Book of Common Prayer* the case is extreme, but the lesson is universal.

> *Benjamin Stein, "Dinner in the Rain Forest," in* National Review *(© National Review, Inc., 1977; 150 East 35th St., New York, N.Y. 10016), June 10, 1977, p. 678.*

The theme of Joan Didion's famous collection of essays and muscular reportage, *Slouching Towards Bethlehem,* was that things fall apart. There were two very good reasons why the book worked. The first was that things in 1968 very obviously were falling apart, in America at least, and any new, young and accurate cultural diagnostician who said so was to be thanked; and the second was that Joan Didion made no attempt to disguise the extent to which she was falling apart in sympathy. . . . Joan Didion is back in California. But things go on falling apart, all over the world; and it is in Joan Didion's nature to try to make sense of this, to put some system in it. . . .

Perhaps there is too much system in [*A Book of Common Prayer*]. The suffering in it is organized (in view of the title one might say litanized, though as a matter of fact the title doesn't seem all that appropriate) with such implacable firmness that one's imagination cannot move around in it at all. Part of the trouble is the chosen form, that of a first-person "testimony" sifting evidence and weighing probabilities with an explicit doubtfulness of its own capacity to come up with the truth of the matter. . . . In *A Book of Common Prayer,* it's as though [Didion] saw, in her mind, connections between the confused, revolutionary future and what one might call the rhythmic, natural chaos of womanhood, and felt unwilling to spell them out. . . .

There is . . . a heavy throb of disillusionment in the verbal texture of the book, its patterns of call-signs and repetitions, which do, at odd moments, resemble the *sotto-voce* recitation of private and habitual prayers:

> Tell Marin she was wrong. Tell
> her that for me.
> Goddam you all.
> She remembers she bled.

> *Russell Davies, "On the Verge of Collapse," in* The Times Literary Supplement *(© Times Newspapers Ltd., 1977; reproduced from* The Times Literary Supplement *by permission), July 8, 1977, p. 821.*

*   *   *

DONOSO, José   1924?-

Donoso is a Chilean novelist, essayist, and short story writer who in his fiction seems captivated by the bizarre and the grotesque. *The Obscene Bird of Night* **catapulted Donoso into international prominence. He is presently living as an expatriot in Spain. (See also** *CLC,* **Vol. 4.)**

The Obscene Bird of Night, Donoso's third novel and the culmination of everything the Chilean author has done so far, is a phantasmagoria chronicling the decay of family, church and social system. What marks it as literature, though, is the brilliant handling of the narration in such a way that the book, like *One Hundred Years of Solitude,* advances "in an opposite direction from reality" and ends up as pages being burned by a hag. The novel comes to its own end, like Garcia Márquez's, as a physical text both *in* the book we are reading and *as* the book we are reading. Throughout, confusions and confluences predominate as the narrator, a deaf mute, records what he hears and writes down what he says in the course of a monstrous, mythic metamorphosis where a legend in the first part becomes the informing reality of the second. . . . *The Obscene Bird* is at once a parodic life of Buddah and a modern version of both Dante's *Inferno* and Bosch's *Garden of Earthly Delights.* A popularized surrealism, it might also be seen as *The Childhood of Rosemary's Baby,* but Donoso often brings Gothic fright to the pitch of Lookingglass sublime. . . . Donoso's imagination is so proliferating that at times he seems about to deliver a thalidomide novel, but his perpetual transmogrification of characters, events and places into the mute's text, which is the text you read, discovers a dark intelligence, which you may call baroque, as opposed to the transparence of reason. Ultimately, the book is the carrying of an idea to its bewildering conclusion—the text of a text as a text in a text—and the novel is a vast black mass of the written word. (pp. 484-85)

> *Ronald Christ, in* Partisan Review *(copyright © 1974 by Partisan Review, Inc.), Vol. XLI, No. 3, 1974.*

Donoso's work emanates from a childhood spent in the midst of senile, bedridden relatives. Indeed, this element of his youth marked him for life with an intense awareness of death and decay. His short stories, as well as his more mature fiction, exhibit this preoccupation. In addition to the world of the old and the dying (often insane aristocrats, as in *Coronation*), there is the universe of children and the constant intimation of infant cruelty. Such stories as "Veraneo" and "El güero" hint at the mysterious and often perverse quality of infancy; others, notably "El hombrecito" and "China," as well as the novel *This Sunday,* are

adult evocations of distant childhood. However, it is the world of servants, another recollected facet of his early life, that particularly attracts the author. Although ignored by their masters, female servants in Donoso's works seem to shape their lives secretly from within. Donoso sees these women as possessing witch-like powers, as in the case of Peta Ponce in *The Obscene Bird of Night.* She is the embodiment of the archetypal nursemaid and sorcerer.

Donoso's characters emerge from three distinct social classes: the senile aristocracy, the manipulative maids and the amoral pariahs of society. He purposely ignores those complacent years of human experience, particularly among the privileged classes, when the fears of imminent death and self-confrontation are not paramount. For the underprivileged or the old, life and death have an immediacy never suspected by the contented upper classes, which ignore chaos by veiling it under an appearance of order. Thus, beyond the social reality and its multiple stratification, Donoso probes into life's duality of good and evil, order and chaos, life and death, and examines man's inability to reconcile both sides of existence. Therein lies the tragedy; for, despite man's effort to build an illusion of order, life's anarchy eventually overcomes him. Madness, abdication to chaos, becomes the only alternative. (pp. 249-50)

Love is absent from Donoso's universe. Men approach one another to destroy and to be destroyed, never to attain plenitude of being. Furthermore, if man cannot redeem his fellow man through love, neither can God. The games the children play in *This Sunday* provide a clue to Donoso's conception of God: an arbitrary divinity who creates man solely to destroy him, just as the children create an imaginary character, Mariola Rocanfort, only for the purpose of killing her. The title of this section, "The legitimate games," seems to justify the ways of God to man.

The tragic nature of Donoso's characters stems from their inability to alter their condition. In *Coronation,* Donoso's first novel, Andrés Abalos is ultimately forced to the conclusion that "if there is a God, he has to be mad." The only alternative to this helplessness is "to join the cosmic madness." Thus we perceive a glorification, a symbolic crowning of insanity. (p. 250)

[The] recurrent themes in Donoso's fiction [are] the dissolution of self and the resulting madness. The abundance of costumes and disguises in Donoso's novels marks this process of disintegration and emphasizes the many personalities or symbolic masks that the characters assume in their futile attempts at self-integration.

If madness is glorified in *Coronation,* then *Hell Has No Limits,* Donoso's third novel, exalts the mask. By presenting Manuel or Manuela as a homosexual transvestite, the author succeeds in conveying the anguish of a consciousness fluctuating between two opposing realities, alternately male and female; yet the protagonist, constantly torn by his own ambiguity, is unable to find a permanent shelter in any one self. (p. 251)

Throughout the novel we sense an imminent doom. . . . Beyond the objective reality of a marginal town, we detect a reiteration of the image of a crazed God (a divinity who creates the world only to destroy it) through man's enslavement and exploitation by a social and cosmic order that ultimately annihilates him, an order represented here by the image of the brothel. The characters in *Hell Has No Limits,* most prostitutes and drunkards, are immobilized by their indulgence in sex and wine. Like Manuel, they are tormented by the dread of sinking into nothingness; but unlike Manuel, they are never moved to action.

In the midst of this stagnant world stands the grotesque transvestite, the aging Manuel. Even though eventually unsuccessful at self-integration, he nonetheless seeks ontological affirmation by struggling to identify with his preferred mask—namely, that of a young female dancer. . . . Manuel's death recalls Cerberus, and we are indeed at the gates of Hell. The title of the novel, a line from Marlowe's *Dr. Faustus,* underlines the hellish quality of life, a life "without limits" where man is doomed to remain and disintegrate and from which there is no escape.

The conception of life as an immanent hell underlies *The Obscene Bird of Night.* In fact, Donoso's masterpiece constitutes a reductio ad absurdum of the themes stressed in *Hell Has No Limits:* the donning of the mask and the disintegration of personality. However, in *The Obscene Bird,* the masks multiply as the narrator's self dissolves into several conflicting personae. The novel portrays the mind of a madman who surrenders his reason to chaos. Becoming a multifaceted, monstrous personality, he is nobody because he is each and every creature of his phantasmagoric world. (This brings to mind the image of a many-headed beast recurring throughout Donoso's fiction.) The first-person narrator of *The Obscene Bird,* Humberto Peñaloza or Mudito, is, in essence, a man bewitched by the irrational powers he has conjured up. He is a captive of the charms of sorcery, a situation symbolized, toward the end of the novel, by his being smothered under a seemingly infinite number of burlap bags. This notion suggests another recurrent image, that of the *imbuche.* This term, which recalls a superstition (among the Araucan Indians) whereby small children are robbed, choked and disfigured by old wizards, ultimately signifies possession by an act of sorcery. Not surprisingly, then, the presence of Peta Ponce, the archetypal witch, haunts Humberto throughout the book. (pp. 251-52)

The fantastic world of *The Obscene Bird* revolves around two locales: the Rinconada, run by Humberto Peñaloza, and the House of Incarnation of the Chimba, an old convent now serving as a home for the aged, under the supervision of Mother Benita. Because he feels threatened . . ., Humberto, transformed into Mudito (the deaf-mute), escapes the Rinconada and seeks refuge in the House. Although most of *The Obscene Bird* is an interior monologue (interspersed with dialogue), its narrator frequently seems to address Mother Benita, who is presented as his imaginary confidante. Mudito's mental labyrinth, filled with obsessions which result in the proliferation of selves, is paralleled by the labyrinthine structures of both houses, in which the rooms, corridors and galleries also proliferate.

In the Rinconada the teratological materializes in misshapen beings in the form of hunchbacks, dwarfs and lizard-like creatures. To dramatize the absolute supremacy of chaos, even the inanimate statues that decorate the gardens and the parks at the Rinconada have been stripped of their classical proportions and converted into grotesque parodies of their originals. Anarchy also prevails in the House of Incarnation, but in the form of decrepitude, imbecility and imminent death. This impending end is further reinforced by the fact that the House has been condemned. The name of the place, Incarnation, suggests the advent of a Savior; and we discern, in effect, a parody of the birth of Christ. One of the girls, Iris, bears the miraculous child whose coming promises deliverance from death for the se-

nile women. As the novel moves toward its end, Iris is transformed into Inés and enthroned and worshipped in another parody of the Virgin Mary, for Inés is also identified with Peta, the eternal witch, and Mudito himself with the miraculous child.

Thus, through parody, Donoso has succeeded in revealing "le monde à l'envers" (the world turned upside-down), a distorted and estranged universe in which everything has been, in Donoso's words, "monstrified" to present the grotesque irrationality of existence. By revealing the obverse and reverse of reality . . ., Donoso has further underscored man's inability to reconcile the dualities of life. Because this inability is a direct consequence of a cultural nourishment that has for centuries exalted reason at the expense of the dark powers of life, "the obscene bird of night" eventually and ironically prevails. Thus, the archetypal Mother is not the eternal Virgin but, rather, the eternal Witch; and the Savior, the son of that irrational God whose presence is all-pervading in Donoso's universe, is born to "redeem" the world not through an act of love but, instead, through an act of madness. Throughout *The Obscene Bird,* Donoso reiterates his primary intuition, earlier expressed by Andrés Abalos in *Coronation,* that man's sole alternative is to partake of and unite with the cosmic madness.

The Obscene Bird of Night closes, appropriately, with a vision of an old woman emptying a parcel (made of burlap bags), which represents Mudito's mental world. Thus, the narrator's lapsing into non-consciousness climaxes the dissolution of his subjectivity. At the end, "there is no writer, no Mudito, no nothing, only papers, and garbage, filth collected by the old women. The eternal witch: Inés de Azcoitía and Peta Ponce, the yellow bitch." This witch is Woman, the eternal sorcerer; she is the embodiment of irrationality, the very essence of existence. In the final analysis, the character's multiple identities merely mask his ontological vacuum. . . . Deaf, mute and eventually blind, Mudito represents man as an alienated and solitary being, impotent before the irresistible chatter of the bewitching "obscene bird of night," doomed to absurdity and irrationality. (pp. 253-55)

> *Z. Nelly Martínez, "José Donoso: A Short Study of His Works," in* Books Abroad *(copyright 1975 by the University of Oklahoma Press), Vol. 49, No. 2, Spring, 1975, pp. 249-55.*

In "The Boom in Spanish American Literature," José Donoso says that he left his native Chile to escape the social realist or slice-of-life parochialism that dominated the novel there. Like many another literary expatriate, he went abroad in search of a deeper desolation, a more universal unease. On the evidence of "Sacred Families," which consists of three novellas, I believe he both gained and lost by the move.

In "Chattanooga Choo-Choo," the best of these three, a Barcelona playboy erases his mistress's face every night with vanishing cream so that he can create her anew each day, in the ultimate male chauvinist dream of perpetual novelty. Sometimes he removes her arms as well, to prevent her from clinging to him or importuning him with endearments. In revenge, she detaches and hides his genitalia, which turn out to be just as precariously situated.

"Green Atom Number Five," the second piece in "Sacred Families," is less interesting. Again, the theme is loss or dispossession, but this time it is the furniture not of the self but of an apartment that disappears. The victims are a smug couple who have made a fetish of their pretentious décor, people for whom things substitute for feelings. This notion of objects displacing emotions is neither a new nor a fertile one. . . .

"Gaspard de La Nuit," the third novella, tries to make the best of an idea that strikes me as arbitrary and unconvincing. A teen-age boy who is visiting his divorced mother rejects all her overtures and occupies himself with whistling a melody by Ravel. Donoso tries to persuade us that only in this way can the boy express his true self, the inner music that only he hears. The premise is rather mechanically carried out, and the story whistles itself away.

In ["The Boom in Spanish American Literature"], which is more a personal chronicle than analytic interpretation, Donoso observes that his works have been influenced by authors from other countries rather than from his own. One result of such crosscultural orientation is that his writing has, for me at least, in these latest collections a rather touristic or anthropological detachment. He sounds like a man without a country or a history of his own. Men like Kafka or Faulkner experienced or suffered their subjects, while Donoso appears to have been led to his by books, like a literary comparison-shopper. The whistling boy is a thin echo of Kafka's "Josephine, the Songstress." "Green Atom Number Five" recalls Robbe-Grillet's obsession with inanimate objects. Only "Chattanooga Choo-Choo" establishes a territory of its own.

Perhaps, too, Donoso has overlooked certain possibilities in his own country. His account, in "The Boom in Spanish American Literature," of a timid and ironic young woman hawking her own books in the trolley cars of Chile is more Kafkaesque than any story Donoso has written. In these same pages, he describes his native tongue as "rich . . . naturally Baroque, protean, exuberant"—yet in his novellas, the language is meager, fussy, deracinated and marred by clichés. Perhaps in moving from Chile to Barcelona he has lost his tongue. In escaping what he regards as a prison, Donoso may have become a fugitive from his past. Rhetoric, the conspicuous surface of a language, often becomes the voice of the expatriate, but here too I miss in Donoso the wide-eyed, open-mouthed excitement in response to what Hart Crane called "new thresholds, new anatomies." It may be that this has nothing to do with expatriation, that Donoso simply does not have much feeling for words. In "The Obscene Bird of Night," the novel that made him famous, the language is feeble compared with Borges, Fuentes, Márquez or Cortázar. And in that book, Donoso is still in Chile, on his own home ground.

"Charleston & Other Stories" is a less venturesome collection than "Sacred Families." Donoso cannot seem to get up much impetus in the space of a short story. In each of his novellas, he is a slow starter. There are other difficulties too: Like so many writers with "metaphysical" leanings, Donoso assumes that every dislocation of the ordinary is extraordinary. He also confuses dreariness with ominousness. These stories read like slices of life that have dried out and lost their vitality. A boy spends all his spare time sleeping, pursuing some ineffable revelation: this is the whistler again, still less convincing. A neglected child runs away with a neglected old man, but these two negatives do not make a positive. A highly intellectual couple produces an incorrigible son who eventually drowns: Is this a baptism of humility? Only the title story, "Charleston," achieves a certain tricky equilibrium.

"The Obscene Bird of Night" was a fat book, in both senses of the word, and in these two new collections of stories, Donoso is living off his fat. I believe we would have to turn to sociology rather than literary criticism to explain the success, if that is the word, of the earlier book. It is superficially grotesque—like primitive statues carved for foreign consumption—opaque, and exasperating, and it sometimes pleases a part of the American public to seize upon such qualities as signs of profundity. It is easier to romanticize such a book as the spectacular cultural artifact of a country cousin than to read it.

> *Anatole Broyard, "The Exile Who Lost His Tongue," in* The New York Times Book Review (© *1977 by The New York Times Company; reprinted by permission), June 26, 1977, p. 14.*

What is clear from José Donoso's *Charleston & Other Stories* is that, in pursuit of his own demons, his agile, sometimes hypertrophied imagination was off and running in the morning. After his first three novels, all variously portraying the decay of Chile's antiquated, rigidly structured society, Donoso was pegged as a *criollista*, a writer in the tradition of Chilean regional realism. Yet of the nine pieces in the *Charleston* volume . . . , only three tales are rooted in *criollista* realism. . . . Although skillfully done, these tales are the weakest of the lot, perhaps the only signs that Donoso ever served a literary apprenticeship.

The other stories in *Charleston* reveal Donoso at his typical best, which is when he moves step by step from our real world toward a realm of dream, magic, fantasy, and mystery, exposing no telltale footprints as the transition occurs and gradually winning over a reader to an acceptance of fictional incredibility. Not unexpectedly in a collection of early work, a number of the tales exorcise youthful demons as their heroes and heroines first experience—and reject—the indifference, dullness, and cruelty of grown-ups. More important, however, is the haunting, self-contained isolation of Donoso's characters, who, driven by obsessions and supernatural powers, hover constantly on the brink of either salvatory revelations or imminent destruction. (p. 30)

Perched on an edge between reality and fantasy, the mundane and the visionary, rationality and insanity, order and chaos, Donoso's protagonists in *Charleston* inhabit a dark, grotesque world of their own making.

Separated by more than two decades from the earliest *Charleston* stories, the three novellas in *Sacred Families,* all set in the expensive glitter of today's Spanish bourgeois society and unified by overlapping characters, show Donoso so entirely in control of fictional unreality that he can joke about it. . . . Where the earlier stories often present a closed world inhabited by people distant from our norms, and hence threaten to be a bit stagy, even tricky, *Sacred Families* deals with our most recognizable concerns and brazenly displays fantasy as a mode of playfulness and humor. (pp. 30-1)

[Representing] his beginnings and where he is now, [*Charleston & Other Stories* and *Sacred Families*] allow one to see the constants in Donoso's work: his gripping power as a storyteller; his grotesque vision of experience; and his dark, terrifying account of human existence, lying just beneath the surface of the normal, the orderly, and even the humorous. Donoso has said it was after reading Ernest Sábato's novel *About Heroes and Tombs* that he realized how "the irrational could have intellectual signifi-

cance equal to or even greater than the rational." That realization, however, was not so much a shaping force for his
fiction thereafter as it was a description of the writer he'd
always been. (p. 31)

Robert Maurer, "Unbridled Pegasus," in
Saturday Review (© *1977 by Saturday Review Magazine Corp.; reprinted with permission*), *July 9, 1977, pp. 30-1.*

*   *   *

DOS PASSOS, John   1896-1970

**An American novelist, Dos Passos is best known for his
U.S.A. trilogy. Disturbed by the social and economic conditions faced by Americans in the twenties and thirties, Dos
Passos pictured his country as a wasteland. A self-proclaimed
"middle-class liberal," Dos Passos was concerned with individual freedom in an increasingly repressive society. (See also
CLC, Vols. 1, 4, and *Contemporary Authors*, 1-4, rev. ed.;
obituary, Vols. 29-32, rev. ed.)**

Dos Passos, in *U.S.A.*, focused entirely on the "widening
gyre" [as in Yeats' "Second Coming"]. He obliquely explored the physical and social landscape that West symbolized in *Day of the Locust* by viewing the period leading up
to the depression through one set of intellectual and emotional lenses of the thirties. There is no "green light," Hollywood vista, Daisy Buchanan, or Faye Greener in
U.S.A., no symbolic goal—only a gyre continually widening beyond reach. And there is no vehicle, only the collective life of all the characters. The real subject is the motive
power, or the force that drives the characters in the "widening gyre": America's aimless and uncontrollable energy,
the spirit of *laissez faire* and the melting pot, which the
style so fully and palpably embodies. The style (which Dos
Passos mistakenly considered the "speech of the people"
in his appended introduction to *The 42nd Parallel*) drives to
include everything in an apparently indiscriminate and shifting mixture. And the style finally levels all human action,
motivation, and destiny—turns action into movement, reduces motivation to conditioned response, converts destiny
into blueprint. If we see the style, which embodies America's destructive energy, as the subject, the trilogy is a success. Still, Dos Passos' Marxist materialist determinism
intrudes, and the overall pattern is consecutive and causal.
Dos Passos finally simplifies his vision by showing the
"widening gyre" to be the cause of the "centre's" destruction. (p. 133)

Richard Pearce, in Criticism (*reprinted by
permission of the Wayne State University
Press; copyright 1971 by Wayne State University Press*), *Vol. VIII, No. 1, (Winter,
1971).*

Dos Passos' USA . . . remains the most ambitious work of
fiction attempted by any writer in English during the Thirties, and technically it was extremely influential, and not in
English writing alone. It was an attempt at w̄hat used to be
called the Great American Novel, a kind of epic of the
American experience during this century. It fails, I think,
because in the end Dos Passos cannot fuse it into a unity;
and though it is complicated it is not complex. What I am
tempted to call the novel proper—and that one can extract
from a novel something one speaks of as the novel proper is
surely a sign of the author's failure—is, despite all the documentation, curiously lifeless, a result partly of Dos Passos' extremely flat style of rendering his characters. The

vivifying quality, the poetry, goes into the other elements of
the novel, the biographies of eminent Americans with
which it is interspersed, and the sections of what Dos Passos calls Newsreel, and the device, which certainly arouses
aesthetic problems, called the Camera Eye. These seem to
me brilliant, the biographies outstandingly so. But they also
appear as so much husk around the novel proper. When
one compares *USA* with *Ulysses*, one can only say that, by
comparison with Joyce, Dos Passos was an amateur. (p.
248)

Walter Allen, in Twentieth Century Literature (*copyright 1974, Hofstra University
Press*), *October, 1974.*

Most of [Dos Passos's] experience, in personal evolution,
politics, and technique, is distilled in *U.S.A.*, the triumphant point of his career. The novel isn't only a massive
vision of America corrupting itself over Dos's own lifetime
. . .; it's also a great technical enterprise in which the attempt is made through presentational tactics to relate personal psychology to the historical process. But the personal
life of the author, given in the 'Camera Eye' sections, exists in a pained isolation of images, self-dwarfing and self-
abnegating. In unstylised form we get this sensibility in the
letters [in *The Fourteenth Chronicle*]: the self is uneasy and
not very assertive, and the gestures outward toward principles and process seem, here, like efforts to contact reality
and wholeness which can't quite succeed, though there's no
doubting the fervent radical indignation. . . .

Where he mainly differs from his lost generation peers is in
his personal withdrawal and loneliness and the scale of his
pessimism, which starts early and persists as if as a character trait, however vindicated by circumstances. The letters
lack intensive confession, and you feel back to an unease
with self further behind them; the novels are the justification for reading them, as well as a proper curiosity about
the mental movements of an important figure in a crucial
generation of American writers and thinkers. They have
not that kind of immersed involvement in history that Fitzgerald's have: for Dos Passos, history was outside the self,
pulling and pushing it. But this is a significant accounting,
carrying a lot of the experience of a total culture inside it.
(p. 509)

Malcolm Bradbury, "Inside U.S.A.," in
New Statesman (© *1974 The Statesman &
Nation Publishing Co. Ltd.), October 11,
1974, pp. 508-09.*

If you are a Dos Passos fan (as I am), then you will appreciate [*Century's Ebb*, his] posthumous fiction-history. It is
in the mature Dos Passos manner: a complex intersection
of fiction, social history, biography, blank verse, and sermonizing, the whole interspersed with bits and pieces of
headlines, popular tunes, and slogans intended to evoke the
texture and subliminal meaning of the passing scene.

Dos Passos bore witness to the chaotic complexity of the
twentieth century in much the same manner as monastic
historians of the patristic period chronicled the fall of Rome
and the birth of Christian Europe. Monk and novelist felt
themselves in the presence of a social situation so multitudinous and so intrinsically chaotic that the only appropriate
response was to open up the forms of narrative itself, so
that it might reflect the teeming confusion of an age in
which fact and fiction, legend and event, prose and poetry,
myth and statistic melted together in the crucible of crumbling orthodoxies and social transitions. . . .

The closer Dos Passos came to the present (and we are speaking here in terms of decades and half-decades) [in *Century's Ebb*], the more his narrative method came under strain. Implicit in his earlier chronicles—and underpinning them as ontological—were correct acts of selection in the matter of who and what was most representative. No matter how unstructured and unassessed was the history of the 1890-1930 period, it already had for Dos Passos an underlying myth and an agreed-upon cast of characters. Dos Passos's chronicles were, in their own way, mixed-media events: in dialogue with, and sustained by, a sense of history already brought to semi-coherence by the triaging of newspapers, magazines, and motion pictures.

I am afraid that, in completing *Century's Ebb*, Dos Passos knew that his earlier method had come under strain in dealing with the 1935-1969 period, both as a matter of substantive vision and literary technique. . . .

A dedicated conservative in his later years, Dos Passos in *Century's Ebb* has the perennial problem of conservatives: to come up with heroes and mediating symbols. Did he, when he put aside his manuscript, suspect that John Foster Dulles, Joe McCarthy, and the astronauts just weren't compelling enough as public figures to sustain a conviction of enduring American tradition amidst the chaos? Did he realize, as he meditated upon this incomplete and uncompleted book, that the experiences of so many of its fictional characters were, in the last analysis, inconclusive, a faint puttering in comparison with the lives of his previous protagonists?

Or did he intend it that way? Did he intend that his last chronicle be one long, grand anticlimax, because, being a Jeffersonian conservative, he felt the Republic sadly detached from its founding ideals, and that American lives were being led to no purpose?

Century's Ebb, in short, suffers not from a lack of scale, but from a certain subtle fatigue, a weariness with it all. . . . *Century's Ebb* will not add an iota to the reputation of John Dos Passos, which is already enduring. It will not offer much in the way of either satisfying narrative or compelling moral vision. It will give greatest satisfaction to those familiar with the Dos Passos oeuvre—and especially to those familiar with the conservative philosophy of Dos Passos in the years since the Second World War. It is a plaintive coda to a major canon in the corpus of contemporary American literature.

> *Kevin Starr, "A Plaintive Coda," in* Harvard Magazine *(copyright © 1975, Harvard Magazine, Inc.; reprinted by permission), October, 1975, p. 69.*

Century's Ebb is not a very good book; it would not reward serious interest outside the context of the chronicles and were it not the last gesture—I assume—of its author. It's appropriate that the work looks like a Dos Passos novel. . . . The fiction as always is supposedly naturalistic, but is betrayed here by its stiffness. . . . The essays—for want of a better word—are impressionistic, cranky, and lively, the occasional vulgarity (liberals are "nervous Nellies") really only the ideological obverse of the style of *U.S.A.* But, especially since *Century's Ebb* is a "chronicle"—a word suggesting enormous significance—the inconsequentiality of some of the fictional episodes and essays taxes one's patience, and the forced relationship between the fiction and the essays compels one to wonder if Dos Passos's method hasn't always been a safe one—since such a separa-

tion exists between the old-fashioned storytelling and what is thought "experimental" in his work. (p. 16)

Dos Passos fictionalizing direct experience is, of course, not new, but there is something—I don't know—*coy* about it here, a sort of peek-a-boo quality that undercuts and diminishes the supposed intention of *The Thirteenth Chronicle.* (pp. 16-17)

Joseph Kennedy and Bernard Baruch play themselves, but . . . did the two old gentlemen have the conversation heard here? (Note, for contrast, E. L. Doctorow's *Ragtime,* where improbable meetings are given an artistic truth this probable meeting is without.)

My point is that *Century's Ebb* amounts to much less than a "chronicle." In the absence of a sustained vision—some large historical sense—that draws the disparate elements into a web of consequence and inevitability, it becomes a kind of invitation to a quiz game (dressed up with some provocative essays futilely assuring us there's something epic here), a release for the reader's own frustrated investment of attention and energy, little more than a *roman à clef*—in my book a trivial form of literature, if an elevation of gossip. The earlier novels, before Dos Passos thought of the formal term, *were* chronicles—so why the degeneration? Many possibilities, I'm sure, but I'd like to sketch one.

To write fiction that stands as a serious historical account of the time-spirit, a witness, one must control the writing, it seems to me, by either conviction or wonder—exploration or awe—not by defensiveness, self-justification. Dos Passos consistently has his eye on a liberal audience—the substance and tone betray that fact. . . . I'm not suggesting any automatic and necessary connection between such a tone and a *roman à clef* specifically—of course not. But surely what's left of a "chronicle," deserted by graceful conviction or naive wonder, is merely pop costume-fiction of one kind or another. (p. 17)

> *Samuel Hux, "Pignatelli's Progress," in* Saturday Review *(© 1975 by Saturday Review/World, Inc.; reprinted with permission), October 18, 1975, pp. 16-17.*

Like the author of *Ulysses,* who circulated the word *claritas*—the radiance that attends intellectual apprehension—Dos Passos wanted multifariousness to cohere, and trusted that a cunning interplay of literary techniques would make that happen. He was willing to outwait the impatience of readers who thought the techniques themselves incoherent, mainly because they fragmented the orderly *look* of print. . . . Using "newsreels," meditations, chunks of prose-poetry, fictional interludes, biographies like *Time* covers, he composed Chronicle after Chronicle: a twentieth century American reader's own life and times. . . .

Century's Ebb, . . . Chronicle Number 13, is a posthumous book never really firmed up by the author. . . . Its focus is the Spanish Civil War and Truman-Era leftism. Its three fictional sequences, intercut, chronicle a fiscal hotshot on the lam in South America, a pair of left-wing True Believers, an attorney whose experience of Stalinist chicanery in Spain swings him rightward. . . .

What works, works thanks to Dos Passos' gift for stepping efficiently through clutter. (p. 1247)

What's most evidently missing, from end to end of the book, is any sense of anyone *experiencing* those years. A lot of pop-lecture clarification occurs, and much pointing of facts the current mythology forgets (though Dos Passos' mythology forgets different facts). . . . Don't mistake it for real fiction, . . . nor, above all, for the sort of literary cubism it masquerades as. . . . (p. 1248)

> *Hugh Kenner, "Methadone Fix for Experience Addicts," in* National Review *(© National Review, Inc., 1975; 150 East 35th St., New York, N.Y. 10016), November 7, 1975, pp. 1247-48.*

*   *   *

DRABBLE, Margaret   1939-

An English novelist, short story writer, essayist, and playwright, Drabble uses traditional style and form in a revolutionary attempt to reconcile the established patterns of marriage and motherhood with the lifestyle of the contemporary woman. (See also *CLC*, Vols. 2, 3, 5, and *Contemporary Authors*, Vols. 13-16, rev. ed.)

The star of [*The Realms of Gold*] is a heroine perfect for those people who prefer to 'identify' rather than to read. Frances Wingate is an archaeologist, reasonably intelligent, reasonably successful, reasonably attractive, and in her 'thirties, too. She begins her fictional life by suffering one of her recurrent bouts of depression in a European hotel, and the novel ends back in her native village in England. This is the reverse of the usual progress of such things and, in such a lengthy novel . . . , there are naturally some recognitions, reversals, and coincidences on the way. . . .

[Beneath] all this is a note of futility which becomes the dominant tone of the book. It is no mere accident that the three central protagonists . . . [are all] looking for "realms of gold", a period or place in which everything has its significance, taking its place in the scheme of things. As it is, the other characters of the novel peep through the narrative only to get carried away down the meaningless but relentless succession of present moments. . . .

All of this book is written in this bland but effective reportorial style, principally as a device to keep the narrator close to her heroine but not *that* close. Margaret Drabble is too intelligent and painstaking a narrator not to take advantage of that situation, and Frances Wingate eventually emerges as a rather more complex creation than the mythical creature with which I opened this review.

The direct transcription of emotional details has its pitfalls, though, as well as its rewards. Its virtues are that, in a writer who is as faithful a recorder as Margaret Drabble, passages of strong feeling spring unimpeded to the front of her narrative. . . .

But the problems of this slow attention to tone and to mood is that, in a book of this length, it's necessary to be very interested in the role and the character of Frances Wingate before the book can carry full conviction. Margaret Drabble sometimes dabbles in the still waters of tedium, with a misplaced seriousness hovering over some sections of the narrative: it is only her strong sense of reality . . . coupled with the bleak, weary note at the bottom of everything, which keeps some of the excesses of the modern novel in check. They are enough, at any rate, to make the novel a more complete statement than her wordy heroine would have been able to make herself, and the *Realms of Gold* has a calmness and a sanity which eventually shine through.

> *Peter Ackroyd, "Per ardua . . . ," in* The Spectator *(© 1975 by The Spectator; reprinted by permission of The Spectator), September 27, 1975, p. 412.*

With Margaret Drabble's *The Realms of Gold* we come to full realization that her title is the true name for fiction. In reviewing her last three books in these pages I have had occasion to remark on some flaws that began to seem so persistent that it felt foolish to keep pointing them out when obviously she could do so much in their despite: a weakness of plot, a heavy reliance on not very interesting male characters, an excessive willingness to settle for superb parts and inferior wholes. But here all that has been wiped away. This long novel is wonderfully and carefully worked out, rich in pretension, detail, and execution so that one really needs to read right through to the end to see all she has conceived. There are at least two places where the book seems to lose its way, to become attenuated, but finally one sees it is all needed, not just to make the theme full but to make the story clear. (p. 625)

I believe [this novel], every word. The joy at the end overwhelms disbelief. Drabble knows. Having suffered a life that led to years of novels of hiddenness and unfulfillment, having touched down with Arnold Bennett and perhaps thereby discovering she was suffering only from a curable if lingering case of Midlands illness, she can create that stable and those Jaguars, the smell of straw and apples, the private history of an England that, if only in this beautiful novel, is becoming a realm of gold. (p. 628)

> *Roger Sale, in* The Hudson Review *(copyright © 1975 by The Hudson Review, Inc.; reprinted by permission), Vol. XXVIII, No. 4, Winter, 1975-76.*

"Omniscience has its limits," Margaret Drabble tells the reader in her seventh novel, "The Realms of Gold". . . . Having taken upon herself the voice and manner of an omniscient Victorian novelist, she seems rather frequently to be appealing to the reader to help her out, to write the novel with her. Her particularizations suggest multiple-choice problems: "Something in her finally rebelled—pride, conscience, something like that"; "she ached, with either sympathy or envy for them: she was not sure which." A disarmed, if not disarming, vagueness afflicts her especially in the vicinity of male characters. . . . Like a housewife quite overcome by the complexity of her household tasks, yet confident of her feminine charm, the author in amiable dishevelment apologizes for the thinness of some scenes and the fullness of others. . . .

Miss Drabble in some ways bears comparison with Iris Murdoch and Muriel Spark; she is as intellectually serious as they, though not as witty, and warmer than either. But, in sharp contrast to these two plotmakers, she does not *encompass* her material; rather, she seems half lost within it—mystified by her characters, ruminative where she should be expository, expository where she should be dramatic, shamelessly dependent upon coincidence, lackadaisical about locating her theme, and capable, for long stretches of blocking in episodes devoid of dynamic relevance to what one takes to be the action. . . .

The heroine, Frances Wingate, is a divorced archeologist enjoying the aftermath of celebrity that has followed her discovery and excavation of the ancient Saharan trading city of Tizouk. The amount of archeological detail and theory Miss Drabble has worked up attractively adorns her portrait of this mistress and mother, drinker and lecturer. Archeology brings a wealth of metaphors and incidental illuminations to the book, and in a sense informs its very structure; we have less a plot than a lode of prose and description, through which, as he reads, the reader digs down toward some underlying message about kinship, ancestry, vitality, and life's meaning. An ingenious interlocking of academic disciplines broadens and unifies the terrain of significance. (p. 88)

The moments in "The Realms of Gold" that do not feel trivial tend to be those showing women alone: in hotel rooms, in suburban living rooms, in isolated cottages, wherever they are removed from the clutter of men and mating and freed to concentrate upon the silent solemn tasks—cooking and childrearing, withstanding pain and depression—that seem to be their essence.... English critics have already remarked, with raised eyebrows, [Miss Drabble's] fiction's concern with motherhood; she has here broadened her family to include all the earth, described geologically, topologically, archeologically, botanically (her background of vegetation is luxuriant and precise). Her love scenes take place in the mud; Karel and Frances gravitate to ditches, and in the end fall into one. Along with this earth-sense goes a naturalistic pessimism—"there never was a golden world, there was never anything but toil and subsistence, cruelty and dullness"—and something inchoate and defiantly, jauntily casual about the organization of at least this novel. The conversations, the dinner parties, the conferences (all trendy, flirtatious, and desultory) feel superficial, perhaps because they appear so to the author—a crust over the earthy realities.... Deeper than its scattered, diffident surface as a novel of manners, "The Realms of Gold" celebrates the human as a department of the natural. (pp. 89-90)

> *John Updike, "Drabbling in the Mud," in* The New Yorker *(© 1976 by The New Yorker Magazine, Inc.), January 12, 1976, pp. 88-90.*

The best drawn of Margaret Drabble's characters have lives of their own; they are unpredictable, and they are believable. Their limits are those of their author. The female characters are treated in greater depth than the males, the males tend to be seen through female eyes, and when an effort is made [in *The Realms of Gold*] to get inside a male character—David the geologist—the result is one-dimensional and wishy-washy; we see him in nothing like the same relief. (We are taken into a ladies' lavatory with Frances, but modesty forbids a woman novelist from going inside a gents'.) Although there are some distracting and, I believe, mistaken distancing devices in the narrative, the author's resting-place in the book is in the consciousness of her main character, Frances. We are given Frances's history, feelings, perceptions and opinions in profuse detail, in so much detail, in fact, that one longs for a little reticence, for some sense of economy of means, for a meaning to be given through the narrative rather than simply being stated. It is a narrative eye with a wide-angle lens, getting in all the peripheral goings-on which make for naturalism. The result is ... a novel not unpleasingly old-fashioned in its methods, a novel which means to be read and enjoyed and understood; but in the last resort, I feel, it is not a novel which breaks new ground for its author. (p. 70)

> *James Price, in* Encounter *(© 1976 by Encounter Ltd.), February, 1976.*

"It is interesting," wrote Charles Darwin at the end of The

Origin of Species, "to contemplate a tangled bank, clothed with many plants of all kinds, with birds singing on the bushes, with various insects flitting about, and with worms crawling the damp earth, and to reflect that these elaborately constructed forms, so different from each other, and dependent on each other in so complex a manner, have all been produced by laws acting around us. ..." ...

[To] my knowledge no novelist, certainly no comic novelist, has taken [*The Origin of Species*] and the image [of the tangled bank] so explicitly for text as has Margaret Drabble. She does not quote the passage directly ...—remarkable restraint for someone who calls on Shakespeare, Milton, Wordsworth, Arnold, Clare, Shaw, T. S. Eliot, and Darwin himself with far too much EngLit facility—yet it is the invisible epigraph for an ambitious work whose theme is nothing less than the survival of the human species.

Drabble has been preoccupied with the subject ever since the heroine of her second novel, *The Garrick Year,* concluded: "I, being different, and being what I am, am made for survival." ...

Drabble's women usually decide in the end not to act against their natures, but most of them take some time to discover just what their natures are. Frances Wingate, the much traveled archeologist in *The Realms of Gold,* already knows hers, and it is a formidable force: She has "amazing qualities of survival and adaptation." (p. 17)

Given Drabble's rich descriptions of physical and social landscapes, and her capacity to entertain, it may be churlish to predict that *The Realms of Gold* will become dated before any of her earlier, smaller books. It is not the mod extensions of '70s London—where people "chat people up"—but the book's earnest received wisdom, its academicism, that makes it old before its time.... The realms of gold in Keats' poems were literary of course, and so are they—too literary by half—in this novel.

Traditions, received ideas, are not so much criticized here as simply assimilated into conventions of the novel and life. The confrontations between people become formulaic.... (pp. 18-19)

With the intrusive narrative voice, another natural law seems to be in effect: The wider the range and the longer the perspective, the greater the chance of banality. Drabble is far better when she shows than when she talks and tells. The discussions of survival and adaptation, of Freud, of psychology in general, of the Woman Question, are generally trite, although Drabble captures down to the last crumb of the baby's Weetabix the damp life of a trapped young housewife....

Still, Drabble is a natural-born storyteller, always delivering the party after the preparations, the reunion after the separation, the funeral after the death. The pleasures to be found here and there in *The Realms of Gold* make me hope that in her next work she will forsake her reach and return to the grasp she has long secured. (p. 19)

> *Ruth Mathewson, "A Tangled Bank," in* The New Leader *(© 1976 by the American Labor Conference on International Affairs, Inc.), April 26, 1976, pp. 17-19.*

The Realms of Gold is Miss Drabble's seventh novel, and she is enormously comfortable in her role of storyteller. At first glance she seems almost to be a throwback, a female Rip Van Winkle who slept through the clever things that

James and Joyce and all the others taught us. She intrudes herself into her own narrative as shamelessly as Thackeray, but as one comes to see, she knows the new techniques as well and pulls them out when they are needed. Miss Drabble's main character is an archaeologist named Frances Wingate, a figure of such splendid dimensions that she dominates the novel totally: she is the star around which all else revolves. (p. 119)

In its basic delineations *The Realms of Gold* is a sort of modern picaresque: it wanders over England, the continent, Africa; characters interesting in themselves but often of no significance to the major action are introduced, exploited, and allowed to fall from view, their ultimate fates of no consequence to the author or reader. But there is art at work here, and the larger sense of history, of the cycles of civilizations that Frances Wingate possesses as an archaeologist, informs and deepens the changes and absurdities and small tragedies of modern existence. (pp. 119-20)

[The] serious moments toward the end of the story, the introduction of mortality near the climax, enhance the comic resolution, the world brought right at last. Miss Drabble writes with remarkable candor. Cry here, she seems to be telling us, laugh now. This is a dangerous way to go about things, but her light touch and the enormous energy that infuses her writing carry her through. (p. 120)

> *Walter Sullivan, in* Sewanee Review *(reprinted by permission of the editor, © 1977 by The University of the South), Winter, 1977.*

* * *

DUBERMAN, Martin   1930-

American playwright, essayist, and editor, Duberman is best known for his plays which combine fact with fiction, as, for example, the documentary *In White America* or the quasi-biographical *Visions of Kerouac*. (See also *Contemporary Authors*, Vols. 1-4, rev. ed.)

In White America [is] a documentary of the Negro's trek through the jungle of white American injustice (and occasional decency), from his arrival here to this very day which is, if not a day, at least a dawn. From letters, journals, journalistic accounts, trial records, and similar sources, Martin B. Duberman has assembled a piece of history that makes good theater because it is true, interesting and overwhelmingly important. And it is theater—even if not art—in the best sense: moving, funny, humane, genuine and, best of all, unflaggingly provocative, coming as it does from sources most of us would always have been unaware of, and the worse off for it. (pp. 36-7)

> *John Simon, in his* Uneasy Stages: A Chronicle of the New York Theater, 1963-1973 *(copyright © 1975 by John Simon; reprinted by permission of Random House, Inc.), Random House, 1975.*

The life, as seen by Martin Duberman in his fine new play, *Visions of Kerouac* . . . is a moving and disturbing one. Duberman has changed the names of Kerouac's colleagues (Allen Ginsberg becomes Irwin Goldbrook, Gregory Corso becomes Raphael Urso), but the raw life is there; the testaments of poets stoned on physical love, on hard and soft drugs, on America, on raw literature, on spiritual journeys to the East are all vividly there. . . . [The] play, at its best, is like a series of kicks from a high-strung horse. . . .

The play has its mannerisms; there is some windy writing, but it is that rare thing in today's theatre—it's alive. In its gut and its head. (p. 110)

> *Arthur Sainer, in* The Village Voice *(reprinted by permission of* The Village Voice; *copyright © by The Village Voice, Inc., 1976), December 20, 1976.*

Martin Duberman's didactic play [*Visions of Kerouac*] uses Kerouac's life and world, as he wrote about them, to prove that Kerouac was a man who suffered and died because he was unable to express sexually his love for his male friends, and claims that he was emblematic of the Beats and the counterculture they established: this, too, is a simplification.

There are two difficulties: the basic idea is reductive, and it's reductively expressed on stage. However seriously Duberman may be attempting to reinterpret the sexual doubts, fears, and ambiguities of that period—let alone the whole fabric of a major cultural upheaval—he fails. Intellectually, because he relies on a very partial theory; artistically, because he uses a tensionless and sentimental episodic form, and as a historian (and he is, when not writing drama, a distinguished historian) because his primary source is Kerouac's own novels. (p. 110)

But it's not true that Kerouac typifies those days. He reflected and popularized the ideas of his heroes, while originating only the subjective slap-dash style of his own sentences. The movers, those he wrote about, don't fit Duberman's thesis: Burroughs and Ginsberg were accepted (by themselves and their friends) as homosexual; others in the play (Snyder, Corso) were heterosexual; probably most people, then as now, occasionally made love across their "preference," for reasons of affection or loneliness. It was a sexy subculture, though not easy for women; and Kerouac's discomfort in it was quite personal.

The play ignores the religious, poetic, ecological, and political ideas of the Beats, who activated almost every counter-cultural notion that has fermented over the past 15 years. They were serious, knowing, brave, intellectual. Kerouac, however, lacked imagination and wrote only about people he knew and events that happened in his presence. Being simple, he described complex issues and people simplistically. In real life, the men he idolized could write and think rings around him. Duberman seems to have relied on Kerouac's portraits for hs characterizations; as his own style is flat and obvious, without Kerouac's vigor, the stage is stalked by cartoon phantoms about whom one is only sure that they never had the spirit to write *Howl* or *Bomb* or *Naked Lunch*.

Kerouac is similarly diminished. In his books he has a lumbering, melancholy, lovable self; he's a kind of prose bear among the poet foxes and butterflies, as well as an ascetic though lapsing Christian mystic. Egocentric, too—but not characteristically so self-pitying as in this play's repeated line: "Oh, what am I doing here, is there some way I am supposed to feel?" (pp. 110-11)

The often paradoxical, complicated relations of macho, misogyny, and homosexuality are diminished here. In his volume of collected plays, *Male Armor*, Duberman uses Reich's concept of character armor (though Reich was violently anti-homosexual) to investigate the question: "What does it mean to be a 'man'?" His answer: it means being a homosexual man. The one woman in these plays whom the playwright, according to his introduction, thinks of as "changing" and "generous" arranges for her husband to become a male whore, and, when he takes to the work more enthusiastically than she expected, tells him she's pregnant, wishes him well, and exits tearfully. In all respects except the man's job she's like one of the beatniks' barefoot broads. In *Visions of Kerouac,* the portrayal of Kerouac's lover Ruthie is meek and simpy compared to that Kerouac drew in his own work: and the mother he seemed wholeheartedly to adore turns weirdly Jewish and, at the end, horrible and demanding.

Duberman ends up using the same evidence to prove Kerouac's repressed gayness that a biased heterosexual would muster: he feared women and thought they were stupid, was celibate for long periods, alternated misogyny and idealization, hung around with gay men, idolized macho men, drank too much, was poetical and sensitive, loved his mother, and had a sentimental overwrought prose style. If a straight critic used these aspects of Kerouac's character as proof of gayness, she (or he) would justly be accused of simple-minded stereotyping.

In his novels, at least the ones I have on hand, Kerouac talks about his affection for his gay friends, his rejection of gayness for himself, and his love and fear of women. . . . I don't know why Duberman should spin a theory when there's a web of meaning like that available. (p. 111)

> *Erika Munk, in* The Village Voice *(reprinted by permission of* The Village Voice; *copyright © by The Village Voice, Inc. 1976), December 20, 1976.*

*   *   *

DUHAMEL, Georges   1884-1966

A French novelist, essayist, short story writer, playwright, and poet, Duhamel is a seriously neglected writer (outside of France) whose novel sequence *Salavin* is a classic of world literature. Duhamel's outstanding characteristics are his compassionate understanding of society's outcasts and his psychological depth. His simple and lucid writing is enriched by an abundance of strikingly original metaphors and infusions of warm humor. It is Duhamel's humor, in fact, which tempers an essentially tragic view of humanity. Dostoevski was an obvious influence, while today's existentialists might well claim Salavin as a forerunner of the modern anti-hero found in the works of Camus and Sartre. Duhamel has written under the pseudonym Denis Thevenin. (See also *Contemporary Authors*, obituary, Vols. 25-28, rev. ed.)

Georges Duhamel enjoyed the advantage of clear prose and an apparently effortless and smooth narrative, which designated him as the successor to Anatole France. His work, however, wore thin after he had drawn on his war experience and on his postwar vision of men bound by friendship and a kindly desire to rebuild a better world. His long and facile saga-novel, *Chronique des Pasquier,* in spite of occasional charm and freshness, fails to hold the attention of readers; Duhamel's one determined attempt to renovate his inspiration, after World War II, with *Le Voyage de Patrice Périot* (1951) resulted in an unconvincing picture of a doctor's family torn by ideological feuds and of naïve scientists becoming the playthings of political exploiters. These novels start auspiciously and are delineated in pleasing and precise outlines, displaying a gift for draftsmanship, which has become a rarity nowadays. They breathe a human warmth that is also rare in the pessimistic literature of our

age. But they fail to expand and to be sustained to the end by sufficient creative fire. It is sad to nourish an author's energy more persistently than pity and love. (p. 46)

Duhamel tempers his picture of man with humor. His sentimentality is closer to the tragic kind that is found in Russian fiction. His characters lay their hearts bare with humility and a passion for abject confession of their weaknesses and sins; but they do not revel in it with the pride of sinners who wish to unbosom their secrets so as to make room for more sins in their unburdened souls.

The lifelong concern of Duhamel, apparent in all his essays, reminiscences, and novels, is one that he shared with Charles Péguy, Romain Rolland, Jules Romains, and other writers of his period: an idealistic impulse to save men. Duhamel, like young Péguy, then an unbeliever, turned all his meditations around the categorical imperative inspired by Joan of Arc: 'One must save.' But save whom? For men are stubbornly reluctant to be saved. . . . Duhamel smiles at the men and women whom he wants to continue loving in spite of themselves. He is not blind to the disappointments that an optimist must endure, and all his novels display the gradual collapse of a rosy dream. He will not seek a solution in an easy catchword, tendered by Christianity, which he respected but never professed, or in science, which he always admired, though he was aware of its limitations. Friendship is the feeling of which he spoke most nobly (in *Deux Hommes* especially); like Romains, Vildrac, and later Malraux and Saint-Exupéry, he would have liked to build a virile and warm regeneration of mankind upon friendship, that is, upon the most beautiful of all words and ideals proposed by humanism and by Christianity—fraternity. (p. 48)

> *Henri Peyre, in his* French Novelists of Today *(copyright © 1967 by Oxford University Press, Inc.; reprinted by permission), Oxford University Press-Galaxy, 1967.*

Though his novels are mainly concerned with the adventures of individuals supposedly seen in terms of their situation in the twentieth century, the climate of Duhamel's work is clearly related to the traditional values and beliefs of a pre-World War I "petite bourgeoisie"; this may explain both its wide appeal and its fundamental insignificance in the development of the novel. Duhamel's humanism is sincere and his concern with the frustrations and joys of the man in the street is real, but the rather facile sentimentality of his approach, the naïve ethical evangelism of his attitude, based on vague spiritual values, hamper the creative artist he might have been. The long list of his essays and articles, their monotony and increasing self-righteousness, reveal Duhamel's intellectual limitations. (p. 63)

"Georges Duhamel or the Bourgeois Saved" is the apt title of a critical essay on Duhamel. The bourgeois may or may not need salvation, but his salvation as a bourgeois is not a very potent theme in a novel. Duhamel's faith in the values of honesty, affection, hard work, art, selflessness and devotion to humanity is above reproach, as is also his faith in the capacity of individuals to achieve ethical and spiritual greatness. He wants to put his readers into contact with those realities. But Duhamel's so-called realism moves out of the realm of objectivity. Ethical judgments are given as facts and a personal moral view as an objective truth. It is actually a form of personal idealism that imposes its limitations on the novelist. It rejects, a priori, whole segments of human experience, just as Duhamel rejects our mechanically conditioned age. Busily engaged now in putting old wine into old bottles, Duhamel becomes increasingly conventional. His books, after the Salavin cycle [*Vie et aventures de Salavin* (1920-32)], lack that generous and total involvement in life that characterizes the living novel. In a sense Duhamel is the Anatole France of his generation, but a France in whom earnestness has displaced whimsicality. The violence of the times proved too powerful for Duhamel to cope with. (pp. 66-7)

> *Germaine Brée and Margaret (Otis) Guiton, in their* An Age of Fiction: The French Novel from Gide to Camus *(copyright © 1957 by Rutgers, The State University; reprinted by permission of the Rutgers University Press), Rutgers, 1957 (and reprinted as* The French Novel: From Gide to Camus, *Harcourt, 1962).*

As a short-story writer Duhamel donned his magnifying lenses, sharpened all the tools at his disposal which would help him observe his surroundings more accurately, and became a devotee of *le mot juste*. In each of his stories, he first outlined the situation in general, then set about filling out the various phases of the action. Uppermost, however, were the characters. These were pertinently described, in short, pithy sentences. Exteriors were focused upon first; then the surgeon-writer reached deeply into the interior of his creatures and, from there, viewed the world about him, discovering a more profound and meaningful reality: "This region of reality has its believers, of which I am one. It can even boast of having its fanatics, which I prefer not to be." Once the characters had come into full view, they lived their existence boldly or fitfully, pitifully or cruelly, according to their natures and environments.

Duhamel . . . was particularly interested in studying the human heart in its most sordid, cruel, and tender aspects. His vision of human suffering, noted in his war books, is again brought to the fore in his short stories, but in a different manner, frequently through satire and irony. He displays, moreover, a great flair for building suspense, a talent for creating an atmosphere of fright and awe. These devices were virtually unnecessary in his war books, since the subject itself was sufficiently horrendous and gruesome.

The title, *The Abandoned Men (Les Hommes abandonnés)* (1921), which Duhamel chose for his first volume of short stories, is indeed apt. The men whose lives he depicts and etches so forcefully on paper are all "abandoned" souls, rejected by society in some way, incapable of relating to others, solitary, inexplicably aggressive and introverted. . . . They are, for the most part, either evil in intent or the victims of some cruel act. . . . What is of extreme interest . . . is Duhamel's preoccupation, in this period, with questions of *evil*. (pp. 80-1)

Stylistically speaking, Duhamel's talent for storytelling is never better displayed than in *The Abandoned Men*. The humble lives of ordinary people are dramatized with objectivity yet with great warmth, but the treatment is never maudlin, even under the most gruesome of circumstances. The contrast in personalities, as well as the nature descriptions which frequently mirror the characters of the protagonists, make for powerful effects. (p. 81)

Literary endeavors are to be based on real-life experiences, Duhamel suggested, this being the only authentic manner of writing. The world, filled with infinite mysteries, is rich enough, he maintained, to be an eternal source of nourishment for the creative mind. Reality, however, must not be presented as is; it must be offered readers with artistry, sobriety, and reserve. Duhamel further elaborated: everything introduced into a novel must be related and intertwined and must create a type of *fondu* from its disparate parts, of which truth becomes the alpha and omega of the entire work. A literary endeavor must grow like a tree, have a solid foundation, give off strong shoots which eventually grow into firm and beautiful branches.

Duhamel never set down any detailed techniques for writing. Each author, he believed, must find his own reality and express it in simple and forceful terms. Prose, he intimated, should follow the rhythms of respiration, and since each writer is possessed of his own mechanism and personality, his work will have its own individual tempo. The sound of prose must likewise be varied, as is its meter. Tonal structure should include the variegated ranges implicit in the human voice. Prose, consequently, must possess the differences present in nature as well as its measured harmonies.

The Prince of Jaffar (Le Prince de Jaffar) (1924) is a work difficult to categorize. Strictly speaking, it is not a novel, nor is it an essay or a travelogue. It has the trademarks of each of these types. In it Duhamel relates, with clarity and objectivity, his impressions of Tunisia and the influences that country has undergone. (pp. 83-4)

Duhamel's intention is not to underline the differences existing between Occidental and Oriental civilizations but rather to depict man and his customs as he observes them, both outwardly and inwardly. When watching a veiled woman walk about the marketplace, for example, or a man in a burnoose, Duhamel leads his reader on—ever so gently—to examine the inner realm, thoughts, beliefs, the very souls of these people. (p. 84)

Duhamel succeeds in arousing his reader's interest through his sensitive portrayals of so many types ranging from the penurious to those wallowing in luxury and joy. His local-color tones, his images so sharply incised, enhance the meaning and flavor of this volume. It might be added that Duhamel's compassion, as always, comes to the fore, in his feelings of pity for the suffering and his anger directed at the oppressors who take advantage—everywhere and at all periods—of the less fortunate, the weak, and the ignorant. (p. 85)

What stands out most vividly in this novel is Duhamel's ability to depict his protagonist's feelings of solitude in terms of nature. . . .

Though *Horeb's Stone* is in many ways autobiographical since it describes Duhamel's own school days, his work in the laboratory, his rapport with his co-workers and co-students, it gives, nevertheless, an impression of artificiality at certain times. A contrived tone is most apparent when dealing with love episodes. Duhamel seems hampered, even prudish, when trying to depict feelings of love and sensuality. This may be due to his lack of experience in writing about this aspect of life. Because he fails to yield to a spirit of abandon, the novel as a whole is marred and does not seem authentic.

The Stormy Night (La Nuit d'Orage) (1928) which varies considerably from Duhamel's previous novel, is one of his most fascinating works up to this time. It is exotic in nature and, because of the excitement it generates, it brings to mind Théophile Gautier's *The Romance of the Mummy* and Balzac's *Wild Ass's Skin (La Peau de Chagrin)*. More than titillating the senses and the imagination, however,

The Stormy Night dramatizes a certain psychological state which we refer to today as psychosomatic illness. (p. 86)

The essay form . . . served Duhamel well. It became a splendid vehicle for his biting irony, satire, and jocularity. (p. 88)

Whether Duhamel levels his sarcasms at orators, who are so narcissistic as to have become infatuated with their own voices; or at those who are overly gullible and believe anything and everything, falling victim, thereby, to the stentorian voices of self-proclaimed gods; or at those who are convinced that life's problems can be answered with simple formulas and so succumb immediately to various political groups (whether leftist or rightist), without applying reason and logic to their attitude—his slings and arrows always penetrate deeply. (pp. 88-9)

Though the literary and scientific world always attracted Duhamel, he never once forgot his war experiences. These had so traumatized him that they had altered his entire attitude toward life. Indeed, he felt that the horrendous aspects of the war—as gruesome and painful as they might be—should be kept before the public's eye. He was convinced that torture, blood, gore could be instrumental in helping pacifists such as he to avert another conflagration. Who would want to suffer? Who would want to inflict pain? For this reason, every now and then, Duhamel produced a work treating of the war and its aftermath. Let man contemplate his own destructive side, the devastation he has wrought, then perhaps he will work for peace.

In *The Last Seven Wounds* (*Les Sept dernières plaies*) (1928), Duhamel takes his readers back to the World War I periods, to a hospital at the front where he had been a surgeon. He recounts, with an irony and a bitterness tinged with pathos—always with extreme understanding—certain case histories. . . . (p. 89)

Duhamel . . . was never one-sided. Whenever depicting the sordid aspects of modern society or humanity in general, he always counterbalanced his literary endeavor with its opposite, man's eternal search for serenity, his notions of joy and well-being. Duhamel, who reacted so deeply to the beauties of nature, responded equally forcefully to the canvases of Maurice de Vlaminck. He appreciated the turbulence and the violence which his friend, Vlaminck, injected into his landscapes, and noted these in an essay, *Vlaminck* (1927). (p. 90)

Scenes from the Life of the Future is probably the most violent attack on overcommercialization and overindustrialization that Duhamel ever wrote. It was completed shortly after he had returned from a brief visit to the United States (1928), a visit which included stops at New Orleans, Chicago, New York, and several other cities. In many respects this anti-American diatribe, as many people have labeled it, is quite a superficial work in that there is no attempt to evaluate the positive and negative accomplishments of a young people. Furthermore, it reveals an utter skimpiness of knowledge of both the country and its inhabitants. (p. 92)

Duhamel began the cycle of the Pasquier family in 1933 and terminated it, ten volumes later, in 1944. Though he invented nothing new in terms of structure, his work remains fascinating because he succeeded in enticing his readers into the heart of a bourgeois milieu. There, he permits each of the individuals to burgeon forth, to develop, and at the same time to beguile or anger the reader who is forever re-

sponding to the various acts, ideas, longings, and quixotic antics presented him. With extreme simplicity and dexterity, Duhamel depicts the workings, both psychological and intellectual, of each member of the Pasquier family. These characters are never static, but rather evolve as they normally would in the workaday world—positively or negatively. Duhamel does not describe a character just once and then permit him to vanish. Rather, he proceeds in an impressionistic manner. Each time the reader confronts a certain personality, the descriptions are slightly altered, depending upon who views the protagonists, as well as upon the action involved. In this manner Duhamel succeeds in creating a feeling of fleeting time, of life as in a state of flux.

Duhamel ushers his reader into an everyday world, in which *feelings* are uppermost. Though the author is the supreme manipulator of his characters, they seem to move according to their own dictates. Duhamel never compels them into one path or forces them to adopt a certain and intransigent point of view. On the contrary, one feels that they are free individuals in their own right, that the author experiences their pathos, anguish, anger, moods of all types. Their daily life, therefore, becomes accessible to the reader through a variety of techniques adopted by the author: portraits, analyses, dialogues, descriptions, and narrative devices. Scenes are frequently described in order to lure the reader into a state of direct participation. He then considers the event in question, in terms of his own world; the characters' *presence,* both visual and psychological, conveys within him the impression of actuality. (pp. 104-05)

The Notary from Le Havre is a tightly woven work. Every aspect of this novel—from the fleeting descriptions of friends and neighbors to the family scenes, from the outer world of matter to the inner realm of feeling, from the rueful to the hilarious situations—is dexterously connected to the body of the saga. There is not one extraneous element to mar the general pattern drawn by the author. (p. 106)

There is another important protagonist in this novel: the city of Paris. Duhamel had brought this city to life in the Salavin series, thereby forming an important nucleus for the novel. He does likewise for the Pasquier works. The city thus becomes an intrinsic part of the Pasquiers' daily existence. The tortuous streets and avenues with their particularly pungent odors take on a life of their own as do the dismal parks and their shabby trees and stunted bushes. The various domiciles of the Pasquiers' also emerge as living beings—the Impasse Vandame, for example, with its lower bourgeois families, and the many abodes into which they are forever moving, both comfortable and distressingly small, sunny and dismal. Paris, as described by Duhamel, imposes itself in an utterly human manner upon the reader. (p. 108)

The Garden of the Savage Beasts [1934] is primarily a drama of adolescence. It describes the pain a young lad [Laurent Pasquier] experiences when first confronted with the world about him, when just emerging from the protective realm of innocence and childhood into the *imprévu* world at large, filled with ugliness and terror. "The world order was imperiled and my position in the heart of this world, perturbed; it seemed rather frightening." (p. 109)

Duhamel's detailed account of [Laurent's sister] Cécile's performance of a Mozart sonata is not only accurately transcribed, but the sensitivity and the impression the notes make upon Laurent as he listens is most unusually portrayed. All the senses, including the visual, are aroused.

Duhamel infuses the reader with his own sentiments concerning music: that it is beyond description, that it nourishes and is a faithful companion at all moments of life, in joy as well as in sorrow.

One is always impressed in Duhamel's novels with his great feeling for nature in all of its phases. His finely etched portraits of clouds, as they move their massive hulks to and fro, of a solitary leaf, of the sounds emanating from foliage, from the onrush of water, those which cajole or jar the ear —all are imbued with depth and feeling. Indeed, the opening paragraph of *The Garden of the Savage Beasts,* a description of fish imprisoned in an aquarium, might accurately synthesize or symbolize everything that will transpire during the course of the novel. The Pasquiers are looked upon as a microcosm of the world, prisoners within its fold.

> Exiled from native sands, captives in some glass aquarium, at the bottom of a laboratory . . . the small coastal animals continue, by means of a secret warning, to obey the rhythms of the tide, descending at floodtide, rising when the ebb uncovers the distant coast.   (p. 112)

A View of the Promised Land, [1934, third volume of the Pasquier story] is centered around Laurent's glimpse of the promised land, that is, of independence and maturity. With infinite finesse, it recounts his inner struggles, his development, and his final break with his adolescent world and the subservient existence he has previously lived out vis-à-vis his family. . . . (p. 113)

The fourth volume in this series, *Saint John's Eve (La Nuit de la Saint-Jean)* (1935), is narrated by Justin Weill. A victim of World War I, he has left a diary which his mother finds and sends on to Laurent. After certain changes, the manuscript is published. . . .

Saint John's Eve is probably the least interesting of the Pasquier series. There is little or no development of personality but rather a restatement of what we already know concerning the protagonists. . . . (p. 115)

The remainder of the characters introduced in this volume seem contrived, as though especially invited to [Laurent's brother] Joseph's home in order to hurt Laurent even further. None is sharply delineated nor sympathetic in any way. (p. 116)

It is Duhamel's extraordinary ability to re-create the excitement of youth—the ardor, the passion to succeed, even the disillusionment—which makes for the interest of [*The Bièvres Desert* (1937)]. With great tenderness, coupled with feelings of nostalgia and whimsy, Duhamel recounts the step-by-step change which each of the protagonists experiences. "We want to restore purity," they say. "Manual labor is in a way a type of sacred law." (pp. 118-19)

[*The Masters'* (1937)] main theme is the portrayal of the dichotomy existing between two types of individuals: the cold, rational and objective scientist who thinks only in terms of his work and not the people involved [personified in the character of Laurent's superior, Rohner]; and the other type, which includes objective but tender and understanding workers who are involved in humanity's problems [personified by the scientist Chalgrin].

Duhamel attempts and succeeds in examining both types of men, who exist not only in scientific groups but in all walks of life. (p. 119)

[In *Cecile Among Us* (1938), as in Duhamel's work as a whole,] music is such an intense experience, such an integral part of his being, that [Duhamel] translates or transposes the effect of these tonal modulations in terms of his own senses and ideas: the notes caress his soul; they gnaw at his vitals; they soothe or arouse him as the case may be; they inflame or bring forth feelings of pathos, despondency —even anger. It is through music that both Duhamel and his characters, Laurent most particularly in this volume, are transported into another world, a realm of infinite beauty—and also sorrow. The manner in which Duhamel recounts the transition from the musical note to the emotion is valuable and meaningful. (p. 122)

The Struggle Against Shadows [1939] takes us into a world thoroughly familiar to Duhamel: that of the laboratory. In this instance, he takes an intransigent attitude and speaks forth clearly through Laurent. Scientists devoted to their professions, he maintains, should not become involved with any political group. Their lives should be devoted to science. There is no room in any laboratory for a political appointee interested merely in self-aggrandizement, in ego-building. The researcher's task is to help humanity as a whole; he should, therefore, be above the petty concerns of routine living and move steadily toward the scientific goal he has set for himself. In a way, the laboratory in *The Struggle Against Shadows* is comparable to the community described in *The Bièvres Desert*, in which each individual is dedicated to some artistic endeavor. The outstanding difference, however, is that the material problems of those working in a laboratory are taken care of, whereas in *The Bièvres Desert* these arose to plague the group. The scientist is concerned with the application of methods and the work involved. (p. 123)

Though interesting in the main for broaching the problem of a girl in love with the theatre, there is remarkably little suspense in [*Suzanne and the Young Men*]. The characters are not drawn in depth, the action is repetitive and tedious. The idyllic situation depicted has already been created and more forcefully in *The Bièvres Desert*. . . . It is more a subjective recounting of Duhamel's ideal than a well constructed novel. . . .

Joseph Pasquier's Passion (La Passion de Joseph Pasquier) (1944), the last of the Pasquier series, analyzes Joseph's world and his downfall. (p. 124)

In this final volume of the Pasquiers, Duhamel is in the process of tying all the strings together. A sense of doom and futility reigns in the novel. Laurent stands out as the only one who has found true happiness in life and in his work. Joseph, who has spent his years amassing a fortune, gathers nothing more into his orbit than problems. (p. 125)

Certainly the writing of these ten volumes was a fulfilling experience for Duhamel, perhaps even more satisfying than the Salavin group. With the latter, Duhamel's range had been sharply restricted: one main character, his foibles and development; a series of peripheral characters who appeared most frequently in one volume and disappeared as rapidly thereafter. The central anecdotes were also limited in scope, since Salavin's abilities were far from varied. The Pasquier volumes, on the contrary, take the reader into various métiers and trades, several strata of society, which are all described in detail, as is every member of the Pasquier family. Moreover, Duhamel introduces absolutely intriguing [peripheral characters] who are drawn with depth and finesse. In this manner the author could better express his own ideas concerning science, politics, literature, the theater, music, and children.

Though Duhamel had his own social and moral code, the Pasquier series cannot really be looked upon as "thesis" novels. Quite true, Duhamel denigrated the materialism of anyone who, like Joseph, believed money to be the *sine qua non* of life; he believed fervently in honor and integrity as virtues capable of bringing one fulfillment and happiness; he was certain that love and kindness, man's most admirable gifts, should be central to one's relationships throughout life. Yet he did not fly the banner of the "thesis" novel as did Emile Zola and the Goncourt brothers. Duhamel's intention was limited in this respect to the creation of a family and the dramatization of its course through life. . . . (pp. 126-27)

> *Bettina L. Knapp, in her* Georges Duhamel *(copyright 1972 by Twayne Publishers, Inc.; reprinted with the permission of Twayne Publishers, A Division of G. K. Hall & Co., Boston), Twayne, 1972.*

* * *

DURRELL, Lawrence   1912-

Durrell is an Indian-born English novelist, poet, translator, travel writer, playwright, and critic. His works reflect his love for the Mediterranean: the Cyclades, Egypt, and Cyprus are among the settings used in his verse. He is known as a poet of "place"; his sensuous imagery is some of the finest in modern poetry. Durrell has written under the pseudonyms Charles Norden and Gaffer Peeslake. (See also *CLC*, **Vols. 1, 4, 6, and** *Contemporary Authors*, **Vols. 9-12, rev. ed.)**

Once upon a time the first words of a story used to be "Once upon a time." But these are the last words, or almost the last words, of Lawrence Durrell's "Alexandria Quartet," which suggests that we may have come to the end of a literary cycle, or rather to the beginning of a new loop in the spiral of literary history. You remember the passage which closes "Clea," the last volume of the "Quartet":

> Yes, one day I found myself writing down with trembling fingers the four words (four letters! four faces!) with which every storyteller since the world began has staked his slender claim to the attention of his fellow men. Words which presage simply the old story of an artist coming of age. I wrote: "Once upon a time. . . ."
>
> And I felt as if the whole universe had given me a nudge!

In reading the passage we feel very strongly a kind of duality which pervades Durrell's work: we are pulled in the direction of the primitive by those four magical words and by the description of the artist as a mere story-teller, but we are also made aware of the modernity of the work; we are pulled in the direction of the sophisticated by the preoccupation of the passage with the art of story-telling. Like so many modern works, this is a portrait of the artist, a Künstler Roman, about a character in a book who is writing a book in which he is a character. And the shades of Proust and Gide, among others, hover between our eyes and the page. What is new in Durrell, however, is neither the primitive nor the sophisticated but his peculiar combination of the two. (p. 411)

[The "Alexandria Quartet"] is wild, exotic, romantic. Yet its main interest is not life, but art. It is really a little essay in esthetics, presented in the form of a dramatic scene. It reminds us of the moments in "Don Quixote" when there is a pause in the adventures of the Knight of the Mournful Countenance to allow for a literary discussion involving the Bachelor and the Curate or some passing stranger. And the resemblance is not a chance one. Cervantes' work was written as an anti-romance, and became, via Fielding and Smollett in English tradition, a major ancestor of a new literary form—the novel. Durrell's work, as the passage quoted above indicates, is an anti-novel in the same sense as Cervantes' work was an anti-romance. Both men were faced with a constricting literary tradition and revolted against it. (p. 412)

Durrell's revolt is not an isolated and magnificent gesture of defiance to an entrenched and flourishing literary tradition. The tradition he finds thin and constricting is the very one started by Cervantes—the tradition which begins as anti-romance and gradually insists on more and more scientific treatment of life: the empirical tradition which in its theoretical formulations calls itself first realism and finally naturalism. . . . Lawrence Durrell is the heir of Proust. For it is Proust who explodes the empirical notions of characterization so essential to realistic and naturalistic fiction, by demonstrating the artificiality of the real and the reality of the artificial. (p. 413)

The "Alexandria Quartet" is alive with mirrors. The prismatic facets of character glitter, unreconciled, in our imaginations. Appearance and reality are continually confused, and the line between life and art is continually blurred. . . . What we took for fact in one volume is exposed as false in another, and the exposé itself is proved incorrect in the third. . . . [For] Durrell fiction is a whirling prism reflected in a liquifying mirror. . . . [In "Justine"] Durrell attempts on the one hand to establish in the reader's mind his version of the new, Proustian esthetic, and on the other to blur the line between the real and the artificial in order to make it harder for the reader to begin applying his disbelief, even if he refuses to suspend it. Durrell seeks to confuse and bewilder the reader, to separate him from his habitual reliance on probability and verisimilitude, so as to offer him something better. *Behold,* he as much as tells you, *you thought you could not walk without that crutch of realism. I tell you you can fly!* And he nearly convinces us that we can. Using the modern esthetic of Proust, and a narrative technique which, with its multiple narrators and dislocations of time, seems also typically modern, Durrell takes us on a journey—a magic carpet ride not only through space but through time as well—a return to Alexandria. (pp. 415-16)

The "Ethiopica," richest and most elaborate of the Greek romances, stands very much in the same relation to the Homeric epics as Durrell's "Quartet" does to such great realistic novels of the nineteenth century as "Anna Karenina" and "Middlemarch." Both the epics and the great realistic novels present events as ordered by an omniscient narrator whose controlling mind not only shapes the events but colors them and comments on them. But in Heliodorus much of the narrative is conveyed to us directly by characters in the story. Furthermore, Heliodorus is not content simply to imitate the "Odyssey" and have one man narrate much of his own tale. In the "Ethiopica" we have as many narrators as in the "Alexandria Quartet." Indeed, one of the first stories we are told, a brief résumé of her life by the heroine, turns out to be a tissue of falsehoods designed to deceive her captors (and also the reader, who only afterwards learns the truth). In the hands of Heliodorus the romance is characterized by a multiplicity of narrators and tales within tales like a sequence of Chinese boxes; by a consequent dislocation of the time scheme, as the narrative moves backwards and forwards from its beginning . . .; and by a fondness for elaborate set pieces of a spectacular nature, involving such things as battles, rituals, necromancy, and celebrations.

The general resemblance of the "Alexandria Quartet" to the "Ethiopica" should be obvious. Some of the action of the ancient story even takes place on the shores of Durrell's beloved Lake Mareotis. But the point is not that the resemblance indicates any direct indebtedness; rather, it is that the two works are so similar in spirit. Durrell is not so much a descendant of Heliodorus as a reincarnation of him in the twentieth century. When Durrell speaks of his characters in an interview as "puppets," he reminds us not only of Thackeray's insistence on the artificiality of literature but also of the way in which Heliodorus manipulates his characters in a virtuoso display of sustained and integrated form. And form, for Durrell, is nearly everything. . . . [There] can be little doubt that the spirit which presides over the "Alexandria Quartet" is Proust's. And in turning to Proust Durrell brought himself into contact with a tradition of sustained form which was fundamentally opposed to the "slice of life" technique characteristic of empirically oriented mimetic fiction. The tradition of elaborate form in fiction leads back through the romances of the seventeenth century to the European rediscovery of Heliodorus himself in the sixteenth, whose influence on the subsequent development of prose fiction can hardly be exaggerated.

Of course, the purely melodramatic side of the Greek romance has been greatly modified in its modern reincarnation. In the old romances the characters were mainly highly stylized extremes of virtue and vice, and the plot was always subservient to the decorum of poetic justice. In the "Alexandria Quartet" the characters and the prevailing ethos are as elaborate and complicated as the plot and the setting. The thinness of characterization which, for the modern reader, relegates the "Ethiopica" to that secondary level of works whose influence surpasses their interest would be inexcusable in a modern work of serious intent. But even richness of characterization, which we think of as a peculiarly modern attribute of fiction, has its roots in Alexandria. The Alexandrians and their followers, especially Ovid and the Greek romancers, introduced the arts of rhetoric into narrative literature. The combination of psychology and rhetoric, which characterizes the crucial monologue of Medea in the Third Book of the "Argonautica," works through Dido and the Ovidian lovers into the mainstream of narrative literature. . . . The novel may indeed be dying, but we need not fear for the future. Durrell and others are leading us in a renaissance of romance. (pp. 418-20)

> *Robert Scholes, "Return to Alexandria: Lawrence Durrell and Western Narrative Tradition," in* Virginia Quarterly Review *(copyright, 1964, by the* Virginia Quarterly Review, *The University of Virginia), Vol. 40, No. 3 (Summer 1964), pp. 411-20.*

The general appreciation of Lawrence Durrell's *Alexandria Quartet* has been blurred by discussions about the validity of the author's preface to *Balthazar*, the second volume of the quartet:

> Modern literature offers us no Unities, so I have turned to science and am trying to complete a four-decker novel whose form is based on the relativity proposition. . . .

So much attention has been focused upon Durrell's handling of the concepts of relativity and indeterminacy, upon his belief in the impossibility of communication, that his work has come to be regarded as solipsist. Yet in *The Alexandria Quartet,* key concepts such as the mutability of truth, the endless intercalation of realities, the disintegration of "the old stable ego of character", are counterbalanced by a search for transcendental values, by a belief in some basic (universal) harmony [, as he says in *Justine*]:

> Somewhere in the heart of experience there is an order and a coherence which we might surprise if we were attentive enough, loving enough, or patient enough.

The fact that the first three volumes of the quartet depict the gradual dissolution of everything stable might easily lead to the assumption that this dissolution is the very subject of the novels. Some critics have therefore been baffled by the unexpected change of emphasis in *Clea,* a novel that is purely affirmative in tone, and in which, by a curious shift of the plot, the tensions created in *Justine, Balthazar* and *Mountolive,* are resolved. This development, however, is not only justified, but almost imperative: the negatives through which the first three novels move constitute a preparatory stage necessary to the final discovery of a new, transcendental set of values, of "the order and coherence in the heart of experience". "The Negative Path" towards enlightenment, insight, and knowledge, is exemplified throughout the quartet. (pp. 134-35)

From one point of view *The Alexandria Quartet* is a *Bildungsroman.* Darley, the narrator in *Justine, Balthazar* and *Clea,* wants to become a writer. At the end of *Clea* his artistic faculties find full expression, and the tetralogy is, amongst other things, a record of this development. Art is one of the main themes in the quartet, and since, according to Durrell, "The theme of art is the theme of life itself", Darley's artistic development and his psychological growth are indissolubly linked. . . . Darley's record of the past is an attempt at establishing his own identity. . . . [We] should bear in mind that Durrell, who has made a thorough study of psychoanalytical theories, distinguishes between the "ego" and the "self". The former denotes the conscious part of man's personality, whereas the term "self" refers to the totality of the psyche and embraces both conscious and unconscious. Darley's search for his "proper self" is therefore an attempt at integrating his personality. . . . As the unconscious contents of the psyche can never be drawn up to the conscious level, Darley must needs confine himself to his "ego": he must understand all that consciousness yields in order to grasp the impact of the unknowable behind it.

The ego is the articulate part of the psyche, the field that has been domesticated by language; hence, in the last resort, it is a classifying entity, a "catalogue raisonné" which tends to impose a rationally conceived pattern upon life. As Darley penetrates further into his experiences in Alexandria, he is tormented by a sense of insufficiency, by a growing awareness of the relativity of the "reality" consciousness perceives. Even so-called absolutes are ambivalent; all motives, emotions, thoughts, judgments are relative and open to question. What troubles Darley most of all is the fact that human personality turns out to be basically unstable, volatile and merely potential, a "huge, disorganized and shapeless society of lusts and impulses". . . . This leads him to deny the possibility of attaining some unequivocal "truth": all our observations, interpretations, conclusions, are distorted by the limitations of our vision. There is no stable, tangible "reality" to be deduced from our observations, from "the classifications of the ego," for everything is perpetually moving, changing, and forever unattainable. . . . Darley's self-realization will not be complete until the end of *Clea*, and the atmosphere of utter uncertainty and ambiguity which permeates *Justine* and *Balthazar*, is essential to his further development. In this respect there is a very appropriate and illuminating phrase in Durrell's poem "Alexandria":

> As for me I now move
> Through many negatives to what I am.

(pp. 135-37)

It is interesting to note that, in *Clea*, Darley has become a "Knowbody" in the sense that he has reached a high degree of self-knowledge (though, in accordance with the pun, he has also become a "No-body" through the utter disorientation described in *Justine* and *Balthazar*). If we assume that "poetic illumination" now changes him into a "Sunbody", the phenomena depicted in [Jung's] *The Integration of the Personality* and [in] *Clea* appear to be strikingly alike. (pp. 138-39)

It should be noted that Darley reaches "poetic illumination" partly through his love for Clea. In *The Alexandria Quartet,* the sexual act is of the utmost significance, because the awakening of man to the mysterious substance behind ordinary experience, his growing awareness of the ubiquity and wholeness of life itself, is kindled by "the coupling which unites the male and female ends of knowledge merely—a cloud of unknowing". This is another paradox: heightened consciousness—always in the sense of awareness of the mystery—can be attained only through the partly, or even mainly "unconscious" knowledge disclosed by the sexual experience. . . . If we keep in mind that Durrell, in accordance with psychoanalytical theory, has tried to restore "the double-sexed Eros of Plato", it should be clear why love plays an essential part in Darley's search for his "proper self". (p. 140)

Obviously there is no place for [logic] in *The Alexandria Quartet,* where the intercalation of realities, the multiplicity of aspects and truths, are constantly emphasized and focused upon. . . . Since there is no single, "objective" kind of reality, the true meaning of life will always elude our most painstaking observations, mocking every effort to domesticate it in a system. For this reason, any kind of inquiry which aims at explaining, at classifying instead of understanding is rejected in the quartet. This also explains why the Cabal, and hermetic science in general, are held in high esteem throughout the four novels. (p. 141)

The experience of the "poetic illumination" is not recorded at once: if the artist (or the mystic) wants to recapture it in words, he must re-work it, and words are seldom adequate to the task. As, in *The Alexandria Quartet,* the "poetic illumination" becomes a sine qua non of art, it is not surprising that the novels abound in passages where language is said to be inadequate, incomplete and distorting. Moreover, in trying to reveal in language what remains forever "beyond capture", Durrell becomes the prey of his own words. Darley is in the same predicament. . . . (p. 142)

Ratiocination is replaced by "the act of dreaming". In *The Alexandria Quartet,* however, this rather vague and misleading term merges into the more specific "imagination", which is an active, creative kind of dreaming. Unlike logic, the imagination does not rely upon . . . verifiability or objectivity, but upon subjective significance. As it is not confined within the boundaries of a formal, objectified system, the imagination is "free" in that it is able to play upon itself, upon the mind, upon the dictates of reason and objectivity. In fact, Durrell has been more rational than he wants us to believe, for he has carried the importance of the imagination in the context of the quartet to its logical extreme: if everything is perpetually moving, changing, and indeterminate, "To see is to imagine". The next step leads him to assert that to imagine is to make reality. Life remains a disconnected tangle of potentialities until man's creative imagination shapes it into coherence and significance [, as expressed in *Justine*]:

> Life, the raw material, is only lived *in potentia* until the artist deploys it in his work.

Since an artist is usually endowed with a highly developed imagination, he comes to be regarded as the centre from which life and reality radiate, as the "creator" of life in the most literal sense of the term. Already in *The Black Book* the protagonist had spoken about "the people and their makers—the artists", and in *The Alexandria Quartet,* Pursewarden is never tired of proclaiming that "it is only the artist who can make things really *happen*".

All art is a product of the imagination. If we want to grasp its full significance in the quartet, we must consider "poetic illumination", art and imagination, within the same transcendental (non-logical) field of experience. They are equally important, they have the same roots, they are interdependent, yet it is possible to describe their mutual relations in the following way:

a) Only by a perfecting of the imagination (which yields a non-assertive kind of knowledge), can "poetic illumination" be attained.

b) The illumination itself is an apprehension which can neither be analysed nor recorded; it takes place on an intermediate level between conscious and unconscious, being and not-being, hence it is "religious" in the purest sense of the term.

c) Art, or—to be more specific—poetry, is an attempt at translating the reality disclosed by this experience into language, yet the stress is never on the latter, but again on the impalpable reality "beyond", at which the words only try to hint. . . .

[The artist's] proper field of information is the field of mysticism and religion. His object is to reach a region where he is in contact with the Inarticulate. Durrell has labelled this region "The Heraldic Universe", the transcendental, archetypal or mythical substratum behind reality. He calls it the "plus-side" of reality. . . . In *The Alexandria Quartet,* Pursewarden is at first the only one who seems to have some knowledge of the Heraldic world of poetry (Darley will succeed him only at the end of *Clea*). . . . Pursewarden's saying [in *Justine*] that "God's real and subtle nature must be clear of distinctions: a glass of spring-water, tasteless, odourless, merely refreshing", comes very near to the account of a genuine "mystical" experience quoted by William James in *The Varieties of Religious Experience*.... God is thus regarded as the original vital force in man—the unconscious if you like—which is neither living nor inanimate, neither time-bound nor eternal, but beyond everything. And this is yet another reason why self-exploration, self-knowledge are so essential in the quartet.... Writing —or any other kind of art—is a "technique of self-pursuit", hence it is never an end in itself. Once the stage of self-realisation has been reached, art ceases to be important, or, to put it more accurately, art is carried into another field of operation: it becomes an inherent attribute of living instead of a separate category.... The struggle for artistic achievement coincides with a struggle for wholeness as a human being. Every man is therefore potentially an artist, and many passages in *The Alexandria Quartet* emphasize this idea. (pp. 143-46)

Real life, as we have seen, lies on the other side of "the poetic illumination". The world beyond, or Durrell's "Heraldic Universe", is an archetypal world. I have chosen the word archetypal because it seems to me a fairly accurate indication of the ambiguous state half-way between time and eternity. An archetype, being a collective unconscious substratum, is not eternal in that it does not stretch from infinite past to infinite future, but it is timeless because, as an *a priori* content of the human mind, it stands above time. It is therefore "static" (cf. Durrell's description of the Heraldic Universe, where the adjective static is also used). If we keep in mind that myth is one of the actualizations of the archetype in the collective consciousness, it will be clear why Lawrence Durrell has seized upon the significance of myth. Throughout the four novels, individual characters are represented as if they were "exemplars" rather than "identities".... Alexandria is viewed as a mythical city, and the characters in the novels are part of its mythology; they are "exemplars", hence symbols....

Durrell calls "The Heraldic Universe" "that territory of experience in which the symbol exists". His distinction between symbols on the one hand, and emblems and badges on the other, is partly based on the fact that the symbol does not try to describe, partly also on the peculiar "neither-nor" character of the symbol. (p. 146)

The act of creation is ... essentially "joy"; the discovery of a timeless and pure substance behind reality is an affirmation of life as it is, in its wholeness. In *The Alexandria Quartet,* art becomes a purifying medium; by hinting at the unalterable, "the still, tranquil, motionless, odourless, tasteless plenum" which underlies the apparent formlessness of life, it makes the formlessness of life itself meaningful and worth-while. (p. 147)

> *Roland Decancq, "What Lies Beyond?" in* Revue des Langues Vivantes, *Vol. 36, No. 2, 1968, pp. 135-50.*

In "Sicilian Carousel" [Durrell] gives us a picture of most of the historic sites of Sicily, an account of Sicilian history, some knowledge of what it's like to take a group tour of the island—it's rushed—and some inspiring passages about writers—Aeschylus, Pirandello, Sekilianos—whom the island brings to his mind.

While Durrell tours Sicily he often thinks back to Greece, where he lived for some 10 years. Sites on Sicily remind him of ideas he has about Greek history; a thought about an ancient Sicilian writer takes him back to a reverie about a modern Greek writer he has known. Durrell seems like a man preoccupied with his past. Though he is on Sicily, he

seems distant from it, and his most vivid passages are those about his own memories and dreams. He writes as though he were going through the motions of the kind of travel writing he has done better before.

Durrell's other travel writing—his many articles, his poetry, his three island books and his "Alexandria Quartet" all are marked by a mystical passion for union with place and by a belief that landscape, as powerful as a god or a parent, shapes character: "We are the children of our landscape," he writes in the "Quartet." "I can think of no better identification."

In "Prospero's Cell," his book about Corfu, where he lived for four years, Durrell wrote a shimmering, ecstatic prose poem to an island he felt led him to discover himself.... In "Reflections on a Marine Venus," about Rhodes, where he lived for two years after the war, he drew a compassionate portrait of an island whose "spirit" taught him how "to outlive the savage noise of wars and change." "Bitter Lemons," his book about Cyprus, where he lived for two years, traced the drama of Cypriot nationalism, as it came to dominate his otherwise idyllic island life.

In these books, as in his many poems about place, there is a sense of being possessed, of identification—the image of a man seeking to surrender to landscapes he finds nourishing to his psyche and his art. "Writers each seem to have a personal landscape of the heart," Durrell writes, "which beckons them."

But in "Sicilian Carousel" this "landscape of the heart" is missing, perhaps because Durrell's mission is not one of identifying or of being nourished, but rather of touring. His companions are not other island residents—as in his other books—but tourists, who, after two weeks, will scatter and go home.

So Sicily never comes alive for the reader, unlike Corfu, Rhodes, Cyprus, Egypt and Greece. And Durrell's characters, in quest of some kind of spiritual realization, here are stereotyped tourists, mainly out for a good time. (pp. 7, 18)

One of the sadder aspects of looking back at the past work of Lawrence Durrell, which spans some 40 years, is that in the 16 years since he completed the "Quartet," he has written nothing that evokes the importance of its themes or the originality of its art. (In fact, much of his work after the "Quartet" seems to be more strained and obscure than anything he wrote before it.) The "Quartet" concluded with the triumph of a writer taking possession of his power to create and to love; that is, coming into his full maturity. Ironically Durrell's work has not yielded the triumph promised by the "Quartet." Perhaps the reason has to do with Durrell's celebrity; for, after the "Quartet," in his novels, "Tunc" and "Nunquam" he often seemed to be writing almost in imitation of himself. Or the reason may have to do with the fact that Durrell is now 65. There is about his most recent work a sense of weariness, of melancholy, as if he had not yet found the expression for the experiences of oncoming old age....

[At the end of "Sicilian Carousel," Durrell] takes off for a short trip on his own which, as if he were unknowingly revealing the advantages of a travel writer going off on his own, evokes some of his most intriguing passages. Though he realizes that Sicily's "variegated history and variety of landscapes simply overwhelms the traveller who has not set aside at least three months to deal with it," this realization makes him feel only "rather irresponsible and lighthearted." He leaves Sicily to write a book about it. From a writer who has given us profound explorations of love and creativity, as well as intensely poetic evocations of place, it should have been better. (p. 18)

> *Joan Rodman Goulianos, "Guided Tour,"* in The New York Times Book Review (© *1977 by The New York Times Company; reprinted by permission), September 4, 1977, pp. 7, 18.*

* * *

DÜRRENMATT, Friedrich 1921-

Dürrenmatt is a Swiss dramatist, novelist, short story writer, painter, and essayist. Next to Max Frisch, he is conceded to be the most celebrated dramatist writing in the German language. Dürrenmatt's grotesque tragicomedies have been compared to the phantasmagorical art of Hieronymous Bosch, as well as painters associated with German expressionism. Dürrenmatt also writes excellent detective fiction. (See also *CLC***, Vols, 1, 4, and** *Contemporary Authors***, Vols. 17-20, rev. ed.)**

Friedrich Dürrenmatt, by far the most significant playwright [writing in German] after Brecht, has written several high caliber detective novels, successful movie scripts, and a whole series of noteworthy radio plays. The author's main interest centers on the stage, however. His plays break away from the theater of illusion and often display characteristics of the literary cabaret for which Dürrenmatt wrote many texts at an earlier stage of his career. His dialogue is often farcical, his protagonists are exaggerated prototypes, and his scenes may exhibit burlesque elements. Yet Dürrenmatt is not an innovator of forms. Rather, he uses forms of the theater introduced by Brecht and Thornton Wilder, both of whom had great impact on German dramatists after the war. Wilder's technique of destroying theatrical illusion by letting actors frequently step out of their roles and his ability to blend farce and metaphysical symbolism made their mark on Dürrenmatt's plays as did the parable character of Brecht's later plays.

In 1955, the Swiss author formulated his dramatic credo in an essay entitled "Problems of the Theater." He declares the traditional laws of drama unacceptable for the modern author, for the modern times are void of tragic heroes. The recent catastrophic events of history appear to him as monstrous disasters caused by madmen. Hitler or Mussolini cannot be seen as tragic heroes like Wallenstein. Dürrenmatt claims tragedy is impossible in our modern world of bureaucracy and overadministration in which the individual has become invisible and "Creon's secretaries handle the case of Antigone." Only in comedy does Dürrenmatt see a chance to depict the complex problems of modern man.

Dürrenmatt's first plays after the war, *Es steht geschrieben* (*It Is Written*, 1947) and *Der Blinde* (*The Blind Man*, written in 1947), concern the theme of religious belief in revolutionary times and do not fully reveal the author's dramatic potential. The protagonist of his first comedy, the Roman emperor *Romulus the Great* (1950), takes a greater interest in chicken farming than in ruling the empire. He confesses to "love people more than the idea of a fatherland" and feels quite relieved to turn Rome over to the barbarian conquerors without bloodshed. *The Marriage of Mr. Mississippi* (also translated as: *Fools Are Passing By*, 1952) scored the first international success for Dürrenmatt. He

puts four main characters on the stage, each of whom, in the manner of a morality play, personifies an abstraction.... The stage becomes the battlefield of different world views. (pp. 399-400)

The historical comedy *An Angel Comes to Babylon* (1954) is a parable showing how greed for power corrupts people. The tragicomedy *The Visit* (1956) ranks among the best plays of the century....

The Physicists (1962) are inmates of an insane asylum who believe themselves to be Einstein and Newton.... Together with Brecht's *Galileo*, Frisch's *Chinese Wall*, and Kipphardt's *Oppenheimer, The Physicists* reflects the moral conflict of the modern scientist whose discoveries can either ease or terminate human existence.

Dürrenmatt's love for the grotesque culminates in his last comedy, *The Meteor* (1966). The protagonist, the Nobel laureate Schwitters, dies and experiences an immediate resurrection. In biting scenes Dürrenmatt displays the reactions of the "survivors."

Dürrenmatt's comedies do not echo the bitter laughter of a despairing and disillusioned author. They often show the perversion of man through power, greed, and money, and mirror the wretched situation of the world. But Dürrenmatt also presents heroes who, often masked as fools, encounter this world with courage and firmness. His comedies are an attempt to regard the world from a critical distance. "Seeing the senselessness, the hopelessness of this world, one might despair," says Dürrenmatt, "yet despair is not the result of this world. It is an answer one gives to this world. A different answer might be: not to despair, but to decide to accept the world in which we often live like Gulliver among the giants. But he who wants to evaluate his opponent, who prepares himself to fight or to escape his enemy, has to step back a little in order to create distance. It is still possible to present the courageous man." (pp. 400-01)

> *Diether H. Haenicke, "Literature since 1933," in The Challenge of German Literature, edited by Horst S. Daemmrich and Diether H. Haenicke (reprinted by permission of the Wayne State University Press; copyright © 1971 by Wayne State University Press), Wayne State University Press, 1971, pp. 350-404.*

There is in [Dürrenmatt's humor] a touch of the Pirandellian "*umorismo*," with its emphasis on the accidental character of all the so-called "great" events which determine the life of man and the course of his history; with its fierce dedication to the task of tearing masks off faces and façades off ideologies; and its acceptance of the relativity of all concepts and values. Like Pirandello, Dürrenmatt would present to us the emperor in his nightgown, rather than wearing imperial purple—and the result is both ludicrous and pathetic. His strong point is the grotesque, applied to social satire. The use of grotesque techniques in no wise represents a purely negative attitude. On the contrary. Like all great writers of comedy, Dürrenmatt considers himself a moralist—an admission which in itself constitutes no small act of courage in the twentieth century.... (pp. 28-9)

Dürrenmatt's little-known radio plays are definitely superior to most of his serious drama; and as for producing a "serious" novel, he has never even tried, preferring to restrict himself to the minor genres in his fiction. It is tantalizing to speculate upon the reasons for Dürrenmatt's obvious preference for these minor genres—"*Trivialgat-tungen,*" as they are called, even more derogatorily, in German. Aside from the very realistic fact that these works represent for the artist valuable "*Brotarbeit,*" that is, a source of income, I think they could be interpreted as a threefold escape: escape from the critics; escape from the pressures of the avant-garde; and escape from nihilism and the philosophy of the absurd. He could, then, be defined as an artist who escapes into escape Literature. (p. 29)

It is also safe to assume that Dürrenmatt has gone underground into the minor genres, which still allow at least outwardly, for a conventional approach because of a deep distrust of the extreme avant-garde. His one venture into a technically contemporary, what might be called a Beckett-type work, *Play Strindberg* (. . . 1969) represents, in my opinion, a dismal failure (although it does bring out quite successfully the monstrous marriage theme). Dürrenmatt is too much of a humorist and too much of an individualist to fall into a pattern of any sort. Rather than join an avant-garde, he prefers to retain conventional trappings, reserving to himself the privilege of revealing their absurdity through grotesque alienation.

Finally, and most important, I suggest that Dürrenmatt's light novels represent an escape from the nihilism and the philosophy of the absurd which permeate all "serious" contemporary literature. In spite of his Calvinistic background and a youthful bout with nihilism, Dürrenmatt essentially remains an optimist. . . . This in no wise invalidates the writer's serious concern with, and full awareness of, the metaphysical anguish of modern man; it means only that he refuses to give himself up to total despair. . . . The heroism which Dürrenmatt advocates (he himself prefers the term "courage") resembles that advocated by Camus in *Le Mythe de Sisyphe,* a heroic resignation and acceptance of life in spite of its absurdity. In fact, Dürrenmatt was at one time considered another "romancier de l'absurde" in France. He himself, however, quickly disclaimed any such categorization. Beyond the realization of the absurd, he wishes to show the paradox in human life, and the quixotic quality to which our age has reduced any attempt at heroism.

In his early works, he alternates between Promethean rebellion and the facile consolations of religion. A despairing nihilism breathes in the expressionistic fragments of his early prose, such as *Weihnacht (Christmas), Der Folter-knecht (The Torturer)* or *Die Falle (The Trap)*—the latter originally entitled *Der Nihilist.* In the epilogue to the collection, written several years after the stories themselves, Dürrenmatt mentions that these fragments represent an attempt: "To fight a battle which can be meaningful only if it is lost." He did not remain a nihilist long. His involvement with the Christian religion was a more deep-seated one, and for a time brought him peace and respite from despair. . . . [The] religious themes of his early plays and his general preoccupation with the problems of evil and guilt have led to the mistaken assumption that Dürrenmatt is essentially a religious writer. The bulk of his mature work, as well as his own pronouncements, speak against such a view. Neither absurdist, nor religious writer, nor *engagé* in any way, Dürrenmatt remains entirely *sui generis,* a paradox among contemporary authors, an artist capable of turning the most tragic truths into grotesque farces. . . . Rather than feeling totally hemmed in, Dürrenmatt believes that a limited number of artistic modes of expression remain open to the artist in the twentieth century, foremost among them the possibility of dealing with serious facts in a flippant manner. Courage remains a possible quality in the world of Dürrenmatt because he tempers it with a tinge of the ridiculous. . . . (pp. 29-31)

Dürrenmatt sees the injustice of any social order as inherent in the paradox of social organization as such. . . . There is no way out of the dilemma: Man craves both justice and freedom, but the two terms are mutually exclusive. Any social order, whether it be the capitalistic "wolf game" or the socialist "sheep game" represents a compromise solution which must remain unsatisfactory. This does not mean a total rejection of either system on Dürrenmatt's part, but rather a cautious detachment and, above all, categorical refusal to posit absolute ideologies. . . . His ideas on how to effect the proposed improvements, however, remain vague, although he includes a strong warning against the emotional force of ideologies, "the cosmetics of power politics." He suggests that in politics, as in literature, it may be beneficial to look at reality with critical imagination, rather than ideologically. . . . Like Böll, he sees an unchecked continuation of current trends leading to the disaster of a fully automatic machine age, an age where computers and other complex hardware would turn the world back from civilization into a barbaric jungle, with an elite of technicians and scientists functioning as the medicine men of the spage-age savages. It is this threat of imminent barbarism which most concerns him in his fiction; already, he sees us living in a state where a technological accident can set off a cosmic cataclysm and where man has lost all of his grandeur and most of his dignity. His laughable, pathetic and grotesque heroes are the last upholders of a civilization on the decline, his escape into a "still possible" humanism.

Such a "hero" is Arnolphe Archilochos, hot-milk-and-Perrier-sipping central character of the satirical little novel *Grieche Sucht Griechin* (Once a Greek). Under the guise of light entertainment literature, Dürrenmatt here presents us with a scathing satire on political, social and moral orders, bringing out their paradoxical quality. At the same time, he uses grotesque alienation techniques in a brilliantly successful attempt to turn the True-Romance-type love story into a caricature of itself. (pp. 32-3)

[The] novel brings out the interchangeability of social and moral value systems. At the outset of the book, the line of distinction is clearly drawn; the social and moral establishment is represented by the eight pillars of society, who together form Archilochos' "ethical universe," while the anti-establishment invades the story in the form of brother Bibi and his clan. As the book proceeds, the towering personages of Archilochos' ethical universe begin to totter, revealing all the weaknesses of ordinary mortals. Meanwhile, brother Bibi and his good-for-nothing family have become converted into hardworking, law-abiding, church-going citizens. . . . Archilochos cannot escape the uncomfortable feeling that somehow things have cancelled each other out, that nothing much was accomplished after all. And this realization fills him with melancholy—a melancholy which can be cured only, as the author points out in an ironic digression into Hollywood *Kitsch,* by the ever-present power of "Love."

However, the main interest of the book rests with Archilochos himself and the monstrous story of his venture into matrimony. There are traits of both Candide and Parzifal in Dürrenmatt's hero. Candide in reverse, he is catapulted from misery into what appears to be the best of all possible worlds; but his strokes of good luck turn out to be as disastrous for him as the original Candide's bouts with misfortune. . . . Archilochos strikes one as a latter-day Parzival: a middle-aged, slightly overweight Parzival, to be sure, forever cleaning his thick-lensed glasses, a grotesque travesty of the original, but a Parzival figure, none the less, in his absolute purity and innocence. Archilochos, indeed, is the "pure fool" of the legend, like Parzival too shy to ask the necessary questions when he encounters mysteries beyond his ken. True to his calling, he emerges a conqueror—though in keeping with the cynicism of our age, he wins the town courtesan, rather than the Holy Grail, an achievement which, as Dürrenmatt would be quick to point out, has the advantage of remaining in the range of what is "still possible."

But the use of the grotesque goes far beyond the characterization of Archilochos himself. Dürrenmatt achieves some outstanding effects by clever plot manipulation, which involves alienation in two directions: an originally harmless event is alienated into a finale of horror, and, in contrast, a monstrous happening is turned into the most innocuous affair. The result is in both cases is grotesque and tinged with ambiguous humor. . . . In spite of the fairytale quality of much of the book, Dürrenmatt's grotesque developments are sufficiently rooted in reality, both psychological and social, to make it impossible for the reader to achieve a safe distance and with it, emotional detachment. (pp. 35-6)

Rather than selecting one victim for ridicule, the author throws a benignly satirical light on all the participants. . . . The author emerges as a man who is able to smile at the absurdities of the world he depicts.

Another element in the book serves to temper its pessimism: the author's occasional digressions into Hollywood-style fantasies. These are particularly apparent in some of the descriptions, descriptions which clearly reveal the fact that their author has worked on film scenarios more than once. These excursions into the never-never lands of *Kitsch* and soap opera stand in stark contrast to the feeling of futility expressed at the end of the book, and take away much of its impact—an escape into escape literature. Perhaps the most interesting example of this type of description occurs on the occasion of Archilochos' first visit to his bride's home. Dürrenmatt, who normally uses great restraint when it comes to erotic fantasies (food fantasies are more along his line) here indulges himself in a full flight of fancy. The result is the kind of sequence typical of the movies of the 40s and 50s, where sex is discreetly hinted at by luxurious settings and carefully selected props. . . . The Bower of Bliss, rediscovered. A similar concession to the public's love of luxury is made in the description of the upper regions of the Petit-Paysan office tower where Archilochos works. This top floor is a fantasy world of space, warmth and light, with baskets of flowers everywhere, soft music replacing the clatter of office machines, and delicate period furniture, lending a cultured air to the premises. It is a tongue-in-cheek description of the executive suite, to be sure. The incongruity reaches its peak, as Petit-Paysan, himself, emerges from his office, a volume of Hölderlin's esoteric poems in his hand. Nevertheless, descriptions of this sort represent temporary escapes from the ultimate conclusion of the novel, which is anything but gay.

The detective novels represent another form of Dürrenmatt's escape into escape literature. They contain less social satire than *Once a Greek*, and the grotesque element in them leans more heavily towards the monstrous. First and foremost, they testify to the author's love of story-telling. But they all contain the basic features typical of Dürrenmatt's work and Weltanschauung: ambiguous treatment of the hero, ambiguous treatment of the genre, and heavy use of the grotesque. The stories all center around a quixotic hero, a detective *sans peur et sans reproche*, who brings the full force of his intellectual acumen and moral conviction into an absurd and lonely battle for justice. . . . A courageous man may still assert himself in the face of a hostile and callous world—in fact, Dürrenmatt posits such assertion as a moral imperative. . . . (pp. 37-8)

Nevertheless, the ultimate absurdity remains, equally shocking whether it is caused by the transcendent fact of death or simply by one of the unfortunate and accidental combinations of circumstances which determine the life of man. With the help of cleverly constructed mystery plots, however, Dürrenmatt manages to temper the pessimistic impact of his novels.

Although conventional at first glance, Dürrenmatt's detective stories subvert the basic principle of the classical mystery, namely, that events must be developed by the rules of logic, as in a chess game. In so doing, the author again turns the genre into a satire of itself, a dead-end street, as he was well aware when he subtitled *The Promise* a "requiem to the detective novel." Arbitrary, accidental occurrences, rather than logical developments, become the pivots which determine the development of his plots. . . . The principle is effectively illustrated in the story line of *The Promise*. Inspector Matthäi really is a genius whose superb tactics prove fully successful—but a stupid accident prevents him from cashing in on the success of the manoeuver to which he has sacrificed his career. When the truth finally does come out, and Matthäi appears fully vindicated, he is too far gone in absinthe even to register the news. (pp. 38-9)

[*The Promise* reflects] two of Dürrenmatt's favorite grotesque themes: the monstrous nature of extreme old age, and the monstrous meal. . . . Not surprising for a diabetic, Dürrenmatt tends to link together surfeit of food and impending judgment and catastrophe. (p. 40)

It is perfectly clear that Dürrenmatt is a writer who thrives on paradox at all levels. A great believer in the power of art, he goes underground into genres which normally escape this classification. A profound pessimist, he makes us laugh; an unalterable optimist, he points out to us the absurdity of our universe. A cynic, he insists on creating images of courageous men; a humanist, he reduces his heroes to caricatures. He, himself, is fully aware of his own paradoxical nature. (pp. 40-1)

Renate Usmiani, "Friedrich Durrenmatt, Escape Artist: A Look at the Novels," in MOSAIC V/3 *(copyright © 1972 by The University of Manitoba Press), Spring, 1972, pp. 27-41.*

[The] plays of . . . Friedrich Dürrenmatt . . . are marked with the grandeur of an almost Jacobean excess. When we enter his fantastic world there can be no doubting that we have come into a realm where the impossible has become probable. Like those writers whom he most admires—Aristophanes, Wycherley, Nestroy, and Thornton Wilder—Dürrenmatt is the master of the dramatic conceit. He invents a bizarre and improbable situation and exploits it for all it is worth, and then some. However, just beneath the apparently absurd lunacy of the surface conceit we discover a stern moral vision which shapes all that he writes. Like

Ibsen, only with a somewhat better sense of humor, Dürrenmatt has a Lutheran conscience much like that of a Protestant pastor who has defrocked himself because he has lost his belief in the possibility of a salvation. He is a stern judge of the world, but his harshest judgments are directed against himself. Like a cynical Shaw, we sense he is ever ready to turn the stage into a pulpit from which to preach about the evils of a world turned sour. But until *The Physicists* he has always stopped short just in time. His troubled agnosticism would reassert itself at the final moment, and with awkward protestations that his sermons would be of little use, he returns to the theatricality with which he began, once more ironic and aloof.

It is this constant struggle between the zealot and the cynic which finally accounts for all the contradictions in Dürrenmatt's theatre. He appears misanthropic, but he cares deeply for human-kind; he claims the world is beyond hope, while he desperately searches for the strategies of salvation; and, in spite of his insistence that art doesn't teach any lessons, he has a tendency to be hopelessly didactic. . . . His usual dramatic method is to set up a grotesque fantasy world and then step back and watch with the audience as his invented fate works itself out with a ferocious inevitability. But this Olympian detachment is more apparent than real. He is, in fact, a puppeteer-god, and there are times when we sense he wants to change the script or is on the verge of getting involved in the action himself.

Dürrenmatt's chief protection against this tendency for over-involvement is his remarkable grasp of theatrical technique. His dramaturgy, like that of his fellow countryman Max Frisch, can best be described as "Biedermeier." he employs a hodgepodge of theatrical style and will try any device or theatrical convention if he feels it will work on the stage. Such disregard for consistency is not the amateur's lack of discipline, but the result of Dürrenmatt's fervent desire to put the richness and manifold diversity of the world on the stage. It is his strong conviction that the theatre should present "not the potential of a situation, but its rich harvest." The total effect of such an idea of the theatre is not confusion, but a baroque lushness. But he combines this penchant for amplification with the techniques of romantic irony, and as a result he achieves a

toughness of tone as well as a richness of style. His use of bizarre and macabre situations, the chatty comments to the reader in the stage directions, the bits of buffoonery and grand guignol, and the constant employment of anachronism and irreverent parody all contribute to the creation of an ironic fairy-tale world which captures our attention, but at the same time keeps us at a distance. (pp. 247-48)

The two major themes in all that Dürrenmatt has written are guilt and helplessness. He is painfully conscious of men's collective sense of guilt for the disasters of global upheaval, but he is perhaps even more aware of the sense of helplessness people feel living under the shadow of imminent atomic destruction in a world that seems too difficult and too complex for even the wisest or wiliest of men to control and govern. Like Kafka, Dürrenmatt describes the human condition as that of victims trapped in a tunnel (one of his most powerful short stories is called "The Tunnel") with no beginning and no end, in which there can be no meaningful action, and from which there can be no escape. (p. 249)

With *The Physicists*, Dürrenmatt seems to be entering a new stage in his development as a playwright. His fantastic imagination and his unrivaled powers of invention are still very much present, but they seem to be completely under control for the first time. This play has a concentration which all of his earlier plays except *The Visit* have lacked. In his important essay, *Problems of the Theatre*, Dürrenmatt bemoans the fact that the modern dramatist is incapable of achieving that tightness of form which characterizes the classical Greek theatre. *The Physicists* indicates that Dürrenmatt can, and we only hope that his achievement will persuade other playwrights that theatrical richness and a rigorously controlled form need not be considered mutually exclusive or incompatible in the contemporary theatre. (p. 252)

> *Robert W. Corrigan, "Dürrenmatt's 'The Physicists' and the Grotesque," in his* The Theatre in Search of a Fix *(copyright © 1973 by Robert W. Corrigan; reprinted by permission of Delacorte Press), Delacorte Press, 1973, pp. 247-52.*

E

EASTLAKE, William 1917-

An American novelist, short story writer, and poet, Eastlake uses the background of the present-day rural West in his often wonderfully comic fiction. He is, however, a serious artist who utilizes mythic and literary allusiveness in a manner more reminiscent of Hemingway and Faulkner than of local colorists. (See also *Contemporary Authors,* Vols. 5-8, rev. ed.)

Eastlake's novels are neither the stereotyped "Westerns," nor are they regional Southwestern novels any more than William Faulkner's novels are "Southern" or regional novels of the South.

Just as Faulkner created his Yoknapatawpha County out of the area surrounding Oxford, Mississippi, William Eastlake is creating a fictional area in the "Checkerboard" region of the Navajo reservation and its adjacent areas in northern New Mexico. His characters live and die in a physical setting that often has dominated the works of lesser writers, turning their expressions into regionalistic descriptions. D. H. Lawrence once received a letter from Leo Stein which described the New Mexico landscape as the most "aesthetically satisfying" he knew, and Lawrence commented in an article for *Survey Graphic* that "To me it was much more than that. It had a splendid silent terror, and a vast far-and-wide magnificence which made it way beyond mere aesthetic appreciation. . . . [It gives] one the greatest sense of overweening, terrible proudness and mercilessness; but so beautiful, God! so beautiful!"

It is a dangerous country for novelists. Because of its very magnitude, its terror, its magnificence, its beauty, its fascinating history, and its mingling of cultures, it has a tendency to overpower the artist. He becomes so involved with the "romance" of the country or its history or its people that his resulting work can be thought of only as regional—as "local color"—literature. But this is not true of Eastlake and his novels. Eastlake is a writer who, like the Ernest Hemingway of *The Sun Also Rises* and *A Farewell to Arms,* keeps a tight rein on his materials, using physical descriptions to suggest or enlarge ideological content. He *uses,* then, the New Mexico landscape, history, and people not for ornament but for the enhancement of meaning. Reading Eastlake, one is always aware of the desert, the mesa, the mountain, the sky, in all their color and beauty, their proudness and mercilessness, but one is also aware that they may be the symbol of "home," or of the "cradle," or the "coffin" of civilization.

It is not by accident that Faulkner and Hemingway have been mentioned, for Eastlake appears to have been shaped by both writers. His first novel, *Go In Beauty,* shows the Hemingway influence at its strongest. (pp. 188-89)

[It] is the mystic interrelationship between man's sins and nature that proves most interesting in [*Go In Beauty*]. Both sins are against the land. The prediction of the Navajo medicine man, Paracelsus, that a "theft" will cause a drouth, and the drouth that results, are central to the novel. Although there are chapters devoted to the satirical treatment of modern society, the mood of Greek tragedy is felt as an undercurrent throughout the novel—a mood which Lawrence had felt, and which Eastlake creates through his treatment of the land and the oracle-like Paracelsus. (p. 190)

Perhaps no other concept reveals more adequately Eastlake's break with modern "objective naturalists" than his concept of time. It is a break from the "traditional" objective handling of sequential events into a recognition of both the reality of the continuum and also the validity of the subjective or Romantic treatment of the moment as forever —that everything which is, has been and will be, is now. . . . In *The Bronc People,* [Eastlake's most ambitious and successful novel], the Indian, My Prayer, [says], . . . "They call everything by a different name but it's the same thing. And they call everything by a different time but it's the same time. Everything repeats. It would be no different if everything in every language and every time was called Cowboy's Delight."

But this concept is most successfully handled through description. For example, . . . : "The mesa here was eroding away in five giant steps that descended down to the floor of the valley where the abandoned hogan lay. Each of the five steps clearly marked about twenty million years in time. In other words, they had been laid down twenty million years apart, and were so marked by unique coloration and further marked by the different fossil animals found in each. It took the four boys about twenty minutes to descend these one hundred million years but they didn't think that was very good going." (pp. 191-92)

There are other Romantic elements to Eastlake's novels,

for example, his use of what Jungian critics might call archetypal symbols to suggest or to explore the mythic consciousness of the human race. Little Sant Bowman, son of the owner of the Circle Heart, is at the rodeo. Traditional to the cowboy, the rodeo is the traditional and symbolic expression of a way of life. Like the Olympic games of ancient Greece, it is the place where only the best compete. Or perhaps it might be likened to the Roman arena before it was corrupted. And certainly it may be compared to the bullfight, traditional and meaningful to the Spaniards. Or, it is as meaningful as the annual hunt in Faulkner's "The Bear." The primitive but religious nature of the rodeo is suggested in a description of one of the events. "What they did with these was to put a clutch of pigs in a pickup truck out at one end of the field, then all the horse-mounted men came hell for leather, dismounted, grabbed a greased pig, remounted, held the flashing object high, like Montezuma's men the golden mantle, like offerings to the god, the animals flashing and screaming, fighting along the arms, upward to the sun."

As at the bullfight and the Olympic games, there are judges, "pulling on their chins as wise men will." (pp. 192-93)

Eastlake's writing is a controlled mixture of realistic detail (to the point of being specific about the exact number of shells a Winchester .30-30 will hold), and of allegorical symbol (the "marvelous," as Hawthorne would have called it)—the whole conditioned by a humorous treatment that makes it all credible and thus acceptable. (p. 193)

[The theme of *The Bronc People*]—the destruction by civilization of nature and a way of life that was in harmony with nature—is a theme that runs through much of Southwestern and Western literature. Mr. Peersall [the character who functions as Eastlake's spokesman for the Western spirit] also reflects the skepticism toward law and order in the civilized community that is traditional with the Westerner. . . .

But it is not just the Western philosophy that Mr. Peersall espouses. It is deeper than that, and more consistent with the main stream of American literature and thought. Mr. Peersall often sounds like a Western Thoreau. He is a naturalist with a love for, as well as a curiosity about, nature. He is an individualist, and a proponent of moral courage. And in civilization, he sees the loss of freedom for the individual. His action during the Tularosa school dispute is Thoreau-inspired, though active instead of passive. (p. 196)

That "no man is an island" is perhaps true, but in another sense we are all alone. Eastlake, the unmodern—or perhaps the more modern—accepts that condition. The modern tendency has been to merge with the herd, to conform to the "other-directed" society, to be forgotten in the mass. American writers, from the twenties on, have elaborated on that tragic aspect of man's nature—his physical and spiritual (or psychological) isolation from his fellow man. Eastlake's answer is a return to certain important aspects of frontier individualism. . . .

In Eastlake's novels, the triumphs are the momentary, and often illusory, achievements of man; the tragedy is in the land, and in nature—the continuum. Perhaps no other writer has used the New Mexico landscape so artistically and meaningfully to point up the timelessness of the earth on which man lives. (p. 197)

Portrait of an Artist With Twenty-six Horses is marred by

more technical difficulties than either of the earlier novels. It appears to be a loosely constructed collection of episodes, some previously published as short stories, held together by an incident that, in itself, might make another fine short story but that does not provide a satisfactory structure for a novel despite Eastlake's ability to provide transitional materials to blend the stories together. The situation of the sinking man reflecting on his life is obviously rather trite, but, strangely enough, the treatment is not. Nor, on closer examination, does the structure seem so loose. The novel does center around the meaning of the portrait by the young Indian artist named Twenty-six Horses. (pp. 199-200)

One can . . . overlook the unevenness of tone—say, from the comic-pathetic episode of the Jewish refugees who seek revenge on a former Nazi to the unhappily slapstick characterization of a between-the-breasts gun-toting Texas schoolmarm and wife of a timid atom-bomb worker—and recognize that *Twenty-six Horses* contains some of the most brilliantly and humorously satirical passages of all the Eastlake novels. . . . [The] foibles of modern man [are] reflected through the mirror of the Indian.

In *Go In Beauty,* there is the wonderful speech of Paracelsus, who tries to convince his fellow Navajos that the white man is not completely inferior. In *The Bronc People,* there are My Prayer, and President Taft, and The Other Indian. But none of these can match, for example, the mother of Twenty-six Horses, who, when she feels that she is losing her son, buys a restaurant in the village of Coyote and hangs up signs like "REAL LIFE WHITE PEOPLE IN THEIR NATIVE COSTUMES DOING NATIVE WHITE DANCES" and "WE RESERVE THE RIGHT TO REFUSE SERVICE TO EVERYBODY." (pp. 200-01)

[Although] the Indian is not the only mirror [for satire], he is the most effective. And he is most effective because Eastlake has broken from the realistic treatment of the Indian. Eastlake's Indians are closer to Faulkner's Ikkemotubbe, Herman Basket and Craw-ford than to Oliver La Farge's Laughing Boy and Red Man. In other words, they are not realistic Indians, although they act and speak more like Indians than the real ones. . . . [Eastlake has constructed] Indian characters that reflect the most ridiculous aspects of the twentieth-century Anglo's frantic need for material progress with its resulting destruction of the Anglo's own psychological balance. The important point is, of course, that Eastlake has not been content with describing the Indian as he is, but has used the Indian for an artistic purpose. (p. 202)

Of contemporary Southwestern writers, only two seem to have been able to break from a description of the land, its people, and its traditions to interpret them in the novel form in a manner that breaks from the restrictions of regionalism. These two are Edward Abbey, in *The Brave Cowboy* and *Fire on the Mountain,* and William Eastlake in all three of his novels. Of the two, William Eastlake is the more complex and the more interesting. There has been no other Southwestern writer, certainly, who has used the Southwestern land, its people, its traditions, and then added the symbolic undertones that lend the depth of universal meaning; who has created a new mythology out of the old; and who has treated all this through a full use of tone that includes the comic, the tragic, and the satirical. It will be a serious loss to American literature if Eastlake's novels are neglected because they happen to be set in the country where there are cowboys and Indians. (p. 203)

Delbert E. Wylder, "The Novels of William Eastlake," in New Mexico Quarterly *(copyright, 1965, by the University of New Mexico Press), Summer, 1964, pp. 188-203.*

William Eastlake is the funniest, most profound, most musical writer I have read in years. He has the greatness of soul not only to kid the characters in ["Dancers in the Scalp House"] . . . but also to kid himself and his own style and thought as a writer. He has the confidence, in other words, of a man half-bard and half-bum, yet undeceived as to the truth in all the confusion. Eastlake is wise: a poet in the best sense. . . .

The subject of the book is the impending doom of the Indians and the Indian land by eagle-killers, sellers of 50-foot "ranchettes," and the Atlas Dam; which looms over the whole movement of the book. . . .

The true subjects of the book are America and William Eastlake's plenitudinous mind, but the vantage from the Navajos in New Mexico and Arizona offers an especially glaring and rich theater for our diseases. . . .

But do not think that Eastlake riots in the sentimental. His mind is tough, reasonable, and crawls simply everywhere in the connections he makes. Funniness, last resort of the Indian, he has aplenty. His humor ranges from middlebrow easies like the President staring "unimpeachably" out of his limousine, to ranges of wit so complex you would have to be at the top of your class to appreciate.

I was at first put off by, then agreed with, Eastlake's wildly mobile point of view. It is hard to get used to the thought of the eagles named Sun and Star, because an eagle can't think, as we all know. The book, however, accustoms you to their vision and feeling. We remember that several of the people the Indians are fleeing from cannot think either, and that along with the Indian we would do well to eliminate much of our human pomposity in these last days for pure air and unspoiled beauty.

No, humor doesn't get you through everything. Eastlake is a fine American humorist, and he is wise. The last beautiful passage strikes in no uncertain tones one of the finest dirges I've seen. (p. 43)

Barry Hannah, in The New York Times Book Review *(© 1975 by The New York Times Company; reprinted by permission), October 12, 1975.*

New Mexico has been a fount of inspiration to many writers. D. H. Lawrence, Willa Cather, Paul Horgan and Oliver La Farge were among those moved to write about the land and its people. But most writing about New Mexico has focused either on the beauty of the landscape or events of the frontier period. One of the few authors to write about the Indians of the present is William Eastlake. . . . Eastlake is most sensitive to the language and life of the Indians. His novel deals with a fundamental conflict in the Southwest, the struggle between those who want to despoil the land—speculators, bureaucrats, drive-in entrepreneurs—and those who want to preserve it—the Indians and a few Anglos.

Dancers in the Scalp House is the story of some Navajos and an Anglo couple who are trying to prevent their homes and way of life from being washed away in the waters of a new dam. The story gathers force as it broadens into the larger theme of the spiritual death of white Americans.

Unlike his earlier books about New Mexico, which include *Go in Beauty, The Bronc People* and *Portrait of an Artist with Twenty-six Horses*, Eastlake's latest novel is more fanciful than realistic. (p. 57)

Eastlake uses the confrontation between the Indians and white America to jab at parts of American society that he considers ephemeral and pernicious. For example, the Playboy clubs are represented by a huge outdoor advertisement of a naked, neon girl which is torn down by the Indians, and the Governor of California wears a small sign advertising Disneyland, "a parlor of entertainment in California."

In contrast, the Indian way of life is described as a function of the natural order, shared by the eagle, the coyote, the sun and the moon. The Indian world "is a circle that contains all the rhythms of the poetry of life." It is a "continuity in time and place and person."

Caught between the world of the whites and the world of the Indians is Tom Charlie, called Thomas Charles by the whites. He is described as the "man who did not know who he was." Tom Charlie symbolizes the dilemma faced by most Indians: whether to accept white civilization and lose an important part of themselves or reject white civilization and remain outcasts from the larger American society. (pp. 57-8)

[The] dilemma of the Indians is related to the lives of all Americans, Eastlake suggests. . . . The struggle between progress and nature becomes a struggle for the soul. The plastic men in the novel have died spiritually and they are determined to add the Indians to the casualty lists. . . .

Drawing on the belief in the power of nature to rejuvenate us spiritually, Eastlake is following in the tradition of Chateaubriand and Wordsworth as well as Americans such as Thoreau and Whitman. The theme is still important today. Unfortunately, some of the comic passages in the novel dilute the theme. The reader is tempted to dismiss the antics of the characters with a wry smile, and that response can easily be transferred to the novel's profounder elements.

In *Go in Beauty*, Eastlake wrote that "if the Indian Country ever fell to the advancing ravages that civilization called progress," he would set it all down. *Dancers in the Scalp House* is a continuation of that effort, the recital of a "dream, a white nightmare, a phantasmagoric and contemporary white frolic and farce in which the Indian is victim and buffoon to the white man, but played out on the real Indian land, not stage, of Indian heritage and hope." (p. 58)

John Friedman, "Another Great Good Place Going," in The Nation *(copyright 1976 by The Nation Associates, Inc.), January 17, 1976, pp. 57-8.*

It was inevitable after all the bogus historical novels of the Bicentennial that someone would show the Revolution from the other side—not just the British side, but that of the fence straddlers who regarded the events with an eye to main chance. . . .

[Readers] will recognize . . . William Eastlake's time-, space- and brain-warped terrain. It is littered with eight-horse, double-wide mobile homes and populated by publishers like Big Brown who want to bring out edible books under the imprint of the Digest Reader.

As the comic scenes increase both in number and hilarity, "The Long Naked Descent Into Boston" reads like history as recorded by Woody Allen. . . .

But too often the laughs seem to leave Eastlake lightheaded and he repeats variations on lines as old as burlesque "so Paul will be back here in a trice. . . . And he started out on a horse." At other times he overuses clichés and colloquialisms, apparently with the intention of poking fun at them. . . .

Finally, however, the book is buoyant. It makes a few low passes, looking as if it might crash, but like Poxe's balloon it keeps rising again to new heights, light, dizzying and funny. (p. 10)

> *Michael Mewshaw, in* The New York Times Book Review *(© 1977 by The New York Times Company; reprinted by permission), July 10, 1977.*

*   *   *

EMPSON, William   1906-

An English poet and critic, Empson is best known for his seminal contribution to the formalist school of New Criticism, *Seven Types of Ambiguity.* **As a poet he is noted for his concern with style and form, as well as his wry wit. (See also** *CLC,* **Vol. 3, and** *Contemporary Authors,* **Vols. 17-20, rev. ed.)**

[William Empson] writes poetry demanding a great deal of miscellaneous and sometimes abstruse information, such as the domestic arrangements of ants and beetles, the incidence of chairs in Chinese art, some implications of the theory of relativity. His literary references are as unexpected as they are various. A poem dealing with the absurdities and cruelties at work in a society that calls itself Christian is entitled "Reflection from Anita Loos": to the effect that "A girl can't go on laughing all the time." Naturally, the man who explored *Seven Types of Ambiguity* through their most labyrinthine passages writes what he calls a "clotted kind of poetry", thick with multiple meanings. He has, however, composed a "Poem About a Ball in the Nineteenth Century" that moves as airily and chimes as gaily as the event it describes. Learned, witty, and ironical, Empson is not incapable of directness. A difficult poem on some of the uses of the imagination ends on the memorably plain admonition to "learn a style from a despair." (pp. 232-33)

Admiring the restrictions of Empson's forms, notably the villanelle, the quietness of his tone, the lack of extravagance in his diction, [younger poets] have produced wryly melancholy, witty poems, wanting in the intensity of which this complex poet is capable. (p. 233)

> *Babette Deutsch, in her* Poetry in Our Time *(copyright © 1963 by Babette Deutsch; 1963 by Doubleday; reprinted by permission of Babette Deutsch), revised edition, Doubleday, 1963.*

Trained as a mathematician . . . Empson was responsible for introducing relativity into poems. Previously they had seemed, like space and time, to have solid, respectable internal structures. But Empson showed that, especially if you discounted their punctuation, they could be made rich and runny inside like jam, or like dissolving toothpaste which, as he observes in 'Camping Out', is itself like a constellation approached at a speed greater than the speed of light. *Seven Types of Ambiguity,* the work that reshaped English literature, he wrote in a fortnight as an undergraduate. A mighty gaggle of ambiguity-hunters has waddled in its wake since then, and from that angle it might seem to have a lot to answer for. But what Empson's imitators have consistently failed to match up to, apart from his genius, is his tone, which is intricately bound up with his insights. (p. 926)

His alertness to multiple points of view deepens his humanity, as well as making his critical procedures endlessly subtle.

The Structures of Complex Words, their subtlest outcome, represents, in a sense, a lifetime's work—Empson has said that he felt *Nunc dimittis* when he'd finished it—and the reaction can't be rare that it would take more than a lifetime to understand. (pp. 926-27)

> *John Carey, "Kippering," in* New Statesman *(© 1974 The Statesman & Nation Publishing Co. Ltd.), June 28, 1974, pp. 926-27.*

More than any other criticism I know, Empson's throws us back upon the text. Eliot, say, tends to leave you feeling you ought to take another look at Dante when you next get the chance, and Leavis often creates the comfortable impression that you have already read everything worth reading. But Empson has you chasing off *now* to see whether what he says is in the poem can really be there. . . .

The commonly assumed connection of Empson with the New Criticism is a curious affair. Certainly he is a great believer in what he calls "verbal analysis," and the New Criticism owes him a great deal. But he is as concerned to engage history as his American followers were to elude it. He insists on the local, concrete situation of poet and poem, and he is an almost militant devotee of the intentional fallacy, always telling us what Milton or Shakespeare "must have" felt or thought. The general effect of this is no doubt not as historical as Empson wants it to be, but neither is it as fanciful as a rigorous opponent might suggest. What Shakespeare must have thought is not, with Empson, romantic speculation about Shakespeare's psychology, but a form of metaphor for what Shakespeare actually wrote, a way of seeing words on the page as continuous with an individual human life.

Of course, *Seven Types of Ambiguity* is a mischievous book . . . , which delights in multiplying complicated meanings. But then Empson tells us that this is what he is doing ("I have put down most of the meanings for fun," he says of his discussion of a line in Chaucer, "the only ones I feel sure of are . . ."), and I don't see how what seems to be a standard accusation against him . . . can possibly be supported. The accusation is that Empson thinks that a word *does* mean anything it *may* mean, which is plainly nonsense. But all Empson says, as I understand him, is that we had better look at some of the meanings a word *might* have before we decide which meaning or meanings it *does* have. (p. 31)

[There] is a danger, not in Empson's critical method, but in Empson's continuing critical subject, which is always irony, in one form or another. But this is not now a question of the baleful influence of *Seven Types of Ambiguity.* Throughout his career, . . . Empson remains a student (and indeed a distinguished practitioner) of irony, experienced as a complicated response to a life seen as riddled with contradictions. "The notion is," Empson says in a note on his poem "Bacchus," "that life involves maintaining oneself between contradictions that can't be solved by analysis." . . . There is a difficulty. . . . We tend to . . . forget what all this equilibrium is *for,* and the result is a very cosy variety of stasis. If you're a critic, you discover that your poet has said a lot of perfectly opposed things about life, and therefore can't have *meant* anything. The political expression of this position is a very relaxed form of sitting on the fence. . . .

Empson's own ironies, for example, usually suggest a vigorous common sense doing what it can in the midst of a terrible muddle, or perhaps even, to quote Empson's own phrase about Milton, "a powerful mind thrashing about in exasperation"; but they can also be read as rather bland invitations to give it all up and go home. . . .

Empson's poems are generally, as he says of Shakespeare's use of the word *honest* in *Othello,* "a very queer business." He published verse steadily between 1928 and 1940, but since then, apart from a sonnet, a Chinese ballad, a lumpish masque for the Queen's visit to Sheffield, and a couple of short pieces added to the *Collected Poems* in 1949, has published no verse at all. Everyone points out that most of the poems belong, in their preoccupations, to the universe of *Seven Types of Ambiguity* (1930) and *Some Versions of Pastoral* (1935), but given their dates, it is hard to see how they could belong anywhere else; and the most striking thing about the poems for me is their radical difference in tone and feeling from the criticism. They are cramped, clogged, and diffident where the criticism is reckless and easy. The reason for this may be simple enough: it's exciting to discover fruitful complications in a great writer, but it's no fun to face and articulate oppressive contradictions in your own life.

Still, the contrast is remarkable, and I wonder whether its real source is the contradictions being faced in the poetry or a certain hampered, mechanical approach to the actual writing of poetry. Empson speaks of "my clotted kind of poetry," and it is clotted, thick with allusions and odd, mathematical-sounding words. Its rhythms literally slow the tongue ("No, by too much this station the air nears"), and its elliptical syntax ("It is Styx coerces and not Hell controls") creates a sense of intense crowding. Empson has said that although most of his poems "turned out to be love poems about boy being too afraid of girl to tell her anything, the simple desire to think of something rather like Donne was the basic impulse"; and perhaps all I mean to say is that at this distance in time the manner seems very faded, a brittle ghost of the Twenties.

But I am speaking of the collected poems as a whole, and half a dozen pieces remain amazingly good—as good as Auden at his best, say, which is very good indeed—and there are marvelous musical lines scattered about poems that themselves don't come off. The lasting works are the obvious, recurring anthology items ("To an Old Lady," "Homage to the British Museum," "Notes on Local Flora," "Aubade," "Let it go"), but "Letter II" and "Autumn on Nan-Yueh" seem to me just as fine. There is tremendous poise and wit in these poems, there are all kinds of jokes and graces, and above all they are generous and moving. Whatever shallow impulses started them off, they found their way into profound life. The old lady visible only in darkness, lovable only at a distance, respected although she is so distant, is a kind of paradigm for Empson's respect for the right of others to be themselves. And [the] closing verses from "Autumn on Nan-Yueh" . . . express

with the utmost delicacy a sense of personal loss in the midst of losses all around which are considerably greater. (p. 32)

"The masterpiece is *Some Versions of Pastoral,*" Denis Donoghue wrote . . . , and Roger Sale says the same thing in his excellent essay on Empson in *Modern Heroism.* I think this is true in the sense that the book contains the biggest doses of careless Empsonian wisdom about the larger structures of literature, like tragedy, pastoral, irony, plot, and so on, and also in the sense that it has an elegance and a flow and a sense of ongoing argument which are lacking or obscured in the other books; and the chapter on *Alice* is probably the most brilliant thing Empson has ever done. Yet *Seven Types of Ambiguity* is a more exciting, in many ways richer, work and provides me at least with more sheer pleasure; and there is nothing in either of those two early books that quite comes up to the essay on *Lear* in *The Structure of Complex Words* (1951), or even to the essay on *Tom Jones.* (pp. 32-3)

These essays answer and defuse a suspicion which I think must lurk in the mind of anyone who has been reading Empson for a while: the suspicion that this wonderfully subtle and intelligent man has too much of a taste for the bushes and byways of culture, a taste not for minor works but for the back entrances to major works. A great deal of *Some Versions of Pastoral* is devoted to finding pastoral where no one else would think of looking for it, and the great, musical statements which appear now and then in the early books . . . come across as something like slips of the tongue, moments of negligence in which Empson allowed himself to say something that sounded important.

But the essays on *Lear* and *Tom Jones* tackle major works in a direct, major way, present themselves calmly at the front door. . . .

The Structure of Complex Words . . . shifts attention from the ambiguities of literature to the ambiguities of language. Empson is interested in usages which suggest that the whole language is behind a speaker, not that the speaker can do wonderful things with language, and these are the terms on which he distinguishes this book from his earlier ones. It is a question now not of showing what Shakespeare could do with English, but of showing the riches of English on display in Shakespeare. . . .

[*Milton's God* is a] brilliant business, right about God, often right about Milton, full of good jokes, it has a feverish, strident note not heard before in Empson. The Christian God, Empson says, "is the wickedest thing yet invented by the black heart of man," and I would want to demur only at the tone of that judgment and its exaggeration (the Indian Kali and the Mexican Tezcatlipoca were not exactly a bundle of smiles). What seems wrong is not Empson's view of Christianity, but his strained insistence that we have to have a view of Christianity. . . .

We are wrong to look to Empson for dignity or doctrines, and probably wrong to look to him for complete, satisfying books, for masterpieces. . . . What Empson gives us are repeated instances of an incomparable mind at play. He enhances for us, even restores if we feel we are losing it, the pure, dizzying exhilaration of *reading,* and anyone who thinks this is not important doesn't care about the life of the imagination in any of its forms. (p. 33)

*Michael Wood, "Incomparable Empson,"
in* The New York Review of Books *(re-*

printed with permission from The New York Review of Books; *copyright © 1975 by NYREV, Inc.), January 23, 1975, pp. 30-3.*

* * *

ENRIGHT, D(ennis) J(oseph) 1920-

Enright is an English novelist, poet, critic, and editor. His poetry is characterized by its humanism and intelligibility. Enright has written four novels set abroad, which he disparagingly calls travel books. (See also *CLC*, Vol. 4, and *Contemporary Authors*, Vols. 1-4, rev. ed.)

["The Terrible Shears" is] grimly entertaining. . . . Enright is really a writer of light verse, and he tells the quite horrible events of his childhood in a jaunty tone not devoid of its own brisk gruesomeness. Odd, but distinctive, owing a good deal to Lawrence, but with an enabling, and also disabling, common sense, Enright's verse admits that by the standards of world suffering, his "wasn't a bad life":

> No one was dragged out of bed by
> Armed men. Children weren't speared
> Or their brains dashed out. I don't
> Remember seeing a man starve to death.

True, but at the same time, to the truest poetry, which must be the poetry of the single soul, irrelevant. Enright's baby sister was seen to "quietly disgorge a lot of blood" and disappear, his father's death certificate remarked that "a Contributory Cause of Death was Septic Teeth," and his grandmother, after being "pushed into" a car, shouted "with a dreadful new voice: / 'I know where you're sending me, / You're sending me to the Workhouse!'" Enright's tone of the worst-below-the-worst polishes off the poem ("Geriatrics") about his grandmother:

> She was found to be deranged on arrival,
> And they sent her on to another place.
> So she didn't go to the Workhouse after all.
> She died soon after.

The banality of suffering suggests that none of us can write any longer about our own versions of it without irony. If the only alternatives to irony are bathos or false heroics, as Enright's poems imply, we have lost a great deal. (pp. 4-5)

> *Helen Vendler, in* The New York Times Book Review *(© 1975 by The New York Times Company; reprinted by permission), April 6, 1975.*

D. J. Enright, like Philip Larkin, is very English: they have the most recognisably English tones of any poets writing today. . . . [One] would distrust anything a foreigner said was 'very English,' and it is probably either complacent or vulgar or both to claim a different sort of inside knowledge. But it would not seem apposite to call Auden English, or Frost American: they write in Audenian and Frostian—lordly dialects of the international vernacular. Larkin and Enright have their own idiom, of course, quite individual to themselves, if at times mutually comparable; but poetically speaking they are also distinctively English as well—their idiom appearing to distil in poetic and linguistic form the contemporary state of the nation. These assertions lack precision, but are about as near to the question as I can come.

In many poems, as in prose works like *The World of Dew*, Enright has explored the nature of foreignness, our reactions to it and its reactions to us. That helps to achieve

negative definition, as in 'Reflections on Foreign Literature' from . . . *Addictions*. . . . The exactness there could only be put in poetry, indeed only in Enright's poetry; but, for that reason, its virtues seem splendidly contemptuous of the ingrown solipsism we are accustomed to in so much contemporary poetry. Its intelligence, that is, does not seem there for the sake of the poem, but for the sake of the point it makes, which is the great virtue of Enright's poetry. . . . He writes reports and messages in poetic form on real situations; indeed, it would not be unduly fanciful to see many of the best poems as despatches from the guardians of an ideal diplomacy, the sort of despatches that the Duke of Wellington (that very English hero) might have written if—as he put it when apologising for the length of one—he had had the time to make them shorter.

Enright is an extrovert in the refreshing sense that when he writes about himself he does so with a mild curiosity, as if he were writing about something else. This non-attachment in an odd way parallels the sharp little point made in 'Reflections on Foreign Literature': for many poets, to write about themselves is a kind of journey into the permanently exotic, a holiday from the corruptions and discriminations exacted by what is familiarly and grindingly quotidian. . . . That is the foreign country in which Enright toils with unseduced clarity and genial amusement, but he never allows himself to go native in it: the self must not be used like a foreign country, though it is the greatest indulgence of contemporary poetry so to use it. (pp. 681-82)

[He] has never, it seems, taken himself seriously to the point of manufacturing a style for himself; and knocking about the world generally and the mysterious East in particular, though it has given his verses something of the accomplishment, in movement and metre, of the oriental and demotic, has in no way affected its native and marrowy pith. The dimension of *Sad Ires,* in which urban humours and spectres of Earl's Court replace, for the most part, the experiences of an old China hand, contains poems on an even higher level of achievement than those in previous collections. (p. 682)

> *John Bayley, "Word of an Englishman," in* The Listener *(© British Broadcasting Corp. 1975; reprinted by permission of John Bayley), November 20, 1975, pp. 681-82.*

[D. J. Enright's] earlier poems can be seen as attacks on large gestures of almost any kind. His characteristic assertions have been for the rights and individualities of the common man; mishaps perpetrated on ordinary citizens are seen as the consequences of those who "thought big." He has never paid much attention to the possibility they "thought wrong."

For all their avowed certainties, Enright's points of view now begin to look a shade more controversial than they were in the 1950s and early 1960s. Wisdom, which Enright has—or it is an attractive ploy for him to pretend he has it—can, when showing itself as satisfied with its "own reward", act as little more than a warning that it is dangerous to be anything other than cunning, reserved and cynical. His stoic, shifty fortitude might be nothing more than a consistent overstating of the negative side of his mind's conclusions. He writes as a Machiavellian soliloquiser speaks; except, of course, that this soliloquiser also wears motley, a partnership which is responsible for the marvellous readability of his poems. (p. 77)

Enright's tone of voice, which is important in his poems, is usually called "laconic" or "mordant." It could be said to be much more than these so-called "anti-poetic" terms generally mean. In an epoch when those who maintain liberal, humane values have been constantly on the defensive, his tone sounds representative of that defence, bemused and indignant but careful not to overdo either. Elsewhere I've said Enright's tone is like Brecht's in his poems. A coincidence of that sort leads me to believe Enright is as political a poet as we've got, a poet of suspicions, of sly counter-jabs, a poet who points out exceptions the political rules are unprepared to include.

Technically, Enright is adroit. On the other hand he can be mistaken by some as a poet devoid of technical interest; he seldom turns in a sustained metrical performance, or indulges in pan-American experiment. His technique is guided by and supports tones of voice needed for his slyly offensive and defensive patterns of thought. *Sad Ires* marks no new stage in his writing, which is a disappointment after *The Terrible Shears* seemed to promise a more bruisingly local treatment of his themes. The book is good enough, and two poems ("R-and-R" and "Meeting a Person") are among his best. (pp. 77-8)

> *Douglas Dunn, in* Encounter *(© 1976 by Encounter Ltd.), February, 1976.*

While varied in subject, Enright's poems usually concern chance episodes and characters on the fringes of society who are observed with a keen but sympathetic eye as they hopelessly live or helplessly meet their fate.... Enright's chronicle of ineptitude and inevitability usually avoids sentimentality by virtue of his discriminating intellect and his sense of humor; to maintain one's poise while recording scenes likely to evoke ineffectual sympathy is no small achievement....

[The] transposition of attention to the particular from its native habitat to alien cultures affects more than subject matter. In their diffident criticisms of English life, poets of the Movement could assume the values of the liberal tradition within the context of Western civilization. Enright, as [William Walsh] points out [in *D. J. Enright: Poet of Humanism*], is engaged in the implicit affirmation of a liberal humanism that others have been able to assume. Enright forces us to recognize that this tradition has not taken root elsewhere in the world and that we must face up to a massive amount of human suffering without being able to palliate it. These considerations may help explain his "uneasiness as to some of the things poetry can do, together with misgiving at how skilfully it avoids doing other things" ..., as well as the ascetic spareness of the later poems (it is almost as if Enright denies himself indulgence in his own talent). The moral concerns of [F. R.] Leavis' criticism have left their mark on Enright. (p. 568)

The problems facing Enright and his generation are not exclusively literary in nature, as Leavis himself has argued. Enright is in some respects a test case for contemporary British poetry because he allows us to see what happens to the best part of the British tradition when it is sympathetically engaged with other literatures and cultures. Sympathy, based on [contemporary Anglo-American] liberal humanism, shows us not only the intolerable political practices of other nations but the fundamental faults of entire civilizations as well.... From this point of view, we are helpless to change the world, certain of what is wrong with it, and sorrowful or ironic as a result. Enright's admiration of Goethe and Thomas Mann suggests that it might be possible to escape these melancholy alternatives; an attempt to understand other civilizations on their own grounds, rather than judging them in the belief that ours are in fact "human grounds," might provide an even more liberating escape. (p. 569)

> *Wallace Martin, in* Contemporary Literature *(© 1976 by the Board of Regents of the University of Wisconsin System), Vol. 17, No. 4, Autumn, 1976.*

F

FARRELL, James T(homas)   1904-

Farrell is an American novelist, short story writer, poet, and critic. Influenced by his Catholic background, Marx, and the novels and stories of Dreiser, Anderson, and Joyce, Farrell won for himself a permanent place in American letters with his early masterpiece, the *Studs Lonigan* trilogy. To this day Farrell continues to write in the objective, naturalistic style that brought him his fame. At the age of seventy-four he is hard at work writing a panoramic fictional study of American society that is projected to total approximately thirty volumes upon completion. (See also *CLC*, Vols. 1, 4, and *Contemporary Authors*, Vols. 5-8, rev. ed.)

In an age of such mind-boggling changes as ours, it's a shock and a pleasure to find something that hasn't changed, to see once again the old familiar landscapes and inscapes, signs and portents. This was my reaction on reading James T. Farrell's *Judith and Other Stories,* his forty-seventh book and his fourteenth collection of short fiction. . . .

I've frequently tended to think about Farrell [that] anyone that prolific really can't be much good. Obviously this kind of judgment should be avoided. It's easy, and at one time it was very popular, to overemphasize Farrell's shortcomings —the lack of humor, the prolixity, the repetitiveness—all of which have been present in his work since *Studs Lonigan* (can it really have been forty years ago?) and which are present here in these stories and novellas, whether they be set in the late thirties or in the contemporary period. In spite of this *Judith* is a good book. Farrell at seventy is impressive, towering, almost monolithic; it is difficult to believe there was a time when he and his fictional world didn't exist. His sincerity, his intelligence, his gravity, his knowledge of his people are formidable, and though Farrell can still write some bad lines, his prose is surprisingly good: simple, direct, uncluttered. And he has a couple of brief, single-episode anecdotal pieces that may surprise and confound those who tend to take him for granted. "On a Train to Rome" and "On the Appian Way" are very nice indeed; so too is "Sister," a relatively short piece about the effect of a nun upon one of her students. Farrell has always been effective in depicting the pangs and aspirations of the young, and "Sister" is one of his best. (pp. 724-25)

> *William Peden, in* Sewanee Review *(reprinted by permission of the editor,* © *1974 by The University of the South), Fall, 1974.*

Farrell's *Studs Lonigan* . . . has the obvious quality of ambition. It is, I suppose, the most intransigent work of naturalism ever written, and its defects come from this. In this novel at least Farrell is the true heir of Dreiser. If he lacks Dreiser's tragic sense, he has an icily relentless passion that transforms *Studs Lonigan* into a formidable indictment of society. It is, apart from George Gissing's *The Nether World* and for similar reasons, probably the most depressing novel ever written, and as it is synopsized in the *Oxford Companion to American Literature* it appears the *reductio ad absurdum* of naturalism. But its impact is extremely powerful; if we laugh at the *Oxford Companion's* synopsis, we do not laugh at the novel. It is a passionate work. To it Farrell prefixes a quotation from Plato: "Except in the case of some rarely gifted nature there never will be a good man who has not from his childhood been used to play amid things of beauty and make of them a joy and a study." A most important statement: it explains Stud's fate. But epigraphs are luxuries for a novelist: they are not a part of the novel itself; and my criticism of *Studs Lonigan* now is that somehow—I don't know how he could have done it—Farrell ought to have woven Plato's words, translated into dramatic action or symbolism, into the texture of the novel itself. All the same, I still see *Studs Lonigan* as an heroic work. (p. 249)

> *Walter Allen, in* Twentieth Century Literature *(copyright 1974, Hofstra University Press), October, 1974.*

[*The Dunne Family* is] a very slow-moving, ponderous book which lacks freshness, narrative drive, and dramatic intensity. About ninety per cent of it develops through dialogue, and this dialogue is constantly dull, ordinary, circular, and repetitious. The novel has been padded beyond all legitimate limits; in fact, it is doubtful if the material and characters are meaningful enough to make even an effective short story. So obvious a potboiler is a distressing experience.

A reviewer, however, can applaud a sense of dignity about this work which must be attributed to Farrell's maturity. Studs Lonigan Farrell appears to have mellowed a good bit and come to acknowledge that not all his Chicago Irish are essentially primitive monsters. Apparently not all problems are to be blamed on society, the clergy, the government, and other bugbears of Farrell's youth. He seems to have caught humanity's eternal note of sadness, and while he has not, alas, developed a complete recognition of matters beyond a feeble Naturalistic level, there are indications that perhaps the depth of philosophical perception is expanding. Farrell still has little awareness of the real meaning and importance of Catholicism to the Irish. Having a character say the Rosary in the way he presents it is a prop and a verisimilitude stunt rather than a meaningful act of piety with links to the goal of heaven. (p. 348)

> *Paul A. Doyle, in* Best Sellers *(copyright 1977, by the University of Scranton), February, 1977.*

*   *   *

FAULKNER, William   1897-1962

An American novelist, short story writer, poet, and screenplay writer, Faulkner is one of the greatest writers America has produced. While his themes are many and have been subjected to conflicting interpretation, his major fictive concern is with the inevitability of individual responsibility and the absolute necessity of compassion and humanism. Faulkner's southern experience provided the material for the creation of his own fictive world, Yoknapatawpha County. An experimentalist, Faulkner wove together myth, oral tradition, symbol, and allegory in some of his most complex and admired works, including *Absalom, Absalom!*, *The Sound and the Fury, As I Lay Dying,* **and** *Light in August.* **Yet he was also a very successful Hollywood screenwriter and several novels, such as** *Sanctuary,* **have been read as compelling thrillers. Faulkner was awarded both the Pulitzer and Nobel Prizes. (See also** *CLC,* **Vols. 1, 3, 6.)**

[If] one thing is more outstanding than another about Mr. Faulkner—some readers find it so outstanding, indeed, that they never get beyond it—it is the uncompromising and almost hypnotic zeal with which he insists upon having a style, and, especially of late, the very peculiar style which he insists upon having. Perhaps to that one should add that he insists *when he remembers*—he can write straightforwardly enough when he wants to; he does so often in the best of his short stories (and they are brilliant), often enough, too, in the novels. But that *style* is what he really wants to get back to; and get back to it he invariably does.

And what a style it is, to be sure! The exuberant and tropical luxuriance of sound which Jim Europe's jazz band used to exhale, like a jungle of rank creepers and ferocious blooms taking shape before one's eyes—magnificently and endlessly intervolved, glisteningly and ophidianly in motion, coil sliding over coil, and leaf and flower forever magically interchanging—was scarcely more bewildering, in its sheer inexhaustible fecundity, than Mr. Faulkner's style. Small wonder if even the most passionate of Mr. Faulkner's admirers—among whom the present writer honors himself by enlisting—must find, with each new novel, that the first fifty pages are always the hardest, that each time one must learn all over again *how* to read this strangely fluid and slippery and heavily mannered prose, and that one is even, like a kind of Laocoön, sometimes tempted to give it up. (p. 200)

Mr. Faulkner's style, though often brilliant and always interesting, is all too frequently downright bad. . . . But if it is easy enough to make fun of Mr. Faulkner's obsessions for particular words, or his indifference and violence to them, or the parrotlike mechanical mytacism (for it is really like a stammer) with which he will go on endlessly repeating such favorites as "myriad, sourceless, impalpable, outrageous, risible, profound," there is nevertheless something more to be said for his passion for overelaborate sentence structure.

Overelaborate they certainly are, baroque and involuted and in the extreme, these sentences: trailing clauses, one after another, shadowily in apposition, or perhaps not even with so much connection as that; parenthesis after parenthesis, the parenthesis itself often containing one or more parentheses—they remind one of those brightly colored Chinese eggs of one's childhood, which when opened disclosed egg after egg, each smaller and subtler than the last. It is as if Mr. Faulkner, in a sort of hurried despair, had decided to try to tell us everything, absolutely everything, every last origin or source or quality or qualification, and every possible future or permutation as well, in one terrifically concentrated effort: each sentence to be, as it were, a microcosm. And it must be admitted that the practice is annoying and distracting.

It is annoying, at the end of a sentence, to find that one does not know in the least what was the subject of the verb that dangles *in vacuo*—it is distracting to have to go back and sort out the meaning, track down the structure from clause to clause, then only to find that after all it doesn't much matter, and that the obscurity was perhaps neither subtle nor important. And to the extent that one *is* annoyed and distracted, and *does* thus go back and work it out, it may be at once added that Mr. Faulkner has defeated his own ends. One has had, of course, to emerge from the stream, and to step away from it, in order properly to see it; and as Mr. Faulkner works precisely by a process of *immersion*, of hypnotizing his reader into *remaining immersed* in his stream, this occasional blunder produces irritation and failure.

Nevertheless, despite the blunders, and despite the bad habits and the willful bad writing (and willful it obviously is), the style as a whole is extraordinarily effective; the reader *does* remain immersed, *wants* to remain immersed, and it is interesting to look into the reasons for this. And at once, if one considers these queer sentences not simply by themselves, as monsters of grammar or awkwardness, but in their relation to the book as a whole, one sees a functional reason and necessity for their being as they are. They parallel in a curious and perhaps inevitable way, and not without aesthetic justification, the whole elaborate method of *deliberately withheld meaning,* of progressive and partial and delayed disclosure, which so often gives the characteristic shape to the novels themselves. It is a persistent offering of obstacles, a calculated system of screens and obtrusions, of confusions and ambiguous interpolations and delays, with one express purpose; and that purpose is simply to keep the form—and the idea—fluid and unfinished, still in motion, as it were, and unknown, until the dropping into place of the very last syllable.

What Mr. Faulkner is after, in a sense, is a *continuum.* He wants a medium without stops or pauses, a medium which is always *of the moment,* and of which the passage from moment to moment is as fluid and undetectable as in the life itself which he is purporting to give. It is all inside and underneath, or as seen from within and below; the reader must therefore be steadily *drawn in;* he must be powerfully and unremittingly hypnotized inward and downward to that image-stream; and this suggests, perhaps, a reason not only for the length and elaborateness of the sentence structure, but for the repetitiveness as well. The repetitiveness, and the steady iterative emphasis—like a kind of chanting or invocation—on certain relatively abstract words ("sonorous, latin, *vaguely* eloquent"), have the effect at last of producing, for Mr. Faulkner, a special language, a conglomerate of his own, which he uses with an astonishing virtuosity, and which, although in detailed analysis it may look shoddy, is actually for his purpose a life stream of almost miraculous adaptability. At the one extreme it is abstract, cerebral, time-and-space-obsessed, tortured and twisted, but nevertheless always with a living *pulse* in it; and at the other it can be as overwhelming in its simple vividness, its richness in the actual, as the flood scenes in *The Wild Palms.*

Obviously, such a style, especially when allied with such a *concern* for method, must make difficulties for the reader; and it must be admitted that Mr. Faulkner does little or nothing as a rule to make his highly complex "situation" easily available or perceptible. The reader must simply make up his mind to go to work, and in a sense to cooperate; his reward being that there *is* a situation to be given shape, a meaning to be extracted, and that half the fun is precisely in watching the queer, difficult, and often so laborious evolution of Mr. Faulkner's idea. And not so much idea, either, as form. For, like the great predecessor whom at least in this regard he so oddly resembles, Mr. Faulkner could say with Henry James that it is practically impossible to make any real distinction between theme and form. What immoderately delights him . . . and what sets him above—shall we say it firmly—all his American contemporaries, is his continuous preoccupation with the novel *as form,* his passionate concern with it, and a degree of success with it which would clearly have commanded the interest and respect of Henry James himself. The novel as revelation, the novel as slice-of-life, the novel as mere story, do not interest him: these he would say, like James again, "are the circumstances of the interest," but not the interest itself. The interest itself will be the use to which these circumstances are put, the degree to which they can be organized.

From this point of view, he is not in the least to be considered as a mere "Southern" writer: the "Southernness" of his scenes and characters is of little concern to him, just as little as the question whether they are pleasant or unpleasant, true or untrue. Verisimilitude—or, at any rate, *degree* of verisimilitude—he will cheerfully abandon, where necessary, if the compensating advantages of plan or tone are a sufficient inducement. The famous scene in *Sanctuary* of Miss Reba and Uncle Bud in which a "madam" and her cronies hold a wake for a dead gangster, while the small boy gets drunk, is quite false, taken out of its context; it is not endowed with the same *kind* of actuality which permeates the greater part of the book at all. Mr. Faulkner was cunning enough to see that a two-dimensional cartoon-like statement, at this juncture, would supply him with the effect of a chorus, and without in the least being perceived as a change in the temperature of truthfulness.

That particular kind of dilution, or adulteration, of verisimilitude was both practised and praised by James. . . . It was for him a device for organization, just as the careful cherishing of "viewpoint" was a device, whether simply or in counterpoint. Of Mr. Faulkner's devices, of this sort, aimed at the achievement of complex "form," the two most constant are the manipulation of viewpoint and the use of the flashback, or sudden shift of time-scene, forward or backward.

In *Sanctuary,* where the alternation of viewpoint is a little lawless, the complexity is given, perhaps a shade disingen-

uously, by violent shifts in time; a deliberate disarrangement of an otherwise straightforward story. Technically, there is no doubt that the novel, despite its fame, rattles a little; and Mr. Faulkner himself takes pains to disclaim it. But, even done with the left hand, it betrays a genius for form, quite apart from its wonderful virtuosity in other respects. *Light in August* . . . repeats the same technique, that of a dislocation of time, and more elaborately; the time-shifts alternate with shifts in the viewpoint; and if the book is a failure it is perhaps because Mr. Faulkner's tendency to what is almost a hypertrophy of form is not here, as well as in the other novels, matched with the characters and the theme. Neither the person nor the story of Joe Christmas is seen fiercely enough—by its creator—to carry off that immense machinery of narrative; . . . for once Mr. Faulkner's inexhaustible inventiveness seems to have been at fault. Consequently what we see is an extraordinary power for form functioning relatively *in vacuo,* and existing only to sustain itself.

In the best of the novels, however—and it is difficult to choose between *The Sound and the Fury* and *The Wild Palms,* with *Absalom, Absalom!* a very close third—this tendency to hypertrophy of form has been sufficiently curbed; and it is interesting, too, to notice that in all these three (and in that remarkable *tour de force, As I Lay Dying,* as well), while there is still a considerably reliance on time-shift, the effect of richness and complexity is chiefly obtained by a very skillful fugue-like alternation of viewpoint. Fugue-like in *The Wild Palms*—and fugue-like especially, of course, in *As I Lay Dying,* where the shift is kaleidoscopically rapid, and where, despite an astonishing violence to plausibility (in the reflections, and *language* of reflection, of the characters), an effect of the utmost reality and immediateness is nevertheless produced. Fugue-like, again, in *Absalom, Absalom!,* where indeed one may say the form is really circular—there is no beginning and no ending properly speaking, and therefore no *logical* point of entrance: we must just submit, and follow the circling of the author's interest, which turns a light inward towards the center, but every moment from a new angle, a new point of view. The story unfolds, therefore, now in one color of light, now in another, with references backward and forward: those that refer forward being necessarily, for the moment, blind. What is complete in Mr. Faulkner's pattern, *a priori,* must nevertheless remain incomplete for us until the very last stone is in place; what is "real," therefore, at one stage of the unfolding, or from one point of view, turns out to be "unreal" from another; and we find that one among other thing with which we are engaged is the fascinating sport of trying to separate truth from legend, watching the growth of legend from truth, and finally reaching the conclusion that the distinction is itself false.

Something of the same sort is true also of *The Sound and the Fury*—and this, with its massive four-part symphonic structure, is perhaps the most beautifully *wrought* of the whole series, and an indubitable masterpiece of what James loved to call the "fictive art." The joinery is flawless in its intricacy; it is a novelist's novel—a whole textbook on the craft of fiction in itself, comparable in its way to *What Maisie Knew* or *The Golden Bowl.*

But if it is important, for the moment, to emphasize Mr. Faulkner's genius for form, and his continued exploration of its possibilities, as against the usual concern with the violence and dreadfulness of his themes—though we might pause to remind carpers on this score of the fact that the best of Henry James is precisely that group of last novels which so completely concerned themselves with moral depravity—it is also well to keep in mind his genius for invention, whether of character or episode. The inventiveness is of the richest possible sort—a headlong and tumultuous abundance, an exuberant generosity and vitality, which makes most other contemporary fiction look very pale and chaste indeed. It is an unforgettable gallery of portraits, whether character or caricature, and all of them endowed with a violent and immediate vitality. (pp. 201-06)

> Conrad Aiken, "Faulkner, William" (1939), in his Collected Criticism (copyright © 1935, 1939, 1940, 1942, 1951, 1958 by Conrad Aiken; reprinted by permission of Oxford University Press, Inc.), Oxford University Press, 1968, pp. 200-07.

Reduced to an outline, Faulkner's stories are like many others: a contingent unfolding of events whose fatal aspect may simply be the illusion of those involved. That is why his plots never appear too easily as unified structures, as geometrical sequences of moments, events, and feelings. Much remains hidden from the reader, and it is this very obscurity of plot which weighs so much upon all that happens and exists. One of the purposes of Faulkner's apparently disordered narrative is to show that [the] sense of fatal oppression is not a device of cohesive narration, but that it subsists, and that by suggesting it the novelist is obeying the nature of things. . . . We must . . . not look for the explanation of Faulknerian destiny in any supposedly deterministic time structure. (p. 79)

[Through] the persistence of past impressions, especially childhood impressions, Faulkner shows that the present is submerged in the past, that what is lived in the present is what was lived in the past. In this case, the past is not so much an evocation as it is a constant pressure upon the present, the pressure of what has been on what is.

Consciousness, therefore, is mostly memory. But not the kind of memory which attaches the present to a past known as past and no longer existing. For memory is so much a part of what actually exists that it does not know itself as memory, does not know itself as anything but the sense of reality. Since, however, memory cannot possibly be anything but the sense of the past, we must conclude—and this lies at the core of Faulkner—that it is the past which is real. (p. 80)

Faulknerian past is extra-temporal. The fact that an event slips into the past does not mean that it becomes pure memory labeled with a date, but that it sheds temporality, inasmuch as time is change and dispersion.

These ideas are difficult to express and not at all explicit in Faulkner. The past is not a temporal past, that which no longer is and can only be remembered. It is something here and now, present in the proper sense of the word. Inserted into time, the past *was* and is therefore past, but inasmuch as it subsists, it is present. This is why we can say it is extra-temporal—not, however, that it resides in a superior realm, because a timeless past accompanies each chronological present. It receives its significance from the present and at the same time incorporates the present into itself (the present becomes past, as Temple becomes the girl already raped whom he had just seen being raped). All this is certainly not supposed to constitute a theory on Faulkner. It only applies to his characters' manner of living, since time is nothing outside someone's consciousness of time. So

when we say that present means past, that the past recaptures the present, we are speaking of the hero himself who feels bound to a past he cannot dismiss. This is when fate appears. (pp. 80-1)

The future does not seem to enter into a novel like *Light in August* or *Sanctuary*. In *Light in August* the end of the story, the murder, is already indicated at the beginning, so that the entire novel is but an exploration of the past. In *Sanctuary* there is indeed a progression of events, a very normal one in fact, and yet we are never given the impression that the various characters really have a future. They advance, but backward. They are not lured by a feat or fascinated by a certain type of behavior into which they madly throw themselves, as are Dostoevsky's heroes when they feel the call of destiny. Christmas has no concept of his future. Even though he vaguely knows he will kill, this murder is simply an advent of the past to which he adds nothing. He feels the meaninglessness of his performance even before he acts. The future can be compared to the present: we cannot say it is determined by the past since there is no reason why such and such a thing must happen. Anything might happen. But whatever does happen, the event immediately assumes the colors of the past without changing them in the slightest. . . . Being the past, it is untouchable, and that is why it is also destiny.

The past, therefore, not only was but is and will be; it is the unfolding of destiny. Note, though, that this development is not rendered either necessary or imperious. It little matters what happens, since Faulknerian destiny does not depend on the realization of a particular contingent event. The course destiny chooses is in a sense superfluous, for we are not dealing with the kind of fatality which manifests itself in a dramatic progression of events, from which we cannot add or subtract a single one without changing its entire passage, for to do so would be like saying that someone has not fulfilled his destiny because of a premature death. In this case destiny is recognized as life's term, whereas in Faulkner destiny is at the source of life. . . . (p. 81)

For Proust, too, the past is a present reality and the fundamental dimension of time. Even the title of his novel announces that the present has no consistency and is not really a presence, that it only becomes real in a past which purifies it, in a past which must be recaptured. Does not Proust, on an intellectual level, resemble Quentin in *The Sound and the Fury*, this being who can live only in the past? . . .

With Proust [the past] is strictly individual, made up of personal habits and sensations. The adventure of the little cake dipped in the cup of tea applies only to him. With Faulkner, on the other hand, it is not only my past that emerges and adapts itself as best it can (for Proust, not too well) to an exterior present, it is everybody's past, the pasts of all his characters. Faulkner's people are real only in their pasts. . . . [Proust's past is] distinct from a perfectly real present. Christmas lives his memories, whereas Proust relives them. . . . Proust lives in two times, in chronological time and in recaptured time. His analysis is born in the confrontation of the two, when subjective reality interferes with objective reality. But since Faulkner refuses chronological time, he has nothing to analyze. Subjective reality absorbs everything and becomes fate, intensified by the annihilation of all opposition. (p. 82)

Without warning the reader, he places one moment into another and shuffles all habitual order because, according to him, lives are not lived chronologically. This is what the interior monologues try to make us understand.

Chronological order would ruin the past for two reasons. First of all, there would be but a succession of mutually exclusive "nows," valid in themselves alone and not in their identification with the past. . . . Secondly, chronology would chop up the past into fictitious pasts, presents, and futures. The past which Faulkner's heroes feel weighing upon them is a detemporalized unit. Whereas the present is fragmented, dispersed, and not really experienced, the past forms an undecomposable whole. The entire novel is but an attempt to make this known, but not, however, through some sort of administrative report. We reach this past through a succession of plunges. The order of the plunges is determined by the appearance of those characters who know a certain past of a person from the exterior or from hearsay and are thus able to relate it. (pp. 82-3)

One might accuse Faulkner of artifice, for we all know that in fact things do happen in a certain order, that this order is still real for whoever lives these things. This of course is quite true, but we will never understand Faulkner's point of view unless we distinguish between consciousness and knowledge. Faulkner places himself on the level of the former. Consciousness is inevitable, knowledge only a possibility. Since one does not necessarily attain knowledge, Faulkner can omit it without deforming human nature, especially in the kind of characters he chooses. Chronology, being a posterior organization of a life, belongs to the domain of knowledge. It is a kind of intellectual liberation from destiny; it assures us that the past is indeed past even if we feel its pressure on our present. Faulkner's heroes enjoy no such liberation, which is itself a free rather than necessary category of the human mind. All this goes to confirm what we said before: destiny in Faulkner is the opposite of a geometrical relationship between chronologically situated moments. (p. 83)

[There] is nothing artificial in Faulkner's technique. He has merely emphasized and generalized the psychological reality of omission. After all, everything that takes place has passed as soon as it happens, and can therefore only be told as a recollection, even in direct narration.

The nature of Faulkner's vision converges here with his concept of time: he never "sees" the important events for he is "with" his heroes (he "sees" one "with" the other), with these heroes who see only their past. Let us make an unexpected comparison with French classical tragedy: here too the tragic events are only related; we never see them happening. The tragic is what has been (or, to use one of Sartre's expressions, what "is been") and cannot be seen directly. If we find this principle in two forms as different as Racine's theater and Faulkner's novel, it must be of a fairly general nature. (p. 84)

Faulkner's people are not "blind puppets of Fate" as Coindreau erroneously names them in his preface to *Light in August*. Faulkner's is undoubtedly "a world where man exists as a crushed being" as Malraux writes in his preface to *Sanctuary*, but the pressure comes from within, not from without. Faulkner's man crushes himself more than he is crushed.

If this is true, if destiny is in fact an inner force, and if Christmas is dominated by himself more than by things, the hero must constantly feel fate's affirmation.

The feeling of inner fatality is expressed very clearly in the account of Christmas' attempt to escape in *Light in August:* "But there was too much running with him, stride for stride with him. Not pursuers: but himself: years, acts, deeds omitted and committed, keeping pace with him stride for stride. . . ." When we say that the hero feels his destiny from within himself, we of course do not mean that he *knows* it. Faulkner places himself on the level of his heroes' immediate consciousness of themselves and of things, not on the level of their knowledge of them. They feel in some way responsible for their fate since they have a vague foreboding of what is going to happen to them. . . . Consciousness without knowledge of destiny means that the heroes sense what awaits them without knowing it distinctly. They are not surprised by what happens because they at least know that no future can deliver them from their past. This is evident in the way they act. Faulkner always tries to give us the impression that they already know what one normally would not be able to foresee. . . .

Since they have a dim but constant awareness of the destiny they bear, it is quite normal that Faulkner should reveal this consciousness by using interior monologues and by placing himself "with" his characters. There is an important connection between this manifestation of destiny, his conception of time, and his way of regarding his characters, which it will be necessary to clarify if we are to understand the psychological significance of destiny. We sense perfectly well, without knowing exactly why, that Dos Passos' manner would not suit Faulkner. Perhaps it is because Faulkner makes his characters appear in their own present and implies the reality and importance of this present. But why should the classical type of psychological analysis, where the author is "behind" his heroes, be equally ill-suited? Analysis presupposes, of course, an author and reader superior to the characters, on the level of omniscient reflection, and this again Faulkner refuses. But why?

We could analyze the feeling of destiny from such a vantage point—in fact, that is what we have just done, abstractly. But then we reduce consciousness to an illusion: we take a hero who believes he is a plaything of fate, we examine this belief from above, and in doing so, we transcend the feeling of oppressiveness which is the very nature of fate. Fate would thereby lose all reality except as a subjective impression. Perhaps it is nothing more. But Faulkner has no intention of presenting his reader with a theory of fatality. Rather, he wants to communicate to us those very impressions that strangle his characters, and to do this, the reader must not be entitled to privileged knowledge, he must not understand the characters any more than they understand themselves—it is the error of many novelists to imagine that an impression is strengthened when it is justified. Thus Faulkner, and, as a result, his reader stay "with" the hero.

Faulkner might have been confronted with an antinomy, because in certain cases there is no opposition between feeling and knowing. Perhaps there is even a mutual reinforcement—this certainly was Proust's idea. But then one must choose: destiny dissolves as soon as it is understood, as soon as it has been reduced to psychological causes which bear no relation to what one thinks destiny is while subjected to it. Destiny is real only while it is endured—that is to say, while it is not known but only felt. . . . Past time—that is, time which was lost the moment it was lived—dissolves as such when it has been recaptured and analyzed. Experience is reduced to causes in a kind of Spinozian liberation, and time loses its mysterious fatality. The example of Proust proves what we were saying: understanding destiny is its undoing. (pp. 84-6)

Jean Pouillon, "Time and Destiny in Faulkner," in his Temps et Roman, *translated by Jacqueline Merriam, Gallimard, 1946 (and reprinted in* Faulkner: A Collection of Critical Essays, *edited by Robert Penn Warren, Prentice-Hall, Inc., 1966, pp. 79-86).*

[Faulkner's] novels are the books of a man who broods about literature, but doesn't often discuss it with his friends; there is no ease about them, no feeling that they come from a background of taste refined by argument and of opinions held in common. (pp. 132-34)

Faulkner is a solitary worker by choice, and he has done great things not only with double the pains to himself that they might have cost if produced in more genial circumstances, but sometimes also with double the pains to the reader. Two or three of his books as a whole and many of them in part are awkward experiments. All of them are full of overblown words like "imponderable," "immortal," "immutable," and "immemorial" that he would have used with more discretion, or not at all, if he had followed Hemingway's example and served an apprenticeship to an older writer. (p. 134)

Faulkner's mythical kingdom is a county in northern Mississippi, on the border between the sand hills covered with scrubby pine and the black earth of the river bottoms. . . . It sometimes seems to me that every house or hovel has been described in one of Faulkner's novels, and that all the people of the imaginary county, black and white, townsmen, farmers, and housewives, have played their parts in one connected story. (pp. 135-36)

Sartoris . . . is a romantic and partly unconvincing novel, but with many fine scenes in it, such as the hero's visit to a family of independent pine-hill farmers; and it states most of the themes that the author would later develop at length. (p. 136)

Just as Balzac, who may have inspired the [Yoknapatawpha] series, divided his *Comédie Humaine* into "Scenes of Parisian Life," "Scenes of Provincial Life," "Scenes of Private Life," so Faulkner might divide his work into a number of cycles: one about the planters and their descendants, one about the townspeople of Jefferson, one about the poor whites, one about the Indians, and one about the Negroes. Or again, if he adopted a division by families, there would be the Compson-Sartoris saga, the continuing Snopes saga, the McCaslin saga, dealing with the white and black descendants of Carothers McCaslin, and the Ratliff-Bundren saga, devoted to the backwoods farmers of Frenchman's Bend. All the cycles or sagas are closely interconnected; it is as if each new book was a chord or segment of a total situation always existing in the author's mind. (p. 137)

All his books in the Yoknapatawpha cycle are part of the same living pattern. It is the pattern, not the printed volumes in which part of it is recorded, that is Faulkner's real achievement. Its existence helps to explain one feature of his work: that each novel, each long or short story, seems to reveal more than it states explicitly and to have a subject bigger than itself. All the separate works are like blocks of marble from the same quarry: they show the veins and faults of the mother rock. Or else—to use a rather strained figure—they are like wooden planks that were cut, not from a log, but from a still-living tree. The planks are planed and chiseled into their final shapes, but the tree itself heals over the wound and continues to grow. (p. 138)

Although the pattern is presented in terms of a single Mississippi county, it can be extended to the Deep South as a whole; and Faulkner always seems conscious of its wider application. He might have been thinking of his own novels when he described the ledgers in the commissary of the McCaslin plantation, in *Go Down, Moses*. They recorded, he says, "that slow trickle of molasses and meal and meat, of shoes and straw hats and overalls, of plowlines and collars and heelbolts and clevises, which returned each fall as cotton"—in a sense they were local and limited; but they were also "the continuation of that record which two hundred years had not been enough to complete and another hundred would not be enough to discharge; that chronicle which was a whole land in miniature, which multiplied and compounded was the entire South." (p. 139)

More or less unconsciously, the incidents in [*Absalom, Absalom!* come] to represent the forces and elements in the social situation, since the mind naturally works in terms of symbols and parallels. In Faulkner's case, this form of parallelism is not confined to *Absalom, Absalom!* It can be found in the whole fictional framework that he has been elaborating in novel after novel, until his work has become a myth or legend of the South. . . .

Briefly stated, the legend might run something like this: The Deep South was ruled by planters some of whom were aristocrats like the Sartoris clan, while others were new men like Colonel Sutpen. Both types were determined to establish a lasting social order on the land they had seized from the Indians (that is, to leave sons behind them). They had the virtue of living single-mindedly by a fixed code; but there was also an inherent guilt in their "design," their way of life; it was slavery that put a curse on the land and brought about the Civil War. (p. 142)

After the war was lost, partly as a result of the Southerners' mad heroism . . . , the planters tried to restore their "design" by other methods. But they no longer had the strength to achieve more than a partial success, even after they had freed their land from the carpetbaggers who followed the Northern armies. As time passed, moreover, the men of the old order found that they had Southern enemies too; they had to fight against a new exploiting class descended from the landless whites of slavery days. In this struggle between the clan of Sartoris and the unscrupulous tribe of Snopes, the Sartorises were defeated in advance by a traditional code that kept them from using the weapons of the enemy. As a price of victory, however, the Snopeses had to serve the mechanized civilization of the North, which was morally impotent in itself, but which, with the aid of its Southern retainers, ended by corrupting the Southern nation. In a later time, the problems of the South are still unsolved, the racial conflict is becoming more acute, and Faulkner's characters in their despairing moments foresee or forebode some catastrophe of which Jim Bond [a half-witted mulatto from *Absalom, Absalom!*] and his like will be the only survivors. (p. 143)

Faulkner presents the virtues of the old order as being moral rather than material. There is no baronial pomp in his novels; no profusion of silk and silver, mahogany and moonlight and champagne. . . . What [Faulkner] admires about [his Southern aristocrats] is not their wealth or their manners or their fine horses, but rather the unquestioning acceptance—by the best planters—of a moral code that taught them "courage and honor and pride, and pity and love of justice and of liberty." (pp. 143-44)

The old order was a moral order: briefly that was its strength and the secret lost by its heirs. But also—and here is another respect in which it differs from the Southern story more commonly presented—it bore the moral burden of a guilt so great that the Civil War and even Reconstruction were in some sense a merited punishment. (p. 144)

The men [Faulkner] most admired and must have pictured himself as resembling were the Southern soldiers—after all, they were the vast majority—who owned no slaves themselves and suffered from the institution of slavery. The men he would praise in his novels were those "who had fought for four years and lost . . . not because they were opposed to freedom as freedom, but for the old reasons for which man (not the generals and politicians but man) has always fought and died in wars: to preserve a status quo or establish a better future one to endure for his children." One might define the author's position as that of an antislavery Southern nationalist.

Faulkner's novels of contemporary Southern life [those written before 1945] continue the legend into a period that he regards as one of moral confusion and social decay. He is continually seeking in them for violent images to convey his sense of outrage. *Sanctuary* is the most violent of all his novels; it has been the most popular and is by no means the least important (in spite of Faulkner's comment that it was "a cheap idea . . . deliberately conceived to make money"). The story of Popeye and Temple Drake has more meaning than appears on a first hasty reading. . . . Popeye himself is one of several characters in Faulkner's novels who represent the mechanical civilization that has invaded and conquered the South. He is always described in mechanical terms: his eyes "looked like rubber knobs"; his face "just went awry, like the face of a wax doll set too near a hot fire and forgotten"; his tight suit and stiff hat were "all angles, like a modernistic lampshade"; and in general he had "that vicious depthless quality of stamped tin.". . . [He] was a compendium of all the hateful qualities that Faulkner assigns to finance capitalism. *Sanctuary* is not a connected allegory, as George Marion O'Donnell [see excerpt above] condemned it for being—he was the first critic to approach it seriously—but neither is it a mere accumulation of pointless horrors. It is an example of the Freudian method turned backward, being full of sexual nightmares that are in reality social symbols. It is somehow connected in the author's mind with what he regards as the rape and corruption of the South.

In his novels dealing with the present Faulkner makes it clear that the descendants of the old ruling caste have the wish but not the courage or the strength to prevent this new disaster. . . . Faulkner's novels are full of well-meaning and even admirable persons, not only the grandsons of the cotton aristocracy, but also pine-hill farmers and storekeepers and sewing-machine agents and Negro cooks and sharecroppers; but they are almost all of them defeated by circumstances and they carry with them a sense of their own doom.

They also carry, whether heroes or villains, a curious sense of submission to their fate. "There is not one of Faulkner's characters," says André Gide in his dialogue on "The New American Novelists," "who properly speaking has a soul"; and I think he means that not one of them exercises the faculty of conscious choice between good and evil. They are haunted, obsessed, driven forward by some inner necessity. (pp. 145-47)

Even when they seem to be guided by a conscious purpose, like Colonel Sutpen, it is not something they have chosen by an act of will, but something that has taken possession of them: Sutpen's great design was "not what he wanted to but what he just had to do, had to do it whether he wanted to or not, because if he did not do it he knew he could never live with himself for the rest of his life." In the same way, Faulkner himself writes, not what he wants to, but what he just has to write whether he wants to or not.

It had better be admitted that most of his novels have some obvious weakness in structure. Some of them combine two or more themes having little relation to each other, as *Light in August* does, while others, like *The Hamlet,* tend to resolve themselves into a series of episodes resembling beads on a string. In *The Sound and the Fury,* which is superb as a whole, we can't be sure that the four sections of the novel are presented in the most effective order; at any rate, we can't fully understand the first section until we have read the three that follow. *Absalom, Absalom!* though at first it strikes us as being pitched in too high a key, is structurally the soundest of all the novels in the Yoknapatawpha series—and it gains power in retrospect; but even here the author's attention seems to shift from the principal theme of Colonel Sutpen's design to the secondary theme of incest and miscegenation.

Faulkner seems best to me, and most nearly himself, either in long stories like "The Bear," in *Go Down, Moses,* and "Old Man.". . . That is, he has been most effective in dealing with the total situation always present in his mind as a pattern of the South, or else in shorter units which, though often subject to inspired revision, have still been shaped by a single conception. It is by his best that we should judge him, as every other author; and Faulkner at his best—even sometimes at his worst—has a power, a richness of life, an intensity to be found in no other American writer of our time. (pp. 148-49)

Moreover, he has a brooding love for the land where he was born and reared and where, unlike other writers of his generation, he has chosen to spend his life. . . . Here are the two sides of Faulkner's feeling for the South: on the one side, an admiring and possessive love; on the other, a compulsive fear lest what he loves should be destroyed by the ignorance of its native serfs and the greed of traders and absentee landlords. (p. 149)

Faulkner's novels have the quality of being lived, absorbed, remembered rather than merely observed. And they have what is rare in the novels of our time, a warmth of family affection, brother for brother and sister, the father for his children—a love so warm and proud that it tries to shut out the rest of the world. Compared with that affection, married love is presented as something calculating, and illicit love as a consuming fire. And because the blood relationship is central in his novels, Faulkner finds it hard to create sympathetic characters between the ages of twenty and forty. He is better with children, Negro and white, and incomparably good with older people who preserve the standards that have come down to them "out of the old time, the old days."

In the group of novels beginning with *The Wild Palms* (1939), which attracted so little attention at the time of publication that they seemed to go unread, there is a quality not exactly new to Faulkner—it had appeared already in passages of *Sartoris* and *Sanctuary*—but now much stronger and no longer overshadowed by violence and horror. It is a sort of homely and sobersided frontier humor that is seldom achieved in contemporary writing (except sometimes by Erskine Caldwell, also a Southerner). . . . In a curious way, Faulkner combines two of the principal traditions in American letters: the tradition of psychological horror, often close to symbolism, that begins with Charles Brockden Brown, our first professional novelist, and extends through Poe, Melville, Henry James (in his later stories), Stephen Crane, and Hemingway; and the other tradition of frontier humor and realism, beginning with Augustus Longstreet's *Georgia Scenes* and having Mark Twain as its best example.

But the American author he most resembles is Hawthorne, for all their polar differences. They stand to each other as July to December, as heat to cold, as swamp to mountain, as the luxuriant to the meager but perfect, as planter to Puritan; and yet Hawthorne had much the same attitude toward New England that Faulkner has to the South, together with a strong sense of regional particularity. . . . Like Faulkner in the South, [Hawthorne] applied himself to creating [New England's] moral fables and elaborating its legends, which existed, as it were, in his solitary heart. Pacing the hillside behind his house in Concord, he listened for a voice; one might say that he lay in wait for it, passively but expectantly, like a hunter behind a rock; then, when it had spoken, he transcribed its words—more cautiously than Faulkner, it is true; with more form and less fire, but with the same essential fidelity. . . . Faulkner is another author who has to wait for the spirit and the voice. He is not so much a novelist, in the usual sense of being a writer who sets out to observe actions and characters, then fits them into the framework of a story, as he is an epic or bardic poet in prose, a creator of myths that he weaves together into a legend of the South. (pp. 151-52)

In Faulkner's later novels, the Yoknapatawpha story is traced backward to the founding and naming of Jefferson, as well as being carried forward almost to the time of his death. Those novels might be regarded as sequels to the earlier books, yet they almost seem to be written by a different man. The sense of doom and outrage that brooded over the early ones has been replaced by pity for human beings, even the worst of them ("The poor sons of bitches," Gavin Stevens says, "they do the best they can") and by the obstinate faith, expressed in the Nobel Prize address, "that man will not only endure; he will prevail"—all this combined with more than a touch of old-fashioned sentiment. In Faulkner's case, as in those of many other writers, there had been a return to the fathers. I respect the later author, with most of his demons exorcised, but the younger possessed and unregenerate Faulkner is the man whose works amaze us, as they never ceased to puzzle and amaze himself. (pp. 153-54)

Faulkner in his early novels is indubitably a Southern nationalist and an heir of the Confederacy—for all his sense of guilt about the Negroes—but he is something else besides. . . . What he regarded as his ultimate subject is not the South or its destiny, however much they occupied his mind, but rather the human situation as revealed in Southern terms—to quote from one of his letters, "the same frantic steeplechase toward nothing everywhere." He approached that steeplechase in terms of Southern material because, as he also said, "I just happen to know it, and dont have time in one life to learn another one and write at the same time." There was of course another reason, for it was the South that aroused his apprehensions, that deeply engaged his loyalties ("*I dont. I dont hate it!*"), and that set his imagination to work. He dreamed, however, that his Yoknapatawpha story might stand for the human drama everywhere and always. (pp. 154-55)

> *Malcolm Cowley, "Faulkner: The Yoknapatawpha Story," in his* A Second Flowering *(copyright © 1956, 1967, 1968, 1970, 1972, 1973 by Malcolm Cowley; reprinted by permission of The Viking Press, Inc.), Viking, 1973, pp. 130-55.*

According to Faulkner, with the introduction of slavery into the South, a culture that had wanted to imitate pastoral ideals was destroyed before it had an opportunity to function. As such the South had experienced its fall long before the Civil War, and from his earliest stories through the cycle in *Go Down, Moses* the author was preoccupied with the loss of an earthly paradise.

A brilliant formulation of the South's failure to establish an Arcadian ideal—to resurrect an Eden on earth—appears in Faulkner's early short story "Red Leaves." Of the more than seventy-five short stories that Faulkner published, "Red Leaves" is his finest. It is also, by any legitimate standards of excellence, a masterpiece of American short fiction: the conception and execution of the story are striking, the prose is beautifully cadenced and devoid of those violations of grammar and syntax for which Faulkner has been excessively praised, the moral force is impressive, and the subject is great. Given the remarkable calibre of this short story, and the proliferation of Faulkner criticism in the past two decades, it is curious that this story remains unexplicated; to a large extent, this failure is a reflection of the cursory treatment of Faulkner's short fiction in most major studies of his work.

In "Red Leaves" Faulkner is dealing with the earliest history of Yoknapatawpha, that transitional period in which the last vestiges of Chickasaw culture were being corrupted by the plantation South. The story, which is divided into six sections, traces the efforts of the Chickasaw community, which had incorporated the South's peculiar institution into its own culture, to hunt a runaway slave, a black servant of the deceased chief Issetibbeha, who cannot pass into the far country without his dog, his horse, and his retainer. This is the literal level of the story, but Faulkner had a pronounced tendency to allegorize human experience, and consequently the world in "Red Leaves" serves as an area of conflict in which moral and spiritual problems are projected in mythic form. (pp. 243-44)

The story begins in a manner typical of Faulkner's short story technique, which relies for its effect upon the device of withholding information and building a rich impression through the accretion of detail. Consequently it takes the reader a few paragraphs to discover the astonishing similitude that Faulkner is erecting in this story. For rather than attacking the cultural ethic of the Old South directly, he creates a parable on slavery by casting the Indians in the role of plantation masters, while the blacks, rather than being an economic asset, become useless chattel. In short, he develops a startling conceit in which plantation culture and the institution of slavery that supported it are reduced to decadence and parody. (pp. 244-45)

Nostalgia for the past is a quality which permeates "Red Leaves," but this feeling involves more than the memory of happier times; it is also symbolic of human perfection and spiritual harmony. Thus it is no accident that Three Basket and his companion, Louis Berry, are described in a twofold manner: as belonging inevitably and tragically to the present, but also as mirroring the divine past. . . . Three Basket, with a snuff-box clamped through his ear, is an effete parody of the white plantation aristocracy that hovers over the story like an inescapable afterthought. But at the same time he and his companion are treated as diminished gods who have been cast into an uncomfortable drama. (p. 245)

The dehumanizing essence of this culture is seen in the hunt for the slave, who eludes his oppressors for six days, only to discover that "there was nowhere for him to go." . . . This sense of entrapment lends a nightmarish quality to the flight of the Negro. He is cast adrift in a world that he did not create and which he cannot control. He is trapped by circumstances and he eventually succumbs to a process of attrition that deprives him of his physical strength. For him, and for the Indians, movement through what was formerly a natural paradise becomes a hellish torment. He runs to the extremities of this fallen world, and then is forced to retreat towards its center, frequently passing his pursuers as they follow his trail outward toward the far reaches of a diabolical kingdom. The transformation of Eden into hell for all participants is crystallized in the agonies of the inert Moketubbe, who is so diseased and flaccid that he must be carried by members of the clan during the hunt: "To Moketubbe it must have been as though, himself immortal, he were being carried rapidly through hell by doomed spirits which, alive, had contemplated his disaster, and, dead, were oblivious partners to his damnation." . . .

The Negro, too, makes repeated passages through this secular Inferno, and at one stage in his torment he encounters the Tempter of Souls, embodied in the form of an aging cottonmouth moccasin snake. Here Faulkner presents a highly stylized ritual of man confronting death with courage and nobility. (p. 247)

Faulkner, however, does not grant the Negro an acceptable death. It is not accurate to say that the Negro suffers and endures in "Red Leaves," for Faulkner's critique on slavery is far more rigorous than this and does not admit to sentimentality. . . . It is true that Three Basket compliments the Negro for the excellent race he ran at the end of the fifth section and again at the conclusion of the sixth, just before the Negro meets his death, an event that occurs outside the context of the story. Yet by this time the Negro has lost all semblance of humanity; between the endings of these last two sections a radical alteration in his character has occurred. He still looms taller than his captors, who throughout the story are depicted as grotesque travesties of Indian toughness and resilience, but he has been reduced to subhuman form. (pp. 247-48)

The ritual of human sacrifice is not seen by the reader, but it is apprehended by him and made all the more horrible because he is forced to reconstruct it imaginatively. He is also forced to recognize the chilling fact that a shadow hangs over the world, that the once sacred communion of men has been replaced by a satanic one, and that the metaphorical wilderness, which is Eden, is no longer capable of regeneration. Within the miasmic gloom of this tale there is only a slight hint of the world's former glory, expressed in one of the most poignant images in Faulkner's fiction: "Dawn came; a white crane flapped slowly across the jonquil sky." . . . This vision of a bright golden day is all the more striking because it is counterpointed against manifold images of an abrasive sun and of swamp-like decay; but it is never forgotten, because Faulkner carefully intimates that

his earthly garden, fallen to ruin, is a dim reflection of that original Garden that man lost when evil came into the world. The wilderness depicted in the story is no longer the incarnation of spiritual beauty because the generation of men that now populates it has forgotten its sacred origins and its chosen status. By embracing a pernicious institution, these men have become voluntary exiles in a disordered and fallen land. They have sacrificed their territory to the devil, and they are now horribly trapped in his dominion.

The idea of closure, or entrapment, is a primary concept in Faulkner's fiction. In "Red Leaves" existence is decidedly constricted because the inhabitants of this world have lost any capability of moral and spiritual growth. Through a variety of operations they effect a diminution of consciousness; like the Negro, they constantly retrace their steps rather than expand their field of vision. Practically all of the stories in *These Thirteen*, including the best—"Red Leaves," "A Rose for Emily," "That Evening Sun," and the chilling war story, "Crevasse"—present this skeptical and essentially distopian vision of a tightly compressed universe. But only in "Red Leaves" is this closed world expressly equated with man's fall from grace. Man has lost sight of the holy Garden and this failure of vision estranges him from the possibility of salvation.

The theological statement of the human predicament in "Red Leaves" is rendered with a force and a complexity that no other short story by Faulkner matches. In subdued apocalyptic fury, the malefactors in this story invent rituals that attest to their imperfection. They engage in a drama that is both temporal and eternal, and consequently the narrative operates on two levels, as a brilliant critique on racism, and as a parable on Paradise Lost. Whether or not an alternative to Eden can be found is a possibility that lies beyond the frame of the story, yet the tone of "Red Leaves" suggests that the agonies of the characters will persist as long as men's actions are negative and repetitive. (pp. 248-49)

> *Gilbert H. Muller, "The Descent of the Gods: Faulkner's 'Red Leaves' and the Garden of the South," in* Studies in Short Fiction *(copyright 1974 by Newberry College), Summer, 1974, pp. 243-49.*

[A] probable source for and a key to the emotional core of William Faulkner's little-discussed but fine and moving short story (or, more precisely, short chapter or section of *Go Down, Moses*) "Pantaloon in Black" may be found to reside in an old southern black and white country blues song which Faulkner probably knew and which very likely exercised a pervasive influence in the writing of this section of the novel [keeping in mind that any reading of this section is ultimately significant in terms of *Go Down, Moses*]. The song or songs in question are really two separate pieces, each of which has many versions and variants. . . . Of the many versions and variants of "Easy Rider," or "C. C. Rider," or "See, See Rider," which in one form or another has been very well-known through much of this century, in oral tradition, in "race recordings," and, most recently, in "rock and roll," the refrain which seems most nearly common to all is: "Easy Rider, now see what you done done." Less familiar, but more compelling and more directly to the point for a reading of "Pantaloon in Black," is the related blues sometimes called "I Know You, Rider," sometimes called "Circle Round the Sun." . . . In spite of differing versions and variants, what folksong scholars would call the "emotional core" of this particular folksong remains strikingly consistent: love, loss, bereavement, as expressed through the woeful iteration of the key line "I know you rider, gonna miss me when I'm gone" and through such highly charged imagery and curiously effective lines as the following: "She throws her arms around me like a circle round the sun." I would suggest, then, that we consider this song as a kind of objective correlative for the prose-poem, "Pantaloon in Black," the function of which within the novel is essentially non-novelistic; that is, "Pantaloon in Black" has no direct narrative or dramatic relation to the movement of the larger fiction of *Go Down, Moses* but exists as a poetic image which serves to crystallize and to universalize certain fundamental aspects of the McCaslin family story.

We know already that Faulkner knew "Easy Rider," from his use of the lyrics in *Soldier's Pay.* There would appear to be no hard evidence for his knowledge of "I Know You Rider." Yet certain scenes in Faulkner's novels, such as the scene in which young Bayard Sartoris goes out troubadoring and serenading with the black musicians in *Sartoris,* have the ring of autobiographical authenticity to them and suggest that Faulkner probably was well-acquainted with blues and folksong from oral tradition. . . . Of course, if we know something of Faulkner's life and of the country and the fashion in which he lived it, his frequent exposure to the blues and to folksong in oral tradition is precisely the thing which needs the least documentation.

Moreover, the strategy of allusion, especially with reference to song titles and random images and catch-lines, was a standard and increasingly conspicuous device with novelists and poets from the 1920s on. In fact, the device was overused; thus by the time Faulkner came to write *Go Down, Moses* his strategy was that of more or less oblique allusion. For example, he used song titles or images for short story ("That Evening Sun") or novel titles, but he avoided the use of song as direct and insistent echoic refrain throughout a given work. The title of the novel, *Go Down, Moses,* is of course taken from the spiritual as is the name of the final chapter or section of the novel; yet in that final section we do not have community choruses chanting lines from the spiritual as we might have had from a novelist with a heavy hand. Likewise, in "Pantaloon in Black" we have the underlying form of the powerful blues, fully assimilated imagistic echoes, and the central presence of Rider in profound bereavement, but we do not have the kind of bathetic spectacle that a less sure novelistic hand might have shaped with similar circumstances and materials; we do not have the "pantaloon" crooning the blues on the occasion of his wife's death. That curious title does, however, suggest the performer, the blues singer as "pantaloon," cast in a grotesquely comic role, perceived as caricature by the detached audience of whites, yet transcendent in grief and loss and ultimately escaping—or fulfilling?—the role through violence. (pp. 241-44)

While [there] seem to be fairly close verbal and situational parallels [in the song and in the story], even more telling to the reader who has pondered the story and the listener who knows the song, is the central feeling of both: love, loss, grief . . . (p. 244)

Just as this curiously evocative name [Rider] rings throughout "Pantaloon in Black," so the sun of the blues shines pervasively in the prose. When Rider sees Mannie's ghost and moves toward her, it seems strangely akin to the paradoxical act of throwing one's arms around the sun. Or,

to reverse the perspective, Mannie, gone, lost, throws her arms around Rider, "like a circle round the sun" [as in the song]. (pp. 244-45)

I would hasten to reaffirm that [a] more significant connection [than textual parallels] is the way in which the deep form of the song and the story is shared. Love, loss, grief are indeed difficult to write about or to sing about with such directness, without sentimentality, without excess. The mode of discourse is essential to the blues, as to the fiction, and here each enriches the other.

Finally, the business of "Pantaloon in Black" is much more than a frozen moment of the blues, a resonant but disconnected "circle round the sun." Viewed in the larger context of the novel, the reading outlined here suggests that the deep form, the profound and essential music of the novel which defies discursive analysis, exists in a tension between the blues and the spirituals, between the love and grief and violence of Rider and the exaltation of the full vision of *Go Down, Moses,* the song as well as the novel. (p. 245)

> *H. R. Stoneback, "Faulkner's Blues: 'Pantaloon in Black'," in* Modern Fiction Studies *(copyright © 1975, by Purdue Research Foundation, West Lafayette, Indiana, U.S.A.), Summer, 1975, pp. 241-45.*

*   *   *

FAUST, Irvin   1924-

American novelist and short story writer, Faust created something of a sensation with his first book of stories, *Roar Lion Roar.* **The collection revealed Faust to be a writer of psychological depth, who, in addition, possessed a good ear for the idiosyncratic speech patterns of New York City youths. The stories were followed by his first novel,** *The Steagle,* **the study of an incipient psychotic breakdown. Unfortunately, Faust's subsequent novels have not quite matched his earliest efforts. (See also** *Contemporary Authors,* **Vols. 33-36.)**

"Foreign Devils," Irvin Faust's fifth book, probably needs two reviews. Or three. But one, two or three they would have to be applausive. Irvin Faust impresses.

Let me clarify. This novel is side-saddle astride one of the tiredest premises in fiction: a fouled-up, wife-and-family-separated, past-fixating writer with a block. And, yes, also Jewish. So what else is *nu?* For this impacted personal and artistic life the hero writes a laxative-therapeutic novel, while arguing with Captain Bligh, his Wasp conscience, with which sort of conscience a Jewish novelist shouldn't get stuck. It doesn't sound promising? No, I didn't think so either. But the character Benson (né Birnbaum) actually writes his novel—about the Chinese Boxer Rebellion—while Faust is writing a Chinese box or two of another novel and an extended short story around it. Both are valid and whole. At the end, as organic, live fiction must, they integrate with fine aptness. It's one hell of a concept, and executed.

"Boxers," the core novel, Benson-Birnbaum's novel, is a splendid exercise. Benson selects a character of energy and confidence. He expects to draw on it vicariously. Norris Blake is an old-boy newspaperman of the Hearst-Pulitzer age. And Faust has mastered the written language of that age—pompous, romantic, flowered, yet effective and easy. . . .

Faust has a terrific ear. And, mind you, this isn't cheap

parody. Faust (or Benson) appreciates the very real power of Blake's archaic style. Until the end, when Blake's narrative breaks down—preparing then to meld with Benson's narrative—"Boxers" itself claims attention. It is well-researched, painstakingly placed in China, in its particular time. Faust has taken no short cuts. And, throughout, the Blake narrative adjusts to, is influenced by, the mood and experiences of Benson, who, presumably, has been influenced by Faust's moods and experiences. It's a small, sharp lesson in the metabolism of creativity. . . .

Benson-Birnbaum has some difficulty with Jewishness. He denies energy and confidence to people of his ethnic stock, looks for self-assurance in Christian masks. . . . Birnbaum wins an algetic health: It's a moving climax; the foreign devils in him have been exorcised.

A superior performance altogether. I recommend it. Irvin Faust does things here that will not easily be done again. Or as well. (p. 7)

> D. Keith Mano, in The New York Times Book Review (© 1973 by The New York Times Company; reprinted by permission), May 20, 1973.

The stories in Roar Lion Roar (1964) had all the wry, crazy skepticism of Malamud in The Magic Barrel, but they had an added dimension as well, a kind of hard-edged, street-smart view of experience that took them beyond their carefully mapped, predominantly New York settings and into a relationship with America.

Roar Lion Roar defined the themes that have occupied Faust—in gradually increasing complexity—ever since. "Into the Green Night" was a tribute to the warm world of childhood movie fantasies. "The Duke Imlach Story" was about a cipher of a young man who expected life to come to him. "The Madras Rumble" illustrated our American confusion of values: how we believe in fighting for power, but only in the right place at the right time. In "The World's Fastest Human" a track star was obsessed with victory and victory over women. "Roar Lion Roar" drew the equation between winning and belonging in America. "Jake Bluffstein and Adolf Hitler" turned an elderly New York Jew into a Nazi—because the war had been exciting and peace was not.

It's but a short step from these stories to The Steagle (1966), and the wild odyssey of Harold Aaron Weissburg, New York English professor. Weissburg leads a conventional American life of conventional American obligations. And then it is the Cuban missile crisis and he is careening across the country, fulfilling his childhood movie fantasies, living out his fantasies of victory in the sports arena and the bedroom. Weissburg was in the army during World War II. War, he knows, is a liberating experience. Responsibility can go by the board when there may be no tomorrow. Why not get what you want when the time is right? All that power. All that glory.

Which leads us directly into the urban warfare of The File on Stanley Patton Buchta (1970). Here some New Left students, black militants, and a right wing police group are brought together in a confrontation that has more to do with our American idea of power and victory and the glories of war than it does with liberty and justice. And in the middle, shuttling back and forth between the adversaries, is Stan Buchta: Hofstra graduate, Vietnam veteran, New York cop, girl chaser, cipher totally without commitment.

Which provides a contrast to the commitment of Willy Kleinhans in Willy Remembers (1971). Willy is ninety-three now. . . . The experience that shaped his life was the Spanish-American War. When he discovered his own heroism in "human-type warfare." When "it sure was something grand to see, all that thrilling and chilling American power sounding off," and they "had to plunge America into world powership." When his world was simple and intact.

Now we have Foreign Devils, and for the first time all the themes and obsessions have been brought together. They've also been taken further—into a vivid exploration of the agonies of the creative process. (p. 459)

[It's] a book well worth reading. Not only for its continued Faustian insights into our ambiguous American natures. Not only for its ability to document that tenuous, perilous relationship between the writer—his moods, his fears, his uncertainty—and the work he produces in the midst of it all. . . . This is a novel that can be read for its humor and richness of language as well.

Over serious questions of identity, Irvin Faust's characters have frequently indulged in impersonations. . . . But over them all stood the author—perfecting various ethnic voices in Roar Lion Roar, concocting the whole series of old movie routines in The Steagle, stringing together the historical—and not so historical—one-liners in Willy Remembers. Following a New York tradition, Faust has always been something of a stand-up comedian in print. And now we have a Sidney Benson who identifies with Lenny Bruce. . . .

All of Faust's novels have been flawed. The Steagle gradually slid out of control. Stanley Patton Buchta never quite made sense out of Stanley. Willy Remembers couldn't entirely reconcile the blurring of history with the clarity of remembered personal experience. Foreign Devils can't quite make it all add up either. But you will laugh, and you will cry. It's Irvin Faust's best book to date. (p. 460)

> Steven Kroll, "More New York 'Awareness'," in Commonweal (copyright © 1973 Commonweal Publishing Co., Inc.; reprinted by permission of Commonweal Publishing Co., Inc.), August 24, 1973, pp. 459-60.

I have always been fascinated by the terrible passion of the stand-up comic, a man whose monstrous confidence is matched only by the fixed, abject conviction that he stinks. . . .

So, I came to Irvin Faust's new novel, "A Star in the Family," ready to be enchanted by the familiar told in a new way; to be vouchsafed insights (outside of the kind of two-bit Freudian insights applied these days to any phenomenon); to find literature made of the stand-up comic, as West made literature of Hollywood, and Celine of the lower depths, or, yes, as O'Hara did with Pal Joey. . . .

In the Faust novel (as in [Wallace Markfield's "You Could Live if They Let You"]), I found this: absolute accuracy, absolute fidelity to the milieu; a rendering of conversation without a false note; an exact estimate of who represents what on any level of show business; an impeccable story line moving inexorably from bright beginning to dismal end; technical devices not new but used expertly; in short, a thoroughly professional performance.

And that was all. The reader could as well have pieced together the story himself from a year's issues of Variety ("N.Y. to L.A.") and the personal memoirs of a writer born in the same year . . . that his protagonist, the stand-up comic, was. The reader begs to be transfixed, to be made dizzy with revelations of the universal. He is given, instead, smooth competence and a set of computer print-outs. He is impressed by that but he is not moved, neither exhilarated nor depressed; occasionally amused; put off by the failure of a number of fantasy passages. (p. 13)

> *Gilbert Millstein, in* The New York Times Book Review *(© 1975 by The New York Times Company; reprinted by permission), March 30, 1975.*

* * *

FEIFFER, Jules   1929-

A widely syndicated cartoonist, Feiffer is also an American playwright and novelist. Known in literary circles for his play *Little Murders,* **which John Simon called "a bloody-minded play, boldly proclaiming that our irrational and vicious society turns ordinary people into maniacal murderers," Feiffer possesses a style of writing which rests between absurdist farce and satire. (See also** *CLC,* **Vol. 2, and** *Contemporary Authors,* **Vols. 17-20, rev. ed.)**

What gives [*Knock, Knock*] its humor—and a great deal of it is screamingly funny—is the incredible accuracy of [Feiffer's] language, and his use of it to paint the urban neurosis in exact colors. This we know from his cartoons, and we learn it anew from this endearing, congenial theater piece. . . . There isn't a sincere or honestly felt moment in his play. Let him darken his tone for a moment, and immediately he demolishes the mood with a gallumphing surge of breast-beating and spatterings of guilt. Better even than in the admirable *Little Murders,* he has learned to aim his pen into the heart of life's absurdity, and direct it unerringly to its target.

> *Alan Rich, "Pie-Eyed Feiffer," in* New York Magazine *(© 1976 by NYM Corp.; reprinted by permission of New York Magazine and Alan Rich), February 2, 1976, p. 64.*

In his classic early cartoons Jules Feiffer carried on the tradition of James Thurber and William Steig in their rueful dissection of middle-brow idealism. At the same time he was the link between the burgeoning idea of "popular culture" and writers like Bellow, Malamud and Roth. In his later plays and movies—"Little Murders," "God Bless," "Carnal Knowledge"—Feiffer moved closer to these writers while keeping his comic's license. You could say that Feiffer is the comic muse of the urban Jewish artist-intellectual.

His charming, mournfully hilarious new play, "Knock, Knock", is a very personal work. Using the same velvet scalpel that soothes as it draws blood in his cartoons, Feiffer depicts two middle-aged dropouts from our pre-apocalyptic state. His shambling, seedy heroes, called Abe and Cohn, have retired to a little house in the country, from which they haven't moved in twenty years. . . .

Abe is a retired stockbroker and Cohn a long-unemployed musician, but they're really one character split into two dialectical poles—the two sides of Feiffer's own spirit. Ironically, Cohn, the musician, is the realist, believing only in things he can touch. Abe is the romantic, hedging his bets "just in case" there's a prince inside the frog of reality. . . .

Cohn wishes for a new roommate and his wish is promptly granted in the form of a mad magus named Wiseman who is a mixture of Mephistopheles and Groucho. This leads to another invader, none other than Joan of Arc, who calls Abe and Cohn to join her in a pilgrimage to Heaven before the coming holocaust. This cute kid from the realms of sainthood causes Abe and Cohn to switch credos—Abe becoming the skeptical realist and Cohn the true believer. All of which allows Feiffer to create some tenderly sardonic comedy about idealism and the female as male fantasy. . . .

"Knock, Knock" is a laughing elegy for the gently demoralized humanist spirit represented by Feiffer himself. He sketches this screwed-up but still hopeful spirit in a mad mélange of echoes from Pinteresque colloquies to Grouchoid semantics to Shakespeare's Lear.

> *Jack Kroll, "Feifferland," in* Newsweek *(copyright 1976 by Newsweek, Inc.; all rights reserved; reprinted by permission), February 2, 1976, p. 68.*

[*Knock, Knock*] is a kooky, laugh-saturated miracle play in the absurdist tradition. It is as if someone had merged *The Odd Couple* and *The Sunshine Boys* and peppered the mix with Kierkegaard and the Marx Brothers. Nor is that all. The unifying element is Jewish humor—skeptical, self-deprecating, fatalistic and with an underlying sadness that suggests that all the mirth is a self-protective mask hiding imminent lamentation. . . .

The words are manic—puns, syllogisms, answer-and-question games, in that order. Some scenes are animated versions of Feiffer's cartoon strips. Basically one-line throwaways, they lack dramatic continuity, but they sputter with hilarity.

> *T. E. Kalem, "Kooky Miracle," in* Time *(reprinted by permission from* Time, *The Weekly Newsmagazine; copyright Time Inc. 1976), February 2, 1976, p. 55.*

One should distinguish between Feiffer the crafter of theatrical moments and Feiffer the dramatist. "Knock, Knock" so effervesces in its parts—the first wishing sequence, Abe's soliloquy, the card game with Joan as the stake (no pun intended)—moves one along from joke to joke so briskly that it is easy not to notice that the play lacks continuity, that the sum of its parts is no whole.

Feiffer's genius as a cartoonist is for dramatic moments—establishing and comically concluding a situation in eight still frames. His characters have personality only for the purpose of making the point: They do not have, as breathing dramatic characters must, the freedom to develop, to grow away from their status as idea-bearers.

"Knock, Knock" is easily divisible into moments, routines, the connections between which are awkward, unnatural acts of determination. It is as if Feiffer, intent on writing a play, had concocted a plot to hang his ha-has on. The more artificial and fragmented the plot, the less the chance that anyone would notice the discontinuity. But Abe and Cohn, the two protagonists, are supposedly the same persons throughout, and we should be able to recognize their dramatic evolution, even if we cannot describe it. Instead of sliding from one state of mind to the next, though, they jump, or are jumped. One day Cohn is a disbeliever, the next a believer, but we miss the minute increments of change, the drop by drop growth which makes up a life or a sand castle. As in movies, where the rapid display of stopped moments produces the impression of real motion, so in all dramatic art, where instant by instant must combine to make a man. . . .

"Knock, Knock" must be commended as a witty, brilliant evening with a cosmos-conscious comic, but not as a play. (p. 110)

> *Carll Tucker, in* The Village Voice *(reprinted by permission of* The Village Voice; *copyright © The Village Voice, Inc., 1976), February 2, 1976.*

Jules Feiffer's . . . novel [*Ackroyd*] isn't always fun to read, but it is fun to figure out. *The Murder of Roger Ackroyd*, you'll recall, was the Agatha Christie mystery in which the crime was perpetrated by the narrator himself. . . .

It's no accident that this Rags-to-Roger saga is set in the years between 1964 and 1971. The reference points include the New York status scramble, antiwar activism, JFK (who may be the real ghost haunting both men), and, of course, the ultimate private investigation of psychotherapy. Unfortunately, the best clues are buried under long, dull stretches of dialogue that are all too reminiscent of Woody Allen's Sam Spade parody—with the funny lines omitted. Feiffer can't bring himself to act out his own madness. Instead he picks away at it like an overscrupulous analysand. The result isn't a very satisfying story; just a fascinating bundle of neuroses that uncannily mirrors our own. (p. 35)

> *Joyce Milton, in* Saturday Review *(© 1977 by Saturday Review Magazine Corp.; reprinted with permission), May 14, 1977.*

My strongest reaction to Jules Feiffer's new novel ["*Ackroyd*"] is to wonder why he wrote it. We have to remind ourselves, every now and then, that a novel is a *transaction* between author and reader, and I'm tempted to ask Mr. Feiffer: "What did I do to deserve this?"

Feiffer has a reputation as a funny man, and this, in effect, exonerates his work from sober consideration. If at first you don't laugh, try, try again. Wit works in mysterious ways, and the burden of proof has somehow come not to be the writer's, but the reader's.

Many are the disguises of wit: irrationality, gratuitousness and negativism are only a few of its masks. Didn't Freud teach us that truth is often an inversion of what we feel? So convoluted is the modern reader's gullibility that the spectacle of Feiffer being *unfunny* will probably be taken for precisely such an inversion, a meta-joke. The deadpan need never dissolve into the uncool grimace of laughter. . . .

"Ackroyd" is about a young man who changes his name because, as he puts it, "I don't respect myself. It was not a rejection of my family—my father—when I took on this joke of a name, Roger Ackroyd. It was a rejection of *me*. Self-mockery. A recognition that I was not a serious person, so did not deserve a serious name." Among the other things Ackroyd did not deserve, apparently, is a prose style, and the reader of his story has to slog through 349 pages of the kind of pidgin English such self-deprecation imposes on its subjects.

Ackroyd has borrowed the name of an Agatha Christie character because he is "going into the detective busi-

ness." Symbolism: the first obligation of all honest men is the search for clues to the meaning of life. Most of the book consists of a tangled and interminable investigation of the commonplace neurosis of a character named Rags Plante, who consults a detective instead of a psychoanalyst so that he can control the pace of revelation. What is revealed reminds me of Edmund Wilson's remark to the effect that reading certain detective stories is like ransacking a crate of straw in order to discover a rusty nail.

If I were to hazard a charitable guess, I'd say that "Ackroyd" is intended to be a morality tale on the subject of identity. At the end of the book, the private eye laments the fact that he is still working on Rags's case when he should be investigating his own. However, it is the reader, at this point, whose lament should be heard: If "Ackroyd" has a moral, it is not that the characters should look to themselves, but the author. (p. 12)

> *Anatole Broyard, in* The New York Times Book Review *(© 1977 by The New York Times Company; reprinted by permission), May 15, 1977.*

     *   *   *

FOX, Paula 1932-

Fox is an American novelist who also writes fiction for children. She has been praised for her realistic characterization in *Poor George* and *Desperate Characters*. (See also *CLC*, Vol. 2.)

["*Desperate Characters*"] has one little fault: a tendency to use brand names and other handy totems to suggest the character (rather than the circumstances) of the person the objects are attached to. This is journalistic shorthand—using Pucci and Gucci to cut and run from the hard work of revelation. But apart from this mannerism, "*Desperate Characters*" does precisely what it sets out to do. It takes as axiomatic that life in the city is almost intolerable. Not because the streets are dirty, but because some craziness is epidemic behind the locked doors. In a wonderfully controlled way it identifies the craziness, and its cause. And best of all, it does this without reference to "us" versus the "others." It does not lay blame. In Miss Fox's persuasive world, Thoreau's "mass of men" includes us all, includes herself as well. Her imagination is exact and rigorous, like her language. But it is not exclusive, and that is her rare virtue.

> *Geoffrey Wolff, "The Evil City," in* Newsweek *(copyright 1970 by Newsweek, Inc; all rights reserved; reprinted by permission), March 16, 1970, p. 108.*

The great American novel strikes again; these 333 pages [of *The Western Coast*] are very tightly stacked with tiny type. There is a sense of uncertainty at the beginning which makes it a touch difficult perhaps for the reader to acquire much immediate interest in anyone presented to him. But I would advise those with time and tenacity to stick with it. In her stride Paula Fox is good value, spinning a narrative thread that tightens in unexpected places. Moments or incidents that have passed return to create an overall texture of life and lives going on. . . .

The Western Coast is neither indictment or praise; it comes over as factual and real, a straightforward statement of a country at a certain time. Here and there one may pick out hints, beginnings, forebodings of America's contemporary malaise. (p. 77)

Roger Baker, in Books and Bookmen (©
*copyright Roger Baker 1973; reprinted with
permission), March, 1973.*

For most novelists, there is a special constellation of fiction
elements that works best. Alas, novelists are not born
knowing what that constellation is, and the body of work of
individual writers is often a series of trial-and-error efforts,
interesting because of the gifts that are seeking, like water,
their true level. In Paula Fox's new novel, ''The Widow's
Children,'' her special brand of unemphatic, perceptively
detailed writing, along with her penchant for life-benumbed,
will-less characters, struggles to make its mark. (p. 6)

Within this story of death and burial, the motif of Death-in-
Life weaves its way. At intervals throughout the story's
progress, various characters feel themselves to be numb,
nearly asleep, half-dead; or they are observed to be that
way by others. . . .

Everyone in the book, in fact, at some time looks at everyone else with disgust. Because the point of view moves
about to different members of the group, the characters are
continually diminished by having bits of themselves sliced
off by new pairs of observing eyes, uniformly hostile. When
we feel we ought to be warmly inside the very bosom of the
character on whose responses the moral authority of the
book at that moment rests, we are kept coolly on the outside. . . .

And therein lies what may be a central problem of this
book: the characters are in the stocks, imprisoned in the
narrow allotted space of their assigned personalities,
trained to non-response. (p. 7)

As in Paula Fox's earlier novels, ''The Western Coast''
and ''Desperate Characters,'' will-lessness is again the
motif. But here the novel centers about a key incident that
demands distinct response—conscious, moral. Why else
have we been led to this moment? But the moment is undercut, blurred, muffled. Evil and good are both drowned.

With considerable skill, the author has moved her characters through the long, continuous scene that makes up the
main body of the novel. From a room in a hotel, through its
corridors, into streets and thence into a restaurant, this
tightly stuck-together group performs a kind of dance of
death from which now an arm protrudes, now a leg or a distorted face. Because of her skill, the reader reads and
hopes. But alas, these dead will not awaken. (p. 18)

Norma Rosen, in The New York Times
Book Review (© *1976 by The New York
Times Company; reprinted by permission),
October 3, 1976.*

The adventures of literary orphans, who are liable to be
both cast out and imprisoned, locked out and locked in, can
resemble a certain experience of family life: the experience
of those who feel themselves excluded and who wish to
escape. To think about orphans can look like a way of
thinking about the family, whose members will sometimes
be exposed, and imagine themselves exposed, to the orphan's double trouble of coercion and neglect. . . .

The Widow's Children is a drama of rival presences and
outlooks. . . .

[Real] or imaginary, the orphan may be an outcast, but he
may be more like an outlaw, or he may experience, as Jane
Eyre occasionally does, a ''sense of outlawry.'' And the
outlaw is capable of constraining the outcast, as happens in
Paula Fox's book.

Her remarkable novel describes a grisly family reunion,
summoned by Laura as a send-off for her husband Desmond and herself, who are leaving on a trip to Africa, and
sited in a New York hotel room, over drinks, of which
Desmond flings back implausible quantities. Laura is a
monster—impulsive, domineering. Her daughter Clara,
whom she rarely sees, is at the party, and so are her
brother Carlos, homosexual, once a music critic, and her
friend Peter Rice, a dry, mild publisher. . . .

Rice imagines Clara as a kind of orphan, and conveys why,
in the books which uncover the latent witness of the outsider, the situation of the pathetic outsider who nonetheless is
or has been in the bosom of a family has never been neglected. . . .

It's not always easy to think of Clara as Laura's daughter,
even as her rejected daughter, or to think of Laura as anybody's mother, or even as a woman at all. (p. 30)

It is as if the novel as we have it has partially suppressed a
novel about a literary world, and the protective treatment
of homosexual life might lead one to imagine that Laura the
rich bitch has been painted over the portrait of a certain
type of outrageous male writer or cultural partygoer. Unless I am inventing this element of transvestism, it may be
that the author wanted to write about her profession—the
etiquette of launches and lunches, about publishing, editors, interviews, leather, the world of literature—but was
then won over by a competing subject matter. You might
say that publishing is a somewhat childless profession: the
novel as we have it is largely about children and the orphan's plight.

That plight has often induced shows of sensibility and a
floridity of language, from neither of which the novel is altogether free. Clara declares that her birth was ''a consequence of Ed Hansen's momentary insistence,'' which is a
bit high-flown, and perhaps, in general, there is something
like an excess of awareness on the part of the characters—
Clara especially. We tend to call that kind of thing novelistic, and to a number of readers it may seem novelistic to
make so much of the issue of attendance at the funeral,
considered as a means of escape. No great harm, though, is
done by any of this. *The Widow's Children* is a compelling
and satisfying book. The critique of kinship and the world's
law is intelligent and far from sentimental: it has in it, especially apparent in the wit, a worldliness which it could not
do without, and which is that of someone who has lived
long enough to have learned a good deal, for example,
about brothers and sisters. (p. 31)

Karl Miller, in The New York Review of
Books *(reprinted with permission from* The
New York Review of Books; *copyright ©
1976 NYREV, Inc.), October 28, 1976.*

The Widow's Children is an exceptionally well-made novel,
elegantly written and technically accomplished, with a rigorous regard for the classical unities of time (less than 24
hours elapse in the course of it) and place (a few rooms in
and a cemetery outside New York City). Its plot, character, setting and structure are skillfully integrated. This is
the novel as art, and the distinction between it and life is
never blurred. . . . Aristotle would understand *The Widow's Children,* and use it to illustrate the second edition of
his *Poetics.* (p. F1)

In all her books [Paula Fox] displays a lapidary talent, polishing each phrase until it glistens. Her eye and ear are

unerring. . . . Such evocative, limpid and accurate writing is not so simply achieved.

Yet it is quite possible to admire Paula Fox's style and to appreciate her talent without feeling much more affection for this novel than its characters feel for one another or for themselves, which is very little indeed. Estranged from the world and abandoned by one another, they seem unable to fulfill either their own needs or the needs of anyone else. In the same way, the reader, too, is estranged; his own expectations, heightened by the form of this very formal novel, unfulfilled.

This may strike some as less a criticism of the novel than a questionable if not actually illegitimate response to it, a response less cerebral than visceral. Perhaps so, but as a barometer of aesthetic response, gut feelings are not to be distrusted entirely. Ultimately, *The Widow's Children,* like the night Paula Fox describes, seems not so much illuminated as "diluted by a pale but ruthless artificial light." (p. F3)

> *William McPherson, "The Family That Preys Together," in* Book World—The Washington Post *(© The Washington Post), October 31, 1976, pp. F1, F3.*

"The Widow's Children" [is a] strange, bilious novel about a violent family gathering that leaves none of its participants unharmed. . . . Mrs. Fox allows her characters brief outbursts in which they seem to rise above their contempt for each other, but these flashes of levity or optimism are soon quashed. Despite the fact that the book is well written, it is somehow difficult to respond to, perhaps because the author has battened down each character so tightly in his or her misery that they all seem like dead souls—almost beyond comprehension or curiosity. (pp. 164-65)

> The New Yorker *(© 1976 by The New Yorker Magazine, Inc.), November 1, 1976.*

Not until we have finished *The Widow's Children* . . . do we realize how aptly [Fox's] intention is expressed by the epigraph she has taken from Rainer Maria Rilke. With characteristic economy she quotes only the beginning of his poem "Widow": "Deprived of their first leaves her barren children stand, and seem, for all the world, to have been born because she pleased some terror. . . ." The rest of the short poem moves away from the children to the mother, but Fox is a novelist, not a poet, and her characters—a widow's aging offspring with willful perversity of their own—have made demands on her quite as urgent as Rilke's larger vision. Yet it is a measure of her impressive ambition that his lines stand sentinel over her work—that she dares in this short, rather brittle social novel, to be judged by their implications. . . .

Karl Miller [see excerpt above] came [close] to grasping the scope of the book in quoting Stuart Hampshire on "the genealogy of misfortunes that pass across the generations as an inherited punishment," and in speaking of all the characters, whatever their age, as "outcast" and "outlaw" orphans. Nevertheless, it is their entanglement in family ties, more than their forlorn freedom from them, that shapes their destinies. . . .

[Fox's originality] consists of an odd combination of traditional elements (with her puritanical Jamesian ambassador in a transplanted European scene); a stylish appreciation of contemporary urban life; and appeals to our long-standing fascination with the witch, the family curse, the changeling. . . .

Fox's narrative is neither obscure nor cryptic. The foreground story follows the Maldonada family (the name suggests their deprivation; they are "badly bestowed") for 24 hours in New York City. (p. 16)

[Their] mother, Alma—the widow of the title—has just died in a nursing home. . . .

Fox's design . . . is straightforward—indeed, with its party at the outset and its funeral at the end, the novel is conventionally structured. Still, such resolution as she offers is not of itself enough to rid the reader of his disgust for the three Maldonadas—"like dinosaurs sinking into the tar pits, flailing about," Clara says. They and their friends would be unbearable if Fox did not provide the background of their youth and beauty, when they were vigorous and optimistic. Constantly, and with great emotional force, she moves from their aging bodies, "warm, sweating hands," drunken maundering, to a time when everything seemed possible.

But, in summoning up the past, the author falters in precisely the command of detail and concrete reality that is her greatest strength when rendering the present. It is as if concentration on the contemporary scene had exhausted her. She is under no obligation, of course, to provide a genealogy; memories fail, legends take over, these dreamers of lost wealth are unreliable narrators. It is not in this gray area that we sense the past falls apart, rather on occasions when Fox has been unnecessarily specific, with someone's age given here, a date or two there, until the most unobservant reader is disturbed by anachronisms and improbabilities. . . .

Fox has earned the right, though, to leave larger mysteries unanswered, to proceed by indirection in suggesting what set the childrens' teeth on edge, how Alma, in the words of Rilke, "pleased a terror" in order to give birth to her barren brood. . . . Yet I think the terror lay not there, but in the Maldonadas' denial of their [Jewish] faith. As a child, Alma liked to visit churches and synagogues; perhaps in death, Carlos jokes, she "was returning to the bosom of Abraham."

An ambitious novel, as I have said, with a larger intention than I had at first realized. In its purpose, and in execution when Paula Fox remains on the scene she knows so well, *The Widow's Children* is remarkable. (p. 17)

> *Ruth Mathewson, "Family Entanglements," in* The New Leader *(© 1976 by the American Labor Conference on International Affairs, Inc.), December 20, 1976, pp. 16-17.*

The intelligence and sensibility in which Paula Fox's fiction is steeped sets it distinctively apart. Moreover, her narrative skills are considerable, her dialogue is engaging and authentic, and an appealingly wicked humor often glints beneath the appraisal of one of the characters who crowd her pages. Having said this, one cannot help fretting that her latest novel, *The Widow's Children,* leaves behind a great sense of dissatisfaction. For although she displays in it all the qualities that have distinguished her earlier novels, somehow, in *The Widow's Children,* they do not combine to the same striking effect as before. In fact, they do not combine at all, which may be part of the problem.

A more significant part may lie in the nature of the people who pass through this story. On the whole, they are a wearisome lot, far too self-absorbed to be able to respond dramatically to each other. Yet it is their effect on one another that provides the focus of the book and that should—but doesn't—provide the momentum of the plot as well. Mrs. Fox's interest lies in an examination of the nature of the family's claims on the individuals who compose it. But the family she has created for this purpose, although linked by birth and chained to the same disabling memories, is not up to her intentions. Its members are not just improbable, singly and as a group; they are unusable as a lens through which the reader may scrutinize either the society or himself. The book suffers an additional handicap: its story is told from no single viewpoint but from several simultaneously, a device which, in this case, serves only to dissipate the reader's sympathies. With everyone talking at once, points are hard to make and meanings are apt to get lost in the babble. (pp. 217-18)

[There] is a cryptic conclusion to a cryptic book, a book with much to recommend it, but one whose deepest meaning seems to have been buried under too many levels of implication. (p. 218)

> *Rene Kuhn Bryant, "Painted Veils," in* National Review *(© National Review, Inc., 1977; 150 East 35th St., New York, N.Y. 10016), February 18, 1977, pp. 217-18.*

* * *

FUCHS, Daniel   1909-

An American novelist, short story writer, and screenwriter, Fuchs was born in New York but has lived in Hollywood since the thirties. While he won an Academy Award for writing the screenplay for the movie *Love Me or Leave Me*, Fuch's literary reputation will survive on the basis of three novels written in the thirties that were rediscovered in 1961. *Homage to Blenholt*, *Low Company*, and *Summer in Williamsburg* depict the lives of Jewish slum-dwellers with humor and pathos. In retrospect Fuch's three novels are significant forerunners of the modern Jewish novel associated with Malamud, Roth, and Bellow.

One of the most talented of novelists to emerge during the Thirties, [Daniel Fuchs] had the least heartening of receptions. Richly original and humorous as the books were, the first, "Summer in Williamsburg," sold four hundred copies; the next, "Homage to Blenholt," sold exactly the same amount, and the third, "Low Company," reached a high point of twelve hundred copies sold. Fuchs can certainly be forgiven for taking what seemed to be a hint on the part of the public, and turning to short stories for *The New Yorker* and other magazines, and eventually to screenwriting. . . .

[He] slowly became known, mostly to fellow writers, and to serious critics like Alfred Kazin and Irving Howe. Secondhand book dealers began quoting high prices for the available copies of the three volumes. And now they are brought together in one volume. . . . They go very well together, for the *milieu* of all three is Brooklyn of the mid-Thirties, and taken together they represent the solid achievement of an author of high stature. . . .

I was fortunate enough to encounter the novels at a relatively early age, being introduced first to "Homage to Blenholt". . . . At first I thought Fuchs might be one more member of the school of social realism, prevalent at the time, but though the book was firmly rooted in the tenement life of Brooklyn it was not trying to say that life was terrible and that the class struggle was the answer, but rather that life, wherever it was, had beauty and terror and comedy. The comedy in "Homage to Blenholt" was the

best kind, funny and pathetically human at the same time. Poor Max Balkan, living in Williamsburg, dreaming of the fortunes he will someday make and disburse, is to be found everywhere and in every time, and when his dreams of empire—based on an idea for bottling onion juice—are shattered, he becomes every man who must make his sad, compromising adjustment to reality. The homage he pays to Blenholt, the dead Commissioner of Sewers, is the homage paid by the sensitive man to those hard-hearted and insensitive enough to get what they want.

As vivid as young Max Balkan is his old father, once a Yiddish actor, now walking the streets dressed as a clown, carrying the sandwich boards that advertise Madame Clara's Beauty Salon. He doesn't say much, but he knows the tragedy of his son, and philosophically and gently suffers for him. If I have implied that all this is sad, it isn't really. A warm glow of humor, rising at times to hilarity, plays over [these people]. . . .

A darker vein of violence ran through ["Low Company"], but the wild humor and the richness of characterization were still there. Fuchs again managed to find a profound and delectable irony in the most unprepossessing of places, nothing less than a Coney Island soda fountain. Here was a new and marvelous gallery of people. . . . (p. 17)

I came to "Summer in Williamsburg" last, because of the difficulty of obtaining it, and was not prepared for it to be as good as it is. The vogue for young literary geniuses had not yet begun, and it was hard to imagine that anyone at the age of twenty-four could be so mature and comprehending and at the same time so fully formed as a novelist. Very few writers are able to evoke anything out of the environment that depressed them as they grew. Fuchs has been compared to James T. Farrell, but it is clear now that he had greater gifts than Farrell, and did much more than transcribe. His dialogue, from the very beginning, had a flavor of its own; while seemingly realistic it is as artful as Hemingway's or O'Hara's, and read aloud it usually makes one laugh. In this book, as in the others, there are the sensitive and the brutal; they encounter and are astonished by each other, and Fuchs judges not, for they are all human.

Reading the novels again, I was fearful that they might not hold up, but time has neither dimmed nor darkened them, and I suspect they are more readable and compelling today, if only because the problems are different now, and we can meet all of the author's wonderful people simply as people and not as representatives of a condition. They are fixed now, the nice ones, the evil ones, the old, the young, as a wonderful tapestry of "low life" captured with unsentimental warmth. "These three novels," the jacket tell us, "constitute a minor American classic." What exactly, I find myself wondering, is so minor about them? (p. 18)

> *Hollis Alpert, "The Southside Story," in* Saturday Review *(© 1961 by Saturday Review, Inc.; reprinted with permission), September 23, 1961, pp. 17-18.*

When Fuchs's novels were reissued in the early sixties much was made of the fabulistic, "poetic" side, as if they could only be appreciated in the wake of a moral allegorist like Malamud. Actually, the great strength of the books is their feeling for the life of the streets, the Runyonesque "low company" of youthful gangs in Williamsburg and Jewish mobsters in the Catskills, a chapter of social history quickly forgotten when the Jews became more respectable and the Jewish novel more morally austere. In Fuchs the moral temperature is low—he is notably ham-handed in portraying the religious life of his Jews, a more inward subject. He is a folklorist, an anthropologist of street life rather than a purveyor of moral parables. For all his freedom from the cant of proletarian writing he remains in essence a 1930s realist; for him life is with the people. (p. 42)

> *Morris Dickstein, in* Partisan Review *(copyright © 1974 by Morris Dickstein), Vol. XLI, No. 1, 1974.*

In his prose of glimmering diffidence, Fuchs tells the story [in *West of the Rockies*] of Adele Hogue, a movie star, and Burt Claris, a handsome nobody who works for her talent agency. The beginning of their romance is tersely sketched indeed: "He had taken up with her, had gotten into her good graces, slept with her. Claris was no better than most. She was accessible." (One of the book's incidental mirages is that Fuchs always refers to the hero as "Claris," which sounds feminine, and often to the heroine as "Hogue," which seems masculine.) The novel centers upon a Palm Springs resort to which Adele Hogue has fled after bolting the set of a movie in production; Burt Claris, on behalf of the agency, has chased her there. The action generally observes the unities of this place in these few days of crisis. . . . (p. 445)

What might be faults in another novel feed this one's dreamlike, movie-like glow. Gentle improbabilities hurry events along. Servants are remarkably obliging: a Filipino hotel steward volunteers his room as a love nest, and a baby's nurse spontaneously tells Burt where his wife has hidden her love letters. The imperfectly guessed motives and sketchily summarized lives give a mysterious largeness to the world beyond the plot's circumference. Los Angeles becomes a nostalgic presence. . . . (p. 446)

Contracts, erotic as well as financial, take effect in an arid atmosphere purged of any Old World notions of honor or noblesse oblige. The dreams of success and love are acted out against a hard awareness of the "they" who control destinies—the bankers, the gangsters, as implacable and irrational as Greek deities. The women who populate Palm Springs form an ominous chorus of Furies. They lie in the sun discussing girdles and beauty operations, they make love with necklaces on, they fly decorators in from New York and Texas, they are not unkind, having "all been in the business at one time or another, as stand-ins or stock girls," but with men their ardor is "overwhelmingly tender and solicitous and at the same time impersonal, a kindness which they could discontinue seemingly without an instant's feeling or trace of remembrance": they are all, Wigler tells Burt Claris, "secret agents." They have all made their "adjustment," and in this they differ from Adele Hogue.

Fuchs's portrait of a star is masterly. He seems to do everything to diminish her. She appears frightened, sick, vulgar, and foolish, callous to her children and destructive wherever she can reach. Even her body is seen sadly. . . . Since neither beauty nor skill ("She didn't know anything about acting, never had, would be the first to say so") has lifted her up from the high-school malt shops through the petty prostitutions and mismarriages and neurotic ailments into stardom, what has? Fuchs answers, "Fanatic energy." Adele explains it to herself: "Her special effectiveness with the audience was spontaneous, something organic, beyond control. She believed it was the product of the nervous system you were endowed with, and she was convinced her

nerves were used up, that you were given just so much." So "star quality" exacts an exceptional toll, and reader and author and lover together come to adore anew this exasperating and worse-than-average woman. Using as his material the shabbiest truths, Fuchs rebuilds the Hollywood myth; a happy ending evolves in an atmosphere of exhausted illusion. When, at the end, Adele Hogue stands with Burt on the edge of a marital partnership perhaps—who knows?—as profitable as that of Doris Day and Marty Melcher, and turns to him in the mass of reporters and mouths "I love you" as if on a sound stage, her sincerity is beyond gauging; we are dazzled by her courage, her real will to go on living her life of unreality. (pp. 446-48)

> *John Updike, "Phantom Life," in his* Picked-Up Pieces *(copyright © 1975 by John Updike; reprinted by permission of Alfred A. Knopf, Inc.), Knopf, 1975, pp. 444-48.*

[A] claustrophobic actuality [is present in] a trilogy—*Summer in Williamsburg, Homage to Blenholt, Low Company*—that Daniel Fuchs wrote in the thirties as a *comédie humaine* of Brooklyn immigrant life. Set in a gray slum at the foot of the Williamsburg Bridge, Fuchs's novels take the immigrant story a generation further, to the American-born sons and daughters growing up in the early thirties, ready to flee their parents but without purpose or possibility. The cramped life of the slums is to be decisive, even traumatic, in shaping Fuchs' work. There can hardly have been another American writer, except perhaps James T. Farrell, whose image of life has been so tightly bound by his adolescent years, whose entire creative effort is so painful a struggle to come to terms with memory and its costs, yet whose achievement, in the bruised serenity that shines through his best work, seems finally much more than the growl or whimper which a young writer brings to his unhappiness.

If it makes sense to speak of American Jewish writing as a regional literature, Fuchs is one of the most regional—even provincial—among these writers. Rarely does his horizon extend beyond the slum: it is there that he finds his truth and his sadness. All of Fuchs's novels are dominated by a sense of place as it grasps a man's life and breaks him to its limits. *Summer in Williamsburg* may seem at first like still another study of an unhappy, sensitive youth, but it soon becomes clear that Fuchs is not merely prey to a dilemma, he is actively developing a novelistic idea. And that idea is the way the power of environment, the tyranny of conditions, can take over a life.

The power of the Jewish past fades, there is hardly even a conscious rejection of it; all that remains in these novels is the children of the immigrants, scurrying through Williamsburg streets, seeking ways of escape and avenues of pleasure but soon learning that escape is unlikely and pleasure brief. And that, insists Fuchs with a quiet but self-tormenting passion, is the law of Williamsburg life. From first to last he is obsessed with this single theme: escape and trap. At the end of *Summer in Williamsburg* the central figure sadly reflects on what he sees about him:

> That was the choice . . . Papraval [his uncle, a racketeer] or his father. Papraval, smoking cigars, piled up money and glowed with sweat and happiness, while his father sat with his feet on the windowsill in the dimness of a Williamsburg flat. . . . He was

heading in his father's direction. . . . Look at him, Philip said, he's old, he's skinny, and all he has after all the years is a cigarette and a window.

What Fuchs brings to the immigrant experience is a wry and disenchanted tenderness, perhaps because he possesses that capacity for accepting the "given," that stoicism which, like an underground river, winds through both Jewish faith and Jewish rebellion. It is not exactly love for his world or his people that is at stake here, but something that for a writer like Fuchs is more important: a total absorption in his materials, so that his rendered world creates an illusion of coming not from craft or contrivance but from some deeper, shared necessity.

Fuchs's best book, *Homage to Blenholt,* releases a gift for exuberant comedy, a sweetly mocking play with Jewish daydreams. Untroubled by the vice of abstraction, Fuchs is the most novelistic of all the American Jewish novelists. No theories concerning the destiny of the Jews weigh upon his books; he seems quite indifferent to those modern notions which transform Jewish characters into agents of the human condition, symbols of estrangement, heroes of consciousness. He writes about quite unremarkable people, Jews in the slums, neither larger nor smaller than life; he writes as a young man enjoying the discovery of his mimetic powers but also as an older man, Jewish to the marrow, who is never able to forget the essential sadness of things. Two generations speak through his work, that of the father, the ridiculed "Mr. Fumfotch," and that of the son, a Brooklyn Harold Lloyd aflame with dreams of grandeur. Moving past ideologies as if some blessing of fate had made them invisible, Fuchs is closer to such Yiddish storytellers as Sholom Aleichem than are most of the later, more intellectualized American Jewish writers, since for him, too, the life of the Jews is a sufficient subject, a universe into itself. The past has been lost, the future seems inaccessible, but the immigrant present encloses everything: a cigarette and a window. (pp. 590-91)

> *Irving Howe, in his* World of Our Fathers *(© 1976 by Irving Howe; reprinted by permission of Harcourt Brace Jovanovich, Inc.), Harcourt, 1976.*

*   *   *

FUENTES, Carlos   1928-

Fuentes is a Mexican novelist, playwright, short story writer, and critic. An internationally acclaimed author, he has proven to be an erudite and highly innovative writer, with the potential to be one of the great writers of the twentieth century. His major drawback, giving some critics reason to pause, is his cosmopolitanism, which can cause his writing to appear too facile or even slick. (See also *CLC*, Vol. 3, and *Contemporary Authors*, Vols. 69-72.)

The goddesses of myth have had two faces: mother earth, the mother goddess, the creative, on the one side; the seductive devourer and destroyer of men on the other. . . . [For] Carlos Fuentes, woman is always the second aspect of this duality. Woman is the destroyer, and love is a kind of death.

For Fuentes, love is abnormal, a violation of the innocence of man. His stories are filled with incestuous unions or the desire for them . . . with endless reworkings and manipulations of the basic theme, and woman always the corrupter. The woman is almost always the older in the union; the man is the one who suffers the loss of innocence.

Age is the second theme that fascinates Fuentes. His heroines are sometimes dual, the same personality existing simultaneously at two different ages, as in the surrealistic novela *Aura.* In this story the protagonist falls in love with the beautiful servant girl, only to discover that she is a recreation of the past youth of his employer, an ancient, dying widow. Or two individuals are closely related, such as those in his short story, "Las Dos Elenas," in which one man is in love with his wife, a young, liberated woman, and his wife's mother, who evokes the nostalgia for the past.

One of his most telling explorations of the theme of age is in the novel *Zona Sagrada (Sacred Zone).* The protagonist is an aging movie star, Claudia Nervo, who is possessively attached to her son, already in his twenties, but at the same time repelled by him as a reminder of the falseness of her pretense at youth.

Claudia, who has left her son with his father when he was very small, has returned at some time during the son's young boyhood and stolen him from his school. The feeling of violation along with corruption is heightened by Fuentes's use of the term "Robachicos," child-snatcher, which links her with gypsies, witches, thieves who steal children to make them into tamales to sell at the market. At the same time he emphasizes the son's delight in her smell of perfumed furs and the likeness of her face to the one he had seen in his own mirror. The slow, warm pace of Guadalajara, where he had been living with his father and his grandparents, contrasts sharply with the Mexico City of his adulthood. The woman has brought him out of the womb of Jalisco into the turbulent world of Mexico City.

She has brought him forth to destroy him. Her love must be strangling rather than creating. He is slowly driven mad because he is in an untenable position; he may have no identity because, though she expects filial love and devotion, she cannot acknowledge it or him without risking the loss of what has given her power: her beauty and her youth. Therefore, he cannot be her son or not her son. He has no place, but he cannot be released. (pp. 246-47)

The theme of incest runs throughout, . . . but with a dizzying number of variations. The mother constantly denies the sexual maturity of her son, calling him "*santito,*" little saint, and denying his masculinity. Nevertheless, she either frustrates his love affairs or possesses his lovers, both male and female, so that he is unable to feel conjunction with anyone and is left isolated, fractionated. He feels the pull between his humanity, his temporality, and her existence as goddess, myth, legend, beyond time. As he is losing his mind, he contemplates a return to the womb, which he feels she has promised, but realizes that it is impossible. He then considers cannibalism. . . . (pp. 248-49)

Having realized the impossibility of any change, as Claudia is rooted in the present and must exist as a being outside time, eternal, he loses his mind, his sanity dissolved in her myth. (p. 249)

In one of his most successful stories, "The Two Elenas," Fuentes explores yet another sort of unnatural family relationship, that of the man who is his mother-in-law's lover. Pursuing a plot which might easily have become absurd, Fuentes draws the reader slowly into an awareness of the brittle childishness of the liberated wife, the delicate sensuousness of the mother, and the man as a contented cuckold. (p. 250)

Gradually the reader [of the surrealistic novel *Aura*] comes to realize that Aura and the widow are two aspects of the same personality, as Aura ages from twenty to forty in [a] period of days. . . . Montero continues to pretend to himself that the widow is holding Aura prisoner with some sort of secret, and he goes to meet Aura for an assignation to discover what the hold may be and to rescue her from it. Seeing a woman in the darkness, he approaches her, fearing that at any moment the widow may return. . . . The final shock comes when he recognizes in the moonlight the nude figure, not of Aura, but of the old woman, "thin, wrinkled, small and old, shivering lightly because you touched her, you love her, you have returned, too." Aura has been a creation of the widow's will, the will that she had to create children—the will to recapture, through sixty years of widowhood, her lost youth. . . . (p. 252)

With *Aura*, Fuentes moves toward his most penetrating but most difficult exploration of the theme of woman, *Change of Skin*. In *Aura* the atmosphere is one of magic; in *Change of Skin* it is one of nightmare and madness. The device of having a madman as the narrator, as well as the alter ego of the major male characters, allows a constant interplay of reality and magic, real events with symbolic and mythical nightmares. These illuminate all aspects of the relationships between the four principal characters. . . . However, though the characters are well developed as individuals and have distinct backgrounds which are related in flashbacks, the characters often blend into one another until the reader is again aware that he is looking at different aspects of two personalities: archetypical woman and man, at once both victimized and destroyer. It is only in this book that Fuentes admits that man may conspire to destroy himself at the hands of woman, and he explores the capacity for self-destruction which each possesses through the interplay of different aspects of the personality as distinguished by the different names.

The two women, Elizabeth and Isabel, are more clearly aspects of the same personality than are the two men. . . . Javier is the link between them—married to Elizabeth, but lover to Isabel, who has been one of his students. Javier is also both victim and victimizer; he and Elizabeth destroy each other, and he seduces and shames Isabel. The links between the two female characters are many. It is no accident of Fuentes's writing that Isabel is the Spanish for Elizabeth. Javier finds pleasure with them only by calling them both Ligeia, again associating them with a female archetype and denying them separate identities. (pp. 252-53)

Javier, Elizabeth, Isabel, are all at once victimizers and victimized; each relationship between two people is that of "Two tiny animals. Each wrapped around the other and each quietly, patiently, eating the other alive. . . . We can still hear the whimpering, the tiny moans, the choking sounds." (p. 254)

Change of Skin, through the interplay of characters and times, is a novel about love and death. As Javier says, "Ligeia will be beside me, forcing me to understand that in loving all life we also loved all death." Love is a dying, a humiliation, a release of self which is always destructive of the individual. The woman, by desiring permanent union, possession, is desiring the destruction of the lover, and to submit to love requires a relinquishment of the self which Fuentes calls dying. Thus, for Fuentes, woman symbolizes a cycle of love, humiliation, and death; and submission to her will mean disaster. Woman, though destroyed, remains always the destroyer.

However, *Change of Skin* goes beyond this theme of Fuentes's earlier works to involve man in his own destruction. Relationships of love are seen as destructive, not because of the malevolence of woman, but because of their inherent nature. Moreover, *Change of Skin* shows both men and women as self-destructive (through the interplay of the two aspects of each personality, Isabel and Elizabeth, Javier and Franz) as well as destructive in their interrelationships. Thus, Fuentes has moved from a condemnation of woman as evil to a pessimistic statement about the nature of man and woman and the possibilities for human love. Though his characterization of women in his novels has become more sophisticated and understanding, love remains a kind of death. (p. 255)

> *Linda B. Hall, "The Cipactli Monster: Woman as Destroyer in Carlos Fuentes," in* Southwest Review (© *1975 by Southern Methodist University Press), Summer 1975, pp. 246-55.*

The year Columbus first landed in America, say the history books, was the same year Ferdinand and Isabella, soon to be titled "the Catholic Kings" by Pope Alexander VI, conquered the last of the Moorish kingdoms of Andalusia and expelled the Jews from Spain. One act opened a new world; the other two, argues Carlos Fuentes in [*Terra Nostra,* his] massive, brilliant and frequently grotesque novel, destroyed a civilization and assured that the order later transplanted from Spain to the new realms would be rigid, sterile and suffocating. . . .

Terra Nostra is no more a historical novel than Thomas Pynchon's *Gravity's Rainbow* is a World War II adventure yarn. Throughout it, the fantastic becomes commonplace and history is altered. . . .

What Fuentes has created here is another history, a hidden, occult, symbolic history in which past, present and future converge in hallucinatory splendor. The time separating epochs melts, the barriers between continents disappear. . . .

The outcome of this other history, however, is ultimately the same as our own. . . .

Fuentes, . . . has been building to [a] confrontation with the heritage of Tenochtitlan and El Escorial ever since his first book, a collection of short stories called *The Masked Days,* was published in 1954. That book took its title from the last five days of the Aztec calendar, nameless days in which time was suspended and activity ceased; later, in *Where The Air is Clear,* he was to create Ixca Cienfuegos, whose very name joins Mexico's Spanish and Aztec strains. And in *Change of Skin,* his last novel before *Terra Nostra,* four modern travelers journey to the pyramid of Cholula—where, in 1519, Cortes massacred thousands of Montezuma's priests and warriors.

But in *Terra Nostra,* Fuentes probes more deeply into the origins of Mexico—and what it means to be a Mexican—than ever before. That inevitably takes him beyond Mexico and even beyond Spain. Egyptian, Greek and Roman prophecies, the mystical doctrines of the Hebrew Kabbalah, Zohar and Sephirot, and the rites of the heretical Christian sects of the Middle Ages are all a part of . . . "a-rithmythic," the peculiar brand of numerology that unites the new world, the old world and the other world and permits characters to slip from one time and place to another.

Masterful in his manipulation of history and legend,

Fuentes is no less accomplished in his manipulation of language and narrative. Though a torrent of words, translated faithfully, descends on us in *Terra Nostra,* the book is not overwritten. The subject itself is rich and immense, demanding verbal invention and structural experimentation. . . .

It may well have been Fuentes's intention to make *Terra Nostra* the supreme, all-embracing piece of modern Spanish-language fiction: the Great Latin America Novel, as it were. That is certainly the impression conveyed by the apocalyptic finale of *Terra Nostra,* in which characters lifted from novels by Cortazar, Garcia Marquez, Mario Vargas Llosa, Jose Donoso and Alejo Carpentier sit around a table in Paris ("all good Latin Americans come to Paris to die") on December 31, 1999, playing "C.I.A. Poker" ("I have five of a kind: United Fruit, Standard Oil, Pasco Corporation, Anaconda Copper and I.T.T.") while they await the end of the world.

If that was indeed his aim, then Fuentes has come very close to succeeding. *Terra Nostra* is at once savage and erudite, as complex and contradictory as Latin America itself, and Fuentes's audacity in appropriating for his book the figures who symbolize the best writing of an entire continent is fully justified.

> *Larry Rohter, "A Vision of Justice, A Vision of Tragedy, A Vision of Decadence," in* Book World—The Washington Post (© The Washington Post), *October 26, 1976, p. F-1.*

Deep within, while writing ["Terra Nostra"], Carlos Fuentes seems to sense that he might be making a mistake. "Terra Nostra's" axial event is the construction of the Escorial, Spain's 16th-century monastic palace and royal mausoleum near Madrid. . . .

Fuentes clearly does not himself believe in such grand ambitions. . . .

Yet, sooner or later, the irony must have hit him: he was himself into just such an undertaking. "Terra Nostra" is a colossal 350,000-word opus, a kind of panoramic Hispano-American creation myth. . . . [Like the Escorial] the book seems largely to have been a labor more of duty than of love.

Carlos Fuentes is a world-famous author, serious, provocative, controversial even, inventive, widely considered Mexico's most important living novelist, maybe the greatest ever—but the world is full of doubters and perhaps Fuentes wished to silence them once and for all, burying them under the sheer weight and mastery of his book. More likely, though, it is the familiar case of a committed and conscientious writer being overtaken and captured by his own metaphor. From his earliest stories, Fuentes has always aspired to instructive all-embracing overviews, especially historical and mythical overviews (he is as much a Hegelian and a Jungian—not to mention a Cleanser of the Temple—as a Marxist) that might explain once and for all what it means to be a Mexican; and he has always been willing to take any risk. So, if the ultimate metaphoric set occurred to him, how could he refuse to pursue it?

Most of the predominant elements in "Terra Nostra" are present in his earliest work. His first novel, "Where the Air Is Clear," published nearly 20 years ago, is an expansive, vivid, densely populated, kaleidoscopic portrait of mid-20th-century Mexico City, brash and ruthless yet highly lyrical, something like a surrealistic "Manhattan Transfer."

It established Fuentes immediately as an extraordinary new voice in Latin American fiction, and, after a conventional dues-paying second novel, his third, "The Death of Artemio Cruz," projected him upon its publication in 1962 into the front rank of the world's best-known avant-garde novelists. Though he has written other novels since then—as well as stories, essays, experimental theater pieces, filmscripts, and journalism—it is "The Death of Artemio Cruz" that people still tend to remember him by 14 years later.

Much more tightly controlled than his first novel, "The Death of Artemio Cruz" draws a kind of time-line, as it were, through the spatial plane of the earlier book, capturing in the retrospective details of one man's life the essence of the post-Revolutionary history of all of Mexico. Both books make use of experimental narrative techniques (especially variations on person and verb tense), propaedeutic sex, Aztec mythology, long interior monologues, and the themes, among others, of betrayal, cultural determinism and a national way of life that is, as he is to say later in "Terra Nostra," "nourished by the arts of death." (p. 3)

The plot, or *mythos,* [of "Terra Nostra"] . . . is a kind of hortatory dialogue and revelation in the style of the Hermetic Magi of the Renaissance.

There is no room in this review to discuss . . . the Magi. . . . But suffice it to say, their impact on this book has been enormous, providing—or at the very least reinforcing—most of its binding images: all the numerologies, the circles, the transformations and interlocutions, such conceits as Cities of the Sun and Theaters of Memory, the invocation of demons, the colors, archetypes, dreams, pilgrimages, beasts, exhortations, mirrors, magic, even the *furores* of eroticism, scatology, murder and blasphemy.

The writings of the Magi commonly took the form of a dialogue between Magus and Adept, and similarly these are the two principal characters—indeed virtually the only characters—of "Terra Nostra." They have many names throughout the book . . . but ultimately they are all engaged in the same exercise, even taking turns at playing the two roles: interrogatus and respondit, ancient and pilgrim, chronicler and hero. They all seek through dialectic to pierce what [is called] in the book that "veil drawn across a world moving rapidly and silently from some unknown center, issuing from some subterranean force," and thence to apprehend the true reality behind the tear, the Ideas behind the Shadows, the demonic flow of Life beneath the world's mausoleums, charnel-houses, sacrificial altars and other holy debris.

Moreover, Fuentes seems to share with the Hermetics (whom he perhaps discovered during his acknowledged research into the Renaissance art of memory) a belief in cyclical history. . . .

To press home his lessons, Fuentes has everybody repeat them, revise them, work variations, etc., and though this chorus can be impressive, it is not often very moving. . . . Even moments of vivid action seem, often as not, to get turned into mere vehicles for extended rhetorical monologues and dialogues, such that the plot, though elaborate in its conception, becomes static and pictorial in the telling: just the opposite of that free open-ended flow the book is supposedly celebrating.

The book itself is closed, circular and tightly structured. Devoted as it is to the creative and synthetic power of the number three, it is quite naturally divided into three major sections; the Old World, the New World, and the Next World (an unfortunate mistranslation and hardly the only one in this largely trustworthy but pedestrian and sometimes downright quaint translation—it should be the Other World). The middle section is the young Pilgrim's tale of his voyage through the New World. . . . This pilgrimage is a kind of blend of the likes of the Gilgamesh and Percival stories with the exotic imagery of Aztec mythologies, though all the characters in it seem to be interchangeable with those of the Old World.

Rippling outward from this central pilgrimage are circles of past, present and future time, with fore and aft parallel images, rituals, narrative devices, thematic variations, numerologies and so on, all carefully balanced. (pp. 48-9)

[If] "Terra Nostra" is a failure, it is a magnificent failure. Its conception is truly grand, its perceptions often unique, its energy compelling and the inventiveness and audacity of some of its narrative maneuvers absolutely breathtaking . . . , the variations on themes and dreams, the interweaving of rich, violent, beautiful, grotesque, mysterious, even magical images—not without reason has this book been likened to a vast and intricate tapestry. (p. 49)

Fuentes's second person is not one overheard on a stage: the book itself, rather than the author or a character, becomes the speaker, the reader or listener a character, or several characters in succession. . . . The reader, then, becomes—together with the author—the Adept, playing the roles within the story that help them to learn together, watched by the book that reads them. . . . I know of [no other writer] who so intimately activates the otherwise dead space between page and reader. (p. 50)

> *Robert Coover, in* The New York Times Book Review *(© 1976 by The New York Times Company; reprinted by permission), November 7, 1976.*

[In] ways impossible to illustrate in brief (or even in fairly lengthy) quotation, *Terra Nostra* really is an Old Novel. Nightmare or not, Fuentes's Spain is too scrupulously fixed and predictable. If Donoso and García Márquez are like Dostoevsky, say, writers in a fever, seeking to catch us up in a plausible hysteria, then Fuentes and Vargas Llosa are like the Flaubert of *Salammbô*, naturalists of the dream, so that Fuentes's sixteenth-century Spain becomes less fantastic than Fuentes's modern Paris, and the Peru of Vargas

Llosa's novels is merely everyday Peru broken up by technique.

This is intentional, of course, an artistic and no doubt a temperamental choice. But it does turn the writer back toward that always dying animal, the novel grounded in the seen world and public experience. All good stories are slow stories, Thomas Mann said, but one of the implicit rules of phantasmagoria seems to be that it must move fast, however long it takes. And *Terra Nostra* moves like a pavane. When phantasmagoria reproduces not the feel of material reality but only its remorselessly stable appearance, then the liberation proposed by the New Novel is rejected, and we are back sleeping in the nightmare within which, at least, it had seemed possible to be awake. History, that is, can be confronted or evaded, but there is very little to be said for converting an evasion into a prison more confining than the one you've just got out of.

But this, in the end, is Fuentes's point. *Terra Nostra* is about escapes which can only be longed for, about a new world which is merely a grimace of the old, about flights into time which are simply flights into predetermination. (p. 60)

Insistently, throughout the book, . . . Fuentes insists on the promising properties of the number three, which will save us from the strife represented by the number two. Yesterday, today, tomorrow are more than mere past and present; life, death, and memory (for which another name might be fiction) are more than living and dying. The city founded by triplets will be spared the devastations that come upon cities founded by twins. And in anticipation, perhaps, Fuentes has divided his book into three parts: the old world, the new world, the other world. But the book, like reality, keeps sliding back into warring pairs: then and now, old and new, men and women, memory and oblivion. And it is the solidity of these pairs, the purely wishful quality of the liberating trinities, that gives the novel its final flatness, as well as its moving last chapter. It is flat not because Fuentes can't imagine a way out of time and history, and not because history congeals to such thickness in his hands, but because Fuentes, in spite of his own good intentions, really does seem to prefer the tidiness of despair to the disorder of faint hope. (pp. 60-1)

> *Michael Wood, in* The New York Review of Books *(reprinted with permission from* The New York Review of Books; *copyright © 1977 NYREV, Inc.), January 20, 1977.*

G

GADDIS, William 1922-

Gaddis is an American novelist. Although *The Recognitions* initially received harsh criticism from the literary world, the novel has enjoyed a steadily growing reputation and is now considered a contemporary American classic. His second novel in twenty years, *J.R.*, won the 1975 National Book Award. (See also *CLC*, Vols. 1, 3, 6, and *Contemporary Authors*, Vols. 17-20, rev. ed.)

Homogenization, confusion, intermingling of realms constitute the core of *J.R.* . . . [Gaddis is skilled] at depicting the intrusion of the corporate world into the worlds of education and the arts. Aphorism follows brilliant aphorism follows devastating image with a controlled abandon that will provide fodder for cocktail party paranoias of corruption for months to come. But that notion of corruption which rests upon the implicit acceptance of some master villain does violence to the complexity, artistic force and strand of genuine despair of Gaddis' work. An honest to God villain would make things much easier. In fact, Gaddis offers us no scapegoat, and I think his Gibbs must be taken with deadly seriousness when he says there is no wise man who vanished with the truth. (p. 29)

Gaddis has mastered the absurd logic of corporate society. Thus one of the themes of *J.R.* charts the accelerating deterioration of education from school as custodial institution, to televised teaching, to the packaging of communications skills, to advertisements in textbooks, to money for grades, to school personnel turning up as hospital personnel. And the novel ends with a child still trapped in a vast statue on a wind-swept cultural plaza, victim of the combined forces of purchased art and cultural-hegemony-seeking purchasing power. . . .

Gaddis [also] plays skillfully, although never glibly, with the tortured tangle of human existences. Child and parents, husband and wife, lover and lover meet each other, pass each other, use each other, lose each other. . . . The confusion and pain of human contact twists through the novel, people never sure if they love or whom or why. Their love never moves directly from one individual to another; it passes inexorably through the social nexus. . . .

This novel does not make for easy reading; nor does it end in some reassuring grand design. The 700-odd pages of almost uninterrupted conversation, unrelieved even by chapter breaks, capture the pervasive plasticity of a social experience that blends imperceptibly with mindless technological necessity. God is not in his heaven, all is not right with the world. Even the human facsimile of divine purpose, artistic creation, is fighting a desperate rear-guard action against the lack of purpose. The theme of creativity, like that of love with which it intertwines, twists in and out. . . .

The levels of meaning defy any succinct rendering. The wider one's knowledge, the more numerous the opportunities for discrete interpretations. . . . At least by the second reading, if not the first, even the untrained ear will begin to pick up the haunting melodies, the phrases that recur periodically in old and newly absurd context. Gaddis has more than proved himself a master of his craft, and that craft is sheer delight. After indulging in taking the pieces apart, one must return to listening to the whole. (p. 30)

> *Elizabeth Fox-Genovese, in* The New Republic *(reprinted by permission of* The New Republic; © *1976 by The New Republic, Inc.), February 7, 1976.*

JR does for American business what James Joyce did for Dublin, and Joseph Heller for World War Two. The eponymous hero belongs to that peculiarly North American line of hustling go-getters which includes Milo Minderbender, Sammy Glick and Duddy Kravitz, except for the fact that JR . . . [is] only 11 years old!

Dreiser and Dos Passos are William Gaddis's literary brethren. He reworks their canvases in experimental, contemporary colours, producing a gigantic and overpowering jigsaw of American megalomania. A charivari of characters parades through the book as their stories cross and interweave with bewildering intricacy. . . .

As the book is written almost entirely in dialogue—and nobody ever seems to finish a sentence—the only clue the reader has as to who is speaking is the speech pattern itself: but so finely is each character observed that, eventually, that is all one needs. The author makes very few concessions and demands careful reading: there is minimal punctuation; dialogue suddenly becomes narrative without warning, and these occasional narrative passages—at odds with the naturalistic dialogue—maunder into Faulknerian obfuscation. But, happily, the narrative accounts for a minute percentage of the book.

I am lost in admiration for Mr. Gaddis's achievement: in encompassing the worlds of business, government, education, the arts and music, journalism and public relations, while sustaining the rhythm and pace, the humour both high and low, the puns and wordplay, and counterpointing these with extremely moving scenes and romantic ones, Mr. Gaddis has marshalled enough material for half a dozen novels, fashioning a satiric vision of contemporary America that can only leave you breathless. (p. 717)

> *Tony Aspler, in* The Listener *(© British Broadcasting Corp. 1976; reprinted by permission of Tony Aspler), June 3, 1976.*

In 1955 William Gaddis published his first novel, *The Recognitions,* a perplexing, anagramatic, massive book which speculated on the themes of forgery, falsity and cash, and the place of art in the modern technologised world. Recognition was, in fact, what the book was slow to get. But it subsequently made its way as one of the contemporary American classics of experiment, and it has some real claim to have influenced the development of the massive, modern, post-psychological novel as this has evolved latterly in the United States. John Barth and, especially, Thomas Pynchon have been running with the same baton; and Pynchon's *V* and his *Gravity's Rainbow* have shown much the same obsessions, with the creation of plot and verbal text in a world of science and technical energy which has tipped irretrievably over the edge into entropic decline. The 'technetronic' novel has indeed become an American species; highly regarded, but nonetheless requiring of its readers a certain specialised tolerance. Heavily lexical, given to massive textual proliferation, elaborated learning, and complex inner ciphering, evolving through characters who do not so much make as suffer a plot evolving itself for plot's own sake, it invites the reader to a kindness not always easily granted to fiction.

It is, then, only fair warning to say that with his second novel Gaddis has, 20 years later, come back to enjoy the salad days of the species. *JR* is 726 pages of decidedly hard reading, a work of minimalist conventions, heavy on inventions and play. Modern America, according to the now very recognisable conventions of this species, is metaphorised as a universe of cybernetics and capital. (p. 820)

The first word of the text is 'money,' spoken in 'a voice that rustled,' and money, spawning, interconnecting, dividing, dominates and plots the book. It is an ancient theme of fiction, but Gaddis wants it for a total vision; *JR* is packed with learned financial elaborations so dense that the work is surely ripe for serialisation in the *Wall Street Journal*. . . . (pp. 820-21)

> *Malcolm Bradbury, "Hello Dollar," in* New Statesman *(© 1976 The Statesman & Nation Publishing Co. Ltd.), June 18, 1976, pp. 820-21.*

[*JR*] is about money—its power, its pervasiveness, its curious progression toward the unreal as its quantity increases; it is also and inseparably about the waste of talent, substance, love, and ultimately lives, and the base misuse and destruction of art and intelligence. The literally hundreds of materials used by Mr. Gaddis to deploy and elaborate his themes take their shape as accreted layers of data and innumerable threads, twisted and tangled. It is a magnificent work that is at once savagely comic and drenched in bitter pathos. While it is not tragic, it surely exists at the edge of despair. By a painstaking marshaling of

detail, the major characters are given us finally as exhausted, beaten, and desolate. (p. 613)

[Everybody] and everything in the novel is interconnected in what might justly be called a perfect if insane logic of possibility. *JR* does not work on the level of a meager naturalism, but supposes a world that exists of and for itself and in which all the characters are rigidly predestined to play out their roles. It is a claustrophobic world that works, within itself, like a syllogism. The author insists on a closed system: that this system plunges, with maniacal precision, toward denouement *within* that greater system that we may label the "real world" makes it no less a creation of supreme effectiveness and fictional truth.

JR, a sixth grade pupil at a gadget-ridden, computerized, and flagrantly intellectually bankrupt public school on Long Island, sits at the center of the novel, a boy who is the epitome of greed, the quintessential product of twentieth-century culture run to seed, plastic, and decay; at the same time, he is vulnerable, alone, touching—a castoff of his society and of his broken family within it. From this center, he sets in motion a chain reaction of financial wheeling-dealing that touches the seats of power where the decisions that affect the structure of the world—its politics, culture, social priorities—are formulated. He is, in his precocious strivings toward acquisition for its own sake, for the sake of attaining whatever, God help him, he may take to be the good life, a perfectly formed miniature of the macrocosm that he imitates. (p. 614)

Mr. Gaddis has entwined [his] characters' lives in such subtle and elaborately complex ways that "answers" or suggestions of possible answers as to their motivations and relationships are not so much given as they are strewn across the novel's pages. . . . The complexities are endless and ironic and shattering. Minor characters function in odd, neurotic, yet precise ways, elements of data in this enormous investigation of avarice and waste and their casualties.

Painters are cheated of their money, used and exploited as producers of saleable goods; writers are blocked, thwarted, duped, or twisted into shiny and agreeable hacks; lovers are sacrificed to fates that function as cosmic jokes; a school is perverted, drained, and finally sold; groves of ancient trees are paved over in a "deal" and in another a house is moved; marriages are smashed and soldiers sent to their slaughter carrying toy guns; and all of this (and dozens of more instances of perversion and corruption) is not only inevitable, it is logical, legal, and normal. The cause for this socially acceptable devastation is the quest for profits. On its simplest and most obvious level, *JR* is a compendium of those things that have been done, over the past half-century, to the people of the world by their governments and those whom governments truly serve. It is also, as I hope I have suggested, an investigation of the artist in a society that not only has no need for him but that despises him, and a mordantly limned picture of the "common man"—armed with his manipulated opinions and his jest of a "voice" in public affairs. (pp. 614-15)

Mr. Gaddis's ear is the perfect one of all first-rate novelists, by which I mean his speech as here recorded is beautifully crafted so as to appear to be "real" speech. His characters speak in cadences as precisely stylized as those of, say, Hemingway or Henry Green. It is not the product of the tape recorder that we are given, but the carefully selected and shaped materials that reveal each character as definitely as physical description. The patterns and tics of each character's speech are so brilliantly molded, so subtly and yet totally different one from the other, that the reader, after his first introduction to a character, has no difficulty in identifying that character in subsequent passages. It is a remarkable achievement and, I think, a stroke of genius on Gaddis's part to have structured his novel [mostly in dialogue]. Not only do we stay in absolute touch with what is being said by everybody, we begin to hear not *only* what is said, but what is *meant*. The "time" of the novel is of course rigorously restricted to the actual time it takes the characters to say what they have to say. Perhaps most importantly, this method of composition allows us to see the surfaces of things—what is really there, what people really appear to be to each other and to eavesdroppers (like the reader). This jettisoning of tawdry and banal "psychological" probing and the "hidden motivations" of characters allows Mr. Gaddis a clean surface, blessedly free of bunkum masquerading as the profound. What we know is what we hear.

JR strikes me as one of the very few distinguished and *written* American novels published in the last decade; indeed, it makes most other novels of this period seem watery or pretentious or both. Its comedy is that of all excellent comic artists—it conceals the ultimately absurd hopes and pretensions of life. It is a brilliant work—a great novel. (pp. 615-16)

> *Gilbert Sorrentino, in* Partisan Review *(copyright © 1976 by Partisan Review, Inc.), Vol. XLIII, No. 4, 1976.*

Winning the 1975 National Book Award for his second novel, *JR,* partially compensates William Gaddis for the neglect and incomprehension accorded his first novel, *The Recognitions.* Perplexed readers needing a guide and hesitant readers needing a goad will do well to realize that Gaddis, far from being a long-winded aberration, is a worthy follower of a tradition begun, say, by James Joyce and continued by many others, including Thomas Pynchon. Like his cohorts, he employs vast erudition to clarify inchoate but interesting reality, thereby contrasting the intellectual life with the quotidian. Gaddis, like the others, is fascinated by language and his own literary patterns. He also tries to find an ethical theory that will make sense in the contemporary world and to see whether love can still endure. He addresses these issues with a skill sufficient to justify the effort required to read his two thick books.

The Recognitions is difficult partly because its characters are slightly peculiar. Its hero, Wyatt Gwyon, slips away like a Cheshire cat, leaving behind only his grimace. For hundreds of pages, that is, he has no name, and at the end he is called Stephan Asche. Many of the minor characters, like those in such works as *Candide, Gulliver's Travels* and *Gargantua and Pantagruel,* are little more than vaguely dramatized intellectual positions. The action of *The Recognitions* is comprehensible section by section, even though it does not proceed coherently throughout. Accounts of Sinisterra, a counterfeiter of money, and Wyatt, a counterfeiter of paintings, alternate with satiric vignettes of pseudo-intellectual life. All these scenes work like mirrors to reflect light on Wyatt's search for understanding, which, because of the important religious theme, appears to be a search for salvation. Wyatt finds it in Spain as *The Recognitions* ends. (pp. 1-2)

Gaddis, like T. S. Eliot, looks to Dante for a viable system

of ethics, hoping that in the past he can find an order transferable to the chaotic present. His method of using Dante is Joycean, however; in his novel *The Inferno* reverberates with contemporary life, as *The Odyssey* does in *Ulysses.* (p. 2)

[A] series of clues identifies the section of *The Inferno* that is most relevant to *The Recognitions.* Gaddis refers occasionally to an elderly art collector, the Conte di Brescia, and at the end of the book Stanley sails to Italy on the *Conte di Brescia.* Gaddis thus alludes to Dante's passage about Adamo di Brescia, a counterfeiter who resides in the tenth and last Bolgia of the eighth circle of hell. Here suffer persons who have committed four types of simple fraud: alchemy, false witness, counterfeiting and evil impersonation. Analysis of these four sins is the most important compenent of the ethical theme in *The Recognitions.* . . .

Valentine is guilty of fraud, although not of alchemy specifically, because he sells Wyatt's counterfeit paintings and because he plagiarizes. Like other characters, Valentine for his own advantage desecrates things by transforming them and rejects transcendental judgment for a paltry kind of rationalism, mystery for magic, and art for profit. Some of the false witnesses, the fraudulent with words, in *The Recognitions* are the reviewers whom Gaddis mocks. Here his borrowing from Dante resembles using a cannon against gnats. . . . The counterfeiters, particularly Sinisterra and Wyatt, require little comment. Gaddis' meticulous description makes them the most vivid instances of fraudulence. (p. 3)

The other sinners in Dante's tenth Bolgia are evil impersonators. Gaddis, like Dante, includes literal examples. Sinisterra sometimes poses as a Rumanian, Mr. Yák, and he induces Wyatt to call himself Stephan Asche. Most of the instances, however, are figurative and contribute to the satire of pseudo-intellectuals: persons who impersonate real intellectuals. . . . On the topic of pseudo-intellectuals Gaddis . . . drifts away from his Dantean perspective and writes conventional satire against easily ridiculed targets.

Recktall Brown, the wealthy leader of the art counterfeiters, is the Satan who presides over this hell and thus Gaddis' embodiment of contemporary evil. His name is a scatological pun that recalls the medieval belief in the devil's association with the anal regions. Brown's name also reminds one of Freud's and Norman O. Brown's analyses of the anal-retentive character type. Revealing another source of his satanism, Brown appears in circumstances like those in which Mephistopheles appears in Goethe's *Faust.* A dog runs in circles around Otto and Wyatt, gradually moving closer, and a dog circles Faust and Wagner. Wyatt inadvertently identifies it when he says, "'damned . . . animal out of hell'." Brown, the dog's owner, soon appears, as Mephistopheles does in *Faust.* According to his notes, Gaddis originally intended this novel to be a parody of *Faust,* apparently with Brown trying to win Wyatt's soul, but the echoes of Freud and Brown seem more relevant to Gaddis' purposes, because they indict materialism as a cause of moral squalor. (p. 4)

Alive in a hellish world, denied the traditional comforts of art and religion, which have their own troubles, Gaddis' sensitive characters suffer. As an analogue of their suffering, several times Gaddis mentions Rilke's suffering. Even one of the pseudo-intellectuals claims, "'I understand Rilke, I understood him because he understood suffering, he respected human suffering, not like these snotty kids who are writing now'.'' . . . Gaddis' references to Rilke show his recognition of suffering, but when he is examining contemporary problems he uses most of his energy for satire, not for empathy. . . .

Although some reviewers have accepted Valentine's comments [connecting *Faust* with the Clementine *Recognitions*] . . . they are misleading. Gaddis has said that he discovered *Faust's* connection with the Clementine *Recognitions* by reading *The Golden Bough,* but the closest relation I can find with that legend is that three of the characters have names that sound like Faust. Gaddis probably did discover the Clementine *Recognitions* while he was writing a parody of *Faust* and then began to write a different kind of book, a more serious one, to which Valentine's comment is not a reliable guide.

A better understanding of this ancient book will clarify Gaddis' novel. Two of the Clementine books, *The Homilies* and *The Recognitions,* tell essentially the same story. Clement, a non-Christian, hears Barnabas and follows him to Palestine, where he meets Peter and becomes his secretary. The members of Clement's family have become separated, he tells Peter, who later finds them. A standard history of early Christian literature calls these works Ebionite: heretical because they emphasize the Mosaic covenant and Peter at the expense of Pauline Christianity. Of the two kinds of Ebionism—Essene and Gnostic—the latter is evident in the Clementine *Recognitions,* which advocates "gnosis" (intuitive knowledge or recognition) and direct religious experience unencumbered by the theology of Paul, the fathers of the church and later thinkers. Like the Clementine *Recognitions,* Gaddis' book extols direct experience and intuition and denigrates experience mediated by so much knowledge or artificial behavior that it provides neither meaning nor comfort. (p. 5)

Gaddis' frequent allusions to James Joyce suggest that recognition is analogous to Joyce's idea of epiphany. One can also define recognition as transcendence of ordinary perception, about which Esther thinks like a scholastic philosopher: "substance the imperceptible underlying reality, accident the properties inherent in the substance which are perceived by the senses." In these terms, perceiving substance is thus recognition.

Some characters understand recognition by creating and theorizing about art. . . . Statements about painting, about copying painting, and about counterfeiting painting—the most important threads in this plot's tangled skein—illuminate the meaning of artistic originality and thus illuminate recognition in both the aesthetic and general senses.

By all these means Gaddis clarifies recognition, but the things that his characters recognize are more important. Wyatt arduously learns the most important lesson near the book's end, although hints about it appear much earlier. At first he, like Otto and other characters, admires Flemish painters of the fifteenth and early sixteenth centuries— Memling, Van der Goes, the Van Eycks, and others—because they filled their canvases with accurately portrayed discrete objects. At that time Wyatt attributes their completeness and meticulousness to faith in God's concern for all things. In contrast, Basil Valentine argues that medieval painters and Van der Goes demonstrate by their obsession with separate details not faith but doubt. Wyatt later agrees with Valentine and attacks separation in painting and in other things. . . . He attacks science's analytic method, the method of separation, and he praises Titian, who taught

Navarette, and another of Titian's students, El Greco, because they '''learned not to be afraid of spaces, not to get lost in details and clutter, and separate everything'.'' Wyatt later echoes Valentine's critique of the Flemish painters and says that separation is '''what went wrong'.''

Wyatt finally accepts unity as a way of life, not only as an aesthetic principle. . . . [He] eats bread that because of a peculiar series of circumstances contains his father's ashes. This bizarre symbolism signifies a union of father and son. The reality that Wyatt through tortuous ways had sought in art lies open to him in love's unification. About half way through the book he mentions love's relation to reality: '''it's as though when you lose someone . . . lose contact with someone you love, then you lose contact with everything, with everyone else, and nobody . . . and nothing is real anymore'.'' He quotes to Ludy some advice that puts more positively and succinctly love's importance: *'''dilige et quod vis fac'''* (love, and do what you want to). This conversation so moves the obtuse Ludy that he becomes "a man having, or about to have, or at the very least valiantly fighting off, a religious experience." Gaddis thus, by means of a long, learned explication of aesthetics and ontology, arrives at a traditional advocacy of love.

If Wyatt had pondered something his wife said to him, he could have discovered much earlier that love connects people with reality. Otto tells Esther about Fichte's belief that '''we have to act because that's the only way we can know we're real, and . . . it has to be moral action because that's the only way we can know other people are. Real I mean'.'' Esther paraphrases this idea for Wyatt: '''because this is the only way we can know ourselves to be real, is this moral action, you understand don't you, the only way to know others are real'.'' The characters whom Gaddis satirizes do not understand this simple principle; they neither act morally nor acknowledge the reality of others. Indeed, they act little in the sense of performing functions, though very much in the sense of performing roles, so they do not have much reality. Gaddis' methods of characterization—his dependence on speech habits, his caricatures and his occasional decisions not to identify and distinguish characters—support his point that these people are barely real. Here is the nexus between Gaddis' satiric methods and his theme of love.

In short, despite the overwhelming theological allusions, the impossibility of separating and distinguishing all the characters and the often anonymous or pseudonymous hero, *The Recognitions* makes sense. Gaddis' characters sometimes make testy remarks about less intellectually ambitious writers, such as '''they write for people who read with the surface of their minds, people with reading habits that make the smallest demands on them, people brought up reading for facts. . . . Clarity's essential'.'' Here he sounds like many modernist writers. Gaddis does sometimes seem too intent on dazzling his readers, on exercising his technical skills, but he deserves considerable credit for attacking important moral issues, recognizing suffering and seeking ways to alleviate it and to bring order out of chaos. (pp. 6-7)

In many ways *JR* is more accessible than *The Recognitions,* so readers may be wise to begin with it. One should realize that in addition to the moral centers of this book— most notably Amy Joubert, Edward Bast and Isadore Duncan—Jack Gibbs is the intellectual center, because he knows a principle vital to its meaning. This is the concept of entropy that Clausius formulated in the Second Law of

Thermodynamics: entropy is a measure of the energy inevitably lost in closed systems. . . . *JR* is filled with conversations that communicate nearly nothing and thus illustrate entropy. The primary inhibitor of communication in *JR* is jargon, such as "'in terms of tangibilitating the full utilization potential of in-school television'."

Thermodynamic analysis is appropriate for Gaddis' characters because many are virtually mechanical. Vogel teaches about the human body by making an interminable analogy with a machine, and he later quits the school to try to freeze and transmit human speech and to ship people by cable. Gibbs cites a German anatomist who attempted to make sounds by blowing through human larynxes with strings and weights attached, and Cates has had so many transplants that he is nearly a mechanical man. Gibbs, too, has noticed this fearful dehumanization and is writing a book about "'order and disorder more of a, sort of a social history of mechanization and the arts, the destructive element'." The insights that Gibbs includes in his book do not explain very well the rest of Gaddis' novel, but his main theme is revealing. He is attempting, in fact, to write the kind of book that Gaddis accomplishes.

The pathetic school and disastrous marriages indicate the rapid deterioration of the society that Gaddis depicts. In this novel the concept of entropy seems to apply to society as well. J. R.'s school is easy prey for the corrupt, full of costly but unused equipment, run by administrators unable to clear their minds of cant, the scene of violence and drug dealing but of little education. . . . Gaddis' satire on the school attacks obvious targets, but his use of a child-tycoon as the central character is ingenious and puts the adults' machinations in a revealing context. . . . Gaddis' accounts of educational and domestic failures are often humorous. The large number of instances, however, suggests that fraudulent education and marital failures are pervasive, and their cumulative effect is tragic. Gaddis' comedy thus gradually turns into moral indictment and an expression of pity for contemporary humanity. (pp. 8-10)

[The] situation sounds even more desperate than the situation in *The Recognitions*. Art offers relief to some, but it is no panacea: a boy trapped in a sculpture waits days for release not only because of the insurance companies' entanglements but also because some art lovers object to breaking it. As in *The Recognitions*, love is the most effective solution that the characters find. Unfortunately, however, they rarely make it work. (p. 11)

[The] confusion about Amy's marriage is by no means the only one in *JR*. It takes some ingenuity to discover that Cates is the executive whose monologues comprise a large part of the book, and the business transactions constitute an enormously twisted web. One does not need to unravel them, however, in order to realize that according to Gaddis business is inhumanly complex. At other times he toys with the reader. . . . Gaddis often does not identify or distinguish characters, thus making them disturbingly non-separable and in consequence attacking the faith in unity he expresses in *The Recognitions*.

A reader can easily endure some confusion, even some useless confusion, if he or she finds redeeming qualities in a book. By now Gaddis' insights should be evident, and in this novel his wit is diverting. J. R., for example, is an amusing combination of the quintessential schoolboy—sneakers perpetually untied, arms full of free pamphlets, nose running—and a hard-driving tycoon. . . .

Unlike many contemporary writers, especially experimental ones, [Gaddis] knows and cares that people suffer. His two books provide considerable evidence that he spent so much time writing them, and wrote the second even though the first sold poorly, in large part to work out for himself and others the reasons why human suffering occurs and the means for alleviating it. His expenditure of more time documenting dehumanization and suffering than describing the traditional—but now severely threatened by rampant dehumanization—antidote of love indicates his pessimism. His literary prestidigitations, however, suggest that he, like many other modernists, finds solace in literary creation. (p. 12)

John Stark, "William Gaddis: Just Recognition," in The Hollins Critic *(copyright 1977 by Hollins College), April, 1977, pp. 1-12.*

*   *   *

GARCÍA MÁRQUEZ, Gabriel   1928-

Colombian novelist, short story writer, and journalist whose works, including the monumental *One Hundred Years of Solitude,* **are noted for their blending of the real and the surreal. (See also** *CLC,* **Vols. 2, 3, and** *Contemporary Authors,* **Vols. 33-36.)**

It is to be hoped that [*One Hundred Years of Solitude*] soon gets established as the Great Latin American Novel, for it will mean that Latin American literature will change from being the exotic interest of a few to essential reading, and that Latin America itself will be looked on less as a crazy subculture and more as a fruitful, alternative way of life. For this novel shines in its abundance—of obsession, eccentricity, fantasy, magic, myth, comedy, whimsy, political satire, archetypical beings, romances, folk tales, cycles, and tragedies—all in the amazing single, continuing story of the Buendía family, in the town of Macondo, Colombia, Latin America, the world. García Márquez restores storytelling to the anaemic, motivation-ridden context of the novel; and the combination of his sheer humanity and Rabassa's marvelous English recreation under the guise of translation establishes this work as a green milestone, which makes our fiction shrivel by comparison. The book is an imperative; its quality is that of restoring health—to dreams-in-life, to the language, to the reader. (p. 129)

The Antioch Review *(© 1973 by The Antioch Review, Inc.; reprinted by permission of the editors), Vol. XXX, No. 1, 1970.*

Gabriel García Márquez is a man who has so far dedicated his entire literary career to the writing of one novel. That is not to say that he has written only one book. It is rather that [all his earlier works] . . . can be seen now as warming up exercises for his masterpiece, *Cien años de soledad* ('One hundred years of solitude', 1967). Nearly all his works explore a remote, swampy, imaginary town called Macondo, a backwater in the Colombian *ciénaga*, the region where García Márquez was brought up. The richly charted town of Macondo is García Márquez's fictional 'world', his contribution to Latin American literature. Yet the Macondo whose hundred years of solitary history is recorded triumphantly in *Cien años de soledad* had to be built, brick by brick, in its creator's imagination. The earlier works serve this purpose of meticulous construction. For this reason I shall concentrate on the definitive novel. Indeed there is nothing of importance that can be said of it that cannot be applied to the previous works.

Of all contemporary Latin American novels, none has captured the public imagination more than *Cien años de soledad*. It has sold hundreds of thousands of copies in Latin America and Spain, and many more in numerous translations. In Latin America it appears, remarkably, to appeal to most people who can read. Enthusiasm for it comes readily from university professors, but also, for example, from ladies who normally read Spanish translations of Agatha Christie. The enthusiasm, moreover, appears to be genuine. Why?

The main reason for the book's success may be that it can be read on many levels, and there is a superficial level on which it can be read of very obvious appeal. For this town of Macondo that García Márquez has been inventing for so many years is an extraordinarily dotty place, populated by endearingly eccentric people whose antics are, above all, *funny*. The novel is full of comic caricatures. (pp. 144-45)

The dead-pan depiction of extraordinary people and extraordinary events is indeed one of the principle stratagems the book employs to achieve its comic effects. Events and personal characteristics are spectacularly *exaggerated*, made quite absurdly larger than life, yet in a style that takes the hyperbole for granted, as though it were a meticulous fact. (p. 145)

There is plenty of satisfaction to be derived from this book simply in the savouring of his joy in whimsy and much of the novel's appeal lies in the sense of liberation it inspires in one: liberation from a humdrum real world into a magical one that also happens to be funny. It also happens to be exotically tropical, of course, and part of the novel's success in France or Argentina, for example, may be due also to its differentness.

Yet the novel functions at far deeper levels. Like several other contemporary Latin American novelists García Márquez has discovered that it is possible to tell a compelling story in a novel yet also convey complex thoughts in it which do not disturb the story's rhythm.

A clue to one of the novel's more complex aims can be found in its occasional references to other Latin American novels. . . . For the moment it should be merely stressed that these references show that García Márquez is assiduously *aware* of other Latin American writers. We shall see that *Cien años de soledad* is almost as much a reading of them as an exercise in original creativeness.

Sometimes García Márquez seems deliberately to be invading the 'territory' of other writers. There are scenes which could almost have been written by Alejo Carpentier, others which could almost have been written by Borges or by Juan Rulfo. (pp. 146-47)

Messages to Borges are numerous in *Cien años de soledad*, and there are many others directed at Alejo Carpentier. What, then, is their purpose? Is García Márquez merely engaged in some Nabokovian game to be deciphered by some Latin American Mary McCarthy? I don't think so. I believe that he is attempting to suggest to his readers that one of the novel's fundamental aims is to tell us something about the nature of contemporary Latin American writing on which we shall see that it acts as a kind of interpretative meditation. For the novel places many of the obsessions of contemporary Latin American writing in an illuminating context.

This it does in particular with regard to fantasy, which we have noted is one of the central ingredients of contemporary Latin American fiction. In the works of Borges, Bioy Casares, Sábato, Cortázar, Rulfo, Jose María Arguedas, Asturias, and Juan Carlos Onetti, to name but a few, fantasy is spectacularly evident. Why? It would seem to be one of the roles of *Cien años de soledad* to suggest several plausible reasons.

In the first place, the novel shows how there can be no continental agreement on what is real and what is fantastic in a continent where it is possible for a palaeolithic community to reside at an hour or two's flight from a vast, modern city. Backwardness of course need not be palaeolithic. A wholly isolated village in a Colombian swamp with religious beliefs almost unchanged from those imparted by the Spanish medieval Church is sure to have an appreciation of reality somewhat different from the one entertained by the inhabitants say of Bogotá. The Assumption of a local girl, the ability of a local priest effortlessly to levitate, a rain of yellow flowers—all these things are less astonishing for the people of Macondo than the 'modern inventions' that reach the town from time to time, such as ice, magnets, magnifying glasses, false teeth, the cinema, and the railway. One's distinctions between fantasy and reality therefore depend a great deal on one's cultural assumptions. And in an isolated community, such distinctions are likely to be perceived from a particular *ex-centric* perspective, should one wish, arbitrarily perhaps, to take modern Western civilization as a centre of reference. (pp. 147-48)

For the Government and for the Americans reality is something then that you can cavalierly fabricate at your own convenience. So who can blame a mere citizen of Macondo for believing in the Assumption of a local beauty? And who can blame García Márquez for choosing to liberate himself from official lies by telling his own lies, or otherwise for choosing to exaggerate the Government's lies *ad absurdum*? Many of the fantasies of *Cien años de soledad* are indeed absurd but logical exaggerations of real situations. (pp. 148-49)

Has the novel . . . any universal interest at all? I think it has, in the first place for the simple reason that Latin America has no monopoly of biased historians and mendacious politicians. Similarly, with regard to the dependence of our perception of reality upon cultural assumptions, it may be conjectured that an inhabitant of a Cotswold village has a view of what is real that is different from that of, say, the Queen. The differences may be greater in Latin America than in Europe. But in the end García Márquez may be writing a hyperbolic parody of a continent that looks itself from Europe like a hyperbolic parody—of things that are nevertheless all too familiar. (p. 150)

Borges demonstrated that even the most realistic writing is fictive because all writing is. He showed, in his poem 'El otro tigre', that a tiger evoked in a poem is a very different thing from the beast that paces the jungles of Bengal. So if you cannot reproduce a real tiger in a book why not write about a tiger with three legs, say, that reads Sanskrit and plays hockey? Both are fictive, but is one necessarily more fictive than the other, or less real within the fictive reality of a book? We may know that yellow flowers do not suddenly pour from the sky to carpet the streets in normal life but we cannot deny that they do in *Cien años de soledad* and, because they do, we have to recognize that they are a legitimate part of that book, of the world that book seeks to create and which is signified in its language. It follows, of course, too, that that world, the world of Macondo, is neither bigger nor smaller, lasts neither longer nor shorter than the sum of the book's pages. Macondo *is* the book, and when the book ends, so does Macondo. (p. 151)

History, in the end, is words; events in the past are confined to the words written about them. Since we cannot 'remember' events that took place centuries ago, we must rely entirely on what is written about them. Those events *are* what is written about them. (p. 156)

Colombia's past is as much a fiction as *Cien años de soledad,* all the more so of course because it is contained in words that were written . . . [sometimes] with the deliberate aim to deceive. So the final pages of *Cien años de solidad,* by showing us how Macondo can exist only within the pages of the book that depicts it, also symbolizes the fact that Colombia's past only exists within the books that have been written about it. Like the history of Macondo, the history of Colombia is a verbal fiction. The 'city of mirrors (or mirages)' is in the end a symbol of a 'country of mirrors (or mirages)'. (pp. 156-57)

The novel's built-in reminders that what one is reading is a fiction, its disturbing suggestions that life may be no less of a fiction, its vision of the world as endless repetition, its deployment of messages to other writers, particularly of messages that deliberately confuse 'fact' and 'fiction', its conversion of writing into a sort of 'reading' of other literatures—all these things are Borges's familiar stamping ground. Yet García Márquez is no plagiarist, not only because his novel, in its every detail, *feels* so different from Borges's work, there being little similarity between García Márquez's Caribbean exuberance and Borges's rather English understatements, but also because though García Márquez follows Borges very closely, he somehow modifies him and throws fresh light upon him. As he does with contemporary literature of fantasy in general, he provides him with a very Latin American context. *Cien años de soledad* is a very Latin American *reading* of Borges, for it discovers Borges's relevance to Latin America—the relevance of his cyclical vision of time to the cyclical nature of Latin American history, the relevance of his sense that life is a dream, a fiction, to the dream-like nature of Latin American politics, the relevance of his sense that the past is inseparable from the fictive words that narrate it to the tragic fact that Latin America's past is inseparable from the deliberately distorted words that have claimed to record it, the relevance, finally, of Borges's demonstrations that our perceptions of things depend on our previous assumptions about them to the fact that in a continent shared by so many cultures there can be no common continental perception of anything. (p. 163)

> *D. P. Gallagher, "Gabriel García Márquez," in his* Modern Latin American Literature *(copyright © 1973 by Oxford University Press; reprinted by permission), Oxford University Press, 1973, pp. 144-63.*

["The Autumn of the Patriarch" is] a stunning portrait of the archetype: the pathological fascist tyrant. . . .

The book, as is to be expected from García Márquez, is mystical, surrealistic, Rabelaisian in its excesses, its distortions and its exotic language. But García Márquez' sense of life is that surreality is as much the norm as banality. "In Mexico surrealism runs through the streets," he once said. And elsewhere: "The Latin American reality is totally Rabelaisian."

And so his patriarch, the unnamed General (his precise

rank is General of the Universe) of an unnamed Caribbean nation, lives to be anywhere between 107 and 232 years old [and] sires 5,000 children. . . . (p. 1)

The novel is unendingly bizarre and fevered, but ultimately not difficult. Yet it is difficult to enter: a densely rich and fluid pudding that begins at the end and makes Faulknerian leaps forward and backward in time. Sentences at times run on for three pages, with dialogue neither quoted nor paragraphed. García Márquez has compounded the problems by making the novel a puzzle of pronouns, consistently changing narrative points of view in mid-sentence. (pp. 1, 16)

The narration is largely within the General's mind, but García Márquez also enters other minds with brief intensity, often speaks in the collective voice of all people in the blasted nation; and so, through relentless immersion of the reader in these exquisitely detailed perspectives, he illuminates the monster internally and externally and delivers him whole.

As with "One Hundred Years of Solitude," the reader also bathes luxuriously in panoramic prose, this work even more poetic than the last. There is no conventional plot, only chronologically scrambled episodes that take the General from birth to death through an unspecified modern era in which the king and queen of Babylonia co-exist with closed-circuit television. . . .

A reader grows somewhat weary at times over the excesses, the repetition and predictability of certain sections . . . and there is a yearning for some pithy understatement. But García Márquez is as exorbitant as Melville and Dostoyevsky. He believes not only that excess is good for you, but that it is essential, that a book must have an immensity about it in the same way life is enormous—and dense and mysterious and as repetitiously predictable as the General's vengeance for an affront. How else, his novel implicitly asks, could the story of interminable dictatorship be told?

This novel, of necessity then, has none of the life-celebrating quality that made "One Hundred Years of Solitude" so universally embraced. There is nothing to celebrate in the General's long and tortured life. He is given endless opportunity to persuade us that his anguish and grief and bafflement are real. But we are never persuaded. He is not even pitiable. He is a spectacle, the embodiment of egocentric evil unleashed, maniacally violent, cosmically worthless and, despite pretentions to eternity, as devoid of meaning as anything else in an absurd world. His main contribution to life, finally, is fear; but fear such as thunder, cancer or madness may provoke, fear based on irrational possibility, on the oblique ravages of a diabolical deity.

The book is a supreme polemic, a spiritual exposé, an attack against any society that encourages or even permits the growth of such a monstrosity. García Márquez objectifies the monster and at novel's end attempts to explain it as the consequences of the General's incapacity to love. . . .

But the monster is not reducible to a single cause, any more than civilization is explainable through the invention of the wheel. . . . Could lovelessness alone explain such blood-drenched misanthropy?

The incapacity to love seems to stand, rather, as another fact of the General's life, like the whistle of his hernia, or the seed of his unknown father, or his discovery that a lie is more comfortable than doubt. And these facts, under the hand of this master novelist, accumulate not to explain anything simply, but to embody a most complex and terrible vision of Latin America's ubiquitous, unkillable demon. (p. 16)

William Kennedy, in The New York Times Book Review *(© 1976 by The New York Times Company; reprinted by permission), October 31, 1976.*

The Autumn of the Patriarch is a novelist's revenge for the political abjection of his native continent. The subject is grey, and basic: the tyranny of a nameless Latin American republic by its vicious, decrepit president; but the form of Gabriel García Márquez's novel is sophisticated and its language is luxuriant to a degree. Style and subject are at odds because García Márquez is committed to showing that our first freedom—and one which all too many Latin American countries have lost—is of the full resources of our language. The Patriarch does not like writers, they are the one class of person whom, even when launched on a rare and sinister fit of clemency, he refuses to amnesty. "They've got fever in their quills", iş his paranoid belief, "so that they're no good for anything except when they're good for something." The fever here is in the flushed, anarchic prose of García Márquez, a man who wants socialist revolution in Latin America and who now says he is giving up fiction for blunter forms of incitement.

The unhappy republic of *The Autumn of the Patriarch* is perfectly unreal, a grim confusion of facts and fantasies. It is more fantasy than fact because the Patriarch—or General —has kept it in such ignorance and isolation that data are hard to come by; it is underdeveloped in every way imaginable, morally, culturally and economically. It is a fact that the General is a bestial and vindictive man, but the rest is mostly rumour. He is a one-man dynasty: having captured power—we are not told how—from the bickering *caudillos* of some distant federal past, he hangs on to it for roughly two hundred years. He is far too regressive to stomach anything as risky or progressive as chronology: his rule is one of equal terror and lethargy. . . .

The book amounts to a sort of demented obituary notice, a breathless report of the Patriarch's feats and the absurd legends that go with them. It is not the report of an individual but of a nation: the "I" who now and again takes charge of the narration is an unstable, migratory presence, identifiable with all classes and conditions of a suffering population.

The novel relies—too heavily in the end—on García Márquez's will to invent the alternately bizarre and satirical circumstances of a monstrous life. As with that earlier epic of stagnation, *One Hundred Years of Solitude,* some of the inventions are vivid and surprising. . . .

The General is a grotesque, recognizable by his hugely herniated testicle in its jangling truss, his solitary gold spur, his denims. And García Márquez would have done well to stop there, to leave him as an empty bundle of instincts, without an inner life. But he has tried to give him a psychology too, and this means that *The Autumn of the Patriarch* is also going to be read as an explanation of such regimes. It is not a good explanation. The General has a fixation on his mother and, when she dies, on mother-substitutes; he is lonely and insecure; he cannot, above all, stand very much reality. He behaves like a murderous, autistic child, and gets no obvious pleasure from his authority beyond the easy, instant satisfaction of his elementary lusts.

There is a strongly optimistic ending to the novel. The General may have kept reality out for all these years but he never killed it; it was always there, threatening him, outside the defences of his palace. It is exclusive to the people, who can now celebrate their deliverance; truth and reality are free to return. As an insight into political pathology, this is worryingly primitive. Why should the powerful, or even the tyrannical, have any weaker a hold on reality than their victims? Unlike the Patriarch, they may be both happy and gregarious men. In this novel, tyranny is identified as a disease of the tyrant's personality and not of the body politic, which is surely defeatist.

The merely wishful conclusion apart, however, *The Autumn of the Patriarch* is the desperate, richly sustained hallucination of a man rightly bitter about the present state of so much of Latin America.

John Sturrock, "The Unreality Principle," in The Times Literary Supplement *(© Times Newspapers Ltd., 1977; reproduced from* The Times Literary Supplement *by permission), April 15, 1977, p. 451.*

* * *

GARDNER, John   1933-

American novelist, short story writer, and critic, Gardner, an Old and Middle English scholar, is a superb storyteller, intertwining modern-day realism with medieval fantasies. Frank McConnell credits Gardner with creating the genre of "protest fantasy" in *The Wreckage of Agathon*. (See also *CLC*, Vols. 2, 3, 5, 7, and *Contemporary Authors*, Vols. 69-72.)

[In John Gardner's novels and stories] there is an element of the arbitrary, of the willed, that too often interrupts the natural momentum of his material and produces an odd dryness in those very places where the flow of feeling should be most spontaneous and life-giving. Gardner's work gives the impression of having proceeded from a *too* well-stocked mind, a mind that cannot resist the temptations arising from its own cultivation, that must bring to bear the whole weight of Greek mythology, Western philosophy from Plato to the present, medieval allegory, English literature and Protestant theology upon the quotidian lives of farmers, police chiefs and piano teachers.

"October Light" is a lavishly talented, often impressive work, clearly his best book since "Grendel." It does not however, finally allay my suspicion that Gardner's powers are more histrionic or mimetic than instinctively novelistic. The book is really composed of two novels—one serious, one "trashy"—that coexist in uneasy counterpoint. The main novel, the "true" novel, takes place in granitic Vermont, around Bennington. It concerns the desperate struggle between an octogenarian widow, Sally Page Abbott, and her brother, James L. Page, a hard-bitten, cantankerous and violent old farmer. . . . (p. 1)

In attempting to do full justice to the story and its main characters, I am aware of having to contend with a mild prejudice induced by a surfeit of crusty, strong-minded New Englanders who either struggle to wrest a living from rocky soil or else lead "old-American" lives in picture-book villages. The setting of "October Light" is Ethan Allen country, heavy with the lore of two hundred years; in another aspect, it is the country of Norman Rockwell, who is several times mentioned in the book. Its inhabitants live not very far west of "Our Town" and not very far north—

as one is reminded by the unyieldingness of the central struggle—from the landscape of "Desire Under the Elms" and "Ethan Frome." Still, Gardner must be granted at least squatter's rights to his new territory. More important, he has been remarkably successful in animating his two archetypal Yankees and in dramatizing their conflict, which reaches into the depths of what might be called, loosely, the Protestant soul.

The novel is no mere psychomachy, with the Puritan virtues (resourcefulness, optimism, a hunger for improvement) on one side and the vices (a nearly mindless dedication to hard work, an incapacity to express any deep feelings except anger, suspiciousness, xenophobia) on the other. Sally's ruthlessness can be startling. . . . And James, for all his orneriness, is fully and deeply humanized. . . . James stands before us as a figure of almost tragic dimensions—pitiable, moving and perversely admirable.

The lesser characters, too, are carefully rounded, lovingly observed. (pp. 1, 16)

Another prejudice of mine is aroused by the fact that "October Light" is heavily theme-ridden. What I am willing (with some inconsistency) to accept in the stories of Hawthorne or in "Moby Dick," I tend to deplore in contemporary American fiction. Symbolic meanings, obvious and occult, abound in Gardner's novel, ready to be gathered like mushrooms from the forest floor. . . .

The variations on locking are endless, ranging from the literal locking of Sally's door to the fact that James has been locked in icy remorse since the death of his son and is "unlocked"—able to thaw into tears—near the end. Much of the lavish and often beautiful natural description, and most of the historical references and quotations from the Founding Fathers ("October Light" is very consciously a Bicentennial book) present themselves for symbol-plucking. This indulgence in thematic cross-referencing impeded my enjoyment of the novel; other readers may find it enriching. In any case, its occurrence within the main story does no great harm to the book, whose characters and central situation are strong enough to generate a significance of their own that glows through all the symbolic encrustation.

The inclusion of the sub-novel is another matter. A third or more of "October Light" is consumed by the mangled text of the paperback, "The Smugglers of Lost Souls' Rock." . . . I suppose Gardner included this boring and exasperating farrago as a counterweight to the old-American, narrow Yankee world of the true novel, as a surrealistic projection of the crazed new world of America. All sorts of thematic connections between the two can be discovered, if one is so inclined. Perhaps he included it as self-parody, an elaborate joke. . . . Whatever the case, the sub-novel badly gets in the way of the main story and seriously wounds the novel as a whole. If Gardner were a first novelist, I suspect his editor would have insisted that the sub-novel be excised, or at least reduced to a harmless paragraph or two.

The wound is serious but, happily, far from fatal. Whatever its excesses and miscalculations, "October Light" remains a powerful and often admirable performance. . . . (p. 16)

> *Robert Towers, in* The New York Times Book Review *(© 1976 by The New York Times Company; reprinted by permission), December 26, 1976.*

The more of John Gardner I read, the more he seems to me a kind of Evel Knievel at the typewriter, confronting in his novels the enigma of a universe that won't explain itself, hurtling himself through that narrative space, but acting on faith that he will, at the end, land upright and affirmatively on the solid terrain of significance. But a significance not merely "personal." He simultaneously thwarts our engagement *and* gets us to love the monsters and the near monsters, the graceless and grotesques who people his random accidental worlds.

The struggle for meaning, often in the face of demonic absurdity, is what is in store for most of Gardner's protagonists. How is one to make sense of a suicide or murder, as in *The Sunlight Dialogues* (1972) or *Grendel* (1971)? How is one to make sense of a terminal illness? In *Resurrection* (1966), Gardner's first novel, the solution is traditionally Christian. A young philosophy professor, James Chandler, learns he is dying. In his final weeks, he befriends—almost accidentally—a young neurotic woman named Viola. He dies, the sacrifical lamb, and she is left "beautifully changed," redeemed. Chandler, of course, does not take such a Christlike view of himself, but he, too, comes to his own peace. "It was not the beauty of the world one must affirm, but *the world,* the buzzing, blooming confusion itself." Gardner's brilliance is that in the telling, the tale does not sound like an article in *Reader's Digest;* whatever affirmation we come to is dignified and difficult, not sentimental.

In later novels, particularly *Grendel* and *The Sunlight Dialogues,* Gardner has more to say about the nature and sources of meaning. Like the mystics, he asserts not that the universe is meaningless but that what most of us construe as "reality" is too limited and therefore useless and false. . . .

One possible corrective to our limited vision, suggests Gardner, is the monster-hero, the outlaw or social outcast who, by choosing to live beyond the social system we take for "real," bears witness to our lack of metaphysical comprehensiveness. As one character in *Grendel* says, "Except in the life of a hero, the whole world's meaningless. The hero sees values beyond what's possible. That's the *nature* of a hero. It kills him, of course, ultimately. But it makes the whole struggle of humanity worthwhile." . . .

In *Grendel,* the verse of the Shaper—a kind of court poet—is beautiful, but an illusion. "He knows no more than they do about total reality," says the dragon. "But he spins it all together with harp runs and hoots, and they think what they think is alive, think Heaven loves them." And this may be why Gardner deliberately creates gothic worlds which are not beautiful, and why he deliberately uses the novel to remind us it's only a novel. . . .

Within *October Light* is another novel—150 pages of *The Smugglers of Lost Souls' Rock,* Gardner's "trashy" and yet serious spoof of the blockbuster adventure novel (set in and around California). . . . (p. 70)

The effect of interspersing the two novels is to keep us *continually* aware that each is an artifact and not a world we can settle into (and, lest we forget, the characters in both novels are forever comparing themselves to characters in novels). But, even more significantly, the juxtapositioning of the two stories allows us to see beneath the accidental circumstances of each set of lives to the essential connectedness of both.

In addition, each novel serves as a foil to or gloss on the other, and so Gardner is free to have his characters do less explaining and analyzing than they have in the past, though ironically, the "trashy" novel is far more self-conscious, and contains more intentionally coy literary and philosophical allusions than *October Light*. In this way, and in its deliberate attention to form and formula, *Smugglers* is more like Gardner's earlier novels than *October Light* is, and perhaps it is Gardner's private joke on himself to insist repeatedly on *Smugglers's* trashiness.

What the counterpoint finally reveals is that in Vermont [the setting of *October Light*] as in California (at times Gardner's mock symbol of decay and dissipation) lives are violent, suicidal, lawless, but also loving, affirmative, collaborative—perhaps more so (in both extremes) in decadent California than in contained Vermont. . . .

Gardner this time around suggests that meaning is apprehended through feeling, that the present moment acquires its legitimate resonance through the reflections of a sensibility that is willing to know and accept its own history, and willing to welcome its own future—loves, hatreds, victories, failures. . . .

His concerns still are those of the philosopher and theologian, but in this novel he has found a way out of the explicit didacticism that occasionally made his novels read like *Plato's Republic*, and a way into that is not an announcement but an enactment of what in this life continues to move him. (pp. 70-1)

> *Elizabeth Stone, "John Gardner Writes Two Novels for the Price of One," in* The Village Voice *(reprinted by permission of* The Village Voice; *copyright © by The Village Voice, Inc., 1976), December 27, 1976, pp. 70-1.*

Whatever else may be said about [*October Light*,] John Gardner's rich and fragrant Indian pudding of a novel (soaked in apple jack and stuffed with juicy raisins), it ought to be said first that it does tell a good and rather old-fashioned story—rollicking, ribald, truly imaginative the way Dickens, for example, is imaginative, and real. . . .

Philosophically—and Gardner's readers know there is always a *philosophically* in the fictional underbrush—*October Light* is a hopeful novel, as if the author believes that life in America will continue beyond the bicentennial year and not be cut off by an angry God, the Symbionese Liberation Army, or terminal despair, any one of which may threaten and even claim a victim or two from time to time. . . .

"It's as if God put me on earth to write," [Gardner] remarked a few years ago, and there is indeed a deep theological cast to his fiction, which deals essentially with the question of how a man should live his life caught "in the trench warfare between freedom and order," as the critic and fellow Vermonter Geoffrey Wolff once wrote.

John Gardner is one of the eight or ten "major" novelists of these times, and *October Light* is a rich example of his art. (p. G1)

> *William McPherson, in* Book World—The Washington Post *(© The Washington Post), January 2, 1977.*

[John Gardner] wants to suggest that many clichés are true, which I suppose no one doubts. The question is how useful their truth is, and the difficulty is how to make them *seem true* in a book.

We are told of a character in *October Light* that he is "not so naïve as to doubt that the trashiest fiction is all true, as the noblest is all illusion." But the only serious way for a writer to act on this notion, I suspect, would be to write trashy fiction unrepentantly, and Gardner can't bring himself to do this. It is also very hard to write trashy fiction when you don't believe in your own trash. What Gardner has written (in collaboration with his wife, he informs us) is a playful philosophical take-off of trashy fiction, which is about as lighthearted as the Declaration of Independence, and which an old lady in *his* novel finds and reads, with us peeping over her shoulder. . . .

The fact that [Gardner's] people are clearly parodying themselves doesn't really help, it merely freezes them in their limbo between coyness and pretension. The same goes for the clumsiness of the device of having this story found and read in the novel. It is an intended clumsiness, no doubt, but what is it intended to do? When the old lady reading the story thinks of its "impishness" and the "delicate way" it works, we can't really smile at the old lady's literary taste, because if the story isn't impish and delicate (and it isn't), it certainly isn't anything else. (p. 59)

October Light is a bicentennial tour of old Vermont, all brisk weather and cold light and Yankee orneriness, the account of a feud between two old people, brother and sister, neatly illuminated by quotations from Jefferson, Franklin, Washington, John Adams, and their contemporaries. This is a novel in which people say, "By thunder," "By tunkit," and "Heavens to Betsy," and are described as being "meaner than pussley broth" and "crazy as a loon." However it is not a novel which places any faith in this vocabulary, and when it wants to say something it reaches for another one: "and the image before him he would have called, if he'd known the word, symbolic." There must be dozens of Vermont farmers who are more at home with the word "symbolic" than they are with pussley broth.

October Light is also full of artful symmetries and juxtapositions and prophecies. . . .

[Gardner offers] up allegories by the handful and just [lets] them drop: the brother and sister are England and America, America and the Third World, men and women, whites and blacks. When a character protests against this projection of a private wrangle on to history by saying, "Oh Sally dear, what's the *country* got to do with it," Sally, the sister, smartly replies, "The country's got everything to do with it. It's the haves and the have-nots, that's what it is." Again, as with the impishness and delicacy of the inserted story, we are no doubt meant to feel Sally's got something wrong here. But what is it she has got wrong?

Her perspective is backed up by the whole novel, the whole heavy investigation of the divided American character, angry nostalgia on the one hand and sloppy liberalism on the other. Certainly these factions do exist in America now, and do loom large; the cliché is true to this extent. But it is not a cliché that Gardner can properly animate in his novel, and it seems to me too crude anyway, too flat and too big to do anything except squash the discussion it is supposed to start. Can we really take another long debate about whether television scatters the mind and whether workmanship is what it used to be?

And yet *October Light* doesn't altogether fail. There are all kinds of rooms in the house of fiction, and missing the truth of trash and the truth of good novels, Gardner still manages to get across what I'll call the truth of allusion. I can't believe in Gardner's cut-out characters as they stand, but I don't feel they're simply fakes. Sally says of the tale she's reading that "it came close enough to life to remind her of it," and I would say much the same about *October Light*. Gardner understands the loneliness of stubborn people, and the violence that apparently simple and stable lives may contain. . . . [What] has crept into *October Light* from the real world is Gardner's loyalty to people and lives he can't quite catch in fiction, and to the apparently dying, old-fashioned form he can't believe in and can't let go. (p. 60)

> *Michael Wood, in* The New York Review of Books *(reprinted with permission from* The New York Review of Books; *copyright* © *1977 NYREV, Inc.), January 20, 1977.*

In *October Light* a Bennington coed asks her dance partner if he has read anything by John Updike, Gardner's nod of recognition to a fellow practitioner of spirit-flected realism. With Bellow, Gardner and Updike have resisted both language games and the apocalypse of fact by continuing with narrative leavened by the possibility, at least, of transcendence. In *October Light* and *Marry Me,* they write of men "born in an age of spirits" (Gardner's phrase) but living with few visible reminders of this past, anachronistic men in consciously anachronistic novels. Gardner and Updike are skillful and necessary resisters. I wish they had written better books.

Like Bellow's *Mr. Sammler's Planet, October Light* is about the "unlocking" of an old man with hard opinions and little charity. . . .

Gardner's materials are the familiar ones of family chronicles—marital problems, parental failures, the twining of guilt and love—but with an interesting perspective of place, a Vermont small town where memory is long but the growing season is short. This perspective and its attendant language, the not quite Rockwellian minor characters, and the unlocking of James Page's armored self in his late October would have sufficed very nicely. But Gardner is defensive about this kind of fiction, and it is this defensiveness that spoils the book. (p. 89)

[A] beat-up paperback entitled *The Smugglers of Lost Souls' Rock,* [a] Pynchonized *Dog Soldiers* with a sci-fi ending, . . . kills much of [Sally's] time and about a third of Gardner's novel. Sally believes *Smugglers* is "trash," yet it begins to influence the way she thinks about her brother and the past. Gardner's point here and elsewhere in the novel is that literature (along with other media) *does* affect behavior and, implicitly, that the novelist has a responsibility to tell an ennobling truth.

Even if this is true, the novel within *October Light* is a ham-handed way of demonstrating it. And perhaps inconsistent too, since *Smugglers* is hardly affirmative. Too long to work as parody, [it is] too meager to be taken seriously. . . . In his attempt to defend the out-of-fashion fiction that is the strength of *October Light*, Gardner ends up writing a contemporary cliché. (pp. 89-90)

> *Thomas LeClair, in* Commonweal *(copyright* © *1977 Commonweal Publishing Co., Inc.; reprinted by permission of Commonweal Publishing Co., Inc.), February 4, 1977.*

John Gardner is a genuinely eclectic novelist whose books consistently display an impressive range despite their determined articulation of a repeated constitutive theme. (p. 520)

One may say the message is existential. The voyage traveled by Gardner's heroes and villains constitutes man's search for meaning and permanence in a universe which asserts their irrelevance and ignores him. Successive books examine the idea of ultimate absurdity from the viewpoints of wildly differing individual seekers; their creator appears to be examining the consequences, in a variety of social and historical contexts, of the lessons they learn. Some of Gardner's people (and nonhumans as well) are destroyed by what they come to know; others persevere in spite of it. Their author's own opinion must be inferred. My guess is that he is obsessively interested in the tension between social order and individual freedom, that he has decided that civil utopias are unmanageable, and that he therefore poses for his readers situations which ask them whether the alternative of isolated personal freedom may be substituted for these as a desirable goal. . . .

Characters, structural devices, and thematic preoccupations from biblical, classical, and medieval poetry and drama prominently figure in [Gardner's] fiction (within that blanket term I include Gardner's sassily hubristic version of the classical epic, his *Jason and Medeia*). (p. 521)

The employment of conventional forms imbues Gardner's chronicles of thwarted aspiration with a contrary groundswell of optimistic idealism. His stories assert that even plain and timid men are heroes who are forced to embark on quests during which they encounter symbolic personified forces that test their endurance and ingenuity. I read his books as attempts to reconcile values implicit in traditional literatures with the psychological uncertainty bequeathed to us by a universe that now looks nonrational. Religious faith removed, there is no longer reason for contemporary knights-errant to feel assured that the monsters they slay are their enemies, or that the goals they pursue are unambiguously good.

Some sources for these confusions and tensions may be glimpsed here and there in Gardner's scholarly essays. He has written . . . on Chaucer, on the mystery and miracle plays (viewing the Wakefield cycle, for example, as a coherent single work, not a hodgepodge of unrelated plays), on numerous Old English poems—riddles, runes, *Beowulf* (of special interest, since Gardner has produced his own *Grendel*). He has "modernized" *The Alliterative Morte Arthure, The Owl and the Nightingale,* and five other Middle English poems. Most interesting of all is his translation of *The Complete Works of the Gawain-Poet,* graced by a long introduction which speculates incisively on the ironic deployment of medieval themes in that bafflingly faceted gem "Sir Gawain and the Green Knight." Gardner emphasizes the sorely tried Gawain's "failure to be perfect," as well as the gap between his buoyant idealism "and the nature of this fallen, traitor- and monster-ridden world." In the afterglow of irony, the grandiose architecture of feudalism looms up as only one among many alternatives to anarchy; chivalry and courtly love seem nothing more than gorgeously brocaded arrangements which foolishly presume to imitate some overarching divine order. (pp. 521-22)

The medieval poets' assertion of man's imperfect nature is the clear precursor of medievalist Gardner's fictional patterns. All his stories concern themselves with initiatory journeys toward knowledge. Each journey resolves itself into a humbling acceptance of man's limitations. All the more reason why we may wonder at the puzzling alternation, throughout his books, between crushing pessimism and optimistic stick-to-itiveness. His books read in sequence do not seem to move in a discernible direction or reveal a design. This is explainable: Gardner's novels have not been published in the order in which they were written.... Both [*The Sunlight Dialogues* and *Nickel Mountain*] show unmistakable signs of apprentice work as well as numerous incidental resemblances to the first of his novels to be published, *The Resurrection*. And I find reason to surmise that Gardner's new novel, *October Light,* may have originated in conception some years ago and been only recently revised. The best way to argue such speculations is to examine Gardner's fictions in the order in which I believe he wrote them.

In *The Resurrection* (1966) the elements of all its successors inhere, though the novel itself is an abstract young writer's production: it is forced and clumsily erudite. Its protagonist, James Chandler, is a professor of philosophy who has discovered he will soon die of leukemia. (pp. 522-23)

The Resurrection is overloaded with philosophical allusions, but they yield—as Chandler's "education" progresses—to a parade of sharp surprising images.... Reason cannot account to the philosophical man for the mysteries that surround him. The gain in visionary power lets him understand how others, who grieve for him, struggle to smooth his passage toward death. Still there is no suggestion that life's alarming turbulence has been contained or mastered....

Nickel Mountain . . . is another fable of aheroic regeneration. (p. 523)

Gardner surrounds [Henry, his protagonist,] with garish and lively personalities, events, and portents. An unusually hot summer is "a sure sign of witchcraft at work, or miracles brooding." "Jesus" and "the devil" are so frequently evoked (by expletives) that it would be ingenuous *not* to recognize the simplistic contours of pastoral morality play. Right and wrong, optimism and pessimism struggle for the soul of Henry Soames. The novel moves so well that it disguises its sentimental overstatements: the growth of complex awareness in its hero's modest mind seems a natural process, emanating, sensibly enough, from his refusal to accept despair.

There is a pleasing richness in these novels, though neither *The Resurrection* nor *Nickel Mountain* completely overcomes its overdependence on eccentric situations and characters (virtuosity displayed for its own sake, perhaps) and on a rigid thematic framework in which a single central figure undergoes a series of trials to earn new knowledge and to emerge from the experience a better man. *The Sunlight Dialogues,* a major step beyond these fictions, is a work of rare ironic complexity and is one of the most ambitious American novels of recent years. For once Gardner has written an ambitious novel whose crosshatched plots and intersecting characters are pulled together in a relationship dictated by the overruling exposition of an encompassing central theme: man's need to know that the world he inhabits makes sense and that his own actions matter....

[A] climate of imbalance breeds several confrontations between opposites. In the central conflict Batavia's police chief Fred Clumly is baited by a bearded anarchist who calls himself "the Sunlight Man" and mocks the irrelevancies of Law and Order while lecturing his confused pursuer on metaphysical principles....

This simple opposition rests at the center of a labyrinthine many-leveled plot which confirms Fred Clumly's hunch that "it's all connected. There can't be order otherwise. It's all some kind of Design." (p. 524)

The novel's surface events—all parts of interrelated separate mysteries, each requiring its own solution—absorb so much attention that one can only guess at the patterns intimated by Gardner's profligate use of literary sources.... There are direct allusions, within the narrative proper, to the "recantation" from Chaucer's *Troilus and Criseyde,* Plato's Allegory of the Cave, Dante, the Ceres-Proserpina myth, and I dare not guess how many others. A contretemps in front of an outdoor barbecue clearly suggests a journey to the underworld. A sexual temptation scene is observed occurring beneath an apple tree.

Remarkably enough, these troublesome added dimensions never disengage our attention from the ordeal of Fred Clumly, and the two crucial subplots which echo and reinforce it.....

Too much happens in *The Sunlight Dialogues.* Characters are not always clearly delineated, and we keep forgetting things that we have been told about them. But we accept the prolixity and keep reading avidly through it *because* Gardner keeps returning the focus to Chief Clumly—a plodding, unpretentious representative of an Ideal he feels privileged to serve. (p. 525)

In Gardner's next three books the conflict between social order and individual freedom is experienced not by unheroic average men but by historical or legendary figures that he has wrenched from their original literary contexts and has reimagined into amusingly contentious rebels and ideologues. His protagonists are no longer innocents: they take positions, espouse systems of thought. And very frequently the events that overtake them put their philosophies in doubt.

Like the medieval poets (specifically Chaucer) Gardner finds fresh approaches to the problems which preoccupy his fiction in retelling "olde stories," reshaping formal dialogues and tales of heroic adventuring into wry iconoclastic questionings. Imitative exercises stimulate Gardner's originality: he is at his best when devising ways to make conventional expressions of the old values prove that those values are undependable. It becomes the burden of all his later books to argue that the accepted certainties cannot hold—that man's experience is more menacing than he can know upon plunging into it.

As the intent of his work becomes more assured, then, Gardner loses some of the appealing undirected energy that animates his early novels. In its place there is a clear gain in concentrated irony—when his personae are credible as individuals (not just as states of mind), and when the plots which contain them do not too nakedly reveal the diagrams beneath the outlines of their actions.

The Wreckage of Agathon (1970), set in Sparta in the sixth century B.C., takes the form of a twin monologue spoken alternately by the philosopher and seer Agathon and his wary apprentice Demodokos, nicknamed "Peeker" (i.e., "Seer Jr."). (pp. 525-26)

The flashbacks to Agathon's unrestrained tenure as an Athenian freeman, his (tiresome) tribulations with wife and mistress, prove that Gardner does not have enough material for a novel. But the book works wonderfully as a dialogue. Though it makes explicit correlations (optimism/

freedom, pessimism/restraint), it does not permit us the comfortable illusion that Agathon is a humanitarian hero. . . . (p. 526)

[Agathon] can't accept theories of any kind, for he suspects truth is findable. . . . Perhaps . . . the "wreckage" of Agathon is both his unpretentious humanity and his refusal to hope for ultimate knowledge.

The narrator and protagonist of *Grendel* (1971) informs us bluntly that the universe is absurd. (p. 527)

Grendel is Gardner's best novel—ingenious, concise, crystalline, furiously funny. . . . By putting his inhuman protagonist through a recognizably human succession of intellectual crises, Gardner makes Grendel's savage relativism credible, even beguiling. Still we should remember that it is a monster who has convinced himself that "things come and go. . . . That's the gist of it."

The same theme floods [*Jason and Medeia*]. . . . [It] is an epic poem, a retelling in twenty-four "books" of a story pieced together from Euripedes' *Medea,* the *Argonautica* of Apollonius of Rhodes, and several other sources. It is a tragedy of betrayed faith and deluded idealism, heavily weighted with satirical gibes against the virtues which epics are wont to celebrate. . . . Vividly etched characters loom before us, only to pronounce variations on the poem's relentless central theme: "the gods' deep scorn of man," the heroes' realization that "all our convictions, all our faith in each other, [are] an illusion." (pp. 527-28)

This darkest of Gardner's fictions is perhaps most interesting for its energetic blending of literary influences. Earthly struggles are paralleled by scenes set in the palaces of the gods. Allegorical personifications parade by. . . . [The] downward momentum is irreversible; the gods remain blandly nihilistic, and the game must play itself out.

The rhetorical splendor of *Jason and Medeia* is dulled by dozens of flat or wordy passages, but the boldness of its conception alone should keep the book alive, to be fairly judged by later generations. I doubt that any other contemporary writer will attempt such a work in our lifetime. At the very least this truly herculean effort is an admirable companion to the novels it joins in its stark suggestion that men's ambitions are nonsensical games. But again there is the problem centered in the narrator: why should we believe him capable of telling us the entire truth?

There are some interesting adjuncts to these chronicles of wreckage and waste, among the children's stories gathered in *Dragon, Dragon* . . . (1975) and *Gudgekin the Thistle Girl* . . . (1976). Fanciful and clever as they are, the tales remain ironic jokes which assert a breezy relativism. . . . (p. 528)

His most recent books reveal Gardner's virtues and defects in unruly profusion and in almost equal measure. *The King's Indian* (1974) includes most of his short stories. They are artful redevelopments of themes and situations borrowed from Poe, Browning, Kafka, Melville, and other writers. Even allusions to Lewis Carroll appear in the three "Tales of Queen Louisa," rambunctious Graustarkian romances which liken the "accidents" of status and rule to the kind of unexplainable sorcery that can make a rosebush bloom in winter or transform a monarch into a toad (and back again).

Several stories ("The Temptation of St. Ivo," "Pastoral Care," "The Warden") mislead their protagonists into an-

ticipating that their traumas will conclude in some kind of sensible comprehension—then reduce them to dejected frustration when meaninglessness asserts itself. (pp. 528-29)

The protagonist of "The King's Indian" has "learned early in life that any man not firmly committed to a single point of view is as apt a philosopher as anybody else." . . . It teases us with the information that the "King's Indian" is a classic chess move—but also lets the title phrase imply an ideal composite, mingling orderly intelligence with unlettered instinct: the double strength derived from the matched excellences of master and servant. The man who surfaces above these confusions and lives to tell us of them has done so because he accepts knowing there are no paradises, earthly or celestial; that, in spite of such knowledge, "a wise man settles for, say, Ithaca." (p. 529)

[*October Light*] reads like a close cousin to *The Resurrection* and *Nickel Mountain*—which it resembles in its use of a rural setting, broadly drawn characters who embody symbolic oppositions, and dreadfully clumsy ironies (a theological discussion carried on over the interruptions of people passing by to use the bathroom; an argument on race relations shouted through a locked door). I think this is a rewritten version of a novel which has been around Gardner's workroom for several years. . . .

October Light is ambitious and reasonably sprightly but fails to satisfy the expectations it raises. The epigraphs are reverberant quotations from Founding Fathers. . . . [However] this bicentennial salute implies that America's battle for independence was not rewarded by any dramatic increase of vision. Gardner's personified forces perceive things in "October light"—a phenomenon native to New England late in the year: a sharp autumnal clarity which arranges hitherto blurred objects in unambiguous focus. The point is that it arrives late in the year; that the clarity (if it be such) is relative in the eye of the beholder. (p. 530)

When John Gardner uses his characters as mouthpieces, his readers must feel like sinners who encounter at the gateway to Hell a three-headed dog who doesn't guard against intruders but instead tugs them headlong into the place. The impulse behind his early novels was preferable: to show uncertain protagonists swept up in life's confusion and struggle, surviving their ordeals with an understanding that experience is a mystery not to be too easily understood. Therefore I hope that the unevenness of his recent work reflects an ongoing process of choosing how best to dramatize his characters' assumption of ironic pessimism. It is difficult to believe in the reality of characters who are seemingly born knowing that whatever happens to them will end up being of no consequence. We care more for the ones who live life and learn from it.

There is a real (and I think disturbing) mystery about Gardner's fiction. Are the stories which show his people growing into knowledge newly published work in an early mode that he unwisely has now abandoned? Or is he relaxing his thematic hold on characters, permitting them to be persons as well as ideas and symbols? I choose the latter alternative and will await further stories (like *The Sunlight Dialogues, Grendel,* "The King's Indian") told, or retold, for the purpose of reminding us that we have no choice but to accept our burden of incompleteness and study the outrageous ambitiousness of stubborn humans through the imperfect human medium: "not the sunlight, but the sunlight entrapped in the cloud"—October light. (p. 531)

Bruce Allen, "Settling for Ithaca: The Fic-

tions of John Gardner," in Sewanee Review (reprinted by permission of the editor; © 1977 by The University of the South), Summer, 1977, pp. 520-31.

* * *

GARRIGUE, Jean   1914-1972

American poet, critic, novelist, and short story writer, Garrigue was an elegant stylist whose poetry, according to Howard Nemerov, illustrated a "small world but one absolutely brought into being." (See also *CLC,* **Vol. 2, and** *Contemporary Authors,* **Vols. 5-8, rev. ed.; obituary, Vols. 37-40.)**

Intrepid explorer of intensities that she is, [Jean Garrigue] wants . . . regard for limits, whether of form or feeling. Nevertheless, . . . [in] poems about the slum, the park, or the forest, [she] unites accuracy of observation with clear moral judgments. There are pictures in her "False Country of the Zoo" that might have been drawn with Marianne Moore's delicate pencil. . . . Miss Garrigue finds her subject matter in the give-and-take between the physical presence and the ideas, or more often, the emotions that attach to it. If she wears her feelings upon her sleeve, the embroidery can dazzle. And with what unembarrassed ecstasy she proffers the key to a foreign city or to the gate of a secret garden. (pp. 103-04)

> *Babette Deutsch, in her* Poetry in Our Time *(copyright © 1963 by Babette Deutsch; 1963 by Doubleday; reprinted by permission of Babette Deutsch), revised edition, Doubleday, 1963.*

Miss Garrigue has often irritated me with her mannerisms of fashionable femineity. She seemed to belong to the world of Colette (to whom the first poem in [*Country without Maps*] is addressed), a world suffering, no less in the blatancies of *Vogue* than in Colette's chief novels, from a profound emotional stoppage, basically sexual. The manner is recognizable anywhere: a too involved Jamesian syntax that is inclined to burst predictably into pseudoecstasies, exclamations which are not really exclamations at all but simply coynesses. . . . Yet after all I am not sure that Miss Garrigue's connection with this world amounts to more than her manner, and even this disappears in her best work. Leaving aside the poems about Colette, cats, country gardens, etc., her work contains a core of intensely and I should say fully humane poems, which are increasing in proportion to the whole. If they never rise to anything that can be called a pitch, they nevertheless perserve the attractive quietness of steady intellectual warmth. At the same time there can be no doubt that she has a splendid lyrical gift and uses rhyme and meter elegantly. This is a less rare attainment than her others; some of her poems could be transposed to volumes she never wrote and no one would know the difference; but in the best poems her softly modulated rhymes and assonances together with unexpected variations in the length and pace of her lines produce what she (elegantly) calls "a little native elegance": the effect is right and original. The most ambitious poem in her book, called "Pays Perdu," is a meditative travelogue eleven pages long, a considerable effort by modern standards. In the best sense it is a Wordsworthian poem, an emotional intertexture of landscape and idea that we can read with pleasure while we recognize its philosophical limits. Indeed the poem suggests that this form of "thinking" is as indispensable as any in an age when all mental activity has become an expression of the pathos of self-limitation. (p. 134)

> *Hayden Carruth, in* The Hudson Review *(copyright © 1965 by The Hudson Review, Inc.; reprinted by permission), Vol. XVIII, No. 1, Spring, 1965.*

I had thought of Garrigue as a poet of rich, baroque, rather exotic and remote poetry; poems of travel, as I chiefly remembered, with the elaborate descriptive texture of such poetry. [*Studies for An Actress and Other Poems*] is rather different; though it contains a certain kind of high rhetoric that I wish had been cut-through, it cleaves much closer to the bone of personal experience, and specifically that of living in this particular society at this particular time. In a poem like "For Such A Bird He Had No Convenient Cage" she evokes a sense of contemporary helplessness, not merely before shattering public events, but individual reticence and disrelation. Perhaps the most beautiful poem in the book is "On Reading 'The Country of the Pointed Firs'"—a pure, hard-edged poem, as good or better than most of Frost, about a woman surviving through the refrain of *change and loss.*

> *Adrienne Rich, "Caryatid: A Column," in* The American Poetry Review *(copyright © 1973 by World Poetry, Inc.; reprinted by permission of Adrienne Rich), September/October, 1973, p. 43.*

[Many] of Jean Garrigue's poems are so moving in their bitter-sweet elegance that my interior tuning fork hummed to their sometimes painful beauty. (p. 371)

The symbiotic relationship between the artist and reality is the key for Jean Garrigue to the dynamism at the heart of life. If it is lost "The light is out, all is inert and stony,/ What's loved is not known one loves." Such knowledge can be shared only analogically and each of Garrigue's subsequent poems explores from the ground of her being images for meaning in the contemporary world. (pp. 371-72)

Her characteristic poems are long (although she writes a few short and poignant lyrics) and ratiocinative but illuminated with meticulously controlled metaphor. Garrigue also writes for the ear. The exquisite melody of her verse counterpoints the simple exposition of such a poem as "On Reading the Country of the Pointed Firs."

Jean Garrigue's achievement in *Studies for an Actress* is considerable. (p. 372)

> *Claire Hahn, in* Commonweal *(copyright © 1974 Commonweal Publishing Co., Inc.; reprinted by permission of Commonweal Publishing Co., Inc.), January 11, 1974.*

["Shining"]is—has always been—the word for [Jean Garrigue's] poetry, whose brilliant surface glimmers with seductive coruscations that do not conceal but invite the exploration of even more shimmering depths. Here, in other words, is poetry in what I suppose we must call the "grand manner", art that displays its artifice with pride but without arrogance, consciously incorporating "motifs from the dark wood", the *"pays perdu"* of the past, "moonstuff, lawn and tissue of it", and "myth-making mist and resurrecting light". Significantly, the title poem of her . . . posthumously published book is *Studies for an Actress:* her own art is deliberately, gravely or wittily, theatrical; she strives, like a *diva,* to sing so that she *is* her subject, to impersonate and illuminate all the people and things she encounters. (p. 45)

Occasionally, perhaps because she does see herself as a virtuoso performer through whom the past as well as the present speaks, Garrigue's influences seem to me to overwhelm her. The ghost of Yeats, almost always present throughout this book which begins with a *Song in Sligo,* becomes too assertive in *Dialogue* and a few other poems. Archaisms ("There is a binding element / The which when had, sustains . . .") and inversions ("And walked we by the harvests of the light") mar certain of her melodies like mannered inflections or injudicious trills in a baroque aria. For the most part, however, this graceful performer exploits her heritage skillfully: the *Song in Sligo* rewrites Yeats with *élan* and bespeaks no anxiety of influence; *For Jenny and Roger,* a delightful occasional piece, might have been written by the fire at Thoor Ballylee ("For those who talk the night away, / What makes that pride so sweet . . .") but the Yeatsian mask glitters like Garrigue, and was, besides, wonderfully contrived. And the elegant *To Speak of My Influences,* civilized as Marvell ("Straw-in-the-fire love, / It's no morality play we're in / Nor can we trick time / Nor end where we began"), makes me reflect, with pleasure, that this woman poet, anyway, would have been as accomplished a metaphysical as many seventeenth-century gentlemen.

To speak of her other influences: a few of the very best poems in the book, for instance *The Smoke Shop Owner's Daughter* and *Country Junction,* have a notably Rilkeesque depth and compassion. But again, those qualities are hardly faults. For to say that Garrigue's new poems sometimes echo men—or, more accurately, reinvent male modes —is not to say that, as some feminists might fear, she repudiates her own self, her own femaleness. On the contrary, her finest pieces are written out of a distinctively female consciousness, in Jong's sense. (p. 46)

> *Sandra M. Gilbert, in* Poetry *(© 1975 by The Modern Poetry Association; reprinted by permission of the Editor of* Poetry*), October, 1975.*

Jean Garrigue was a wildly gifted poet, the most baroque and extravagant of spirits, whose art took the road of excess that leads to the palace of wisdom. She was our one lyric poet who made ecstasy her home. Her world of angels, demons, ghosts, moon and roses, fabulous beasts and birds, fireworks and fountains would seem Gothic and artificial if a real anguish, countered by the most sumptuous of joys, did not hold its ingredients together. The flushed and impulsive quality of her poems and even their flaws reflect her lifelong pursuit of the romantic ideal. Of all the writers and artists I have known Jean Garrigue most vividly embodied, in her person, the ardor of the poetic imagination. Another generation may be better tuned to the freshness of her lines. . . . (p. 256)

> *Stanley Kunitz, in his* A Kind of Order, A Kind of Folly *(© 1935, 1937, 1938, 1941, 1942, 1947, 1949, 1957, 1963, 1964, 1965, 1966, 1967, 1970, 1971, 1972, 1973, 1974, 1975 by Stanley Kunitz; reprinted by permission of Little, Brown and Co. in association with the Atlantic Monthly Press), Atlantic-Little, Brown, 1975.*

*   *   *

GASS, William H(oward)   1924-

Gass is an American novelist, short story writer, philosopher,
and essayist. An experimentalist, Gass works out his philosophical and literary theories in both the formal and thematic aspects of his prose. It is often said that his novels and short stories read like poetry rather than prose. He is probably best known for *Omensetter's Luck.* **(See also** *CLC,* **Vols. 1, 2, and** *Contemporary Authors,* **Vols. 17-20, rev. ed.)**

It was [easy] for the novelist William Gass, a brilliant but exhaustingly self-conscious theoretician of the novel, to get attention with a showy construction, *Omensetter's Luck,* a book that showed every sign of great personal intelligence, curiosity, mimicry, but was brilliantly unconvincing—an act. Gass was a restlessly inventive, loquacious writer whose sharp critical writing showed that he knew as much about different minds operating in fiction as a philosopher is likely to know. But as a fiction writer Gass could stimulate many other critics without conveying any honest necessity about the relationships he described. He was like the man Kafka described who walked just above the ground. Everything was there in *Omensetter's Luck* to persuade the knowing reader of fiction that here was a great step forward: the verve, the bursting sense of possibility, the gravely significant atmosphere of contradiction, complexity of issue at every step. But it was all in the head, another hypothesis to dazzle the laity with. Gass had a way of dazzling himself under the storm of his style. In a book of essays, "Fiction and the Figures of Life," Gass called for a fiction in which his characters, "freed from existence, can shine in essence and purely Be." Perhaps Gass was, then, a mystic or absolutist of the novel? To have one's characters "freed from existence" is not a sensible wish for a novelist. The seeming unlimitedness of the novel as a form does tempt extraordinarily bright people into identifying their many "figures" for life with life itself on the page.

Gass was an event in the boggy history of the postwar novel. The overpowering classroom demonstrativeness of his skill at "construction"—of argument, of situation with voices—showed insight into the human mind and its fictions, in the current style that so much stressed the secret compartments of the mind, the counterfeit, the duplicity. But Gass's own fiction was make-believe fiction, not the real confidence game which takes in, to his supreme delight, the confidence man himself. (pp. 293-94)

> *Alfred Kazin, in his* Bright Book of Life: American Novelists & Storytellers from Hemingway to Mailer *(copyright © 1971, 1973 by Alfred Kazin; reprinted by permission of Little, Brown and Co. in association with the Atlantic Monthly Press), Atlantic-Little, Brown, 1973.*

William H. Gass is both a novelist and a professor of philosophy, and the two vocations seem to wage a kind of lover's quarrel in his fiction. They do, indeed, have much in common, [as Gass wrote in *Fiction and the Figures of Life*]: "Novelist and philosopher are both obsessed with language and make themselves up out of concepts. Both, in a way, create worlds." The novelist creates a world of people and things, while the philosopher creates a world of abstractions. On the one hand, Gass points out that theology, for instance, "is one-half fiction, one-half literary criticism" . . .; on the other, a successfully created, living fictional world will imply the philosophy or theology ordering that world. Yet for Gass, "Fiction and philosophy often make most acrimonious companions," because philosophy too often demands that fiction philosophize—that is, present ideas rather than people and life. . . . In *Omensetter's*

Luck, his first novel, Gass creates a world in which the lover's quarrel can perhaps be resolved. In his fictional world, however, the quarrel between philosophy and fiction also involves such other basic human conflicts as those between mind and body, reason and emotion, experience and innocence, and word and deed. All of these conflicts are, of course, as old as mankind; so Gass, like many American writers before him, refers to the myth of Adam and Eve and the Fall of Man and uses it in his own way to bring these conflicts to life.

The events of Gass's novel can be quickly summarized: Brackett Omensetter, "a wide and happy man," moves his family to the late nineteenth-century village of Gilean, Ohio. His careless, happy personality and his apparent harmony with nature immediately begin to affect the townspeople of Gilean, and his "luck" incites both admiration and envy among them. Henry Pimber, Omensetter's henpecked landlord, sees in Omensetter's happiness the lost potential of his own life and hangs himself from the top of a tall tree. Jethro Furber, a clergyman, sees in Omensetter's animal naturalness a denial of the spiritual truths which he defends, and he attempts to destroy Omensetter by casting the suspicion of Pimber's death on him. Eventually, the townspeople's suspicion drives Omensetter out of town, but not before Furber feels the effect of his naturalness. At the end of the novel, Furber also leaves Gilean. (pp. 5-6)

Omensetter is like Adam before the Fall, still in harmony with nature, almost totally lacking self-consciousness and confident in the "promise" of happiness in Gilean which he feels has been given to him. He is not merely an observer or conqueror of nature but a part of it.... To his post-lapsarian neighbors, however, Omensetter's naturalness makes him seem almost subhuman, merely a higher animal or worse.... "That man ... lives like a cat asleep in a chair.... Is it attractive in a man to sleep away his life? take a cow's care? refuse a sparrow of responsibility?" (pp. 6-7)

Omensetter's wife tempts him to mingle with men, first to support his family and later to save his infant son's life. As Gass's Eve, she is more earth-mother than temptress; we see her through Furber's eyes as she lies pregnant, sunbathing on a rock, and later as she nurses her newborn son. In Furber's theology such fertility led to Eve's fall; her desire for procreation—not for knowledge—led her to bite the apple. In the story of Genesis according to Furber, the Fall was already inherent in the creation of Eve, for God created by division.... (p. 7)

The effect of the Fall on Omensetter-Adam is knowledge, which divides him from his instinctive harmony with nature.... With knowledge to separate the mind from the senses come its main tools: observation to replace touch, and language to replace emotion.... Omensetter's fall from innocence starts to show when he begins to observe his life rather than live it. It begins to affect him when the townspeople label his naturalness "luck." Omensetter for the first time allows himself to question whether or not his happiness might be merely luck.... In *Omensetter's Luck,* then, the Fall of Man consists of the tragic separations of man from woman and knowledge from sensation, separations accompanied by a dependence on observation and language. (pp. 8-9)

Pimber [seeks] Omensetter's secret, which Gass explains elsewhere as "to feel at home in our body, to sense the true *nostos* of it, ... to have it move to our will so smoothly we

seem will-less altogether.".... Yet the Fall of Man has made such a condition impossible, for "Thought seems to remove us; we cannot enjoy life.".... To deny thought would be to deny our humanity, our very essence; thus, Pimber seeks a solution to the most basic human dilemma: to enjoy our bodies fully, we must eliminate or at least subordinate thought; yet to be human, we must cling to perception and thought. We seem not to be able to have it both ways.... Pimber thinks at first that Omensetter's "stony mindlessness" offers the "sweet oblivion" of escape from self. As he sees even Omensetter being made self-conscious of his luck, he realizes that the return to Eden, to the animal delight in body, is impossible. He sees Omensetter becoming like everyone else.... Omensetter could save Pimber from lockjaw but not from his own humanity.

Pimber's predicament is man's, as Gass elsewhere describes it: "We have fallen out of our bodies like a child from a tree...." Unable to climb back into the life of the body, Pimber escapes instead by a symbolic climbing back into the tree. (pp. 11-12)

With the gates of Eden locked against man's return to his body, is the quiet darkness of death [like Pimber's] the only escape? Perhaps not. In the character of Jethro Furber we see another alternative.... Indeed, in spite of his varied and disgusting faults, the diabolical Furber proves at last to be the holiest and most whole character in Gilean.

Gass's Satan wishes to return to Heaven. Furber wages within himself a kind of Manichean war between Spirit and Body, which he equates at first with Good and Evil.... (pp. 12-13)

Furber, like Pimber, has fallen not only out of Heaven but out of his own body; he has fallen, like all men, into the uniquely human predicament of perception.... The Fall leads to knowledge, and knowledge leads to perception, the recognition of our own otherness, our separation from the world we inhabit.... The danger is that our perceptions may become more real to us than the things we perceive. (p. 14)

The principal tool of perception is language, and Furber, "the wondrous watchman," is a master of language. He recognizes that we can no longer simply live as Omensetter does, without observing. Having fallen into perception, man finds that "Experience must mean".... Furber uses words to substitute principles for people and sound for sex. He is a master of what Gass calls "protective language".... (pp. 14-15)

Furber becomes so absorbed in the world of watching and words that words not only protect him from actuality, they become his reality. We find him, like the narrator of Gass's story, "In the Heart of the Heart of the Country," living totally within his own mind and the words that order its world.... The Fall has indeed made man god-like, for Furber has become a god creating his own world out of words.

The world of words, though it has a reality of its own, isolates man from the actual world of deeds and makes him a lonely god. Furber recognizes and regrets man's lonely position, between two worlds and imprisoned behind his words.... He asks God, "Why have You made us the saddest animal?" ... (pp. 15-16)

The confrontation between Omensetter-Adam and Furber-Satan is an ironic one. Instead of Furber tempting Omensetter into a Fall (Omensetter, as we have seen, has already fallen), Omensetter tempts Furber out of his world of words and back into life. At first, Omensetter fills Furber with envy, fear, and hatred of his physical naturalness; Furber sees Omensetter as the evil champion of the body against the spirit.... Furber perceives correctly that Omensetter's threat to his congregation lies in the temptation to abandon human perception and go back to the life of the wholly physical, a dead end. (p. 16)

He finally recognizes the beauty of Omensetter's innocence.... What Omensetter ... reveals to Furber is love, an ability to accept the life and people around him with complete trust, to care for people rather than principle. Omensetter offers completely unconditional love, and Furber feels the full effect of his grace. (p. 17)

Huffley is, however, only a representative of man's present mediocre condition, not his potential. In the world of *Omensetter's Luck* the Fall of Man is a kind of *felix culpa*, a fortunate fall. Pimber, not realizing it, mistakenly tried to revert to Omensetter's pre-lapsarian innocence. Furber, recognizing the danger of such total innocence, at first denied it completely in favor of the experience of human perception. Only later, through Omensetter's grace, does he recognize that both innocence and experience are necessary. Furber learns the full potential of his humanity; he truly knows himself. The discovery is crucial, as Gass says elsewhere:

> Nothing keeps us back from nothingness but knowing; knowing, now, not necessarily in the sense of squeezing what we know into a set of symbols and understanding those [Furber's first error]; but knowing in the sense of seeing—seeing clearly, deeply, fully —of being completely aware and consequently of being perfectly our selves.   (pp. 18-19)

The same unkind vision which was the curse of man's Fall becomes also the means of his salvation. Perception and language can imprison man, but they can also free him. As Gass suggests, for instance, "protective language" can isolate a person but can also create a different, perhaps better and higher, reality. (p. 19)

Furber's theology is, then, Gass's inferred literary criticism. Gass warns us that the language of fiction can imprison us.... He also suggests that the same language can free us by taking us into a world different from (though related to) our own and thereby expanding our own consciousness, our own "knowing," and our imagination. The novelist's task is not merely to talk about such worlds but to create them. The novelist or artist, Gass tells us, "is not asked to construct an adequate philosophy, but a philosophically adequate world, a different matter altogether, ... from whose nature, as from our own world, a philosophical system may be inferred; but he does not, except by inadvertence or mistaken esthetic principle, deem it his task to philosophize".....

Nevertheless, Gass does philosophize in *Omensetter's Luck;* indeed, many readers will object that he philosophizes too much. Before hastily accusing him of literary hypocrisy, however, we must notice that the philosophizing is deliberately done through characters who fail to live— Pimber and Furber. Both discover that philosophy without both life and love can only fail. When Furber has his change of heart, he also begins to come alive fully as a character. On the other hand, Omensetter, despite his vitality, remains rather vague and elusive until he is forced by

personal tragedy into the kind of knowledge with which philosophy attempts to cope. He finds that love and trust are not enough to heal his dying infant son; knowledge must be accepted also. As Gass implies, the chaos of life and the orderly systems of philosophy can, indeed must, co-exist in fiction; however, fiction is ultimately about life. Through his characters, Gass suggests that any philosophic separation of spirit from body, reason from emotion, experience from innocence, and words from deeds is destructive of life. He reminds us (and we need reminding) that fiction, like poetry, should not merely mean but, above all, be. (pp. 19-20)

> Richard J. Schneider, "The Fortunate Fall in William Gass's 'Omensetter's Luck'," in Critique: Studies in Modern Fiction (copyright © by James Dean Young 1976), Vol. XVIII, No. 1, 1976, pp. 5-20.

Like all metafictions, *Willie Masters' Lonesome Wife* deals with writing and its own construction in a self-conscious manner. The work proves to be especially complex and ambitious, however, because Gass brings to it not only a literary viewpoint, but a background in the philosophy of language.... *Willie Masters'* deals with the building-blocks of fiction—words and concepts—in a more direct and sophisticated fashion than most other metafictions; it is more explicitly experimental than just about any other work of fiction which comes to mind and can serve as a virtual casebook of literary experimentalism, since it appropriates almost every experimental device used by writers in the past and suggests a good many possibilities for future development as well.

Interestingly enough, *Willie Masters'* is actually only one section of a much longer and more ambitious book which Gass worked on periodically during the 1960's. Before he abandoned the longer work as being impractical—it was originally to have dealt metafictionally with almost every Western narrative mode—two other short excerpts appeared, "The Sugar Crock" and "The Clairvoyant." Like *Willie Masters'*, these pieces are metafictional reflections on the nature of fiction-making, with self-conscious narrators pondering their relationship to their creations. They do not provide much background for *Willie Masters'*, although they introduce a few of the people who appear in the later work. (pp. 23-4)

Gass never allows the reader to forget that literature is made of words and nothing else; here the words themselves are constantly called to our attention, their sensuous qualities emphasized in nearly every imaginable fashion. Indeed, the narrator of the work—the "Lonesome Wife" of the title —is that lady language herself. Although the narrative has no real plot, the "events" occur while Babs makes love to a particularly unresponsive lover named Gelvin—suggesting the central metaphor of the whole work: that a parallel exists—or should exist—between a woman and her lover, between the work of art and the artist, and between a book and its reader. The unifying metaphor is evident even before we open the book: on the front cover is a frontal photograph of a naked woman; on the back cover is a corresponding photograph of the back-side of the same woman. Gass, thus, invites one to enter his work of art—a woman made of words and paper—with the same sort of excitement, participation, and creative energy as one would enter a woman's body in sexual intercourse.... Unfortunately, as we discover from Babs, all too frequently those who enter her do so without enthusiasm, often seemingly unaware that she is there at all. (pp. 24-5)

Gass uses the color and texture of the page to indicate subtle alterations in Babs' mind rather than relying on traditional chapter divisions and pagination. Even the page itself is not ordered in the usual linear fashion; instead, typographical variations establish a different visual order for each individual page. (p. 25)

By far the most intricately developed device used by Babs to call attention to her slighted charms is the wide variety of type styles and other graphic devices with which she constructs herself. (p. 26)

In addition to mimicking typefaces, Gass presents many other typographic conventions, often with parodic intent. One amusing example is found in the Olive Section (2) in which a one-act play is presented with all the rigid typographic formality usually found in a written transcription of a play. Babs provides asterisked comments and explanations about stage directions, costumes, and props. These remarks begin in very small type, but as the play progresses the typeface becomes larger and bolder. Gradually the number of asterisks before each aside becomes impossible to keep up with, and the comments themselves become so large that the text of the play is crowded off the page—to make room for a page containing only large, star-shaped asterisks. Gass thus pokes fun at a typographic convention in much the same way as John Barth did (with quotation marks) in "The Menelaid." Gass also uses the asterisks for reasons we do not usually expect—for their *visual appeal*. (pp. 27-8)

In addition to drawing attention to how words look, Babs makes us examine the way we read words. In particular, she reminds us that the Western conventions of reading—left-to-right, top-to-bottom, from first page to last—are all merely conventions.... In *Willie Masters'*, especially in the Olive and Red Sections (2 and 3), Gass typographically makes ordinary reading impossible.... Like Joyce who forces us to page backwards and forwards to check and cross-check references, Gass is taking advantage of what [Hugh] Kenner has termed "the book as book"; the book's advantage lies in the fact that we can go backwards and forwards rather than being forced to move ever forward—as we are with a movie or a spoken narrative. The use of asterisks and marginal glosses indicates Gass's willingness to take advantage of the expressive possibilities of Babs' form as words on a printed page; he uses a typographical method to deflect the eye from its usual horizontal/vertical network. (pp. 28-9)

The last—and most significant—method used by Babs to call attention to herself is also probably the least radical of her strategies. It is produced by the sensual, highly poetic quality of the language which she uses to create herself. This non-typographic method of focusing our attention on the words before us is often used by poets. In ordinary discourse and in the language of realistically motivated fiction, words do not usually call attention to themselves.... In ordinary discourse and in most fiction, words are used mainly as vehicles to refer us to a world (real or imaginary), and the words themselves remain invisible: as Babs says, "The usual view is that you see through me, through what I am really—significant sound".... Babs, however, resembles the stereotyped woman in being vain about her physical qualities and resentful when she is used but not noticed. Babs shares with Valery (to whom Gass seems to

owe much of his esthetics) the view that when words are placed in an esthetic context (as in a poem) their utility is sacrificed in favor of a unity of sound and sense.... (pp. 29-30)

Like Barthelme's Snow White, who wishes "there were some words in the world that were not the words I always hear," Babs is bored with her own existence as she usually finds it: "Why aren't there any decent words?" she exclaims at one point in the Blue Section (1); and in a footnote to the play in the Olive Section (2), she compares the "dreary words" of ordinary prose to ordinary action, which often loses all subtlety and beauty as it strains to make itself understood to an audience "all of whom are in the second balcony." Too often, claims Babs, writers—and readers—seem unaware that words make up the body of all literature. (p. 30)

If poetry is the language which Babs is trying to realize herself in, she admits that she rarely finds lovers appreciative enough to create her properly. When Gelvin leaves, she says: "he did not, in his address, at any time, construct me. He made nothing, I swear. Empty I began, and empty I remained".... The main problem, as Babs observes, is simply that we have forgotten how to make love appreciatively.... Today readers and writers alike approach lady language in the wrong spirit. The pencil, the writer's phallic instrument of creation, grows great nowadays only with blood, never with love. (p. 31)

Babs confers upon language the same magical potency which Stephen Dedalus gave it in *A Portrait of the Artist as a Young Man:* she exalts the habit of verbal association into a principle for the arrangement of experience. Of course, she is right—words help arrange our experience and often exhibit the power to make us "feel more at home, more among friends." Naming something gives us a sort of power over it, just as we become the master of a situation by putting it into words. (p. 32)

Because of her envy of poetic language, Babs is especially interested in circumstances—as with the language of Shakespeare or any great poet—where words become something more than simply Lockean devices for calling to mind concepts. Babs thinks a good deal about the "poetic ideal": the word which lies midway between the "words of nature" (which constitute reality) and the words of ordinary language (which are nothing in themselves but arbitrary symbols which direct our minds elsewhere).... Nearly all the strategies of *Willie Masters'* are closely related to the idea that in literature words should not merely point somewhere else but should be admired for themselves.

Willie Masters', then, is a remarkably pure example of metafiction. As we watch "imagination imagining itself imagine" ..., we are witnessing a work self-consciously create itself out of the materials at hand—words. (pp. 32-3)

As the best metafiction does, *Willie Masters' Lonesome Wife* forces us to examine the nature of fiction-making from new perspectives. If Babs (and Gass) have succeeded, our attention has been focused on the act of reading words in a way we probably have not experienced before. The steady concern with the *stuff* of fiction, words, makes Gass's work unique among metafictions which have appeared thus far. (p. 34)

Larry McCaffery, "The Art of Metafiction: William Gass's 'Willie Masters' Lonesome Wife'," in Critique: Studies in Modern Fiction *(copyright © by James Dean Young 1976), Vol. XVIII, No. 1, 1976, pp. 21-34.*

The title story, "In the Heart of the Heart of the Country," is composed of reflections of a poet-teacher on his situation in Middle America and on his failed love affair. It is also a fiction about the relation between poetry and false consciousness. The protagonist of "Icicles" [in the same collection] was a type in whom poetry and false consciousness met; while Fender seemed to accept Pearson's view that everything is property, which was "the power of [Pearson's] imagination," his own invention created "a princess in her tower" out of the icicles—a kind of objective correlative for his feeling of entrapment. The narrator of "In the Heart of the Heart of the Country," explicitly a poet, suffers from the same kind of narcissistic withdrawal: on the one hand he says, "I would rather it were the weather that was to blame for what I am and what my friends and neighbors are—we who live here in the heart of the country" . . .; on the other he says, "Who cares to live in any season but his own?" . . .—the climate being an objective correlative for his inner state. If lovers, poets, and madmen are, in fact, near allied, we can see that Fender is more the madman, the narrator here more the poet—and both are frustrated lovers.

The story opens with an echo from "Sailing to Byzantium": "So I have sailed the seas and come . . . to B . . ." . . . . Yeats' assertion that "Once out of Nature I shall never take/My bodily form from any natural thing" is echoed ironically in Gass's observation: "Tell me: do they live in harmony with the alternating seasons? It's a lie of old poetry. The modern husbandman uses chemicals from cylinders and sacks, spike-ball-and-claw machines, metal sheds, and cost accounting. Nature in the old sense does not matter. It does not exist." . . . Here again poetry and false consciousness are near allied—the artifice of Yeats' Byzantium echoed by the anti-nature of Gass's technology. The narrator of Gass's story calls into question poetry's "lies" (or fictions), among which are man's harmony with nature and the whole and immediate experience of childhood. . . . (pp. 47-8)

The relationship between sex and writing is elaborated at length in the story. Fender's narcissistic fear of castration in "Icicles" is a fear everywhere diffused in "In the Heart of the Heart of the Country." (p. 49)

The real caress in "In the Heart of the Heart of the Country" is "fearful," the caress of flies: "No caress could have been more indifferently complete. . . ." (pp. 51-2)

[After the title character of "Mrs. Mean"] has denied the narrator's "preternatural power" as an idol . . . the narrator feels that he does not exist. . . . The aggression and exclusion suggested by Mrs. Mean's denial are characteristic of the "mirror stage" of our development, where we achieve a coherent image of ourselves—particularly of the topology of our body—through imaginary identification with another. . . . (p. 53)

That the mirror stage of imaginative identification is involved [in "Mrs. Mean"] is revealed by the massive patterns of identification and mutual aggression. Consider the theme of swallowing: the narrator as a spider swallows others, Mr. Wallace as a whale swallows the narrator, and Mrs. Mean's "beak" of a hand swallows the bolls of dandelions—also identifed with her children. . . . As a god, the narrator can observe without being observed; he can objectify the others and play with their possibilities; as an

idol, however, whose eyes are treated like "marbles" by them, he seems desirous of impressing his objective being in the wax of their subjectivity. . . . Such intersubjective process is revealed also in the narrator's observation: "Mrs. Mean is worse for witnesses. She grows particular" —more and more the essence of meanness to be penetrated. . . . That the narrator is trapped in his mirror image is revealed by his having withdrawn from purposeful activity, measuring time by playing Achilles to the Other's tortoise. Mrs. Mean's "reality" is not only mechanical; it is geological. . . . Meanness has density, although the paradoxical density of an abstraction. Its increasing density corresponds to the narrator's increasing compulsion to penetrate it, a compulsion that he calls "prophecy" since his future is the distance he can create in order to cross it, the shadow he can cast in order to enter it. (pp. 54-5)

From a cosmic point of view, both creation and destruction are equally necessary; from a human point of view, an orderly love—particularly between men and the gods—must be fostered. Through sacrifices one can appease the gods and even improve them. In "Mrs. Mean" the narrator creates beings of gigantic proportions: the Goliath, the Polyphemus, the whale of Mr. Wallace, and the Mrs. Mean whose "anger is too great to stand obedience"—embodied by the narrator in a malevolence that gives her density, an inside to penetrate. Since he uses divination in order to penetrate and torment them, all he discovers (like the reversal of fisherman and fish in the Puritan poem he remembers) is his own otiose tyranny. . . . The narrator's discovery of his same in the other—his trap in an imaginative identification—inevitably leads to paranoid aggression since he is not the other that he is. (pp. 55-6)

The dynamics of Gass's narrative are revealed by the narrator's view of the Means' Calvinism: "Their meanness must proceed from that great sense of guilt which so readily become a sense for the sin of others and poisons everything." . . . That the narrative is a projection of the narrator's guilt and fear of castration is clear. . . . (p. 56)

While the theme of Calvinism suggests the way in which the poet's *pathos* is translated into *poiesis*, the story's Orphic theme takes us back to the force of instinct. The poet's Pegasus is the most sublimated example of the force —but toads, bears, cats, insects, and bleached animals inhabit the interior of the Means' world, as does the following mythical creature: "his cow-chested, horse-necked, sow-faced mother." . . . Despite his ambition for transcendence, [the narrator] also has the desire to be engulfed by the Other. . . . The narrator, having sacrificed his concrete freedom, wants to recover a sense of existence by being the responses he stimulates in the Other, whose gigantism makes the secret meaningful. Being swallowed, however, is a return to primal unity, and being swallowed by one's own creation is the narcissistic gratification of art. (p. 57)

Bruce Bassoff, "The Sacrificial World of William Gass: 'In the Heart of the Heart of the Country'," in Critique: Studies in Modern Fiction *(copyright © by James Dean Young 1976), Vol. XVIII, No. 1, 1976, pp. 36-57.*

Metafiction's stance is necessarily anti-Platonic. Both ideal forms on high and underlying schemes are harmful illusions. Here, it should be noted, Gass departs from other writers of the metafictive mold. Gass's fiction indicates the existence of an underlying order which is separate from the individual. For example, in "Order of Insects" a house-wife, who apparently speaks with Gass's own voice, over-comes her squeamishness toward roaches and is able to say, "When I examine my collection now it isn't any longer roaches I observe but gracious order, wholeness, and divinity." It is because of this belief in something beyond the self that Gass criticizes Nabokov for writing novels which reflect only Nabokov. It is the reason he abhors what a Nabokov or Beckett would treasure: "Imagine that a mirror, nothing falling into it, began reflecting itself: what a terrifying endlessness and mockery of light—merely to illuminate its own beams."

Because of Gass's inclination toward wholeness and harmony, he prefers the concept of reader as brother to that of reader as opponent. This is close to Kierkegaard's hope that his works could bring about reconciliation with the world (of which the reader is part) rather than the obliteration of it. On the other side are writers who cut into the carefully woven fabric of narrative suspense to give the reader a lecture on the art of creating narrative suspense, who gain reader sympathy and credibility for a character only to later reveal that character's madness, who undermine their narrator. . . . (pp. 216-17)

The main difference between Gass and writers such as Barthelme, Nabokov, and Barth is that Gass takes life more seriously. (p. 217)

> Margaret Heckard, in Twentieth Century
> Literature (copyright 1976, Hofstra Univer-
> sity Press), May, 1976.

William Gass's *Willie Masters' Lonesome Wife* is a study of the creative process from a particular philosophical point of view; it exemplifies [Wolfgang Kayser's] analysis [in *The Grotesque in Art and Literature*] of an important modification in aesthetic theory of fiction which began in the eighteenth century and in which fictive structures were not measured extrinsically, but intrinsically, on the basis of their own inherent aesthetic form and content. This transvaluation shifted emphasis from the reliable Lockean world of primary substances to the unreliable and confusing subjective world of secondary substances. According to Kayser, this philosophical turnabout has led to such effects as a grotesque "fear of life rather than fear of death." . . . It also expresses the division between the intellectual view of reality and that of the accepted public concept of the real world of primary occurrence and subject. In terms of structure, the grotesque visually models disorder, mutation, impish perversity, and eternal change in a world of constant variability governed by no single principle: the public view of structure would be that the world contains specific and identifiable, reliable and stable forms which are in themselves scientifically verifiable and never-changing. As Gass points out, the average consciousness is unable to enjoy works of art as pure sensation, because literature must *mean,* it must be significant of primary facts and intentions. To the average consciousness the idea of eternal change would be an offense, a radical impossibility.

The grotesque represents the image of our disorientation in a strange world; it structures our failure to understand such lately amorphous concepts as finitude and concrete substance. In this realm of strangeness one finds both the grotesque and the ironic as negative rejoinders to final truths. The ironic can be considered the verbal, discursive, and demonstrative equivalent of the grotesque, which itself is less concerned with the persuasiveness of a discursive argument than with depiction in visually demonstrable terms of cosmic ambivalence, unresolvability, and distortion. The two principles are complementary.

In Kayser's terms, *Willie Masters' Lonesome Wife* can be considered as "a scene or an animated tableau" which is an ingenious commentary on the artistic process and the structural grotesque. It is at the same time a reflection of Gass's Platonic and Socratic view of reality. Unlike romantic irony, whose negative vision of reality leads to a kind of heightened spiritualism and subjectivism, and unlike rhetorical irony whose vision of the world is didactic change, Gass's irony and his consequent structuring principles are from a particular Socratic position. Like Socrates, Gass believes that we can really never know anything at all about our finite existence and the impenetrable cosmos. . . . It is quite certain, however, that Gass would not accept the Socratic notion of transcendent absolutism, that the ideal lies archetypally outside the realm of the finite. It is his denial of absolutistic ends, and his acceptance of creativity as "play in necessity," that constitute Gass's aesthetic conglomeration of Socratic, Nietzschean, Symbolist and Wittgensteinian ideas. Gass maintains an art-for-art's-sake "ethic" of infinite aesthetic value, in a structure of the sublime grotesque, as his principle of creativity. His interest lies in the pleasures of the imagination, in model making, and in aesthetic projections composed in the face of an all-pervasive determinism. (pp. 306-08)

The actual threefold process of fictional creation in conjunction with Gass's own epistemology and ontology is the subject matter of *Willie Masters' Lonesome Wife;* it is also mimetically and philosophically reflective of Plato's idea of the work of art and the creative process itself as a shadowy metaphoric grotesque thrice removed from reality. Gass agrees with Plato and Socrates that "there are no descriptions in fiction, there are only constructions, and the principles which govern these constructions are persistently philosophical."

Although this "essay-novella," as Gass refers to it, is less well-known than his novel *Omensetter's Luck* or his now famous and frequently anthologized "In the Heart of the Heart of the Country," *Willie Masters' Lonesome Wife* stands, along with his fascinating, impressionistic literary criticism, as perhaps his best work to date. . . . Structurally, it is clear from the beginning that the subject of this book is the act of creation, and that Babs is William Gass's "experimental structure" composed of language and imagination. The book *is* literally Babs. It is not about her; it is her whole essence and being. The book is a woman from beginning to end. The covers are the extrinsic flesh, the pages are the intrinsic contents of Bab's consciousness—her interior world. It would be difficult to find a better example of the use of structural principles than in Gass's stylistic combination of form and content in his book. There are photographic illustrations of Babs in various positions throughout the text, but perhaps the most significant and humorous picture is on the title page, where one sees Bab's left arm extended and pointing to the title, *"Willie Masters' Lonesome Wife,"* in a parody of Michelangelo's Sistine Chapel painting of God creating Man.

Babs Masters, a whore, is the interior monologue narrator who, throughout the larger portion of the narrative, is in the throes of sexual intercourse with Phil, the act in itself being an analog for artistic creation. Phil is analogous to the perceiver, or co-maker, of the artifact, or work of art. The ontological correlative to the fictive is Babs herself who is being literally made—that is who is making herself known through her interior monologue while she is being "made" in a physical sense by friendly Phil. She is exposing herself completely, giving herself entirely—though she knows that the act itself is purely sensual, creative only in the provocation and delectation of her senses. Her body is the work itself, her mind the aesthetic structure of the work; she is literally in the process of self-creation. Babs is "imagination imagining itself imagine." The work is an illuminating view of the interior world of the narrator as well as a remarkably diversified, inventive, and cosmic description of the consciousness; it is a self-contained poetic.

Gass has attempted to create a work of pure sensation whose reception will be based upon the immediacy of the response to the act and the ruminations appearing on the page before the perceiver's eyes and mind. The act of sex and Babs's often poetic reflections are a process of sensory excitation which is illustrative of the transitoriness of experience and expression, the fleeting notion, the emptiness of retrospect. All of these events and results are tacit verifications of Gass's aesthetic ideas, at the same time being a rejection of the general belief that one must convey or receive a "message" in literature, an idea that both Gass and Plato would find ludicrously innocent. Gass's play with structure and his parody of traditional social theses include his own satire of Gogol's satire, "The Nose," typographical eccentricities and jokes, etymological games, plays within plays, noncausal insertions, and brilliant descriptions of the artist as *homo ludens*. At the same time all of these devices illustrate the validity of Kayser's statement that the grotesque is "our failure to orient ourselves to the physical universe," . . . that the grotesque is "a play with the absurd," . . . and that it is "an attempt to invoke the demonic aspects of the world." . . . In Gass's position the "demonic" describes the boundaries of a deterministic cosmology. To Gass the artist is a liar, a player, and a gamester; he has the capacity to imagine sensibilities and to create mirror worlds—shadow worlds of possibility—through the creation of his various fictions which have fiction as their collective subject matter and ontological model. (pp. 308-10)

To paraphrase the title, perhaps Gass has, in his successful mastery of this particular model, indeed mastered the subject of the lonesome wife as a fictive probable. She, in turn, though being laid by many, is mastered by none; sexual intercourse only triggers her freedom of imagination instead of binding her to another's possession. Intercourse initiates Babs's creative sense. Artistic creation is the only equivalent man has to giving birth, as Socrates points out in *The Symposium*. (p. 311)

The narrative is consistently first person interior monologue, a soliloquy reminiscent of Molly Bloom's, but Babs is the more intelligent and self-perceptive of the two. As the text of her monologue becomes increasingly more complex, so does the typescript, being set in various styles meant to represent the diversity of Babs's many levels of consciousness existing simultaneously, and proportionate to her sexual excitement and her mental imaginings. The act of procreative sex has commensurately triggered her consciousness, freeing it from the burden of time and place and locating it in the creative, non-selective and random past, present, and future. (pp. 311-12)

Babs, once a common stripper, now a whore, is at the same time an abstract and complicated universal sort of woman; she is the illusion that language can create, and she is the manifestation of Plato's world of illusory flesh, shadow and

substance. She is the imagination turned through language into creation. . . . (p. 315)

In *Willie Masters' Lonesome Wife,* William Gass takes the aesthetic position that the world is both determined and illusory. In this grotesque world which is ironically sublime as well as ugly, the conditions are consistently confused, demonstrating that, as Gass suggests, "*from any given body of fictional text, nothing necessarily follows, and anything plausible may.* Authors are gods—a little tinny sometimes but omnipotent no matter what, and plausible on top of that, if they can manage it." (p. 316)

Reed B. Merrill, "The Grotesque as Structure: 'Willie Masters' Lonesome Wife'," in Criticism *(reprinted by permission of the Wayne State University Press; copyright 1976 by Wayne State University Press), Vol. XVIII, No. 4 (Fall, 1976), pp. 305-16.*

William Gass is not only a philosopher in the business of posing paradoxes but a writer (*Omensetter's Luck, In the Heart of the Country*) to whom words matter. Blue, for instance. [In *On Being Blue: A Philosophical Inquiry*] Gass notes that "a random set of meanings has softly gathered around the word the way lint collects." Gass would like to know why, and he is writer enough to make his inquiry far more entertaining than just another academic trip through the wild blue yonder.

Not since Herman Melville pondered the whiteness of Moby Dick has a region of the spectrum been subjected to such eclectic scrutiny. . . . He squints at past authorities on physics (Democritus, Aristotle, Galen), the better to glimpse the essence of this protean color in the corner of an eye. The mystery remains, more mysterious because Gass so thoroughly exposes its complexities. Yet the humanist does not visit nature for facts but for creative suggestions, and these Gass offers in abundance: "Blue is the color of the mind in borrow of the body; it is the color consciousness becomes when caressed."

The erotic overtones of this surmise tinge Gass's entire argument. For he is not finally interested in pinning "blueness" to the wall, but in suggesting what is truly "blue" in the realm of art. Not, he insists, the vivid depiction of sexual activity. . . . Instead of their lovers, Gass wants writers to caress their language: "It's not the word made flesh we want in writing, in poetry and fiction, but the flesh made word." In Gass's view, the truly "blue" writers are not those who flaunt explicitness but those whose works demonstrate "love lavished on speech of any kind, regardless of content and intention."

This is a polemic, although the author does not alert the reader to the argument on the other side. His approach leads to a hermetic absorption with words as objects rather than signs pointing outward—precisely the premise that makes so much "experimental" writing so ghastly and unreadable. (pp. K10, K12)

Yet by his own definition Gass has produced a very blue book, both in the sinuous beauty of its language and in the passion for argument his words radiate. He gives philosophy back its old good name as a feast that can never sate the mind. He also has the common sense not to run on until he is blue in the face. (p. K12)

Paul Gray, "Hue and Cry," in Time *(reprinted by permission from* Time, The Weekly Newsmagazine; *copyright Time Inc. 1976), November 15, 1976, pp. K10, K12.*

William Gass probably thinks more than any other living novelist about the nature of fiction, its ability or inability to "make statements" or reveal truths or evoke a sense of the physical world. Gass's concern comes partly, no doubt, from the fact that he is a philosopher first and novelist second, more disposed than most of us to inquire into the nature of what he is doing in abstract, systematic ways. It comes also from the kind of pleasure Gass obviously finds in staking out a polemical position eccentric enough to what most people believe so that it causes small shock waves every time he articulates it. It comes, also, from the nature of Gass's talent, a virtuoso talent for exploiting the richness of language not exactly in the service of fable but as its own end. The title story of *In the Heart of the Heart of the Country,* for example, has struck most readers as being wonderfully evocative of the texture of lived experience in small-town Indiana, a response that Gass professes to disapprove of, insisting that small-town Indiana is not like that at all, his story being a made thing, an invention, answerable not to Indiana but to the implicit laws of its own art. After the fact, one can see how inevitable it is that Gass should now have produced a "fiction" that escapes fable altogether, being a meditation on words, or rather a meditation on a word, the word being "blue." (pp. 118-19)

What the premise sets in motion is an attempt to gather, "celebrate" as Gass puts it, the things of the world which are blue, the things which are called blue, some of which are really blue, some of which are not, the feelings evoked by both seeing and being blue, observations on the aesthetic value of blue, above all speculations on erotic words, books and works of art, since they all arrange themselves under the epithet blue. Gass subtitles his book "A Philosophical Inquiry," but the austerity and the pretense at method stop there. If it is to be judged as philosophical inquiry, the book is grotesque, without rigor or system, self-indulgent in its arrangement, not even very inclusive. (Gass seems almost totally innocent of the musical uses of blue.) The book does, on the contrary, implicitly ask us to respond to it as a fiction, a strange, crabbed, stylized, lyrical, involuted meditation, true not to any abstract principles of orderly inquiry but to the contours of Gass's own mind. Still, there is a kind of method to the book, a miming of philosophical rigor, that gives it much of its charm. . . .

The encyclopedic range of the book *is* extraordinary. The word "blue" is as rich, diverse, and unpredictable as Gass says it is. . . . It is perhaps on its sexual content that Gass's book finally invites judgment since he, finally, makes that its most prominent aspect. . . . Gass's insights into blue words are the most stylish and ingenious I know, the most consistently interesting, but I am not sure that they can be trusted, either on such matters as the covert meaning of sexual insults or the power of a sado-erotic passage from Hawkes. Still, Gass's discussions of erotic language are not so much meant to be trusted as observed, being the fluid, impressionistic, sometimes crotchety, often arresting opinions of a character, named William Gass, in a fiction by William Gass, which masquerades as philosophical treatise and which finally amounts to an eccentric and ingratiating book, like no other before it, full of grace and wit, displaying a mind in love with language, the human body, and the look of the world. (p. 119)

> *Philip Stevick, in* The Nation *(copyright 1977 by the Nation Associates, Inc.), January 29, 1977.*

GODWIN, Gail   1937-

An American novelist and short story writer, Godwin focuses on the perception of self as well as of the physical world. Her interest in writing, she says, is precipitated by a need "to expand awareness of the possibilities of experience." Joyce Carol Oates comments on Godwin's work, "in exploring extremities of human behavior . . . such art saves us from these experiences and is cathartic in the best sense of the term." (See also *CLC*, Vol. 5, and *Contemporary Authors*, Vols. 29-32, rev. ed.)

As a novelist whose books tend to pivot on classic feminist issues, Gail Godwin will undoubtedly be shelved as yet another women's writer. But this would be a gross injustice. Godwin's appeal goes far beyond feminism, and the basis for this is her talent. Godwin is an extraordinarily good writer. . . . "The Odd Woman" could be compared, in sensitivity and brilliance, to the best of Doris Lessing and Margaret Drabble (two writers who have vociferously rejected the feminist categorization of their work). . . .

"The Odd Woman" is written with a light, witty touch. It is a cerebral, reflective novel—most of the action takes place in Jane's mind—and a pleasure to read. Godwin's prose is elegant, full of nuance and feeling, and sparkling with ironic humor. At times it feels like a 19th-century novel. Godwin has the self-consciousness of an author who knows her characters well, maneuvering them through this long, complex book with skill and grace. . . .

"The Odd Woman" is Gail Godwin's best and most ambitious book. It is not only twice as long as her previous novels, but far more complex, spanning several generations and a remarkable range of female characters, all successfully realized. While Godwin never tells us what women really want, her exploration of their longings and desires is fascination enough. (p. 4)

> *Lore Dickstein, in* The New York Times Book Review *(© 1974 by The New York Times Company; reprinted by permission), October 20, 1974.*

[*The Odd Woman*] is about the past and its relation to the present, about the relationship between literature and life, about [the protagonist's] living more in the nineteenth century (her teaching speciality) than in the present. For Jane's essential problem is her inability to live in her own "real life." Her only "letting go," her only abandonment, is to her imagination. . . . [Neither] Jane nor Gabriel [her lover] can create the paradoxical union of motivations Godwin sets up as ideal in her epigraph: consciousness of human limitation and of the infinite.

Like other contemporary women's novels, *The Odd Woman* points toward a future which will resolve some of its female ambivalence. And stylistically, it reads more like life than fiction. It is an important woman's book, one which is mature and quietly intelligent. (p. 121)

> *Dianne F. Sadoff, in* The Antioch Review *(copyright © 1975 by The Antioch Review, Inc.; reprinted by permission of the editors), Vol. 33, No. 2, 1975.*

[For] Jane, the lucidly intelligent figure at the centre of *The Odd Woman*, words retain true power, from the brilliant opening stream of thoughts on insomnia, through the miseries of death, failed love, and disappointing friends; they are the ultimate means of her survival. For her, to name is to control, and ultimately to exorcise. At first sight, Gail Godwin's subject-matter seems well-worn; but even familiar campus territory can be illuminated by strong light: *The Odd Woman* is a most unusual novel. . . .

At the key point in the book she truly fears to melt her 'beautiful frozen mind'; and even naming the possibility feels like magic, the spring thaw beginning, which is only a metaphor for the dangers of her central proposition: 'If you believe in words, you had better be careful which words you say and how you say them.' . . .

But it is her grandmother Edith's words that count. In her heroine's last dream before relapsing into insomnia at the end of the book, a young version of Edith (remembered from an old photograph) appears who 'just wants to understand this lesson'.

There isn't a lesson, however. Nothing, except the effort of trying to organise 'loneliness, and the weather and the long night into something of abiding shape and beauty'; as indeed Miss Godwin has. (p. 204)

> *Elaine Feinstein, in* New Statesman (© *1975 The Statesman & Nation Publishing Co. Ltd.), August 15, 1975.*

In "The Odd Woman" (1974), her best-known work so far, Gail Godwin attempted a fleshed-out portrait of a beleaguered but plucky modern woman; the novel virtually sagged under the weight of the author's earnest sympathies and attentions. "Dream Children," her first collection of short stories, now returns to the bloodless control of her first two novels ("The Perfectionists," 1970, and "Glass People," 1972), with their internal psychological naturalistic landscapes. While broadly representative human experience continues to elude, or perhaps simply not to interest her, Godwin at least recovers here from the oppressive gabbiness of that last book. . . .

Notwithstanding such occasional flashes of affirmation and melioration, Godwin is essentially a chronicler of life on the edge, where isolation and alienation move toward the extremes of nihilism and madness. To be sure, figures reminiscent of the super-wife-mother-career-woman who befriends Jane Clifford in "The Odd Woman" crop up here and there in "Dream Children," intimations of consoling orderly spheres, but these serve primarily to heighten, by contrast, the dark and dangerous atmospheres of the stories. In the end, the grim unwelcoming and fantastic hold sway here. . . .

All but two or three of the stories in this volume in some way amplify, extend or reiterate the themes of Godwin's novels; she is preoccupied with the nature of womanhood—its particular desires, disappointments, distresses. There has been, needless to say, much largely autobiographical, and unworthy, fiction generated by women writers in recent years, devoted to the sundry woes of their sex; it should be pointed out that certain refinements of style and sensibility clearly distinguish Godwin's work from this Mad Housewife school of novel writing. Still, with less serious and talented authors, she shares an essentially reductive image of women, seeing them as almost universally passive and feckless. Whatever impulses of charity or compassion may prompt the creation of these "loser" heroines, the net effect is simply to deprive them of consequence and substance. True, a kind of independence attaches itself to Nora in "Notes for a Story". . . . (p. 5)

But this work, significantly, is styled as "notes for a story," the narrator jotting reminders to return at some later time to supply details, dialogue, carefully evoked emotional climates. All but moments of hysteria have an unfinished feel to them, almost as if to say that the narrator is uneasy about the possibilities of a competent woman who's also troubled and complicated.

Nowhere are Godwin's women less convincing that when she tries to say something about women in love. Although hardened readers of contemporary fiction might be expected to be inured to notions of human love as mere victimization, entrapment, quagmire, it is still irritating to have to come across, once again, a celebration of the rootless, no-risk kind of emotion that Nora claims as the reward for her "stubborn sense of self." From the earth-mother in "The Woman Who Kept Her Poet" to the elegant maneater in "indulgences," these stories are ready to investigate every sort of relationship except those usually complex, difficult and animated ones that real human beings spend most of their time coming to terms with.

When Godwin's people have disconnected from themselves and from the selves in others, drift in dream worlds whose contours threaten dissolution and violence, the author can be chilling. There is a virtuosity to her craftsmanship, and it isn't very often that even the most elaborate schemes run away with her. On a first reading, "Dream Children" arrests and engrosses. But on closer inspection, the reader recognizes that the deepest and most consistent response the writer elicits is really no more than a sauna-like self-pity, and that the special effects are rather frequently too *outré* for genuine resonance.

Ultimately, the very idiosyncrasy and detachment of Godwin's characters and the worlds they marginally inhabit lend to her writing a tedium and inconsequence that paralyze even her deftest effects. As one reads through the *longueurs* that take up so much room in these stories, one becomes increasingly impatient for some breakthrough to the real world, for news of its happenings, for representations of engaging destinies acted out by men and women capable of variegations of feeling and action. (pp. 5, 22)

> *Jane Larkin Crain, in* The New York Times Book Review (© *1976 by The New York Times Company; reprinted by permission), February 22, 1976.*

Dream Children, Gail Godwin's first collection of stories, may disappoint or even dismay readers who admired *The Odd Woman.* My own admiration for that novel was a little uneasy; though Godwin can be eloquent and witty, her effects depend mainly on amassing incidents and thoughts, and her work can be ponderous and sentimental. In *The Odd Woman* the accumulation adds up, finally, even though it is not a continuously active or engaging book.

The stories, I'm afraid, expose further deficiencies that aren't evident in the longer and denser novel. A number of them seem exercises in fantasy-making which ought not to be memorialized in hard covers. . . . Some themes recur in these stories—dead children and lost lovers, female gigantism, sexual attraction to and damage from older men, writers constructing fictions out of life or life out of fiction or dreams—but Godwin's use of the short story form doesn't succeed in giving them clear meaning.

Goodwin can be very good—and sometimes very funny—when she attaches her characters' feelings to the conditions of their culture. . . . (p. 34)

When she confines herself to relatively conventional modes, where inner feeling and outer circumstance each have their rights preserved, she does quite well, as in "False Lights". . . .

"Dream Children" . . . remains a little too close in tone and intensity to the emotional conventions of a familiar kind of commercial women's fiction to earn its professions of seriousness. I much prefer "Notes for a Story," which, though done mostly in outline, mixes emotional intensity with intelligent ironic control.

[The ending,] in effect the climax of a longer story which hasn't fully been written and suggesting a novel's greater amplitude, reminds us that Gail Godwin is a very considerable writer indeed. (p. 35)

> *Thomas R. Edwards, in* The New York Review of Books *(reprinted with permission from* The New York Review of Books; *copyright © 1976 NYREV, Inc.), April 1, 1976.*

To find one of Gail Godwin's stories in an anthology or magazine is a pleasure, and equally a challenge. She possesses an enormous command of technique, together with a much rarer command of appropriateness: like Donald Barthelme, Gail Godwin will use any means necessary, but only what is necessary, to her purpose. Also like Barthelme, she demonstrates that the methods of 'experimental' fiction are out of the breadboard stage and available for normal use.

Why is it, then, that reading straight through *Dream Children* is noticeably enervating? Qualities emerge that were not visible in individual stories: to begin with, a cloying, insistent rhythm of incantation, a lilting prolixity used to bridge tricky caesuras of plot and feeling. This is the clue to a deeper evasiveness which, once suspected, is confirmed. . . .

The recurring theme of *Dream Children* is the *aperçu* that collapses in upon itself if one tries to make it do everyday work; as with the Sussex vicar in 'An Intermediate Stop' who turns his epiphanic vision into a book, then into a lecture tour—and finally stares uncomprehendingly at meaningless lecture notes. Gail Godwin is a mystic, with a mystic's cunning in pointing at the inexpressible. *Dream Children* should be read one or two stories at a time: to avoid the jadedness from too many words about silence. (p. 21)

> *Nick Totton, in* The Spectator *(© 1977 by The Spectator; reprinted by permission of The Spectator), January 15, 1977.*

*   *   *

GOLDING, William   1911-

A British novelist, poet, playwright, and short story writer, Golding is most famous for his *Lord of the Flies* which, according to Steven Marcus, is the "only recent novel of imaginative originality that I am aware of which implies that society, insane and self-destroying as it undeniably is, is necessary." (See also *CLC*, Vols. 1, 2, 3, and *Contemporary Authors*, Vols. 5-8, rev. ed.)

William Golding has just turned sixty, an age when a man has made his life, done the best of his work, shaped and expressed his mind if he is ever going to. In Golding's case the work is modest in quantity (he has written a good deal less than Forster, for example), and has come out of a creative career of less than twenty years; nevertheless, it is all of a piece, a unified and impressive accounting of a unique

imagination. When those first novels appeared, the originality of their conception was so great that many readers (and some critics) never got beyond the invention to the imagination; the astonishment with which one discovered the minds of the pre-human, or the ego of a dead man was blinding. And to find such an imagination functioning in the 1950s, in England, was even more extraordinary. Golding seemed to belong to no school, to exist quite outside fashion; one could not even be certain that he had read Joyce.

Now that the shock is past, we can see that Golding is in fact a very conservative novelist, as he is a conservative thinker. This is not to say that he is not original, but only that his originality has not needed more than the traditional novelistic tools to express itself. He does not play with reality, and he does not, like many novelists since Joyce, hold his readers on the arid level of language. He is concerned to tell a story, to engross, and to render experience. But he is also and above all concerned that experience should reveal its meaning, that fiction should tell truths; that is to say, he is a serious moral artist.

Golding has never been much concerned with the immediate present, and certainly seems to have no feeling that the present moment in human history is unique. His classical training, and his amateur interests in Egyptology and archaeology have encouraged him to see man's story as an evolving one, and have fed that quality of his mind that is most individual, and that makes him irreplaceable—his sense of the human *species*. His humanity reaches back beyond history, and finds us there; he is an anthropologist of the imagination. He is primarily interested in the cruxes in the evolution of consciousness, and the childhood of individuals or the childhood of races serves him equally well, providing those points at which a mind opens imaginatively to knowledge, learns to use fire or to impose discipline, learns evil or love or the nature of death. His courage in attempting such subjects is admirable, and when he has failed, he has failed courageously. . . .

Golding has said that he wrote *The Inheritors* to refute Wells's *Outline of History,* and one can see that between the two writers there is a certain filial relation, though strained, as such relations often are. They share the fascination with past and future, the extraordinary capacity to move imaginatively to remote points in time, the fabulizing impulse, the need to moralize. There are even similarities in style. And surely now, when Wells's reputation as a great writer is beginning to take form, it will be understood as high praise of Golding if one says that he is our Wells, as good in his own individual way as Wells was in his.

> *"Origins of the Species," in* The Times Literary Supplement *(© Times Newspapers Ltd., 1971; reproduced from* The Times Literary Supplement *by permission), November 5, 1971, p. 1381.*

[In *Pincher Martin*] Golding used [the traditional Robinson Crusoe formula, or *Robinsonade*] to establish in the reader's mind a sense of the ideal vision of natural and divine benevolence that its formulaic embodiments sustained. With the formulaic story in mind, the reader is made aware . . . of the ironic discrepancy between the ideal vision of benevolence sustained in the formula and the harsh reality of man and nature as Golding saw it. Golding is thus able to make both incident and diction ironic through the use of conventional elements from the formula. . . .

The hero of *Pincher Martin,* Christopher Hadley Martin,

is, as one might by now expect, shipwrecked upon a desert island. Nature on the island is, in a very limited and a very harsh sense, if that is possible, benevolent, in that food and water are available, even on an island that turns out to be composed of pure rock. Mussels attached to the rock provide food, along with something odious that Martin refers to as "red sweets." Obviously, the benevolence of nature in Golding's world is scarcely that which prevails in [earlier *Robinsonades*]. The island provides housing for Martin, a shed formed by a slab of rock under which he is somewhat protected from the elements. Unhappily, no goats, nor pigs, nor any animal, for that matter, have been left there by altruistic ship captains, and their absence is as important to Golding's vision as their presence was within the traditional *Robinsonade*. Martin is, like so many of his predecessors, a wily survivalist; he is capable of using his tools intelligently, and of applying a very rational mind to his dilemma. (p. 46)

Like his predecessors, the mastery of his environment is Christopher Martin's aim. . . . Of course, unlike the efforts of heroes of traditional *Robinsonades,* who do indeed dominate their environment, Christopher's efforts do not lead to survival, nor, as they do for most, to spiritual salvation. Once again, the formulaic expectations are violated for ironic ends. (pp. 46-7)

Golding's use of the *Robinsonade* formula enables a relatively direct ironic inversion of plot and language in order to propose a naturalistic explanation for the human condition. The ways in which the fiction relates to ideological shifts are made more explicit through the study of Golding's fiction along with the formula from which it derives. One may also see in the comparison aspects of the relationship between serious and popular literature. Golding's novel serves as a commentary upon the meaning of the fiction from the popular realm, and thereby, of course, a commentary upon the belief of a great number of people. On the other hand, the popular fiction provided plot, specific incident, and metaphor for the serious author. (p. 48)

> *Tom R. Sullivan, in* Journal of Popular Culture *(copyright © 1974 by Ray B. Browne), Summer, 1974.*

*   *   *

GOYEN, (Charles) William   1915-

American novelist, short story writer, playwright, and translator, Goyen, whose style and subject matter place him in the tradition of the southern Gothic novel, has been largely overshadowed by the more prominent authors associated with that tradition, such as Flannery O'Connor and Carson McCullers. His relative neglect has little to do with his ability, since he is a fine writer in his own right. His first novel, *House of Breath*, is considered by many to be his best. (See also CLC, Vol. 5, and Contemporary Authors, Vols. 5-8, rev. ed.)

It is hard to believe that these two books were written by the same man. One, the "Selected Writings," shows William Goyen to be an extraordinarily rewarding and exciting writer. The other, "Come, the Restorer" is an embarrassingly bad echo. Of course, Goyen's fiction technique is by its nature a fail-safe gamble. He approaches the problem of fiction in such a way that he can only win or lose—he cannot produce a middling good book. (p. 73)

Goyen is usually classified as a Southern writer, but his regionalism sits lightly on him. He superficially resembles

Flannery O'Connor and the early Truman Capote ("Other Voices, Other Rooms"). But the similarities are misleading. Capote and O'Connor were truly regionalists, drawing their support from their background. Goyen is very nearly a completely placeless writer, his landscape the mind's interior.

The "Selected Writings" shows Goyen to be an eccentric, difficult writer. Because of his great concern with his own inner perspective, he is often jumbled in his words and tangled in his wildly grotesque visions. He is primarily a writer of despair, of hopelessness, of pain. There is no relief, no shadow of comfort in his vision, only a kind of frenzied dance of death performed with a curious desperate elegance. A stylish apocalypse, as it were.

Goyen always seems far more interested in expression—the recording of his own visions and thoughts—than in communicating with the reader. And this is basically the reason for the failure of ["Come, the Restorer"].

"Come, the Restorer" is a long private dream of good and evil, of life and death, of man the angel and man the beast, of creation and destruction. It is like a canvas of Hieronymus Bosch but without Bosch's unifying esthetic tensions. "Come, the Restorer" is a novel without pattern, without plot (except in the crudest sense), without forward motion. Everything is symbolic, and every symbol alters its meaning many times. It is a book in which conventional logic is of no use, no value. This fragmentation is of course quite deliberate. In his freewheeling fashion Goyen pyramids his shifting symbols (a white rattlesnake, a grave in the Garden of Eden, an exploding chemical factory, etc.), relying on their cumulative effect, their overall impression on the reader's emotions rather than his intelligence. Randomness produces unity—at least in theory.

"Come, the Restorer" is a foolish novel. There is, for example, a long passage in a tropical Garden of Eden (where elemental male and female forces engage in a battle of sexuality) that is embarrassingly silly. It is as if "Green Mansions" were being replayed with Xaviera Hollander in the part of Rima the bird girl.

The novel suffers, moreover, from being too clever. It dies of its own intricacy. Its grotesques are just possibly exaggerated. (pp. 73-4)

Still, in this day of written-to-order novels, of fiction tailored to meet the expected demands of the market—like a new breakfast cereal or an after-shave lotion—it is encouraging to find a novelist who has enough faith in himself as a writer to be difficult and obscure and inevitably limited in his sales. The serious American novel is still alive. (p. 74)

> *Shirley Ann Grau, in* The New York Times Book Review *(© 1974 by The New York Times Company; reprinted by permission), November 3, 1974.*

["The Collected Stories of William Goyen"] will make an excellent introduction to the haunting, intensely poetic fictional world of William Goyen, whose best-known work is probably the novel "The House of Breath.". . . Though the stories are all distinctly Goyen's—possessing that curious blend of the surreal and the tender, the nightmarish and the visionary—they range from "The White Rooster," originally published in 1947 . . . to the extraordinarily mysterious "Bridge of Music, River of Sand," published this year. . . . The only "development" in Goyen's prose is toward the lyric, the understated; it seems that, from the first, he was already a master of the form of the short story. One can see, for instance, how Flannery O'Connor must have learned from "The White Rooster," and it is quite likely that many other writers have learned from Goyen to seek out what he calls "the buried song" in their characters, "the music in what happened." Goyen is one of our finest American writers. . . .

His particular interest has always been, as the stories attest, the teller-listener situation; he has thought of his stories as folk song, as ballad, as rhapsody. . . .

Any skillful writer who wishes to satirize Americans can make their speech sound flat, ugly, banal and outrageous. It takes a truly gifted writer, like Goyen, to seek out the deeper, subtle beauty, to liberate the poetic possibilities of ordinary speech, to give life to characters whom the world seems to have left behind. (p. 4)

Because these stories are so close to poetry, they may not yield their "meanings" at a first reading. They should be read again; ideally, one should read them aloud. (They would make excellent recordings.) Only by reading the stories over several times did I feel that I had approached an understanding of them, an appreciation of their musical, delicate authority, their evocation of transient, visionary moments that might otherwise be lost in that large "disorder" of the world. (p. 14)

> Joyce Carol Oates, "William Goyen's Life Rhythms," in The New York Times Book Review (© 1975 by The New York Times Company; reprinted by permission), November 16, 1975, pp. 4, 14.

William Goyen's short stories and novels, most of which are based upon his East Texas roots but written over many decades of wandering far from home, are rich with the bizarre and wildly tragic quality that we have come to associate with Southern fiction. Not unexpectedly we find the plethora of hopelessly entangled families in which no member can escape the inadvertent wounds caused by the onward life course of the others, the familiar abundance of itinerant evangelists wandering forever homeless in search of the holy energy that cannot be truly found, the multitude of deformed and mutilated people who are stared at and exploited, the cold metal shotguns hidden under pillows of the mad, and even the relentless white roosters crowing until disaster comes, the plagues, the flagpole sitters and the immense Biblical birds of doom. But as we read further and allow ourselves to be captivated by Goyen's recurring song-like sorrowful refrains, his very personal transformation of his local dialect to poetry, we realize that despite the expected images and icons, the similarity in the situations and stories explored, William Goyen's work is strangely lacking in the cruelty and violence common to most other writing from the South. Although, like Flannery O'Connor, his focus is upon redemption, his vision is much gentler and he seems to substitute compassion and a loving human healing for O'Connor's cleansing by intense hellfire and clear sight of sin. (pp. 296-97)

Very often William Goyen's writing seems to speak on an almost sublingual level, his words becoming vehicles for something else more primitive in resonance, akin to folk music in stark simplicity of impact. His novels and even his shorter tales do not conform to our standard notion of plot, but rather are circular in form, the slow unfolding of the stories arising in waves which swell from recurring thematic refrains reminiscent of the choruses of ballads, the rhythmic repetition of these often plaintive calls drawing the reader ever backwards in time and memory, like undertow against the forward motion of the tale. (p. 297)

It is [an] intuitive grasp of the extraordinary within our ordinary experience, the cosmic within the simple, that is very characteristic of William Goyen and his work. (p. 298)

"A Shape of Light," an early story in which Goyen retells the local folk myths which grew up around the famous "ghost light" in the thicket begins relatively simply: ". . . So the record reads: 'If on an evening of good moon you will see a lighted shape, much like a scrap of light rising like a ghost from the ground, then saddle your horse and follow it where it will go. . . . Some old timers here call this Bailey's Light and say that it is the lantern of a risen ghost of an old pioneer, Bailey was his name. . . .'"

At first this seems to be merely a collage of legends superimposed upon one another and made human in the telling by Goyen's personal entry into them. However, gradually as the fusion of the layered tales intensifies, we realize that we are being asked to follow not just one man's mad pursuit of an illusionary glowing made of light of moon on dust motes, but the search of every human being for the radiance of life and hidden meaning in the darkness. In his slow and seemingly simple retelling of these superimposed stories, William Goyen is taking us on a spiritual voyage in the quest for God and for illumination, ever so gently, hardly telling us where he is taking us and why. (p. 299)

One of William Goyen's earliest stories, "Nests in a Stone Image," ends with the description of a man who lies "like a star, in a kind of new curious steadfastness, feeling himself calm purity, deep clarity, clear cold star. . . ." William Goyen considers this stellar luminosity, this "coming out clear," one of the most vital functions of art. He believes that art is redemption, that salvation comes through clarifying and resolving other people's suffering and "coming out whole, in a way." For him, writing has eased the suffering of entering other people's pain, has given him a missionary sense of healing, "Let me take your pain because I will be able to use it and transmute it." (pp. 300-01)

William Goyen . . . believes all art is about the absence or presence of that power of love which he discovered in the writing of A Book of Jesus. Come the Restorer, the novel which immediately follows A Book of Jesus, is both a return to his older works, rich in the legends of East Texas and the local folk tales, and a branching out into something slightly freer, more surreal, more mythic, and more whimsical. In place of much of the old pain and sorrow that only the telling of the tale could heal, we find a quality of hope, of sexual energy, and of regeneration. Although, like Goyen's earlier works, this book reverberates with plaintive cries for the lost past which cannot be, there is a constant quality of partial mending, of rebirth and human trying from which the redemption comes. (p. 302)

For William Goyen, the act of writing, the telling of the tale, becomes a "keeping" in the most sacred sense, a way of retaining not only those ghosts of the actual past, but the spirit ghosts of the unrealized loves and longings that haunt us all. Throughout his work one hears the calling of vanished voices, both from the past which is irreparably gone and from the wished-for future which can never be. His writing is an act of restoration and retention in words of that which can never be truly restored or kept, yet stays with us in the deepest recesses of our souls, the lingering memory within which calls us from our life of doing and of flesh, towards the earlier echos we both fear and crave. (p. 302-03)

> Erika Duncan, "Come a Spiritual Healer: A Profile of William Goyen," in Book Forum (copyright © 1977 by The Hudson River Press), Vol. III, No. 2, 1977, pp. 296-303.

* * *

GREENE, Gael

An American novelist and journalist, Greene has written *Don't Come Back without It, Sex and the College Girl,* **and** *A New York Restaurant Strategy.* **She is currently a restaurant critic and contributing editor for** *New York Magazine.* **(See also** *Contemporary Authors,* **Vols. 13-16, rev. ed.)**

Though this novel has been touted . . . as an erotic zinger that "makes *Fear of Flying* look sick," it's not lust so much that the book seems intent to incite but envy of the Beautiful Life. The sex scenes are a trifle overcooked *à la* potboiler ("Floating, tumbling, exploding, coming apart again. . . . His cock is steel battering into me"). And the dialogue is dabbed with purée of cliché ("I am thinking what you would be like in bed," says Kate's rich, sexy cattleman, Jason, "no mask, no veneers, the makeup rubbed off, everything exposed"). (p. 44)

There's a lot of tonic self-mockery between the lines of Gael Greene's restaurant reviews. But that very irreverence is what's missing in her novel. Perhaps this is a conscious bid for paperback buyers in the heartland. Perhaps you need a lovable loser, not a lovable winner, to yield the bite of parody. The tone of *Blue Skies* is peculiarly self-impressed, the wit more coy than lancing.

Which just goes to show that pulp can be ground even from imported bonsai trees at Bloomingdale's garden shop. And that, as Greene herself knows, there's as much schmaltz in *pâté de foie gras* as in the humblest can of chicken soup. (pp. 44-5)

> Sheila Weller, "A Glutton for Sex, or: A Bad Case of Heartburn," in Ms. (© 1976 Ms. Magazine Corp.), October, 1976, pp. 42, 44, 47.

Gael Greene, who writes about food for "New York Magazine," now writes about sex for the readers of "Cosmopolitan." It will take sex a while to recover.

"Blue Skies, No Candy" is fantasy unleavened by art. Beyond that it is a recurring rather than a serial fantasy; the author simply keeps returning to the same basic dream, with virtually no narrative complexity. The fantasy is this: I am a tall, slender, bright, extremely attractive woman, a famous screenwriter who dines with David and Helen Gurley Brown, who is wanted by Ingmar Bergman, who is being considered for the cover of "Time," and who is in bed with a fantastically erotic man not my husband.

This is the old Olympia Press formula, in which a woman has sexual relations with a series of men, sans plot development. Each man in turn is a better, more varied lover than his predecessor; he is bigger, lasts longer, performs more often and introduces the heroine to a greater variety of stimuli. And of course there are the obligatory lesbian and masturbatory scenes. According to this book, not only are women's sexual fantasies as banal and repetitive as men's, they *are* men's.

Except for the brand names. It isn't her pants Miss Greene's heroine drops, it's her St. Laurent pants. Out of the boutiques, it's directly to the fun places of the world. . . . Seldom have so many backgrounds been used to such ill effect. A consciousness-raising session among Manhattan West Side ladies (a stock set-piece in the current measles of Sisterhood books) is an intermittently good sequence, and the only hint that the author is capable of observing anything beyond merchandise labels.

Mostly, though, observation is at a minimum, and a craven craving for status reeks through the pages. Following this year's fashion, real people are mentioned *en passant,* thousands of them, in tones of unearned intimacy. It's a slender line that separates the tacky from the gross, and Miss Greene has crossed it. (p. 20)

> Donald E. Westlake, in The New York Times Book Review (© 1976 by the New York Times Company; reprinted by permission), October 10, 1976.

[For] a while I thought my trouble getting through [*Blue Skies, No Candy*], or even into it, might indeed be sexism. The novel is frequently devoted to celebrating (sometimes criticizing) the male body as a sexual object from the viewpoint of a presumably liberated woman, and it's been suggested that male readers cannot cope with that. Bothersome. I'm accustomed to being susceptible to porn, and not totally exclusionary in such tastes. The erotic focus in *Blue Skies* is even refreshing—after all those bouts of lesbianism that seem requisite to proper feminist fiction. (Sexism still does prevail: Male homosexual eroticism remains pretty much a no-no outside of books for gays.) But here, even the dirty parts failed to intrigue; I found the book confusing however I tried to get into it, and thus lacking a reason for caring, found it boring. Still, the hideous possibility of prudishness nagged—until I asked an acquaintance who had read *Blue Skies* how *he* had gotten through it.

"Oh," he said, "you've got to know the people. It's a *roman à clef,* and the fun is figuring out who is who."

"Are those famous people, the characters in her book?"

"Oh, no. You probably wouldn't know them. I just happen to, some. But I can't see anyone who doesn't know them being very interested."

Ah, I thought *so that's* what friends are for. Capote could have told me.

> Eliot Fremont-Smith, "What Are Friends For?" in The Village Voice (reprinted by permission of The Village Voice; copyright © by The Village Voice, Inc., 1976), November 29, 1976, p. 92.

* * *

GUARE, John 1938-

American playwright and recipient of several distinguished awards, including the New York Drama Critics Award for the Best New Play of the Year, Guare is generally thought to be the most promising playwright to appear in America since Edward Albee. He excels at writing Strindbergian domestic dramas and savage farces.

"Rich and Famous" . . . is a vengeful attack on commercial show biz, Absurdist in tone, masquerading as a commercial comedy about eccentric theatre people. A young playwright named Bing Ringling (Guare's taste in character names tends to be garish) has his deeply personal poetic drama about the first Emperor of China gutted and jazzed up, overpraised and bad-mouthed, followed up by talent-hunters and put down gently by failure-freaks, until the climactic rug is pulled out from under him (the production never opens), and he goes off somewhere to "try and be a writer".

Shaky as this is at the core—because Guare never delves into what gives his hero the ability to become a commercial success, or the desire to do so—it triumphs onstage because Guare, a sharp sociologist who appears to have taken his degree in the subject at the College of Pataphysics, is largely content to let his hero, like many a soulful Candide before him, play straight man to a gallery of Dickensian zanies that includes a grandly gay black actor, a compulsive lady producer, Bing's starstruck parents, and in the play's most cutting scene, a young movie actor, Bing's closest boyhood friend, who has sold "the rights to his death," to evade the terror of trying to top his current hit movie. (pp. 67, 70)

> *Michael Feingold, "Are the Lean Years Over?" in* The Village Voice *(reprinted by permission of* The Village Voice; *copyright © 1974 by The Village Voice, Inc.), August 22, 1974, pp. 67, 70.*

John Guare, the author of "Marco Polo Sings a Solo," . . . has one of the most fertile, magpie comic imaginations in the theatre today; his "House of Blue Leaves" and "Muzeeka" . . . are indelible. "Marco Polo" is as full of incidents and jokes and surprises as an old George Abbott farce, but it is actually a science-fiction comedy. . . . The play, like so much else in science fiction, is based on the premise that the future will be the present in italics (a theory that I have always considered at least arguable), and the dramatist seems to have gleaned his teeming brain of all the emotional and intellectual detritus of the twentieth century. Overflowing though it is, however, the play is never chaotic or pointless. In fact, Mr. Guare has points to make —though it cannot be denied that he is easily diverted from them, to our benefit, by his invariably funny routines. (pp. 53-4)

> *Edith Oliver, in* The New Yorker *(© 1977 by The New Yorker Magazine, Inc.), February 14, 1977.*

John Guare's "Marco Polo Sings a Solo" explodes like a piñata, littering the stage with fragments, some bright and delightful, some torn and frazzled. (p. 66)

John Guare has thrown so many ideas, notions, themes, schemes and dreams into his play that you can practically hear it burp. . . . Guare can be very funny, sometimes jejune. But his real strength is the genuine sorrow in his view of our world as a technological runaway, spewing cultural and intellectual debris all over the universe as it careens toward slapshtik apocalypse. (p. 69)

> *Jack Kroll, "Slapshtik," in* Newsweek *(copyright 1977 by Newsweek, Inc.; all rights reserved; reprinted by permission), February 14, 1977, pp. 66, 69.*

Although steeped in Ibsen (frequent references to *A Doll's House*) and Chekhov (one notably funny diatribe against *The Three Sisters*), [*Marco Polo Sings a Solo*] recalls nothing so much as the play Kurt Vonnegut would have written if he could write plays; the same affectionate loathing for humanity, the same manipulation of preposterousness in

event and language, the same comic ability to grab a cliché and twist it into life by taking it literally. Above all, the same despair, splashed across an otherwise good-humored farcical entertainment, too thinly to rank as a deep artistic vision but strong enough to put a chill on the jollity, to scatter it across the stage in tiny beads of freeze-dried horror. You feel that, packed into a test tube, Guare's view of life would indeed be powerful enough to freeze the whole world, like Vonnegut's ice-nine. We probably ought to be grateful that he has the kindness to dilute it with sheer playfulness, that his mind cannot resist a purely comic or nonsensical diversion, that he follows so many tracks off in so many directions that returning to the main point becomes a tour de force.

The forces that keep *Marco Polo* from falling apart are the characters' obsessions, carried almost to the degree of Jonsonian humors: one with heroism and planthood, one with the glow of someone else's family life, one with his stature in the pop-political world of diplomacy. And the glamorous female around whom these three creatures revolve, drained of any feeling at all, sublimates her disgust by going to endless productions of *A Doll's House*. The end is stasis, an emotional icing over that reflects the ice-palace setting. The characters wait, frozen, for the new century, wondering if they have actually lived through any of this one.

> *Michael Feingold, "John Guare's Freeze-Dried Despair," in* The Village Voice *(reprinted by permission of* The Village Voice; *copyright © by The Village Voice, Inc., 1977), February 14, 1977, p. 43.*

The decline of [John Guare, a] once promising writer, from *Muzeeka* and *The House of Blue Leaves* to last year's *Rich and Famous* and now this latest uninspired lunacy [*Marco Polo Sings a Solo*], is something for Mr. Guare to explain, if he can, and at least to ponder. . . .

Marco Polo is a sad study in non-discipline. Somewhere under all the college-boy overwriting, the *Mad*-magazine sci-fi spoofery, there is something of an idea in the play: the failure of people to deal with present or future realities. But nothing comes together, nothing in this futuristic phantasmagoria makes sense. (p. 62)

> *Alan Rich, in* New York Magazine *(© 1977 by NYM Corp.; reprinted by permission of* New York Magazine *and Alan Rich), February 21, 1977.*

* * *

GUEST, Judith 1936-

Guest is an American novelist. Her first book, *Ordinary People*, was highly acclaimed for its realistic and sensitive portrayal of family relationships. *Ordinary People* was the first unsolicited novel to be accepted by Viking Press in twenty-seven years.

Ordinary People . . . is a rather bland and far from ironic novel, yet its title hints at a complicated irony. On the one hand, the book suggests, there are no ordinary people; people are all extraordinary in their way, both finer and feebler than we think. And on the other hand, ordinary people are what we may become, if we can conquer our fear of being extraordinary. In a novel, that fear has to be acted out. In *Ordinary People*, it *is* the novel, the trace of a season of exile. . . .

[The] whole novel is subtly implausible . . . because problems just pop up, get neatly formulated, and vanish, as if they were performing a psychoanalytic morality play. "I think I just figured something out," Conrad [the protagonist] says to his psychiatrist, and he has. It's a milestone on the road to reason.

The psychiatrist, a wisecracking cross between Groucho Marx and Philip Marlowe, is perhaps Judith Guest's major contribution to current mythology. . . .

But . . . Conrad's psychiatrist, like most of the characters in the book, is very charming and very intelligent. Judith Guest has a good eye for social detail and a good ear for turns of phrase, and the breeziness of her manner . . . goes with her brisk good sense. . . . She measures health by a capacity for jokes, which means both a faith in shared meanings (people understand you when you say the opposite of what you think) and a sort of independence within a community (your wit pulls you out of the rut of routine).

It is a shallow notion, but not a dishonorable or an unsympathetic one, and *Ordinary People* is not a book to be condescended to. . . .

Ordinary People is . . . a snappy, proficient novel that reads a little too smoothly for its subject; skates on thin ice without managing to give us any real sense of how very thin the ice is. (p. 8)

> *Michael Wood, in* The New York Review of Books *(reprinted with permission from* The New York Review of Books; *copyright © 1976 NYREV, Inc.), June 10, 1976.*

"Ordinary People" is a fine and sensitive novel, if small and not completely successful.

"Ordinary People" is a strong, honest portrait of a troubled boy: 17-year-old Conrad Jarrett, grade-A student, member of the choir and swim team, a typical Midwestern kid from an ordinary American family. What changes the routine of normal life of these conventional people is Conrad's suicide attempt and a subsequent eight-month stay in a mental hospital. The effect of Conrad's breakdown and recovery on the people around him is the mainspring of the novel.

There are the usual reactions: He doesn't look crazy, is mental illness catching? . . . The forms of civility become all important: freak out politely, please; mind your manners. But Conrad feels the "air is full of flying glass," the order and control that once served as stability for him no longer work. We suspect from the very beginning the genesis of Conrad's problem—his older brother died in a boating accident and he survived—but even this kitschy Freudianism does not detract from the novel's strength.

Guest portrays Conrad not only as if she has lived with him on a daily basis—which I sense may be true—but as if she has gotten into his head. The dialogue Conrad has with himself, his psychiatrist, his friends, his family, all rings true with adolescent anxiety. This is the small, hard kernel of brilliance in the novel; the rest is deeply flawed. Guest is an unsure narrator: there are jarring shifts of tone, and confusion about who is speaking (and this is not experimental fiction); the devices for presenting characters are crude and unimaginative. (Twice we are introduced to people as they examine themselves in a mirror.) But these are tricks of the trade that can be learned. Judith Guest has a raw, unpolished talent, but she also has a passionate honesty and sen-

sitivity that cannot be bought from a mail-order Writer's School. (pp. 14-18)

> *Lore Dickstein, in* The New York Times Book Review *(© 1976 by The New York Times Company; reprinted by permission), July 18, 1976.*

There are not many first novels like Judith Guest's *Ordinary People*. It tours through the stereotypes of much contemporary fiction so precisely and so humanely that the reader cares—in the same way that he cares, for example, for the family in Joseph Heller's *Something Happened*. The stereotypes include the adolescent-with-problem, the mother-with-social-activities, father-with-sensitivity, psychologist-with-accent. In the usual run of contemporary fiction, the stereotypes are plugged into equally stereo-typical social themes—the decline of the family, the loss of values, the banality of modern life. Mrs. Guest works with her characters as persons. . . .

The tone of the novel is splendidly controlled, the sentences a pleasure to read. . . . It is the kind of multi-valued prose seldom found in first novels—it sets the scene, establishes the tone, shows the character, and poses the problem; each element contributes to the combination of effects.

Despite the grimness of the subjects—death, insanity, difficulties in human relationships—Miss Guest manages to suggest that people do indeed survive and may even thrive. And because of her skill, the suggestion is as plausible as it is reassuring.

> *Lee L. Lemon, "First Novel," in* Prairie Schooner *(© 1977 by University of Nebraska Press; reprinted by permission from* Prairie Schooner), *Winter, 1976/77, p. 380.*

Guest's experiences as a mother, her sensitivity to the painful uncertainty of adolescents, lie behind [*Ordinary People*, her] often moving story of the tentative, groping re-entry into human society of a seventeen-year-old boy who attempts suicide and spends eight months recuperating in a mental institution. But this bare summary suggests a book more melodramatic than the actual novel, which . . . is unusually restrained in its careful descriptions of the boy's struggle with the ordinary routines of his life. . . . There are passages, even whole chapters, that declare themselves as apprentice-work, worthy in intention but uncertain or awkward in the actual writing. Guest is less effective with the boy's parents than with the boy himself, and the mother, especially, seems more a dramatic convenience than a fully realized character, her own guilt and sense of inadequacy emerging rather too schematically as a parallel or counterpoint to the pattern of her son's experiences. But the boy and his pain are rendered with great insight; Guest's ear for teenage dialect is acute, and her prose achieves an unflamboyant eloquence. . . . (p. 589)

Sanity is truly a profound moral option for this troubled young man, an urgent conscious labor against the smallest gestures and choices and flarings of memory. But neither he nor his creator would think to say such an explicit thing, much less to diminish his vividly particularized anguish by absorbing it to some modernist paradigm of universal malaise. (p. 590)

> *David Thorburn, in* The Yale Review *(© 1977 by Yale University; reprinted by permission of the editors), Summer, 1977.*

H

H(ilda). D(oolittle). 1886-1961

American poet connected with the Imagist school, H. D. wrote poetry possessing the rhythm of emotionally-charged speech. Greatly affected by the terror of the Second World War, H. D. reveals a tone of desolation in her poetry, notably the group of poems known as her "War Trilogy." (See also *CLC*, Vol. 3.)

The publication of *The Flowering of the Rod* brings to a close H. D.'s war trilogy.... "War trilogy" (the publisher's phrase) requires some qualification. It is true that the poem, which will be considered here *in toto,* begins amid the ruins of London, in the flaming terror of the Blitz, but it is equally true that it ends in an ox-stall in Bethlehem. The war was the occasion, it is not the subject-matter of the poem. Neither is "trilogy" wholly satisfactory, since it implies more of temporal continuity and progressive narrative line than the three parts possess. The relation between the parts seems to me more that of a triptych than of a trilogy, each book being a compositional unit, though conceptually and emotionally enriched by association with its companion units; each composition, furthermore, embodying a dream of vision. This formal arrangement is particularly suited to H. D., whose art has unmistakable affinities with the pictorial.

Pursuing the triptych analogy, we find the second book, *Tribute to the Angels* (1945), falling naturally into place as the central composition; in the background "a half-burnt-out apple-tree blossoming," in the foreground the luminous figure of the Lady, who carries, under her drift of veils, a book.

> her book is our book; written
> or unwritten, its pages will reveal
>
> a tale of a Fisherman,
> a tale of a jar or jars.

The left side-panel, titled *The Walls Do Not Fall* (1944), shows the ruins of bombed-out London. They have an Egyptian desolation, like the ruins of the Temple of Luxor. The ascendant Dream-figure is Amen, not as the local deity of Thebes, ram-headed god of life and reproduction, nor even in his greater manifestation as Amen-Ra, when he joined with the sun-god to become a supreme divinity incorporating the other gods into his members, but the Amen of Revelation . . . with the face and bearing of the Christos. . . . The background figure recording the scene is Thoth (to the Greeks, Hermes Trismegistus), scribe of the gods, in whose ibis-head magic and art married and flourished.

The interior of an Arab merchant's booth is represented in the foreground of the right side-panel *The Flowering of the Rod*. Half-turned towards the door stands a woman, frail and slender, wearing no bracelet or other ornament, with her scarf slipping from her head, revealing the light on her hair. ("I am Mary of Magdala, / I am Mary, a great tower; / through my will and my power, / Mary shall be myrrh.") The noble merchant with the alabaster jar is Kaspar, youngest and wisest of the Three Wise Men, transfixed in the moment of recognition, of prophetic vision, before he will present her with the jar containing "the myrrh or the spikenard, very costly." In the background he is seen again, making his earlier gift, also a jar, to the other Mary of the manger.

Much has been omitted in this simplified presentation, but enough has been given at least to suggest the materials of the poem and its psychological extensions out of the modern world into pre-history, religion, legend, and myth. "This search for historical parallels, / research into psychic affinities, / has been done to death before, / will be done again," writes H. D. in a self-critical passage. No hint of staleness or weariness, however, blemishes the page. On the contrary, the poem radiates a kind of spiritual enthusiasm. (The composition-period for two of the books is given: a fortnight apiece.) What H. D. is seeking for, what she has obviously found, is a faith: faith that "there was One / in the beginning, Creator, / Fosterer, Begetter, the Same-forever / in the papyrus-swamp, / in the Judaean meadow"; faith that even to the bitter, flawed Mary is given the gift of grace, the Genius of the jar; faith in the survival of values, however the world shakes; faith in the blossoming, the resurrection, of the half-dead tree. (pp. 204-06)

The modulations and variety of effects that H. D. achieves within [a] limited pattern are a tribute to her technical resourcefulness and to her almost infallible ear. Her primary reliance, orally, is on the breath-unit; aurally, on assonance, with an occasional admixture . . . of slant or imperfect rhyme. . . .

Like Yeats, though with a different set of disciplines, founded on her Imagist beginnings, H. D. has learned how to contain the short line, to keep it from spilling over into the margins. For straight narrative or exposition she usually employs a longer, more casual line that approaches prose without becoming, in context, fuzzy or spineless. . . . (p. 207)

The lyric passages have, at once, purity and tension, delicacy and strength, seeming to rejoice in the uncorrupted innocence of the worshiping eye. . . . (p. 208)

One of H. D.'s innovations is a form of word-play that might be called associational semantics. "I know, I feel," she writes, "the meanings that words hide." She sees them as "anagrams, cryptograms, / little boxes, conditioned / to hatch butterflies." To a large extent her poem develops spontaneously out of her quest for the ultimate distillations of meaning sealed in the jars of language. ("Though the jars were sealed, / the fragrance got out somehow.") . . . Most of [the word-play] passages impress me as being too self-conscious, too "literary," in the bad sense, though I recognize their catalytic function.

Although the significant fusion, the mutation into a new kind of experience, a new large meaning, does not take place in the body of the poem, it would be wrong to say that this ingenious, admirably sustained, and moving work fails because it does not achieve monumentality. H. D.'s is not a monumental art. Her poem remains as precise as it is ambitious. It is like the vision seen by the Mage on the occasion of his meeting with Mary of Magdala:

> and though it was all on a very grand scale
> yet it was small and intimate.

(pp. 208-09)

> *Stanley Kunitz, "H. D.'s War Trilogy"* (*originally published under a different title in* Poetry, *April, 1947), in his* A Kind of Order, A Kind of Folly (© *1935, 1937, 1938, 1941, 1942, 1947, 1949, 1957, 1963, 1964, 1965, 1967, 1970, 1971, 1972, 1973, 1974, 1975 by Stanley Kunitz; reprinted by permission of Little, Brown and Co. in association with the Atlantic Monthly Press), Atlantic-Little, Brown, 1975, pp. 204-09.*

First published in 1944-45-46 in separate volumes, [*Trilogy*] is really one long poem in three sections, a working out of H. D.'s mystical and optimistic religious vision in the face of World War II and Freudian psychology. . . .

Trilogy has many sections of delicate craftsmanship, where the imagist virtues of clarity, concentration and flexibility shine forth. . . .

Trilogy is religious poetry without Yeats' "odour of blood." Written in free-verse couplets, the *vers* no longer seems very *libre*, but that's not the problem. The main problem is that there is little drama, little tension. The "essential harmony of all religions" and the compatibility of war with a good God are pretty much just given to us, not imaginatively rendered. (p. 33)

> *Peter Meinke, in* The New Republic (*reprinted by permission of* The New Republic; © *1974 by The New Republic, Inc.), February 16, 1974.*

Trilogy republishes . . . three hermetic poems . . . in which destruction and the ripping open of life reveal the rebirth and renewal of spiritual life. However, the question—as with all poetry—is not what these poems are about, but

what they are. The last of the three was dedicated by H. D. to Norman Holmes Pearson: he writes an introduction telling us that in these poems H. D. "made the not known known". That again isn't helpful, and has to be reduced, poetically, to how and what: "How does she make the not known known?"

Postponing the answer for a moment, one must say that experience of H. D.'s earlier (and later) poems, coupled with a general experience of the poetry of ancient wisdom (or of ancient wisdom made known in poetry) does not make one hopeful. H. D. wrote what was within her power. It would be wrong to say that she reduced verse to versicles. She wrote versicles, and then said that was the way verse should be, an hygienic, anaemic imagism, with all too little incarnation. Add to that limitation, that the esoteric uses words only because it must, reluctantly. The thought is its substance, the symbol conveys thought; and poetry can stand only so much philosophy if it is to remain poetry; and H. D. was no Yeats or Blake, no Spenser or Pontus de Tyard. She does not take possession of words, she only cuts down their number. If a poet of her kind takes to the ancient springs (though dabbling or paddling in them is safe enough), the result is likely to be the poetically dilute still further diluted; which describes *Trilogy*.

Each of the three poems consists of forty-three sections (4 + 3 = 7 = the Seven Planets = the Seven Planetary Angels, etc) or constituent poems, written in narrow couplets of unrhymed free verse. They are full of symbols. They are full of words and phrases adequate for a subject, but otherwise ordinary and inert—full of such lines as "So we reveal our status", "yet he was not out of place / but perfectly at home", or "we are at the crossroads, / but the tide is turning", or "here is the alchemist's key, / it unlocks secret doors", or "what new light can you possibly / throw upon them?"

In the first poem a section attacks the poetic for exactly what H. D. herself proffers, "disagreeable, inconsequent syllables . . . under-definitive". . . . All in all, it is not that these poems are ludicrous, only that they are, as poems, colourless, tasteless, insensitive, unearthy, indefinitive, bare, and useless. They are only length and wordage.

> *"Maximum Dilution," in* The Times Literary Supplement (© *Times Newspapers Ltd., 1974; reproduced from* The Times Literary Supplement *by permission), March 15, 1974, p. 267.*

Which phase of H. D.'s poetry one likes best is perhaps a matter of taste. All her work is of a very superior, possibly the most superior, order, transcending questions of merely technical success or failure; this much is clear. Hence one's judgment rests on intangibles and is subjective and variable. For my part her early poems have sometimes seemed *too* well written and *too* exactly conceived to be altogether convincing—since perfection of a kind does verge on preciosity—while her late poems, searching deeper into the configurations of her private spiritual and cultural vision, have seemed too specialized, though this last is surely a function of the literary epoch and not of the poems themselves: one has simply been subjected to more of these great mythological collocations than one can absorb, each with its new burden of the unknown and its straining for coherence. I have preferred her war-time poems. Now, having just reread them [in *Trilogy*], I feel justified in my preference, though I emphasize that it is not a point I should wish to insist on and that all her poems, when looked at from another angle of vision, undoubtedly do make a consistent progression from first to last, in spite of the gaps of time which occurred in her writing of them. (p. 308)

The three poems [*The Walls Do Not Fall, Tribute to the Angels,* and *The Flowering of the Rod*], written so closely after one another, written with great speed and in the heat of a particular moment of vision, make a complex but single thrust of the poet's imagination, and they are well enough integrated; if by nothing else, then by the quality of her writing. (pp. 308-09)

In short, writing under the pressure of war in London, the bombs falling around her, H. D. brought together all her powers in one marvelous synthesis: her verbal power in its superbly workable maturity, her spiritual and cognitive powers, the power of her concern for the humanity of the world. (p. 311)

> *Hayden Carruth, in* The Hudson Review *(copyright © 1974 by The Hudson Review, Inc.; reprinted by permission), Vol. XXVII, No. 2, Summer, 1974.*

The genesis of *Trilogy* lies in the catalytic effect on H. D. of living in war-time London: in that sense, although the poems carry no impedimenta of that period at all in their imagery, Trilogy grows out of the threat of violence and the sense of a shared destruction, particularly with the civilisation of ancient Egypt. Her sense of living at a turning point in time led her to these meditations on the nature of the poet's role, the correspondences between Christian belief and the Egyptian pantheon, the presences of the spiritual world and the healing and unifying visions of reconciliation. She attempts to find answers, in her own symbolic terms, to the eternal questions: Where do we come from? What are we doing here? Where are we going? Her intensities move towards the unity expressed at the close of *Little Gidding,* where 'the fire and the rose are one.' . . . Technically [the first section, *The Walls Do Not Fall,*] is built, as the two subsequent sections are, out of a linked sequence of numbered lyrical passages. Each passage is written in unrhymed couplets or triplets and each wanders down to a final full-stop, usually its first. H. D. can handle this form with unmistakable power . . . , but too frequently the tensions drop, and the language falls into flat dogmatic statement or that vague abstraction of imagery which is the danger of symbolic discourse. Sword, word, cup, wheat, Lamb . . . such words, which seem to certain temperaments the basic vocabulary of spiritual wisdom, lose their numen if handled as counters and embodied in language itself flaccid. A further danger H. D. does not always escape is to write in the tone of the adept, the secret-sharer, the citizen of a world which issues few visas to travellers and where the poets (of her own persuasion) are the spiritual aristocracy. (pp. 40-2)

There is a kind of mandarin spirituality here which opposes itself to worlds of utility and common sense, and which hardly cares to be fair to them. . . . *Trilogy* could, at times, do with more of the H. D. . . . and rather less of such tricksy etymological juggling in the name of spiritual correlation as the identification of the Egyptian Amen-Ra with the Hebrew Amen.

The second section, *Tribute To The Angels,* combines the arcane and the simple; the arcane element derives largely from the Book of Revelation, and elaborates on John's an-

gelology and the themes of guardianship and power. More beautiful and direct are H. D.'s own images for a world poised between death and resurrection. (pp. 42-3)

The final sequence, *The Flowering of The Rod,* which brings the work to reconciliation, is the strongest and most coherent. The dedication to spiritual truth is imaged in the action of Mary Magdalene in anointing Christ's feet. Her myrrh comes from Kaspar, who as Mage had brought his other jar to Bethlehem. In the interplay and resolutions of this fable comes, unlooked-for, a redemptive vision for Kaspar and an interlocking of ends and beginnings. . . . *Trilogy* grows purer and more concentrated after a rather quirky and shaky start, and there are passages of grave and fluent beauty. Perhaps the major failing is that H. D. shows little concern with changes of pitch and tone, and the lack of technical variety leads to a kind of crystalline monotone throughout.

Archibald MacLeish, writing of St-John Perse, said that '. . . the farther a poet lets himself go into the world of the mysterious—the farther he follows . . . those paths which lead by analogy, by association of ideas, by the echo of one word with another, into the undiscovered and yet ancient continent—the farther he penetrates that country, the greater becomes his need of memory and will.' *Trilogy* is a map of such a country, but the world discovered there is a world of silences, cut-glass, embroidery and enamelling: a world where a drink is distilled too pure to quench thirst. The roughness and intractability of life is worked in silk. Antaeus could, perhaps, have taught her more than Osiris. (pp. 43-4)

> *Peter Scupham, "H. D.," in* Agenda, *Autumn, 1974, pp. 40-4.*

H. D. is one of the most elusive writers of the century, and she has in fact eluded many readers who might find pleasure in her work. Her work is scattered among a score of volumes, most of them slight. There is no *Collected Poems;* the volume so named dates from 1925 and most of her best work was done after that. The work itself is elusive, and the reader might easily wonder, when he has run some slim volume to earth, whether he has really caught anything. In fact he has, if he can hold it. It is tenuous but not absolutely a ghost. A living spirit, running like quicksilver among sparse verses. (p. 85)

There was no doubt a great awareness, among the more teachable in Pound's circle, of the web of interrelationship in Renaissance literature, Italian, French and English, and of their dependence on Greek and Latin originals. . . . This background is to be remembered in considering the work of H. D. People say 'Imagist' and they say 'Greek' when her name is mentioned. They should think also of the Renaissance—Pater's as well as Spenser's—and recall that T. E. Hulme, who was killed in 1917, had made a case for thinking that the significant work of the twentieth century would turn its back on that period. It is not to the anti-humanistic art which Hulme saw or foresaw that H. D.'s work belongs. Nor does it belong to that movement of taste which has put Donne so near the centre of our understanding of the seventeenth century and displaced the more pastoral Elizabethans, including Spenser himself. (pp. 85-6)

However harmless, or even useful, when it was first applied, the [Imagist] label has certainly served to obscure the nature of H. D.'s development. There is, even in [the] early verses, a psychological as well as an objective element. The rapidity of movement answers to a breathless apprehension of the external world. . . .

H. D.'s early work is well illustrated—and readily accessible—in Peter Jones's Penguin, *Imagist Poetry*. It is evidence of the high degree of training of which her temperament made her capable. A person so fastidious as she was was no doubt glad of a formula which relieved her of the necessity of saying more than she had to say, and invited her to efface herself before appearances. (p. 86)

[*Bid Me to Live*, her autobiographical novel,] is certainly unusual in its kind. There is none of the fluttering and showing off of *The Waves*—if Virginia Woolf's book is to be included as another uncharacteristic member of the *genre*. There is none of the special pleading inseparable from D. H. Lawrence's recordings. Most of the book shows a quiet, almost withdrawn, observation. H. D. carries her fastidiousness into the midst of the most personal observation. There are many—all too many—books of reminiscences by women who have slept with or otherwise known writers of notoriety enough to make the reminiscences publishable. They are usually horrible, less for what they record than for the lack of perception they betray. It needs more talent to venture into a book than into a bed. One peculiarity of the H. D. book, which indeed makes it unique, is that the observer is herself a woman of original, and not merely reflected, literary talent. Her observation may be partial but it is veridical. (p. 87)

On a small scale, much of the work in *Hymen* has considerable formal merit. There is the imagist trick, learned long before. There is also what is perhaps best described as a sort of rhetoric, elegant enough, but which leaves the reader in the end with a sense of emptiness. (p. 88)

Pound talked of 'Hellenic hardness' in connection with H. D.'s work. There is certainly a persistent use of Greek sources, and of Greek allusions. . . . Behind this there was no doubt a good deal of work. . . . [The] impression left by much of H. D.'s earlier work is, after all, of a certain emptiness, as if not much was found in all this fumbling among Greek deities and Greek islands. The elegance of manner is often striking, and it is no small thing. But the twentieth century is not a happy time for a writer who has formal gifts but has to seek his material. So many conventions have become unusable. H. D.'s notes on Elizabethan and seventeenth-century poets, in the prose part of *By Avon River*, indicate where her sympathies lie. Her taste, sure in its way, veers from the more energetic poetry to the more formal celebration of beauty and death. There is, in her own work of this period, a lack of intellectual content. (pp. 88-9)

There is a marked development in depth in the later poems, in particular the (second) wartime sequence of *The Walls Do Not Fall*, *Tribute to Angels*, and *The Flowering of the Rod* and the poems in *Hermetic Definition*. The long poem *Helen in Egypt* (1961), has its place in H. D.'s *oeuvre* but is less satisfactory, truth to tell, partly on account of its length. There is a surging to and fro over the legend of Helen—that she was in Egypt and that only an illusion appeared on the walls of Troy. That the confusions of H. D.'s own past are as much in her mind as the fate of Helen could not be in doubt for anyone who has read her work at all extensively. There are passages between Helen and Achilles which are certainly not free of allusion to the personal history recorded in *Bid Me to Live*. The successful long poem is an extreme rarity, and one can say of H. D.'s attempt that it is creditably near to a style in which a long poem *could* be written in the twentieth century—the long

poem conceived not as having, on an impossible scale, the quickening of the lyric but the combination of sobriety and movement which carries us on in Drayton or in Golding. But H. D.'s poem, as a whole, has not quite these qualities. The impression is often of a mulling over of old worries—and old Greeks—and the sense of direction is not sustained.

The change in the character of H. D.'s later work, as compared with the earlier, may be related to her exploration of those distresses which took her to Vienna as a patient of Freud in 1933-4. . . . H. D.'s interest in Greece took her back to Egypt and muddling among the pattern of ancient mysteries, so obscurely known as to allow more room for fantasy than Christian theology, with its vulgar links with rationalism and the crudities of social structure. H. D. carried her interest in magic and ancient mumbo-jumbo into the world of her analyst. . . . [*Tribute to Freud*] is a masterpiece of its kind, accurate and inconclusive, the work of an observer immensely gifted and profoundly trained to record her impressions. It is a little classic in its own right, however one may rate the contribution it can offer to the understanding of H. D.'s verse.

The verse of the later period is continuously concerned with interpretation of experience by the dark help afforded by ancient cults. There is, however, much of a more overt and accessible character. (pp. 89-90)

The poems in *Hermetic Definition* take up a number of themes. . . . But the life of these poems—what makes them unique, perhaps—is the delineation, with the precision her long training allowed her, of the reflections of an old woman, still thinking of love, still with her habitual lack of restraint as to what needs to be said, and complete restraint as to what does not. (pp. 90-1)

Where does one place H. D.? It is perhaps imprudent to try to place her firmly in relation to her contemporaries. Her preoccupations, as well as the superficial severity of her verse, have kept her out of the main flow of interest. The Greek carapace may seem forbidding. But it should not be. In her essence H. D. is a slight, extremely feminine figure, whose battles are all inward, and who scarcely sought to link her thought with the public preoccupations of the age. She lived obscurely with the illusion—which is not entirely an illusion—that if the artist gets on with his art all will be well. For her this was not a personal thing, but a thing which took her, through and beyond current social necessities—as she saw it—to the permanent concerns embodied in the ancient religions, including our own. The connections she established were exploratory, not dogmatic. The point for the prospective reader is merely that H. D. offers far more than the formal virtues which are usually allowed to her work, and that that work abundantly repays the not very strenuous labour of reading it. (p. 91)

C. H. Sisson, "H. D.," in Poetry Nation *(© Poetry Nation 1975), No. 4, 1975, pp. 85-91 (the full text of this essay appears in C. H. Sisson's* Collected Essays, *Carcanet Press, Manchester, England).*

* * *

HALEY, Alex 1921-

An American journalist, essayist, and historical novelist, Haley first earned his reputation as a prominent black writer in the mid-1960s with the publication of his *The Autobiography of Malcolm X*. Haley's next major effort, *Roots*, required twelve years of intense personal research in the United States

and Africa, and it is the enormously successful chronicle of his own family's history from slavery to freedom.

The world of ["Roots"] begins in Gambia West Africa in 1750 with the birth of one of [Haley's] ancestors, Kunta Kinte, born of Omoro and Binta Kinte, of the Mandinka tribe, and of the Muslim faith. In the re-creation of this time and place, Haley succeeds beautifully where many have failed. He must have studied and sweated hard to achieve such ease and grace, for he would appear to have been born in his ancestral village and to be personally acquainted with everybody there. The public ceremonies of this people are revealed as a precise and coherent mirror of their private and yet connected imaginations. (p. 1)

We know that Kunta will be kidnapped, and brought to America, and yet, we have become so engrossed in his life in the village, and so fond of him, that the moment comes as a terrible shock. We, too, would like to kill his abductors. We are in his skin, and in his darkness, and, presently, we are shackled with him, in his terror, rage, and pain, his stink, and the stink of others, on the ship which brings him here. It can be said that we know the rest of the story— how it turned out, so to speak, but frankly, I don't think that we do know the rest of the story. It *hasn't* turned out yet, which is the rage and pain and danger of this country. Alex Haley's taking us back through time to the village of his ancestors is an act of faith and courage, but this book is also an act of love, and it is this which makes it haunting.

The density of the African social setting eventually gives way to the shrill incoherence of the American one. Haley makes no comment on this contrast, there being indeed none to make, apart from that made by the remarkable people we meet on these shores, who, born here, are yet striving, as the song puts it, "to make it my home."

The American setting is as familiar as the back of one's hand. Yet, as Haley's story unfolds, the landscape begins to be terrifying, unutterably strange and bleak, a cloud hanging over it day and night. Without ever seeming to, and with a compassion as haunting as the sorrow songs which helped produce him, Haley makes us aware of the disaster overtaking not the black nation, but the white one. . . .

"Roots" is a study of continuities, of consequences, of how a people perpetuate themselves, how each generation helps to doom, or helps to liberate, the coming one—the action of love, or the effect of the absence of love, in time. It suggests, with great power, how each of us, however unconsciously, can't but be the vehicle of the history which has produced us. (p. 2)

> *James Baldwin, "How One Black Man Came to Be an American," in* The New York Times Book Review *(© 1976 by The New York Times Company; reprinted by permission), September 26, 1976, pp. 1-2.*

It was in the midst of [the] mass assertion of black/African identity that a remarkable literary claim made the international press: Alex Haley, a writer who was greatly admired for his meticulous rendering of *The Autobiography of Malcolm X,* actually had traced his ancestry back to Juffure, a village in The Gambia, to the very captive slave who started Haley's family in America. . . .

It was a unique claim. . . . The odds were so against it. More than 40 million Africans had been dragged off the Continent over a period of 300 years. The African diaspora now spread clear around the globe. . . . Had the claim been

made by anyone with a reputation less than that of Alex Haley, it would have been dismissed out of hand as an inevitable fanciful claim of the sort born in cultural revolution. And when years passed without anything between hard covers, tongues wagged and jokes were common about Haley's claim.

Now, a decade after his story first made the papers, Alex Haley's *Roots* is a reality. The book is here to be judged for itself. I picked it up in suspicion and put it down so overcome by the power of the narrative that my first reaction was to wonder how much it mattered whether every detail of Haley's lineage had been precisely established. Overwhelmingly, this is the story of how Africans became Afro-Americans; the connection Haley seeks to make gives the narrative a certain tension that would be difficult to maintain otherwise, but I found myself not really caring as much about that as about an extremely engaging young Mandingo named Kunta Kinte who was stolen from the outskirts of his village at the age of 17 and shipped across the middle passage. I have read a bit of village life and about the middle passage, but never has either been brought to full-life scale as in the masterful hands of Alex Haley. And by the end, as he tells how he made all the connections necessary to establish that Kunta Kinte was his ancestor, I found myself persuaded of his claim. I would have preferred a book loaded with footnotes and other documentation, but that is not this book. I am told . . . that Haley's next book, *The Search for Roots,* will provide us with detailed resource material. What is surprising to me now is how much less important that documentation became as I moved through the story of seven generations of a family. I found myself disturbed by something, but lack of documentation wasn't it.

I kept wondering whether there are large number of black people in America today who feel they would like to trace their genealogy as Haley has—to find the place where their ancestors were held as slaves, and work their way back and back until they came to some village in Dahomey or Ghana or Senegal and looked some villager in the face in the conviction that but for the brutal advent of slavery, this might be immediate kin. The reason that question disturbs me is the awareness of the pain so many people feel at the realization of how much of their past has been—and continues to be—robbed. (p. 1)

Haley's accomplishment is a far-fetched dream for practically all Afro-Americans. We are African villagers no more, but part of a unique formation in history, the Afro-American people.

Just as Haley says, we began on the slender shoulders of such as Kunta Kinte. . . . Very few of those in the African diaspora, whether Afro-Cuban or Afro-American, have been able to thread back through the maze to a specific point of origin. Since that number is so small, Haley means for this book to stand as all our story, a summary of all our experience, not just the story of his own family. And so it does, while taking nothing away from those of us who cannot duplicate the feat. The more important point is that black Americans and all Americans will find in Kunta Kinte the personalization of a slavery whose dimensions are so monstrous that its full meaning can be only approximated through the moving account of one person. It is in that sense that this book is bound to have a lasting impact on American culture. It was worth the wait. (p. 2)

> *Robert C. Maynard, "The Making of an*

American," in Book World—The Washington Post (© The Washington Post*), September 26, 1976, pp. 1-2.*

Roots: The Saga of an American Family is [Alex] Haley's memorial to [the] past. (p. 109)

[The book] most closely resembles a historical novel, a form that Haley does not seem to have studied too carefully. His narrative is a blend of dramatic and melodramatic fiction and fact that wells from a profound need to nourish himself with a comprehensible past. Haley recreates the Old South of mansions and slave shacks, fully aware that chains and blood ties were at times indistinguishable. The book dramatically details slave family life—birth, courtship, marriage ("jumping the broom"), death and the ever present fear of being sold off and having to leave your kin. (p. 109, K11)

In general, the more verified facts that Haley has to work with, the more wooden and cluttered his narrative. Yet the story of the Americanization of the Kinte clan strikes enough human chords to sustain the book's cumulative power. Haley's keen sense of separation and loss, and his ability to forge a return in language, override *Roots'* considerable structural and stylistic flaws. The book should find a permanent home in a century teeming with physical and spiritual exiles. (p. K15)

R. Z. Sheppard, "African Genesis," in Time *(reprinted by permission from* Time, The Weekly Newsmagazine; *copyright Time Inc. 1976), October 18, 1976, pp. 109, K11, K15.*

When asked whether and how true *Roots* is to life, Haley is reported to have responded that it is "factional," a strange term that suggests that the primary incidents and historical moments are true, but that in reconstructing the emotions of his personalities in the grip of their fates, in supposing their motives, indeed, in filling their mouths with conversation, he has done the best he could, as other writers of historical fiction try to do.

Roots is not precisely a historical novel, because the main carriers of the story were indeed true people. Although it is clear that Haley has few specific facts about the three Africans, Omoro, Binta, and Kunta, even they are more than exclusive constructions of the author's imagination. Nevertheless there is as much fiction as fact in *Roots,* some of it designed to lift the spirit, some to amuse, and all of it to tell the collective story of a people. *Roots* hasn't the plot of a novel but in following the generations it has instead the spirit as well as the form of a saga. . . .

Haley has no trouble beginning his saga, and getting it moving. But the problem of characterizing the individual people of so many generations, of making more than a score of persons come alive in the special circumstances of two vastly different cultures, and over a span of two centuries, challenges Haley the artist, and taxes Haley the historian. There are long sections in the book that will cause the historian to call *Roots* fiction, when literary critics may prefer to call it history rather than judge it as art. For *Roots* is long and ambitious, and all of its parts are not as good as the best parts.

The splendid opening section on African life is beautifully realized. It is an *artistic* success. But that the real Juffure of two hundred years ago was anything like the pastoral village Haley describes is not possible. (p. 3)

Conveying the passage of time becomes a serious problem, both aesthetically and historically, after Kunta Kinte reaches America. Haley writes with power, and often with lyrical effect, but his feeling for the probable talk of slaves is often marred by a too-exposed mechanical purpose. He puts these conversations up to little lessons in history that are more distracting than informative. He has difficulty showing how the information picked up at the white man's dinner table, or from the driver's seat of the massa's buggy, or from a surreptitiously read newspaper, is relayed in the kitchen and the quarters. . . .

Kunta Kinte's own life poses no such problems about time for Haley, for the process of assimilation is one of the strongest and subtlest themes in *Roots*. For the miseries of Kunta in the land of "*toubob*" (white man), the reader will not only feel a vivid sympathy; he may even laugh a little at the incomprehensible ways of Kunta's captors. . . . Especially effective is the inner contempt the African hero (for that is his role) feels for those of his color who shuffle and scrape when they say "Yassuh, Massa." Those who had learned this manner of dealing with power returned Kunta's contempt with a predictable suspicion, for they saw in the African's wild ways the courage of desperation, and its dangers.

It is all convincing, for we are made to feel that inevitably this is how things happened. . . .

But the account of the external conditions in which Kunta lives in Virginia before, during, and after the American Revolution is disconcerting. The reader of any basic book on Southern history will be startled to learn that Kunta was put to work picking cotton in northern Virginia before the Revolution (or ever, really), under the whip of an overseer, in fields loaded with the white stuff "as far as Kunta could see." Surely this is Alabama in 1850, and not Spotsylvania County, Virginia, in 1767. . . .

These anachronisms are petty only in that they are details. They are too numerous, and chip away at the verisimilitude of central matters in which it is important to have full faith. . . .

Haley's sense of historical setting becomes more surefooted in the pre-Civil War decades, and after Reconstruction, when the whole family moves under the guidance of the steady blacksmith Tom to Henning, Tennessee. . . . Sagas must have many persons and many stories, many deeds. But there should be one dominant soul, and in *Roots* it is Kunta Kinte, whose gloomy intelligence inspires the action through three-fifths of the work. Kunta's final departure from the book (and not by death) is its most poignant moment, and the subtlest statement on the finality of slavery that this reviewer has read. (p. 4)

Willie Lee Rose, "An American Family," in The New York Review of Books *(reprinted with permission from* The New York Review of Books; *copyright © 1976 NYREV, Inc.), November 11, 1976, pp. 3-4, 6.*

Prior to its publication date, [*Roots*] was billed as "an epic work destined to become a classic of American literature." Upon a perusal of *Roots*, it is clear that this advance judgment was not far off track. Haley has managed to weave incredible details about West Africa during the 1750s—the cultural habits, values, rituals, and myths of the people—

into a narrative. This mode of historical recall seems to be as valid as any other one might think of, but it does raise some questions: How much of the narrative is historically accurate? How much of it is the result of Haley's fictional plotting? These questions vary in importance, depending, of course, on the perspective of the reader—that is, whether the reader is interested in the book as historical record of Haley's lineage, or if he is interested in it as a symbolic attempt to capture the lost heritage of Afro-Americans. Insofar as I am concerned, the first perspective is not a valuable one, as it shares in common many of the problems which surround the search for the historical Jesus. The latter vantage point, however, comes closer to seeing *Roots* in terms of its significance to Afro-Americans, to cultural historians, and to American civilization.

Within this latter perspective, it is important to take into account the manner in which Haley chooses to tell the story. He borrows techniques from the novelist—setting, narrative voice, flashback—to give his story imaginative form. Specifically, Haley tells the story from the perspective of an omniscient narrator. This gives the narrative an authoritative posture, and brings the reader closer to an intimate understanding of the culture of West Africa in 1750, of the physical and psychological problems incurred by, first, kidnapping Africans, second, transporting them in an inhumane manner across the Atlantic Ocean, and, finally, selling them into slavery. This perspective also allows Haley to interweave historical facts together with fictionalizations in fluid prose. There is one unfortunate side effect in all of this: When Haley finally moves the reader through the various generations of his clan to the point where he is born . . . , his narrative voice shifts suddenly from omniscient narrator to that of first-person participant. The last two chapters of the book relate the process by which Haley became intimately involved with the project, and by which he came to discover the story he tells in the book. This sudden change affects the unity of the story; the narrative may be construed at this point as discontinuous and sketchy. That there are one hundred and twenty chapters in *Roots* adds to this problem.

Yet these objections to Haley's process are not enough to devalue *Roots* as history, as literature, or otherwise. This book stands as the first thorough attempt by an Afro-American to come to terms with his African heritage. Its significance to scholars and critics is that it solidifies the view that African oral traditions are rigid cultural forms; that they are valid historical records. (pp. 98-9)

> *Chester J. Fontenot, "Radical Upbringing," in* Prairie Schooner *(© 1977 by University of Nebraska Press; reprinted by permission from* Prairie Schooner*), Spring, 1977, pp. 98-9.*

*   *   *

HANDKE, Peter   1942-

Austrian-born novelist, playwright, poet, and essayist, Handke emerged in the sixties as the leading practitioner of the experimental novel in Germany. Then, with the translation of *The Goalie's Anxiety at the Penalty Kick,* **Handke's literary reputation took hold in America. To date, he has had five plays published in this country. Handke's novels reveal the influence of the existentialists, particularly Sartre, while aspects of the French "new novel" are also discernible in some of his writings. (See also** *CLC,* **Vol. 5.)**

Human loneliness, human identity and personality, memory, feelings, indoctrination—all these emerge as leading themes in [*Die Unvernunftigen Sterben aus*], which is set in a modern business world totally stripped of every human and humanitarian element. In extremely fast-moving dialogues periodically interrupted by obscenities, economic practices designed to tighten control of the market and the consumer are discussed with a ring of reality and brutality by a group of businessmen. . . . The realistic details and factual discussions . . . take on a grotesque and phantasmagoric air, conveying through Handke's "assembled sentences" the breakdown of personality in characters that are motivated by the dictates of business and are only residues of what once were men.

[They] also discuss feelings, but these are material for dreams and leisure time and would ruin their financial world if not transformed into business methods. [Handke shows their] inner emptiness and inability to communicate on any human level other than that of business. . . .

Handke apparently demonstrates this time that personality is in danger, if not obsolete or lost altogether, in a class that possesses power. (p. 315)

> *Maria Luise Caputo-Mayr, in* Books Abroad *(copyright 1975 by the University of Oklahoma Press), Vol. 49, No. 2, Spring, 1975.*

A Sorrow Beyond Dreams is Peter Handke's precise, inspired tribute to his mother who killed herself at the age of fifty-one. Subtitled *A Life Story,* the book is spare, less than seventy pages, but as rich in its configurations as a Brancusi or Balanchine's *Movements for Piano and Orchestra.* Handke, who is always coolly brilliant, is here full of an emotional purpose: his sorrow. The arresting intellectual games of his plays and his two previous novels are beside the point. . . . Handke is so absorbed in the definition of his mother's life he is self-effacing, untroubled, in the writing of it. He argues nicely that his mother's unique story can only be of interest to him, and when he extends his theme the individual is forgotten—"like images in a dream, phrases and sentences enter into a chain reaction, and the result is a literary ritual in which an individual life ceases to be anything more than a pretext."

A good point, and one that he takes to heart. None of his theories in *A Sorrow Beyond Dreams* takes up much room. They never exist as the author's explorations by and about himself. They compose the mimetic line. . . . Handke's speechlessness in the face of [his mother's] sorrow and his, brings him to write this memoir. His feelings become so palpably close to hers that he tells us "I experience them as doubles and am identical with them. . . ."

The only poetic lament that compares to Handke's is Allen Ginsberg's *Kaddish.* Peter Handke's tone is reserved, the cadence strict as tears held back, but the sense of bringing the dead mother to life through communion with the son's voice is as strong. If the religious wailing of Ginsberg has moved us, I believe we will be equally moved by Handke's sacred rationale. (pp. 409-11)

> *Maureen Howard, in* The Yale Review *(© 1976 by Yale University; reprinted by permission of the editors), Spring, 1976.*

Handke is generally unknown to American audiences and students of the drama; his plays have baffled and antagonized American critics who, for the most part, have grasped neither the radicalism of his theatre nor its contemporary significance. (p. 52)

Handke's creation of the *Sprechstücke* (translated into English as "speak-in") is his original contribution to dramatic form. The five speak-ins he has written (*Offending the Audience, Self-Accusation, Prophecy, Calling for Help,* and *Quodlibet*) are not plays as we are used to defining them but virtually public addresses to an audience. Non-representational in their approach, they are *completely lacking in stage pictures* but are instead composed of incantatory words. Frequently they are simply language games; dialogue is entirely absent. They are presented by performers who function as "speakers" rather than actors playing roles.

The creation of speakers is crucial to the conception of the *Sprechstücke* because it allows Handke to eliminate from the drama character which is necessarily limited by a linguistic structure (dialogue), and to give full play instead to the presentation of words-in-freedom. Thus, *Sprechstücke* lack setting, plot, dialogue, and character—all the elements of traditional drama.

A chief component of the speak-ins are "ready-mades" (like the "found" objects in painting and sculpture), material from the language of daily existence: maxims, honorifics, slogans, officialese, advertisements, greetings, etc. With these language materials Handke has constructed a kind of literary environmental art in which the dramatic structure demonstrates the regimentation of the individual by his language-conditioned perceptions. Like many twentieth century artists, Handke recycles "popular" forms to create a work of radical art. His is an art of radical juxtaposition—a collage of "found" words which carries on an inner dialogue with the newly created structure of words (speak-in). What Handke has done, in effect, is take the language of an ordered reality and turn it on itself to provide a critique of reality, with the speakers functioning as negative physiognomies on which Handke "writes" the contradictions of human behavior.

From the recognizable language of reality presented by the speakers the spectator can extract the proclamations that pertain to his existence. The link, therefore, is anthropological—all members of a given society are checked within its linguistic perimeters. The presence of the audience is the *sine qua non* of the *Sprechstücke*. "They need a vis-a-vis, at least *one* person who listens; otherwise they would not be natural but extorted by the author," Handke says. (pp. 52-3)

The audience is as important as the speakers in the *Sprechstücke,* particularly in the participatory language games that compromise *Calling for Help* and *Quodlibet.* In *Calling for Help* (1967) several speakers—and the audience—play at trying to guess the word "help" which is being sought. Built on the principle of collage it is a collection of sentences, phrases and words—a series of clues conveyed by the speakers (as in the game "Password")—clearly recognizable from ordinary social discourse.

In this brief linguistic construct speakers only play the need for help acoustically, that is, by varying the deliverance of the clues to the word. Though they need help in finding the word "help," once they have found it they no longer need "help"—the word has lost its meaning. *Calling for Help* is grounded in the neo-Positivism of Wittgenstein who viewed the use of language as the playing of language games in which meaning is contained in the use of the word. . . . Handke, like Wittgenstein, has turned language inside out and measured it against reality. In *The Ride Across Lake Constance* (1971) in which a part of the discussion centers on naming emotions that derive from familiar poses, he seems to be carrying on his own philosophical investigations—and in Wittgenstein's familiar question and answer format!

Quodlibet (1969), like *Calling for Help,* is a word game. Both pieces operate on the principle of association. They put forth word and sentence clues—codes—which trigger certain predictable (often automatic) responses in the audience. Both pieces have musical as well as game structures. Aural tableaux, crescendo and decrescendo patterns, fluctuations in pitch and tempo—in general, the orchestration of sound—define their presentation.

Quodlibet, more expansive than the essentially one joke *Calling for Help,* is a highly sophisticated "play on words" which offers those whom Handke calls "figures of world theatre" (general, bishop, politician, etc.) in random social intercourse. The audience (over) hears only bits and pieces of their conversations, enough to let the imagination run wild with associations. (pp. 53-4)

From the cliches and repeated expressions of political, sexual and social attitudes, the speakers' improvisational "assemblage" of personal stories and perceptions, and news from daily papers, a picture of (false) reality is created in the audience's imagination—by the audience. Of all the *Sprechstücke Quodlibet* is the one which most demands the audience's active participation; its open structure allows the audience to enter it and actually partake of its presentation. No two people will experience it in the same way. Hence, Handke's playful Latin title "Quodlibet" which, translated into English, means "as it pleases you."

Prophecy (1966) doesn't offer the multiplicity of experience that the more complicated *Quodlibet* does, but is instead a simplified example of Handke's characteristic serialism (the dominant style of his dramatic works and poetry). (pp. 54-5)

Self-Accusation (1966) extends beyond the limitations of a language game and the fundamentally simple proof that language is an inept tool of communication to demonstrate the socialization of the individual through his acquisition of language. In this speak-in the theme of domination-submission, the focus of full-length plays *My Foot My Tutor* (1968), *Kaspar* (1967) and *The Ride Across Lake Constance* (1971), is expressed in the structure itself. The message *is* the structure of the play, and it unfolds as it traces the movement of the individual from the beginning of consciousness to the loss of it through social regimentation. . . .

Between the first and second parts there is a refrain of twenty-eight questions exposing possible violations against the state and social order. This refrain—a verbal aria in which all questions but one end with the word "violate"—bears the same relationship to the whole structure of the speak-in as the songs in a Brechtian *Lehrstück* do to its entire structure. As the dialectical frame of the piece it expands the themes and perspectives of the text, and breaks the flow of the piece by turning from the declarative sentence to the question form. By throwing the problems of the speak-in into relief, as it were, it also singles out the dominant issues of the structure. (p. 55)

In their focus on either the relationship of the audience to the theatre event, or the relationship of reality to the language an individual uses to describe it, *Sprechstücke* are essentially consciousness-raising pieces. They attempt not so much to revolutionize the audience, but to make the audience *aware*. They are concerned more with the thinking process than ideas.

Sprechstücke are didactic in the broad sense of the term but Handke, unlike Brecht, does not suggest solutions to social problems. He merely presents the problem. (p. 56)

Handke it seems has taken a more subtle, cerebral step forward from Brecht's *Lehrstück*, the dramatic antecedent of the *Sprechstücke*. Both forms of drama are "teaching plays," yet one important difference between Brecht and Handke is in each's use of the dialectic. In Brecht's work the dialectic operates within a montage of images; in Handke's it functions in a collage of words. In Brechtian dramaturgy the dialectic remains in the sphere of the stage and the characters on it whereas Handke has situated the dialectic in the relationship of the audience to the stage itself, further radicalizing the theatre event and consciously activating moment-to-moment audience response. Finally, if Brecht formalized situations drawn from reality, Handke merely formalizes the language of reality. (p. 57)

[Peter] Weiss is the link from Brecht to Handke; each has progressively taken character out of the drama and put history in its place, and in the process stripped away the dialogue. But, Brecht and Weiss never abandoned the illustration of a narrative on stage to point out social contradictions. They always use images to complement or contradict the language in their plays. The most radical of the three, Handke creates a "picture" of social contradictions entirely through words: his is not a theatre of images but a universe of words. . . . It is also interesting to note that in their attempt to devise a non-literary drama—and renovate the notion of dialogue—all three dramatists turned to musical structures, each to varying degrees.

Of the three Handke is the most concerned with man as an existential rather than political being. He enlists the aid of language to expose the existential situation of all individuals in society which reduces reality to words. More subtle in effect than the plays of Ionesco, Handke's plays, nevertheless, make one aware, through their evocation of the platitude, that language is incapable of serving as a sure mode of communication, that it, in fact, distorts reality.

Handke carries this line of thinking to its *reductio ad absurdum* conclusion in his full length play *Kaspar* by dramatizing the disintegration of its hero through his mastery of language. When one compares *Kaspar* to *Self-Accusation* the latter seems a more hopeful work simply because it dwells on an awareness of the situation rather than demonstrating its tragic end. Partly, however, *Kaspar* carries on the confessional mode of *Self-Accusation*. (pp. 58-9)

In the American theatre, the work of Richard Foreman (Ontological-Hysteric Theater) parallels Handke's in several ways. Both write dialogue-less (totally self-referring) consciousness-raising pieces which attempt to make the audience aware of the theatre event while experiencing it. Built into their pieces is an inner dialogue with the history of Western theatre. Both use characterless characters—actors as mouthpieces of the author—in a lecture-demonstration form: Handke is concerned with the acquisition of language, Foreman with the acquisition of knowledge. Both have situated the dialectic in the relationship of the audience to the theatre event. Where Handke and Foreman

differ—and this point separates Handke from both his predecessors and contemporaries—is the latter's highly image-oriented theatre, and the former's refusal to create images in his *Sprechstücke*. (pp. 59-60)

Handke's work easily identifies him with the rebellious youth of the rock generation. His "Rules for the Actors" which precedes *Offending the Audience* mocks Brecht's stricter Rules. Instead of analyzing acting techniques, he suggests that before performing the speak-in actors should listen to certain Beatles' songs, to chanting at demonstrations, to street noises, etc. All of his "Rules" have to do with becoming aware of acoustical textures in social situations. From this vantage point Handke seems very close to the aesthetics of John Cage in suggesting that noise form the basis of the "music" of *Offending the Audience*.

There is even a trace of Dadaist good humor in the piece. . . . Notwithstanding, it is only fair to state that Handke's philosophical temperament is far removed from that of the Dadaists, though his abuse or shock of the audience has aesthetic antecedents in Dadaist performance. But, Handke is much too serious, his pieces too schematic to be content with mere offense against the audience. He gives his audiences much more—a framework for philosophical thought.

Indeed Handke's rigorous intellect is among the best we have in contemporary theatre, his plays among the most important in post-Beckettian drama. In their uncompromising look at the function of theatre and the audience's problematical relationship to it, and their vigorous examination of language at its deepest and most subtle levels, Peter Handke has given us new dramatic form and a new mode of consciousness as well. (pp. 60-1)

> *Bonnie Marranca, "The 'Sprechstücke':*
> *Peter Handke's Universe of Words," in* Performing Arts Journal *(© copyright 1976 Performing Arts Journal), Fall, 1976, pp. 52-66.*

Manheim has been a bit tender toward American readers' feelings in his translation of the title [*A Sorrow beyond Dreams*]: A *Wunschloses Unglueck* is not a sorrow worse than anything you ever dreamed of ("dreams," though not strictly inaccurate, is the misleading word), but the nicest sorrow you could possibly ask for. "A Satisfying Misfortune" would be another way of translating it—a rancorously ironic title, since the volume is Handke's description of the life and suicide of his mother, written in the deepest grief as a memorial tribute to her and, as a test of the whole art of writing, i.e., of his whole occupation in life. That is the sense in which the misfortune is satisfying: What writer could ask for a better opportunity? At the same time, how can a writer be truthful to that occasion, of all others?

Two struggles take place in the book, both ferocious: One is the struggle of Handke's mother to be a person, in the face of Austrian farm society, Western marital mores, the mass pressures of Nazism, and her own inner confusions. The second is her son's struggle to put her life on paper without in some way betraying it, without turning the facts into generalities, the real woman into an archetype "eternalized" in prose, like a bronzed baby shoe.

The mother . . . weakened by childbearing (and three abortions), by a lifetime of woman-slavery, and by a nerve disease that brings spells of temporary insanity, cuts her losses and opts out of the struggle. The son, alternately dazzled and horror stricken by her choice (at one point he actually says he feels proud of her for committing suicide), goes on fighting, winning at the end the most slender and unsatisfying of victories. (The last sentence is, "Someday I will write about all this in greater detail.") In their tenacity, the two figures keep reminding me of Jung's devastating description of James Joyce and his mad daughter (in whose schizophrenic ravings Joyce found similarities to his own writing): "two people going to the bottom of river, one drowning, the other diving."

> *Michael Feingold, "One Is Drowning, the Other Diving," in* The Village Voice *(reprinted by permission of* The Village Voice; *copyright © by The Village Voice, Inc., 1977), January 24, 1977, p. 75.*

The Austrian, Peter Handke, who writes poetry, novels, plays and memoirs, is concerned with a familiar subject— the loss of authenticity or innocence. For Handke, this loss characterizes modern life. He thinks we no longer experience things directly, no longer truly feel. All our experience is mediated by cultural formulae, established ideas, clichés of language and manners. Hence, we are alienated from others and ourselves and left only with the knowledge that everything valuable is gone.

This loss of authenticity remains Handke's subject in his new novel, "A Moment of True Feeling," which, as one critic has said, is too much like Sartre's "Nausea," in its ideas, moods and sentiments. Handke's novel literally contains much that is nauseating, even a moment of truly felt vomiting. I'm not making a joke. In an obvious way, "A Moment of True Feeling" is ridiculously reminiscent of Sartre's novel. But it probably intends to be. That is, Handke probably intends his novel to be consistent with our day, fundamentally inauthentic.

Even the name of his hero, Gregor Keuschnig, recalls another hero, Kafka's Gregor Samsa, who wakes one morning to find himself metamorphosed into a dung beetle. Handke also thinks of his contemporary Gregor the way Kafka thought of his own, as a kind of loathsome psychological bug. Because Gregor thinks of himself this way, too, it must seem that if he and Handke are not exactly the same person, they are also not very different. The hypothetical man and the real writer are both understood as creatures of fiction. One lives in the novel; the other merely writes it.

Specifically, Gregor Keuschnig (notice Kafka's K) lives in Paris with his wife and child. He works as press attaché to the Austrian Embassy. One night he dreams that he has become a murderer. His whole life changes thereafter, but the plot of the novel does not in itself become more exciting. It couldn't, because it concentrates on Gregor's spiritual condition, his ennui; it is not too concerned with what wonderful things happen next. As any reader soon guesses, Gregor's dream means that he no longer loves his wife. Thereafter, he thinks, because he doesn't love her he wants her dead. Some might call this a sort of infantile omnipotence, but Handke makes his hero less a victim of unconscious logic than one who exploits such logic.

Late in the novel, when the marriage breaks up, Gregor actually says to his wife: "I want you to die." We knew that all the time. Furthermore, we suspect that Gregor's marital situation—the opposite of unusual—is a pretext, not really a plot, and it is there only to help the novel engage its proper subject, Gregor's loss of authenticity and fall into the literary condition of ennui.

Between his dream and the breakup of his marriage, Gregor ennuis around Paris and thinks about what he sees and feels in different quarters, rooms, cafés and playgrounds. His impressions and thoughts are indeed often interesting. These are the novel's chief virtues. . . .

The real order [of life] is isolation and meaningless persistence through quotidian rituals: shopping, eating, working, making nice conversation, taking care of children, etc. Marriage and everything else that speaks for human solidarity merely represents authenticity, but, according to Gregor's view, all of it is a morbid delusion, a mystification, a concession we make to death, a polite commitment to organized, expedient, lethal inauthenticity every day, every minute.

Gregor blames himself for thinking this way. He yearns for a normal life that he could authentically live. Unfortunately, he has ennui. He cannot help but gaze into the abyss with Sartre, Nietzsche, Kafka and others who presently stand at the brink, as if at some literary cocktail party, where, between groans they chat about their royalties. . . . The world is a crazy soup in which all things swim, dreaming of meaning and forever, inevitably drowning. . . . Handke hates clichés, but they are as much the object of his hatred as they are his medium. He makes them the very substance of his imagination. (p. 7)

Handke, who thinks authenticity is gone, not only feels free to imitate anyone he chooses, he might even argue that one has no choice but to imitate even when the thing said is strictly personal. In any event, he lacks Kafka's sense of humor and moral weight, and, sometimes merely flaunts a kind of adolescent petulance. Kafka manages to say terrific things terrifically. Handke at times seems to say things intended as terrific, but, unlike Kafka, he requires us to participate in the experience of his intention, not the amazing convergence of language and sense. In brief, Kafka manifests, Handke exhibits. Like a little Kafka. Also, to repeat, some Sartre, Bertolucci, et al.

Where then is the man called Handke? In the library and movies, I suppose, with all the rest of us, collecting postures, attitudes, clichés and matching them more or less well with personal realities. When Handke's match is good it is very good. This is particularly true when his subject is pure pain. The lie Handke discovers in all meanings and every aspect of human solidarity tortures him into extreme gestures. For example, notice how Handke abruptly separates himself from his hero in the last paragraph of "A Moment of True Feeling": "On a balmy summer evening a man crossed the Place de l'Opéra in Paris. Both hands deep in the trouser pockets of his visibly new suit, he strode resolutely toward the Café de la Paix. Apart from the suit, which was light blue, the man was wearing white socks and yellow shoes; he was walking fast, and his loosely knotted necktie swung to and fro. . . ."

For an instant you wonder who is this fellow? Then one realizes *that* is Gregor. After 131 pages of relentless intimacy, Handke releases him as if he were indeed some gaudy bug. The effect is sad and a little frightening. It is also severely moral. Handke's power as a writer comes from this, his courage and honesty, which makes him reject and despise his modern hero who is, at least in part, himself. (p. 29)

> *Leonard Michaels, "Intendedly Inauthentic," in* The New York Times Book Review

(© *1977 by The New York Times Company; reprinted by permission), July 31, 1977, pp. 7, 29.*

*   *   *

HANLEY, James   1901-

Irish novelist, essayist, and playwright who presently resides in England, Hanley is acknowledged to be a writer of crude energy and power. He spent ten years at sea, and some of his best novels take place aboard ship. His is a bleak, sombre vision that bears comparison with Hardy as well as Dostoevski. (See also *CLC,* **Vols. 3, 5.)**

Sometimes one can dislike a novel for excellent reasons, but still wonder if perhaps somehow the point has been missed. For this reason I do not want to attack *A Dream Journey,* but simply to report my fallible response of boredom and irritation. . . . [*A Dream Journey*] seldom or never departs from a single tone of nauseous misery, the repetitive dull thud of two people very slowly banging their heads together, for a lifetime, the ringings in their ears in perfect harmony.

There are perhaps circumstances in which boredom can reach an acuteness which transcends boredom; but what is more alarming than boring is that Mr. Hanley really seems to regard this harmonised vertigo as the heart of marriage, and to approve of it. There is an implication that Lena, spending her life coin by coin in support of her husband Clem's delusion that his art is worthwhile, is a heroine; that terror and admiration are somehow the appropriate response to the three last dreadful years of drink and bickering when both know, but neither admits, that Clem's paintings are mediocre and aimless.

If I understand Mr. Hanley correctly, then his thesis is pernicious and should be directly opposed by a clear statement that avoidable suffering and unending dishonesty are not a price worth paying for the illusion of security. But when, for instance, one can reach no opinion as to whether two inconsistent versions of the same event, a character's arrival at a house, appear deliberately (and pointlessly) or through oversight—it is clear that one is irretrievably out of sympathy with the author and unlikely to understand anything. 'Who destroyed who? Was it a waste? What did it mean *now*?' Yawn. (p. 22)

> *Nick Totton, in* The Spectator (© *1976 by* The Spectator; *reprinted by permission of* The Spectator), *October 16, 1976.*

There are people who deliberately seek out the front rows of movie theaters. Risking headache and distorted vision, they find pleasure in the sheer intensity, the claustrophobic immersion that sitting close to the screen provides them. Something like this engulfment in a rush of images comes to mind when one tries to describe the fictional world of James Hanley. . . .

[Hanley] is that rarity of rarities: a genuine original. No one has ever quite used the English language with such bruising abrasiveness, nor quite worked out the same vision of human existence. Forty-five years ago T. E. Lawrence found in Hanley's novels a "blistering vividness"—and that will do as a preliminary description. Trying to place Hanley, one thinks of George Gissing or Theodore Dreiser or Arnold Bennett, but soon such comparisons collapse.

Hanley has never won a large public and in the United States he is barely known, even among people who read serious fiction. Perhaps for understandable reasons. He yields nothing to sentiment or fantasy; and while not difficult in the way avant-garde writers can be, he demands a highly charged attention. He has perfected a gritty, plebeian realism that leaves one emotionally exhausted yet persuaded that here is a writer of high integrity and considerable achievement.

Hanley's new novel, "A Dream Journey," is one of his best, a study of two people, Clem Stevens and his mistress Lena, as they slip into middle age. The book focuses on their shared realization of failure, their sufferings during the London blitz in World War II, and, nevertheless, their clinging together with such a fierce absoluteness as to make the word "love" seem a mere trifling. . . .

As in some of his earlier novels, the characters are loners, people sliding off the margin, grappling for a bit of space. Hanley turns repeatedly, in book after book, to the theme of exhaustion, the exhaustion that comes from the sheer fact of having managed to hang on for a certain number of decades. Consciousness turns in upon itself, becoming obsessive and clogged. Yet Hanley's characters, with an underdog stoicism, cling to their days, still wanting to taste a bit of life's stuff or pursue some end they know is beyond their reach. The career of human will is Hanley's great theme, the will to keep blundering through circumstance and time. . . .

The customary attitudes of the novelist—either covering up too much or uncovering too much—Hanley leaves far behind. Life taken in close-up has no need for judgment of pity. . . . (p. 1)

Hanley's novels demand to be read slowly, in order to protect oneself from his relentlessness. It's like having your skin rubbed raw by a harsh wind, or like driving yourself to a rare pitch of truth by reflections—honest ones, for a change—about the blunders of your life.

Hanley piles rough slab of language upon rough slab. The usual connectives and transitions are often dropped, the usual "rests" between units of speech denied us. Words rub against one another, bleeding in friction. There is no point in quoting, since the effects are accumulative, not local. Sentences can seem ugly, paragraphs like a shapeless rockpile; but the book as a whole is a work of beauty, a capture of truth.

Inevitably there are also serious flaws in this sort of prose. Overfocused language can lead to incoherence, and at times one wants to beg for a shift in voice, an easing of pressure. What keeps Hanley from being a great writer (though he is a very fine one) is the absence of that copiousness of tone, perspective and voice one finds in the masters. By comparison, he seems rigid, stiff.

Still, let me urge anyone at all interested in contemporary writing to give Hanley a try. Even those readers who will dislike his work or find it too oppressive are likely to acknowledge its seriousness and worth. Reading Hanley, I found myself thinking about the sheer silliness of recent fashionable criticism about "the death of the novel." A Parisian critic is said to have called for "breaking the back of the novel." Well, I should like to see him try it with Hanley. It would be like beating a giant with a feather. (p. 25)

> *Irving Howe, in* The New York Times Book Review (© *1976 by The New York Times Company; reprinted by permission), December 19, 1976.*

James Hanley's *A Dream Journey* considers with painful, grinding closeness the relationship—they aren't married and hardly can be called lovers—of Clement Stevens, a very unknown painter, and Lena, who has lived with and sustained him for many years. . . .

The slow-moving story comes alive in a long middle section which shows Clem and Lena, in the same house, enduring the air raids of World War II. . . . Hanley beautifully orchestrates the small and self-centered concerns of people driven into closeness, but not understanding or affection, by disaster.

Under pressure, Clem and Lena were given something they never had before or since, an almost Wordsworthian sense of ordinary life as heavy with intimations, glimpses of apocalyptic strangeness beyond the grasp of "meaning." . . .

If youth, for all its pain, is a classically attractive subject for fiction, old age and unredeemable failure lend themselves less easily to the genre, since the pleasure of speculating about outcomes is foreclosed. *A Dream Journey,* though quite conventional in method, is a hard book to learn to read, being resolutely unamusing, severly undecorated, unresponsive to expectations of "story." It is to be liked, if at all, only on its own intransigent terms, and I see why Hanley's long career has brought him the admiration of other novelists but not of a wide audience. . . . Hanley's [novel] is . . . troubling and profound. (p. 32)

> *Thomas R. Edwards, in* The New York Review of Books (*reprinted with permission from* The New York Review of Books; *copyright © 1977 NYREV, Inc.), March 3, 1977.*

Most novelists give their characters words, actions, and settings that gradually reveal who they are, allowing the reader soon to feel that he knows more about them than they know about themselves. James Hanley works the other way around. From the start, the reader is privy to his characters' innermost thoughts, and little facts about the outside world filter in like falling leaves. . . . Technically, [*A Dream Journey*] suffers from all sorts of weaknesses—contrived plot devices, a blurriness when it isn't focussed on the two main characters, and a few too many of the choked exchanges ("'We . . . we . . .' He turned round, suddenly stuttered it out, 'I . . . he . . .'") that form the bulk of Clem and Lena's conversation. But few writers dig as deeply into people's spirits as Mr. Hanley does, and although his stiff, flat sentences take a bit of adjusting to, the rewards are well worth the effort. (pp. 118-19)

> The New Yorker (© *1977 by The New Yorker Magazine, Inc.), March 7, 1977.*

*   *   *

HECHT, Anthony   1923-

A Pulitzer Prize-winning American poet, Hecht is a technically ingenious and accomplished craftsman who writes in an elegant, baroque style. A common theme of Hecht's—the ironic contrast between harsh reality and artistic (hence false) versions of reality—can be found in one of his frequently anthologized poems; the highly satirical "Dover Bitch." (See also *Contemporary Authors,* **Vols. 9-12, rev. ed.)**

Anthony Hecht's collection, *A Summoning of Stones,* is a first volume of sustained charm and elegance. Mr. Hecht's most individual style, a sort of reflective effervescence set in variable mood-keys, is seen to its best advantage in "La Condition Botanique":

> The Mexican flytrap, that can knit
>   Its quilled jaws pitilessly, and would hurt
> A fly with pleasure, leading Riley's life in bed
> Of peat moss and of chemicals, and is thoughtfully fed
>   Flies for the entrée, flies for the dessert,
>   Fruit flies for fruit, and all of it . . .

A Baroque exuberance in the medium characterizes Hecht's poetry; the words whirl and perform their curves. The verbalism shows his confidence in his *métier.* In the poem cited above, in "Japan", "Divination by a Cat" and "The Gardens of the Villa d'Este", the poet is reminding us of something we have too long forgotten: that poetry is a profession, that one can rejoice in pure professionalism. An artist who has mastered the possibilities of his talent hopes to catch our attention, like Bernini, with grand curves and plungings and soarings. In the drabness of a self-conscious age, licking our wounds in corners, we have forgotten the plasticity of the High Baroque, the "abounding, glittering jet" of man rejoicing in his own condition, to the envy of the gods.

This sets the dominant tone, the individual note of Hecht's writing. He is a poet, for example, who is not afraid to produce a pure exercise, as in "The Place of Pain in the Universe", where all is craftsmanship held up for our admiration, and the subject merely a device, as in an étude of Chopin. Language is meant to be enjoyed. The "Songs for the Air" show the same quality, an astonishing virtuosity, as if the language were a thousand genii. Echoes of Stevens at the beginning of the poem give way to language considered purely for itself, as a Roman square is functional only in the sense that it attracts onlookers. . . . In "A Poem for Julia" Hecht shows a propensity and a noble ability to discuss the various conditions and situations of man, shown in historical perspective; at the same time a tendency to draw a moral which seems an appendage to what had been some pretty live language.

I imagine the best poems are "At the Frick" and "Alceste". Here tough subject-matter has given his exuberance and vitality considerable bite. . . . It is a fine performance; and throughout his book Hecht shows himself to be a poet of much talent and many possibilities. (pp. 307-08)

> *Joseph Bennett, in* The Hudson Review (*copyright © 1954 by The Hudson Review, Inc.; reprinted by permission), Vol. VII, No. 2, Summer, 1954.*

A Summoning of Stones is Mr. Hecht's first volume of poetry. It shows him to be a poet of great charm, possibly even too great charm, for when these poems fall below Mr. Hecht's highest standard, as of course they occasionally do, it is always because his witty fancy gets out of control. This may be partly the fault of the period style, of which Mr. Hecht has a remarkable mastery.

We have, after all, been living for nearly half a century in an almost continuous poetic revolution, a preservation of the dialect of the tribe by drastic surgery. During the last decade or so, this revolution seems to have been slowing down; as it does, poets become more interested in mastering the established style and using it than in making an entirely new style for themselves. In poets like Mr. Hecht and, say, Richard Wilbur, the period style seems to be emerging pretty clearly. It is an eclectic style, a composite of means developed by various earlier 20th Century poets; you can hear the echoes, as you hear Yeats in Mr. Hecht's

So that pale mistress or high-busted bawd
Could smile and spit into the eye of death,

and Stevens in

Deep in the phosphorous waters of the bay,
Or in the wind, or pointing cedar tree,
Or its own ramified complexity,

and Crane in

as the gulls hover
Winged with their life, above the harbor wall,
Tracing inflected silence. . . .

Such a style offers the poet a great range of resources for "extending his remarks"; indeed, its mastery almost forces such an extension on him, whether his subject calls for it or not, just as Milton's style forced grandeur on him even when the occasion—no fear lest dinner cool—hardly required it. This is the danger of our period style. But it is a fine style when the occasion is right and the poet's remarks are good enough and sufficiently controlled. (p. 479)

[It] is not the established style which makes Mr. Hecht's poems interesting; it only determines their kind. Mr. Hecht makes them good. The distinction is clear in "La Condition Botanique." This is a poem "about" botanical gardens; it belongs to what is by now almost a conventional kind, a poem in which, while apparently making meticulous and even scientifically accurate observations about the obvious subject, the poet gradually builds up a system of assertions about life as a whole. . . . How complicated and yet how clear and controlled the structure of this sentence [from "La Condition Botanique"] is: "The Romans and the rest knew nothing of the sweat of plants, plants which breathe on the greenhouses, which are run so to the pleasures of the plants, so to their happiness—which spreads to the ground where pipes do this and that—so to the pleasures of the plants that. . . ." The clause which follows upon "that" runs to eighteen more lines of equally complicated and equally controlled sentence structure. This syntactical virtuosity is what the period style provides for the poet if he can learn it. Its use is to provide the maximum syntactical opportunity for what is the main interest of this kind of poem, the only apparently incidental detail. The poet has to be able to make such detail good enough or the poem becomes a monumental bore. Mr. Hecht is able to; in spite of the apparent randomness of his observations, they all fall together finally. Satan remains below; the flowers thrive "as in the lot first given to Man, / Sans interruption . . .". (pp. 480-81)

Mr. Hecht likes to apply this style to such subjects as botanical gardens, and he has poems on "The Gardens of the Villa d'Este," on "A Roman Holiday," and on the Frick Museum. He also likes abstract elements like Air or Water. But he knows too how to make this style work for "A Discourse Concerning Temptation" or pain, for narrative, like the one of Samuel Sewall's wooing, for a soldier's soliloquy ("Christmas Is Coming") or an elegy for dead companions ("Drinking Song"). He has considerable range, but he is committed to the established style, of which he might have said what he actually says of something slightly different:

This was not lavish if you bear in mind
That dynasties of fishes, swimming before mankind,
Felt in the pressure of their element
What Leonardo charted in a brook:
How nature first declared for the baroque
In her design of water currents.

(p. 481)

Arthur Mizener, in The Kenyon Review *(copyright 1954 by Kenyon College), Summer, 1954.*

Anthony Hecht belongs to the courtly tradition, and is our latest and happiest answer to Baudelaire's libel that "The protestant countries lack two elements indispensable to the happiness of a well-bred man: gallantry and devotion." In addition to its wit, its complexity and its high musical qualities, Mr. Hecht's poetry is notably generous and open. The gentlemanly virtues are sublimated into gesture. To maintain this spirit in our acid atmosphere, a poet needs the gift of radical irony. All his truths must be provisional on the conditions and premises established in the poem. . . . In no other young poet has it a wider or more cheerful range than in Hecht, nowhere is it more blithe or baroque. . . . Poise, weight, variety, ease, wit, economy and unforced distinction of phrasing—all these things are present in Hecht to an unusual degree. Best of all, I should say, is the sense of spaciousness and reserve. A poem like "Alceste in the Wilderness," with its Websterian *mortisme,* manages to balance a (probably) insoluble obscurity against such a rich texture of image and sound that our normal demands for coherence are satisfied. This is a rare achievement in any poet and puts Hecht in the highest modern company. (pp. 679-80)

R. W. Flint, in Partisan Review *(copyright © 1954 by Partisan Review, Inc.), November-December, 1954.*

[There] is the intriguing possibility that the older Auden will be as influential in the U.S. as the young Auden was in Britain—and to just the same effect: making the newest American poetry Parnassian, provincial, even Tennysonian. Anthony Hecht is surely a case in point. Nothing is so immediately Audenesque about his poems as their insolently perfunctory attitude to subject matter. "Think of a subject, and verify it." Doubtless at all times indifferent poems have been written to this recipe. What distinguishes recent Auden poems is their bland refusal to conceal the fact, and just as the "Bucolics" in his last collection displayed what Auden called to mind when some one in the audience called out "Mountains" or "Lakes," so Hecht has a poem called "Japan" constructed on just the same principle. Five intricately regular rhyming stanzas present the author remembering that Japanese are little, that they are acrobats and jugglers, that they make ingenious toys, and that on the other hand they were fierce and treacherous in war yet afterwards eager to be friends, that now they are "very poor." We wait for the resolution into harmony. Instead the poet remembers something else—that (apparently) the use of human dung in the paddy-fields produces a disease called "schistosomiasis japonica." By a virtuoso-feat these Latin syllables are accommodated into the stanza without flawing its glassy surface, and this glittering expertise is the true climax of the poem which needs only to be rounded off by a last stanza saying that the poet will have to revise his ideas about Japan. There is no pretence that the ostensible subject exists for the poet except as a peg on which to hang the embroidered robe of style; and style, thus cut loose of any responsibilities towards what it offers to express, degenerates at once into virtuosity, frigid accomplishment. Thus all we can say if asked to distinguish the good poems from the bad in [*A Summoning of Stones*], is to point out that some are less accomplished than others —that, for instance, in a poem called "The Gardens of the Villa d'Este," the intricate regularity of the rhymed stanza is achieved, as it isn't in "Japan," with no respect for the stops and starts of syntax or the natural pauses of the speaking voice. (pp. 43-4)

It's the provincialism that needs insisting on, for the poems are full of erudite and cosmopolitan references, epigraphs from Molière and so on; and the diction is recherché, opulent, laced with the sort of wit that costs nothing. Here and there too the poet knowingly invites what some reviewers have duly responded with, the modish epithet "Baroque." But if that is an accurate description of the style, it has nothing to say to the crucial question of how the style is related to its ostensible subject. For that the right word is the much less fashionable "Victorian."

Trying to find one poem that can be exempted from these strictures, I choose "A Deep Breath at Dawn," a poem in much simpler stanzas, altogether too Yeatsian for comfort both in diction and feeling, yet possessing what the more polished pieces so disastrously lack—a true development, unpredictable yet natural, of a subject which one thereby knows to be truly, not just ostensibly, the subject of the poem. (p. 44)

> *Donald Davie, in* Shenandoah *(copyright by* Shenandoah; *reprinted from* Shenandoah: The Washington and Lee University Review *with the permission of the Editor), Autumn, 1956.*

"The Hard Hours" . . . releases with dramatic completeness a talent that was only hinted at in "A Summoning of Stones." The truth is, the weak poems in the earlier book, and a few in the present one, are weakened by a mechanical sense of form. The strong and spacious poems that give the new book its character—poems like "A Hill," "Behold the Lilies of the Field" and "More Light! More Light!"—demonstrate how well Hecht understands the economy of his vision. He brings these poems to book by the most intense lyric control. Only in two poems in the new book do I feel the kind of cookie-cutter use of stanza that gave his first book a slightly frivolous effect. These are called "Ostia Antica" and "The Origin of Centaurs," and perhaps the very concerns of the poems suggest the brittleness of form. (pp. 24-5)

> *William Meredith, in* The New York Times Book Review *(© 1967 by The New York Times Company; reprinted by permission), December 17, 1967.*

At first acquaintance, Hecht's art may seem to be a retreat, or withdrawal, from modernism. In his method, he leans more to realism than to symbolism, and he is an insistent moralist—his poems carry an unfashionably large freight of message. (p. 602)

Whereas the symbolist's difficulty is the risk of moving too far from literal experience to be intelligible, Hecht's art takes the risk of moving in too close. We see the events as clearly as through the camera eye—there seems to be no blurriness, even at the edges of the scene imaged, no ambiguities. In contrast with the ornate style of many of Hecht's

earlier poems, the new work [in *The Hard Hours*] is characterized by starkly undecorative—and unpretentious—writing. He relies, to a valiant degree, on the power of quiet overtones to transmit the intense emotional experience hidden below the casual surface; the undemonstrative vocabulary, low-keyed meters, and rhythms often accumulate, as in the closing lines of "The Hill," into a withering revelation of truth and pain.

At times, Hecht's new style grows too flat and prosy, onetoned. All verbal tension is dissipated by the studied dullness of rhythms. In an extreme effort to pare down his verse to essentials, and to omit any embellishments of style that might attract the reader's attention to themselves and away from the serious human statement, the technique backfires. . . . When the line flows too easily and unobtrusively, it offers no settling resistance to the reader—the hesitations that significant form always imposes on the mind's ear—to free him from style and release his thought into the urgencies of subject. This is the risk Hecht takes when he trims his style too close, but only rarely does he overrefine.

Hecht's most consistently masterful device is to juxtapose stories from history, ancient and contemporary (or scenes from his personal life, present and past), generating a powerful religious and political moral from collision between them. . . . The scissoring movement between story and story provides the reader's nervous system with a series of shocks, a jackknifing of emotions, comparable to that produced by the interplay of plot and subplot in *King Lear*, and in some story sequences of the Old Testament. I don't know any other poetry in English, outside poetic drama, that creates anything like this effect. (pp. 602-03)

> *Laurence Lieberman in* The Yale Review *(© 1968 by Yale University, reprinted by permission of the editors), Summer, 1968.*

Mr. Hecht, unlike other poets, has not cried *mea culpa* and kicked over the traces of one discipline in order to embrace another. He has discarded the baroque, decorative elements of his earlier verse; he no longer writes the poem which is essentially one long, dazzling, conceit; he has a new simplicity and strength. But he is still brilliant; he still employs literary sources; his poems are still tightly woven, excellently constructed forms. Fortunately. For Mr. Hecht is surely one of the most accomplished practitioners of metrical verse around. His rhythms are invariably energetic and his rhymes manage never to be clumsy or obtrusive. The overall effect is one of classical balance and vigor, admirably suited to his themes and their treatment. . . . Most of Mr. Hecht's poems are dramatic rather than lyrical, in the sense that he sets up situations in which characters move and act. Some are in a ballad style, including the tough and powerful "The Man Who Married Magdalene," after a poem by Louis Simpson (with whose verse Mr. Hecht's has a good deal in common). (p. 71)

> *Lisel Mueller, in* Shenandoah *(copyright by* Shenandoah; *reprinted from* Shenandoah: The Washington and Lee University Review *with the permission of the Editor), Spring, 1968.*

[*The Hard Hours*] represents Hecht's career from its beginning (the earliest copyright is 1948) and allows us to see the basic argument that underlies most of his poetry: facing the biological conditions of decay and destructiveness and the historical facts of mass savagery, man tries to construct "rites and ceremonies" by which to know his condition, combat his weakness and despair, and achieve civility. Hecht's favorite images for man's biological condition come from the insect world, an insidious and yet microscopically elaborate world in which man sees his own reflection. In "Alceste in the Wilderness", for example, he imagines Molière's misanthrope escaping to the jungle and finding there a microcosm of the hypocritical world he has fled:

> Before the bees have diagrammed their comb
> Within the skull, before summer has cracked
> The back of Daphnis, naked, polychrome,
> Versailles shall see the tempered exile home,
> Peruked and stately for the final act.

The analogous image from history is the slaughter of the innocents. In "'It Out-Herod's Herod. Pray You, Avoid It'", a father, seeing himself reflected in his children's eyes as a television hero-protector, muses:

> Yet by quite other laws
> My children make their case;
> Half God, half Santa Claus,
> But with my voice and face,
>
> A hero comes to save
> The poorman, beggarman, thief,
> And make the world behave
> And put an end to grief.
>
> And that their sleep be sound
> I say this childermas
> Who could not, at one time,
> Have saved them from the gas.

The horror of historical chance is all the more concentrated for the nonchalance with which it is mentioned; and the "childermas", even if ultimately insufficient, is quietly noble.

Hecht is a highly accomplished formalist, but form is not an ultimate value. "Nothing," he says in "Three Prompters from the Wings", "is purely itself / But is linked with its antidote / In cold self-mockery—/ A fact with which only those / Born with a Comic sense / Can learn to content themselves." This describes the broadest use of form in Hecht's poems: it holds together, in harsh comic fusion, the self-mocking opposites; it rarely resolves them. Often the tension issues from a comic inappropriateness of rhetoric, as in the description, in "A Vow", of a miscarriage ("In the third month, a sudden flow of blood. / The mirth of tabrets ceaseth, and the joy / Also of the harp"), or as in the liturgy, in "Pig", to the swine into whom a thousand demons were driven ("O Swine that takest away our sins / That takest away"). Whatever the tactic—and his approaches are many—the strategy is basically the same: Hecht works against the grain, but so smoothly that we almost fail to notice. He gives us valved emotion; rather than direct expression of feeling, he presents, in magnificent variety of forms, the artifices we construct in the face of our historical and biological condition. Thus we get both formal brilliance and intense, often bitter, irony—and, more difficult to trace, a humane and kindly sympathy for man, inadequate as he struggles against destruction. (pp. 684-85)

> *Richard A. Johnson, in* Sewanee Review *(reprinted by permission of the editor, © 1968 by The University of the South), Autumn, 1968.*

Anthony Hecht's first book of poetry, "A Summoning of Stones," was published in 1954, his second, "The Hard Hours," in 1967. . . . Thirty new poems make his third collection, "Millions of Strange Shadows."

If there is a genteel tradition in American poetry, Mr. Hecht is commonly supposed to belong to it; he is regularly esteemed for precision, wit, craft, inventiveness—the virtues which a poet is required to practice in the absence of passion. . . .

Generally, . . . Mr. Hecht is content to be urbane. Not a poet of the incandescent line, he loves the linkages of a stanza, where he has room to move and breathe. If he had lived four centuries ago he would have composed himself by writing madrigals. As it is, he writes long, shapely sentences and sends them through an entire stanza, eight or ten lines for good measure. Fluent without being garrulous, his tone accommodates nearly every effect within the limits of high conversation, including certain excesses of diction which would be offensive on a more informal occasion. (p. 6)

In his new book Mr. Hecht is more abstemious. . . . Effects of diction no longer call attention to themselves. Mr. Hecht speaks of poetry as "governed by laws that stand for other laws," and he prefers laws that are self-evident to those that need to be explicated and enforced. . . . In "Dichtung und Wahrheit" Mr. Hecht puts "the freshness of the text" beside "the freshness of the world / In which we find ourselves," an allusion to Wallace Stevens's poetry, presumably, in acknowledgement of an old affiliation. . . . In another poem he invokes "some shadowless, unfocussed light" in which "all things come into their own right." The same poem speaks of "the cool, imperial certainty of stone" and of pebble, weed and leaf seen "distinct, refreshed, and cleanly self-defined, / Rapt in a trance of stillness." The composure is not deemed to be impregnable: when rain comes things run to flux again. But meanwhile we have hovered upon Mr. Hecht's central mood, where the state of blessedness is "deep" and "unvexed."

The new element in these poems is a sense of the cost of such felicity. Trances of stillness are expensive. Roman motorcyclists have to "put much thinking by" to become "as Yeats would have it, free and supple / As a long-legged fly." In another poem one's "negligence and ease" are earned by another's "sunken hideousness." (pp. 6-7)

It is my guess that the poet of these new poems is no longer confident that to know the world in little is to know it at large or well enough. He is now weighing the cost, in these weighted poems, of the order and finality they appear so effortlessly to achieve. (p. 7)

> *Denis Donoghue, in* The New York Times Book Review *(© 1977 by The New York Times Company; reprinted by permission), March 27, 1977.*

*   *   *

HECHT, Ben   1894-1964

American dramatist, novelist, journalist, and screenwriter, Hecht is probably best known for having written highly popular melodramas for the stage. His most successful play, *Front Page,* **was written in collaboration with Charles MacArthur. From 1933 until his death, Hecht wrote for the films.**

It is difficult for a writer to sustain a 654-page autobiography if he thinks [as Hecht purports to in *A Child of the*

Century] that "ideas lie on a perpetual rubbish heap." He is not equipped to give any clear sense of the meaning of his life and time or of the century of which he is a child. . . .

Hecht's iconoclasm about and his contempt for ideas does not mean that he is devoid of them. He isn't. But generally his ideas are banal. They repeat what he has said in the yesterday of his own youth. His autobiography is a concoction, an improvised literary cocktail. Everything in life is an occasion for Hecht to sound off, and he fills too many pages with the wind of his prejudices. (p. 70)

[*1001 Afternoons in Chicago*] ranks in my opinion as Hecht's best book. It consists of sketches Hecht wrote for the *Chicago Daily News* and is full of charm, color, and exciting phrases. Hecht's best talent is that of coining metaphors, and he was at his peak when he knocked off *1001 Afternoons in Chicago*. His subjects are usually grotesque. The grotesque has usually interested him and to it, he brings a sense of the mordant. . . .

1001 Afternoons in Chicago helped me to become more aware of, let us say, the poetry of the street. Its high-voltage figures of speech attracted me. Frequently, the young and aspiring writer sees the use of figures of speech, the coining of phrases, as the sign of literary talent. I did. Ben Hecht could make phrases. Harry Hansen, in *Mid-West Portraits*, characterized him as a Pagliacci of the fire escapes. *1001 Afternoons in Chicago* consists of sketches. They are short and Hecht's talents were fresh; he had an exuberance and flair. His novels *Erik Dorn* and *Humpty Dumpty* were frustrating. They exuded a sense of the present, of life going on immediately in one's own time, and there was some excitement in this. . . . There was a frankness about sex but the cynicism, the iconoclasm, the verbal posturings, the lack of empathy frustrated me. A newspaper man can look at people and happenings; he can cast a cold and jaundiced eye at politicians; he can watch hangings; he can dig into tales of rape and murder; and he can do a good piece of reporting without having to identify deeply with the people who are subjects of his stories. A fair number of journalists tend to develop what sometimes seems to be an occupational trait—they tend to regard what happens as though it occurred so that they could do a story. The world is a show made for them. Hecht often gives the impression that this is an integral feature of the way he looks at life. . . . *Count Bruga* was an exception but it is a special kind of book. The chief protagonist is a poet who acts and talks much like a once well-known Chicago poet. The character is bizarre and Hecht has a lively and enthusiastic feeling for the bizarre.

Behind the frustration I found in Hecht's early novels, there was not only a limited power to identify; there was too little sympathy. Sympathy is usually significant because it is the means of making human emotions important. I discovered Sherwood Anderson and Theodore Dreiser after Hecht. In them, I found not cleverness or a keenness for a grotesque surface of life or an iconoclasm that helped me feel a false sense of superiority to others; but rather, in them, I encountered a seriousness of feeling about human emotions, human tragedies, about the struggle, often so blundering, which we all make to live out our life span. There are some writers who can produce out of negative emotions, who can arouse and move us. . . . Ben Hecht doesn't hate; he flings out phrases of contempt. He laughs. He falls into quick scorn; is facilely negative. (pp. 71-3)

A Child of the Century echoes Ben Hecht's other writings,

including his plays and movie scenarios. There are remembrances of *1001 Afternoons in Chicago, The Front Page, Erik Dorn, A Jew in Love,* and of many motion pictures jumbled up with readily given offhand judgments on almost all of the complicated world of today. By being so confidently judgmental, Ben Hecht does damage to his book; he reduces the effect that he might have achieved. Frequently, he asserts a dislike for people. "The greedy little half-dead" of the twenties are redescribed as "the half-alive ones." (p. 73)

[In his autobiography] Ben Hecht writes with warmth and love of his family, his parents, aunts and uncles. He describes touchingly a scene when he went to dine with his parents and to tell them that he had left his first wife and was living with another woman. Here, convention was flouted, and his parents were conventional people. But how differently he handles the flouting of convention in recounting this scene from the way he does when he flings out worn-down banalities of the twenties. He becomes a man of perception; he senses his parents' feelings.

Reading this scene, we know that the author is a man of talent and perception, as well as one who speaks of serious problems with shallow cynicism. (p. 74)

Seen now and in the past, Ben Hecht appears a man of talent, of easy prejudices, and without values. Unlike in the twenties, he cannot today stimulate youth. He has seen and reported the grotesque and sordid but it now appears on his pages as something too familiar.

He writes: "Except for my relation to God, I have not changed in forty years. I have not become different as an adult."

It seems a shame that man of talent who has had the opportunities in life that Ben Hecht has had would be pleased to keep sitting on what he styles as his "Pedestal of Sameness."

This comes as a strange boast from a man who defends—even rants against—the destruction of individuality in our country. Iconoclasm can be as conventional as conventionality. And this child of the century appears to be a conventional iconoclast. The "half-alive ones," the mob, the people drowned by the "tidal wave of education"—they have not changed. But here is one of the not-half-alive, here is one of the alive ones; and he does not give us a great outpouring of his aliveness.

Talent could be better used. (pp. 75-6)

> *James T. Farrell, "The Mind of Ben Hecht" (1955), in* Literary Essays, 1954-1974, *edited by Jack Alan Robbins (copyright © 1976 by Kennikat Press Corp.; reprinted by permission of Kennikat Press Corp.), Kennikat, 1976, pp. 70-6.*

If a man writing a story decides to bring himself in as a character, there is no reason why he shouldn't. If he puts a certain amount of energy into implying that he, the storyteller, is a man of the world, moves in circles unknown to his desk-bound brethren, gets around and meets people generally, that is simply one more ingredient in the flavoring of the story.

Mr. Hecht generally manages to give his stories a topdressing of this kind, and usually it doesn't come amiss, especially when he is in his O. Henry vein, writing about the teeming and shifting world of Manhattan. O. Henry is the basis here, with flecks of Hemingway in the constant reminders that the writer is a man of action and no mere word-merchant. But neither of these two influences goes at all deep. Mr. Hecht's heart is elsewhere. His eyes, for all their shrewd Manhattan glitter, are in reality fixed far away, on a vision he had once and has never ceased to stare after.

In a word, Mr. Hecht is a romantic. Not just any kind of romantic, but a Wildean romantic, a man of the nineties. If, instead of being a mid-twentieth century New Yorker, he had been a *fin de siècle* Londoner, he would have been faithfully present, week in and week out, at the Cheshire Cheese. His figure would have been a familiar one in the bars of Fleet Street, where he would have made an attentive listener to the monologues of Lionel Johnson. Possibly Mr. Hecht's would be the hands that raised Johnson's lifeless body after his last fatal fall from a stool in one of these same bars. He would have known Yeats, Beardsley and Richard le Gallienne.

That is Mr. Hecht's misfortune. Owing to an unaccountable kink in the time-corridor, he slipped sixty-five years and landed on the wrong side of the Atlantic into the bargain. (pp. 343-44)

At the center of his imagination lurks the romantic sardonic dandy, like a carp in a pool; and one cannot watch for long without seeing him rise.

Like his fellow aesthetes, Mr. Hecht is a good deal preoccupied with "the artist" as a human type. (p. 345)

> *John Wain, "The Case of Ben Hecht," in* The New Republic *(reprinted by permission of* The New Republic; © *1959 by The New Republic, Inc.), September 28, 1959 (and reprinted as "Ben Hecht," in* The Critic as Artist: Essays on Books 1920-1970, *edited by Gilbert A. Harrison, Liveright, 1972, pp. 343-50).*

Mr. Winkelberg is a jeweler, a repairer of watches; Jonathan Winkelberg is a poet, a searcher for a beautiful memory. These two characters with the same last name appear in two different works by Ben Hecht, and the radical difference in their attitudes and life styles suggests not only Hecht's tendency to draw polarized figures but also the consistent location of the poles. One represents what is dead through constant exposure to and participation in dullness, stupidity, and ignorance; the other shows what is killed for trying to live despite the overabundance of the negative forces in the world.

In *Humpty Dumpty* (1924) Mr. Winkelberg stands for almost everything that is oppressive and deadening in society. What is worse, this Winkelberg is unaware of his condition, having been submerged in it for so long. In the entire novel no hint is given of any elevating spiritual or mental qualities left in him: "Mr. Winkelberg was no more than this—a paunchy, bald-headed, undersized man scratching his nose in front of his darkened store as if he were thinking of something. . . . Of what was he thinking? Of nothing. Another day had been." (p. 103)

Hecht never allows the reader to forget that Mr. Winkelberg is pathetic and incomplete, one of the many dead people who walk the streets:

> He had confronted life with a character.
> And this character had put an end to all such

dangers. This motley of ideas, prejudices, routines and emotions which was Winkelberg answered back to the mysterious urgings and fumblings in his head somewhat as follows . . . "enough. I am complete. No use trying to make me think my way into empty places. This is the end of the line. All out. Far as we go.". . .

The distance is very short, indeed, for the "complete" unfinished Winkelberg is soon contrasted to Kent Savaron, a young writer sickened by the lifelessness of the world, a condition with which he quickly associates the jeweler, eventually equating the two. When introduced, Savaron is only nineteen, aware of "almost nothing beyond the fact that there was a noise inside of him". . . . The difference is obvious and striking. Savaron is the opposite side of Winkelberg, the expression of life that has not been suppressed and forgotten. The "noise" inside the watch repairman can only carry on a monologue with itself:

> "Poor Winkelberg, walking alone in the street," said life, "you and I no longer know each other. And I must sit like this, meaningless and futile, inside your head and mourn for something that has not yet existed.". . .

Savaron, however, hears the "noise inside him," the life that cannot make Winkelberg hear but only make him inexplainably sad. "Poor Winkelberg walking alone in the street, you no longer know who you are or what has happened. Something warm and important slipped away, something strange and shining vanished". . . . Hecht's repetitions even become monotonous as he constantly describes Winkelberg and Savaron as opposites, for he seems to want to insure that the reader cannot fail to miss that Savaron represents the natural self that Mr. Winkelberg has forgotten, the self that still retains warmth and original thought.

In order to understand fully the consistency of such polarization in Hecht, one should turn next to a later play entitled, appropriately enough, *Winkelberg* (1958). In the play Jonathan Winkelberg is a poet, consistently opposed to everything that Mr. Winkelberg supports. He is, in fact, another Savaron who listens to the life inside him, keeping his individuality, though eventually discovering that the price is enormous. Hecht apparently resurrected the character name from the Twenties and gave it to a figure most unlike the mediocre jeweler in all his fiction. Jonathan Winkelberg is as close to an exact opposite of Mr. Winkelberg as possible.

Having been killed before the action of the play begins, Jonathan is sent in search of a beautiful memory in order to create his own heaven, for afterlife is simply a continuation of dominant attitudes. . . . The structure of the play is Winkelberg's reliving a series of scenes of treachery, cruelty, greed, drunkenness, lust, and stupidity—each episode adding another reason for his eventual cynical posture. . . . (pp. 104-05)

Jonathan's adversaries are more brutal than the Winkelberg people whom Savaron must deal with, but their self-complacency is the same. Tony Riggs, a literary critic, dismisses the poetry he cannot understand with an easy one-line rationalization: "I have no memory for hogwash". . . . Abramovitch demonstrates even more obviously how Hecht tends to place people at one extreme or the other, for although he supposedly shares artistic inclination with

Jonathan, he can dismiss him in as off-hand a fashion as Riggs: "I can't eat my soup! For God's sake, I don't want to hear about a dead bum named Winkelberg". . . .

More obvious, though perhaps more expected from his upper middle-class position as publisher, is the opposite pole figure of Horace Williger. His alliance with the compromisers, the jeweler Winkelbergs, is discernible as he seeks to appease the critic who influences sales, not the artist working with life. "By God, Johnny—your apologizing to Tony Riggs revives my faith in you—as a human being—as well as a poet". . . . When Jonathan eventually refuses to apologize, Williger naturally dismisses him, for he is so submerged in compromise that he cannot understand the point of view of someone who is "alive."

The result of such polarization is predictable. Mr. Winkelberg muddles through *Humpty Dumpty,* plodding unchanged to the end. Kent Savaron dies young and disillusioned, confused by the contradictions of peoples' lives without "life." Jonathan is killed senselessly in a petty argument by an unthinking brute; the world goes on without caring about his absence or even being concerned about his futile exit.

The realization that Hecht employs such polarities is important: many of his works emphasize extreme opposites toward similar conclusions, especially his most important novel, *Erik Dorn* (1921), in which the title character is introduced as the finished product of exposure to the emptiness of a Winkelbergian world. . . . Cool, calculated, Dorn is a Savaron and Jonathan Winkelberg who lives long enough to resign himself to the nothingness: "At thirty he had explained to himself, 'I am complete. This business of being empty is all there is to life. Intelligence is a faculty which enables man to peer through the muddle of ideas and arrive at a nowhere.'"

As would be expected, Dorn is contrasted to an opposite. George Hazlitt, who maintains a fanatic naive belief in Mr. Winkelberg's assorted mediocre virtues. Hecht's description of Hazlitt is again strikingly similar to the portrait of Mr. Winkelberg given earlier:

> For the paradox of Hazlitt was not that he was a thinker, but a dreamer. His puritanism had put an end to his brain. Like his fellows for whose respect and admiration he worked, he had bartered his intelligence for a thing he proudly called Americanism, and thought for him had become a placid agitation of platitudes. . . .

Dorn kills the Mr. Winkelberg figure instead of being killed; the act is the triumph not of awareness over lifelessness but merely of instinctive self-preservation, having little effect on the attitudes of Dorn.

In Hecht's short stories more figures are Jonathan Winkelberg/Kent Savaron/Erik Dorn cynic-philosophers. For instance, in "The Philosopher's Benefit" Lefkowitz's son, the philosopher, is described in a now familiar manner: "Everybody is to him a commercial maniac. And everybody else is to him a low brow and a fool. . . . Speeches insulting people, that's his philosophy writing." Although the reader never meets Lefkowitz's son, the philosopher is described consistently as an "alive" character who is set against the suppressed masses of watch repairers. (pp. 106-08)

Hecht's opinion of books, given in 1958 on his television show, points out, along with the play *Winkelberg* of the same year, that his polarized view of life did not diminish after the Twenties. Commenting on the value of Joyce Cary's *The Horse's Mouth,* he said, "An Englishman who wrote the best account of a non-conformist at bay before a conformity-demanding world." (p. 108)

Hecht was still putting figures on widely different sides, even in other writers' books, and the poles are the same as they are in Hecht's works. Winkelberg against Winkelberg, cynical artist against mediocre business man, free life fighting to release suppressed life. Just as consistent are the conclusions: disillusionment or death, or both. Perhaps an oversimplification on Hecht's part, but the consistency of his polarized vision should be understood when reading his serious writing. (p. 109)

> Gary Fincke, "Polarity in Ben Hecht's Winkelbergs," in Critique: Studies in Modern Fiction *(copyright © by* Critique, 1973), Vol. XV, No. 2, 1973, pp. 103-09.

Like [Tom Sawyer], Hecht and his major heroes, Erik Dorn (1921) and Kent Savaron, the central character of *Humpty Dumpty,* have excessively literary imaginations. But whereas Tom gets most of his ideas from Sir Walter Scott, Hecht and his characters, as he explains endlessly, both in his autobiography, *A Child of the Century* (1954), and in his novels, are readers of the later romantics, of Dumas and Maupassant, of Gogol, Gorki and Dostoevski (especially, *The Idiot*) and of Richard Harding Davis, Bret Harte and Stephen Crane. (p. 908)

Stuart Sherman, as early as 1926, in a study called *Critical Woodcuts,* revealed the essential sentimentality which characterized Hecht's attitude toward his reading. "He does not find in literature any sobering body of classical experience or any human conclusions," wrote Sherman. . . . "He seeks only secrets of stylistic expressiveness, stimulus for his fantasy and assistance in getting his mind beyond good and evil." Hecht, himself, summed it up succinctly, but with all the superficiality of his feeling for literature exposed, when he wrote in his autobiography . . .: "I worked in Chicago, but I lived, a little madly, between book covers," or when he has Erik Dorn . . . refer to reading as "the last debauchery." One is certainly reminded of Tom's fantastic plans to rescue nigger Jim (in *Huckleberry Finn*) and of his equally elaborate dream of "a crusade to recover the Holy Land from the paynim" (in *Tom Sawyer Abroad*). The chief difference of course is that Tom had a companion of rare distinction, Huck Finn, whose living voice raised their adventures to the level of that sublime original, *Don Quixote,* whereas Erik Dorn and Kent Savaron had no such associate. They had only the feeble pen of Ben Hecht, "a word slinger rather than a stylist, master of invective rather than wit, poetaster rather than poet, crackpot philosopher and calculating crackpot, romantic cynic and cruel sentimentalist, third-rate Mencken and fifth-rate Rochefoucauld" (the description is by Louis Berg in his October, 1954 *Commentary* review of *A Child of the Century*).

And if these words seem too harsh, let us remember that Hecht was a contemporary during those wonderful years in Chicago of Dreiser, of Sandburg and of Sherwood Anderson, yet he never seems to have truly recognized the qualities of these writers, nor indeed of many other contemporaries; he reminds one of teachers of literature who seem to feel that the art ceased to be practiced with the coming of prohibition. (p. 909)

Mark Twain not only endowed Tom Sawyer with a boy's outlook on literature (and a tendency toward fantasy and action, and a lack of understanding of the significant meaning of the literary work), but he also made him a paradigm of eternal youth: Tom never grew up. Twain knew what he was doing. In the Conclusion to *The Adventures of Tom Sawyer,* he indicates that since his story is "strictly the history of a boy," it must stop while Tom is still a youth; but he leaves open the option: "Some day it may seem worthwhile to take up the story of the younger ones again and see what sort of men and women they turned out to be." Mark never really took up that challenge.

Ben Hecht did. One result is that his characters, Erik Dorn and Kent Savaron, remain boyish; for all their adventures and romances, they seem immature. The reason may lie deep in the American character (and it may also have been a difficulty for Hemingway); it may somehow be related to a fear of women or to that phenomenon called "momism" (Twain cleverly allows neither Tom nor Huck a mother) or to something in the American experience which on the frontier led men to trust and love one another while regarding women merely as objects for sexual pleasures or as agents of the confining forces of civilization. (pp. 909-10)

[What] continued to attract [Hecht's] attention, in Chicago, in New York, in Germany and in Hollywood, were the Tom Sawyer-like antics of the human race, a series of catastrophes which he witnessed and then described in a section [of his autobiography] with the revealing title, "Boy about Town" . . .; many of these paragraphs were later expanded into the nine episodes which make up *Gaily, Gaily* (1963). A distinction here must be made, however: what for Twain were the essentially joyful and humorous recollections of childhood and youth in nineteenth-century rural America became for Hecht the joyless absurdities of twentieth-century urban U.S. The loss was almost unendurable. But . . . Twain was a giant reflecting an end-of-the-century malaise with which one would have to couple Melville's *Billy Budd.* Hecht could sense these troubles, but he couldn't find the plots or the characters to embody them. As he confesses in his autobiography . . .: "I have written much fiction. The characters I made up are still alive, but they inhabit no world—only a closet. A foot beyond is limbo. They do not walk or caper in people's minds. They continue to utter their many fine sentences, to weep, joke and make love—but in the closet always." And there it is: he undoubtedly means the closet image to be taken in the theatrical sense of a lifeless drama, but it could as well refer to the child, punished and alone, languishing in the dark. Such seems to me the way he treats his characters even in his most ambitious novels, *Erik Dorn* and *Humpty Dumpty* (the childish metaphor in the title is pathetically revealing). (p. 910)

In a very real sense Ben Hecht was unlucky. He arrived on the scene a little too soon, like the butler who starts the play, polishing the silver, answering the telephone and then retreating when the leading actors appear. The figure of Erik Dorn, in his first . . . and most successful novel (1921), is the same kind of forerunner. Both Hecht and Dorn retreat from stage center in the face of the competition: Fitzgerald's [and Hemingway's overwhelming protagonists]. (p. 911)

But Hecht was overshadowed in another sense as well. Always the reporter, with the mind set and the emotional make-up of the clever journalist out for a scoop or a good newspaper yarn, he never moved away from those preoccu-

pations. (A good case could be made for maintaining that *Gaily, Gaily,* published in 1963, made up of newspaper stories, expanded from a chapter in his autobiography and in turn developed from the columns he wrote for the Chicago *Daily Journal* in the 20's, is his best work.) Now many American writers, both in the nineteenth and twentieth centuries began as journalists of one sort or another. One thinks of Howells and Twain, of Bret Harte and Stephen Crane and then of Sherwood Anderson, Hemingway, Faulkner. In each case, the journalistic experience was a means to an end, a preparation and a trying-out, both in terms of ideas and style. And although there are sentimental edges even to the mature writings of many of these authors, they all pushed ahead to genuine creativity and to stylistic distinction. Hecht seems not to have learned anything from his days as a reporter. . . . [He] stands surprised by life, by brothels, homosexuals, lesbians, murders, vice and corruption; and he became a voyeur rather than a novelist, a point of view he never relinquished. . . . [A] fault, which he was unable to correct, was the sheer pretentiousness of his "literary" writing. . . . [His] novels are filled with high-sounding, "poetic" phrases ("into this emptiness of spirit, life had poured its excitements as into a thing bottomless as a mirror" is a typical sentence from *Erik Dorn* . . .). (pp. 911-12)

Erik Dorn . . . has some of the qualities which do mark superior reporting. The book does reflect the anguish and the search for values of young Americans in the immediate post-war years. And although Dorn is not, like Jake Barnes, an ex-aviator suffering from a real wound, he shares the disillusionment both of those who returned to these prohibition-controlled states and those who sought meaning in more glittering activities in less commercialized European settings. His emptiness and his cynicism, however, have no outlets in action, especially in symbolic action, which would allow for continued reinterpretation. . . . [He] is the observer of life, rather than the participant; he has eyes, but no heart. . . . The novel does catch and hold some of the aspects of the decade. . . . But it remains a document rather than a novel. Even its overblown prose and simplistic psychology only set it more firmly in its time and place. Again, Hecht himself offers an excellent critique. Kent Savaron, the writer hero of *Humpty Dumpty,* finally finishes his novel, only to remark about it . . .: "It's incomplete. There's no life in it. There's disillusion and a curious ecstasy. But no pain."

Humpty Dumpty, like *Erik Dorn,* is, at its best, journalistic and autobiographical. . . . Again, the story stresses the emptiness of life in mid-America in the 20's, an emptiness summed up in the nursery rhyme about "Humpty Dumpty"; like Erik . . . , Kent on occasion has vivid memories of his childhood. . . . But the nothingness which Kent feels is given a wider application . . .: Hecht lambastes youthful fashions ("bell bottom pants" and "short skirts") and behavior ("drinking moonshine, dancing in phallic embraces to the melancholy, aphrodisiacal strains of the 'St. Louis Blues'") as well as "barbarism" (the cult of the primitive), the "caterwaulings and stupidities" of the radio; in addition, he roasted religious movements and revivals, but he reserved his greatest contempt for jazz songs and "nigger" singers and he even particularized the symbols of disintegration: Valentino, Fairbanks, Synthetic Gin, F. Scott Fitzgerald, "Shuffle Along," Gilda Gray, and, strangely, Nicholas Murray Butler. In such a world Humpty Dumpty was, undeniably, King, And for Kent "art" (such as practiced by Picasso, Brancusi and Gertie Stein) "is the obituary of passion . . . decorations in an endless cemetery.'' No wonder Hecht's novels have not survived: in them he treats his times with a shallow contempt; he could neither rise to satire nor sense with sufficient passion the essential meanings. As readers, we respond as we do to newspaper accounts: that's the way of the world. We are left without either intellectual or emotional depth. (pp. 912-13)

Ironically, today, his reputation may turn out to rest more upon such scripts as *Underworld* (1927), *Scarface* (1932) and *The Scoundrel* (1935) (both *Underworld* and *The Scoundrel* won Academy Awards, a factor of aesthetic as well as monetary significance, but Hecht mentions neither occasion in *A Child of the Century*) than upon the novels which he was able to write in the free time his Hollywood fees bought him. Here, too, journalism is the key. These gangster films are documents of the Chicago he could never forget or get out of his system. It is an interesting fact that his career, like that of Fitzgerald and Faulkner, to name only two, involved participation in the significant art form of the twentieth century. But he never recognized the power or the cultural importance, let alone the aesthetic qualities, of the cinema. Nor did he note that the imposition of certain values on films (''the triumph of virtue and the overthrow of wickedness'') was not merely the result of the profit motive of the moguls, but also a cultural fact of the greatest significance. (p. 914)

> *Marvin Felheim, "Tom Sawyer Grows Up: Ben Hecht as a Writer," in* Journal of Popular Culture *(copyright © 1976 by Ray B. Browne), Spring, 1976, pp. 908-15.*

* * *

HEINLEIN, Robert 1907-

American science fiction novelist and short story writer, Heinlein established his reputation writing stories for *Astounding* in the forties. Today he is, along with Isaac Asimov, the dean of American science fiction writers. His *Stranger in a Strange Land* became a cult novel among the college youth of the mid-sixties, drawing attention to science fiction as a literary genre warranting more serious consideration than had previously been granted it. Heinlein has also written under the pseudonyms of Anson MacDonald, Lyle Monroe, John Riverside, and Caleb Saunders. (See also *CLC*, Vols. 1, 3, and *Contemporary Authors*, Vols. 1-4, rev. ed.)

[*Stranger in a Strange Land*] is the story, told in detail with sardonic humor, of Valentine Michael Smith, a Mars-born earth child. Raised by Martians after the death of his parents and all other members of the first Martian expedition, Smith is returned to earth by crewmen of the second expedition twenty-five years later. Having been nurtured by the Martians, who are so non-earthly as to confound earthly analysis, Mike Smith is a Martian in an earth body. He thinks in Martian.

The rest of the novel is well-written—perhaps ''slick'' is the best adjective to describe Heinlein's style—as a variation on the noble savage theme, coupled with some intriguing variations of the Whorf-Sapir theory of linguistic relativity. You can't really appreciate Mike Smith or the Martians until you learn to think in Martian, and you begin to think in Martian when you begin to grok. As one character put it, ''I grok it. Language itself shapes a man's basic ideas.'' *Grok* is the only Martian word used in the novel, but it is so basic to the Martian character, according to Heinlein, that an understanding of *grok* comes before an understanding of every other word in the Martian tongue.

As Heinlein handles the concept, the notion of grokking is crucial to the enlightened pantheism which is the religious construct of *Stranger in a Strange Land*. *Grok* means *drink* in basic Martian, and on a desert planet the sharing of water, or drinking together, becomes almost the highest, the only, religious sacrament. Those who share water become ''water brothers,'' a unity so elevated that mistrust is impossible to one so internally baptized. . . .

By a process of extension of meaning drawn from its earthly context, Heinlein adds a number of Terran modifications to the wildly alien Martian concept of *grok*. *Grok* seems first to mean *know, understand, appreciate, comprehend*. It resembles the hipster ''dig.'' Gradually it comes to include *love, cherish, create*. [The] unsexual Martian *grok* becomes modified in the minds of the living Terrans: it broadens to include the fullest and most intimate communication humanly possible, the very essence of life itself, sexual intercourse. Thus transmuted, *grok* becomes a quasi-assonantal surrogate for its common Anglo-Saxon equivalent, and it revitalizes the archaic meaning of the Biblical *know* as well as emphasizes the ambiguity of the Terran word *intercourse*.

There are several further extrapolations of the term as Heinlein handles it. *Grok* also means *life*, as a logical extension of its meaning *drink*. In a most logical Martian way, all that groks is God. This concept leads Heinlein to build a quasipantheistic religious system with Mike Smith, man by ancestry but Martian by environment and thought processes, as its major prophet. The water ceremony is the sole sacrament: ''Share water, drink deep, never thirst.'' In basic Martian this translates, approximately, into ''Grok, grok, grok.'' (p. 4)

[The] central message of the novel [is] . . . , ''All that groks is God.'' Alternately, God groks, in every sense of the word thus defined: God loves, drinks, creates, cherishes, infuses every being.

Heinlein carries the religious message of the novel even further by advancing the thoroughly Martian concept of ritual cannibalism. . . . The custom on Mars is formalized and deeply religious. The survivors would, by eating the discorporated one, thereby acquire some of his characteristics, attributes, or even eccentricities. . . . Of course, Heinlein does not evaluate any qualitative or quantitative differences between the symbolic cannibalism of most Terran religious sects and the actual cannibalism of the Martians. He leaves those discussions to his readers. (pp. 4-5)

Heinlein has apparently read his [Benjamin Whorf] well, because this concept of temporal discontinuity is another of the major theses of *Stranger in a Strange Land*. . . .

[This is] the Whorfian conclusion inevitable in the novel: the realities of time, space, and matter are almost totally dependent upon the verbal system one uses to speak of time, space, and matter. When we learn to think in another language, our entire perception of reality changes. What is more important, reality itself changes. Grok?

Accomplished literary craftsman that he is, Heinlein skillfully utilizes almost every technique to communicate his ideas. One specific device is Mike Smith's constant use of the participle or progressive verb form to indicate the eternal present of the Martian now. ''I am been saying so.'' ''We are growing closer.'' ''I am savoring and cherishing.'' Further examples could be multiplied, but only one more need be cited. It is used so often in the novel that it becomes almost a ritualistic theme song: "Waiting is." Not "Waiting is necessary," or "Waiting is important," or "Waiting is inevitable." Simply, "Waiting *is*." The phrase, a curious juxtaposition of tense forms, implies that one will wait, until eternity if necessary, before grokking in fullness.

In one of the most moving parts of the novel, Mike comes to understand that merely speaking about love is meaningless. If all that groks is God, Mike must demonstrate this truth, not simply repeat it. . . .

[This] is not the place to note the number of Christian parallels in *Stranger in a Strange Land,* nor to evaluate if they are wholly successful. From a standpoint of linguistic relativity, however, similarities of Martian grokking and English thought find a union in Mike's last benediction as he is being stoned to death. He says in a striking parallelism with the Crucifixion, "I'm ready to show them now—I grok the fullness. Waiting is ended". . . .

Implicit in this Martian-Terran-Christian-Buddhist-Hindu benediction is the ultimate concept that "Love," however extrapolated from whatever widely divergent culture, will find an identity of expression. Many anthropological linguists will find this thesis highly debatable. In fact, the identity of expression seems to contradict the thrust of the novel: that a language "map" will alter reality—any reality, including that of love.

The appeal of *Stranger in a Strange Land* is not limited to its intriguing development of Martian thought, or even to its more than adequate descriptions of the "growing closer" ceremony. The sugar-coated, over-simplistic romanticism of the story has become almost a cult in certain areas of the country. . . .

There is no doubt that the sense of alienation or anomie which troubles the flower children has caused many of them to turn to *Stranger,* as the cult calls it, with the same emotion that causes them to wear buttons reading "Frodo Lives" or "Go, Go, Gandalf!" Heinlein is almost Swiftian in his attack on some of the same American folkways that the hippies reject. His analysis of the hypocrisies of religion, politics, economics, and, explicitly, the Protestant ethic, seems to supplement the strictures which the flower children themselves maintain against our society. Whether grokking is an adequate substitute for involvement or commitment is conjectural, but a certain vociferous element in our society has seized upon it as a way of life. Fiction has become reality.

Stranger in a Strange Land may not be a great novel. Perhaps science fiction has yet to produce one. Yet when a writer skillfully combines the varied themes of any work as well as Heinlein has done, science fiction has at least come of age. (p. 5)

> *Willis E. McNelly, "Linguistic Relativity in Middle High Martian," in* The CEA Critic *(copyright © 1968 by The College English Association, Inc.), March, 1968, pp. 4-5.*

Heinlein assumes that technology will continue to develop and thereby change society. The cosmos is infinite. With increased scientific knowledge man may roam the universe and even the fourth dimension. Unlike many science fiction writers who express an uncritical faith in technology or, like C. S. Lewis, who express a distrust of materialism and science, Heinlein's view shows more balance. He recognizes that technology may threaten the existence of independence and individual integrity, but . . . he expresses a

belief in the individual's ability to cope with strange conditions and to act in an independent, non-deterministic fashion. The portrayal of modern man's ability to shape his own destiny accounts in large part for Heinlein's continued popularity since this view is expressed concretely through fast-moving action and appealing situations. (p. 33)

> *Diane Parkin Speer, "Heinlein's 'The Door into Summer' and 'Roderick Random'," in* Extrapolation, *December, 1970, pp. 30-3.*

Although circumstance made him temporarily a sort of guru, Heinlein is best as a teller of fairly straightforward adventure stories. He has a gift for believable, concrete detail and he knows how to stretch suspense to its proper length, two gifts that do not quite add up to a blinding glimpse of hidden realities but can be parlayed into enjoyable reading. *Starman Jones* is good, average Heinlein adventure; *The Past Through Tomorrow* is both better and worse: a massive collection of short stories, novelettes and one novel *Methuselah's Children* mostly written in the '40s and each adding its mosaic bit to the fragmentary but consistent "history of the future" which has been a framework for much of his work. (p. 4)

> *Joseph McLellan, in* Book World—The Washington Post *(© The Washington Post), May 11, 1975.*

*   *   *

HELLER, Joseph   1923-

An American novelist and playwright, Heller rocketed to literary prominence in 1961 with the publication of *Catch-22*. A hard-hitting indictment of war, free enterprise, and the American way of life, *Catch-22* is a satirical farce, utilizing black humor in the vein of Waugh in *Men at Arms* and Mailer in *The Naked and The Dead*. Heller has also written a play, *We Bombed in New Haven*, and a second novel, *Something Happened*. (See also *CLC*, Vols. 1, 3, 5, and *Contemporary Authors*, Vols. 5-8, rev. ed.)

Heller's vision of the horrifying absurdity of service life in World War II is, as the constant references in [*Catch-22*] to its wider implications indicate, merely an illustration of the absurdity of the human condition itself. *Catch-22* reflects a view of the world which is basically that of Jean-Paul Sartre and the early Albert Camus. The world has no meaning but is simply there; man is a creature who seeks meaning. The relationship between man and his world is therefore absurd; human action having no intrinsic value is ultimately futile; human beings have no innate characteristics. Reason and language, man's tools for discovering the meaning of his existence and describing his world, are useless. When a man discovers these facts about his condition he has an experience of the absurd, an experience which Sartre calls "nausea." But there are innumerable contemporary novels which are fundamentally Existentialist. What is interesting about *Catch-22* is that the experimental techniques Heller employs have a direct relation to Existentialist ideas; they are an attempt to "dramatize" his view of the human condition rather than merely describe it. (pp. 75-6)

The question of authority is central to the novel. God certainly no longer runs the organization, though He lingers on in certain distorted images some characters still have of Him. (p. 76)

Duty is now owed to such vague abstractions as patriotism and free enterprise, which have become exactly the tyrannous absolute values that Camus talks of in *L'Homme révolté*. The old man in the brothel in Rome exposes patriotism as illogical: "Surely so many countries can't all be worth dying for".... Capitalism and free enterprise lead Milo to bomb his own unit and he excuses his action with the old slogan that what is good for money-making interests is good for the country. "Incentive" and "private industry" are "goods" and their evil results cannot change anyone's attitude towards them.

Such assertive values as patriotism, then, are merely words, words which have become divorced from meaning. Heller's awareness of the separation of word and idea, which Sartre talks of, is apparent in several places in the novel. General Peckem who "laid great, fastidious stress on small matters of taste and style" ... has lost all sense of what words *mean* and writes his directives in a manner which combines impeccable grammar and trite adjectives. Language no longer communicates but serves to confuse things further. When Yossarian makes a game of censoring letters, declaring one day "death to all modifiers," the next declaring a "war on articles" and finally blacking out everything except "a", "an", and "the", he finds that it creates "more dramatic interlinear tensions ... and in just about every case ... a message far more universal".... (pp. 76-7)

Catch-22 is, of course, Heller's illustration of the irrational nature of the world. Any attempt to argue logically and reasonably ends in a paradox; one reaches that point where thought reaches its confines, which Camus talks of....

Catch-22 is composed of rules which apparently operate to make it impossible for a man to find a reasonable escape from them. They do not exactly contradict each other, but are continually inadequate to the occasion and always disregard the individual human life. They are intended to impose order upon chaos, but life so exceeds these rules that they only serve in the end to create more chaos. One of the clearest examples of this is the firemen who leave the blaze they are attempting to control at the hospital in order to obey the rule that they must always be on the field when the planes land....

Since the rules do not work, anything may happen. There is no reasonable justice. (p. 77)

In a world where philosophical ideas, traditional morality and reason itself are apparently useless, all man has to hold on to is his own physical body. The value which Heller supports throughout the novel is that of human existence, the individual human life.... There is no talk of love or even of close friendship in the book; the pleasures of life are purely physical—food, liquor, sex—just as the only real horror is physical pain and ultimately death. "In an absurd universe," writes Frederick Karl, "the individual has the right to seek survival; ... one's own substance is infinitely more precious than any cause" [see *CLC*, Vol. 1].

The view of the world in *Catch-22*, then, is the same view as that presented by Sartre and Camus, and the aware individual in this world comes to very much the same realizations about it as do Roquentin and Mathieu in Sartre's novels. He realizes that there is no ultimate reason for doing one thing rather than another.... (p. 78)

The aware individual realizes, too, that there is "no way of really knowing anything." ... [We] learn that there are always two widely divergent official reports for every event that takes place.

When everything is questionable, it is a small step to questioning one's own identity.... Names, uniforms, marks of identification are all a man has in Heller's world to assure him of his own identity.

Yossarian and the chaplain, probably the two most aware characters in the novel, both have experiences of the absurd very similar to those of Roquentin in Sartre's *La Nausée*. The chaplain experiences "terrifying, sudden moments when objects, concepts and even people that the chaplain had lived with all his life inexplicably took on an unfamiliar and irregular aspect that he had never seen before and made them seem totally strange." ... Yossarian's experiences also have the effect of alienating him from his environment, but are less concerned with the strangeness of objects than with their profusion and gratuitousness. (pp. 78-9)

Heller, like Sartre and Camus, is not however totally pessimistic. Valid action is possible for the individual; there is even the suggestion of a sane universe which Sweden may represent. The hope of Sweden is perhaps a false note in the novel, but it is important to remember that it is only a possibility, a state of mind rather than a real place. Although Orr has, at least reportedly, reached Sweden, ironically by pretending to be "crazy," Yossarian at the end of the novel does not really expect to get further than Rome.

In a discussion of the techniques which Heller has employed to convey his view of the world it would be easy to ignore the obvious. *Catch-22* is a very funny book. It would be easy to ignore this because, in spite of the laughter it evokes, the overall impression is as much of horror as of humor. The laughter evoked is not of the kind that unites us warmly in sympathy with the human race as we enjoy its foibles, but rather that which serves to alienate us by exposing the bitter ironies of existence. Nevertheless I believe that humor is a way of understanding the techniques of the novel. Laughter, as Bergson suggests, is caused by incongruity, by a frustrating of our expectations of a certain result, and it is a failure to fulfill certain of the reader's expectations which is the link underlying the so-called absurd techniques of the novel. (p. 79)

[When] the reader is confronted with the juxtaposition in one sentence of references to several unrelated events about which he so far knows nothing, we cannot say that it is not like life. Actually it is; we often overhear conversations which are meaningless to us because we do not understand to whom or to what they refer. Yet we are surprised to find it in a novel. In this instance, obviously, it is our expectations about the nature of the novel, not about life, which are not being fulfilled. This is, I think, the key to defining the absurd techniques. In some way each of them plays against and frustrates the reader's expectations of a novel, the illusions, one could say, that he has about the nature of the novel....

It is obvious that the narrative technique of *Catch-22* does not fulfill the expectation of the reader for a continuous line of action in which one episode is related to the next, at the very least chronologically, and in which events are life-size and probable. Situations which are initially familiar enough to the reader may be gradually exaggerated to the point of absurdity. (p. 80)

The futility of all human action is suggested by Heller in the number of times events or conversations are repeated so that the reader, like Yossarian, eventually has the feeling that he has "been through this exact conversation before." ...

The narrative technique serves to confuse the reader about time and to destroy any certainty he may have about what has taken place, thus creating in him the same doubts about reality that Yossarian experiences and that Sartre and Camus speak of. Heller employs three basic methods of disrupting the expected chronological flow of the action. The first is a simple one. He often makes a statement about an event which has taken place and deliberately omits the clarification which the statement requires. Therefore many of the major events in the novel are referred to two or three times, sometimes in increasing detail, before the full account is given. . . .

The second device creates confusion in the mind of the reader by presenting him with two apparently contradictory statements about the same event before providing a clarification. (p. 81)

The third method is an extension of the second: contradictory accounts are given of an event and no solution is provided. The reader is left uncertain of the truth and in some instances asked to believe the incredible. . . .

As well as confusing the reader about the time or exact nature of the events in the novel, Heller also frequently shocks him by adopting attitudes to objects or situations opposite to the expected ones. By introducing these unexpected attitudes in a very casual way, he not only challenges the traditional value system but suggests through his tone that nothing unusual is being said, thus doubling the shock effect. . . .

Heller's methods of characterization, like his narrative techniques and his use of tone, depend upon a frustration of the reader's expectations. (p. 82)

There are two possible ways . . . of failing to fulfill a reader's expectations about character in a novel: one is to change the character's identity, provide multiple personalities for the same name, or one name for various figures, and thus disturb the reader's whole conception of identity, as do John Barth and Samuel Beckett; the other is to provide caricatures, figures who are no more than puppets and in whom the reader is not expected to believe. Heller occasionally appears to experiment with the first method, as, for example, in the scene where Yossarian pretends to be a dying officer whose parents fail to recognize him, or where Yossarian and Dunbar discover they can change identities by changing hospital beds. But although in these scenes the characters experience doubts about their identities, the reader is always quite clear about the identity of the character and no real confusion is created.

Most of the characters in *Catch-22* are, however, caricatures, cardboard figures who are distinguished for the reader by their particular obsessions. Each lives with an illusory view of the world which isolates him and makes the results of his actions very different from his expectations. Each is, in his way, the unaware individual who, as Camus illustrates in *Le Mythe de Sisyphe,* believes that he can operate in the world as he imagines it and that his actions will achieve their purpose. (p. 83)

Most of these characters are introduced to us in deceptively explanatory paragraphs which appear to sum up their personalities in a few adjectives, but which really provide the reader with irreconcilably opposite traits. . . . Gradually the characters become increasingly absurd as the personality traits of each are seen to be one, an obsession. It is believable that one of Milo's moral principles was that "it was

never a sin to charge as much as the traffic could bear," . . . but by the time his activities have taken over Europe and North Africa in one vast syndicate and he has bombed his own men, he has become little more than a personification of greed. Scheisskopf's enjoyment of parades may be initially credible but his childish delight in calling off parades that have never been scheduled is not. These characters may have names, parents, heredity, professions and faces, but we cannot very long sustain the illusion that they are "real" human beings.

The most important device a novelist has to suggest an irrational world is, of course, the treatment of reason itself. Reasoning, in *Catch-22,* invariably ends up in some variation of Catch-22; apparent logic is used to destroy sense. The reader is led into following an argument which progresses logically, but which arrives at an absurd conclusion. (pp. 83-4)

Sentence structure is used throughout *Catch-22* to add to the reader's confusion about characters and events and contributes to the impression of an irrational world. The novel is full of complex sentences in which the individual clauses and phrases are not related to each other or are related at a tangent. . . . (p. 84)

Frederick Karl describes Yossarian as "the man who acts in good faith to use Sartre's often-repeated phrase," and claims that all Yossarian "can hope to know is that he is superior to any universal force (man-made or otherwise), and all he can hope to recognize is that the universal or collective force can never comprehend the individual." He goes on to call Yossarian's final decision "a moral act of responsibility," "reflective, conscious and indeed free," while the other characters are not free, he considers, because they are unaware. This is all true; it is obvious that Yossarian is a man of whom Sartre would approve, but it does not go far enough. Certainly awareness is a prerequisite to the right action as Heller sees it. It is proved useless to be simply good like the chaplain or merely innocent like Nately, unable to detach himself from his father's values. And certainly Yossarian acts in freedom, but in the name of what? I do not think that it is only in the name of his own individual life, although this is his starting point. What most critics have overlooked is that Yossarian changes, is the one character who learns from his experience in the novel.

At the beginning of *Catch-22* Yossarian attempts to exercise his reason to escape from the situation he is in. "Everywhere he looked was a nut, and it was all a sensible young gentleman like himself could do to maintain his perspective against so much madness." . . . He soon learns, however, that everyone considers everyone else "a nut" and that when he attempts to argue logically against flying more missions he comes up against Catch-22. He realizes that to use reason in the face of the irrational is futile and that the way out of Catch-22 is simply to rebel, in Camus' sense, to take a stand, to say "no." He refuses to fly any more missions. This is, of course, the way the problems of Catch-22 have been solved earlier in the novel: the young officers solve the problem of the "dead man" in Yossarian's tent simply by throwing out his possessions; Major de Coverley solves the "great loyalty oath" Catch, which is preventing the men from getting their meals, simply by saying "'Give everybody eat'." . . .

Until the final episode in the book, Yossarian is the great supporter of individual right. . . . "That men would die was a matter of necessity; which men would die, though, was a matter of circumstance and Yossarian was willing to be a victim of anything but circumstance." . . . Yossarian indeed realizes, as Karl suggests, "that one must not be asked to give his life unless everybody is willing to give his," but by the end of the novel he has come to realize the logical extension of this concept, that, if what is true for one must be applied to all, then one cannot attempt to save one's own life at the expense of others. One cannot give tacit acceptance to other people's deaths, without giving everyone the same right over oneself. (pp. 85-6)

Yossarian is given the chance to save his own life if he lies about Colonels Cathcart and Korn to their superior officers. He will, in accepting the offer, probably act as an incentive to his fellow officers to fly more missions in which many of them may be killed. He is given a chance, in Camus' terms, to join forces with the pestilences. After accepting the offer he is stabbed by Nately's whore and realizes perhaps that by joining those who are willing to kill, he has given everyone the right to kill him. If one rebels, one must rebel in the name of a value which transcends oneself, human life is the value for which Yossarian rebels and runs off to Rome, but it is not merely his own individual existence. (p. 86)

If we look back at the novel in the light of what Yossarian's decision reveals, we can see that Heller has presented us with a series of character studies of selfish men and has shown how their actions for their own gain have involved death for others. They are all like Major Major's father, "a long-limbed farmer, a God-fearing, freedom-loving, rugged individualist who held that federal aid to anyone but farmers was creeping socialism." . . . Milo, another "rugged individualist," bombs his own men; Colonel Cathcart, aiming at impressing the Generals to obtain promotion, keeps raising the number of missions his men must fly. To claim as Karl does, that these characters "are not really evil in any sinister way" but just "men on the make" is inaccurate. The "man on the make" is evil to Heller, since he gains at the expense of others and asks them to do what he is not willing to do himself.

The last ten pages or so of the novel may be sentimentally handled, as critics have suggested, but they present the key to a full understanding of what Heller is saying. In an irrational and gratuitous world the aware individual has to rebel, but his rebellion must be a free act and in the name of a value which can be applied to all men and does not limit their freedom.

The style of *Catch-22*, like the narrative technique, the tone and the methods of characterization, serves to frustrate the reader's expectations. . . . The reader expects to be drawn into the world of a novel, then, but *Catch-22*, while initially providing him with familiar human situations, ends by rejecting him. The novel itself becomes an object which provides the reader with the experience of the absurd, just as the trees provide it for Roquentin in Sartre's *La Nausée*. After attempting to relate his preconceptions about novels, his "illusions" about the form, to this novel, the reader is finally stripped of them. *Catch-22* simultaneously shows man's illusory view of the world, employs techniques to suggest the irrational nature of the world and is itself an object against which the truth of its statements may be tested. (pp. 86-7)

"Jean E. Kennard, "Joseph Heller: At War with Absurdity," in MOSAIC IV/3 *(copyright © 1971 by the University of Manitoba Press), Spring, 1971, pp. 75-87.*

"Something Happened" . . . is, I'm extremely sorry to say, a painful mistake. I've read that Mr. Heller spent twelve years on this very large novel; perhaps that is one of its problems. For "Something Happened" resembles nothing so much as a fifties story of anxiety and despond among the corporate worker bees in the honeycombs of New York and the flowery fields of Fairfield County.

"Something Happened" is a novel of anomie, of the imminent disintegration of the social and moral order, and Mr. Heller puts his considerable talents (this is a well-written novel) at the service of his point. So much so, in fact, that he indulges in overkill. When we have seen Bob Slocum [the narrator] suffer a failure of nerve (or a failure of common humanity) in a dozen different situations, we do not need to see him fail a dozen times more; when we have heard a score of hateful, baiting conversations among the Slocums *en famille*, we do not need to hear a further score. Yet the book plods ponderously on for nearly six hundred pages, building a Watergate-size mountain of evidence against this society (or is it *that* society—the America of the late fifties, in which this novel must surely have its roots?) before a new note of menace is sounded: gradually (and skillfully, in terms of technique), Slocum's dogged, despairing monodies become more ravelled and disjunctive, and long before he suspects himself of going mad we see that that is what's happening. Now, at last, the long, slow buildup of the earlier pages seems to promise a dividend. Once the stage has been so painstakingly set, we think, we are to witness the self-destruction of an incipient madman as it happens from *inside*—from his internal point of view. But no: in an inexplicable flinging away of all he has built, Heller permits an unconvincing cataclysm—the death of one of Slocum's children by his own inadvertent hand—to arrest Slocum's fall and, amid double incredibility, to restore him to purpose and respectability, if not to real manhood.

One of the reasons this books is (or was for me, at least) so difficult to read is that its characters—Slocum in particular—do not command respect or empathy. And this in turn is because they are too often archetypes or paradigms and not real people. It is discouraging to learn that Slocum's friends, enemies, and overlords in his anonymous company possess such deliberately anonymous names as Green, White, Brown, and Black; it is destructive of the humanity of the novel and of its ultimate purpose when we discover that there are never first names for his wife, daughter, and young son. (Perversely, his other son, the idiot, is referred to by his first name. This is but one example of the playing with paradox that allowed "Catch-22" to work but is utterly out of place—and false—in this utterly different novel.) The flatness, the blankness, the non-humanity of these characters makes the book tractarian, and it is a tract for other times. Too much has happened since 1960 for Bob Slocum's trials and miseries to seem quite apposite today. (p. 193)

L. E. Sissman, in The New Yorker *(© 1974 by The New Yorker Magazine, Inc.), November 25, 1974.*

Although *Catch-22* is a war novel, the death in it is not just a result of war; the logic of death that Heller establishes early in the novel makes his ending false. . . . (p. 14)

[Ultimately] Heller suggests that the absurdity of dying in war is only in degree greater than the absurdity of dying anytime, anywhere. . . . Heller shares with the other Black

Humorists, then, an interest in death as an element of existence, both as it affects the living and is a result of stupid policy decisions by a self-serving bureaucracy. For Heller, as for Donleavy and others, death is an absolute end . . . which forces men into closed survival systems or desperate flight. That Heller felt the need to lessen the burden of survival in the ending of *Catch-22* illustrates . . . that affirmation for the writer who knows and presents death's potency is desired but difficult to achieve.

In his more recent *Something Happened*, Heller treats paranoia and survival anxieties within a peacetime context. . . . A profound study of domestic life and the ramifications of death anxiety in our time, *Something Happened* extends the primal (and social) insights of *Catch-22*. (pp. 16-17)

> *Thomas LeClair, in* Critique: Studies in Modern Fiction *(copyright © James Dean Young 1975), Vol. XVII, No. 1, 1975.*

Mr. Heller seems to me to accede, in [*Something Happened*] at least, to the view that American society is incapable of direction or restraint. Taking up such a position has not only affected the content but the form of his novel. His main character, Bob Slocum, is not in control of his environment and realising this, is unable to act positively. Not only American society, but Bob Slocum himself, avoids Mr. Heller's control, leaving us with an overlong and shapeless novel. . . . The tones of anxiety and despondency so dominate his novel (more so than his black humour) that he cannot direct, even within the novel, what makes him so despondent. (p. 68)

Bob Slocum . . . is the only consciousness in Mr. Heller's book and he always sounds as if he were speaking to an audience. . . . I find not only the content of Slocum's talk but his mannerisms (ha, ha) annoying, particularly bearing in mind that he goes on in this way, without change of pace, for 569 pages. The reader has to rely solely on Slocum who is completely self-indulgent; there are no other lenses and this leaves not only the reader but Joseph Heller in Slocum's hands. Does Heller intend to annoy the reader or does he himself think the mannerisms genuinely funny or fruitful?

For me, the most interesting sections of the novel are 'My daughter's unhappy' and 'My little boy is having difficulties.' Despite their faults they are remarkable for their portrayal of intense, irrational (at least as much so on the part of parent as child), and extraordinarily wounding conflict. One cannot but recognise that many of the pressures on Slocum are generated by the nuclear family itself and by the establishments in which the family is trained; thus children reflect one's own worth; and competiveness, rather than co-operation, is valued. Although Slocum's son, for instance, is a fast runner, he is unable to win races. His sympathy for slower children makes him slow down in order to allow them to catch up. Such behaviour angers both his peers and his teachers. His father, unlike the others, can understand his son's behaviour and is sneakily proud of it though he would prefer the boy (for his sake as well as his son's) to act conventionally. It does not occur to him to help the boy weigh up alternatives nor does he support the boy's unaggressive stance. Indeed, he adds to the pressures the boy feels. Mr. Heller presents such concrete episodes memorably, indeed brilliantly, but he cannot stop Bob Slocum who keeps referring to the same incidents, remembering others, and piling detail upon detail without a con-

comitant extension of range or purpose. I was left with mixed feelings about *something happened*. I do not think it is a novel which will survive (if one wants to talk about survival). Mr. Heller's unwillingness or inability to distinguish between his own aims and values and those of Bob Slocum, the wordiness which he seems as incapable as his character of staunching or shaping, has too seriously injured his book. Yet it is, at the same time, an extraordinarily interesting novel both because of the problems explored and the problems exhibited in the execution. (pp. 68-9)

> *Elaine Glover, in* Stand *(copyright © by Stand), Vol. 16, No. 3 (1975).*

Something Happened is an apparently problematic work. Most of the seeming difficulties, however, can be attributed to three basic features of the novel: the extremely limited mode of narration, the unheroic nature of the protagonist, and the ostensibly pessimistic quality of the novel's message. (p. 74)

The entire book is narrated by the protagonist, Bob Slocum, a middle-management executive. . . . Consequently, Heller is not at liberty to indulge his own considerable powers of verbal agility and satirical humor that were so evident in *Catch-22*. *Something Happened* has none of the linguistic inventiveness or antic authorial satire that so distinguished the earlier novel. Slocum, a businessman rather than a man of letters, is by necessity a limited narrator. Although articulate and aware of the fundamentals of grammatical expression (which he sometimes touches on in his numerous parenthetical asides), he is not a *writer*. His mode of speech—and the book has the feel of being spoken, rather than written—is flat, ordinary, and unexciting, and is an accurate reflection of his personality. (pp. 74-5)

Additionally, Slocum is completely unheroic, a conventional man. Worse, he is not even a *good* man. . . . Slocum's failure as "hero" becomes clearer when he is contrasted with Yossarian, the waggish protagonist of *Catch-22*. Yossarian is concerned not simply with surviving but with preserving his honor in what he perceives to be a dishonorable world. To Slocum, however, survival is everything. He is an integral part of the unacceptable situation in which he finds himself—the ruthless, cutthroat, immoral realm of big business. Further, Yossarian is the embodiment of that time-honored American literary conception, the individual. . . . Not so with Slocum, who conforms rigidly, punctiliously, to the system that he despises.

Accordingly, Yossarian is an outsider, as even his Assyrian cognomen implies, while Slocum's name is indicative of his WASP origins, which render him more acceptable in an environment that is distrustful of ethnic minorities. (pp. 75-6)

Perhaps the essential difference between these two protagonists can be best explained as the conflict between innocence and experience. Yossarian, although no *naif*, maintains a high-minded sense of individual responsibility to self, while Slocum—older, lacking in illusions, and basically corrupted—has long since relinquished any such idealistic notions. . . .

If a principal theme of *Something Happened* is the bankruptcy of the contemporary middle-class American experience, it finds its most effective expression in Slocum's preoccupation with lost innocence and integrity. Although Slocum's ideas on sex are badly askew, he is nevertheless capable of entirely appropriate responses in many other areas. If he sometimes waxes inordinately maudlin over relatively inconsequential matters, he addresses himself just as often to topics of legitimate concern, and his three children serve to dramatize his being upset with certain distressing realities, especially lost innocence.

His older son, for example, functions as a living metaphor for the idea that artless virtue is doomed in a hostile, antagonistic world. (p. 77)

Slocum's daughter, a sullen, contentious teenager, seems to have lost her innocence practically at birth and serves almost as an updated version of the Greek chorus, as she constantly goads her parents while delighting in their unceasing domestic strife. . . . In view of the novel's underlying concerns, that the daughter survives while the son does not is hardly surprising.

Slocum's other son, hopelessly brain-damaged, further exemplifies the notion that innocence has no fully realizable potential in a corrupted world. Like Faulkner's Benjy, he personifies the idea that total innocence is conceivable only in harshly qualified terms. (pp. 78-9)

This, then, is the raw material of *Something Happened:* an unexciting narrative style, a flawed protagonist, and a decidedly depressing set of "givens." How, one might reasonably ask, does Heller finally manage to surmount these potentially overwhelming obstacles and engage and hold the reader's attention? *Does* he so succeed? . . .

Heller is certainly not breaking fictive ground in his choice of a pusillanimous protagonist; numerous instances of this sort of main character come to mind, Dostoevski's Raskolnikov and Stendhal's Julien Sorel being just two. Moreover, strictly moral considerations aside, Slocum evinces a number of minor personality quirks and personal habits that we can all relate to, bits of ourselves that we recognize and draw us to the character in spite of (because of?) his very fallibility and unattractiveness. (p. 79)

The resulting sense of identification that the reader experiences is related to one other aspect of the novel which lends it additional impact: Heller's skill at playing upon the reader's indulgence of morbid curiosity. . . . The novel capitalizes upon the unwilling but very human fascination for the painful and grotesque. . . . *Something Happened* is to an alarming degree an accurate social documentary that mercilessly captures some very real elements of the contemporary American situation.

Preoccupied with the irremediable emptiness of a certain segment of modern life, the novel offers none of the stated affirmations that we sometimes get from, say, Bellow or Malamud and none of the comic relief that characterizes Vonnegut's books or *Catch-22*. The novel, however, conveys an *implied* affirmation; it is a relevant, affirmative, ultimately moral book—clearly an indictment and a recommendation for something better. (pp. 79-80)

Something Happened is . . . in one important respect a better book than its predecessor. *Catch-22* depends for its effects upon boisterous exaggeration that does not always convince, and the novel too often verges on self-parody. *Something Happened* is actually far more sophisticated in its method. Heller has turned from hyperbole to implication; in opting for a less strident, less obvious statement, he has produced a more mature work. (p. 81)

> *George J. Searles, "'Something Hap-*

pened': A New Direction for Joseph Heller," in* Critique: Studies in Modern Fiction *(copyright © by James Dean Young 1977), Vol. XVIII, No. 3, 1977, pp. 74-81.*

* * *

HELLMAN, Lillian 1906-

American playwright, screenwriter, and director, Hellman has also published three highly successful memoirs. Hellman's plays and memoirs are characterized by a scrupulous diction, an economy of language, and an objectivity that consistently rejects sentimentality. (See also *CLC*, **Vols. 2, 4, and** *Contemporary Authors*, **Vols. 13-16, rev. ed.)**

Pentimento deals mainly with people other than its author, but there is still a good deal of Lillian Hellman in it—possibly more than she intended—and it's hard not to think of the book as finishing off *An Unfinished Woman,* a memoir which was inundated with laurels but left at least one reader doubting its widely proclaimed first-rateness. Meaty details about Dorothy Parker, Hemingway, Scott Fitzgerald and Dashiell Hammett were not quite compensation enough for a garrulous pseudo-taciturnity—distinction of style, it seemed to me, was precisely the quality *An Unfinished Woman* had not a particle of. The very first time Hammett's drinking was referred to as 'the drinking' you knew you were in for a solid course of bastardized Hemingwayese. The drinking got at least a score more mentions. There were also pronounced tendencies towards that brand of aggressive humility, or claimed innocence, which finds itself helpless to explain the world at the very moment when the reader is well justified in requiring that a writer should give an apprehensible outline of what he deems to be going on. . . . What we needed to hear about was what she *thought,* and it appeared that what she thought was, as usual, a sophisticated version, decked out with Hem-Dash dialogue, of 'I don't understand these things'. . . .

The 'I don't understand these things' syndrome came in depressingly handy whenever she wandered on to the scene of an event about which she might have been obliged to say something analytical if she had. . . .

Lillian Hellman was an early and impressive example of the independent woman, but she never completely forsakes feather-headed femininity as a ploy, and her continuing ability not to comprehend what was going on in Russia is a glaring demonstration. In a section of *An Unfinished Woman* dealing with a later trip to Russia, she finds herself tongue-tied in the presence of a Russian friend. We are asked to believe that her own feelings about the McCarthy period were welling up to block her speech, just as the Russian friend's experience of the recent past had blocked hers. The two communed in silence. That this equation was presented as a profundity seemed to me at the time to prove that Lillian Hellman, whatever her stature in the theatre, possessed, as an essayist, an attitudinizing mind of which her mannered prose was the logically consequent expression. One doesn't underrate the virulence of McCarthyism for a minute, and it may well be that such goonery is as fundamental to America's history as terror is to Russia's. But the two things are so different in nature, and so disparate in scale, that a mind which equates them loses the ability to describe either. For all its Proustian persnicketiness of recollected detail, *An Unfinished Woman* was a very vague book. . . .

I certainly agree [with other reviewers] that the perceptiveness [in *Pentimento*], such as it is, is closely linked to the style. What I can't see for a moment is how trained *literati* can imagine that the style is anything less than frantically mannered and anything more than painfully derivative. (p. 88)

[There are passages in *Pentimento* that] read like E. B. White's classic parody *Across the Street and into the Grill*, in which White established once and for all that Hemingway's diction could not be copied, not even by Hemingway. Nor are these echoes mere lapses: her whole approach to moral-drawing is Hemingway's—the excitations, the pacing and the intensifications. (p. 89)

To have been there, to have seen it, and yet still be able to write it down so that it rings false—it takes a special kind of talent. . . .

On Broadway Lillian Hellman took her chances among the men, a pioneer women's liberationist. Her plays were bold efforts, indicative social documents which are unlikely to be neglected by students, although as pieces for the theatre they will probably date: they are problem plays whose problems are no longer secrets, for which in some measure we have her to thank. She is a tough woman who has almost certainly not been relishing the patronizing critical practice—more common in America than here, and let's keep it that way—of belatedly indicating gratitude for strong early work by shouting unbridled hosannahs for pale, late stuff that has a certain documentary value but not much more. She says at one point in *Pentimento* that in her time on Broadway she was always denied the benefits of the kind of criticism which would take her properly to task. (p. 90)

> *Clive James, "Stars and Stripes," in* The New Review *(© The New Review Ltd., 11 Greek Street, London W1V 5LE), May, 1974, pp. 88-90.*

It is easy enough to find a place in the short and simple annals of the poor American stage, but is that any reason for an author who is so clearly a melodramatist rather than a dramatist to usurp a position of prominence? Certainly Miss Hellman knows how to construct a play, just as a tailor knows how to make a suit, but unless that tailor is also a designer, unless he creates a style, are we to call him a *couturier*? The fact is that *Watch on the Rhine* is a good piece of melodrama, and *The Children's Hour* a sometimes brashly effective broadside, but as plays they are inferior to *The Little Foxes* by almost as much as it is inferior to Chekhov, whom, in its best moments, it tries to resemble. But unfortunately its best moments—I mean its attempts at psychology, language, drama—are really its weakest. Only when villainy snarls or smiles as it stabs does the work come to life—and then only to the second-rate life of melodrama. (p. 117)

> *John Simon, in his* Uneasy Stages: A Chronicle of the New York Theater 1963-1973 *(copyright © 1975 by John Simon; reprinted by permission of Random House, Inc.), Random House, 1975.*

[Even] though Miss Hellman is scrupulously specific in what she says in *Scoundrel Time*, carefully limiting her text to what she herself experienced, thought, said, and did, this memoir nevertheless applies directly to the essential experience of her time—in other words, to history. There are a couple of good reasons for this. First, and probably most important, is that this is a work of *literary* quality. As with her two previous memoirs, *An Unfinished Woman* and *Pentimento, Scoundrel Time* is a triumph of tone. No writer I know can match the eloquence of her ah-what-the-hell as she looks back over the whole sorry spectacle and tells with restraint and precision just what she sees. Lillian Hellman is a woman given to truth-telling as a kind of benign neurosis. She spares neither her friends nor herself. . . .

Surely another reason that *Scoundrel Time*, within its set limits, is of real historical importance is that its author had such an important role in the continuing drama (about equal parts farce and tragedy) played out before the House Committee on Un-American Activities. Not only was she the most eminent unfriendly witness to be called before the committee when she appeared in 1952—the author of *The Children's House, The Little Foxes,* and *The Autumn Garden* among other plays—but she was the only one up to that time to score even a limited victory against it. (p. 28)

There are those, however, she cannot forgive—not, perhaps surprisingly, those who cooperated with the committee and actually gave names of those known, or sometimes only thought, to be Communists. There are sad, vivid, touching portraits of a couple of these on the eve of testifying. She shows us Clifford Odets at dinner with her, truculently proclaiming his defiance, pounding the table so hard he knocks over a glass, promising he would "show them the face of a real radical man." He appeared before the committee the day before she did, and he gave names. Not long after her meeting with Odets she had another dinner, this time with Elia Kazan. He talked in such circles that he only managed to confuse her. Thinking that if she gave him a few minutes to collect himself he might make more sense, she left their table to make a phone call to someone who happened to be a mutual friend. In passing, she mentioned her difficulty understanding what Kazan was getting at. She was told: "He is telling you that he is going to become a friendly witness. I know because he told me this morning." Kazan and Odets named one another as former members of the Communist Party; neither implicated Lillian Hellman. (p. 29)

> *Bruce Cook, "Notes on a Shameful Era," in* Saturday Review *(© 1976 by Saturday Review/World, Inc.; reprinted with permission), April 17, 1976, pp. 28-9.*

At the opening of "Scoundrel Time," Lillian Hellman's memoir of the McCarthy era, she says that there is no mystery why this, the most painful episode in her life, was never told in two previous autobiographical works, "An Unfinished Woman" and "Pentimento." . . . This story, of artistic necessity, had to be singled out from the polished memoirs that preceded it: it is a beautiful work of self-definition.

Twenty-five years after the fact Lillian Hellman is still angry, but the villains are not, as one might expect, the leading players in the perfidious spectacle of that time—McCarthy, Nixon, the whole sick crew—but the many writers, movie people and academics who found patriotism an easy refuge. "Simply, then and now," she writes, "I feel betrayed by the nonsense I had believed. I had no right to think that American intellectuals were people who would fight for anything if doing so would injure them. . . ." Hellman stands witness to all of her time: "then and now" are the operative words here. She would like to demythize the hysterical red-baiting days of Joe McCarthy, the Hollywood Ten, the blacklists, the friendly witnesses, the opportunism of Nixon; and her method is to match each public personality and event with a corresponding inner reality that she is still willing and able to verify.

"Scoundrel Time" is compelling, quite wonderful to read: we see her then, a young woman sitting on the bed with Dashiell Hammett in the beginning of their days together, listening to his confession of a difficult time in his past: we hear her react with the pious absolutism of the inexperienced. . . . Her life, as we know from the autobiographies, always did contain the material of drama. From the start of her career as a playwright she knew how to arrange her scenes.

"Then" is skillfully told, but the "now," the alert, tough mind of Lillian Hellman watching herself, is what gives life to her story. (p. 1)

"Scoundrel Time" is not a confessional book. Hellman has seldom told more than her work required. Hiss, Chambers, the pumpkin, the boozy demise of Joe McCarthy are sketched in, and she gives us the details of her own bewildering sadness during those hard times. . . . Her stories are guarded and spare by design. It is clear from much of Hellman's work in the theater that she is good at staging her arguments and can even be—in "Watch on the Rhine" and "The Searching Wind"—comfortable as a partisan. In her later prose she is equally disciplined and fervent, but memory has become a liberation: as she speaks directly to us her voice, unshared with her characters, has a new freedom. For a mind like Hellman's the imagination is enlarged not limited by the facts of her life. She has forged a remarkable autobiographical style which relates the emotionally charged moment to a wide cultural reference. The precedent for "Scoundrel Time" is "Julia," the resonant story in "Pentimento" of a girlhood friendship, which seems to extend itself almost effortlessly as we read.

It is the personal quality of this book which preempts argument: one cranky, strong-willed lady had expected, wrongly that smart people would behave decently. She is clearheaded; by her own admission it took her "too long to see what was going on in the Soviet Union." Yes, she "mistakenly denied" the "sins of Stalin Communism," but the last thing she asks is our support or sympathy for her political positions. The question which she puts to all of us now and to all of those who more or less collaborated then is: "Since when do you have to agree with people to defend them from injustice?" (pp. 1-2)

The great risk that Lillian Hellman takes is in playing her own heroine. There are two scenes on the grand scale in "Scoundrel Time" where, if we don't read carefully, she is almost too fine. The narrative builds to her day in court. Her letter to the Committee (given in full earlier in the book) is read into the record. Her words. "I cannot and will not cut my conscience to fit this year's fashions," rings with conviction in our minds as it must have in the hearing room. But just as the morality play becomes too simple, the underlying drama unfolds, a legalistic comedy of errors which she does not understand, and she is excused. She will not, in fact, go to prison but is free to have lunch and a few too many drinks with her lawyers. For years after, she recomposes the letter and restages her performance in her mind, where most of us play our bravest roles. Shortly after her Washington appearance Lillian Hellman went on stage, literally, to read the narrative for Marc Blitzstein's opera

version of "The Little Foxes." Before a word was spoken she received a standing ovation from the New York audience. . . .

[Hellman] doesn't care whether her readers like her or not. She is not waiting up for the notices to come in. The final pages of "Scoundrel Time" are a sweeping and fierce indictment of our past and present passivity. . . .

In the wake of Watergate, Lillian Hellman has made the necessary connection between 1952 and our recent disgrace. Her self-reliance is extraordinary; in her insistence on writing her story "then and now" she has, in Camus's terms, dedicated herself to the duration of her life. She has not been content with the success of the past but has gone on to a new career, and in writing her memoirs she remains responsible for everything that happens to her. (p. 2)

> Maureen Howard, in The New York Times Book Review (© 1976 by The New York Times Company; reprinted by permission), April 25, 1976.

What is . . . distinctive about Scoundrel Time is the voice behind the words—that voice we first heard with such startled pleasure in An Unfinished Woman . . . then with deepening gratification in Pentimento . . . and now with moving intensity in this third volume of Hellman memoirs. It is the voice of a writer who seeks to describe in measured sentences as precisely as possible the imprecise flow of life as it has moved through her and all around her. It is the voice of a writer who reveals great courage of spirit because that voice, quite plainly, says: Make no mistake, there is much about myself I do not know, much that remains a dark and painful mystery I cannot face unflinchingly because if I do I will lose control and fall apart all over these pages, and that I'm damned if I'll do. But much that seems painful is often merely difficult. I know the difference between pressure and pain, and pressure I can take. I will force my pen, my actions, my life down on those pressure points to the utmost of my ability—even unto the point of pain.

It is quality that makes Lillian Hellman the remarkable writer she is. The measured gravity of her sentences coupled always with the sudden, earthy directness reveals a steadiness and independence of mind, heart, and spirit that induce nothing but uncritical admiration; a welling-up of warmth and gratitude in the face of such a civilized intelligence. (pp. 46-7)

Scoundrel Time is a valuable piece of work. The kind of work that stands alone, untouched, in the midst of foolish criticism and foolish praise alike. (p. 47)

> Vivian Gornick, "Neither Forgotten nor Forgiven," in Ms. (© 1976 Ms. Magazine Corp.), August, 1976, pp. 46-7.

* * *

HEMINGWAY, Ernest   1899-1961

A novelist and short story writer, Hemingway is regarded by many to be one of America's greatest authors. Known for his abbreviated style and stories which picture men proving their worth in situations of conflict, Hemingway attempted to live what he wrote. An associate of F. Scott Fitzgerald, Ford Madox Ford, and James Joyce in Paris during the 1920s, Hemingway fought in World War I, the Spanish Civil War, and led resistance action against the Germans in France during World War II. A recipient of the Nobel Prize for Literature, Hemingway committed suicide in 1961. (See also CLC, Vols. 1, 3, 6.)

As critics have pointed out, *The Torrents of Spring* satirizes [Sherwood] Anderson's experimental novel *Dark Laughter* (1925), in which he had gone pretty far out. Straining for new effects, he had drifted uncertainly. Especially tempting to the shark-like instincts of the satirist were some of Anderson's experiments with impressionism and stream of consciousness.... There are whole paragraphs in *The Torrents of Spring* exaggerating the jerky, noun-heavy style which resulted from [Anderson's] experiments.... (p. 488)

In addition to parodying the older author's flickering, impressionistic presentation, Hemingway also zeroed in on Anderson's unsuccessful attempts at stream-of-consciousness narrative....

It is risky to apply the stream-of-consciousness elements of the parody exclusively to Anderson, for Hemingway was also sniping at Gertrude Stein. Although *Dark Laughter*'s attempts at stream-of-consciousness narrative and its catalogs are definitely Joycean, Hemingway's profound and lasting respect for Joyce rules out satire. (p. 489)

[Hemingway's story "My Old Man"] provides evidence of Anderson's influence. Although it is Hemingway's only known experiment with a naïve, colloquial, adolescent narrator, other elements of the story, such as colloquial devices and a new, subjective way of describing things, persisted and can thus be traced back to Anderson, particularly to "I Want to Know Why." (pp. 490-91)

As Hemingway said in defending the originality of his story, it does include the father-son dimension not present in Anderson's tale.... But in matters of style, there are parallels of far-reaching significance, parallels which can be extended to vernacular elements found throughout the body of the authors' works. (p. 491)

[A] fundamental characteristic of the colloquial style, *polysyndeton,* or the linking of simple sentences with *and,* is ... found in both stories.... (p. 492)

Hemingway ... made extensive use of the construction in work following "My Old Man." It is especially evident in his early writing: *The Sun Also Rises* (1926), "Now I Lay Me" (1927), and *A Farewell to Arms* (1929). Polysyndeton is less prominent in his later prose, although *Green Hills of Africa* (1935) provides a few good examples. He was at the same time beginning to forsake the coordinated sentence for more involved ones. Two outstanding stories appearing in 1936 continued the movement toward a new style: In "The Snows of Kilimanjaro," a fondness for polysyndeton is still discernible, but even the compound sentences manifest an increasing amount of subordination. "The Short Happy Life of Francis Macomber" provides further illustration of this change in emphasis. The trend toward two widely divergent styles accelerates in *For Whom the Bell Tolls* (1940), which has on the colloquial side Pilar's account of the massacre of the Fascists, but is more typically represented by denser, more complexly subordinated sentences.

The thrust of Hemingway's stylistic development after *A Farewell to Arms,* then, may be seen as being toward greater complexity and increased subordination. Overall evaluations of Hemingway's style have always been complicated by eccentric works such as *Death in the Afternoon* (1932), *To Have and Have Not* (1937), and *Across the River and Into the Trees* (1950), which are sometimes interpreted as being his attempt to attain that "fourth and fifth

dimension" in prose. With his last two books, *The Old Man and the Sea* (1952) and *A Moveable Feast* (1964), it seemed that Hemingway was trying to return to his proven vernacular strength. Although not specifically colloquial, yet providing examples of polysyndeton, the style of *The Old Man and the Sea* is nonetheless simpler than the middle works, if rather mannered. It is in returning to Paris, appropriately, in attempting to recapture the simple pleasures, that Hemingway most closely approaches the style he was writing thirty years before.... Comparing *A Moveable Feast* with *Across the River and Into the Trees,* it occurs to the reader not only to question Faulkner's widely shared opinion that Hemingway never experimented, but also to lament that he ever sought any other than the third dimension of prose he found in Paris.

While he employed it ... Hemingway apparently made more extensive use of polysyndeton than did Anderson. Influence is difficult to ascribe here, but it should be noted that Anderson did not really use polysyndeton as much as appearances suggest. Also, it is unwise to overlook possible sources of influence on both. (pp. 493-95)

[It] would seem that, although Anderson did provide some models, the relationship was more one of parallel development than of direct influence. And it is Hemingway who made the most of the legacy left by vernacular pioneers such as Mark Twain and Gertrude Stein. (p. 495)

Perhaps the most significant link between [Anderson and Hemingway], one which grows out of their common vernacular heritage, but which ultimately transcends it, is the colloquial habit of *understatement,* the deliberate use of simple modifiers like *nice, fine,* and *good* in place of more descriptive words. (p. 498)

Both stories ["I Want to Know Why" and "My Old Man"] utilize vague adjectives which convey states of feeling rather than concrete details. This *subjective descriptive technique,* which later came to be associated with Hemingway, is very evident in "I Want to Know Why." (p. 500)

Beginning ... with the inspiration of British and American colloquial understatement, Hemingway followed Anderson's lead in developing this technique for conveying the maximum amount of emotion with the least possible fuss. It would seem from the evidence of "I Want to Know Why" and "My Old Man" that this was Anderson's clearest technical gift to him, the others bearing to varying degrees the mark of Gertrude Stein. Whereas in matters of syntax and repetition, Anderson was in a way his fellow pupil, in this stylistic area above all others, he showed Hemingway the way to convey immediacy with emotional intensity. (p. 503)

> *Paul P. Somers, Jr., "The Mark of Sherwood Anderson on Hemingway: A Look at the Texts," in* South Atlantic Quarterly *(reprinted by permission of the Publisher; copyright 1974 by Duke University Press, Durham, North Carolina), Autumn, 1974, pp. 487-503.*

As a man [severely wounded in World War I], Hemingway lived every day in the full knowledge of his own death; and as a writer, he sought, at the deepest levels of his art, to confront this knowledge and to shape its meanings. In the process, he highlights the flowering of the tremendous and probably irreversible change in the direction and content of human consciousness which began in the twelfth and thirteenth centuries and culminated in the middle and late nineteenth century: the secularization and internalization of reality which is the true significance of those much misused terms, realism and naturalism. Then as now, the most characteristic and influential thinkers and artists increasingly saw reality in, and only in, this world and man and in the dynamic interrelationship between them. Then and since, the shifting glow of the magical, the supernatural, the transcendent, the absolute increasingly flickered out in those remote and mysterious mental processes we call human consciousness.

So it was too with Hemingway. The beliefs and values implanted by his childhood . . . were shredded in the explosion of the trench mortar. For Hemingway, death and its implications for life became entirely existential realities to be confronted existentially—though, to be sure, with a small rather than with a large *e*. In his writing, religion appears only as an empty echo of what once was but is no more; and men turn to objective nature and to themselves and each other for meaning and solace. (pp. 176-77)

In such a universe, reality for Hemingway is entirely and only secular and human: objective nature and the external world as man perceives them with his senses and learns from them through experience. The famous and extraordinarily eloquent concreteness of Hemingway's style is inimitable precisely because it is not primarily stylistic: the *how* of Hemingway's style is the *what* of his characteristic vision.

Tortured to the edge of insanity by a world gone mad in war, Nick Adams keeps his hold on reality by returning to the pure and absorbing sensuousness of camping and fishing on the Big Two-Hearted River. . . . Waiting to be killed by Fascist cavalry, Robert Jordan in *For Whom the Bell Tolls* finds meaning not in religious or philosophical abstractions but in the people he loves and is dying for and in his sensuous perceptions of nature. "He was completely integrated now and he took a good long look at everything. Then he looked up at the sky. There were big white clouds in it. He touched the palm of his hand against the pine needles where he lay and he touched the bark of the pine trunk that he lay behind." Santiago in *The Old Man and the Sea* prays for divine aid in catching his great fish, but he does so mechanically: "I am not religious," he thinks; and reality for him is the sea with all its creatures, the birds above it, and himself and his fellow fishermen upon it. (pp. 177-78)

Hemingway recognizes that with the disappearance of the transcendent and the absolute from man's consciousness, the universe becomes empty of meaning and purpose. . . . Santiago doesn't understand a universe in which he must kill the great fish he has come to love. "I do not understand these things, he thought. But it is good that we do not try to kill the sun or the moon or the stars. It is enough to live on the sea and kill our true brothers."

In such a universe, the ultimate truths of man's condition are existential and creatural: whatever else life may be or become, it is first of all a matter of violence, pain, suffering, and death. These are the characteristic terms of Hemingway's world, these and his conviction that man must confront them directly. Moreover, in addition to nature, Hemingway's richest source of imagery and symbolism is Christianity; but for Hemingway, the meaning of Christ is not martyred God but suffering and enduring man. It is a rare story of Hemingway's which does not center in some way on violence, suffering, or death; and nearly all his novels end in death. (pp. 179-80)

If Hemingway sees man trapped in a void, he is also convinced that man is not without resources in the trap. "Light was all it needed," he writes, "and a certain cleanness and order." For Hemingway, the central problem of man is how to live in this world; and he believes devoutly that man has the capacity and the will to recognize the existential and creatural truths of his condition and yet to find or to create within it meaning, order, and beauty.

The first thing man must do, Hemingway suggests, is to discard the illusions which lie to him about reality. A powerful current of disillusion flows through Hemingway's writing, especially in his early works, a feeling that little or nothing in the human condition is what he had been led to believe it is. Not surprisingly, therefore, many of his characters undergo a stripping away of all illusions. (pp. 181-82)

Once man has recognized the truth of his condition and accepted it, he can, if he will, Hemingway believes, live in it with meaning, order, and beauty, finding or creating them in the processes of life itself. Experience in this world is the key: "Perhaps as you went along you did learn something," Jake Barnes tells himself. "I did not care what it was all about. All I wanted to know was how to live in it. Maybe if you found out how to live in it you learned from that what it was all about." For Hemingway, learning to live in this world means turning to the sensuous beauty of nature, to sequential processes with immediate goals to be found in or imposed on nature and society, and to meaningful personal and social relationships. . . . Hemingway's fascination with bullfighting stems largely from his view of it as an art form, a ritual tragedy in which man confronts the creatural realities of violence, pain, suffering, and death by imposing on them an esthetic form which gives them order, significance, and beauty.

But learning to live in this world also implies for Hemingway a meaningful involvement with other people. (pp. 182-83)

By living in [this world], then, man can find or create meaning, order, and beauty; and working increasingly at the deepest levels of Hemingway's thought and art is the conviction that man's fullest source of meaning and value lies in his relationship to all those who share life with him. Friendship, love, and empathy: these are man's finest triumphs over an existential and creatural human condition he can neither escape nor change nor ultimately understand. Hemingway's writing is rich in memorable friendships: Jake Barnes and Bill Gorton, Frederick Henry and Rinaldi, Robert Jordan and Anselmo, Santiago and Manolin. Equally important in Hemingway's world is sexual love. Love may be only secular and natural, not the spiritual absolute of the romantics; and its highest, not its lowest, expression may be sexual; but it is none the less for Hemingway a life-transforming experience. (pp. 183-84)

The fullest measure of meaning and value which can come to man through living in this world, a consequence of experience that appears increasingly in Hemingway's middle and later works, is a profound empathy, an acceptance of life in all its paradoxical imperatives and a deep compassion for those creatures who share them with him. In Hemingway's earlier writing, nature is primarily objective reality to be experienced sensuously; and hunting and fishing are principally important as sequential activities with immediate goals. In *Green Hills of Africa*, however, his love of nature deepens into a profound harmony with it; he feels love and compassion for the creatures he hunts, and he identifies with them and shares their pain. These responses to life become the central experience of *The Old Man and the Sea*. (p. 184)

The high seriousness of Hemingway's writing evokes an essentially tragic vision of man. His characters can and do transcend the conditions which hurt and destroy them: in an empty and indifferently maleficent universe, they confront the human condition directly and by living fully within it find or create meaning, order, and beauty. "Man is not made for defeat," says Santiago, "A man can be destroyed but not defeated." But Hemingway's vision and his art, in all their greatness, look backward to a time still able to evoke and sustain them: he has something of the rationality and the stoicism of a classical age, something of the harmony with nature of the Romantics, a largely positivistic epistemology, much of the concept of character of the realists, and much of the subject matter of the naturalists. He is, then, in most respects a thinker and artist with his roots in the nineteenth century, a great writer of the recent past. (p. 191)

> *Clinton S. Burhans, Jr., "Hemingway and Vonnegut: Diminishing Vision in a Dying Age," in* Modern Fiction Studies *(copyright © 1975 by Purdue Research Foundation, West Lafayette, Indiana, U.S.A.), Summer, 1975, pp. 173-91.*

Hemingway . . . learned one role early, that of Special Correspondent, professionally detached from public horrors which he owed it to his readers to write down. . . . This role, in the inter-chapters of *In Our Time*, established a center from which to write of private horrors as well, and we can tell from the swept and tidied prose of those stories how readily it could blend into another role, that of the martyr to literature, starving while he sought to write One True Sentence. (p. 144)

The quest of the one true sentence leads to wordlessness; that is the irony of Hemingway's aesthetic. And if, to get a novel written, wordlessness must be filled with words, they will verge on the parodic. Joyce began *Ulysses* in naturalism and ended it in parody, understanding more profoundly than any of his followers that naturalism cannot end anywhere else, and a law like the hidden law that governs the unfolding of styles in *Ulysses* brought Hemingway to self-parody at last, as though, not understanding the history disclosed by Joyce, he was condemned to repeat it. (p. 155)

[His] drive, he thought, [was] to recapture perfect moments: to put down "what the actual things were which produced the emotion that you experienced." But that drive was menaced, perfect moments were encroached on, by a . . . small word, which he preferred in its Spanish form, *nada*. We see it surrounding "A Clean Well-Lighted Place," and the light holding it at bay.

Fighting off *nada* was his conscious drive, but only a small part of his achievement. His achievement, seldom vouchsafed to the novels but often to the stories, consisted in setting down, so sparely that we can see past them, the words for the action that concealed the real action: Nick Adams fishing, not thinking, very deliberately not thinking of the shadows, or the protagonist of "After the Storm" withheld by the very limits of the body from satisfying his almost bodily greed for the rings on the fingers of the submarine Venus, her dead face afloat amid its floating hair beneath that impregnable glass between what is quick and what is still. (pp. 156-57)

> *Hugh Kenner, in his* A Homemade World: The American Modernist Writers *(copyright © 1975 by Hugh Kenner; reprinted by permission of Alfred A. Knopf, Inc.), Knopf, 1975.*

[*Islands in the Stream*] consists of material that the author during his lifetime did not see fit to publish; therefore it should not be held against him. That parts of it are good is entirely to his credit; that other parts are puerile and, in a pained way, aimless testifies to the odds against which Hemingway, in the last two decades of his life, brought anything to completion. It is, I think, to the discredit of his publishers that no introduction offers to describe from what stage of Hemingway's tormented later career *Islands in the Stream* was salvaged, or to estimate what its completed design might have been, or to confess what editorial choices were exercised in the preparation of this manuscript. Rather, a gallant wreck of a novel is paraded as the real thing, as if the public are such fools as to imagine a great writer's ghost is handing down books intact from Heaven. (pp. 422-23)

Carlos Baker's biography speaks of a trilogy about the sea that Hemingway, amid the distractions of Cuba, the cockfights and double Daiquiris and proliferating hangers-on, carried forward with enthusiasm in late 1950 and early 1951. The third item of the trilogy, "The Sea in Being," was separately, and triumphantly, published as *The Old Man and the Sea*. The first part, "The Sea When Young," seems to have been an abridgment of an earlier, disastrously long and gauche novel called *Garden of Eden*. The middle section, "The Sea When Absent," has for its hero an American painter named Thomas Hudson and, in the form that Hemingway announced as "finished" by Christmas of 1950, answers the description of the section entitled "Cuba" in the present book. "The Island and the Stream" (*sic*) had become, by mid-1951, the working title of the first section, presumably the revamped *Garden of Eden*. (p. 423)

What we have, then, is a trio of large fragments crudely unified by a Caribbean setting and the nominal presence of Thomas Hudson. "Bimini" is a collection of episodes that show only a groping acquaintance with one another; "Cuba" is a lively but meandering excursion in local color that, when the painter's first wife materializes, bizarrely veers into a dark and private region; and "At Sea" is an adventure story of ersatz intensity. Hudson, if taken sequentially, does not grow but dwindles, from an affectionate and baffled father and artist into a rather too expertly raffish waterfront character into a bleak manhunter, a comic-book superhuman containing unlooked-for bubbles of stoic meditation and personal sorrow. (pp. 423-24)

Whereas an achieved novel, however autobiographical, dissolves the author and directs our attention beyond him, *Islands in the Stream,* even where most effective, inspires us with a worried concern for the celebrity who wrote it. His famous drinking, his methodical artistic devotions, his dawn awakenings, his women, his cats, even his mail (what painter gets anything like a writer's burdensome, fascinating mail?) are all there, mixed with less easily publicized strains, dark currents that welled into headlines with his last illnesses and shocking suicide. The need to prove himself implacably drives Thomas Hudson toward violence and death. His enemy, pain, has become an object of infatuation. (p. 424)

Hemingway of course did not invent the world, nor pain, mutilation, and death. In his earlier work his harsh obsessions seem honorable and necessary; an entire generation of American men learned to speak in the accents of Hemingway's stoicism. But here, the tension of art has been snapped and the line between sensitive vision and psychopathy has been crossed. The "sea-chase story" is in many ways excellent, but it has the falsity of the episode in Hemingway's real life upon which it was based. (p. 425)

The new generations, my impression is, want to abolish both war and love, not love as a physical act but love as a religion, a creed to help us suffer better. The sacred necessity of suffering no longer seems sacred or necessary, and Hemingway speaks across the Sixties as strangely as a medieval saint; I suspect few readers younger than myself could believe, from this sad broken testament, how we *did* love Hemingway and, pity feeling impudent, love him still. (pp. 426-27)

> *John Updike, "Papa's Sad Testament," in his* Picked-Up Pieces *(copyright © 1975 by John Updike; reprinted by permission of Alfred A. Knopf, Inc.), Knopf, 1975, pp. 422-27.*

The difficulty of deriving a single, coherent understanding of the political theme of *For Whom the Bell Tolls* is a result of the major value of the novel—that it refuses to simplify events, motives, or politics, but insists on rendering the complexity of what was a very complicated historical and political event. In fact, the novel seems to do a number of paradoxical things: while Jordan praises the organizing and disciplining power of the Communists, he also reveals their corruption and divorce from the Spanish people; while defending the Republican cause, Hemingway renders sympathetic portraits of several Nationalist soldiers; while portraying the bravery, and communal unity of the guerilla fighters, he also indicts their lack of discipline and responsibility; and, finally, although the novel supports the Republican cause and makes a number of warning statements about fascism, it also indicts the dehumanizing effects of power politics, Falangist and Communist alike. (pp. 269-70)

[The] Jordan that we see at the narrative beginning of *For Whom the Bell Tolls* is a wounded romantic hero, a man who has become an emotionally alienated, pragmatic instrument of those who are conducting the war. All that he really has to sustain himself is his craft and his current assignment. When Pilar asks him what he believes in, he replies, "In my work." . . . His reply is uninvolved, mechanistic, emotionally detached from the cause; it defines the insulated mental discipline that Jordan has shored up against his profound disillusionment in order to continue to function. But if this were the primary subject of the novel's political theme, then *For Whom the Bell Tolls* would not be a great deal different from the political novels of Silone, Koestler, and Orwell—all of whom have dramatized the liberal-humanist disillusionment with power politics. However, Hemingway is interested in doing something different than just showing this classic disillusionment. The novel is primarily concerned with retrieving Jordan from the abyss of his disillusionment and restoring the values which he has lost—for Hemingway's concern is not with saving his hero from the mucky world of politics, but with preserving both Jordan's personal authenticity and his ability to function as a political man.

With his entrance into the Sierra del Guardarama and the community of the partisans, Jordan undergoes a process of reorientation that reawakens his humanist sensibility. . . . The effect of this community, then, is to reawaken Jordan to the values of personal relations and personal conscience, both of which he has tried to hold in abeyance. This almost simple re-education of the disillusioned Jordan is the method by which Hemingway dramatizes what he sees as the dichotomy between power politics and the basic struggle of the common people—asserting, like Orwell, that the war against fascism must also be concerned with the preservation of personal and the individual values. (pp. 272-74)

While Hemingway seems to make more of the underlying humanity that connects . . . men than of the rival ideologies which separate them, he also realizes that in the face of fascism men must act as political men. And this is precisely the problematic political sensibility behind the novel.

I think we can now see that although *For Whom the Bell Tolls* rejects both power politics and ideological rhetoric, the novel is by no means without a clear political commitment. The conclusion of the novel is concerned with exposing the very real danger imposed by the threat of fascism and with suggesting what must be done in order to avoid the domination of power politics. Hemingway offers a simple, almost naive panacea for a world that has become increasingly ideological: education. (p. 276)

If this political vision seems to be fundamentally simplistic and expressive of a conservative-bourgeois standard, it nevertheless defines the political sensibility of the novel. The final political message of the novel is the need to combat both fascism and power politics in the name of such simple human virtues as individual freedom and dignity—for it is finally just such bourgeois-humanist language that expresses Hemingway's political commitment in *For Whom the Bell Tolls*. (p. 278)

> *David E. Zehr, "Bourgeois Politics: Hemingway's Case in 'For Whom the Bell Tolls'," in* The Midwest Quarterly *(copyright, 1976, by The Midwest Quarterly, Kansas State College of Pittsburg), Spring 1976, pp. 268-78.*

In recent years, . . . several critics have referred briefly to similarities between [Hemingway and Henry James]. Their tremendous dedication to their craft is generally acknowledged, for example, as is their at times almost obsessive interest in style, an interest which sometimes goes beyond their desire to describe "the way it was." Arthur Mizener has observed [in *Twelve Great American Novels*] that both men "wrote in styles that to some extent exist independently of what they are being used to express in order that they may display certain purely stylistic qualities that have some sort of false but irresistible appeal for the writer." . . . Their handling of dialogue has been compared—the almost stichomythic quality of much of their conversation, for example, and their use of what Carlos Baker calls [in *Hemingway: The Writer as Artist*] the "hovering subject": conversation which proceeds along two planes—the overt and bland, the covert and significant. They create dialogue which reveals even as it attempts to conceal, a fact which helps to explain the tension that a reader feels in scenes from both writers in which the surface subjects are trivial. . . . [Critics have] noted important thematic similarities between the two men: . . . their common interest in the themes of the American in Europe, the artist in society and

. . . their mutual efforts to dramatize ways of life in which the physical, the aesthetic, and the ethical are fused. (pp. 155-56)

Perhaps the most effective way of convincing critics of the remarkable and interesting similarities which exist between the visions of both writers (particularly between the work of the early Hemingway and that of James from *The Portrait of a Lady* on) is to compare two novels ostensibly very different. Hence, my focus on *What Maisie Knew,* James's story about a little English girl whose parents are divorced, and on *The Sun Also Rises,* Hemingway's tale about post-war expatriate life in Paris and Spain. Both are excellent novels, and both possess cogent likenesses which can be found in other works by the two men.

That the world of Jake Barnes and his coterie is, for the most part, a moral wasteland, is obvious to any reader of the novel. The fine causes seem dead; the values of church, state, and middle class spurious to the Hemingway characters. . . . All this is clear and need not be dwelt upon.

It is equally clear that the world of James's child heroine in *What Maisie Knew* is also squalid, something which James stresses satirically in the prologue to the novel when he describes the effect on the child of her parents' divorce. . . . (pp. 156-57)

In *The Sun Also Rises,* the possibility of family life does not even exist for the central characters; the sexual relationships are often sado-masochistic. In *Maisie,* the family is a chameleon, shifting identities almost as soon as the child begins to recognize an old one or feel comfortable in it; and in James's story the men and women also engage in relationships which are at times exhilarating, but more often either subtly or patently destructive. . . .

Perhaps the most crucial similarity between the worlds of the two novels is that both are ravaged, metaphorically, by war. . . . It is a commonplace of Hemingway criticism, of course, that the threat of sudden physical and psychological violence and death pervades Hemingway's fiction. What also must be stressed, however, is that the drawing room world in many of James's novels can burst equally, frighteningly into war—a fact suggested in *Maisie* by several scenes in which hostility crackles and by the martial imagery which pervades the novel. . . . (p. 158)

[The] question which James poses paramountly—as does Hemingway—is not the why of the situation (although causes are implied), but "how to live in it." Jake Barnes, looking backward at the experience from which he has emerged, tries to find meaning in the heap of broken images which assault his memory, attempts to impose shores against his ruins. James, looking forward as he dramatizes the growth of Maisie's consciousness, watches while she seeks clues in her "domestic labyrinth" . . . and tries to learn how to live well as she plummets toward the death of her childhood. (p. 160)

In view of all these conditions, the most remarkable aspect of both *The Sun Also Rises* and *What Maisie Knew* is that, within the waste land worlds, values exist which, however evanescently, can transform games of war into games of love. Jake learns the values, of course, by observing Count Mippipopolous and Pedro Romero, the "code heroes." Thus he discovers not only the essentially negative virtues (because their worth is primarily defensive) of endurance, self-discipline, and courage; but also the positive ones—joy, love, the ability to suck from the marrow of the smallest piece of existence the goodness which is always there. Jake knows the values, although he is not very successful in living by them. Perhaps it is only through the telling of his story, thus reliving the events in memory and shaping them into meaningful form, that he is able to achieve Hemingway's peculiar blend of stoicism and hedonism—to live his life "all the way up, like the bullfighter." (p. 161)

> *W. R. Macnaughton, "Maisie's Grace Under Pressure: Some Thoughts on James and Hemingway," in* Modern Fiction Studies *(copyright © 1976, by Purdue Research Foundation, West Lafayette, Indiana, U.S.A.), Summer, 1976, pp. 153-64.*

Critics agree that Ernest Hemingway's "After the Storm" is about the narrator but disagree on how the reader is supposed to regard this scavenger of the Florida keys. Most critics have seen him as an exemplary Hemingway hero, representing "man's victory over himself and adjustment to the world in which he lives." Concomitant with this sympathetic view of the narrator is the idea that his values and behavior are moral, or at worst amoral: the scavenger acts and feels as he does in order to survive in a jungle-like environment. Recently, however, Anselm Atkins, calling attention to the loss of human life that the scavenger observes and reports totally dispassionately, has suggested that the narrator should be treated ironically, not sympathetically. This note aims first to point out a literary allusion hitherto unnoticed in Hemingway's story, and second to suggest tentatively how awareness of this allusion helps to determine which of the two prevalent approaches to the story is more valid.

The very title of Hemingway's story implies the kind of world into which the fiction seems to lead us: a world where the primary relationship between events is a temporal one ("*After* the Storm"), but also a world where being first does not guarantee a claim on buried treasure. (p. 374)

By far the most memorable portion of the story is the description of the narrator's discovery and examination of the wrecked liner. . . . This picture of a man excluded from wealth and, symbolically, from feminine companionship by the unyielding glass is an excellent instance of vivid naturalistic writing. That the narrator is close enough to note even the rings on the woman's hand emphasizes the painful near miss of fortune. But the scene can give us still more. Hemingway here employs an allusion to a passage from Plato, an allusion so subtle and so well-integrated into the narrative that it has escaped previous observation.

In the second book of *The Republic,* Glaucon, discussing with Socrates whether or not justice is intrinsically good, relates the myth of Gyges, a Lydian shepherd:

> after a great deluge of rain and an earthquake the ground opened and a chasm appeared in the place where he was pasturing; . . . he saw and wondered and went down into the chasm; and . . . he beheld other marvels there and a hollow bronze horse with little doors, and . . . he peeped in and saw a corpse within, as it seemed, of more than mortal stature, and . . . there was nothing else but a gold ring on its hand, which he took off and went forth.

Gyges subsequently discovers that the ring has the power to make its wearer invisible, and so, relieved of the possibility of detection, he seduces the king's wife, slays the king, and usurps the throne. Glaucon's point is that "no one is just of his own will but only from constraint".... The allusion seems indisputable.... But how does recognizing the reference help us to understand Hemingway's work?

To state the obvious, the semi-educated sponge fisherman is oblivious of the reference to Plato. This in itself creates a distance between the narrator on one hand and the author and the audience on the other, thus introducing the possibility of ironic treatment. Moreover, the critical disagreement over how the narrator should be regarded is indicative, I think, of the issue Hemingway knew his story would arouse: how does man reconcile selfishness and self-survival with concern for the well-being and survival of others? Perhaps the reference to a passage in *The Republic* which debates the very same question shows us Hemingway taking a Joycean perspective and laughing at those who would delve too deeply into his story in search of a solution. Or perhaps, and this is the answer I prefer, just as Glaucon's temporary argument in favor of moral relativity gives way eventually to Socrates' moral absolutism, so we are meant to see, indeed, that the narrator does not express Hemingway's last word, that the cold and ruthless scavenger's lack of an ethical system must give way to one which places a price other than salvage value on human life. (pp. 374-76)

> Robert G. Walker, "Irony and Allusion in Hemingway's 'After The Storm'," in Studies in Short Fiction (copyright 1976 by Newberry College), Summer, 1976, pp. 374-76.

The title of *For Whom The Bell Tolls* demonstrates that Hemingway was aware of the notion of men as islands, and in spite of that novel's apparent implication that no man is an island, the story of Thomas Hudson [*Islands in the Stream*] is a clear demonstration that at least one kind of man, in a psychological sense, is an island. Hudson, in fact, is only one island of an archipelago within Hemingway's fiction. Beginning with Nick Adams and Jake Barnes his characters are consistently isolated (from the Italian word *isola,* island), alone in the stream of human society. They occasionally make contact with others and experience a certain degree of communion and attachment, but these contacts are temporary.... The famous Hemingway code, after all, is a technique for coping with the island condition.... From Nick Adams's solitary and deliberate trout fishing to Santiago's lonely test with the great fish, Hemingway's characters are island men who confront loneliness and isolation by a ritual of disciplined physical activity. But the exterior toughness of these characters and their preoccupation with physical activity are masks for personalities that are essentially emotional, sensitive, and even tender. (p. 75)

Wright Morris once pointed out [that] the real "subject" of Hemingway, pushed to its extremity, is nostalgia. Hemingway himself was markedly prone to nostalgia and even as a young writer was beginning, in Carlos Baker's words, "To make fictional capital of the remembrance of things past." Nostalgia was at the very center of the process by which he created art from his own experience; and within his fiction it not only contributes to subject matter, but functions as an artistic device for developing characteri-

zation, vivifying settings, and producing a dramatic rhythm and intensity. He learned to make time past work in a special way in time present. (pp. 75-6)

The future never has a significant place for Hemingway. His concern is with the past and the present. His main interest in the future is in storing up experiences and memories which will later be recollected and savored. (p. 80)

Hemingway [sometimes used nostalgia] as an artistic device, as a distinct method of narration. Many of the conventional ways for revealing and developing character were unavailable to him because he had committed himself to the principle of showing rather than telling, to objective narration in which the author is self-effacing. This method has the advantage of dramatic immediacy, but the disadvantage of preventing the author from telling about subtle inner emotions and experience. Hemingway, by exploring a quality of his own temperament, was able to transcend this limitation. Islands of nostalgic recollection can be presented with an objectivity consistent with his chosen impersonal method of narration, but at the same time, nostalgia has an evocative power which awakens within the reader a rich and emotionally understood knowledge of the character's inner life. Hemingway seemed to believe that a man is his nostalgia—that is, what he remembers about the past and how it affects him in the present constitutes his essential personality. In Hemingway's naturalism a man is what he has experienced, and nostalgia seems to be the process by which the most meaningful of those experiences are selected to be actively remembered. As Hudson says to himself while looking over favorite paintings he bought long ago, "*Nostalgia hecha hombre*"—a man is formed or shaped by nostalgia. (p. 81)

> Stephen L. Tanner, "Hemingway's Islands," in Southwest Review (© 1976 by Southern Methodist University Press), Winter, 1976, pp. 74-84.

Hemingway has a hard time imagining beginnings but an easy time inventing ends. Middles challenge him most of all. His novels constantly anticipate, when they do not prematurely achieve, the sense of an ending.... Living from birth to death through a long life proves difficult of depiction for a writer trying to stave off death by continually adumbrating it. Hemingway's beginnings have the uncanny effect of raising the very specter of the end against which they are so concerned to defend. In the attempt to forestall annihilation by preempting it, Hemingway loses hold on the present. His moments of immediate experience unshadowed by future loss are rare indeed. His present tense, abundant as it is, registers itself as the tension of a consciousness caught between the trauma of the "before" and the fear of the "after." Hemingway's pleasure in the "now" is a largely apocryphal experience. Short stories, consumed in the limit of a single sitting, can protect us from the gathering sense of doom which becomes, in all but one of Hemingway's five major novels, his central effect. For writing novels of any length excites as much tension as it releases. The sense of option felt while beginning to write (or read) proves to be an oppressive irony when all that can be foreseen is the outstretched interval of time that must be filled. (pp. 476-77)

The major obstacle to understanding *In Our Time* is ellipsis. Do the spaces between the stories and vignettes connect or separate? Life emerges here as a series of gaps punctuated by crises. Reading *In Our Time* trains us to infer, to search for patterns of continuity underlying seemingly disjointed episodes. The continuity of the book reveals itself as psychological rather than structural. What we uncover is a life history obsessively unified. The reader's attention weaves together Nick's story as the true plot of the book.... ''Indian Camp'' is the true beginning of Nick's story and of Hemingway's novelistic career:

> At the lake shore there was another rowboat drawn up. The two Indians stood waiting.
>
> Nick and his father got in the stern of the boat and the Indians shoved it off and one of them got in to row. Uncle George sat in the stern of the camp rowboat. The young Indian shoved the camp boat off and got in to row Uncle George.
>
> The two boats started off in the dark. Nick heard the oarlocks of the other boat quite a way ahead of them in the mist. The Indians rowed with quick choppy strokes. Nick lay back with his father's arm around him. It was cold on the water. The Indian who was rowing them was working very hard, but the other boat moved further ahead in the mist all the time.
>
> ''Where are we going, Dad?'' Nick asked.

The darkness which shuts off sight does more than disorient. It presents departure as risky. Origins are murky here, just as ends will prove too certainly known. The one thing we will see clearly in ''Indian Camp'' is death; the one thing Nick cannot look at is birth. Our not being able to see where we start sharply contrasts with his being able to see how all of us must stop. Yet for all its obscurity about specific contours, this opening makes us confront the fact of priority. We enter a world already filled with objects. ''Another'' has gone before us. Repetition of definite articles (as in ''the Indians'') suggests that this is a place with which we are already familiar. Hemingway never questions the givenness of reality. He refuses to deal in epistemological angst. The world is not unknowable; it is just unpredictable. Parataxis conveys the sense that event follows event by only the slimmest logic. ''And'' reflects Hemingway's honest ignorance of how one thing leads to another. It is not an ignorance he cherishes. Hemingway's project becomes to predict as well as to know.

The casualness of this narrator contrasts with the ignorance of the reader and encourages us to pretend that we are, in fact, at home here. Yet no one is at home here. A relaxed and knowing tone acts as defense against a wholly unfamiliar scene. Hemingway approaches the terror of the sublime through the uncanny, the *umheimlich*. In ''The 'Uncanny,''' Freud points out that the German synonym for the ''uncanny'' derives from the word for home *(heim)* and that its original meaning was ''familiar.'' Hemingway's career follows a similar evolution: what begins as familiar becomes unfamiliar, and yet is sought for as if it were still desired as much as feared. So his goal turns out to be at once ''mysterious and homelike.'' The uncanny is the opposite of the ''good place'' Nick will spend his life trying to recover, and yet the ''good place'' (the womb) becomes for Nick the most uncanny place of all. (pp. 477-78)

Nick asks two questions just before the story ends: ''Do ladies always have such a hard time having babies?'' and

''Is dying hard, Daddy?'' These are the central questions in Hemingway's novels. To ask one is to ask the other, since to confront any kind of birth is to confront one's mortality. What has a specific beginning very likely has a specific end. But Nick confronts not only the facts or origins and ends—he witnesses them as violent. From this night on, Nick's psyche begins to play the violent extremes of human life against its uncertain middle. Love emerges as the fleeting center of a parenthesis. It only lasts in fantasy. (pp. 478-79)

While there is nothing new in calling Hemingway's basic fantasies regressive, we need to look more closely at how difficult this makes it for him to conceive of going forward as satisfying. The recurring experience in *In Our Time* is of anticlimax. Narrative pathos constantly collapses into bathos: ''He loved the mountains in the autumn. The last I heard of him the Swiss had him in jail in Sion.'' (p. 479)

The story which brackets [Sam Cardinella's] execution is Hemingway's most ambitious flight from the world of death. [''Big Two-Hearted River''] cannot be understood apart from the personal history necessitating it. An elliptical return to the darkness of ''Indian Camp,'' this regression to origins proves how little Nick has moved beyond them. He lives but he does not develop. Nick's initial trauma either predicts or preempts future experience.... The recurrent limitations of this composite character is an ability to adapt. None of [Nick's] experiences lead to emotional development. Nick's life has no middle. It emerges as pure reaction. It is not by accident that Nick suffers wound after wound. Some inner compulsion leads him to put himself in the way of disaster. Nick's fate reflects his author's lack of faith in life after birth. (p. 480)

Nick transforms his anxieties over stopping and starting into a despair over middles. A lack of closure thus becomes more intimidating than foreclosure. A known death menaces less than unpredictable life. This anxiety originates, as we have seen, in a premature exposure to the dark and uncertain place from which life emerges and of which living and loving must therefore be a part. Sex and birth cross the hard fact of personal limitation with the harder facts that our limits are vulnerable, that we are not the original possessors of our first source, and that our first source must be lost. This anxiety terminates in Nick's confrontation with the swamp, that evokes the boundary where sexuality merges with mortality. (p. 481)

Every book is an invitation and a challenge. *The Sun Also Rises* begins by inviting us to believe [Jake Barnes] and challenges us to despise Robert Cohn.... Cohn emerges as a massive projection of the speaker's anxieties.... The dominant emotion here is rage at Cohn's inability to appreciate a potency that he possesses and the narrator lacks. Jake's uncanny fantasy becomes explicable once we realize that it reflects a universal fear which for Jake has become a realized fact. So by the logic of Jake's fantasy (mutilation points back to the mother), it is not Cohn's birth he libels, but his own.

This is the only one of Hemingway's major novels which does not begin at a specific season or time of day. Its action will remain the least constrained by rhythms other than those the characters themselves impose. This generation is ''lost'' to any connection with earlier or later generations and hence to the primary vehicle for forwarding life. *The Sun Also Rises* is a novel about wasting time. Jake's castration has made him unable to participate in the natural rhythms of life. He can never consummate experience; resolution is always withheld from him. Sexual impotence becomes a metaphor for the inability to enter the flow of duration. (pp. 482-83)

Style here focuses the repetitiveness which is necessarily Jake's fate. Chapter V opens with a new morning, but the prose soon confines any sense of option within a recurring formula for Jake's movement: "I walked," "I read," "I got," "I walked," "I passed," "I stepped," "I walked," "I walked." Anyone who narrates his experience through such unvarying syntax experiences motion as anything but discovery. Jake's two experiences of *déjà vu* provide the strongest evidence that he feels himself caught in an uncanny pattern of repetition beyond his control. His most promising attempt at love collapses into "the feeling as in a nightmare of it all being something repeated, something I had been through and that I must go through again." After Jake fights Cohn and begins to cross the Pamplona square, he experiences a *déjà vu* about returning home: "I felt as I felt once coming home from an out-of-town football game. I was carrying a suitcase with my football things in it, and I walked up the street from the station in the town I had lived in all my life and it was all new. They were raking the lawns and burning leaves in the road, and I stopped for a long time and watched. It was all strange." Jake can never beat Cohn, for he has lost the organ which would permit him to consummate, rather than endlessly repeat, the attempt to get "home." Here the *déjà vu* gets dangerously close to exposing the original experience for which the feeling of "something repeated" acts as a screen memory. Jake . . . remembers a homecoming experienced as a dream. It is a *déjà vu* about *déjà vu*—an uncanny repetition of the feeling of the uncanny. If Hemingway's fiction continually strives to get back home, the greatest irony awaiting it would be to achieve the return only to find it "all strange." (pp. 483-84)

It may be more appropriate, then, to read Jake's actual castration as a literalization of the original castration-anxiety that threatens to make home feel unhomelike. Jake's conscious drive toward competency expresses his author's unconscious anxieties about potency. Jake's narration is an instruction manual—how to drink, kiss, fish . . . and pimp. Technique culminates in the bull ring. Bullfighting is the great orgy of a repressed culture: competence killing potency. What makes this more than just another "how to" is the prospect of death. Hemingway finds here a game like life, one played for mortal stakes. And yet in *Death in the Afternoon* he admits that it is the opposite of a truly existential sport: "Rather it is a tragedy; the death of the bull, which is played, more or less well, by the bull and the man involved and in which there is danger for the man but certain death for the animal." As Jake teaches Brett, bullfighting is something "with a definite end." Watching a bullfight, Hemingway unconsciously identifies with the doomed animal. He has no more sense of hope for his own end than for the bull's. Jake's irony is to be granted the comparative immortality of a "steer." He drifts onward in a life promising no final climax. By insisting upon the analogy between the tragedies of the ring and the ironies of the café ("It's no life being a steer"), Hemingway again confounds anxieties over death and sex. *The Sun Also Rises* can be read as the story of an impotent animal submitted to repeated gorings. (p. 484)

Our belated disgust with the book's beginning exemplifies . . . morality [as after-thought] at work. Hemingway so skillfully gets us to "go along" with Jake that only afterward do we learn "how to" understand what his beginning

is all about. If we do not resist the opening, the increasingly simple demands the novel makes on us—just to go along—become more and more easy to accept. The moral contexts which permit judgment are precisely those that the book tries to tease us out of. It finally asks us to abandon all prejudices except the love of style. The obsession with "how to" do something is the only forethought Jake allows himself. We tardily realize that the novel opens with a display of Jake's skill at how "to get rid of friends." While the middle does not justify the tone of the beginning, it explains it. We come to understand that Jake is jealous of Cohn for his unmistakable potency. His symbolic castration of Cohn (flattening his nose) attempts metaphorically to convert a bull into a steer. Language is the only weapon Jake has left.

Yet this first person narrator, upon whom the prolonging of the narrative depends, finally disbelieves in language: "You'll lose it if you talk about it." Jake talks because he has already lost everything. Yet he expresses a theory that where language is not necessary as a defense, it is not necessary at all. For whom, then, does he speak? We can speculate that Hemingway invents an impotent male who is still the "hero" of the novel in order to establish that impotency is a crisis that a man can actually survive. Yet his project ends in a draw, for it appears that in the case of this wound, talking or not talking finally makes little difference. Hemingway begins by marshalling his best rhetorical skills in a sneak attack on the threat, and ends once he realizes that even direct talk "about it" will only confirm the loss of what has been already lost.

A Farewell to Arms is Hemingway's most fatal book. While it promises the most life, it delivers nothing but loss. The imagination of disaster intrudes even into the strenuously pacific opening:

> In the late summer of that year we lived in a house in a village that looked across the river and the plain to the mountains. In the bed of the river there were pebbles and boulders, dry and white in the sun, and the water was clear and swiftly moving and blue in the channels. Troops went by the house and down the road and the dust they raised powdered the leaves of the trees. The trunks of the trees too were dusty and the leaves fell early that year and we saw the troops marching along the road and the dust rising and leaves, stirred by the breeze, falling and the soldiers marching and afterwards the road bare and white except for the leaves.
>
> The plain was rich with crops; there were many orchards of fruit trees and beyond the plain the mountains were brown and bare. There was fighting in the mountains and at night we could see the flashes from the artillery. In the dark it was like summer lightning, but the nights were cool and there was not the feeling of a storm coming.

At first this voice appears simply to report what it sees. it sounds in touch with seasons and elements. We stand aside here and conserve ourselves. The water flows, the troops pass, the leaves fall. Everything else spends itself. Yet high summer—a time of ripeness—somehow becomes late fall. We are manipulated into the season of loss. Parallel syntax presents an army of falling leaves. Men are "marching" and leaves are "falling," and through this parataxis they become all too easily confused. The leaves last; the men disappear. What remains is the emptiness of landscape—"a road bare and white"—which the human presence interrupts but cannot master.

The narrator subtly repeats this involvement of the reader in a fall that is at once natural and human. To say that "the nights were cool and there was not the feeling of a storm coming" is to protest too much. Yes, the storm is denied—but why is it ever envisaged? In *A Farewell to Arms* potential turbulence has more presence than actual peace. What Frederic Henry anticipates, Hemingway actually precipitates. A storm is exactly what Catherine fears: "I'm afraid of the rain because sometimes I see me dead in it." The storm looms over the entire novel, and inevitably breaks.

Yet this is not the only disaster the beginning obliquely foreshadows. More striking is Frederic's projection of pregnancy. As he watches the troops march by he notices "under their capes the two leather cartridge-boxes on the front of the belts . . . bulged forward under the capes so that the men, passing on the road, marched as though they were six months gone with child." . . . [The] metaphoric leap from carefully measured cartridges to carefully measured pregnancy is so idiosyncratic as to reveal more about the mind of the beholder than what he beholds. Even before Frederic conceives a child, he seems to "feel trapped biologically." Projection allows him to assign to others what he feels as threatening to himself. Yet he no more negates this possibility than he does the chance of a storm. (pp. 485-88)

The storm is upon us before we have time to feel it coming. Yet we will learn to get ready. The novel educates us in anticipating the worst.

Such presentiments are uncanny. They make us uneasy because they so often come true. They express a fascination with death that recurs throughout Hemingway's work. Such recurrence suggests that every encounter with death aggravates rather than allays the fear of it. It is a repression which continually fails and so must repeat itself—a repetition compulsion. (p. 488)

Caught in the middle, Frederic is a man with no belief in middles. His one memory of childhood defines this sense of limbo:

> The hay smelled good and lying in a barn in the hay took away all the years in between. We had lain in hay and talked and shot sparrows with an air-rifle when they perched in the triangle cut high up in the wall of the barn. The barn was gone now and one year they had cut the hemlock woods and there were only stumps, dried tree-tops, branches and fireweed where the woods had been. You could not go back. If you did not go forward what happened? You never got back to Milan. And if you got back to Milan what happened?

Here Frederic's inability to go either forward or backward proceeds from one anxiety. Later, his thoughts about his dead child show how a fear of dying derives from an ambivalence over the conditions of birth:

> He had never been alive. Except in Catherine. I'd felt him kick there often enough. But I hadn't for a week. Maybe he was choked all the time. Poor little kid. I wished

the hell I'd been choked like that. No I didn't. Still there would not be all this dying to go through. Now Catherine would die. That was what you did. You died. You did not know what it was about. You never had time to learn. They threw you in and told you the rules and the first time they caught you off base they killed you.

Frederic renounces Jake's hope that learning to live in the world might help one to know what it was all about. In this world, dying is what one learns how to do. (p. 489)

[The] book is stillborn. Like the child, "it had never been alive." It never knows an interval of time free from intimations of mortality. We do not experience its middle as a discovery of its end. Nothing is allowed to seem lasting. Our insecurity is founded on untimeliness. . . . Our disappointment with *A Farewell to Arms* comes less from fastidious omission . . . than from Hemingway's refusal of this "splendid chance to be a messiah." Love is always something had on leave, stolen from fate. Throughout, Frederic treats his love for Catherine as something already over—as recollection. His "mistake was this," Kierkegaard argues in *Repetition,* "that he stood at the end instead of the beginning." Yet he goes on to admit that

> the man who in his experience of love has not experienced it thus precisely at the beginning, has never loved. Only he must have another mood alongside of this. This potentiated act of recollection is the eternal expression of love at the beginning, it is the token of real love. But on the other hand an ironic elasticity is requisite in order to be able to make use of it. . . . It must be true that one's life is over at the first instant, but there must be vitality enough to kill this death and transform it into life.

Frederic has . . . irony but not . . . elasticity and so begins and proceeds by "seeing it all ahead like the moves in a chess game." Would we begrudge Hemingway his oft-criticized romance were it not betrayed from the start to so bitter an irony? If books can be defined by how they end—tragedy with the death of the hero, comedy with the birth of a new society—then romance never ends and irony ends before it begins. The two modes are simply incompatible. *A Farewell to Arms* might have been Hemingway's best novel had he opened himself more to the awkward and sometimes silly lovemaking many readers find so embarrassing. Embarrassment is precisely what Hemingway dreads and what he must overcome. But he cannot imagine a future that is not foreclosed in advance because he cannot trust in the basic facts of human continuity: procreation and married love. While Hemingway remains capable of depicting a series of carefree sexual encounters, he fails to invent a hero who truly domesticates the uncanny place. (pp. 490-91)

Across the River and into the Trees returns to the mode of "Indian Camp." Darkness and uncertainty dominate. As before, we are belated—"other boats had gone on ahead." We travel in someone's wake. The narrator knows no more about this world than the reader. Things are just "somewhere." Directions are given which do not direct. We are not only cut off from shore but from the action. "They started" makes the novel's beginning simultaneous with a fictive moment of beginning but leaves us ignorant of and distant from these third persons. Movement goes on here, but only its aftermath—broken ice—testifies surely to its presence. Human presence is once again an interruption. After that presence turns aside "there was no broken water," and the world becomes quiet, still, seamless again. (pp. 491-92)

If the beginning of the novel establishes the uncertainty of going forward, it is because there is so little to go forward for. This is a book about going back. The Colonel is a man without a future. All that is left to him (except one more day of love) is cleaning up old messes, paying old debts, opening old wounds—"merde, money, blood." (p. 492)

Unpracticed in the presentation of ruminative consciousness, Hemingway must rely on the awkward device of having Renata ask the Colonel to remember. No narrative requirement governs these forays into the past. . . . This is not a novel but an essay about impending death. All the action (with the exception of one "act") is past. Hemingway, against his best impulses, chooses to tell rather than show, and thus the book is as revealing about how Hemingway thinks as about who its hero is: "Death is a lot of shit, he thought. It comes to you in small fragments that hardly show where it has entered." The threat as usual is less death than consciousness of dying. Hemingway here replaces death with a metaphor and reduces it through synecdoche. (pp. 493-94)

Though the book itself is not a spatial form, it does contain one—Renata's portrait. The Colonel responds to "the static element in painting" as a stay against the confusion of dying. Yet this nostalgia for a life arrested by art Hemingway's art cannot requite. The Colonel is a man who has made fatal decisions at every stage in life: "I made them early. In the middle. And late." His life has nevertheless decomposed even while exhibiting the classic and neatly punctuated contours of a composition. Only one more decision awaits him—to opt for the present one last time. He must turn from the portrait toward the actual woman:

> The Colonel said nothing, because he was assisting, or had made an act of presence, at the only mystery that he believed in except the occasional bravery of man.
>
> "Please don't move," the girl said. "Then move a great amount."
>
> The Colonel, lying under the blanket in the wind, knowing it is only what man does for woman that he retains, except what he does for his fatherland or his motherland, however you get the reading, proceeded.

Hemingway here steps out of the novel to challenge his reader in one of the most self-conscious moments in his fiction. If it is not well done it is bravely done, for it admits that this writer can no longer create meaning alone in a world of death. And it implies one of his guiding premises—that language separates us as surely from experience as death does. When one is present to an act, one says nothing. Speech testifies to the absence of immediacy, to the death of the moment. (p. 494)

For Whom the Bell Tolls is a long book about a short time. It reverses the mode of *In Our Time* by leaving nothing out. . . . [Reading] fuses intensity and duration into an experience where every moment brims with value. This is a book that fills rather than kills time. . . . Robert Jordan's story not only consummates Hemingway's development but takes great and welcome exception to it. (p. 495)

The novel begins on a summer morning. We see a man seeing at a distance. Nothing is melodramatically foreshadowed or withheld. The scene is both familiar and strange. The landscape is known; the mill is new. Yet far from producing an uncanny effect, the scene unfolds as one more stage in its viewer's education. An old man gives information to a younger one. It is a scene of instruction innocent of any resonance of a primal scene. Knowledge passes from an older to a younger generation with no apparent loss of power.

The relaxed tone of the opening contrasts sharply with the ultimate objective of the book: the proper timing of an explosion. As usual, Hemingway gives away the end at the beginning: "To blow the bridge at a stated hour based on the time set for the attack is how it should be done." We also learn—or are encouraged to expect—that Robert Jordan will be killed. (pp. 495-96)

How then does Hemingway help us to live through the book rather than anticipate the end of it? By encouraging us to commit an act of presence, of forgetting. . . . [It] is less the overt instruction to enter into the passing moment than the patient recording of the least remarkable of them that commands our attention. Certainly the novel can be read as apocalyptic, but we are allowed throughout to participate in a sense of reprieve. While we remain torn between the impulse to finish and the impulse to prolong, it is making the most of time which truly distinguishes character here. (p. 496)

Hemingway knew that he carried his fortune in his hand. When he could no longer write with it, he turned it against himself. What had made him was used to break him. Yet the novel literalizes this metaphor in order to reject it. Pilar literally reads Robert's palm to give the ending away a second time. But he refuses to believe this prophecy. Pilar has already given Maria better advice: "She said that nothing is done to oneself that one does not accept." . . . "In this sack will be contained the essence of it all": [in this line spoken by Pilar] all of Hemingway's fantasy material coalesces. It is a lurid triumph of the uncanny. But it is also a triumph *over* the uncanny. Hemingway presents this less for effect than for scrutiny. The fantasy is unique in its explicitness, its self-consciousness, and its patent absurdity. (pp. 497-98)

For Whom the Bell Tolls divests love of all its vestigial uncanniness. The first thing Robert must learn about love is to make time for it. From believing only "in my work" Robert moves toward believing in "making believe." He gives in to "a complete embracing of all that would not be." This reverses Hemingway's typical attitude toward the future. To embrace what will not be is to embrace a fiction, not a fate. Love is the supreme fiction. If it has previously been left out of the novels, here it is consciously brought back in. The two notorious and extended descriptions of "*la gloria*" mark important stages in Robert's (and his author's) development. During the first lovemaking Robert repeatedly goes "nowhere." He experiences love as a recurring "dark passage" toward the unfamiliar. But in the second love scene Robert is carried into the "now." A Hemingway hero finally becomes present to the act of love, finally has time to become familiar with the woman he loves. A new kind of heroine emerges here—one both pure and impure. Maria is an experienced virgin. Her rape is a fact; her sense of newness, a shared fiction. Both Robert and Maria must face her past before they can share a true present. They cleave to the liberating principle "that nothing is done to one that one does not accept and that if I loved some one it would take it all away.'' Forgiven is the guilt Maria carries from her traumatic past. Her story couples catharsis with the insight that resolves the aftereffects of the trauma. Hemingway breaks through here, against the entire history of his defenses, to the freedom implicit in love, the great fiction of reversal. (pp. 498-99)

[Robert's] recurring response to his father is embarrassment. He is ''embarrassed by it all'' when his father says good-bye at the train, apprehensive lest at any future meeting ''both he and his grandfather would be acutely embarrassed by the presence of his father.'' This embarrassment is authentic and difficult to criticize. Embarrassment is a minor version of the uncanny: shame at something familiar which ought to have remained hidden and secret, and yet comes to light. What is striking is that Hemingway *chooses* to bring it to light. Robert is distinguished from Nick Adams not by his traumatic upbringing—Nick's is traumatic too—but by the chance he is given to work directly back through it. Robert's overt rehearsal of his embarrassing past (his father proves a ''coward''; his mother, ''a bully'') helps him to understand it, and ''to understand,'' he ventures, ''is to forgive.'' He can contemplate the forgiveness (of himself and his origins) which will integrate his past with his present and free him to grow into the future. A past no longer repressed loses the power to return as an anxiety experienced as unavoidable fate.

This marks the victory of insight over repression. The potentially crippling force of Robert's past is not denied its return but openly assimilated to a more inclusive imaginative scheme. The single obsession which has dominated Hemingway's fiction—waiting for the end—is absorbed into a multiplicity of truths. The ending of *For Whom the Bell Tolls* celebrates the power of ''making believe'' over fantasies which the traumas of our personal history make us believe. . . . The power of the imagination over a sense of fate culminates in Robert Jordan's good-bye to Maria. When he says ''I go with thee,'' he gives his entire life up to a saving fiction. Metaphor here *is* truth. Robert will always ''go'' with her in her heart. Wounded and lying alone at the very end, he knows that truth comes down to getting the tenses right. ''I have tried to do with what talent I had. *Have, you mean. All right, have.*''

Robert Jordan is alive until the end. His novel does not end —it recommences. Its last words carry us not into loss but return us to the first sentence: ''He could feel his heart beating against the pine needle floor of the forest.'' This is a repetition which knows nothing of the uncanny. These words are familiar; we have heard them before. But they return us to a point of origin unshadowed by loss. The book draws a circle and thus spatializes our sense of return. It overcomes the sense of being bound by unwilled recurrence and creates instead a sense of eternity, of being still in the place and time where we began. Of course between the first and last sentence everything has changed, but these words *say* the ending as if it had not. Here Hemingway's end truly does create the fiction of recovering his beginning. Robert Jordan refuses to take his life by his own hand: ''I don't want to do that business that my father did.'' He understands his father and forgives him but will not emulate him. That Hemingway ultimately chose to emulate his father's final act suggests that the vision of possibility held out by his greatest novel did not at last help him to live until he died. Yet however Hemingway ended, his most generous novel authorizes us to remember him not as the man who

took his own life, but as the creator of Robert Jordan, who can say, facing certain death, ''I wish there was more time.'' (pp. 499-501)

> *David M. Wyatt, ''Hemingway's Uncanny Beginnings,'' in* The Georgia Review *(copyright, 1977, by the University of Georgia), Summer, 1977, pp. 476-501.*

*   *   *

HILL, Geoffrey   1932-

Winner of the Gregory Award for Poetry in 1961, Hill, a first-rate English poet, belongs to no particular ''school'' or movement. In some respects a traditionalist, Hill's preoccupation has been with eternal themes: war, death, and human suffering. (See also *CLC*, Vol. 5.)

Hill is, in the judgment of some of us, the best poet now writing in England (and I am not sure that I should except Philip Larkin). ''Somewhere Is Such a Kingdom'' comprises his three books, ''For the Unfallen'' (1959), ''King Log'' (1968) and ''Mercian Hymns'' (1971), a sequence of extraordinary prose-poems, humorous and ursine, which burgeon from the imaginative meeting of the legendary King Offa from the 8th century with a 20th century childhood. Many of Hill's poems are deep and bitter doubtings as to whether the imaginative life can't too easily become an indulgence in factitious high concern. There are ''Ovid in the Third Reich'' and ''September Song,'' with their poignant rebuke to glib evocations of death-camp compassion. And there is the love-sequence ''The Songbook of Sebastian Arrurruz,'' a fictitious Spanish poet whose first name cries out for the arrows of martyrdom which are then supplied by his second name. Hill's poetry is a rooted herb, culinary and medicinal, as strange as arrowroot, the tubers of which were used to absorb poison from wounds, especially those made by poisoned arrows. But then so perhaps is all poetry; not the wound and the bow, but the wound and the arrow and the arrowroot. (p. 6)

> *Christopher Ricks, in* The New York Times Book Review *(© 1976 by The New York Times Company; reprinted by permission), January 11, 1976.*

Geoffrey Hill . . . is easy to consider in American terms because he reflects the influence of American poets. Hill refers directly to Ransom and Tate. So one is not surprised that his early poems have something in common with those of the young Robert Lowell. Unlike Oppen, Hill finds no contradiction between witty writing and authentic emotion; and he desires richness of style. Like Yeats and Lowell, he seizes on intimate, private experience and tries to endow it with public meanings. Like Swift he possesses a deep sense of tradition and community which is (as Hill has wisely observed of Swift) ''challenged by a strong feeling for the anarchic and the predatory.''

In most of his poems Hill tries to convey extreme emotions by opposing the restraint of established form to the violence of his insight or judgment. He uses savage puns, heavy irony, and repeated oxymorons. He uses bold, archetypal images and religious symbols while complaining of their inefficacy. He deals with violent public events. . . . Appalled by the moral discontinuities of human behavior, he is also shaken by his own response to them, which mingles revulsion with fascination. . . .

Hill dismisses the way of transcendence and the way of

withdrawal from the world: he will not blame the devil for our villainy or look to the realm of pure spirit for salvation. Integrity is meaningless for him apart from experience, and experience must involve him in the corruption he loathes. Ideally he would be a priest-king-poet, one who could order the chaos, sanctify the routines of communal life, and celebrate the goods of the natural world. . . .

Hill tries to stir the reader up with strong rhythms, a mingling of coarse and sublime particulars, and a tone of ridicule pierced by sorrow. He strains to be compact and explosive, gnarled and bruising. The effect is not fortunate. One gets the impression of muffled outcries rather than furious eloquence. (p. 4)

Nobody who reads [*Somewhere Is Such a Kingdom: Poems 1952-1971*] will doubt that he has the attributes of an excellent poet. But his desire to produce stormy emotions with a few calculated gestures seems wrong for his technical resources; the quasi-sublime rhetoric does not move one, and the poet probably knows it. I suspect that his anger and self-mockery are due as much as anything to the frustration he feels over his lack of an authentic voice.

Geoffrey Hill thoroughly understands the dialectic of good and evil within the self, and its relation to the moral ambiguities of history and society. He is well on the way to a moving poetic style—less powerful, I think, than he would like it to be, but strong enough for his purposes. "Mercian Hymns" probably brings him to the edge of his best work, which is still to come. (p. 6)

> *Irvin Ehrenpreis, in* The New York Review of Books *(reprinted with permission from* The New York Review of Books; *copyright © 1976 NYREV, Inc.), January 22, 1976.*

[Hill] exhibits a kind of literacy and comprehensive imagination. . . . He is in command of a profound moral sophistication and maturity rare among poets writing in the language anywhere.

On first reading any of Hill's poems one is struck by his fresh and functional use of forms, and by the almost incredibly dense connotative textures. There is little that is obvious in either his best rhymes or his meaning. Beginning *Somewhere is Such a Kingdom,* his collected poems through 1971 and the first trade edition of any of his books available in America, the surprise is how early he achieved his style. . . . [The first poem, "Genesis,"] is a haunting poem ("There is no bloodless myth will hold."), and the last few lines present the kind of charged ambiguity, the grim paradox sensually posed, that Hill so much delights in. . . . It is this early work which contains the grain of truth leading [Harold] Bloom to assert erroneously in the introduction that "Hill has been the most Blakean of modern poets." This would be accurate had he written nothing but "Genesis," but almost immediately, as we shall see, he became another kind of poet entirely.

In this early work Hill is obsessed with the metaphor of the drowned, of the sea giving up its dead at the Resurrection. . . . Not only does Hill have an unromantic distrust of nature and "generative process," he seems suspicious, even ashamed, of art which cultivates and feeds on the violence, waste, and suffering of human experience. At the same time he keeps returning to the gesture of calling out of time and drowning and decay into the permanence of form and language. The poem seems for him a kind of verbal garden where the expulsion is reversed by hard-won saying.

Though he is not sure how far he should trust it, the gesture is made again and again, is a deep structure he finds wherever he turns, as he will later make of the concentration camps of World War II an inverted Eden.

The other major theme of the early poems is marriage, closely related to the drowning image and perhaps as complex. In at least one poem, if I read it correctly, "Asmodeus," the demon from the *Apocrypha,* is recognized as the true Cupid who cannot be expelled or tamed into a hearth deity without destroying the marriage. "The Turtle Dove" could be an eloquent and concise telling of Dylan and Caitlin Thomas' most stormy years. In Hill's poetry there is always a "distant fury of battle," the title of a poem here and a phrase he uses later in a note for one of his most important sequences. Wherever he looks the battle, the same battle, is being fought, in history, theology, love, politics, nature, art. (pp. 31-4)

A motif that begins to emerge more and more clearly in the later poems of *For the Unfallen* is a sharp-edged ambiguity about art, including the art of words. This could best be described as a suspicion, with at once reverence and contempt. It appears in the carefully selected phrase "artistic men" which appears twice, first describing the Magi in "Picture of a Nativity" and later in "Of Commerce and Society." What the poet has begun to suspect is that art, no matter how well executed, begins to betray what it would uphold. The prime example of this for him, both here and in the later poems, is language's and a culture's, inability to prevent, even comprehend, the atrocities of Nazi Germany. . . . There is the fear that art, even when trying most conscientiously, evades and subverts, because of its very nature. Realizing the full impossibility of Milton's stated task (and hence his or any poet's), he offers the poem as apology rather than as justification. In fact he becomes so unbearably conscious of the limits and falsifications of poetry in the actual world that he feels guilty for his own gift to make art, but only art, of the agony of others. (p. 35)

Hill is not just a stoic, he is a fallen stoic, and his salvation, which is his formidable power as a maker, throws him always back into the tragedy of the actual world, which language must amplify. . . . The poems from *King Log,* Hill's second book, are at once some of his finest and most infuriatingly obscure. . . . Contrary to Bloom's statement in the introduction to this Collected Poems, what we find in *King Log* could be called unromantic, unBlakean, and certainly un-apocalyptic. Not only has Hill taken over the tortured, overloaded line from Tate, he has been deeply stirred by his ideals and strictures. Perhaps the word is not influence but a recognition of kinship. I suspect that Hill used Tate's ideas at an important time to clarify his own, and what he made of that agonizingly conscientious line and allegiance to form, the guilt of history, the sad failure of American progressivism, and his love of the "Mediterranean," the catholic, the lucid, and controlled, is something very much his own, and unique in modern poetry. We would have to go back to Baudelaire and maybe classical antiquity to find the precision, depth, and ease of surface this all leads to in "The Songbook of Sebastian Arrurruz." (pp. 36-7)

The title of *King Log* comes from Aesop, the fable where the frogs are given a log for king. When they complain to Zeus that their monarch is unresponsive to their needs, he gives them a stork for king instead, which eats them. It is a brilliant choice of title for Hill at this point because it expresses his skepticism of social and religious progress, and idealistic reformation in general. History is the correlative of guilt and reformers at best fail to comprehend its burden, at worst aggravate and fuel its cruelty. Yet, in such a world, no bystander is innocent, and "innocence" is a liability, even at times a threat. In these poems Hill is a master of clear and two-edged irony. "Ovid In the Third Reich," a confession of helplessness to alleviate or even understand evil, self-justifying, must be read as accusation. Hill plays on the disarming sophistry of the modern intellectual, the use of irony to avoid responsibility, self-incrimination. In the poem "Annunciations," when the Word returns from abroad "with a tanned look" we know that any "announcing" can be taken ironically, and that the "announcer" will plead seriousness or jest, depending on the accusation, and beyond that will plead the times, and the world which tends to corrupt what it hears. (p. 37)

["Locust Songs"] show as much as any poems here the impact of Tate and his revulsion for Emerson, Whitman and populist rhetoric. Going back to Jonathan Edwards and forward through the Transcendentalists and Whitman we find an obsession in the New World with discovering divinity in everything, from the most commonplace and humble to the continent itself and the destiny of the new nation. To Tate and Hill this is a manifestation of insanity, or at best a crippling heresy, the leveling of all being so the mud and detritus of the riverbank and sewer are infused with deity same as the rituals of the Church; and the miracles are denied any special significance or efficacy, given no greater importance than the annual resurgence of the grass or the copulation of birds. To Tate the refusal to recognize the fallen tragic condition of man deepens suffering and invites madness. (p. 38)

One of the best marks of Hill's greatness as a poet is his attention to the conscience of and for history. His confessions are not confessional poetry in any personal sense only, but speak for the race and species. What seems to alarm him most is looking into the fallen world and seeing people pretend not to know they are fallen, though he grants they may be helpless to act on that knowledge. At one extreme is self-righteous preaching and at the other a satisfied surrender to corruption. The concentration camp is the world itself, an island of the condemned. To pretend the sentence has not been passed is the gravest blasphemy.

But the martyrdom to nihilism, the particular sainthood of the modern intellectual, is equally offensive. Of what use is intoxication with one's insight into nothingness, the celebration of negative triumph? . . . The visionary void is no more authentic than the visionary plenitude of Whitman, and it is that emptiness, Hill would say, on which the transcendentalists of the Twentieth Century have built their gospel, as confused and misled as the romantics of the century before. To seize on the void as the unifying metaphor is, in Hill's mind, to evade the whole question. The nothingness is certainly there, but will not suffice now any more than four thousand years ago.

In the tradition of Yeats' "The Scholars" and Roethke's "Academic" Hill gives us "The Humanist," lest anyone think he is advocating that failed movement. The humor here arises from the scholar's blindness to the carnality, carnage, even cannibalism, of his surgical enterprise. The schoolman by the tedium of his manner, the sense of superiority to his subject, denies the full-fleshed reality of what he examines. He denies by his rhetoric and gesture that he shares the common clay. (pp. 39-40)

The first of the two great sequences of *King Log* is "Fu-

neral Music." In a short essay appended to the collection he describes the group as attempting "a florid grim music broken by grunts and shrieks." . . . These blank verse sonnets are an homage to the reign of King Stork. The language wallows and revels in violence, intrigue, betrayal, gore. Passages anger by their very complexity and obscurity. Others are among the best Hill has ever written. Some remind me of Hopkins' bitter sonnets, and of Dickinson's indictments of God. A priest at the scene of a beheading prays, his "voice fragrant with mannered humility." A participant, perhaps one of the condemned, meditates, "we are dying / To satisfy fat Caritas, those / Wiped jaws of stone." Soldiers dying in each other's filth on the battlefield—and the image seems to include us all in the mortal combat of conscience with experience—"Tup in their marriage-blood, gasping, 'Jesus.'" Tup means to come into heat, and to copulate, and the Christian connotations of "marriage-blood" are clear.

Among this brutality and meaningless conflict the speaker turns with wrenching nostalgia toward the Platonic world of Mind as the exclusive reality. But he cannot believe it, though, as always, it is the nonbeliever who can apprehend the full glory of what he rejects. (pp. 41-2)

A key entry in *King Log* is the short lyric "History as Poetry." More than any modern poet in English Hill feels a deep responsibility to address the reality of history. Where most of his contemporaries stay with their personal experience for subject matter, or play with fantastic and vague textures, practicing an emotional nominalism, Hill works with the biography of state and race, language, the neuroses of empire, the actuality of wars. His title here reverses the well known equation of the Marxists and phenomenologists, that all relevant literature participates in and clarifies history. "History as Poetry" says something entirely different, bringing collective events sharply into the foreground of his text. We already know of Hill's awe of his own and others' gifts, how the imagination through "the knack of tongues" will always salute and celebrate, perhaps can only praise and celebrate, no matter what the case, the suffering and waste. As the world of experience is pathetically undeserving of praise and salutation, so the human spirit may be unfit for the "resurgence," the turnings over and renewals out of the carnage of history. Poetry with its love of the dramatic, the violent paradox, may be the truest image of history, and "the tongue's atrocities." Hill is baffled by the practice of his own art. Even when attempting the opposite, trying to present truth, indictment, not praise, the craft subverts the intentions. (pp. 42-3)

The second sequence, and the crowning work of *King Log*, bears the unlikely title, "The Songbook of Sebastian Arrurruz," and purports to be a translation from the work of a Spanish poet of that name, dates 1868-1922. It is with this group that Hill came to his full powers as a poet, shedding the labored obscurities of many of the early poems. Whereas before his lines were often clogged and tangled in both syntax and meaning, were loaded so heavily with ironies they sometimes collapsed, he now writes with a classic simplicity of surface. According to some of the reviewers of the original volume in 1968 the name "Sebastian Arrurruz" is meant to suggest first the martyrdom of St. Sebastian and then the arrows that kill him, as well as arrowroot, which is an herb for drawing out poison from wounds made, for instance, by venomed arrows. Playing that game further I would say that "Arrurruz" embodies the hum of the released bow string and the whisper and thud of the arrow going home. But I believe it far more worthwhile to go immediately to the poems themselves, and the martyred lover who is their speaker and subject. In the group of eleven poems he meditates on his loss of a mistress to someone else a few years before. As the title implies he is still receiving and trying to heal his wounds. This may sound sentimental when summarized, but the sequence reads dry as *rioja,* and crisp as a cool sea wind on glaring rocks. They could be the finest erotic poems since antiquity.

One of the things I have admired most about British poets such as Larkin and Hill is their ability to choose the inspired adjective. This genius is used to better advantage than ever in the "Songbook." The choices are always startling, always accurate, "refreshed trivia," "glandular bloom." This is one of the reasons that Hill can write at such a high level of generalization and connotation. His statements are sensuous, his images significant, often because of a happy modification. . . . I don't want to leave the sequence without quoting the final tercet from "A Song from Armenia."

> Why do I have to relive, even now,
> Your mouth, and your hand running over me
> Deft as a lizard, like a sinew of water?

Here all of Hill's best talents come together at once, with none of his worst. His tendency toward the tropical and sensuous is controlled by astringent wit, like a dry desert wind across the Mediterranean. There is a wholeness to the imagination here, a luminous classic quality, catholic in the best sense, a demonstration of what Tate had in mind all along but had not realized in poetry. The sequence reads like a short novella, distal yet vivid. The poems remind me a little of Machado, but no one has ever translated anything like this into English. This is the original.

The last section of this volume is *Mercian Hymns,* originally published in 1971 and Hill's most accessible book. It is the one that is making him widely known, even popular. Luckily it also contains some of his best poetry. It could be described as a fantastic autobiography, a revery of historic scope. . . . The "hymns" are in a kind of dense, clear prose, colored with unexpected humor and astonishing juxtapositions in terms of time, superimposing the present on medieval landscape, creating a deep texture of history and language. There is lightness, and thickness with regard to reference and association. The ambience created is at once modern, medieval, and timeless. You could say the sequence redacts something of *The Anathèmata* in thirty sharply etched miniatures, but that would not be completely fair to either David Jones or Hill. The distances of history melt inside the powerful field of Hill's linguistic energy. Like many of the early works, the diction, the substitutions, the modifications, are stunning and masterful. But it is the overall effect, incorporating comic relief, that is most memorable, and is not found in the earlier grim poems. Though there is no narrative there is a sense of sweep, of leaping into obscure corners of history and the psyche and discovering crucial documents. The poems thrill, not with patriotism exactly, but with a loving knowledge of the physical, linguistic, cultural hearth on which we live. Both the peripheral and direct vision are coordinated and focused. *Mercian Hymns* is a sign that Hill has at least partially won his struggle with his own talent and hypersensitivity to experience. His field of vision is amazingly wide and these poems consolidate the fullness of his talent realized in the "Songbook."

Again the fabric here is woven of brutality and beauty twisted tightly together, but remaining distinct. Though at one point the speaker seems to feel that the poems are a kind of grave-robbing of language and psyche, Hill has learned better to live with his ugly fascinations and obsessions. I think a better analogy here would be archaeology or numismatics. There is a digging out and cleaning into definition of objects such as coins from old wells, from the mould and bone-heaps. Hill successfully rejuvenates the cliché of "coining," by striking from the ancient but permanent substance both new and ancient features. In fact, Hymn XIII is about examining old "coins" from Offa's time. "Draw, one by one, rare coins to the light. Ringed by its own lustre, the masterful head emerges, kempt and jutting, out of England's well."

If there is a central image to the book it is grubbing into the compost and refuse, among "night-soil, tetanus," plowing, grave-digging, archaeology of flues from Roman times, root systems, tearing out stumps, shoveling into the detritus of empire and church. "Their spades grafted through the variably-resistant soil. They clove to the hoard. They ransacked epiphanies, vertebrae of the chimera, armour of wild bees' larvae. They struck the fire-dragon's faceted skin." And after the great ceremonies of state, what is left on the land? "Wine, urine, and ashes."

There is a wonderful honoring of craftsmanship, the anonymous artisan, "this master-mason as I envisage him, intent to pester upon tympanum and chancel arch his moody testament, confusing warrior with lion, dragon-coils, tendrils of the stony vine." This is followed directly by one of the masterpieces of the group, an attack upon the industrial parody of craftsmanship. Here again Hill makes the historical personal, summoning to the forefront fragments of modern ugliness. (pp. 43-7)

Hill is one of the two or three best poets writing in English and he seems to be getting better. The poems I have seen in magazines since *Mercian Hymns* seem original even for him. This is especially true of the group of sonnets published in *Agenda* called collectively "Lacrimae." (p. 47)

> *Robert Morgan, "The Reign of King Stork," in* Parnassus: Poetry in Review *(copyright © by* Parnassus: Poetry in Review), *Spring/Summer, 1976, pp. 31-48.*

Somewhere Is Such a Kingdom collects Geoffrey Hill's three books of poetry—*For the Unfallen* (1959), *King Log* (1968), and *Mercian Hymns* (1971)—for an American audience. . . . He is one of the three or four most important English poets of the past twenty years—an anomaly of recent literary history, a direct heir to a religious and visionary tradition that runs from Donne's Holy Sonnets through Eliot's "Ash Wednesday" and Tate's "Sonnets at Christmas." His fierce angular lyrics, decidedly angry and compressed, recall the sensibility of an Eberhart crossed with the passionate Christianity of an early Lowell. Yet Hill's voice is all his own—violent, sexual, lacking indulgence for art. He is a craftsman of the first order, continually telescoping his vision through a short rhyming stanza which resembles a high-intensity lamp. The clenched line and clotted syntax of his poetry are the perfect analogues of a staunch and difficult voice. . . . [To] my knowledge he is the only poet of a presiding Christian imagination still writing poems of the first order.

Though I suspect that Hill has little patience for religion as such, he is compelled by the sacrifice of Christ, and continually he witnesses the reenactment of that blood submission in the atrocities of war.... And the apparent meaninglessness of sacrifice, the abandonment of those who suffer, the erosion of the logos, in fact the impotence and impossibility of speech in the face of wholesale destruction seem to undercut the very possibility of poetry. (pp. xcvi-xcvii)

The relentless paradox at the center of Hill's work is the sense of a linguistic responsibility to a reality which evades language. Speech may be impotent and bereft of meaning, but it is the only weapon that the poet-as-bewildered-survivor can rely on. And so he is left with the irony of his own helplessness, the promethean task of reinfusing the shod Word. It is a task which Hill faces squarely, questioning his own enterprise but mustering great strength.

What truly distinguishes Hill's poetry is not his subject but the intensities of that subject brought under the energetic light of a "bleak skill." His chafing at the restraints of speech is infused with the strength of his impacted line, the formal way he assaults the subject of atrocity and language.... Hill's imagination does owe something to the exotic influence of the southern Fugitives—their poems, their religious preoccupation, their study of the metaphysical poets.

Mercian Hymns is a stylistic departure from his earlier work and is his most ambitious book to date. It is a syntactically varied sequence of thirty prose poems, intermittently colloquial and archaic, which relies heavily on a schoolboy's (and poet's) historical reveries. As the voices merge and subdivide, the poem combines and plays off the legendary exploits of Offa, eighth-century king and "the presiding genius of the West Midlands," against the reality of a West Midlands childhood. Most of Hill's familiar deities are present, but they are generally emptied of religious impulse: the inexplicable necessity of pain and suffering, the longing for heroic sacrifice, the distance between event and document, the passion required to bridge that gulf. One dimension of *Mercian Hymns* is the attempt to confront the necessity of an early suffering. Another is the poetic opportunity of expanding the line and image of the first two books. Although I prefer the rigors of his formal lyric, Hill's prose poems do have a music and range not found in his earlier work. (pp. xcvii-xcviii)

> *Edward Hirsch, in* Sewanee Review *(reprinted by permission of the editor; © 1976 by The University of the South), Summer, 1976.*

*   *   *

HOCHMAN, Sandra   1936-

Hochman, an American confessional poet, has recently been writing novels that chronicle the growth of consciousness of the female protagonist. Her first novel, *Walking Papers*, was quickly embraced by the feminist movement. (See also *CLC*, Vol. 3, and *Contemporary Authors*, Vols. 5-8, rev. ed.)

The tone [of *Walking Papers*], set by the tension between the crazy fragments [the central character] Diana collects from life and the unifying, sane love she hopes for, would be ironic were it not hysterical. The mode is vaudeville, Diana is a stand-up comedian, and the problem is age-old: when Alan King tells the one about his wife, we know he doesn't really mean it. When Diana tells her marriage joke, it removes her finally from the events: she is so much caricature, so much super-hyped female Portnoy, that we never believe she lives. If Hochman told us, for instance, why

and how Diana, at some point vulnerable, fell in love with her husbands, the book might have a chance; as it is, we are so smothered with volleys of lefts and rights that we can't see who's punching, much less care whether the problem is men or women or their combinations. (pp. 283-84)

> *The* Antioch Review *(copyright © 1971 by The Antioch Review, Inc.; reprinted by permission of the editors), Vol. XXXI, No. 1, 1971.*

[Wanting] to *be* a poet, and writing *poetry* are two utterly different things. One feels Miss Hochman has made her career out of the wanting alone....

Miss Hochman's poems [in "Earthworks"] have been written by a sort of tourist in life, whose travels began at boarding school and continued through, say Bennington College; they resemble nothing so much as a collection of postcards, their thought and observation no more profound or exciting or comprehensive than the messages sent home by an unhappy traveler who has moments of pleasant personal insight that occur in bazaars or temples or hotel bathrooms or beds.

Like postcards, these poems are self-centered, focused on a lonely, wistful existence and spoken by a very "bright" daughter, whose emotional tone is flaccid, discouraged and awkward even when she speaks of her joys. (p. 6)

> *Jascha Kessler, in* The Los Angeles Times *(copyright, 1971, Los Angeles Times; reprinted by permission), January 1, 1971.*

From beginning to end [in *Futures*], it's clear in every poem that the Hochman Circus is back in town with all those tragical-comical acts we remember from *Walking Papers* and from the earlier collections: the violinist-husband, the mad lover, the ineffectual father, the nurse, the uncles, and of course the ringmistress—sensitive, tumultuous, "barefoot tough-girl Sandy" herself. Only now the costumes are a bit frayed, and the glittery sets have been set up too often before. In many of the poems the artful, self-celebrating delight of, say, *Love-Letters From Asia*, seems to have given way to a sort of gossipy logorrhea, as if the poet-ring mistress had merely become a voice at the other end of a telephone, endlessly rehearsing the old woes, the new woes, the old woes. In particular, *Children's Court* and *Secrets of Wonder Women* have this *nudgily* solipsistic quality. The first [is] soggy with serio-comic memories.... The second, a piece about dieting that might make it as a confessional number in *Vogue* or *Glamour*.... (pp. 48-9)

Well, to the extent that she permits herself to publish stuff like this, it's obvious that success has spoiled Sandra Hochman. Poetry really isn't a stand-up comedy routine, a gossipy confession, a worn-out circus act, or even a documentary about women of the year, although those are all illuminating analogs sometimes. But then no one knows this better than Hochman at her best.... I suppose from such poets we can't—or shouldn't—expect eternal prudence. It's perhaps our problem if we have to sit through a lot of distracting and tedious reminiscence to get to the real point.... And at least the title of the book, *Futures*, suggests a semiconscious longing to exorcise the old bogeys once and for all, and get on with the business of inventing new dreams. (p. 49)

> *Sandra M. Gilbert, in* Poetry *(© 1975 by The Modern Poetry Association; reprinted by permission of the Editor of* Poetry *), October, 1975.*

Sandra Hochman's second novel ["Happiness is Too Much Trouble"] is the latest installment in the continuing saga of the liberated New York divorcée. As followers of the genre already know, the heroine, after a privileged childhood and great success at high school (private, progressive) and college (same), moves on to analysis, the arts and a series of disastrous relationships with men. At least one lover is a certifiable lunatic, another is an incorrigible woman-hater, and another is simply impossible. None of them pays her enough attention, even though, she is quick to tell us, she is sensational in bed and has a terrific sense of humor. Questions the reader is not supposed to ask: would *any* amount of attention satisfy this person? Are her men really so dreadful, or is she maybe not telling the whole story? Would the reader like to have her over for dinner?

Hochman's first novel, "Walking Papers," was one of the best of these books, because it was an exploration of its heroine's obsessions and not just an apologia for them. Diana Balooka's need to be loved was so overwhelming that she put up with real misery for the sake of the constant romantic turmoil she required. Lulu Cartwright, the much less endearing heroine of "Happiness Is Too Much Trouble," rejects Diana's bargain. Love, she decides, just isn't worth it, and she goes after power as representing both good feminism and a safer bet. . . .

Lulu has all the faults she criticizes in men: she is boorish, insensitive, self-absorbed and fond of impersonal sex. Although she claims to have tried love and found it wanting, her choice of men precludes all but the shallowest sort of involvement. . . . Next to them, she can't help but look good, which may be what attracts her to them.

Lulu's story is a fantasy, of course, and in lighter, defter hands could have been a funny and illuminating one, a "Putney Swope" of the sexes. But as her leaden, joyless prose makes clear, Hochman is in dead earnest. She really believes that Lulu is the blameless victim of men she sincerely loved, and that she is right to covet prestige, a huge salary and the ability to boss others around. The line between Hochman's feminism and plain old materialism is extremely thin. It's all very well to say that power is necessary for "self-realization," but what kind of power? What kind of self? Interestingly, Hochman never wonders why, if power is so beneficial, the male executives Lulu confronts are so grotesque. I suspect it's no accident. (p. 5)

Katha Pollitt, in The New York Times Book Review (© *1976 by The New York Times Company; reprinted by permission), March 7, 1976.*

*   *   *

HOLLANDER, John   1929-

American poet, critic, and editor, Hollander is a formalist poet of considerable merit, a neo-Scholastic who looks to the seventeenth century for his poetic models. Along with Frank Kermode, he edited the *Oxford Anthology of English Literature.* **(See also** *CLC,* **Vols. 2, 5, and** *Contemporary Authors,* **Vols. 1-4, rev. ed.)**

John Hollander's poems [in his second volume, *Moviegoing and Other Poems*], even at their most frivolous and perverse, explore the shifting barriers between semblance and reality with a sort of chuckling irony, but never with a very high inner seriousness. His irony has no satirical thrust behind it, little melancholy, no compelling joy. These are poems whose major emotion lies in their own clever-

ness. It is worth taking poetry more seriously—as in their ways Creeley and Levertov do—and perhaps in his third book Hollander will find his way. (p. 87)

Peter Davison, in The Atlantic Monthly (*copyright* © *1962 by The Atlantic Monthly Company, Boston, Mass.; reprinted with permission), November, 1962.*

Vision and Resonance, John Hollander's first critical book since *The Untuning of the Sky* (1961), proves to have been well worth waiting for. The earlier work was a comprehensive study of ideas about music, and the interrelation between music and poetry, in English verse of the 16th and 17th centuries. The shifting dialectic of attitudes toward music and verse is still very much part of Hollander's subject in his new book, but now he moves beyond literary history to a general analysis of how sound in poetry interacts with syntax, generic convention, and the visually scanned shape of the printed poem, to produce the complexities of poetic statement.

Vision and Resonance is the most subtle, convincing account I have seen of the operation of accentual syllabic verse in English. Hollander is meticulous in the use of concepts and terms where others have variously perpetuated a centuries-old legacy of vagueness, and the key distinctions he develops—such as between meter and rhythm, or between performative and descriptive scansion—seem not only precise but demonstrably valuable as he applies them. This enormously learned, technical study is a model of lucidity and, often, even of witty liveliness. The analysis of a variety of poetic texts from Donne to Blake to William Carlos Williams not only illustrates the general observations being made about English prosody, but also demonstrates how a discriminating approach through prosody can illuminate difficult or semantically dense poems. Hollander's readings of brief passages from Donne, Milton, and Blake have an Empsonian brilliance, without Empson's abrasive quirkiness: they impress one not as exercises in ingenuity but as fuller perceptions than previous readers have enjoyed. (p. 94)

[In] his final chapter, Hollander suggests that any poem must be located along the two axes of the eye and the ear, the former locked into meter, generic identity, tradition, collective literary experience, the latter associated with rhythm, the particular objects of representation, individual talent, the intuition of the moment. "The ear responds to the dimension of natural experience, the eye to that of convention." The distinction is so sweeping and simple that at first one suspects it cannot be altogether true, but it is surprising how sturdily the generalization holds up under scrutiny, as Hollander's own abundant illustrations from a variety of poetic texts make clear.

This way of conceiving two intersecting axes of poetry has one important consequence for literary ideology: in even the most radically iconoclastic poetry, tradition and convention remain an ineluctable dimension of the poem. Modern poets may wilfully ignore the old boundary lines of poetic genre, but none can escape from the convention-bound axis of the eye. (pp. 94-5)

Hollander stresses what he calls "the modality of verse"; a poetry which avowedly elects long-established forms of expression works toward "creating discourse in an ideal community, within which the literary dialect would be as speech." Modern poets have often rejected all notions of the modality of verse, breaking down genre and decorum in the effort to forge a uniquely personal, purely *expressive* style. Some, however, like W. H. Auden, have actually reaffirmed modality, adopting from the tradition a variety of forms and styles through which they implicitly assert a public realm of literary discourse more durable than the transitory idiom of individual experience. (p. 95)

[The] reaching for modality explains, I think, the strength, the limitations, and the peculiarity of John Hollander's own poetry. It is heartening to discover in the scholarly analyst of prosody a poet who is himself a technical virtuoso, but Hollander's recurrent problem from the beginning of his career has been to escape the aridness of mere virtuosity. His first volume, *A Crackling of Thorns* (1958), is astonishing in the variety of styles so finely controlled by a young poet, but there is something ventriloquistic and frustratingly oblique in the way the poet treats his own experience. This continues to be true, I find, though in less obtrusive, more complicated ways, of Hollander's five subsequent volumes of verse. There are, to be sure, some notable exceptions, like the evocative title-poem of *Movie-Going* (1962), or the poems dealing with memory and childhood and adolescence in *Visions from the Ramble* (1965). The persistent problem, however, of Hollander's poetry is illustrated on almost every page of . . . *The Night Mirror* (1971). Poem after poem reads like a distanced, abstractly conceived "treatment" of some idea or situation, a set exercise in rendering a quality or effect. The poet who had imitated the Elizabethans, Marvell, Dryden, Wordsworth, and many others finally seems to have arrived at a kind of accomplished voicelessness, in which the poem becomes an elegant arabesque of studied (sometimes precious) images concluding in a deft cadence with a word like "dust," "dark," or, alternately, "light."

This disembodied virtuosity continues to dominate many, though fortunately not all, of the poems in *Tales Told of the Fathers*. The difficulty, I would suggest, is that modality as Hollander tries to carry it out in his verse is no longer feasible because of what has happened to literary tradition and the language of poetry. . . . For a modern poet . . . to invoke or revive a whole mode of earlier poetry seems like a strenuous experiment in willed atavism.

One frequently feels the problem on the level of diction in *Tales Told of the Fathers*. Without a doctrine of sublime style for "lofty" subjects, phrases like "diurnal panache" and "the reservoir's onyx water" seem like mere preciosity, and the attempt, imagistically and lexically, to resuscitate a mythic mode in lines like "A Deus in the graciousness day,/Drunk with skyeyness," is inadvertently comic. And for a generation accustoming itself to no-frills flying, a poet cannot quite get away with rendering travel by plane in terms like these: "Huddled in silver/Pinions of his steel eagle,/ He drops not down, but/ Plummets forward into clouds. . . ." Milton could do this for Lucifer falling—syntactic inversion, high-diction "pinions," obtruded enjambment, and all—but as a rendering of an airplane flight it seems an affectation.

Yet, in poetry so conspicuously assembled out of antecedent poetry, there is one subject on which poet and manner can sometimes fall into the lovely alignment of illumination, and that is when the poem deals with the perplexing nature of poetry itself. There are several striking pieces of this sort in *Tales Told of the Fathers*, where Hollander's play of verbal and situational wit, his love of allusion and multiple styles, seem fully integrated with what he means to say. In the scary playfulness of "Cohen on the Telephone," the poem moves in a rapid allusive sweep from Exodus and Milton through Keats and the Elizabethans to *Tales of the Hasidic Masters* and the talmudic Celestial Echo. . . . "Mount Blank" . . . wryly glances back at Shelley's "Mount Blanc," Wordsworth's "The Simplon Pass," at *King Lear* and *Paradise Lost,* in order to point up its own predicament after those primary masterworks, caught in a late self-conscious moment of literary history where all objects of representation prove to be "pictures of pictures,/ Or views of noise: postcards of roaring."

Finally, "Kranich and Bach," the concluding poem of this volume, combines a brooding meditation on art and mortality with for once, concretely realized personal memory. (pp. 95-6)

> *Robert Alter, "The Critic as Poet" (reprinted from* Commentary *by permission; copyright © 1975 by the American Jewish Committee), in* Commentary, *September, 1975, pp. 94-6.*

[It] remains a characteristic of New York poetry (not just Hollander's) that it may look north and south, and certainly east across the Atlantic, but very seldom west, into that continental hinterland on which it mostly turns its back. And that eloquently uninterested back turned upon Midwesterners and Westerners can make us—even an adopted and latecome Westerner like myself—not so much alarmed as daunted and irritated. Are we such hicks, so provincially incapable of keeping up with the speed and gloss of the metropolis? Near the end of *Tales Told of the Fathers,* for instance, there is a series of five poems called "Examples," each one concerned with a philosopher's dilemma about language; and a reader like me is divided between shamefaced awe at the thought of a society where particular passages of Descartes, Russell, J. L. Austin, G. E. Moore, and Immanuel Kant are part of the common change of party conversation and a mutinous suspicion that no such society exists, even in Manhattan, and that the whole illusion has been fabricated as a putdown for us country cousins.

The odd thing is that this terrifying knowledgeability in Hollander is something that he has seen, from time to time, not just as a block between himself and his potential public, but as a block between himself and his "best self." Thus, in "Upon Apthorp House," when he said goodbye to Harvard and thankfully returned to New York, he regarded it as a goodbye also to one sort of knowledgeability, specifically a literary sort. . . . But knowledgeability or (why fool about?) sheer *knowledge* is not so easily abandoned or concealed. All Hollander's later collections have betrayed this, as does *Vision and Resonance,* [a] collection of his critical essays. . . .

As a critic, then, Hollander is very learned—and in a field where learning is in short supply, to just the degree that unwarrantedly confident assertion, and by serious characters like Williams, Pound, and Olson, is embarrassingly plentiful; that's to say, in the area where poetry and music overlap, or seem to. From the twelve carefully interlinked essays that make up *Vision and Resonance,* one thing that emerges, even for such a musically obtuse reader as me, is the arresting and indeed momentous contention that in English, far more than in French, Italian, or German, the marriage of music with poetry—of chords or notes with verbal sounds—has been, for four centuries and for readily ascertainable reasons, exceptionally difficult; so that a potent notion like "the music of poetry" has been in English for several centuries, without English-speakers recognizing it, a merely metaphorical or figurative expression, as it has not been over the same period for French-speakers, Italian-speakers, German-speakers.

The implications of this are very far-reaching. But it must be said that in his essays Hollander doesn't always wear his learning lightly. And this is lucky for him; since his writing is so much more sprightly in verse than in prose, at least he is spared the torment reserved for the doubly damned—of having his poems regarded as the spin-off from his criticism. (p. 30)

As an elegant romantic Hollander has, of course, at least one distinguished American predecessor: Stevens. And Stevens's idiom—even, sometimes, Stevens's mannerisms—lie up closer below the surface of Hollander's style than do even the idioms we might call "Audenesque." Accordingly readers who have less trouble with Stevens than I have will respond without my querulous hesitations, for instance, to fifteen formally identical poems in a sequence called "The Head of the Bed." That the inside is the outside, that dreaming is as true as waking, that daybreak and nightfall are therefore interchangeable, that imagination and reality switch places as soon as you think about it—these are propositions to which I give assent under the persuasion of nice diction and cadence, but reluctantly, because they don't give me what I most hunger for: the fact (or the illusion, if that's what I must settle for) of some fixed and stable points in the flux of living as I experience it day by day and night by night.

One may say of such a world that in it everything rhymes—inside with outside, night with day, sun with moon; and some people find a comfort in that. Strikingly, Hollander can sympathize with those of us who don't. . . . [Very] often, Hollander's word games are played for the highest stakes. . . . For Hollander's romanticism differs from Stevens's, I think, precisely in aching, in *yearning* (the corny word is the right one) for a region of nonnegotiable fixities which resist even the cleverest mind's attempts to turn them into their opposites. And often enough—as in the admirable "Rotation of Crops," for the moment my favorite Hollander poem—that region has an image for him, one that generations of romanticism have sanctified, as the region of the fixed stars. (pp. 30-1)

Hollander, who in the past has been a gay and insouciant writer, is here on page after page experiencing a sort of desolation, at its bleakest in a series of nine poems called "Something About It," where the central and indeed sole character is one Doctor Bergab. Bergab: gabber. The talkiness that Hollander was struggling to be rid of in 1962 is what enmeshes him still. He can see this as clearly as we can, and most of these poems are preoccupied with just that. Talkiness, mere gab; that's to say, breath, that's to say, air. And of the four archaic elements—earth, water, air, and fire—it's the third dimension, air, whose terrors these poems especially explore, though one of the wittiest of them, "The Ziz," tells us that the fourth element, fire, is comprehended also. The wit, in any case, is Prince Hamlet's; deployed to keep terror at bay, it thereby witnesses how real the terror is. And the metaphysical terror is in the possibility that the air we incessantly expel as we incessantly articulate is never bounced back to us off any surface whatever; that there is no being—human or other—that listens, let alone responds. . . .

Merely to turn the pages of *Tales Told of the Fathers,* seeing how—except for certain interlinked sequences—each page presents a new shape to the eye, is to realize that this is a poet for whom the idea of *genre* is meaningful and precious. Only the *idea,* of course; for the old system of once canonical genres has been dismantled and will not be put together again. What is held open by Auden or Hollander is the possibility of a different system of genres one day emerging. Hollander might prefer to "genres" the more flexible "modes"—a word that he uses with a musicologist's unusual exactness. Whichever word we use, we are talking of something important; for discrimination between kinds of stylistic behavior in writing reflects and may even enforce discriminations in other kinds of behavior, and it is surely on discriminations of that kind that rests any idea of civility, of mutual consideration. There may or may not be a Being who listens to the little gouts of air, called words, that we expel toward him; but if there is, the least we can do is to address him not always in the same tone of voice, whether a manic shout or a querulous grumble or a precarious suavity.

And if this is what a New York poet like Auden, or Hollander in his more constricted way, is saying, than the rest of America—at whatever cost to its currently cherished preconceptions—needs to listen. (p. 31)

> *Donald Davie, "Gifts of the Gab," in* The New York Review of Books *(reprinted with permission from* The New York Review of Books; © 1975 by NYREV, Inc.), October 2, 1975, pp. 30-1.*

Hollander is unquestionably one of the most skillful versemakers around, and the qualities of his imagination are most evident at the verbal level. Music, in his work, is just as much an agent of meaning as discourse, and the sonorous textures of his poems compel us to read with our ears as well as our eyes. Intelligent to a fault, rational even in his darkest broodings, Hollander nevertheless achieves distinctive emotional effects through his subtle use of the technical resources at his command. Rhyme and meter, word-play and allusion, a keen sense of the line: these are not ornaments in Hollander's poetry, but essential, binding forces, and they reveal to us that language is not merely a systematic organization of signs, but a magic soil in which the pre-history of the human unconscious can be traced. . . .

Hollander is chiefly known as a poet of wit, learning, and charm—and these are qualities that should in no way be underestimated. . . . Hollander's is an art of control rather than passion, but his work is never cold or severe, and he is by no means a man of few words. From poem to poem it is a sense of playfulness that dominates, an ebullient delight in the generative possibilities of language. . . .

Hollander dazzles us with his language, but inside this sphere of human imagining he knows there is a core of void, a center that resists all utterance. (p. 109)

Hollander tries to seize the thing for which there is no word, the otherness of the inhuman. It is not a religious confrontation, but a metaphysical gesturing toward that-which-is-beyond, and more often than not his approach to the problem is ironical, even intentionally silly, as if he were saying to us: here it is again, the old question that cannot be answered, even though it is the only question that must be answered. The dilemma leads to a highly inventive kind of non-sense. . . . (pp. 109-10)

Hollander has never been what could be called a private poet, and in *Tales Told of the Fathers* we find few personal references or confessional impulses. Each piece stands so solidly by itself and is so smoothly perfected according to its own inner logic that it almost seems independent of the will of its creator. But if this prevents his work from attaining a vivid personal dimension, it is also one of Hollander's greatest strengths, for it frees him from unnecessary restrictions and enables him to roam to the full extent of his considerable talents. . . . *Tales Told of the Fathers* . . . [is] a collection of remarkable diversity. Hollander's range is enormous, and he writes in all modes with equal virtuosity and panache. Few poets have ever communicated such delight in the making of poetry, and few books in recent years have been able to make the act of reading so purely pleasurable. (p. 110)

> *Paul Auster, in* Harper's *(copyright 1975 by Harper's Magazine; all rights reserved; reprinted from the November, 1975 issue by special permission), November, 1975.*

Hollander's *Tales Told of the Fathers* . . . , more even than his previous work, indicates the movement of another American poet into the bitterness of strength. Hollander's burden is that his verse somehow combines Ben Jonson and Shelley in a single body, an uncanny and unique blending that in Hollander has the force of a fatality. . . . The wonder of *Tales Told of the Fathers* is that Hollander now integrates all the diverse strains of his poetic nature. At his best, as in the long poem or sequence, "The Head of the Bed," Hollander can be compared to Ashbery as being in the line of Stevens without merely yielding to the precursor's power. But Hollander also is emerging into a plangent voice related to Yiddish poetry, movingly evident in the title-sequence, "Tales Told of the Fathers," as in a parable of Hillel taken from the Talmud. . . . This voice of erudite lament, troubled by a final knowledge, and intensely sad when it intends to be most stoical, is Hollander's true voice of feeling, and prophesies a major phase to come. (p. 25)

> *Harold Bloom, in* The New Republic *(reprinted by permission of* The New Republic; © *1975 by The New Republic, Inc.), November 29, 1975.*

John Hollander's new book, *Vision and Resonance,* is a selection of essays written at different times, dealing with various topics, but still pretty well integrated around one central question: how to account for the "music," or musicality, of lyric poems that have been written specifically to be read and not sung. What do we mean when we speak of the music of verse? Hollander seeks the answer mainly through historical explorations. . . . [All] of the book is vague; or worse—confused, difficult, and not very important. At least that's how it strikes me.

I must qualify my discontent immediately by acknowledging that I am a poor reader for this sort of book, certainly not the reader Hollander had in mind. I have neither a classical education nor a firm grounding in recent technical criticism. Hollander, on the other hand, has spent years thinking about the problems of historical and analytical prosody, which obviously are topics as valid for the activity of human intelligence as any other. Perhaps his book *is* important; the prosodists must decide. As for me, since I cannot evaluate the main technical drift of his argument or the thoroughness of his documentation, I shall limit myself to aspects of Hollander's book that may be, though I think not necessarily, tangential.

First, the confusion and difficulty. To some extent they spring from Hollander's writing. Without doubt it is disappointing to find a poet who is so bound-up, not to say tongue-tied, in his prose. Bad style isn't obligatory. Granted, Hollander's topic is complex; but Saintsbury wrote three volumes about the prosody of English verse and wrote them in long elaborate sentences, without ever losing his grip on lucidity. Hollander's book, though much shorter, took me three days to read, and the reading was painful. His polylingual and frequently jargonistic diction and his arch rhetoric lead him into sentences like this: "By continually manipulating word sounds in lexical contexts, their suggestive quality is forever enhanced, it being remembered that—and this is a cardinal rule for the discussion of the effects of sound in any poetic environment—words can only 'sound like' other words, and it is thereby that they sound like nature if at all." I quote the whole thing to show that no matter how patiently you trek through it you never come to a grammatical resolution. And the book is full, crammed full, of sentences just as hard to read.

Secondly, the "sense" of that sentence, namely that words can only sound like other words. Hollander is led by his emphasis on the conventional aspect of poetic language, and perhaps by his respect for linguistics, to the idea that language is functionally conventional. All right; but then he presses it to the extreme, to the point of nonsense. (pp. xcviii-xcix)

The main point I still wish to raise, my third, concerns Hollander's use of the word *form.* . . . [He] uses it to mean the abstract, conventional pattern of a poem, the scheme, the plan, the structural graph—call it what you will. But this doesn't make sense. Can the form of a poem, or of anything else, exist apart from the thing that is formed? We know it in and only in its object. Hollander is speaking continually in terms of definitions, not forms, and this is more than a terminological dispute. Definitions are good for making classifications; sometimes they may be aids to abstract understanding; but they do not show us forms, which are the functional aspects of objects. In short, Hollander's book is a modernized version of criticism by genre, and we know what to think about that. It doesn't work. It can't work. Every genre that has ever been erected in literature has broken down, and the "rules" governing it have evaporated. (pp. c-ci)

I kept hoping, as I read Hollander's book, that I would come to a discussion of recent poetry, but except for passing glances at Stevens, Williams, and one or two others, Hollander concentrates on the poetry of the past. (p. ci)

> *Hayden Carruth, "John Hollander's Prosody," in* Sewanee Review *(reprinted by permission of the editor, © 1976 by The University of the South), Summer, 1976, pp. xcviii-ci.*

Hollander's long narrative [*Reflections on Espionage: The Question of Cupcake*] is a Kafkan tour de force, a virtuoso performance to match Merrill's that "reprints" the "regular, encoded radio transmissions" of the master spy Cupcake to the agent Image or to his director Lyrebird. The transmissions, "copies of which were eventually recovered by sources in his native country ['an altogether inconvenient little republic which ceased to exist a good time ago'], have only recently been deciphered. . . ." The work consists of 101 dated sections beginning with 1/14 and ending with 10/1. They range from one line to nearly 100; they average about 30. Their ingenuity is astonishing, the energy behind them never lets up. They form a composite picture of a brilliant, sad, witty man whose antecedents (in addition to Kafka) are Dostoevsky's underground man, Melville's Bartleby, and all those 19th century clerks whose unimportant agonies went unnoticed except by those who saw them as archetypes. The book is devilishly well-made (the clue to Cupcake's fate is Et Glpkx Et V di Vxnt, and is also all-too-human, for its theme has to do with an anomie so acute and a distrust so pervasive that one only puts his faith in the work-derived attachments subsisting between a few individuals, no other moral structures being available. By contrast the scenes in *All The President's Men* between Bob Woodward and Deep Throat in the D.C. garage were moments of all but union. Here, everybody (literally) checks up on everyone else so that in the end we find that even the minimal faith one thought one had fails. The last line is (. . . XXXXXXXXXXXXXXXX). Instructions are provided for deciphering this. You won't like what you learn. (p. 365)

> *Stanley Poss, in* Western Humanities Review *(copyright, 1976, University of Utah), Autumn, 1976.*

Hollander, whose poems always suffer the burden of knowing perhaps more than poems should, is at his all-but-best in the delightful *Reflections On Espionage: The Question of Cupcake.* . . . I say "all-but-best" because his two great longer poems are *The Head of the Bed* (in the volume *Tales Told of the Fathers*) and the even more Kabbalistic *Spectral Emanations,* recently and now appearing under the heading of different colors in various magazines. *Reflections On Espionage,* like the erotic *Town and County Matters,* is written by Hollander's left hand, but this gives it the freedom to be an outrageous parody-poem, mocking the whole condition of contemporary poetry under the guise of a spy-thriller. Cupcake is Hollander, done with shattering wit and deep sorrow, while nearly everyone in current verse is marched before us with an almost Popean accuracy and compassion. As a parable of poetic belatedness, and a commentary upon the way poets live and write now, this is without rival. (p. 23)

> *Harold Bloom, in* The New Republic *(reprinted by permission of* The New Republic; © *1976 by* The New Republic, Inc.*), November 20, 1976.*

Reflections on Espionage . . . is, in effect, a narrative about the act of converting sensation to art. I imagine the entire work deriving from Browning's "How It Strikes a Contemporary," a narrative poem that pictures the poet as a sort of secret agent communicating with God. There is no God in John Hollander's story, and the secret messages are communications from the self to the self, but nonetheless, the resemblance is there. I suspect that the cover design of *Reflections on Espionage,* showing the poet reflected in a full-length mirror, is meant as a hint to help us along in this kind of interpretation, as are the many references to reflections and mirrors in the poems. (p. 89)

The writing in *Reflections* is graceful, smooth, easy to read. Sometimes it is arch and playful—not an unusual quality in a poet who has written books like *Types of Shape* and *Town and Country Matters.* It is also sometimes tired and flat, but it is always skillful. The danger in this sort of game —and it is a game—is that the telling has become more

important than what is being said. The lyric impulse to speak about poetry and the creative act has been strung together through the benefit of a doubtful "story," the narrative details of which are sometimes quite boring, since it is not the tale we care about, but only the central point of the entire poem. I won't say that Hollander has failed to achieve his purpose in this poem, but I do feel that *Reflections on Espionage* teeters on the edge of vacuity, good as its writing is. (p. 90)

> *John R. Reed, in* The Ontario Review *(copyright © 1976 by* The Ontario Review*), Fall-Winter, 1976-77.*

John Hollander's *Reflections on Espionage* is an extended metaphorical treatment of a special sort of conspiracy— "Us," the milieu of art, vision, understanding, the "altogether inconvenient little republic" of letters, against "Them," the philistines. Beginning with this neat analogy for the marginal state of contemporary poets, Hollander's long poem establishes several more equivalences: the verse is presented as a series of encoded messages, identified by month and day, and transmitted to other agents or to a "control" (who may be understood as a sympathetic critic). The "Work" undertaken by Hollander's group of master-spies is nothing less than the writing of the poetry of our own day; and it is all done under the direction of a topflight commander styled "Lyrebird," viz., Apollo or the Muse.

The poem's agent-narrator, code name "Cupcake," is, I assume, based on Hollander himself, and I believe "real life" prototypes for most of the other agents could be found. (p. 537)

What Cupcake and his creator have in common is that they both seem to know everything. John Hollander holds, surely, the Monsieur Teste chair in American letters. His earlier poetry and criticism frequently and usefully allude to many kinds of learning—scientific, historical, musical— when these might throw light on the issues under consideration. *Vision and Resonance,* his study of poetry as a sonic and visual entity, is the most informative and infectiously interesting treatise to date on that subject. And Hollander's learning serves him well in his poetry, both as stimulus and substance. . . .

Amusement will probably be most readers' first reaction to Hollander's parodic spy-thriller, but I doubt it will be the last. The humor and wit so apparent in these pages suggest that the poet is dealing with matters too important to be presented with unrelieved earnestness, too urgent to risk leaving the reader in the detachment of pity or polite toleration. (p. 538)

Some of Cupcake's most interesting reflections turn around the relationship between espionage (poetry) and the agent's "cover" (his ostensible profession), since in our day most poets must make their living by doing something besides writing poetry. . . . During the nine-month period recorded, something seems to be gestating; this proves to be Cupcake's death or rather his "Termination," the order for it coming down from Lyrebird. No definite reason for the "termination" is given—but it is implicit. When Hollander's Muse stops being stimulated by the persona of "Cupcake," it's time to drop him and for the book to end. Of course, there may be more to it than that, for *Reflections on Espionage* is a richly textured work, multilayered, and evocative of meanings leading in several directions. (pp. 538-39)

Anyone who knows modern poetry will almost reflexively decode Cupcake's aspirations toward a Final Cipher as the Supreme Fiction Stevens made notes toward, or, again, as the final book Mallarmé asserted the world was destined to become. Mallarmé appears to be Hollander's most telling precursor in French. . . .

Cupcake . . . , among recent American voices, seems to have the clearest sense of the Mallarméan imagination. And Mallarmé's notion of the *azur* he seems very much at home with. The most characteristic Hollander moment has always seemed to be one captured in an environment at high altitudes and low temperatures, with cloudless, ultramarine skies. (pp. 539-40)

Among English poets probably the most important for Hollander is Ben Jonson. Certainly Jonson has had few critics as sympathetic as Hollander. The two are alike in their complete possession of poetic tradition; and Hollander also seems to share Jonson's healthy attitude toward the classics, which the English poet termed "Guides, not Commanders." (p. 540)

In the twentieth century the poet most resembling Jonson is Auden; and some of the typical concerns of both—reasonableness, loyalty, and an interest in writing in many different poetic genres—have been inherited by Hollander. The association between Hollander and Auden was personal as well as literary, of course; and here I will quote the first but one of Cupcake's transmissions, which details the death of "Steampump," an agent unquestionably based on Auden:

> Steampump is gone. He died quietly in his
> Hotel room and his sleep. His cover people
> Attended to everything. What had to
> Be burned was burned. He taught me, as you surely
> Know, all that I know. . . .

I hazard that one of the germinating impulses for *Reflections* was a desire to present, in code, a portrait of what remains of Auden's influence in American poetry. The "covers" that I can identify all seem to have at least a tenuous relationship to Auden, either as poets he chose for the Yale Series, or as his friends, his disciples, or disciples of his disciples. This group, *mutatis mutandis*, is a fair equivalent for the celebrated Tribe of Ben that accounts for most of the important early seventeenth-century poetry in England after Jonson's death. Perhaps this parallel struck Hollander. Certainly it seems to be the case that, with the passing of Auden, we lack any figure of international stature in poetry. Greatness in the poetry of this moment is probably best judged as a joint achievement, the sum of a group effort.

The assertion of a real—though not pious—sense of community in Hollander's rendering of the present milieu of poetry is one of the book's most attractive features. He allows us to see how poets, at least some of them, must view each other's work and careers—not as a mad, competitive scramble, but as a kind of teamwork. . . . The world limned out in this book has broader implications than its immediate reference, of course. It could serve as a model for an imaginative community on any scale, one whose members were all respectfully conscious of the others' lives, work, and "signifying" capacity. In such a utopia, citizens specifically designated as poets might vanish. Cupcake seems to be aware of the possibility: "as if the whole world perhaps were/ At the work? What then? Why then there would be no/ Need of it." But we are far away from that, I think. A book like *Reflections on Espionage* is still very necessary, nor could anyone but a poet have written it. (pp. 540-41)

Alfred Corn, in The Georgia Review *(copyright, 1977, by the University of Georgia), Summer, 1977.*

*   *   *

HUXLEY, Aldous   1894-1963

A British-American novelist, essayist, short story writer, poet, critic, and playwright, Huxley was noted in his early works for a satiric tone, while his later works express a concern for the political and social problems of contemporary society. The grandson of Darwinist T. H. Huxley and brother of scientist Julian Huxley, Aldous Huxley retained a central interest in science. His concern with societal problems and his continuing interest in science coalesce in his most famous work, *Brave New World*. (See also *CLC*, Vols. 1, 3, 4, 5.)

[Huxley's] excursions into political philosophy were most notable for the uncompromising pacifism which drove him into his self-imposed Californian exile. He was, most of the time, miserable there during the war years, unavoidably prone to feelings of guilt in the bad years. He had brought the misery on himself because he remained to so large an extent the prisoner of the Victorian rationalism in which he had been brought up and against which he constantly rebelled. In true rationalist style, he seems never to have believed in evil as a positive force. This seems to have made him incapable of grasping the significance of Hitler, and of the inevitability through him of World War Two, and allowed Huxley in his last years to divert his enormous talent into the unreal and fatuous Wellsian serenities of *Island* (written in 1960). . . .

One might have supposed that Huxley's self-exile, his separation from his normal environment—and in Los Angeles, of all uninspiring places—would have had a damaging effect on his talent. This did not happen. Some of his best writing belongs to these years. *Grey Eminence*, written in 1940 and 1941, is a masterly performance. His first novel since 1936, *Time must have a stop* (published in 1944), was Huxley's own favourite among his fiction. It is a brilliant invention, though . . . I cannot believe that it is more than that. *The Perennial Philosophy*, published in the next year, 1945, is perhaps the book by which Aldous Huxley will be best known to future generations. The most horrifying of all his novels, *Ape and Essence*, was published in 1948. It is a book of great and terrible power. . . .

After 1950, he wrote books which are better described as brilliant pieces of controversy rather than masterpieces, with one exception. One of them, *The Doors of Perception*, is still a matter of lively controversy today. At the risk of sounding prudish, I give my opinion that it would have been better if he had not published this book. If one reads it, one quickly appreciates that Aldous Huxley's attitude to drug-taking was responsible, reasonable and morally justifiable. He saw the dangers in his tolerant view of the use of certain drugs. What he did not see was that the fact of his name appearing on a book which, superficially viewed, seemed to approve of drug-taking, would give enormous encouragement to pushers of pot and suchlike. . . . He underestimated, even though aware of the possibility, its harmful latency. He continued to think of evil as a negative force.

Christopher Sykes, "The Unhappy Pacifist," in The Listener *(© British Broadcast-*

ing Corp. 1974; reprinted by permission of Christopher Sykes), October 17, 1974, p. 511.

[Aldous Huxley] was haunted by the vision of two possible futures. One, the most likely, was of destruction, war and ever-increasing tyranny in an overpopulated world. The other was that of the "pragmatic dream" that he advanced in his last essay-novel, *Island:* psychologists must be given power to disqualify certain types of people from ever getting into positions of power. The economic system must be cured of overproduction and the world of overpopulation. Scientists, psychologists, educators who have mustered techniques which could bring life closer to the "pragmatic dream" should be given every opportunity to do so. This is the Huxleyan Utopia of a happiness brought about by scientific techniques. It is the opposite of his somber vision of a world made miserable by its abuse of these techniques in the hands of power maniacs.

Stephen Spender, "A Pilgrim's Progress," in Book World—The Washington Post (© The Washington Post), November 17, 1974, p. 1.

There is not a character who speaks on his author's behalf in Huxley's novels—Gumbril, the timorous inventor of pneumatic trousers for men of sedentary habit, in "Antic Hay"; Quarles; Anthony Beavis in "Eyeless in Gaza"—who fails to share his affliction of non-feeling. As a man Huxley is remote and unresponsive. As a writer he lacks the all-encompassing humanity of the real novelist.

But if there was this always-visible inherited disproportion between his capacity for thought and feeling, at least Huxley's intellectual endowment was an uncommon one. . . .

[One] can think of no other writer who was as personally implicated as Huxley in the break in traditional thought between the 19th and 20th centuries; in important part it had been the work of his own grandfather. Under the general burden of social uncertainty and the peculiar burden of being a Huxley, he turned to satire as his instrument of social and personal renovation and, during the years in which he made the contribution for which he is best remembered, wrote the brightest, most mercurial books of his generation. (p. 1)

[Despite an enormous] output it was actually to a small handful of early novels . . . that Huxley owed the special reputation he had in his contemporary literary world; and even among these only "Antic Hay" blended charm, erudition, humor, intelligence and narrative interest with an entire ease and success. Never did a writer who worked in so many different fields, from poetry to playwriting, from travel reporting to sociology to politics to spiritualism, impress himself so particularly in but one field, satire, and even in that one field produce really only a single completely satisfactory book. And certainly never did a satirist flash so coruscating a wit over so vast a field of learning: not alone the range of his study—history, ancient and modern literatures, philosophy, the social sciences, all the physical sciences, music, art—but his competence at whatever he undertook was staggering. . . .

Man's greed, his folly and selfishness, his concupiscence, his inability to use his skills to his own best purposes: all of this in Huxley's best work became his good-natured joke behind which there loomed, of course, his great fear. Fifty years ago in his early satiric fiction the issues which today

press upon us so relentlessly—pollution, the uncontrolled growth of populations, the destruction of cities, our insane waste of the world's natural resources, social and racial inequity, national ambitions and prides—were already given first sharp statement.

An advantage which Huxley shared with his literary contemporaries Lawrence and Joyce—it made his despairing view of the universe also an enlivening one—was the possibility of shocking his readers. Looking back on Huxley from our present circumstances it is difficult to suppose that it required much daring to write about sex as he did—the most he ventured in erotic overtness was an occasional gaping blouse or the rhythmic strokings of a female arm and shoulder. It was not, however, what happened on the pages of his novels that made Huxley famous for "sophistication," that poor sad accolade now lost to us; it was what he suggested as taking place off-page, especially the compulsions and deviations of sexual desire. For Lawrence sex was a metaphor for burgeoning life. For Huxley it was among the plainer manifestations of the tyranny of selfhood. The erotic sphere might be only one area in which to observe the infinite gradations of human gracelessness, but for someone of Huxley's disposition it was an inescapable one. . . .

Death, ugliness, decay: he brings these repeatedly into juxtaposition with sensuality.

As a countervailing principle to sensuality Huxley proposes the religious transcendence of self. He speaks of a self simultaneously discovered and lost in one's spiritual unity with one's fellow man. . . .

For Huxley, . . . who was a writer of the twenties and thirties [in contrast to today's writers], society was still *there,* faulty and perhaps doomed but still decipherable; a sum of discernible parts, not an undifferentiated and undifferentiating hostile mass. Its intimate patterns of waywardness and perversity, even of possible beneficence, were still available to description. Huxley might himself choose not to describe in the manner of the traditional realistic novelist. "My life . . . is not so long," he has a character protest in "Antic Hay," "that I can afford to spend precious hours writing or reading descriptions of middle-class interiors." But as solidly as he rested his portraits of the people in his books on their unexplained or certainly unspoken inner lives, he accounted for their conduct in terms of their membership in a society of class, money, custom, an English society, indeed, of establishment, education and taste. (p. 2)

Already in "Crome Yellow" in 1921 Huxley had made it clear that faith is the necessary attendant on our worldly programs, their sole reliable source of proper content and direction. . . . But it is not until the final section of "Eyeless in Gaza," the novel published in 1936 with which Huxley followed his very popular "Point Counter Point" and his very disturbing "Brave New World," that we are introduced to the "miracle," his first didactic statement of the nature of the spiritual quest which he will from this time forward increasingly urge upon us. (pp. 2, 42)

Following "Eyeless in Gaza" only one other novel of Huxley's, "After Many a Summer Dies the Swan" (1939), would even partially attract his old enthusiastic audience. The times had changed; Huxley had changed too but not with the times so much as several decades in advance of them; good humor and charm were gone. There are several passages in this novel where Huxley mocks with mordant vividness the California search for panaceas; he describes, for instance, the road signs on a Los Angeles highway: "Astrology, Numerology, Psychic Readings. Drive in for Nutburgers." It seems not to occur to him that it is the satirist who himself now requires to be satirized; that *he* has now in significant part become California. (p. 43)

Diana Trilling, in The New York Times Book Review (© *1974 by The New York Times Company; reprinted by permission), November 24, 1974.*

The relation of *Brave New World* to Wells's fantasies is (with the exception of a number of technological details to be dealt with later) of a rather general nature. Though it may have started out as a parody of *Men Like Gods,* Huxley is quite right in insisting that *Brave New World* ended up as something quite different. It is no *Shamela* to Wells's *Pamela.* The only major areas at which the two novels intersect concern the emotions and the Savage. In Wells's utopia, as in Huxley's dystopia, deep feeling is either non-existent or reprehensible. (p. 265)

It is clear that Huxley borrowed a number of the technological aspects of his Utopia from Wells [especially from *When the Sleeper Wakes*], but it would be dangerous to assume that Wells was Huxley's only or even primary source of scientific information. In the immediate Huxley background, one should remember, were his brother Julian and various sometime friends such as J.B.S. Haldane, Bertrand Russell and J.W.N. Sullivan. And in any case, the technological details, whether Wellsian or no, are not what matter most. They are only the most superficially memorable aspects of Huxley's novel, and as he himself soon realized, he had blundered badly by missing out on one of the most obvious ones, atomic energy. But while this omission is surprising, it certainly does not vitiate the continuing force of his satire. Is Swift's *Gulliver's Travels* no longer of interest because a thorough exploration of the globe has turned up no islands inhabited by Houyhnhnms? (pp. 267-68)

Despite all the gadgetry, . . . the proper study of the novelist remains man. That is why a remark like Gerald Heard's about *Brave New World* being "obsolete because of the growth and findings of subsequent research" seems quite beside the point. So, for that matter, is Hillegas' conclusion that Huxley "is against Utopia not only because it would mechanize human life but because it would give abundance and leisure to everyone, making these no longer the special privilege of people like Huxley himself." Huxley, it is true, made no secret of his suspicion of democracy and of the machine, especially when in combination. . . . After his first traumatic experience of the U.S.A. in 1926, that suspicion grew even more intense. But surely not, as Hillegas asserts, for selfish reasons. After all, a great deal of Huxley's intellectual and artistic life prior to *Brave New World* (and following it) was taken up with the effort to find an adequate solution to the wearisome condition of this chiefly gregarious but intermittently anti-social creature called man. *Brave New World* is no exception. It is no mere what-would-it-be-like-if-pigs-could-fly fantasy, but a bitter attack on a kind of mentality which was seeking to destroy man and replace him with an anthropoid beast or an anthropoid machine. That after all was the point of the epigraph which Huxley had chosen for his novel from Berdyaev's *The End of Our Time* (1927). (p. 268)

Lawrence bears a considerable, if indirect, responsibility for the figure of Mond/Wells in *Brave New World.* Nor is that his only responsibility. For just as behind Mond and behind the whole technological world which he controls stands H. G. Wells, so behind the Savage and the New Mexican Pueblo stands D. H. Lawrence.

When Huxley began work on *Brave New World,* he had never been to New Mexico. That he had not seems in fact to have troubled him, since nearly thirty years later he recalled having "had to do an enormous amount of reading up on New Mexico, because I'd never been there. I read all sorts of Smithsonian reports on the place and then did the best I could to imagine it." . . .

If, however, Huxley had not been to New Mexico and if, for that reason, he had to do a good deal of boning up on it, one wonders why he bothered. If it was underdeveloped or non-Western societies he was after, he had already seen several such during his travels in the Far East in 1926. Why then? . . .

The real answer is Lawrence. By the time Huxley came to know him intimately, Lawrence had already, to be sure, closed the New Mexican chapter of his life, but he had by no means forgotten it. . . . New Mexico, it seems safe to assume, existed for Huxley (that is, before he delved into the Smithsonian reports) only insofar as he had heard about it from Lawrence. (p. 272)

There are signs that Huxley was debunking Lawrence even when their friendship was at its height. Lawrence must have been at least partly on his mind when Huxley wrote in "The Cold-Blooded Romantics" (1928) that "the modern artist seems to have grown down; he has reverted to the preoccupation of his childhood. He is trying to be a primitive. So, it may be remembered, was the romantic Rousseau. But whereas Rousseau's savage was noble, refined and intelligent, the primitive our modern artists would like to resemble is a mixture between the apache and the fifteen-year old schoolboy." Reading this, one is reminded of the scene in "Indians and the Englishman" where Lawrence is confronted in the dusk by an Apache who, he is convinced, wishes to murder him. Here they are, the twin spirits of Lawrence: Natty Bumppo and the primitive blood-consciousness.

Certainly, by the time Huxley was writing *Brave New World,* he was sure that Lawrence's primitive Utopia no longer cut any ice, or certainly no more than Wells's technological one. . . . [In a 1931 essay,] Lawrence's Utopian vision is degraded (or should one say debunked?) to the point of being just another literary stone piled on an already ruinous edifice. Later on in the essay, Lawrence is degraded even further, to the level of a fad (as he is in *Eyeless in Gaza*). "With every advance of industrial civilization," Huxley predicts, "the savage past will be more and more appreciated, and the cult of D. H. Lawrence's *Dark God* may be expected to spread through an ever-widening circle of worshippers." Now Lawrence is the fashionable cultist, no longer the prophet of a new religion. And now the connection is made explicit: Lawrence *is* the savage past.

The savage past or the Fordian future? That is the question which *Brave New World* poses. The Malpais (literally "bad country" in Spanish) of prehistory or the ironically "Buen-pais" of post-history? The choice is between two evils. Not that Lawrence is to be exclusively identified with the one or Wells with the other; that would be to simplify excessively the complexity of Huxley's vision—and to err by trying to make a partial truth do the work of a whole one. Huxley's

Pueblo Indians, closely related as they are to Lawrence's, also have other ancestors. The fragmentary tales they tell derive, for instance, not from Lawrence, but from Frank Cushing's *Zuñi Folk Tales* (1901), which seems also to be the source of many of Huxley's Indian names, including Mitsima and Waihusiva. Not to mention the Smithsonian reports. . . .

No, though Lawrence's experience of New Mexico and Lawrence's antipathy to science, to social regimentation, and to promiscuous sexuality surely helped shape the spirit of the Savage, it would be wrong to identify him with Lawrence too completely. For one thing, it is important to note that Huxley transformed the Pueblo Indians, in one respect at least, almost as much as he did our own world. The Pueblo Indians—as the Smithsonian reports, among others, make clear—are anthropologically a separate entity from the Penitentes. . . . [There] is no mingling of the two, certainly nothing like the fusion that exists in *Brave New World.* Huxley was, of course, aware of this fact and in his foreword described the religion of his Indians as "half fertility cult and half *Penitente* ferocity."

The fertility cult is Indian, and as one might expect, the snake dance is part of that cult. How closely this feature of Pueblo Indian life was linked with Lawrence in Huxley's mind may be appreciated from H. K. Haeberlin's observation that "the Great Serpent of the Pueblo is commonly known as the 'plumed serpent.'" So too with the *sipapus,* the openings in the floor of the *kiva,* which play an important part in Huxley's description of the snake dance. It is there that the deities of germination and fertility reside. And associated with these deities are also the wargods, "Püükon" and his less important [twin] brother."

"Püükon" is obviously Huxley's Pookong, but in *Brave New World* his twin brother has been replaced by Christ, and along with Christ have also come the Penitentes. . . . The Pueblo Indians would certainly never tolerate sadism of the kind which climaxes the snake dance in *Brave New World.* Their whippings take place at initiation ceremonies only and then always in groups, with each youth accompanied by an adult sponsor who is sometimes also whipped. The maximum number of strokes is usually four, and there is no attempt on the part of the person being struck to conceal pain. Furthermore, no Pueblo Indian would go out alone into the desert and commit an act such as the Savage describes. "'Once,'" he tells Bernard Marx, "'I did something that none of the others did: I stood against a rock in the middle of the day, in summer with my arms out, like Jesus on the Cross,'". . . . (pp. 274-76)

What is Huxley's point here? Why does he insist on combining an Indian fertility cult with a Christian penitential ritual? If it is merely to suggest that the forces of life are balanced by those of death—Huxley, one remembers, is often accused of Manicheanism—then he could have portrayed that balance with much less effort by means of the Aztecs of the Old Mexico. Sir James Frazer's *Sacrificial God* is full of horrific examples.

Then why? Because, I suspect, he wishes to make a point about the relation of life and death which he could not have done using the Aztecs. The Aztecs practiced human sacrifice in order to preserve the life of their gods; for them death was merely another aspect of fertility. This is one of the chief reasons why Lawrence rooted his dark god in the

old Mexican soil. But here again Huxley is debunking Lawrence. Life, Huxley implies, is life, never to be confused with death—unless it is the everlasting life, the life beyond death. Lawrence, as Huxley knew, disliked Christianity and may have feared it. Characteristically, he tried to shut himself off from all contact with the Penitentes during his stay in Taos. (pp. 276-77)

There is another and perhaps more important reason why Huxley may have chosen to put the Penitentes into his novel. *Brave New World* portrays a future as well as a past which differ from the present in that they have no history. Our Ford's remark that "History is bunk" applies with equal force to the Pueblo and to the London of AF 632. Both are stable societies which can tolerate no change and therefore possess no history. Now, the one relatively stable institution known to the West in modern historical times is the Church. Significantly, Christianity is the most important shared element of both the Fordian and the Pueblo societies.

This may be less apparent in the new world, but it is no less true. The Solidarity Service which forms a counterpart to the Pueblo Snake Dance is an obvious parody of the mass. (p. 277)

Christianity is an essential element in both of the worlds Huxley depicts. But—and this is a crucial distinction—it is not the same Christianity. In the one instance, it is the Christianity which maintains that we inhabit a value of tears and that we should mortify the flesh in this life in order to store up credit in the next; on the other, it is the Christianity which promises a paradise on earth. The one is Christianity in rags, with flagellation and retreats into the desert; the other Christianity in riches, with everybody "happy" and the peace of the world insured by ten semi-apostolic World Controllers. "Suffer little children," Mustapha Mond admonishes the DHC who has disturbed the little girls and boys at their erotic play.

At the end of *Brave New World,* secular and fanatic Christianity meet and join. The Savage's flagellation of himself and Lenina, echoing the dance at the Pueblo, merges with the orgy-porgy dance of the visiting Fordians and culminates in a fertility-sterility rite in which the Savage finally yields his principles and himself. The only purification for that sin, he realizes on the following day, is death. Such is the result of the Controller's "experiment." Pueblo is Pueblo, and Ford is Ford, and ne'er the twain shall meet, for if they do disaster ensues. Stability lies at the extremes, not at the middle; in machine and in monster, not in man. The choice is between the chiliastic horrors of the Wellsian future or those of the Lawrentian past, both of which exclude the (by comparison lesser) day-to-day trauma of the Huxleyan—or human—present.

And what does Huxley mean to suggest by all this? Perhaps, as he once wrote to his brother Julian, "all's well that ends Wells." To which he might later have added that finishing off Lawrence, as a social philosopher at least, was not a bad idea either. (pp. 277-78)

Peter Firchow, "Wells and Lawrence in Huxley's 'Brave New World'," in Journal of Modern Literature (© *Temple University 1976*), April, 1976, pp. 260-78.

I

INGE, William 1913-1973

An American playwright, screenwriter, and novelist, Inge is the author of, among other plays, *Bus Stop* and *The Dark at the Top of the Stairs*. Inge presents ordinary lives; their horror, in his view, rests in their banality. Like the plays of Tennessee Williams, Inge's dramas frequently focus on women. He was a recipient of the Pulitzer Prize in Drama. (See also *CLC*, Vol. 1, and *Contemporary Authors*, Vols. 9-12, rev. ed.)

William Inge the playwright, like William Inge the gentleman from Kansas via St. Louis, uses his good manners for their proper dramatic purpose, which is to clothe a reality which is far from surface. It is done, as they say, with mirrors, but the mirrors may all of a sudden turn into x-ray photos, and it is done so quietly and deftly that you hardly know the moment when the mirrors stop being mirrors and the more penetrating exposures begin to appear on the stage before you. All of a sudden, but without any startling explosion, it happens, and you're not sure just when and how. This nice, well-bred next door neighbor, with the accent that belongs to no region except the region of good manners, has begun to uncover a world within a world, and it is not the world that his welcome prepared you to meet, it's a secret world that exists behind the screen of neighborly decorum. And that's when and where you meet the talent of William Inge, the true and wonderful talent which is for offering, first, the genial surface of common American life, and then not ripping but quietly dropping the veil that keeps you from seeing yourself as you are. Somehow he does it in such a way that you are not offended or startled by it. It's just what you are, and why should you be ashamed of it? We are what we are, and why should we be ashamed of it more than enough to want to improve it a little? That's what Bill Inge tells you, in his quiet, gently modulated voice that belongs to no region but the region of sincerity and understanding. No, don't be ashamed of it, but see it and know it and make whatever corrections you feel able to make, and they are bound to be good ones.

X-ray photos, coming out of mirrors, may reveal the ravages of tissues turning malignant or of arteries beginning to be obstructed by deposits of calcium or fat. This is God's or the devil's way of removing us to make room for our descendants. Do they work together, God and the devil? I sometimes suspect that there's a sort of understanding between them, which we won't understand until Doomsday.

But Inge reveals the operations of both these powerful mysteries in our lives if you will meet him halfway, and therein lies his very peculiar talent. (pp. vii-viii)

> *Tennessee Williams, in his introduction to* The Dark at the Top of the Stairs, *by William Inge (copyright © 1958 by William Inge; reprinted by permission of Random House, Inc.), Random House, 1958, pp. vii-viii.*

The Dark at the Top of the Stairs, considered both as a play and a production, had all the ingredients of the masterpiece which its author has repeatedly been on the verge of writing. But these ingredients were not blended by a sufficiently determined intent. Whatever his actual intention in *The Dark at the Top of the Stairs,* [Inge] appears to have been most deeply concerned with traumatic family rifts and their devastating effect on children. But his group play technique tends to dissolve this central drama in favor of peripheral themes, chiefly the mistakes that women make in trying to run men's lives. Everything Inge shows us here seems to be authentic, but his several truths weaken the one truth. A play about family trauma would have produced a more gripping and fully realized drama, a successful or unsuccessful *major* drama rather than a successful minor play. As it stands, *The Dark at the Top of the Stairs* is successful because it is many things to its audience. It moves the public without shattering it, and provokes middle-aged relief when the errant husband returns, is reconciled with his wife, and comically beckons her upstairs. (pp. 172-73)

William Inge needs a larger and more original vision than psychotherapy affords if his fine symphonic gifts are to come completely into focus. Even when the psychoanalytical motivations on which he relies are absorbing and compelling in the dramatic action, he does not carry them to the ultimate tragic conclusion. Instead he contents himself with such questionable solutions as the return of the father in *The Dark at the Top of the Stairs* or the successful exorcism of a fixation by one night of love in *A Loss of Roses.*

Whatever psychiatry can do, it cannot take the place of *dramatic* logic and *tragic* vision. (p. 173)

> *John Gassner, "William Inge and the Subtragic Muse: 'The Dark at the Top of the*

Stairs'," *in his* Theatre at the Crossroads: Plays and Playwrights of the Mid-Century American Stage *(copyright © 1960 by Mollie Gassner; reprinted by permission of Holt, Rinehart and Winston, Publishers), Holt, 1960, pp. 167-73.*

[*Overnight*] is one of a series of Inge's plays in a different vein from that of his accredited hits: *Picnic, Bus Stop, The Dark at the Top of the Stairs.* The later plays have little of the gentle humor and amelorativeness of the former. The first in Inge's more severe manner was the 1959 *A Loss of Roses,* and the last one vouchsafed an off-Off Broadway production in 1970, was *The Last Pad.* . . . Nearly all these "unpleasant" plays take place in a sordid atmosphere—which is perhaps the chief reason for the reviewers' and public's aversion to them. They require a subtly superior kind of acting and direction to make them more acceptable. But what I wish to stress here is that these plays reveal the sorrow, pain and protest which were always latent in Inge's spirit but which for a while he succeeded in tempering with benign comedy and with perhaps too heavy a dependence on the therapeutic aspects of Freudian psychology.

The American theatregoing public more than any other is repelled by the expression of raw hurt, the anger of wounded souls—especially when, as in Inge's case, it sometimes lacked clear focus. The original title of *The Last Pad,* which deals with prisoners awaiting capital punishment, was *Don't Go Gentle,* to signify the character's (and Inge's) need to cry out in violent desperation against the cruelty in man's fate.

Of these plays (several are still unproduced) *Overnight* is perhaps the most balanced and assimilable. It does not go to the savage extreme that *The Last Pad* does. But before I speak further about *Overnight* I believe it appropriate to say something more about Inge's work in general.

For all the good notices in the dailies, the box-office success and the Pulitzer Prize the first plays won, I am convinced Inge was underestimated. Serious critics thought the early plays too sweet, sentimental, facile. But whatever justification there may have been in such pejorative judgments, they were rarely set in a just perspective. Fault was found with Inge for not measuring up to standards he never set himself.

Inge was the dramatist of the ordinary. He plumbed no great depths, but this limitation does not negate the honesty or genuineness of his endeavor. Inge really knew and felt his people; he was kin to them. His plays provide insights into their childlike bewilderment, their profound if largely unconscious loneliness. His touch was popular, but never "commercial." His plays reflect a perturbed spirit modestly but nonetheless authentically groping for alleviation from the burdens of our society, particularly as they affect simple or unsophisticated citizens outside our big cities or on their fringes. As such, Inge's plays are perceptive and touching. The narrowness of their scope, their American "provincialism" is in his case an asset rather than a liability. There was very little synthetic in what he had to say; his plays were born of his own distress. (pp. 91-3)

Harold Clurman, in The Nation *(copyright 1974 by the Nation Associates, Inc.), August 3, 1974.*

Come Back, Little Sheba was probably the late William Inge's best play, certainly the most sturdily crafted, smoothly functioning, and universally meaningful. In passing, it may bear a casual resemblance to soap opera, but it is much too honest and down-to-earth a work, far too concerned with existential truth, to be glibly downgraded. Of all the plays about addiction in which the past quarter-century has abounded, this one may ring truest; it provides some modest answers without falling into the trap of pretensions to omniscience. Even more interestingly, it examines with sympathy the marriage of complementary failures: a woman who had conventional beauty but not enough brains, and a man who allowed his conventional propriety to get the better of his talent. . . .

Inge was haunted by the pathos of the beautiful but dumb woman (who may or may not have been a stud in dehomosexualizing disguise), but neither in *Picnic* nor in *Bus Stop* did he focus in on it with such devastating straightforwardness. . . . [The] quintessential drama [of the play is] the portrayal of the terrible battle between waning good looks and time with its scorched-earth policy, and of the heartbreaking fragility that only women whose one defense was allure can display when they must finally shiver in a nakedness of soul for which the nakedness of flesh is no longer adequate covering. . . .

Universal catastrophe becomes visible beneath the diminutive drama. . . .

John Simon, "The 'Sheba' of Queens," in New York Magazine *(© 1974 by NYM Corp.; reprinted by permission of* New York Magazine *and John Simon), September 9, 1974, p. 67.*

[Inge's] early plays have a richness of incident and humor that endows with audience-winning appeal even minor roles as he felt the surging of his powers. In contrast, the last plays and the two late novels he wrote are suffused with despair and self-pity; moreover, the characters who exhibit these traits lack the dramatic depth of the self-sufficient, if psychologically tortured, small-towners of the early works. (p. 439)

Beginning in 1950, he achieved four consecutive Broadway successes. These plays, *Come Back, Little Sheba, Picnic, Bus Stop,* and *The Dark at the Top of the Stairs,* gained other vast audiences as motion pictures, although Inge did not write the adaptations. These four plays, along with his Academy Award winning script for the movie *Splendor in the Grass,* have earned a respectable place in contemporary American literature as reflections of the way Midwesterners spoke and behaved in the first half of the twentieth century. They continue to intrigue new audiences with each community theater revival or television rerun.

In contrast, Inge's later works were in large part rejected by audiences and members of the theatrical profession as well as by critics. Brooks Atkinson's evaluation of the phase that began with the playwright's first Broadway failure in 1959 is typical: "It was as if Mr. Inge had lost his gift of seeing living truths in obscure places. For all practical purposes his career was over." A friend of long standing, the playwright William Gibson (author of *The Miracle Worker*), observed that Inge's "work did change, over the next three flops [Broadway productions] the real and simple folk of his Midwest settings turned into big-city neurotics, modern, super sexy, violent—thin fantasies. . . . Still writing plays, he couldn't get them produced now, they went begging; one of our top three playwrights had simply been liquidated." (pp. 439-40)

It was when Inge, numbed by urban living and by artistic failures at a relatively advanced point in his career, began giving attention to social issues that his work wore a glaze of topical narrowness. (p. 441)

There was much diligent courage in Inge's attempts to come to terms with the modern idiom in the last plays and novels. He knew he was on shaky ground, having recognized in his commentaries on his own plays the danger of mutability in works drawn around ideas or events rather than character development. "All attempts to deal with men in groups, or as objects of time and environment, I think, fail," Inge wrote in the introduction to *A Loss of Roses,* the production of which in 1959 broke his string of successes. (p. 442)

[Inge's plays reveal] his nostalgia for the past and ability at portraying family life; the extraordinary ability to capture middle-class speech patterns; a preference for individuality and popular culture as subject matter; and a colloquial rather than esoteric approach to writing. (p. 451)

Inge's conviction that [Tennessee Williams's] works and will helped him to find his own way is borne out by relatively frequent references to [Williams] in plays and novels where anachronism would not result. He dedicated *The Dark at the Top of the Stairs* to Williams. Textual references to Williams in other Inge works are couched in such a way that they often seem to express a defense of the function and scope of literary art. The most notorious passage is in *Natural Affection,* in which the lines are spoken by a nymphomaniacal wife and her near-impotent, bisexual husband.... [Their] dialogue really is an ironic position statement on the right and obligation of an author to use his creativity to interpret aspects of modern life, including the unsavory. Unfortunately for this new consciousness in Inge, he lacked the poetic and cosmopolitan touch that has enabled Williams to present naturalistic material in a way acceptable to many critics and audiences. (p. 454)

Inge [had] something of the attitude of a dispassionate observer to both physical and spiritual violence—including some in his personal life.... [The courage to endure emotional quandaries] is evident in many characters in Inge's best plays, as acquaintances say it was in his own life. (p. 456)

Creativity gave some catharsis to Inge. There is verisimilitude in his treatment of both tragic and comic elements of alcoholism in the drawing of such characters as Doc Delaney in *Sheba,* Howard in *Picnic,* Professor Lyman in *Bus Stop,* and Vince in *Natural Affection.* He approached homosexuality in his characterizations more cautiously; except for Professor Lyman's pursuit of schoolgirls (largely alluded to rather than demonstrated), characters with deviate sexual tendencies do not appear straightforwardly until the fifth Broadway play, *A Loss of Roses,* in the minor role of Ronny Cavendish. Inge's plays of the 1960s presented homosexuals in major roles to an audience conditioned by that decade to accept such stage characters. Vince of *Natural Affection* and Pinkerton (Pinky) of *Where's Daddy?* are well-rounded tragicomic figures in somewhat weak plays, even carrying some of the burden of defending conventional values.... The most fully developed character in Inge's last New York play, *The Last Pad,* carries the comedy lines despite his status as a convicted murderer awaiting execution for killing his mother and grandmother. One of the few notices of the play called it "another slice of the Inge landscape—full of strong women and suffocating men."

This unpublished play, set on "death row," is the most graphic of Inge's works in which incarceration is a real, remembered or anticipated trauma. Inge had experienced it as a result of depression and alcoholism from time to time, from his youth until a few days before his suicide. Tennessee Williams and William Gibson learned that the end for Inge came after he checked himself out of a sanatarium and proceeded to combine excessive sedation and drinking in his last days. "He suffered from extreme claustrophobia, a fact that explained his inability to accept hospital confinement for more than two days," Williams has written. Gibson remembered that in the late 1940s Inge "was worried that he was drinking too much" and inquired about admission to an Eastern clinic for therapy, but cancelled the request when *Sheba* went into rehearsals.

It is little wonder that breakdowns, of one sort or another, form a species of resolution in most of Inge's plots. (pp. 456-57)

Teachers, particularly intellectual professors, provide a goodly share of the comic pathos in his plays. They are invariably disturbed in some way, although capable of courageous self-discipline as he himself was.... Inge's treatment of boardinghouse-dwelling high school teachers in *Good Luck, Miss Wyckoff* and *Picnic* often is devastatingly and pathetically funny. The sardonic futility expressed by *Picnic*'s Rosemary could be close to Inge's own view of the profession: "Each year, I keep tellin' myself, is the last. Something'll happen. Then nothing ever does—except I get a little crazier all the time".... (pp. 458-59)

The loss of youthful illusions is a great tragedy throughout Inge's works—plays and novels which demonstrate that he had almost total recall of his boyhood. The disappointments of his maturity are reflected in the depression of Miss Wyckoff, experiencing premature menopause, when she finds that "only her memories of childhood seemed real to her. Her life since then had no substance nor reality. She was a total failure. She wished to God that he would take her life, but that was useless, too".... Inge himself was able to cope with the erosion of self-worth for a time, as he said in the brief foreword to *A Loss of Roses,* by holding to the view that "man can only hope for an individual peace in the world." (pp. 459-60)

Front Porch-Picnic-Summer Brave represents some of Inge's memories of the sunstruck prairie towns of his youth with "all the variety I could find of character, mood, pathos and humor." By contrast, *Come Back, Little Sheba* is a rendering of the interior autumnal gloom of a barely respectable urban Middle West.... Considering a title, Inge remembered the tiny black Scottie he had been forced to give up when he changed living quarters.... The pet lost in reality in St. Louis becomes the symbol of vanished innocence and happiness in the play; even the name of the principal female character, Lola, appears to be a modification of the Scottie's name, Lula Belle. (p. 466)

Although the setting of the play is urban, the main characters really are not departures from the bedeviled villagers of Inge's other strong plays, as Harold Clurman has pointed out: "It is a realistic portrait of small-town people cramped almost to extinction by their repressions, their shallow spiritual horizons, their mechanical Puritan prejudices, their ignorance." Doc and Lola have been uprooted, because of reaction against their indiscretions, from the town of their youth, [Green Valley].... Throughout Inge's works, childhood environments are given names symbolizing rural placidity and lost innocence; other examples are Maple Grove of *Bus Riley's Back in Town* (the nearby metropolis called Midland City obviously is drawn from St. Louis), and the Belleville of *Good Luck, Miss Wyckoff*. In the urban situation brutally portrayed in *Natural Affection,* a place of childhood security is longed for by even such a city-sated sophisticate as Claire: "Sometimes I wish I was back home in Bloomfield with my Mommy and Daddy. But I just love Chicago. I wouldn't leave Chicago for anything in the world. I just wish I didn't get so lonely." (pp. 466-67)

Charles E. Burgess, "An American Experience: William Inge in St. Louis 1943-1949," in Papers on Language and Literature *(copyright © 1976 by the Board of Trustees, Southern Illinois University at Edwardsville), Fall, 1976, pp. 438-68.*

J

JHABVALA, Ruth Prawer 1927-

Jhabvala is a novelist, short story writer, and screenwriter who was born in Germany of Polish parents, was educated in England, and has lived primarily in India since 1951. A perceptive, often satiric, observer of Europeans living in India and of the lifestyle of middle-class urban Indians, she portrays with wit and irony both Eastern and Western sensibilities. (See also *CLC,* **Vol. 4, and** *Contemporary Authors,* **Vols. 1-4, rev. ed.)**

Like her last novel, *Travellers* (and like her seven earlier novels), Ruth Jhabvala's new work [*Heat and Dust*] is distinguished by a rapier wit and subtlety, in a blend altogether unique to her. Invariably, Mrs. Jhabvala refuses the flat satiric thrust, the temptation to have the last word about her characters settled and done with, however cleverly. Rather, even the most callow-seeming and predictable of them have their moment of expansion and mystery; it is the mark of these characters that they should be, hilariously and unforgettably, both what they seem and yet more. *Heat and Dust* is set alternately in the India of the Twenties and the present, its main characters Englishmen and women who, like all Mrs. Jhabvala's Western protagonists, find themselves willingly or otherwise on a voyage of discovery in India. Indeed, it is the fate of the Westerners that in their encounter with India they perceive that which, clearly, they would wish not to perceive: that which makes the lives, the assumptions, the loves they already have less tenable than before. . . . It is, particularly in its delicate chartings of passion and of the growth of consciousness, a superb story, a gift to those who care for the novel, and to the art of fiction itself. (p. 30)

> *Dorothy Rabinowitz, in* Saturday Review
> *(© 1976 by Saturday Review/World, Inc.;*
> *reprinted with permission), April 3, 1976.*

Unlike any other foreign novelist in English, Mrs. Jhabvala writes from within the extended Indian-family structure, an affectionately satiric observer of the conflict between traditional passivity and Westernized ambition within individuals battered by the indifferent tides of change in present-day Indian life. Though there are inescapable echoes of Forster when she writes about the reckless English innocents who these days "come no longer to conquer but to be conquered," her sharpest and most fully realized portraits are those of Indian parents and children, masters and servants,

husbands and wives, whom she knows with the unthinking familiarity of an insider, but scrutinizes with the frequently amused detachment of a privileged stranger.

In her most recent work—"Travelers," published in 1973, and the new novel "Heat and Dust," which won the coveted Booker Prize in England—Mrs. Jhabvala has been struggling admirably to break away from the dubious contentments of the minor novelist who prefers not to make things too difficult for herself or her readers, and has tried to place her experience of India in less conventionally realistic, more demanding forms than she chose for her many domestic comedies of manners. In serious writers such deliberate assaults on habit are of course not a matter of esthetic whimsy but a way of coping with a changing point of view, and it is clear that Mrs. Jhabvala's attitudes toward India have been growing more ambivalent. (p. 7)

Mrs. Jhabvala moves nimbly between the two generations and the divergent points of time and sentiment between a vanished English past that was arrogant and unyielding and a venturesome English present that is mainly confused—in brief precipitate scenes, laconic but remarkably evocative. . . . Writing with austere, emphatic economy, she does not belabor the parallels and dissimilarities between the two levels of narrative—at least not until the very end. Like Forster, she renders the barriers of incomprehension and futility that persist between English and Indians with witty precision. . . .

"Heat and Dust" is an obscure and somber novel, tense with undisclosed judgments and meanings that crouch and whisper just beyond one's reach. Mrs. Jhabvala stubbornly resists the brisk and tidy accommodations of satire that came so effortlessly to hand in her earlier work. And though there is no firm reason for thinking so, beyond a chillingly outspoken essay that she wrote a few years ago, a *cri de coeur* in which she declared "I am no longer interested in India. What I am interested in now is myself in India . . . my survival in India," I suspect that she is becoming tired of the literary burden of India she has carried for so many years. No longer in India, she may be ready, as novelist, to move on. (p. 8)

> *Pearl K. Bell, in* The New York Times
> Book Review *(© 1976 by The New York*
> *Times Company; reprinted by permission),*
> *April 4, 1976.*

Ruth Prawer Jhabvala continues her series of Indian short stories with a collection, *How I Became a Holy Mother*. She is a . . . complex operator, not in the sense of character motivation . . . but in the proper sense of the orientation of her psyche. The title story for example is brilliantly shifty as an English girl goes guru-hunting round the ashrams and is eventually deified for the public when she couples with a beautiful holy boyfriend.

The trouble with India is its volume, mental and physical. It is very easy to be angry or sentimental about it. Mrs. Jhabvala isn't either of these things. She is tough, clear and unusual. She has no propaganda to push on behalf of the Red Earth. Nor does she set herself up as one touched by the Wand of Knowledge, although knowledge is what she demonstrates with every inflection. Her Polish origins, English education and Indian husband must have something to do with the acute independence of her style and the feeling of confidence which accompanies it. Throughout the tone is dry and slightly sardonic, a writer of an economy somehow filled with events, beautiful to read. (p. 24)

> *Duncan Fallowell, in* The Spectator *(© 1976 by* The Spectator; *reprinted by permission of* The Spectator*), July 3, 1976.*

[In "Heat and Dust" the] alternation between parallel plots drains both of momentum, or of the substance that lends momentum; the two stories are shadows each of the other, conveying an ambience of reincarnation but also of inconsequence. Above the two planes of the plot, we feel a third, that of a supervisory manipulator, be it author or god. . . . A cyclical cosmology makes all stories essentially endless.

Perhaps Mrs. Jhabvala grew so tired of being reviewed in terms of "A Passage to India" that she deliberately set a tale in the era of Forster's classic novel. Olivia's world [of the 1920s], as reconstructed by the narrator in today's "Indianized" India, has a formal grandeur that supports her stylized romance and preordains it from the first page to its pattern of fascination and fall and flight and unutterable disgrace. Its vanished time seems enchanted—the men in evening dress, the servants silently barefoot, the monuments in the English cemetery freshly carved, the Nawab's pearl-gray palace still inhabited, its fountains flowing and its rooms full of mischief. . . . The cosmos may be cyclical, but the local demographic trend is all one way. The historical past in India seems not so much discarded as crowded out of being. (pp. 82-3)

The theme of a transcendent happiness recurs in Mrs. Jhabvala's short stories ("The Old Lady," "My First Marriage") and apparently declares a crucial aspect of her Indian experience. This happiness seems to be especially accessible to women. . . . The female characters, in 1923 as now, draw strength from this teeming land. . . . [The] god behind Mrs. Jhabvala's artful shuffle of Indian scenes and moments is female. (p. 83)

> *John Updike, in* The New Yorker *(© 1976 by* The New Yorker Magazine, Inc.*), July 5, 1976.*

It might seem [from her fiction] that Mrs Jhabvala leaves no hope for the European in his quest for a satisfying experience of India. But she does not, I think, destroy all optimism. Although she obviously feels that East is East and West is West and that when the twain do meet the air soon thickens with misunderstandings, she does point out that people unlike herself could stand a better chance of being

'truly merged with India'. 'To stay and endure,' she says, 'one should have a mission and a cause, be patient, cheerful, unselfish, strong. I am a Central European with an English education and a deplorable tendency to constant self-analysis. I am irritable and have weak nerves.'

Even more encouraging is the total effect of her own work. Full as it is of warnings, of descriptions of social dangers and emotional disasters and marriages gone sour and holy grails that turn out to be will-o'-the-wisps, it is *in toto* a highly successful and understanding experience of India, however she herself may have deprecated it and written it off as failure. Indeed, the stories in *How I Became a Holy Mother* show that Mrs Jhabvala has mellowed since her earlier forebodings and 'Keep Out!' messages to the aspiring immigrant. She has, I believe, left Delhi recently and gone to live in the States, and it may be that these stories were conceived in the light of that decision, an instance of intended absence making the heart grow fonder. In this collection she seems gentler, more compassionate, and in most of the stories she leaves her characters forgiving one another or finding that minor virtues can outweigh major faults. For example, the wife in 'In a Great Man's House' knows her husband, the pompous Khan Sahib, to be utterly domineering and inflexible, but when she hears him singing a romantic song, his voice and interpretation full of feeling and insight into a woman's suffering, she is quite happy—because, not in spite, of him. . . . In 'Two More Under the Indian Sun' Mrs Jhabvala seems at first to be as waspish as ever to the two English women, particularly to the dogmatic, energetic do-gooder, Margaret, but in the last two pages of the story it is on Margaret, not on the more sympathetic Elizabeth, that the author bestows her charitable insight.

Heat and Dust . . . struck me as rather too contrived a novel, the parallel vicissitudes of the narrator and of her grandfather's first wife too obviously a literary ploy; but there is nothing contrived about the stories in *How I Became a Holy Mother*. Mrs Jhabvala is a still developing and maturing short story writer, and is now using all her skills of satire, irony and humour, together with that formidable knack of catching a tone of voice and outlook on the world so different from her own, to penetrate further and further into the most intimate relationships between friends, lovers, husband and wife, disciple and teacher, Hindu and Moslem, and Indian and European. To have lived in India for twenty-four years and still to be adding to her *comédie humaine* of Western sense and Eastern sensibility does not strike me either as an example of waste or as an admission of failure. Whatever she may say about herself, in her books if not in her life she *has* 'truly merged with India'. (pp. 96-7)

> *John Mellors, "Merging with India," in* London Magazine *(© London Magazine 1976), August-September, 1976, pp. 96-7.*

Ruth Prawer Jhabvala is an excellent short-story writer with a natural sense of the comedy available to those who keep their eyes open to Indian society. She is also good at showing the essential difficulties of Europeans assimilating the culture of India. Recently she has been expanding her territory by writing serious multilayered novels which, as part of their significance, allude to earlier fiction about the English in India. *Heat and Dust*, her latest novel, tells two related stories. In the 1920s a young, newly married Englishwoman, bored with the confinement of provincial colonial life, leaves her husband for an unscrupulous but charming local prince, whose family rejects her. The remainder of her life is shrouded in mystery. . . . [The] story is a classic tale of the colonial period, warning of the dangers of exotic attractions abroad. The significance can also be inverted to show the early twentieth-century liberal message, as exemplified by E. M. Forster's novels, that it is necessary to reach out across social and national borders to experience life fully. . . . [The second] story, representative of the modern era, is as delphic as the older tale: [this protagonist's] history can be that of either spiritual discovery or frivolous illusion, not unlike that of the foreign hippies and drug addicts who are noticed as part of modern Indian scenery. Presumably the two histories show the timeless European fascination with India and Hindu culture.

Heat and Dust is a well written novel, carefully put together, but contrived. . . . The events are parallel between the two narratives throughout the novel, which has been influenced by the recently popular cinematographic techniques of jump shots and intercutting scenes. The juxtaposition of two diaries is fleshed out by interviews, descriptions, and the voice of the narrator. Unfortunately the contrast between the highly stylized life of the past and the cold, unrevealing modern narrator appears a mechanical device to create irony and ambiguity. One feels left on the surface of the experience. We see an India which has decayed from past grandeur, which was built upon now unacceptable exploitation of the poor; and we see young inarticulate Europeans seeking a spiritual refuge in India, but we feel neither India in any depth nor the inner emotions of those who have rejected European society. There is a sense in which this is an outsider's novel in which romantic infatuation with the exotic has been made to appear disciplined through narrative techniques carrying associations of paradox and puzzlement. . . . I suppose *Heat and Dust* is meant to show that we cannot judge the attraction of India to the Europeans and that they never in fact can assimilate a culture so different from their own. (pp. 131-32)

Each of the ten stories [in *How I Became a Holy Mother*] recounts the experiences of women in India. As the stories progress, social satire is infused with intimations of deeper revelations of character which unfortunately are not developed. Each of the stories is an example of the craft of writing: characters are so well sculptured as first to appear stereotypes, but when put into motion are found to have deeper, less clearly articulated emotional lives; often the main plot leads to a secondary character who is found to be the real interest of the story; the main characters' habits of thought are reflected in the author's narrative style, which grows more supple as the characters develop. Such craftsmanship should produce great art; it does not because the emphasis is on irony, pacing, and paradox instead of the rich inner life that the stories imply after the original stereotypes have been demolished. (pp. 132-33)

Bruce King, in Sewanee Review *(reprinted by permission of the editor, © 1977 by The University of the South), Winter, 1977.*

Ruth Prawer Jhabvala's [stories in *How I Became a Holy Mother* are] Chekhovian in that they are anti-climactic and non-dramatic, more concerned with stasis than with change even when there is the appearance of change. The first sentence of 'Desecration', one of her best stories, mentions the suicide of the central character, Sofia, but the rest of the story, while describing the adulterous affair that leads to her death, scrupulously avoids the obvious dramatic, even sensational, potential of the narrative. By announcing the suicide at the outset, thus removing the possibility of

suspense, Mrs Jhabvala can concentrate on what interests her about the affair, Sofia's growing awareness of her inner contradictions which eventually become too unbearable to live with. 'Desecration' ends before Sofia's suicide, and there is no description of the events immediately preceding it or of its manner. Even in this story, which is more intense and sexually explicit than Mrs Jhabvala usually is, her restraint is very considerable.

Mrs Jhabvala is noted for her sense of nuance, emotional delicacy, and sympathetic sensitivity rather than for her technical adventurousness. As a story writer she is content to be a descendant of Chekhov and . . . shows little interest—perhaps it is a typically American interest—in stretching the genre. Yet her formal conservatism is probably an advantage considering the comparative novelty of her subject matter, the contemporary muddle (as opposed to mystery) of India—human muddle, not political. In this book she is principally concerned with Indians themselves rather than Europeans in India, although European influence is usually a factor. The title-story, however, is a wry, ironic narrative about the current Western flirtation with Eastern religion written from the viewpoint of one of the flirts, a twice-married English ex-model in her early twenties who is not overburdened with either intellect or common sense and who is looking more for a relaxing change than a spiritual nirvana. With its portrayal of a bizarre, free-sex ashram and dubious gurus, seemingly as interested in Western holes as in Eastern holiness, this story is untypically satirical for Mrs Jhabvala, but is too soft-pedalled to be wholeheartedly so. If the humour had been broader and the satire sharper, the story might have been even better, but satire is not her forte.

Where she excels is in rendering the ambiguities of Indian life, including the tensions between traditionalism and progressivism, during a period of social change. She does this not in general terms but by exploring particular individuals in their relationships with their husbands or their wives or their parents or their children or other people with whom they are involved. . . . The ambiguities can produce tragedy as in 'Desecration' or comedy as in 'Picnic with Moonlight and Mangoes'. Mrs Jhabvala is never in danger of repeating herself, but what most of her characters have in common is an essential loneliness, whether they realize this or not. Many of these stories are really about alienation, the failure of communication, the difficulty of making genuine human contact, and the near-impossibility of fulfilment—themes that receive their most complex treatment in 'In a Great Man's House', arguably the best story. Mrs Jhabvala casts a cool, but not a cold, eye on life, and a tone of melancholy pervades much of the book. She writes about India, but her India is as universal as Yoknapatawpha. (pp. 68-9)

Peter Lewis, in Stand *(copyright © by Stand), Vol. 18, No. 2 (1977).*

*   *   *

JONG, Erica   1942-

An American novelist and poet, Jong belongs to the "confessional/personalist" school. She is best known for her controversial works of sexual frankness, *Fear of Flying* and *How to Save Your Own Life*. (See also *CLC*, Vols. 4,6.)

To those who found her first in the poem collections *Fruits & Vegetables* and *Half-Lives*, Erica Jong was a fresh presence, a poet with a flair for creating striking imagery and evoking gut responses. What with the subsequent publication of her first novel *Fear of Flying*, however, that earlier impression seemed threatened by a newer, coarser one—that of a badmouthed blonde appearing on national TV, frequently being bleeped and carefully cultivating book sales, and an image. In the new collection, *Loveroot* (the word is Whitman's), Jong carries the quest for sexual frankness and poetic license even further; if Sexton is Plath diluted, then Jong is diluted Sexton—diluted, I mean, in terms of control—but a Sexton determined to survive. Her poems are printed shouts, chants; they are oral, and encourage recital. They are genuinely Whitman-influenced, yet bear within them the dangers inherent even in Whitman's own work, that of descending to an open, formless rant, the work of readings' darlings. (pp. 99-100)

Loveroot is adorned, perhaps burdened, with an excess of quoted texts; often enough, they are excerpts from authors to whom Jong writes poems (Whitman, Keats, Colette), as well as others whose presence moves in subtler ways through these pages. In other sections ("In the Penile Colony," "Hungering") Jong is more clearly personal, less "easy" in the achievement of effects dependent upon construction of abstract mosaics of the works of the subject him/herself. (p. 100)

[Is Jong's poetry narcissistic?] Of course, but refreshingly healthy in the context of the "school" to which Jong nominally belongs, the confessional/personalist group of Lowell and Snodgrass, but especially Plath and Sexton and Berryman. We all know what the last three have in common, and forgive Jong the *chutzpah* that staves off a like fate. . . .

Jong is more than a feminist, she is a woman, and her personality translates into poetry as naked as any written. She knows that

> Terror writes poetry,
> hope, prose.

and though the presentation of her terrors has thus far to be taken on her own recognizance, their effects are universal enough, and intermittently poetry of a high order. (p. 101)

> *John Ditsky, in* The Ontario Review *(copyright © 1975 by* The Ontario Review*), Fall-Winter, 1975-76.*

Erica Jong writes not so much novels as almost breathlessly up-to-date confessional bulletins. When last seen in *Fear of Flying,* Jong (who calls herself Isadora Wing on paper) was soaping up in her psychiatrist-husband's bathtub, waiting rather ambiguously for him to return and forgive her for the 340-page sexual excursion that made up the novel.

It didn't work out. At the start of *How to Save Your Own Life,* Erica/Isadora is slipping out of the Wing/Jong Upper West Side co-op apartment for the last time, leaving the doctor to his patients and, as Isadora says, "his hatred of women." . . . In Jong's wall-poster philosophy, today is the first day of the rest of your life.

Fear of Flying possessed a bawdy exuberance. John Updike even found it Chaucerian [see *CLC,* Vol. 4]. But *How to Save Your Own Life* is marinated in sour juices: dissolving marriage, curdled fame, Hollywood's treachery. "Ain't it awful?" the reader mutters. Erica/Isadora uses the book to settle old scores against her husband ("I married a monster, I think") and a hustling Hollywood producer who, she says, flimflammed her on the film right to the bestselling first novel. Before she gets around to making the final break with Dr. Wing, Isadora has a lesbian affair, checks in with a brace of former lovers (male), flies West to work on her

film, and there finds the vacant, curiously dippy Josh, a 27-year-old aspiring screenwriter who is to be the love of her life. For now, anyway. Isadora composes lines to him that read like hard-core Kahlil Gibran: "My soul is mine; / My mouth belongs to you."

How to Save Your Own Life is written in six or seven different styles, ranging from academic hauteur (she says she was "amanuensis to the Zeitgeist") through *Cosmo* cute ("Bed reared its ugly headboard") to bewildering lifeless porn. The author's mind seems to have been softened by too many hours in a Malibu Jacuzzi. As if searching for a new definition of vulgarity, Jong writes that hostile criticism of her first novel makes her think of "Jews gassed at Auschwitz." (Actually, *Fear of Flying* was extravagantly overpraised.) She also contrives to turn the tragic suicide of Poet Anne Sexton (named "Jeannie" in the book) into a kind of posthumous blurb for herself.

The woman is enough to make readers think that sex really *is* dirty. She describes remarkably unpleasant oral activities with her female lover; if a man had written that, feminists would have beaten him unconscious with a copy of *The Hite Report.* (pp. 74-5)

> *Lance Morrow, "Oral History," in* Time *(reprinted by permission from* Time, The Weekly Newsmagazine; *copyright Time Inc. 1977), March 14, 1977, pp. 74-5.*

There is one hilarious scene in "How to Save Your Own Life," when Isadora Wing takes a fling at lesbianism. There is also a nice orgy. . . . And, of the 18 erotic poems batched at the back of the book, several are quite good, especially "We Learned."

That, perhaps, is the news about Erica Jong's second, surprisingly tiresome novel, unless we want to sit around in the Jacuzzi dilating on what constitutes fiction, or autobiography, or "myth." Like "Fear of Flying," "How to Save Your Own Life" advertises itself as a novel, with Isadora Wing as heroine. But in interview after interview, ever since she burst upon us as a sort of Mary Poppins of female sexuality in 1973, Erica Jong has insisted that "myth" is what she's really after. . . .

[It] is hard to believe that the author of "Fear of Flying" wrote "How to Save Your Own Life." Whereas the author of "Fear of Flying" was looking inside her own head, shuffling her fantasies, and with a manic gusto playing out her hand, the author of "How to Save Your Own Life" is looking over her shoulder, afraid that the critics might be gaining on her. Instead of neat one-liners, she specializes in pious philosophizing. Not insincere, but pious, hectoring, self-important.

The prose in "How to Save Your Own Life" bogs into cliché alarmingly. . . .

Along with this laziness there are slapdash summaries, not embodiments, of her characters. They amount to little more than lists of ingredients, recipes for people. Besides, if we spent much time with the other characters, we might miss Isadora's next exhortation. Jong insists when she should persuade. . . . She has . . . thumped us on the head with the "really subversive" affirmation that "Love *is* everything it's cracked up to be." One hopes so. And one hopes she's happy in Malibu. And one hopes she makes a lot of money, because writers ought to have some.

But what happened to the energy and irreverence of "Fear

of Flying,'' the Huck Finnishness, the cheerful vulgarity, the eye for social detail? Whence this solemnity and carelessness—not in the poems, because ''Loveroot'' (1975) is an advance from ''Fruits & Vegetables'' (1971) and ''Half-Lives'' (1973)—that make ''How to Save Your Own Life'' so sententious? Why, in her book, must we do most of the imaginative work? . . .

As she told ''Mademoiselle'' last June, ''I'm one of the most interviewed people in the world.'' Being interviewed demands very little from a celebrity—much less a myth— but time and canned opinions. It is as if, in ''How to Save Your Own Life,'' Erica Jong had interviewed herself, when she should have been, sentence by sentence, writing a book. Sincerity is no excuse for sloppy craft. (p. 2)

> *Leonard Michaels, in* The New York Times Book Review (© *1977 by The New York Times Company; reprinted by permission),* March 20, 1977.

There is no point in talking about *How to Save Your Own Life* as a serious didactic work, despite the title, or as art, or as entertainment. . . .

There are in fact some good or at least interesting things about the book. In some respects it is an improvement on life. . . . Jong's book, which resembles in every way the ramblings of the deserted friend who has taken to the tape recorder and submitted the unedited transcript, has the virtue that we can abandon it without hurting her feelings or damaging our own self-regard. . . .

[*How to Save Your Own Life* is] a plain, wholesome American story, containing . . . that peculiarly American and purely literary substance Fulfillment, modern equivalent of fairy gold, so gleaming and tangible you can even put it in your pocket and carry it from coast to coast. The novelist is adroit in combining all the clichés of two types of regional novel which had formerly seemed distinct, the Manhattan and the Hollywood, in such a way as to reveal that Hollywood is simply a cultural mutation of New York. She says, with characteristic delicacy, ''California is a wet dream in the mind of New York,'' which perhaps we ought to have seen all along, though from the Western point of view certain differences seem to persist, which are not discoverable if you get no farther than the Polo Lounge. East or West, the nature of her prescription for saving your own life is finally unclear: divorce? lesbian encounters? love? best-sellerdom? So it is hard to say of what use the unfulfilled will find it. (p. 6)

> *Diane Johnson, in* The New York Review of Books *(reprinted with permission from* The New York Review of Books; *copyright* © *1977 NYREV, Inc.),* April 28, 1977.

I'm treed; it irks me no end. I have to—have to—ravage Erica Jong's new book. Irksome, because this is just what Erica wanted all along: the barracuda treatment. I mean, a man and a Gentile blitzing her: oh, pogromsville and joy. Despite the hitter-chick sex, *Fear of Flying* was cute as baton-twirlers: likable, humorous, adroit. Erica expected suffering and outrage and at least one honorary FBI tap; instead she got whacking great success. Life is cruel. She'll relish this flop the way Al Goldstein secretly relishes going to Leavenworth for public lewdness. Discipline is love; American society has been too permissive. Erica, I love you: *How to Save Your Own Life* is Christ-awful. An aphid could have written it.

What we get here is Erica Jong writing a ''novel'' about Isadora Wing, who has written a ''novel'' about Candida Wong, who is really her: let that pronoun refer back where it will. . . .

In *Fear of Flying* Isadora had charm: probably the first female Malamud character, a Jewish clown. But Isadora II takes herself so seriously: fem-lib emblem now, not shnook. . . .

Enthusiasm, not crankiness, is the most accurate gauge of talent. Even C+ writers can engross while being bitchy or snide. And Isadora II enthuses often: on love, on most-unforgettable author friends, on the fearsome responsibility one has to upper-case Art. Her enthusiastic writing is sump gush: a smell of sulphur dioxide in it. You want to look away. . . . Erica writes, Lord, just like a *woman*. And that's my very best pejorative. (p. 498)

Worse yet, she has cheapened the art of fiction. *FoF* was attractive, yes, but it sold in pallet-loads because it was expressly autobiographical. Erica turned herself into a side-show geek. Look, there's the woman who has to masturbate three times per day. Look, fiction (unless it can be read for *People* magazine gossip) has no contemporary relevance. Her success did just a little bit more to invalidate the novelist-imaginator. Erica Jong has clout: Holt, Rinehart, & Winston would've published anything she wrote. Even a real novel with, excuse the oxymoron, real imaginary characters. Literature is risk. Erica didn't accept the risk: unsurprisingly, she had no balls. Isadora may have fled her husband for a younger man, but, as far as literature is concerned, Erica Jong still fears flying. (pp. 498-99)

> *D. Keith Mano, ''The Authoress as Aphid,'' in* National Review (© *National Review, Inc., 1977; 150 East 35th St., New York, N.Y. 10016), April 29, 1977, pp. 498-99.*

Romance is back! Erica Jong's publishers clearly understand. They describe *How to Save Your Own Life* as a ''remarkably romantic love story'', and Isadora herself boasts of being a ''romantic''. What they mean is that within the world of this novel, and the literary tradition to which it belongs, sexual love is the only thing, ultimately, that matters. It is this that women desire above all else: it is this that gives meaning and justification to their lives. . . .

The sexual freedom that Isadora enjoys seems neither liberating nor degrading. It is largely irrelevant: ''I suddenly realize that I could fuck a different man every weekday afternoon and still not feel contented.'' Adultery is no solution, only a diversion. Many diversions, in fact, and all leading to true love. . . .

How to Save Your Own Life is not, however, merely confessional: it is a novel with a message, and this also is something it shares with the great tradition of romantic fiction. It would be hard to imagine admirers of Henry James, or Conrad, or Harold Pinter, writing to them for advice on how to live, but Rhoda, and Elinor, and Edith were expected to guide and govern the lives of their more daring or lonely readers, and so is Isadora. The success of *Candida Confesses* makes Isadora realize that for all her own feelings of guilt and inadequacy, the heroine of her novel has become a model, an inspiration, for countless women. . . . When a close friend and fellow poet commits suicide, leaving behind her a blank notebook and the suggested title ''How To Save Your Own Life'', Isadora is determined to conquer her fear of flying.

The message is: be happy, be joyful, reject cynicism, seek for true love—"Fly and live to tell the tale!" The moment when Isadora decides on this is a turning point of *How to Save Your Own Life;* it is the main theme of the love poems addressed to Josh which are appended to the novel, and it recurs in the new volume of Erica Jong's poems *Loveroot.* . . .

It is not being cynical to say that Isadora's experiences as a "wise-ass Jewish girl" would not be so possible if she were not sexually attractive, famous and rich. She is, of course, a poet as well, but the poetry is as confessional as the best-selling novel. . . .

Here, and in *Loveroot,* every activity takes second place to sexual love:

> The sky is clearer when I'm not in heat,
> & the poems
> are colder.

The advice is, cast off cynicism and experience joy, but too often this comes over as find your man and all will be well. It is not simply a matter of the words being colder when the writer is "not in heat". Quite the contrary really, for humour tends to disappear when romantic love is taken too seriously. Erica Jong trying to convey unhappiness is no more believable than Isadora in her moods of sadness: "I'm forever trying to convince my friends and family that I bleed when stabbed—but no one believes me because I look so jaunty."

And how could she expect anything else? Isadora irreverent, cynical, outrageous, or jaunty, is delightful. She is at her most convincing when she portrays the ridiculous or bizarre; when she is classifying the lavatories of Europe, or trying to convey an adolescent girl's bewilderment at the "hiddenness" of her body, or, in one of the funniest episodes in *How To Save Your Own Life,* as she strives desperately, and inexpertly, to bring off her lesbian friend. . . .

Erica Jong's [sense of the ridiculous is highly developed], and it would be sad if she goes on allowing it to be suppressed.

Peter Keating, "Erica, or Little by Little," in The Times Literary Supplement *(© Times Newspapers Ltd., 1977; reproduced from* The Times Literary Supplement *by permission), May 6, 1977, p. 545.*

K

KAUFMAN, Sue   1926-

An American novelist and short story writer, Kaufman writes of the plight of the American housewife in a male-oriented society. Her best known novel is *The Diary of a Mad Housewife*. (See also *CLC*, Vol. 3, and *Contemporary Authors*, Vols. 1-4, rev. ed.)

Sue Kaufman's *Falling Bodies* . . . reminds you of how much a novelist's work can have in common with a bricklayer's: the awful distance between the stuff in the hands—bricks, mortar, dialogue, detail—and the idea of the edifice. Miss Kaufman works hard to render upper-middle-class Manhattan life: lists and letters, private school scenes, mums at the playground, endless conversation in dialect from a Colombian maid. And she succeeds. By a third of the way through I'm there, but unsure *why* I'm there. Her gift is for comedy, with a special endowment for the description of pompous and somewhat deranged husbands (as in *Diary of a Mad Housewife*). . . . But the novel wants to be something more: in the person of Emma Sohier there's an effort to mix comedy with a chronicle of a genuinely "rough year" and heavy questions about her life. It comes to little, and as if she doubted the worth of the enterprise, the author pitches the book into farce at the end. Too bad; I was all set to care. This is a muddled book by a writer with a good eye but not much, it seems, in mind this time around. (p. 128)

> *Richard Todd in* The Atlantic Monthly *(copyright © 1974 by The Atlantic Monthly Company, Boston, Mass.; reprinted with permission), May, 1974.*

"Under the Trees" is the richest and most affecting piece in Sue Kaufman's "The Master and Other Stories." And for an ironic reason: Mr. Morgan [the protagonist] is, in fact, almost the only person in the book who remains *un*placed. Nearly all of the other characters in this collection have hardened into their roles long before we meet them. They are victims, mostly—victims of unfeeling mothers, weak fathers, selfish friends or lovers. Their sense of themselves as victims colors every thought and act. Like those tiresome fellow-passengers on airplanes who manage to bring any topic around to their own diseases, these people see all of life through a haze of affliction. Some of the stories end with a momentary lifting of the haze, but the effect

is dimmed because we have long since lost hope for the heroes.

There are three characters in this book for whom we do hope. First, [Mr. Morgan]. . . . Second, the new mother in "Icarus," sifting her way delicately but unerringly through a handful of memories to discover the cause of her so-called post-partum depression. And third, the son in "The Jewish Cemetery"—a self-possessed man who finds himself weeping at a graveside for reasons far more complicated than the death of an uncle. These three are creatures of possibility. Unlike the flat, crabbed victims in the other stories, they give us a sense of layers unexposed, mysteries unsolved that we ourselves (we imagine) might solve if we consider them long enough on our own. We are reminded that even the most ordinary situation can suddenly take a quarter-turn and assume a whole new meaning. . . .

What Sue Kaufman tells us in "Under the Trees" is that we take reassurance from the assigning of a person to an identifiable place—however superficial, or even false, that place may be. (p. 7)

> *Anne Tyler, in* The New York Times Book Review (© *1976 by The New York Times Company; reprinted by permission), July 11, 1976.*

[Sue Kaufman writes] within the conventional boundaries of the modern story, creating a story which is straightforward, direct, dramatic, economical, and solidly built around a single central point, a single dominant mood. The teller of this kind of tale aims at a firm yet quiet and shadowy authority, the focus of attention being maintained by a clear, clean, unselfconscious prose. The stories [in *The Master*] are various, set in memory or in the present, freely ranging in place. In each case the author is an exact master of the vanishing art of literary decorum—the rule that all things, language, rhythm, imagery, the whole sensuous affective surface should derive from the characters and context of the story. . . . Kaufman's special reserve of strength is in the precise evocation of a particular sensory world. Here she has such authority and authenticity that it follows that the events of the story must have happened just that way to precisely those people. In [this] the art is, then, to disguise itself and to stress the reality of the story. . . . Kaufman [makes] this strenuous and difficult way look easy and graceful. (p. 107)

George Garrett, in Sewanee Review *(reprinted by permission of the editor;* © *1977 by The University of the South), Winter, 1977.*

*   *   *

KENEALLY, Thomas 1935-

Keneally, an Australian novelist who once studied for the priesthood, has shown a preoccupation with religious themes in his novels. He is appraised as a serious but flawed artist. Keneally's work appears to be influenced most by Evelyn Waugh and fellow Australian and Nobel Prize-winner Patrick White. (See also *CLC,* **Vol. 5.)**

[*Bring Larks and Heroes*] is passionate and fluent. The author's approach to language is aggressively determined. But the result is uneven and, for a medium-length novel, oddly diffuse.... Mr Keneally writes brilliantly but he does not organize his material well, either in the novel taken as a whole or in the smaller units of paragraph and sentence. His narrative shifts in and out of character, abruptly: at one moment a character is being lyrical or reflective or ironic, at the next the author is editorializing in the same or a different vein. The narrative also changes focus when there is an episode outside the immediate experience of Halloran [a protagonist]. Such episodes are relevant and other devices to incorporate them in the main line of narrative would doubtless be cumbersome; but Balzacian omniscience requires Balzacian authority and technique.

Perhaps it is Mr Keneally's very brilliance, his abundance of ideas and facility with words that suggests self-indulgence. Good phrases—and there are scores of them—seem to go down regardless of their aptness in context. And there are several horrors.... Some of the consciously fine writing is fine in spite of itself; the rest is consciously fine.

Most of Mr Keneally's faults would have been excusable in a first novel: *Bring Larks and Heroes* is his seventh. Treated with more austerity and discipline, it might certainly have been a very considerable novel.

          "Nasty, Brutish, and Short," in The Times Literary Supplement *(©* Times Newspapers Ltd., 1973; *reproduced from* The Times Literary Supplement *by permission), October 26, 1973, p. 1299.*

Thomas Keneally has written a "documentary" novel ["Gossip From the Forest"] about the behavior of the Allied and German signers of the Armistice in the forest clearing at Compiègne on Nov. 11, 1918, and I started it with misgivings. Did we really need another "Ragtime" or "Travesties," reducing the great to dolls? ...

[When] I finished I was persuaded that Keneally's book belongs not with historical fictions that patronize the past and thus set it aside, but with those like Solzhenitsyn's "August 1914," books that delineate the past in sympathetic depth and so urge the reader to enter it....

It is odd to have to say of a novel that it is a "study" of something, but that must be said here. "Gossip From the Forest" is a study of the profoundly civilian and pacific sensibility beleaguered by crude power. Erzberger [the pacifist and liberal member of the Reichstag who led the German delegation] is intelligent, hopeful, studious, unpretentious, absent-minded and easily bored, and Keneally depicts him as a doomed negotiator with no leverage but

personal decency, a knack at sympathy and a flair for language. He is the type of the Weimar Liberal. His victimhood is completed in 1921 when he is shot to death on vacation by two vengeful young officers for the crime of signing the Armistice at all. We are to understand that obscenities like private armies and the youth movement are only a few years away. By the end of the novel we are deeply sympathetic with Erzberger's fate and with Keneally's point, that the 20th century will not tolerate Matthias Erzbergers. They are civilized, and they are sane. (p. 7)

"This account is not scholarly," says Keneally, "but merely gossip from the forest." Whatever it is, as fiction it is absorbing, and as history it achieves the kind of significance earned only by sympathy acting on deep knowledge. The tradition of the historical novel is that it is about cavaliers and bosoms. But recent historical novels, by George Garrett and Thomas Pynchon and Solzhenitsyn as well as Keneally, have been about suffering, or failure, or the world's discomfort when confronted by intelligence and probity. I think that's an improvement. (p. 8)

          Paul Fussell, in The New York Times Book Review *(©* 1976 by The New York Times Company; *reprinted by permission), April 11, 1976.*

Serious-minded readers have ignored historical fiction for so long that when a historical novel became critically fashionable last summer many of them gasped in ignorant delight. [E. L. Doctorow's] "Ragtime," they said, was a new breed of book: real people like Henry Ford and Harry Houdini mingled with the made-up people. What daring, what imagination. Sir Walter Scott, in his corner of the empyrean, could be heard to sigh. Writers since Shakespeare's day (or Dante's, if you want to stretch a point) have thrust historical figures into fictional situations—to entertain us or to a moral. Thomas Keneally does it [in "Gossip from the Forest," a] distinguished book that is nothing like most historical novels but seems a fictional meditation on history instead....

Such drama as the novel affords is entirely psychological. There is a lot of waiting in this book, all of it highly charged. The [characters] dream, tell stories, write letters, quarrel among themselves. Keneally is a patient, exploratory writer, content to poke at his characters, to let antagonisms, develop. His forest is a fateful place, fit to get lost in, and his characters are all lost one way or another—in stupidity, delusion, desperation. His book is about the crushing effect past attitudes have upon present emergencies. It is not a cheerful story, nor is it hyperventilated like most successful fiction today. I hope its intelligence and measured pace will not prevent it from finding an audience. (pp. 90-1)

          Peter S. Prescott, in Newsweek *(copyright 1976 by Newsweek, Inc.; all rights reserved; reprinted by permission), April 19, 1976.*

In "Gossip from the Forest" ..., Thomas Keneally, one of the most talented of current Australian writers, has made the task of writing a historical novel almost intractable for himself. He has chosen to narrate from inside, as it were, one of the most complex and massively archivized scenarios in the whole of modern history: the armistice negotiations conducted in a railway carriage in the forest of Compiègne for four days in November, 1918.... Mr. Keneally, whose motives in the enterprise are suggestively indistinct, aims to get at the "true truth," at perceptions more persuasive than the historian's within a stringently factual framework. The current vogue for "fact-fiction," for the montage of real happenings and celebrities on an invented background, is plainly at work here. But Mr. Keneally's range is higher. He is after that poetry of order, of inward transparency, which enables the classic novel to say not merely "This is how it might have been" but "This is how it must have been" given the raw material of human sensibility, which only serious art can lay bare. (pp. 80-1)

Mr. Keneally's presentation is as stylized as a Balinese dance-drama. Much of the dialogue is direct. Short sentences and terse paragraphs hammer away to simulate confinement. Epithets are mannered in the extreme.... A precedent suggests itself for this artifact. It is a novel that few today will have heard of, let alone read: George Meredith's "The Tragic Comedians," of 1880. In it, Meredith tells the histrionic, bathetic tale of the last days of Ferdinand Lassalle, the German radical Socialist and demagogue who perished in an absurd duel in obese Geneva, his genius floundering in a risible affair of the heart. Meredith and Keneally produce a comparable omniscience and posturing irony.

I do not know that Keneally has looked at Meredith, but one source is certain. In 1931, John Maynard Keynes read to a circle of friends an exquisitely subtle and poignant memoir of his negotiations with Dr. Carl Melchior, who in 1919 had met with Allied economic officials to plead for a delay in reparations and for a more humane view of Germany's desperate domestic plight. This memoir, published later in Keynes's "Essays and Sketches in Biography," inspires not only Keneally's treatment of Erzberger but many touches of material and atmospheric detail. The honors stay with Keynes. Himself a party to the high business, and expertly equipped to judge the strategic motives and national sensibilities implicit in the situation, Keynes keeps his narrative reticent and his verdicts on person and motive provisional. "Gossip from the Forest" has a damaging knowingness. Behind the pointillist technique rumble great portents of foresight and allegorical finality. There is a tactical coyness even to the title. In short: an interesting failure, quite like the parleys at Compiègne so many (or was it so few?) Novembers ago. (p. 82)

> *George Steiner, "Petrified Forest," in* The New Yorker (© *1976 by The New Yorker Magazine, Inc.), August 23, 1976, pp. 80-2.*

Thomas Keneally ... puts his characters through some pretty heavy paces. Emotions run large in his novels, and so do events: violence often predominates, and you can count on a good deal of blood running in the streets. Yet he is a serious writer and and accomplished one.... *Season in Purgatory* is a good if gruesome entertainment that readers of popular fiction might well like.

The central character is David Pelham, a young British doctor serving in World War II....

At its most superficial level, the novel is a cross between *M*A*S*H* and *A Farewell to Arms*—operating-room humor all mixed up with ill-fated wartime lovers—and at that level it is rather predictable, scarcely as powerful as such earlier Keneally novels as *A Dutiful Daughter* and *The Chant of Jimmy Blacksmith*. But Keneally is not merely an entertainer telling a bloody and exciting story. He is also a writer of formidable skills and resources; ... he has a visceral feeling for physical action and his prose conveys it powerfully.

When all the blood has dried, *Season in Purgatory* is about the conversion of David Pelham from warrior to pacifist. At last he sees more blood than he can stomach: "In his bloodstream were two simple propositions: that the savagery of the Germans did not excuse the savagery of the Partisans: that the savagery of the Partisans did not excuse the savagery of the Germans...."

It is not, as Keneally readily admits, a novel idea. But what the story of David Pelham argues is that to one discovering it for the first time, it has the force of revelation. It changes lives.... Keneally does not go so far as to say that lives thus changed will eventually change the world, but he leaves no doubt that is his hope. For one who writes with such violence he comes to gentle conclusions—and therein hangs the tale.

> *Jonathan Yardley, "Bloody Good Novel," in* Book World—The Washington Post (© *The Washington Post), February 20, 1977. p. N1.*

[Keneally] is an honest workman. He will not probably end up in future anthologies of 20th-century prose, but he has the secret of narration well in hand, as well as a gift for filling in his scenes with absorbing details. Surgical minutiae, infighting with partisan bureaucrats, eccentric British fellow officers, the refurbishing of an ancient generator—all these [in "Season in Purgatory"] blend into a plausible world. Keneally may have painted in too much gore and violence for some readers, but this naturalism is more than a primitive appeal to our bloodlust. Blood is the proper medium for surgeons in battle. If it runs freely here, so does the tale. (p. 30)

> *Raymond A. Sokolov, in* The New York Times Book Review (© *1977 by The New York Times Company; reprinted by permission), February 27, 1977.*

*   *   *

KENNEDY, Joseph Charles
See KENNEDY, X. J.

*   *   *

KENNEDY, X. J. (pseudonym of Joseph Charles Kennedy)   1929-

Kennedy is an American poet, critic, and editor. He is a minor talent who has written very little poetry since his first volume of poems won the Lamont Award in 1961. Generally regarded as a traditionalist, Kennedy's cleverness and wit tend to limit the emotional range and depth of his poems.

[Kennedy is essentially a serious poet] with a strong sense of humor and the wit to display it gracefully. Kennedy's prodigious technical gifts often lead him into light verse, which he is able to raise above the usual level; in this respect he is in the tradition of Auden and William Jay Smith....

[He tries] to free subjective images from hermeticism, and [in *Growing into Love*] is successful in his own way. The world [he] creates and inhabits arises out of a confrontation with today's world, not out of withdrawal from it. (p. 122)

Like Auden and Smith, Kennedy can tune the music of his forms precisely to the various attitudes of his speakers, and so can avoid, in his serious poems, the cloying cuteness which often invades the dead-pan poems of such light-verse virtuosos as Phyllis McGinley and John Updike. Even within the same poem, Kennedy can make successful shifts of tone by increasing or decreasing his dependence on light-verse techniques. In a long poem called "Reading Trip," he recounts an experience which many poets have had, but which few have seen so clearly. The poem is wildly playful in spots, as when the poet encounters, during the question-and-answer session, a young man who asks, "Don't you find riming everything a drag?"

> A drag, man? Worse than that! Between the eyes,
>   I take the blade of his outrageous stare.
> Whoever crosses him, the varlet dies,
>   Trapped Guest to his unancient Mariner:
> "Get with it, baby, what you want to be
> So artsy-craftsy for? Screw prosody . . ."

The trip is recounted in familiar detail, which is partly the source of the humor—Kennedy's typed characters and situations are funny because we know them. But the familiarity also imparts a wistful quality to the poem. A poet's intensity may be heightened by the experience of being a "trapped Guest," but even the intensity becomes routine after a while. . . . Kennedy captures the wistfulness and the cyclical nature of the process. . . .

This poem is not as slight as it may at first seem; the playfulness is part of a serious vision.

Most of the poems in this collection exhibit a remarkable control, though few of them pull together so wide a range of tones. Of those which are more obviously serious, the best are in "Countrymen," the middle section of the book. Here Kennedy has assembled several character sketches and dramatic monologues; these poems best demonstrate his imagination, compassion and involvement with contemporary life.

Through all the forms and voices of his monologues, there comes Kennedy's own quite distinctive voice, which is characterized by a high degree of tension and an astonishing ability to absorb and revivify the flat rhythms and colloquialisms of contemporary American speech. (p. 123)

> *Henry Taylor, in* The Nation *(copyright 1970 by the Nation Associates, Inc.), February 2, 1970.*

There is a tendency in some of Kennedy's weaker poems to write mere society verse—superficial, imperceptive pieces like the account of his "Reading Trip" or his cliché of the "Scholar's Wife." This is not, I think, a vein that Kennedy really ought to pursue. His best work lies in his sympathetic apprehension of the actuality of the world that lies around us. (p. 260)

> *Louis L. Martz, in* The Yale Review *(© 1970 by Yale University; reprinted by permission of the editors), Spring, 1970.*

[Kennedy is] not passionate enough about poetic pleasure, not committed enough. The world is still before [him]. Consequently, even though Kennedy is an obvious admirer of some masters of poetic style and consciously seeks after their secrets of power, his worldliness too often distracts him from his proper art. . . . His view of the poet's role is too ethically oriented, as his ironic manifesto *Poets* [in *Growing into Love*] makes clear. . . . The wry gestures of self-depreciation cannot conceal the ritual sentimentality of this poem. Yeats brings off this sort of poetry because the romantic elements, in his work, will bear the weight of his attacks. (pp. 197-99)

Kennedy aims for wit and discipline in his verse, and the success of the final stanza of *Poets* only highlights the weakness of the lines it should be counterpointing. In general, *Growing into Love* scatters its achievements, though not by design. (p. 199)

> *Jerome McGann, in* Poetry *(© 1970 by The Modern Poetry Association; reprinted by permission of the Editor of* Poetry*), December, 1970.*

Kennedy, in any first reading, seems clearly of the order of Classical ironists: worldly, satirical, wry, astringent. . . . Kennedy's little witticisms . . . place *Growing into Love,* like his earlier book, in the light verse tradition of what A.J.M. Smith has called "the worldly muse."

Some of Kennedy's work, though, is so passionate in its sense of life and art that, despite his surface amusement at romantic mystification and its magical symbols, he exposes himself as vulnerable and sympathtic to their magnetism after all. (p. 90)

> *M. L. Rosenthal, in* Shenandoah *(copyright by* Shenandoah; *reprinted from* Shenandoah: The Washington and Lee University Review *with the permission of the Editor), Fall, 1972.*

With impish glee [Kennedy] borrows Emily Dickinson's epigrammatic style to debunk current follies. Insistent little pecks—measured in short phrases separated by dashes—chip away at the bronzed and brazen images of our modern Lotus Land, home of the beach-combers, Hollywood heroes, razor-blade barons, and hapless prisoners queued for miles on what are euphemistically termed "freeways". (p. 347)

For those who view our current overpopulation of fools and ask, Where are Dryden and Pope, now that we need them? Kennedy provides a partial answer. Though his concise couplets usually lack Augustan polish, they precisely hit the mark. Unlike his devastating mentors' Kennedy's attitude . . . is, however, more amused than outraged. (p. 348)

> *Joseph Parisi, in* Poetry *(© 1974 by The Modern Poetry Association; reprinted by permission of the Editor of* Poetry*), September, 1974.*

In *Celebration After the Death of John Brennan,* X. J. Kennedy has written an extended elegy for a former student. It is painful, and properly be, so full of rigorous metrical struggle with itself. Its conscientiousness is also a topic of the elegy, and part of what is celebrated in the dead young poet. Poetry is *cura,* solicitude, concern. The interpolated quotes from the student's own poetry enhance this book and give it a formally interesting dramatic structure. The poet seems to be carrying on a last painful dialogue with the dead. . . . Here, quotation is no mere device and Kennedy frames the poet's words and with them contrives a discontinuous unity.

My problems with the book are practical ones. Sometimes the poet seems to overwrite. . . . Slang does not always convince when it arrives out of some Dictionary of New English. . . . Sometimes, too, an archaic diction is equally obtrusive: "Dissolved, those fugitive songs". A clotted melodrama intrudes: "Trussing me to / In dried umbilical cords". Apostrophes to the dead are less convincing than the felt quotations: "Swept from your Rockies, John, did you find home?"

Still, the poet is capable of a sudden concreteness: "Some egocentric homemade Buddhist Mass? Word stops me as I'm climbing Medford Hill. / Trivial Rocky patched with ice-fringed grass." A fine enjambment reminds one of the disorderly vitality of didactic decorums: "That was one hell of an opening / Pedagogue-student conference!" Eliot was correct that the experience ripening us most is at once both sensuous and intellectual, and Kennedy sometimes yields us an image simultaneously cognitive and concrete: "Fragments of mirror ranged along a strand / For the arisen sun to time-expose." With its modest diction, its formal poise, Kennedy's praise most moves us as a complex pastoral. . . . (pp. 226-27)

> *David Shapiro, in* Poetry *(© 1976 by The Modern Poetry Association; reprinted by permission of the Editor of* Poetry*), July, 1976.*

*   *   *

KING, Francis   1923-

King is a British novelist, short story writer, poet, and editor. He has been writing subtle, atmospheric novels about the human condition for some years now, yet his name is hardly known outside of England. Perhaps the combination of a rather grim pessimism and a subdued, conservative writing style have mitigated his appeal. (See also *Contemporary Authors*, Vols. 1-4, rev. ed.)

Travellers' tales, of a modest kind, the two stories which make up *Flights* are evidently intended to relate to one another. The first, set in Hungary, is called "The Infection". The second, set in Greece, is called "The Cure". Both evoke a mood of insecurity, of unease with foreign ways, of helpless dependence upon airline staff, chauffeurs, interpreters and the supposed good will of unpredictable strangers. Passengers' tales, perhaps, rather than travellers'. . . .

Plausibility and technical skill are what it is natural to admire in these stories. The author has set himself difficult tasks and succeeded: a mass of information about imagined people, real places and customs, is offered with a neat and graceful economy. But the stories can fairly be called modest, whetting curiosity rather than satisfying it. One feels that Mr King is wary of conjecture, that he describes nothing he is not pretty sure of. There is a real pleasure in following the work of a writer so firmly in command of his material.

> *"Tales of Travel," in* The Times Literary Supplement *(© Times Newspapers, Ltd., 1973; reproduced from* The Times Literary Supplement *by permission), October 19, 1973, p. 1269.*

Francis King is the sort of writer who deliberately underplays his material, letting each small incident and revelation make its own, often devastating point; and he is a master of the style appropriate to this narrative restraint. The balance and complexity of his writing, which seems simple, are constantly fresh and bracing. Of course it is never simple at all, nor is his subject matter. In the tight world of *A Game of Patience,* set in the Surrey countryside during the last months of the war, bombs fall, an old man dies and an old woman loses her reason, a tense CO commits two acts of terrible cruelty, a party of servicemen discordantly interrupts village life. A persistent sexual undercurrent flickers throughout. An entire network of relationships is explored

and clarified with no authorial pushing or nudging, each response authentic and beautifully placed.

The exact sense of pace and touch means that King never has to violate his matter by sensationalising it. His selection of a 17-year old girl as principal foreground figure—all of the action is subtly filtered through her mind—distances the events of the book from the reader, who must fill in the chinks in her perceptions. This novel makes no easy choices and, in its cold, rather comfortless way, demands much more of the reader than its very English elegance seems to suggest. (p. 355)

> *Peter Straub, in* New Statesman *(© 1974 The Statesman & Nation Publishing Co. Ltd.), September 13, 1974.*

[*The Needle*] goes for an info-packed intro, lobbing in a wordy image before you even know what it will refer to:

> Like strangers thrown together fortuitously at the same table in an overcrowded café and determined not to be invaded by each other's indentities [*sic*], brother and sister breakfasted in the dark, high-ceilinged, old-fashioned kitchen above the surgery.

Even without the tiresome misprint, there's a lot to be getting on with here: time of day, location, mood, 'intriguing' personnel, and the additional worry of wondering quite why this evidently bleak and Sundayish tableau suggested an overcrowded café to Mr King's mind.

It's such an honest opening, however, that you might say the whole book is in it. Certainly the brother/sister tension stated here is the life of the narrative. Almost at once, we know that the brother, Bob, dunnit. What we want his GP sister Lorna to find out is what he dun. . . . [A] vaguely disgusting, semi-incestuous state of affairs sets up a whole series of sympathetic minor revulsions in the middle of the book, when Mr King dwells queasily on dog hairs, fleas, household muck, bowel trouble, a senile neighbour known as 'the grub', and Lorna's crippled partner Matty, who slurps tea and makes execrable slimy mousse.

All this suburban nausea is, of course, part of the build-up for Bob, who has to come through with something pretty sick in the way of a guilty secret to justify it. Mere queerness won't do. But guilt does finally explode into revelation (in a series of lugubrious pops); and Mr King shows a short-story writer's cunning. . . . The mood of the piece . . . swings almost right over to Bette Davis Gothic in the last pages. . . . [What] depresses me slightly, in the end, about books of this kind is that they drop back so snugly into the world they depict. *The Needle* is just the kind of book lonely women like Lorna will be reading this winter. (p. 285)

> *Russell Davies, in* New Statesman *(© 1975 The Statesman & Nation Publishing Co. Ltd.), September 5, 1975.*

There has always been a dark side to Mr King's novels, somewhat contradicting the conventional view of him as one of our more placid writers; although he is no Poe, and would not want to be, he is adept at casting various forms of terror and unease within his apparently calm, collected prose. (p. 316)

[His novel, *The Needle,*] is no mere pot-boiler, since Mr King never dabbles in over-statement. He is also too fastidious to bother with the thoroughly modern under-statement;

he is, rather, a master of the precise statement—going very well with his constant effort to keep up appearances: the appearance of his characters, of his prose, and of the neatly but tightly formed shape of his narrative. But beneath this surface, some dark fantasies swoop and glitter. The novel is invaded by images of decay. Sexual violence—aptly suggested by the title of the book—and physical decrepitude . . . are somehow connected in Mr King's mind, and his darting imagination is only barely kept in check by the iron discipline he imposes upon his own writing. But order and control, however self-willed, have their disadvantages.

I wish that Mr King would take a leap into the dark—the real dark: not the dark of fantasy and imagination, but the dark of language—and although he would run the risk of massive failure . . ., he might also in the process add to his considerable powers of observation and description. The plot of *The Needle,* for example, is carefully and cleverly developed but it is just a little too neat. . . . It is all very intriguing, very well told, very plausible, and I admire the way in which he manipulates his narrative; but, it may be that Mr King is putting his points too well, and manipulating too cleverly. The darkness within should become visible on the surface, too. (pp. 316-17)

Peter Ackroyd, in The Spectator (© *1975 by* The Spectator; *reprinted by permission of* The Spectator), *September 6, 1975.*

No one could accuse Francis King of flaunting his consciousness or even of imposing a slanted attitude towards the Human Condition on his readers. His best novels—of which *The Needle* is certainly one—are like chamber pieces for their delicacy of tone and clarity of line, but also for their apparent lack of a conductor. *The Needle* has a third-person narrator, not a participant in the action, who unobtrusively sets scenes and times, moves characters from bed to bath, offers a little personal history where necessary, describes a gesture here, a facial expression there, reads the mind of a character when there is no occasion for dialogue. He combines the functions of reciter and attendant in a Japanese Noh play, moving the story along between incidents and stepping forward from time to time to rearrange the actors' costumes.

If King's London seems grey and seedy (though never apocalyptically so, as in *Our Father*), it is because the characters happen to live in grey and seedy circumstances rather than because King has got it in for London or contemporary society. When his heroine, a G.P. with a practice in Parson's Green, says: "That's life—a perpetual state of vague worry, or at least, that's what it is for me", the sentiment stops with her, not spilling over into the relation between writer and reader. Her partner's warning: "There'll always be mess and inefficiency in this country. More and more of it. So you'd better reconcile yourself" is belied as a counsel of despair by the speaker's own sturdy efficiency in the surgery. Belied, but not entirely cancelled, since she is physically crippled and her home is squalid. King is adept at introducing little knots of complexity like this into the clear line of his narrative. They neither impede nor advance it, but belong somehow to a separate level of the book, the observation of character.

Our unobtrusive attendant is more of a tyrant than at first appears. Though he never uses settings to convey attitudes, one begins to suspect that he loves his settings more than his characters. He certainly loves his plot best of all. *The Needle* sounds nasty and it is. What seems, to begin with,

ordinary and sad turns twisted and sharp. The early impression of independence in the main characters is an illusion caused by not knowing them well enough and they cannot be properly understood until the plot has tightened round them. For this reason the novel's after-taste is stronger than its taste in the mouth. What one goes away with is no substitute for biography but a real sense of place and a *frisson* from the virtuosity of the plot. (pp. 78-9)

John Spurling, in Encounter (© *1975 by* Encounter Ltd.), *December, 1975.*

There are alarming signs in *Hard Feelings* that Francis King admires his own undeniable deftness and economy rather more than is good for his writing. At the end of several stories, there is a suspicion of a faint sigh of self-satisfaction—'is there no end to the man's resourcefulness?'—which is unutterably irritating and, in fact, not always excused by the work's merit. Some of the plot devices creak with old age and over-use; sometimes the reader gets restless waiting for the smashing—and predictable—blow of dramatic irony. Mr King is capable of combining extreme flashiness with an air of sober craftsmanship in a fashion reminiscent of Annigoni.

None of which denies that there is much to admire in *Hard Feelings.* Mr King has an appallingly accurate ear, eye and nose for hypocrisy, and teeth to match. He also has a somehow unexpected capacity for tenderness towards his characters, when he can break clear of his deep rooted contempt for their failure to see their situation as clearly as he does himself. In stories like 'A Nice Way to Go' or 'The Brothers', he tempers justice with mercy, so to speak, remembering that an author is a member of the human race, too, despite his temporary advantage of omnipotence. (p. 22)

Nick Totton, in The Spectator (© *1976 by* The Spectator; *reprinted by permission of* The Spectator), *October 2, 1976.*

*   *   *

KOCH, Kenneth   1925-

Koch is an American poet and playwright identified with the "New York School." Poetry seems to be a form of play for Koch—a way of making people feel better about the world and themselves. His best poetry is delightfully childlike and highly imaginative. A teacher as well as a writer, he has been successful in instructing both children and the aged to write verse. (See also *CLC,* Vol. 5, and *Contemporary Authors,* Vols. 1-4, rev. ed.)

The surreal absurd has a mystical intensity which one recognizes in the poetry of Ginsberg, Bly, Wakoski, Simic, Lamantia, Knott. It is a quality which lacks entirely in Kenneth Koch's poetry. Koch plays on the quirks and mannerisms of surrealist language; he is a virtuoso of the absurd image. There is an air of provocative non-sense in his work which echoes the French poets with a lightness of touch verging on coquetry. . . . Koch makes surrealist poetry into a field of fun; but his wit, en route, moves closer to the absurdist snicker than to the intensity of a Breton. Although such distinctions are difficult to make, it is possible that Koch is not as much a surrealist as he seems. His humor has an edge of satire; his ebullient absurdity slides into an original form of social and cultural criticism, as in "The Artist" and "Fresh Air," both enormously funny epics about the impossibility of art. With Koch . . . the elements of surreal language are often put to a more circumscribed use, as absurdist jokes. (p. 279)

Paul Zweig, in Salmagundi *(copyright © 1973 by Skidmore College), Spring-Summer, 1973.*

Kenneth Koch's work is always entertaining and usually enlightening. [*The Art of Love,* his first] . . . collection of poems . . . in over five years, is no exception. His playfulness, in tone and technique, has often caused him to be underrated. But it is just his great capacity for humor, based on so much more than mere irony, that makes him important. He has reclaimed the humorous for serious writers of poetry and for that we are in his debt. . . .

He is . . . known as one third of the trinity labeled the founding generation of "The New York School of Poetry," John Ashbery and the late Frank O'Hara being the other two-thirds. . . .

Ashbery and O'Hara have come to be recognized finally as the major poets they are, while Koch has perhaps been more liked than appreciated.

All three can be playful and witty and surrealistically bizarre in their work. But it is Koch who remains the most direct, and therefore most accessible. His sense of humor seems quirky, and at times even kinky, but it is closer to the quick hitting humor of kids and nonsophisticates than either of the other two.

Michael Lally, "Playtime at the New York School," in Book World—The Washington Post *(© The Washington Post), August 3, 1975, p. 1.*

[Although] Koch's sense of humor is certainly one of the irrefutable delights of ["The Art of Love"], it is one among many. Other qualities these poems embody are—at random —the ability to move the reader, plain but beautiful language that should appeal to a wide audience, a general graciousness of spirit that has long been an unremarked-on hallmark of Koch's writing, and last but not least, outright wisdom. . . .

[His] work, while sharing in the surface charm and facility common to all the writing of [The New York School of **Poets**], has a range of interest and grasp that seems to me unique. "The Art of Love" is the best of his books to date. To be able to state this of the new work of an American poet of 50 is, to state the least, unusual. Poets in our country have very short creative life spans, for the most part: in many instances they seem not so much to mature as to ferment. . . .

If his predecessor, Ovid's poem of the same title, tends to a purity of detail that Koch's poem can't help but parody by going to the opposite extreme, the final effect of both poems is remarkably similar: a heightened sense of mortal innocence engaged in the mysteries of Love. . . . (p. 16)

Aram Saroyan, in The New York Times Book Review *(© 1975 by The New York Times Company; reprinted by permission), September 28, 1975.*

Koch's delicate, persistent irony [in *The Art of Love* is] necessary to his poetic self-definition. . . . It's clear, for instance, that there's an enormous gulf between the author of *The Art of Love* and its mad speaker, whose grotesque lecture not only parodies but seriously subverts ency-clopedists of sexual self help from Andreas Capellanus and the author of the *Kama Sutra* to Havelock Ellis and Alex Comfort. "The days of / Allegory are over. The Days of Irony are here. / Irony and Deception", Koch says (only half ironically, I believe) in *Some General Instructions,* another long bravura poem in this volume, adding "But do not harden your heart. Remain / kind and flexible." Kind, flexible, winsome, soulful irony—irony appreciated as an intelligent voluptuary might appreciate fine chocolate or good wine—is one of the arts (pleasures? sciences?) at which Koch and other poets of the so-called "New York School" seem to me to be most adept. Its purpose is generally commendable: to enable both poet and reader to distance feelings, ideas, experiences, so as to perceive them strangely, freshly, as if they were rare or even alien curiosities, *objects d'art,* perhaps, in some great Bloomingdale's of the imagination. "A reader", says Koch in *The Art of Poetry,* still another of the *tours de force* in this collection, "should put your work down puzzled, / Distressed and illuminated, ready to believe / It is curious to be alive."

If there's a drawback to this literary theory, it's that the detachment it presupposes from both poet and reader isn't always easy to sustain. . . . When, for instance, Koch's mad speaker—no doubt wildly embroidering upon that notorious "Fly me" ad—advises the (male) reader to make his girl into an airplane, I can't help wanting to say, "Please, be serious, this is no laughing matter!" And in fact it's plain that Koch himself really agrees. Studiedly emerging from behind the parodic, lunatic mask, from time to time he breaks into seriousness, wondering "What reasonable substitute, in love's absence, could be found for love?" or noting, in a passage that gradually detaches itself from detachment, that there are

> Ten things an older man must never say to a
> younger woman:
> 1) I'm dying! 2) I can't hear what you're saying!
> 3) How many fingers are you holding up?
> 4) Listen to my heart. 5) Take my pulse. 6) What's
> your name?
> 7) Is it cold in here? 8) Is it hot in here? 9) Are you
> in here?
> 10) What wings are those beating at the window?

No doubt the tension between funny and serious parody is intentional, judicious, but I'd have preferred a less careful balance. For which reason, I guess, my favorite poem in this book is *The Circus,* the only piece not at all in the detached, parodic mode of *The Art of Love.* Grave, naive, nostalgic, *The Circus* is—among other things—a poem about Koch's earlier poem *The Circus,* and hence a poem about mutability. Its distinctive freshness and directness reminds us that its author, besides being the connoisseur of irony who composed *The Art of Love,* is the inventive teacher of *Wishes, Lies, and Dreams* whose "poetry ideas" have defined "the true voice of feeling" for many children and adolescents. That Koch himself can speak in that voice, controlling its nuances without the expensive tool of irony, is made quite clear in this poem. When he says, riskily, "I wonder how long I am going to live / And what the rest will be like I mean the rest of my life", he places the line in its unsentimental context so expertly that I am simply moved. Despite some of the problems his self-definition may involve, despite the ways in which his use of parody occasionally verges on self-parody, *The Circus* assures us that Koch is truly at ease with his art. . . . (pp. 292-93)

Sandra M. Gilbert, in Poetry (© 1976 by
The Modern Poetry Association; reprinted
by permission of the Editor of Poetry), August, 1976.

[In "The Duplications" Koch] has completed a long poem,
somewhat arbitrarily divided in half by an autobiographical
section. Using mostly rhymed octets, he sets out to abolish
space, time and historical experience in order to create
exuberant images that entertain, and occasionally (though
with a light hand) instruct. The narrator is a rather sensuous, symbol-prone itinerant, at once rhapsodic and skeptical. He clearly sympathizes with those "Students dreaming up some pure Havanas / Where love would govern all,
not francs or dollars"; but he worries that new tyrannies,
announced with messianic slogans, keep replacing their
predecessors—one of the "duplications" intended by his
title, which more broadly refers to the cyclic rhythms of
life. He is, always, very much an individual—someone who
might not bother Fidel Castro, but who certainly would
arouse the suspicions of his bureaucratic henchmen: "O
Liberty, you are the only word at / Which the heart of man
leaps automatically."

Koch has a delicious sense of ironic detachment running
through his rather lyrical, if not ecstatic, celebrations of the
flesh. On a Greek island, contemplating the serene beauty
of the Aegean, he thinks of the life underneath: ". . . Fish
are nice / In being, though we eat them, not revengeful / I
think that we would probably be meaner / To those who
washed us down with their retsina!" It is an observation
utterly worthy of Pueblo or Hopi children, who, like Emerson or Thoreau—speaking of duplications—are not especially inclined to what in the 19th century was called "human vainglory." (p. 26)

Robert Coles, "Teaching Old Folks an Old
Art," in The New York Times Book Review (© 1977 by The New York Times
Company; reprinted by permission), April
10, 1977, pp. 1, 26.

*   *   *

KOESTLER, Arthur   1905-

**Hungarian-born British novelist, essayist, journalist, and his-
torian, Koestler reflects in his works a concern with politics,
ethics, philosophy, history, and psychology. His *Art of Creation* explores the creative/destructive dichotomy of human
nature, a continuing theme throughout his work. (See also
CLC, Vols. 1, 3, 6, and *Contemporary Authors*, Vols. 1-4, rev.
ed.)**

[The] Koestler of *Darkness at Noon* is a genuinely great
imaginative writer who has changed the direction of the
flow of thought on political matters, and it is as such that he
will live and continue to be read; . . . he is not a scientist,
though he has had some good ideas in the tradition of what
Germans call nature-philosophy, and he is not nearly critical or tough-minded enough to be a creative philosopher.
Nevertheless, Koestler has been accepted as a scientific
philosopher by a number of serious and able scientists. . . .
I believe that the real trouble with Arthur Koestler is that
he writes and acts as if he thought that the high inspirational origin of a theory and the sheer intensity of the conviction with which it is held to be true are somehow evidence of its authenticity. . . . [Quite the opposite,] in
science we are taught, or come painfully to learn, that to
fall in love with a hypothesis is one of the roads to ruin. . . .

Sometimes one can watch the inspirational elements in
Koestler taking over from, and damaging, his thought. . . .
(p. 22)

Koestler is . . . a superbly accomplished journalist. He is an
enormously intelligent man with a truly amazing power to
apprehend knowledge and grasp the gist of quite difficult
theories. Above all, he is a master at telling a story. One
story that seems to attract him is that of the brilliant genius,
the true original, who is cold-shouldered and misunderstood
by the Establishment. This is an important element of the
high-romantic view of scholarship; another is that the
"creativity and pathology of the human mind are, after all,
two sides of the same medal." Or, alternatively, that genius
and insanity are somehow cognate.

I very much doubt if either opinion would stand up to critical scrutiny. Nearly all great geniuses are recognized in
their own lifetimes, but of course we tend to remember only
the exceptions. Moreover, high genius is distinguished by a
high, clear sanity that casts its light all around it. In the
absence of any conceivable "control experiment," we cannot say for certain, though we may very well surmise, that
Nietzsche and Schumann, for instance, would have risen to
even greater heights if their minds had been unclouded by
manic or depressive tendencies.

Koestler is a great campaigner, too. Very often I have got
the impression from his writings that, where they should by
rights be cool and deeply analytical, they are, in reality,
Koestler's part in a dialogue with an unseen disputant—
someone who takes a bit of convincing and needs all of
Koestler's considerable persuasive powers. (pp. 22, 24)

Peter Medawar, "Doing the Honors," in
Saturday Review (© 1976 by Saturday
Review/World, Inc.; reprinted with permis-
sion), March 6, 1976, pp. 22, 24.

The comparatively sudden appearance of large communities of Jews in Eastern Europe during the twelfth and thirteenth centuries is generally attributed to the migration
eastward, because of discrimination and persecution, of
Jews from France, England, and Germany. In *The Thirteenth Tribe*, Arthur Koestler argues that this theory has
been accepted primarily because of a lack of any alternative
explanation. . . .

The Thirteenth Tribe, a study of the Khazars, attempts to
prove that the majority of modern Jewry . . . is in fact descended from this Turkic tribe that settled in the Caucasus
in the sixth century, built up an empire in the seventh and
eighth centuries that preserved Eastern Europe from the
advances of Islam and defended Byzantium from the ravages of the nomadic peoples of the steppe, and converted to
Judaism in the eighth century. (p. 1248)

Despite the intriguing nature of the thesis put forth by
Koestler, it has no firmer factual foundation than the theory
it seeks to supplant, and the manner in which it is presented
does incalculable harm. Historical accuracy is discarded
where it impairs the symmetry of his argument; and, in an
attempt, one presumes, to attract a popular mass audience,
Koestler abandons the dispassionate and exact language of
his earlier works for clichés. Phrases such as "no news is
good news in history," "the Khazars had their fingers in
many historic pies," "it was good psychology" abound.
The reader is also confused by the endless use of twentieth
century terminology to describe Khazar society: Koestler
discusses the influence of the Khazar princesses on Byzan-

tine "haute couture" and the Khazar's "Brains Trust." What could have made a fascinating and thought-provoking article was instead stretched to book length through the introduction of extraneous and misleading information and a great many unnecessary asides. The result is a work that has neither the value of a well-executed, honest piece of scholarship nor the emotional appeal of a polemic—only the earmarks of a poorly researched and hastily written book. (p. 1249)

Jane Majeski, "Chutzpah," in National Review (© *National Review, Inc., 1976, 150 East 35th St., New York, N.Y. 10016), November 12, 1976, pp. 1248-49.*

Arthur Koestler has long been depersonalizing himself; he has now achieved practically complete self-extinction. Twenty years ago he drew the conclusion that only two choices were possible for Jews: to abandon their Jewishness (or what passed for it) and to assimilate into the mainstream of the nations in which they found themselves—or go to Israel. For himself, he sewed leather patches on the elbows of his worn-out cardigans and became (he thought) a true-blue Englishman. But the transition from Jewish-Hungarian exile to John Bull elicited only nods of pity from the Jewish community. . . .

In the process, he came across some marginal references to the Khazar Jews of medieval Russia, especially those references that depicted *their* descendants as being of non-Semitic origin, of being not really Jews at all, but a mongrel mixture of dubious origins and with no racial, moral, juridical, or even theological right to "return" to the Holy Land. He persuaded himself, in short, that neither he nor the Jews of East Europe were Jews at all, as the world understood that term. . . .

In this tortured effort to come to grips with the problem—it must be stressed, it is largely *his* problem—he takes tortuous routes to unravel bits and pieces about the Khazars, some of it real, much of it fanciful, and most of it—sheer speculation. (p. 69)

In the eighth century (740 AD) the king of the Khazars (and his court) "embraced the Jewish faith, and Judaism became the state religion of the Khazars." Thus Koestler writes in his opening statement on the subject [in *The Thirteenth Tribe*] except that he is a hasty "historian," contradicting even this early in his text (page 15) what he had written a page earlier, namely, that this Jewish state had achieved "the peak of its power from the seventh to the tenth centuries AD." How this "Jewish state" achieved "the peak of its power" a hundred years before its birth is not further elucidated.

The history of the Jewish Khazars is known to both scholars and informed readers. . . . [There] is . . . historical evidence, gleaned from early correspondence, travelers' observations, philosophical dissertations . . . , plus much other relevant material from Arabic and Hebrew sources [to prove the existence of a Jewish state in Southern Russia].

But Koestler is not content with the evidence; he must concoct a theory to suit his own notions that the overwhelming majority of the world Jewish community are not authentic Jews at all. They, he argues without a shred of genuine authority for his vagrant opinions, are not Semites, but stem in toto from their Turko-pagan ancestors of the Middle Ages who, when dispersed in the thirteenth century, provided the bulk of the "Jewish" populations in Poland and Lithuania.

This concoction is so fanciful it has been repudiated by every known scholar in the field. (pp. 69-70)

So, the question remains: What is Koestler up to? Ever since the publication of his fictional account of why the Old Bolsheviks at the "Moscow Trials" of 1936-8 confessed (*Darkness at Noon*), he has been engaged in an intellectual adventure that has led him to speculate on such recondite subjects as parapsychology, and to flirt with the discredited theory of the inheritance of acquired characteristics (*The Case of the Midwife Toad*). In these endeavors *vox populi* (actually the voice of the popular critics) has been kind to him, while the professionals (the scholars) have tended to dismiss him as an often irresponsible amateur. But so long as his rhetoric did not seriously affect the lives and fortunes of an entire people—as is the present case—one could pass it off as trivial. With *The Thirteenth Tribe,* however, we are confronted with a situation where the informed scholar disdains to take him on . . . for fear of sullying his own credentials. . . .

[Thousands] of people who never read a word about the ancient Jewish kingdom of the Khazars, who never heard of Yehuda Halevi, who never looked into the subject at all, will be beguiled (and misinformed) about a chapter in Jewish life that needs understanding. Such books have been written, good books, brave books, scholarly books—but *The Thirteenth Tribe* is not one of them. It is a book that when it doesn't insult the intelligence, helps in the eternal defamation of a people which seems helpless before the kind of plain and fancy ignorance deployed by the uninformed "critics" of the daily press who have combined to catapult this misguided nonsense onto the best-seller lists of the popular book media. And that is a shame. (p. 71)

Max Geltman, "Koestler's Contortions," in Midstream (*copyright © 1977 by The Theodor Herzl Foundation, Inc.), February, 1977, pp. 69-71.*

*   *   *

KONWICKI, Tadeusz   1926-

Konwicki is a Polish novelist, short story writer, and film director. Although he has written many novels, he is known to an English-language audience on the basis of a single translated work, *A Dreambook for Our Time*. This novel, with its continuous flashbacks, nightmarish images, and shifting realities, is a terrifying study of a war-shattered mind.

[Neither] Konwicki nor his novel [*Wladza* (The Power)] differ in any significant way from the clichés of socialist-realist fiction produced on a mass scale in Poland in the early 1950s and modeled on Soviet novels of the same period. Despite the fact that *Wladza* was never finished, it won the [State Prize] and was most favorably reviewed by the critics, who encouraged the young author to continue along the same path, which brought success for political rather than artistic accomplishment. (pp. 485-86)

When *Rojsty* (The Marshes) appeared in print in 1956 it did not win a state prize; nevertheless, we should consider its publication a turning point in the novelist's literary career. (p. 486)

In *Rojsty* Konwicki gives a fictitious, often self-mocking account of the year he spent with the guerrillas. Superficially satirical, in fact it pronounces a sad post mortem tribute for the young men who opposed the Soviet invasion, fighting for their native land, taking no orders, expecting no help, hoping against hope that "at least their courage would be remembered by someone some day." And indeed, while the official Polish historiography either remains silent or dismisses that chapter in the country's postwar history, Konwicki's novel provides an almost unique literary document of it.... [It] begins with a rather satirical picture of a young man desperately trying to become a hero, but as the political situation changes so does the style of the novel. The narration grows more dramatic, the scenery more somber, and the characters undergo a dramatic transition, emerging as mature, embittered men whose idealism and hopes have been shattered. Konwicki's style, initially light-hearted and casual, changes too, evolving toward a more complex, symbolic vision of reality. The image of *rojsty,* the local name of quicksands and marshes, dominates the novel as a symbol of doom for all hopes, sacrifices and aspirations. *Rojsty* provided the young Konwicki with fictional themes and motifs which have gradually emerged and taken over and finally created Konwicki's own nightmarish world. (pp. 486-87)

The motifs of an impending doom, the impossibility of sharing one's own past, and the futility in seeking lasting happiness—enhanced with images and visual symbols, which Konwicki as a film director [in the late 1950s] was able to realize perhaps more clearly than he could have at that point as a novelist—all come to the fore in his major novel *Sennik współczesny* (1963; *A Dreambook for Our Time,* 1969). Virtually everything Konwicki's world has been made of appears in that novel in a new and revealing light of sudden understanding of those internal and external forces which have created it. The very first lines of the novel set up the weird atmosphere of suspense made up of the dreams and reality experienced by a nameless protagonist who narrates his own story:

> I didn't open my eyes, and, like a man awakened from an afternoon doze, I did not know where or who I was. The venomous taste of bile burned my mouth, the ticklish centipede of pulse ran across my temples. I was lying in a ponderous sack of pain and sweat.

As it turns out, he is an escapee from the frustrating hustle of urban life in contemporary Poland, a temporary settler in a symbolic valley whose days are numbered, for it will be flooded as soon as a new water reservoir is completed. The new construction project, the sign of a new era, threatens the very livelihood of the valley, where a strange collection of phantomlike characters vegetates suspended between bitter recollections of the past and inevitable destruction in the immediate future. The protagonist, whose memory is constantly tormented by his terrible war experiences, lives among them trying to find his own place in that strange world, but, as Czesław Miłosz correctly remarked, "this is a novel about guilt, and since the feeling of guilt oppresses men with distorted, even monstrous recollections, everything bathes in an aura of torment; situations, people, landscapes create a nightmarish web of metaphors." That feeling of guilt, as it will be explained later, which emerges in *Sennik współczesny* as the main motif, also appears in Konwicki's subsequent novels, threatening the very fabric of human existence, or at least its sanity. Although the protagonist eventually seems to get rid of his obsession with the past and hopes to return to "normal" life, it is obvious

that the psychological wounds inflicted by the war and the years of horror immediately following it can never be healed.

Such a dramatic change in the novelist's philosophy is clearly reflected in the style of the novel. Every scene and every character acquires a deeper, symbolic meaning, the descriptions and dialogues become more metaphorical than ever before, making the novel tense and coherent. The initial image of a man submerged in a half-dream eventually changes into a more conscious quest as expressed by the protagonist: "What I've lived through up to now is like a handful of stones brought up from the riverbed. Now I shall forever be fitting them into new configurations and search for the meaning behind all this." (pp. 487-88)

His movie *Salto* (1964) presented virtually the same problem—a man entangled in a nightmarish web of haunting memories, fears and terror with no escape, no hope and no redemption. *Salto* signifies a further step into the exploration of the existential night descending upon the world, which Konwicki has been painstakingly creating since 1948 —or perhaps the world which created Konwicki and his fiction in the years preceding that date.

His novel *Wniebowstąpienie* (Ascension), published in 1967, seems to point it out quite eloquently. Set in contemporary Warsaw, the novel introduces another uncanny cast of characters for whom the capital of Poland serves as a purgatory they have to pass through before being doomed forever.... Konwicki leads his [ghostly] characters through the streets, restaurants, parks and jails but most frequently gathers them together in the empty marble halls of the [Palace of Culture], ... juxtaposing their enormous size and deserted spaces with the ugliness and pettiness of everyday life in contemporary Poland. Such an ironic twist adds a grotesque flavor to that somber and masterfully written novel, in which realistic presentation of characters and scenery achieves another dimension of supernatural and symbolic vision.

In a manner resembling that of Bulgakov's *Master and Margarita,* Konwicki succeeds in combining the realistic, often humorous scenes of contemporary Warsaw with a terrifying vision of evil reigning over all human lives. Now the horrors of war memories give way to the torments of life in the corrupted post-war society, life frustrated in an inescapable trap of human bondage. Ever-present, suspicious policemen replace the oppressors of the past while victimized people either seek forgetfulness in drunken stupor or turn into ghostlike phantoms populating the city. The protagonist, a man who has lost his memory and in a series of flashbacks tries to imagine who he could have been had the circumstances not prevented him, moves among the drunken crowd of human wrecks. (p. 488)

Konwicki ... comes from those regions Poland lost to the Soviet Union in the aftermath of World War II, and therefore the accute sense of irreparable loss of his native land has always been present in his writings. The land of his childhood, that paradise lost—in this case quite literally—to which he constantly returns has grown into [a] haunting motif of major proportions. Parenthetically one might remark that the Eastern territories, which Polish writers had not been permitted to write about for almost fifteen years after the war, recently have been making a dramatic comeback in Polish literature.... Konwicki, [like other Polish writers], makes a sentimental journey to that land of his youth in one of his minor novels, *Dziura w niebie* (A Hole in the Sky, 1959) but only in his major works does he transform it into an everpresent image of major importance.

It has become a basic structural motif in what so far is his best and most ambitious novel *Nic albo nic* (Nothing or Nothing, 1971), the winner of a readers' plebiscite for the best novel of the year. (pp. 489-90)

Nic albo nic epitomizes Konwicki's haunted world more and better than anything he has ever written, for it explores all the passions, obsessions, fears and complexes he has inherited from the violent past and which he sees in the present. In that novel, perhaps more violent and cruel than his previous works, the guilt complex comes to the fore, transferred into an image of sexual violence leading to death. Death appears in that novel as a dominating force, an ultimate culmination of all those motifs he has explored before. It is always there, in the novel's imagery, in its scenery, in the minds of its characters, and one may safely assume that the protagonist in *Nic albo nic* has become the author's porte-parole when he says:

> I know . . . how to sense the nearness of those who have departed, how to get in touch with their existence, how to be swamped in their silent presence. I do not have to call them in. They are always around me, near me, in me. Some of them I love, some I respect, I hate some of them, and some I despise. They participate in my daydreams and in my dreams at night, in my memory and in my premonitions, in my hopes, and in the spasms of terror.

And indeed, that acute sense of terror transposes Konwicki's world into a nightmarish, haunted realm. Philosophically close to existential thought, Konwicki, not as a moralist but as an accomplished artist, has put his finger on the very source of the anxieties and fears of the modern world, laying them bare in a relentless exploration.

The road he has covered in the last twenty years exemplifies the direction of contemporary Polish literature perhaps better than any other writer's work in the same period. From a superimposed interest in political power to an almost complete defiance of the values established by that power, a nothingness, an all-embracing *nada*, Konwicki's haunted world has become an important part of modern literature, the literature of our violent, cruel and yet uniquely fascinating century. (p. 490)

> *Jerzy R. Krzyzanowski, "The Haunted World of Tadeusz Konwicki," in* Books Abroad *(copyright 1974 by the University of Oklahoma Press), Vol. 48, No. 3, Summer, 1974, pp. 485-90.*

[*A Dreambook for Our Time*] is a deliberately unapproachable fable of contemporary Polish life. (p. 31)

The difficulties of Konwicki's *A Dreambook for Our Time* stem from the dreamlike vision of the contemporary world in which the narrator finds himself, a vision predicted by [Tadeusz Borowski in *This Way for the Gas, Ladies and Gentlemen*. Like Borowski's narrator], this man is also a guilty survivor. In the war, which in Poland involved a bloody civil conflict (partisans against Communists) as well as the defense against the Nazis, the narrator like many other young men betrayed and murdered his countrymen for causes which were increasingly confused. When he wakes after an unsuccessful suicide attempt at the begin-

ning of the novel 20 years later he wakes into another dream where the present is still clouded by the confusions of the past. In one last effort to sum up the meaning of his experience he sets about investigating his surroundings; they are his only materials. The village and its environment are thick with the unorganizable fragments of history. Its inhabitants come from all over Poland, but they are presently caught up in a deracinated religious cult which seals off their pasts from his investigations. The township itself has been destroyed and rebuilt so often that no trace of history or tradition survives. Its forest is crowded with the unmarked graves of centuries of war, and its monastery's museum displays a ragtag collection of minerals and fish from foreign climes, all of which points to nothing except a tradition of transience and destruction, a dumb randomness out of which a man tries vainly to wrest some explanation.

The plot moves back and forth between the narrator's recollections of the war and the events of his current life. The connections he does manage to make between landmarks here and in his past or between persons then and now do nothing to control the randomness of his findings. Events and landscape duplicate and reduplicate themselves in the narrative without leaving any trace of a pattern. And suppose he does correctly identify a man or a place from his past, will he gain any explanation beyond the baldness of the coincidence itself? Apparently not as each of these coincidences swells in importance distorting itself as it does so, and then bursts. The novel ends with his wilting hope to wake at last into an "ordinary, commonplace day, with its usual troubles," and one thinks that Tadeusz Borowski too would have settled happily for something like that. (pp. 31-2)

> *Elizabeth Pochoda, in* The New Republic *(reprinted by permission of* The New Republic; © 1976 by The New Republic, Inc.), *April 10, 1976.*

Polish writing of the last two centuries has a coherence and relevance that are without parallel elsewhere. In consequence, it is for the foreigner both difficult and private, intricately traced with historical and literary allusions. There is no comparison with the lucid humanism of the modern Czech novels. With the exception of the experimental theater of Witkiewicz and Mrożek—and not all of that—there are very few first-class works of Polish literature that do not require an explanatory introduction.

Dreambook is given such an introduction by the philosopher Leszek Kolakowski. While it is not autobiographical in a precise way, its themes are the themes of Konwicki's own life and Kolakowski summarizes them. . . .

[Konwicki's] narrator awakens after a suicide attempt, surrounded by inquisitive faces in the remote village to which he has drifted. We understand that he is a solitary, crushed and bewildered by memories of the war and the postwar years to which, although some fifteen years in the past, he can still give no meaning. But the other inhabitants are in the same pass. Nothing is happening in this somnolent place, malarial with sinister memories of violence and mystery. From the forests, an occasional shot resounds. The legend is that "Huniady," a last survivor of the anticommunist bands, still wanders there with his rain-rusted weapon. (This background—the forest which harbors a mythical partisan, part-menace and part-savior—is a Polish convention: it is, for example, the setting of Kazimierz Brandys's marvelous novella "The Bear.")

Gradually, the narrator begins to associate with the people of the village. . . . Three personalities stand apart from them. One is Szafir, the silent and contemplative party secretary, who lives ostracized in his own house and broods on the coming fate of the valley. The others are Joseph Car and his wife Justine. From his house down by the river, Car brings the people of the village together in a strange redemptionist cult.

We begin to learn more about the unnamed narrator, as he is drawn close to Car and attracted to Justine, herself an orphan from forgotten massacres. His own past, hideously vivid and yet meaningless as a dream which cannot be banished, is materialized by flashbacks, disordered and out of sequence but slowly coming together as the novel develops. . . .

Still poisoned by guilt and hatred, he is searching. He is obsessed by one man, one swarthy face: the face of a man whose arrest during the occupation he failed to prevent, of the man whose execution after the war he failed to carry through. The narrator is still fighting in these dead struggles, like Huniady. It comes to him that the mythical Huniady is perhaps one Korvin, his sergeant in the Home Army and then his commander in the anticommunist guerrillas. And it comes to him that Joseph Car is that swarthy man, his victim and his betrayer, the man who must be confronted if his own torment is to be resolved. Delicately, Konwicki indicates that this man—or two, or three men: the dream is never explicit—is a Jew. The appearance, the persecution, the detachment converge with Joseph Car's remark: "It isn't easy to be an alien among your own people." But in fact all the villagers, and the narrator, have become such aliens, and Car through his cult seeks to release them from the original sin of the past.

Soon, the waters will cover everything. Since the fall of Stalinism after the war, the Poles have had the longest period of stability that the nation has been granted since the First Partition. Men and women born since the occupation are entering their thirties. The generation of those who survived the apocalypse, for whom all was decided by which forest you fought in, what color of brother-Pole you fired on, whether your exile was in Russia or the West, is beginning to pass away. At a party in Warsaw last year, one of that generation said to me: "At last, the age of biographies is over." Konwicki was in the room, his sharp face closed behind heavy spectacles, offering no comment. But his many novels, of which I believe this to be the best, are helping to terminate that age with the mercy and ceremony he allotted to Joseph Car. (p. 14)

> *Neal Aseherson, in* The New York Review of Books *(reprinted with permission from* The New York Review of Books; *copyright © 1976 NYREV, Inc.), May 27, 1976.*

Punishment deferred is the theme of . . . Tadeusz Konwicki's *A Dreambook for Our Time,* which is directly about the psychological costs of war and the fate of survivors. (pp. 761-62)

This is indeed a dreambook for not only does the past inhabit the present with inescapable recollections but present events themselves dissolve in a dreamlike haze of uncertainty. Here, as in Borowski's stories, the terrors of war lead to emotional anesthesia, though here too is a blurring of perception. As in a play by Beckett, the simplest acts are performed with maddening difficulty, and the most routine thoughts and recollections are achieved only through a tedi-

ous grappling with the will to forget. Mental life is involuntary while the present is suffocated in folds of anesthetic cotton.

And it is no wonder that Konwicki's hero reports back from within such a haze of sense, for the history he has witnessed is a rebuke to the senses. His generation was one that saw and felt too much, for which one remedy is the mortification of sense and the comparative comfort of autism. Comparative, since life also issues commands and they too must be satisfied: . . .

> The road of sterile vegetating, a state of dullness brought on by the biological rumination of days, cheating the memory by senile little pleasures in pushing checkers about. Is this the only alternative?

The book doesn't really answer that. . . . (p. 762)

> *Mark Shechner, in* The Nation *(copyright 1976 by The Nation Associates, Inc.), June 19, 1976.*

The past holds [all the characters of *A Dreambook for Our Time*] prisoner, for their attitudes toward the present have been conditioned by their experiences before and during the German occupation. The hero's consciousness is permeated by a double sense of betrayal. On the one hand, he has "betrayed" his mother (arrested in his stead during the war) and his fellow countrymen (in bloody reprisals against Communists after the German retreat). On the other hand, he has felt himself "betrayed" by the superior officer who expels him from his partisan unit for insubordination.

After the end of hostilities we know only that the narrator has joined the Communist Party, but he seems to have lost his affiliation with it by the time the novel's action begins. Tormented by guilt and traumatic memories, he is led to commit self-destructive acts which serve only to intensify his sense of alienation. Doomed to relive the frustration and failure of wartime days, he seeks understanding and possibly expiation through attempts to relive the past. Fragments of his earlier life are shown in unchronological flashbacks. These alternate with a somewhat fragmented succession of events in the present. A witness to evil, he finds himself drawn into the role of participant, then victim. Human relationships can offer him little solace; indeed, his sense of hopelessness is only intensified by a desultory and morbid love affair.

The main characters are defined in terms of certain recurring types who seem familiar to the narrator but whose personality traits are often blurred and contradictory. It is a universe basically hostile to any notion of Christian or romantic love. Nature—brooding, sinister, occasionally poignant—mirrors in its own excesses (a heat wave in November, followed by a cold and torrential flood) the perverse and obscure emotions of the actors. Superstition, myth and longing for the past sustain their feelings of resentment toward the new social order. Even Szafir, the local Party official (who is presented as a decent enough humanitarian), dies a victim of the pointless and irrational universe around him.

All in all, Konwicki's *Dreambook* projects a gloomy and nihilistic view of humanity. His grim caricatures perturb and sometimes amuse the reader, although they evoke little sympathy. This was possibly the author's intention: in any case, the novel's message is highly symbolic. The dream atmosphere, visual, pungent, yet impressionistic, inclines us to accept the work for what it is: a montage of apocalyptic events seen and relived by an obsessive and guilty imagination. (p. 464)

Reuel K. Wilson, in World Literature Today *(copyright 1977 by the University of Oklahoma Press), Vol. 51, No. 3, Summer, 1977.*

* * *

KRLEŽA, Miroslav 1893-

Krleža is a Croatian dramatist, novelist, short story writer, essayist, and poet. The most important Yugoslav writer, surpassing Ivo Andrić in the eyes of most critics, Krleža, a Marxist, has been chiefly concerned with the downfall of the Austro-Hungarian empire in his writings. A master stylist, Krleža has been compared with the great writers of Western Europe: Proust and Joyce. It is to Krleža's credit that he has not permitted the doctrine of socialist realism to limit or inhibit his creativity.

The volume and scope of Krleža's writings is vast and impressive. He has written more than fifty volumes of prose and poetry. Among his plays, the best known are *The Glembays, In Agony,* and *Leda,* all published in 1929. These plays constitute an organic entity, along with the short stories of the *Glembay* prose cycle. Here we meet the Glembays and the Fabriczys, two patrician families who marry, give birth, and die on the soil of Austria, Hungary, and Croatia between the days of Empress Maria Theresa (1717-1780) and those of the Auschwitz, Buchenwald, and Jasenovac concentration camps (1941-1945). (p. 10)

The geographical setting of almost all of Krleža's fiction is Pannonia, once a Roman province, today a territory encompassing western Hungary, eastern Austria, and northern Yugoslavia, bordered on the north and east by the Danube. The fact that Krleža refers to a modern region by its ancient name must be seen as both an attempt at universalization and as an ironical device: we are confronted with a part of the world that has been stagnating for many centuries. It is a real and at the same time mythical region, like Faulkner's Yoknapatawpha County, obeying the specific laws of the author's imagination. Nothing changes in Pannonia's utter desolation, where pigs eternally grunt, horses neigh, and somber women creep about in muddy hovels. (p. 12)

With Voltairian irony, Rabelaisian laughter, and Orwellian satire, Krleža ridicules the degraded Pannonian intellectual and moral climate. He bombards bourgeois respectability and every kind of oppression of the free expression of man's thoughts. He analyzes the origins of wealth among the Pannonian rich and somewhere on each genealogical tree he finds a murderer or a swindler. The first accumulation of capital reeks with the stench of blood. (p. 13)

A Funeral in Teresienburg is a long procession of impressive names and titles—Krleža's funeral oration over the dead body of a condemned system. What is being buried in *A Funeral in Teresienburg* is not only the body of a young first lieutenant but, more generally, everyone who walks behind the coffin: the dignitaries with heads devoid of a single intelligent thought, dentured and coifed waxlike figures in cloaks, helmets, straps, chains, bronze lions' heads, two-headed golden eagles—all the pomp and ceremony of a crumbling empire. (pp. 13-14)

Krleža portrays the peasants, the bourgeoisie, and the nobility who live in and around those small Pannonian towns

with poplars along the roads, the blacksmith shops and taverns, the steeples in the distance, and the brickyards on the edge of town where, when the bus returns at a monotonous pace from the hotel on the main square, everybody already knows who arrived that afternoon: a new officer or a traveling tie salesman. . . . But there is a fourth group in his fiction; the Pannonian Don Quixotes—the seekers, the dreamers, the prodigal sons, the neurotic artists and vagabonds who refuse to succumb to the Pannonian mentality, fighting to the very last to escape it. These heroes are Krleža's fallen angels who seem to have retained the memory of a former paradise they seek to recapture. Through them Krleža castigates and brilliantly illuminates the Pannonian mode of existence while at the same time criticizing the heroes' lofty dreams and attitudes. Some of these dreams glorify a particular woman, others an escape to a foreign country, still others the return home after futile wanderings abroad. . . . All are defeated and end in suicide or abandon or are completely shattered and full of remorse for their initial folly. (pp. 14-15)

In *Banquet in Blithuania* the liberal politician Niels Nielsen confronts the dictator Barutanski. The battle may appear at times to be futile; the ideal may seem weak compared to the political reality of the day. But Nielsen will continue to fight because—and this aptly illustrates one of Krleža's fundamental beliefs—against stupidity, violence, and arbitrariness the printed word still remains the most prestigious and effective weapon.

There are many more rebels, protesters, fantasts, and dropouts in Krleža's fiction. Leone, for instance, in the play *The Glembays,* is the prototype of Krleža's oversensitive, critical intellectual who denies his patrician family and the social order of his time. Krleža is fascinated, too, by Juraj Križanić, a seventeenth-century Croat who one day, laughed at by all his neighbors, set out from his village for Moscow in a horse-driven carriage full of books and documents, intent on alerting Russia's rulers to the historical obligation of Russia toward their Slavic brethren—only to be scorned and thrown into Siberian captivity where he remained for seventeen years—time enough to ponder his sin of idealism and imagine what his life could have been instead. (p. 16)

Krleža is attracted by tortured men whose lives are manuals of self-destruction. The same holds true for Krleža's women. If there be some general truth in the saying that women of twenty are crude, like Africa; women of thirty full of hope, like Asia; women of forty generous, like America; and women of fifty wise, like Europe, then it can be advanced that Krleža shows a predilection for portraying women in their forties, former beauties full of autumnal charm, rich in experience, open, hurt by life, with nothing to hide.

Only with these women can his equally tortured heroes find a few moments of deep understanding and meaningful respite. In describing such relationships Krleža has written some of his most beautiful pages, as, for instance, when Philip and Xenia Raday console themselves by attributing their sufferings, the deep wounds and beatings they have taken from life, to some ancestral, primeval force, feeling as if someone else's life is streaming through their hands, revealing itself in chance touches. Xenia Raday in *The Return of Philip Latinovicz,* Yadwiga Yesenska and Wanda in *On the Edge of Reason,* are all women whose very names evoke something languorous, and strangely attractive. And Laura Warronigg, the silly "twenty-year-old goose" in *The Love of Marcel Faber-Fabriczy for Miss Laura Warronigg,* becomes interesting only twenty years later when, as the tired, disappointed, and anxious heroine Baroness Lenbach in the play *In Agony,* she slowly but inevitably slips into suicide, struggling in vain to retain her last lover, Dr. Križovec. Time is dealing out poetic justice; the old wounds have been cauterized; life goes on. The rich texture of Krleža's prose integrates the swelling of memory, the nostalgia for childhood dreams and for a time of life and an epoch that are no longer. . . . (pp. 17-18)

[Krleža illuminates his fictional edifice] in his remarkable book of reminiscences, *A Childhood in Agram.* As a child Krleža slept under a baroque ceiling, gazing at it intently before closing his eyes. Later, when he began to write and throughout his career, he was to translate into literature that rich ceiling with its fallen and not-yet-fallen angels, devils, saints, warriors, trumpets, flutes, cymbals, drums, bows, arrows, candles, banners, horses, eagles, prayer books, and wreaths. (pp. 19-20)

In a broad sense, Central Europe is Krleža's literary territory, and Pannonia is part of Central Europe. He has peopled it with extravagant characters, corrupt and refined. He has ferociously attacked the Central European, Austro-Hungarian Pannonian bourgeois culture, but cannot help also admitting that this culture was able to produce a material civilization that on the whole compared favorably with that of the French. To understand Krleža one must bear in mind his own ambivalence. Along with his violent negation there exists a strong affirmation. He is in love with what he denigrates, just as he cannot help tearing apart the ideals of his dreamers for which, in the same breath, he voices profound nostalgia and admiration. When asked whether his Glembays and Fabriczys ever existed, he retorted: "Of course not. Had they existed, Zagreb would today be another Florence." They grew out of the baroque ceiling of his childhood and he made them live.

In *A Childhood in Agram,* Krleža recalls how, forty years later, the odor of old church books would bring back long-passed sensations of his earlist youth. . . . Krleža recalls the stillness of a room, the deep perspective formed in the shadow of a burning candle, the distant echo of thunder, the muffled roar of guns, the outpost with the young soldier who must kill for the first time, the penumbra of a church where one hears the twittering of swallows outside. All of these scents, noises, colors, perspectives Krleža weaves into the rich texture of his fiction.

One thing Krleža sensed from the very outset, deeply and intuitively—the existence of two different realities: One, a brute reality, used, abused, fragmentary, and diminished by the rational ideas of the man to whom the tree he observes hides the forest; the other, a pure, fantastic, virginally untouched reality that is fresh, childlike, and immediate, more real than the reality divided by reason. Consequently there are two kinds of people: First, men who have completely lost the link with their childhood, members of a molded and deformed humanity, actors reconciled to their parts, men turned gray and inert, fodder for statistics and consumer reports; the other, the poets, all those referred to by average talentless man as dreamers and schizoids, individuals who want to live life with the intensity of their childhood, for whom reality remains the prickly warm ball of a porcupine slowly moving in the dust under moonlight. The poet, the artist, the creator, the seeker is the man who remains, in the innermost core of himself, a child. And from the out-

set of his career Krleža has sided with that child against all the forces intent on annihilating him. (pp. 19-20)

Krleža has lived through a succession of isms—fascism, communism, and socialism, among others, and knows both sides of the coin only too well. He is equally suspicious of the right and the left. He expresses as does no one else in today's letters the wisdom of a third world that has demystified many consecrated historical, political, and artistic cults (p. 20).

Krleža's denials of certain ways of living rest on a deep personal faith from which they derive their strength and conviction. "To refuse the world is a way of accepting it," says Krleža in a statement that permits us better to understand the negative universe he creates in order to transform it through the very power of negation into its opposite.

There is something insufferable about a hot Sunday afternoon in August in one of the many Pannonian small towns with "gray, dusty, unwashed windowpanes, bare curtain rods, mothballed rugs, paper lanterns in the windows of stationery stores." It is on such a Sunday afternoon that the narrator in *The Cricket Beneath the Waterfall* runs into his old acquaintance Dr. Siroček and in a tavern tells him about the unusual things that have been happening to him recently—of how, for instance, he has been hearing voices of people who are no longer. Dr. Siroček listens with interest and sympathy. He invites the narrator into the latrine where once, beneath the waterfall, he heard the voice of a cricket. Ever since, Dr. Siroček carries bread crumbs in his pocket in case the cricket is heard again. The mere possibility of hearing its voice from out of the heart of the Pannonian wasteland transforms the loneliness of two people into a shared experience of human understanding.

Since the early part of the century when he began writing, wherever he has gone—in classrooms and in military barracks, in hospitals and prisons, behind coffins and on devil's islands, on trains and in hiding—Krleža has been following that voice into the darkest recesses of the night and of the heart of man. (p. 23)

> *Branko Lenski, in his introduction to* The Cricket beneath the Waterfall and Other Stories *by Miroslav Krleža, edited by Branko Lenski (copyright © 1972 by Vanguard Press; reprinted by permission of the publisher, Vanguard Press, Inc.), Vanguard, 1972.*

Aside from the novel *The Return of Philip Latinovicz . . .* and a few stories here and there, the prolific work of the leading contemporary Croatian writer Miroslav Krleža, a repeated nominee for the Nobel Prize, is still largely unknown to the English-speaking reader. As the first collection of his short stories in English, *The Cricket beneath the Waterfall and Other Stories* goes a long way toward rectifying this omission. (p. 185)

[The six stories comprising this book] are among the best of Krleža's stories. Written over a span of several decades and varying in length from a few pages to a short novel, they display the rich repertoire of a seasoned writer: a keen interest in what is important to the contemporary reader, a skill in creating unforgettable characters and above all an ability to understand and recreate the specific atmosphere of his milieu—Croatia of the last two centuries. A Marxist practically all his life, Krleža has always felt that literature should have a social function. That he has not fallen prey to the deadening dicta of a didactic and propagandistic literature inherent in such a method as socialist realism—against which he has always fought vigorously—can be attributed largely to his immense artistic talent. For Krleža is first an artist and then a social revolutionary. In a very informative introduction to the book the editor Branko Lenski says that Krleža "expresses as does no one else in today's letters the wisdom of a third world that has demystified many consecrated historical, political and artistic cults" [see excerpt above]. Thus by keeping a proper balance between his art and his views he has succeeded in remaining an always fresh and pure writer.

The stories depict Krleža's favorite environment—a corner of Central Europe comprising parts of Croatia, Austria and Hungary, which he mythically calls Pannonia. Skillfully translated by various hands, they abundantly show Krleža as a very contemporary writer even though some of them were written almost half a century ago. (pp. 185-86)

Vasa D. Mihailovich, in Books Abroad *(copyright 1974 by the University of Oklahoma Press), Vol. 48, No. 1, Winter, 1974.*

A few casually uttered home truths change the course of a man's life in ["On the Edge of Reason," a] mordant parable about social convention, injustice, and hypocrisy. Mr. Krleža is a Croatian writer who examines human folly under a microscope, and all varieties seem to repel him equally. The main character is a respectable middle-aged lawyer who scandalizes a dinner party and eventually gets thrown in jail for insulting his host, a pious profiteer who has been boasting to his guests about how he once shot four peasants who were attempting to steal his wine. In rapid succession, everyone the lawyer knows turns against him, and he loses his wife, his friends, his job, and, eventually, his sanity. The story is narrated by the gradually less sane-sounding lawyer, and, though his plight is horrendous, it is hard to feel much about him, perhaps because the author garlands his martyrdom too lavishly. (p. 140)

The New Yorker (© 1977 by The New Yorker Magazine, Inc.), April 11, 1977.

L

LARKIN, Philip 1922-

British poet, novelist, essayist, and jazz critic, Larkin is a poet of disillusionment, of timid, inhibited characters easily resigned to defeat. If his concerns appear too narrow and his style too conventional, Larkin more than compensates for his limitations by his wit and his intelligence. Many critics consider him the finest poet in England today. (See also *CLC*, Vols. 3, 5, and *Contemporary Authors*, Vols. 5-8, rev. ed.)

High Windows has been allowed to set the terms of its own discussion, as if there were no criteria beyond its own criteria, as if it was a book above criticism.

If only Larkin had given us another collection on the level of *The Less Deceived* or *The Whitsun Weddings,* we would indeed have cause to be grateful, deeply so. *High Windows,* alas, is not nearly so consistent an achievement as they were, and for reasons which are important, and seem to contradict Larkin's own avowed belief that a poet does not need to develop. For the lesson of this book seems to be that in poetry you cannot stand still: if you do not move forwards, then you begin to move backwards, or slip sideways.

Larkin himself has said that he doesn't know how he writes well, and looking at the best poems in *High Windows* one can see to what an extent the impulse is involuntary. The title poem gives us the clue:

> And immediately
> Rather than words comes the thought of
>   high windows:
> The sun-comprehending glass,
> And beyond it, the deep blue air, that shows
> Nothing, and is nowhere, and is endless.

Rather than words, the image. Perhaps Larkin's most distinctive poems are those which achieve themselves by a sudden dislocation of the argument into a visual image that 'leaves / Nothing to be said.' In *The Less Deceived* 'Wedding Wind', 'Next, Please' and 'Deceptions' all use this technique, in very different ways. In *The Whitsun Weddings* a visual image initiates the movement of 'Dockery And Son': in 'Days' another sharply concludes it. In his new collection Larkin relies on this technique more than ever before, and the conclusive images of 'High Windows', 'Friday Night in the Royal Station Hotel', 'Money' and 'The Explosion' are, I suspect, what we will chiefly re-

member from it. Other poets, Auden, for instance, can conjure up any number of apt, illustrative images, snap-shots and vignettes, as Larkin himself can: but only Larkin produces, as if by a jerk of the unconscious, images at once so plangent and so final. (p. 112)

Larkin's previous work should remind us how much is missing. Looking back to 'Here', 'The Whitsun Weddings', 'An Arundel Tomb', one sees that the visual haunting was there alright, but as part of a much broader, more inclusive structure. The effort of style that this implies, supporting and extending, even, perhaps, evoking the involuntary impulse, is central to Larkin's achievement in his best work. The procedure of these poems is as much metaphysical as visual. Indeed, they have a strong sense of being thoroughly argued through. Their assimilation of the reality that surrounds them is equally thorough. It was these poems, after all, that altered our awareness of poetry's capacity to reflect the contemporary world. As deliberate as Larkin's self-restriction to idiosyncrasy elsewhere is his assumption here of a communal voice, which continues through such poems as 'Ambulances', 'Faith Healing' and 'Essential Beauty'. Wasn't there, in fact, a very real development from the totally private world of *The Less Deceived,* only falteringly foreshadowed in 'Church Going', and stylistically perhaps in 'I Remember, I Remember'? 'The Whitsun Weddings' could almost be seen as a translation into contemporary speech of the final sonorities of 'Church Going'. Perception, colloquialism, and humour are welded together into what is, as much as anything, a triumphant technical resolution.

Where in *High Windows* would one look to find anything approaching this marriage of humanity and technique? Only to 'The Old Fools' or 'Vers de Société', and they're unequal marriages. One should be able to look to 'To the Sea' or 'Show Saturday', but set either of those beside 'The Whitsun Weddings' and they look pretty inert. Or compare 'Ambulances', whose verse form binds its ironies so tightly, with the pedestrian pace of 'The Building'.

That the weakness of *High Windows* should reveal itself as a technical weakness is not surprising, though it is surprising that it hasn't been the subject of comment. Technical advance, surely, results from a poet's engagement and recalcitrant material, and there's abundant evidence in *High Windows* to show that there's been no such engagement. In this respect, the way in which 'Show Saturday' fails to clinch its 'regenerate union' is symptomatic. Larkin's stylistic unity, of the colloquial and the sacramental, is falling apart, because his two mental worlds have fallen apart. We are either among 'the rusting soup-tins', with a strong sense of *déjà-vu,* or, more often, we are back pre-1914, before innocence had left the country.... 'The Trees', 'Dublinesque', 'How Distant', 'Cut Grass', 'The Explosion' all suggest a quick answer to the old charge that Larkin is a neo-Georgian: one can discard the neo-, and simply say Georgian. This is a step back in every sense: compare the stiff monotone of 'Forget What Did' or 'Cut Grass' with the subtlety of 'Coming' in *The Less Deceived.*

Nowhere, outside the journeyman 'Going, Going', do the England of Larkin's imagination and the England in which we really live come into the sort of conflict that could generate further advance. *High Windows* shows a talent in retreat to the edges of its concern. The edges of a talent are strange regions. 'Solar' or 'The Explosion' suggest that Larkin may continue to write poems in whose quality there is an element of the miraculous: but he will no longer be, he is not already, the Larkin we have valued up till now, a man writing out of the centre of his talent, making poetry from the world in which he and his readers actually live. (pp. 113-14)

> *Roger Garfitt, in* London Magazine *(©* London Magazine *1974), October-November, 1974.*

Larkin is really one of the best poets now writing, a somewhat bitter swan plunging down the waters of the so sad Thames. He is a dangerous satirical poet, killing where Betjeman is comfy. And yet he is an inheritor of the sweetest strains of English poesy, at times as lucid and airy and heartening as Wordsworth, Spenser, or Shakespeare. He deserves to be, human and lovely as he is, a classic. (p. 50)

> Virginia Quarterly Review *(copyright, 1976, by the* Virginia Quarterly Review, *The University of Virginia), Vol. 52, No. 2 (Spring, 1976).*

Philip Larkin describes ["Jill," his] first novel, originally published in 1946, as "in essence an unambitious short story." This is a modest remark, and the modesty is not misplaced, for "Jill" is indeed a quiet, gray, inconclusive little book, with a gray hero, and a plot so slight that readers might be forgiven for thinking, as I did, that the final blank pages of the volume were a mistake of the printers, and that some dramatic denouement had been accidentally omitted. But this is not so: the inconsequential ending is deliberate. Some might expect this of Larkin, the poet of half-tones and gray moods, suburban melancholy and accepted regrets, but in fact the poet is much better at conclusions than the novelist: most of Larkin's poems, at least in his last three volumes, are remarkable for their devastating and bitter punch lines. In "Jill," there is much of the gloom, little of the bitter precision of wit.

Nevertheless, it is an interesting book for several reasons. It was written when the author was 21, and has some most accomplished passages of descriptive prose—notably the hero's visit to his bombed hometown, Huddlesford. (Larkin's own birthplace was Coventry, one of the most heavily bombarded towns in Britain.) At the least, it is a noteworthy piece of juvenilia by one of England's finest poets. It also has, according to the American critic James Gindin, the first example of "that characteristic landmark of the British postwar novel, the displaced working-class hero."...

As a working-class hero, in fact, John is singularly spineless: unlike the defiant and ambitious characters that people the novels and plays of Amis, Wain, Braine, Osborne, Wesker, he seems all too keen to learn the ways of his social superiors, even when those ways [are] repulsive.... None of the joys, all the embarrassments of youth are carefully catalogued. Maybe this is Larkin's point. Being young was not much fun in those days, for that kind of boy. In a poem published recently, "Annus Mirabilis," the older Larkin deplores the fact that the younger Larkin missed out on the good times, and was too old for the wonderful year of 1963, when the Beatles and sexual intercourse were invented. Times have changed, and "Jill" is certainly a useful sociological record by which to date those changes.

But perhaps the most curious section of this volume is Larkin's own introduction. There are, in fact, two introductions, one written in 1963, and a postscript to it, composed specially for this edition in 1975. Anyone interested in the history of attitudes and ideas will find these compelling reading. In the 1963 section, Larkin sets out, ostensibly, to explain wartime Oxford to the American reader. This was not, he says, the rowdy lavish Oxford of Evelyn Waugh's "Decline and Fall," where young bloods threw champagne parties and threw one another in fountains: it was a more serious, sober place, and was far less concerned with class distinctions. This seems a curious preface to a novel in which people do indeed drink too much (admittedly beer), throw one another in fountains and appear to be more class conscious than would seem conceivable to the average 18-year-old today. Larkin then goes on to tell us that he himself was not at all like his protagonist John, and that he had a lot of lovely friends. This passage I found wholly mystifying. Until I read it. I thought I knew what Oxford was like; after finishing it, quite bemused by a string of Christian names—Norman who? Bruce who? Kingsley who? Ah yes, thank goodness one can spot *that* one, Kingsley Amis—I felt that Oxford was, after all, an exclusive clique about which the outsider could never learn a thing. So much for explanations for foreigners and youngsters.

In the 1975 addendum, Larkin remarks that despite all efforts to dissociate himself from the feeble John, he still finds readers identify him with his own creation. This annoys him, as does, apparently, the passing of the collegiate system that his own novel renders so unattractive. And, finally, he disclaims the myth that he was himself a scholarship boy: "thanks to my father's generosity," he says drily, "my education was at no time a charge on public or other funds." This may be a dry joke: it may be a genuine disclaimer of virtues of effort he never possessed; but it is worth remarking, (in Larkin's words "American readers may need reminding") that it is an extraordinary thing for an Englishman to say. The phrase "a charge on public funds" rings very oddly. One wonders what the 1984 introduction will have to say about British education. (p. 5)

> *Margaret Drabble, in* The New York Times Book Review *(© 1976 by The New York Times Company; reprinted by permission), May 16, 1976.*

No living poet can equal Larkin on his own ground of the familiar English lyric, drastically and poignantly limited in its sense of any life beyond, before or after, life today in England. Within these limits the life is registered with superb economy and immediacy. So much so that when reading Larkin one often feels that no poet could write much closer to the quick of post-Christian, post-imperial England without also surrendering to those of its elements (mainly commercial but civic and political too) which, a few years ago in a poem called 'England', Davie was attacking with clipped invective as obscene, false and vandalistic. . . . Yet in spite of 'lapses' which outside their ironic context sound like total capitulations to the enemy ('Books are a load of crap'), Larkin shares just as much of Davie's lower-middle/professional-class sense of *pudeur* and care for politeness as is consistent with his, less frontal, way of caring for social truth—that is, by not respecting sacred cows or underwriting any promises of pneumatic bliss. The most 'common' feature of his work is a recurrent cautionary tale of frustrations beforehand and desolations afterwards which we all suffer because of the expansive fantasies we pay, twice over, to share with our various pundits and image-makers. If in Larkin's England the fantasies are unusually timid and cozy (as compared with those of, say, Emma Bovary or Jay Gatsby), they just as often, and more cruelly, betray. At the same time, though, Larkin frequently exposes the funny Walter Mitty side of the picture and discovers not merely a few minor beans-and-bangers satisfactions in the only life we have but also, in himself and others, shy tendernesses and risible family likenesses which *do* help brace one for the inevitable one-way excursion down Cemetery Road.

Larkin himself is now the nation's most successful maker of poetic images, and his work surely must become increasingly important and consolatory for an England of still-diminishing expectations. For within the limits of his expectations of poetry and people, Larkin is a great and even national poet, and few poets who work outside those limits —Ted Hughes is a partial exception—can hope to match his popular value and appeal. (pp. 45-6)

George Dekker, in Agenda, *Summer, 1976.*

Philip Larkin's most irreverent revision of John Keats rejects the famous dichotomy of the "Ode on a Grecian Urn." "I have always believed," Larkin writes, "that beauty is beauty, truth truth, that is not all ye know on earth nor all ye need to know.". . . Yet Larkin's achievement as a poet demonstrates a more profound reappraisal of romantic values than is evident in any of his wryly dogmatic critical pronouncements. In particular, "The Whitsun Weddings" may be viewed as a searching revaluation of Keats's art in the "Ode on a Grecian Urn."

Larkin himself discourages such comparative treatment of his work. He has stated that one of the pleasures of writing poetry is the release it bestows "from reading poems by other people," and that "experience makes literature look insignificant beside life.". . . Life would seem to have wholly displaced art as a source for this poet's inspiration.

Yet his persistent choice of traditional poetic forms creates an undeniable link between his work and that of previous poets, even as his comments disclaim any connection. . . . Especially in so highly accomplished a poet as Larkin, traditional form actively contributes to the poem's experience, enlarging its range of meaning instead of acting merely as a "transparent" means of expression. Thus, when Philip Larkin chooses to write "The Whitsun Weddings" in the stanzaic form that Keats evolved for his great odes, his decision allows a wider frame of reference to enrich and interact with the experiences that his poem conveys—

whether or not that frame of reference is uppermost in his reflections about the process of composition.

This characteristic resonance of traditional form gives warrant for an interpretation of "The Whitsun Weddings" that takes account of its distinctive formal context. I take further warrant from a critical principle that is more appreciative than formalist, one voiced most memorably by Eliot in "Tradition and the Individual Talent": "No poet, no artist of any art, has his complete meaning alone. His significance, his appreciation, is the appreciation of his relation to the dead poets and artists. You cannot value him alone; you must set him, for contrast and comparison, among the dead." The approach may represent what Larkin derisively calls "poetry as syllabus," but I believe that it allows us to achieve a fuller valuation of at least one of his poems. (pp. 529-31)

[Keats's odes] share a common goal: the attainment of timelessness through art, a romantic theme that they carry to its highest pitch. . . . For Philip Larkin, however, "our element is time." Instead of inhabiting some untrodden region of the poet's mind and encouraging him to "leave the world unseen," poetry has the task of recording and reflecting on the imperfect, transitory experiences of the mundane reality that the poet shares with his readers.

Like his acknowledged master, Hardy, Larkin roots his poems deeply in the world of time, and documents its effects on us. For Keats's images of pastoral detachment and transcendent ecstasy, he substitutes material sights and sounds: sixty-watt bulbs, jabbering (TV) sets, tin advertisements, cheap suits, and man caught for good or ill in the middle, laden with his "depreciating luggage." Given this extreme difference in emphasis, it is remarkable that Larkin should have chosen to adopt Keats's form for one of his poems; but what is more remarkable is the extent to which he has both subtly answered the form's romantic challenges and made it assume, with great vitality and appropriateness, a shape that expresses his own values. A detailed comparison of the "Ode on a Grecian Urn" and "The Whitsun Weddings" reveals the complexity of Larkin's revision.

The ode has traditionally been an atemporal form, tending to remove its subjects from specific contexts of time and place, and to celebrate them in structures whose organization is spatial or musical rather than temporal. The organization of Keats's stanzas reinforces this characteristic. . . . Such stanzas accord perfectly with Keats's desire to present an ideal of beauty beyond the reach of time, and they condition us to accept it through their own playing of a kind of timeless "music," "For ever piping songs for ever new."

The Keatsian stanzas of "The Whitsun Weddings" underline that poem's thematic concerns in an equally masterful way, but Larkin's structure is as different from Keats's as his themes are. A succession of similarly rhymed stanzas (all *ababcdecde*) leads the reader on an unbroken movement through time that mirrors the narrator's progress on the train. The unfolding of this narrative action links the stanzas into a tight sequence, and this effect is furthered by Larkin's characteristic habit of running his stanzas into each other. . . . As both narrator and newly married couples are picked up and carried along on a fixed, timetabled journey—over whose speed and direction they can exercise no control—so the reader is drawn by these stanzas into a steady temporal progression. We become predisposed towards viewing time as "our element," rather than as a frame that can be transcended.

The presence of a foreshortened line in each stanza would break this pattern if Larkin used it as Keats did in the "Ode to Psyche" and "Ode to a Nightingale." But where Keats introduced shorter lines towards the ends of his stanzas, which quicken through this overturning of our expectations, Larkin shortens the second line of every stanza. This burst of energy, offering the possibility of other directions, loses itself in the seven pentameter lines that follow; its life is absorbed into the regular flow of each stanza, soft sift in an hourglass. "A slow and stopping curve southwards we kept": Larkin's stanzas direct us to the unrelenting flow of time as surely as Keats's proclaim the remoteness of art from its course. (pp. 531-33)

Keats approaches the urn's supramundane essence through a mode of description that, appropriately, abounds in unanswerable questions (seven in the first stanza) and paradoxes; and the word "ever" sounds a constant leitmotif to remind us that the urn or, by implication, art itself, does not essentially belong to our world of time.

"The Whitsun Weddings" roots us at once in time ("That Whitsun") and manifests a concern with time ("I was late getting away"). Larkin sets the train in a context of precise calculation ("One-twenty," "three-quarters-empty") appropriate to this central symbol which is both poetically and literally a vehicle in motion rather than a fixed mark. In opposition to the mysterious otherworldliness of Keats's first stanza, Larkin's involves our senses in a situation: "we" feel the hotness of the cushions, are blinded by the glare of windscreens, and smell the fish-dock. Soon a noise of "whoops and skirls" appeals to yet another sense, in contrast to the silence of the urn's unheard melodies. The train proceeds on its journey, advancing by means more solid than Keats's questions and paradoxes: it picks up a cargo of sympathetically observed human details—uncles shouting smut, children frowning, girls gripping their handbags tighter. These details represent what John Wain has called a "connoisseurship of the particular," and they show how much this poet has learned from the novelist he once was.

Larkin realizes, however, that we must pay a price for such full involvement in the world of time: the urn exists in a perpetual morning, but the train moves gradually from "short-shadowed cattle," past the "Long shadows" of poplars later in the afternoon, until finally walls of blackened moss "Came close, and it was nearly done." The wedding days are coming to an end, and the train's progress realizes the full emotional ambiguity of a word—prominent in the titles of two earlier Larkin poems—that captures this mingling of happy beginnings and poignant endings: departures. This poem's leitmotif consists not of "ever," but of words and phrases that recall us to the ticking of the clock: "late," "hurry," "At first," "next time," "at last," "in time," "long enough," "this hour."

Keats instead suggests, through a series of references to the supernatural, that the urn's proper sphere is more divine than mortal. . . . The constant renewal and transcendent permanence of religion suggest and symbolize that of art.

Nothing like this overtly religious setting appears in Larkin's poem, even though its title refers to both a holy day and a sacrament. Faithful to his own vision and the values of his age, Larkin places us "out on the end of an event": his brides and grooms emerge from cafés and banquet halls

rather than from churches. . . . "The Whitsun Weddings" would seem to testify not only that art serves life, but that life serves a time unquickened by transcendent impulses; and the contrast between this view and that of the ode is so great that Larkin's poem would seem to share only a rhyme scheme with Keats's. Near the end of the poem, however, we witness an experience that transforms this impression.

In the last stanza of "The Whitsun Weddings," Larkin creates his version of the vital moment of fulfillment at the center of the ode, where Keats conveyed an ecstatic vision of ideal beauty. . . . Larkin's dénouement is as much descriptive as visionary, yet it does not lack intensity. Instead of being animated by the thought of permanence, it gathers strength from "the power / That being changed can give." As the train journey comes to an end, the poem fills with words that generate an image of consummation: "loosed," "tightened," "took hold," "swelled," "sense of falling," "arrow-shower." But to pick out these words and list them is to distort the poem's effect while trying to explain it: in its context, the sexual symbolism moves us profoundly without calling attention to itself; it works as inconspicuously as Larkin's syntax in the last sentence, which carries us effortlessly from literal brakes to metaphorical rain:

> We slowed again,
> And as the tightened brakes took hold, there swelled
> A sense of falling, like an arrow-shower
> Sent out of sight, somewhere becoming rain.

The train's entrance to the tunnel and arrival at its destination carries, ever so gently, overtones of the most personal and lifegiving of human "arrivals." This beautiful fulfillment resolves a slight element of suspense created by the poised images of the previous stanza's landscape, where "An Odeon went past, a cooling tower, / And someone running up to bowl." More important, it releases the "power" of the marriages that the train has steadily taken on during the course of the afternoon and informs that power with shape and purpose.

The connotations of this fulfillment are not only sexual. As one responds to the swelling sense of falling that envelops the "dozen" couples "sitting side by side," one recalls with a sharp tender shock that these are *Whitsun* weddings; and the recollection confirms one's feeling that another kind of consummation is also being imaged here. . . . The "power" that Larkin depicts in the final stanza is a profoundly spiritual one, like the "power" bestowed on the apostles at Pentecost, after Christ had been taken "out of their sight". . . . That the poem should turn towards a religious experience after portraying the wedding parties in overwhelmingly secular terms, may be explained in part by Larkin's own conclusion in "Church Going":

> someone will forever be surprising
> A hunger in himself to be more serious,
> And gravitating with it to this ground. . . .

> (pp. 533-36)

Keats conceives an absolute separation between the visionary and mundane experiences. . . . Larkin's vision is not one which fades, however, when we step back into the world of time. Rather, it is a product of that world, and the structure of "The Whitsun Weddings" underlines its nature by letting us experience it at the end of the poem—as a destination, not a flight.

Probably no other aspect of "The Whitsun Weddings" reflects more clearly the extent to which Larkin has revised the romantic outlook of the "Ode on a Grecian Urn." When Keats set stanzas 3 and 4 apart from the rest, even giving them a different rhyme scheme, he emphasized the remoteness of the visionary moment from the world around it. Larkin's final stanza moves through the same rhyme scheme as all those before it; by making the stanzaic pattern that of the poem's liberating vision he expresses a belief that the moment of fulfillment comes about *through* time rather than in spite of it. Even though the short second line of each stanza has subsumed its freedom and energy into a steady temporal progression, it turns out that the latter movement brings "all the power" of the incomparably greater sense of release which concludes the poem and informs its passengers. Time has transfigured them. (pp. 536-37)

[The] whole experience depicted here, of arrival at a terminus, points to the most irrevocable of "departures." All of these associations both qualify and accompany the poem's vision of fulfillment. The last stanza unfolds as a moving elaboration of an oxymoron formed earlier: "happy funeral." The poem brings us to an awareness of time as simultaneously both a destructive and a creative force. The ecstasy of Keats's "happy, happy boughs" is achievable, but such happiness is inseparable from the recognition that the boughs *do* shed their leaves.

The magnitude of Larkin's revision of Keats may perhaps be best appreciated by comparing it with one more widely celebrated. In the last stanza of "Sunday Morning," Wallace Stevens echoes the ending of Keats's ode "To Autumn.". . . The great strength of Stevens' revision derives from its use of a similar landscape to capture and convey a mood of mixed ripeness and decay that masterfully approximates the mood of Keats's poem, even as Stevens varies the tone to emphasize not so much the poignancy as the voluptuousness of the scene. Larkin sets himself a still more formidable task. While Stevens chose to echo a poem that expressed ideas rather close to his own, replaces the more typical romantic urge towards transcendence with an acceptance of mutability that strikingly anticipates Stevens' more modern view; but the "Ode on a Grecian Urn" embodies in every respect the romantic viewpoint repudiated by both Stevens and Larkin. "The Whitsun Weddings" is a revision in the fullest sense of the word, a critical second look at the validity of an earlier approach.

One might ask what Larkin gains from formally associating his poem with Keats's ode. Besides acting as a contrasting ground against which Larkin can define his own position, the ode offers an ideal of ecstatic fulfillment for him to aim at—and to approach from a different direction. By leaving "All breathing human passion" behind, the ode's central stanza arrived at one of the most perfect romantic expressions of visionary joy; but "The Whitsun Weddings" shows how an acceptance of the world abandoned by Keats can bring a profound spiritual fulfillment that stands the test of comparison with Keats's. In Larkin's poem, joy is found in the consummation of love rather than in an infinite postponement always "near the goal" but never reaching it. In keeping with its leitmotif of temporal allusions mentioned above, "The Whitsun Weddings" rejects both the ever ("For ever wilt thou love") and the never ("never canst thou kiss") of Keats's poem; instead it accepts without reservation the "changes" that time brings to its fresh couples. These couples are living, breathing mortals (*"I nearly died"*), not marble men and maidens. (pp. 538-39)

His art incorporates far more of that world than did Keats's

exclusively "sylvan" historian; yet the movement and details of "The Whitsun Weddings" revitalize Keats's form— what other modern poet has used it so successfully?—as they criticize its purpose. Larkin has shone new light on a traditional form, and in doing so, has illuminated and probed some of the most moving experiences of contemporary life. Far from selling poetry short [as some critics claim], such an approach redefines and, for many readers, widens the boundaries of the art. (p. 540)

*John Reibetanz, "'The Whitsun Weddings':
Larkin's Reinterpretation of Time and Form
in Keats," in* Contemporary Literature (©
*1976 by the Board of Regents of the University of Wisconsin System), Vol. 17, No. 4,
Autumn, 1976, pp. 529-40.*

Between *The Less Deceived* ([Philip Larkin's] first mature collection) and *The Whitsun Weddings* there had been no essential change in either thematic material or style. Yet, despite the success of *The Whitsun Weddings,* one wondered whether Larkin could go on like this, working the same thin vein. How long could he make poetry from the conviction that none of the choices of life is really preferable, that all the ways one spends a life are not ways of living but "ways of slow dying"? Already in *The Whitsun Weddings* a few of the poems had seemed a little too familiar. Would not the problem become more severe now that there were even more poems behind him? Without some major breakthrough, would not Larkin become entrapped in sterile repetition and self-imitation? But what development was possible? The very condition of Larkin's success was his rejection of most of the materials of poetry, his conviction that there were only a few subjects worth talking about and that these subjects might leave, in the words of one of his poems, "nothing to be said."

A new collection, *High Windows,* has now appeared and it is at once exciting and disappointing: exciting because Larkin, by viewing his familiar materials from a slightly different perspective, has found a way to renew his poetry; disappointing because that new perspective at times reveals a distasteful side, hitherto concealed, to all Larkin's poetry. This new perspective may be described by the words ritual and habit. Larkin's central theme has always been survival in a world without value, a world with all coherence gone. His strength as a poet has been his ability to confront this world and describe it without lament. Behind the modest surface of his poems there was always an intellectual fearlessness. In *High Windows* Larkin explores the ways in which ritual and repeated domestic events may give some slight meaning and coherence to the world. In the best poems in this volume, this sense of ritual exists side by side with Larkin's earlier, unflinching vision; in the weaker ones, ritual becomes an escape and Larkin becomes nostalgic, launching simplistic attacks on the commercial values of modern England and lamenting the loss of the aristocratic and hierarchical values of merry old England. Fortunately, the good poems in *High Windows* far outweigh the weak ones. (pp. 481-82)

In his overinsistence upon the commercialization of the modern world [as in "Show Saturday"] Larkin betrays a hankering for an idealized past that is disappointing after all those earlier poems in which he faced the empty present so courageously. (p. 483)

[In the title poem] there is an implicit lament for those "Bonds and gestures" now lost which once made life coherent. Instead of presenting this as positive doctrine, Larkin crystallizes it in a beautiful and terrifying image:

> Rather than words comes the thought of high windows:
> The sun-comprehending glass,
> And beyond it, the deep blue air, that shows
> Nothing, and is nowhere, and is endless.

The pristine image comes as a shock after the brutal concreteness of the earlier stanzas (a device Larkin has used successfully in the past). Those high windows may indeed be part of an Anglican church but the image renders the emptiness of a world without value-giving ritual in a way unattainable through explicit social commentary.

The concern of *High Windows* with the survival of ritual is by no means a totally new element in Larkin's poetry. In a sense, it has always been present as the obverse of Larkin's conviction that all our *individual* hopes prepare the way for disappointment. As early as the poem, "Church Going," he had predicted that the meaning of the church and of the rituals it held, "marriage, and birth, / And death, and thoughts of these," would never be completely lost. In the title poem of *The Whitsun Weddings* Larkin handled these themes in a way which foreshadows "Show Saturday" and the present volume generally. But in the earlier collections, the concern with the shared experiences of life is a minor note and is balanced by the fear that death empties even these moments of their meaning. In *High Windows* the poet, either with increased confidence or in increased desperation, concentrates again and again on the possibilities offered by vestigial ritual.

Through this concentration, Larkin escapes the mere repetition of his earlier achievements. Indeed this new focus seems to free his imagination as he develops an impressive series of strategies for exploring his ideas. In "To the Sea," the first and one of the best poems in the volume, Larkin follows a format similar to that of "The Whitsun Weddings," observing "the miniature gaiety of seasides" and speculating

> It may be that through habit these do best,
> Coming to water clumsily undressed
> Yearly; teaching their children by a sort
> Of clowning; helping the old, too, as they ought.

Through such habit, no matter how clumsy, the parts of life are drawn together once more. In the first and third parts of the triptych, "Livings," and again in "The Card-Players," historical vignettes are used to contrast the security of an habitual present with the sort of cold, empty exterior seen through the high windows. In "Friday Night in the Royal Station Hotel" the same contrast is made in a contemporary setting.... With a deceptive lightheartedness the same themes are developed in "*Vers de Société*" in terms of the unpleasant partying of social occasions. Even of these trivial occasions the poet can ask:

> Are, then, these routines
>
> Playing at goodness, like going to church? . . .

From poem to poem, Larkin shifts his angle of vision, presenting new sides of his central concern. The result is a volume even stronger as a whole than as separate poems.

Not all the poems in *High Windows* focus on these concerns but most of the best do and where others appear, such as "The Old Fools" and "The Building," which

harken back more completely to earlier stances, they are made more interesting by the juxtaposition. (pp. 484-86)

Stephen David Lavine, "Larkin's Supreme Versions," in The Michigan Quarterly Review *(copyright © The University of Michigan, 1976), Fall, 1976, pp. 481-86.*

Admittedly, Larkin's laconic, scaled-down, wryly pessimistic poems are not to everyone's liking, and there are times when his determinedly plain style comes to seem rather forced; but the achievement of such collections as *The Whitsun Weddings* (1964) and *High Windows* (1974) is incontestable. I know people who can quote passages from "Church Going" and "The Whitsun Weddings" with a zest that would have astonished Dylan Thomas, and must now astonish those who believe that poetry, in order to be loved, must celebrate rather than condemn, and must strive to approximate music rather than to give us back, with very few distracting flourishes, the rhythms and nuances of "ordinary" speech. (p. 38)

Willing himself to be unexceptional, taking for his own a provincial English landscape writ painfully small, Larkin has created a number of nearly perfect poems and two very interesting novels which address themselves to the question of what to make of a "diminished thing" (to use Frost's helpful terminology). Larkin might say that the "diminished thing" is life itself—

> What are days for?
> Days are where we live.
> They come, they wake us
> Time and time over.
> They are to be happy in:
> Where can we live but days?

—but an impartial observer might speculate that the true subject of Larkin's poetry is England: the waning of English civilization: the paralysis of the spirit when it is confronted by historical changes beyond its ability to gauge. In his preface to *Jill* (1946), Larkin's first novel, he has said: "At an age when self-importance would have been normal, events cut us ruthlessly down to size." Though he is speaking of wartime England in this case, his sentiment holds true for present-day England, and both *Jill* and *A Girl in Winter* will strike readers as absolutely contemporary—perhaps even prophetic.

A Girl in Winter . . . is a highly sensitive, rather meditative and slowly moving novel, a work of deliberately modest proportions reminiscent of Virginia Woolf and the early Elizabeth Bowen: a poet's novel, one might be inclined to say, in which a not-extraordinary provincial town in the depths of winter is lovingly reconstructed. Perhaps not lovingly: Larkin is never sentimental. But there is an unmistakable pleasure in his descriptions of ugly old buildings and wan, joyless people and crowded buses and insufferable dentists' offices and the futile, hopeful, and ultimately doomed gestures people make toward one another. His heroine, a young woman named Katherine Lind, shares with the Larkin of the poems a readiness to accept limitations and even to welcome the frustration of desire—a perverse eagerness to celebrate the failure of the world's enchantment. It is not other people, after all, who disappoint us, but rather our own foolish expectations: and so we are better off when, like Katherine, we turn resolutely aside from the entanglements of human emotion. We should make of the deadening winter an ally, and see in its relentless chill our own icy souls. (pp. 38-9)

The novel's central weakness lies in its characters, who are so without motivation and purpose that one finds it difficult to care very much for them. Katherine Lind is shadowy and vaporous, lacking distinctive features.... Unless the young woman is a zombie, or a near-catatonic, her failure to think or feel *anything* is quite improbable.

It is possible, of course, to read *A Girl in Winter* as a prose-poem in which nothing happens, and to insubstantial people, because such is the nature of life in the 20th century in England. Larkin has the ability to evoke, in a few bleak images, a sense of waste and disillusion and emptiness that is as profound as the similarly barren vision of Beckett; but one might argue that so minimal a vision is perhaps best rendered in non-naturalistic terms, in parody or absurdist drama or in brief poems. The fleshing-out of a novel requires human blood and warmth, the interplay of personalities, the possibility of change and surprise. At the conclusion of "Church Going" the poet concludes that "the place was not worth stopping for" and—whether this cynical observation strikes the reader as true or not—a place not worth stopping for is best investigated, if investigated at all, as quickly as possible.

The negation of feeling so brilliantly dramatized in Larkin's poetry stimulates the reader to believe that here, at last, in these drab merciless terms, is life driven into a corner and justly assessed: less is not more, surely, but it is at least more *truthful* . . .? Yet the conviction is a false one. Larkin's studied nihilism is as florid in its way as the too-generous affirmation of a Whitman, and there is no reason to think that there is more "truth" in diminished things than there is in inflated things: for the poet expresses his interior landscape primarily.... [It] does not seem surprising that Larkin himself never attempted another work of fiction. "Novels are about other people," he has said, "and poetry is about yourself." One might amend that to allow for the probability of his poetry being about his nation, his culture, his heritage: which accounts for the enthusiasm with which his poetry is always received in an England ready to believe that it has been at last cut down "ruthlessly" to size. (pp. 39-40)

Joyce Carol Oates, in The New Republic *(reprinted by permission of* The New Republic; © 1976 by The New Republic, Inc.), *November 20, 1976.*

Larkinolatry is an easy condition to succumb to; I have suffered bouts of it myself. During a time in which so many English poets have assumed American mannerisms, Larkin's style has remained stubbornly indigenous. His poems have not been made for export; his achievement, his attitudes, and his deliberation in pursuing a career out of the public eye, all have for us the charm of unfamiliarity. Formal perfection has not been foremost among our poets' concerns since the middle fifties; a poet like Richard Wilbur, who has not significantly altered his style since then, seems an astonishing survivor halfway through the seventies. Larkin has the same sort of tenacity, maintaining standards of craftsmanship whose rigour seems enhanced by an infrequency of publication. One book every decade, a pile of mature poems numbering less than a hundred—what American poet over fifty has been as scrupulous an editor of himself as Larkin has been? If the finish and relative scarcity of these poems seem alien to us, the world view many of them express is even more so. Thoroughgoing pessimism in the manner of Hardy has generally seemed unadaptable to American minds.... If an all-embracing pessi-

mism were to appear again in American poetry (and perhaps it may, in response to our Asian empire's dissolution) I expect it would be a noisier, more histrionic attitude than it is in Larkin's handling of it. The surfaces of his poems are so quiet, the depths of the best so profound, that one might reread them for a lifetime without having distilled their last drop of melancholy.

The bleakness of Larkin's vision, present in his writing from the beginning, has intensified through time. The almost bottomless bitterness expressed in some of the pieces in *High Windows* may be taken, depending on one's taste, as signalling either the perfecting of an artist's individual focus or the surrender of his imaginative flexibility. *High Windows,* like Larkin's other mature collections, is a problematical achievement, and is more readily assessed after a glance back upon its predecessors.

The early verse collected in *The North Ship* (1945) has almost nothing of the poet's characteristic voice. The poems, as Larkin notes disarmingly in a preface written twenty years after their original publication, are mostly mouthpieces for the 'potent music, pervasive as garlic' of the middle Yeats. Moonlight, drumtaps, and ominous horsemen are frequently and floridly introduced. What now seems prophetic in these pieces is the recurrent appearance in them of the theme of loneliness as a fact of life, a given, against which any struggle can only end in exhausted defeat. (pp. 100-01)

The maturing of his gift was evident in his prose earlier than in his poetry. *Jill* (1946) and *A Girl in Winter* (1947) are admirable novels, authoritative in style without borrowing any other writer's rhetoric—altogether remarkable productions for a novelist under twenty-five. Both written in the third person, they pursue the theme of loneliness with a satisfying blend of earnestness and amusement, detachment and sympathy. In the traumas suffered by the protagonists of these novels we see vivid anticipations of the disillusionment to be voiced in the later poems. (pp. 101-02)

I wonder if Larkin will not in the end come to be esteemed as much for his novels—especially *A Girl in Winter*—as for his verse. The persistence of his single prevailing theme allows us to tally the relative advantages each genre has tendered him. The novels are rich in circumstantial detail, in clear, true-coloured depictions of settings (Kemp's Oxford, Katherine's unnamed provincial city) which provide a telling depth to the emotional experience of the characters who inhabit them. In the poems some of this descriptive density has necessarily been sacrificed; and there is, in a deeper sense, less background supplied. The speaker in the poems, whether observing others or himself, spends little time examining the reasons for a malaise which he views as all-pervasive. There is no explaining why the vessels in the 'sparkling armada of promises' we see approaching us never drop anchor. We have picked up 'bad habits of expectancy', the poem tells us.... There is no positing of causes, no attempt to trace unhappy effects meaningfully back to a source. The powerful, blank absoluteness of [his] pronouncements goes beyond anything in the novels. John Kemp's experience of class prejudice, and Katherine's of exile, are credible as provocations of their emotional disorders. The novels partake of a larger, less subjective view of life than the poems attempt or desire to assume. *The Less Deceived* and *The Whitsun Weddings* lose something in breadth as they reduce to an eloquent, personalized shorthand the estrangement that is adumbrated in Larkin's fictional prose.

Yet Larkin's poetic material remains more novelistic (to speak of the novel in its classic form) than any other contemporary poet's. The poems frequently present life histories condensed and calcified. Plot and character are dominant elements, however Larkin's mastery of verse technique may enhance the total effect of a poem. One feels that a century ago he might have been a brother in arms of Dickens or Trollope, rivalling them in his cunning exploitation of the unconscious, at times grotesque comedy of which humanity is capable. 'Mr Bleaney', 'Dockery and Son'—these are Dickensian names, Dickensian titles. (The name Dockery appears, offhandedly, in *Jill*—a sign that Larkin's imagination was very early attracted to a traditionally English [or at least Victorian] poetry of proper names.) Of the poems in his first two mature volumes one's initial question might be: do they successfully realize their narrative impulse within the confines of verse?

In some cases yes, in others no. There are times at which one feels that the dooms of Larkin's characters have been unduly and insistently contrived. At their least convincing the poems recall Hardy's *Satires of Circumstance,* which lead one to reflect that it is not the Unknown God who has dealt such a miserable hand to the hapless folk involved, but Mr Hardy himself. Recurrently annoying is the busy stage-managing by which Larkin will lull the reader into a false security only to pull the rug out from under him in a last stanza, or a last line. (pp. 102-04)

The finest work . . . occurs when argument is consistently carried through not by didactic statement but by a wondrously expressive imagery or scenic description—as in the title poems, 'The Less Deceived' and 'The Whitsun Weddings'. . . .

The tone throughout [*High Windows*] is consistent and convincing, without the selfconscious drops into didacticism or defensiveness that at times discountenanced the earlier poems. The pieces expounding Larkin's brand of pessimism have become less stagy; it is as if he has fully grown into an attitude which in a younger man had the appearance of being overly willed. (p. 106)

There are two things before which Larkin will relax his toughly critical stance: the beauty of nature and what might be called democratic social rituals. For these subjects he reserves his gentlest tones: the earlier pastorals, 'At Grass' and 'Wedding-Wind', and the brilliant panoramas, 'Here' and 'The Whitsun Weddings' are notable instances of this benignity. Nature is celebrated in two small, impeccable lyrics in the new book, 'The Trees' and 'Cut Grass'. The more considerable poems 'To the Sea' and 'Show Saturday' offer engaging pictures of, respectively, a seaside resort and a rural fair. The poet observes the zest and resilient traditionalism of common people on holiday: 'Still going on, all of it, still going on!' he exclaims with delighted wonder in 'To the Sea'. . . . Perhaps because he is so sparing of affirmations, Larkin's moments of expansiveness seem totally felt, and are as moving as they are rare.

Expansiveness of a different sort is operative in the book's title poem and its last piece, 'The Explosion'. One sees in these how Larkin has got beyond reliance on the nervous, over-determined climaxes criticized above. It is not that his treatment has become optimistic—the content of both these poems is vividly sad. But Larkin has provided each with a startling final image, which points beyond all emotion,

whether of joy or grief. The marvellous close of 'The Whitsun Weddings' may have provided the cue for this tactic: there, the poet crowns his catalogue of the sights and sounds of his train journey with [a] vault into featureless, inscrutable distance. . . . In 'High Windows', the envy of age for youth, and the supposed pleasures envied, are alike transcended and reproved by a stark conclusion which comes out of nowhere and yet seems perfectly in place. . . . This chilling mixture of numbness and exaltation has few counterparts in poetry of our own or any time; this is one of Larkin's finest and most unusual poems. On the level of meaning his latest work is as austere and uncompromising as ever, but it is subtler in structure, and more flexible in the means by which it makes a difficult, unappealing view of life accessible to the common reader. Instead of being led down corridors to come up against a locked door, we find the door swinging giddily open on to an absolute void. The effect is at once appalling and exhilarating. . . . (pp. 107-09)

> *Robert B. Shaw, "Philip Larkin: A Stateside View," in* Poetry Nation (© Poetry Nation *1976), No. 6, 1976, pp. 100-09.*

Philip Larkin, like Tennyson, has the power to make poetry out of material that might seem to be unpromising and intractable. Most of us live in urban or suburban landscapes among the constructions and the detritus of an industrial society. Larkin distills poetry from the appurtenances of this society—an Odeon cinema, advertisement hoardings [British billboards], scrap heaps of disused cars, hospital waiting rooms, cut-price stores—which he presents without falsification or sentimentality. And, again like Tennyson, he delineates with considerable force and delicacy the pattern of contemporary sensibility, tracing the way in which we respond to our environment, plotting the ebb and flow of the emotional flux within us, embodying in his poetry attitudes of heart and mind that seem peculiarly characteristic of our time: doubt, insecurity, boredom, aimlessness, and malaise. (p. 131)

Larkin is, like Tennyson, an artist of the first rank, who employs language with a rare freshness, precision, and resonance, and whose verse records with lyrical purity his experience of loneliness and anguish. He is both the unofficial laureate of post-war Britian and the poet who voices most articulately and poignantly the spiritual desolation of a world in which men have shed the last rags of religious faith that once lent meaning and hope to human lives. (p. 132)

The 1966 edition of *The North Ship* is a reprint of the 1945 edition, plus one poem, numbered "XXXII," of which Larkin writes: "As a coda I have added a poem, written a year or so later, which, though not noticeably better than the rest, shows the Celtic fever abated and the patient sleeping soundly." The first stanza of this poem leads us at once into a world far removed from the artificial, literary stage set of *The North Ship:*

> Waiting for breakfast, while she brushed her hair,
> I looked down at the empty hotel yard
> Once meant for coaches. Cobblestones were wet,
> But sent no light back to the loaded sky,
> Sunk as it was with mist down to the roofs.
> Drainpipes and fire-escape climbed up
> Past rooms still burning their electric light:
> I thought: Featureless morning, featureless night.

Already in this stanza we can observe many of the hallmarks of Larkin's mature poetry: the ability to evoke not only the specific appearances of things but the atmosphere that surrounds them; the power of discovering poetry in objects or in situations that most people would regard as dull or unremarkable; a rare skill in making slight, unobtrusive departures from the dominant metrical pattern—the last line deviates from the expected beat of the iambic pentameter and, despite its irregularity, paradoxically conveys the impression of weariness and monotony: "I thought: Featureless morning, featureless night."

It is instructive to compare this poem with Poem XX from *The North Ship,* which begins, "I see a girl dragged by the wrists / Across a dazzling field of snow," and speedily moves on to the contemplation of the poet as "a sack of meal upon two sticks," and of "two old ragged men," before concluding with an "image of a snow-white unicorn." The girl exists merely as a prologue to a brilliant evocation of Yeatsian cadences and personae.

The theme of poem "XXXII" is also Yeatsian in its speculation about the poet's being forced to choose between the Muse and the mortal girl, but although there is no description of her physical or emotional characteristics, we are convinced that, like the young lady in the photograph album, "this is a real girl in a real place." It is not easy to determine to what extent the poem reflects Larkin's newly-born admiration for Hardy. The diction and the tone are quite unlike Hardy, and indeed Larkin seldom imitates or verbally echoes him. Yet he is present in the poem, even though we cannot locate him precisely, for as Larkin himself remarked, "Hardy taught me to feel rather than to write." From 1946 onward Larkin has remained faithful to the belief that poetry can be made out of any situation or incident, however odd or trivial, that genuinely stirs the poet. Conversely, he must write only about those matters that move or excite him and not about subjects that he feels ought to form the themes of his poetry. This belief Larkin owes in part to his study of Hardy. (pp. 134-35)

The awareness of suffering and the brooding spirit of compassion that inform so much of Hardy's poetry are widely diffused throughout *The Less Deceived.* I believe also that there is a close kinship between the emotional pattern of this collection and the complex attitude of mind delineated by Hardy in the Apology, dated February 1922, with which he prefaced *Late Lyrics and Earlier.* Poems such as "Deceptions" and "Myxomatosis" embody Hardy's desire that "pain to all upon [the globe], tongued or dumb, shall be kept down to a minimum by loving-kindness." And the best introduction to "Church Going," the most celebrated poem in *The Less Deceived,* is Hardy's Apology, with its conviction that "Poetry and religion touch each other, or rather modulate into each other; are, indeed, often but different names for the same thing." Although Larkin has remarked of "Church Going" that its tone and argument are entirely secular, the power of this poem is largely generated by the tension between the ironical mistrust of orthodox Christianity expressed by the poet and his intuitive reverence for the church as a place where our intimations of mystery and destiny are enshrined. . . . Hardy, despite his atheism, regarded himself as a "churchy" man, and in the Apology acknowledges the potentialities of the Anglican Church. . . . Although Larkin is, like Hardy, an unbeliever, he suggests in "Church Going" that "this accoutred frowsty barn" of a church will continue to be worthy of respect. . . . (p. 138)

If *The Less Deceived* can be called Tennysonian because of the notes of lyrical intensity, loneliness, and longing that resound so plangently in its pages, *The Whitsun Weddings*

(1964) reveals the other side of the Tennysonian medal on which the lineaments of contemporary England are depicted. Larkin evokes for us, in poem after poem, the postwar English landscape, rural, urban, and suburban; and his verse takes on the central, representative character that marks the poems of Tennyson in the years after 1850 and of Auden in the late 1920s and throughout the 1930s. (p. 139)

Whereas T. S. Eliot regards the modern world with horror and catalogues, with a mixture of disdain and disgust, golf-balls, abortifacient pills, women's underwear, false teeth, cigarette ends, and "other testimony of summer nights," Larkin is moved to a wry tenderness. . . . Even the enormous hoardings that most of us find so distasteful awaken in Larkin a rueful compassion, since he sees them as the media whereby the urban masses are led to contemplate ideal Forms in the Platonic sense, (although they are deluding Forms). The title of the poem, "Essential Beauty," in *Whitsun Weddings* is not entirely ironical: the figures on the hoardings transport simple people into a pure, otherworldly realm, and in an age when the Christian pantheon has lost its power to comfort and uphold, they may bring a kind of consolation to those on their deathbed. . . . (pp. 139-40)

The volume's title poem, "The Whitsun Weddings," evokes a series of impressionist pictures that capture the appearance and the atmosphere of our heavily urbanized landscape. Larkin manages to combine a curt exactness with a Tennysonian delicacy and amplitude. . . . Larkin's eye is acute and unsentimental; his portrayal of the wedding guests clustered on the railway station platforms is so accurate that it verges on cruelty. . . . Yet these rather coarse, ridiculous figures are aware that marriage, like birth and death, has a sacred quality. . . . And as the train approaches London the poet feels that in some mysterious way the Waste Land of the metropolis is fertilized not by a dying god or a mythical redeemer, but by the newly married couples sitting in the railway carriages. (pp. 140-41)

High Windows contains more overt comment on the state of England than any of Larkin's previous volumes. Twenty years earlier he had remarked that "the impulse to preserve lies at the bottom of all art," and such an impulse colors his entire political and social philosophy, which is profoundly conservative and pessimistic. Larkin's feeling for tradition and continuity is very strong: one of the most beautiful poems from *The Whitsun Weddings,* "MCMXIV," is an elegy for those who rushed to volunteer at the outbreak of the First World War, and for a vanished England; another poem from that volume, "Naturally the Foundation will Bear Your Expenses," flays a literary intellectual who despises the London crowds on Armistice Day. (p. 141)

"Homage to a Government," written in 1969 and included, like "Going, Going," in *High Windows,* has angered some readers by its reactionary sentiments. Just as "MCMXIV" is a lament for lost innocence, "Homage to a Government" is a lament for a sense of responsibility submerged beneath a tide of materialism. . . . It is a mark of Larkin's superb technical skill that in "Homage to a Government" he can make a virtue of monotony and give tonelessness a strong flavor. (p. 142)

The poems on public themes in *High Windows* are counterbalanced by poems that evoke a world transcending the contingencies and imperfection of daily existence. Larkin has always been aware of such a world, which corresponds to the needs of human loneliness and longing, and whose nature can be hinted at by the medium of images drawn from the inexhaustible realm of nature—sun, moon, water, sky, clouds, distance. (p. 143)

[Although Larkin] has repeatedly deplored the post-Symbolist revolution inaugurated by Eliot and Ezra Pound, [there is] a quality that has been present in his poetry from the very start, a quality that manifests itself in *High Windows* with an intensity of feeling and of utterance fiercer than Larkin has ever previously attained. The language takes on at times a concentration and density so intricate and compressed that they incur the charge of obscurity, a vice strongly reprehended by Larkin in twentieth-century poetry:

> By night, snow swerves
> (O loose moth world)
> Through the stare travelling
> Leather-black waters.

This kind of concentrated lyrical purity coexists in certain poems with vulgarisms and obscenities that have become more frequent and more coarse with every successive volume. There are precedents for this in modern English verse. Eliot's "Sweeney Among the Nightingales" foreshadows the strategy, though not the vocabulary, of Larkin's more outspoken poems; and Yeats shocked some of his older admirers with his Crazy Jane sequence and with *Last Poems* (Larkin still owes more to the rhetoric of his first master than he may care to admit). The collocation of musical intensity and poignant longing with the employment of four-letter words more commonly found in taprooms and barracks than in poems occurs in several places in *High Windows.* The title poem opens with a brutal reflection on youthful sexuality, but ends in a meditation that transcends the impulses of sweating carnality.... The title of another poem, "Sad Steps," lulls us into a mood of high romance where Sir Philip Sidney looks questioningly at the heavens: "With how sad steps, O Moon, thou climb'st the skies!" We are in for a shock:

> Groping back to bed after a piss
> I part thick curtains, and am startled by
> The rapid clouds, the moon's cleanliness.

Then, after a precise delineation of the cloudy sky through which the moon dashes, the poem modulates into a series of invocations that might be the climax of a Symbolist poem, were it not for the irony underlying the apostrophes. The moon shifts again, the rhetoric is dispersed, and the poem ends with a bare statement that, like so many of Larkin's closing lines, strikes home with unerring accuracy and gravity:

> One shivers slightly, looking up there.
> The hardness and the brightness and the plain
> Far-reaching singleness of that wide stare
>
> Is a reminder of the strength and pain
> Of being young; that it can't come again,
> But is for others undiminished somewhere.

I began this essay by suggesting that Larkin is, like Tennyson, at once the public laureate of contemporary England and the solitary poet of human isolation, fear, and longing. One poem in *High Windows,* "The Trees," is more reminiscent of Tennyson than anything else that Larkin has written. This is partly because it employs the metrical and stanzaic form of *In Memoriam,* but mainly because it recalls and re-creates the older poet's extraordinary responsiveness to the emotional significance no less than to the sensuous properties of the English landscape. (pp. 143-45)

We find in Larkin as in Tennyson an awareness of the way in which the utter perfection and abundance of the natural world accentuate our sense of its mortality as well as of our own. The whole poem is so perfectly ordered that it is unrewarding to point out individual felicities, but it is worth drawing attention to the consummate artistry and deep awareness of complex emotions displayed in the last line. The word *afresh* normally evokes images of greenness and of hope. So it does here; but Larkin somehow contrives to suggest that sadness and transience are mingled with joy and affirmation. The effect is akin to that achieved at times by Mozart and Schubert at their most tender and poignant:

> The trees are coming into leaf
> Like something almost being said;
> The recent buds relax and spread,
> Their greenness is a kind of grief.
>
> Is it that they are born again
> And we grow old? No, they die too.
> Their yearly trick of looking new
> Is written down in rings of grain.
>
> Yet still the unresting castles thresh
> In fullgrown thickness every May.
> Last year is dead, they seem to say,
> Begin afresh, afresh, afresh.

(pp. 145-46)

John Press, "The Poetry of Philip Larkin," in The Southern Review *(copyright, 1977, by John Press), Vol. XIII, No. 1, Winter, 1977, pp. 131-46.*

*   *   *

LE GUIN, Ursula K(roeber)   1929-

Le Guin is an American writer of science fiction and fantasy whose primary genre is the novel. She has also published a compilation of short stories, *The Wind's Twelve Quarters,* **and a volume of poetry,** *Wild Angels.* **Le Guin has likewise extended her creations of fantasy to the world of children's literature. The** *Earthsea* **trilogy is her most noted contribution in this field. (See also** *Children's Literature Review,* **Vol. 3, and** *Contemporary Authors,* **Vols. 21-24, rev. ed.)**

The Dispossessed belongs right in the middle of the literary genre announced in its subtitle [*An Ambiguous Utopia*]. Le Guin creates for us a society that is in her view significantly better than our own, but one not beyond our capacity to achieve. We see how the people of this society live, work, play, love, hate; how they are organized politically, exchange their produce, educate their children, manage their sexual relations; we see what they value and disvalue and we witness how their values stand up under extreme stress. The book is organized so as to display the virtues and (uncharacteristically for the genre) the weaknesses of a "good place." In another traditional function of the genre, just as Thomas More's *Utopia* is a slashing satire on the sixteenth-century European social order, so *The Dispossessed* constitutes a severe critique of twentieth-century industrial society. In these respects and in others *The Dispossessed* is close kin to most utopian fictions one can think of from More to H. G. Wells.

The story concerns a people who have voluntarily left the fertile mother planet Urras to live on Anarres, Urras's barren and desolate moon. Urras is a transparent stand-in for Earth in the twentieth century.... Anarres, on the other hand, is a stand-in for no existing country or government; it represents possibility only. (pp. 256-57)

Le Guin has not tried to depict the "just" or "perfect" or "happy" society that utopian theorists have from time to time evoked. Life on Anarres is hard; people suffer; some are selfish, narrow, power-loving. There is conflict and the anarchistic ideal is flawed. Still, the principles are there in action; and despite a lynching mob and encroaching bureaucratization, the moral level of Anarres, its success as a humane society, is high. (p. 257)

It is as though Le Guin had set out to test Socrates' contention in *The Republic* that the ideal state is one in which people lead hard, simple lives, producing only necessities. . . . These are recalcitrant materials for a writer: how does one show, how does one make interesting, a truly simple happiness? . . . Utopian writers have always found it easier to define the good life by showing what it is not.

The genre is full of traps. For example, how does a utopian society come into being? More's King Utopus simply founded Utopia by decree. Edward Bellamy's Americans slid into it by accident. Marxists tend to like William Morris's *News from Nowhere,* an otherwise rather delicate book, because it faces the question of how revolutionary violence can give birth to the good life. Plato was most forthright of all: the philosopher who is to create the ideal society will "take society and human character as his canvas, and begin by scraping it clean." The image has given liberal commentators fits. Le Guin's way of scraping the canvas is to have her anarchists abandon not only their native planet but their native language as well. They create, and use exclusively, an artificial language, with all the losses that entails, in order to start afresh.

Another trap, source of much tedium in utopian fiction, is that of exposition. "Tell me," say innumerable visitors to Utopia, "how your society is organized," and the flat expository prose rolls on endlessly before us. *The Dispossessed* avoids this as much as possible, showing instead a non-authoritarian communist society in operation; not in detail, of course—this is not a blueprint—but in selected scenes and episodes so that we get a feeling, if by no means a full understanding, of how such a society might work. It is a measure of Le Guin's seriousness and honesty that with all its negative advantages the society has its full quota of moral complexities and human failure.

The genre, of course, has advantages as well as traps. A visitor from Utopia to our world brings unexpected perspectives to the familiar and commonplace. [The protagonist] Shevek's first view of Urrastian landscape, a grove of trees with the land falling away to a fertile valley—nothing dramatic—has vivid impact because we see, with heightened visual powers, through his unaccustomed eyes. Used negatively, the device provides a built-in satiric blade. Le Guin has only to place Shevek on the Madison Avenue of A-Io for a process of estrangement, of "defamiliarization," to take place. Shevek looks in shop windows, the show places of our culture. . . . The Anarresti have a saying: "Excess is excrement." From that perspective the simple enumeration [of merchandise] becomes fierce social commentary.

Melodramatic doings in A-Io are handled less deftly than the smaller episodes on Anarres. Le Guin's talent is in imaging the remote, the extreme, life pared down to the thing itself. . . . Le Guin loves her Anarresti, who by choice and by the iron force of environment have reduced

their lives to what is essential: "a people selected by a vision of freedom, and adapted to a barren world, a world of distances, silences, desolations."

Any work powered so overtly by moral and social energies can hardly avoid a certain fictional thinness. H. G. Wells recognized the problem. "That which is the blood and warmth and reality of life is largely absent" from utopian fiction, he said; "there are no individualities, but only generalized people." *The Dispossessed* does not entirely escape the difficulty, but in the character of Shevek, the Anarresti physicist, Le Guin achieves something new. Starting with richly imagined scenes from childhood (a chilling episode, for example, in which Shevek and three other youngsters enact a prison experience), she creates the kind of character one associates with the novel proper. A believable scientist, a complex human being tormented by competing obligations, Shevek has some of the functions of the traditional apologist for Utopia; but the functions have been complicated almost beyond recognition and Shevek comes from another literary kind. Thus generic expectations are confounded and a genre enriched. (pp. 258-60)

In ordinary terms the proportion of science fiction to utopia in *The Dispossessed* is very small indeed. The book is set in the future, but so, of course, are many utopias. The Hainish, a people from Le Guin's science fiction novels, play a small but crucial role, and Shevek's great theory is straight out of the science fiction repertoire. But this is about all. Thus the bloodlines of the book are, as always, mixed; but the dominant strain cannot be in doubt.

The ghetto experience of science fiction has prompted it to imperialistic ventures: science fiction now lays claim to all forms of speculative fiction, emphatically including the utopian. I think this is a mistake, tactically as well as strategically. Had reviewers recognized *The Dispossessed* as a newer, more interesting *Walden II* or *Island,* instead of categorizing it as they did and missing its central thrust, we would already be having the discussions—literary, political, generic—a work of this importance is certain to generate. (p. 261)

Robert C. Elliott, "A New Utopian Novel," in The Yale Review *(© 1976 by Yale University; reprinted by permission of the editors), Winter, 1976, pp. 256-61.*

Unlike many science-fiction writers [Le Guin] is exhilarated less by "probable causes" than by "future experience," less by the gadgetry of the future than by the quality of life and the psychic consequences of social and technological change.

Much science-fiction works roughly along the same principles as science itself: can the problem or its solution be duplicated? Le Guin often begins with a scientific possibility, as in the story "Nine Lives," one of the finest in the volume [*The Wind's Twelve Quarters*], which dramatizes what happens when two technicians on a far-off planet are visited by assistants, a 10-person clone. Here is duplication personified. Le Guin is fascinated with what it would feel like to be a member of such a clone, sexually and emotionally self-sufficient. . . . And she moves from this concern to the insight that future experience is still human experience. For all of us the distance between the stranger and oneself is absolute, but we learn to negotiate it so early that we may forget the negotiation is learned. . . .

A kind of cultural relativism is implicit in many of these stories. . . . (p. 28)

The stories are not so impressive as the best Le Guin novels, for Le Guin is superb at suspensefully sustaining long narrative sequences impossible in short fiction. Nevertheless "Nine Lives" and "The Field of Vision" need not be condescended to.... Like Doris Lessing, who has several times recently crossed in the other direction the traditional line between fiction and science-fiction, Ursula Le Guin is capable of a healthy blurring of genres. (p. 29)

> *Joan Joffe Hall, in* The New Republic *(reprinted by permission of* The New Republic; © 1976 by The New Republic, Inc.), *February 7, 1976.*

[Ursula Le Guin's] fiction is closer to fantasy than naturalism, but it is just as grounded in ethical concerns as [John] Brunner's work, despite its apparent distance from present actualities. Though some would argue that her political novel, *The Dispossessed* (1974), is her best work, and others might favor her ecological romance, *The Word for World is Forest* (1972, 1976), or her young people's fantasy, *A Wizard of Earthsea* (1968), today's critical consensus is still that her best single work is *The Left Hand of Darkness* (1969).

In *The Left Hand of Darkness* Le Guin moves far from our world in time and space, to give us a planet where life has evolved on different lines from our own.... [The] major effect of Le Guin's imagining such a fictional world is to force us to examine how sexual stereotyping dominates actual human concepts of personality and influences all human relationships. (p. 39)

I know of no single book likely to raise consciences about sexism more thoroughly and convincingly than this one. And that this is done gently, in a book which manages also to be a fine tale of adventure and a tender story of love and friendship, makes the achievement all the more remarkable. There are few writers in the United States who offer fiction as pleasurable and thoughtful as Ursula Le Guin's. It is time for her to be recognized beyond the special provinces of fantasy and science fiction or feminism as simply one of our best writers. (pp. 39-40)

> *Derek de Solla Price, in* The New Republic *(reprinted by permission of* The New Republic; © 1976 by The New Republic, Inc.), *October 30, 1976.*

Ursula K. Le Guin, one of the most accomplished of contemporary science fiction writers, has written a provocative collection of short stories that are not science fiction by any conceivable definition of the term. Having said this, I must add that these "Orsinian Tales" share many of the virtues of her best science fiction. As in her novels "The Dispossessed" and "The Left Hand of Darkness," she writes in quiet straightforward sentences about people who feel they are being torn apart by massive forces in society—technological, political, economic—and who fight courageously to remain whole. In her science fiction, these struggles take place in a vaguely defined future on imaginary planets, where everything from the shape of continents to the flux of social conventions has been created to frame, mirror and, at key points, force the action. Readers who feel uncomfortable with objective correlatives on this scale may dismiss the creation as mere "fantasy."

But no one is likely to fix that label on the "Orsinian Tales." Most of the stories are set in an unnamed Central European country with a long and typically somber history;

the "progress" from feudalism to industrial capitalism to Soviet-dominated Communism does nothing to alter the odds against individual freedom. (p. 8)

The chronology of the tales is deliberately mixed; the dates of the first six stories are 1960, 1150, 1902, 1920, 1956 and 1910. By turning history inside out in this manner, Mrs. Le Guin forces the reader to piece together a picture of the country and its people bit by bit. And only as the bits accumalate does the underlying strategy become clear: The country is unnamed because it is "imaginary." It is not simply Yugoslavia or Czechoslovakia or Hungary with the names and faces changed, nor is it a generalized Kafkaesque nightmare. Like the allegorist (or the science fiction writer), Mrs. Le Guin has carefully constructed an entire country to suit her needs.

Of course, she has not given her imagination the same loose rein as she does in her science fiction novels; all the details have the ring of reality. There are no anachronisms in the "Orsinian Tales," no *deus ex machinas,* nothing that clashes with the broad outlines of European history as the textbooks know it. But even within these bounds she succeeds in putting her special mark on the material. Most authors achieve verisimilitude in historical fiction through a display of documentation; well-researched descriptions of specific locales somehow vouch for the authenticity of characters and plot. Despite the superficial resemblance, Mrs. Le Guin's method is entirely different; what breathes life into each of her tales is not documentary pretense but the primary act of imagination underlying the whole book.

Not surprisingly, the two most successful stories deal directly with the claims of the imagination. (pp. 8, 44)

There are no easy choices in Le Guin's "made-up" world. The imagination, she tells us, destroys as well as redeems. It is not even clear that we can influence the outcome; yet freedom consists of acting as though we could. (p. 44)

> *Gerald Jonas, in* The New York Times Book Review *(© 1976 by The New York Times Company; reprinted by permission), November 28, 1976.*

* * *

LEM, Stanislaw   1921-

Polish science fiction and fantasy novelist and short story writer, Lem has been called a genius, a titan of Eastern European literature. He is one of the few writers of science fiction to have transcended the limitations of the genre, gaining international recognition. In his fiction Lem welds a wildly comic imagination to a darkly surrealistic vision of life. In 1973 his work was acknowledged by the Polish Ministry of Culture and in this country he became the recipient of a special honorary Nebula Award for science fiction.

Solaris is a strange and fascinating exploration of memory and reality, a story about events on a space station hovering over a bizarre ocean that covers a distant planet.... [Lem's] *Invincible* ... exhibits the emotional range of man's dedication to science and exploration, a range from curiosity to courage to a thirst for vengeance; the story is about an expedition to discover what catastrophe (or enemy) destroyed the men of an earlier expedition. Lem's talent is for the sensitive and sensuously precise rendering of the mind's struggle to understand an unimaginably alien reality. His spacemen remain men; their equipment finally matters less than the emotions, imaginings, ideas, commitments they can muster. *Cyberiad* . . . is quite different, short pieces in classic fairy-tale, moral-fable form, though with machines and their constructors as heroes and with feats of engineering and computer science as their plots. The poetry writing machine and the machine that can create anything that begins with the letter "n" are curious inspirations wonderfully conducted. . . . [The] tales provoke thought and laughter in equal and ample measure. (p. 489)

Donald Marshall, in Partisan Review *(copyright © 1976 by Partisan Review, Inc.), Vol. XLIII, No. 3, 1976.*

Stanislaw Lem is a Polish writer of science fiction in both traditional and original modes. . . . [His] books sell in the millions, and he is regarded as a giant not only of science fiction but also of Eastern European literature—as well he should be. Lem is both a polymath and a virtuoso storyteller and stylist. Put them together and they add up to genius.

Lem's marriage of imagination and science creates various intricate worlds. Some are just around an indeterminate corner from our everyday one; some are just beyond the horizons of our own space age; some are far distant, parabolic extrapolations of the folklore of the past into a legendary future of statistical dragons and microminiature kingdoms, of psychedelic utopias that mask universal suffering, of autobionic mortals who persecute monotheistic robots—as though the tutelary spirit of Lem's fantasy were a mingling of Jonathan Swift and Norbert Weiner. . . .

[He] has been steadily producing fiction that follows the arcs and depths of his learning and a bewildering labyrinth of moods and attitudes. Like his protagonists, loners virtually to a man, his fiction seems at a distance from the daily cares and passions, and conveys the sense of a mind hovering above the boundaries of the human condition: now mordant, now droll, now arcane, now folksy, now skeptical, now haunted and always paradoxical. Yet his imagination is so powerful and pure that no matter what world he creates it is immediately convincing because of its concreteness and plentitude, the intimacy and authority with which it is occupied.

If there is any dominant emotional coloring to Lem's vision it is the dark surreal comedy that has flourished in this century in Eastern Europe, the principal charnel house and social laboratory of the modern age. (Indeed, Eastern European history seems like a scenario for science fiction in which a peaceable pastoral planet with centers of high culture is repeatedly invaded by lethal, authoritarian robots.) What gives Lem's writing its regional signature is its easy way with the grotesque—as in the corpse with a rose behind his ear, the stonefaced bureaucratic chief with a wink-like tic, the community that is inanely proud of the cement factory that is destroying their environment and lungs, and so on throughout the postwar literature and films of Poland, Hungary and Czechoslovakia. (p. 1)

[A] clarity and richness of detail pervades Lem's accounts of [the] far-fetched worlds [in "Solaris" and "The Invincible"], so that they become in time just as credible and coherent in their strangeness as, say, Thomas Mann's biblical Egypt or Nabokov's Terra. Further, the behavior of the beleaguered earthmen is so finely attuned to their characters, particularly in "Solaris," and so powerfully dramatized that we believe in their experience because of the depth at which it is perceived and suffered. These books

are not just told, they are imposed—minutely, completely and irrevocably. (p. 14)

Lem, in his characteristic way, works out the situation [in "The Investigation"] by carrying it to a deeper level of enigma than the one on which it began. His science fiction and mystery novels are renovations of genres, much like Fowles's "The French Lieutenant's Woman," which exploit their conventions to uncover what they conceal: the problematic universe that underlies their assurances and any others. (p. 15)

One can read "Memoir Found in a Bathtub" as a spy novel that takes its conventional involutions to absurdity, as a cold war satire, or as another Lemian experiment with his Möbius strip of randomness and design. But in its dizzying depths . . . lurks the dark side of Lem's paradoxical attitude toward the man-machine relationship that dominates his fiction. Is Pentagon III a perversion of humanity produced by the further evolution of computer technology? Or is this evolution being perverted by the uses to which human folly puts it? And beyond this lies the further problem that humanity and technology are locked into a symbiotic relationship that progressively amplifies its consequences of good and evil. . . .

Lem's queasiness is not simply that of an old-fashioned humanist. Some of his most inspired and charming writing is produced by his feeling for the interchanges and interfaces of humanity and technology. This writing comes mainly in an original form that Lem has been developing for the past 20 years, best described as the futurist folktale. . . . (p. 16)

A few of the stories at the beginning of "The Cyberiad" are a bit coy, but they grow in power and implication and culminate in an extraordinary series, "The Tale of Three Story Telling Machines," including the Beckett-like story of "Mymosh the Self-Begotten," who comes together by pure accident on a cosmic junkpile of tin cans, wire, mica and "a hunk of rusty iron which happened to be a magnet." Mymosh is immobilized by further accidents and, since his only reality is his thoughts, he uses them to create a "Gozmos . . . a place of caprice and miracles."

In much the same spirit, "The Star Diaries" relates the adventures of Ijon Tichy, who in his one-man space ship goes whizzing around a universe that seems about the size of Poland. By and large, Lem seems to use these stories to satirize and parody the interests and themes of his darker books; thus there is a lot of horseplay about pseudo-scientific space- and time-travel, about the folly of an anthropocentric view of the universe, about the habitual tendency of mankind to abuse its technology. In Tichy's cosmos, as he reports, robots have a "natural decency" and "only man can be a bastard." Also, perhaps because he is writing in a comic way, Lem feels freer to play with Iron Curtain satire, as in Tichy's encounter with a planet that coerces all of its citizens to believe that water is their natural element and to behave accordingly. When an editor makes the mistake of writing that water is wet, he is purged. "You have to look at it from the fish's point of view," he confesses to Tichy. "Fish do not find water wet—ergo, it isn't."

The major story in "The Star Diaries" deals with robot theologians who are forced to live in catacombs because they insist in maintaining a religious faith that their mortal masters have long since abandoned in their delight in changing into whatever forms science enables them to assume. The theology of the monks proceeds from the paradox that "faith is, at one and the same time, absolutely necessary and altogether impossible." In the pages of explication and argument that follow, as subtle and precise as Lem's account in "Solaris" of the history of "Solaristics" (which also terminates in a purely religious conception of the "sea"), there is plenty of reason to believe that Lem is enunciating the grounds of his own faith. It is a faith that proceeds and returns to the indeterminacy of all that surrounds and retreats from the structure of human consciousness. This indeterminacy is God. Without it there is only a treacherous eschatology of freedom, of which the autobionic mortals are grisly examples. God is the mind's necessary constraint.

In these pages, among the most fascinating that Lem has written, possibly lies his resolution of the central paradox of cybernetic man and his future. But read Lem for yourself. He is a major writer and one of the deep spirits of our age. (pp. 18-19)

> *Theodore Solotaroff, in* The New York Times Book Review *(© 1976 by The New York Times Company; reprinted by permission), August 29, 1976.*

Mortal Engines . . . shows [Lem] mainly in a jovial mood, as a light-hearted would-be La Fontaine of the cybernetic age. . . . There are several stories which insist on the shiftiness, vengefulness, and general nastiness of human beings, who thus take on the mean, imperialist role which used to be assigned to Martians and Venusians and the like in Fifties science fiction. This is a worthy enough revision, but it has become a standard gesture in recent science fiction, and good science fiction, in any case, has always known it was *us* and not *them* who caused trouble, indeed has always known that *they* could not be anything other than versions of ourselves, mirrors of our favorite fears and wishes.

Lem's special field, the theme which brings out his most vivid writing, is the puzzled relation between men and robots. And even here *vivid* is perhaps not the word. It is impossible to judge the texture of prose in translation, and Polish is no doubt fiercely difficult to render in English, but even apart from the tiresome and insistent whimsy, there does seem to be a jerkiness in Lem's writing, an unsteadiness of focus or of inspiration, which is probably more a quality of mind than an accident of style or the casualty of travel between languages. Fine touches are constantly dissipated by a manner which simply marks time and misses chances. (pp. 36-7)

Nevertheless, Lem has interesting things to say about men and robots. In "The Hunt," a man out to catch a robot gone berserk begins to feel a kinship with it, because he can guess its movements, and because for a moment he pretends to be its ally rather than its pursuer. He destroys the robot and accomplishes his mission, but is haunted by the sense that he has done away with a creature who was more his fellow than most of his fellow men—than the people who shot at him by mistake, for example, and against whom the robot actually defended him. . . .

What is attractive in Lem is his view of humanity not as a matter of organic life or biological development, but as a matter of freedom—even if it is a freedom we may not in fact be able to exercise. . . . We are brethren whenever there are even flickers of freedom, and the political implications of this view, in the work of a writer who lives in Poland, are clear. . . . Lem seems to feel that reality is . . . a system of betrayals, and in an interesting displacement of

his concern from politics to metaphysics, it is the universe, not the world, which comes under attack: "this state of things that merits only derision and regret, called the Universe." (p. 37)

> *Michael Wood, in* The New York Review of Books *(reprinted with permission from* The New York Review of Books; *copyright © 1977 NYREV, Inc.), May 12, 1977.*

Throughout his accounts of his adventures, the disparities between what [the central characer of *The Star Diaries*] Ijon Tichy is, what he says he is, what he says the universe is and what we know it to be provide scintillating humor and entertainment while at the same time subtly hinting at how time- and space-bound we all are in our imaginations.

The other half of Lem's oeuvre is quite unlike these works. It appeals to lovers of science fiction and, because of its superior quality, has won a large following. The most admired, *Solaris* (1961), explores in an artful way the difficulties—and ultimately the impossibility—of man's establishing communication with a "sentient ocean," a one-celled organism that is found to cover the entire surface of a distant planet, about the size of the earth, to a depth of several miles. This is quite an impressive and original novel, one which may serve as the epitome of the science fiction genre for some time. (p. 465)

The Star Diaries belongs to that half of Lem's work devoted to humor, satire and parody, most of which is directed at the pettiness and vanity concealed within the motives behind human endeavors of all magnitudes. . . . [These works] are all rich in hyperbole, fantasy, humor and wordplay. . . .

> *Tom J. Lewis, in* World Literature Today *(copyright 1977 by the University of Oklahoma Press), Vol. 51, No. 3, Summer, 1977.*

*   *   *

LEVERTOV, Denise   1923-

Levertov is an English-born American poet. During her long career she has evolved from early verse influenced by the romanticism prevalent in Britain during World War II, through the influence of the Black Mountain poets, to become a unique poet whose verse consistently reflects her concern with the relation of form and content. The material for her poetry is drawn from her own experience, evoking both outward reality and inward response. (See also *CLC*, Vols. 1, 2, 3, 5, and *Contemporary Authors*, Vols. 1-4, rev. ed.)

Through clean, simple, precise language [Levertov] seeks to record in terse pictures the vivid present, though not for its own sake so much as for the sake of a mystical vision of life. . . . In her fourth collection, *The Jacob's Ladder* . . . , the poems rise to greater heights, burn with a brighter light than Creeley's. At best they embody a humble immolation of vision, reveal beauty emerging from objects like a butterfly from its chrysalis, cause a transformation of the events of everyday life into the words of a message from somewhere far beyond it. They are songs of praise, rendered in a proselike free verse in terms of the present moment. . . .

Yet by their nature Denise Levertov's poems suffer from limitations much like those which ultimately sterilized the imagist movement. Too often her insistence on the present tense, the present participle, the present perception necessitates a narrow, mannered way of speaking, particularly since she dispenses with meter and has no recurrent heartbeat to broaden and unify the rhythm. Too often her poems, anchored in the present, cannot move out of it unless the reader, independently, can make the same mystical connection that the poet has made.

This is the risk inherent in depending only on unconnected images: the poet leaves it to the reader, not to the power of language, to guide the connection between image and idea. It is like a conversation whose silences are as meaningful as its words; such conversations do not take place between strangers. (p. 86)

> *Peter Davison, in* The Atlantic Monthly *(copyright © 1962 by The Atlantic Monthly Company, Boston, Mass.; reprinted with permission), November, 1962.*

What struck me first on reading *The Poet in the World*, which is a collection of Denise Levertov's prose writings about art, politics, and life in general,—what struck me first, and what still strikes me in my reconsideration of the book . . . is the force of the author's good sense and practical wisdom. To many readers this may seem surprising. Levertov's base, both philosophical and temperamental, is in Neoplatonism, as I think is well known; certainly it has been more than evident in her poetry for twenty years. But unlike many writers who share this broad neoplatonic provenance, she never, or hardly ever, steps outside her role as a working poet aware of the practical and moral relationships between herself and her poetic materials: her experience, her life, her humanity. She keeps her mind on the reality of imaginative process. She rarely veers into mystical utterance for its own sake. (p. 475)

["The Poet in the World," the centerpiece of her book], should be read by every poet in the country—in the world! Written from the working poet's point of view, out of Levertov's own active experience in the recent period of collaboration between poetry and politics, it has the immediacy and efficacy that my own more scholastic arguments, not to say tirades, doubtless lack.

Has Levertov solved the paradox of the poet as a specialist of sensibility in the practical human world? Not entirely. Her book contains many statements, and her poems many more, in which [the dangerous view of the poet as a person apart and special, somehow superior,] is at least implicit. . . . Often she invokes The Poet in a role essentially vatic or ideally prophetic. Her affinity with Neoplatonism, from Plotinus to Swedenborg to Hopkins—a devious thread —is clear. My own base, which is not, whatever else it may be, Neoplatonism makes me shy away from such statements. But always in her prose, and often in her poetry, there is this saving complementary strain, awareness of the poet as a craftsman engaged in a psychologically reasonable endeavor; ultimately her affinity is with makers more than seers, with Wordsworth and Rilke, Williams and Pound. The title of one of her essays gives it in a nutshell: "Line-Breaks, Stanza-Spaces, and the Inner Voice." Moreover, in her basic humaneness Levertov often realizes, reaches out to, and celebrates the poet in Everyman, at least *in posse,* thus incorporating a necessary disclaiming proviso among her attitudes. She does it best, I think, in the essay that deals with sensibility as a moral and political instrument. The paradox remains, of course. It cannot be glossed over. . . . But the point is that Levertov does not . . . well, I was going to say that she does not recognize it, but of course she does. Yet I think she does not *feel* it. She is not stopped by it, not boggled. She works through and beyond it, in her writing and in what we know of her life, conscious

only of the wholeness of her vision. And she succeeds. She is practical.

This is the heart of the matter, I think. At any rate it is what I am interested in now: not the larger verities but her own work and the way her theoretical writing applies to her own work, particularly to her recent poetry. Undoubtedly her best known statement about poetry is the brief discussion of "organic form" that was originally published in *Poetry* in 1965, then reprinted a couple of times elsewhere before its appearance in her new book. . . . [It] asserts that forms exist in reality as natural, or possibly more than natural, immanences, and that the poet perceives or intuits these forms through acts of meditation, which issue, once the perception has acquired a certain intensity, in the creation of verbal analogies; that is, poems. This is not simply the pathetic fallacy at work in a new way, because the analogy between poem and object is not superficial; there may be no resemblance whatever in exterior structures, textures, and styles. The resemblance is indwelling. Levertov refers to Hopkins and his invention of the word "inscape" to denote intrinsic, as distinct from apparent, form, and she extends this denotation to apply not only to objects and events but to all phenomena, including even the poet's thoughts, feelings, and dreams. She emphasizes the importance of the quality of meditation, speaking of it in basically religious language. Meditation is the genuine but selfless concentration of attention upon phenomena, the giving of oneself to phenomena, from which proceeds the recognition of inner form; it is, to use another of Hopkins' inventions, the disciplined or ascetic submission to "instress." And I must point out also, with equal emphasis, that although at times Levertov speaks of the poet as no more than an instrument of a larger "poetic power," and although more than once she implies that the poem as a verbal analogy may occur in part spontaneously in a sensibility which is thoroughly attuned to its object through a sufficient act of meditation, nevertheless she insists as well on the element of craft in the poetic process, the part played by verbal experiment and revision in bringing the poem into proper analogy to its phenomenal paradigm. The poem is a *made* object.

I don't say there aren't questions—risks, qualifications, paradoxes by the bucketful—and of course the entire complex is . . . conventional, having appeared and reappeared at many times and in many places; yet Levertov's reformulation is very evidently her own, a personal vision, personal and practical; that is, *it comes from her practice*. One can't miss, either in her prose observations or in her poems, the way her understanding of what she is doing is instinctual at base, ingrained in her whole artistic personality. Look at her poems up to about 1968. They are what we call "lyric poems," mostly rather short; they fall into conventional categories: nature poems, erotic poems, poems on cultural and esthetic themes, and so on. Their style is remarkably consistent from first to last, changing only to improve, within its own limits, in matters of expressive flexibility, subtlety of cadence, integration of sonal and syntactic structures, and the like. But if the style is consistent the form is various, the *inner* form. From poem to poem each form is its own, each is the product of its own substance; not only that, each is the *inevitable* product—we sense it though we cannot demonstrate it—of its own substance. . . . It has been customary to speak of the musicality of Levertov's poetry, and I have done so myself. But I think this is the wrong term. I doubt that she has been aware of music, e.g., as Pound was aware of it. But she has been deeply aware of formal consonance, of the harmony of inner form and vision; and certainly this, rather than the facility of artifice some critics have ascribed to her, is what lies at the root of her "musical" language. (pp. 476-78)

["Staying Alive"] is, first, a sequence about the poet's life as a political activist from 1966 to 1970; second, an exploration of the sense and temper of those years generally; third, an attempt to locate and express the poet's own complex feelings, particularly with regard to questions of artistic responsibility; and fourth—and most important—a creation of poetic analogues to the inner form, the *inscape,* of that momentous "historical present." Remember the elements of poetic process as Levertov conceives them—perception, meditation, making—and then apply them to the *substance* of this long poem, those enormously intricate social, historical, esthetic, and moral *gestalten.* A whole nation, even the world, is involved here. No wonder the poem is multiform. It contains, what so annoys the critics, highly lyric passages next to passages of prose—letters and documents. But is it, after *Paterson,* necessary to defend this? The fact is, I think Levertov has used her prose bits better than Williams did, more prudently and economically; she has learned from *Paterson.* And aside from that, if one grants the need, in a long poem, for modulations of intensity, as everyone must and does, then why not grant the further modulation from verse into prose? It is perfectly feasible. Much of "Staying Alive" is what I call low-keyed lyric invocation of narrative; not narrative verse as such, not "thus spake mighty Agamemnon" or "the boy stood on the burning deck". . . . Brilliance is not wanted here, nor musicality (the superficial kind), but rather a strong supple verse, active and lucid; and this is exactly what we have. It changes; heightens and descends; turns soft or hard as the evolving analogy demands; it does the job. I repeat, the poem must be read whole. And readers who do this, as they easily can in one sitting, will see, I believe, or hear, precisely the consonance I spoke of in connection with Levertov's shorter lyrics, but now greatly enlarged and more varied: a just analogue for a complex phenomenon, unified in its whole effect, its vision, and its inner, "organic" form.

I don't say the poem succeeds in every line. That would have been a miracle. Sometimes the poet's perception or meditation apparently flagged; she tried to make up for it with acts of simple artistic will (as when she writes about her English friends whose lives "are not impaled on the spears of the cult of youth"). But such lapses are few. They do not disturb the unity of the poem.

As for the recurrent accusation of self-indulgence, who except the self can perceive, meditate, and create? Would the poem have been different if the poet had remained "anonymous" and "omniscient"? No, except for a possible loss of authenticity. Was De Tocqueville self-indulgent? Was Mrs. Trollope? Montaigne wrote: "I owe a complete portrait of myself to the public. The wisdom of my lesson is wholly in truth, in freedom, in reality"; and reality in this poem is in part the exemplary, very exemplary, responses of the poet to the perplexities of a time of rapid social disintegration. Clearly Montaigne was right for himself in his more moderate circumstances, and I think Levertov is equally right in the extremity of her (and our) circumstances. I also think that "Staying Alive" is one of the best products of the recent period of politically oriented vision among American poets.

Denise Levertov and I are good friends. Writing "Lever-tov" repeatedly where I would normally write "Denise" has seemed peculiar to me, even painful in a way. . . . I believe our friendship, which I suppose is rather well known, makes no difference and should make no difference to what I have written here. . . . If my view of Denise's work were antipathetic, obviously in the circumstances I would choose to say nothing about it. But the fact that my view is, on the contrary, sympathetic does not seem to me to detract from its usefulness. I have omitted many things about *The Poet in the World* that would have been said in the customary review. It is, for instance, a miscellaneous volume, springing from many miscellaneous occasions, and its tone ranges from spritely to gracious to, occasionally, pedantic. It contains a number of pieces about the poet's work as a teacher; it contains her beautiful impromptu obituary for William Carlos Williams, as well as reviews and appreciations of other writers. But chiefly the book is about poetry, its mystery and its craft, and about the relationship between poetry and life. It is an interesting and valuable book in general, and in particular it is an essential commentary on the poet's own poems and her methods of practice. It should be read by everyone who takes her poetry seriously. (pp. 478-80)

Hayden Carruth, "Levertov," in The Hudson Review *(copyright © 1974 by the Hudson Review, Inc.; reprinted by permission), Vol. XXVII, No. 3 Autumn, 1974, pp. 475-80.*

In the last twenty years Denise Levertov has given us ten volumes of poetry, a body of work that insists on passionate formal clarity and on the dailiness of the activity of writing. This first collection of her prose [*The Poet in the World*] is as good as the poems might make us hope. It is, certainly, the best and most valuable writing on the craft that we have from an active poet. Its value derives not only from what it tells us about her own art, but also from her rather special connection to the traditions of English and American poetry. She is a disciple of Williams and an associate of Creeley, Olson, and Duncan, who began her career in the style of the British "new Romantics" of the forties and had actually grown up in an English vicarage where she acquired a "curiously Victorian" education by browsing in her parents' library. The essays do not tell us how an imagination as Anglican and romantic as hers was drawn to objectivism or the austerities of Black Mountain, but they demonstrate why. Levertov is able to show us that, in her own art, Wordsworth's dictum that language is the embodiment not the dress of poetry comes to mean that there are no ideas but in things. In doing so, she makes lucid the relation between romanticism and the American experimental tradition. (pp. cxxxi, cxxxiv)

The Virginia Quarterly Review *(copyright, 1974, by the* Virginia Quarterly Review, The University of Virginia), *Vol. 50, No. 4 (Autumn, 1974), pp. cxxxi, cxxxiv).*

Levertov, through her forceful and compassionate presentations of urban lives, has been associated with the work and traditions of William Carlos Williams and Walt Whitman. She also has been praised for the beauty and sensuousness of her nature poems. By nearly unanimous agreement Levertov was well on her way to becoming one of our leading poets. The onset of the Vietnam War began the decline of her reputation, coinciding with the reemergence of the genteel tradition of polite and ultra sophisticated writing, a fantastic paradox in the face of the disaster of the war. Levertov, like so many other poets socially and personally involved, began to write her passionate Vietnam poems and to help lead large demonstrations against the war. In midst of our terrible spirtual dilemmas, nationwide, we can no longer afford to ignore her.

In "The Freeing of the Dust," her power to move us has not diminished. If anything, it has gone into new, vital areas. Poems against the Vietnam War are still present, several of superb pathos, but beyond that are poems of a way of looking at life that we never before met in her work. She has changed. I am referring to her poems of love and divorce, for instance. At her center there now seems to be an acceptance of imponderable limits, yet without the bitterness one would expect from a disillusioned humane idealist. Rather there is a sweetness, a tenderness towards life; a change rises from her poems that is inspiring to read. For Levertov the circle of human frailty has been completed and forgiven and even blessed, because of life. . . . (pp. 54-5)

> *David Ignatow, in* The New York Times Book Review *(© 1975 by The New York Times Company; reprinted by permission), November 30, 1975.*

*   *   *

LOWELL, Robert   1917-1977

Though also a playwright, critic, and translator, it is preeminently as poet that Lowell distinguished himself in American letters. Lowell relentlessly probed the dark side of the human condition through symbol, myth, and history using rich imagery and highly descriptive language. His raw honesty, especially displayed in *Life Studies,* is said to be the origin of the contemporary confessional movement. The theme of history, both personal and national, runs throughout his works. Lowell's self-avowed goal was to "deal with all experience in a variety of styles, without a conflict of form and content." Lowell was the recipient of the Pulitzer Prize in 1947. (See also *CLC,* Vols. 1, 2, 3, 4, 5, and *Contemporary Authors,* Vols. 9-12, rev. ed.)

Robert Lowell . . . is one of the most history-conscious American writers of our time precisely because he has a quarrel with history.

If history is the past, and the past is unchangeable, then Lowell's quarrel with it is futile. [Lowell's philosophy of history is close to Henri] Bergson's conception of time past as impinging on time present in the dramatic duration of the experiencing mind. Now his relation to this past is extremely tense, and also complex; to understand it is to see how his poetry comes *toward* our history, and how our history painfully procreated it in its own inverted image.

As an American, Lowell is the heir of the New England past; this shows clearly in so many poems that . . . project family history into public history. On the other hand, to inherit New England means to inherit a secession from Europe, from that older past and wider cultural horizon in which Lowell feels involved as a Westerner: "I write the Wonders of the Christian Religion, flying from the Depravations of Europe, to the American Strand. . . ." (pp. 219-20)

His direct inheritance was a promise, but a disinheriting one. The Pilgrim Fathers were indeed "children of Light," but of a blighting light, the light of Lucifer:

> Our fathers wrung their bread from stocks and stones
> And fenced their gardens with the Redman's bones;
> Embarking from the Nether Land of Holland,

> Pilgrims unhouseled by Geneva's night,
> They planted here the Serpent's seeds of light;
> And here the pivoting searchlights probe to shock
> The riotous glass houses built on rock,
> And candles gutter by an empty altar,
> And light is where the landless blood of Cain
> Is burning, burning the unburied grain. . . .

Few people would miss here, as in so much else that Lowell wrote, the forceful way in which history begets poetry, and poetry in its turn accuses history, through the alchemy of metaphor: the puns on the Netherlands, on Lucifer, on the searchlights, on the "riotous" houses built on Biblical rock, but too brittle to stand the coming quake, are not clever word play, but a structural device bent on eliciting its fearful meaning from the landscape of history, down to our own time. . . . Humor is not absent from this flash of telescoped vision [from *Life Studies*], or, for that matter, from all of [the volume] with its affectionate family sketches, or from its predecessor, *The Mills of the Kavanaughs.*

But the earlier volumes—*Land of Unlikeness, Lord Weary's Castle*—have little or no humor, being attuned to a mood of bitterness that might well make them offensive to whoever refuses to share Lowell's fiery conversion. Who is, after all, this New Englander who repudiates his spiritual lineage? Isn't he simply a renegade? If so, the poetry will have to be accepted as a merely private expression of troubled genius in a historical context to which it is irrelevant. A personal conversion to the long-abandoned dogmas of Papist Rome, even if it results in magnificent verse, cannot have any bearing on the realities of Protestant Yankeedom: can you abolish three hundred years of history by a stroke of pen?

At this point the historical sense will intercede for the "unhouseled" poet by reminding us that his secession from his secessionist forebears actually continues their own attitude, whatever the motivating ideology. (pp. 220-22)

Lowell, like other American writers of note, stands apart from his native land within his native land, and thus takes up the posture of the prophet. It would seem that America is one vast community of "sinners in the hands of any angry God;" will it mend its way and avoid the threatening doom? The conscientious objector cannot tell; he sees what he sees, and he feels it is his mission to awaken, not to soothe. In "Where the Rainbow Ends," his native Boston swings dangerously between salvation and destruction:

> I saw my city in the Scales, the pans
> Of judgment rising and descending. . . .
>
> (p. 223)

Christ is envisaged as the liberating force behind the accusing violence of the prophet; Lowell is an apocalyptic believer, like Blake or Hopkins, and "Colloquy in Black Rock" embodies to perfection his imaginative thrust from the machine-like rhythm of an earthbound beginning to the transcendent lightning of the crowning line:

>   . . .—my heart,
> The blue kingfisher dives on you in fire.

It is this moral tension, translated into a uniquely taut compactness of style, that enables Lowell to sustain a successful dialogue with formidable literary ancestors like Melville. "The Quaker Graveyard in Nantucket," one of the modern poet's highest achievements, is precisely such a dialogue. (pp. 224-25)

Lowell's sense of history is eschatological and not, properly speaking, "historical," for he speaks like an angry prophet, not like a Hegelian historicist or hopeful humanist. Later poems concerned with Rome, such as "Beyond the Alps," "Falling Asleep over the Aeneid," "For George Santayana," develop in a . . . meditative tone, but still questioning history in the alternatives of power, reason, and faith; and the eschatological note is not wanting either.

Because his commitment to spiritual values is so thorough, whatever direction his religious allegiance may have taken since his conversion to Catholicism, Robert Lowell can sustain his poetry at a declamatory pitch that would prove dangerous to a less gifted imagination. There is despair in his faith, and cruelty in his love; but he agrees with his countryman Robert Frost that fire is better than ice. If rebellion is the best way an American has to establish a connection with his tradition, then Lowell's New England ancestry counts for something. The sociologist, the scientific historian has to do with facts and laws; who but the poet can afford to have "a lover's quarrel" with history? This is his way of being available to history-ridden mankind. (p. 228)

> *Glauco Cambon, "Robert Lowell: History as Eschatology" (originally published in a slightly different version in* Papers of the Michigan Academy of Science, Arts, and Letters, *Vol. XLVII, 1962), in his* The Inclusive Flame *(copyright © 1963 by Indiana University Press), Indiana University Press, 1963, pp. 219-28.*

It is difficult to know how anyone actually relates to a man like Robert Lowell. Certainly, for many of us, he is more than the sum of his poems, more a palpable presence than a tissue of convictions and doubts. We are aware of him always in his role as poet, but our notions of this role have distinctly expanded under the influence of his example. If Robert Lowell would not presume to accept Shelley's designation as "unacknowledged legislator of the world," he might lay claim to the office of unofficial spokesman to that small portion of the human brain we manage somehow to preserve against the clamor and violence that wither consciousness. Steadily, Robert Lowell has shown us not what it means to be a man in our time, for this we can know all too clearly by looking at ourselves, or at those around us; no, he has given us a portrait of a sensibility in retreat, in part from the world, but chiefly from the self he has become in response to that world. What we have come to expect from Robert Lowell in his poems and in his appearances before us as a man is a rather graphic demonstration of how little we have left that we can try to preserve. (p. 36)

Those who have sought in Lowell's poems for strategies to ward off intimations of disaster, or metaphysical dread, have no doubt come away disappointed. When a fine poet-critic like Robert Bly [see *CLC*, Vol. 4] complains about the failure of Lowell and his friends to achieve "a clear view of modern literature or politics," and about "their insistence on the value of alienation," he betrays expectations which measure the great distance between his own view of what is possible in the modern world, and Lowell's. In the view of Robert Bly and the gifted people around him, one decides either for or against alienation. One's poetry is either reducible to or suggestive of a program. One's emotional commitments are firm, rather than ambiguous, and doubts will disappear at the behest of will. Really, it is a most attractive way of looking at things, only of course it is

but one way among many, and it is in the nature of human experience that those who believe such propositions as Bly's viable, will have an inordinate capacity for self-deception, or dishonesty. These are qualities conspicuously lacking in Robert Lowell, as even his severest critics have had to agree. And their absence has not made him or his work more appealing. (p. 37)

What is it then that has so drawn a generation of literate people to Robert Lowell? . . . Robert Lowell has been "our poet" because he has had trouble getting through each day, and told us why. We do not identify with him, we envy him, foolishly, sentimentally, but definitively. He sees, and suffers, and we would suffer with him if only we could convince ourselves there were something in it for us. Ultimately, we decide, it is enough that Robert Lowell sees and suffers for us all, a distinction we might have permitted him to share with Sylvia Plath had she lived to a riper age.

It is an extraordinary relationship for a poet to have developed with his audience, and to maintain this relationship, Lowell has had to violate the integrity and unity of his personality. . . . [The] man has become the posture, and nothing in the poems or utterances rings false—but it is a posture that addresses us, a role, not a man. So perfect has been the assumption of this role that we rarely notice how it dictates gestures and commitments wholly at odds with the man's temperamental indisposition to indulge such things. What most of us applaud when he publicly insults the President of the United States, or counsels young men to resist the laws of their country, or storms the Pentagon, is his temerity and conscience. What we are less likely to consider are the doubts, the irony that are so much a part of the commitment, and which in fact call into question the very meaning of the various enterprises. But then, nothing has become more paradigmatically demonstrative of purity of intention in our time than failure, and those of us who have found even the lesser failures a bit more costly than we are willing to allow ourselves must often have silently thanked Robert Lowell for permitting us to deplore and pity his. He is our truest victim, for we have together cast him in such a way that he can only assuage, never goad. And if he has been a witting and willing accomplice in the entire operation, by so much has it been the worse for him. (pp. 37-9)

[What] is new in *Notebook,* beyond the concern with power and health, the relation between personal vigor and political commitment, is the relative delight Lowell is able to take in things, in people, in the procession that is history, replete as it is with murder and disaster. He no longer seems to want to turn away from the gaudy spectacle, and the boredom that is consequent upon the turning in of all experience upon the relatively static responsiveness of the self has largely disappeared. There will never be anything remotely playful in Lowell's work, we may suppose, nor could we ever desire such a thing. But the degree to which he has here given himself to the contemplation and vivid evocation of realities beyond the twistings of his old self surely speaks optimistically of Lowell's own health and satisfaction with the fact and manner of his survival. If anything, his poetry has become a more comprehensive and essential document of civilized consciousness in the twentieth century, and its registration of fluctuations in conviction and hope is surely testimony to the relentless honesty of Lowell's work. (p. 44)

> *Robert Boyers, "On Robert Lowell," in*

Salmagundi (copyright © 1970 by Skidmore College), Summer, 1970, pp. 36-44.

Lowell may never strike us as possessing Miltonic magnitude; the status of poetry in our time leaves open the question whether any mid-twentieth-century poet can, while Milton's contemporaries still believed in the importance of epic. But in the political sonnets, in *The Readie and Easie Way*, in more than one passage of *Paradise Lost*, Milton's motive is his own political distress; poetry and rhetoric, though fine, are secondary. And Lowell is of this sort. (pp. 118-19)

There may be some danger here of confusing art and life. On the one hand, there are relatively few explicitly "political" poems in Lowell's output to date. . . . On the other hand, Lowell's public image is largely political, compounded of his imprisonment during World War II as a conscientious objector, of his association with such semi-political movements as PAX, of his much-publicized refusal to participate in President Johnson's White House Festival of the Arts on the grounds of his dismay at Mr. Johnson's Vietnam policy. . . . [The] temptation to second-guess the poems, to detect the politics of dissent where there may be nothing but personal relations and personal feelings, must be considerable.

I do not propose to resist that temptation; it seems to me that, with Lowell as with Milton, the practical distinction between the personal and the public, the private and the political, does not hold. To put it another way, perhaps a simpler way than circumstances warrant, both political events and personal events take on the same patterns, become aspects of the same historically and morally conditioned forces. (pp. 119-20)

The effect of adding "Colonel Shaw and the Massachusetts' 54th" to [a later edition of] *Life Studies* can be described, it seems to me, in either of two ways. It may say that, however much of the Lowell malaise can be accounted for in terms of family history and personal trauma, such terms cannot account for the unsettling past or the still more unsettling destruction of that past by an overblown technology—that the source of the malaise is in the world and its past, not simply in the individual and his. Alternatively, it may say in effect the *all* experience is in some sense public, political, conditioned by and answerable to history—*haunted* by history, in fact, whose burden can be escaped only by saints and monsters. I think that the latter formulation is the more rewarding of the two.

The past haunts the present. This has been apparent in Lowell's work from the start, as "Children of Light," "At the Indian Killer's Grave," or "The Quaker Graveyard in Nantucket," all from *Lord Weary's Castle,* sufficiently testify; and in *Lord Weary's Castle* the results are characteristically splendid, disturbing, and unclear, with a particular sort of unclarity. "At the Indian Killer's Grave" ends with a prayer for release from the burden of history, for the transformation of the speaker's nightmare vision of the dead King Philip mocking dead colonials and their descendants into Mary's ecstatic reception of God. . . . We recognize that angst is transformed into ecstasy, that in some fashion the terror of Indian attack merges into the divine visitation; the final line carries overtones of both. Rhetorically, the effect is magnificent, and it may seem merely querulous to ask questions; yet it is not really clear how the Mary vision relates to the rest of the poem except rhetorically. It is as though Lowell's concern with the historical

and moral problems raised in the poem has not so much resolved itself into a position, a moral attitude, as it has been given up. And yet the poem's logic seems to be concerned with the establishment of some sort of moral attitude, with the problem of how the descendant of John and Mary Winslow is to bear his inheritance, of what he must *do.* In fact, one could describe the dominant tone of *Lord Weary's Castle* as a baffled will for action, for finding a meaningful stance, with the bafflement characteristically translated or transformed into rhetoric.

To a degree, the magnificence has faded in *Life Studies* and *For the Union Dead.* The voice of these later poems is a smaller voice than that of *Lord Weary's Castle,* less prophetic in its resonance, and less resonant; but compensating for that diminution by a kind of moral clarity, as though Lowell, or Lowell's speaker, knows better who he is and what his stance must be, or at least what stances are possible for the uneasy individual in a world of history. Colonel Shaw, of course, exemplifies one such stance. . . . It may as well be called the heroic, and though it appears rarely in Lowell's work to date, it appears impressively—in Colonel Shaw, whose poem is used as the final statement in two volumes, and more starkly in the "Epigram" in *For the Union Dead.* . . . The point, I suspect, is that for Shaw and Leonidas the heroic gesture was final, enabling them to escape history's tendency to chop things down to size. The purity of their gestures is more or less accidental—though to be sure such commentary is niggling and does nothing to reduce the nobility that Lowell is concerned with, perhaps especially so in a historical context involving Medgar Evers and James Reeb.

But Shaw and Leonidas are Samsons; Lowell's speaker knows that he is at best Adam, for whom the heroic stance is the unlikely possibility at one end of a scale. The other end appears in "Caligula," also from *For the Union Dead.* . . . Caligula is the authentic human monstrosity, possessed by

> the lawlessness
> of something simple that has lost its law,

and devotes its efforts to trying to live without law, to destroying what it cannot have. I want to linger over this point, because it seems to me that Lowell's feeling for the past—and consequently for much else—does in fact have, as its lowest depth of possibility, the blindly paranoid violence of a Caligula. One can see, or suspect, something of this sort in the treatment of his parents, particularly his father, in *Life Studies.* (pp. 122-25)

And, of course, what he does to his father, or to himself through his father, he has also done to the American past. In "My Kinsman, Major Molineux" (in *The Old Glory*), Lowell discredits revolutionary enthusiasm quite as uncompromisingly as he does his father's manliness and character in "91 Revere Street"; *Lord Weary's Castle* includes "Children of Light" and "At the Indian Killer's Grave," in both of which the fathers' sins rather than their excellences survive, to haunt the present like an inherited curse. . . . And in such poems as "Rebellion" and "The Blind Leading the Blind," cryptic though they are, ancestral accumulation of goods and acres, even without murdered Indians or lynched Tories, erupts in strange violence involving fathers. . . . (pp. 125-26)

On the one hand, the will to discredit and destroy the past; on the other, prophetic denunciation of or sorrow over that destruction. Our past destroys us, but we must not lose the past. Here, it seems to me, is the tragic center of Lowell's work, the moral stance that dominates his later writing, brings the political and the personal into a single perspective, and perhaps accounts for the elegiac tone that, in *For the Union Dead* and *Near the Ocean* particularly, has largely displaced the erupting violence of *Lord Weary's Castle*. In "At the Indian Killer's Grave," the vision of Mary simply obliterates the historic past in a manner not wholly unlike Caligula's wish to obliterate Rome: "You wish the Romans had a single neck!" In *Lord Weary's Castle*, to be free of the past is to experience ecstasy.... In *Life Studies*, it is to drift like the convicted and imprisoned Lepke, of Murder Incorporated.... And in *For the Union Dead*, it is at best a quiet sense of some final loss, as in "Those Before Us".... (pp. 126-27)

It seems to me that ... Lowell expected more of his religion, or of himself as religious, than in fact happens.... [For] the man who is neither hero nor monster, who for whatever reason cannot disavow the "ordinary" world, and for whom history is real and often terrible, [his] expressions of belief, attempting some final and affirmative resolution, leave out too much of the factuality of existence that, for all but the utterly single-minded, constitutes most of life's meaning. If *For the Union Dead* finds its polar types in Caligula and Colonel Shaw, it has its human center in "Hawthorne" and more especially "Jonathan Edwards in Western Massachusetts." Hawthorne experiences no final transforming ecstasy.... For Edwards, bafflement and frustration and failure—and for Edwards even the transforming experience of the Great Awakening had failed—are the realities he has to live with. (pp. 127-28)

What both men have done, it seems to me, is to survive, at much cost to themselves to be sure, and without the heroic self-abnegation of Leonidas or Colonel Shaw, but equally without either the maniacal violence of a Caligula or the flabby drift of a Lepke.... They do what they can; they cultivate their own baffled honesty; they survive. That honest survival does not eliminate Endecott's dilemma, but it does provide an alternative—even, perhaps, a categorical imperative, in its undramatic, low-keyed *non serviam*.

"Low-keyed" and "undramatic" are the words for it. After the violence of *Lord Weary's Castle* and *The Mills of the Kavanaughs* and the sometimes shocking confessionalism of *Life Studies*, *For the Union Dead* is predominantly elegiac, as is *Near the Ocean*. Something has been resolved, if only in the sense that the poems of these late volumes admit of no resolution, whether in religion, in psychotherapy, or in a moral understanding of history. These things remain important, in their way; but their way is not, as in "At the Indian Killer's Grave," to transform circumstances or to provide answers. The past is irrevocable, as it was for Milton in his later years; as with Milton, human history is a record of disasters, and the problem is to survive, remaining sensitive to both personal and public terror but resisting those forms of destruction that can be resisted. Such resistance characteristically appears as ironic acknowledgment and rejection of various modes of self-deception—nostalgia for the past, for childhood, or for moments of personal love, the various Eden images visible in *For the Union Dead;* over-simplified versions of history emphatically denied in the plays of *The Old Glory;* belief in one's own innocence or, conversely, in one's special and particular evil, as in "Middle Age," "Eye and Tooth," "The Neo-Classical Urn," or again "Caligula."

Lowell's real subject in these later poems is, finally, the difficulty of remaining individually human and morally responsible in a world that offers increasingly compelling occasions for surrendering either or both. The ideologue wants to be innocent in a guilty world, and can prove his innocence out of dialectical materialism or Calvinist theology or genetic determinism; the sentimental immoralist wants to be guilty in a world whose innocence he has destroyed, like Byron's Manfred, the paranoid variety of white liberal, or perhaps the speaker of "Skunk Hour." Lowell has been persistently aware of the temptations and consolations offered by both positions, and it may be true that he has not always successfully resisted those temptations—the first in *Lord Weary's Castle*, the second in *Life Studies*. But this late work—low-keyed, often flat, sometimes even approaching the banal—gives us, regularly and under firm control, at least two parts of T. S. Eliot's notable triad of the boredom, the horror, and the glory that lie beneath beauty and ugliness, innocence and guilt.

And perhaps the third part as well, though "glory" may seem a dubious term for Lowell's later work. Whatever glory he provides lies not in the world he looks at nor in the vision through which he sees that world, but in the man who looks. Few poets would risk the flatly pitying last stanza of "Waking Early Sunday Morning," from *Near the Ocean:*

> Pity the planet, all joy gone
> from this sweet volcanic cone;
> peace to our children when they fall
> in small war on the heels of small
> war—until the end of time
> to police the earth, a ghost
> orbiting forever lost
> in our monotonous sublime.

(pp. 129-31)

Like [Wilfred] Owen, Lowell warns; like Owen's, Lowell's effort is to be truthful; and like Owen's, Lowell's primary concern is less poetry than pity. But Owen's subject was explicitly limited to "War, and the pity of War." Lowell's, like Milton's, is larger. His achievement is involved with a transforming of private experience into a reading of the American present. That reading may be grim, or lopsided, or eccentric, or simply wrong. But the painful honesty with which Lowell has arrived at it, has worked his way through its sources in historical, family, and personal experiences, serves to make of it something more than poetry. (p. 132)

George W. Nitchie, "The Importance of Robert Lowell," in The Southern Review *(copyright, 1972, by George W. Nitchie), Volume VIII, No. 1, Winter, 1972, pp. 118-32.*

When *The Old Glory*, Robert Lowell's trilogy of plays, was first produced in 1964, it appeared to offer a new direction in American theater. Concerned with the materials of American history and literature, brooding, intellectual, yet punctuated by eruptions of violence, *The Old Glory* promised to satisfy the requirements of both intellectuals and theatergoers. Moreover, as Robert Brustein put it at the time, Lowell's plays also seemed to fulfill the requirements of literary modernism. They had "the thickness and authority of myth." In them, "ritual and metaphors abound; traditional literature and historical events begin to function like Greek mythology, as the source and reflection of contemporary behavior." Lowell, Brustein predicted, "may very well come to revolutionize the American theater."

Viewed at its recent revival . . . , *The Old Glory* proves to have been prophetic enough, and not only of developments in the American theater, but of cultural life in general. In fact, it anticipates the bitter anti-Americanism that seized hold of American writing for the remainder of the 1960's. Felt in these plays is the first shock of liberal guilt in response to the black protest movement and the beginning of the Vietnam war. Though inevitably, for a modernist like Lowell, the favored vehicles of expression remain those of ritual and myth (along with the verse techniques of T. S. Eliot's poetic dramas), *The Old Glory* gives evidence of an abandonment of the modernist values of difficulty and complexity in favor of espousing a cause.

In *The Old Glory* Lowell adapted three short stories by Nathaniel Hawthorne and a short novel by Herman Melville. Interestingly, all of the tales represent attempts by two writers of the mid-19th century to comprehend "contemporary behavior" by exploring American history and myth. Like Lowell, Hawthorne and Melville adapted their sources, but, on the whole, they also adhered to them with remarkable fidelity. Just as the changes they imposed have long served scholars as measures of their intentions and accomplishment, so the changes made by Lowell in *his* materials serve to measure his intentions and accomplishment. (pp. 64-5)

In each of his plays Lowell introduces . . . an extra character to provide an interlocutor for his protagonist. Instead of using figures to draw out the moral complexities of the American character, however, he conveniently makes each of them an exacerbated reflection of the protagonists' ugly Americanness. . . . In [the] first play, as in the last, a violent ending serves to display a prototypical American as the murderer of a subject race.

The contrasts [in *Endecott and the Red Cross*] between the humorless Puritans and the playful Merry Mounters, between the wintry prayers of the former and the summery dancing of the latter, all come from Hawthorne. But where Hawthorne looks at his oppositions with a questioning eye, Lowell points a finger of accusation. . . .

Hawthorne shows the Merry Mount flower children to have been as fanatical as the Puritans. . . . In Lowell's version, which is filled with innocent dancing, there is no hint of Hawthorne's reminder that "it was high treason to be sad at Merry Mount." The fate of America, for Hawthorne, lay in the manner in which its combination of cruel and admirable qualities would work themselves out. . . . In Lowell the contrast is black-and-white, with the Puritans representing American greed and racism. His dramaturgy returns us to the manichean spirit of the Puritan imagination he had set out to reject. (p. 65)

[In *My Kinsman, Major Molineux*, Hawthorne depicts] a kind of personal coming of age that is at the same time historically predictive. Its cruelty is the cruelty both of revolution and of the break from one's parents. . . .

[In this story] Hawthorne . . . presents a ritual of *succession*: the transfer of power in the family and the state from one generation to the next as a process with built-in elements of revolution. This is a profound and troubled way to conceive of revolution. It attempts to probe the dark, unconscious side of the American Revolution, just as the Endecott stories examined both sides of Puritanism.

This second play of Lowell's trilogy, by contrast, expresses the flirtation with violence that was indulged in by politi-cally frustrated intellectuals in the 1960's; in omitting the ambiguous significance of the young man's experience [in Hawthorne's story], it turns Hawthorne's study into a celebration of youth, of going into the streets and humiliating the establishment. The literary result is a play uncritical of violence and prophetic of the literary mode of the rest of the 60's.

The last play in *The Old Glory* is about race, with Lowell again making explicit what is implied in his source: Melville's *Benito Cereno*. Here too there is a mystery, with an innocent American unable to plumb it until at the end it violently stares him in the face. . . . An American captain, Amasa Delano, brings a gift of provisions on board a Spanish ship in distress off South America. The Spaniard is a trader and a slaver. Drifting practically out of control, its human cargo strangely lolling about the decks, and its captain, Benito Cereno, apparently ill, the ship presents a mystery. The truth is that it has been taken over by the African slaves, whose leader, Babo, is pretending to be Benito Cereno's body servant in order to keep next to him and control what he says. (p. 66)

Lowell occasionally departs to good effect from the unemphatic language of the earlier plays, conveying the languid, threatening atmosphere with versifications of Melville's own magnificent rhetoric.

But it is Captain Delano who speaks the poetic lines, and herein lies the problem with the play. The audience is not permitted to respond to Delano's language or sympathize with his perplexity because Lowell has transformed him into an object of ridicule. Melville's Delano is a forthright, unsophisticated American whose faith in the rightness of things prevents him from recognizing the danger he is in. Lowell's Delano is deceived because he is a smug bigot. . . . The audience is held at bay from this Delano, for the purpose of the play is not to enable us to share his experience, as in Melville, but to condemn him as a representative of American racism.

Like Hawthorne, Melville offers a number of paradoxes regarding the American character. . . . There is a dark side of American life that must be brought to consciousness, Melville seems to be saying, yet there is also much to be said for its optimism and generous naiveté.

No such duality is suggested by Lowell's captain. His open-handed provision of goods is ridiculed as a gesture of American superiority. When at one point he nearly divines the mystery of the ship, it is not by beginning to contemplate the dark side of things, but as a result of his own greed. (pp. 66-7)

Typically for the 1960's, evil is here conceived not in moral but aesthetic terms. To climax his trilogy, Lowell presents in Captain Delano a figure to be despised chiefly for his vulgarity and his involvement in business. From these crimes it is but a short step to the racist murder with which the play ends. . . .

The Hawthorne and Melville tales selected by Lowell have for some time been recognized *loci* of modern literary criticism. By 1964, when he adapted them, they were well-known as "Kafkaesque," 19th century predecessors of the literature of the absurd. It is remarkable, therefore, that Lowell, rather than building on the proto-modernist subtleties of his sources, chose to flatten them out. It would seem that at its very moment of triumph, the modernist ideal of complexity was being abandoned by a leading modern poet.

And others quickly followed Lowell in announcing their own conversions in the 1960's: from fiction to nonfiction, from abstraction to representational pop art, and from criticism to a position "against interpretation." . . .

[One] cannot help thinking in retrospect that *The Old Glory* marked the beginning of a willful return to art as agit-prop —and the beginning of a period that Richard Hofstadter was to call an age of rubbish. (p. 67)

> *Peter Shaw, "'The Old Glory' Reconsidered" (reprinted from* Commentary *by permission; copyright © 1976 by the American Jewish Committee), in* Commentary, *June, 1976, pp. 64-7.*

Robert Lowell, that literal and spiritual scion of New England, has a thoroughly historical mind, which is to say that he has chosen a venerable mode—the mode of Gibbon, Carlyle and Marx—over a capitulation to scientific modernism. . . . [There] have been "surprising conversions" of poetic form and ideology that no one could have foreseen at every step of this remarkable career. Nevertheless, both the Catholic pacifist of the '40s who resurrected the heroic couplet, and the '60s antiwar liberal who invented the "unrhymed sonnet," are classicists, striving to reconcile a passion for the past with a lively modern voice.

It is fitting, then, that Lowell's long anticipated *Selected Poems* . . . should appear during the Bicentennial, when reevaluation of history is the national sport. For here past and present live together in a familiar yet uncomfortable marriage, from Pulitzer Prize-winning *Lord Weary's Castle* (1946) to the recent *History* (1973). . . . As in his later books, many poems go to make up one long one, so *Selected Poems* may be read as a single composition about Lowell himself.

Lord Weary's Castle has lost none of its startling power in 30 years. Although many personae speak the poems, the overriding tone is drunk with outrage and inspiration. Lowell's great originality allows him to be apocalyptic without reminding us of Blake. (p. 15)

A greater quietude is achieved in *The Mills of the Kavanaughs* (1951). The spire of Lowell's conversion to Roman Catholicism still points on the skyline: In Calvinist Concord, "Virgil must keep the Sabbath; but Apocalypse is giving way to Stoicism." An old nun reminisces about the late "Mother Marie Therese":

> Our world is passing; even she, whose trust
> Was in its princes, fed the gluttonous gulls
> That whiten our Atlantic, when like skulls
> They drift for sewage with the emerald tide.

These worldly nuns, a wonderful metaphor for Lowell's early poetry, have cloistered themselves from the "Canuck" of New Brunswick to indulge their love of Cato and French classicism. The aging sister now muses, "The Good old times, ah yes! But good that all's forgotten . . ." She is the only one strong enough to remember the past's foolishness and terror along with its beauty. This is Lowell's swan song to neoclassical narrative poetry, and to Christian themes as well. (pp. 15-16)

The famous "confessional poems" of *Life Studies* (1959), very often and badly imitated by others, examine raw and conflicting feelings about Lowell's own early life and family. . . .

Life Studies has its champions, and Lowell has included a

greater percentage of it than of any of his other books, but I do not think it shows him at his strongest. Certain poems are undeniably effective. "Sailing Home from Rapallo" for example, is skillfully built on associative contrasts, as the poet, traveling with his dead mother's coffin . . . leaves the flowering Italian spring for the family graveyard in Dunbarton. . . . Yet even in this relatively powerful poem there is a lack of directive, and the whole seems smaller than the sum of its parts.

Lowell's mature attitudes are nowhere better expressed than in "The Neo-Classical Urn" (from *For the Union Dead*, 1964). An ironic look at his passion for classicism, it parodies the vocative—"Oh neo-clasical white urn, Oh nymph, Oh lute!"—and mocks Orphic pretentions. . . . The shell is the body of the lute, traditional symbol of lyric poetry; it also represents the carapaces of turtles the poet, as a boy, left to die in a garden urn. The poet elegizes them in wrestling with the moral predicament of guilt. Finally, Lowell can identify his sufferings as an instinctive animal with the creatures whose "crippled last survivors pass, / and hobble humpbacked through the grizzled grass." It is an unflinching recognition that the artist's impetus can come from hurting or destroying others. . . .

[In *History* past] blends fluidly into present. . . .

History is actually a kind of novel, and much more like the post-*Finnegans Wake* product than most current fiction. The flexible sonnet form has the immediacy of modern speech, although Lowell has worked to attain this effect as carefully as Lawrence Sterne labored on the rambling monologues of *Tristram Shandy*. . . .

Robert Lowell is not really apologizing for doing what he sees as the artist's job. . . . The language is today's, but the voice has become old and weary. Alas, despite Lowell's craft, the muse of history's oracles are as obscure and unsatisfying as oracular utterances usually are. Perhaps it is time for our great American poet to remember with Aristotle that "Poetry is something more philosophic and of graver import than history." (p. 16)

> *Phoebe Pettingell, "Robert Lowell and the Muse of History," in* The New Leader (© *1976 by the American Labor Conference on International Affairs, Inc.), October 25, 1976, pp. 15-16.*

Going through Robert Lowell's *Selected Poems*, one realizes again how funny and witty his work can be—"With seamanlike celerity, / Father left the Navy, / and deeded Mother his property." Lowell's comic power was manifest in *Life Studies*. But as the poet moved into middle age, humor became a subtler element of his work, displacing the vindictive sarcasm of his early books.

The effect of Lowell's comedy is reductive: Clytemnestra becomes a figure not unlike the poet's mother but with a simpler sexuality—"our Queen at sixty worked in bed like Balzac." Lowell takes persons or situations that threaten one with anxiety. But rather than immerse himself in the primitive response, he stands outside like an independent observer, and sees the danger as (after all) finite: it shrinks into the commonplace, fades into the trivial, or vanishes into the unreal. . . .

In general, the threat of the dangers is to confine the poet, to deprive him of dignity, power, life—above all, of freedom. But the comic element releases him and gives him a feeling of magical transcendence. Often the danger springs from his own unmanageable emotions, the frightening impulses drilled into him during childhood, impulses that now seem predetermined and external, beyond control. But the source may also be perfectly natural, like the coming of death.

So, as the poet starts many poems, he sounds hemmed in by psychic traumas, the deteriorations of age, or the resistance of language to art. He should be too old for love, too tired to write. Yet the turn of the poem is repeatedly comic: he remains productive, and he is loved. The fate that seemed ineluctable is softened or avoided, because life defies theory.

One way of framing and therefore controlling the peculiarly human dangers is to set them off against the condition of animals. Guilt-free, untroubled by our conflicting emotions, the beasts and birds of Lowell's poems attract the smiling sympathy we extend to very young children. At the end of "Skunk Hour," the mother skunk feeding her young is absurd as well as admirable when she "jabs her wedge-head in a cup / of sour cream." So is the seal swimming "like a poodle" in "The Flaw."

But Lowell builds his most elaborate comedies around the personality of the poet, especially as the inner man confronts the outer. "Near the Ocean" is a remarkably involved, essentially comic meditation on the ego's fight to deliver itself from lust and guilt. Here the poet seems to smile at the antitheses connecting his public and private character.

In the poem he pictures himself first as a theatrical Perseus, heroically freeing mankind from the tyranny of the Medusa. But then he quickly revises the scene and appears as an indecisive Orestes, about to kill his own mother. The two deeds become absurdly equivalent: liberation of oppressed victims and betrayal of a parent; or else, love for Andromeda and hatred of Clytemnestra. . . .

[The poet] draws a witty contrast between the Mediterranean world and our own Atlantic seaboard. The one possessed myths and institutions to absorb the more wasteful passions of humanity. . . .

But in our own, troubled nation, the causal ties between character and action, past and present, are fading. . . . In "Near the Ocean," . . . the poet treats the Atlantic as an emblem of moral chaos, and seesaws his way to its edge in contrasting episodes of restraint and abandon, innocence and exhaustion, night and day. . . .

Pondering the fact that every involvement with a lover means a betrayal of an earlier love, the poet can only forgive himself for his trespasses after shriving and the penance of self-ridicule. . . . Oceanic passions have worn away his attachment to ritual and tradition. Ambiguous love remains. . . .

Behind the ambivalent attitudes one detects a friendly ribbing of Matthew Arnold's "Dover Beach". . . . "Ah, love, let us be true / To one another!" said Arnold in the face of a world meaningless and chaotic. Lowell suspects that the recipe is too simple, that love cannot be true either, and that perhaps the chaos within us requires betrayals even as the chaos without deceives our hopes and dreams.

"Near the Ocean" is a difficult poem. One of the simplest poems Lowell ever wrote suggests the ideal that floats, like Eden or Atlantis, above the humor. This poem is "Will Not Come Back.". . .

[The poet] celebrates his love in his common way of transferring emotion from the principals to their surroundings: the swallows, the honeysuckle, the season. And in the manner of Ronsard's similar sonnet, *"Quand vous serez bien vieille,"* he also moves the sense of loss from the lover to the beloved. Yet even in such earnest, conventional circumstances, the poet cannot resist a dash of ridicule. Knowing birds rather better than most poets, he observes that the insectivorous swallows who looked in on the couple were not simply to-ing and fro-ing: they were feeding in flight (as usual), and snapping up the romantic nightflies, even as reality must devour the illusions of the middle-aged seducer. . . .

The swallows of "Will Not Come Back" reappear in Lowell's best play, *Benito Cereno,* which mingles the bitter ridicule that marks his early poems with the reflective humor of his later. . . .

In the play . . . an ironical relation exists between the bleak natural setting and the grim human drama. Ordinarily good omens, the swallows here join the prophets of evil. (p. 3)

The whole line of action is conceived in harshly ironical terms; ambiguities and puns reveal the complex absurdities that line the conscience of Captain Delano; and if the visible form is a melodrama, the inner design is a bitter farce. The playwright's own sympathies seem divided between the melancholy Spaniard and the rebellious black: disillusioned age and New Left youth. For the question is whether one is determined by the other.

Among the matters that most deeply underlie Lowell's poetry is this dilemma of free will and determinism. . . . Determinism (whether Christian, Marxist, Freudian, or metaphysical) fascinates Lowell as joining men to the rest of nature and offering us relief from guilt. Free will fascinates him because he knows life loses its point when men take no responsibility for their actions.

So in his excellent poem "The Flaw" he treats human existence as a picnic in a graveyard, and sees our peculiar nature as the flaw in a universe where every other creature feels at home—as much at home as a seal in the sea. Here he compares free will to a fault in one's vision, a lopsided way of seeing reality: "if there's free will, it's something like this hair, / inside my eye, outside my eye, yet free." By imposing moral choice, it spoils our simple response to instinctive desires.

Such attitudes deeply influence the form of Lowell's work. He loves to give a theatrical setting to his meditations on the human condition. The reason is not so much the ordinary contrast between appearance and reality as Lowell's peculiar sense of playing an assigned part. Reading over a book like *Imitations,* or *History,* one is struck by the poet's habit of casting himself and his intimates as historical figures. . . .

[An] ironical comedy lies in the contrast between a "great" man's feeling of power or freedom, and history's judgment that he only conformed to a prepared script. Lowell does allow a few exceptions like Thomas More and Colonel Robert Shaw—men who consciously chose their fate. But that choice was self-sacrifice; and the poet seems to intimate that one realizes freedom best when one dies for a noble ideal.

For Lowell, even nations fit the deterministic scheme. So in "Near the Ocean," ancient Greek myths are reenacted on our side of the Atlantic, and a Greenwich Village Orestes succumbs to his own mother's depravity. Or in *Benito Cereno* the founding fathers of the United States seem to enjoy the vices of the tyrants they had denounced, while their young republic willingly inherits the criminal character of the Spanish and French monarchies.

In the making of his verse, Lowell shows his humor by incongruities that run parallel to his sympathies. Like many innovators, he has the admirable custom of adapting the material of other authors to his own purposes. When the old source shows unsuspected affinities with the new subject, we hear reverberations that are not only comic but instructive. For example, Lowell gives Caligula the voice of Baudelaire . . . and we realize that the same gloomy boredom that sends a dictator to his sadistic pleasures can also propel the creative imagination of a genius. The final joke of course is that Lowell, elsewhere, not only describes himself as subject to fits of spleen but also uses "Caligula" for his nickname, and that he has been compared with Baudelaire.

A subtler aspect of comic technique is Lowell's use of the rough sonnet form. . . .

By fixing on a much-used form, Lowell puts himself in the same position as the persons who inhabit his works; for the innovator and iconoclast must now accept the technical assignment bequeathed him by his predecessors. (p. 4)

So in the poem on Cleopatra, reduced from his translation of Horace's ode, Lowell wittily preserved the Latin opening but magically transformed it from the original Alcaic meter into the pentameter normal to a sonnet, even fitting the line into a rhyme (bought at some sacrifice of grammar). He turned the poem neatly in the traditional way, between the first eight lines and the last six. But as if to draw a mustache on the familiar face, he also insisted on reversing Horace's admiring picture of Cleopatra, and made her finally not "unhumbled" as in the Latin, but "much humbled," with an epithet that draws more sympathy from the modern reader.

Even wittier is the way Lowell miniaturized his old translation of Villon's *"Dames du temps jadis."* He got the three and a half octaves down to fourteen very short, irregular lines; but he rhymed all except the last, with only three rhyme sounds, thus producing the ghost of a sonnet for the ghosts of dead ladies. (pp. 4,6)

Pathos and comedy reach their mingled intensity of effect in Lowell's poems about the literary career. In these the self-ridicule depends on a double image: the man in his ambitious youth, planning to throne himself on Parnassus, and the older, established but dubious personage, only too conscious of the gulf between public recognition and true accomplishment. . . .

[In "The Nihilist as Hero"] Lowell faces the mutually incompatible desires of the modernist poet: to give us the experience of immediate, unrefined life, and to create something indestructible in its perfection: "to live in the world as is, / and yet gaze the everlasting hills to rubble." The poet says he wants "words meathooked from the living steer," and so opposes his own writing to the conventional idea of polished versification. . . .

On the same page is "Reading Myself," in which Lowell's patent mastery of form quarrels with the fear that he has not fulfilled his promise. The charming, witty imagery is related to that of the matching poem, and some of the lines are almost mellifluous. But the design elegantly reverses the old shape of a sonnet (i.e., description followed by reflection), for it has six lines of reflection followed by eight of a single, elaborate metaphor. . . . It seems plain that "The Nihilist as Hero" through its eloquent coarseness conveys one-half of the poet's ambition, while "Reading Myself" conveys the other, and that Lowell illustrates by his technique a yearning to reconcile art as process with art as product.

[In] "Fishnet," the opening poem of *The Dolphin*, . . . Lowell brings together the terms of love and art. The lines carry a tribute to his present wife as not only the muse who inspires him but also the dolphin that preserves him from drowning in psychotic disturbances. By relying on metaphors from fishing, it touches a current of autobiography, because that solitary pastime (as solitary as writing) provided one of the constant pleasures of Lowell's boyhood and some of the striking images of his poetry early and late. The reductive humor of writing conceived as a sport deflates the poet while sparing his beloved and his art. . . .

For all [its] free variations from traditional sonnet form, the poem clings to an underlying pentameter beat, and has a coherence of imagery that keeps it focused. . . . In design and in theme, therefore, the poem brings out his fundamental poise between liberty and determinism. (p. 6)

> *Irvin Ehrenpreis, "Lowell's Comedy," in* The New York Review of Books (*reprinted with permission from* The New York Review of Books; *copyright* © *1976 NYREV, Inc.), October 28, 1976, pp. 3-4, 6.*

Lowell ought to have been, with Elizabeth Bishop, the unquestionable strong poet between Warren and Roethke, and a younger generation of Merrill, Ashbery, Ammons, Merwin and James Wright. I am aware that a consensus of critics has so canonized Lowell, but my already intense doubts have been increased by reading his *Selected Poems,* and so I don't believe that time will confirm the age's verdict upon Lowell. The early work, in *Lord Weary's Castle,* is not often so finely wrought as the verse of Allen Tate from which it clearly derives, and its savage indignations are hollow compared to Tate's furies. Readers should test Lowell's *The Quaker Graveyard in Nantucket* against Tate's more eloquent and authentic *Ode to the Confederate Dead,* and Lowell's *Where the Rainbow Ends* against Tate's more intellectually founded savagery in *Aeneas at Washington.* Lowell's middle-period, in *Life Studies,* does not differ greatly, in degree or kind, from the bad "confessional" (actually one should say "hysterical") school which it fostered, though there are some moving exceptions in the book. My judgments may seem harsh, but at least Lowell up to that middle-phase still provokes judgment. From *History* on to the present, there seem to be no poems at all, but only drafts of the same sonnets, none of which quite earns the status of being called an actual "revision." Either the age is very wrong about this poet, or I am, and so I am willing to record myself against the age, in order to await later verdicts. I prophesy though that Lowell will be another William Vaughn Moody, and not an Edwin Arlington Robinson. (p. 22)

> *Harold Bloom, in* The New Republic (*reprinted by permission of* The New Republic; © *1976 by The New Republic, Inc.), November 20, 1976.*

Whatever else it may signify, the fact that there have now been published more books about Robert Lowell than by him testifies to his rank as our preeminent contemporary poet. And the appearance of his *Selected Poems* is summary evidence of his further position as our representative national poet—not in the sentimental manner Frost was so designated, but in the sense that the work of Auden's career once captured the shifting currents of his time, both in its public manifestations and its unconscious motivations. In much the same way, Lowell's successive volumes have not only displayed the character of our generation, most often revealed in the details of his own personality, but have also transcended that character to embody, in his art's voice and vision, its animating conscience. He is, in Richard Poirier's decisive phrase, "our truest historian." (p. 34)

What makes his *Selected Poems* so intriguing is that the book provides Lowell's own sense of his career.... *Selected Poems* affords us an adjusted vantage on his extraordinary art. His impulse toward existential narrative, his calculated use of surreal imagery, his deployment of historical allusion—all of these emerge with a heightened resonance. Likewise, his confessional method, first announced in *Life Studies* and later reaffirmed in *The Dolphin,* is revealed with new force.

As in his career, so too in his *Selected Poems* is *Life Studies* given a centering pride of place.... Not only has the book been regarded as a profound influence on American poetry generally and as both the origin and sanction of the confessional movement, but it has been represented as the radical, decisive reversal of Lowell's early style and subject, so that the poet discovered significance at once in and for himself.... His earliest and best critic, Randall Jarrell, quickly perceived the pattern of concern in the poet's development, and his judgment of *Lord Weary's Castle* [see *CLC,* Vol. 1] was prophetic for the career itself: "Anyone who compares Mr. Lowell's earlier and later poems will see this movement from constriction to liberation as his work's ruling principle of growth." ... That progress is at once tortuous and simple: a king's through the guts of a beggar. Its literary modes of expression—from the symbolic to the mythological to the historical—reflect his personal deconversion from faith to fiction to fact. In his *Notebook,* there is a line that could be used to graph the intention and effect of all his work: "I am learning to live in history."

In his Introduction to Lowell's first book *Land of Unlikeness* (1944), Allen Tate offered an important observation about the early poems—one that applies equally to *Lord Weary's Castle* (1946) which incorporates the best of *Land of Unlikeness* and so is the convenient focus for a discussion of Lowell's beginnings. There are, Tate noted, two types of poems in the collection, "not yet united." The first are "the explicitly religious poems" with their intellectualized and often satirical Christian symbolism, and the second are those "richer in immediate experience," "more dramatic, the references being personal and historical and the symbolism less willed and explicit." Together, they comprise what Hugh Staples calls a "poetry of rebellion." ... But rebellion was less the reason for than the result of the informing vision and voice of these poems. The epigraph from St. Bernard affixed to *Land of Unlikeness* offers the cause in a comparison: *Inde anima dissimilis deo inde dissimilis est et sibi* (As the soul is unlike God, so is it unlike itself). This alienation, suspended from "the jerking noose of time," is masked behind a Catholic mysticism that holds the poet apart from both unredeemed nature and the burdens of history. (pp. 34-5)

Lowell's militant faith served him also as a defiance of and defense against the "sewage" that "sickens the rebellious seas" ("Salem")—his own past and that of his family, which emerge only emblematically in *Lord Weary's Castle.* (p. 35)

The *Selected Poems* rather self-consciously minimizes the impacted apocalyptic aspect of *Lord Weary's Castle,* in favor of those poems Tate referred to as "richer in immediate experience." ... Stripped of its mystical contortions, it is easier now to see the book's treatment of concentric alienations as the prelude to Lowell's versions of the theme, under different guises, in subsequent collections. But what disturbs me is that the same argument that may have resulted in that decision may also have occasioned the poet's grievous cuts from his next book, *The Mills of the Kavanaughs* (1951). Perhaps Lowell has come to agree with the majority of his critics who, unlike myself, seem to consider the book an uncertain exercise in verbal self-indulgence.... Though these mythic monologues remain dramas of remission and evasion, they indicate that Lowell no longer wished to transform or transcend his personality, but to integrate its conflicting motifs. Poems like "Falling Asleep over the Aeneid" and "Mother Marie Therese" ... seem self-absorbed in a gorgeous display of the form itself, but generally in this book Lowell, like one of his characters, has "gone underground / Into myself." The voice is subdued to a new control, the scope narrowed from cultural to personal decline, from civilization to the family, from the Church to a marriage.... Each poem in *The Mills of the Kavanaughs* deals with a present relationship to the past, and as one critic says, the book "shares with *Life Studies* this intensity of memory." ...

During the eight years that intervened before his next book, *Life Studies* (1959), Lowell's philosophy of composition underwent a radical revaluation. The influences on that process were multiple: some of them personal (the death of his mother in 1954, and his subsequent hospitalizations and private psychotherapy), some of them literary. The poet himself began to think that the style of his early poems was "distant, symbol-ridden, and willfully difficult," and occluded their sense. His exposure to the Beats and to the peculiar responsibilities of communication demanded by reading poetry aloud, interested him in a more colloquial approach to diction and the dynamics of narrative, while his simultaneous immersion in prose studies—especially the subdued, realistic precision of Chekhov and Flaubert—confirmed him in the need for a more relaxed rhythm and line, for a syntax responsible to voice and a tone that would both prompt and project his subject.... Replacing the strictures of imposed form, Lowell's new voice worked with subtle modulations of stanza, varying rhythm, unobtrusive rhyme and sharp detail, to achieve an effect of "heightened conversation." ... So the mystical commitment of the early symbolist verse becomes a moral commitment in the confessional verse; honesty replaces devotion, fact replaces faith, in the poet's shift from ideology to history, from Catholicism to psychoanalysis as a method of self-interpretation, from apocalyptic rebellion to ironic detachment....

Life Studies begins with a renunciation of the consolations of culture and religion that had previously sustained Lowell's art and life: "Much against my will / I left the City of God where it belongs." Will surrenders to experience, eternity to history, as Lowell sets out to discover where *he* belongs. In this modern, parallaxed *Prelude,* the poet arranges his significant spots of time, pausing at moments of crisis like infernal circles, into the definition of himself that presents a life in which the only innocence is insanity, the only resolution a scavenging survival. (p. 36)

The sins of the father revisited in *Life Studies* revealed a helpless and ironic repetition in his life that Lowell was determined to avoid in his art.... *For the Union Dead* (1964), with the grand public manner of its title poem, is the "more impersonal matter," the retreat from self to sensibility: "I am tired. Everyone's tired of my turmoil".... His guilts become figures in an "unforgivable landscape," his neuroses change the studied confessions into impulsive, lyrical meditations. The therapeutic and critical success of *Life Studies*'s revelations seems to have occasioned a self-consciousness that demanded both release and restraint.... *For the Union Dead*, in other words, is the effect of *Life Studies*. (p. 37)

The political poems that are the positive achievement of *For the Union Dead* are the reason for Lowell's subsequent book, *Near the Ocean* (1967), which draws on his previous talents for elegy and imitation to complete—along with his staged poems *The Old Glory* (1965) and *Prometheus Bound* (1967)—his Juvenalian indictment of mid-century American political and spiritual failure. Written during the period of Lowell's own most active political involvement, the book sheds a good deal of personal malaise coincident with the national.... [Critics] were disappointed by *Near the Ocean*—except for its interesting reversion to a strict prosody, presumably to emphasize the severe moral tone these poems adopt. After *Life Studies,* Lowell seems to have experienced a difficulty—or possibly a diffidence—in combining the confessional and political modes. The large experiment he next undertook to overcome that difficulty—*Notebook 1967-68* (1969)—created difficulties of its own, as evidenced by the constant recycling of its format and contents, first as *Notebook* (1970) and then as *History* (1973).... The poet here resumes history by recording it, not by narrowing it to the slant of private vision but by opening his vision to the rush of outer accidents, tempered only by the seasonal cycle that underlies it and the involuntary memories that intrude upon it. It is his effort to accommodate a life in history and the life of history—though many of its first readers found it merely one damn poem after another....

It is an unfortunate necessity that the present book cannot reproduce *History*'s convulsive particularity and sacrifices its scope to a fine sample from his catalogue of tyrants and saints, artists and criminals, each a variation on the type of the monster, so that his meditations are really personalizing studies of the themes of will, authority, breakdown, and recrimination in his own history....

His portrayal of a discontented civilization derives from the late Freudian model, whose sense of instinctive aggression is finally suicidal—itself an illuminating comparison with Lowell's confrontations with both himself and his society....

[The] more congenial if painful struggles of "becoming" are the subject of his most intimate and controversial book, *The Dolphin,* an account of his divorce from [Elizabeth] Hardwick, his remarriage to Caroline Blackwood and the birth of their son Sheridan.... With the melodrama diluted, we are not offered glimpses of the wrenching affair, which leaves it with an appropriate immediacy yet lends it a retrospective quality of accomplishment....

[Lowell has said of] his own acknowledged precursors—Pound, Eliot, Williams, and Hart Crane among them— ... [that they wrote] in "styles closer to the difficulties of art and the mind's unreason." There is no better descriptive praise for Lowell's own work than that, and his *Selected Poems* are both the abstract and particulars of the successful risks he has taken to bring the mind's unreason to the orders of art, to bring the difficulties of art to the history of human experience. (p. 38)

> *J. D. McClatchy, "Robert Lowell: Learning to Live in History," in* The American Poetry Review *(copyright © 1977 by World Poetry, Inc.; reprinted by permission of J. D. McClatchy), January/February, 1977, pp. 34-8.*

[The] sense of loss [at Lowell's death] will be all the greater —for some of us, anyway—with the passing of this poet, in whose poems we were obliged to relive so much of the history and so many of the terrible emotions of our time. These he often stated with a violence that seared our sensibilities and made the poet seem, at times, an ally of the very impulses he castigated, and that, too, is something we are now left pondering. Lowell was never an easy poet, even in his most accessible poems, and he was never a decorative poet, even in those poems that were encased in the "ponderous armor," as he once called it, of an elaborate and gorgeous artifice. His verse offers us no escape from the world we know, no zone of neutrality or reprieve—no Cythera or Parnassus or pastoral repose. When, in his last book, "Day by Day," he wrote—with the nervy egotism we had learned to expect of him—that "The age burns in me," he was only stating what many of his keenest readers had long been made to feel, and what some of them, certainly, recoiled from. Especially if we are old enough to have read these poems as they appeared, year by year, first in the magazines and then revised in books, then often in further revisions in still later books, as if even the poet himself could not quite keep their asperities firmly in place, we feel compelled now to see what it is we have lived through in this poetry. (pp. 3, 36)

It is difficult now to describe the effect of "Life Studies" on its first readers in 1959. Not only Lowell's own earlier achievements but an entire poetic culture seemed, at one inspired blow, to be shattered—the whole edifice of metaphysical and ornamental verse so carefully nurtured over a period of decades in the universities, in the quarterlies and in the very bosom of the literary family from which Lowell himself had sprung and whose most eminent heir he had unquestionably become. We all know that "Life Studies" created a new idiom for a whole generation of poets—and indeed, that it was obliged, like many original works of art, to suffer the ignominy of attracting an army of vulgar imitators whose energies, to this day, produce an unending stream of noxious poetic effusions about every sort of random obsession and malevolent confusion. The vogue of "confessional" verse became for a time so firmly established—so much the normal convention of contemporary poetic discourse—that we tend to forget how divisive and disruptive and raw "Life Studies" was on its initial appearance, a book of poems that halted careers, severed friendships, probably marriages too, and caused many people to feel that they had to choose up sides in some imminent Armageddon of literary struggle.

Overlooked for the moment—they are always overlooked at such moments—were all the elements of continuity that connected the themes and materials of "Life Studies" with the poems that had preceded it and already, in some cases, become established classics, as if a mordant dissection of family history and the dislocations of the psyche had not been at the very heart of "Buttercups," "In Memory of Arthur Winslow," "Between the Porch and the Altar" and even the magisterial sweep of "The Quaker Graveyard in Nantucket." Only the differences separating the new poems from the old were felt to matter, and they mattered a lot.

The poet who, in "The Quaker Graveyard," all but choked his readers with the cadence of his terror-stricken images . . . and closed his elegy for a cousin lost at sea with a line that removed us from the cares of earthly existence, "The Lord survives the rainbow of His will," now addressed himself to his earthly family in a radically different accent:

> "Anchors aweigh," Daddy boomed in his bathtub,
> "Anchors aweigh."
> when Lever Brothers offered to pay
> him double what the Navy paid.
> I nagged for his dress sword with gold braid,
> and cringed because Mother, new
> caps on all her teeth, was born anew
> at forty. With seamanlike celerity,
> Father left the Navy,
> and deeded Mother his property.

American poetry was never the same after that.

And neither was Lowell. The poet who described himself, in the very first poem of "Life Studies," in that line about "the blear-eyed ego kicking in my berth," with its two (or is it three?) insolent and unembarrassed puns, more and more made of this kicking ego and its domestic vicissitudes the central focus of his verse. The rage to record the pulse-beat of every private emotion, to encompass every turn of current history, to deal with public events as if they were personal and the personal life as if it were ineluctably public, overtook him, and the very rhythm and texture and structure of his poetry changed again as a result. "Notebook," in its various versions, was as hard for some readers to take as "Life Studies" had been. (pp. 36, 38)

The problem was well stated by Robert Boyers in the preface he wrote for the special Robert Lowell number of the magazine "Salmagundi" marking the poet's 60th birthday. . . . "How is one to judge a sequence moving only in parts, sometimes casual almost to the point of un-caring?" Mr. Boyers wrote. "Lowell 'trained' his audience to expect classics, which he nicely provided in book after book for more than 20 years. Most of his readers could not be asked to shift gears and read the later volumes—'Note-book,' 'For Lizzie and Harriet,' 'The Dolphin,' and others —as though a brilliant poetic graph of lived experience were ample substitute."

Evidently the poet himself did not regard such observations as irrelevant to his ambitions, for he made the matter the very subject of the poem "Epilogue." . . .

> Those blessèd structures, plot and rhyme—
> why are they no help to me now
> I want to make
> something imagined, not recalled?
> I hear the noise of my own
> *The painter's vision is not a lens,*
> *it trembles to caress the light.* voice?
> But sometimes everything I write
> with the threadbare art of my eye
> seems a snapshot,
> lurid, rapid, garish, grouped,
> heightened from life,
> yet paralyzed by fact.
> All's misalliance.
> Yet why not say what happened?
> Pray for the grace of accuracy
> Vermeer gave to the sun's illumination
> stealing like the tide across a map
> to his girl solid with yearning.
> We are poor passing facts,
> warned by that to give
> each figure in the photograph
> his living name.

He remained, then, difficult—and central—to the end, the writer who gave a "living name" to more things in our lives than any other poet of his accursed generation. (p. 38)

Hilton Kramer, "The Loss of a Poet," in The New York Times Book Review (© *1977 by The New York Times Company; reprinted by permission), October 16, 1977, pp. 3, 36, 38.*

M

MacLEISH, Archibald 1892-

An American poet, playwright, editor, and political adviser, MacLeish has been continually involved in literature, art, government, and other facets of American cultural life. Often taking the political as his subject matter, MacLeish is, as James Southworth says, "not political in the party sense of the word, but in its larger connotation of the problem of man's relation to society." The scope of MacLeish's themes also encompasses nature, love, and reminiscences. MacLeish has won three Pulitzer Prizes. (See also *CLC*, Vol. 3, and *Contemporary Authors*, Vols. 9-12, rev. ed.)

Not only his journalistic but his poetic and especially his dramatic writings in the 1930's manifested the extroverted temperament which equipped MacLeish for the role of "communicator," or public spokesman. This was no new attribute: his poems of the 1920's and earlier could only have come from a man of this type, but in technique they resembled works of introspective writers, symbolists and impressionists, who were very different from MacLeish. In the 1940's he proved perhaps all too well extroverted, in the sense that his public duties left him less time for poetry. . . . If MacLeish can be said to have had a mission as distinguished from a vocation, it has been to integrate the role of poet with that of public man. (pp. 7-8)

The themes [of much of his early poetry] are amatory and visionary, mainly in the Aesthetic tradition: there is some superficial paganism, sometimes yoked with Christian symbols, and a great deal of hedonism and a rather Yeatsian preoccupation with an enchanted realm of dream. Antiscientific or at least antipragmatic sentiments, characteristically late-Victorian, come out in the dream poems "Jason" and "Realities." A time-worn motif of mutability, devouring Time, and Death the inexorable recurs abundantly. Yet, even with their intellectual representations, most of these poems seem to achieve more through music than through argument. Often the sound is more *interesting* than the sense. Imagery appears not be be handled deliberately or for the sake of symbolic possibilities, but to be mainly decorative. (p. 10)

After a few years' fascination with [Swinburnean] music, MacLeish reacted against it. It seems that his reaction was a vehement one: his later poetry has, if anything, avoided musicality and has often been downright unmusical. At any rate sense and argument reasserted themselves strongly; an

intricate, even devious, rhetoric began to dominate. For a time the sonnet retained his favor, as in the title piece of the volume *The Happy Marriage, and Other Poems* (1924). That long poem (a sort of nontragical *Modern Love*) is made up partly of sonnets and partly of other regular forms, and the verbal effects produced with these are very skillful. (p. 11)

Between 1917 and 1924 MacLeish's style acquired the features of its maturity—conscious symbolism; witty, almost metaphysical strategies of argument; compressed and intense implications—all of these owing much, though quite certainly not everything, to Eliot's example. MacLeish was usually able to resist the Eliot rhythms. His cadences were to have great diversity and to echo many predecessors. His voice, moreover, did not have much in common with the self-conscious orotundity of Eliot's middle period (it had something in common with the Prufrockian tones), and he seldom undertook vocal productions such as dramatic monologues. Indeed, a lasting mark of MacLeish's work has been the weakness of the persona. At times the diction is remote from speech; at other times it may be close to speech but bare of individuality, diffuse, as though spoken by a chorus. For this reason, despite his partial debt to Eliot, MacLeish belongs not only outside of the Browning-Tennyson traditions of monologue but also outside of the American schools which have stemmed from those. . . . MacLeish's poetry, for the most part, is not introspective, and this is why indeed no persona is wanted. According to its own purposes, its diminution of the persona is a strength: by this means it turns the reader away from the endless labyrinths of subjective illusion and irony, the "echoing vault" of the poetic self, and invites him to contemplate the phenomenal world. It does not vocalize that self: it can and often does fabricate a kind of disembodied speech, or speech whose origin need not be known. It aspires to be, and sometimes becomes, a poetry of spectacle —not always, but especially when, as in the near masterpiece "Einstein" (1926), it is wholly under the control of an intellectual concept. Then the images arrange themselves as objective counterparts of the progress of an idea—Eliot's "objective correlative" intellectualized.

MacLeish in the 1920's increasingly took pains with the formal structure of his poetry. Only through form could the swelling rhetoric be channeled. After the 1924 volume, the sonnet was neglected for a while, but it was not discarded even in *Streets in the Moon* (1926), where free verse of a highly regulated type alternates with blank verse and stanzaic patterns. Blank verse, with a few rhyming lyric passages, was used also for his symbolistic poem *The Pot of Earth* (1925) and his closet drama *Nobodaddy* (1926). (pp. 11-13)

The idea that human feelings meet nothing like themselves, no sympathetic responses, in nature, and that nature governs the life of the body as if the desires of the mind did not occur, is present in *The Pot of Earth*. But the theme of this poem is the bitterness and pity of those desires so subjected to the Gardener's indifference. Here is the case of the toad beneath the harrow. The poem was published three years after *The Waste Land* of Eliot. The two works are of roughly the same length. They have much similarity, in technique and symbolism alike. In certain notable ways they are dissimilar. *The Waste Land* is a first-person monologue to which are subordinated various genre adaptations. *The Pot of Earth* is mainly a third-person narrative, though with some first-person stream-of-consciousness effects. Stylistically *The Waste Land* is by far the more experimental and radical. Both poems, however, draw upon Sir James Frazer's work *The Golden Bough* for vegetation symbolism which, mythologically and ceremonially, represents the death and resurrection of a fertility god (e.g., Adonis) as a type of the seasonal decay and revival of nature. Both also, in applying this symbolism within a modern context of life, emphasize not the victory of life over death but the reverse of this. On the other hand, they again differ most significantly in what they apply such symbolism to. *The Waste Land,* exploring a gnostic and "spiritualized" sense of death and rebirth, uses a special myth (the Grail legend) concerning an *arrest* of fertility, whose equivalent in the poem is the male protagonist's state of emotional aridity and despair. *The Pot of Earth* applies the vegetation symbolism to its female protagonist's organic functions: the biological cycle takes place in her, as if in a plant springing up, flowering, being fertilized, bearing fruit, and dying. Or, more exactly, the girl or woman herself can be regarded as such a "pot of earth," or Garden of Adonis described by Frazer in the passage which MacLeish prefixed to his poem as a general epigraph. For, like those shallow-rooted plants forced into brief and hectic life under the Syrian sun, only to wither and to be thrown into the sea as symbols of the god bewailed by his sectaries, she leads a transient existence, devoid of any lasting meaning except the biological one. The resurrection of the fertility god means new life for nature, not for the individual. At the conclusion of *The Pot of Earth*, the woman has borne a child and has died; a chestnut tree is in flower; but she rots in the earth. Here the Adonis myth becomes the vehicle for a realization of the inextricability of life and death. MacLeish's second epigraph to the poem (later transferred to part I) is the "god kissing carrion" passage from *Hamlet;* and part III is called "The Carrion Spring." In *Hamlet* "carrion" is the prince's coarse designation for Ophelia: evidently the woman in *The Pot of Earth* has a sacrificial role like that to which the Ophelia personage is doomed in *The Waste Land.* But she has been sacrificed by the indifference of nature, not the brutality of man.

The 1925 text of *The Pot of Earth*, several pages longer than the text printed in *Poems, 1924-1933* (1933) and thereafter, adopts the *Waste Land* technique of making the past and present interpenetrate, so that the modern woman's life cycle is depicted in timeless fusion with that of a primitive world: its incidents are abruptly juxtaposed to details from the Adonis ritual. But the three principal passages in which this effect is created have been omitted from the later printings, leaving the poem free of the startling "intertemporal" counterpoint typical of Eliot, and with a contemporary texture purely. Yet, beneath this, continual allusions to the Adonis ritual remain to suggest a theme of unending recurrence. Perhaps recapitulation, rather than recurrence, is the universalizing motif in *The Pot of Earth . . . .*: this woman is eternal woman, and eternal woman typifies reproductive nature, whose dream is her life. She, like the Garden of Adonis in antiquity, blossoms as an emblem, a signature, of some omnipresent and all-involving archetype of cyclical life and death. Her anonymity is as profound as that of Tiresias, the *Waste Land* persona; but whereas he is obscured by Eliot's pretentious legerdemain with literary cross references, she has a constant, though shadowy, identity.

There seems to be a philosophical difference between *The Pot of Earth* and *The Waste Land* in the ways they pose their protagonists against the world. Eliot's poem is very much in a "psychological" tradition; that is, starting from an Idealist's assumption that the individual point of view is of paramount importance because it uniquely focuses knowledge of externals, *The Waste Land* attains form by offering a view from a single point, or through a single narrow peephole. It recalls Bergsonian and stream-of-consciousness fiction. MacLeish's poem seems to start from a Realist's assumption that there is nothing special in point of view as such; that the law of things is common to all. It depicts a *typical* relation of the natural to the human, indeed choosing to examine the fate of someone quite average. Whatever the resemblance of MacLeish's techniques to those of subjectivists and symbolists, his *fond* was otherwise. His poem, like Eliot's, uses Aesthetic and symbolist procedures to assist naturalistic statement, but his is closer to a philosophical naturalism which assumes the total subjection of man to time and chance.

There was much of the eighteenth-century rationalist in the MacLeish of the 1920's and in his political character later; much, also, of the scientific observer of life. He had made an almost complete break with his antiscientific and aesthetical beginnings as a poet. He now accepted the scientists' description of reality—only boggling at its falsification of experience. The external world he confronted was the one described by the astronomers, by the biologists, and above all by the mathematical physicists of his own day. Whereas Eliot and Pound and Yeats were ancients, MacLeish was a modern. One may believe that Einstein's space-time-energy continuum receives, in the work of MacLeish, its most important poetic treatment to date—a treatment not through casual allusion for contemporary color, but through exact intellectual integration with the subject matter of felt life. A thematic carry-over takes place from *The Pot of Earth* to later poems—the conflict between personal hopes and natural law, developed first, perhaps a little less pessimistically, in *Nobodaddy.* (pp. 16-18)

The central paradox of "Ars Poetica" [from *Streets in the Moon*] is that it makes sense only when the reader accepts its sense as a function of form. It then survives as the aesthetic object it approves—with the proviso that the approval must be held as an utterance *in vacuo*, a silence. . . . The real subject of "Ars Poetica" is itself, by a sort of narcissism of the written word as "pure poetry"; this poem exhibits aestheticism circling round, as it were, and returning like the equator upon the round earth. The result contrives a stasis indeed, free or nearly free of time's rotation. . . . "Ars Poetica," somewhat Yeatsian like various other short poems in the volume, looks also Keatsian: the whole poem speaks with a voice which, like that of the Grecian urn when it equates beauty and truth, belongs to a realm of ideality and is relevant only to that. Such a realm, proper to poetry, conflicts with nature; MacLeish's long poem "Einstein" reviews the naturalistic conception that man, at least, cannot quite escape the prison of his time-bound flesh. That, too, is a Keatsian thought.

"Einstein" in theme recalls *Nobodaddy;* the resemblance proves useful in the unraveling of its complexities. Not only is the subject difficult (like most subjects) unless one already understands it, but the rhetoric lumbers in obscurity. Nevertheless the poem operates compellingly upon the emotions, and it ought to be one of the best known philosophical poems of the period. The Einstein of the title is modern intellectual man, scientist, represented microcosmically as a sort of Leopold Bloom, atomic and entire (*ein Stein*, perhaps—a stone, or at least a pebble!), who has inherited the problem and the mission of MacLeish's Cain, the mission of rationality. The Einsteinian universe is rationality triumphant, as indeed it is the triumph of the modern spirit. The poem (a narrative showing the process of "going back," by reason, to a condition which seems to repeal Adam's alienation from nature and to reunite his posterity with the primal creator—i.e., in effect deifying man) reveals the way back by recapitulating the way forward, from any infancy to full consciousness. (pp. 21-2)

Those critics are surely wrong who see "Einstein" as antiscientific; rather, the poem, like *Nobodaddy,* affirms the necessary destiny of man to subdue everything to his knowledge—everything but the stubborn, atavistic ape within, which *must* refuse to yield. The anecdotal poem "The Tea Party" says all that need be said about man's sense of his primitivism; "Einstein" says something further, that the animal residuum is man's very life. The tragic fate awaiting this life has already been revealed in *The Pot of Earth.* "Einstein" is not tragic; it is not even precisely critical. It is an intellectual celebration of an intellectual triumph, attended by a voice bidding the *triumphator* remember that he is dust. (p. 23)

The gloom pervading *The Hamlet of A. MacLeish* is left behind in the next collection, *New Found Land: Fourteen Poems* (1930). Here the over-all tone is one of acceptance—not the unreflecting acceptance urged but resisted in the closing part of the earlier poem, but something urbanely detached. There is a return to the meditativeness of an even earlier period, in poems about memory and time; along with this there is an advance toward a new theme of affirmation, for which a tone of optimism comes into being. (pp. 26-7)

The hallmark of [*Conquistador* (1932)], unfortunately, is an unrelieved sense of enormous confusion. In the memory of the speaker, the successive episodes are crowded with detail; and an effect of "nonlinear" construction is heightened by the frequent use of parataxis. That is, the language depends a good deal on coordinated statements, whether or not with conjunctions. That this device was intentional is evident from the special use of the colon as a divider; it is made to separate phrases of all kinds. The elements which are thus compounded stand in any order: logic seems not to be in question, since free association controls largely.

If the influence of St.-J. Perse dominates the larger framework of the poem, affecting the shape of its "grand sweep," still another influence, that of the Ezra Pound of the *Cantos,* often prevails at close quarters. The arbitrary juxtaposition of "significant" details is Poundian. So, too, is one ingredient of MacLeish's subject matter, the use of Book XI of the *Odyssey* in the "Prologue," where Bernál Díaz is given a role like that of the Homeric Tiresias, summoned from the dead along with fellow ghosts to speak to the living. . . . Though more in key with the biblical rhapsodies of Perse than with the social grumblings of Pound, *Conquistador* lacks optimism. For one thing it is based on one of the bloodiest and most barbarous exploits in history, one which destroys the empire it conquers and which ends in a retreat. Furthermore it is set forth by a spokesman for the dead and disillusioned, himself aware, in his very book, that death hangs over him. At the last he longs for the impossible resurrection of youthful hope. . . . In general this poem, far from acclaiming the origin of the New World as the harbinger of American civilization, is negative as well as confessional. Díaz, like MacLeish's Hamlet, is a wastelander, and what he longs for is a lost innocence that in fact was never real at all: certainly it did not dwell in the Aztec priestly slaughterhouse or in the hearts of the Spanish butchers either. In the poem it only tantalizes like a gilded dream of El Dorado. (pp. 29-30)

The short volume *Public Speech: Poems* (1936) is strong in social implication, like MacLeish's plays in the same decade; but for part of its length it is different in manner from the usual "public" poetry. . . . [The] adjective *public* is not synonymous with *national* or with *political* or with *cultural* in a social scientist's sense; it connotes all that is common, all that touches everyman. Those of MacLeish's poems that treat of the individual in society, or of society in history, do seem public in a more "communal" sense than is possible to a lyric commemoration of love; but this subject, too, can be so treated that its private values become general meanings. Moreover, the first poem in the volume, "Pole Star," celebrates social love, the observance of charity for all, as a guiding principle in an age of misdirections; almost the whole collection is about human bonds of feeling. What *public* meant to MacLeish at this juncture seems to have been dual: in one aspect it came close to our present slack sense of *relevant;* in another it rather implied *impersonal* in something like Eliot's sense, that is, marked by avoidance of self-absorption. In "The Woman on the Stair," personal subject matter becomes archetypal.

"The Woman on the Stair" is really about the psychology of love. The Eros who rules here is the god of maturity; it would be instructive to set beside this another group of lyrics, also a sequence and also a chronicle of love's progress, but focusing on youthful love—Joyce's *Chamber Music.* There the intensities of feeling wear romantic disguises which in turn undergo transformations into fabrics of symbol. Here, viewed alike from the masculine and the feminine sides, are the great intensities—need, selfishness, shame, jealousy, fickleness, boredom—and time's deadly gift, detachment, all of them functions of a pragmatism that often governs human relations in the mask of the romantic spirit. This sobering vision culminates in the remarkable closing poem , "The Release," a meditation on past time as stasis. What "The Woman on the Stair" projects as a "cinema" sequence, a passional affair involving two people only, becomes in projection a far-reaching commentary on behavior and motivation. (pp. 32-4)

[*Land of the Free—U.S.A.* (1938)] is hard to judge as poetry because, as published, it was tied to a series of eighty-eight contemporary photographs in order that (according to a note by MacLeish) it might illustrate *them*. The photographs were already collected before the poem was written. (pp. 34-5)

America Was Promises [1939] is indisputably the most eloquent of the "public" poems. It contrives an absolute alliance between theme and voice; actually the theme helps to flesh the voice so that it surmounts its usual anonymity and acquires the solidity of a persona. Who the persona is, is unclear, but what he is, is obvious, a prophet but contemporary, a liberator but traditionalist, a revolutionary but sage.... In its intellectual ambiguity *America Was Promises* had much in common with the philosophy of the national administration at that period. So seen, of course, the poem is milder than the rhetoric of its conclusion: it is simply urging people to remain loyal to New Deal doctrines at home and American policy abroad. Really it is much better as a poem than as a message: for once, MacLeish's adaptation of St.-J. Perse's geographic evocations seems precisely right. (pp. 35-6)

[*Actfive and Other Poems* (1948)] is fully postwar, and it contains the perceptions of a man who had worked within government and who now had a far more exact idea of the gulf between political dreams and reality. It is the book of his second renaissance. A number of the poems, quite apart from the title piece, are of immense interest technically. (p. 36)

The title piece, "Actfive," was the most significant poem by MacLeish since the publication of his *Hamlet*. It does what a major work by a developing poet has to do: it clarifies the meaning of his previous major works in relation to one another, and it subjects to new form the world which his art is trying now to deal with. This poem relates to *The Pot of Earth*, to "Einstein," and to *The Hamlet of A. MacLeish;* and though quite intelligible independently of those, it gains depth and complexity by the relation.... "Actfive" continues, in a manner of speaking, the actions of that nightmarish poem [*Hamlet*], advancing them beyond the circle of a single protagonist's mind and showing that they involve all men. (p. 37)

Part III, "The Shape of Flesh and Bone," identifies the sought hero at last; it is flesh and bone, unidealized, existential man, instinctive, physical, able to define the meaning of his universe to himself—man the transitory but in spirit indomitable.... The closing lines reaffirm the unutterable loneliness of man in his universe of death, but, like "Einstein," leave him with his inviolate creaturehood. It is ironic that "Actfive" should so circuitously return to the point insisted upon in "Einstein"; for it steers by the opposite pole, assuming that man's lordly reason, far from having subdued nature to its understanding, has been dethroned utterly. Equally, the animal self here, which can still "endure and love," is all that preserves man from destruction; whereas in "Einstein" it is the only thing that debars him from godhead. (p. 38)

Clearly the leading theme of *Songs for Eve,* the whole book, is man's ordering function; the collection is closer to "Einstein" and the other space-time poems of *Streets in the Moon* than are the works in between. Here much is made of the origin of the human soul within space-time, particularly in "Reply to Mr. Wordsworth," where the proposition that the soul "cometh from afar" is refuted by an appeal to Einsteinian physics and —paradoxically—to the felt life of the emotions. The poems "Infiltration of the

Universe," "The Wood Dove at Sandy Spring," "The Wave," "Captivity of the Fly," and "The Genius" are emblematic, and they happen also to compose a miniature bestiary. The volume pays tribute impartially to matters of intellect and of feeling; these compressed parables divide between them.

The Wild Old Wicked Man (1968) explores the whole scale of MacLeish's concerns, still optimistically. Old age and youth, time, domesticity, contemporary manners, love, death—these predominate. Introspection is not overworked, but two of the most arresting poems in the volume are "Autobiography," on childhood vision, and "Tyrant of Syracuse," on the subliminal self.... [The elegy to Edwin Muir] quotes "The Linden Branch," applying to a *green memory* the graceful conceit of the green bough as a musical staff with leaves for notes. Yeats furnished the title of the volume; and the title poem, placed at the end, closes on the theme of

> ... the old man's triumph, to pursue
> impossibility—and take it, too,

which is a signature for MacLeish's poetry, restating the theme of Adam victorious, fallen upwards into a stasis of art and eternity. (pp. 40-1)

Herakles and *J. B.* show Janus faces of the human struggle to neutralize the blind sentence of death passed upon mankind. Their two scales of poetry, exemplifying MacLeish's maturest talents, correspond to extremes of lyricism and tragic realism in speech. (p. 45)

> *Grover Smith, in his* Archibald MacLeish, *#99 in the University of Minnesota Pamphlets on American Writers (© copyright 1971 by the University of Minnesota), University of Minnesota Press, Minneapolis, 1971.*

It is to the art of poetry that Mr. MacLeish has given the best part of his mind and heart, and it is to the poetry that we must turn—and return—for a sense of his true accomplishment....

The writer who gave us the lengthy "Conquistador" and "Frescoes for Mr. Rockefeller's City" and "America Was Promises" will always, perhaps, have a place in the cultural history of the 1930's, but it is not primarily as poetry that such works survive today.

Given Mr. MacLeish's taste for large mythic endeavors of this sort, it is not surprising to find the results occupying a good deal of space in his "New and Collected Poems, 1917-1976." But the real interest of the book lies elsewhere, I think—in the discovery (as it will be for many readers) or re-discovery (as it will be for some) that he is, and always has been, an engaging and often moving lyric poet, a poet of tender emotions and fastidious ethical yearnings, a very personal poet who has found in love, in friendship, in poetry and in nature, even in death, the subjects that inspired his purest and deepest writing.

This gift for a delicate and inward lyricism has by no means diminished with age. He had it in his 20's and 30's, and it is there, if anything even stronger, in the poems he has written in his 70's and 80's.... The elegiac note that is sounded in ... so many of the later poems was there at the beginning, too—in the poem about his college years, "Baccalaureate," written 60 years ago, and in the memorials to his brother, a casualty of the First World War—but there is a clarity of language and feeling in the later poems that we do not find in the earlier ones. Age has brought, if not superior wisdom, a more concentrated perception.

Some of the most moving of the later poems are written as memorials to dear friends who were poets ("Mark Van Doren and the Brook," "Cummings"), others deal with death itself ("Conway Burying Ground") and with love, marriage and age in relation to death ("The Old Gray Couple," with its haunting last line: "We know that love, like light, grows dearer toward the/dark."). They are very much the poems of a survivor, and "Survivor" is the title of one of the most beautiful of them (beautiful, too, in its skill as well as its emotion). (p. 27)

Reading such poems, one has no doubt that it was in the lyric mode, with its inward examination of private experience, that Mr. MacLeish found his true vocation. The poems addressed to public issues are simply not in the same class, and not only those of the 1930's but the recent ones, too. The voice of civic rectitude in his verse is pious, stentorian, false—less so in the later poems, perhaps, but it is still a voice that is a poor surrogate for action or impotent rage. And the odd thing about Mr. MacLeish's career is that two of his most famous poems—"Ars poetica," written in the 20's, and "Invocation to the Social Muse," written in the 30's—are eloquent warnings against precisely this sort of tendentious sermonizing. . . .

Archibald MacLeish is, then, a contradictory and paradoxical poet, and his "New and Collected Poems, 1917-1976" is a book, a big book, very much divided against itself. One would like to see some day a slenderer volume of short lyrics culled from this large book—a book made up of the poems of the "man alone"—for it looks very much as if it will be by those poems that this writer will live. (p. 28)

> *Hilton Kramer, in* The New York Times Book Review *(© 1976 by The New York Times Company; reprinted by permission), October 3, 1976.*

MacLeish is a gracious, civilized, humane and genuine poet who has never been able to dispel wholly the shadows of Pound and Eliot. His elegiac language is Eliot's; his language of history Pound's; his attitudes as a citizen and a humanist are opposite to theirs, but a poet's stance *as poet* is always a matter of language. (p. 22)

> *Harold Bloom, in* The New Republic *(reprinted by permission of* The New Republic; *© 1976 by The New Republic, Inc.), November 20, 1976.*

It saddens me to think that MacLeish, whom I know to be a gentle, decent man, should be disheartened or even disgruntled reading a young nobody denigrating his life work [*New and Collected Poems, 1917-1976*]. But uncritical veneration is disrespect. The only compliment one can pay a poet is to compare him to the greatest.

The problem with MacLeish's poems is that they are almost all quite good. Prompted by a quick intelligence and sensitivity, there are few poems or lines one can extract and dangle as damaging evidence. Always level-headed, unlike Eliot, Pound, Frost, or Yeats, there seems to be nothing in MacLeish's politics or aesthetics with which one can take strong issue. Most of his poems are well made. The index to my copy is littered with the check marks by which I record my moderate interest in a poem.

But I find only four asterisks—my mark for especial interest—and only one double asterisk, to remind myself of an indispensable poem. Nor, when I am reading or after I close the book, is there a particular voice, an unmistakable tone, a personality, ringing or echoing in my head. What MacLeish has said has seemed true, intelligent, rhythmic, not unoriginal, and yet I have not heard *him,* felt that trembling that makes a great artist seem better known to one than one's best friend. When one reads such lines as "Now as at all times I can see in the mind's eye"; or "When I see birches bend from left to right"; or "At the first turning of the second stair"—instantly one is drawn into worlds whose clarity makes them somehow mysterious: One senses a peculiarly obsessive observer.

By contrast, three MacLeish openings—"Under an elm tree where the river reaches"; "From these night fields and waters do men raise"; "Who is the voyager in these leaves"—chosen moreorless at random, suggest a diligent poet, but no person—a desire to write a poem without the obsessive need to do so that will give it life.

I wish I could be more precise. With stories or expository prose one can explain effect on the basis of logical development of idea, image, plot, character. It is not difficult to understand why Miss Havisham continues to creak in our consciousness long after we've forgotten her fictional context. But a poem depends on a conjunction of sound and sense, a tug of syllables that keeps the rope of meaning taut. Subtract a suffix—"At the first turn of the second stair"—and the whole velocity and mystery of the line is lost—the sinuous-seeming sliding of the stair—though it is not easy to explain how the meaning has been changed.

Time and again, MacLeish has good ideas for poems, but the poems themselves flap their wings like penguins. . . .

In "'Dover Beach'—A Note to That Poem," a vivifying metaphor, that generations resemble successive waves, is hobbled by an unmusical realization: "Let them go over us all I say with the thunder of/What's to be next in the world. It's we will be under it!" Time and again, one yearns for MacLeish to be less diligent, less complete, to remember that a poem is not just its words, but also the silences it creates, the hollows that suck us in.

Perhaps his ablest poem, for which he was awarded his first Pulitzer Prize, is *Conquistador,* a book-length recollection of Cortes's Mexican expeditions by one of his soldiers, Bernal Diaz. In his "preface," Diaz movingly declares his right to recall his experience and the thrill of remembering. His language, there and following, is sensuous and particular. If one lacks a sense of the characters, one feels the locales and the fatigue and exaltation of the troups. One is conscious that the poem is written well, that MacLeish has reined the Dantean terza rima into an obedient English verse form. One admires—and wonders: What is the point of the story, the reason for its telling? Pleasant as recollection may be, it is insufficient cause to tell a tale. . . .

MacLeish's weakness as a poet may be his strength as a man: his level headedness, which saves him from having to invent and believe in an imaginary order to protect himself from actual disorder. No Michael, wrestling with meaning, MacLeish reacts and feels as much as, but no more than, every man. To change metaphors: He sinks his fishhook as deep as any fishhook and catches what we all catch—that death is serious, that time passes, etc.—but none of the marvelous monsters that greatness yanks from the deeps. His poems come from life but lack lives of their own.

That said, it is a pleasure to report that the best poems in this volume are the "New." By surviving, MacLeish has entered into unfamiliar poetic territory. His love is no longer conventional: Everyman dies at 65, and most poets sooner. Neither could the knowledge or tone of "The Old Gray Couple (2)" (my index's only double asterisk) be faked by a younger man. Eliot's "Gerontion" is a poseur by comparison....

Despite their competent composition, almost none of MacLeish's collected poems enlarged my insights. I found myself constantly (a bad sign) noticing the "good parts" in individual poems, wishing like anything that the parts would coalesce into an elevating whole. "The Old Gray Couple (2)" is not just a fine poem, but a promise, an occasion for hope. What a golden irony if art, which delights in ironies, should allow MacLeish posterity for work done after most men cease being productive.

May he live, laureate of senescence, forever.

> *Carll Tucker, "Intelligent Craftsmanship, but Where's the Damaging Evidence?" in* The Village Voice *(reprinted by permission of* The Village Voice; *copyright © by The Village Voice, Inc., 1976), November 29, 1976, p. 90.*

*   *   *

MAILER, Norman   1923-

A novelist, essayist, critic, and film-maker, Mailer is one of America's most controversial literary personalities. The subjects of Mailer's writings vary tremendously from war, in *The Naked and The Dead*, **to artistic creation, in** *Barbary Shore*. **A recurrent concern is the psychological forces at work in each American's daily life, and, to Mailer, these forces reflect a nation that is often immature and irrational. Mailer has received the Pulitzer Prize and the National Book Award. (See also** *CLC*, **Vols. 1, 2, 3, 4, 5, and** *Contemporary Authors*, **Vols. 9-12, rev. ed.)**

I could not, with the best will in the world, make any sense out of *The White Negro* and, in fact, it was hard for me to imagine that this essay had been written by the same man who wrote the novels. Both *The Naked and the Dead* and (for the most part) *Barbary Shore* are written in a lean, spare, muscular prose which accomplishes almost exactly what it sets out to do. Even *Barbary Shore*, which loses itself in its last half ... never becomes as downright impenetrable as *The White Negro* does.

Now, much of this, I told myself, had to do with my resistance to the title, and with a kind of fury that so antique a vision of the blacks should, at this late hour and in so many borrowed heirlooms, be stepping off the A train. But I was also baffled by the passion with which Norman appeared to be imitating so many people less talented than himself, i.e., Kerouac, and all the other Suzuki rhythm boys. From them, indeed, I expected nothing more than their Pablum-clogged cries of *Kicks!* and *Holy!* It seemed very clear to me that their glorification of the orgasm was but a way of avoiding all of the terrors of life and love. But Norman knew better, had to know better. *The Naked and the Dead*, *Barbary Shore*, and *The Deer Park* proved it. In each of these novels, there is a toughness and subtlety of conception and a sense of the danger and complexity of human relationships which one will search for in vain, not only in the work produced by the aforementioned coterie, but in most of the novels produced by Norman's contemporaries.

What in the world, then, was he doing, slumming so outrageously, in such a dreary crowd?

For, exactly because he knew better and in exactly the same way that no one can become more lewdly vicious than an imitation libertine, Norman felt compelled to carry their *mystique* further than they had, to be more "hip," or more "beat," to dominate, in fact, their dreaming field; and since this *mystique* depended on a total rejection of life, and insisted on the fulfillment of an infantile dream of love, the *mystique* could only be extended into violence. No one is more dangerous than he who imagines himself pure in heart; for his purity, by definition, is unassailable.

But *why* should it be necessary to borrow the Depression language of deprived Negroes, which eventually evolved into jive and bop talk, in order to justify such a grim system of delusions? Why malign the sorely menaced sexuality of Negroes in order to justify the white man's own sexual panic? Especially as, in Norman's case, and as indicated by his work, he has a very real sense of sexual responsibility, and even, odd as it may sound to some, of sexual morality, and a genuine commitment to life. None of his people, I beg you to notice, spend their lives on the road. They really become entangled with each other, and with life. They really suffer, they spill real blood, they have real lives to lose. This is no small achievement; in fact it is absolutely rare. No matter how uneven one judges Norman's work to be, all of it is genuine work. No matter how harshly one judges it, it is the work of a genuine novelist, and an absolutely first-rate talent. (pp. 73-4)

> *James Baldwin, "The Black Boy Looks at the White Boy" (first published in* Esquire *Magazine; copyright © 1961 by Esquire, Inc.), in* Esquire, *May, 1961 (and reprinted in* Norman Mailer: A Collection of Critical Essays, *edited by Leo Braudy, Prentice-Hall, Inc., 1972, pp. 66-81).*

[The] seriousness of *An American Dream* involves a denial of certain kinds of novelistic seriousness, of social probability and relevance, as well as of so-called intellectual depth. It is an intensely private novel, and one key to what has offended or puzzled the reviewers is probably in the way Mailer allows his hero to treat himself, in that peculiar blend of self-concentration and self-deprecation which, in fact, largely accounts for the originality of his language. The expectations of a political novel which might be set up by the joke that begins the story are rapidly destroyed. Mailer in *An American Dream* is somewhat like Balzac in his attitudes toward social maneuvering and power: he seems just as naïvely melodramatic in his notion of what goes on at the top, and the images of political power in both novelists should be immediately recognizable as private mythologies expressing private obsessions and dreams of power ideally demonic. Both are impatient with the specific strategies for gaining and keeping power, as distinct from the excitement of exercising it.... Mailer, like Balzac, is better at suggesting some of the sexual impulses that perhaps account for the enjoyment of power than at detailing the more prosaic and conscious calculations that pave the way to it.... [In Kelly's] brutal, simultaneous appeal to impulses of anality, homosexuality, necrophilia and cannibalism, the magic of his power is made marvelously concrete by the energy of his indulgence in bodily fantasies, an energy so great that Rojack begins to share the fantasies, to feel "unfamiliar desires."

It is power of this sort that both fascinates and terrifies Rojack; the murder of Deborah and, perhaps more significantly, the story of that murder are his attempts to free himself from it. If Rojack responds like an electric coil to multitudinous "invasions" from the outside world, it is because he is pathologically convinced that what he calls his "center" may be stolen from him at any moment, at the same time that he feeds on this sense of constant threat as a kind of substitute for a sense of self. This fantasy provides what could be called the psychological theme, or obsession, of the novel. . . . *An American Dream,* at any rate, records a dramatic and exhilarating struggle with [an] "empty dread," an attempt to fight the vampire complex that makes Rojack both fear and need a world of devouring bitches, telepathic powers and omnipotent smells. The novel, for all its apparently complacent acceptance of magic, is a continuous attack against magic, that is, an attack against fantasies of the self as both all powerful and totally vulnerable.

The strategy of resistance is, inevitably, literary, and the power of *An American Dream* is in its demonstration of verbal tactics which finally make what I have called the psychological theme irrelevant. The "courage" which is made so much of in the novel, and which the reviewers have found lamentably banal as a moral philosophy, is much more of a brilliant and difficult trick than a virtue in the ordinary sense. While it is often merely the bravery born of a superstitious compulsion, as when Rojack forces himself to walk along the parapet of Kelly's terrace, it involves, more profoundly, a willingness to entertain the most extravagant fantasies and hallucinations in order to change their affective coefficient. . . . Rojack discovers fantasy as a source of imaginative richness in himself instead of fearing it as an ominous signal from mysterious, external powers. He moves, in other words, from fantasy as a psychological illusion about the world to the use of fantasy as a somewhat self-conscious but exuberant display of his own inventive powers. Every menace becomes the occasion for a verbal performance, and his fluttering nervousness about being deprived of his "center" is rather humorously belied by the incredibly dense and diversified self which his language reveals and creates. Nothing in the book (not even Rojack's moving attempt to know love as something sane and decent with Cherry) except the virtuosity of the writing itself indicates a way out of the nightmare Rojack seems to be telling. The nightmare would be nothing more than a nasty story if Mailer, like his critics, had allowed it to separate itself from the virtuosity, from, especially, the metaphorical exuberance which is, I think, a way of mocking and outdoing the dangerous inventiveness of a magic-ridden world. This means, of course, that the *playfulness* of the novel is by no means a frivolous attitude toward "dirty" or "ugly" events, but rather the natural tone of a man for whom events have become strictly literary-novelistic situations to be freely exploited for the sake of a certain style and the self-enjoyment it perhaps unexpectedly provides.

It is, then, irrelevant to complain of improbable situations or unreal dialogue in *An American Dream.* Rojack's playfulness, his verbal exuberance, is the sign of a confident use of power, and it involves an occasionally reckless indifference to the probability of his own experience. The telling of his story becomes *Rojack's* invention as well as Mailer's once his life confronts him as choices to be made about language and novelistic form. The plot of *An American Dream* is, therefore, nothing more than a mode of Rojack's inventive exuberance, and, while it is perhaps understandable that the anecdotal aspect of fiction should trick us most eas-

ily into confusions between art and life, we should be admiring the power of extravagance in Rojack's tall story instead of upholding the faded banner of verisimilitude. . . . And much of the novel's humor is in the unexpected shifts from one kind of writing to another. . . . (pp. 121-24)

This free play of virtuosity in the narrative structure of *An American Dream* also characterizes Rojack's similes, which the reviewers have pounced on with a comical solemnity about stylistic propriety. . . . But Mailer in *An American Dream,* unlike Flaubert, never uses metaphor for the purpose of arresting our attention, of making us stop to admire a tiny verbal island, an exquisite *trouvaille.* Rojack's similes *make* a self of enormous, even fantastic imaginative range, and their power lies in a kind of dialectical reference to, and denial of characters and events in the novel. They change the story, as it is being told, into a challenge to the resources of fantasy; their complexity is not in their farfetched nature, but lies rather in the dramatic burden they carry of transforming oppressive experience into tokens of stylistic play. The plausibility of Rojack's similes is irrelevant; what matters is that he makes us feel his associations as spontaneous, irresistible fantasies, and that we accept his most elaborate verbal constructions as illustrating the elaborateness of immediacy rather than of development toward an idea. For no intellectual strategy could explain the humor or justify the casual difficulty of Rojack's style. It is, in a sense, his very absence of thought (an absence deplored by [critics]) which creates Rojack's "system" of defense, his refusal to conceptualize sensation and to be reasonable about the accumulation of metaphor which makes of his writing an act of total responsiveness. (pp. 124-25)

[The] irrelevance of what has been said about *An American Dream* must perhaps be explained by the shock and resentment produced by a work that would force us to admit the self-indulgence, the particularity and even, in a certain sense, the irresponsibility of interesting art. Mailer's admirers are already hard at work making him responsible and relevant to all sorts of things, but to read *An American Dream* is, happily, to see the hopelessness of their good intentions. Nothing, after all, could be more typical of the marvelous lightness of imagination than to test, in the most scrupulous detail, the possibility of a grown-up love, built on tenderness and respect, with Cherry, and then to end the whole thing on the frivolous note of that charmingly nonsensical phone call to heaven. (p. 126)

> *Leo Bersani, "Interpretation of Dreams," in* Partisan Review *(copyright © 1965 by Partisan Review, Inc.), Fall, 1965 (and reprinted in* Norman Mailer: A Collection of Critical Essays, *edited by Leo Braudy, Prentice-Hall, 1972, pp. 120-26).*

Mailer is at once the most intrinsically relevant and the most inventively original of Fitzgerald's inheritors, and thus a most valuable writer in whom to study the reaches of Fitzgerald's tradition both intensively and, as it were, from the inside. (p. 120)

Hemingway is the writer most frequently cited in Mailer's prose, of course, and usually with admiration. But Fitzgerald, who turns up only a little less frequently, he often treats with condescension, sometimes even with scorn. (Though in his introduction to his recently published collection of short fiction Mailer speaks of Fitzgerald as "another favorite" in the short story game.) And yet in the important ways Mailer's fiction is much more like Fitzgerald's than like Hemingway's. The kinds of men and women inhabiting their fictional worlds, and the archetypal relationships obtaining between them—the women as promissory images of value and possibility, the men as agents of motive and choice—are clearly similar. Like modern versions of Spenserian knights, their heroes move through mazes of sexual ambiguity inhabited by true and false goddesses, by restorative earth-mothers and half-mad Cassandras, by tyrantesses and simple girls, who lead or mislead them in their uncertain quests for fulfillment or aliveness or goodness. "Mate the absurd with apocalyptic," Mailer once said of his own imagination's susceptibility, "and I am captive." This self-description could as easily have been Fitzgerald's as Mailer's. But it could never have been Hemingway's. Questions of "influence" aside, the least one could say about the relation between Fitzgerald and Mailer is that *The Deer Park* and *An American Dream* seem to derive from a sensibility with much the same essentials as that which produced *The Great Gatsby, Tender Is the Night,* and *The Last Tycoon.* (pp. 128-29)

An American Dream seems startlingly to be the kind of novel Fitzgerald might have conceived had he lived through the Second World War and the McCarthy era into the Cold War years of Korea and Eisenhower, Cuba and Kennedy.

[Their] striking likenesses and continuities extend to the non-fiction. For both writers the conventional distinction between fiction and fact, or between fiction and something like "journalism," was likely to vanish under the stress of creative intensity. Though both have viewed themselves primarily as writers of fiction, both have also been naturally adept at vividly personal essays on the contemporary scene. But this non-fiction feeds back, for both writers, into their fiction, and is in fact hardly distinguishable from it in either substance or art. . . . [Sounding like] Fitzgerald, who tended in the long run to equate artistic achievement with the moral aliveness of the artist as a human being rather than with the sophistication of his skills as a craftsman, Mailer once expressed the conviction that for the writer "keeping in shape" morally and intellectually is much more important than "craft". . . . (pp. 129-30)

The contemporary essays of both writers, always highly personal, tend to take the form of quasi-autobiography, even confession, with the authors speaking as representative men who have been carried by circumstances and sensibility into the existential center of the life of their times. (p. 131)

The exhaustion of a creative gift of personality by the sheer weight of unformed reality which it confronts Mailer conceives in much the same way Fitzgerald did—as an inevitable overexpenditure and final bankruptcy of vital spirits. . . . Such fated exhaustion of masculine power, grace, and faith is the substance of one kind of modern tragedy. And in most of the work of both writers this inherently tragic matter is characteristically distanced or conserved by being rendered in an essentially comic perspective. (p. 132)

Mailer's characterization of America as "the country in which the dynamic myth of the Renaissance—that every man was potentially extraordinary—knew its most passionate persistence, . . . the land where people still believed in heroes: George Washington; Billy the Kid; Lincoln; Jefferson; Mark Twain, Jack London, Hemingway; Joe Louis, Dempsey, Gentleman Jim . . ." is almost pure Fitzgerald, or Fitzgerald essentialized. . . . [And] where the impetus of

the Fitzgerald vision begins to transcend Fitzgerald's experience, we are aware of passing beyond him without really leaving him behind. . . . [In his] long *Esquire* piece on the 1960 Democratic convention, Mailer takes his sweeping prospect into a new historical dimension, the age prefigured in the pattern of developing strife between fascist temperament and communist will which lurks behind the landscape of general breakdown in *Tender Is the Night* and *The Last Tycoon.* This new age is our own, with its multiple covert totalitarianisms, its prevailing violence, its proliferation of techniques of mass dehumanization. Though their conscious minds and wills repelled its orgiastic solicitations, the coming age had already begun to express itself in the chaotic passions and self-destructive instincts of the disintegrating Dick Diver and Monroe Stahr, and indeed in Fitzgerald himself. Mailer is not only a post-Kinsey, but a post-Hiroshima Fitzgerald as well. (pp. 133-34)

[Their] appetite for solutions to problems pertaining to the general human good not only signifies the temperament of the idealist, but also that of the hero, or the idealist in action. . . . As Fitzgerald's career develops, . . . his choice of protagonists tends to shift from aspiring and representative types like Amory Blaine to active and exemplary ones like Dick Diver. An analogous pattern of development can be seen in Mailer, but with the crucial difference that as his protagonists become increasingly active and exemplary they also become more deracinated and anarchic. (pp. 135-36)

But there are some lively images of the traditional hero in Mailer's work. They live primarily in his non-fiction, however, and from that immediately "real" context they have the effect of confirming the positive, and often covertly traditional moral significance of his anti-heroes. (p. 136)

Mailer's evocations of Kennedy as nominee, candidate, and president are studded with effects of style and imagery that echo Fitzgerald's portraiture of his own heroes. (p. 137)

In Fitzgerald's late work, as his traditional idealism moves closer to its inevitable demise, the final instinct of his heroes is virtually to court and further their threatened destruction, as if they sense that from the death of their own worn-out life-forms fresh life may be released.

Mailer shows a similar ambivalence of vision, similar in the way a white design on a black ground is like the same design in black on white. In *Advertisements for Myself* he writes of "authority and nihilism stalking each other in the orgiastic hollow of this century." And he exhibits this pattern of contemporary experience everywhere in both his imaginative writing and his personal life—between which two there is as little substantive distinction to be made as there was in Fitzgerald's case. . . . In his famous essay on "The White Negro" and its succeeding addenda, Mailer, like Yeats, not only defines but woos and invites his personal image of the "rough beast" of this apocalyptic time—the hypersexual hipster anarch. Yet in an interview in the same volume he eloquently defends chastity and true love and attacks promiscuity, masturbation, the use of contraceptives, and modern atheistic rationalism, as forms of sacrilege. Speaking almost as a conservative guardian of traditional values in the arts, Mailer writes an essay on Jean Genet in which he condemns the surrealist impulse in modern literature for artistic vanity and moral nihilism. . . . [In an essay on *Waiting for Godot,*] the directness, almost the "realism" with which history's dark message is read in the social and political "facts" of the contemporary moment, and the casual, almost slangy way in which not despair but acceptance, confidence, even a kind of "gaiety," declares itself as the final meaning of this dark night of knowledge, gives its author, in the end, a closer affinity with Fitzgerald's vision than with anyone else's.

It is a doubleness of vision, then, rather than an inconsistency or even an ambivalence, that characterizes the imaginative responses of Mailer and Fitzgerald to history's drift from tradition and order toward anarchy and chaos. Paradoxically, because they welcome life they must also welcome such diseases, violences, and deaths as make more life possible. (pp. 138-39)

[Fitzgerald wrote]: "To be useful and proud—is that too much to ask?" And Mailer writes, near the end of his odd, funny, poignant, utterly serious Patterson-Liston piece on the psychodynamics of failure and death, "To believe the impossible may be won creates a strength from which the impossible may indeed be attacked." "To be useful and proud . . ."; "To believe the impossible may be won . . ." —this pattern of affirmative and idealistic impulses reflexively renewed or reborn in the face of disillusioning experience, plus the contemporaneous American subject matter which is the characteristic substance of their imaginative visions, not only connects Fitzgerald and Mailer importantly, but puts both of them in the main stream of American writers for whom the beauties and ambiguities of the "American dream" have been the inescapable motifs. (p. 142)

> *Richard Foster, "Mailer and the Fitzgerald Tradition," in* Novel: A Forum on Fiction *(copyright © Novel Corp., 1968), Spring, 1968 (and reprinted in* Norman Mailer: A Collection of Critical Essays, *edited by Leo Braudy, Prentice-Hall, 1972, pp. 127-42).*

In Norman Mailer's hyperbolic world it will no doubt seem like a putdown to say that his new book [*The Armies of the Night*] is a fine, exciting piece of work, flawed but immensely interesting, a literary act whose significance is certain to grow. Mailer never lets us forget that he wants it all: all the kudos, all the marbles, honorary degrees in every field, a status that can best be described in a phrase from the adolescence he has never wholly shaken off: King of the Hill. All estimation of him is affected by his having always wanted, in the worst way, to *count,* the ferocity with which he attacks everything that stands in the way of his being seen to count having its roots in the fact that, as he says in this book, "the one personality he finds absolutely insupportable [is] the nice Jewish boy from Brooklyn."

That a nice Jewish boy from Brooklyn simply can't be a representative American figure, much less a mover and shaker, is the principle of much of Mailer's acrobatics and histrionic movements. He has willed himself into pertinence and power, and it is one of the most fascinating and instructive episodes of our recent cultural history. More than any other of our writers Mailer has intervened in the age so that he has come to count, more securely as time goes on, and if it isn't exactly in the way he wants, if it still seems ridiculous to call him the *best* American writer, he nevertheless matters in a way that only a man with so mighty and precarious an ego as his could find disappointing. He long ago made it out of niceness and Jewishness and Brooklyn; with this book he makes it into a central

area of the American present, where all the rough force of his imagination, his brilliant gifts of observation, his ravishing if often calculated honesty, his daring and his *chutzpah* are able to flourish on the steady ground of a newly coherent subject and theme and to issue in a work more fully *in our interests* than any he has ever done.

Mailer's subject, as it has always been in some measure, is himself, but this time a self balanced between objective events and private consciousness in a riper way than ever before. And his theme is just that relation of antipathy but also fertile interdependence between the self and history, the ego and actuality, which he has always strenuously sought—with greater suggestiveness than substance it's often seemed—to make the arena and justification of his work. In writing about his participation in the anti-Vietnam demonstrations in Washington . . . (most particularly the march on the Pentagon), Mailer has finally succeeded in laying hands on the novelistic character he has never quite been master of before, and at the same time succeeded in finding a superbly viable form for his scattered, imperfect and often greatly discordant gifts.

I don't think it's been clearly enough seen how Mailer's talents and strengths have for the most part been disjunctive if not wholly contradictory. Such contradiction may be a mainstay of his energy, but it's also an element of his fretful anarchy. His rather old-fashioned novelist's inquisitiveness about the behavior of men in society has, for example, often been diverted by his utopianism, his extra-literary hunger for things to change and change *now,* in palpable ways rather than in the imaginary, alternative ways, in which most artist-novelists deal. His ambition for guruhood, prophetic status, has run up against his violent need for immediate action. His repertorial gifts have been charged with novelistic daring but also corrupted by novelistic license. And his sense of writing as the expression and progress of personality, less a rigorous art than a style of public appearance, a way of counting, has kept him from achieving the full mastery of language, the hardwon grace of a conquest by which previously nonexistent realities are brought into being, that we associate with writers we call great.

In *The Armies of the Night* Mailer's talents come more than ever into working agreement and, moreover, move to ameliorate his deficiencies. Antinomies are resolved: the artist who has to invent and the observer who has to prey on facts merge into the same person; the transcendencies of art and the imminences of action move toward each other's replenishment; the excesses of personality find a new and strangely valuable use in the face of the opaque excesses (and history has come to be almost nothing but excesses) of our public days and years.

This is the central, rather wonderful achievement of the book, that in it history and personality confront each other with a new sense of liberation. By introducing his ego more directly into history than he ever has before, by taking events which were fast disappearing under the perversions and omissions of ordinary journalism as well as through the inertia we all feel in the face of what is *over with,* by taking these events and revivifying them, reinstating them in the present, Mailer has opened up new possibilities for the literary imagination and new room for us to breathe in the crush of actuality.

I don't think anyone who is more purely an artist than Mailer could have brought this off; but neither could any kind of journalist, no matter how superior. This is the conjunction of Mailer's special being—half artist-half activist, half inventor-half borrower—with what the times require: an end, for certain purposes, of literary aloofness on the one hand and of the myth of "objective" description on the other. . . . Mailer, by making himself the chief character of a "novel" whose truth doesn't have to be invented and by making history reveal an "esthetic" dimension has helped bridge gaps of long standing, has brought some ordinarily sundered things together in a revelatory book whose nearest counterpart in our literature, for all the obvious differences, is Henry Adams' *Education.* (pp. 158-60)

Much of Mailer's appeal has always lain in his stance vis-à-vis the powers that be; the Jimmy Cagney of literature, he has especially been a model for youth, who have always admired him perhaps more for being a welterweight taking on heavies than for being a heavyweight himself. And as Mailer moves on into the actual events of those four days in Washington this cocky stance—the self as the equal of all large intimidating public opponents, yet also the self aware of its small size and internal divisions—becomes a representative posture for all of us. More than ever, Mailer's embattled ego is seen to be the troubled, sacrificial, rash and unconquerable champion for all of ours. (p. 161)

In the last quarter of the book Mailer turns from "History as a Novel" to "The Novel as History." What he means by these phrases isn't always clear, nor are his claims for what he's done convincing in the way he intends. In dividing his book this way . . . he hasn't succeeded in nailing down the distinctions he's after. . . .

The trouble lies in Mailer's notion of "novel" and "novelist." The idea has always ruled him—and is, I think, the source of his erratic and inconclusive performance as an imaginative writer—of the novelist as someone whose gifts of intuition and prophecy enable him to see more deeply than other men into society or human organizations. From this follows the notion that novels are superior reports on social or psychic or moral phenomena and that fiction is therefore a superior way of agitating for change and helping bring it about. I think this a rather outdated conception of fiction and that his possession of it, along with his retention of the Hemingwayian policy of style as performance, has kept Mailer on certain wrong, if for him inevitable, tracks. (p. 165)

What Mailer has done is not to have written a novel in the form of history or history in the form of a novel, not to have produced any startlingly new forms, but to have rescued history from abstraction and aridity by approaching it with certain "novelistic" instruments at the ready and in a certain large, general "novelistic" spirit. They are rather old-fashioned things, constituents of an older idea of fiction, the kind of qualities we associate with Balzac and Zola and Maugham and textbook notions of the novel. A more advanced novelist than Mailer, one less interested in getting at social or political reality, wouldn't have been able to bring it off; that Mailer is only imperfectly a novelist, that his passion for moving and shaking the actual has prevented him from fully inhabiting imaginary kingdoms, is the underlying, paradoxical strength of this book.

The important thing is that Mailer has refused to leave history, actuality, to historians and journalists. Writing *as he can,* as part-inventor, part-observer, part-intervener, writing with gusto and vigor and an almost unprecedented kind of honesty, writing very badly at times . . ., but writing always with a steady aim: to do for our present situation and, by implication, all our communal pasts and futures, what our traditional instrumentalities of knowledge and transcription haven't been able to do—place our public acts and lives in a human context—Mailer has put us all in his debt. In the light of that, whether or not he's the best writer in America, the best novelist or the best journalist would seem to be considerations out of a different sort of game. (p. 166)

Richard Gilman, "What Mailer Has Done," in The New Republic *(reprinted by permission of* The New Republic; *(© 1968 by The New Republic, Inc.), June 8, 1968 (and reprinted in* Norman Mailer: A Collection of Critical Essays, *edited by Leo Braudy, Prentice-Hall, Inc., 1972, pp. 158-66).*

Beginning with *Advertisements for Myself* (1959), Mailer has so concertedly placed his personal character and beliefs at the center of his work that the disentangling of work and man, a process that seems so important to our current definition of lasting literary value, becomes an almost impossible task. Propelled by the dynamic of personal reference, Mailer does not stand still to be evaluated and critically categorized; tags hung on him at various stages in his career, such as "war novelist" or "Jewish novelist," seemed peculiarly irrelevant when they were first minted and are even more misleading now.

Mailer himself has been little help to his prospective critics. Although he is often accused of excessively seeking fame and publicity, Mailer has paradoxically enough pursued this success by successively alienating whatever audiences he had achieved by his earlier work. (p. 1)

[He] abandons completely the literary good manners that lie in developing a single theme, style, or set of characters. Mailer instead forces the interested reader and critic to accept this seeming discontinuity as essential to an understanding of his career. . . . His effort to grapple continuously with his work, setting up a constant interplay between himself and whatever project he is engaged in, has made him at once the most protean and the most archetypal of American authors. . . . It was twenty years before *The Armies of the Night* brought Mailer anything like the literary success and understanding that greeted *The Naked and the Dead.* Yet in the meantime Mailer never compromised his own sense of what ought to be done in a particular work. (p. 2)

Barbary Shore, in content, is an ideological novel more in the European than the American tradition, although its allegorical landscape may be reminiscent of Hawthorne and its amalgam of politics and dream akin to *The Blithedale Romance.* Through an atmosphere of political allusion, *Barbary Shore* implicitly attacks the dogged anti-ideological stance of *The Naked and the Dead,* with its freight of Dos Passos-like distancing devices, such as the "Time Machine" flashbacks and the playlet interludes. But if *Barbary Shore* is a novel concerned with ideology, it is also a novel in flight from ideology, at least from any institutionalized ideology associated with a particular party or any group outside the searching individual. Prophetically charged with the sense of political romance that becomes so important in America during the 1960s, *Barbary Shore* is Mailer's first attempt to bring together his interests in both politics and psychology. In *Advertisements For Myself* he will describe this imaginative synthesis as an effort to build a bridge between Marx and Freud. In *Barbary Shore* neither politics nor art can exist apart from the individual's engagement with them. Mailer is not pessimistic about the inclusiveness of art that fueled *The Naked and the Dead* as it fueled the work of Dos Passos, Farrell, and Steinbeck; but he does reject the bland assumption that the novelist's vision will triumph.

From *Barbary Shore* onward Mailer attempts to merge his ideological and philosophical interests with the more anti-intellectual tradition of American naturalism, bringing together the meditative European intellectual with the craftless American *naïf,* Malraux's scholar-adventurer with Faulkner's stay-at-home social criticism, Fitzgerald's innocence, and Hemingway's commitment to unmeditated action. . . . Mailer's own interpretation of "naturalism," as it develops through his work, tends to view the novel as social solipsism rather than social panorama, a private vision each of us has of our world. . . . Instead of narrative detachment and an encyclopedic effort to encompass American life, with *Barbary Shore* Mailer begins to develop his own more subjective mixture of description and metaphysic, social criticism and personal reference, journalism and fantasy. A Marxist analysis of society could stand in the wings behind the naturalistic novel, but Mailer wanted also to include Freud, to emphasize the actor beneath the makeup, the imaginative and psychological effects of ideology. Individual novelists might have political interests and individual novels might spring from a radical or Marxian critique of American society. But until *Barbary Shore* (unless one counts the Hearn-Cummings sections of *The Naked and the Dead*) ideology was one thing in America and literature was something quite different. Mailer authenticates the place of ideological controversy in American literature, not because he is the first to use political themes, but because he fuses these themes with the psychological preoccupations that had distinguished American romance from the English and European social novel in the nineteenth century. From *Barbary Shore* on, thinking, ruminating, and philosophizing become an essential characteristic of Mailer's work, whether it appears in the form of non-fiction or fiction. (pp. 3-5)

[In] *An American Dream* . . . [Mailer decides] that comic-book paranoia and melodramatic excess more clearly mirror the present realities of the American experience than either the careful social explorations of Henry James or the homey, nation-spanning detail of Dos Passos, Farrell, and Steinback. (p. 5)

Literary naturalism often assumed that the sociological makeup of society was a key to problems of self-definition within the individual. The true life of a nation could be found in the interminglings of class and job. But Mailer characterizes almost all of his heroes as men who attempt to fulfill several jobs or social roles, cutting across the conventional divisions of society. . . . To deepen this sense of variety and apparent contradiction within individuals, Mailer's heroes often have polyglot, polynational backgrounds. . . . Mailer's long digression in *Of a Fire on the Moon* about the various national backgrounds of his wives and what he has learned from them seems a conscious attempt to supply himself with the varieties of experience he gives to his characters.

In older terms, the pluralistic background and vocation of such characters might make make them paradigmatic Americans. But Mailer emphasizes instead the uncertainty,

the lack of coherent identity, involved in having such a nature. After the detached omniscience of *The Naked and the Dead,* in the later works it is Mailer's heroes who have become his narrators. For the easily accessible past of *The Naked and the Dead,* Mailer in *Barbary Shore* substitutes a world in which the past and its meaning are uncertain. (pp. 5-6)

No matter what their small success, Mailer's heroes are essentially bottled up, doomed by their own weaknesses and inadequacies to use their creativity with little effect. But the creative potential does persist in such characters, however repressed it may be. After the overpowering fatality of *The Naked and the Dead,* in which accident seems to dominate human affairs totally, Mailer, in *Barbary Shore,* makes the first of many affirmations of the power of human will. But these affirmations are imaged, paradoxically enough, in this and later novels by a weak and fallible central character and in his so-called journalism by the comic device of a narrator named "Norman Mailer."

The two largest stumbling blocks in the way of deeper appreciation of Mailer's work—personal reference and ideological polemic—are therefore tugged into position by Mailer himself. Typically he is indicted for too much autobiography in his nonfiction and too much ideology in his fiction. But Mailer in fact controls these two important elements in his work by a romantic irony that involves self-consciousness first about the position of the writer and then about the individual created work. . . . Mailer has made the difficulties of being a writer in America one of his most powerful themes because he has seen its inseparable relation to the difficulties of being a human being in America, filling contradictory roles, being asked to believe contradictory things. Self-consciousness has always been Mailer's way of dealing with literary tradition. His decision to write in what resembles a personal voice expresses a particularly literary self-consciousness rather than the arch candor of the confessional writer or the mannered innocence of the *naïf* so often imitated by Hemingway. (pp. 7-8)

[In] *Advertisements For Myself* autobiography and personal publicity become the means to a meditation on the meaning of his own life that Mailer believes every reader could write for himself: "Let others profit by my unseemly self-absorption, and so look to improve their own characters." *Advertisements For Myself* makes Mailer's own life and career a laboratory for his examination of American life. In it and in his later works he carries on a gradually developing exploration of himself as a paradigmatic American personality (in the same way that every American sees himself to be typical) but with little self-congratulation. The harsh clarity of Mailer's self-examination is mitigated only by the wry humor he pokes at his own pretensions, a rich and mellow wit that receives its fullest expression in *The Armies of the Night.* (p. 9)

The critical attack against the "egotism" of Mailer's work may be in fact the projection of a belief that the self is one of the most trivial topics for literature, inferior especially to the social world that preoccupied the great nineteenth-century novels. But Mailer is fascinated with the dialectic between faceless destiny and individual will, whether destiny be the capricious island world of *The Naked and the Dead* or the interlocking directorate of power in *An American Dream.* Action, for Mailer, is something stolen from necessity, even in the face of human weakness. (p. 10)

At its best, and it is frequently on that level, Mailer's journalism is his own reaction, always a little earlier than anyone else's, to the emphasis on the validity of personal experience that in the 1960s brought the Left in America closer to the more libertarian and antigovernmental Right than to the corporate and rational liberal Middle. Mailer's search for an authentic point of view in his journalism, as well as his search for an authentic connection to his past and his traditions, is an attempt to make some relation between the individual and the nation. (p. 12)

Mailer's journalism plays most heavily on the secret enmities in the old naturalistic entente between observer and detail. His factual material, such as the documents of *The Armies of the Night* or the technical information in *Of a Fire on the Moon,* is neither a correlative nor an authentication of his perspective. It becomes instead a base on which he builds his own interpretation of the meaning of the events he describes, not as a congeries of otherwise isolated facts, but as part of both a historical tradition and a personal metaphysic. "Mailer" within events becomes both our surrogate and our scapegoat, taking risks and exposing personal foolishness and fallibility that no reader would dare reveal. Through such self-exposure Mailer comes to understand both the external events themselves as well as the place of the individual consciousness within a society where such events can occur and within a history grown irremediably complex. *The Armies of the Night* gains much of its power from the perfect melding of the public author and the private foolish individual, the public event and the limited individual perspective. All of Mailer's impotent and weak heroes culminate for a moment in this "Norman Mailer," whose double consciousness, as detached author and participating actor, can understand the Pentagon march, both in its immediacy and its history, its moment-to-moment nature and its ultimate meaning. (pp. 12-13)

The American character, in Mailer's view, is torn between . . . two possibilities of self-definition; in literary terms, it might be expressed as a conflict between journalism and romance. But in the twentieth century, Mailer implies, there is no longer any possibility of a Thoreauvian retreat. Stephen Rojack can go to Guatemala and Yucatan only as part of a fantasy solution; Mailer himself must turn to a deeper exploration of the possibilities of the world around him. Each individual, he implies, must steal something from the fear of what lies outside himself. Paradoxically, in the face of its "objective" billing, Mailer's journalism actually serves to develop his sense that the main business of the novel is exploration of the defects and beauties of character. Public and private pressures on individual character move together in Mailer's eye in the same way as many other seemingly opposed concepts.

It is in fact very difficult to discuss Mailer's work without mentioning his fondness for antinomies or simple opposites —for example, the conceptual pairs mentioned above, the Stevensonian linking of such characters as D. J. and his friend "Tex" Hyde in *Why Are We in Vietnam?,* and, by extension, Mailer's own efforts to merge journalism and fiction in his literary nature. . . . All three of Mailer's books of reportage—*The Armies of the Night, Miami and the Siege of Chicago,* and *Of a Fire on the Moon*—move between event and background, impression and detail, to work out themes of contradiction or dialectic that are replicated in Mailer's own point of view. *The Prisoner of Sex* acts as a coda to this trilogy because it asserts what has been implicit all through them: the primacy of the writer who attempts, however subjectively, to understand the world around him and convey to his audience some sense of its complexity.

The interplay between Mailer's fictional and nonfictional work satisfied his need for a realistic base while releasing him for more melodramatic and fantastic speculations. To complement his discovery of new creative power in this interplay, he was also building a new style. The first inklings of it come in the final sections of *The Deer Park* and in a few places in *Advertisements for Myself,* where Mailer first explores the themes the style is meant to express. But it appears full-blown only with *The Presidential Papers.* It is long-line, sinuously rippling, filled with reference and allusion, very different from the more clipped and spare manner of his earlier work. Paradoxically enough, as Hemingway begins to fascinate Mailer more and more as one type of the American author, Mailer's own style departs further and further from Hemingway's parataxis. Instead it moves toward a hypotactic style more characteristic of Hawthorne, Faulkner, or the Robert Penn Warren of *All the King's Men,* a style that is unsure of the meaning it searches for, rather than a style, like that of more realistic writers, that contains meaning and dispenses it in tight droplets. Mailer's new style implies that much less is known than the clarity of naturalistic description assumes. Metaphors are picked up, their uses assayed, and then they are discarded for more appropriate ones. Language becomes a medium for meaning rather than merely a convention to be rendered as transparently as possible. (pp. 14-15)

In its panorama of different kinds of Americans, *Miami and the Siege of Chicago* may come closer than any of Mailer's works since *The Naked and the Dead* to a total vision of society. Mailer's America is inclusive, not exclusive. It has no "real self" encrusted with bad habits or bad heredity. Only the formulaic views of America are wrong. From *The Presidential Papers* on, Mailer indicts American "schizophrenia." But his growing counterassumption and undertheme . . . is that schizophrenia rightly understood can be health rather than disease, a dialectic of renewal rather than a deadend of hateful contraries. A bitter-sweet patriotism scents all of Mailer's journalism. . . . In his vision of America, [Mailer] . . . has half-found and half-created an arena capacious enough for his imagination.

In parts of *Of a Fire on the Moon,* however, and especially in the short "King of the Hill," the vitality of journalism for further defining Mailer's themes seems to have run dry. In many places the language does not flow; it is wrung out. (pp. 17-18)

Blinded by his polemical style, many do not pause to examine what he is polemical about. They are content to condemn his manner, without perceiving that it springs from a belief that a novel or a film or any work of art should have the potential to change the reader's life. Such a commitment to the power of art has impelled his whole career. Following his sense of what is most appropriate to a particular situation, Mailer has often catered to what is worse in his audience even while he has tried to make them more sensitive to the nuances of his work. The two may be inexorably connected, for his invention of and grappling with his public self have allowed him insight into the cultural movement of America since World War II that few writers have shown and fewer still have expressed with the same style, wit, and grace. (pp. 18-19)

Leo Braudy, "Norman Mailer: The Pride of Vulnerability," in Norman Mailer: A Collection of Critical Essays, *edited by Leo Braudy (copyright © 1972 by Prentice-Hall, Inc.; reprinted by permission of Prentice-*

Hall, Inc., Englewood Cliffs, New Jersey),
Prentice-Hall, 1972, pp. 1-20.

Mailer's view of the underlying pattern of American history is not particularly original, but it places him firmly in line with many major American writers from Emerson and Melville to Faulkner: the belief that American development is the product of a confrontation with virgin nature on a vast scale; the rapid and accelerating rate of social and psychological change that results from the American attempt to fill such large natural space with a burgeoning machine technology; the heterogenous background of the Americans —immigrants all—partly melting into a new composite American, partly exacerbating social tensions as they whirl around the white Protestant center. The "revolution of consciousness" he calls for in *Advertisements for Myself* is primarily a call for a psyche capable of confronting its own wilderness of possibilities.... The goal of the American novelist, Mailer believes, is not only to dramatize [the] schizophrenia in the national psyche—to remain true to a vision of the essential doubleness at the heart of the American dream—but to affirm that the creative implications of this doubleness are ultimately more worthy of faith than the destructive implications.... Mailer proposes that an American's best chance for salvation depends on treating the conflict at the center of the national psyche as an epic battle.

In light of such concerns, it should not be surprising that, of all nineteenth-century American writers, the one from whom Mailer most obviously draws strength and lessons is Herman Melville. No doubt one reason for his appeal to Mailer lies in the immensity of Mailer's literary ambitions. (p. 144)

Another reason for Mailer's attraction to Melville is implied . . . in his *Esquire* essay on "Some Children of the Goddess" [in which he calls *Moby Dick* "a book whose action depends upon the voyage of Ahab into his obsession"].... Mailer's own response to the inward voyage of the self into its own obsession is traceable in his fictional protagonists, and certainly in the self-image that he presents in *Advertisements* and other works. Whatever sense of himself that Mailer has gleaned from Hemingway or Malraux or other "artists of action," he has certainly discovered an equally powerful model in the oceanic depths of *Moby Dick.* (p. 145)

Mailer's characteristic advocacy of Americans' need for adventurous voyages into the dangerous frontier world of the self seems, by Mailer's own statements, to find a strong counterpart in Melville. (p. 146)

As *The Naked and the Dead* suggests, Mailer mines *Moby Dick* not only for major analogues to the adventures that he has constantly stressed as an essential component of America's psychic and social health but, equally important, for a major symbol of the ambiguities and dangers that attend such excursions. Significantly, since Mailer has taken on the mantle of "Historian," he has found Melville's book also a useful reference point for determining how far his countrymen have departed from their "organic" heritage.... Whereas the American Renaissance's major symbol of power, Moby Dick, combined not only essential ambiguity with dignifying epic drama, contemporary America's major symbols of power, such as the Pentagon, have become not only faceless but utterly without dramatic personality, have become, in fact, "anonymous" signs of the failure of the adventurous symbolizing imagination in

American public life. As Mailer treats it in *The Armies of the Night*, the Pentagon becomes almost a travesty on Melville's mighty leviathan. . . . The easiest way into the Pentagon, he reminds us, is through its shopping center and cafeteria, and he finds "something absurd" in this possibility. . . . The decline in the power of the epic symbol is thus not only a reflection of a degeneration of national value but a terrifying reminder of how difficult it is for a contemporary American writer to create an image that again will move his countrymen to heroic action. (pp. 149-50)

Loving America too much to leave it, he must dig for redemptive metaphors in his native soil.... Watching the overwhelming battle at the Chicago Hilton between the protesters and the police, Mailer searches for a mighty image appropriate to the dramatic occasion and finds one in *Moby Dick.* . . . What is interesting about [Mailer's comment from *Miami and the Siege of Chicago* in which he compares the Democratic Party's split to "Melville's whale charging right out of the sea"] is not merely that Mailer is searching for an epic symbol with which to give weight yet another time to the dialectic of American life, but that he has self-consciously chosen to do so by means of a traditional symbol transformed for his own purposes. Melville's Leviathan, as Mailer treats him, is no longer merely a natural force against which the American must wage his epic and perhaps tragic frontier wars. It has become a symbol of the split at the center of the American's sense of identity. Moby Dick is not merely a frontier threat, but a humanized resource from the past that the American imagination can use in its never-ending struggle to redeem the present. Without denying the existential value of remaining true to the "perpetual climax of the present," Mailer affirms also that such a present is not a break with but outgrowth of the past, and that the frontiers of the modern consciousness require not only existential resources but in addition the creative adaptation of tools offered by a historical tradition. (pp. 150-51)

In [Melville, Hawthorne, and Faulkner], an essentially romantic sensibility proposes that high tragedy is more worthy of the human spirit than a divine comedy turned facile, that the individual can often show more dignity in suffering the defeat of his greatest dreams than in winning mundane victories, that guilt is as essential an ingredient as pride to the mature man's self-respect and sense of essential identity. If anything, this traditional stance has become more marked in Mailer's non-fiction since the early sixties. (p. 151)

Like [Henry] Adams, Mailer has increasingly treated his work as the rather ironic story of an education whose value as preparation for succeeding in or at least understanding a rapidly changing modern world is at best ambiguous. . . . Mailer seems a nineteenth-century romantic (with a trace of the puritan) trying to straddle the twentieth century in order to seize a twenty-first century that has arrived before its time. Like Adams, Mailer sees history as an accelerating movement from unity to multiplicity. . . . Like *The Education*, Mailer's most recent work is in important ways a poet's search for a metaphorical structure that will at least bring the illusion of order to the multiplying contradictions of modern experience. (pp. 152-53)

[In *Of a Fire on the Moon*], Mailer rather wryly takes on the kind of role that Adams finds for himself in the latter part of the *Education*—that of a senior American statesman and philosopher whom the world has by-passed and who therefore must make a virtue out of being an important if detached observer of the rapidly changing scene. (pp. 153-54)

American technology ... has attempted to harness the forces of nature which Melville had symbolized by Moby Dick, and Mailer is willing as detached observer to leave ambiguous the question of whether the launching of Apollo II shows man taming nature or nature's revenge on man—further, whether the rocket is a "Sainted Leviathan"—Moby Dick canonized by the American dream—or "a Medusa's head" whose only powers are those of death. . . . (p. 155)

As a Brooklyn-born "Nijinsky of ambivalence," Mailer, like Whitman, has been exasperatingly eager to contradict himself in order to keep open a multitude of possible approaches to modern American experience. His major works are hymns to incompletion and openness and rarely conclude so much as continually begin. . . . [Critical] opinions . . . have not dampened Mailer's zealous and constant search among the common as well as spectacular materials of his nation for new launching pads. No matter how impressive or awkward Mailer's soaring through the painful but stimulating ambiguities of contemporary American life and thought, the irrepressibility of his flight is itself a demonstration of the Americanness of his dream. (pp. 156-57)

> Michael Cowan, "The Americanness of Norman Mailer," in Norman Mailer: A Collection of Critical Essays, edited by Leo Braudy (copyright © 1972 by Michael Cowan; reprinted by permission of Michael Cowan), Prentice-Hall, 1972, pp. 143-57.

If one ignored the history of the last twenty-five years and drew one's conclusions strictly from a reading of [Burrough's *Naked Lunch,* Kesey's *One Flew over the Cuckoo's Nest,* and Mailer's *An American Dream* and *Why Are We in Vietnam?*], one would be misled into thinking that the reciprocal enmity between the creative and conventional factions of society were still as intense as ever. . . . Mailer's case seems particularly symptomatic, since in the sixties he was ambitiously trying to make his fiction a testing ground of the historical and social forces of his age. What obstructed this effort was Mailer's inability to arrive at an analysis of history or society that went beyond crude schematization or mere confusion. On the one hand, Mailer reduced contemporary history to an apocalyptic myth of liberation, counterposing the hipster and the square, the id and the rational consciousness, the "existential" individual and the plastic, life-denying power of "Technologyland." The content of the social criticism contained in this scheme was summed up in Mailer's statement, in *Advertisements for Myself* (1959): "The shits are killing us." Transferred to the novels, this simplistic diagnosis became the principle of characterization of such corporate establishment figures as D. J.'s "asshole" father, Rusty, and his "medium asshole" associates in *Why Are We in Vietnam?* Scatology, in other words, tried to do the work of sociology. On the other hand, the element of schematic moralism in Mailer's fiction —as in that of Kerouac and Burroughs—was confused, though not really mitigated, by the frequent expression of a diffuse, semi-mystical enthusiasm over the vibrating, electrokinetic dynamisms of technological society itself. Thus Mailer's point of view was simultaneously remote from the actual society which he sought to understand and unable to separate itself from the confused processes of that society. (p. 313)

In *Advertisements for Myself,* Mailer writes that obscenities are "our poor debased gutterals for the magical parts of the human body, and so they are basic communication, for they awake, no matter how uneasily, many of the questions, riddles, aches and pleasures which surround the enigma of life." Obscentities, in other words, having been protected by taboos from the contamination that results from general social use, remain an uncorrupted way of speaking about what Mailer calls "the mysterious dualities of our mysterious universe," a phrase suggestive of the vague Manichaean theology which is never far from the surface of his writing. . . . Mailer's attempt [in *An American Dream*] to elevate Ruta's private parts into symbols of the metaphysical axes of reality results in one of the more memorable examples of unintentional comedy in American literature, and in the process illustrates the difficulty a writer encounters when he attempts to make a wholly private typology take the place of a plausible system of concepts. (pp. 314-15)

In Mailer's journalistic works, which have drawn his energies away from fiction since the late sixties, many of these problems persist. In *The Armies of the Night,* the most successful of these works, Mailer gets around them by openly acknowledging confusion and building this acknowledgment into the texture of the work. Instead of the imposition of dualistic myths—as in the improbable antithesis of "honestly" violent Chicago versus "plastic" Miami Beach, which organizes *Miami and the Siege of Chicago,* or the hoked-up theories of schizophrenia in *Marilyn*—coherence in *Armies of the Night* is attained through the confessed bewilderment of the point of view of the observer. . . . (p. 316)

> Gerald Graff, in TriQuarterly 33 (© 1975 by Triquarterly), Spring, 1975.

Mailer . . . —and this is well below the often eccentric bravado and fustian of his rhetoric—appears to be at his deepest root a soul in a fiery religious search, an experimenter in an erratic pursuit of the Absolute, a writer with a powerful moralistic sensibility, intolerant of any compromise and insidiously attracted to categories of experience such as Sex and Time, God and the Devil. (pp. 162-63)

Mailer's search . . . has aimed inexorably at discovering or creating some *holiness,* or "wholeness," in a world perversely governed by entropy. His novels and journalistic ventures have tended to become dramatized exercises in testing or groping for that stance of moral muscularity that may release an essence of purity in a plastic world—that may create some bastion of permanence that will withstand the cancerous corrosions of change. Thus, whereas Bellow's struggles to arrive at a workable moral identity have led him inevitably into the ambiguous modes of comic and grotesque irony—that style that is the last-ditch defense against despair—Mailer, like a compulsive ascetic, has been impervious to humor and tolerance and ambiguity, adopting the sometimes visionary and the sometimes tedious role of the artist as seer, pundit, egotistical crank, and Establishment scourge. (p. 163)

Although he has never repeated the wholesale naturalistic doctrine that informed *The Naked and the Dead,* and although he has hurtled out of the somewhat doctrinaire Marxist Darwinism of his first novel into a thrilling steeplechase over the barriers of Reichian revisionism, and in and out of the thickets of Existentialism and New-Left Apocalypticism, he has remained more or less true to his first view of the universe. It strikes me as significant, for example, that after the Gothic failures of *Barbary Shore* and *The Deer Park*—failures in part dependent on the curious inability of either book to locate itself in reference to reality—Mailer turned to journalism. And what he has done in his brilliantly original reportorial adventuring is to reembrace covertly that solid objective reality that structured his first novel. In other words, by placing himself aggressively in front of the historically real and actual—a heavyweight prize fight, a national nominating convention, a march on the Pentagon, a moon launching, or the poignant career of a Hollywood sex symbol—Mailer is able to cope with a world he himself never made. Because he has not created and is not responsible for that world, he can attempt to transform it (along with his own self) interpretatively into his own special fictions. In this sense, his earlier abortive attempts to project a persuasive illusion of reality in *Barbary Shore* and *The Deer Park* may be seen as symptomatic of a double refusal on his part: on the one hand, Mailer may be stubbornly refusing to recant the dogmas of naturalistic determinism that he had first proclaimed in *The Naked and the Dead;* on the other hand, he may also be refusing to accept the bleak condition of creative impotence that these very dogmas impose upon him. There is no MOS for a creative artist in the Table of Organization that sustains the cosmos of Anopopei, and Mailer is clearly frustrated by the necessary passivity that realism requires of his surrogate narrator-heroes, Mikey Lovett (*Barbary Shore*) and Sergius O'Shaughnessy (*The Deer Park*). Artist *manqués*, they are burdened with the obligations of creating the worlds of their respective novels and acting in those worlds at the same time; they manage neither task particularly well.

Mailer's attempts to resolve this dilemma delineate the volatile shifts in direction that his career has taken since the 1955 publication of *The Deer Park*. His emergence as a journalist can thus be understood as an action entirely consistent with his well-publicized disgust with "victim-literature," and with his theatrical struggles—personal, political, and novelistic—to invent or incarnate a "hipster-hero" who will prove immune to the paralysis of living in a universe of cause-and-effect determinism. In *An American Dream* and *Why Are We In Vietnam?*, novels that become increasingly extreme in their departures from realistic reference, Mailer appears to be trying to avoid the strictures of naturalism without confronting them head-on. Such a procedure strikes me as highly exciting and even more highly dangerous for a committed realist to undertake. For if *The Armies of the Night* or *Of A Fire on the Moon* succeed in communicating the personality of a creative passion and intelligence (Mailer's), they do so through the agency of the world that we all share undeniably with Mailer. In his last two novels, however, that world is radically distanced, and the projected worlds of Rojack and D. J. may simply be outside our capacities of recognition.

Mailer's metaphysics—or as much of it as I can understand —seems to be founded on an inexorable either-or basis: Hip or Square, cancer or schizophrenia, victim or rebel, God or the Devil, nothingness or wholeness. Intellectually absolutistic and prone to solipsism, Mailer will either have his cake and eat it too, or insist that everyone must do without cake. And though this attitude can be amazingly useful in forcing a reader to attend to a brand-new pattern in a familiar landscape (even in *The Prisoner of Sex* and *Marilyn*, Mailer captures at moments the entire attention of his reader), it has severe disadvantages as the basis of

structuring a novel. Bestowing a totalitarian authority on the consciousnesses of Rojack and D. J., Mailer eludes the responsibilities of realism without endorsing an alternate position. Rojack's world is as vivid and puerile as a crude animated cartoon, and despite the occasionally brilliant verbal texture of *Why Are We In Vietnam?*, D. J.'s world evokes no dimension beneath or beyond its own volubility. When fiction casts off the supports of realism, it must strive to sustain itself as parable, parody, urgently rooted fantasy, or as an aesthetic structure self-defined by its own created metaphor. To my mind, Bellow's one nonrealistic novel, *Henderson the Rain King,* manages this transition with great effectiveness, but Mailer's last two novels float narcissistically free from the grip of human experience. Rojack and D. J. are narrator-minds deliberately swollen into states of mindlessness in order that they may posture as successful rebels. Mailer is still unwilling or unable to deny the formative pressure of history, but in *An American Dream* and *Why Are We In Vietnam?* he pretends to ignore it. Engorged by the sweet taste of their own egos, his free-swinging (but far from "dangling") rebel-heroes comport themselves in a never-never land located between the past and the future—a mythical pseudomystical *now* of super-sensuous immersion and courageous instinctual response. (pp. 165-67)

Mailer's work . . . [is] difficult to view as a whole. In a sense, each of his books is a brand-new beginning; and any one of his novels could be mistaken for the dazzling debut of a highly promising young first novelist. All his books share an uneven virtuosity in style, an interest in focusing on men facing extreme crisis-situations, an unflagging concern for the proper measure of courage, and a razzle-dazzle breathlessness in their presentation—a histrionic sense of the hero-magician yanking the absolutely newest and most relevant rabbit of all out of his tall, black, inexhaustible hat. How or if Mailer will find a way of resolving the knotted dilemma that seems to me to lie at the very core of his work —his unnegotiable demand that man be creative in a deterministic universe—I do not know. Perhaps the compromise accepted by his naturalistic predecessors such as Steinbeck, Dreiser, and Norris—the reluctant or enthusiastic embrace of some unorthodox variety of mysticism—may still be an open option for Mailer. (Apparently, a temperament that is beguiled by the theoretical comprehensibility of a completely ordered and completely meaningless natural universe is equally beguiled by the potential revelation of a completely ordered and completely meaningful supernatural universe. It would seem that it is not the problem of *meaning,* but that of *mystery,* that challenges such a temperament.) At any rate, all readers of Mailer are well aware of his frequent references to states of expanded consciousness, telepathic communication, electromagnetic forces, the more-than-human power of the will, and the knowledge that the glandular and olfactory organs can impart to man if he has the creative courage to expose himself to their uses. There is some indication that Mailer is willing to weigh these matters at more than metaphorical seriousness, and he may yet move assertively into a full-fledged membership in Godhead. It is also possible, however, that his dalliance with the occult is just an aspect of the rhetorical fireworks that are his stock in trade. It would be foolhardy to predict Mailer's next moves or jumps, but I think that until he makes a significant attack on his central unresolved "problem," his novels *as wholes* will lack that sharp realistic edge that is always present in the best passages of his writing. (pp. 167-68)

Earl Rovit, in Saul Bellow, *edited by Earl Rovit (copyright © 1975 by Earl Rovit; reprinted by permission of Earl Rovit), Prentice-Hall, 1975.*

*   *   *

MALAMUD, Bernard   1914-

An American novelist and short story writer, Malamud employs his Jewish heritage to explore the themes of sin, suffering, and redemption. His style is characterized by the imaginative, mystical, and symbolic, and is reflective of his moral optimism. In 1959 Malamud won the National Book Award and in 1967 received his second National Book Award and the Pulitzer Prize. (See also *CLC,* **Vols. 1, 2, 3, 5, and** *Contemporary Authors,* **Vols. 5-8, rev. ed.)**

The Assistant, like *Crime and Punishment,* is a novel of guilt and expiation. The nature of both Frank Alpine's crime and his final redemption are of course different from Raskolnikov's, and it is in this difference that one of Malamud's major social criticisms can be discerned. For at the end of the novel, despite the fact that his crime is smaller and his attempt at expiation far more tangible than anything Raskolnikov achieves prior to confession, Frank Alpine is left very much alone, and in this isolation is embodied a condemnation of that society which has driven him to both crime and penitence. This is not to say that Malamud is writing a naturalistic or didactic novel, but simply that the internal struggles of his characters, like those of Dostoevsky's, are set in a clear social context, and that this context affects the nature of their ambivalent personal responses. (p. 90)

Along with the pattern of guilt and expiation, Malamud uses two major devices from *Crime and Punishment* in order to evoke a comparison with the earlier novel and some of the expectations which it raises. The first of these is a broadly-shaded character dualism, underlying the entire novel, but in the case of the hero gradually diminishing toward the end. And the second is the intense recognition of similarity between two characters, the sensing that one is in part an echo of the other. Both devices emerge out of a dualistic psychology, and assume a personality at war with itself, and they are each a part of the larger theme of the double. Explicit in this theme, which appears so often in Dostoevsky's work, is the notion of the divided self, and the attraction of two characters who mirror a part of each other, and are therby drawn together as doubles. The dualism of the characters is thus manifested both internally and externally, and there is the sense of a self, partially aware of its own fragmentation, and seeking to resolve itself, to become whole again, through relationship with its double. As used by Dostoevsky, the double theme arouses and often fulfills expectations that a resolution of inner conflict will occur, that this resolution will emerge in part through recognition of one's double, and that this recognition, if based on morally valid qualities, will lead to affirmation of a transcendent unity that supersedes human conflict and fragmentation. As used by Malamud, however, only some of these expectations are fulfilled, and the disparity between expectation and reality creates the irony by which he can comment on the possibilities of relationship and the structures for redemption in our inconclusive world.

Although both Frank Alpine and Raskolnikov are similar in their dualism, Malamud intentionally makes Frank's crime less serious, his dualism less pronounced, and his desire for self-renunciation more extended in time, in order to make much more ironic the incompleteness of his resolution. (pp. 91-2)

Malamud apparently wants to make Frank seem less ethically alien all through the novel in order to emphasize the irony of his final social alienation. At the end of *Crime and Punishment,* Raskolnikov is able to move into a socially meaningful religious structure and to renew his ties to a community of men. This is something that Frank is unable to do, and his failure is due less to his own faults than to the fact that his society embodies no clear moral structure and that Frank himself, by finding one which separates him from the social norm, simply transcends it. (p. 93)

By reducing Frank's ethical dualism in comparison to that of Raskolnikov, by showing Frank to be unsuccessfully drawn toward two fragments of what for Dostoevsky was a unified ethical pole, and by showing this fragmentation of personal love and social ethic in his other major characters, Malamud creates an irony that underlies his entire novel. The world of *The Assistant* is impersonal and competitive. Ethical commitment of the kind represented by Sonia's Christianity and Morris's Judaism is no longer a social but a personal alternative. Such commitment lacks context and expression in a society that is the antithesis of everything for which it stands. Because of competition, alienation, and the general disintegration of traditional social values, human relationships are virtually impossible. Where they exist at all, they are marked by fear and distrust rather than open acceptance. In such a society, self-definition is even more difficult than it was for Raskolnikov, and any definition that is achieved is likely to be an isolated one. Morris, Frank, and Helen have all been damaged by their world. Their patterns of ethical action and response to one another have become confused, and there is no clear redemption. There is only longing, partly fulfilled, and at the end an ironically hopeful conversion for the novel's self-renouncing hero. (p. 94)

[Morris is established] as the living embodiment of a self-renouncing ethic to which Frank himself can eventually adhere. The concept of reciprocal obligation expressed through the Law is of course antithetical to the competitive spirit manifested by society; and when Morris says that a Jew suffers for the Law he indicates the tragedy of his own position. By building his life around the Law, the grocer has cut himself off from a world that is scarcely reciprocal and relegated himself to a life of suffocating poverty. His own suffering has made him weary and somewhat bitter, and the resulting distrust makes him unable to sympathize with Frank at the very time when the assistant most requires his help. (p. 96)

The recognition which Frank and Helen feel is based on a mutual sense of loneliness and need for love, but the same tensions and dual responses that existed between Frank and Morris are evident here. Helen moves between attraction and distrust, and her inconsistency only arouses in Frank an unsatisfied hunger and a desperate need to force himself on her, which culminates in an impulsive rape. Throughout the novel, however, Frank is far more willing to give and compromise than is Helen, who cannot even free herself to the point of acceptance. As the embodiment of Frank's desired love, Helen is an inverted symbol; she appears as the broken mirror image of a disconnected world. (p. 97)

[In] Dostoevsky's novel, the heroine is marked by her almost intuitive sense of Raskolnikov's dualism, and a fidelity to him that is governed by trust and faith. In his reading of Dostoevsky, Frank has not as Helen wished become more like herself; he has been affected by the insights of the sympathetic prostitute and transcended those of the repressive grocer's daughter.

The difference between Sonia and Helen can be seen by their contrasting roles in the confessions which Raskolnikov and Frank are finally able to make. Helen does little to encourage Frank's final revelation of himself; in fact he is driven to it out of a desire to regain her understanding and show her that he has changed. Sonia, on the other hand, in the underworld context of prostitution which Raskolnikov finds so like his own crime, encourages him to confess by her very evidence of faith and compassion. Rather than wanting to draw her back to himself, he wants to become like her; that side of him which is compassionate is drawn towards her sympathy and piety. Frank's confession emerges out of a relationship that is already on the decline, already rather hopeless, while Raskolnikov's is the beginning of a close relationship and is filled with hope. (p. 99)

In contrast to Raskolnikov, Frank is unable to find love and ethical commitment at the end of his struggle. Helen's rejection of his two last attempts to reach her has left him very much alone. Despite brief and intermittent suggestions in the last few pages that Helen, even after the confession, may be reconsidering her position, Malamud gives us nothing conclusive and purposely leaves the impression that the relationship remains an unsolved and perhaps insoluble problem. It is not for Frank and Helen to experience such an encompassing sense of each other as Raskolnikov and Sonia feel at the end of Dostoevsky's novel. . . . [Frank's] growing understanding of Morris's ethic of the need to suffer, as well as the perceptiveness that he has gained through figures such as Raskolnikov and Sonia, have allowed him to confront his dualism, to assume the grocer's role, and to embody through this role a commitment that he cannot find in human love. (p. 101)

Frank . . . had been rent by distrust and a sense of alienation, but he was willing to risk commitment, to open himself to a degree greater than either of his partial doubles, and thereby he was able to move beyond them to the self-definition that marks him in the end.

It is in the disparity between the loneliness of this final definition and the expectations aroused through the Dostoevskian devices of dualism and recognition, as well as through the implied comparison with *Crime and Punishment* itself, that the novel's irony lies. And through this irony, through the concluding sense of Frank's isolation and definition, Malamud is able to make a telling comment on the difficulties of individual regeneration in a competitive and fragmented world. (p. 102)

Norman Leer, "The Double Theme in Malamud's 'Assistant': Dostoevsky with Irony," in MOSAIC IV/3 *(copyright © 1971 by the University of Manitoba Press), Spring, 1971, pp. 89-102.*

Malamud offers us . . . [in his obsessive moral fables] narrow, suffering Jews, unwilling victims of a heritage they thought to reject. In the short story "The German Refugee," for example, the title character flees to America from Nazi Germany and his non-Jewish wife, and then commits suicide after learning that she embraced Judaism and was executed in the gas chambers. Malamud's characters are old, even the young ones—old and tired and bitter and

complaining about a world set against them by definition and which asks them to endure more of the same and keep on shrugging benignly. And, surprisingly, mostly they do, and achieve in the process a crummy but miraculous dignity which allows life to go on going on and meaning to remain a potential. (p. 52)

Alan Warren Friedman, in The Southern Review *(copyright, 1972, by Alan Warren Friedman), Vol. VIII, No. I, Winter, 1972.*

[One wonders] why so accomplished, so esteemed and ultimately successful a writer as Malamud . . . should concern himself to such a large extent with struggling, frustrated novelists or failed artists. Typical of the former was the novelist rather too obviously named Lesser, dreaming of "writing a small masterpiece though not too small" in *The Tenants*. No doubt recognition came to Malamud comparatively late, his first novel, *The Natural,* appearing when he was in his late thirties. Moreover, in twenty years or so he has published five novels and four collections of short stories (some of these stories, dealing with the tiresome failed painter, Fidelman, featuring more than once), an output which an ambitious writer might consider small. One guesses extreme care, intense self-scrutiny and ready elimination.

Underlying Malamud's work is the dilemma of the conflicting claims of art and life which preoccupied the writers of the nineteenth and early twentieth centuries as much as the question of truth and illusion bothered the artists of the High Renaissance and the Baroque. The conflict was amusingly summarized in the epigraph to *Pictures of Fidelman:*

> The intellect of man is forced to choose
> Perfection of the life, or of the work. . . .
> W. B. Yeats.
> Both. A. Fidelman.

There seems little doubt that Fidelman here presents one of the bizarre masks of the author himself who, if correctly reported, once told an interviewer somewhat awkwardly, "I want my books to contain a feeling for humanity and to be a work of art." . . .

So passionate and fearful a concern with art—already adumbrated years ago in "The Girl of My Dreams", where long before *The Tenants* a manuscript is awesomely burned in a (non-magic) "barrel", an Ibsenite image of the death of a spiritual child or self that haunts Malamud's imagination —may surprise those who tend to think of him largely in terms of what a critic once called his "rather unconvincing fiddling-on-the-roof pastiche".

Paradoxically, however, it is when Malamud is most vigorously fiddling on the roof amid lit candles that he seems (to the present non-American outsider at least) to be at his most American. His magic barrels and silver crowns, whatever their scale, firmly belong in the moral, allegorical realm of scarlet letters, white whales and golden bowls. "The Silver Crown", with its wonder rabbi, tells us less perhaps about any specifically Jewish predicament than about the universal opposition of spirituality and materialism. It also turns upon an unsatisfactory father-and-son relationship, that theme beloved of American writers which is to be found in "The Letter", in "My Son the Murderer" and, by extension, in "Notes from a Lady at a Dinner Party" with its betrayal of the father-figure or father-substitute. (p. 35)

On the one hand he conveys distaste for self-pitying Jewish

exploiters (the self-pity is a nice touch); on the other he exalts Jewish spirituality while feeling doubts about certain manifestations of it. The Dostoevskian symbolic doubles in his fiction can be seen as representing two contradictory inner voices. The relentless pursuit of one figure by another would imply the secret urge to escape and remain uninvolved as well as the call (through a sense of guilt) to the conscious and willed acceptance of responsibility. . . .

[Beneath] much of Malamud's earlier fiction there lay his personal experience of the depression during the inter-war years and the intractable fact of Nazi genocide. But now he tends to speak of social and racial injustice in a broader sense. (p. 36)

> *Renee Winegarten, "Malamud's Hats," in*
> The Jewish Quarterly (© The Jewish Quar-
> terly *1974), Autumn, 1974, pp. 35-7.*

Even when Malamud writes a book about baseball, *The Natural,* it is not baseball as it is played in Yankee Stadium but a wild, wacky game, where a player who is instructed to knock the cover off the ball promptly steps up to the plate and does just that: the batter swings and the inner core of the ball goes looping out to center field, where the confused fielder commences to tangle himself in the unwinding sphere; then the shortstop runs out and, with his teeth, bites the center fielder and the ball free from one another. Though *The Natural* is not Malamud's most successful book, it is at any rate our introduction to his world, which is by no means a replica of our own. There are really things called baseball players, of course, and really things called Jews, but there much of the similarity ends. The Jews of *The Magic Barrel* and the Jews of *The Assistant* are not the Jews of New York City or Chicago. They are Malamud's invention, a metaphor of sorts to stand for certain possibilities and promises, and I am further inclined to believe this when I read the statement attributed to Malamud which goes, "All men are Jews." In fact, we know this is not so; even the men who are Jews aren't sure they're Jews. But Malamud, as a writer of fiction, has not shown specific interest in the anxieties and dilemmas and corruptions of the contemporary American Jew, the Jew we think of as characteristic of our times. Rather, his people live in a timeless depression and a placeless Lower East Side; their society is not affluent, their predicament is not cultural. I am not saying—one cannot, of Malamud—that he has spurned life or an examination of its difficulties. What it is to be human, and to be humane, is his deepest concern. What I do mean to point out is that he does not— or has not yet—found the *contemporary* scene a proper or sufficient backdrop for his tales of heartlessness and heartache, of suffering and regeneration. (pp. 127-28)

> *Philip Roth, in his* Reading Myself and Oth-
> ers *(reprinted with the permission of Farrar,
> Straus & Giroux, Inc.; copyright ©1961,
> 1963, 1969, 1970, 1971, 1972, 1973, 1974,
> 1975 by Philip Roth), Farrar, Straus, 1975.*

Seen against the crumbling of Yiddish culture, Bernard Malamud is the most enigmatic, even mysterious, of American Jewish writers. In his best stories he writes as if, through some miraculous salvage, the ethos of Yiddish has become an intimate possession. At such moments, something happens in his stories that one cannot pretend to explain: Malamud not only draws upon Jewish figures and themes, not only evokes traditional Jewish sentiments regarding humaneness and suffering, he also writes what can

only be called the Yiddish story in English. There is something uncanny about this, leading to a greater respect for the idea of transmigration of souls. Malamud can grind a character to earth; but in his best stories there is a hard and bitter kind of pity, a wry affection preferable to the wet gestures of love, which makes him seem a grandson—but a grandson without visible line of descent—of the best Yiddish writers. For, as far as one can tell, he does not work out of an assured personal relation to Yiddish culture; he seems to have reached out for the *idea* of it rather than to possess its substance. Perhaps the moral is that for those who wait, the magic barrel will be refilled.

In his failures, the connection with the past is not made, and instead there is a willed, inflated Jewishness, a sentimentalizing of Yiddish sentimentalism, which he takes out of its homely setting and endows with a false vibrato. For this Malamud, Jewishness seems a program rather than an experience.

But a story like "The Magic Barrel" seems in its characters, its ethos, its unembarrassed yielding to melodrama, like an extended finger of Yiddish literature moving not from left to right but from right to left. Here the question of influence becomes acutely provoking, and one wonders whether Malamud knew, or how precisely he knew, that he was employing standard materials of Yiddish culture. The matchmaker, or *shadkhn,* is a stereotypic Yiddish figure: slightly comic, slightly sad, at the edge of destitution. (p. 595)

Did Malamud know of such materials? Had they reached him directly, or, what seems more likely, did he hear conversations at home about a newspaper read, a play attended? Perhaps there was a direct influence, the result of inner knowledge, but it seems more likely that such figures and motifs of the past, lost for a time in the silence of cultural repression, came to him (as Yiddish critics like to say) "through the air," particles of culture floating about, still charged with meaning and potent enough to be reshaped in American fiction. (p. 596)

> *Irving Howe, in his* World of Our Fathers
> *(© 1976 by Irving Howe; reprinted by per-
> mission of Harcourt Brace Jovanovich,
> Inc.), Harcourt, 1976.*

*   *   *

MARKANDAYA, Kamala (Purnalya)   1924-

Indian novelist Markandaya is particularly skilled at analyzing human relationships, which she does in a clear, delicate, and richly metaphorical prose style. Although her works have been translated in many languages, she is generally regarded as a minor talent.

["Two Virgins" is a] simple, moving story about two adolescent Indian sisters, their closely knit, impoverished family, and the backwater village they live in. Miss Markandaya writes in a forthright, almost breakneck style that could have been paced a little less relentlessly but could not be more precise or lucid. From the minutiae of the girls' lives we learn a great deal about the fabric of life in India today. They are constantly choosing between Eastern and Western ways of looking at the world—in their school, at home, in their language, and in their attitudes toward their own ripening sexuality, of which they are both keenly aware. One sister dares all, moves to the city, and is brought low. The other dares nothing but observes everything, and quivers like a tuning fork. Both their stories are fascinating and demonstrate that Miss Markandaya writes as well about such universal feelings as lust, friendship, envy, and pride as she does about matters idiosyncratic to her country. (p. 174)

> The New Yorker (© *1973 by The New Yorker Magazine, Inc.), October 22, 1973.*

Since [the publication of *Nectar in a Sieve* in 1954] Markandaya has published seven other novels that place her with other talented Indo-Anglican novelists like Raja Rao, R. K. Narayan and Mulk Raj Anand. Unlike them, unlike *most* writers, there has been no deterioration in her work. She has been writing better and better novels during the course of her 20-year literary career. [She has continually expanded] her interests and the geography of her writing. . . . It is, however, with *Two Virgins,* her most recent work, that she reaches the pinnacle of her achievement. (p. 30)

In its entirety *Two Virgins* is a story of mythic proportions, an archetypal story of the loss of innocence. It embodies a journey—a going forth and a return. . . . Kamala Markandaya has written a novel of quiet resignation. The first revolution for India ended years ago, with independence. Now a more difficult aspect of nation-building is beginning, rooted in the simplicity and dignity of traditional life. *Two Virgins* is superb fiction. (p. 31)

> *Charles R. Larson, "Honored Novel," in* The New Republic (*reprinted by permission of* The New Republic; © *The New Republic, Inc.), June 1, 1974, pp. 30-1.*

Miss Markandaya's eighth novel [*Two Virgins*] is one of those unpretentious books which require a little time to make their impact: their unique perfume, as it were, is of the slow-release variety. . . . I would guess that, apart from native influences on her writing which the Westerner can only guess at, she has learned something from the art of understatement as practised by the great American novelists of the middle decades of this century. The book opens on a rather low key, and very gradually rises to a climax; the only exciting action is reserved for the last fifty pages. But the slow climb of the dramatic interest is very skilfully managed, and the beginning linked to the end with a deftness that can only have come with long practice. . . .

This penetrating study of the awakening of sexuality in a young girl (who, like Ernestina in *The French Lieutenant's Woman,* had "seen animals couple, and the violence haunted her mind" . . .) is also a sensitive account of the impact on a rural community of city mores. (p. 80)

> *John Fletcher, in* The International Fiction Review, *January, 1975.*

The Golden Honeycomb is the major novel of Kamala Markandaya's literary career. An Indian who writes in English, she is still best known in this country for her first novel, *Nectar in a Sieve,* published in 1954, although she has written works of far greater significance than that first one: her two more recent books, *The Nowhere Man* (1972) and *Two Virgins* (1973), for example.

The outer parameters of *The Golden Honeycomb* circumscribe the golden age of the Indian Princes—roughly from about 1870 until World War I. . . .

Though the outer framework of *The Golden Honeycomb* is historical, it would be difficult to classify this work as historical fiction. Markandaya, rightly, places her emphasis on

her characters: Bawajiraj, Mohini, Rabi, the Dewan, the British. We are privy to their thoughts, projected into their innermost desires. Bawajiraj is a likeable person, totally human, because of his multiple weaknesses and excesses. Herein lies the core of Markandaya's achievement: she has written a humanistic account of the princely oppressors—a subject which must certainly be anathema to Indian intellectuals.

Moreover, Markandaya is a rare kind of magician—she knows how to control the tension in every scene, in every incident in the narrative, often by nothing more than a word or two which cancel out everything that has been said in a previous scene or conversation. Early in the story we want things to hurry up, so we can discover what is going to happen next. Later, as we approach the end of this lengthy novel and the ending which we expect will be violent, the author achieves a certain mellowness. We want things to slow down, so we never have to turn that last page.

> *Charles R. Larson, "The Prince and the Paupers," in* Book World—The Washington Post (© *The Washington Post), February 6, 1977, p. F10.*

The author of *Nectar in a Sieve* has set [*The Golden Honeycomb*] in the declining years of the Raj, before Gandhi's influence pushed India irretrievably toward independence. With language as ornate, detailed, and slow-moving as the court life she describes, Markandaya weaves a rich tapestry in which subtle shifts of power and the nurture of illusions are the primary pursuits. Her characters are essentially from stock; overt action is minimal; dialogue, when it comes, can be intrusive, teetering on the brink of modern idiom. The art of the book lies in the author's command of the sometimes humorous, sometimes threatening nuances in formalized relationships, and in her considerable gift for irony, which is relentlessly plied.

Indian and Englishman both are treated with a compound of charity and scorn; they are rendered almost quaint by historical distance and by Markandaya's aloof yet precise depiction of them. One can't help wondering how much her barbs would sharpen if they were turned against the monumental irony of India's present administration. (p. 116)

> *Martha Spaulding, in* The Atlantic Monthly (*copyright © 1977 by The Atlantic Monthly Company, Boston, Mass.; reprinted with permission), March, 1977.*

The story of "The Golden Honeycomb" may not be full of surprises . . . once you have got the characters down. . . . A certain historical inevitability leaves no room for surprises in the interplay among the characters. . . .

But what, you may ask, about the "glittering backdrop" of this "rich, colorful dynasty novel," as the blurb calls it? Well, if you know nothing about the period, when you finish "The Golden Honeycomb" you will probably know more about it than the British Viceroys did. The author's research has been prodigious, and the historical details, I am sure, are faultless. . . .

But Kamala Markandaya seems to have been affected by the elaborately ornamented world she is describing. This is her first foray into the past; her other eight novels are set in contemporary India. . . .

I don't know whether Mrs. Markandaya thought the theme of Princely India merited a more ornate style, but in her new novel the chapters grow as encrusted as a Maharajah's turban. Sentence inversions, strings of clauses, obscure words and tense changes accumulate throughout the 468 pages until the reader gasps for air. The author evidently loves the sound of English (unlike some Indians, who urge its abolition as the national language on the grounds of its British Imperial overtones and fossilization), but her writing here is overwrought. In her embellishments the characters flounder and India seeps away.

You may want to read this book for its absorbing historical detail. Afterwards, if you feel up to it, read Ruth Prawer Jhabvala's "Heat and Dust" for the real flavors, resonances and deeper meanings of Anglo-India, delivered with an economy of characterization and language altogether exemplary.

> *Caroline Seebohm, "Class and Caste in India," in* The New York Times Book Review *(© 1977 by The New York Times Company; reprinted by permission), April 3, 1977, p. 42.*

The sustained grip of this novel about princely India derives from the quality of the writing. . . . In *The Golden Honeycomb* the writing has become almost an object in its own right, a structure so exquisite and so highly wrought that its purpose seems to be less the transmission of life than of artistic experience. . . . [Kamala Markandaya's] subject is wildly fanciful though not lacking in plausibility. A third of the Indian subcontinent was left by the British as protected states, and Devapur, where her scenario is laid, is no bad fictional representation of a sizable Rajput state in the days of British paramountcy. . . .

If her purpose was to write a historical novel, then her chosen setting certainly provides the quintessential mixture of the real and the exotic. Yet her studied inattention to details of time and place and her comparative indifference to plot suggest that her interests lie elsewhere. She seems fascinated by patterns of emotional response towards the constraints imposed by historical situation. Her characters have all manipulated their immediate environments so as to give their apprehension of the world an aesthetic dimension and to immure their personality in a pleasure dome of sensuous mental feelings. It is this which enable them to come to terms with reality while holding it at bay. "Life", to quote Rabi, the central figure, "was intended to be ravished by the senses".

Lady Copeland, the Resident's wife, creates a world of ordered beauty in house and garden to enable her to cope with the bitterness of exile and lend her courage against neurotic fears of a racial massacre. The Maharajah and Resident revel in subtle traditions of civility and ceremony which permit them to form a restrained friendship and screen the naked facts of power. All this is depicted so well, with so much understanding that it seems to testify to some instinctual belief on the author's part that any genuine political, social or even artistic culture must be an artefact of this kind. Yet the historical theme of the book is the recovery of reality and the overcoming of estrangement, hypocrisy, and alienation. This is the function of Rabi, the heir-apparent born out of wedlock.

Reality is to be found in the people, in the harsh actuality of their poverty, in British imperial oppression and in princely greed and self-indulgence. But in the novel it is kept in the wings and never possesses the stage: the author's own aesthetic sense is too strong for her to get close. She cannot

manipulate stench, filth and violence, or transmit other than an ordered and tidy image. No blood is spilt, the gathering personal and political tension is readily dissipated by British concessions. There is no climax since there is no drama being staged. At the end both the British Raj and the Indian princes pass into historical limbo.

If this is not a historical novel, neither does it properly succeed as a character study. The leading figures gain shape and body but the minor ones like the Copelands and the Dewan possess a stronger internal consistency. All have to play a double role as individuals and as historical symbols. Rabi is too difficult a character to bring off entire. The double pull of East and West, of rags and riches, woven into his relations with the Dewan's daughter, with the sweeper-girl, the Bombay prostitute, the Resident's daughter, the Resident's wife and finally his parents, leaves him a powerful but uncertain quantity.

A novel which seeks to register the broken immediacy of life rather than to pursue the ordered purpose of tying and untying a dramatic knot has to be held together by a constant renewal of sensation. Here there is a wealth of incident and situation, and Kamala Markandaya is resolutely fashionable in serving up her dish of sweetmeats with some well-sugared titbits of sexual delight, although (strangely) it is the purblind but lovable Maharajah rather than his intense hero son for whom sexual love has the profoundest spiritual significance. Similarly we are presented with a few four-lettered obscenities to show that the author is up with the times and down to crude reality when it comes to recording the conversations of Rabi with the common folk. We must forgive these concessions to contemporary fashion which sit self-consciously and awkwardly on the page, for this is a beautifully and tightly written book. It is built up out of short separate sections, each carefully and delicately worked to achieve an exact economy of statement. The sections fit together like cells in a honeycomb, although the honeycomb itself lacks determinate dimensions.

> *Eric Stokes, "Generally Ravishing," in* The Times Literary Supplement *(© Times Newspapers Ltd., 1977; reproduced from* The Times Literary Supplement *by permission), April 29, 1977, p. 507.*

*   *   *

MARKFIELD, Wallace (Arthur)   1926-

American novelist and short story writer, Markfield combines experimental techniques borrowed from Joyce with a subject matter of Jewish-American urban life to produce a distinctive, and often underrated, fiction. (See also *Contemporary Authors*, Vols. 69-72.)

One of the reasons we read novels is to learn about the exotic world: how do Portuguese priests go about seducing their parishioners, why are the Japanese forever injecting themselves with vitamins? Wallace Markfield's first novel, *To an Early Grave,* is about a way of life just as exotic and glamorous as those, if one can stand away from it for a while: the life of New York Jewish intellectuals. Jewish? Indeed, to paraphrase Nietzsche, all too Jewish. The book is broad satire, wonderfully funny and mean. . . .

I do not think that *To an Early Grave* is a work of major importance, or that Markfield intended it to be. It is a small comic triumph, the sunniest novel about death that I know. The book deals with one Sunday in the life of Morroe Rieff, during which he and three other friends of Leslie Braverman, a gifted writer dead at 41, attend Leslie's funeral in Brooklyn. Markfield makes only the most perfunctory effort to unify the incidents: Morroe finds that he cannot cry over Leslie's death; everyone else cries at the funeral, but instead Morroe embarrassingly gets an erection at the sight of Sandra Luboff, Miss Social Welfare, and his memory of their dalliance; finally, at the end of the long day, rubbing his wife Etta with insect repellent, Morroe is able to cry. But this is less a serious development than Markfield's final irony: the tears come just as inappropriately as did Morroe's earlier reaction. (p. 214)

The other three mourners are broad caricatures. Holly Levine, a most pretentious literary critic, owns the Volkswagen that takes the four to the funeral. Levine's Volkswagen is introduced with a marvelous soliloquy that begins: "To own a car in Manhattan is like towing a camel across the Sargasso." A seven-page scene in which Levine tries to write a review should be enough to drive anyone of decent impulse, susceptible to shame, out of the profession. Levine's form of mourning for Leslie is to say to a friend at the funeral: "We must first determine whether we want memoir or critique."

We first see Barnet Weiner, poet and critic of the arts, spending his Sunday morning in bed with a thin Bronx girl named Myra Mandelbaum, who had previously refused to stay the night, she explains, because her hair is oily and he has such hard water. Weiner "used to correspond with Gide in French and call him *Cher Maître.*" In his criticism Weiner is fastidious and delicate, in reality he is a lecherous vulgarian, calling Morroe's attention to a girl walking by with the comment: "That little *tochiss.* I could bite into it like a piece of hot pastrami."

The fourth mourner, Felix Ottensteen, is an older man (the other three are about Leslie's age) who writes literary articles for a Yiddish daily and lectures to Hadassah groups. . . . Ottensteen is a refuser, but he is the most likable of Morroe's companions, he is the one most loyal to Leslie, and his rhetoric about Jewish woes is a relief from the culture-faking of the rest of them.

The most interesting character in *To an Early Grave* is of course the dead Leslie, who is endlessly resurrected for us. He was a small fat man, who walked like "a little *bubbe* loaded down with shopping bags." Leslie was dirty, tirelessly promiscuous, and a shameless sponge; he was a ruthless exploiter of his wife, who eventually evicted him; before his death he lived by writing pornography. But Leslie was also a brilliant critic and fiction writer, a conscientious stylist, and a man who saved his integrity for his work. (pp. 215-16)

The women in *To an Early Grave* are all minor. Morroe's wife Etta comes through as a nagging voice and "absurdly large breasts." Leslie's widow, Inez, a Yiddish-speaking Gentile, is made "radiant, positively radiant" by her grief, and she is masterful at the funeral, inviting the mourners back to her apartment and instructing them to bring two large pizzas, "one all cheese, one cheese and anchovy." Sandra, Myra, and the other girls described or mentioned, are interesting only in their ready horizontality. The other women in the novel are ludicrous figures overheard in restaurants, or comic storeladies. This is accurate sociology: women are insignificant in the novel because they are insignificant, instrumental housekeeper-bedmates, in the Jewish intellectual subculture—to its shame. (p. 216)

Markfield's comic descriptions are marvels of economy.

He can compress all of Flatbush into a few words: "Kids gumming zwieback in wading pools." Here is an unfriendly Gentile: "She had on a narrow fur piece; its little beast jaws gaped open as though from great pain or rage." As for the cemetery, "even the young maples that lined the street seemed trimmed and pruned to the shape of menorahs." Here is a remark overheard in the washroom: "He was never a normal personality. A normal personality is not going to set fire to his mother's bathroom curtains when he's a big boy already."

Some of the funniest parts of *To an Early Grave* consist of tribal lore. The only art that truly interests Leslie's circle is popular culture. During the trip, Weiner challenges Levine to identify the nemesis of Bim Gump, the Green Hornet's driver, the words that Hop Harrigan radios to his announcer, and so on. (p. 217)

The book bubbles over with comic rhetoric. In Leslie's apartment "the very walls dripped troubles! You could peel them off with the laths and tiles, they hung from the clothes dryer in the kitchen, they stuffed up the drains, they killed the plants, they brought in roaches!" (pp. 217-18)

At times there is too much rhetoric, and the topical and popular culture references overpower. But mostly the richness of language amuses and delights. Markfield has clearly taken *Ulysses* as his model, but instead of trying to duplicate that encyclopedic masterpiece, he has aimed more modestly at writing just Mr. Bloom's Day in Brooklyn. As such, *To an Early Grave* is brilliantly successful. . . . (p. 218)

> *Stanley Edgar Hyman, "Jewish, All Too Jewish," in his* Standards: A Chronicle of Books for Our Time (© *1966; reprinted by permission of the publisher, Horizon Press, New York), Horizon, 1966, pp. 215-18.*

"Teitlebaum's Window" is an ethnic musical comedy—it hasn't opened yet, but it will—about Brighton Beach Jews in the 1930's. It has a large cast, all of whom are indistinguishably "Brooklyn Jewish," and all of whom do comic turns that are based on Wallace Markfield's marvelous ear for a pretension. But these comic bits are usually artificial, implausible, repeated without mercy, and always identify the characters as Brighton Beach Jews in the 1930's. This was a very hilarious thing to be.

Mr. Markfield is a parodist, a relentless jokesmith, a gifted improviser in the Nichols & May tradition. Most of all he is an expert on old issues of "Photoplay" and "Liberty," on Ronald Colman, high-school yearbooks, the prices of dairy products in 1938, ladies' undershirts, matjes herring, Dolores Del Rio, Dorothy Lamour, and the best B.M.T. routes to Times Square. . . .

[Memories] are used in a movie technique ("they panned and picked out Gelfman") and as a comic strategy by which things represent people—and finally replace them. Mr. Markfield has a ferocious energy for the trivial. If old copies of "Liberty" and "Photoplay" had wit, they would resemble "Teitlebaum's Window." His gifts of mimicry are used to make not believable human emotions but a warehouse of Brooklyn Jewish folklore. There is not the slightest hint of human conflict, for Mr. Markfield is everybody. All the characters—hero, father, mother, girl friends, teachers, storekeepers—are without exception used by the author as vehicles for his own jokes. (p. 5)

The trick of unrelated dialogue is used in this book over

and again, and usually never gets us very far, for Mr. Markfield's interest is mimicry, not drama. . . .

The sound of one voice clapping alone is Mr. Markfield's star bit. When he abandons the unrelated conversation, he gives us Simon's school years entirely through Simon's notebook. In a book so full of unregarded people and perished tidbits, only one voice, one person stands out—the author. Simon, his mama and papa, his girl friend, Yenta Gersh, Mrs. Harlib, all get ground up with the Spanish Civil War, the Depression, Dick Tracy, Louella Parsons, and the tops of old Dixie ice cream cups. (p. 40)

> *Alfred Kazin, "Brighton Beach Was God's Country," in* The New York Times Book Review *(© 1970 by The New York Times Company; reprinted by permission), October 18, 1970, pp. 5, 40.*

[In] Wallace Markfield's novel, *Teitlebaum's Window,* one will find at last what O. Henry called "the composite vocal message of massed humanity. In other words, of the Voice of a Big City." What it amounts to (in O. Henry's story) is the tender, eloquent, heartrending silence of a municipal spectrum of vibrations, heart beats scaling into a vast, sweeping thunder. Markfield stands with the biggest innovators, the most colorful Jewish interpreters of our most important, our Old/New City: Montague Glass, Abraham Cahan, Michael Gold, Henry Roth, Daniel Fuchs, Bel Kaufman, Bernard Malamud. [Markfield's book is a] screamingly funny, outrageous (in places it out-Portnoys *Portnoy*), vibration-filled saga of the city. . . .

The hero, the big-boy growing-up, in Markfield's bildungsroman, is Simon Sloan, eight years old when the story opens in June, 1932 and old enough to go to war when the story ends in April, 1942. . . .

All through the ten-year period of the novel, as Simon makes his way upward to Brooklyn College, Markfield develops a memorable group of thematic melodies. The changing signs in Teitlebaum's grocery window, saying in effect: "The World Looks Like It's Blowing Up—Buy Now Before It's Too Late." The Knishe Queen's incredible letters to the world's Greats, soliciting their knishe testimonials. The sadistic treatment by the family, of Hymie's *bubbee,* senile and helpless but possessing all kinds of valuables for them to extract. Simon's father's ambivalence: his wife nags him to "go make like a Daddy," and when he does, it's so upsetting to him that he becomes furious with his unoffending son. Beyond all the rich themes and vignettes that enhance this marvelous book are the ever-present mass media, especially the movies, which taught the Jewish immigrants their language, made them High Verbals, and reshaped their thinking. *As it was said on the screen* . . . And at a time when most books have little (at best) to say any more, Markfield has written one that will be speaking to us for a long time. (p. 33)

> *Samuel I. Bellman, in* Congress Bi-Weekly, *December 25, 1970.*

[*You Could Live if They Let You*] is much more than its collected lines. It's a concise portrait of a streetwise wit and the cloistered academic who hopes first to immortalize him (on the conceit that large audiences count for less than small footnotes) and then to be saved by him (on the discovery that exegises is a chancier way to redemption than laughter). And it's an enormously funny and often rather brutal study of, uh, the-way-we-live-now. Or at least the way some people do.

But mostly it's a book about being a Jew. That topic obsessed the hero, Jules Farber, who's idealized on the dust jacket as a clown chained to a microphone with a target pinned to his chest. Ponderously assailed by the narrator, who wonders if he hasn't been "painting on the face of the imaginary Jew what Ezra Pound calls 'the image of our accelerated grimace,'" Farber retorts, "Who needs the imaginary Jew? Believe me, the real Jew is beyond my imagination." (p. 2)

The notion that popular art deserves serious study calcified into doctrine in the late '60s, when pop and avant-garde became the same. It is just one of the ideas revivified in this well-made work, which carries the author a long step beyond his earlier preoccupations. (Theodore Solotaroff called Markfield, not altogether in praise, one of those Jewish writers who "seem to possess virtually total recall of their adolescent years, as though there were still some secret meaning that resides in the image of Buster Brown shoes. . . .") Farber is still saddled with that half-desperate recall, but Markfield has brought him into being in order to go beyond it. Like *Portnoy's Complaint,* the book is a breakthrough. And it's even sadder, and funnier. (p. 3)

> *William C. Wood, "Kosher Ham," in* Book World—The Washington Post *(© The Washington Post), November 17, 1974, pp. 2-3.*

* * *

MARKHAM, Robert
See AMIS, Kingsley

* * *

MERRILL, James   1926-

Merrill is an American poet, novelist, and playwright. Throughout his distinguished career his poetry has grown more ambitious and his explorations of the human mind more intense. His exquisite, meditative poems have won for him both the Bollengen Prize and the National Book Award. (See also *CLC,* **Vols. 2, 3, 6, and** *Contemporary Authors,* **Vols. 13-16, rev. ed.)**

Auden would have liked ["Divine Comedies"]—in fact, he is mentioned in it as one of the spirits who, from the next world, act as "patrons" of the living. A spirit named Ephraim tells the narrator, J. M., and his friend, D. J., that spirits must return to earth repeatedly, as to a school, until they have worked through their ignorance. (p. 6)

Ingenious? Witty? Merrill's writing is all of that. But the reader who wants to be gripped by strong feelings or a plot will be disappointed. Merrill has staked out his claim very nicely, thank you; I have the impression that he would think the demands made upon poetry by a certain kind of reader—for example, the reader who is looking for strong feelings—irrelevant if not absurd. There are two kinds of poets. The first believe that poetry is a language-skill, that poems are constructed with words, not emotions. Auden was of this opinion and said so more than once. He said that if a young man wanted to write poetry in order to say something important, then there wasn't much likelihood of his being a poet. On the other hand, if he wanted to see what he could do with words, then there was a possibility. James Merrill and one or two other American poets—John Ashbery and W. S. Merwin come to mind—have taken Auden's way. For these writers, poetry is a word-game of a high order. It is a matter of style. It is not circumscribed by nature and, in the long run, it may adopt some form of religion. For Auden toward the end of his life, Pope was a great poet and Romantic poets of any kind were anathema.

The other kind of poet believes that poetry is a product of feeling rather than wit. He believes that words are not chosen by the poet's rational mind but, to the contrary, may be forced upon him, and the best writing is done this way. . . .

For getting through life with sense and charm, even with some Sybaritic pleasure, as Merrill's narrator evidently does, the first kind of writing is the kind to choose. It can be worked at intelligently and it leads somewhere. It is likely to wind up with the prizes. Auden was a brilliant writer of verse, unfailingly articulate and witty. I suspect, however, that his way of writing will be of interest to fewer and fewer people as time goes by—especially in the United States where life is not witty and does not aim to be articulate.

James Merrill, too, is a brilliant writer, operating on a level of high style. A society of cultivated readers might give his "Divine Comedies" a high place. At its best, as in the poem titled "Chimes for Yahya," his writing is exotic and picturesque. The tone of easy, intimate conversation is a stylistic achievement. It is hardly the poet's fault that there are few readers of this kind of poetry. For that matter, there are few readers of poetry of any kind—people seem just as oblivious of the poetry that intends to render "feelings" or describe "real life." So Merrill may as well please himself and his friends, and be as capricious as he likes. (p. 7)

> *Louis Simpson, in* The New York Times Book Review *(© 1976 by The New York Times Company; reprinted by permission), April 4, 1976.*

Misunderstanding his gifts, James Merrill has written a long, a very long, poem, "The Book of Ephraim." He is not one disposed to call things deeply into question; nor does he wield a comic whip. He is a thoroughly personal poet with a gift for appreciating his own life, pains and all. The epic size is too coarse and ambitious for him. As it is, he has written a poem neither imposingly public nor poignantly personal. "The Book of Ephraim" is made out of the stuff of conversation among intimates. To read it is at best a desultory pleasure, like treading agreeable water. . . .

"The Book of Ephraim" has neither thought nor plot, and its casual record is made still more desultory by references to a lost and uncompleted novel that of course means more to Merrill than to us. We shuttle between the aimless and the scant. And occasionally the poet's musings twist and preen themselves into defeating abstraction. . . .

[Merrill] is a man with an almost crippling, almost enabling love of his own past, his old loves. He needs the deep place, the small pool, to find how close he is, how far after all, from the ecstasy of being self and other, actor and his own audience, simultaneously. (p. 22)

Merrill's modesty and tact are almost a vice of privacy. As if invented by Henry James, he has often been self-effacing without quite displacing himself with the objects of his love, objects made autonomous. They live by their refraction in his feeling. Still, "Chimes for Yahya" has sufficient detail to give firmness (and finely exotic detail it is). The poem triumphs typically, too, through the Jamesian "quality" of the poet's mind and the related sweet radiance of his words.

This radiance does not show well in brief quotation. It has no flash. Steadily, as in the best poem in the volume, "Lost in Translation," it shines through many words, part warmth of attitude, part grace of motion. Here no line is brilliant, none is dull. The subject of the poem—a memory of putting a puzzle together with his "French Mademoiselle"—is likewise unremarkable, save that, in remarking it, the poet makes it live. The slight materials do not feel slight. Here is a child's loneliness, his capacity for absorption in puzzling representations of life, his romance with those who care for him, with history, with what is known only by hearsay and by wish. Here is the man that child fathered trying to father the child through completeness of memory and the magic of verse. It is nearly done. Perhaps it is done. The child is rephrased by the man and nothing seems lost in translation. (pp. 22-3)

> *Calvin Bedient, in* The New Republic *(reprinted by permission of* The New Republic; *© 1976 by The New Republic, Inc.), June 5, 1976.*

Our situation as readers [of *The Book of Ephraim*] is not unlike that of the Wedding-Guest before the Ancient Mariner; and, like him, we must eventually be able to see through the strangeness of the tale, and our captivation by the teller, to the more this-worldly lesson they bear. If James Merrill is without a "glittering eye," he is not without equally dazzling devices for holding and enchanting the reader, but unless we can see through the poetic effects to the "unsteady ground" . . . for which they exist, they will have been created in vain. And we, as I believe, will be the worse for it.

The basic strategy of the poem is Romantic, the recreation of experience and its recollection in relative tranquillity, but the terms of the enchantment are distinctly modern: what is asked of the reader, as it is exemplified by the poet, is both submersion in and resistance to the other-worldly revelation in the poem. We are, by now, perhaps all too ready to suspend disbelief, and it is one of the poet's chief concerns to guard against this possibility, to muffle credulity even as he attempts to unbutton skepticism. His diffidence as to the reality of Ephraim and as to the particulars of Ephraim's revelation is, however, neither more nor less than the strongest of the strands in that net of enchantment from which we must at last free ourselves—in order, that is, to see the poem for what at least in part it is: an instance of the admission of the Other. (p. 64)

The Book of Ephraim is composed of something approaching 2500 lines of fine unto exquisite poetry; and the achievement of the poem everywhere weighs on the reader, particularly the reader who would ask more—or other—of a poem, especially one of such ambitious length, than evidence of poetic mastery. . . . [The] suspicion that while little can be done in poetry without a master's skill, that skill alone guarantees nothing, [makes] the poem's accomplishment *as poetry* all the more, if I may put it so, insidious. Or captivating: for the attention the verse calls to itself is attention drawn away from the poem's matter. . . . *The Book of Ephraim* is a particular case for [a] general principle . . . appropriate to the poem's theme; namely, art is a place where the human and the divine meet. The verse, then, would partake of and give insight into that relationship that is the explicit matter of the poem. More, the verse's variations will prove to be revealing in ways that the language of the poem *as statement* will not be, for if it were the spell the poet is concerned to cast would be badly damaged if not absolutely torn. In other words, we must neither be taken in nor put off by the mastery of the poetry; we must resist even as we give ourselves over to its dazzling shallows, for beneath lie profundities indeed.

Similar difficulties, and opportunities, are presented us by the paraphernalia of the poem's revelation—ouija board, familiar spirit, mediums, the "whole/Fantastic monkey business of the soul/Between lives, gathered to its patron's breast".... Whatever our preconceptions about such things, the poet is continually at our ear counseling by exhibiting tentativeness, the steering of a course between "Milton" and Auden (between, that is, "ghastly on the spot/Conversion" and "Impatience with folderol"), and it is just this advice that is meant to enchant us. For we know, or seem to remember knowing, that while the extremes of fanatic commitment to or contemptuous disdain for anything may be avoided, there is no third alternative to belief or disbelief. But the poet's own apparent uncertainty, his care to give more attention to the pros *and* cons than most would ever have thought themselves interested to hear, invites just that suspension of fixed ideas that once upon a time was taken to be poetry's peculiar genius.

Another inducement to tentativeness, part of the weaving of the spell, is the possibility that what is revealed in *The Book of Ephraim* is simply the poet's invention.... [It] may occur to us, and will nowhere be explicitly denied, that the "Projection" might as well be artistic as psychological, in which case we would be dealing not with delusion but with metaphor. That Ephraim is a character in the poem, not in the cosmos, and that the paraphernalia is figurative for what is occult in love are suggestions tendered to both the credulous and the skeptical in order to disarm them.

The main attraction in all of this, the spell-binder, is the poet's persona, a character whom I shall call the Gentleman Tempter. In attempting to define this character, Coleridge's "bright-eyed Mariner" will prove useful—and more useful still, perhaps crucial, will be recollection of the matter and the mode of *The Rime* itself if we are to recognize *The Book of Ephraim's* Romantic roots, for the profusion of Neo-classical foliage might otherwise lead us to mistake its genus.

Alexander Pope's presence in the poem is, in fact, felt as quite substantial; and, more important, his relation to the material and composition of the poem is complicated where Auden's, say, even for the space given it, is relatively straight-forward.... [Beyond] suggestions of arcane ties between [Pope and Merrill] (difficult as it is to imagine Pope thinking of couplets as bedeviling) and, what is implied, their firm footing in Locke's rendition of the Real as that which is sensuously and commonly experienced, there is the obvious relation on one of *The Book of Ephraim's* recurrent themes: the place of Man between Angel and Beast. I know of no other work, and certainly no contemporary work, that is so preoccupied by the conundrum at the heart of "An Essay on Man." ... However, especially but not solely in terms of characterizing the Gentleman Tempter, Pope's value will be almost entirely by way of contrast. James Merrill's inclination to self-criticism, for example, opens an abyss between him and Pope, while the latter's indignation (which if not savage was by no means genteel) finds no correspondence in the former. In addition, and as a means for moving more confidently to *The Book of Ephraim's* Romantic lineage, where Pope was social, James Merrill is eremitic; where the one was moralistic, the other is psychological; where the great 18th century poet

held that Taste and Value are objective categories, the contemporary poet's preferences are explicitly instances of his temperament. Crucially, it is in the matter of tone, where the two poets seem so much alike, that they are most diverse; for while both are urbane, I do not know that anyone has ever called Pope bewitching. Lastly, where Pope the man and Pope the speaker in his poems are not easily or even necessarily to be differentiated, it seems to me decisive that we see the seam that separates even as it joins James Merrill and the Gentleman Tempter.

That a "glittering eye" is the appropriate analogue for the speaker's wiles will be clearer in the reading of the poem's first Section ..., so long as it is remembered that the polish and serenity of the verse are as important to effecting the enchantment in *The Book of Ephraim* as the incantatory ballad stanza is to generating that of Coleridge's *Rime*. Sirens are to be found in drawing rooms as well as on open seas. (pp. 64-7)

The function of the Gentleman in [the first Section] is, as I take it, to make the reader feel comfortable, to draw him into (an albeit one-sided) conversation in familiar and worldly surroundings. We are made privy to a literary confidence, the poet's failure with his novel, treated to a number of nicely turned literary and social observations, and presented with the opportunity to hear a story as distinct from any vital or immediate concerns as *The Arabian Nights*. In commercial jargon, a soft sell; in ethical terms, a temptation—or hard bargain. For the prologue to *The Book of Ephraim* constitutes not only an invitation to read, but also a temptation to learn, and what the Gentleman promises is, as ever, that knowledge will do us no harm. (pp. 71-2)

There are three formal devices that characterize the Gentleman Tempter's pitch, but while each of them might be understood as no more than a functional utensil for so large a meal (that is, something the poet was forced to use because of the poem's length rather than something he chose to use because of the poem's nature), taken together they will be seen to be indicative of that resistance to making a pitch that is characteristic of the Gentleman. I refer to 1) the muting of poetic effects, 2) the eschewing of riddles and hidden meanings, and 3) comic relief. A Gentleman does not 1) show-off, 2) play practical jokes, or 3) take things *too* seriously.

The basic poetic line of *The Book of Ephraim* is iambic pentameter, the preferred poetic unit the couplet. But only for short stretches does the poet make continuous use of either, and, still more rarely, both. While variety in metrics, rhyme-scheme etcetera is perhaps "necessary" in a poem of this length (hundreds of exceptions notwithstanding), the refraining from the preferred measures is felt in the poem as restraint that proceeds from other than formal considerations. (In Elizabethan drama, a couplet was sometimes used to close a speech delivered in blank verse, and the straining for that couplet is often felt; in James Merrill's verse, to the contrary, the straining is to escape the couplet —the bedeviling couplet.) That the poet will virtually identify rhyme and contact with the absolute in Section 'X' ought to further establish the degree to which the poetic variations are either more than functional or so profoundly functional as to disabuse us of the shallower uses to which the term is put.

The Gentleman also provides occasional reminders, or padded elbows to the ribs, so as not to appear enigmatic—

or vulgarly so. Section 'R' is composed of five sonnets, for example, but they are broken into quatrains and tercets in order to conform with other stanzaic usage in the poem, so we may miss the fact that they are sonnets. Worse from the Gentleman Tempter's point of view, as I take it, is the possibility that this arrangement is meant to signal something more, or other, than the poet's love for Eleanora Deren (the "Maya" to whom the sonnets are addressed, see Section 'D'), so the fifth sonnet begins, "Leave to the sonneteer eternal youth" ('R'). The impression intended is that the reader will be met honestly.

A more important example of the disinclination to uncouth mysteriousness, to whatever might encourage occult communication between the poet and cognoscenti, is the name Ephraim is given in the poem's version of the lost novel. Ephraim is called "Eros." When the Gentleman Tempter tells us, in Section 'A', that his theme is "the incarnation and withdrawal of/A god" and then spends the first half of the poem relating this to the efflorescence and withering of a love affair, we may well imagine (since Gentleman Readers are not made in a day) that we know what "god" has come and gone. But just in case we did not know, the god's name appears in the first Section of the second half of the poem. Laying all his cards on the table, even playing the ace that many writers might have kept up their sleeves, convinces the reader of the Gentleman's high-mindedness, his candor. More important, though, this bringing of everything into the poem's mix discourages the reader from looking beyond the poem for resolution of its difficulties—in fact, from looking beyond the poem at all—and so constitutes a kind of insulation, is itself an image of that insulation from the Other that is precisely the Gentleman's mission in art. (pp. 73-5)

The Gentleman Tempter would, like the Ancient Mariner, hold us until his story is told, a story whose fluency carries as well the current of compulsion (cf. the Mariner's "strange power of speech"), and then more or less shrug us off. The telling of the story, that is, completes the circuit which, while it may be driven by contact with the supernatural, is not meant to electrify—much less, electrocute—the reader. Thus, the purpose of the enchantment, woven out of those materials described above, is as much defensive as it is attractive, and the captivation is meant to be temporary (the Ancient Mariner does not use his glittering eye to harm the Wedding-Guest, but to hold him *and* release him at the story's close). (p. 76)

The Book of Ephraim is composed of 26 Sections lettered A-Z; in one sense the ABC's of Ephraim, in another his Alpha and Omega. If, in terms of the poem's structure, the first image suggests a kind of primer in which the introduction to Ephraim and his revelation will be incremental and progressive, the second image suggests a compendium in which the sequence of the poem's elements will count for less than their eventual interrelatedness and the coherence of the whole they go to make up. The distinction may also be seen as that which (I believe) exists between *living through* an experience as it reveals itself in successive and temporal shapes and *thinking about* the experience, once it has been constituted as past, that may see it as whole and atemporal. I do not mean to imply that thought is ever suspended, nor that there is a change in the kind of thought involved, but that the shapes with which we are presented alter from, in the first case, something more than less serial to, in the second case, something more than less complete. (pp. 76-7)

The overwhelming majority of the poems' action flows into two pools of time (Lethe and Mnemosyne, say): the first is the period of two years from the summer of 1955 through that of 1957 (Lethe), the second is January through December, 1974, during which time *The Book of Ephraim* is composed (Mnemosyne). Sections 'B' through 'L' are, with two or perhaps three exceptions, largely taken up with the recreation of the experiences of the first time period; their movement, even when it is interrupted, depends upon a chronological line, and we are gradually and progressively introduced to Ephraim's cosmography. We get the sense of a primer from these Sections, and their progressive character is all the more emphatic for their narrative form, Ephraim's news being embedded as it is in the story of a love affair. But something stops in Section 'L'. Looking back on these Sections (roughly the first half of the poem) from the perspective of Sections 'M' and following, we find that they seem to constitute an action whole and complete because it is past.

If there is a narrative to action, if experience is sequential, there is as well a narrative to thinking; itself an experience, thought is successive because we can only think of one thing at a time. But the narrative line of thought, so to speak, is liable to be more complicated geometrically—at least in the record of it—than the narrative line of action, and I should say that this is particularly true when the object of thought is taken as past, is thereby understood as whole and complete in itself, and is thereby felt as resistant. (Something of the distinction I am arguing may have simply to do with conventions of literary rendering, but the conventions themselves may be well-founded.) So, in any case, we may account for the movement of Sections 'M' through 'U', which are a record of the poet's *thinking about* experiences that have been *lived through* and are understood as irremediably past. Sections 'M' through 'U' are occasionally dated, but their sequence is not based on chronology; in fact, they seem to depend for their power and coherence as a group on the suspension of time. For these Sections too, when seen from the vantage point of those ('V' through 'Z') that follow them, show themselves as a complete unit. (pp. 77-8)

[The] two pools of time mentioned earlier spill over into one another in Section 'L', where . . . the narrative of the two years' (1955-1957) love ends and the narrative of the year of the poem's composition (January through December, 1974) goes underground. After the series of meditations that occupies Sections 'M' through 'U', the second narrative surfaces to plain view in Section 'V' and continues to the poem's end. The trip taken in those meditative Sections is so arduous that a reminder of the more literal excursion is perhaps necessary, which is why we get the padded elbow in Section 'U'. The return to a sequence based on chronology, in Sections 'V' through 'Z', is what lets us see the speculative group as a whole—which is not to say that the poet stops thinking, and wondering, in the poem's final Sections, but that thought is once again presented with fleeting (time-unbound) images. We feel, I think, these final Sections as a return to earth. . . . Time, as we are abruptly reminded in Section 'V', does not stop; nor can it be, except perhaps in artful images of it, suspended. The return to earth—and Venice at that—from the apparently timeless reaches of wonder cannot but be felt as the formal or structural counterpart to the poem's inquiry into matters human and divine. And time will also prove to be only one of many things that, however much they seem to end, continue. (pp. 78-9)

Section 'F' [is] the second of the three displaced Sections in the narrative that ends in Section 'L'. That the Section is out of its place in the poem's chronological order I think we should take as extraordinarily telling: where, in certain pathological contexts, a slip of the tongue may reveal more about the gist of what is said than what is deliberate in the saying, in art a slip (or displacement) will be supremely indicative of what we read as the artist's intent. (The first of the displaced Sections is 'D', "a partial list" of the poem's Dramatis Personae; the narrative, however, is picked up at its close, and its place seems to be no more than simply functional.) Section 'F', then, is a "Flash-forward" in time; the chronicling of the events of two years is abrupted—as it could not be in fact, but can be in fiction—just at the cresting of love's wave. The intent, as we take it, is to celebrate that love before (in the poem's reliving of it) it breaks and sizzling, hissing, sinks into the sand (see Section 'L'). (p. 80)

I should note that some of *The Book of Ephraim*'s difficulties may not be the reader's alone; there are questions that go unanswered perforce because the poet is as much in the dark as we. (p. 83)

Section 'L' (el, 'el, Hell?) is *The Book of Ephraim*'s most important. It is made up of four parts, the first of which brings to a close the love story begun in Section 'B', or, better, the chronological narrative of two years in the love story. For we know that the love began before 1955 ("*Second* summer of our tenancy"; my italics), and we have had a parenthetical indication, in Section 'J', that it extended to at least 1958. But the sense that something begun in Section 'B' ends in Section 'L' is . . . strong. . . . (p. 86)

[In the] effortless transition from July, 1957, to July, 1974, another transition has taken place. The narrative of the year of the poem's composition moves from January ('A') through March ('E'), April ('F'; for the visit to Temerlin, as we can see by this scheme, is almost certainly in 1974), and May ('H'), but then it skips in Section 'L' to July—omitting June. And it is in June, 1974, as we do not learn until Section 'U', that the break with Ephraim and the SCRIBE's "Edict" come. Chronologically, Section 'U' comes before Section 'L', and the sense of finality, and even dread, that pervades 'L' is in large measure to be attributed to the events described in 'U'. The displacement of Section 'U' is *The Book of Ephraim*'s most pronounced formal feature; and therefore . . . we will read in it the poet's most profound deliberation. . . . Moreover, we can measure the terror that attached to the break with Ephraim in Section 'U' if we read the fourth part of Section 'L' as its emotional equivalent. (p. 88)

The break with Ephraim comes in Section 'U'. The poet makes one last attempt to give a this-worldly name, and place, to those powers that have withdrawn, "Jung says . . . That God and the Unconscious are one" ('U'), but the struggle of these Sections to come to terms with and for those powers, like the effort of Sections 'B' through 'L' to see them as aspects of a waxing and waning love, fails. Leaving us? In Venice, with the poet, in the Augumn of 1974 and of his life.

The return to earth in *The Book of Ephraim*'s final Sections comes as a relief; the world is, as it were, returned to the reader and to the poet. (pp. 90-1)

> *Henry Sloss, "James Merrill's 'Book of Ephraim'," (Part 1), in Shenandoah (copyright by Shenandoah; reprinted from Shen-*

andoah: The Washington and Lee University Review with the permission of the Editor), Summer, 1976, pp. 63-91.

To be delighted by a poem's wit or moved by its emotional force is rare enough; to be delighted and moved simultaneously is exceptional. One could rewrite Ben Jonson's line on the "adulteries of art" for James Merrill's new poems [*Divine Comedies*]: they strike our eyes *and* our hearts as well. Merrill is a leading poet of wit who raises sophisticated humor to its highest level since Pope, a poet of whom he is fond, and who is unafraid to build from lowly puns and spoonerisms a proper setting for themes which are the concerns of a serious poet: "the incarnation and withdrawal of a god"; the search for salvation in this world through love and in the next through a ladder of souls progressing upward; the attempt to amass, out of the mind's imagings and the heart's shadowy feelings, a sense of purpose in a shockingly transient world. The elegant *objets* and artifacts which used to be more in the foreground of Merrill's work have surrendered the center stage to the mature poet's humane worries. Cozy and intimate in tone, like Pope, Merrill transcends mere coterie verse. The very audacity of his title prepares us for both an amused chattiness, as if he were saying "the comedies, my dear, were simply divine," and his serious reconsideration of Dante's traversal of a universe ordered by divine love.

With this volume Merrill has realized the promise of his earlier autobiographical poems by becoming a major narrative poet. He develops in verse the suspense, human depth, and social complexity which are the stuff of fiction. More than half of *Divine Comedies* is a single narrative, *The Book of Ephraim*. . . . The machinery of the poem (complete with a consideration of biological evolution as a complement to progressive reincarnations toward divinity) is as delicious as anything Pope or Yeats could have contrived, and like their sylphs and spirits, is meant to be taken lightly and seriously at once.

The Book of Ephraim is novelistic in its feeling for society and in its characterization (it also gives glimpses of a lost unfinished novel of Merrill's whose characters mingle freely, in the poem, with the real people in his life); it is epic in its spatial and temporal dimensions. . . . The presiding spirits of the book, apart from Ephraim of course, are Proust and Dante, the first (according to Ephraim "a great Prophet throned on high") because the major question in all of Merrill's work is "Where has time flown?" and the second because the answer wherein he finds his major compensation for time's thefts is "love that makes the world go round." These clichés, from the shorter "Verse for Urania" at the beginning of the volume, cannot do justice to the depth of Merrill's effort to integrate the pieces of the past into the present. . . . With its interlacings of past and present, otherworldly visitors, fictional characters, and friends and family, *The Book of Ephraim* is more than a jigsaw puzzle. It is like life ("This World that shifts like sand, is unforeseen/Consolidations and elate routine), full of delightful surprises and solace. It is also a statement of faith, like the *Divine Comedy*. (pp. 333-34)

> *Willard Spiegelman, in Southwest Review (© 1976 by Southern Methodist University Press), Summer, 1976.*

[What] we must attend to now is Ephraim's revelation. To do so will involve some guesswork, for a number of reasons. The most important of these is that whatever else the poem is, it is not a delivery system for dogma: the revelation is put resolutely at the service of the poetry, not vice versa.

According to Ephraim, who as we shall see is not omniscient, Heaven consists of "NINE STAGES" ('C'); he is at Stage Six. The Stages are graduated, the lowest containing "the curates and the minor mages" ('C'), the highest more "PERFECTED SOULS" of "RARER & MORE EXPERT USEFULNESS" ('Q'). Although we are not told for what precisely those at the highest Stages are more useful, we do know that work is done in the next world. Ephraim's job, for example, is to judge the newly dead, with the help of "his staff," in order to see which are fit to enter Heaven (see Section 'E'); Maya's, once she gains Paradise, is to "DIRECT SOME AVANTGARDE HALLUCI/NATIONS ETC FOR HEADS OF STATE" (the enjambment allows a 'Hail Lucy,' and Maya works for St. Lucy, to be discovered in the first three syllables of 'hallucinations'), the upshot of which is to be found in Section 'R'. Of the Stages above his, Ephraim either knows little (which seems likely) or is not allowed to speak of what he knows, except on one occasion [in Section 'P']. . . . (p. 84)

There is upward movement among the Stages, but when he is asked if there is travel in both directions, "Ephraim changed the subject/As it was in his tactful power to do". . . . Ordinarily, we gather, progress upward is made one Stage at a time through the displacement of a "Patron" by its "Representative."

Each human being, we learn in Section 'C', is the "REPRESENTATIVE of a PATRON," the latter being a spirit who lives on one of the Stages. . . . While every human being has a Patron (an exception will be noted in due course), we do not know if each spirit has a Representative; that is, we do not know the proportion of the dead to the living. Ephraim does say that "Power's worst abusers" (like Hitler and "MY POOR RUINED LOVE CALIGULA") "are held . . . stricly INCOMMUNICADO" ('P'), so we may assume both that the next world is more populous than this one and that not all its members serve as Patrons. It seems, nonetheless, to be one of the standard tasks of the Heavenly hosts.

The Patron is responsible for the training of its Representative between lives, the point of the instruction being to permit the soul to escape life (or another life) and gain Stage One. The content of the Patron's lectures in "savior vivre" ('C') may be gathered, in a rough and ready way, from certain suggestions that Ephraim lets fall about the conduct of life. Among these is his comment, in Section 'S', that for a Patron there is "NO PUNISHMENT LIKE THAT OF BEING GIVEN/A GROSS OR SLUGGISH REPRESENTATIVE." The Patron's own "upward mobility" ('P') depends upon the Representative's achievement of Heaven (the maintenance of Heaven itself may depend on it), but we may well read in these two terms something equivalent to specific sins. . . . [What] the poet calls "plain old virtue" ('P') is not much rewarded in or by the Beyond. . . . Only between lives may the Patron "DO" anything for the Representative other than worry and, as Ephraim puts it in another context, "LOOK LOOK LOOK LOOK" ('K'). . . . The immediate incentive for all the Patron goes through, however, is plain enough, for when the Representative succeeds to Heaven and becomes a Patron in turn, the (we may imagine) triumphant mentor

moves up a "notch" ('C') in Heaven's Stages. . . . (pp. 85-7)

[Let us] see what more can be learned about the Heavenly scheme in the specific cases of W. H. Auden, Charles Edward Merrill (the poet's father), and Eleanora Deren ("Maya"), each of whom dies in the course of the twenty years the poem spans. In each instance, Ephraim gets in touch with the departed (by whatever means is not explained) and communication [is] . . . as always via the ouija board. (p. 88)

Although we are not explicitly told so, we may assume both that W. H. Auden is not to be returned to earth for another life and, I think, that his Stage in Heaven is higher than One. When Hans is at Stage One, it is described as "that of vision pure/And simple" (see Section 'D'), so the *pleasure* Auden takes in his "NEW" body would argue for his being at a Stage where more complex sensuous apprehension is possible; the distinction of his life and work would, as well, suggest a Stage above that of "the curates and the minor mages." That he is anxious about just that which has been left irrevocably behind will, perhaps as much as anything else, assure us that he has spent his last spell on earth, but the contrast with Charles Edward Merrill's passage through the heavens should show itself decisive.

The poet's father, "CEM," died in 1956 . . . (see Section 'K'), but what unhappiness the poet feels, even as it is called in question by an other-worldly observer, is difficult to sustain given Merrill Sr.'s mood when he "gets through" to Ephraim's mediums. He is "high-spirited," and "incredulous" presumably as much about where he finds himself as about his contacting his son. . . . [He] explains, "Some goddam fool/Hindoo is sending him to Sunday School" (his Patron, we understand, is trying to teach him the ropes that he has evidently not learned). In what is probably the same conversation, although the phrase is placed elsewhere in the poem (Section 'D'), CEM characterizes his Patron as a "DAMN POOR ADMINISTRATOR," and we may guess that the latter has very little "PEACE FROM REPRESENTATION." (pp. 88-9)

Maya, as Ephraim had informed her during her visit to the "Boys" (see Section 'G'), was in "her FIRST LAST ONLY/Life"; she had had no Patron, was herself the Patron of "The cat she felt kept dying in her stead" ('G'). Maya's case, then, is . . . exceptional, . . . and it might be noted that the Gentleman Tempter is not shy of presenting exceptions to even the sketchiest of rules, credibility being precisely what he would strain. Maya now works for St. Lucy, . . . but when she describes her assignment a curious note is struck: St. Lucy

> IS LETTING
> ME DIRECT SOME AVANTGARDE HALLUCI
>
> NATIONS ETC FOR HEADS OF STATE
> U SHD HEAR THEM MOAN & FEEL THEM
>   SWEATING
> WE GIRLS HAVE STOPPED A WAR WITH CUBA
>   Great! ('R')

Here is an indication of Intervention which, far from being disapproved, is solicited by Heaven, and it will be well to keep this episode in mind. Again, as in Auden's case, we are not told Maya's Stage, but we feel it to be high, perhaps because of her effectiveness in the work described above as well as the very real sense that she is at home in Heaven. Perhaps, too, we get this sense from the high spirits of the verse.... It may also be that Maya's knowledge is what convinces us of her high Stage, but that there are limits to what Maya knows will also be seen.

If the information that can be gleaned from these episodes raises more questions than it answers, and, further, if the questions we would ask seem hardly ever to be those the poet asks of the Beyond, explanations are not wanting. For the first, the poet explains that "huge tracts of information/ Have gone into these capsules flavorless/And rhymed for easy swallowing" ('C'), so what raw data we do get represent perhaps only a fraction of the total received.... For the second, there is the long Hymn to Nonchalance that closes Section 'I', "Nonchalance," that is, with regard to "... who or what we took Ephraim to be,/And of what truths (if any) we considered/Him spokesman" ('I'). But, as I believe, these explanations give off of the Gentleman Tempter; the poet's motives are far more solemn, far more serious. For now, it may suffice to say that James Merrill's handling of this material is not to be confounded with the way a not terribly diverse material is handled by Carlos Castaneda.

However little of Ephraim's revelation is simply presented for inspection, one thing that can be gathered from what we are shown is that some way of replenishing the supply of Representatives, as each becomes a Patron, will be required by the Heavenly scheme. And wondering from whence come those "brand-new little savage souls" (see the passage from Section 'C' quoted above) will return us to one of the poem's main preoccupations—the relations between man and animal.

Here is Ephraim, in 1970, on the reasons for a change in what might be called Evolutional Policy: because there are "TOO MANY CHATTY STUDENTS" and "TOO FEW DUMB/TEACHERS ..., THE SCHOOLS/ARE CLOSING SO TO SPEAK" ('O'). While we may remember the closing of many Universities and Colleges following the announcement of the Cambodian air strikes in the Spring of that year, the "SCHOOLS" to which Ephraim refers are those in which human beings are the inattentive students to the instructive behavior of animals.... When we understand that these "SCHOOLS" are those from which Heaven's graduates are drawn, we may also see that "CLOSING" is portentous; for, evidently, the generalized upward motion in the other world, that is from lower to higher Stages, depends in part on pressure from below, the force that is exerted by Representatives achieving Heaven and pushing their Patrons higher. The extinction of some species (and their lessons) plus the devil-may-care comportment of human beings appear to have caused a kind of crisis, a stasis perhaps in the upward movement. (pp. 90-2)

Ephraim's ministrations as design are plainest in a poem which precedes The Book of Ephraim in the Divine Comedies ..., a poem called "The Will." ... Nowhere in The Book of Ephraim are things made quite so explicit [as in this poem]: Ephraim wants what he has taught his mediums writ large ...; he wants, in short, that "baldest prose/ Reportage ... that would reach/The widest public in the shortest time" ('A') that the poet renounces at the beginning of the latter poem. Ephraim is still more explicit, apparently too explicit (for one of those indicative "pauses" follows), when he explains why he wants his "TEACHINGS" set down.... [The] poet responds. "Why, Ephraim, you belong to the old school—/You think the

Word by definition good," to which an almost angry familiar spirit returns

IF U DO NOT YR WORLD WILL BE UNDONE
& HEAVEN ITSELF TURN TO ONE
    GRINNING SKULL....

[What] is revealed here is so grave as to be taken as the proximate occasion for the writing of The Book of Ephraim; the interview may well be where and why the "prose/Reportage was called for" (my italics). The urgency of this crisis differentiates it from that associated with evolution, although the two may be related, and might thereby be understood as leading to the evocations of Time in Section 'A'.

In Section 'P', the nature of this crisis receives its name, Götterdämmerung. Ephraim's anxiety about the state of the "SCHOOLS" (in Section 'O') leads to a grisly note:

NO SOULS CAME FROM HIROSHIMA U
    KNOW
EARTH WORE A STRANGE NEW ZONE OF
    ENERGY
Caused by? SMASHED ATOMS OF THE
    DEAD MY DEARS. ('P')

No wonder then that Patrons are often "DUMB WITH APPREHENSION" ('Q'). In the context of the Section, we can see that Ephraim is trying to warn, perhaps even trying to scare, the "Boys," but although the "SMASHED ATOMS" was "News that brought into play our deepest fears" ('P'), they continue to play.... Ephraim's rebuke takes, for they suddenly understand what their familiar spirit is talking about.

Wait—he couldn't be pretending YES
That when the flood ebbed, or the fire burned low,
Heaven, the world no longer at its feet,
Itself would up and vanish? EVEN SO

Götterdämmerung.

The "flood" we may well take as referring to the "FLOOD" ('Q'), the "fire" to "DEVOTION" ('Q'), and in this way we can see the relation between the two crises mentioned above. (pp. 95-7)

[A] kind of escape clause from the holocaust seems to be included, for among the few things that we learn of Ephraim's superiors is that they are "SOULS FROM B4 THE FLOOD B4 THE LEGENDARY/& BY THE WAY NUCLEAR IN ORIGIN/FIRE OF CHINA" ('P'). The latter part of this is eagerly seized upon, by the Gentleman Tempter:

New types, you mean, like phoenixes will fly
Up from our conflagration? How sci-fi! ('P')

The hopeful proposition does not follow from what Ephraim has said, and, more important, he makes no answer to it; the exclamation anticipates, and disarms, skepticism.

That all of this is not playful appears in the final interview with Ephraim, in June, 1974.... Here, too, despite the possibilities suggested by Ephraim's remarks in Section 'Q' that he is operating more or less on his own ("SO FEW UP HERE WISH TO THINK ... I WANT TO DO MORE THAN RIDE & WEAR & WAIT"), the more awesome likelihood that his Intervention is, like that of Maya (see Section 'R'), sanctioned if not ordered by his superiors shows itself. (pp. 97-8)

None of the parties to this final call knows why the break was made, whether in anger or desperation or neither, but the very character of the corrections administered by Heaven's higher-ups testifies to a twilight of the gods. (p. 98)

A feel for the poem's movement will, as I have tried to suggest, convince the reader that there is something "drastic" about Section 'L', something in addition to its content —or anterior to it—that is in part imaged in the equally "drastic" displacement of Section 'U'. The energy or force represented in the remove at which Section 'U' is found might best be measured in mechanical terms, were the poem a machine. The strain, and mechanics would be useful here as well, endured by the intervening Sections finds its likeness in the reader's (at least this reader's) straining to make them out: not only is the line of thought difficult, individual lines and groups of lines have about them an opacity that distinguishes the writing in and of these Sections from that of those preceding and following them. May we not imagine, then, that the poet himself was straining? I think that we should like to know something the poet will not, in so many words, tell us—what the strain was.

The explanation that comes most readily to hand is that the poet was rushed. He tells us so, after all, in *The Book of Ephraim*'s first Section, but that Section was ostensibly written five months before the "SCRIBE" gave him six months in which to finish his "WEORK." (p. 99)

[However, the theory] that one of the constraints under which the poet worked was time, specifically the time dealt him by the SCRIBE, . . . ignores the fact that all work is accomplished under that universal constraint, and, more important, it figures necessity as a father instead of as a mother. The invention of the Sections cannot be accounted for in terms of a shortage of time, even if the choice of some of their raw material can be; neither, I should say, in general, nor in the case of that particular that seems to be so prominent, the displacement of Section 'U' and its replacement by Section 'L', will appealing to time much help us to understand *The Book of Ephraim*. (pp. 100-01)

I take it . . . that *The Book of Ephraim* is of the genre spiritual biography, of the particular type "Confessions," and for all that it chronicles a love story and carries the elements of revelation . . ., what the poem is about—its meaning—is the conversion of the poet. (p. 101)

The difference between JM as he is represented in the poem's early Sections and the poet as we find him on the Accademia Bridge, in Section 'V', does not lack for other images in the poem. For example, the difference may be that as between a younger and an older man. We feel about the younger man his freedom and his power; about the older, definition of his freedom and severe limitation of his power. (p. 102)

Prior to *The Book of Ephraim*, the fullest representation of an unregenerate JM is to be found in a poem called "Voices from the Other World," first printed in 1957 by the *New Yorker*. . . . The date will be important in permitting the reader to hear directly from that period which is recreated, after more than a decade and one half, in *The Book of Ephraim;* but it should also be noted that the lack of subsequent treatment of the material, prior that is to *The Book of Ephraim*, might itself be thought an image of unregeneracy. . . . [The] undertaking of [*The Book of Ephraim* constitutes a] powerful change of heart—from "nonchalance" [of the earlier poem] to "commitment."

When in Section 'I' of *The Book of Ephraim*, the poet says of "Ephraim's revelations—we had them/For comfort, thrills and chills, 'material'," we can see from "Voices from the Other World" just what he means; and the nonchalance mentioned in the lyric links up with the Hymn to Nonchalance that concludes Section 'I', although by now I suppose that the importance of its past tense as well as its situation (leading to or provoking the infernal Section 'J' and the ominous Section 'K') will be plain. But where the nonchalance is declared in "Voices from the Other World," it is argued in Section 'I' as though it is in need of justification: the difference consists in, so to put it, unregeneracy and a representation of his former self by a convert. (pp. 103-05)

With the assistance of "Voices from the Other World," then, we can now characterize the voice of that younger man as we have it in *The Book of Ephraim*—it is Brünnhilde's.

It is a voice much chastened by the time we hear it in *The Book of Ephraim*, but that it is the voice of Brünnhilde— whom her creator made "spurn/Heaven's own plea" and "ecstatically cling/To death-divining love" ('W')— we can be sure from the lyric's evidence. Even in "Voices from the Other World," however, the "commitment" the Heavens clamor for is not gainsaid: it is postponed.

That the "commitment" had been made by the poet before he began composition of *The Book of Ephraim* we can tell from the Gentleman Tempter's refined version of the unregenerate self, but just when the change of heart took place is difficult to know. (p. 106)

Whatever the poet had in mind for his poem in January, 1974, whatever it was to have been, was changed by the break with Ephraim in June. How great the change was, though, I suppose we shall not be able to tell. The poet's "surprise" ('U') when he learns that what of the poem had been written by June (he specifically mentions Section 'K') was well received by his other worldly readership suggests that he was worried. . . . But that "surprise" was as nothing compared to the shock of what followed. For if, as might be conjectured, the poet had intended to write an however transmuted account of his conversion in *The Book of Ephraim* (conversion, that is, to belief in the reality of Ephraim and his revelation . . .), he suddenly found himself cut off from just that to which the poem would attest. Section 'L', then, and particularly its final part, will have to bear the weight of *two* "drastic" changes: one from skepticism to belief, the other from initiation to literal excommunication. In such a dreadful context, the strain of the Sections that follow 'L' will be the poet's trying to understand why. His answer, at least in part, is to be found in the equally dreadful aspect of Ephraim's revelation that Sections 'O' and 'P' contain—Heaven's desperation. *If* the poet's "commitment" in *The Book of Ephraim* had been to some image of his conversion, the poem now holds as well an image of his state. JM is indeed a new man in Section 'V'—a man twice changed, a man exalted and humbled. (p. 107)

In Section 'X', the poetic line varies to an eleven-syllable, non-metrical measure. The feminine endings, which is how we first feel the line, we associate with the Section's introduction of the poet's mother ("she's here/Throughout, the breath drawn after every line"); then a climactic variation on the absence/presence paradox is rung, one that makes us feel that communication with the Spheres has, far from having ended, simply changed media—from the ouija board to poetry. . . . For how but in terms of inspiration are we to account for that image of the presence of the Other—even as it is absent . . .? Inspired, too, we may well believe the choice of poetry as the medium of revelation: for not only do "The twinklings of/Insight hurt or elude the naked eye" (the pun enforces the lesson), but "as to Composition, few had found/A cleaner use for power" ('W'). That last . . . answers the question the poet asks after Ephraim reveals the wages of an however metaphorical "DRUNKEN-NESS."

> How to rid Earth, for Heaven's sake, of power
> Without both turning to a funeral pyre? ('P')

Composition—even of his "Confessions"—is the best James Merrill can do, and the composition of *The Book of Ephraim* offers us, after all, an image of just that "DEVO-TION" upon which, according to Ephraim, Heaven and Earth depend. (pp. 108-09)

> *Henry Sloss, "James Merrill's 'The Book of Ephraim'," (Part 2), in* Shenandoah *(copyright by* Shenandoah; *reprinted from* Shenandoah: The Washington and Lee University Review *with the permission of the Editor), Fall, 1976, pp. 83-110.*

James Merrill . . . had convinced many discerning readers of a greatness, or something like it, in his first six volumes of verse, but until this year I remained a stubborn holdout. The publication of *Divine Comedies* . . . converts me, absolutely if belatedly, to Merrill. Technically, Merrill began as a master, but even *Braving the Elements* (1972) seemed to stay within a too-conscious control, as though Merrill were too fine an artist to accept ultimate risks. *Divine Comedies* is an astonishing return-of-the-repressed, an American book that dares everything in order to achieve what Emerson called the essential American trope of power: *surprise*. The book's eight shorter poems surpass nearly all the earlier Merrill, but its apocalypse (a lesser word won't do) is a 100-page verse-tale, *The Book of Ephraim*, an occult splendor in which Merrill rivals Yeats' *A Vision*, Stevens' ghostly *The Owl in the Sarcophagus*, and even some aspects of Proust. I don't know that *The Book of Ephraim*, at least after some dozen readings, can be overpraised, as nothing since the greatest writers of our century equals it in daemonic force. Merrill has written an uncanny romance of dallying with the spirit-world that moves with the dangerous persuasiveness of an excessive fiction, yet nevertheless interprets itself as though it had, for its author, proper as well as figurative meaning. Directly autobiographical, the poem creates an obsessive cosmos of mediums, singular reincarnations, and preternatural voices which uncomfortably have a social plausibility that is quite overwhelming. The penultimate section ends with a quietly sinister epiphany: "Young chameleon, I used to/Ask how on earth one got sufficiently/Imbued with otherness. And now I see." Otherness, or the overcoming of solipsism, henceforth for Merrill will be an occult journey, and the poetic results, should they equal or go beyond *The Book of Ephraim*, will make him the strangest, the most unnerving of all his country's great poets. (pp. 21-2)

> *Harold Bloom, in* The New Republic *(reprinted by permission of* The New Republic; © *1976 by* The New Republic, Inc.), *November 20, 1976.*

["The Book of Ephraim"] can . . . be read as an account of the nature of poetic activity. [Like John Hollander in *Reflections on Espionage*], Merrill is the poet communicating with his source of inspiration, but unlike Hollander's vague and phantasmal poem, "Ephraim" develops a genuine personal history. . . . [It] is half game, like the play on the Ouija Board; at the same time it is intensely subjective. . . . The whole adventure with Ephraim is a process of self discovery. It makes a good story and contains the substance of a novel. (pp. 90-1)

Briefly, "The Book of Ephraim" is a *tour de force*. It is splendidly written. It is filled with moving, witty, funny, evocative lines. It has the richness of an exotic novel bound to the intensity of poetry. But it is not about what it seems to be about. Rather it is . . . a study of the individual artist's contest with his own talent and with his art. (p. 91)

> *John R. Reed, in* The Ontario Review *(copyright* © *1976 by* The Ontario Review), *Fall-Winter, 1976-77.*

*　　　*　　　*

MERWIN, W. S.　　1927-

Merwin is an American poet, playwright, short story writer, and translator. He has written poetry eliciting much praise from critics, but relatively little attention from the reading public. He is a cerebral, often difficult poet, writing as one critic, Gunderson, has said, "at the margin of intelligibility." Nevertheless, Merwin is one of America's greatest living poets. He is the recipient of the Pulitzer Prize and the National Book Award. (See also *CLC*, Vols. 1, 2, 3, 5, and *Contemporary Authors*, Vols. 13-16, rev. ed.)

In [*W. S. Merwin: The First Four Books of Poems*], . . . there are no lapses of taste, no humor qualifying the often tedious certainty of the poems. The risks these poems take are technical, not personal. They leave you impressed with Merwin's skills but frustrated by his remoteness. The best, or perhaps the most thrilling, poems are those that reveal not only the talents of the poet, but the poet as well. It is that intimacy of the poet with his work that makes Merwin's later writing so interesting and it is missing in much of this early poetry. In the poems published since 1960, when the last book in this collection appeared, artifice serves to reveal the poet's voice, rather than disguise it.

But it would be wrongheaded to deny the significance of this collection. The four books represent almost a decade in the output of one of America's greatest living poets. All but the last volume, *The Drunk in the Furnace*, have been out of print for some time and until now there has been no convenient way of measuring the notable changes that took place in Merwin's writing after 1960 when he abandoned the poetic conventions and traditions that mark the first phase of his career for the openness of his more recent poetry.

His first book, *A Mask for Janus*, includes one of Merwin's greatest poems, "Dictum: For A Masque of Deluge." The poem is written in a language of "shocked speech" that avoids the mannered literary diction of much of these poems and sounds at times like a poem by Frank O'Hara. It is also an announcement of the purpose of Merwin's work: "to seek / An affirmation . . . and to find only / Cities of cloud already crumbling." This tension between what he calls in another poem the "immortal season" of stillness and the crumbling mortal world is crucial to Merwin's early work. But this poem stands as an exception among many others in these first four books that describe a sensibility that the later poems simply demonstrate. The second book, *The Dancing Bears,* published in 1954, provides more examples of Merwin's repertoire of demanding literary forms, the most prominent being "East of the Sun and West of the Moon," written in 39 stanzas of 13 lines each. But more successful is a short poem entitled "You, Genoese Mariner" in which the poet speaks of "A grammar of return" through which, as in the example provided by Columbus, mistaken notions can lead to imaginative discovery.

The solitary, disembodied "I" that has become Merwin's true voice in his later work rarely speaks in these early poems. In *Green with Beasts* (1956) and *The Drunk in the Furnace* (1960) he seems to be testing out different voices in an attempt to discover his own. In both of these books he uses the dramatic monologue frequently but not very successfully.... The attitude the language takes towards itself is so authoritarian that the credibility of the poems is threatened. The two best poems in *Green with Beasts* work because they avoid authoritarian postures....

In Wordsworth's terms, [in *The Drunk in the Furnace*] he is beginning to write in the "language really used by men."

But it was not until the work that followed these books that Merwin's new style and power took shape.... He describes himself in *The Lice* (1967) as "I who have always believed too much in words," but what he repudiates in his mature work is not words but the formal poetic expertise of his first books. His new poems are shorter, more fragmented. The structures have loosened and opened. The language is intense and intimate, not ornate. Merwin's mastery of words is still a crucial factor in the success of his work, but his greatness is in allowing his skill to serve him rather than itself.

Merwin's translations have played a conspicuous role in the changes that have taken place in his work. His extensive involvement with the languages of many cultures and ages introduced a new spirit of artlessness, of fidelity to what he has called "the spoken idiom" rather than "the written convention." The title of his last book, *Writings to an Unfinished Accompaniment* (1973), is itself a clue to the tentative, modest claims his new work makes. He speaks of the need to "empty out," to simplify. This emptying out has completely transformed his work: the wisdom now comes out of Merwin, rather than down from him.

> Terence Winch, "*A Master Poet's Early Art —and Artifice,*" in Book World—The Washington Post (© The Washington Post*), August 31, 1975, p. 3.*

W. S. Merwin has gotten along well for several volumes now without punctuation, putting the burden of sense on the verse and the stanza structure—and the burden of understanding on the reader. This quirk he carries along in *The Compass Flower.* The verse is still elegant, the vocabulary plain, and the punctuation absent. This new book is somewhat more concrete; here and there a face emerges, a scene can be identified, the poet detected as a living man. A father appears, a lover, an especial fig tree, once (in "The Windows") a fully-fleshed child, observing the world upside down from between his knees. Merwin has traveled and translated in many countries, Eastern as well as Western, and his allusions are not easy to trace. The most ambitious poem here, "Kore," is clearly a reworking of the Demeter-Persephone story (though nothing like Tennyson's version!) with hints of Psyche and Eros added, and

each of the twenty-four stanzas given a letter of the Greek alphabet as side-note. Perhaps it is overweighted; it never quite floats. But the book in general is vintage Merwin and no doubt many of its pieces will reappear when he collects his poems. As he concludes: "before and after / in house after house that was mine to see / the same fire the perpetual bird." (p. 84)

> Kirkus Reviews (copyright © 1977 The Kirkus Service, Inc.), January 15, 1977.

W. S. Merwin is a poet drawn to see the still essence in this changing, moving world, "the same fire the perpetual bird." This new collection of his poems [*The Compass Flower*], is, in many ways, more open and clearer than many of his books, speaking of hospitals and ferry ports, the particulars of nature, whether the "Saxophone and subway" of the city or the quiet intensity of mountain, apple and snowflake in the countryside. But he remains no describer or annotator, rather a seeker and sayer touching the still life at the center of the chaos of change where "we are bottles smashing in paper bags."

He does speak of change, sees it and recognizes it: "the whole country has changed / means of travel accelerated / signs almost totally replaced traffic rerouted every / love altered...." But out of this change he writes a poetry that does not depend upon the verb, but rather upon the moving accumulation of nouns. He used verbs, of course, but always quietly, almost silently, and more often he transforms even the verbs he uses into nouns, transforming time into an artistic semblance of timelessness, of eternity. The spring, the rebirth in the very fact of death, which he celebrates in this book, is an unchanging, continually present spring, effective in its incarnation into time but pure and free of time's corroding power; he finds it in love (as in the beautiful and strong love poem, "Kore," which is the still point upon which the compass needle of this book quivers) and in the astonishing beauty that hovers in the world like a sturdy and powerful dream or unfailing glimpse into the real.

The Compass Flower is an important book by a fine poet, his best, to my mind, since the appearance of *The Lice* ten years ago. (p. 15)

> R.H.W. Dillard, in The Hollins Critic (copyright 1977 by Hollins College), February, 1977.

Poetic prose? Prose poems? Whichever or neither, the prize-winning poet again [in *Houses and Travelers*] shares 70 or 80 of his hypnotically cadenced secrets: doubts, visions, dreams, puzzles, riddles, recollections—in one-to-ten-page fables, incantations, balancing acts, and a handful of pieces that actually resemble conventional stories. Often starting with a wake-up-and-pay-attention line ("The bottom of the lake is standing on its side" ... "Every railroad station exists in a dream"), Merwin commands the simplest language in the simplest structures to take on the toughest questions: are we really here? do we really see what we think we see? why do we want what we want? In time-honored fabulistic tradition, animals, objects, and abstractions think and feel. The garden and the desert appraise each other, the carpenter and the woodpecker share memories of wood, the worm and the scorpion converse, as do two "goodbye-shirts" that meet at the laundry. The one ant in an hourglass "thought he was a grain of sand. He did not know he was alone." "Everything has its story" and "Some things try to steal the stories of others." A man thinks he has stolen all of the world's laughter, but there's someone else who keeps giving it away. Most of these metaphorical maneuvers require and deserve a stop-and-think, then-think-again reader—only a few register as ponderous blather or hollow wordplay—but their difficulty makes the more accessible, real-people tales especially entrancing. "Remorse," "The Element," "Brothers," "The Invalid," and fragments of seeming autobiography—these connect in the most openly dramatic and emotional ways, while planting as many reverberating images as the more obviously metaphysical pieces. Welcome *Houses and Travellers,* then, for its own seductive sake, and also for its promise of future Merwin stories that will do all that these do—and more. (pp. 594-95)

> *Kirkus Reviews (copyright © 1977 The Kirkus Service, Inc.), June 1, 1977.*

[No] matter how subtle the directions or how keen our own imaginations, ["The Horse," from Merwin's "The Compass Flower"] remains finally less a cognition than a portent. It is vague.

It moves in the direction of expressive silence. I would not link Merwin with the minimalist-conceptualist agitations that seem so conspicuous now in the visual arts, because I think our poets are influenced less by formal considerations than by the substance of other literatures—surrealism, Spanish-American and Oriental writing, etc. But the effect is the same, this movement toward expressive but still vague silence, the written poem that is a guide to an unwritten one.

Does this come from distrust of the medium, distrust of objective reality, distrust of consciousness? Merwin might say it isn't a question of trust at all. But for my part I cannot see why at this moment in time, this of them all, we should be abandoning one of the few good and beautiful things that prior civilizations have striven to create—language. Our condition now needs more explicitness, not less. Must we leave everything to television? Merwin is a terrific poet. In every phase of his writing, and there have been many, he has made poems that affect me deeply, including some in his new book. But I wish he would tell me if he really and truly thinks this is the way American poetry should go, and if so, why. (pp. 15, 37)

> *Hayden Carruth, in* The New York Times Book Review *(© 1977 by The New York Times Company; reprinted by permission), June 19, 1977.*

W. S. Merwin, one of America's most distinguished poets and translators, seems . . . to be evolving his own mythology. This new book of prose, *Houses and Travellers,* along with its 1971 predecessor *The Miner's Pale Children,* consists of a series of imaginative inventions which can be read as the "system" underscoring Merwin's poems. In one of the pieces in this collection, a priest tells stories which "begin to take on the momentous intangibility of legends; episodes echoed from an unknown sacred text; parables." Merwin's stories are like those of the priest.

"Echoes" is a good word to describe the feel of Merwin's stories. In *The Poetics of Space,* Gaston Bachelard writes of the poetic image: "It is not an echo of the past. On the contrary: through the brilliance of an image, the distant past resounds with echoes, and it is hard to know at what depth these echoes will reverberate and die away." In Merwin's work, "the distant past" is not the past of history, but the past of the soul. What is "half-remembered, half-invented" in these fictions is not book learning, but what Bachelard calls the "Forces . . . in poems that do not pass through the circuits of knowledge."

There is no one tone to the work in this book. Some of the stories are poetic, some Gothic, or whimsical, or fantastic. Some are even straightforward and conventional. One of the longer stories, called "Poverty," is a striking, frightening tale that could have been written by Kafka. But certain characteristics do emerge out of the accumulation of stories. The landscape of most of this work is some "other" world that exists side by side with the "real" world and resembles it in many ways. It is not so much that this other world is strange because the intelligence perceiving it sees it as strange; it is, rather, we who are strangers here, in this world of spiritual dimensions and new realities.

Resonating through these tales is a sense that the narrator is after a special kind of unnamable wisdom, an ability "to recognize the sound of the element in which you were living, passing through you" ("The Element") or to become one of the "hearers of the note at which everything explodes into light" ("The Chart"). . . .

[A] principle of light seems to illuminate Merwin's stories—a principle which is neither disconnected from human particulars nor darkened by the blindness of the ego.

The stories in this book are not always convincing. Merwin's attraction to personifications—there are, for example, pigeons, hinges, and locks that talk—can be difficult to accept. And his characteristic disembodied narrator, so comfortable in a world of "resemblances, association, traces, clues, the components of recognitions" ("Path"), can become monotonous. When the rhythm is broken by a piece like "Vanity," a tale that is closer to the conventional short story than anything else in the book, it seems a welcome change. . . .

The last quarter of this book is, for the most part, a series of biographical remembrances of the past, of childhood—as though to suggest that knowledge of the fantastic, of the opening up of consciousness, is rooted in the ordinary. If you can remember your personal history, you are on the path to remembering the secret, marvelous past of the human soul.

> *Terence Winch, "Merwin the Magician," in* Book World—The Washington Post *(© The Washington Post), September, 1977, p. E3.*

* * *

MICHAUX, Henri   1899-

Michaux is a Belgian poet, prose writer, and artist who writes in French. A unique and independent artist of international stature, Michaux is continually exploring the conflict between inner and outer worlds in his writings. Fantasy, surrealism, and comic grotesquery all come together in the works of this enigmatic author. Of late, Michaux has concentrated on his painting and his drawing. The Chaplinesque Monsieur Plume is one of Michaux's more interesting creations.

The clown has become one of the chief heroes of modern art. . . . Most of the paintings of clowns and harlequins have revealed the tragedy behind the comic mask, but Michaux, while exploiting this association, has given the subject a different interpretation.

Michaux's clown is not the tragic man behind the mask. The grotesque mask of the clown is the real man, the whole man shorn of all pretensions and rationalizations, the man as he really is, "ras . . . et visible." There is nothing behind the mask.

Indeed, this is the main source of originality in ["Clown"]. Michaux takes a step farther than the painters in the direction of metaphysical anguish: his clown does not even possess tragic dignity. The absurd figure he cuts is the true picture.

Even more important than the poet's realization of his utter insignificance is his inability to assume his true role as clown before the world. . . . He still clings to his main source of gratification: the fact that a number of people consider him an important man. . . . The real confession in this poem, then, is that of the poet's inability to admit he is a clown. The indefiniteness of "someday" and the future tense gives him away. (p. 153)

"Clown" is the poet's commentary on himself to himself. But the uncomfortable feeling that the poem creates in the reader suggests that the self-directed irony has been subtly generalized. The phrase "mes semblables, si dignes, si dignes mes semblables," for example, leaves no doubt as to Michaux's opinion of the rest of humanity.

"Ma misérable pudeur" is highly suggestive. It reinforces the lack of courage implied in [the line: "Avec la sorte de courage qu'il faut pour être rien et rien que rien"] and foreshadows the appearance of the Clown. "Pudeur" recalls Plume's timidity and Charlie Chaplin's embarrassment. This is not an implicit allusion to either necessarily, but there is nevertheless a connection. One cannot help thinking of the awkward sad smile that Plume undoubtedly assumes while he lets people step on him and of the smile that Chaplin holds too long.

This poem can be easily read at another level. The death-wish is implicit in nearly every line. The insistent repetition of "être rien et rien que rien" and the violent "Vidé de l'abcès d'être quelqu'un" are denials of existence. It is only as non-being that the poet will partake of the "espace nourricier" and the "incroyable rosée" of the grave. In fact, death is the only logical link between these disparate images. It is only by death that he will shake off all ties with his fellow men. The "totale dissipation-dérision-purgation" is not only death but decomposition—a suggestion that reinforces the imagery. The real clown is the dead man whose absurdity is proven by his death. . . .

The courage required by the poet on this level, then, is the courage needed to kill himself.

The overture of a prose poem always presents a problem for the poet. The reader must be warned that he is dealing with poetry and not with strict prose. Michaux solves this problem by opening with two startling stylistic devices. "Un jour" is a verbless sentence with a single term. (p. 154)

These truncated sentences translate an intensely personal reaction, a spontaneous explosion of affectivity, and are addressed to no one in particular other than the poet himself. This device flows effortlessly into the stream of consciousness. At the same time the poet has given his reader a prior conditioning so that the rest of text will be read as poetry, i.e., language invested with a high degree of organization and style. The reader's reaction is a conditioned response.

Strangely enough, the second line attenuates the first despite the repetition. If the double "Un jour" is fairly aggressive, the phrase "bientôt peut-être" suggests procrastination and indecision, as if the poet were actually trying to convince himself. Throughout the rest of the poem there is an interplay of aggression and reluctance. This tonal fluctuation is consonant with all three themes, the poet as clown, the inability to admit it, the death wish. (p. 155)

The frequency of the compound words is the most obvious of the ironical devices employed by Michaux. . . . In *Clown* abstract nouns are linked in such a way that human pretension to knowledge seems to be parodied: "idée-ambition," "infini-esprit," converging with the normal, "sous-jacent," and the triple-decker, "dissipation-dérision-purgation," have a generalizing as well as a comic effect. (pp. 155-56)

Michaux's clowing with language is appropriate for several obvious reasons.

Like *Le Bateau ivre,* the first section of *Clown* is organized around a boat metaphor and likewise ends with the longing for a new energy in the form of "drinking anew of nourishing space," which would be a release from the stifling atmosphere surrounding the poet hemmed in by his own defense mechanisms. The shocking metaphor, "l'abcès d'être quelqu'un," is a generalization that takes us beyond the poet's predicament. The central image is not introduced, however, until the last section, and the typography indicates that the clown represents not only the poet but all humanity stripped of its ridiculous hypocrisies and ambitions. The clown becomes the emblem of the entire human condition. The "espace nourricier" of the opening section is given an implied analogy: "nouvelle et incroyable rosée" —which suggests a feeling of release from the "abcess of trying to be somebody" that can come only from being a nobody.

The thematic unity of the poem is seconded by its structural unity. The use of the future tense throughout (even the past participles are really future perfects) underscores the lack of decisive energy and courage to put on the clown's suit or the shroud. Each paragraph gives a feeling of unattained vacancy: "être rien et rien que rien"; "Vidé de l'abcès d'être quelqu'un"; "dissipation . . . purgation"; "par vide"; "j'expulserai de moi"; "Réduit . . . Anéanti"; "sans nom . . . sans identité . . . Sans bourse"; "à force d'être nul et ras." The Clown represents the perfect vacuum and anonymity—an unmarked grave. He also represents throughout the poem an unassimilated element in a hostile environment by retaining his traditional comic awkwardness: "ma misérable pudeur . . . mes misérables combinaisons"; "A coups de ridicules"; "dérision"; "une humilité de catastrophe"; "une intense trouille"; "la risée . . . l'esclaffement . . . le grotesque."

The length of each verset is determined by psychological considerations, for the poem is an interior monologue, constructed nonetheless along lines of rational logic. (Sometimes thoughts are *not* disconnected.) The first two and the last two lines are the shortest; the intensity of emotion builds up to its climax in the middle stanzas and returns, at the end, to the same level as in the beginning.

Michaux's selection of the clown to embody and translate his pessimism is an attempt at mythopoesis, in particular the universality of myth. . . . The indefiniteness of the poem is likewise an attempt to attain the richness of myth; the poetic ambiguity smuggles in added dimensions. The poem on first reading seems only a self-confession; upon further investigation, it yields a commentary on the human condition, and, finally, an answer to what Camus considered today's most important metaphysical question—Prufrock's "overwhelming question"; suicide. (pp. 156-57)

> *Lloyd Bishop, "Michaux's 'Clown'," in* The French Review, *October, 1962, pp. 152-57.*

Travel journals are very personal things and, by the same token, not everyone likes to read the same sort of thing while travelling. *Ecuador* isn't the book for the traveller who wants the disasters of his peregrinations romanticized. Michaux may let his imagination play if it helps him get in contact with his experiences, but he won't let it embellish the realities of malaria, mosquitoes, and leprosy with illusory heroics. But for the reader—real traveller or armchair—who wants self-discovery as well as geographical discovery, *Ecuador* is a good journey, with an itinerary worth repeating. (p. 182)

> *Judith S. Ruskamp, in* Chicago Review *(reprinted by permission of* Chicago Review; *copyright © 1973 by* Chicago Review*), Vol. 25, No. 3, 1973.*

[Michaux's] drawings, gouaches and watercolors at first seemed to be contributions to the poems in words. But today they appear more independent, a separate means of expression. Like the poems, they are images fearful of taking on a deliberate form, of renouncing the suggestiveness of their lines. The poem and the gouache are the site of a change or a creation taking place, but they do not necessarily reveal the accomplished metamorphosis, the finished art. . . .

Today he appears as one of the truly authentic poetic talents who is taking his place beside those writers who investigate the strange and the unusual and who, therefore, transpose or even upset the literary perspective. The relationship that Michaux establishes between the natural and the unbelievable has created a surreal world that has become the familiar world of his poetry.

> *Wallace Fowlie, "Henri Michaux," in his* French Literature: Its History and Its Meaning *(© 1973 by Prentice-Hall, Inc.; reprinted by permission of Prentice-Hall, Inc., Englewood Cliffs, New Jersey), Prentice-Hall, 1973, p. 287.*

Henri Michaux has written against the poetic tradition, declaring that he does not care if he is a poet or not. He has used a great variety of styles, and if he has often been elliptical and incantatory, he can also be the opposite: he can write a dry, ironic, agile prose, almost like Voltaire's. All this, however, sprang from a single source, which by its nature was infinitely nearer poetry than were Ponge's objects; for Michaux, it was an inner, if also coenesthetic, experience, full of impulses and phantasms intimately linked with the body. But this "inner space," the space of poetic subjectivity, was depoeticized by Michaux's mode of expression. Thus, Michaux's approach was directly opposite to Ponge's; for as Ponge wrote, he turned what had previously been unpoetic into poetry.

Michaux's work has been unusual, and impossible to classify (it is closest to Artaud's, if one could imagine an Artaud who was in complete control of himself). He began his career long before World War II. *Mes propriétés* (My properties) was published in 1929, and *La nuit remue* (The Night in Motion) in 1935. But only since the war has the

true, and considerable, worth of Michaux's poetry been recognized. His early works included diaries of actual travels (*Un barbare en Asie* [1933, A Barbarian in Asia]); logbooks of imaginary voyages in strange lands, such as *Voyage en Grande Garabagne* (1936, Voyage to Great Garabagne), in which the flora and fauna and especially the customs are described in minute detail; and *Un certain Plume* (1930, A Certain Plume), the chronicle of the life and acts of a character called Plume (Pen), who is constantly the victim of an aggressive environment. But these fables, these fictions, these utopias were used mainly to reveal and unfold the same inner world with which *My Properties* was concerned. It is a world of uneasiness and anguish, in which strong external pressures assail the protagonist, who feels out of place but who reacts, struggles, intervenes, destroying what annoys him, trying by force of imagination, by sheer writing, to make up for what he lacks. These works were feverish but simultaneously detached and full of humor. (pp. 154-55)

But Plume broadened his experience. During the war, Michaux wrote poems in a new spirit and a new tone: anathemas, imprecations torn from him by the horror of events. In some of these he achieved a simplicity and a solemn grandeur that reminds one of the Bible (*Épreuves, Exorcismes* [1940-45, Ordeals and Exorcisms]). Michaux's obsession with death and universal emptiness joined forces with the drama of history. And thus, Michaux's work, so deliberately odd at times that it seemed delirious and even pathological, revealed a universality nonetheless.

Michaux's Plume is ultimately only a more comic version of Sartre's Roquentin and Camus's Meursault: the hero of every poem is continually wounded and disappointed, always lacks something decisive to which he cannot even give a name; he is a "pierced" man who feels only emptiness and absence inside him. Nature's infinite multiplicity weighs him down because he yearns for order and unity; but it reassures him, too, because it constitutes the mask before an emptiness that is still more terrifying. He is "between center and absence," haunted at once by obsessive absence and by excessive presence.

Michaux's work, then, is revelation and testimony. But it is something else, too—witchcraft. His purpose is "to hold at arm's length the hostile forces of the world around us." He writes for reasons of "hygiene" (as he says) and "to find a way out." Abandoning the passive Plume, Michaux has increasingly turned to this force of intervention as the motif and directing force of his works. Some of his titles bear this our: *Liberté d'action* (1945, Freedom of Action), *Poésie pour pouvoir* (1949, Poetry to Enable), *Mouvements* (1951, Movements), *Passages* (1950, 1963, Passages). The man on the run demonstrates such prodigious agility and mobility that it is impossible to grab hold of him. For Michaux, this gesture, projecting ever further, beyond the reach of all snares, defines existence and life. It is also the definition of the poem.

But in the last few years, an important development has occurred in Michaux. He has begun to identify the liberating gesture with his painting rather than with his poetry. For him, "action painting" reproduces this mobility most closely; it is mobility in action, whereas literature can never do more than describe it at a distance, after the event.

A number of collections published after 1956 have reflected Michaux's recent experiences: *Misérable miracle* (1956, Miserable Miracle), *L'infini turbulent* (1957, The Stormy

Infinite), *Connaissance par les gouffres* (1961, Knowledge from the Abyss). Artificially but decisively enlarging the domain of imagination by the use of hallucinogenic drugs, Michaux began to see things he had never seen before. He used his drawings to capture his visions instantly, and the written text tended to be an analysis and commentary on events which had preceded it and which it could never entirely reproduce. In *Les grandes épreuves de l'esprit* (1966, The Great Ordeals of the Mind) he rendered still more clearly the process from re-creation to exposition, relating the unforeseen consequences of the disorientation brought about by mescaline: the derangement experienced enabled Michaux to rediscover the marvelous in ordinary experience. Ravaged consciousness can reveal what consciousness really is.

Michaux is now in a position to reply to the question, "What does getting back to normal mean?" But he has not asked us to think of normal and abnormal consciousness as opposites: it is an experience of the unity of the mind that is revealed—both in the order that normal awareness introduces into actual diversity and into emptiness—in the depersonalization of abnormal consciousness. The supreme intercession of the spirit has the power of creating a vacuum. All obstacles are flattened; all closed doors opened.

But Michaux's absolute is always shown as an activity: it is less a vacuum than an ability to produce a vacuum, a disturbed, potential vacuum, a "peace in the midst of disruption." In his latest book, *Façons d'endormi, façons d'éveillé* (1970, Ways of a Sleeping Man, Ways of a Waking Man), he contrasted the passivity and meagerness of the night's dreams to the rich inventiveness of the "waking reverie." Thus, Michaux still seeks salvation, his always-wished-for consummation, in the same direction. But although this latest book still contained the nervous, unexpected, familiar yet dramatic diction that is inseparably Michaux's, it also showed a further development toward analysis and explanation. One can regret that Michaux has reserved the action of poetry mainly to his visual art, important though it may be. (pp. 155-58)

> *Gaëtan Picon, in his* Contemporary French Literature: 1945 and After *(copyright © 1974 by Frederick Ungar Publishing Co., Inc.), Ungar, 1974.*

*   *   *

MONTHERLANT, Henri de   1896-1972

French novelist, playwright, poet, and essayist, Montherlant, an aristocrat in attitude, extolled Spartan virtue, virility, and stoicism in his writings. Viewed by many as a "right wing" novelist and falsely accused of collaborating with the Germans, Montherlant has suffered a diminished literary reputation as a result. Interesting parallels exist between Montherlant and Hemingway. Both writers have been called egotists and both appear to exalt violence. Furthermore, both wrote about bullfighting, Montherlant more authentically, since he actually had experience in the ring. Finally, both men shot themselves—Hemingway because he was physically ill and because he feared going insane; Montherlant because he was threatened by blindness. (See also *Contemporary Authors,* Vols. 37-40.)

In the 1920s and 1930s Montherlant's literary reputation rested mainly on some distinctive novels—*Les Bestiaires, Le Songe, Les Célibataires, Les Jeunes filles*—and several collections of essays which confirmed his markedly individ-

ual qualities of mind and sensibility. From 1942 onwards, with the success of *La Reine morte,* he established and then confirmed a new reputation as a major dramatist. . . . During the 1960s, however, Montherlant has . . . returned to the novel. In 1963 he published the widely praised *Le Chaos et la nuit* and in 1968 the complete version of *La Rose de sable.* He has now written an outstanding new novel, *Les Garçons*—outstanding in its imaginative sweep, its intellectual power, and its quality of sheer writing. Some readers will be irritated by Montherlant's use of footnotes—particularly since some of them are unnecessarily patronizing, as when explains a reference to *Oedipus Rex* and adds: 'Nous croyons devoir l'éclairer, personne aujourd'hui en France ne sachant qu'il y a un inceste dans *Oedipe roi*'—but these are minor blemishes in the lively dialogue with his readers which he maintains in connexion with all his writings. . . .

Purity, selflessness, idealism all play important roles [in *Les Garçons*], and Montherlant's treatment of the whole phenomenon has an authenticity and a delicacy (accurate rather than squeamish) which contrast strongly with a novel such as Peyrefitte's *Les Amitiés particulières.* . . .

Les Garçons fulfils two further ambitions on Montherlant's part. On and off for the past forty years he had meditated on the possibility of portraying a priest (such as he himself had met) who carries out all his duties, punctiliously, yet is in fact an atheist. In his novel, Abbé de Pradts is the *prêtre-athée,* and he gives Montherlant the opportunity of creating a character of formidable intellectual power and intense psychological complexity. However, quite the most challenging task which Montherlant sets himself is to show the priest's final conversion to the faith at a period (the beginning of the Second World War) much later than that during which the other main events of the novel take place. Montherlant does this with remarkable skill, triumphantly avoids the clichés of a deathbed conversion, and steers clear of all maudlin attitudes. His final comment as the priest dies is typical: 'Dieu rappelait à lui l'abbé de Pradts juste à temps pour qu'il ne fût pas collaborateur.'

The third ambition fulfilled by *Les Garçons* is its analysis of two different kinds of reformist movement and of the way in which each fails. . . .

One of the lessons which emerges is that genuine selflessness and highmindedness are dismissed as incredible—and therefore become suspect as covers for selfishness and impurity—by the group which, both individually and collectively, fails to believe that certain individuals can genuinely live at such a high ethical altitude. The elitist assumptions implied by Montherlant's analysis of these two failed attempts at reform will no doubt prove anathema to champions of a blind, unquestioning egalitarianism. Within the terms of this particular novel, however, they have both historical and psychological justification.

In the course of giving fictional form to his three ambitions Montherlant creates a gallery of wonderfully observed characters. Particularly welcome is the fact that these characters are allowed to behave with spontaneity (to the point of self-contradiction and 'uncharacteristic' behaviour) admirably free from the imposition of prior psychological or sociological conditioning of a systematic, doctrinaire kind. . . .

Montherlant writes out of an astonishing abundance of imaginative and intellectual resource; indeed, as he approaches his mid-seventies his creative powers seem to increase. One has throughout this novel the sense of a thoroughly equipped mind working in conjunction with a rich and abundant humanity. . . .

[The] combination of intellectual power and an ability to convey the rich and subtle texture of lived experience makes *Les Garçons* an outstanding novel. To read it is to have one's subsequent attitude to people and events imperceptibly changed for the better.

> *"The Stoic of the Upper Sixth," in* The Times Literary Supplement (© *Times Newspapers Ltd., 1969; reproduced from* The Times Literary Supplement *by permission), October 23, 1969, p. 1226.*

To emphasize the presence of pattern and purpose in Montherlant's life and writings (as he himself did) is to hold a sometimes difficult balance between impressions of external "fate" and of conscious contrivance on his own part. He committed suicide on September 21 1972 and we know that *L'Équinoxe de septembre*—the title of a collection of essays published in 1938—had a special place in his private mythology. The act of suicide, too, was in itself a "Roman" gesture about which he had frequently written with admiration and approval (most recently and at most length in *Le treizième César* of 1970).

On the other hand, it was obviously not his choice, yet also a significant fact, that he was born on April 21 (in 1896), the traditional date of the founding of Rome—as he himself tells us. This date gives additional shape to his life—a "Roman" birth and a "Roman" death. Again, there is an appropriateness which comes close to conscious planning in the titles of the first and last works which he published during his lifetime: *La Relève du matin* (1920) and *La Marée du soir* (1972). But it was patterning beyond his personal control which ordained that he should be wounded, during the Second World War, at a place less than forty miles from where he had also been wounded, and invalided out of the army, during the First World War. These are only a few of many possible examples. They suggest that his life had a significance distinctively and curiously compounded of both spontaneity and volition.

Montherlant was, above all, a man of contrasts and even paradoxes. Not the least important aspect of his life and thought has to do with the contrast between the presence and cultivation of those private patterns just touched on, and his strong sense of lack of meaning or purpose in the general human predicament. . . .

He used his life and writings as a means of keeping the void at bay. In the end, his defence was to prove fragile and vulnerable. (p. 571)

The "équivalence affreuse" to which Montherlant refers is probably the ultimate basis of his doctrine of *alternance* and the source of many of his apparently paradoxical positions. His sense of the final nullity of everything encouraged him to explore the contrasting faiths by which men live—hedonism and asceticism, instinct and rationality, Roman pride and Christian humility—with that curiously dispassionate intensity which distinguished him among his contemporaries. In a world of increasing intellectual monism, Montherlant was an aggressive dualist—even a Manichaean. . . . When his fellow-writers of the interwar period moved closer to a single ideological position—fascism or communism—he exercised an often corrosive intelligence in the service of non-commitment. (pp. 571-72)

[His] sense of the multiplicity of truth, and of its contradictory nature, was succinctly put in *L'Équinoxe de septembre* where he insisted that two opposing doctrines are simply deviations from a common truth. He saw confirmation of this view in the fact that the orthodoxy of one century has so often grown out of the heresy of the century which preceded it. . . .

[Montherlant's] imaginative sympathy with those whose views he does not necessarily share goes a long way towards explaining [his] capacity for presenting apparently contradictory positions with equal persuasiveness. It explains much of the intellectual—and poetic—power inherent in the great "debating scenes" of some of his best plays. (p. 572)

> *"To Keep the Void at Bay," in* The Times Literary Supplement (© *Times Newspapers Ltd., 1973; reproduced from* The Times Literary Supplement *by permission), May 25, 1973, pp. 571-73.*

* * *

MOORE, Brian 1921-

Moore is an Irish-born Canadian novelist living in the United States. Typically, his subjects are self-deceived outcasts in need of self-redemption. His study of a pathetic alcoholic spinster in *The Lonely Passion of Judith Hearne* is outstanding, a minor classic of Canadian literature. Eschewing experimentation, Moore is esteemed for his ability to write convincingly of society's aliens and misfits in a conventional style. (See also *CLC*, Vols. 1, 3, 5, 7, and *Contemporary Authors*, Vols. 1-4, rev. ed.)

The Great Victorian Collection doesn't belong with Moore's finest work. There is too much the feeling of a good idea done to death; the transformation of the Collection into a commercial gimmick is not as funny as it might have been; and the influence of Borges is obtrusive. But the questions it asks about the nature of art and of reality are an inevitable development of the metaphysical preoccupation which lies at the heart of even his most naturalistic novels. (An object, for Moore, is more than the sum of its atoms. It preserves within it the racial memory of its raw material, as a wardrobe might have heard of the Crucifixion.) And there is some rare sorcery here. 'The final belief,' said Wallace Stevens, 'is to believe in a fiction, which you know to be a fiction, there being nothing else.' In its pristine condition, the Collection is Moore's correlative for such belief, a serene statement of purely aesthetic joy. . . .

> *Derek Mahon, "Magic Casements," in* New Statesman (© *1975 The Statesman & Nation Publishing Co. Ltd.), October 17, 1975, p.479.*

Despite its great technical skill and air of timeliness ["The Doctor's Wife"] . . . , about a woman tunneling her way out of an oppressive middle-class marriage with the trenching tool of an adulterous affair involving a lover 11 years younger than herself, is really quite old-fashioned in plot management and quite conventional in its implications. . . .

[The] book is full of contrivances and tricks. . . . Moore frequently provides fail-safe devices in his plotting that reveal his expertise in the manipulation of readers. . . .

When Moore is writing at his serious best, as in "The Lonely Passion of Judith Hearne" or in "Catholics," that small, somber near-masterpiece, he ranks with the finest novelists of today. "The Doctor's Wife" is not serious in that sense. It may appear to raise many important questions about passion, family commitments, woman's self-determination—also about the interconnections of private and public violence and cruelty—yet even in storytelling a parade of appearances must not be confused with the real thing. (p. 7)

> *Julian Moynahan, in* The New York Times Book Review *(© 1976 by The New York Times Company; reprinted by permission), September 26, 1976.*

There is much to admire in Brian Moore's *The Doctor's Wife*, ... the story of ... Sheila Redden.... There are briskly evoked settings in Paris and Villefranche, the scenes of Sheila's affair; discreet descriptions of Belfast, where Sheila's home and married life have been. There are remarkably sharp pictures of the inadequacies of the men in this book, from Sheila's weak, kind brother to her bullying husband, who to his own surprise is inflamed by his wife's infidelity and rapes her in Paris when he thought he had come to talk peace and take her back....

[The troubles of Northern Ireland] seem to have something to do with Sheila's plight, and this is where my doubts about the novel begin. Is Belfast simply a backdrop of violence and despair and confusion, a political stage for a personal muddle, or is Sheila, in spite of her disclaimers, a victim, or even an emblem of her country's ills? When Sheila and her lover are compared to "survivors walking away from a crash," is that an allusion to the bombs mentioned elsewhere in the novel, or merely a bit of careless writing? To change the ground a little, when Sheila is able to give her lover the slip because they were to take separate planes to America, is Moore suggesting a real shallowness in the American, who is prepared to spend the rest of his life with Sheila but not to give up the return half of a charter-flight ticket? Or is this merely the sound of the plot creaking, the squeal of the machinery which will send Sheila off to her loneliness? Similarly, when the narrator, who has access to Sheila's mind and sensations, including the trickling of menstrual blood down her thigh, calls her "Mrs. Redden," is that a distancing effect or merely a clumsy variation on "she" and "Sheila"? ...

The limitations of *The Doctor's Wife* are perhaps simply the limitations of any novel that offers only to observe its characters rather than to animate them or attack them, or engage with them in any one of a dozen other ways. The straightforward imitation of life in literature tends to produce an imitation of literature. Moore's characters are plausible without being entirely convincing—even when the narrator is inside Sheila's head, he seems to be there as a tourist rather than a resident.... (p. 40)

> *Michael Wood, in* The New York Review of Books *(reprinted with permission from* The New York Review of Books; *copyright © 1976 NYREV, Inc.), September 30, 1976.*

Brian Moore's eleventh novel is a literary event in three countries, as are all his books now. He has a public who have come to expect of him what he unfailingly delivers: lucidity, great craftsmanship, and perceptions that evoke our fears, dreams, and shameful absurdities. *The Doctor's Wife* is of such quality that after reading it twice—fervidly the first time, to find out what happens, closely the second, to unpick its subtleties—it took me hours to answer the question, "How come it's so good and yet so far from being what one hoped for in the opening chapters, so affecting and yet so aggravatingly flawed?"...

Moore is taking as his theme the great question of the decade, maybe of the century: the changing state of women, what it is they suffer from, want, and may never, God unwilling, have. Interwoven with this are further thoughts on other themes that are Moore's continuing concerns: Ireland and its pervasive provincialism, which both repels and compels him; Catholicism and the anguish of those who've lost their faith; failure and the awful regrets of the weak.

It's rich material which he treats sparingly. Moore is the master of the small, revelatory moment....

[The] novel is frequently so crafty one nods in admiration. But it's prevented from being more than that by the weakness of the characterization of Sheila Redden.

Moore has a reputation made from two previous novels, *Judith Hearne* and *I Am Mary Dunne*, for being able to transcend the barriers between male and female sensibilities. Better than anybody since Flaubert and Joyce, he has been said (mostly by male critics, it's true) to have gone inside the minds of women and turned them out to be aired.

The transcendence doesn't happen here. (And I'm beginning to wonder whether it ever did. Were we fooled by Judith Hearne and Mary Dunne because women hadn't turned out their own minds? Now that we've had Lessing in *A Golden Notebook* and *The Summer Before The Dark* and Jong in *Fear of Flying*—and a score, no, a hundred other writers, coming out of consciousness-raising into the light, writing, writing about what it's like to be a woman with so much acuity one longs to escape—would we find Judith Hearne so poignant, Mary Dunne so compatible?)

In any case, Sheila Redden is, for me, a male fabrication, put together from a hundred clever details. She's what a self-consciously sensitive man fantasizes a woman to be. Her memories are romantic, her flaws are adorable, her interests are, if not intellectual, certainly "artistic." Above all, she is passive. Almost everything is done *to* her. The passivity is revealed most tellingly in the passages that touch on sexuality—the "love" scenes with both her lover and her husband, scenes that are so masculine in the way they are perceived it is a painful joke.

In sum, she's a man's woman apparently without passions that spring from her own body's needs, desiring only that men desire, her sexuality tuning into theirs like an oboe section tuning into an orchestra as soon as the conductor waves his wand. (p. 68)

Sheila Redden is ... an object. Were she more than that, this might have been a great book instead of just a skilful one, with a message so palatable it's already been sold to the movies. The message is simple: women, don't arise—if you do, you'll wind up alone in a bed-sitter, working in a dry cleaners. (p. 69)

> *Christina Newman, "The Phallic Fallacy of Brian Moore," in* Saturday Night *(copyright © 1976 by* Saturday Night*), October, 1976, pp. 68-9.*

The Doctor's Wife is one of those bad books it's not easy to let slip past. Moore is a writer widely reviewed and often highly praised, a winner of serious and important awards, a writer published by one of the most respectable firms in New York. He's undeniably intelligent and genuinely gifted —few writers are more deft—and he has repeatedly proved his ability to turn out, like plastic Donald Ducks, the much sought-after "good read."

The Doctor's Wife, briefly, is about a woman, Sheila Redden, who falls honestly, passionately in love with a younger man who loves her in return. She decides to abandon her medical husband, her 15-year-old son, and her homeland, Northern Ireland (Ulster, in fact), and start over. The whole idea of the novel, make no mistake, is terrific. The idea of escape from a futile, stupid marriage and the idea of escape from a futile city are perfectly interdigitated. Sheila has all her life loved poetry and fiction, foreign places, the idea of romance, but because she is and has always been a practical woman, she married, long ago, a competent and dedicated but thoroughly insensitive doctor, a man who loves golf and scorns people like Joyce and Yeats. *Ulysses,* to him, is a "dirty book," and when he finds it in her library he looks with filthy interest to see if Sheila has other dirty books. (She doesn't.) He has no idea that the ideals of Joyce and Yeats have something to do with the Troubles now suffered in Northern Ireland, and if you tried to tell him he would shift the conversation to something serious. The truth seems to be that, as a doctor, he unconsciously enjoys the Troubles. Patients die or are maimed. It gives him something to do. It's interesting. . . .

Philosophically speaking, the book is about promises and what happens to them in a world without faith or principle, a world gone absurd. . . .

Moore creates vivid, convincing scenes. He writes clever dialogue that doesn't sound fake. His humor and much of the sentiment is authentic. For instance the scene in which Sheila and her brother meet in Paris, playing wacky Irish jokes though their hearts are breaking, is both hilarious and honestly touching. And Moore knows everything a novelist ought to know, the minutia that makes for verisimilitude and texture. Normally I hate sex and violence in novels, not so much for prudish reasons (though it's partly that) as because they're always so phony and cliche. Moore brings off both magnificently. . . .

Moore is too good to be a cheap entertainer, and too cheap to be an artist. . . .

The Doctor's Wife is a fake work of art. Its technique is cinematic, not novelistic; its characterizations are stereotypic, with the result that its suspense is mere melodrama; its symbolism is designed not to ambush truth but to preach a message; and its message is false and pernicious.

Cinema can be, as in "Cries and Whispers," great art, but it is not the same art as fiction. Fiction seeks out the darkest, most secret whispers of character, sometimes secrets not even the writer understands. Film, objective, tells its story by implication: it has far more to do with the masterful haiku than with the *Iliad.* Moore's scenes are not scenes in Tolstoy's sense, or Melville's or Dante's, but "shots.". . . The past of Moore's characters is invariably presented in cinematic flashbacks. The character remembers an image . . . , then remembers the complete dialogue of that moment, as never happens in life but can legitimately happen in the film cutaway, which is not memory but exposition. . . .

In a really good novel, the reader is seduced into having a dream—the novel's story—more real than the room he's reading in. The moment the writer accidentally makes the reader wake up—by some technique that too clearly calls attention to itself (like cinematic voice overlay), or by some

obvious lie (like oversimplified characterization), or by intrusive preachiness, the novel goes sour. No one can be sure, while watching "Othello," whether Othello or Iago is right. Othello is appealing, though sententious and dangerously innocent; Iago is foul, but what he says makes sense. Brian Moore takes no such risks. Sheila's husband is simply and unmistakably no good, and what the reader feels, watching him, is *That's not what he'd think.* . . . [It's] out of this pure war of good against evil that [Moore] builds his suspense. . . .

All of us, probably, have people we hate, people of whom we say only the worst. The difference between art and life is that art gets to reconsider itself, can revise out the simplified angry opinions. The true artist does this, both as policy and as artistic craft. The fake artist makes hay on dramatically powerful oversimplifications.

Moore's message in *The Doctor's Wife,* though carefully qualified, is a false message, though one enormously popular in our time. The values of the past have failed, Moore claims—Ulster is his example, but he seems to mean all the world—and only an absurd faith in feeling can redeem our misery. The trouble is that Sheila, who escapes, and her brother Owen, who remains trapped, are instances, not universals.

> *John Gardner, "Brian Moore: The Technique of the Film in the Form of the Novel," in* Book World—The Washington Post *(© The Washington Post), October 17, 1976, p. N3.*

A novel whose premise is a passive heroine buffeted by circumstance must be careful: Too much inactivity may prove boring. One line of defense for an author is to produce a gripping psychological analysis, to focus inward. Thus in *The Doctor's Wife* Brian Moore often ventures into the consciousness of his main character, Sheila Redden. . . .

Unfortunately, what emerges is one woman's very dull mind, leaving Moore, already hampered by Sheila's inertia, to contrive potentially interesting situations to keep the reader's attention. (p. 19)

The novel offers several perspectives on this pathetic woman: her husband's, her son's, her brother's, her friend's, a Paris priest's, and even two English tourists' on the prowl for celebrities in Villefranche. The manipulations necessary to let us see Sheila from so many angles would be nothing more than a minor annoyance if any of these people offered insights into the workings of her mind.

On the last page, we see poor Sheila sitting alone on a park bench. Since the beginning she has had nothing to say. The single difference now, after 277 pages, is that she has no one to say it to. (p. 20)

> *Philip Lemmons, "Suddenly and Unexplicably," in* The New Leader *(© 1977 by the American Labor Conference on International Affairs, Inc.), February 14, 1977, pp. 19-20.*

* * *

MOORE, Marianne   1887-1972

Moore, possibly the foremost American woman poet of this century, combined technical virtuosity with a profound moral vision. Her poetry is both vivid and subtle, and often relates the soul in nature. Moore was a recipient of the National

Book Award and the Pulitzer Prize. (See also *CLC*, Vols. 1, 2, 4, and *Contemporary Authors*, Vols. 1-4, rev. ed.; obituary, Vols. 33-36.)

Our only domesticated poet, at least the only one whom we can take seriously, is Marianne Moore. Her vital optimism and good will have a Christian source and an American flavor. She is at home in the community of her imagination, just as "the hero, the student, the steeple-jack, each in his way, is at home." However much we may be tempted to impute an ironic meaning—conditioned as we are by modern verse—to the job of the steeple-jack and to his danger-sign, we must not suppose that [in "The Steeple-Jack"] Miss Moore is, even obliquely, mocking the "simple people" of this town or being acerbic about their faith. It is prudent and right for a man to protect his neighbors against injury. And the church, though it appeals to the townsfolk as a provident and practical institution, is also the house of mystery and transcendence—hence fittingly labeled "dangerous." This fishing town, with its stranded whales and proliferating seaside vegetation, has its elements of fantasy, but we realize in the clear light that, after all, "the climate is not right for the banyan, frangipani, or jack-fruit trees; or an exotic serpent life. . . . They've cats, not cobras, to keep down the rats." Neither is it a town meant for an exotic spirituality, a fanatic religious life. Maybe hope is as much transcendence as it can bear. The last lines of the poem . . . are appropriately matter-of-fact. Miss Moore, indeed, almost never seeks the smash ending. Her poems are not orchestrated for brasses and kettledrums. Suspended at the close, by-passing the full stop, they seem to drift back into life. (pp. 223-24)

Miss Moore's inductive method of composition is not conducive to economy. Generally she needs to accumulate a palpable mass of data before she is willing to let go of her poem. If she seems to be in no hurry to reach her destination, it may be that she has no destination in view. Her mind is like Stendhal's mirror dawdling along a road, enchanted by the succession of unpredictable reflections, which we in turn are permitted to enjoy. She will know, when she gets there, where to stop. If she did not have a conviction about the unity of experience, she would get nowhere. . . .

We need constantly to remind ourselves that Miss Moore's poems are works of the imagination, despite their lack of afflatus. Their quality depends on her gift for picking and choosing. Miss Moore, who does not pretend to be a bard, has a scrupulous sense of limits. On this rock she has built her house. The workmanship is more than honest: it is passionately fastidious. I suspect it will stand. (p. 225)

Miss Moore has made a great triumph by building an art out of a lifetime of trust in small, real virtues. She is our Moral Eye, saved from platitude by accuracy, by honesty, by coolness, and by joy. One of her convictions is that "poetry watches life with affection." She is fond of quoting from Confucius, who taught her, "If there be a knife of resentment in the heart, the mind will not attain precision." (p. 227)

> *Stanley Kunitz, "Responses, Glosses, Refractions" (originally published in* Festschrift for Marianne Moore's Seventy-Seventh Birthday, *edited by Tambimuttu; Tambimuttu & Mass, New York, 1964), in his* A Kind of Order, A Kind of Folly (© 1935, 1937, 1938, 1941, 1942, 1947, 1949, 1957, 1963, 1964, 1965, 1966, 1967, 1970, 1971, 1972, 1973, 1974, 1975 by Stanley Kunitz; reprinted by permission of Little, Brown and Co. in association with the Atlantic Monthly Press), Atlantic-Little, Brown, 1975, pp. 223-27.*

Mistress of quirks and oddities, Marianne Moore writes poems that look like nothing so much as a magpie's nest of precisely fitted trivia and that almost inevitably surprise us by or into abrupt, oblique, and superficially capricious generalizations. Her home truths, her moral assertions seem to relate in something other than a cause-and-effect way to the material she has assembled. Neither pertinent nor altogether impertinent, those outrageous accuracies seem, when she is in top form, really to have animated a world of pure fact until that world, like one of the gods laboring a thought, gives birth to figures that are heroic, intractable, pure. In her characteristic work, the commonplace assumes a regal strut.

Inimitable, she is also unpredictable. Her revisions—such as the spectacular reduction of "Poetry" from an initial thirty lines to a final three—exasperate some readers and delight others. But they also serve to remind us that, for the living poet who sees his work as indigenously part of himself, the poem is likely to continue to change whenever the poet changes. When he no longer wants to tinker with it, it may be dead. There is no doubt at all in Miss Moore's mind that the best thing to do with a poem that is not living is to discard it. (pp. v-vi)

In the face of what may be universal disaster, she offers us primary values, a poetry of plain fact transmuted—at its best—into wisdom. Admiring the unique, the odd, the peculiar, she reminds us that these qualities—conspicuously her own—make life worthwhile. It is these qualities that make Brooklyn's "crowning curio," the Camperdown elm, worth preserving, and that may preserve, if we are lucky enough and curious enough and possessive enough, the world's other crowning curio, us. (p. vi)

It would be absurd to deny that Marianne Moore is frequently obscure, enigmatic, or peculiar; it would be still more absurd, however, to suggest either that such characteristics seriously interfere with an enjoyment of her poems, even those in which the courage of her peculiarities is most in evidence, or that patience and familiarity are any less effectual with her than they are with Eliot, Emily Dickinson, or Donne. And to place Miss Moore among such poets is, in kind if not always in degree, to place her among her peers—among poets of formidable intelligence, formidable wit, and formidable eccentricity, poets who characteristically achieve their effects through surprise and the strategic violation of decorum. (p. 17)

[One] peculiarity of most Marianne Moore poems is that they are symmetrically rigid, if not frigid, that they are "strict with tension" between the prose elegance of the thing said and the verse elegance of formal regularity. . . . Of such tensions, it may be said with absolute literality that "it is not for us to understand art," since whatever it is that makes us respond to such tensions is a matter not of understanding but precisely of response, something probably organic in nature rather than rational—a "beautiful element of unreason." (pp. 25-6)

[Event] and anecdote in Marianne Moore's writing are rarely presented either for their own sake or for the sake of their unadorned intensity. Those happenings that she observes or invents, that seem to her the appropriate stuff of poetry, interest her because they embody or suggest values, ideas, or modes of conduct. Rather than let sleeping cats lie, she finds in them occasion for comment on the life of man, and she is willing to risk a considerable degree of obliquity in the process of making them give up their significance; her moralities are seldom as straightforward and uncomplicated as that of the grasshopper and the ant, for instance. On the one hand, she has, as moralist, a taste for aphorism; on the other hand, the aphorisms tend to appear in contexts that limit their applicability:

As for the disposition invariably to affront,
an animal with claws should have an opportunity to use them,

and this is something less than a categorical imperative, even for animals, not all of whom have claws. Such an interest in ethics is exploratory, conditional, and even experimental rather than absolutist or dogmatic; Miss Moore detects ethical implications in conduct, but she does not necessarily advocate all she detects.

In [addition], the interest in ethics is matched by an interest in art. Art, once more, is "feeling, modified by the writer's moral and technical insights," and it may be worth noting that moral insights modify feeling rather than the other way round; that is to say that when Miss Moore is thinking explicitly of her role as artist, moral insight is not primary. . . . [Ethics] and esthetics have a symbiotic relationship throughout Miss Moore's body of work. There is not much question which of the two is finally prior for her as a person. (pp. 27-8)

Marianne Moore has written poems in traditional metrical forms ("To Military Progress," for example) and others in what may as well be called free verse ("New York"). But more frequent and more characteristic are those written in the peculiar prosody of "Bird-Witted" and "The Monkeys," with stanzas based on syllable count and inconspicuous rhyme working against a cadence that is essentially that of elegant and precise prose. Quite simply, there is no one among her contemporaries who writes in quite this way. The point here is not really that of having a voice and manner of one's own, though Miss Moore surely has one, as characteristic and individual as that of Frost or Auden, for example. But the prosody has little to do with the voice because it is never more than partially heard, and this is not accidental. Miss Moore remarks on "my own fondness for the unaccented rhyme," attributing it to "an instinctive effort to ensure naturalness," and again, "concealed rhyme and the interiorized climax usually please me better than the open rhyme and the insisted-on climax. . . ." [Her] rhyming is eccentric, but there is no question of its not having been intended; it testifies not to a defective ear but to a prickly and rigorous, perhaps almost an obsessive, concern for craft.

Such a concern for craft is risky but not unprecedented; there is in fact a plausible case to be made that sees Marianne Moore as occupying one of the two possible attitudes, at least for poets in English, toward a relatively strict prosody. Roughly speaking, one may cooperate with one's prosody or one may set oneself in opposition to it. (pp. 28-30)

That harmony of form and content evident in [a] Shakespeare sonnet is in Milton, if not a dissonance, at least a radically strained counterpointing. Shakespeare cooperates with his prosody, Milton opposes it.

In this admittedly limited sense, Marianne Moore is more Miltonic than Shakespearean—more Miltonic in fact than Milton. Milton does not bury his systematic rhymes as does Miss Moore in some instances, and while he counts syllables quite as scrupulously as she, he also maintains at least diplomatic relations with an iambic pentameter norm. She does not, nor with any other norm that the ear can detect; her stance of opposition to her prosody is as complete as she can make it. (p. 33)

For Miss Moore, it seems clear that her prosody expresses a fastidious dislike to sprawl, either verbal or emotional; a sense that cadence alone is not a sufficient safeguard against such excesses; a compelling taste for schematic arrangements of things, indicated not only in counted syllables but in orderly patterns of indentation in her left margins; an equally compelling taste for the freer arrangements and patterns of highly skilled talk (like Samuel Johnson and Oscar Wilde, she is herself an extraordinary and eccentric talker); and I suspect most important of all, her moral and esthetic imperative toward discipline, particularly self-discipline, in all things. To Marianne Moore, . . . Pavlova's sense of style was also a moral quality; [her] essay on Pavlova is a praise of discipline, of values that can be achieved through rigorous devotion of oneself to a craft, and that emphasis provides a constant theme of her critical writing. Of gusto as a literary quality, she writes that it "thrives on freedom, and freedom in art, as in life, is the result of a discipline imposed by ourselves.". . . And for a poet, at least for Miss Moore's kind of poet, law means prosody, those regulations and organizations of language that make possible both the exercise of a more or less impersonal craft and the maneuverings of personal insight and ability through which craft may become art. (pp. 34-5)

[Inconsistencies] make it almost impossible to generalize meaningfully about Miss Moore's revisions, especially in their most recent stages. Some need no defense, others admit of no explanation except the impulse to tinker, or perhaps to make sacrifices. (p. 51)

Even her friend William Carlos Williams has testified to her unwillingness to clarify her poems, and Allen Tate detects a similar reluctance to expose herself in her whimsical rejection of Roman Catholicism on the grounds that her sins were too numerous to inflict on a confessor. "Writing," Miss Moore tells us, "is an undertaking for the modest," and modesty evidently precludes a parading of those reservations that have led to her persistent refashioning of her work. . . . [Her] whims presumably operate in defense of something, some feeling of integrity, some "beautiful element of unreason," but it is clearly whim that operates.

Does it matter? To Miss Moore, it evidently does, but without a clearer sense than we are ever likely to get of just what it is that has troubled her in omitted and revised poems, we have little choice but to regard her tinkering as one of those things which an elephant does and which please no one but itself. Lacking that clearer sense, one may wonder whether it need matter to anyone except Miss Moore, and one need not question her genuineness or personal integrity in order to think that it matters a good deal. But it may be difficult to indicate precisely *why* it matters. Randall Jarrell gives part of the answer in his comment on the shortened version of "The Steeple-Jack" that appeared in *Collected Poems:* "The reader may feel like saying, 'Let her do as she pleases with the poem; it's hers, isn't it?' No; it's much too good a poem for that, it long ago became everybody's, and we can protest just as we could if Donatello cut off David's left leg.'' (pp. 70-1)

Jarrell's response is surely sound. And yet it is not precisely, or not simply, a matter of a poem's being too good to be altered. There are, it seems to me, at least two other elements involved. In the first place, for a poem to register itself on one's awareness as a thing, it has to have some sort of shape. This need not be an arbitrary shape, like a sonnet or a five-line syllabic stanza; it may equally well be its own uniquely organic shape, like a chestnut tree or a thumbprint or ''Howl.'' But a poem that is subject to persistent tinkering, that appears first in strict syllabic stanzas, then as thirteen lines of freely cadenced verse, then twice in loosely syllabic stanzas, and then as three irregular lines with a long footnote, that uses double quotation marks in its first two appearances, single quotation marks in its third and fourth, and double again in the footnote to its fifth, and whose third version is identified by its author as original—such a poem is less a thing than an open-ended process; it is Polonius's cloud. Its successive revisions call attention less to the poem, which one can never grasp because it is never finished, than to the poet, who excites one's curiosity. Actually, what probably happens under such circumstances is that one really accepts that version of the poem in which it first called itself to one's attention, and writes off the others as interesting or exasperating aberrations; one can ordinarily neither entertain equally four different versions of a poem nor simply cancel earlier versions when a later appears. Clearly, a poet is under no obligation to concern himself with such problems; but a poem whose history is one of never quite finding its shape suffers because of them. (pp. 71-2)

''The past is the present,'' as Miss Moore reminds us in the poem of that name, but in *Complete Poems* the past comes dangerously close to being what one wishes it had been. Confusion, though perhaps not confusion alone, is well served by a volume that, evidently intended to be definitive, fudges with history in this way. (p. 73)

Miss Moore as poet persistently manifests certain tensions, certain opposed impulses that in large measure determine both her successes and her failures. Briefly, the impulse to generalize, to reduce particularities in the interests of the Johnsonian ''great thought,'' is constantly involved with the counterimpulse to note particularities despite, or even because of, their refusal to lend themselves to application, to be generalized. . . . When the one mode fails, the result is steam-roller stuffiness; when the other mode fails, the result is mere eccentricity, the accumulation of bric-a-brac or the pointlessly cryptic anecdote. Characteristically, they do not fail but help to define those tensions that make their poems objects of interest. Miss Moore's best work, perhaps like all best work, embodies a kind of dialectical tension between theoretically incompatible modes of knowledge and ideas of value. (p. 81)

With hindsight wisdom, one may say that the dominant movement in *Collected Poems,* and perhaps in Miss Moore's work as a whole, is from an attractive but sometimes dreadfully superior concern with life lived, or failing to be lived, in terms of an esthetic of naturalness, fastidiousness, and enlightened self-interest, to an often humble examination of partialities and objects of concern that have no prior obligations to principle and that are valued not because they illustrate a point but because, illustrating only themselves, they liberate emotion. The difference is that between, for example, the cat in ''The Monkeys,'' and the

pangolin; between the snail, whose economy we may admire, and the paper nautilus, carrying its eggs with arms wound around

> as if they knew love
> is the only fortress
> strong enough to trust to.
>
> (pp. 95-6)

Perhaps only a jaundiced eye will detect in Miss Moore's poems of the 1920s a loss of momentum, a tendency to become more and more special, defensive, and somehow lost; but even a jaundiced eye would be hard put to find such qualities in the poems of the early 1930s. They have in some fashion come to terms with the necessities of ordinary life, no longer finding themselves in contemplation of ocean and glaciers, the vast and the inorganic. Even ''the boundless sand, / the stupendous sandspout'' in ''The Jerboa'' is not so much a mere surrounding, a final judgment, or a bleak object of contemplation as it is a place to live. (p. 111)

What Are Years? moves from its opening celebration of the one to its closing insistence on the other, and the dates of first publication for the various poems in the collection indicate that these poles really are poles rather than accidents of chronology. . . . *What Are Years?* is an organized body of work, and its objective is the affirming of values.

''You must not be surprised,'' writes Auden of the poet's moral affirmations, ''if he should have nothing but platitudes to say; firstly because he will always find it hard to believe that a poem needs expounding, and secondly because he doesn't consider poetry quite that important.'' And though the context of his observation is general, he concludes, ''any poet, I believe, will echo Miss Marianne Moore's words: '*I, too, dislike it.*' '' Certainly one can say that the values Miss Moore affirms in these poems—courage, love, humility, patience—are the stuff of platitude, like Auden's ''You shall love your crooked neighbor/ With your crooked heart,'' or for that matter Dante's ''In la sua voluntade e nostra pace.'' When Miss Moore's moral affirmations startle us, it is never by virtue of their exoticism, like those eggs laid by tigers for which Dylan Thomas somewhere confessed to an early love. But startle us they sometimes do, not just by their energy and wit (this at least the earlier work had prepared us for), but by their quiet intensity.

''What Are Years?'' praises courage in such terms. (pp. 120-21)

Miss Moore gives us no sense of a lost power, as does Wordsworth, and she is not prepared, as Wordsworth is, to base her affirmation on details of personal crisis. But the mortality that is eternity, that achieves joy by its capacity to endure misfortune, even death, has kinship with that humanizing of his soul that Wordsworth experienced as a result of his brother's drowning. . . . ''What Are Years?'' may perhaps be described as Miss Moore's ''Character of the Happy Warrior.'' (pp. 122-23)

A powerfully moving elegiac poem, [''Virginia Britannia''] has a sense of place about it that is without precedent in Miss Moore's work, suggestive of Coleridge's conversation poems or Eliot's quartets. . . . Its characteristic strategy is to hold up something that man, particularly white European man, has made of himself and his surroundings in oblique confrontation with something indigenous. . . . [If ''What Are Years?''] is her ''Character of the Happy Warrior,'' this perhaps is her ''Lycidas.'' It is surely one of our great poems. (pp. 125-26)

What Are Years? moves triumphantly from courage to love; *Nevertheless* opens in much the same way, with instances of hindered mortality rising upon itself to demonstrate that even in the vegetable world there is nothing like fortitude. But it is a different book—more troubled, more aware or more painfully aware of the distance between commitment to belief or principle and the uncomfortable facts of immediate emotional experience. It moves from simple praise of fortitude, in the title poem, to something much more complicated and uncertain in the last, "In Distrust of Merits," a poem that, echoing many earlier poems, shifts uncertainly between an effort to assume a burden of responsibility for the Second World War and a sin-ridden sense of the task's impossibility. It is Auden's "We must love one another or die," but without Auden's perhaps unconvincing cheeriness in his poem's concluding lines, and equally without Auden's framework of historical determinism and his clear sense of purpose. The fight to be affectionate is still the central fact of moral experience, the one overriding categorical imperative that Miss Moore recognizes, but here it is supported by no ironic or triumphant rhetoric. This poem, more starkly than Auden's, expresses the abiding fear that the fight may be a lost cause.

Does it sum up its volume? Perhaps not. At least the certainties of "Nevertheless" ("The weak overcomes its/ menace, the strong over-/comes itself") have become uncertain, and the other four poems in the book do little to prepare us for the expense of spirit that "In Distrust of Merits" involves. (pp. 129-30)

"In Distrust of Merits" is the final poem in *Nevertheless,* and deliberately so; in terms of original publication, only "The Wood-Weasel" is earlier; "In Distrust of Merits" comes last because Miss Moore wanted it to come last. And what it does to the other poems is to throw their innocences into sharp relief. Like *What Are Years?, Nevertheless* is a book in praise of courage and love, but its dynamic is less the sense of grace than it is the loss of innocence. To sleep on an elephant may very well be repose, but it is the human condition to have to ride on tigers. (p. 132)

"Beauty is everlasting," says "In Distrust of Merits"; and if mortal aspiration is eternity, as in "What Are Years?," still "dust is for a time" and behaves at its peril—its moral peril—when it attempts to find rest in some timeless absolute. (pp. 132-33)

"In Distrust of Merits" owes much of its special quality in the Moore canon to its conspicuous refusal to simplify the heart's confusions. This of course is not new with Miss Moore; she has always been attracted by dialectically related impulses to generalize and to particularize, but it may be safe to say that as a rule such tensions resolve themselves in some witty synthesis—the image of a steam roller, a statue of Daniel Webster, an imaginary garden with real toads in it. Even "Virginia Britannia" has its great closing image of particularities gradually absorbed into sunset, cloudscape, and gathering darkness as an intimation of glory. "In Distrust of Merits" offers no such synthesizing image, only its final sense of helpless, almost hopeless guilt and inadequacy, like that of Milton's Samson before his testing. Its closing aphorism—"Beauty is everlasting / and dust is for a time"—is less a synthesis than it is a giving up, a taking refuge in the fact that life is finite. As we have seen, Miss Moore has expressed herself as dissatisfied with the poem on formal grounds, and in a way it is perfectly clear that she is right.

I suppose the real trouble is that "In Distrust of Merits" deals with intolerables. "It's truthful," Miss Moore says; "it is testimony—to the fact that war is intolerable, and unjust." And here, as perhaps always in such cases, the statement serves to suppress partially the more disturbing subject of the moral status and responsibility of those, particularly oneself, who tolerate the intolerable, who inwardly do nothing. (pp. 134-35)

"In Distrust of Merits" is a remarkable performance, but in its uninsistent way, a quite different way, the group of nine poems closing *Collected Poems* is equally remarkable, effecting something much like a musical modulation of key and final resolution. *Nevertheless* closes with an almost schizoid sense of personal fragmentation, of formulations that do not work, of duties to be carried out but that cannot be carried out, and of self-loathing. The mind's enchantment, in the destructive sense of the term, is virtually complete; it has looked into itself and found an abyss. (p. 138)

Miss Moore is not Milton, but she shares his tradition in some important ways. Milton's Protestant humanism, with its emphasis on man as fallen but heroic, as responsible for his own desperations but capable of surviving them, and as dependent for guidance largely on *recta ratio* and his own experience—Milton's humanism differs from Miss Moore's with respect to magnitude and to philosophical and theological explicitness. But Pope's humanism differs from Milton's in much the same way, and if these poems of the 1930s and 1940s cannot be thought of as "Paradise Lost" or "Samson Agonistes," they are a more than respectable "Essay on Man." (p. 146)

[The] poems of [the] late volumes in a way seem to matter less to her. The volumes themselves seem less constructions, like *Collected Poems* and its component parts, than collections; *Like a Bulwark,* in which Miss Moore lists dates of publication as part of her acknowledgments, appears to be a straight chronological assembly of poems, without the concern for arrangement evident in *What Are Years?* and *Collected Later.* And though, as Randall Jarrell observes, "it is most barbarously unjust to treat her . . . as what she is only when she parodies herself," nevertheless the tendency to self-parody, if that is what it is, manifests itself in these late poems. "In This Age of Hard Trying, Nonchalance Is Good and" has a sharply defined point, even though one may be quite unclear what that point is; "A Jellyfish," on the other hand, seems perfectly clear, but has very little to be clear about. "To a Snail" was short and brilliant; "O to Be a Dragon" is only short.

There is, of course, another way to regard these contrasts. "In This Age of Hard Trying, Nonchalance Is Good and" may be suspected of pretending to say much more than it really does, of being all machinery and no function, like a Rube Goldberg creation; "A Jellyfish" makes no pretense to delivering more than its own precise but limited observation. "O to Be a Dragon" can enter the same modest claim, exemplifying principles laid down in "To a Snail". . . . In its own way, it is an extraordinarily funny poem, and it sums up certain preoccupations of Miss Moore's, though one must approach it with almost infinite tolerance in order to enjoy it.

That may be the problem with these later poems: they demand tolerance. "Like a Bulwark" . . . seems a case in point. It says that resistance strengthens one and that the strong endure. There would be no point in quarreling with the statement or with Miss Moore's admiration for the person, real or hypothetical, who exemplifies it. Yet the poem is essentially rhetoric, with little indeed of the fine surprise that makes ''Nevertheless,'' for example, something more than its rhetoric. It remains a verbalized thought for the day, admirable in its way, applicable in its way. But it moves one less to admiration than to sympathy.... (pp. 148-50)

Some of Miss Moore's feeblest work is in these late volumes, work about which there is simply nothing to be said except that she wrote it and has found it worthy of being preserved, which may, of course, be all that needs saying. (p. 150)

Up to about the time of *What Are Years?*, with ''The Pangolin'' as critical poem, Miss Moore's animal poems, though looking toward people, clearly preferred the simpler creatures who prefigured them—jerboas, basilisks, frigate pelicans. The hard job of preferring people, sticky and complicated as they are, was accomplished in the thirties and forties; and now in these later poems the animals seem to be coming back. (pp. 153-54)

The later sections of *Collected Poems* seem to have been organized around and to express an emotional and intellectual crisis; *Like a Bulwark* is more loosely organized, ... but it has a kind of center in its persistent concern with tensions between wholeness and multiplicity, change and permanence, between that which can be rationalized into a formula and that which can only be experienced. *O to Be a Dragon* is still more loosely organized, though the evidence provided by dates of initial publication of its individual poems suggests something other than chronology as the organizing principle. (*Tell Me, Tell Me* changes the principle yet again by printing poems in reverse chronological order.) ... [It] contains a number of old poems as well as new work. The title poem, evidently new, concerns those problems of identity that appear in *Like a Bulwark*. No more than the rosemary will its dragon say *''mutare sperno''*; its capacity to be anything or nothing and still to be a dragon expresses, though it does not resolve, a good many contradictions.

Chameleons too change yet remain chameleons, which may account for the reappearance of ''To a Chameleon''; minimally, the same thing can be said of the jellyfish in ''A Jellyfish.'' And ''I May, I Might, I Must'' deals with the necessary changes one must be prepared for if one is to confront such experiential difficulties as crossing fens. I suppose that chameleons, jellyfish, and fen-crossers all exemplify values in use, but the poem of that name seems extraordinarily oblique, a warning against undue abstraction in writing and speaking; someone is evidently being found guilty of violating his own standards. But the bit quoted in the poem, and equally the larger bit quoted in the note, is not hopelessly abstruse, even judged on its own ground; it is not clear that its means defeat its ends, as did those of the ibis in ''To Statecraft Embalmed.'' Hugh Kenner's remark that ''few of the later poems *enact* as did so many of the earlier ones their lesson of probity'' seems precisely applicable. (pp. 157-58)

Tell Me, Tell Me seems a thoroughly mixed grill, even omitting as it does in *Complete Poems* the four prose pieces that appeared when the volume was published separately. The doggerel whimsy of ''To Victor Hugo of My Crow Pluto'' must establish some sort of outside limit of the admissible, even for school mistresses. Yet ''Tell Me, Tell Me'' suggests, at least, that the school mistress is still practicing dippiness according to strategy. I am not sure what this poem is about, but I suspect that it may be about me, about egocentricity that mistakes and misunderstands, that ventures to ask why such flatness as ''To Victor Hugo of My Crow Pluto'' should be set on the cindery pinnacle of publication. The answer is clear: like Mt. Everest, it was there.... And one must add that she chose [''Tell Me, Tell Me''] to provide the title for the volume in which it appeared.

Such a view of one's writing can be faulted only on grounds that have little relevance to the function the writing serves, thus rendering criticism absurd, as perhaps it is anyway. (pp. 163-64)

Miss Moore knows that the world is not good and evil but good-and-evil, as her ironic sense of man in ''Virginia Britannia,'' ''The Pangolin,'' and ''Armor's Undermining Modesty'' makes clear; she knows that Marianne Moore is not good or evil but good-and-evil, as ''In Distrust of Merits'' and ''A Face'' make equally clear. But reticence, decorum, propriety, an unwillingness to foul the nest in however marvelous a way, or perhaps a mere choice of subject matter operate to hold such knowledge at arm's length.... Virtue, rectitude—Miss Moore's work shines with them, but an ideologue might be forgiven for murmuring, ''Bourgeois virtue, bourgeois rectitude.'' ''Art,'' she writes, ''is but an expression of our needs.'' Perhaps one of our deepest needs—politically, morally, personally—is the clear sense of our capacity for reversion, of the inadequacy of our good intentions. (p. 172)

Of the Georgian poets, David Daiches remarks that they ''seem to have their eyes averted from something''; and Marianne Moore, praising moderate heroes, constructing her moralized bestiary, upholding fastidiousness in small things and integrity in large—manifesting, in fact, personal goodness, a daily beauty that needs no defense—leaves a similar impression as part of the cost of her way of art.

What else does it leave? What are the characteristic excitements of that way of art? Tricky prosody contributes something, as do the sometimes astringent wit and the capacity for an almost pedantically precise, and therefore surprising and amusing, observation. (p. 173)

What is a Marianne Moore poem about? It is about the odd and interesting way Marianne Moore's mind works as it moves from object to object and from aspect to aspect.... What attracts Miss Moore, and us, is her mind's very uncertainness, its unpredictable capacity to associate—''the manner in which we associate ideas in a state of excitement,'' as Wordsworth put it in the preface to *Lyrical Ballads*.

For Miss Moore, such associations sometimes approach Wordsworth's experience in the Wye valley near Tintern Abbey, discovering what he did not know he knew—that things have life, that we share in an organically continuous whole, that there is something in existence far more deeply interfused even than the still, sad music of humanity. But Miss Moore's discoveries are characteristically smaller; she knows that the theater she looks into is not the living plenum Wordsworth saw but her own quirky consciousness. (p. 175)

Unlike the romantics, Miss Moore has never overvalued poetry.... Miss Moore, like Pope and with something of his capacity for self-irony, stoops to truth, speaking of a mind that is often enchanting, sometimes intractable, but never nobly vague, never pinnacled dim in the intense inane. (pp. 175-76)

"Humility, indeed, is armor [Miss Moore wrote], for it realizes that it is impossible to be original, in the sense of doing something that has never been thought of before." Humility may be excessive, as may a concern for armor, though there is little to gain from speculating on the imaginable work of a humble Wordsworth or an egotistically sublime Marianne Moore. Nor is there really any need. Marianne Moore's mind, whether walking along with its eyes on the ground or being rebuked for its deformities by John Roebling's catenary curve, grinding its own ax, dealing with pent-up emotion, or wishing it had invented the zipper, is at the very least a worthy counterpart of the Camperdown elm, one of our crowning curios. And Marianne Moore, armored with humility, might well take that to be quite enough.

As perhaps it is. Yet epigrammatic brilliance, intellectual fastidiousness, and an unwillingness to falsify one's sense of one's own limitations may have an exemplary value of their own, in art as well as in life. Marianne Moore does not tell us the meaning of history, the nature of sin, or the right way to conduct our lives. She keeps things in order; she observes and annotates; she exercises the courage of her peculiarities. She gives us imaginary gardens with real toads in them; she also gives us the sick horror of decency trying to confront honestly the fact of modern war, and the undramatic, faintly humiliating, matter-of-fact discovery that decency recovers from that confrontation. Without heroics and without chatter, she tells us that "originality is . . . a by-product of sincerity"—that is, a moral phenomenon, like Pavlova's dancing—and for half a century now she has been demonstrating what that means. As she wrote of Eliot, "The effect of [such] confidences, elucidations, and precepts . . . is to disgust us with affectation; to encourage respect for spiritual humility; and to encourage us to do our ardent undeviating best with the medium in which we work." Auden was right; in reading Miss Moore, one responds as much to a person as to a work. (pp. 177-78)

> *George W. Nitchie, in his* Marianne Moore: An Introduction to the Poetry *(copyright © 1969 Columbia University Press; reprinted by permission of the publisher), Columbia University Press, 1969.*

*   *   *

MORANTE, Elsa   1918-

Morante is an Italian novelist and poet. Her work *History: A Novel* **is considered a major contribution to modern Italian literature.**

The very title of this enormous novel ["History: A Novel"], hailed by its publishers as the most important Italian work of fiction in a generation or more, is something of a provocation. It takes us back to an age when the novelist could confidently assume that he had authoritatively incorporated the actual movement of history into his imaginative inventions—to such a degree that some of the great fictional productions of the time bore subtitles like "A Chronicle of the 19th Century" and "A Study of Manners in the 19th Century." The technique of "History: A Novel" also harks back to the 19th century, particularly to the Naturalist novel, with its near-omniscient narrator deploying a huge cast of characters through a series of lower-class urban scenes. The book also has a distinct affinity—apart

from one significant exception, to which I shall return—with the Italian Neo-Realist films of the early postwar period.

The main action of the novel takes place in Rome between 1941 and 1947. Scarcely anyone higher on the social scale than a pimp or a juvenile delinquent is allowed into the book. . . . Ida Mancuso, the frail, shabby, uncomprehending widow who is the novel's heroine—though it may sound contradictory, I think Elsa Morante thinks of her as that—is an elementary school teacher, but she approaches her work with about the same mental set as if she were a charwoman or a five-and-dime salesgirl; and however she may cling with her fingertips to the brink of bourgeois propriety, she clearly belongs to the realm of the downtrodden and the oppressed that is the whole human world of this novel.

The physical setting through which these personages move is equally reminiscent of the Neo-Realist cinema: a vast war-scarred landscape of rubble, skeletons of bombed-out buildings, shanties crowded with refugees, incessant scavenging for food, black-market transactions, talking over the bad news in the hope things will somehow get better. The whole novel, in fact, is easily imaginable in grainy black-and-white. Actually, only on occasion does it allow itself a splash of color, often symbolic, like blood-red; and it avoids any self-conscious display of technique or personal style as it moves with a more or less fixed focus from one scene to the next.

The plot is a progress of disasters, from Ida Mancuso's rape by a young German soldier in 1941 to the death six years later of the visionary, epileptic child born of that violent union. Compassion, though it gets Morante into certain serious difficulties, is one of her great virtues as a novelist, and so, interestingly, this is a world of victims without any clearly visible victimizers, except for one walk-on appearance of *Wehrmacht* murderers. (pp. 7,34)

Each year of the novel's action is prefaced by a three- or four-page summary of the year's principal events in world politics. These summaries reflect a kind of simplified popular Marxism that has become all too familiar in the 1960's and 70's: Schematically and tendentiously, world disasters are attributed to the sinister machinations of big industry everywhere; and, by the concluding summary, even the clichés of the ecological apocalypticists (the poisoning of the environment with plastics, and so forth) are trundled out. The question is whether there are grains of truth in such formulas but whether they help the novelist in his work—and in this crucial respect I am afraid their effect is calamitous. . . .

It is, of course, pernicious nonsense to reduce all history to such a grossly leveling common denominator simply because at all times in history relationships of power have obtained among men. It is a way of not really thinking about history but of feeling about it, and feeling one thing—blind, seething resentment. . . .

Morante's compassion . . . frequently spills over into pathetic excess, and her tough realism breaks down into a tediously proliferated series of disasters rigged by the novelist against her own creations.

There is nothing beloved in the novel, be it cat, dog, child, man or woman, that does not end up being hideously destroyed, and the novelist will go 20 pages out of her way to catch a good last agony, even pursuing one quite peripheral character all the way to the Russian front in order to evoke his hallucinations as he expires from frostbite. Again and again, Morante is unable to resist a pathetic overload of detail and commentary. . . . (p. 34)

It seems to me that all the great 19th-century novels of politics and history—from ''The Charterhouse of Parma'' to ''Middlemarch,'' ''Germinal,'' ''The Possessed'' and ''War and Peace''—were built on some reasonably complex working hypothesis about what impels man as a political animal and about historical causation. Obviously I do not mean a ''correct'' hypothesis, but one sufficiently probing, subtle and flexible to help the novelist represent men and women in the flux of history with a satisfying psychological and political amplitude. It is because of this that the accounts of people in history rendered by these novels are still powerfully instructive.

When you assume that all history is a variation on the single theme of fascism, and that all evil—even, it would seem, a child's epilepsy inherited from the mother—is perpetrated by monolithic Powers not even allowed access to the scene of the novel, all that remains of historical experience is the pangs of victimhood; and those, after abundant repetition and heavy insistence, are likely to leave readers numbed—and with a sense that the sharpness of authorial indictment has finally been eroded by sentimentality.

For these reasons, ''History: A Novel'' does not really support the weight of all its encrusted details, though if it fails as a whole, it nevertheless has a good many arresting moments. The best of these, I would suggest, have very little to do with the crushing historical fatalism of the overall scheme. There is a peculiar Dostoyevskian visionary quality in Morante's writing that occasionally illuminates her somber Naturalist landscape. At a number of crucial junctures, she manages to carry out wonderful forays into the uncanny, moving from bleak earthbound things to metaphysical vistas. (pp. 34-5)

> *Robert Alter, ''The Setting, Rome 1941 to 1947,'' in* The New York Times Book Review *(© 1977 by The New York Times Company; reprinted by permission), April 24, 1977, pp. 7, 34-5.*

Luigi Barzini, in his book on the Italians, discusses the melancholy aspect of the Italian character which is so little observed by the rest of the world. But the Italian writers seem to wear their melancholy on their sleeves: or perhaps they are so sad that they cannot conceal it. I have often wondered why this is so. One reason may be that in Italy the consciousness of the modern poet or novelist reflects more poignantly than elsewhere the contrast between European Renaissance genius—evidences of which survive so dominatingly in Italy—and the hopelessly degraded vulgar modern scene.

Falling has symbolic force in Elsa Morante's *History: A Novel*. Her heroine, the schoolteacher Ida, suffered when she was a child from *le petit mal;* and her wonderfully poetic child Giuseppe has the epileptic's *grand mal*—which brings on his death. Giuseppe falls in horror as the result of the nightmares, such as deportation, air raids, and other forms of violence he witnesses, that are provided by History. Mussolini's empire was itself a fall into a terrible vulgarity of, alas, a peculiarly Italian kind, for which, alas, some of the Italian writers fell. This may partly explain their sadness. The worst fall of all—abominable even by Mussolini's own standards—forms the subject of this novel. This was the adoption by Mussolini of Hitler's racial laws and his cooperation, through deportations of Italian Jews to German concentration camps, with the program for the extermination of the Jews.

History covers the period of Fascism and takes place mainly in wartime and postwar Europe. Each section of the narrative is prefaced by an italicized summary of the public events immediately contemporaneous with the corresponding period in the lives of the characters. Thus lives are imprisoned within brackets provided by History. These events happened, of course, not just in Italy, but all over Europe, and in Russia and America. They were worldwide. Yet in Elsa Morante's novel they become canalized into Italian behavior, and they assume peculiarly Italian forms. So this is a novel really about things that happened in Italy, not about the outside world except in so far as it affected Italy. . . .

Within or beyond History, and apart from its victims, there is an effort of consciousness, of which *History,* with its almost invisible but omnipresent narrator ''I,'' is a heroic example. . . .

The tragedy of politics, as seen in *History,* is the inability of men to make politics human. This is no doubt a universal problem, but perhaps it is felt most intensely in Italy because of the particularly self-indulgent Italian upper class and bourgeoisie.

However to try to extract a message or lesson from Elsa Morante's book is to follow to literally the clue hinted at in the title. The story that she has to tell stands marvelously on its own. In outline it is extremely simple: being the account of the effects of an almost depersonalized History conducted by leaders who think of war as campaigns and of peace as a matter of ''spheres of influence'' upon the lives of impoverished victims. Elsa Morante's poor are those from whom History takes away even what they possess—their very lives. (p. 31)

Elsa Morante's treatment of Ida, or Iduzza (as she is often called), is close to Flaubert's of his heroine in *Une Vie Simple*. Indeed *History* is throughout written in the tradition of nineteenth-century realism. This may be because Italy, with its late pursuit of empire under Mussolini, had a twentieth-century history continuous with the nineteenth. Germany did not. Elsa Morante contrasts the figure of Mussolini with that of Hitler, writing that while both were dreamers, ''the dream-vision of the Italian Duce was a histrionic festival,'' ''whereas the other was . . . a formless dream . . . [in which] every living creature (including himself) was the object of torment. . . . And at the end—in the Grand Finale. . . .''

Mussolini's Italy, then, can be imagined within the continuity of the nineteenth-century realistic novel. In any case, this is a convention completely suited to Elsa Morante's gifts. She is a storyteller who spellbinds the reader. Like Flaubert she seems a great processional artist who can cover an enormous canvas, introducing, as the plot develops, new characters who are fixed and made convincing in a few swift strokes, and who are caught up in the sweep of the whole narrative. While in the largest tragic sense, *History* is a novel of doomed characters (the external history of the time ultimately destroys all humble and insulted private lives), it is also full of enchanting surprises, showing the immense vitality of the poor and oppressed. This vitality is particularly Italian and finds its place—or refuses to do so —within the pessimistic vision of history. (pp. 31-2)

Elsa Morante sees children in the light of their pathos, as Henry James also saw them. And in its way the portrait of Giuseppe is the most inspired invention in this book. . . .

[She] has an uncanny understanding of Roman boys and of their dogs, and never translates into language signs of childishness or animality beyond the point where they are convincing to us. . . . [Only] fantastic imagination can sustain this story of the crushing reality of the History which destroys so many of its victims. (p. 32)

"Consciousness" in the latter half of the novel is shared by Giuseppe with his amazing gift of happiness and by Davide with his tormented conscience of the anarchist in revolt against his bourgeois forebears. But in them, as in everyone else in this novel, consciousness is doomed to destruction by History. Giuseppe develops the symptoms of a more extreme form of epilepsy than his mother's. This may or may not be inherited from her, but the profounder significance of the attacks which make him fall are the shocks he has received from glimpses of the workings of History in air raids, deportations, and the solitude to which he is condemned. . . .

The form which Davide's personal tragedy takes is also that of a defect which might seem inherited: the drug addiction of a very bourgeois aunt who had been the object of his greatest contempt when he was a child. But the real significance of his auto-intoxication is of course the utter contradiction between his humanist political faith and History. (p. 33)

The point is very strongly made in [Elsa Morante's] account of the lives of her characters that their fates are scarcely affected by the Allied landings, the liberation of Europe, the meetings between leaders cutting up the world into spheres of influence. The reader may protest that although the disasters in the lives of poor little doomed Useppe and Ida his mother and Davide the partisan hero are convincing, the political generalizations drawn from this are too pessimistic.

Here we are brought back to the particular case of Italy, or rather of Rome and the scandal of the Roman bourgeoisie. Reading *History* we are reminded of the preface that an English poet of the First World War, Wilfred Owen, wrote to his *Poems:* "All a poet can do today is to warn." As it bears on politics *History* provides a gravely pessimistic warning. But this is alleviated—contradicted at times—by the immense vitality of the life described. (pp. 33-4)

The novel's last words are, ". . . and History continues. . . ." The tragic end is of course inevitable, imposed by Elsa Morante's view of History and perhaps also by the nineteenth-century form she has chosen. The great virtue of her novel however is that although the reader accepts the inevitable ending, the life conveyed works as much against tragedy as for it. . . .

Elsa Morante creates, paradoxically, more life than death in this tragic and pessimistic novel, whose visionary force lies not so much in the fate of her little band of doomed victims as in the nightmare of a period of history which had no regard for these lives. . . . [and] in altered form still goes on today. Read the news from Italy. "History continues." (p. 34)

> *Stephen Spender, "Melancholic and Magic History," in* The New York Review of Books *(reprinted with permission from* The New York Review of Books; *copyright ©*

1977 NYREV, Inc.), April 28, 1977, pp. 31-4.

      *   *   *

MURDOCH, (Jean) Iris   1919-

An Irish-born English novelist and playwright, Murdoch is a prolific writer concerned with ethics. Her characters struggle to realize their spiritual, psychological, and philosophical beings in an absurd world, which is often depicted through the tragicomic or fantastical. (See also *CLC*, Vols. 1, 2, 3, 4, 6, and *Contemporary Authors*, Vols. 13-16, rev. ed.)

[*The Sacred and Profane Love Machine*] is a dreadful mess. There are some excellent scenes, but much wasteful floundering, too. As she begins a novel, Murdoch seems to commit herself to a central situation and then to rely on her talent to uncover what exciting scenes lie inherent in that situation. If it works out, fine; if not, start another novel. . . .

So there are three or four scenes of bizarre energy about a third of the way through the novel. But then what? Murdoch didn't ask, or if she did, she accepted bad answers. . . . Murdoch must call on one of her typical collection of ghastly misfits to take over, sexually kinky and emotionally scarred to the last person. The last half of the novel is awful, one big and boring scene after another, each taking the novel further from its ostensible interest. . . . Murdoch must finish every novel she starts, she accepts strong feelings for interesting feelings, she prefers scenes to people—so both she and her reader have to take their chances. Murdoch's characters are twenty years older than they were in *Under the Net*, they are occupationally more settled and have grown children and some occasionally die, but they and their author are essentially the same. Yet she could right now be careening blindly and with joy into a masterpiece. (p. 18)

> *Roger Sale, in* The New York Review of Books *(reprinted with permission from* The New York Review of Books; *copyright ©* *1974 NYREV, Inc.), December 12, 1974.*

Not by any means for the first time I marvel at the combination in Miss Murdoch's novels of perceptive realism (and high, really high, intelligence) with absurd gratuitous fantasy. People just do not behave as these people do—but they live where these people live, they endure the same weather and the same electricity cuts, and they even think, in part, the same thoughts. The setting is dominant in [*A Word Child*] and is marvellously pervasive. The weather is uniformly wintry and wet, except for the enchanted flashback to summer in Oxford; the London scenery—Hyde Park, Kensington Gardens, Bayswater Road, the Inner Circle—is lovingly dwelt upon, and geographically detailed. The fantasy, in contrast, is all the more worrying. Perhaps this is the point: a fairy tale set in the familiar backyard, laced, as usual, with quotations from Wittgenstein. (Why? The hero was not even a philosopher in his academic days.)

But the fairytale does not quite work. For besides the plot, there are also questions that are supposed to be raised in reflecting on it. (p. 519)

The best passage in the book comes when the chance of reconciliation, salvation, whatever it will be, is presented to Hilary by the second wife of his new chief. Everything is ambiguous, unclear: not only what the outcome will be, but what he actually has to do is uncertain. [The] language is

Jamesian. The whole scheme is 'magnificent'; but what *is* it? We are given the authentic sense of complexity, significance and infinite possibilities. All the questions are, as they should be, implicit. How long can a man be responsible for the consequences of his acts? Can doing anything let him off? If he does not believe in God, can he properly make use, as he wants to, of concepts such as forgiveness or redemption? Is feeling guilt or resentment just a habit?

But, alas, none of these questions can be considered for long in the context of *A Word Child,* and not only because they have been too crudely brought to our notice. For to answer them one would have to consider them, not in general, but in relation to the particular people in the novel, and how their actions and sufferings arose out of their characters and out of their pasts. No such consideration is possible: apart from the central, Jamesian section, the rest is too fantastic. Too much happens, and in the end we begin to feel that absolutely *anything* could happen. Once implausibility has taken over, once the connection is lost between what happens and what makes sense, then however much we may be urged to raise questions, there ceases to be any point in raising them with regard to *these* people and *these* events. We could answer them any way we pleased. If the book had ended in the middle, we should have been left to reflect. As it is, we are left with some sharpened perceptions . . . of what falling in love can be like, and what it is like on the Inner Circle. Perhaps this is better than nothing. (pp. 519-20)

> *Mary Warnock, "Inner Circles," in* New Statesman (© *1975 The Statesman & Nation Publishing Co. Ltd.), April 18, 1975, pp. 519-20.*

There was a graceful, intelligent completeness to Iris Murdoch's earliest work; and yet it is hard to think of another novelist who has developed so much. Her confidence increases with each book, as she faces and solves new technical problems (and here each technical problem is a moral one), incorporating her achievement into the texture of her writing, always digesting, so that themes which formed the central problematic of one work appear as powerful details or almost invisible underpinnings in another. By now the strongest impression is of great resource, and equally great economy. Iris Murdoch uses precisely as much energy as is called for.

Henry and Cato is not one of the handful which stand out as watersheds among her novels. This must be said for accuracy's sake, but still seems churlish in the face of such a fine book. It could be seen as her *All's Well That Ends Well,* perhaps—a major, mature and characteristic work, but not destined to be anybody's favourite. . . .

For some time now Iris Murdoch has been telling us what all great artists seem to say if they live long enough: that there is nothing to tell. 'The point is one will never get to the end of it, never get to the bottom of it, never, never, never'. We live, as one of her characters does, 'surrounded by mysteries'; the pursuit of that ultimate mystery which might be called perfection will yield many rich by-products, but only when they are known to be worthless in comparison with the infinitely receding perspective that will never be grasped.

The theme of *Henry and Cato* is truth—or better, mystery. Things are seldom what they seem; skimmed milk masquerades as cream. The book reaches a tentative present tense at the conclusion of Part One—'it is the end of the story,'

thinks Cato, 'the end of a story' echoes Henry; then Part Two unmakes the characters' lives and knits them up again quite differently. The Turn, the Pause, the Counter-Turn: everyone's dearest idol shows feet of clay, their image of themselves, or their self-serving interpretations of others. Iris Murdoch ruthlessly demonstrates that we can never see the 'truth' of the situation, that the demand is inappropriate, or made of the wrong reality. She demonstrates also that the transcendent reality on which we consciously or unconsciously call, in making that demand, cannot be caught in the nets of thought.

In *Henry and Cato,* the inexpressible enters the plot perhaps more directly and freely than in Iris Murdoch's other novels. She has the confidence. Her symbols have less Ibsen-like starkness, they no longer so stridently proclaim their crucial rôle, but emerge from the background when internal logic requires them. There is also perhaps a new stylistic playfulness. But by and large, *Henry and Cato* is a characteristic Murdoch novel; and needs no further recommendation. (p. 19)

> *Nick Totton, in* The Spectator (© *1976 by* The Spectator; *reprinted by permission of* The Spectator), *September 25, 1976.*

Henry and Cato is not a startling new development in the work of Iris Murdoch—her essentially 19th-century way of writing and working has an even temper that renders revolution unnecessary. The novel is rather a consolidation, another star for her literary firmament. . . .

Her new book is about two childhood friends, who have drifted far apart, coming to wrenching turning points in their lives. The corner, the sudden turn is a key device in Murdoch's novels to give her characters a hint of what lies behind them and a glimpse of the road ahead. Henry Marshalson and Cato Forbes are no longer young and both face a crisis. For Henry, the death of his hated elder brother precipitates him from peaceful, self-elected exile at a small mid-Western college, to being lord of the manor at Laxlinden Hall. Cato, meanwhile has become a Roman Catholic priest. As Henry flies back to England to assume his new role, Cato faces alone in a decaying London mission house a shattering challenge to his religious calling. His passion for God the Son has been supplanted by his consuming, so far platonic love for Beautiful Joe, the young tough with the shining hair and hexagonal glasses.

In different and diffuse ways both men fail to ride their crises. Both return home to be greeted as prodigal sons, Henry to his scheming unloving mother, and Cato to his domineering insensitive father. The interweaving of the parallel stories is endless and fascinating and it is a measure of Murdoch's superb craft that the effect, like that of classical ballet, is one of effortless grace, the labor and the discipline quite hidden. Henry has a widowed mother, Cato a widowed father; Henry a brother, Cato a sister; Henry rejects his inheritance, Cato his religious faith; Henry lusts for his brother's mistress, a self-styled tart who is actually a typist; Cato lusts for a son of the slums, a small-time Irish crook. The symmetry is part of the complex pattern, yet is never strained or artificial. "The only writer I am sure has influenced me is Henry James," Murdoch has said. "He's a pattern man too."

Cato's failure to repel the assault on his priesthood leads to violence and death. It also sets the stage for some brilliantly executed cerebral discourses between Cato and Brendan, his fellow priest and spiritual mentor, that lay bare the bones of faith and the loss of faith.

The strong religious theme in *Henry and Cato* brings us inevitably to the question of Murdoch and the philosophical novel. She seems to construe the description as pejorative and has herself criticized the novels of Jean-Paul Sartre for being deadened by the weight of the message they carry. Her novels do not, in fact, stand or fall on their philosophy. They are built on the strength of their characterization and this is especially true of *Henry and Cato*. . . . (pp. K3-4)

The philosophical content of the novel, like its intricate patterns, blends into the whole. On rare occasions, when the blending is not complete, there are slight flaws of ommission and some unrounded characters. The scene is not set carefully enough for the happily-ever-after ending for Henry and Colette, Cato's sister. To make Henry's failure significant, his destiny should be more believable. Cato's protege, Beautiful Joe, is almost a caricature of the beautiful body and the rotten soul. It is hard to get any real sense of his deprived background or of the underworld that has molded him. Murdoch, who feels he is an important character, both admits and regrets his inadequacy. "I didn't quite know what Joe was like," she told an interviewer. "I feel if I could have made him a more sympathetic character without being in any way sentimental about him, it might have been a better book."

But fine writers are notoriously perfectionist. Despite the author's reservations, *Henry and Cato* succeeds in both entertaining and in contributing to our understanding of the muddles of mankind. It is a substantial and satisfying book. (p. K4)

> *Brigitte Weeks, "Weaving the Tapestry of the Prodigal Sons," in* Book World—The Washington Post (© The Washington Post), *January 9, 1977, pp. K3-4.*

Certainly the reader of any of Iris Murdoch's other 17 novels finds ["Henry and Cato"] easy enough to negotiate. I myself confess to having read those 17 all the way through (except "The Italian Girl," which was too feeble to finish) but to what apparent purpose or with what cumulative response I cannot say. There are few contemporary novelists who, page by page, perform in such a lively and interesting manner on such a range of subjects and materials; yet who when the pages are taken together and up to so little. (p. 4)

It could be argued that, as in Iris Murdoch's other fiction, we are dealing with the satirist's vision of things, a cold eye cast at how (in language from "Henry and Cato") "human beings are endlessly ingenious about promoting their own misery." Almost 20 years ago in her essay "The Sublime and the Beautiful" she spoke eloquently of how in great novels "the individuals portrayed are free, independent of their author . . . not merely puppets," also of how "The great novelist is not afraid of the contingent." What has happened, with varying degrees of success in the many novels since this reflection, is that Murdoch has been endlessly ingenious about promoting the miseries of her characters; moreover, she has not only not feared the contingent, she has downright cultivated it, dragged it in wilfully and held it under the reader's nose. It is a subtle form of bullying, as if to say "so you thought prudence or common sense *ever* had any effect an *anybody's* behavior, did you? Well, take this!"

At the same time she has been sparing (unlike, say, Amis or Anthony Powell or Mary McCarthy) of witty and trenchant comment on the human foibles she depicts. There is, apart from the machinations of plot, relatively little pleasure to be taken in her narrative voice. And while her unwillingness to exteriorize "some closely locked psychological conflict of [her] own" may be discreet, it makes the novels, for all their preoccupation with ideas and motives, a good deal less psychologically interesting than one could wish.

What is truly entertaining and permanently valuable about her work are its descriptions of place: of an English landscape, a country house's architecture, the inside of a greenhouse, or the abandoned air raid shelter where Cato is held prisoner by Beautiful Joe. One most remembers from the earlier novels events like prying the car out of the river in "The Sandcastle"; the flowers and the Tintoretto of "An Unofficial Rose"; Effingham in the boggy quicksand of "The Unicorn"; stations on the London underground in "A Word Child"—anything that has to do with how things work or how they look to the eyes and mind of an incredibly perspicacious observer. In that sense all her books are literally spectacular; it would be surprising if at the same time, with but a change of focus, she could also produce elegant or humanly touching analyses of individual miseries. The air of the books is all too feverish, the excited pushing of coincidence and contingency all too stage-center, for that. She has chosen, or been chosen, to write a lot —nine longish novels in the last 10 years! Like the rest of them, "Henry and Cato" should be read as engaging and striking work; though I suspect it will seldom be reread. (pp. 4, 24)

> *William H. Pritchard, "Murdoch's Eighteenth," in* The New York Times Book Review (© *1977 by The New York Times Company; reprinted by permission), January 16, 1977, pp. 4, 24.*

N

NABOKOV, Vladimir   1899-1977

Nabokov was born in Russia, educated in England, became a U.S. citizen in 1945, and lived the last years of his life in Switzerland. His eclectic nature is evident in his mastery of many genres, having written, in both Russian and English, novels, short stories, poetry, essays, and plays, as well as biography, autobiography, criticism, and translations. The wit, ingenuity, and genius of his work have earned Nabokov a permanent place in world literature. (See also *CLC,* Vols. 1, 2, 3, 6, and *Contemporary Authors,* Vols. 5-8, rev. ed.; obituary, Vols. 69-72.)

[In *Poems and Problems* Nabokov] not only translates but brings in the theory of translation. He has collected thirty-nine poems written by himself in Russian and translated by himself into English; fourteen poems written in English; and eighteen chess problems. The book is presented in the manner of a "classic," with line numbers for the Russian poems, introduction, some notes, and a "bibliography," which is not really that but a full record of previous publication. Nabokov refuses to apologize for including the chess problems. I welcome them, but refuse to apologize for not reviewing them.

The Russian poems are, we are told, only a small selection from a much larger body. The earliest is dated 1917, the latest 1967, overlapping those composed in English. Nabokov testily deplores émigré poetry and tries not to be wistful, even pleads insincerity, but many of these pieces fail to escape a feeling of lost Russia and lost childhood, the difficulty a Russian poet forever outside Russia finds in writing poetry. . . . What of the self-translation? Here, as elsewhere, Nabokov insists on strict fidelity. With and for this, we have to put up with oddities. There are many, many inverted phrases. For instance: "To my alarm clock its lesson I set." Whatever excuses may be offered, that is a pretty awful line. . . . Foreign idioms and constructions can come into English and generate new dimensions and new English, as in the King James Bible, but these versions by Nabokov seem unassimilated and uncomfortable. Further, anapests, Nabokov's "beloved anapests" have a way (despite the example of Swinburne) of coming out bumpy in English . . ., like driving on a flat. Also, as Nabokov describes the metre, "tra-tá-ta tra-tá-ta tra-tá," the lines are not really anapests, they're amphibrachs.

In most of the English-composed poems (but not in the unaccountable "Ballad of Longwood Glen"), the awkwardness vanishes. Nabokov's virtuosity in English is manifest from his prose, tiresome as that can sometimes be. "Ode to a Model" has charmed me long since, but Nabokov seems really at his best in "An Evening of Russian Poetry" as he lectures to an imaginary girls' school on the qualities of that poetry. . . . Always the one-upman, Nabokov patronizes his imaginary audience and his reader; this poem is, nevertheless, mellow, beautiful, and wise. (pp. 506-08)

Richmond Lattimore, in The Hudson Review *(copyright © 1971 by The Hudson Review, Inc.; reprinted by permission), Vol. XXIV, No. 3, Autumn, 1971.*

Of Nabokov's works, *Lolita* . . . , *Pale Fire* . . . , and *Ada* . . . belong to the Literature of Exhaustion. [Elsewhere in his book, *The Literature of Exhaustion,* Stark defines the Literature of Exhaustion, using a label supplied by John Barth. The identifying characteristic of the Literature, according to Barth, is that writers of it pretend that it is next to impossible to write original—perhaps any—literature. In other words, some writers use as a theme for new works of literature the hypothesis that literature is finished.]

Nabokov constructs Chinese boxes . . . to undermine the conventional distinctions between the real and imaginary domains. (p. 63)

Nabokov uses Chinese boxes most subtly in *Pale Fire,* and in that book he makes them crucial to the meaning. In this novel, Nabokov is the outermost layer, followed by *Pale Fire,* which . . . contains the dividing line between the real and the imaginary. Botkin, the fairly well hidden teller of the tale, is the third layer, and the pseudonym he uses, Kinbote, is the fourth layer. Next come the commentary and the index, which tell the story of Zembla and its king. . . . Most critics have followed one of Nabokov's false trails, deducing from the many references to Pope in *Pale Fire* that the Zembla mentioned in *Essay on Man* is the relevant one. That reference, however, either does not apply or, if a relation is forced, the subject matter of the quotation from Pope puts *Pale Fire* in a moral light, in which it will not be able to live for long. In Swift's *Battle of the Books,* however, "a malignant Deity, call'd *Criticism*" lives on a mountain in Nova Zembla. This malignant deity and its priest, Kinbote, obfuscate the next layer, John Shade's poem "Pale Fire." The last layer is Shade, who belongs inside his poem rather than outside it because he has written an autobiographical work that reveals, and in a sense controls, him. (p. 64)

Actually, the author and his book (the latter in one sense only) are real; any layer inside them—actually *in* the novel —is imaginary, and none of these inside layers has more reality than any other. . . . [Nabokov] claims that the imagination is the supreme, if not the only, reality. Out of these ideas arise the central paradoxes of the Literature of Exhaustion: this kind of literature creates, by using the premise that the imaginary realm of fiction is exhausted, works of fiction that assert the primacy of the imagination and add to the total number of fictional works. (p. 65)

Nabokov's opinion about the reality of [the] everyday world to a large extent determines the kind of literature that he writes. He shares with [Jorge Luis] Borges one of his main premises, that realism is misguided, though he does not hold to this premise quite as rigorously as the other writer. His bluntest statement about the status of reality appears in his *Paris Review* interview, when he says simply that "everyday reality" does not exist. The most important word in this phrase of course is "everyday," for he does not subscribe to nihilism; he merely believes that other kinds of reality have more claim to men's allegiance. Sometimes he uses more clever and more indirect methods to convince readers of this. Readers of *Pale Fire* who can step back and see what kind of responses they have been limited to by the book can understand that they have been tricked into taking their eyes off the everyday world. A reader of *Pale Fire* must choose from among three entities that claim to be real. One is the poem, away from which Kinbote, the second entity, turns almost completely. Once a reader sees the discrepancy between the poem and Kinbote's criticism, he seeks a third entity to serve as a touchstone, and he can find one in the fictive realm that the novel creates. However, this novel has two settings: Zembla and New Wye, and two different actions. This complicated interaction among rival realities demands the reader's attention, so he turns his back on the everyday world from which he emerged to read the novel. At least while he reads *Pale Fire,* if he does not resist the author's pressure, he sets aside everyday reality, and perhaps this will become habit forming. (pp. 67-8)

Among Nabokov's books, *Pale Fire* makes the most persuasive case that genuine reality must be found in unexpected places and can be discovered only by unusual means. (p. 69)

In *Ada* Nabokov less vigorously opposes everyday reality than he does in his two previous books. At least, he hesitates to attack the part of reality that contains nature. His more mellow attitude includes respect for another way of knowing besides literature: science. This new position should hardly seem surprising in light of his fascination, since childhood, with nature. He is a lepidopterist of professional competence and the author of a number of scientific articles. Before his most recent novel, however, he had used his scientific knowledge mainly as a source of metaphors, but in *Ada* the title character is a scientist. Also, she and her lover/brother, Van, a philosopher and writer, represent, for one thing, the two sides of their creator's personality. The incest theme in this novel functions partly to show that scientific and literary interests can exist harmoniously in the same person. It follows from this compatibility that the imagination can also connect with reality, because "reality and natural science are synonymous in the terms of

this, and only this, dream". . . . The dream is the imaginative world of *Ada.*

Nabokov still does not believe that everyday reality and science, and the common domain of both—nature—can replace the imagination as the dominant reality. A writer, however, can make metaphors from them. Ada, because of her scientific training, has a higher opinion than Van of the world of nature, but Nabokov points out her mistake. . . . [Later] in the book Ada herself loses much of her fascination with science. Science commits sins of omission, not commission; within its limits science and its object of study, nature, are wondrous. In this novel Nabokov does not maintain his earlier interest in nature as a freak show, a conception that also denigrates science. . . . Rather, in *Ada* Nabokov draws exquisite, nearly paradisiacal nature scenes, and he uses the full splendor of his prose style to describe a nature that is anything but hostile to man's imagination.

Even in *Ada,* however, nature by itself cannot nourish man. Its beauty serves only as material for the imagination to turn into art. Clearly, Nabokov himself has done this, both in his set-piece descriptions of nature and in the natural metaphors and images that he sprinkles so thickly throughout the novel. (pp. 71-2)

Nabokov's work . . . continually cries out that it is art or artifice. In his recent work he gradually develops from creating quite conventional types of artifice in *Lolita* and *Pale Fire* to creating more original and subtle types in *Ada.* All three novels, however, clearly belong to the Literature of Exhaustion. *Lolita* contains notes purportedly written by proofreaders and included by mistake, and the hand of the master always pokes through holes in his puppets' costumes. He continually suggests that another person is using the narrator as a ventriloquist's dummy; for example, he reveals information that Humbert cannot know. He also has Quilty, too, supply information that this character has no plausible way of knowing. The peculiar form of *Pale Fire*—poem and critical commentary—calls attention to this novel's artificiality, too.

He does not abandon this technique in *Ada.* Ada's marginal notes and interpolated passages of narrative, editor's notes and even study questions and a blurb at the very end of the novel perform the same function that the artificial devices in the other books do. Nabokov also underscores the fact that *Ada* is a novel by frequently referring to other novels and commenting on narrative technique. (p. 77)

Nabokov uses an enormous number of allusions, but unlike Borges, he sometimes misleads with his allusions. Often he plants them in order to lead down wrong paths critics who think they can match learning with him. One must be particularly wary of the allusions in *Lolita,* which can cause many frustrated expectations. Most of the references to Poe's works and to Merimée's *Carmen* create false scents, the latter because they indicate that Humbett will kill Lolita. (p. 79)

Ada, despite its recent publication, has been quite thoroughly searched for allusions. John Updike, Robert Alter, and Alfred Appel have found and explained the references to Chateaubriand, Tolstoy, Marvell's "The Garden," and some less important sources, Carl Proffer has identified many allusions to Russian literature, and other critics have also made useful contributions. (p. 81)

Nabokov does not merely play games with all these allusions. True, because of them and other features, reading him is sometimes exasperating.... He needs these allusions, however, to demonstrate that authors make literature, above all, from other literature, not from life. This belief is, by itself, one of the precursors of the Literature of Exhaustion and, combined with other attitudes, part of that kind of literature. (p. 82)

Nabokov prefers to play games rather than make myths. His work, besides its allusions, contains many puns—sometimes multilingual—anagrams and other puzzles. Most of these produce one of two fleeting effects, depending on whether or not the reader understands them: a feeling of satisfaction and perhaps a chuckle or an annoyed grunt. Many of his puns make fun of Freud: Lajoyeux, Froid, Signy-Mondieu-Mondieu. Once in a while Nabokov plays for higher stakes, as he does when he composes an anagram in *Ada*. The three main characters form three anagrams from "insect": "scient," "incest" and "nicest." It would be possible to organize around these four words a fairly perceptive analysis of this novel, since they introduce the love, nature, and philosophy themes, evaluate them and hint at the tone of the book.

Characteristically, Nabokov plays these games to discredit realism. For one thing, they distract the reader from character conflicts, social background and other elements that would lead him to a realistic interpretation of this novel. To put it another way, Nabokov's novels are to realistic novels as solving chess problems is to playing chess. In *Speak, Memory* Nabokov compares writing novels to composing chess problems, for in both the battle is not between the pieces on the board but between the person who placed them in position and the solver, who tries to see the pattern.... For another thing, these games provide the reader with a glimpse of a plane of existence more fascinatingly intricate than the mundane world. In the world of magic, the most appropriate metaphor for this plane, exotic, law-defying things happen and the magician has total control. Kinbote compares Shade to a conjurer, "perceiving and transforming the world, taking it in and taking it apart, recombining its elements in the very process of storing them up so as to produce at some unspecified date an organic miracle, a fusion of image and music, a line of verse".... Nabokov makes the same comparison between art and magic in *Speak, Memory,* and compares nature to both.... (pp. 84-5)

Depending on his intent, he parodies or imitates a great number of genres: in *Lolita*, the case study, the novel of the double, detective stories and pornography; in *Pale Fire,* the critical edition; and in *Ada*, letters, essays and the drama. He uses other genres most impressively in *Pale Fire*, because his use is probably original and because he keeps it up for the entire book. In it, mere parody soon gives way to creative imitation, and he invents a new hybrid form for future novelists. (p. 85)

Nabokov manipulates genres to attack realism, thereby again exemplifying the Literature of Exhaustion. His most daring imitation of forms—imitating a critical edition in *Pale Fire* and turning philosophy into a novel in *Ada*—imply that the form of the novel has indeed been exhausted and that novels, if they are to be written at all, must now be written in other guises.

Nabokov most frequently develops the theme of time, and of course he does not accept the conventional notions of chronological and chronometric time that form the under-

pinnings of realistic fiction. Rather, he redefines time; in *Ada*, which contains his most significant development of this theme, he yearns to organize time for nonrealistic writers. To understand more fully the theme of time in *Ada*, it probably would be best to double back quickly to its appearance in *Lolita* and *Pale Fire*. The opening of *Lolita* seems to imply that Humbert desperately pursues his nymphet in order to recreate the timeless past of his childhood by recreating Annabel in Lolita.... He tries to achieve timelessness first through his imaginative transformation of Lolita from a rather barbarous little girl into an icon, from pupa to butterfly. Thus, he accomplishes a watered-down version of an artistic transformation; but he also achieves the latter by narrating the book. In other words, he accomplishes two metamorphoses: changing Lolita from pupa to butterfly and changing the story of his first transformation from raw subject matter into art.

John Shade in *Pale Fire* also seeks timelessness, but his motives need to be examined; in fact, he insists on having them examined. Afraid that his fragile heart will give out, he tries in two ways to escape time. First, he strives to attain an eternal afterlife, a task at which he will probably fail, as indicated by his pathetic attempt to check his conception of eternity with someone else who seems to have the same conception. A long trip and a meeting with this other person end in disappointment when he learns that their apparent agreement resulted from a typographical error. His other method, creating poetry, has more promise, but, it, too, probably will not work for him. His kind of art, autobiographical poetry, does not lift him out of the stream of time; it thrusts him back into it. Furthermore, his motive taints his creative work because it turns that work to a nonaesthetic purpose. (pp. 87-8)

Nabokov describes a lost timeless realm more fully in *Ada* than he does in *Lolita*. Ardis Hall exists outside of time, which the comparisons of it with Eden indicate. In the biblical version of an atemporal realm the onset of sexual awareness begins the time sequence, forcing Adam and Eve, following a burning brand, to leave their paradise of timelessness. The opposite happens in *Ada*, because the first sex act brings on a kind of timelessness for Van and Ada by making them invincible to mundane ravages like those of time. And the fire, a burning barn, conveniently removes possible spectators so that the two children can enjoy each other. They even in a sense escape God, because in *Ada* he is Log, the record of time....

One can defeat time also by turning away from the future to the past. If he can recapture the past and link it with the present, he can perceive time with perfect clarity and give the present moment the richest possible texture. Van accomplishes this, or has it accomplished for him, when Ada calls him after they had lost contact with each other for many years.... She is the past he has sought, not, as Humbert sought Annabel, in the guise of another or represented by someone whose reality he denies, but for herself and as she really is. He loves Ada in a way both aesthetically more sophisticated and emotionally more meaningful than Humbert loves Lolita. (p. 89)

Nabokov presents his theory of time in bits and pieces throughout his work, mainly in *Ada*, but when he reassembles it, it proves to be logical and of great use to a novelist. First, he assumes that the proper goal of an artist is to create timelessness; the realists err in thinking that they should recreate time by imitating real, or at least plausible, actions. He, but not the realists, can accomplish his goal because, although the intervals between events exist in time, events are timeless, if they have texture. If an artist adds texture to events, he will add vitality and meaning to them by shaping them aesthetically, putting them into patterns and describing them in all their complexity. Before he can add texture to a present event, it slips into the past, so he must call it up by means of memory, which connects past and present. Memory enables the imagination to work on the event and give it texture. An artist can easily make this retrieval, for the available past consists of images, the perfect raw material for the creative imagination. (p. 90)

Nabokov works much less with the theme of space than he does with the theme of time. He brings it into his books occasionally, however, to show that commonsense ideas are mistaken. He creates a purely imaginative country, Zembla, in *Pale Fire* to attack space, but only mildly. Kinbote, Zembla's creator, uses an old strategy, merely adding facts so that Zembla resembles Slavic countries closely enough to make this invention seem almost realistic like, say, Hardy's Wessex. Nabokov sets *Lolita* in a painfully familiar America and conventionally uses the spatial setting in this novel. Only in *Ada* does he make a determined effort to disrupt his readers' ideas about space. On Terra countries of our world combine and mix in what appears to be an émigrée's view of geography. For example, Kaluga's waters are near Ladore, which from other references like Bryant's Castle (Chillon) can be recognized as equivalent to Lake Geneva, on which Nabokov now lives. But its sound associates it with two other places in the author's life, Lake Cayuga—the waters of which are mentioned in the song of Cornell University, where he taught—and Luga, a town south of the Nabokov estate in Russia. This shuffling of space contributes less to the novel than does the transformation of ordinary space into artistic space by means of dozens of references to painters and descriptions of scenes as if they were paintings. These last two techniques are analogous to his transformation of ordinary time into artistic time. (pp. 93-4)

Nabokov does not propose that life is a dream. He has some trouble developing this theme, because he has to fend off the Freudians with one hand so he has only one hand left to delineate his own theory of dreams. In *Transparent Things* he makes fun of Freudian psychology in a long section about dreams. He handles this subject most cogently in a brief passage in *Ada*. . . . There he answers Freud by claiming that the improbabilities in dreams have little significance; they merely indicate that a person's mind works less rationally when he dreams than it does when he is awake. Nabokov also, in the person of Van, denies dream symbolism as well as other kinds of symbolism and will admit the validity only of metaphors. On the positive side, Van says that the two most interesting kinds of dreams are the erotic and the professional. Again *contra* Freud, he sees nothing remarkable in dreaming about the sexual aspects of women who interest him. His professional dreams mix his roles of writer and dreamer; for example, phrases he has recently composed influence his dreams. This last notion is the closest Nabokov gets to Borges's position, but this analogy between art and dream differs a good deal from the other writer's extensive claims. (p. 100)

Because of its pervasiveness in Nabokov's work, another theme of the Literature of Exhaustion is difficult to isolate and describe. Nabokov argues again and again that reality is purely linguistic. His hundreds of puns and other bits of verbal magic call attention to language as language instead of letting it be a transparent medium through which a reader sees action. Baroque passages—most notably the beginning of *Ada*—have the same effect. . . . In *Pale Fire* he clearly transposes the names of two proponents of the heroic couplet, making Wordsmith and Goldsworth, but this trick is more complicated. Nabokov hides a moral there, too: the worker with words is worth gold. Humbert's cry "I have only words to play with" makes a fine summary of Nabokov's attitude on this subject—if one removes the "only," for, just perhaps, words are everything.

Critics have almost sufficiently analyzed the crucial theme of metamorphosis. It appears most prominently in *Lolita*. The butterfly imagery in this novel and elsewhere is the most interesting example. . . . If anyone has written a modern version of Ovid's *Metamorphoses* it is Nabokov, and he has done it for an involuted purpose: to argue against the world view of the realists. If the world continually changes guises, or can be made to do so by a writer of the Literature of Exhaustion, a realist cannot describe it, much less explain it. It will take an equally Protean art to explain it, an art that, with puns and other verbal and technical tricks, transforms itself constantly before the eyes of the reader. The brightly colored kaleidoscopic world of Nabokov's fiction does exactly that.

This theme of transformation pervades his work and subsumes two other themes. . . . One is process; a world full of transforming objects always changes. The theme of opposites appears somewhat more independently in Nabokov's works, but often these opposites merge, like the artistic Van and the scientific Ada, in incest, or one of the opposites changes into the other, and this theme fades away. In either case the pairs of opposites in his work do not remain stable, which chips away at another cornerstone of realism because it contradicts one of realism's most important modes of thought: dialectics.

Besides artist-layman and realist-nonrealist, Nabokov also contrasts adult and childlike modes of thought. The splendor of the child's dreamlike world more closely resembles the artist's world and is thus superior to adult thought. The most idyllic scenes in *Ada* appear early in the book and describe Van and Ada's childhood at Ardis Hall. Despite their precocity, they see things then through the eyes of children. They try to prolong this existence, and after they, inevitably, lose it, they try to recapture it. Humbert, too, wants to return to his childhood. (pp. 101-03)

Nabokov, however, does not yearn for childhood in itself. Rather, he wants the opportunity to remember a past time, indeed a past that he did not completely understand when he experienced it. Such malleable material attracts an artist. Even Humbert recognizes this. He admits that during his childhood Annabel was not a nymphet; she became one only after twenty-nine years of remembering have shaped his recollection of her. . . . Remembrance of things past is also one of the central experiences in Nabokov's own life. Neither the financial nor political implications of the Russian Revolution make that event disastrous for him. He mourns the premature ending of his childhood. However, he has learned to turn this misfortune into an advantage. In *Speak, Memory* he says, "the nostalgia I have been cherishing all these years is a hypertrophied sense of lost childhood, not sorrow for lost banknotes". . . . His phrasing is significant, for he says that he cherishes his sense of childhood. "Cherishing" is of course positive, and his *sense* of his childhood, not that childhood itself, attracts him. . . .

Sex, like childhood, provides an attractive escape from the everyday existence in which realists immerse themselves. To prove this Nabokov must refute the man who has preempted the topic and enraged him: Freud. Nabokov detests Freud mainly for arguing that not an artist but something else, such as sex, causes art. In *Lolita* he bluntly counters Freud: "sex is but the ancilla of art".... He presents as evidence this book itself, proof, first, that art can subordinate sex to its own purposes, using it for instance to develop themes like memory and metamorphosis. *Lolita* also demonstrates that an artist, if he has enough skill, can describe sexual eccentricities or any other seemingly taboo subject so as to make them at least acceptable to a reader, and perhaps even make the reader see beauty in the descriptions of them. He also uses other methods to make sexual peculiarities acceptable in a novel. For example, he makes them symbolic in order to deflect attention from the sex itself to its meaning in the book.... He uses this method with both Kinbote's homosexuality and Humbert's nymphetomania. Both characters are aliens, Europeans in America, and their sexual anomalies, among other things, symbolize the alien's loneliness. They desire sexual objects that they have trouble attaining, thus isolating themselves, just as the alien inevitably lives to some extent in isolation. (pp. 103-04)

In *Ada* sex, as the combination of art and science and the attainment of timelessness, is truly real, and therefore unlike the false reality of the realists. Van believes that "in his love-making with Ada he discovered the pang, ... the agony of supreme 'reality.' Reality, better say, lost the quotes it wore like claws".... Nabokov treats sex more frankly in *Ada* than he does in *Lolita,* but he still uses it as a metaphor. He thus develops this staple theme of realistic fiction in a way consistent with his other themes and techniques. (p. 105)

Nabokov has repeatedly scoffed at symbolic interpretations of his work, claiming that he merely describes. He of course is not as rigorous about this as he claims; at least one can convincingly attach symbolic meanings to some of his images. In the three novels that belong to the Literature of Exhaustion he shares one recurrent image, the mirror, with Borges, but he rarely uses circles and labyrinths. Instead of the latter two, his other dominant image is the butterfly.

The meanings of his mirror imagery change from book to book. Although some of the many mirrors in *Lolita* have no symbolic meaning, they appear in crucial passages to add an air of strangeness and thereby to make the action seem even more important. Quilty's house is full of mirrors, the most eerie ones being in one room that contains little else except a polar bear rug.... The hotel room in which Humbert and Lolita first sleep together has an incredible number of mirrors: "there was a double bed, a mirror, a double bed in the mirror, a closet door with mirror, a bathroom door ditto, a blue-dark window, a reflected bed there, the same in the closet mirror".... Thus, in *Lolita* Nabokov uses a typical symbol of the Literature of Exhaustion but does not attach to it meanings characteristic of that literature; in fact he attaches almost no meaning at all to it.

By the time he wrote *Pale Fire* he had concluded that mirrors copy reality either accurately or falsely and, as a nonrealist, he had begun to prefer inaccurate copying. (p. 106)

The accurate mirror of realism appears also in *Ada.* In one instance a character uses it not to confuse but to cheat at cards. However, Van wins the game because his sleight of hand tricks are the work of an illusionist and thus superior to any realistic tricks with mirrors. (p. 107)

In *Lolita, Pale Fire,* and *Ada* Nabokov develops the butterfly image even more extensively than the mirror image. In *Lolita* this image is completely positive, appearing in the tennis scene as a sign of Humbert's transformation of Lolita into an exquisite creature of his imagination. It also appears throughout this book in scattered allusions to the species of butterfly the female of which Nabokov discovered.... (p. 108)

In *Pale Fire* Nabokov attacks as too naive complete faith in the power of the imagination. Shade early in the novel can, like Humbert, create a figurative butterfly. The Vanessa he mentions is both a butterfly (the Red Admirable) and a beloved woman and subject of literature (Swift's Vanessa), and he equates her with his wife Sybil. But butterflies have an important quality, their patterns, in addition to their metamorphoses and their beauty. These patterns are negative because Shade finds, rather than creates, them. The completed pattern of his death is signalled by the appearance of a butterfly, appropriately another Vanessa. Kinbote's real name, Botkin, is once compared to "botfly," which sounds like "butterfly" but is a parasite, not a beautiful transformed creature. Kinbote could be like a butterfly, because in his fantasy of Zembla he has achieved a metamorphosis, but in order to tell his story he has to be parasitic on Shade's poem. In *Pale Fire* Nabokov suggests that butterflies are good insofar as they suggest metamorphosis, bad insofar as they suggest a pattern found in the real world instead of an invented pattern.

In *Ada* Nabokov even doubts the value of metamorphosis, as he shows by the way he uses the butterfly image. Ada likes larvae, insects that have not undergone metamorphosis, and she once goes so far as to kill a butterfly that has just metamorphosed.... She apparently feels that any change will be for the worse. She is twelve when she meets Van, the same age that Lolita was when Humbert met her, but Ada has already matured and she attracts Van; she needs no change.... The butterfly images in *Ada* suggest that one cannot depend on being happy with the changes he can make, even artistic ones, if he uses the real world as raw material. It follows from this idea that it may be better for the artist to turn his back on reality and create self-enclosed work.

Nabokov's characterization creates just such a self-enclosed artistic domain. All his major characters in these three books are readers or writers or both. Humbert writes his memoirs, which comprise *Lolita;* Lolita fits less neatly into these categories than the other characters, but Humbert does occasionally mention what she reads, and he lists the books he buys for her. Kinbote writes the notes and Shade the poem in *Pale Fire,* and the poem contains many allusions to Shade's reading. Van and Ada collaborate to write *Ada,* with the former doing most of the work, and a reader learns about many of the prodigious number of books they read. (pp. 108-09)

The increasing importance of the love theme in Nabokov's recent work, culminating in its manifestation in *Ada,* indicates that he may be moving away from the more purely artistic themes of the Literature of Exhaustion. Even if he does return to more conventional themes—such as love—however, he will not develop them realistically, for that would be to renounce both his own past work and his connection with the literary movement described here....

[Nabokov] does not use the artistically dangerous strategy of repetition to refute time and has shown some signs in *Ada* and *Transparent Things* of moving beyond the Literature of Exhaustion. (p. 116)

After dealing with these general matters one can consider his contributions to various genres. It would take a critic fluent in Russian to evaluate his poetry in that language. The English poem he creates for Shade is better than competent; its quality has usually been rated too low. But he does not qualify as a major poet. *Speak, Memory* belongs in the forefront of twentieth century autobiography, partly for his original use of imagery in it and partly for its haunting evocation of a fascinating life. Judging from his *obiter dicta* on other writers and reports of his Cornell lectures, the book that will be made from these lectures could very well establish him as an important critic. His sharp eye and acid wit will certainly make him at least an interesting critic. His translation of *Eugene Onegin* is controversial but fascinating. Despite his theory that translations should be crabbed, much of his verse translation has real grace, and its notes are intriguing.

His novels represent his major work. Among the ones I have covered *Lolita* and *Pale Fire* are great, both for the daring originality of their conceptions—which advance the genre of the novel, especially in the case of the latter—and for the meticulous way Nabokov realizes these conceptions. *Ada* is also impressively conceived, but it falls short of the other two because of the high price paid for the point that its early thick style makes. According to information current about his projects there will be much, much more from him, for which readers can be hopeful.

If one considers all these works together, Nabokov belongs among the major living writers. His ability to use some of the techniques and themes of the Literature of Exhaustion without weakening the other aspects of his work demonstrates his literary ability. (pp. 116-17)

> *John Stark, "Vladimir Nabokov," in his* The Literature of Exhaustion *(reprinted by permission of the Publisher; copyright 1974 by Duke University Press, Durham, North Carolina), Duke University Press, 1974, pp. 62-117.*

Nabokov has changed the adage about old age being a time for reflection into a private bad joke—he's as narcissistic as any adolescent studying the arrangement of mirrors for a portrait of the artist. He's also the greatest living expert on how to weave the webs that join books together, making a gossamer safety net of allusion. All he has to do is pull a string, and the whole structure shivers enticingly, while the author reclines, plump and possibly venomous, in his silken hammock at the centre. In short, the tensile strength of his oeuvre is there in each thing he does (however unfair that may seem. a lot of things about him are unfair) and imparts to even his gestures of languor a grand feel of having energy to spare. (p. 61)

One of Nabokov's most spectacular skills (why he makes re-readers of readers) is the way he manages to inveigle you into complicity with his heroes' struggles to design the world according to their own grandiose, eccentric specifications. And Vadim [in *Look at the Harlequins!*] is no exception: his creative frenzy may produce lousy novels, but the inside story of its working is altogether fascinating. . . .

Death is the theme, . . . as it has been in *Ada* and *Trans-*

parent Things—death's humiliations, and conversely its seductive closeness to certain recherché authorial tricks involving levitation and making yourself seem to disappear. Nabokov's tone about the great leveller is one of bold romantic irony, insidious, agile and elevated like, say, Shelley in 'The Sensitive Plant'—'It is a modest creed, and yet / Pleasant if one considers it. / To own that death itself must be / Like all the rest, a mockery.' There's no substantial solace to be had, only the bitter pleasure of a defiant, snobbish gesture: '"Let us not anticipate," as the condemned man said when rejecting the filthy old blindfold.'

What he's 'up to' nowadays (one always has the rare confidence with Nabokov that he's bound to be up to something) is plugging the leaks, building around his fiction an ever more dense and elaborate maze designed to baffle would-be annotators—to wear them out and keep them busy. *Look at the Harlequins!* is a preemptive strike, a preemptive parody of scavenging biographers and bibliographers, a portrait of the artist he is not. It stands halfway between his memoir, *Speak, Memory* (which deliberately invoked the Muse), and his invented fictions. There is a snug gap in one's bookshelf ready and waiting. (p. 62)

> *Lorna Sage in* The New Review (© *The New Review Ltd. 11 Greek Street, London W1V 5LE), April, 1975.*

There are, very broadly, three types of Nabokov novel: the satires, which are *tours de force* of ingenious (*Pale Fire, Bend Sinister, Invitation to a Beheading*); the black farces, which are gloating treatments of murder, obsession and perverse love (*Despair, Lolita, Laughter in the Dark*); and the histories, which are oblique recreations of individual lives (*Pnin, Ada, The Real Life of Sebastian Knight*). The new novel is fundamentally a history—it calls itself the 'memoir' of one Vadim Vadimovich—but it serves also as a kind of Nabokov anthology, a recapitulation of his standard situations and themes, a scrapbook of his habitual voices and moods. Nabokov being Nabokov, the formula would seem to be unimprovable; and yet *Look at the Harlequin's* is a forlorn and ragged book.

A shrewdly observed life, Nabokov suggested in his *Eugene Onegin* Commentary, can often disclose an artistically satisfying pattern. Well, Vadim's life, as here described, has about as much shape as most lives have—i.e., not much. . . . This is . . . the third novel running that Nabokov has attempted to weld together with a time-space conundrum: it is an image of whatever you want it to be an image of; it is also very boring to have to read about.

Just as *Ada* (1969) contained a portrait of the larval Vladimir and *Transparent Things* (1972) contained a cameo of the old Nabokov, *Look at the Harlequins!* is an appreciative review of the novelist's middle years. Typically, Nabokov both invites and dares the reader to see the book as tricksy autobiography: his own life and works are pseudonymously saluted throughout (Vadim's brother-in-law calls him 'MacNab'; his *The Red Top Hat* is Nabokov's *Invitation to a Beheading*), and you're evidently meant to have a good time assembling these clues—always bearing in mind, of course, Nabokov's stylish warning in *Speak, Memory*:

> I confess I do not believe in time. I like to fold my magic carpet, after use, in such a way as to superimpose one part of the pattern upon another. Let visitors trip.

Thus we have the twin delights of consenting to Nabokov's

self-indulgence and hearing him chuckle about what dunces he has made of us for doing so.

And this is all right. You don't read Nabokov for reassurance—or for any of the 'human interest' perks he derided so expertly in *Strong Opinions*. There is only one incentive to turn his pages: to get more of his sentences. The really unnerving deficiency of *Look at the Harlequins!* is the crudity of much of its prose. One expects some convolution and strain in Nabokov, but one doesn't reckon on coarse reiteration ('what shall never be ferreted out by a matter-of-fact, father-of-muck, mucking biograffitist'), charmless familiarity ('something to do with a roll of coins, capitalistic metaphor, eh, Marxy?') and the dud Georgianisms he himself chastised in *Speak, Memory* ('I must have hung for a little while longer . . . before ending supine on the intangible soil'). In the book's 250-odd pages I found only four passages that were genuinely haunting and beautiful; in an earlier Nabokov it would be hard to find as many that were not.

Such a falling-off has a peculiar pathos in a writer whom we have come to think of as our greatest stylist—and by 'style' I mean more than mere surface fizz: after all, you can write only as well as you can think. The variety, force and richness of Nabokov's perceptions have not even the palest rival in modern fiction. To read him in full flight is to experience stimulation that is at once intellectual, imaginative and aesthetic, the nearest thing to pure sensual pleasure that prose can offer. Confronted with such gifts of expression, it's in some way a relief that Nabokov can neither characterise, pace nor construct. The lesson of *Look at the Harlequins!* is one we have been getting ready to learn all along: if the prose isn't alive, nothing else is. (pp. 555-56)

Martin Amis, "Out of Style," in New Statesman (© *1975 The Statesman & Nation Publishing Co. Ltd.), April 25, 1975, pp. 555-56.*

Look at the Harlequins! is not a capstone novel, though it provides a summing up, a recapitulation in rearranged echoes and guises, of all the wonders that have preceded it. Our word-magus is still at his worldly best, but he is more than ever writing in this book for himself and for his proven followers. As he has said more than once in interviews, Nabokov writes for himself "in multiplicate." If one is willing to become a Little Nabokov, to enter the author's Fabergé world as a ready acolyte, a holder of mirrors, the benefits are considerable. I know of few more entertaining productions than *Lolita* or *Pale Fire,* both masterpieces in anyone's gathering of major twentieth-century novels. Those two novels are the apogee of the master's craft, the best, clearest presentations of his magical construct. With the mammoth *Ada* (= art, artifice, ardis, ardor, and whatever other reflective facets might be brought to bear to expand the possibilities of language beyond its common limitations) that constructed world became more convoluted, more dependent on what was shown before, less concerned with the responses or imaginings of the unwashed. So it is with high art turned inward. *Ada* might in fact serve as the apotheosis of self-concerned art, for even while Nabokov's Van Veen exhibits all the guilt of vanity, so finally does our magician reveal in himself the flaws of the solipsism that he has so assiduously parodied.

It would be easy—as is demonstrated by Nabokov's numerous admiring critics, some of them painfully awestruck —to back off from recognizing the ultimate diminution of

solipsism. It is easy, too easy, to make that other turn in the lane, to imagine roundabout that through minute self-examination the final leap to recognition can be made. These novels from beginning to end are involved with the solipsist artist and his work, to a fine degree; and in this manner of presentation Nabokov is perhaps exceeded only by Joyce. (p. 714)

Nabokov has little use for foolish Freudians (as well he might not) or for the bureaucratic mind in any coloration, and he loves the fritillaries, the hovercraft, only when they feed as critics or sycophants on delectables that he has deliberately laid before them. Thus examination except by the initiate is unwelcome though obviously necessary. *Look at the Harlequins!* is not a very good novel, though it is remarkable enough; it represents too clearly the decline first recognized with the publication of *Ada.* American critics, except for those bent on building an academic career with the bones of Nabokov, have been too generous, just as they have been with literary politicos like Pasternak and Solzhenitsyn. Politics has, or ought to have, as Nabokov would be only too ready to say, nothing to do with real art, but surely politics has had much to do with Nabokov's own gentle reception in this country and in other western clubs. No matter, that will all sift out.

Look at the Harlequins! is laden with all the quirks and keys we have come to identify with Nabokov, the wordplay, the parodic narrator, the vast allusion, the dancing doubles, the mirrors, the godlike intrusive Creator. Ever since we were willingly seduced by *Lolita* to wander with Humbert in his blue Melmoth the dreamy roads of America, enchanted searchers all, ever since we (some of us) recognized the real beauty of Shade's poem of the shadow of the waxwing, of its fluff, we have been beset by romance. Love's generosity led us to let the old man off with triple alliterations as dull and pointless as the one in this sentence, obfuscations that ruin the texture that is all important if Nabokov's art is indeed to fly on. Nabokov demands a careful reader, a poetic reader, but the chase that was such fun in *Lolita* and *Pale Fire,* the enchanted hunt turned ever more inward in *Ada,* becomes even more involuted in *LATH* (Nabokov's acronymic punning on his own latest title).

In this novel within a novel we are treated to recollections of "the life or at least fame" of the "three or four" marriages (or perhaps these unions are merely emblematic of stages of the artist's development) of Vadim Vadimovich, Nabokov's "author," in his mellow, perhaps overmellow, age. We see this author not far from death, from his final transition, surrounded by his mirror creatures, his "three or four successive wives," his many novels, each title reflecting one of Nabokov's own (*A Kingdom by the Sea* doubles for, you guessed it, *Lolita, Ardis* for *Ada,* and so forth). Thus we have books within a book, titles within titles, words and sounds within words. As Vadim's invented great-aunt puts it, "Words are harlequins." "Look at the harlequins." (pp. 714-15)

Small links, jokes, remembrances, but most of the fun is gone. The quick humor, the kaleidoscopic wordplay, the punctured pomposities of Humbert and Kinbote, the verbal delights that made the American novels *Lolita* and *Pale Fire* such a reward are only shadows here. (pp. 715-16)

Hardly a shy violet, Nabokov has placed vanity and the ultimate terrors of solipsism among his major literary subjects, whether showing them in Krug's pride of superiority in *Bend Sinister,* weaving their involved strands completely through *Ada,* or presenting them in the partial or baiting self-parody of *Look at the Harlequins!.* In his own criticism, as with his own public self-laudation, Nabokov will never play second lead, will never allow himself to become a shadow to another or to his own art; the magus is inevitably o'erweening in his presence though in his public pronouncements he usually maintains a disarming playfulness. His self-assumed, and genuine, superiority is seldom so apparent as in his interviews and his own critical essays, many of them collected in *Strong Opinions.* For his interviews Nabokov, pleading inability to improvise, requires that a list of questions be submitted to him in advance; if the interviewer insists on the "bogus informality" of a visit, Nabokov then reads the responses from cards. No real shyness is involved in this procedure, only the unflagging insistence that all of the artist's words, even fragmentary interviews, be honed to a fineness. In the decade of interviews assembled here Nabokov is thus again able to play Prospero, even with the spoken word, to the Calibans of communication. With verbal virtuosity, he invariably shows their questions to be duller than mud, or makes them seem so. And the same questions are put forward repeatedly, most amusingly when the interviewers, particularly the British, try time and again to extract some display of dislike and disdain for his adopted America. Nabokov is doggedly protective of his golden goose.

Two-thirds of *Strong Opinions* consists of these highly aphoristic simulated interviews, as carefully prepared as any manuscript to present the author's thought-out responses to the tumult that rages beyond his tightly ordered world. The other third of the book is made up of letters to editors, all fragments of political or literary fracases, and several essays classified as "articles" that are really major battles in the expansion (I suppose it is that) of Nabokov's sizable literary empire. The pounding of the opposition is at times as heavy as a Russian winter, and as unrelenting. (pp. 718-19)

> *Kenneth Cherry, "Nabokov's Kingdom by the Sea," in* Sewanee Review *(reprinted by permission of the editor;* © *1975 by The University of the South), Fall, 1975, pp. 712-20.*

[A] novel written in a manifestly antirealist mode can still put us in touch with the nature of real forces at work in history. The book I have in mind is Nabokov's *Pale Fire* (1962), a novel that could well be the finest that has appeared in English since the beginning of the 60's. The celebrated intricacy of artifice in *Pale Fire* has been the subject of much solemn explication (including some of my own), but what saves the evident "brilliance" of the book from mere cleverness is that it illuminates the deeper perplexities of art operating in history....

At first thought, any serious connection with real history would seem quite implausible in this novel where all political events are the fantasies of a madman recessed within the structure of a poem by a fictitious poet.... All this delusional material is presented in one of the most elaborately patterned novels of recent decades, the narrative being a complex interweave of recurring images, colors, anagrammatic clues, and literary allusions. The political "reality" ..., moreover, is ostentatiously of a comic-opera variety....

Nevertheless, *Pale Fire* succeeds in creating an evocative

sense of history as a scary but compelling arena in which different options for human enhancement or disfigurement, different levels of consciousness, are generated by shifting events and political systems, by the varying circumstances of individual and national culture. Nabokov keenly understands that there are, after all, qualitative differences between living in a totalitarian state, ... and living under political systems where there is enough freedom of consciousness for the poet, the lover, the madman ... to enjoy immense riches of inner experience even in the painful comedy and the bizarre contradictions of their wayward mental life. The fact that all the central events of the novel are patent inventions has the paradoxical effect of sharpening this ultimately political theme. (p. 50)

Pale Fire's absorbing fantasy of assassination ... is devised to articulate a desperately serious political concern that has haunted the writer for most of his adult life: what validity beyond mere escapism does art possess, seemingly so fragile, futile, and finally impotent in the face of murderous history; and, conversely, what is the inner nature of the politics that systematically subverts and destroys every important value enhanced or fulfilled by art? The self-conscious fictional prism of *Pale Fire* manages to focus a vivid sense of history in which man is not universally vile but both abysmally vile and mysteriously splendid (Kinbote, the mad poet-commentator, is in his own odd way both), and so the fiction finally leads us ... to ponder what it is about the varieties of historical experience that makes possible such contradictory extremes of destructiveness and creation. (pp. 50-1)

> *Robert Alter (reprinted from* Commentary *by permission; copyright* © *1975 by the American Jewish Committee), in* Commentary, *November, 1975.*

To my taste [Nabokov's] American novels are his best, with a fiercer frivolity and a cruelty more humane than in the fiction of his European decades. In America his almost impossible style encountered, after twenty years of hermetic exile, a subject as impossible as itself, ungainly with the same affluence. He rediscovered our monstrosity. His fascinatingly astigmatic stereopticon projected not only the landscape—the eerie arboreal suburbs, the grand emptinesses, the exotic and touchingly temporary junk of roadside America—but the wistful citizens of a violent society desperately oversold, in the absence of other connectives, on love. If the perceiver of John Shade and Charlotte Haze and Clare Quilty and the Waindell College that impinged on poor Pnin devotes the rest of his days to fond rummaging in the Russian attic of his mind, the loss is national, and sadder than Sputnik.

The latest memento confided to the care of Nabokov's American public is a revision of *Speak, Memory,* whose chapters were published one by one in (mostly) *The New Yorker* from 1948 to 1950 and assembled as *Conclusive Evidence* in 1951. As readers then already know, twelve of the fifteen chapters portray an aspect of the writer's happy boyhood as the eldest son of a St. Petersburg aristocrat, and the last three, more briefly but as enchantingly, sketch his rootless years in Cambridge, Berlin, and Paris. Nabokov has never written English better than in these reminiscences; never since has he written so sweetly. With tender precision and copious wit, exploiting a vocabulary and a sensibility enriched by the methodical pursuit of lepidoptera, inspired by an atheist's faith in the magic of simile and the sacredness of lost time, Nabokov makes of his past a brilliant icon—bejewelled, perspectiveless, untouchable. While there are frequent passages of Joycean trickiness, Proust presides in the metaphorical arabesques, the floral rhythms, and the immobilized surrender to memory. Proust, however, by fictionalizing Illiers into Combray, threw his childhood open to everyone; whereas the Nabokov memoir is narrowed by its implication that only an expatriate Russian, a well-born and intellectual Russian at that, can know nostalgia so exquisite.

The revisions which a laborious collation with the 1951 edition has bared to my scrutiny, tend to narrow the memoir further. The author, back in Europe, has consulted with his sisters and cousins, who have chastened his imperfect recollections. Much new information about the Nabokov tribe, bristling with parenthetic dates and hyphenated alliances with the Prussian nobility, has been foisted off on Chapter Three; a tidy dry biography of his father now inaugurates Chapter Nine. (Compare, invidiously, the fabulous epic of filial admiration worked into his novel *The Gift*.) Elsewhere gardeners and dachshunds have been named, tutors sorted out, and apologies delivered to his previously suppressed brother Sergey. Some of the interpolations are welcome (the family tennis game in Chapter Two, the wooing of Tamara in Chapter Twelve, the differentiated drawing masters in Chapter Four); but sentences at times limp under their new load of accuracy and the ending of one vignette, "Mademoiselle O" (Chapter Five), is quite dulled by the gratuitous postscript of some recent personal history. The additions, and the addition of pleasant but imagination-cramping photographs, make the book more of a family album and slightly less of a miracle of impressionistic recall. (pp. 191-93)

> *John Updike, "Nabokov: Mnemosyne Chastened," in his* Picked-Up Pieces *(copyright © 1975 by John Updike; reprinted by permission of Alfred A. Knopf, Inc.), Knopf, 1975, pp. 191-93.*

When a book fails to agree with a reader, it is either because the author has failed to realize his intentions or because his intentions are disagreeable. Since Vladimir Nabokov is, all in all, the best-equipped writer in the English-speaking world (of which he inhabits a personal promontory by the side of Lake Geneva), the opening chapters of his giant new novel, *Ada*, must be taken as intentionally repellent. His prose has never—not even in his haughty prefaces to works resurrected from the Russian, not even in Humbert Humbert's maddest flights—menaced a cowering reader with more bristling erudition, garlicky puns, bearish parentheses, and ogreish winks.... *Ada* is subtitled "Or Ardor: A Family Chronicle," and the central family matter, not easily grasped, concerns the marriage of the two Durmanov sisters, Marina and Aqua, to two men each called Walter D. Veen, first cousins differentiated by the nicknames Red (or Dan) and Demon. (p. 199)

The confusion of America (Estotiland) and Russia (Tartary) into one idyllic nation where everyone speaks French is, more than a joke upon Canada, a metaphor of personal history. Vain, venereal Van Veen verges on V.N.; Nabokov = Van + book. Ada (rhymes with Nevada) is ardor and art —but not, I think, the Americans for Democratic Action. She is also, in a dimension or two, Nabokov's wife Véra, his constant collaboratrice and the invariable dedicatee of his works. Ada's marginal comments on Van's manuscript, reproduced in print, are among the liveliest bits in the book, and offer an occasional check upon the author's rampaging

genius. I suspect that many of the details in this novel double as personal communication between husband and wife; some of the bothersomely exact dates, for instance, must be, to use a favorite word of our author, "fatadic." I am certain that trilingual puns crowd and crawl . . . beneath the surface of this novel like wood lice under the bark of an old stump. Their patient explication, and the formal arrangement of the parallels and contraries that geometricize "our rambling romance," the hurried reviewer may confidently leave to the graduate student who . . . can spend many a pleasant and blameless hour unstitching the sequinned embroidery of Nabokov's five years' labor of love. He might begin with the prominently displayed anagram of "insect" ("incest," "nicest," "scient"), move on to the orchid-imitating butterflies and butterfly-imitating orchids, get his feet wet in the water imagery (Aqua, Marina, "*A l'eau!*" yourself), and then do something with "cruciform," which crops up in several surprising connections, such as mounted moths, the hero's feces, and the arrangement of a mature woman's four patches of hair. Indeed, this book is Nabokov's most religious—his Testament as well as his *Tempest*—and manages several oblique squints at the Christian religion, a previous sketch of a structured supernature. *Ada* is the feminine form of the Russian "*Ad*," for Hades or Hell, and there is a Van in Nirvana and Heaven, for instance. (pp. 200-01)

In a landscape of "Ladore, Ladoga, Laguna, Lugano, and Luga," everything melts into foolery. I confess to a prejudice: fiction is earthbound, and while in decency the names of small towns and middling cities must be faked, metropolises and nations are unique and should be given their own names or none. I did not even like it when Nabokov, in *Pale Fire*, gave New York State the preëmpted appellation of Appalachia. He is, among other titles to our love, the foremost poet of Earth's geography.... His vision and flair are themselves so supermundane that to apply them to a fairyland is to put icing on icing. There is nothing in the landscapes of *Ada* to rank with the Russian scenery of *Speak, Memory* or the trans-American hegira of Lolita and Humbert Humbert.

As with place names, so with face names; we never get over the playful twinning of Aqua and Marina, Demon and Dan, and though Aqua's madness spins a few beautiful pages and Demon makes some noises approximating those of a flesh-and-blood father, the four remain animated anagrams, symmetrical appendages that want to be characters. To be sure, we are in a world of chrysalis and metamorphosis; as in *Invitation to a Beheading* and *Bend Sinister,* the cardboard flats and gauze trappings collapse, and the author/hero, heavy with death, lumbers toward the lip of the stage. This does happen, and the last pages of *Ada* are the best, and rank with Nabokov's best, but to get to them we traverse too wide a waste of facetious, airy, side-slipped semi-reality. (p. 202)

Is art a game? Nabokov stakes his career on it, and there exist enterprising young critics who, in replacing Proust, Joyce, and Mann with the alliterative new trinity of Beckett, Borges, and Nabokov, imply that these wonderful old fellows make fine airtight boxes, like five-foot plastic cubes in a Minimal Art show, all inner reflection and shimmer, perfectly self-contained, detached from even the language of their composition. I think not. Art is part game, part grim erotic tussle with Things As They Are; the boxes must have holes where reality can look out and readers can look in. Beckett shows us the depraved rudiments of our mortal existence; Borges opens a window on the desolation of history's maze and the tang of heroism that blows off the Argentine plain. And *Ada,* though aspiring to "an art now become pure and abstract, and therefore genuine," is full of holes, stretches and pages and phrases whose life derives from life. (p. 208)

Well, a man's religious life is the last province of privacy these days, but it is clear from *Ada* and other evidences that Nabokov is a mystic.... Nabokov has made a church for himself out of fanatic pedantry; the thousand pages of his *Onegin* footnotes are a cathedralic structure where even the capitals that face the wall are painstakingly carved.... His fiction, from its punning prose and its twinning of characters to the elegance of each tale's deceptive design, represents his boyhood's revelation of art-for-art's-sake within Nature. If Nature is an artifact, however, there must be, if not an Artist, at least a kind of raw reality beneath or behind it, and the most daring and distressing quality of his novels is their attempt to rub themselves bare, to display their own vestments of artifice and then to remove them. Hence the recurrent device of the uncompleted, imperfect manuscript; this text embodies not only *Ada's* marginal notes but various false paragraph starts and editor's bracketed notes of the type frequent in proof sheets.... In *Pale Fire,* John Shade showed a surprisingly literal interest in the afterlife; in *Ada,* Nabokov has sought to construct, with his Hades and Nirvana, an Otherlife. Art begins with magic. Though Nabokov operates, it seems to me, without the sanctions, the charity and humility, that make a priest, he lays claim to the more ancient title of magician. (pp. 209-11)

> John Updike, *"Van Loves Ada, Ada Loves Van," in his* Picked-Up Pieces *(copyright © 1975 by John Updike; reprinted by permission of Alfred A. Knopf, Inc.), Knopf, 1975, pp. 199-211.*

Confessions: I have never understood how they saw the woman in half. Any willful child can dumbfound me with card tricks learned from the back of a comic book. Mystery novelists find in me their ideal gull, obligingly misled by the fishiest red herring. In calculus, I never grasped the infinitesimal but utile distinction between *dt* and Δ*t.* And I do not understand Vladimir Nabokov's new novel, *Transparent Things.* This is a confession, not a complaint; the world abounds in excellent apparatuses, from automobile engines to digestive tracts, resistant to my understanding. So be it. I am grateful. I am grateful that Nabokov, at an age when most writers are content to rearrange their medals and bank their anthology royalties, rides his old hobbyhorses with such tenacious mount and such jubilant tallyhos. A new book by him, any new book by him, serves as reminder that art is a holiday, however grim workdays grow in the sweatshops of reality. His exuberance is catching, as readers of this hyperbole-pocked paragraph can at a glance diagnose. Well, to work. (p. 211)

Transparent Things's hero, Hugh Person, is an editor of, among other authors, one "R." (a mirroring of the Russian *R, ya,* meaning "I"), who, though more corpulent and less uxorious than Nabokov himself, does live in Switzerland, composes "surrealistic novels of the poetic sort," and regards the rest of the world as a grotesquely clumsy siege upon his artistic integrity.... Nabokov's is really an amorous style—foreplay in the guise of horseplay. It yearns to clasp diaphanous exactitude into its hairy arms. To convey a child's nocturnal unease, it can toss off the looming meta-

phor "Night is always a giant"; or with tender euphonic trippings it can limn a woman's facial expression during intercourse as "the never deceived expectancy of the dazed ecstasy that gradually idiotized her dear features." Such a yen to evoke, to use the full spectrum latent in the dictionary, would teach us how to read again. If not always a comfortable, it is surely a commendable impulse.

Less so, perhaps, the murderous impulse visible through the workings of *Transparent Things.* Since the book is something of a thriller, its plot should be left its secrets; but, needless to say, almost no character, major or minor, survives its last turn. Strangulation, conflagration, embolism, cancer—these are some of the methods employed. Characters who barely appear onstage have their offstage demises dutifully reported.... (p. 212)

[Another] impulse is to formulate, at the highest level of intelligence and subtlety, some statement about space/time, death, and being. (p. 213)

The central impulse behind the novel remains obscure. At first, it seems that the "transparency" of things refers to their dimension in time—an ordinary pencil found in a drawer is taken back to its birth as a rod of agglutinated graphite and a splinter buried in the heart of a pine tree. Then it seems that the transparency has to do with an artful overlapping of beds, bureaus, carpets catching a slant of sunshine, shuttlecocks, dogs, and so on, as Hugh Person returns several times, between the ages of eight and forty, to the Swiss village of Trux. Other things are transparent, such as book titles "that shone through the book like a watermark," and a loved one "whose image was stamped on the eye of his mind and shone through the show at various levels." But the culminating image of transparency ("the incandescence of a book or a box grown completely transparent and hollow"), though the author presents it as if it were the crown of his life's thought and passion, arrives as the answer to a conundrum that has not been posed. Alas, what we remember of *Transparent Things* are its agreeable opacities: the busy clots of choice adjectives ("frail, lax, merry America"), the erotic peculiarities of Person's charming and difficult wife, Armande (she likes to make love as fully dressed as possible, while maintaining a flow of cocktail chatter), the delicious, glacial scene of a ski resort.... We close the book guiltily, having licked the sugar coating but avoided, somehow, swallowing the pill.

If an artistic life so variously productive, so self-assured, so hermetically satisfactory to its perpetrator could be said to have a failing, Nabokov has failed to get himself taken seriously enough. A sad shadow of modesty touches this narrative.... [The] book abounds, indeed, in wry self-portraits.... Nabokov's own tricky legerity discourages solemn praise; he makes his acolytes and exegetes seem ridiculous as they compile their check lists of puns and chase his butterfly allusions. His aesthetic of gravity-fooling confronts us with a fiction that purposely undervalues its own humanistic content, that openly scorns the psychology and sociology that might bring with them an unfoolable gravity. Joyce also loved puns, and Proust was as lopsided an emotional monster as Humbert Humbert. But these older writers did submit their logomachy and their maimed private lives to a kind of historical commonalty; the Europe of the epics and the cathedrals spoke through them. The impression created by Nabokov's works in Russian, I am told, differs from that given by his spectacular works in English; he can be compared to Dostoevsky and Tolstoy in a way in which he cannot be compared with Thoreau and Twain. In his post-*Lolita* novels, especially, he seems more illusionist than seer. Though he offers us sensations never before verbally induced, and performs stunts that lift him right off the page, we are more amused than convinced. The failing may be ours; we are not ready, we are too dull of ear, too slow of eye, too much in love with the stubborn muteness of the earth to read the meaning behind his magic. He mutters from his sky, this comical comet, and hints, through his masks, of "a new bible." His measure is that we hope for nothing less from him. (pp. 214-15)

> *John Updike, "The Translucing of Hugh Person," in his* Picked-Up Pieces *(copyright © 1975 by John Updike; reprinted by permission of Alfred A. Knopf, Inc.), Knopf, 1975, pp. 211-15.*

Your invitation to Vladimir Nabokov's birthday party reaches me in England, and it was in England, nearly fifteen years ago, in Oxford, that I first read this great man. . . . [It] has been one of the steadier pleasures of the fifteen years since to catch up on the considerable amount of Nabokov then in English and to keep up with the ample installments of reincarnated Russian and newly spawned American. . . . Though I may have nodded here and there among the two volumes of notes to *Onegin*, I have not knowingly missed any of the rest; for Nabokov is never lazy, never ungenerous with his jewels and flourishes, and his *oeuvre* is of sufficient majesty to afford interesting perspectives even from the closets and back hallways. I have expressed in print my opinion that he is now an American writer and the best living; I have also expressed my doubt that his aesthetic models—chess puzzles and protective colorations in lepidoptera—can be very helpful ideals for the rest of us. His importance for me as a writer has been his holding high, in an age when the phrase "artistic integrity" has a somewhat paradoxical if not reactionary ring, the stony image of his self-sufficiency: perverse he can be, but not abject; prankish but not hasty; sterile but not impotent. Even the least warming aspects of his image—the implacable hatreds, the reflexive contempt—testify, like fortress walls, to the reality of the siege this strange century lays against our privacy and pride.

As a reader, I want to register my impression that Nabokov does not (as Philip Toynbee, and other critics, have claimed) lack heart. *Speak, Memory* and *Lolita* fairly bulge with heart, and even the less ingratiating works, such as *King, Queen, Knave*, show, in the interstices of their rigorous designs, a plenitude of human understanding. The ability to animate into memorability minor, disagreeable characters bespeaks a kind of love. The little prostitute that Humbert Humbert recalls undressing herself so quickly, the fatally homely daughter of John Shade, the intolerably pretentious and sloppy-minded woman whom Pnin undyingly loves, the German street figures in *The Gift*, the extras momentarily on-screen in the American novels—all make a nick in the mind. Even characters Nabokov himself was plainly prejudiced against, like the toadlike heroine of *King, Queen, Knave*, linger vividly, with the outlines of the case they must plead on Judgment Day etched in the air; how fully we feel, for example, her descent into fever at the end. And only an artist full of emotion could make us hate the way we hate Axel Rex in *Laughter in the Dark*. If we feel that Nabokov is keeping, for all his expenditure of verbal small coin, some treasure in reserve, it is because of the riches he has revealed. Far from cold, he has access to

European vaults of sentiment sealed to Americans; if he feasts the mind like a prodigal son, it is because the heart's patrimony is assured. (pp. 220-22)

> *John Updike, "A Tribute," in his* Picked-Up Pieces *(copyright © 1975 by John Updike; reprinted by permission of Alfred A. Knopf, Inc.), Knopf, 1975, pp. 220-22.*

Vladimir Nabokov's new collection of his old stories, "Details of a Sunset" (1924-1935), is much concerned with different kinds of loss—exile, failure of romantic love and family love, the death of a wife, the death of a son, the death of one's self—and yet the effects of these stories are mainly exhilarating, even affirmative. In the last story, as if to comment on this paradox, Nabokov says, "human consciousness is an ominous and ludicrous luxury." In other words, if our world were a simple, rational place, then sad stories couldn't be exhilarating, "ominous" wouldn't rhyme with "ludicrous," and there would be no such thing as humor (certainly not black humor) and also no such thing as art. There might even be no consciousness, but only the sort of mental life as exists, for example, in Marxian utopias. (These considerations are more subtle and more elegant in Nabokov's stories.) . . .

Nabokov, a writer whose awesome wit can bludgeon his critics into silence, can demonstrate exquisite good manners in dealing with his fictional characters and his readers. . . .

Throughout the book Nabokov's descriptive genius makes the world—hooves, boards, Atticus moths, etc.—render itself up to us in delicious peculiarities. Sometimes he humanizes things. Sometimes he thingifies humans. . . .

Nabokov seems to have discovered something—ominous, ludicrous, luxurious—operating in the objective world *and* in our minds, as if it flowed between the two and might as soon find residency in one as in the other. . . .

Even if we don't consider the subjects or the events in Nabokov's stories, it must seem that his imagination—simply in what it sees and in the way it speaks—has demonic powers. Therein lies much of its pleasure for readers, a literary experience reminiscent of "Alice in Wonderland," another playfully verbal world where the perversities of plot, wittily qualified by lots of pain and apprehensions of death, full of exotic and subterranean perceptions, leave one thrilled and pleased.

> *Leonard Michaels, "Early Stories, Full of Human Grief and Literary Pleasure," in* The New York Times Book Review *(© 1976 by The New York Times Company; reprinted by permission), April 25, 1976, p. 5.*

Vladimir Nabokov is, of course, the prince of Amoralists. In these early short stories, translated from their original Russian in White émigré magazines, we have no view from Calvary but merely *Details of a Sunset*. Is that 'merely' just a hangover from the criteria of the moralist convention—and is moral fiction, in fact, simply a technical form? In some ways, yes. But the moralist convention does at least encourage writers to recall that language is a mode of communication between people—a form of human solidarity—rather than a range of stylistic gestures with which to load one's palette.

Mr Nabokov was already, in the 'twenties and 'thirties, a

most consummate artist. But one must ask whether he has ever been anything more; and whether this is enough. One of these stories, 'A Letter that Never Reached Russia', ends with the evocation of happiness: 'in the moist reflection of a streetlamp, in the cautious bend of stone steps that descend into the canal's black waters, in the smiles of dancing couples, in everything with which God so generously surrounds human loneliness.' Like God, Mr Nabokov is content to 'surround' human loneliness; a procedure which, like surrounding a crying child with exquisite objects, only intensifies the centre. (p. 23)

> *Nick Totton, in* The Spectator (© *1976 by* The Spectator; *reprinted by permission of* The Spectator), *August 21, 1976.*

Although the shaping power of our greatest formalist, Nabokov, is light-years ahead of [anyone else's], there is in much of his work a self-aggrandizing hostility toward both his characters and his readers that is not unlike Bellow's. Nabokov's best books are "Lolita," "Pale Fire" and "Speak, Memory"; his attempted grand summation, "Ada," and his more recent novels, "Transparent Things" and "Look at the Harlequins!," seem the works of a paranoid magician—megalomaniacal in their effort to fix the world into an artifact and assert the absolute perfection, the unqualified power, of the autonomous imagination. In this effort Nabokov becomes an all-American imperial self (to use ... Quentin Anderson's term), engulfing the world, rejecting society. Nabokov often creates ruthless mechanical forms, "like those Renaissance designs of flying machines," as William H. Gass has written, "dreams enclosed in finely drawn lines—which are intended to intrigue, to dazzle, but not to fly." In Nabokov artistic omnipotence seems to compensate for political impotence; the imaginary kingdom comforts the exiled soul; the danger is always nostalgia, and only comedy and control can ward off the tears. The balance is finest in "Lolita" and "Pale Fire." (p. 37)

> *Richard Locke, in* The New York Times Book Review (© *1977 by the New York Times Company; reprinted by permission),* May 15, 1977.

[The] moral legacy and confidence [of the Nabokov family], like the famous devotion of the Nabokovs to one another, *seem* to be at variance with the novelist's reputation as a wilfully eccentric, perverse and obscure writer with a vaguely shady intent. His most famous and at one time "scandalous" book, *Lolita,* indeed was first published by the sex-obsessed Olympia Press in Paris. The novels Nabokov wrote in Russian and later translated into English (with his son Dmitri)—*Mary; King, Queen, Knave; The Gift; The Defense; Invitation To A Beheading*—the novels beginning with *The Real Life Of Sebastian Knight* he wrote in English—*Bend Sinister; Lolita; Pnin; Pale Fire; Ada*— still are bewildering to many readers, seemingly perverse in content and impish in style.

But Nabokov, the last of the great 20th century modernists, was at heart as deeply traditionalist as Proust, Joyce, Faulkner, Eliot. As we seem to know only now that the returns are in, modernism was experimental in technique and style, provocative in intent, as a protest against mass society and conformism. It was a revolt of individual genius against life without moral definition. There were Russian writers before 1917 whose experimentalism and impudence were their warning against mass standards and the intellec-

tual dishonesty that followed from political authoritarianism in every sphere of Russian life.

Modernism flourished in exile and expatriation. But no other "modern master" underwent such painful uprooting as Nabokov....

Nabokov's ruling faith as an artist was his hatred of the expected, of "mediocrity" (another favorite swear word), of that self-satisfaction in shoddy goods that more and more passes in American education and culture. His hero and hilarious superman Van in *Ada* says, "For him the written word existed only in its abstract purity, in its unrepeatable appeal to an equally ideal mind. It belonged solely to its creator and could not be spoken of or enacted by a mime without letting the deadly stab of another's mind destroy the artist in the very lair of his art." (p. 13)

Nabokov knew with every instinct of his excellent mind and strict conscience that the "advanced" artist has to fight not only for recognition of his originality but against political superstition. A man of relentless mental energy, Nabokov always was outraged by minds that do not fight against the dominant "cliches." He thought that "cliches" stopped the world dead. He had an old Russian belief that the function of art is to open minds, to clear the air, to strip ourselves of all intellectual weakness.

How far Nabokov succeeded in realizing this in *all* his novels is not certain. Working against the grain, against the century, in pursuit of a beautiful private ideal that he hauntingly associated with a homesickness beyond repair, he wrote with the highest possible ambition for himself at a time when his love of surprising effects, of parody and intellectual "leaps," stunned the reader into more admiration of Nabokov's abilities than of his novels. His most obvious fault was an intellectual showiness and self-consciousness, especially in English, that bound the reader to Nabokov's own mind and personality. He was magnetic, irresistible, irreplaceable, endlessly fascinating; the technical wizardry so important to modernism became such a point of pride with Nabokov that it makes a book like *Ada* a brilliant bore. He wanted above all to be "an enchanter." He wrote some wonderful books, but much of his work is more that of a virtuoso than of an enchanter.

The talent, the sense of things, the power of imagination, were prodigious. You have only to see what Soviet writers in exile still gasp for to realize what Vladimir Nabokov enjoyed as his natural right. His long exile certainly helped. The emigration, he once said, was the only freedom that Russian writers ever have known. (p. 14)

> *Alfred Kazin, "Wisdom in Exile," in* The New Republic *(reprinted by permission of* The New Republic; © *1977 by The New Republic, Inc.), July 23, 1977, pp. 12-14.*

*   *   *

NEWMAN, Charles   1938-

Newman is an American novelist. On the basis of his first two novels, *New Axis* and *The Promisekeeper,* he has earned the reputation of being a brilliant, original, and exciting writer. His latest enterprise is to examine various conflicts of contemporary life in different literary styles. Of the twelve projected novellas, three have been published and collected in a volume entitled *There Must Be More to Love than Death.* (See also *CLC,* Vol. 2, and *Contemporary Authors,* Vols. 21-24, rev. ed.)

Read as an intellectual's misadventures in the dimension of the historical, *A Child's History* is fascinating.

Yet it is writing "without genre," as Newman states. And it will probably be misunderstood. For, like Newman's elegant and difficult prose fiction (*New Axis, The Promise-keeper*), it is an attempt to fuse what might be called the "inner" and the "historical" worlds, to present an egoless self that, being both private and cultural, may speak for a good many people without surrendering its aesthetic commitment to what is extraordinary, unique, unrepeatable. Most young American writers who acknowledge their indebtedness to Nabokov, Borges, Beckett and others in that tradition, have totally rejected what Newman seems to be insisting is the central function of literature: a moral, impersonal transmission of the accumulated wisdom of one individual's life in the form of literature that addresses itself to a specific historical, geographical condition—one's homeland. So the book's true, secret title must be *The Education of Charles Newman*, Vol. I, and its philosophical-poetic monologues on the nature of one's relationship to politics, specifically to revolutions of various types, seem to me without precedence in our literature. For if we are to have any philosophy at all in America, it must have the appearance of being something—anything—else. . . .

So the journal is valuable as history, and even more valuable as the first volume in a work of art "without genre." An extraordinary work, which no review could adequately suggest.

> *Joyce Carol Oates, in* Book World—The Washington Post (© The Washington Post), *October 28, 1973, p. 10.*

Charles Newman is one of the most interesting, intelligent, and, I suspect, secretly optimistic prophets of doom now writing fiction. One has the feeling as one reads that, like all prophets, he speaks more darkly than he means, in the almost but not quite forlorn hope that the sinful may even now repent in time. Whatever this may mean for the future of humanity, it produces pure and magnificently beautiful art. The prophetic warning—against our greed and selfishness, callous indifference and arrogance, our willingness to sink without a whimper into the barbarism of governmental, commercial, and spiritual fascism—comes through as a direct and open warning yet has in it no trace of dogmatism because it's firmly grounded in the feelings and experiences of characters. Sometimes the character's cry has the ring of propaganda at its best; in fact, in isolation from the character's reason for crying out it *would* be propaganda. . . .

But the charged language, the orator's rhythms, the irony and mockery are always set as art, too complex for mere slogan, too firmly tied to life's ordinary joys and griefs.

There Must be More to Love than Death . . . presents the first three novellas of a projected 12-novella series, each novella examining a conflict of contemporary life in a different literary style. The first novella here, the title work, tells the story—partly in traditional narrative, partly by court-martial documents—of a morphine addicted soldier who has learned that his mother's advice is obsolete: "You've a chance to go to hell but you have no right to be bored." . . . It's a quiet story—deadly quiet, as the theme demands. It would be crushing and black-hearted except for Newman's gentle wisdom, his occasional touches of startling but authentic humor, and his brilliant metaphors. (No one can spring metaphors more cunningly or naturally, transforming the mundane into poetry.) The central idea—that in the modern world, where impersonal system rules our lives, boredom may be the only option available—is an idea we've heard before many times; but Newman's careful and compassionate scrutiny of characters, and his remarkable knowledge of places and occupations—a striking feature of all his work—gives the idea dramatic force. . . .

In the second novella, *The Five-thousandth Baritone*, Newman stands the idea on its head. Gerald Fox is an excellent young baritone in a world where there are always five thousand excellent young baritones. If he's ambitious and dedicated, so are they; and even when he discovers that he has one unique talent, the ability to produce two tones at the same time, his gift proves no advantage: the music world wants what it's used to. So he gives singing recitals that don't mean very much, and he supports himself by selling door-to-door for a huge, indifferent company (one more heartless "system").

These could be the materials of a Newman tragedy, but here they're turned to glorious farce. . . .

The novella is shot through with a love of life and art, a delight even in meaningless system, since it's by the company's system (tapes which teach the salesman to crack his customer) that the hero falls into the lives of the Baginskis and gets the surprising and touching reward life's mundane old values can sometimes give. . . .

The third novella, *A Dolphin in the Forest, A Wild Board on the Waves*, is poetically and philosophically the most impressive of the three, a story set in the mind of a sensitive, brilliant boy with a photographic memory, a boy who claims "I never made up a thing in my life!" but whose idea of reality is a strange blend of fact and imagination, the material and the spiritual. His whole labor is to apprehend and record only what is real, but what is real turns out to be, for him as perhaps for all of us, highly mysterious: brute fact is shot through with the leftover emotions of the Christmas season no one believes in anymore. . . .

Newman has always been a writer's writer, a poet-philosopher who never forgets that poetry and philosophy are pointless except when their concern is with people. That, as much as the beauty of his prose, is the reason his books work. He has never written better than in these three novellas.

> *John Gardner, "Optimistic Prophet of Doom," in* Book World—The Washington Post (© The Washington Post), *October 31, 1976, p. F3.*

[The three novellas in *There Must Be More to Love Than Death*] are serious, ambitious pieces: nonconformist, they are unwilling to let themselves be limited either in meaning or in scope simply for the conventional reason that they happen to be pieces of short fiction. . . . Their major characteristic is that they continually strive outward; they remain ambitious, extend beyond themselves. At their best, which is most of the time, they take us straight to the heart of the matter.

For what they are really about—beyond their immediate subject matter—is, quite simply, the likelihood of our survival. They are stories woven consciously out of the ominously suspended historical moment in which we happen now to find ourselves not just living but *waiting*. Newman himself . . . has commented on this sense of waiting as a general characteristic in American writing. . . . "As Whitman had it, echoing Matthew Arnold, 'society waits un-form'd, and is for a while between things ended and things begun,' which is, after all, the quintessential *American* sense of history . . . and our dubious gift to the devolution of Western thought.''

It *is* an old theme, it may be a dubious gift, and Western thought may or may not be devolving. But certainly these three novellas have precisely these things as their themes—anxiety, waiting, dread, a simultaneous fear of what may happen and a Beckett-like fear that *nothing* may happen. (pp. 471-72)

The theme can be seen most easily in the initial piece, the novella from which the book as a whole takes its title. Its materials are familiar ones, but they are wrought so skillfully as to provide a good deal more than would readily be expected of them. The piece is about Vietnam. More precisely, it is about characters on their *way* to Vietnam who are never permitted quite to *get* there. The appropriateness of this is clear. The war for these characters (as it was for the nation as a whole) remains something incessantly to fear and dread, something abstract, menacing, guilt-evoking, and terrifying, but not something they are ever permitted actually to *see* and to *know* and therefore, just possibly, to understand and conquer. The war becomes thus the metaphor solely of dread, fear and threat; never is it made understandable, even ironically, in terms of cause, purpose or perceptible meaning. It becomes the gradually intensifying cause of individual self-destruction, of insanity. . . .

[It] is upon his often brilliant use of language that the quality of Newman's achievement finally depends. It is no accident that language itself becomes a central part of his theme: just as in the writing of so many of the "anti-realists" (with whom Newman, as critic and editor, is deeply familiar), Newman's own writing also comes to be *about* writing, his language *about* language. . . .

The final novella ["A Dolphin in the Forest, a Wild Boar on the Waves"] carries the theme [farthest]; for though we may be doomed already to massive self-destruction, a good part of the cause will be our failed reverence for the humble and invaluable truth of language well respected. Our most valuable possession, after all, is the one we treat most crudely. Nor is this merely the hobbyhorse of the teacher of English: for the truth is that only through language does experience gain meaning; and *meaning*—I meet all arguments to the contrary—is made *meaningful* to us only through language. Without language, Newman tells us—*able* language—we are all the more assuredly doomed.

The third novella is in some ways the weakest of the three, perhaps precisely because its aim is the highest, the most elusive. In it there is the strongest element of what may as well be called science fiction, for the piece is set after the atomic holocaust—or some equivalent—has occurred. . . .

Here we find the narrator mistaking video tapes of Jane and Tarzan for "history"; imagining that tapes entitled *MacArthur Returns* are "a family series probably"; and observing that "the government had built amphitheatres" around old missile silos, "declaring them national monuments. . . ." This is the stuff of minor science fiction indeed, and, though it both jars and intrudes, one forgives it in light of Newman's real aim: to create a metaphor for the implicit destructive potential of America's *cultural* failures. (p. 472)

[Like] the others, [the final novella] is a story that lives primarily *in* its language. One of its major themes, as well, is once again language—more specifically, the phenomenon of language, through abuse, neglect, or design, becoming isolated from meaning. . . . Language gives no meaning to experience; it does not translate experience into meaning.

Once language fails in this way, we effectively lose whatever control of our world we might previously have had. Unrooted from meaningful language, experience itself becomes random and gratuitous. The world is no longer directed or shaped: it merely happens, and we, helpless, are cut adrift in it, confused and without direction (notice the odd inversion of the novella's title). The radical premise upon which the truth of the Orwellian nightmare is based becomes conceivable: one thing is *not* more meaningful than another. (p. 473)

And thus we come around to the essence of it: as writers, we must struggle to create meaning out of materials provided us by a world in which "everything seems to smell the same." It is the writer's task, like the thinker's, to make distinctions between things, to evaluate, to study and reveal the differing and related meanings of differing and related experiences. The difficulty of doing this is increased almost insuperably in a world that strives to negate such distinctions, eliminate the relativity of meanings, and that values as one of its primary devices a language increasingly designed to serve, through powerlessness, its ends.

This book, Newman's fourth, will almost undoubtedly be classified by many—even in their praise—as esoteric, unconventional, even abstruse. But it may be that it has never been more difficult to write significantly than it is now—the questions are so big, the available materials within which to approach them so exhausted. . . . [Newman] suggests the nature of the dilemma: the writer's material, the fictional possibilities of his world, are "drained," yet the importance of writing seriously about them is perhaps greater than ever. For our world is one of enervated banality and at the same time one of immense, even unimaginable, dangers and risks. The difficulties are evident, the dangers those of defeat or hysteria. Charles Newman is one of the writers, whatever his weaknesses, who at least shows us a way, in the face of these paralyzing contrasts, neither to go mad nor to give up entirely. In this richly controlled book, he does not resort merely to screams, yet he shows us how not to remain entirely silent. (pp. 473-74)

Eric Larsen, "Language and the Apocalypse," in The Nation *(copyright 1976 by the Nation Associates, Inc.), November 6, 1976, pp. 471-74.*

*   *   *

NIN, Anaïs   1903-1977

Parisian-born American novelist, short story writer, critic, and diarist, Nin is probably best known for her published diary. She became almost a cult figure from her earliest days of publication, and her reflections on the feminine experience made her a leading presence for a faction of the feminist movement. (See also *CLC*, Vols. 1, 4, and *Contemporary Authors*, Vols. 13-16, rev. ed.; obituary, Vols. 69-72.)

Though Colette is a far more comprehensive and satisfying novelist than Anaïs Nin, at least for most tastes, both partake of the consciously 'feminine' tradition in fiction: their work is apt to deal in extended examinations of woman's character and nature, is highly subjective and personal, often autobiographical, is structured in poetic and intuitive ways rather than by any sort of abstract scheme . . . and has nearly as many ellipses as Céline. As with Anna Kavan or Djuna Barnes, their novels have the particular flavour of internality—the compression which comes from a highly coloured, sensitive personality's producing artistic work almost wholly from the self. And, very strikingly in their work, men are mysterious or contemptible outsiders from true communication. Fathers, lovers, husbands, all are objects of love and jealousy, almost emblematic in their separateness. More to be analysed and dreamt over than understood, men perpetually block the moments of flaring empathy which only women can share. (pp. 477-78)

Winter of Artifice joins three autobiographical novellas which anatomise the destructive dependence of women upon men: the heroines and narrators have been crippled by their fathers—elegant worldly artists, unfeeling and emotionally irresponsible. These daughters revere their fathers, fall in love with them again after long separation, and must eventually see that all of their responses to men have been controlled by the image of the father. Both partners in the fantasy are immured in emotional childhood, and the father wishes for nothing else. These three novellas have strikingly parallel movements. Constructed on almost no incidents or scenes but upon the progression of the heroine's self-analysis, the narratives move toward a recognition that beneath the mask of power and knowledge the godlike male is a weak, selfish parasite.

Then what to do? Since this is Anaïs Nin and not Colette, the point of life is to merge with dream, to stop time in the eternal moment intimated by halting, visionary prose. That is the fiction's import: in life, the solution seemed to be submergence in the famous, unstoppable diary, which is much better reading than any of her novels. (p. 478)

> *Peter Straub, in* New Statesman (© *1974 The Statesman & Nation Publishing Co. Ltd.), October 4, 1974.*

Anais Nin! This exquisite lady has pursued her solitary path for over forty years, and is only just emerging as a distinguished public figure. . . .

Nin loves living. Warmth, food, scents, company, conversation, the delights of the flesh. But she is no mere hedonist. The inner life is her preoccupation, and her literary and personal hunting-ground: adding a rich dimension to the outer life.

Her constant exploration of heart, body and soul is enhanced by some of the loveliest prose I have ever read. She is a writer's writer, though her insights will reach a broader audience. She is an exquisite person, physically (judging from her photographs) mentally (judging from her work) and she exudes a personal magic which is recognised by, and draws to her other people. (p. 57)

With Anais Nin we get down to the fundamentals of life, instead of railing at it. She never preaches, she shows. She knows better than most what it costs to be a woman and a writer. . . . [We] will find no bra-burning from Nin, for that is not the way out. The way out, or on, is most diligently to discover yourself and to pursue your chosen road: changing what you can, accepting what you cannot, and learning to tell the difference. (pp. 57-8)

> *Jean Stubbs, in* Books and Bookman (© *copyright Jean Stubbs 1975; reprinted with permission), April, 1975.*

The diaries of Anais Nin, although revised and intensely compressed, and revised—as Nin has said—by the novelist, are, by their nature, a species of autobiography. Although their excellence has caused them to be ranked with works of imagination, a rank accorded few autobiographies in spite of the current popularity of the genre, they are not novels—one has only to put them next to her novels to feel that—and to ignore that fact is to miss out on the special reading experience which they seem to inspire. Nin's diaries are books of wisdom which have elevated their author to the status of a sage and have had a healing effect on many of her readers, an effect which would be altered if the books were semi-fiction, although, clearly, works of fiction can function as books of wisdom. It is unlikely that anyone has bent to kiss her hem as did one adoring reader of George Eliot, but Nin has evoked in her readers a response similar to the tenacious adulation that surrounded Eliot in her later years, and has joined the company of those great teachers—Eliot, Wordsworth, and the savage but salutary D. H. Lawrence—who had a visionary sense of the healing power of feeling. (pp. 96-7)

Nin's power to stir us and change our lives is not in direct proportion to the quantity of information in the diaries, not a direct function of how much she tells us. Although Nin places her deepest expectations in the personal and private sphere, the diaries are not confessional works. Nin was a practicing Catholic until her teens and therefore familiar with the ritual of confession; she was a student of psychoanalysis and herself an analyst, accustomed to the recuperative monologues of the analysand, but her diaries are not confessional in the most common sense of the word. She does not seek to unburden herself of material as if that material is an impediment to her freedom, nor does she pay guilty attention to the more ignoble details of her life as if to absolve herself by virtue of her typicality or detestability. If anything, she is herself the priest or lay confessor, confessing to herself by means of the diary, but also, by means of the diary, absolving herself from raw experience by transmuting it into form—not just any form, but conscious and lucid writing which expresses control even when she is discussing her weaknesses.

In certain respects the diaries are as elusive as the father they are written to—the absence of Nin's husband in these pages, for instance, necessarily leaves a fissure which would make all other relationships undergo a geological shift—and Nin's omissions have been a focus for criticism of her work, some readers asserting that she appears to have led a life less conditioned by circumstance than the diaries reveal, thus giving us a falsely reassuring picture of human abilities (insofar as she comes to stand for human abilities). This is a criticism that becomes more important as her diaries tend to become more and more models of a life and books of wisdom, for if we look to Peter Pan to teach us to fly but do not see the hook and wire holding him to the ceiling we are in trouble, though he may temporarily increase our optimism.

If Nin does omit crucial elements which would change the tone and nature of the diaries as they now stand she is also persuasive in making us comprehend that these elements are not as crucial as the principles of realism have led us to think. For our idea of what a ''life'' is, based on only relative tenets of Western perception, economy, and chronology, does not necessarily match the shape or proportion with which Nin lives hers, and it is her great strength that she has resisted the habituating sets that conquer and form most of us, her vision changing our notions of the plausible and possible. Just as certain yogis dispel our assumption that we need continuous breath to stay alive, so Nin persuades us that it is not impractical to be guided by dreams, not impossible to defy gravity for a few minutes longer than we think. It is important to note that the characters in Nin's novels also have lives which are, in ordinary terms, unconditioned, possessing an anonymity and inconsistency at odds with the crystallized characterization handed down from the nineteenth-century novel, lives which are not Nin's own but which she sees in a similar way.

For Nin, realism is a form of defeat. She craves the idyllic, the supreme version, and her drive toward the perfect, the harmonized, the Utopian, and her impulse to make things as intense, prolific, and beautiful as possible, is a central feature of the diaries. Transforming her optimism into an esthetic, she believes that the role of the artist is to transform ugliness into beauty, in life as well as in writing. Taking her father's desire to be thought perfect and generously inverting it, she wants others to think they are perfect. And if she makes myth of herself and writes herself large, it is not as a narcissist but out of a desire to transform her life by means of discipline and optimism into the most lovely and elevated existence possible.

The supreme version can be a fiction, however, and we do not want diaries to be fiction, nor, for that matter, do we want novels to be fairy-tale. Nin's passion for harmony expresses itself in her distaste for harsh contradiction or polemic. She does not hold the belief that exigence and contradiction are necessary for genuine selfhood. For Nin, logic and argument, all the voices of the head as opposed to the heart, are only translations from an original emotional reality. Feeling and intellect are not different ends of a continuum but exist on separate planes, and she rejects the quality of negation in modernist literature which comes from the hegemony of intellect, for it is the intellect that doubts; the body, the feelings, are usually sure. . . . [In] both diaries and fiction she emphasizes synthesis over antithesis, maintaining a tone that holds everything in the same plane, neutralizing the distinction between figure and ground, muting conflicts in interpretation. Her style determines that people tend to read her either very loyally—moved by faith to relate, unite, and connect rather than to dispute—or not at all.

Nin's occasional neglect of sincerity and candor in the diaries—the lies she tells to others to make improvements or not to hurt, to maintain harmony and dissolve disruption—is directly related to her desire for perfection. She realizes it as a weakness—this tendency to invent or conceal—and she presents her weakness openly, not only in her own person but in figures who reflect and enlarge the problem, living it out to an extreme degree. Lying—her father's, June's—is a deep concern in Diary I, and is a theme that develops richness in *Spy in the House of Love,* where Nin attempts to find relief from it once and for all, creating a final punctuation in the person of the Lie Detector.

Nin's belief in transmutation and alchemy inspires her to alter the surface and style of things and to take adornment seriously, embracing as a pleasure what many people use only as a strategy of defense. She alters her costume to transform the occasion. . . . This passion for adornment is intimately linked to the possibilities of impersonation, for though Nin shows us how impersonation may whittle away selfhood she also makes clear that it can be a temporary but releasing expression of unlived life, truer than rigidly held consistency. . . . Nin (who associates romanticism with

neurosis perhaps because of this pretense of divided consciousness to innocent unity) dons masks and costumes in order to celebrate the complexity of identity, the unlimited truths of personality. She has a sane longing to be whole but does not pretend, sentimentally, to a wholeness she hasn't earned or an innocence that would simplify her life without being true to it. (pp. 97-100)

Notable for a grace and certainty of style, Nin's diary is utterly distinct from the current outpourings of confessional journalism, undigested notation encouraged by the general abolition of etiquette and the preeminence of therapies which encourage and value the public revelation of personal material. She does not give herself away in her writings but serves us by remaining intact even after we have devoured her work.

Perfection of, attention to style is suspect in autobiography, for we tend to feel, almost superstitiously—Romantically—that the genuine self—naked, chaotic—cannot be contained by language, and that inadequacy of language or stress of expression pays homage to the large undefinable self. Kerouac's rough work clothes and associative prose seem more authentic at first glance than Henry Adams' balanced and dressed up coat and tie sentences. Yet Adams' prim, if profound, accuracy is as revealing of personality as Kerouac's often evasive casualness. Nin's distilled style is a part of the personality being revealed by it. She has a sense of style—in dress, in personal relations, in her self-discipline—which makes transmutation of the raw into the fine a natural and constant process in her life. Stylization is not only a task of the social self, as it is for most people; it is, for Nin, instinctive and intimate. The diary is edited to make it a manageable length and to prevent injury to the living; it is also highly appropriate to Nin's stance that the diary emerges first as a distilled version of the original, for her life itself is a highly distilled version of what, with less will and vision, it might have been. (pp. 100-01)

Nin's distilled style allows us more space for ourselves than the confessional outpourings which make accomplices of us. Her diary, perfected and sometimes reticent, becomes a mirror into which we can look and, often, find ourselves clearly expressed. Her polished surface reflects the reader.

Nin's relation to the reader is not unlike her relationship to real people in the diaries, where her personal allure is clearly an overpowering factor in her experience. Her diaries are seductive rather than confessional, extending to the reader a subliminal invitation to fall in love—with her, *and* with the world—and she instinctively knows, having been traditionally feminine in many respects, the importance of concealment to the arousal of desire. Yet she is fascinated by veils actual and symbolic not out of coquetry, or modesty, but out of an appreciation of tact, subtlety, and the more enduring connections these approaches inspire. (p. 101)

The most remarkable thing about Nin is how she revives the wisdom of sympathy in an age which tends to be embarrassed by it.

The spareness and omissions of Nin's diaries result partly from her wanting to ignore—in Virginia Woolf's phrase—the "appalling narrative business of the realist," just as her strategy as a novelist is to wean us from simple curiosity and a hunger for ordinary narrative. But it is more than likely that sympathy and discretion are as responsible as formal considerations for the withholding of information in the diaries. Nin's unwillingness to injure coincides with her doctrine of omission and extends the portrait of her as a women of sympathy. There is in fact a substitution of sympathy for confessional sincerity in the diaries. . . . The apex of Nin's tact is that she creates an atmosphere of intimacy at the same time that she refrains from a policy of open disclosure. We feel, somehow, that the diaries reach into our lives, that they are intimate about *us*, intimating to us our own latent potential, the latent life force in us.

Nin's wisdom fits nicely into the American credo of "Make thyself" and many of her readers have saved and changed themselves through the inspiration of her work. There is a certain innocence and pragmatism about this reception of her diaries which should be distinguished from the character of Nin herself. She is sophisticated, European, not an innocent, though some skeptics might see her sympathetic nature as innocent. Her naturalness is real but hard won against the cold artifice of her father and her warmer inclinations to masks and perfections. She is not broad and candid by nature but tactful, oblique, delicate. It is this complexity—this chord—her given nature and her growth out of it—that makes her diaries interesting. Her openness is earned and the self she discovers and enriches is all the more authentic for being complex and struggled for. (pp. 101-02)

[There] are readers who depend on Nin's diaries to be sincere, straightforward exposition and are then disappointed (or elated) to discover a more complex mix of modes and motives. Others relinquish all the claims and expectations we bring to autobiography and call these novels. But the diaries, however, unconfessional, contain a wisdom in their obliquity and omissions. Nin teaches us to get rid of the dross of our lives, to pursue essence and ignore the masses of ordinary detail we have been trained to think of as necessary or authenticating. She compels us to believe that the supreme version is worth having, and she revives without apology and with panache the importance of sympathy and aspiration. (p. 103)

> *Lynn Sukenick, "The 'Diaries' of Anais Nin," in* Shenandoah *(copyright by* Shenandoah; *reprinted from* Shenandoah: *The Washington and Lee University Review with the permission of the Editor), Spring, 1976, pp. 96-103.*

Nin did not achieve the recognition she thought she deserved until she began to publish her diary in 1966. "The Diary of Anaïs Nin: Volume VI, 1955-1966", . . . brings the work—covering the years 1931 to 1966—to 2000 pages. At least one more volume is expected. It is time to begin to evaluate as a whole this massive output which Nin has come to view as her major work.

One measure of a diary's success is the degree to which it recreates a convincing sense of life as it is really lived. This depends most on whether the author is candid, self-aware, and direct. The first volume of Nin's diary (1931-1934) is the most compelling and coherent. . . . There is an absence of restraint, a straightforwardness in this volume that probably has to do with the fact that the diary was then only a private document not intended for publication. But far, far too often elsewhere in the scrupulously edited pages of Nin's work she fails both to make her life intimately known and to make that life something that readers can care about deeply and lastingly. Ultimately, to judge the diary is to judge Nin's integrity as well as the scope of her understanding. It is impossible to separate the writer from her subject, and the diary has only one real subject: Anais Nin.

The edited versions of the diary nearly all appear to be concealing more than they reveal. There is nothing, for example, about Nin's long marriage. We are left to guess who exactly were and were not Nin's lovers. There is very little about her daily domestic life or the source of the money on which she lives. The concrete, the practical, the material, the thingishness of life bore Nin. As a result, the Nin persona is often a writer who tries to describe the indescribable, a writer who tries to shine in print with the same "incandescence" she assures us she shines with in life. We just have to take her word for it.

It is not that the diary lacks specificity entirely. There are numerous friends described and analyzed, parties described, trips described, emotions described. The diary does have gossip appeal. Nin had relationships, intimate and otherwise, with scores of famous people in the art, film, and literary worlds. Her portraits of the 21-year-old Gore Vidal and the aging seducer Edmund Wilson are irresistible. So are Nin's very perceptive insights into Henry Miller's personality. But gossip is probably the last thing on which Nin hoped the value of the diary would rest. There is nothing snide or unfeeling in her evaluations, and that is one of the problems with the Nin persona. The diary is unbelievably free of direct expressions of anger, because Nin is unbelievably unaware of the indirect forms her resentments take.

Nin writes often, for example, that politics bores her and that the politically committed have shallow and unlived lives in comparison with her own. But boredom is not what Nin feels; rather, she feels threatened, as she admits elsewhere, by a value system that challenges her own. Nin's response to political morality is the assertion that "what is understood is not judged." But denying political reality does not remove the fact of its existence. Nin is unaware of the degree to which, like it or not, all of her perceptions, tastes, values, and ideas are a function of her social class. Oblivious of the implications of what she is saying, Nin can write passages like this one describing her stay with the Baroness Lambert during the Brussels World's Fair of 1958: "The valises had been emptied, the clothes hung up. The bath was filled with perfumed oil. . . . [The house] was filled with unostentatious luxury . . . quite different from the garish American luxury intent on dazzling you all at once with gloss, shine, newness. . . . One evening, after dinner, we walked up the stairs to the large living room. At each curve of the stairs there was a butler in a red uniform, holding a silver tray with a candle, a box of cigars, and a cigar cutter. It was like court life in the 18th century."

The issue for Nin here is American luxury versus the soft, unobtrusive European brand, not what luxury *means*. Although I would respect Nin more if she had observed that luxury in any country amounts to the relatively cheap cost of human service, the diary would not necessarily have been a better book. But if anywhere Nin had recognized that her exclusively psychological perspective was partial, and if anywhere Nin had observed her own class bias, had written about it, and tried to understand it, the diary would then have been a considerably more interesting work. In spite of Nin's desire to penetrate the truth of her experience, and in spite of her acute psychoanalytic analyses and confessions, at her frequent worst Anais Nin is superficial, a writing Jean Brodie striking elegant poses which look ridiculous. (p. 43)

It is probably the Jean Brodie syndrome in Nin that provoked women like Diana Trilling, Elizabeth Hardwick, and

Frances Keene to pen their reviews in blood. Nin was attacked for being more than a bad novelist. She seems to have stood for a certain kind of woman writer who, in her concern above all with the private, her awareness of clothes, her squeamish refusal to look at the unclean and ugly in life, and her overwhelming narcissism, was a threat to all women who had chosen to be intellectual, concrete, and political as a way of being new and free. In spite of her ambition, and in spite of her understanding of the ways in which women suffer in a male-dominated world, Anais Nin rubs irritatingly against the feminist grain.

That fact notwithstanding—and to some extent because of it—Nin's diary is still a unique and frequently engaging document. Nin was among the first to react to the tight-lipped nonemotionalism of writers like Hemingway and to insist that intimacy in fiction is what makes characters real. Although Nin was everywhere limited by her belief in the ideal of the passive, seductive woman, she consciously struggled against these limitations. Publishing her diary was, in many ways, Nin's strongest act of defiance against that ideal. But the ultimate success of that rebellion rests on the worth of the diary.... The full value of the diary will not be measurable until, if ever, we see it in its unexpurgated form. (pp. 43-4)

Laurie Stone, "Anaïs Nin: Is the Bloom off the Pose?" in The Village Voice *(reprinted by permission of* The Village Voice; *copyright © by The Village Voice, Inc., 1976), July 26, 1976, pp. 43-4.*

Anais Nin is passionately fond of "transmutation," finding "correspondences," "analogies," and "identities" with herself, and herself alone, everywhere. The treacly web she began to spin at age eleven [her diary] has reached by now mammoth proportions, its size matched only by its vacuity. Stupefied by the monotonous voice of the diarist, one re-opens a volume once read and does not remember it at all. From the thirties in Paris with Henry Miller to the New York-Los Angeles shuttle of the sixties, from psychiatrists Allendy, Rank, and Bogner to writers Artaud, Durrell, Duras, Young, and James Leo Herlihy, it's all one. It's impossible to discover what progress, in the *bildungsroman* of the psyche, these volumes—so far the distilled essence of over 160 notebooks—are meant to illustrate....

Ever the aristocrat, [Anais Nin] claims for herself every possible distinction. She is the embattled artist unaccountably placed in an oatmeal world of philistines, Marxists, and realists (synonyms in the Nin lexicon). Equally, she is Woman, a shortcut to the psyche, the child of surrealism, and the heir to the future. For each of these roles she offers herself a crown and then looks in vain for her kingdom.

By *consciously* mythologizing the self, she does reach cosmic proportions, those of caricature, and what is equally ludicrous, her conception of the Artist, Modern Woman, et al. is altogether banal....

Unlike the rest of us, Anais Nin for all her talk of psycho-analysis, neurosis, and the divided self—doesn't appear to experience, finally, any second thoughts. Not a word about an integrity that comes from inherited money nor, for that matter, any clue to a "spiritual vision" that she often refers to but never delineates....

[Whenever] "woman" comes up, she turns out to be another name for Anais Nin and the cosmology she champions. By nature, woman is too attuned to the depths to settle for the oatmeal world of Marxists and not surprisingly, she is something of a surrealist (only profounder) and Freudian (only profounder). When she is an artist as well, she must naturally save the world....

The astonishing thing about this kind of drivel ... is that it has been taken up by the women's movement. Despite Nin's reliance on the worst sort of sexual stereotypes, the fact that she reverses the valances so that intuition, emotion, spontaneity, a childlike acceptance, irrationality, even, are now woman's virtues instead of her limitations has been enough to assure her stature among some feminists. She has achieved, after all, one of the crowns she gave herself. As long as there are those who find the sexes to be an either-or proposition, she'll continue to reign.

When Nin isn't occupied with her royal stature in the vanguard of literature and womanhood, she allows for humbler, less cosmic concerns. Thus, the quotidian tasks are good for a few lines along with recurrent attention to her rejecting father and (less so) friends. But even the simplest of chores is only a step from her overwhelming urge to "transform," "transmute," "alchemize." Hence, Nin can say, "I believe something magical happens when I wipe the furniture," and worse, the juxtapositions that result—the diamond of her art to dusting the house—do not (as they are meant to do) evoke the untidy, multileveled way one lives. The organization or editing of the *Diaries* is such that the spontaneous, like everything else, is caricatured. (p. 26)

[A] diary that covered the last four decades by a woman who'd been everywhere and known everyone could have been—as some claim this one to be—a remarkable document. Filtering the cultural life of the West through the sensibility of an extraordinary woman, yes, that would tell us about woman, culture, and life itself. Anais Nin, though, isn't that extraordinary woman—a little of her (say one modest volume?) goes a long way. That her values are not those of Jane Austen, Swift, or Edmund Wilson is not the objection. In itself her distrust of the ratiocinative life and her involvement with the "way we experience things deep down" is easy enough to accept. The trouble is that she hasn't anything to say. Either she passionately embraces the inarticulate, involving us with "depths" and a "vast unconscious" as unfathomable now as when her first diary appeared in 1966, or she mines awfully well-covered ground: art-loving Europe versus nasty, materialistic America, a profound revolution in the psyche versus shallow political change, and so on.

Most damaging of all, however, is her complete epistemological confusion. Despite occasional evidence to the contrary, she engages in a lifelong dialogue of the objective versus the subjective, herself aligned (naturally) with the subjective....

Finally, she hasn't quite accepted that the division is a bogus one. Once obsessed by a distinction that is altogether nonexistent, the chances for making one's life script a cornucopia of phantoms is immense....

Anais Nin tilts at windmills because she's put reality on a scorecard: the meat and potatoes world doesn't match the superior reality her deep-sea diving for essences can produce. And 'objective' knowledge isn't as fine as 'subjective' insight. The result is a frightening irony: no one more than surrealism's child needs Nabokov's caution that reality always requires quotation marks. (p. 27)

Susan Manso, in New Boston Review

(copyright © 1976 by Boston Critic, Inc.), Fall, 1976.

Anais Nin . . . through her fiction and her life shared in her diaries, has given us the gift of the transforming beauty and the spiritual communion that we can experience through art. She has given us also the bravery to chose a vision deeply felt and personal, the courage to defend the artist's striving for the largeness which the world will not allow. Herself a giant in passion and in involvement with the labyrinthian underworlds of writing, a heroic voyager into the shadowy unconscious regions from which all visions and all works of art come forth, she is one of this century's great defenders of largeness and innovative risk-taking in others. . . .

Anais' writing is a deliberate quest for beauty and transcendence, not only for new forms of expression but for new ways of penetrating feelings. (p. 27)

Hers is the search for the new art form which will embody change and hope and expansion of consciousness, the exploration of the world through intimate communion with the self, the creation of a personal poetic vision so intense that it "breaks its own shell and its own obsessions and reaches the whole." . . . Anais [stands] steadfastly against depersonalization and a giving over to despair. She strives in her fiction to fill the dark void left by the existentialists, to rearrange the shards of their shattered reality into new configurations of possibility. (pp. 27-8)

Because the existing literary establishment did not understand her work, she created around herself a whole movement that did, one which has profoundly influenced the place of impassioned writing in America, one which has brought us all into closer touch with symbolism and surrealism. . . .

In an age of smallness, constriction, and fear, at a time when emerging women writers are being encouraged by the male establishment to write small unimportant books that will not seriously alter anyone's vision, male or female, fragmented descriptions of the everyday which threaten no one and do not challenge the existing order, Anais Nin appears before us as a hero of art and aspiration, advocating the largeness of all we may become and all we may create. She offers us the vision of woman, not as biological mother merely, but as the nurturer of the artist, as the great creative force. She offers also a new vision of spiritual friendships based upon deep inner affinities, a role model for working relationships women writers of the past have rarely realized. She offers a challenge to the whole idea of creative isolation, a new view of art as profoundly connected with the most vital forms of communication. (p. 28)

Erika Duncan, in New Boston Review (copyright © 1976 by Boston Critic, Inc.), Fall, 1976.

If you appreciate erotica, Anaïs Nin's work, commissioned by a male client in the 40s may be intriguing. Though she made a valiant effort to lift her made-to-order stories . . . to something out of the ordinary, to endow them with imagination, fresh language and feeling, the word came back from her customer: "Leave out the poetry." She simply couldn't do it. Beauty of language was too much a part of her. Still, erotica is erotica and however talented the writer, sheer physicality has its limitations. It's quite evident that Nin realized them, for she seems to have found that once the scene was set, the action accomplished, there was little

more to say. Thus transitions and endings in these tales are abrupt, often clumsy, the characters pasteboard, the plotting weak. If there is a bit of poetry here, an attempt at a female language for sexuality, it still doesn't save the day. How sad she had to use her talents this way. Redemption comes in that she could never manage to separate sex from feeling. (pp. 73-4)

Publishers Weekly (reprinted from the April 11, 1977, issue of Publishers Weekly, published by R. R. Bowker Company, a Xerox company; copyright © 1977 by Xerox Corporation), April 11, 1977.

Anais Nin's famous erotica (only brief excerpts of which appeared in Diary III), written in the early 1940's for a private collector, have now become public under the suggestive title of "Delta of Venus." (p. 11)

Begun, as Nin writes in Diary III, "tongue-in-cheek," the stories that Nin then thought were "exaggerated" and "caricaturing sexuality" can be read as original contributions to a slowly emerging American tradition of literary erotic writing. They are, furthermore, the first American stories by a woman to celebrate sexuality with complete and open abandonment.

In a postscript to "Delta of Venus," written in September 1976, a few months before her death, Nin noted that in the erotica she was "intuitively using a woman's language, seeing sexual experience from a woman's point of view." She had already noted in Diary III that the "language of sex has yet to be invented, the language of the senses has yet to be explored." Anaïs Nin became the inventor of such a language: the language in "Delta of Venus" is delicate, sinuous, precise and sensual; it is a language that is astonishing as much for its "purity," its freedom from prurience and from the usual "dirty" language of erotica written by men as for its spirited, unsqueamish sexuality. . . . [What] she emphasized in her best stories was not exploitative aggression (common to male erotica) but the pleasures of sexual surrender. . . . Even as Nin, therefore, yielded to her collector's demand to leave out the poetry, she was still able to "concentrate on sex," and write the poem!

The characters in these stories, though occasionally caricatures, as Nin realized, are similar to the Parisian artists and Bohemians of the 1940's that appear in her other fiction. But whereas in "House of Incest," for example, she depicts these characters in a language that is elusive and dreamlike, in her erotica she writes more directly, using language that becomes more poetic for its very precision, even for its naturalism. (pp. 11, 26)

"Pleasure," therefore, is a word that occurs frequently in these stories. . . . The brothel or the opium den, the studio or the Swiss chalet become mythic settings in "Delta of Venus," not only for the fulfillment of love or its failure but for a quest for knowledge through the body. (p. 26)

Harriet Zinnes, "Collector's Item," in The New York Times Book Review (© 1977 by The New York Times Company; reprinted by permission), July 10, 1977, pp. 11, 26.

* * *

NIVEN, Larry 1938-

Niven is an American science fiction novelist and short story writer. One of the most promising of the younger practitioners of science fiction, he has the rare ability to combine stylis-

tic proficiency with a sophisticated awareness of current scientific discoveries and trends. In this respect, Niven writes "hard" science fiction or updated space opera. Niven, who already has three Hugo Awards to his credit, has recently been writing in collaboration with Jerry Pournelle. (See also *Contemporary Authors*, Vols. 21-24, rev. ed.)

["The Mote in God's Eye"] is a big book—537 pages—with a theme that has intrigued writers and readers since the days of H. G. Wells: The first contact between the human race and a race of intelligent aliens. The two authors [Niven and Pournelle] have impressive credentials.... Yet 20 pages into their novel, I found myself asking, with the congenital uneasiness of all reviewers, "Could this be a put-on?" Five hundred pages later, I reluctantly concluded that it was not. What [they] have done is to graft a serious "first-contact" novel onto a laughably bad space opera.

The result is a textbook demonstration of what is wrong with so much modern s.f.: The only believable poeple are the aliens.... [They] are not merely bug-eyed monsters; the best scenes in the book describe the way in which each individual is adapted perfectly—physically and psychologically—to his assigned niche on the Motie world. It turns out that there is an aspect of Motie civilization that the aliens are trying to hide from human eyes, and the fate of the human Galactic Empire hangs on the unraveling of this mystery. Unfortuanately, the human beings who do the unraveling appear to have wandered into the plot from a swashbuckler about some other Empire—Queen Victoria's, perhaps, circa 1898....

The 19th century flavor in Niven's and Pournelle's Galactic Empire does not work as allegory or parody; it simply represents a failure of imagination. Creating a coherent futuristic background is the s.f. writer's hardest job, and borrowing materials from the past is an old and useful trick. But even history rewritten in space-drag must contain a few oblique hints about how things have changed—if only in such superficial areas as clothes, food and sex. (p. 32)

Gerald Jonas, in The New York Times Book Review *(© 1975 by The New York Times Company; reprinted by permission), January 12, 1975.*

There is a certain type of science fiction story that is completely incomprehensible to the non-S.F. reader. Devotees know it as the "hard science" story. A typical plot involves a hero whose survival depends on the proper use of some futuristic mechanical device. After describing the device—spaceship, time machine, air-purifier, etc.—in great detail, the author announces that it has broken down. The hero must fix it quickly or die. Superficially, the hard-science story resembles an old-fashioned detective story. The author takes care to make the general background convincing, and he is expected to scatter enough clues around so that the alert reader can figure out what the hero will do even before the hero does it. But in fact, the reader has no chance whatever of solving the puzzle, because the solution usually depends on some quirk of futuristic science that the author has made up in the first place. The real puzzle is why these stories are so popular. My guess is that they provide a heady illusion of membership in a scientific elite, without making any demands on the reader (but without insulting his intelligence either). Devotees recognize Larry Niven as one of the masters of this rather specialized subgenre; and his most recent collection, "Tales of Known Space," ... is clearly addressed to those who are already familiar with his work. Outsiders need not apply. (p. 49)

Gerald Jonas, in The New York Times Book Review *(© 1975 by The New York Times Company; reprinted by permission), October 26, 1975.*

A case could be made for the proposition that the deepest subject of Science Fiction is not the vision of other worlds it purports to offer us, but rather the demonstration of our own incapacity to imagine such worlds in the first place. It is a failure of imagination that begins, of course, on the physical level, with the appearance of the individual aliens themselves. Locke observes somewhere that, all ideas ultimately deriving from empirical experience, the wildest chimera invented by the human mind can ultimately always be resolved back into the bits and pieces, the basic building blocks, of all-too-familiar earthly realities. So, fatally, the best aliens Sci-fi has to offer ... turn out to be misspellings of more familiar creatures like bugs and ostriches, giant cats, frogs or turtles, or, as in the case of ... *The Mote in God's Eye,* furry monkey-like beings with an arm in the wrong place. (pp. 35-6)

[The] best of recent Sci-fi—*The Mote,* Arthur C. Clarke's *Rendez-vous with Rama,* Stanislaw Lem's *Eden* or *The Invincible*—focus our attention on the procedures by which we explore an unfamiliar planet and make contact with its inhabitants, seek to interest us in the technical difficulties inherent in such an expedition, rather than in the momentary thrill of their first "flesh-and-blood" appearance.

Sci-fi today may be said to have shifted its emphasis from the nature of the individual alien to that of alien culture; hence the disappearance of the monster as a staple (particularly of the Sci-fi films of the 1950s).... Asimov once suggested that the history of Sci-fi could be read in terms of a development from an initial period of adventure and space opera, through the classical ("golden age") science-and-technology stage, to a mature sociological one, which is with us today, and to which we owe works like those of Ursula Le Guin. Not only does this make life more difficult for the Sci-fi writer, however—it's a lot harder to invent imaginary cultures and imaginary social structures than to produce a bug-eyed monster—it also raises the stakes of Sci-fi as a form, and lends the dictum of Locke new and unforeseen consequences. The inability to imagine new senses, multiple dimensions, new colors or organs—what we may call the perceptual function of Sci-fi—is a good deal less serious a matter, perhaps, than its Utopian function, its capacity or incapacity to imagine other forms of collective living. (p. 35)

[The] Utopian imagination itself, that very capability of drafting and projecting alternate ways of life from which the political visions of the past drew their power, has virtually atrophied within the windless closure of an increasingly total system. But if the alien worlds of science fiction fail to embody any genuinely future history or social difference, then it must be supposed that they reflect back stages and forms already known to us, in coded fashion, without our clearly realizing it.

Even more clearly than *The Mote in God's Eye,* Niven's earlier work gives a striking illustration of this process. A "future history" cycle ..., it presents the peculiarity of a radical break in the middle; and the ancient empire of the thrints, a race of feudal overlords who committed galactic suicide in the face of a successful slave uprising, is separated by millions of years from the emergence of humanity, whose near future Niven sees in the more conventional terms of a galaxy-wide colonization. This near future scheme then allows for the double standard of a dystopian earth—with its organ banks and the new legal system generated by them, in which the mildest crimes, such as jaywalking, serve as judicial pretexts for separating the individual from a stock of valuable transplants—side by side with the rugged individualism of a space-age mining and prospecting frontier in the meteorites that ring the outer part of our Solar System (the "Belt").

Niven's first novel, the intelligent and ingeniously plotted *World of Ptavvs*, gives us the clue to the realities behind this imaginary cycle, while ostensibly telling the tale of a "full-grown thrint," who, surviving the destruction of his own world by billions of years in a stasis field, is outwitted in his attempt to take over ours by an orthodox Jewish telepath with an affinity for dolphins and an inclination to practical jokes.

The mode of being of the thrint—a union of personal authority and presence with sheer physical domination—makes it clear that his collision with Greenberg is also a contact with a type of power unfamiliar in the financial and bureaucratic organization of present-day capitalism. It does not seem terribly far-fetched to suppose that the image of the thrint incorporates faint echoes of the feudal predecessor of our own historical world. That earth's bourgeoisie, in its heroic age—the bourgeoisie of the Protestant Ethic, the Reign of Terror and the British Empire—was able to meet and vanquish feudalism on its own ground is a historical fact; that bourgeoisie, however, is now a thing of the past. The anxiety that haunts Niven's little fable would seem to attach to ourselves and our own capacities, to the credit-card suburban bourgeoisie of the consumer society, with its foundation-grant intelligentsia; if so, the novel provides a reassuringly positive forecast as to the outcome of a head-on clash between a bourgeoisie of organization men and a full-grown thrint. Niven's first book thus offers a playful variant on the by-now-familiar Ardrey anxiety-fantasy: have we gone soft in the age of the welfare state? Are we still men enough to meet the enemy . . . on their own terrain and with their own weapons? The difference between Niven's strategy and the radical right Minute-Man or *Deliverance*-type answer to this question lies in the relative efficiency of practical jokes versus push-ups (Niven's hero ultimately concludes that thrints are stupid); but the question remains the same in both cases and it is the question itself which is first and foremost ideological.

Ideology becomes a good deal more insistent and visible in the later part of Niven's cycle, as in *The Mote* itself. The spaceship of *Ptavvs* was named the *Heinlein,* that of *The Mote in God's Eye* the *MacArthur;* and it is doubtless "no accident" that Heinlein should himself have endorsed *The Mote* . . . as "possibly the finest science fiction novel I have ever read." Not, I hasten to assure the reader, that these books have anything in common stylistically with the interminable and self-indulgent 100-percent talk novels of Heinlein's later period. The older writer is something like the John Ford of Sci-fi, his conservatism that of a right-wing New Deal Cold War orthodoxy, something like a Jackson politics, one would think. The sassiness of the Niven/Pournelle *Weltanschauung* sounds more like William F. Buckley, a mixture of wit and provocation the force of which depends mainly on the fact that for so many long years of liberal orthodoxy you "weren't supposed to say things like that."

Still, ideology is mainly the exercise of fantasies about a particular and privileged way of life that has a special symbolic meaning for the subject: the ideological fantasy that Niven shares with Heinlein is clearly that of the all-male locker and club-room existence, the Navy hierarchy, the war-time *esprit de corps* and commando unit solidarity. . . . One of the chief innovations of the Niven/Pournelle *Mote* is indeed that the space ship is here for a change considered to be a Navy vessel rather than something connected to the air force, and thus provides admirals, cutters, the bridge and the watch, regulations, and everything else needful for the proper satisfaction of a Navy mystique. The other, non-Heinlein component of Niven's ideology—a glamorization of the romance of business, of the sudden strikes of lonely prospectors on distant meteorites, of the encounters and adventures of intergalactic merchants among exotic species—is in many ways fresher and more original, but relatively absent from *The Mote*.

The latter novel marks a considerable evolution from the social and historical elements that power the comic space opera of *Ptavvs*. True, mote society is characterized as an "industrial feudalism"; yet the emphasis here is no longer on the self-reliance of the individual knight, but has been displaced onto the hierarchical features of the feudal system as a whole, here embodied in the biological castes of a function-differentiated species. . . . [The] motie life-world comes as something of a shock, being in constant and bewildering flux, the places, vehicles, furniture built by hand ad hoc for specific occasions and then at once dismantled only to be reconstructed into something unrecognizable. Here once again we glimpse the perceptual vocation of Sci-fi, encouraging an imaginative speculation about the nature of experience and in particular of temporality and memory, in a henceforth unstable spatial element from which all fixed coordinates have disappeared. (pp. 35-7)

The Mote in God's Eye can also be read as something like foreign policy Sci-fi, insofar as it raises the basic policy issue: is peaceful coexistence with the Mote desirable or even possible, and at what cost? At this point we can more fully assess the consequences of that shift in emphasis already mentioned from the dramatization of the individual Bug-Eyed Monster (as in *Ptavvs*) to an interest in the very nature and organization of alien culture. The individual monster can stand as sheer evil, inexplicable aggressivity, a will to power ("taking over the world") that needs no further justification; but the minute you begin to describe the functioning of an entire society, you need (or else you apply without being aware of it) a whole philosophy of history: for any narrative about social change—whether it deals in the fact of historiography or journalism, or in the fiction of, say, galactic empires—necessarily presupposes a set of more general propositions as to the way change comes about and the dynamics of history in general. The splendid variety of hypothetical cultures and their exploration in recent SF . . . should not obscure the poverty of their historical presuppositions and the conceptual limits in which all are imprisoned. The explanatory machinery of SF ranges from notions of spiritual failure of one kind or another, or the even more comfortable hypothesis that history happens by cosmic accident or merely by chance (*i.e.,* the empiricist claim that no philosophy of history is possible), all the way to conceptions of the preponderant influence of individual free will and great men, of bureaucracy, of political power or totalitarianism and the more recent ecological or biological theories implied by apocalyptic images of overpopulation, pollution and the like. Yet insofar as a given theory of history diverts us from the causal relationship between the squalor of contemporary society and the irreversible dynamic of capitalism as a system, to precisely that degree it is ideological and a mystification.

The fate of alien society as it is depicted in *The Mote in God's Eye* is certainly no exception to such a trend: if anything, makes such underlying social and historical assumptions inescapable by developing their political implications in an open and explicit way. This is, indeed, a new Cold War literature, differing from the older kind in that we need no longer see the enemy in terms of individual malevolence (as blob or monster), a strategy which increasing press exposure to the Russians and the Chinese has in any case rendered ludicrous and anachronistic. *The Mote* rather sets out to demonstrate that in spite of the possible good will of individual moties, the danger lies in their system itself, in a way that it is quite beyond the power of individuals to remedy. The novel thus seeks quite consciously, by providing a more "objective" account of the red menace, to lend the hard line against coexistence renewed intellectual respectability. Now it is no longer Big Brother's "lust for power" that threatens us, but rather the seemingly more realistic prospect of a submergence of our own society beneath the unchecked proliferation of creatures as alien and objectively hostile to it as are the beings on the Mote. . . . The Niven/Pournelle solution is of course to bottle the moties up inside their own solar system; and the concluding description of a fleet of intergalactic destroyers poised to blast the mote ships as they materialize within the transit points of our own deep space offers a more vivid image of containment than anything proposed by a Kennan or a Dulles. Yet the usefulness of *The Mote in God's Eye* as propaganda is surely outweighted by its value as a symptom: its authors, after all, have remained faithful to the deepest vocation of science fiction, namely, to articulate those buried fantasies by which a collectivity seeks to come to terms with its own future and its Utopian—or dystopian—possibilities. (pp. 37-8)

Fredric Jameson, "Science Fiction as Politics," in The New Republic *(reprinted by permission of* The New Republic; © *1976 by* The New Republic, Inc.*), October 30, 1976, pp. 34-8.*

O

O'BRIEN, Edna 1932-

An Irish novelist and short story writer, O'Brien uses the material from her rigid Catholic upbringing for her fiction which examines the man/woman question in her native country. Because of her frank portrayal of human sexuality, many of O'Brien's works are still banned in Ireland. (See also *CLC*, Vols. 3, 5, and *Contemporary Authors*, Vols. 1-4, rev. ed.)

Edna O'Brien's stories of the past decade [depict] . . . characters [who] are in and of the modern world. Its rootless alien nature at once defines her protagonists and thrusts them into limbo. They are threatened by madness because they can find no enduring place in that world, and they have no values of an older time to fall back upon. They have been deceived by the possibilities of love, and life holds no other meaning. They are immersed in contemporaneity and consequently as uncomfortable and rudderless as Kafka's faceless men. The range of experience is narrow but deep, and one perceives the control and power of "The Love Object" and such later stories as "Over," "A Journey," and "The House of My Dreams". . . . Miss O'Brien tells her stories through a viewpoint character who is always female, . . . [and] lets her viewpoint character (who is often engaged in a monologue) bore still deeper into the meaning of her experience until that meaning has been wrung from it. (In these first-person narratives Miss O'Brien renders her "imitation of a speaking voice engaged in the telling of a tale." This technique stands at the center of Irish fiction, as Thomas Kilroy has insisted. "It is a voice heard over and over again, whatever its accent, a voice with a supreme confidence in its own histrionics, one that assumes with its audience a shared ownership of the told tale and all that this implies.")

"The House of My Dreams" is an instance of Miss O'Brien's writing at the top of her form. . . . [The] author has forged a distinctive style and voice and has gotten out from under Joyce, O'Flaherty, and O'Connor as Mary Lavin did before her in an entirely different way. Edna O'Brien's stories are superb examples of what Garfitt has observed: "Recent Irish fiction has a distinctly individual focus, centring on a single articulate person, questioning existence among others who are less bothered, or too busy to care." (pp. iv, vi)

George Core, in Sewanee Review *(reprinted*

by permission of the editor, © 1976 by The University of the South), Winter, 1976.

The best things in this rather insubstantial book [*Mother Ireland*] are the banal yet magical moments of childhood, 'the passionate transitory' in Patrick Kavanagh's phrase. . . . Miss O'Brien writes as arrestingly as ever. . . . And there are flashes of poignancy that recall her early novels, as when she waits hopelessly on O'Connell Bridge for a fellow who jilted her, while 'the neon with a different gaudy light for each digit announced and re-announced the word BOVRIL'. But there is something premature and factitious about the whole exercise. It might have been a good idea to wait a while longer before giving us the really considered autobiography which may yet be her masterpiece. (p. 747)

Derek Mahon, in New Statesman *(© 1976 The Statesman & Nation Publishing Co. Ltd.), June 4, 1976.*

There is a point of artistry at which the most commonplace circumstances or experiences can crystallise to a kind of super-ordinariness—this is what happens in the stories of Edna O'Brien when she is at her best. She has created characters who are mildly fatalistic: saturated at school in a vulgar Catholicism, their motivations nonetheless are innocently profane. There is a vapid, undirected element in their behaviour, a rural expectancy tempered with underlying stoicism. The life they have to contend with most often is brutal and depressed, and it is to the author's credit that these qualities are conveyed in a style which partakes of neither. Authenticity and restraint are her novels' most valuable characteristics.

Whether imagined or transcribed the childhood evocations of Edna O'Brien are as particular and astringent as Seamus Heaney's, as disabused as those of Patrick Kavanagh. There is some overlapping of fact and fiction of course: episodes that have found their way into the novels are repeated in *Mother Ireland,* but these gain a new sharpness and interest from the context of reminiscence. . . .

Edna O'Brien's prose is sometimes idiosyncratic but always delicately pitched. [In *Mother Ireland*], the style can be faulted only in the opening chapter where certain words and phrases from old school history books are not properly assimilated with the text. The result is an uncharacteristic feyness. . . . But the old lesson books are a part of every Irish child's experience: they are charged with associations that are valid for the author's purpose. Since the history of Ireland is compressed into seventeen pages, only its most picturesque elements can be cited. . . . The dangers of 'personal' writing, laxity, disorganisation, self-indulgence, are avoided here through the author's sense of the particular and her refusal to prettify or speculate. True, the structure is informal and the sequence of episodes sometimes inconsequential—but these minor defects may have arisen spontaneously from the subject-matter. Ireland, after all, cannot be pinned down: traditionally it defies order, resists classification. (p. 76)

Mother Ireland may be unique in the genre, for its avoidance of nostalgia, its disenchantment. Edna O'Brien's Ireland is not inviting or imposing but it is impressive. The book should be read for its honesty and perceptiveness. (pp. 76-7)

> *Patricia Craig, in* Books and Bookmen (© *copyright Patricia Craig 1976; reprinted with permission),* July, 1976.

In "Mother Ireland" Miss O'Brien has been set down to do a brief evocation of her childhood and her country, to go with some splendid photographs by Fergus Bourke. The effort is forced and full of pain and anger. To get through it she puts on her pub Irish, her brogue, her stock irony. She is an artist in hiding; flashes of her come out in a marvelous phrase, a fragment of a portrait, a moment of atmosphere so perfect it is like a Last Judgment; but most of the book is a mask.

"Mother Ireland" rambles in and around six chapter headings. "The Land Itself" is a mixture of history and overview. It has some well-phrased observations. . . .

But most of the history is written in mock-grandiloquent phrases such as "on the morrow," or "they murthered, spoilt, burnt and laid low." . . . Why does the author wrap herself in the language of five centuries of written and oral Irish history? Why doesn't she speak to us? . . .

There are . . . good moments. There is the teacher who wrote out words such as "intenerate" (to make tender). When the children asked what they meant, she would point to the dictionary and command: "Forage, forage." At the end of the day the children vanished noisily and "we would leave behind us oak desks littered with books and jotters and a teacher suddenly quiet, opaque, staring, possibly wondering what she might do for the remainder of the day without the annoyance and companionship of us."

This kind of thing comes intermittently. When she abandons her mock-heroic re-creation of Irish history Miss O'Brien tells of her childhood and her young life in Dublin in stock incidents. . . .

Experience, maybe particularly in Ireland, folds into a stereotyped mold. But Miss O'Brien's tendency is to present it on the stereotypical level instead of bringing the life out of it. She holds her memories up and dangles them and plays them for what they are most easily worth: she keeps them well away from herself.

It is a necklace without a string. Miss O'Brien does not inhabit her memories, she writes at them. There is no remembering, only elaboration. Perhaps she should have waited. In a decade or two the bitterness might still be there but she might have been able to distill and present it without disguise.

As it is, the title, "Mother Ireland," is her private curse arrayed as a joke: it goes right back to James Joyce calling Ireland the sow that eats her farrow. The author has escaped eating but not scarring. (p. 6)

> *Richard Eder, in* The New York Times Book Review (© *1976 by The New York Times Company; reprinted by permission),* September 19, 1976.

*   *   *

OLESHA, Yuri   1899-1960

Olesha was a Russian novelist, short story writer, playwright, poet, and essayist. In his incisive social satires and enchanting short stories, he displays a playful intelligence and an affirmative attitude towards life. However, his love of freedom and his outspoken criticism of post-revolutionary Russia earned him the disfavor of Stalin, and Olesha was arrested and thrown into a forced labor camp. Critics have credited Olesha with the introduction of the element of slapstick into Russian literature. His novel *Envy* is a minor classic.

Olesha, like his young intellectual contemporaries, sided with the new regime and this position was reflected in his early verse and in his novel-length fairy tale *Three Fat Men* about a revolution in a fairy-tale land that ends with a fairy-tale proletariat triumphant. It is a charming story that eventually became a play and a ballet, and it was the only work by which Olesha's name remained known throughout the grimmest years of the Stalin era.

Olesha's fateful moment came in 1927. That year he published his novel *Envy*. It was an immediate sensation. And perhaps just as sensational, considering what the book said, was the unqualified official endorsement by the government-controlled press. The acclaim followed the full course from specialized literary journals like *Revolution and Culture* all the way to *Pravda,* the supreme repository of Soviet literary judgment. (pp. vii-viii)

Despite this early tribute, Olesha was soon neck-deep in trouble. Somehow, somewhere, signals had got crossed: instead of admiring and wishing to emulate the novel's "positive heroes," readers went as far as to identify with the villain, the "negative hero" who displayed the whole spectrum of loathsome, discarded, obsolete "petty-bourgeois" feelings, from bilious envy through slobbering sentimentality and deadening indifference to total degradation.

Obviously, Olesha not only had failed to deliver the proper message but had delivered a perverse one instead. So the literary critics had to revise their original verdict; this time they found Olesha guilty of "formalism," "naturalism," "objectivism," and "cosmopolitanism." These are grave charges in the vocabulary of a Soviet literary critic. (p. viii)

The same accusations were thrown at Olesha's shorter works, which appeared during the immediately following years—"Love," "The Cherry Stone," "From the Secret Notebook of Fellow-Traveler Sand," and others. As a result, Olesha's writings were soon virtually out of print.

For many years Olesha was known to the younger generation of Soviet readers as the author of *Three Fat Men* or of occasional anti-Western articles in *Literaturnaya gazeta,* the journal of the Union of Soviet Writers.

Then Stalin died and literary controls were somewhat slackened. During that period, now referred to as "the thaw," a collection of Olesha's writing, including *Envy* and other "denounced" works, saw daylight again. It was ushered in by a typical Soviet introductory piece, "explaining" to the reader that, whenever life under the Soviet regime appears unattractive in Olesha's stories, either he does not mean what he seems to be saying or he is simply overindulging in paradoxes, or—all other arguments failing—he was mistaken at the time but realized his error later and recanted. But while concluding that Olesha was, after all, on the side of Communism, the author of the introduction to the post-Stalin edition is careful not to stick his neck out as far as the critics in 1927. For who can ever be sure when assessing the whimsical imagery and symbolism of such a writer? (p. ix)

Like his beggar in "Jottings of a Writer," Olesha is "standing in a drafty passage." The beggar stands in a passage between the drizzly street and a brightly lit store; Olesha, between what he loosely calls the nineteenth and the twentieth centuries. The street represents the nineteenth century, the world of his childhood, which was governed by the old, obsolete feelings without which he cannot write. Unlike the throngs of people who rush into the store, banging the door behind them, Olesha and his beggar cannot cut themselves off so brutally. Olesha must take his past with him into the budding new world of industrialization and five-year plans. (pp. ix-x)

That beggar turns up again and again in Olesha's writings and figures even in Olesha's speech to the First Congress of Soviet Writers (1934). (p. x)

When he wrote *Envy,* Olesha was apparently stuck in that passage between the two worlds. The poem-like novel is full of nostalgia for the discarded old world and its feelings. The attitudes of the various characters toward the wholesale eradication of the unwanted but familiar and comfortable sentiments, and their replacement by new, streamlined, and rational relations, range from open rebellion to enthusiastic endorsement. And Olesha conveys these attitudes by a symbolism as subtle and concentrated as is likely ever to be found in a *profession de foi.* (pp. x-xi)

Olesha uses . . . four characters like the stops of a musical instrument and plays a strange tune, woven out of notes of sadness, hope, rebellion, acceptance, and despair. The ending is a grotesquely plaintive tremolo of resignation. The men representing four distinctive attitudes toward the regime are four metaphorical milestones in time. (p. xi)

There is little doubt that, like Kavalerov [his alter ego, in *Envy,*] Olesha was both saddened and frightened by the new world that was taking shape before his eyes. . . .

Olesha pleaded with the nascent world for the right to be admitted into it with his sentimental luggage, without which he could never be anything but a beggar and would be doomed to regret forever his possessions abandoned in the past. (p. xii)

[The] disparagement of the West [in his major play, *A List of Assets,* was] no mere bone Olesha tossed to the Soviet critics to forestall the automatic accusation that he was in the pay of the capitalists. Like George Orwell, he feared the future, not just the Soviet future.

It must be noted that later, in some quarters in the West, Olesha's *Envy* was misunderstood and mishandled. . . . But it was not commercialization in Olesha's case. In fact, Olesha was welcomed with open arms: the literary critics of the psychoanalytical school eyed hungrily the wealth of his symbols. It did not bother them in the least that these were carefully collected devices chosen to convey extremely conscious thoughts referring to very specific situations. They pounced upon them and, using their various textbooks and vying with one another, explained Olesha in terms of phallic symbols, castration fears, and death wishes. (pp. xiv-xv)

Long before most, a man of Olesha's perspicacity must have anticipated the worst aspects of Stalinism. Too lucid to hide them under euphemisms or explain them away as temporary aberrations, as many intellectuals did, Olesha resisted. As long as he could, he argued, pleaded, begged, would "not go gentle into that good night." When, at last, he found protest not only futile but potentially fatal, he simply stopped writing. To be sure, he did come up with some "beautiful little vignettes," as the Soviet writer who reintroduced Olesha to the public put it. But these vignettes were only little masks that Olesha made grin complacently or snarl with affected xenophobia, as the case demanded. (p. xv)

There is a curious parallel between the career of Olesha and that of his contemporary fellow townsman, Isaac Babel. Both reached full artistic maturity in the second half of the twenties; both fell silent in the early thirties. After that, they wrote little and, as far as is known, nothing of comparable value to their early work. (pp. xv-xvi)

All the works collected here, except one, were written between 1927 and 1933. "Natasha" (1936) is the only piece from Olesha's "post-literary" period that could be included without too much apology. Even so, it provides a sufficiently striking contrast to the other writings to give an inkling of what had happened to Olesha during the intervening years. In "Natasha" the former intricate lacework of symbols is no longer there. Instead, we are offered a rather insipid paradox: in the past people used to invent all sorts of stories to cover up their trysts but Natasha, a girl of the young Soviet generation, invents trysts to conceal from her father the fact that she is a parachutist. One can still recognize here Olesha's former theme: the young world does not understand the one that preceded it, and the survivors of the old world feel left out and mortified. How much more honestly, and therefore more subtly, is this theme developed in his early works. (pp. xvi-xvii)

Olesha expresses himself almost entirely through . . . symbols. They are strictly functional, not at all ornamental, as some critics have suggested. Olesha uses them to create patterns of character and emotional environments. (p. xvii)

Olesha's metaphors and symbols, with which he conveys his thought through artistic shortcuts, are so effective because of their freshness. He seems to raise them deep out of his childhood and then integrate them into his narrative with consummate skill, looking on with artistic detachment all the while (Olesha was a great reviser: he wrote, for instance, more than a hundred versions of the first page of *Envy*).

In his essay "On Prevention of Literature," George Orwell describes the fate of a serious writer when he is deprived of freedom:

> The imaginative writer is unfree when he has
> to falsify his subjective feelings, which from
> his point of view are facts. He may distort
> and caricature reality in order to make his
> meaning clearer but he cannot misrepresent
> the scenery of his mind: he cannot say with

conviction that he likes what he dislikes or believes what he disbelieves. If he is forced to do so, the only result is that his creative faculties dry up.

These words sum up Olesha's case. (pp. xviii-xix)

> *Andrew R. MacAndrew, in his introduction to* Envy and Other Works, *by Yuri Olesha, translated by Andrew R. MacAndrew (copyright © 1960, 1967 by Andrew R. MacAndrew; reprinted by permission of Doubleday & Co., Inc.), Doubleday, 1967, pp. vii-xix.*

[With the publication of *Envy,* Olyesha] was catapulted into a foremost place in Soviet literature, and soon everyone was discussing the new comic genius who had taken his place effortlessly beside Gogol. With his three clowns—Nikolay Kavalerov and the brothers Ivan and Andrey Babichev—he brought a hitherto unknown music into Russian literature. The name of the music was "slapstick." It was comedy of the most wanton kind, gay and impenitent, happily indiscreet and wonderfully invigorating, and like all good comedy it had a serious purpose. Its purpose was to question the foundations of the Soviet state and, if possible, to laugh it out of existence.

When *Envy* first appeared, Stalin had not yet achieved absolute power. . . . Laughter was not yet a crime against the state, and it was still permissible to parody high Soviet officials. (pp. xi-xii)

The phenomenal success of [*Envy*] demonstrated that Olyesha had penetrated into the core of the Soviet mystery; he had challenged the hidebound dogmatism of the dictatorship at its weakest point, and suggested an alternative. Slapstick was merely the sugar coating of a deliberate and reasoned attack against the apparatus of the state. He was therefore accused [later, as Stalin grew more powerful,] of "petty-bourgeois individualism" and of a desire to restore the antiquated values which the Bolshevik revolution had obliterated. Unrepentant, Olyesha went on writing.

In the following year he published *The Three Fat Men,* an even more explicit denunciation of the regime, disguised as a fairy tale. (p. xvii)

The fairy tale is told with wonderful gusto and charm, on many levels, with a deftness which permits him to say many things about the Soviet Union which others had left unsaid. The atmosphere of menace and revolt continues throughout the story; we are never left in the least doubt about the power of the Three Fat Men in their heavily fortified palace, with their armed thugs ready to do their bidding, shooting down unarmed people only because it is necessary to inspire terror. Although the revolutionaries bear classical fairy-tale names . . ., and although Olyesha is compelled to employ all the resources of his comic invention in order to keep the story moving at a breakneck pace, the allegory is almost too transparent. By 1929 the power of Stalin was in the ascendant. The wonder is that *The Three Fat Men* was ever published, and that Olyesha survived its publication.

In fact, the novel was even more popular than *Envy,* and over thirty editions were published in the following thirty years. It was made into a film, a play, and a ballet, and although the Soviet critics found fault with the play, where the revolutionary situation was more explicit, they were inclined to pardon the ideological faults in the contempla-

tion of the wild irrelevance of the love story. . . .The adventures of [the lovers] follow the pattern of the medieval *skazki;* they are highly colored, unpredictable, and always mysterious. Nothing happens rationally; everything happens according to the unpredictable logic of the story. Olyesha was quicksilver, and the critics found it difficult to pinpoint his ideological crimes. (p. xviii)

Olyesha returns again and again to the theme of the primacy of the human heart in his short stories, which appeared in two collections . . . under the titles *Love* and *The Cherry Stone.* In these stories he avoided political allegory, perhaps because it was becoming too dangerous. They are stories of his childhood and youth in Odessa, written freshly and cleanly, with great tenderness and an almost childlike innocence. He possessed none of the formidable philosophic equipment of Pasternak, but he had Pasternak's gift of seeing everything with magical freshness and enchantment. . . . Olyesha's world is brighter and more familiar than our own. (p. xix)

The short stories describe the landscape of the lost paradise, himself wandering through it in joy and perplexity. The light and the sea air are continually rushing in, and sooner or later he finds himself in some abandoned wasteland of the heart. All his life he was especially fond of the circus, and so clowns of all shapes and sizes jump through the hoop of his stories. He had a special reverence, amounting almost to adoration, for Charlie Chaplin.

Even when he writes about death, in the most violent and beautiful of his stories, we are made aware of a perfect lucidity. In "Liompa" he describes the death of an old man as seen through the eyes of a child and of the dying man himself, and when we have finished reading the story, we know there is nothing left to be said. He has pronounced the mystery. In a small compass the story tells more about death, real death, the death which men undergo and mysteriously fail to survive, than any story I have ever come across. Tolstoy's "The Death of Ivan Ilyich" is not about death, but about despair in the face of death. "Liompa" is about death stripped of all its passionate adornments.

What is unusual in Olyesha is his clear uncomplicated vision, his certainty and astonishing ease as he walks along his permanent tightrope. With this there went a profound and unrepenting adoration of life. "I write about how life triumphs over everything—yes, over everything," he wrote once. From him the words did not sound like a manifesto, but like a calm and confident statement of purpose.

Envy and *The Three Fat Men* were acts of magnificent daring, and he may have known he would eventually be punished. By 1930 most of the works for which he would be remembered had already been written. For the next thirty years he wrote chiefly "for the drawer," against the time when it might be possible to write freely. (pp. xx-xxi)

Of Mandelshtam, Essenin, and Mayakovsky, the most famous of the literary victims of the Soviet state, it can be said with some confidence that at the time of their death they had written nearly all the work that was in them. The tragedy of Olyesha was that he was silenced when he had just begun to write. . . .

[*A List of Benefits*] was an act of despair, a *mea culpa* spoken over the grave of his own talents. (p. xxi)

A List of Benefits was staged by Meyerhold in 1931, without success. The play was so turgid and repetitive that even under Meyerhold's brilliant direction it was impossible to breathe life into it. A close reading of the play suggests that he was himself very near to suicide when he wrote it. (p. xxii)

Today a new generation of Soviet writers is discovering Olyesha. They find in him those qualities which have been remarkably absent in Soviet literature—gaiety, daring, the power to improvise on dangerous themes, the exaltation of youth and the understanding of the young. Above all they find in him the unregenerate spirit of comedy, a delight in slapstick. At long last Olyesha, the rebel, is coming into his own. (p. xxiii)

> *Robert Payne, in his introduction to* Love and Other Stories, *by Yuri Olyesha, translated by Robert Payne (copyright, ©, 1967, by Washington Square Press, Inc.), Washington Square, 1967, pp. ix-xxiii.*

Envy shares with Evgenij Zamjatin's *We* and George Orwell's *1984* the tragic theme of the individual's revolt against a monolithic, unfeeling society. The philosophy that only what was useful was acceptable spawned the inevitable reaction among many intellectuals, that beauty and feelings were to be valued for their own sake. In *Envy* the contrast is drawn between Andrej Babičev, a representative of the new, purposeful world-outlook, on the one hand, and his brother Ivan and Nikolaj Kavalerov, both representing the poetic and the useless, on the other. There is a similar theme, and a similar contrast of characters, in "Love" (1928), but due to a complex system of symbolic images the meaning of this short story is not immediately apparent.

The main character of "Love," Suvalov, is discovered at the beginning of the story waiting in the park for his girl, Lelja, to arrive. It is a summer's day, and as Suvalov waits he begins to observe the teeming life of nature all around him. First he notices a lizard, and he thinks to himself: "The lizard is vulnerable on that stone: it can be detected immediately." "This makes him think of chameleons, which are able to escape notice by changing colors to match their surroundings. In this opening paragraph the theme of the story is hinted at, as well as the symbolic mode in which it is to be handled. The author is discussing the experience of the individual who fails to conform, or blend with his environment. The symbolism is almost entirely optical. Suvalov discovers that his vision is sensitive to the point where it plays tricks on him. (p. 281)

[Suvalov] asks the color-blind man [seated near him on the park bench] whether he has ever noticed the imaginary architecture of insects' trajectories, and is somewhat taken aback when the other counters with a penetrating question: "Are you in love?" Oleša here connects theme with symbolism for the first time. Suvalov's over-sensitive vision is symbolical of the world of feelings, while the color-blind man's limited vision symbolizes a lack of feelings. . . . [The color-blind man says] something like: "You are on a dangerous road." This ominous warning is not questioned by Suvalov. He does not argue that the color-blind man is the one who is seeing things, but accepts the supposition that his own affliction is the more serious.

The author takes the same view. . . . [The] idea of error, hence of crime, begins to be associated with Suvalov. . . .

The next morning Suvalov wakes up in a new world—the world of love. He gets out of bed, wondering what the laws of this new world might be, and soon discovers, not a new

law, but the absence of an old one, for he is no longer subject to the law of gravity and experiences difficulty keeping his feet on the floor. (p. 282)

If Suvalov's encounter with the color-blind man was a veiled warning that he was heading for trouble, his next encounter may be seen as the fulfillment of that warning. He goes to the park . . . [again. An] elderly man wearing a black hat and blue-tinted glasses . . . introduces himself as Isaac Newton. There is an air of undisputed authority about the great scientist; as he sits down next to Suvalov the whole of nature seems to hold its breath, like an orchestra ready to burst into sound when the conductor gives the signal. . . .

Newton is offended because Suvalov has violated the law which he, Newton, discovered. . . . Newton represents the oppressive environment in which feelings are prohibited. He is the founding father of this environment. As a child, he was unaware of the law of gravity, but having discovered it he now enforces it and demands blind obedience. The same truth is brought out in the symbolism of the blue-tinted glasses. Born with normal vision, at a given point in his life (presumably when he discovered the law of gravity) he adopted the blue spectacles and has worn them ever since. (p. 283)

[The] color-blind man has the innate tendency to see things blue. Both he and Isaac Newton belong to the same system, for both wear the uniform black hats, but the color-blind man was born within it and is a product of it. Whereas Newton could remove his glasses if he chose, the color-blind man has no choice, and will never know any world-outlook but the blue one. Suvalov's outlook clearly does not conform to the society in which he lives, so it is hardly likely his behavior would. If he were a chameleon he could turn blue to match his environment, but he is not. The chameleon is an age-old emblem of hypocrisy and deceit; Suvalov, however, is honest in his feelings and is therefore more like the defenceless lizard whose alternatives are but two: escape or perish. (pp. 283-84)

Suvalov's frightening encounter with Isaac Newton turns out to be a bad dream. . . . But the dream has shown him something important, and he now turns on Lelja as the cause of his problem: "Since I met you something has happened to my eyes. I see blue pears." This last remark is wishful thinking on his part, for seeing everything blue is precisely the affliction that he lacks. But he is beginning to realize somewhere deep in his unconscious that this abnormality is actually the norm, and he desires it.

Having made this ambiguous statement, Suvalov runs away like a frightened doe, "snorting and with wild leaps, squinting and jumping away from his own shadow." One might say he is running away like the lizard that knows it cannot blend with its surroundings. He finally stops his panic-stricken flight and sits down on top of a hill. Oleša says this hill is a prism, with Suvalov perched on the top, his legs dangling down the sloping side.

This metaphor gives a further insight into Suvalov's present situation. The prism is what causes a rainbow, i.e. the total range of possible colors. Since Newton and the color-blind man experience only a limited segment of the spectrum, this hill symbolizes Suvalov's own sphere of existence. The author mentions that from the top of the hill Suvalov commands an extensive view of the countryside, and indeed, by comparison with narrow world-view of the two black-hatted men Suvalov's world of feelings is infinitely more spacious.

It is as though Suvalov has an angle of vision of 360°. Isaac Newton has taken to wearing glasses which reduce his own angle of vision to 20°; and since he is the progenitor of the new society, the color-blind man and all his fellows are born with that same 20° world-outlook. Though he takes no pleasure in the thought, Suvalov correctly identifies the hill when he remarks to himself: "I am living in paradise." The dialogue that ensues brings the political meaning of the story to the surface:

> "Are you a Marxist?" someone said right next to him.
> The young man in the black hat, the familiar color-blind man, was sitting next to Suvalov in the closest proximity.
> "Yes, I am a Marxist," said Suvalov.
> "You are not allowed to live in paradise."
>
> (pp. 284-85)

Oleša's use of optical sensitivity to symbolize the world of feelings reflects his own powers of observation. After all, everything that Suvalov notices . . . must first have been noticed by the author. And besides these things, there are many fascinating observations made throughout the story by the author as narrator. The wasp hums on a plate like a gyroscope. The apple tree, seen from underneath, resembles a Montgolfier balloon, with its translucent covering over a dark framework of ribs. The ladybug takes off from the highest point of the apple on wings "brought out from behind somewhere, as one takes a pocket-handkerchief out from behind one's tailcoat." A kite stands askew in the sky like a postage stamp. It is not always clear whether an image is occurring to the author or to his protagonist, but it makes little difference. . . .

The ending of "Love" could be interpreted as a victory for the minority group, a triumph of feelings over insensitivity, with the color-blind man as a convert to Suvalov's world-outlook. However, if the symbolism of the story is taken consistently, it will be evident that there is no such victory. Suvalov at one point wants to change places with the color-blind man, and at the end the color-blind man wants to change places with Suvalov. But in neither instance is a change possible. The color-blind man has an inborn distortion of vision for which there is no remedy. In the case of Suvalov, he is what he is: a lizard cannot become a chameleon merely by wishing it. They belong to different modes of existence; they are of different species. It happens that in that particular environment or society the color-blind man is considered normal and Suvalov abnormal, and therefore Suvalov is doomed to perish. Suvalov lives in a paradise, but it is a fool's paradise, and his victory, like that of Kavalerov and Ivan Babičev, is ephemeral and illusory. (p. 286)

> *Anthony Hippisley, "Symbolism in Oleša's 'Love'," in* Studies in Short Fiction *(copyright 1973 by Newberry College), Summer, 1973, pp. 281-86.*

*   *   *

OWENS, Rochelle 1936-

Owens is an American playwright and poet who considers her drama an "organic evolution" from her poetry. Her work is characterized by a reliance on primordial character types, which she utilizes to explore the subconscious side of man. (See also *Contemporary Authors,* **Vols. 17-20, rev. ed.)**

"The Karl Marx Play" . . . is an erratic mixture (a *Ro-chelle Owens* mixture) of historical fact, wild fantasy, and bold anachronisms, of songs and dance routines, and of her own peculiar combination of mockery and deep conviction. According to her program note, Miss Owens sees Marx as a latter-day Job—a raging, inspired, sometimes ridiculous Hebrew saint, plagued by boils, money worries, a large, affectionate, and demanding family, and a case of writer's cramp that amounts to paralysis. (p. 58)

The show is not entirely successful. This may be because Miss Owens' style is no longer a surprise, but I doubt it. Somehow, the magnetism seeps away long before the end, and much of the fooling turns foolish and the ardor tiresome. Even so, there is more wit and originality and feeling and good writing here than one finds in many more successful enterprises. . . . (p. 59)

> *Edith Oliver, "Marx to Music," in* The New Yorker *(© 1973 by The New Yorker Magazine, Inc.), April 7, 1973, pp. 58-9.*

If Brecht could make a poem out of the "Communist Manifesto," why shouldn't Rochelle Owens turn the life of Karl Marx into a musical comedy? Indeed, how else can you treat Marx in these topsy-turvy times. . . .

["The Karl Marx Play"] converts Marx and Engels, those titans of Western thought and revolution, into Keystone Cops of history, slapstick clowns whose perceptions, profundities and programs are just bubbles burped forth by their dyspeptic souls. The show pivots around the confrontations between poor old Marx, who is trying to overcome a deep-seated inertia and get on with the writing of his big script, "Das Kapital," and Leadbelly, who represents the rising consciousness of the world's black people. Leadbelly (named after the late great American folk singer) sees Marx as the last flatulent gasp of burnt-out white European thought. Rising from the earth itself (a trapdoor in the stage), dressed in funky African-style beads and colors, shaking a pair of gourds like a salesman demonstrating a witch-doctor kit at Abercrombie & Fitch, he puts down Marx in rich riffs of superfly rhetoric. (p. 117)

Much of this is very funny and very smart. Miss Owens is a true theater poet with an animal shrewdness, an authentic member of the wised-up generation. That is the trouble—Miss Owens is so wised up she has no time to be wise. She sees through everything and everybody—Marx is a self-hating Jew who thinks Germany is the hope of the world, a frustrated poet who turned to economics, a man of the people who lusts after the "aristocratic flesh" of his highborn wife. Leadbelly may be the black wind of the future, but he is as much wind as he is black, and even he hankers for the milky charms of Mrs. Marx. Unlike Brecht, who structured his cynicism into a powerful esthetic and didactic form, Miss Owens finally has nothing to give us but the gleeful energy of disenchantment. (p. 118)

> *Jack Kroll, "On Your Marx," in* Newsweek *(copyright 1973 by Newsweek, Inc.; all rights reserved; reprinted by permission), April 16, 1973, pp. 117-18.*

Futz is a very short play—[Rochelle Owens] cannot sustain dialogue—and what words there are are mostly hollow, uncouth, obscene, or even meaningless grunts. . . .

Miss Owens wants us, I suppose, to see in [*Futz*] the calvary of the nonconforming individual, the greater bestiality of the supposedly normal majority, and society's cowardice in not daring to espouse an animality it secretly craves. But even assuming that we agree with the author's theses—one of which seems to me old hat, one questionable and one ludicrous—they are not couched in a dramatic event, a set of characters, a language that can move any part of us other than the stomach.

The construction of the play is awkward: tiny open-ended vignettes in which the characters burble pretentious nonsense or infantile naughtiness, while the narrator recites the action. The people are all demented, depraved or retarded. . . . As for the language, it has three modes. (1) Pretentious and preposterous: "sticking his fingers out like stone worms," "how can well I go describing on?" "his kneebones high like the two hemispheres," "my choppers say yes to your head under their feet." (2) Synthetic hillbilly, a cross between Dogpatch and Volapük: "You make it wus tan it is mentionin' the pig . . . O o o o so indecent I am, and now the filty dreams 'ill come. O Gods help meee that we shoulda both laid with a sow." (3) Scatolgy, obscenity, baby-talk and grunts: "HAHA-Haaaah-shhhhhushy yeah yeah," 'Yeeeiiiiiey Oyu Big man-bloke!" and much more, less suitable for quoting. Each of these elements is painful in itself; together, they are well-nigh unendurable. (p. 144)

> *John Simon, in his* Uneasy Stages: A Chronicle of the New York Theater, 1963-1973 *(copyright © 1975 by John Simon; reprinted by permission of Random House, Inc.), Random House, 1975.*

* * *

OZ, Amos 1939-

An Israeli novelist and short story writer, Oz gained notice in the United States with the publication of his novel *My Michael*. (See also *CLC*, Vol. 5, and *Contemporary Authors*, Vols. 53-56.)

Amos Oz belongs to the post-independence generation of Israeli writers (he was born in Jerusalem . . .). In a country as young as Israel, "generations" are not counted in years but in periods of time they were born in. There is a difference between pre-state generation of writers, the "Palmach" and the "Post-Palmach" generation, and those whose outlook and make-up were shaped by the fact that they grew up in a country they could call their own, not knowing any other country, even though their parents and grandparents had come from "somewhere else". The mystique of "*the return*", which played such an important role in the works of the earlier generation (from Agnon onwards) became to them the mystery of being, of living in a land full of contrasts and divisions, with the ever-present threats looming from the mountains and hills on the other side of the borders. In Oz's short stories and novels the people are part of the landscape, and the landscape is part of the reality from which there is no escape. Moreover, what singles out this author from most others among his contemporaries is yet another fact: while many of them began their careers as members of Kibbutzim and later moved to the towns and cities, Oz, after completing his education in his native Jerusalem, has exchanged life in the city with that in a Kibbutz. . . .

Life in the Kibbutz has been made the subject of a number of sociological studies of varying merits. Oz's novel [*Elsewhere, Perhaps*] is neither such a study nor is it the history of a particular Kibbutz, but I know of no other book that depicts life in the Kibbutz more vividly, more realistically or with greater insight. The narrator, of whom we know nothing, is obviously someone who is part of this life. He makes us look at it as he sees it, both from the inside and the outside. Occasionally he leaves us standing alone in the middle of the road, as it were, with the promise that he will return shortly to guide us on. This technique is not always successful but it lends the narrative a broader dimension.

There are no single heroes in the story. The characters are mostly ordinary, hard-working and remarkable people bound together by the vision of a new life, a new society, and the harsh reality of living in a world of wars and a hostile environment. Not that the Kibbutz has not had its heroes but, by now, they are dead and belong to the past; they are remembered on solemn occasions. Perhaps they were no heroes either, and only the need for legends makes them appear as heroic figures. Without a past there is no future. (p. 61)

The reader should not be deceived either by the complexity of the story or by the simplicity with which it is told. . . . Nor do I think that the author was aiming at presenting some kind of a new morality. Somewhere in the story someone says, referring to the battle around a stretch of soil in the no-man's land near the border: "There are more important things than land." Someone else agrees but he adds: "You're quite right, there are more important things than land. But without land they can't exist." (p. 62)

> *Jacob Sonntag, in* The Jewish Quarterly *(© The Jewish Quarterly 1974), Spring-Summer, 1974.*

["Touch the Water Touch the Wind"] offers a profusion of delightful passages couched in unfailingly lovely language. Inadvertently, it also offers an elegant proof for the theorem that a novel as a whole can be less than the sum of its parts. . . .

[In] this [third] novel, flying and diabolism remain poetic fancies rather than compelling fantasies, toys in the author's grab bag. The heroine is a *femme fatale* to whom all sorts of charismatic power and penetration are attributed—reported, not realized. Her conversion to Communism and her rise to power are unpersuasive, not because in any way unbelievable, but because accomplished in the fiction by sleight-of-hand. We are given, for instance, a powerfully composed description of her rape at the hands of lascivious demons who, we are presently informed, are "really no more than twilight shades of a period of change." This, surely, is bathos, not symbolism. Even the hero Pomeranz, for all his melancholy profundity, amounts to hardly more than a twilight shade himself, a nebulous trick-star-genius, insufficiently rendered.

It seems querulous to suggest to an accomplished novelist that he show, not tell, especially when the voice that tells is as suffused with genuine poetry, as impeccable, as fascinating in its modulations, as this one. But scenes are treated with high-handed brevity, tangled relationships are snipped and summarized, interesting minor characters are attributed like balloons till they become pointlessly major, major figures are delineated like cartoons till they become interesting abstractions, flavorful thickenings in the plot are at once diluted, and the result, though beguiling, is an exquisite sketch for a grand novel. (p. 7)

> *Alan Friedman, in* The New York Times Book Review *(© 1974 by The New York Times Company; reprinted by permission), November 24, 1974.*

Amos Oz is an extraordinarily gifted Israeli novelist who delights his readers with both verbal brilliance and the depiction of eternal struggles—between flesh and spirit, fantasy and reality, Jew and Gentile. Oz has tried his hand at various types of fiction: psychological realism in *My Michael*, social documentation in *Elsewhere, Perhaps,* historical narrative in "Crusade," one of two novellas making up [*Unto Death*]: but his carefully reconstructed worlds are invariably transformed into symbolic landscapes, vast arenas where primeval forces clash. Oz's is a generous, magic realism; in his tales concrete things are forever on the verge of shedding their physicality, and abstractions yearn for palpable form.

"Crusade," a haunting study of evil, shows how loathsome and maddeningly tentative the real world appears when seen in the distorting mirrors of perverted spirituality. (p. 36)

[This] novella is at once a remarkably successful evocation of a historical period and a powerful allegory, one in which naturalist details become natural symbols.... The grotesque realism of the narrative, as well as its tortured spirituality, is further enhanced by the highly imaginative use of language....

The companion piece to "Crusade," "Late Love," is gloomy without medieval trappings....

What makes both of these novellas so compelling is that the author fully understands his fanatics' paltry delusions and insecurities, and makes us realize that what all these people are really after is peace of mind. (p. 37)

> *Ivan Sanders, in* The New Republic *(reprinted by permission of* The New Republic; © *1975 by The New Republic, Inc.), November 29, 1975.*

English readers have been introduced to the works of the Israeli author Amos Oz in a haphazard fashion which prevents a coherent chronological appreciation of either the writer's concerns or his art. The novel, *My Michael*, Oz's first work to appear in English (1972), was actually his third published volume (1968), following the short story collection, *Artsot haTan* (*Lands of the Jackal,* 1965) and the novel, *Makom Aher* (1966; published as *Elsewhere, Perhaps* in 1973). This problem of chronology is not unusual in the publication of works by foreign authors, but the English reader should be aware of the actual sequence of original publications so as to achieve a proper perspective on the author's creative development as well as an appropriate interpretation of his works.

Unto Death consists of two novellas ["Crusade" and "Late Love"].... Both works signalled a definite shift in artistic direction for Oz, especially in terms of genre; yet both develop in different ways certain stylistic and structural characteristics found in Oz's previous writings. The matter of chronology looms largest, however, in the very *Sitz im Leben* of these two novellas: written in the late sixties, each in its own way embodies Oz's artistic response to the Six-Day War of 1967. The time factor is crucial in interpreting the meanings of these works.... (p. 61)

Nearly all of Oz's writings before "Crusade," from the short stories of the early sixties to *Elsewhere, Perhaps* and *My Michael* (which was completed just prior to the 1967 War) had been of the "engagé" variety. This style of writing was a moralistic critique in fictional guise, aimed in particular at the kibbutz and in general at what Oz took to be Israel's militaristic bent.

In "Crusade," however, Oz is not really so very inconsistent [in his use, for the first time, of historical fiction]. In one of the stock traditions of historical fiction, Oz utilizes time distancing to comment on the contemporary scene. The story is presented as if it were an actual chronicle of a Crusade journey ...; however, the story's central import, rendered obliquely through psycho-symbolic elements, relates directly to the very real fears for survival engendered by the traumas of May-June, 1967.

Two of the work's dramatic focal points depict in literally excruciating detail the cruel, gratuitous murder of Jews at the hands of the roaming Crusaders.... Both these dramatized scenes are rendered with purposefully graphic visual effect. (In general, "Crusade" seems much influenced, in both visual and conceptual terms, by Bergman's *The Seventh Seal*.) The Jews in the story from beginning to end, are the unambiguous victims of a manifestly whimsical and sadistic scapegoatism. Both plot and characters appear to exist only to exemplify and animate this syndrome of prejudicial hatred.

The story's third dramatic focal point reveals the tale's major theme.

> Surely a Jew had mingled with the Christians in disguise, was walking along the way with us, and cursing us. And what is Jewish in a Jew—surely not any outward shape or form but some abstract quality.... Simply this: a terrible, a malignant presence.... There is a Jew in our midst....

The idea of the "secret Jew" (along with the motif of "signs") grows in intensity until the entire cast of characters becomes obsessed with uncovering the hidden Jew. For the Jew is responsible (so goes the extrinsic anti-Semitic libel, and the inner implication of "Crusade" as well) for all the ills in the world: suffering, fear, insanity, "unto death" itself. The search-and-destroy mission sharpens as the Crusaders, forced to spend the winter in an abandoned ruin, either go mad or wander off to die.... The "secret Jew" mystery is Oz's way of depicting the madness of Judeophobia which has underlain much of the civilized world, a madness which, as "Crusade" purports to tell, is so ingrained as to be inexplicable, uncontrollable, and hence ultimately self-destructive.

This rather allegorical interpretation, which casts Oz, in this particular work at least, as a kind of social historian in fiction-writer guise, is suggested by the narrator's musing on the nature of Jerusalem as an abstraction, not as an earthly goal.

> Does Jerusalem really exist ... or is she perhaps nothing but a pure idea ...? [And, in fact, among these Crusaders] Jerusalem ceased to be regarded as a destination, as the arena of glorious deeds ... the Jerusalem they were seeking was not a city but the last hope of a guttering vitality....

"Crusade" thus represents Oz's historical thinking rather than any fictional reality. The minimal plot, the character typology, even the style—a kind of "gothic lyricism" marked by Oz's verbal virtuosity in static background description—appear subservient to the story's central idea: Judeophobia is to this day a powerful, mysterious mania. In its continual attempts to cleanse itself of the Jews, to make it *Judenrein,* the world will stop at nothing, not even at abject lunacy and self-destruction.

The second novella, "Late Love," which appears here in translation for the first time, differs from "Crusade" in technical construction but not in theme. "Late Love" is energized by the rambling diatribes of Shraga Unger, an old self-taught bureaucrat-intellectual who has spent his life lecturing (usually to sparse audiences in Israel's rural settlements) on one pervasive issue: the Bolshevik terror. The Bolsheviks, he claims, aim to destroy the Jews. Their anti-Semitism, however, is merely the first stage of a Hitlerian scheme of world conquest which threatens to overturn and take control of the entire cosmic order. This extreme political viewpoint—or paranoia, if you will—is matched in hyperbole by Shraga's recommended solution: an all-out preemptive war against Bolshevism to be led by the Israeli Army, beginning with a Blitzkrieg of Eastern Europe (including the fantasized liberation of the still extant Warsaw Ghetto) and ending with the conquest of Moscow! The obvious irony is inflated by Shraga's repeated insistence (in mock tribute to Bellow's Herzogian depiction of intellectual frustration) that he will soon communicate this solution to Israel's Defense Minister, Moshe Dayan.

Both Shraga and his plans are ludicrous; yet the story effectively expresses the heightened feelings of anger, frustration and alienation which beset Israel's populace during the Six-Day War. The appalling actualities of late spring, 1967 are transformed in Shraga Unger's monologues into an overwrought, overstated philosophy of doom. As a political activist linked to leftish-dovish platforms, Oz himself surely does not hold to this philosophy. His aim is to project emotions and assertions which arouse the reader, not a willful didacticism. (pp. 61-3)

Though neither a tirade nor an apologia, Oz transmits his own ideas through Unger. This oblique communication occurs during the character's quieter, more meditative moments, when the feverish pitch is toned down and the reader is less reactive and more calmly attentive. . . . Oz is not ridiculing jingoist war fever in this story; nor is he pre-senting fantasies of super-Sabraism or senile chauvinism. He is expressing the breakdown of the myth of normalcy which has been at the center of Zionist longing for decades: the envisioned State of Israel, with its promise of autoemancipation, which would make of the Jewish people a nation among nations. For Oz it is still an impossible dream.

As in "Crusade," broad contemporary problems are seen through fictional narrative in "Late Love." Similar, too, is the use of a recurring motif of mysterious forces at work beneath the surface of events and ideas. Parallel to the "secret Jew" theme in "Crusade" is Shraga Unger's reflection on the world beyond visual perception, the outer, cosmic world of "eternal flux," which threatens perpetually to demolish the lower orb of human activity. Shraga is the only one able to perceive this "circling grip of strong bands, the forces of Earth and Sun, planets and comets, the galaxies, blindly erupting forces"; he is the watchman who has taken on the responsibility to warn all who will listen of the impending danger.

It is Shraga Unger's central role in "Late Love" which makes this story the more interesting of the two. . . . [At the end, Shraga] finds himself suddenly out of character, so to speak: he becomes singularly uncommunicative and no longer in control of the story's verbal action. Only the effete Hugo listens to him, so despite the passion of his notions, manner and purpose, for Shraga it is too late. Now it is Liuba's more mundane complaints about the polluted atmosphere of Tel Aviv—a cleverly ironic parallel to Shraga's cosmic-political vision of collapse—which takes center stage. The sense of dichotomous perdition heightens Oz's quasi-moralistic message of the post-1967 doldrums: beyond the fictive silence of alienation, where do we go from here? (pp. 63-4)

Warren Bargad, "Amos Oz and the Art of Fictional Response," in Midstream *(copyright © 1976 by The Theodor Herzl Foundation, Inc.), November, 1976, pp. 61-4.*

P

PERCY, Walker   1916-

Percy is an American novelist and essayist. His fictive concerns are serious and ambitious; ranging from existentialism to epistemology to language and ways of communication. Percy won the National Book Award in 1962 for his first novel, *The Moviegoer.* **(See also** *CLC,* **Vols. 2, 3, 6, and** *Contemporary Authors,* **Vols. 1-4, rev. ed.)**

[For] seriousness and keenness of mind, Walker Percy has few rivals in American letters. Since the early '60s we've been accumulating evidence that such is the case, the evidence being Percy's three novels. . . . We might also have been aware of these essays [collected in *The Message in the Bottle*]. . . .

[The] first half of the book is the part most readers will learn most from: the essays in the second half, published in specialized journals . . . are pretty tough. Despite his disclaimers, his profession of modesty, Percy is not the amateur he says he is . . . , and he enters the battleground of linguists, semanticists and behaviorists in full battle dress. He knows the adversaries' language and observes their rules of war. But aside from the thorniness of the language, the proliferation of diagrams and arrows (equally dear to the hearts of Percy and his adversaries), these essays in the latter half of the book are an *expansion* of those in the first half: they detail the reasoning that makes possible the assertions put forward in the more literary essays.

The book's subtitle teasingly suggests what the issues are: "How Queer Man Is, How Queer Language Is, and What One Has to Do with the Other." The comic tone here is altogether characteristic and momentarily disguises the fact that Percy is dealing with life and death matters, with final things, as he makes "an attempt to sketch the beginnings of a theory of man for a new age," in a prose recognizable to the readers of the novels—wry, humorous, ironic, diffident, his meaning made ever clearer with perfectly apt, homely metaphor. His theory of man for a new age grows out of an intellectual tradition which seems not to have much affected our scientific-humanist consciousness: Percy's teachers are Aquinas and Kierkegaard, Heidegger and Marcel, Cassirer and Peirce—and with their help he mounts a frontal assault on how we fail to handle the predicament of our being human, on the ways in which we misconceive ourselves and our great, mysterious, unique gift, language.

Percy sees us as having arrived at a new consciousness and having no theory to deal with it, so we turn for comfort to a patchwork quilt of the past—an attenuated Darwinism, which reduces man to mere organism, a stimulus-response toy, grotesquely combined with an empty and secularized Judaeo-Christian ethic. We live in and with a hopeless incoherence. Percy calls repeatedly in these essays for a radical science of being, which will recognize the uniqueness of the human creature, that symbol-mongerer, who alone in creation names the world in his speech and discovers what it is. His invocation is made from a posture that seems to me altogether singular in American letters: he is by training a scientist (with an M.D. degree), an admitted hard-headed empiricist, quite obviously learned in psychiatry, linguistics and philosophy and he is a Christian. An artist with such inclusive credentials writes essays about coherence with an authority few in our culture can command. (p. 28)

These essays—and those gritty, uncompromising forays into alien territory which follow them—have a way of quickening the spirit and cleansing the sight. Perhaps Walker Percy has been the happiest man in America—and we can share that happiness. (p. 29)

> *John Boatwright, in* The New Republic *(reprinted by permission of* The New Republic; © *1975 by The New Republic, Inc.), July 19, 1975.*

[American] novelists have on the whole been inept at handling general ideas, but in this collection of essays on linguistics, psychiatry and existentialism written over the past two decades, Walker Percy shows himself to be as comfortable with philosophical discourse as he is with the creation of character and plot. Moreover, he avoids the self-promotion that afflicts writers like Norman Mailer when they turn to nonliterary realms.

Percy's explorations derive from a sense of wonder about his immediate situation (a feeling crucial to genuine thought and missing from most academic philosophy). This leads him to the basic issues of his book: Why are we unhappy, what does it mean to use language, and what is the connection, if any, between these two questions? (p. 18)

The central pieces in *The Message in the Bottle* deal with language, and give Percy the opportunity to take direct aim at the behavioral scientists' notion of linguistics. Employing a stimulus-response schema, the behaviorists argue that when one hears the word "fire," for example, one reacts appropriately—by warming one's hands, dousing the blaze, leaving the building, or cooking a steak. Yet this model, Percy observes, cannot distinguish speech from animal language codes; it tells us everything about human communication except what makes it peculiarly human. . . .

Percy uses his theory of language to illuminate the therapeutic session. For him the strict meanings of words and syntax are less important in the psychiatric setting than what is sometimes called the "pragmatics" of communication. If, for instance, a patient announces he is going to commit suicide, the analyst does not necessarily take him at his word: The patient may be pleading for mothering, or indicating that the doctor's hopes for a quick cure are overly sanguine. Certainly, whatever is being communicated cannot be determined by studying the structure of the sentences according to Chomsky's ideas. Instead, Percy's approach to this topic inclines toward much of the work being done currently in psychoanalytic theory—such as Erving Goffman's notions of "framing" and Gregory Bateson's contexts of discourse.

But what, in the end, is the connection between man's capacity to name, and the fact that he is often, against all reason, unhappy? While Percy's answer is far from clear, he seems to be saying that because we can symbolize—because we can conceive of things being other than they are—we are never at one with ourselves, like animals. That is, our alienation is necessarily tied to our capacity for language, to our humanity. Percy's entire argument can be read as a secular version of the "Word become flesh," and, indeed, Percy is a committed Christian. Nonetheless, apologetics is foreign to him, and only in the title essay, where he distinguishes between knowledge and news, does he hint at the Christian nature of his thinking.

Knowledge, Percy says, must conform to empirical reality or be deducible from general laws or principles. In the case of news, we are called upon to respond without bringing to bear the standard criteria of verification. If one is on a sinking ship and hears the message, "Come this way and you will be saved," one doesn't wait around in order to test it for possible errors or faults.

Our human condition, Percy continues, is that of castaways on an island. All we can do is recognize our alienation, for "the worst of all despairs is to imagine one is at home when one is really homeless." In short, *The Message in the Bottle* is presented in the form of negative news, whose purpose, it appears, is to prepare us to regain the sovereignty of insight that is the necessary preparation for receiving the Word, the final positive news. (p. 19)

> *Pearl K. Bell, in* The New Leader (© *1975 by the American Labor Conference on International Affairs, Inc.), October 13, 1975.*

Walker Percy's *The Moviegoer* is a classic and compelling account of the power of representation, of re-presentation, and his later novels show the same wry acuteness in describing characters' adventures in the intersubjective space of symbolic representation. *The Message in the Bottle,* a very intelligent if uneven collection of essays which includes, among others, his famous "Metaphor as Mistake," speaks directly of these matters. Man is "*Homo symbolificus,*" the "symbol-monger," distinguished from other creatures by the fact that he dwells in a world of symbols: "The world is the totality of that which is formulated through symbols."

The book's subtitle, "How Queer Man Is, How Queer Language Is, and What One Has to Do with the Other," gives both the direction of his argument and the deliberately "unprofessional" mode in which readings and insights are marshaled. If man is a rational animal, why does he behave so strangely? No sensible animal so insistently courts self-destruction, insists on being unhappy in good circumstances and happy in bad. If man behaves in paradoxical ways it is because he lives in a symbolic order. Indeed, our notions of rational behavior have been produced and elaborated by a behaviorism which works very well for rats in mazes and animals in their ordinary world but which singularly fails to apply to the most complex and interesting aspects of human behavior. (pp. 261-62)

On the other hand, when one turns to linguistics for elucidation of this central mystery, of the characteristically human, one learns a lot about phonemes, distributional regularities, and syntactic transformations, but next to nothing about "what happens when people talk, when one person names something or says a sentence about something and another person understands him." For Mr. Percy the mystery of language is the mystery of the name: "Naming is generically different. It stands apart from everything else that we know about the universe.". . . What is the nature of this connection, he asks, and, placing it at one corner of a triangle whose other points are word and object, he calls it "the Delta phenomenon": a phenomenon that lies at the heart of every linguistic and symbolic event. By the end of the book it is still a mystery, though it is now treated as a "coupler" which relates the visual cortex to the auditory cortex.

The problem of the sign has a history of which Mr. Percy is partially aware, but the most interesting and contemporary moments of that history suggest that his problem is insoluble in the form proposed. What he seeks is a moment of unity, a point of origin where form and meaning are fused; but since the sign is always a *sign of,* however far one tries to push toward a pure and unitary origin, one will always find a dual structure. The problem may be insoluble, but that it should at least be posed in another way emerges if one notes that it is nonsense to ask what was the first sign or word a baby used. It is contrast between signs that allows signs to emerge, so that the individual sign or name is not the unit in whose terms the problem should be posed. Signs are produced by differentiation of undifferentiated noise and differentiation of an affective universe. Differences are what constitute signs, and thus the problem is one of difference and repetition.

Percy offers a forceful, if unnecessarily repetitive, critique of behaviorism, but he is not always aware of the implications of his own insights and formulations, and this can lead to a measure of confusion. Thus, the central fact on which he insists is that man lives in a symbolic universe, and that therefore his experience is mediated by symbolic structures and systems of names. The varieties of symbolic mediation are what explain man's paradoxical behavior: the bored commuter on his evening train becomes less bored by reading a book about bored commuters sitting on trains. And Mr. Percy's superb discussion of the "dialectic of sightseeing" (the way in which symbolic representations or frameworks alter the character of perception) is based on his awareness of mediation. . . . The impossibility of direct, unmediated experience is the basis of this dialectic.

Yet at the same time, direct perception is something Mr. Percy longs for, and not merely with that nostalgia for what is irrecoverable. His remarks on the inadequacy of behaviorism and linguistics are ascribed to a Martian, the hypothetical representative of unmediated vision, and Mr. Percy seems to conceive of his own role in the same way: since I am not a professional scientist/linguist/philosopher/critic, he will tell us, since I am free of these symbolic frameworks, I can, like a Martian, see things in their true nakedness. He goes on to suggest that an inhabitant of Brave New World who comes upon Shakespeare's poems "is in a fairer way of getting at a sonnet" than a student who reads it in a literature course, and he extends this to a general educational principle.... [One] suspects that "see" has taken on a special meaning and that in his enthusiasm for direct, unmediated perception, he has forgotten that outside of symbolic systems [a thing] would be nothing but a lump of undifferentiated matter and certainly unknowable.

In brief, Mr. Percy raises a series of problems which are central to contemporary thinking about signs, representation, and symbolic systems, and though he often does so without full awareness of their implications or of the distinctions which others have raised, his clear presentation and his skill in relating them to little dramas of ordinary experience make this a book to recommend. (pp. 262-64)

Jonathan Culler, "Man The Symbol-Monger," in The Yale Review (© *1976 by Yale University; reprinted by permission of the editors), Winter, 1976, pp. 261-64.*

Walker Percy, a Southern Catholic non-practicing psychiatrist, has published three excellent novels about the spiritual discomforts of well-meaning, educated Southerners. Since 1954, at least, he has been preoccupied with the nature of language and has made himself into an enthusiastic and well-read amateur of linguistics, regularly publishing his thoughts on the subject in intellectual journals.

Reading [*The Message in the Bottle*] ... gives me the impression that Percy has been writing less about language than about religion. He writes in a quasi-scientific style; he seems to be trying to persuade logically, but his insights are essentially emotional, even poetic; and the whole effort seems to be directed toward opening a line of thought leading toward a Christian concept of human existence, which would be all right except that he purports to be writing about language.

Most of the essays deal with the idea that language—or "symbol-mongering," as Percy likes to call it—is the principal quality that distinguishes man from other animals, and, moreover, that the symbolic nature of language is not only a unique phenomenon, but is inaccessible to understanding by present scientific methods.... Percy makes it clear that he detests the idea that man is no more than an "organism in an environment" and can be studied and ultimately known as such. Indeed, Percy's hostility to science is one of the most striking aspects of the book. (p. 209)

Unfortunately, as an expository writer Percy has a serious flaw. He substitutes cryptomystic eloquence for the effective assembling of a logical case. (pp. 209-10)

Percy's essays show him to be an admirable man: serious, kind-hearted, and genuinely worried about the state of human affairs. But he is fundamentally anti-rational, and, for the most part, he fails to convince. (p. 213)

The Message in the Bottle reveals an ingenuousness that I would not have suspected in the author of *The Moviegoer, The Last Gentleman,* and *Love in the Ruins.* (p. 214)

Martin Kirby, "Neither Far Out nor In Deep," in The Carleton Miscellany (*copyright 1977 by Carleton College), Volume XVI, 1976-77, pp. 209-14.*

The Message in the Bottle is a series of reflections on the birth of a human world through the mystery of language.

As an American writer, Percy can hardly lay claim to something called "the tradition" in and through which we encounter Being. Our tradition for understanding man is provided by the social and behavioral sciences, a reductive hermaneutics wherein nothing spiritual is what it seems but is always the expression of something more or less primitive, the id, the chauvinism of sex or race, and so forth. We have bought the whole fabric of scientism as our ideology. American criticism is either a vast *ad hominem* argument or the celebration of an autonomy of feeling and technique, of a sensitivity which is sensitivity to literature alone, reality having been won by the positive sciences. We can sing psychic unsuccess, make a pure music, or perpetrate the latest variant of a scientific ideology. Percy has taken on this scientific tradition and subjected it to the searching light which is the coming-into-being of the *logos* itself and has, on the whole successfully, showed its inherent incapacity to yield understanding. Perhaps in freeing ourselves from the dimensions which constrain us to think of ourselves as this or that, we open ourselves to Being and human reality.

The major hero of Walker Percy's series of essays is the American mathematician-physicist-philosopher Charles S. Peirce. Best known for the pragmatic tradition he founded and repudiated. Peirce was the first to become concerned with semiotics, the way the world enters into the being of language through the mystery of naming....

Percy shows through the act of naming that the truth conditions for the sciences of man are other than what is assumed to be the case on their positivistic and naturalistic foundations. These conditions lie within the dimension of meaning explored by the existential and phenomenological philosophers. (p. 198)

Walker Percy learned his thesis about the intentionality of consciousness, not from Husserl and Sartre, but from such masters as Wittgenstein and Heidegger who found it in the nature of language itself. Beyond this lurks the realism of Aristotle and Aquinas. For Wittgenstein there can be no realm of private meaning and private language; for us reality is the public world of linguistic meaning, meanings which are shared forms of life. For Heidegger transcendental subjectivity is a distortion and perversion of our original prethematized self-understanding of Being. When this understanding is thematized, first as substance and then as transcendental subject, there is a progressively instrumental and technological feeling (mood) toward beings, a feeling which justifies itself in a science that strips objects and ourselves of ontological mystery and makes of them problems for a technique. We are creatures who constitute a world out of a primordial understanding of Being, and the intentionality founded on this structure gives the world its form. Being, not the I, is the ground of a world: it is this, not subjectivity, which is intended or meant in all our cultural and linguistic formations.

Percy intends to cut through Cartesian dualism and its idealistic and materialistic variants by close attention to the act of naming. This is first of all a public act. I am given the name by him who has for me the authority to name, acts

Plato associated with the legislator and dialectician. When something or other is given for me a name, in this original experience of self, world, and other, I encounter a being in its beingness. (pp. 199-200)

It is through [the] epiphany of the *logos* that Percy extends the discoveries of phenomenology to the anthropological sciences; this marks *The Message in the Bottle* as a unique contribution to what has hitherto been a European phenomenon. The mystery of the symbolic event discloses that the problem for man is that he has come to think of himself as a problem, not a mystery. And what have the human sciences done, insofar as they are true to their positivistic foundations, which has taught us anything much worth knowing? Should we not at least try to follow up Percy's lead? Where might we expect it to take us?

If man is, in Percy's paraphrase of Heidegger, "That being in the world whose calling is to find a name for being, to give testimony to it, and to provide for it a clearing," then our responsibility for our world, our relations to nature, to our fellows, and to ourselves, must be a function of the way we talk about Being. That being itself is not much talked about is evident if we look at how we have come to think about talk itself, both in the formal disciplines in linguistics and philosophy wherein speech is made into an object for us, and in more concrete disciplines in anthropology, sociology, psychology, and philosophy where talk enters into our concern for worldly structure and human behavior. (pp. 200-01)

Percy shows us that the originary presencing of self to itself is with and to another through the naming act, the assertion of a word that raises Being to being known. Being is doubtless inexhaustible, but we shall exhaust ourselves and the creative roots of culture itself in avoiding the ontological issue.

When we abrogate our common right to participate in Being and in one another through the *logos* and bind ourselves to some abstractive scheme which renders experience possible (Kant), or at least respectable, we shall fail to note that our own experience is not the dreary, tiresome repetition of saying and knowing the same thing about the same sorts of things. We become programmed calculators. Socrates in the paradigm case of Meno's slave taught that experience is not so much conformal (for Meno was himself so wrapped up in technical jargon derived from Gorgias that he could not recognize a color when he saw one but had to have it "explained" in the nonsense terminology of Empedoclean effluences) as it is negating, a break away from the customary and conventional into an openness for Being. Language is the instrument of this continual re-creation of the world. In talking to one another in serious, passionate pursuit of what is there, so Beautiful and true, in trying to get right about things, we can follow the power of language itself to lead us from our banal and orthodox subjectivity into a participatory encounter, an epiphany. This human act, not Skinner boxes, might well be the proper paradigm for the human sciences. The truth conditions for the human sciences lie within those conditions of language, essentially spiritual, which constitute knower and known, self and other, man and world. This is the great theme of the *logos* itself.

If one is to pick a nit with Walker Percy it is that he has, in freeing us from naturalistic jargon of the social sciences, unwittingly laid claim to the sterile jargon of despair we have inherited from Kierkegaard and romantic existential-

ism. Granted that the intolerable banality of our culture is endurable only through irony, through the hubris of distancing: were there no community with saints and sages, how in God's name could any humanist bear the burden of trying to represent his values in such a world as we are called to serve? And it is the positive value of this participation in the historic fabric of our tradition which Percy ignores. One can in fact read Plato on a train. It is easy enough to pick away at the social sciences and to demonstrate their bizarre consequences for human self-understanding; but the real issue of a hermaneutical philosophy, as we are now learning . . . , is the possibility of a meaningful involvement in culture and the recovery of effective freedom within the scope of ontologically grounded, inherited values. We can now see a way of avoiding historicism, relativism, and subjectivism in the nature of language itself. Given this understanding, despair seems to be a limit situation, not a norm, and we can begin to see the possibilities of a rebirth, a recovery of effectiveness, duration, and power, the marks of human being in a human world. We can develop the human sciences on their spiritual foundations as sciences of meaning.

The final essay, "A Theory of Language," makes a fundamental contribution to our understanding of linguistics. Percy demonstrates that on his account of naming, which says of something what it is, the basic syntactical structure is implicit. To the dispute between Chomsky and Skinner, which as far as it goes is clearly in Chomsky's favor, he proposes an empirical theory of the origin of "deep structure." The asserting structure of the original naming act is rich enough for that structure which Chomsky has to account for on occult grounds, for oddly he recognizes only those semantical and syntactical features which have been handed over by the formal logicians, not the semiotic dimension itself. There is abundant evidence in various studies of how children learn speech to show how syntax develops out of semiotic activities. A semological-phonological model is "transsyntactical," founded on "the science of the relations between people and signs and things—which specifies syntax as but one dimension of sentential theory"; it accords with the data of language acquisition and provides a model for the ontogenesis of speech; it allows the possibility of looking for a neurophysiological correlate of such a model; and it permits the assimilation of linguistic theory to a more general theory of all symbolic transaction, "a theory which in turn must accommodate such nonsyntactical 'sentences' as metaphor, a painting, a sculpture, a piece of music." I think it works.

Most of the essays have been previously published. They should have been rewritten to avoid what becomes when taken together the tiresome repetition of catch words, stock examples, and identical arguments. Also a good index would make this badly produced book even more valuable, for believe me it is very valuable indeed. It is an important work by a major novelist who is also even more impressive as a philosopher, one who lovingly seeks and strives for wisdom in and out of the conditions here and now with us in America. One is reminded of greater ages when culture was in the hands of amateurs, not prostitutes, of a Jefferson or a Hume. Walker Percy is a member of that community of saints and sages without whom life would be unbearable indeed. (pp. 204-06)

Charles P. Bigger, "Logos and Epiphany: Walker Percy's Theology of Language," in The Southern Review *(copyright, 1977, by Charles P. Bigger), Vol. XIII, No. 1, Winter, 1977, pp. 196-206.*

Serious contemporary fiction which might be called religious is not exactly raining down from the American sky. I'm not in the business of exhaustive keeping up; but I suspect that, once you'd read Buechner, Updike, Oates (a full-time job) and me, you'd have only one other sizable assignment—the novels of Walker Percy.

There are essentially two ways to write stories about God and His relations with the world. You can introduce Him as an actor, a tangible presence among His creatures—the method of the Old Testament, Homer, medieval dramatists and Milton. Or you can circle Him as an invisible axis, hint at His shape and gestures by the path of your circumference—God perceived and described by His absence or exclusion from the lives of human actors. No modern novelist known to me has dared the first method; but religious narrators of the recent past—Bernanos, Mauriac, Graham Greene and Flannery O'Connor—discovered in the world and in their own experience a story which has proved adaptable to the inner and outer experience of the few contemporaries named. . . .

Walker Percy's superb first novel, *The Moviegoer,* had its own grave movement toward the sensing and faithful acceptance of a nonhuman invisible spirit who wishes us peace. His next, *The Last Gentleman,* pursued the suspicion to the rim of certainty (despite a tendency to harum-scarum action and occasional lumps of unprocessed Franco-American metaphysics). His third, *Love in the Ruins,* offered a Roman Catholic doctor (Percy is a Roman Catholic doctor) engaged in a quest for spiritual health. Again an inability or an increased unwillingness to secrete sufficiently interesting *story* as vehicle or solvent for *idea* resulted in a set of parts which refused to form a whole.

Now in *Lancelot,* his fourth, he succeeds—powerfully, scarily and funnily—and at something new for him: not an ignoring of God or a chart of the vertigo induced by His absence but a sustained and ferocious attack upon Him *for* that absence. The attack is not mounted by Percy in his own voice but by his central character who speaks all the book except for two words at the end. The speaker's name is Lancelot Andrewes Lamar; and to hear him tell it, his life has driven him to the acts of murder and arson which have landed him in a mental institution. (p. E7)

Tough luck, one might grant and walk on—a dozen such plights are on tap for any of us: our crumbling friends who yearn to tell us of their baffling collapses. And tell us and tell us. But Percy compels me to listen to Lance. His fervent voice—eloquent, reckless, accurate, hilarious and genuinely agonized—is literally the book. His vision of the world, his tale of revenge, his program for the future (he's about to be released) make a straight, lean story that plunges forward through tawdry small bedroom mysteries toward a final grand puzzle—*Why has this happened, this local disaster and the larger encapsulating disintegration of our world?* (The question of whether it is really our world or only Lance's is moot for the length of his tale.) His own tormented answer to the puzzle is a string of other questions—*What is evil now? In a time of exploded values, what is any longer bad? Would any imaginable honorable God have permitted all this or endured it so long?*

Yet he thinks he can answer the questions, once free in the world again. He'll go with his young daughter to the Shenandoah Valley and begin a pure life of old-Roman zeal, a life which he seems to think will lead to a new revolution in the lives of men. His delayed unveiling of the nature of that

New Life—late in the novel—is almost Percy's last surprise: a half-accurate, half-admirable, wholly insane *reductio ad absurdum* of the Puritan republican founding vision.

The last surprise is the novel's last word. Lancelot has raved out his long monologue to a silent audience—Harry, the beloved companion of his riotous youth; now a Catholic priest called John. As he ends, prepared to leave his asylum, he asks his friend, "Is there anything you wish to tell me before I leave?" The friend says, "Yes" and the novel stops.

Or Percy stops. His story though is only half-told—his story, not Lancelot's. The fury with which he has transcribed Lance's wail (binding the comic-awful plot with sheer hot fury) and the daring with which he has left us at the end to imagine the priest's calm answer to the wail—and left us with a gradually implied complete outline for the priest's reply are the measures of his skill and urgency.

Yet he also leaves me wishing that he'd written the reply. I say that he left us with an outline, but how many contemporary readers of fiction are equipped or even prone to provide a sufficient counter statement?—a full intellectual and emotional Defense of the Faith, and in the implicitly fascinating voice of this particular friend and priest.

We may be grateful then for what we're given—a merciless burning-glass aimed at our faces—while we hope for the more which the last *Yes* promises: license to live in the world we've made. Let it be Walker Percy's next offering. (p. E10)

> *Reynolds Price, in* Book World—The Washington Post *(© The Washington Post), February 27, 1977, pp. E7, E10.*

Though he cares about plot and character, making fictions that easily translate into movies, [Walker Percy] is a serious, even moderately philosophical novelist not at all ashamed of his seriousness. Nor should he be: the familiar philosophical questions he raises, and his ways of raising them, are as interesting as his characters and plots, or anyway they would be if he had any idea of how to answer them. He cares about technique, enough so that—as is often the case in the very best fiction—technique is one of the things we watch with interest, though here sometimes with dismay. He's clever, witty, efficient, concerned, and his fictions pass one of the two or three most important esthetic tests: they're memorable. All this I say without much reservation, which is to say I think he's a novelist people ought to read, as they will anyway, since he's caught on.

"Lancelot" is the story of a man, Lancelot Andrews Lamar, who, after years of happy marriage, learns that his beautiful, voluptuous wife has been unfaithful to him. . . . Out of his disappointment and jealousy—and out of his sophisticated modern sense that perhaps there are no evil acts, no good acts either, only acts of sickness, on one hand, and acts flowing from unrecognized self-interest, on the other—Lancelot turns his wife's sexual betrayal into a central philosophical mystery. Question: Is all good mere illusion?—in which case, seemingly, there can be no God—or can we at least affirm that evil exists, so that (as Ivan Karamazov saw) we see God by His shadow? This question sets off Lancelot Lamar's "quest," as he tells his old school chum, now father-confessor, Percival. (The whole novel is Lancelot's "confession," though it reads like writing, not speech.) Lancelot says, "We've spoken of the

Knights of the Holy Grail, Percival. But do you know what I was? The Knight of the Unholy Grail. In times like these when everyone is wonderful, what is needed is a quest for evil." A good start for a philosophical novel. One begins to read more eagerly.

In his pursuit of evil, Lancelot first tries voyeurism, making absolutely certain of what he already knows, that his wife—and nearly everyone around him—is betraying all traditional values, turning life to garbage. Predictably the proofs do not satisfy, and Lancelot takes the next step. He turns himself into a monster to find out how evil feels—if it feels like anything. Even as he commits his most terrible crime, Lancelot feels nothing, so for him as for Nietzsche there can be no such thing as good or evil in the Christian sense, only strength, on one hand, and, on the other, "milksopiness."

The events that dramatize Lancelot's transformation are typical of the Southern Gothic novel at its best, grotesque but sufficiently convincing to be chilling. They flow from the potential of character and situation with deadly inevitability, supported by brilliant descriptions of place and weather—the climax comes during a hurricane, or rather two hurricanes, one real, one faked by a film crew—and supported by the kind of intelligence, insight and wit that make the progress of the novel delightful as well as convincing. (pp. 1, 16)

I've said that technique is one of the things one watches with interest as one reads "Lancelot." Percy uses, throughout the novel, the conventional device of regular rotation from motif to motif, incrementally building toward the dramatic and intellectual climax.... All this is well done, and the rant—much of it true, some of it intentionally crazy—gives the novel rhetorical oomph. (p. 16)

Convinced that Percival's meek Christianity and faith can have no effect and incensed, rightly, by the modern world's obscenity ..., Lancelot decides, slipping into madness, to start up, somehow, a new revolution and, like Christ Triumphant, either purify the world or destroy it utterly. We're encouraged to believe that he and others like him might really pull it off. He's a competent murderer. Lancelot's decision is not quite firm, however. He would like to be answered by his priest-confessor, though faith, we're told, has never been sufficient to answer reason. Percy is content to leave it at that. He suggests in his final line that some answer is possible, but he doesn't risk giving it to Percival. Certainly no answer can be deduced from the novel except Kierkegaard's consciously unreasonable "leap of faith"—a blind, existential affirmation of the logically insensible Christian faith. But surely everyone must know by now that Kierkegaard's answer is stupid and dangerous. Why Abraham's leap of faith and not Hitler's? Lancelot himself makes that point.

The reader has come all this way in critical good will—ignoring Percy's errors of scientific and mythic fact, though important arguments hang on them (human females are by no means, as Percy thinks, the only ones that make love face-to-face, and Malory's Guinevere was by no means indifferent to the betrayal). And from interest in the story and argument the reader has put up, too, with quite gross esthetic mistakes on Percy's part. Even granting the funny way Southerners name their children, the allegory is too obviously contrived; it distracts us from drama to mere message. Also, as I've said, the "confession" sounds written, not spoken—a bad fault, since it shows that the writer

is not serious about creating a fictional illusion but is after only a moderately successful "vehicle," like the occasions of Chairman Mao's verse.

From interest in the drama and argument, we blinked all this, but when the end comes and we see the issue has been avoided and evaded, as it nearly always is in our stupid, whining, self-pitying modern novels, we hurl away the book. When everyone's talking, as Lancelot does, about the world has no values, it's not a good time to rehash "The Brothers Karamazov" (Is there evil? Does it imply God?) or offer a sniveling version of Ayn Rand, that is, "Maybe—just maybe—Lancelot is right." Everybody, these days, is thinking and feeling what Walker Percy is thinking and feeling. Lancelot rages, at one point, "I will not have my son or daughter grow up in such a world. . . . I will not have it." Paddy Chayevsky's mad TV news commentator and his disciples say the same—only better—in the movie "Network." Everybody says it. Over and over, film after film, novel after novel, people keep whining about the black abyss and turning in their ignorance to Nietzsche and Kierkegaard, as if no one had ever answered them. (pp. 16, 20)

Fiction, at its best, is a means of discovery, a philosophical method. By that standard, Walker Percy is not a very good novelist; in fact "Lancelot," for all its dramatic and philosophical intensity, is bad art, and what's worse, typical bad art. Like Tom Stoppard's plays, it fools around with philosophy, only in this case not for laughs but for fashionable groans. Art, it seems to me, should be a little less pompous, a lot more serious. It should stop sniveling and go for answers or else shut up. (p. 20)

John Gardner, in The New York Times Book Review (© *1977 by The New York Times Company; reprinted by permission), February 20, 1977.*

Lancelot . . . is about the problem of faith. I think that is an accurate description, but it may also be an utterly misleading one, since it doesn't go far toward suggesting the book's tone or its events. (p. 113)

All of Walker Percy's fiction has been written in the service of the same theme that animates *Lancelot,* the search for whatever it is that can banish despair. Percy has spent his entire career debriding the same wound. His work is narrow but it cuts deep. In four novels he has essentially created only four characters, and they have much in common: all southern gentlemen, estranged from their world; all on a quest that begins in wistfulness for an imagined past and ends in intimations of the supernatural.

Spiritual journeys are often lonely, and the great limitation of Percy's work is that he has participated in his heroes' isolation; there is no fully formed character in any of the novels besides the central figures. They themselves could be tedious fellows, but they are saved from that by Percy's wit, by his sly social observation, by his affection for the graceful sentence, and by the additional fact that they unpretentiously embody one of the fundamental dilemmas of existence.

It's the great strength of Percy's fiction that he looks about him and sees a landscape of moral and emotional confusion, and refuses to offer handy sociological or economic wisdom by way of comforting explanation for it. He speaks directly and challengingly to the private heart. Despite the antic nihilism of *Lancelot,* despite the devout respect he pays doubt, it seems plain that he means to call attention to the possibility of faith. (p. 115)

Richard Todd, in The Atlantic Monthly (copyright © 1977 by The Atlantic Monthly Company, Boston, Mass.; reprinted with permission), March, 1977.

The Moviegoer remains Percy's best work, a perfect small novel whose themes, though important, are never allowed to overload the fictional craft. It is a book redolent of its time and place, a book with a thickly sensuous texture that can accommodate both the banalities of contemporary New Orleans and the glamorous aspects of Binx's now meaningless heritage. It is full of expertly realized characters. The working out of the complex destinies of Binx and Kate is both believable and moving. I can think of no American novel in which the device of a first-person narrator has been used with finer tact, control, and shading.

The Last Gentleman (1966) is a much longer, more overtly ambitious enterprise. Its literary antecedents are Candide and the picaresque novel of the eighteenth century. Percy chooses a naïf as his protagonist, a young man of twenty-five from an old and honorable Delta family that has over the generations turned progressively ironical until it has finally lost its grip on life. Suffering from various nervous dislocations, including amnesia, Williston Bibb Barrett lives an almost totally isolated life at the 63rd Street YMCA in New York and works as a humidification engineer at Macy's. . . . The . . . adventures of Will . . . are too complicated for a retelling in this essay; it is worth pausing, however, to consider two aspects of the novel that are central to Percy's fiction: the image of the South to which Will returns and the way in which the Catholic theme is handled. . . .

In this novel, as in The Moviegoer, Percy handles the Catholic alternative so subtly, so diplomatically, that it is hardly to be perceived as an alternative at all. Percy is careful not to stack his deck, as Graham Greene often seems to do and as Waugh did so notoriously at the end of Brideshead Revisited. . . .

I do not consider The Last Gentleman a wholly successful novel. It is somewhat like a hurricane swirling around a hollow center. Will Barrett is simply too blank, too passive a character to sustain the role assigned to him. But it is a rich book, with brilliant scenes, some of them marvelously funny.

Love in the Ruins (1971) is also rich and frequently funny, though in other respects it indicates, I think, a weakening of Percy's grip upon his materials. Set in the pre-Orwellian year of 1983, it begins with a middle-aged doctor (the book's narrator) sitting near the ramp of an interstate highway in Louisiana, a carbine on his lap, awaiting what may well be the end of the world. (p. 6)

The Sunbelt world of golf links, marinas, and shopping centers still exists in 1983; but things are now in a bad way; vines are encroaching everywhere; the young blacks have taken to the swamps, where they call themselves Bantus; atrocities occur daily; the Catholic Church has split into three parts, of which only the smallest still recognizes the supremacy of Rome; political divisions have hardened, the Republicans having become "Knotheads" (conservative, evangelical, prone to disorders of the lower bowel), while the Democrats are now the LEFT (advocates of the pill, pornography, abortion, love clinics, and euthanasia). . . . (pp. 6-7)

Love in the Ruins is a sharp-eyed, clever book that goes on much too long and strikes out in so many directions at once that it puts one in mind of a hornet's nest poked by a stick. It suffers, if ever a novel suffered, from the looseness that Henry James saw as a major weakness of long novels in the first-person—from what he called "the terrible fluidity of self-revelation!". . .

In Lancelot the materials of the novel seem to have eluded Percy's control altogether. Yet the book held my interest throughout, leaving me puzzled, disbelieving, but never bored. It is the story—again the first person but told to a specific listener—of a corrupted Louisiana gentleman, Lancelot Andrewes Lamar, who has been confined to a mental hospital in New Orleans after incinerating his adulterous wife Margot and a group of filmmakers in a fire that destroys his ancestral home, a showplace called Belle Isle. . . .

The main action of the story is the sheerest Gothic claptrap, replete with a ghostly visitation, a grisly murder, and a raging hurricane; Percy, whether deliberately or not, handles this stuff in the perfunctory way it deserves. His real concerns are elsewhere—with the symbolic aspects of the situation. . . . (p. 7)

Lancelot . . . has a primarily emblematic function, one which touches interestingly upon the role of the gentleman in Percy's novels from The Moviegoer on. Percy goes out of his way to establish the thoroughly regressed condition of his protagonist. . . . Lancelot is a heavy drinker, a failed lawyer, a failed liberal, a grubby and withdrawn stranger in his own house. . . . What has failed him above all is his inherited vocation as a gentleman.

It is hard for a Northerner or even a native of the Upper South like myself to appreciate the self-conscious emphasis still given to the idea of the gentleman in the Deep South. Presumably it has more to do with the numerical smallness of the old landowning and professional class, with the comparative lack of a substantial middle class in the old Black Belt, than with the ethos of Sir Walter Scott. Percy himself gives every sign of participating in this self-consciousness. . . .

[For] the gentlemen in Walker Percy's novels, the enemy, of course, is nothing less global than the whole modern world, to which they respond by withdrawing into apathy like Binx, stumbling in amnesiac innocence like Will Barrett; or, like Lancelot Lamar (resonant surname!), by igniting a holocaust. . . .

[The] central problem of Lancelot as a novel [is] its ambiguity of tone. It would be easy enough to accept both the postures and opinions of Lancelot as appropriate to a created madman—a character properly at a distance from its creator—if they did not represent in an extreme form attitudes expressed by far more sympathetic characters in the other novels. When Lance states that in the new order he proposes a woman will have to choose between being a lady and a whore, he is echoing a confusion about women voiced by Will Barrett in The Last Gentleman. The satirical thrusts against the contemporary world in Love in the Ruins have given way to Juvenalian invective and rant in Lancelot—with a palpable loss in effectiveness. Lancelot's fantasy of setting out for Virginia ("where it all started"), and there inaugurating a Third Revolution founded upon honor, chivalry, and the suppression of pornography could be enjoyed as comic megalomania if we did not suspect a certain authorial complicity in the protagonist's program.

Percy evidently wants to have it both ways. . . .

Percy is unsuccessful in making Percival carry his assigned weight, just as he is unsuccessful in assembling the different levels of reality—documentary, Gothic, satiric, symbolic—into a coherent structure.

It is too bad that Percy is not content to be a "mere" novelist—and a gifted one at that. His apparent desire to be a philosopher-novelist in the Continental mode leads him, in *Lancelot,* to chase a dozen thematic butterflies at once while his real subject—the haunting of the Sunbelt by atavistic, even pathological, remnants of the old dispensation—lies half-formed and neglected in the mud. (p. 8)

> *Robert Towers, "Southern Discomfort," in* The New York Review of Books *(reprinted with permission from* The New York Review of Books; *copyright © 1977 NYREV, Inc.), March 31, 1977, pp. 6-8.*

There are what appear to be repetitions here: some lines, even passages, are paraphrases from Percy's earlier novels. And the metaphor of the hurricane which worked so well in *The Last Gentleman* (people are happier, and better to each other, during a hurricane) is expanded in *Lancelot:* the climactic action of the novel occurs during a hurricane.

I believe there are good reasons for this, and that finally what we are seeing is not repetition at all. Walker Percy was forty-five years old when he published his first novel, *The Moviegoer.* So what we don't see in Percy's novels is the changing vision of the world that we often get from a writer who publishes while he is young, and then continues to write. With *The Moviegoer* we were in the hands of a mature writer whose theme had already chosen him. He has been possessed by it ever since, and that is why he is not truly repetitious. A repetitious writer is a tired writer, perhaps filling the blank page because there is nothing else to do. Percy is not tired; he is growing stronger; so that when parts of *Lancelot* sound like parts of the earlier novels, it's not repetition we're hearing, but the resonant sound of a writer grappling with his theme. . . .

The question is simple and profound: What is one supposed to do on an ordinary afternoon? Therefore, what is time for? What is a human being for? To ask the questions and find no answers causes despair (Sutter Vaught in *The Last Gentleman*). Not to ask the questions causes a despair that doesn't know it is despair; this is what troubles most of the secondary characters in Percy's novels, which is why they feel better during hurricanes (from *Lancelot:* "Hurricanes, which are very bad things, somehow neutralize the other bad thing which has no name"). Percy's heroes are assaulted by both: they ask the questions and find no absolute answers, and they are surrounded by friends and relatives who don't ask the questions, who are dead while they yet breathe, talk, make plans, carry them out. (p. 86)

In each of [Percy's four novels] the hero is searching; he is searching because he has to, because if he does not search he will join the active dead who move about Percy's joyless landscape, making sounds, making money, making children. The search remains the same from novel to novel, as it must—for how can Percy ever find the answer? And how can he quit without the answer?

With each novel the tone changes. Binx Bolling of *The Moviegoer* is often comic; his struggle isn't, but the way he tells us about it is. . . . *The Moviegoer* keeps a comic tone because young Binx is tolerant of the people whose values

he cannot accept. So is Bill Barrett of *The Last Gentleman:* he knows there is *some*thing wrong in the land, yet he is able to understand and tolerate the people who embody that something. . . . *The Last Gentleman* is largely comic, too, because Barrett maintains a tolerant vigilance of the people around him, though at one moment in the novel he resorts —happily and justifiably—to violence: he hits the right man at the right time. (This moment of certainty in violence becomes, in *Lancelot,* the climactic action of the novel.) In *Love in the Ruins,* things are closing in on Percy's hero; he is literally under attack. Thomas More is older and less tolerant than Bolling and Barrett; his wife has left him and he likes the bottle. Both the search and the struggle are more desperate, more tangible: hippies, racists, militant blacks, sex clinics have replaced the nuances of despair that entered like ghosts the nice conversations with nice people in the first two novels. . . .

In *Lancelot,* Percy is again confronting the forces which make moral choices and live by them. And his hero, Lancelot Lamar, is angry. Because of this, the novel goes further, more deeply, than the three before it. Lancelot cannot be content with amused tolerance of others, while he takes his lady to bed. In a land where so many are devoting their energy to coping, to being like everyone else and surviving it, Lancelot cries out no. It is a different kind of no. It is not the no of dope or booze or television or what we call recreation. It is the no of Jean Anouilh's Antigone, who finally tells Creon that she simply refuses to live in the world as it is; and that no causes her death. Lancelot's no causes death too, and a new world. It is a small world: the world of the soul, of moral choice and action, is always limited to the few who choose it. (pp. 86-7)

[Lancelot] cannot, like the earlier Percy heroes, find a peaceful bemused niche within the world he sees; he must act, and his action is the center of the novel. He struggles against loss of personal worth and values, a history that haunts him, the infidelity of his wife, his own lust and its purpose, the loss of two of his children to the nonvalues of the age, the invasion of his empty life by even emptier Hollywood directors and actors (for a while their emptiness is active enough to make his emptiness even more passive), with women whose liberation, he believes, has further enslaved them to their unique condition of being the only female creatures who are always in heat, and with God.

In all of Percy's novels Catholicism is essential as an alternative. . . . If Catholicism demanded a stoic life in the desert, no doubt Lancelot would happily do it. But, looking at the flabbiness of the modern church, Lancelot decides there is only one way to leave the present world and enter the new one which all Percy's heroes have yearned for. Lancelot, through his own will and action, destroys the present world, and after that cleansing destruction, he starts over. This novel is Percy's strongest counterattack against those forces which I suspect are still shrieking at his door. (pp. 87-8)

> *Andre Dubus, "Paths to Redemption," in* Harper's *(copyright © 1977 by* Harper's *Magazine; all rights reserved; reprinted from the April, 1977 issue by special permission), April, 1977, pp. 86-7.*

Although Walker Percy is a Christian novelist, he refuses to write mere sermons. He recognizes that he must find— or, better yet, create—striking patterns of imagery, structure, and voice to command our attention. Thus if we simply discuss his apparent attitudes toward faith, American violence, etc., we are fragmenting his work, using it as *our* platform for abstractions. (p. 568)

There is a "two-faced" quality to the narrator [of *Lancelot*] (and his listener); and the fact that they move about and change places in the cell—remember that the narrator offers a chair; the listener refuses and stands near the window— suggests the cross-purposes, the doubling, at work in the novel. Even in the first chapter the narrator tries to get straight to his past (and present troubles), but he is trapped by the narrowness of the chapter. He is locked in by short, abrupt *sentences*.

The narrator is named Lancelot Andrews Lamar. The name is double (as he himself informs us); it signifies the "great Anglican divine" and the knight searching for the Grail; fixed *and* uncertain faith. Perhaps there is even another meaning. "Lancet": "a surgical instrument, commonly sharp-pointed and *two-edged* [my italics], used to open boils, etc." The narrator considers himself a wounded man trying to open the wounds of our society—he is doctor *and* patient.

[These] few metaphors . . . occur in the first pages, but I believe they underlie the complete work. Lancelot continually uses words as an *instrument;* he tells his listener (and reader) that he has committed murder and arson because he had discovered that this child doesn't belong to him: "It is a mystery which I ponder endlessly; that my life is divided into two parts, Before and After, before and after the moment I discovered that my wife had been rendered ecstatic, beside herself, by a man on top of her.". . . [Lancelot] seems to be participant *and* creator of his "revenge tragedy."

Whenever Lancelot discusses such things as Evil—his quest for the Unholy Grail—he offers split motives. He tells us at one point: "Things were split." He mentions two scientists "who did the experiment on the speed of light and kept getting the wrong result. . . . It took Einstein to comprehend that the *wrong* answer might be right." He acts many roles—he's perfected the Southern Gentleman for his wife—but he stands outside these very roles. Although he condemns the shallow actors—including his wife —and the fake lightning storm used to create effects (even when a "real" storm is threatening), he refuses to understand that he shares their theatrical lies. (There are some wonderfully comic Hollywood types, but they blend into his duplicitous role-playing and narration. Mirrors within mirrors!) And when he insists that he wants to speak honestly, he is so intent upon his purpose that it also seems a crazy (*and* sane) *performance* for his listener. Perhaps the most sustained use of this kind of "reflective" metaphor occurs when Lancelot photographs the sexual goings-on "off-camera" of the actors (including his wife and daughter). He calls it a "double feature" because what he views is symbolically linked not only to the trashy, pretentious film being shot at Belle Isle, his home, but to his desire to manipulate, to direct, and to create his artistic "mad" pattern: "Lights and darks were reversed like a negative, mouths opened on light, eyes were white sockets. The actors looked naked clothed, clothed naked." (pp. 568-70)

The novel ends ambiguously. Lancelot is now a free man; he will try to be a prophet outside of cell walls. But he persists in claiming to the listener that "one of us is wrong." Yes *and* no. Percy seems, after all the metaphors of dis-

torted (and distorting vision), to emphasize that humanity is always at a midpoint, a crossroad, and that every design (or map), even a heretical, unholy one, is cloudy. I am fond of the priest-psychiatrist's "Yes"—it can mean anything!— and the word does not finally conclude the narration or solve ultimate mysteries enclosed within.

I believe that *Lancelot* is, oddly enough, an *open* book— despite all the imprisonment metaphors—which offers hints, glimpses, omens. It fights the idea of logical patterns, "useful" knowledge. It offers faith as a possible answer, a view of hell and purgatory, but it stops short of final solutions, visions, Paradise itself. (pp. 570-71)

Irving Malin, "Cross Purposes," in Virginia Quarterly Review *(copyright, 1977, by the* Virginia Quarterly Review, *The University of Virginia), Vol. 53, No. 3 (Summer, 1977), pp. 568-71.*

*   *   *

PLOMER, William   1903-1973

Plomer was a South African poet, novelist, short story writer, biographer, and editor whose diversity of interest made him something of a contemporary man of letters while he was living. Esteemed as much for his poetry as for his novels, Plomer mastered just about every literary genre and even wrote the libretti for a number of works by the distinguished British composer Benjamin Britten. As a poet, Plomer had both a serious side and a lighthearted, comic side, and the latter was just about unmatched in modern English literature. His anti-apartheid novel, *Turbott Woolfe*, is still the most authentic depiction of the South African black's situation. (See also *CLC*, Vol. 4, and *Contemporary Authors*, Vols. 21-22; *Contemporary Authors Permanent Series*, Vol. 2.)

[When] one stands back now and looks at the whole body of Plomer's poetry in the light of [the] revised and enlarged edition of his *Collected Poems*, it is difficult not to feel something very like a sense of disappointment, at a talent which much too often seems to take refuge in obliqueness, sidesteps away from confrontation into blandness, too readily takes on a colouring of snobbishness or superciliousness, and even when it leans towards sensuous descriptiveness loses itself in fussy detail. Above all, it seems a poetry of surprisingly icy reserve. . . .

He was fond of quoting . . . a dictum of the early Chinese poet, Wei T'ai, to the effect that poetry presents the thing in order to convey the feeling, and should be exact about the thing and reticent about the feeling. Sound doctrine, when assaulted with the confessions and protestations of some damp contemporary souls; but Plomer's interpretation of it was inconsistent, for in his comic and satirical poems he tends tiresomely to underline and exhaust the macabre jollity, gesturing with a wink and a nod where, say, Auden in "Miss Gee" (which John Betjeman, surely wrongly, sees as a poem influenced by Plomer) gets his effect by being totally straight-faced; while in many of the serious poems— whether specifically grouped by Plomer as "of the affections" or not—a screen (or mask) stands between the experience and the expression, or between the experience and its "meaning".

What, for example, is such a poem as "The Umbrella" aiming to say? Or, later on, "A Casual Encounter" (a poem "In memory of Cavafy")? They seem to be bemused memories of, or meditations on, former passions; in a way, they are full of circumstance; yet they give absolutely nothing away. Their reticence inclines towards character-lessness, or even moral evasiveness. . . . [The] fault is not simply one of tone but of withdrawal into a position which chose to ignore, or at any rate ignored, his own low-pressured emotional drives, except insofar as they could be attached to unexceptionable objects: an old widow, wild orchids, the dead John F. Kennedy—sincere, dutiful, rather ponderous poems of lament and regret. . . .

[Plomer], for all his well-testified human warmth and generosity, was a distinctly chill poet.

> *"A Thing without the Feeling," in* The Times Literary Supplement (© *Times Newspapers Ltd., 1974; reproduced from* The Times Literary Supplement *by permission), January 11, 1974, p. 28.*

William Plomer's *Collected Poems* show a consistency over the years. . . . Plomer has Davie's well-heeled civility, but it's the civility of a poet more comfortably sociable than Davie ever was, and this isn't really a gain. Whereas Davie makes poetry out of the tensions involved in fending off disruptive experience, some of Plomer's work seems to fend it off unknowingly, and the result is a certain literariness about even the most 'socially conscious' of his pieces. His poems haven't a hair out of place, but not many of them seem to have fought hard to preserve their elegance intact. . . . Not much authentic feeling can filter past [his] alliterative and assonantal tics, reducing the world as they do to a literary *mis-en-scéne* for contemplative consumption. Indeed Plomer's poetry seems to me remarkable for the way it consistently deflects complex or disturbing feeling, modulating into social wit or minor verse at the first opportunity. Like Andrew Young, although in a quite different mode, he seems to have achieved his consistency by moving in a world partly sealed from the most significant history of his period. (pp. 73-4)

> *Terry Eagleton, in* Stand *(copyright © by Stand), Vol. 15, No. 4 (1974).*

*   *   *

POWERS, J(ames) F(arl)   1917-

Powers is an American novelist and short story writer. Writing in a sharp, precise, and witty style, he finds much of his subject matter in his Catholic background, for he is concerned with, as F. W. Dupee says, "the contradictions that beset Catholicism, in practice if not in theory, because of its claim to an earthly as well as a divine mission and authority." Powers is a recipient of the National Book Award. (See also *CLC*, Vols. 1, 4, and *Contemporary Authors*, Vols. 1-4, rev. ed.)

[One] cannot help wishing that Powers were open to the risks of imperfection, that he did not keep his shrewd and funny scrutinies so tightly contained. There is always a lingering poignance of unexplored possibility in everything he has written. How much more, we feel, he could do with the hip young sophisticated priests of the '60s and their puzzled elders! Instead, Powers has padded *Look How the Fish Live* with bits of trivia—a misfired joke about moon exploration, some feeble cautionary tales of adultery and hypocrisy—better consigned to oblivion. If only he would engage his brilliant talent and intelligence in a reckless, even outrageous spirit, daring perhaps to move outside his predictable boundaries. (p. 16)

> *Pearl K. Bell, in* The New Leader (© *1975*

by the American Labor Conference on International Affairs, Inc.), October 13, 1975.

Unfortunately for Powers's admirers (and I confess to be one) his new book is a disappointment. "Look How the Fish Live" is a thin collection of stories from a writer who seems not to have grown in the last 12 years. It is literary retread, a return to safe places peopled by safe characters. . . .

In "Look How the Fish Live" the hand of a master short story craftsman is plainly evident, the impeccable form, a precision of rich detail, the tone of gentle, pinprick satire always in perfect control, the admirable indulgence toward his characters that is a J. F. Powers trademark. But Powers has failed to heed an author's primary responsibility: to observe and interpret the real and changing world about him. Powers has not expanded his perimeters, encompassing new realities and ideas, but has merely shifted them about, creating new configurations within the old. The content of the majority of these stories is depressingly familiar, as abstemious as a Roman cleric's sex life is supposed to be. Little—with the exception of one story, "Tinkers," set in Ireland and about "America's thriftiest living author" and his family, and the title story "Look How the Fish Live," . . . —dares venture beyond the inward-looking churchly world. Powers seems determined to codify the rules for an American theocracy, glorifying provincialism, glorifying parochialism, glorifying an archaic place of privilege and prerogative that has set a good many Catholics running away. Turning inward for protection, then? Perhaps. J. F. Powers seems to have put the turbulent, politicized late 1960's and early 1970's—of the Berrigans and other priestly activists who so severely buffeted his beloved Church—on his personal Index. (p. 14)

Powers professes too little, is cautious to the point of exasperation, measures the beat of his world in tiny pats when a good hard slam is what it needs. His real ability to humanize his characters is demonstrated only when he chooses to mark the depths of their personal loneliness. . . . "Look How the Fish Live" mirrors . . . few of the author's marvelous talents. (p. 16)

> *Tom McHale, in* The New York Times Book Review (© *1975 by The New York Times Company; reprinted by permission), November 2, 1975.*

Powers's heart, never large, seems to have shrunk, and the result is an unpleasant combination of triviality and sourness. Most of the stories [in *Look How the Fish Live*] are, like his earlier ones, about priests, most are neat as a pin, but the ritual noncommunication of pastors with curates, of bishops with pastors, becomes thin. . . . He becomes a little untidy only in "Priestly Fellowship" where he lets a priest just sound off—"All this talk of community, communicating, and so on—it was just whistling in the dark. 'Life's not a cookout by Bruegel the Elder and people know it.'" The result is the only interesting story in the book; the ones that aren't about priests are dreadful. Going back to the stories in *The Presence of Grace* (1956) just to check, I found a lot of mere neatness, but there is a saving wit there that is all but gone now. (p. 31)

> *Roger Sale, in* The New York Review of Books *(reprinted with permission from* The New York Review of Books; *copyright © 1975 NYREV, Inc.), November 13, 1975.*

Perhaps when the roll is called up yonder, J. F. Powers' name will assume its rightful place in the ranks of contemporary American writers, but as matters currently stand he is an author curiously without honor in his own country. . . . J. F. Powers is not a name to conjur with precisely because he is one of the most accomplished practitioners of the short story still alive and writing in America today.

Whatever the reasons (and they are many), mastery of the short story constitutes one of the swiftest and surest roads to creative invisibility that this country has ever devised. (p. 33)

[*Look How the Fish Live*] is a book not without its flaws—or, rather, one large flaw, in that five of the ten stories are little more than landfill, evidently stuck in to pad the volume. . . . It is the other five stories that constitute the real book, and they are pure, unalloyed gold.

Centering on a midwestern priest named Joe, his young curate Bill, Bill's modernist fellow-seminarians, and the aging bishop of the Minnesota diocese of Ostergothenburg, they deal with Powers' unique milieu, the Roman Catholic Church in late 20th century America. It is a church where the articles of faith have been reduced to an excuse for an institutionalized Kiwanian hierarchy and are at the best the subject for sophomoric debate, where efficient administration and good PR have taken precedence over the nurture of souls and good housekeeping at the rectory is more important than the pastoral round. . . .

To say that these stories are beautifully conceived and artfully executed is like saying that an elephant has big ears; on his chosen ground, Powers has no competitors worthy of the name, John Updike not excepted. It seems almost gratuitous to add that, in the service of his larger and intensely serious purpose, he is also marvelously funny. Anyone who fails to laugh aloud at the ridiculous revelation (in "Farewell" . . .) that is the closest the diocese of Ostergothenburg can come to a miracle must have a heart of stone. It is when one realizes why one is laughing that the lesson begins. (p. 34)

> *L. J. Davis, in* The New Republic *(reprinted by permission of* The New Republic; © 1975 *by The New Republic, Inc.), November 29, 1975.*

J. F. Powers is at his best with his tales about Midwestern priests and bishops. They wander through the world of Rosary and Altar Guild raffles and parish Cub Scout meetings and wonder about their own spiritual lives. The way Powers has kept up with the times impressed me most in this collection. The territory is now post-Vatican II. (p. 191)

Several of the stories about laymen also have thoughts on spiritual life at their roots—Powers *is* a believer—but they simply aren't as effective. . . . [The] priest stories reaffirm that Powers is a wonderful colloquial raconteur in the noble tradition of Frank O'Connor and I. B. Singer. His clergy tell us something about the stuff of all our hearts. (p. 192)

> *Peter LaSalle, in* The Carleton Miscellany *(copyright 1977 by Carleton College), Volume XVI, 1976-77.*

R

RABE, David   1940-

Rabe, an American playwright, is a Vietnamese War veteran; most of his work, which has been well received by both critics and the theater-going public, concerns the effect of this war on its soldiers and veterans. (See also *CLC*, Vol. 4.)

The Basic Training of Pavlo Hummel [is] a not unrewarding play by David Rabe. It concerns a confused young man who briefly comes to tragicomic life in the Vietnam war, then goes down in it to absurd and anonymous death. Rabe knows the war, having been through it; and knows, what is more, how to write. His able play nevertheless suffers from splits down the middle in two directions. Horizontally, it tries to be as much about the war and the sad and comic grossness of army life as about the peculiarities and tergiversations of a funny little man trying to find himself. It even wants, I think, to relate the home front (or lack of one) to the battlefront. In these dualities and overextensions it often manages to stretch beyond the breaking point. Vertically, though it is in perfect control when dealing with its subject as a piece of artfully heightened realism, it is also drawn into modishly antirealistic devices over which it exercises insufficient control, and which have a way of becoming top-heavy and crumbling. (pp. 347-48)

Rabe impressively avoids easy pathos by making the protagonist anything but prepossessing, and by making the bad guys—smarmy officers, Napoleonic noncoms, and brawling GI's—as human as villains can be, and often are. The play's horror tends to be comic, as is a nightmare that is so outrageous as to be almost amusing, except that it devastates all the same. What is frightening here is the semblance of logic, of benevolence even, about the inhumanity; the cheerfulness, or at least casualness, with which the worst befalls and befouls us. The dialogue has an assurance that gives it historic authority; it is also marshaled in a way that endows it with artistic dignity.

But there remain the problems of the above-mentioned rifts, as well as the difficulty of making a drama about armies, wars, and senseless death differ from other such plays, however superior to them it may be. (p. 348)

While in *Pavlo* Rabe considered the effect of the Vietnam war on its participants, in *Sticks and Bones* he examines the disasters of the home front. A Vietnam veteran, David, comes back blind to his silent-American family—parents and a brother—who manages to be far blinder than he. Their names derive from television: Ozzie, Harriet and younger brother Rick; it is Rabe's double nelson on America. (p. 387)

The play functions on three levels. There is a kind of heightened realism much striven for by Arthur Miller, but more successfully managed by Rabe. Here, for example, belong Ozzie's reminiscences about the great runner he once was (with a double entendre no doubt implied), and his repeated references to Hank, a friend we never see, whose archetypal American values and success drive Ozzie to admiration, envy and despair. Here, too, belong the outbursts of vindictiveness and castration that flash forth from beneath Harriet's placid kitchen-and-church surface. The next level is that of adroit black comedy. . . , and includes Rick's larger-than-life stupidity, [the family priest's] supposedly enlightened obscurantism, and any number of ferociously funny scenes and speeches. Lastly, there is a level intended to be pure poetry for David's scenes of painful self-searching and despair at his family; here the writing fails to rise to its intentions: "And then I knew that I was not awake but asleep, and in my sleep there was nothing and nothing"; or "The seasons will amaze . . . Texas is enormous; Ohio is sometimes green." Most disturbingly, the transitions between any two of these three modes are at times precipitous and jarring. And Rabe is youthfully prodigal of good ideas insufficiently worked out: he brings the Vietnamese girl David left behind onstage as a ghostly image that follows David around fitfully; except at the very end, the figure does not yield anywhere near its dramatic potential.

But the people live and the dialogue works because Rabe is aware of all the tics, absurdities and sadnesses that go into the making of his characters: he does not limit himself to the most obvious imbecilities or nastinesses to be punctured one after the other. Even pigheadedness is allowed to have its pathos. The recital of the horrors of war does not quite come off, though there is a powerful scene in which David projects what he sees as a film of the ravages of war, but the family and we perceive as blank frames coming from the projector, except for here and there a greenish spot. Throughout, the atmosphere of specious solicitude covering up genuine self-absorption is expertly caught. But the real strength of the play lies in its ability to satirize fiercely without losing a residue of sympathy and even compassion. . . . Rabe attacks with wit, passion, fury turning into despair, but not with hate and still less with modish self-righteousness. (pp. 387-88)

When I read that Rabe's *The Orphan* was an Orestes play set in both past and present and featuring two Clytemnestras, I resolved to expect little, but never, never would I have expected the author of *The Basic Training of Pavlo Hummel* and *Sticks and Bones* to contrive such a strained, pretentious, muddled, clumsy and almost completely flavorless piece of claptrap. The idea, if it can be called one, is that Orestes is reincarnated in Charles Manson; that Agamemnon, Aegisthus, Calchas are the forerunners of the present American Establishment and its materialism, militarism and mumbo jumbo. Clytemnestra is America herself, the traitorous mother who becomes identified with the pregnant Sharon Tate. . . . The notion is not only an insult to poor Miss Tate, it may even be unfair to Charlie Manson. Aeschylus I won't worry about; to his peripatetic shade, it is merely a stinkweed among the asphodel.

The parallel between the Manson "family" and the House of Atreus is preposterous enough, but Rabe does not even try to work it out properly. In the first act, he tells the myth more or less straight in the standard contemporary mode of demystification, anachronism and gags, with occasional intrusions of the present, mostly in the shape of one of Manson's girls. In the second act, he deals chiefly with Manson-Orestes and the "family," but accords the mythic figures a few brief entrances and a bloody exit. To fret his scraggy texture further, he adds a microphone-carrying Speaker, who incessantly butts in either with smart-alec jibes or with lengthy disquisitions on the current state of science and technology and the latest scientific data on the workings of the human brain and heart. Meant either as Greek chorus or Brechtian alienation, the device creates only an obtrusive vocal palimpsest.

Rabe hits out against both secular and religious authorities; indeed, against God himself in the person of a slippery and unsavory Apollo; but, much as I sympathize with his thesis, it falls between parallels as surely as if they were stools. In the broad or abstract sense, Agamemnon & Co. are such obvious power figures that to spell out elaborately their contemporary relevance is sheer supererogation. When, however, specific analogues and far-fetched correspondences are forced on the Then and Now, the whole thing becomes ludicrously unconvincing. And Rabe cannot come up with a language suitable to both his Atreids and Mansonites; when he sticks to modern idiom, he does well enough, but his attempts at fusion confound him: "Think of yourself as a Vietnamese, Aegisthus; think of yourself as a duck, a squirrel!" Or: "Clytemnestra, you are too rich to have ever been anything but a whore!" Or: "You are incredible—how can I forget that you are absolutely disgustingly unbelievable?" Rabe stoops even to a rather heavy reliance on street-corner obscenities, which he does not even put into the appropriate mouths. (pp. 462-63)

> *John Simon, in his* Uneasy Stages: A Chronicle of the New York Theater, 1963-1973 *(copyright © 1975 by John Simon; reprinted by permission of Random House, Inc.), Random House, 1975.*

David Rabe's plays are usually what some people deem "unpleasant." They are angry, brutal, obscene, with flecks of compassionate feeling that others may call sentimental, though they are not without streaks of fierce humor. It may

also be claimed that they are wanting in the alleviation of "catharsis."

But all of them have impressed me as strong and, despite reservations, moving; their feeling is almost always inescapably authentic. Rabe seems to have been subjected to the "basic training" of his *Pavlo Hummel,* a play which showed that war bleeds and besmirches all sides and very often destroys the moral fiber in regard to one another or even those on the same side. *Sticks and Bones* was not just the woeful spectacle of a blinded war veteran but rather more about the calloused sensibility of the homes from which the veteran emerges and to which he returns—perhaps the ground for the very outbreak and social tolerance of wars. *Boom Boom Room* pictured ordinary people of lowly estate sunk in the sewers of our civilization, from which a few still attempt agonizingly to climb out.

It would not be very helpful at this juncture to set down the details of events in Rabe's latest play *Streamers.* . . . It takes place in a bare barracks room in Virginia, 1965. But it is not about the war or about the army. One of the room's occupants is a homosexual soldier but the play is not about his "problem," any more than it is about the "black problem" because two black soldiers are involved in the ensuing violence. The combined history of these men and a third—who is just a blandly decent fellow from Wisconsin—along with the sodden sergeants of long professional (military) experience, is not only bloody but a study of long-standing benightedness and misery.

A "universal" inference is evoked: humanity is composed of poor forked animals caught in a trap of which they can never understand the exact identity or the way out. As one of the black men—the most level-headed and innocent of the lot—says of his duties for which he has no more liking than have any of the others: "We're here, aren't we?," and carries on in resigned bewilderment. Rabe sees the bitter joke of this situation but evinces no scorn for any of his characters' ugliest or most shameful actions. There is a certain stoic objectivity (not without its heartbreak) in the depiction, free of any conscious will to shock or gratification in shocking. He simply echoes the pathos of "We're here, aren't we?" One of the play's ironies is that every character is dismayed or "turned off" by the mote in his neighbor's eye but does not consider the beam in his own. Each man has every reason to be considerate of the others, and each hurts the others terribly.

For all the cruel coarseness which agitates *Streamers,* it is a sober play which speaks, after all, in a "small" voice. (p. 574)

> *Harold Clurman, in* The Nation *(copyright 1976 by the Nation Associates, Inc.), May 8, 1976.*

The American theater may be short on lots of things, but one gift it's loaded with—the ability to make mountains out of molehills. A current playwriting molehill is David Rabe. Now that he has written a play that is not as artily imitative in form, not as rankly jejune and shallow as were, in varying degree, *The Basic Training of Pavlo Hummel, Sticks and Bones, The Orphan* and *In the Boom Boom Room,* he is hailed as near-Olympian and garlanded further with prizes. *Streamers* is called his best play and the best American play of the season. Both of those things may in fact be true; but they strike me as mournful.

Rabe has some ability to write dialogue (although it wavers

. . .). He has some instinct for dramatic action and for the revelation of character through contest. But that's like saying of a painter that he understands perspective and can turn form with color. *Then* what? To begin with Rabe's fundamental lack, which would govern even if he were technically and stylistically more accomplished, he has no insights deeper than those of his audience. And his artistic gifts are insufficient to turn his commonplace percepts into strong dramatic emblems for us so that, even if he didn't enlighten, he could at least fix memorably what we've seen for ourselves. Rabe asks for our attention to tell us what we already know about ourselves and our society, and he puts what he has to say in very earnest but rickety form.

In *Streamers* he has at least abjured second-hand expressionism, bloated neo-classicism, melodramatic physical images. It's a linear play in realistic mode. Of course this doesn't preclude symbolism, of an internal "literary" kind, and Rabe hurries to exercise this option, beginning with the title. "Streamers" are paratroopers whose parachutes don't open. This play is set in an Army barracks in 1965, but it's not about paratroopers. So, you see—you quickly see—the title is symbolic. . . .

The key incidents have the smell of matters that Rabe himself saw or heard of in the army, that greatly disturbed him, and that he wanted to make some statement about. But he has merely pushed some accidents into a sack. (Whether they are based on his experience or not, they are just accidents of occurrence.) . . . The incidents in the play remain accidents. The two stories—of homosexual tension, of black disquiet—are arbitrarily pushed together, as if there were some real relation between psychosexual drama and racial bitterness; and the two are hurriedly married at the end by a sheerly insane violent act, unfounded in character. . . .

Outstanding amidst the gimmicks banked for later reference is "Beautiful Streamers," a paratroopers' song given to us early by two drunken old professional-army sergeants. (The tune is Foster's "Beautiful Dreamer.") We get it early, so that we can get it late—in that painful coda—a big windy metaphor which we are supposed to accept as Poetry without question. But what does it symbolize? What does the symbol of an unopened parachute mean to anything we have seen? Alternatively, what would an "opened parachute" have been in any of the lives we have seen tangled? (p.20)

> *Stanley Kauffmann, in* The New Republic *(reprinted by permission of* The New Republic; © *1976 by* The New Republic, Inc.), *June 12, 1976.*

The Basic Training of Pavlo Hummel . . . is the first of David Rabe's angrily talented plays. I liked *Sticks and Bones* even better, and *Streamers* the best. The three constitute a kind of triptych; though they do not all have the same theme, there is, along with the ferocity, a vein of moral hurt and compassion in all of them.

Pavlo Hummel is not an anti-war play in the conventional sense, nor for that matter are the others. It shows an ignorant, unhappy, guileless youth with no harm or malice in him slowly becoming degraded and brutalized by the "basic training" of an environment—in this case the Army—even before he serves in Vietnam. Environment might have had some of the same ugly consequences if he had remained at home with such a family as the one depicted in *Sticks and Bones.* . . .

Pavlo is an innocent, so much so that his fellow trainees regard him as a freak. . . . But the change in Pavlo from the gutter Parsifal of the first act (we hear that he was a virgin at the time of his Army enlistment) to the later soiled and nasty Pavlo is not sufficiently marked. Thus there is a slight monotony in the performance, so that the final scenes, which should be even more bruising than the preceding ones, fall a little flat. (p. 602)

> *Harold Clurman, in* The Nation *(copyright 1977 by the Nation Associates, Inc.), May 14, 1977.*

The Basic Training of Pavlo Hummel . . . produced in 1971 but in the writing since 1968, today seems almost as dated as *Anna Christie*. This interests me particularly because I had, as the book jacket of the published play reminded me, compared Rabe favorably with O'Neill. Time has now come full circle, and I must again compare him to O'Neill, to the disadvantage of both. *Pavlo*'s language begins to have the same literalness that O'Neill's had, and fails to achieve transcendence in its occasional leaps, exactly as O'Neill's failed.

This is the story of a somewhat unbright, somewhat dishonest, yet basically well-meaning bumbler. . . . Though he becomes moderately efficient as a soldier [in Vietnam], he ends up dying a death as silly as his life. Pavlo does, however, have his little decencies, and, finally, he is a human being; seeing him live and die so shabbily is moving, not the least because Rabe wisely refrains from any sentimentality. Nevertheless, I am fairly sure that much of the fervor in behalf of the play stemmed from its coming when it did and from whom it did—a Vietnam veteran writing with the war still on, and managing to capture some of it for us in a way that other Vietnam plays, written by people who hadn't been there, did not. (pp. 27-8)

> *John Simon, in* The New Leader *(© 1977 by the American Labor Conference on International Affairs, Inc.), May 23, 1977.*

*   *   *

ROBBE-GRILLET, Alain   1922-

French novelist, essayist, screenwriter, and critic, Robbe-Grillet is the leading exponent of the New Novel in France. His style has been described as cinematic: it depicts reality in rapidly changing scenes, revealing the flow of mental rather than physical life. He rejects the idea of the writer as social critic, maintaining that his work is a "search" and not an expression of social attitudes. (See also *CLC*, Vols. 1, 2, 4, 6, and *Contemporary Authors*, Vols. 9-12, rev. ed.)

With Alain Robbe-Grillet, fictional perspective takes the final step prepared for by Sartre and Camus of subordinating the entire spatio-temporal field to its *trompe-l'oeil* aspects. Robbe-Grillet's fictional world presents a single microcosmic enigma, a labyrinth in which as many readers are led astray as successfully enter and find an exit. In *Dans le Labyrinthe* Robbe-Grillet introduces and constantly maintains an ambiguous, enigmatic double perspective with unabashed temerity. It is from the labyrinth of its title that this slim volume comes to represent the vision not only of its author, but of the entire group of New Novelists and their disciples who continue to proliferate in France.

Creating a fiction about the creation of a fiction, Robbe-Grillet in *Dans le Labyrinthe* succeeds more completely than either Sartre or Camus, or indeed than any other New

Novelist, in eliminating his personal voice from the novel. Robbe-Grillet's first-person narrator begins and ends the *Labyrinthe* by narrating a story about a soldier, whose third-person perspective determines his story within the story. Although Robbe-Grillet succeeds through this double perspective in eliminating his personal voice from the novel, he does not even attempt to eliminate the narrator's voice from intervening in his narrative so that interventions by the narrator will occur in the place of the more usual interventions by the author. Although such a technique seems simply to replace the author by the narrator, in fact, the author of *Dans le Labyrinthe* controls the fictional domain of the narrator, who in turn controls the fictional domain of the soldier. Robbe-Grillet's peculiar method of depicting an independent narrator in the throes of the creative process at the very outset of the *Labyrinthe* effectively adheres to Sartre's avowed esthetic purpose of setting both author and reader equidistant from the narrator who creates his fiction independent of either, yet dependent to a certain extent on both.

Rather than allow his narrator to discuss the creative process within his own fictional domain, as Proust, Gide, and Joyce have done, Robbe-Grillet introduces a narrator who shows the creative process at work in the construction of a fictional world different from his own, albeit one which is a reflection of his own. Robbe-Grillet's narrator does not reign as protagonist of the fictional field he creates; indeed, whether he is present within his narrative at all has been questioned.

It is Robbe-Grillet's development of reflection as a literary technique which determines the import of his novel. Although consciousness can proceed from author to narrator to character with no reversal in this novel, forms—objects, itineraries, events and persons within their physical limitations—can reflect precisely as in a mirror image, or approximately as in a shadow, from the narrative domain to the narrator's domain, and from both fictional domains to life itself. (pp. 101-02)

Robbe-Grillet's emphasis is upon the reiteration of single forms under various guises within a specific fictional world, so that his work lends itself easily to mythical and archetypal interpretation. Emphasis upon sameness and reflection works toward the unity of the work, the unity of the point of view, and the unity of the fictional world which itself is double in *Dans le Labyrinthe*. . . .

Robbe-Grillet's concern with method, with the functioning of the feverish or creative consciousness, overrides his concern with its end result. . . .

Although critics have maintained that Robbe-Grillet willfully confuses the spatio-temporal framework in *Dans le Labyrinthe* in order to create a dream state, it seems more relevant to say that the work resembles a daydream or a fantasy. (p. 103)

Dreams, daydreams, and thought being in themselves phenomena with a double aspect, Robbe-Grillet's peculiarly physical affirmation of the existence of things, events, and gestures counter-balances the dreamlike metaphysical aspect in this work. Just as these are double phenomena, the point of view in this novel is double; it is a fictional world composed of two domains or sites, each of which corresponds to one of the two perspectives. (p. 105)

By calling up the powerful archetype of the labyrinth as a figure which incorporates chaos within order, by resorting to a theatrical framework which promotes sequences of scenes emphasizing spatial at the expense of temporal coherence, by exploiting reflection both as a literary technique and as a profound esthetic conviction, Robbe-Grillet tries to impose the experience of creating fiction on the individual reader. Robbe-Grillet's vision begins with peace from within the calm center of each individual who, when exposed to the chaotic confusion of life or death or even the unconscious, will find his own individual solution. In fact, if Robbe-Grillet has a philosophy of life and death, an analogy-myth through which the labyrinthine complexity of life and death is to become comprehensible, it is only that there are no valid generic myths—each man's solution is *sui generis* and is arrived at through the static peace in his inner self. (pp. 147-48)

> Betty T. Rahv, "The Labyrinth As Archetypal Image of the New Novel," in her From Sartre to the New Novel *(copyright © 1974 by Betty T. Rahv; reprinted by permission of Kennikat Press Corp.), Kennikat, 1974, pp. 101-48.*

Robbe-Grillet's theories constitute the most ambitious aesthetic program since Surrealism. . . . [In his essays] reasoning is close; his remarks upon other writers, including the classics of the bourgeois novel, are reverent and lively. Because of his training as an agronomist, his understanding of science and of how its truths subvert our workaday assumptions exceeds that of most writers. His pronouncements do catch at something—a texture, an austerity—already present in other, often older French novelists, such as Nathalie Sarraute. To an American, however, there is a hollow ring of Thomism. Robbe-Grillet's concept of thereness looks like the medieval *quidditas;* the attempt to treat existence itself as a quality that can be artistically emphasized seems a formal confusion, a scholastic bottling of the wind. . . . There is a forced naïveté in his vision, a strange inversion of the pathetic fallacy he detests, for in artistic practice his concern with the inviolable otherness of things charges them, saturates them, with a menace and hostility as distortive of their null inner being as an imagined sympathy. One's reservations about Robbe-Grillet's formulations come down to the discrepancy between his description of what happens in his fiction and what actually happens. Far from striking us with their unsullied thereness, the "things" in his novels are implicated in the pervasive flimsiness and inconsequence.

La Maison de Rendez-Vous could have been translated as *The House of Assignation* or *The Blue Villa* or even *Up at Lady Ava's*. It tells of, or circles around, a night at the elegant brothel run by Lady Ava, or Eva, or Eve, in Hong Kong. . . . Through [a] fog of events, or anti-events ("What does all that matter? What does it matter?" the book asks itself, answering, "All this comes to the same thing"), rotates a constellation of repeated and refracted images. . . . True to Robbe-Grillet's credo, the present never accumulates; rather, it unravels. There is a studied false numerical precision. A hand is "about eight or twelve" inches from a serving tray; forty pages later, the distance is given as six inches. Manneret's apartment is on the third floor, or the fifth, or the sixth, or the eighth. Different characters relive the same adventures; a play within the action becomes the action; and twin servant girls have the same name, "pronounced quite similarly, the difference imperceptible except to a Chinese ear." The ingenuity behind all this doubling and shuffling is considerable. The writing is clean and deft and even entertaining, though the reader's interest tends to cling, pathetically, to the excitements of the hackneyed tale of exotic intrigue that is being parodied, fragmented, and systematically frustrated. The popular adventure form underlying the sophisticated *nouveau roman* rises up and revenges itself by imposing upon the book a cliché ending of double-cross and a flat last sentence: "And there is nothing in her eyes." But there has never been anything in her eyes. Upon the basis, I think, of false analogies, Robbe-Grillet has already dissolved, with his "descriptions whose movement destroys all confidence in the things described," the credibility as elemental to the art of narrative as the solidity of stone or metal is to sculpture. (pp. 354-56)

Robbe-Grillet's fiction is almost exclusively cinematic. *La Maison de Rendez-Vous* is not so much written as scripted: "The scene which then takes place lacks clarity." "Then the images follow one another very rapidly," "Now we see the young Eurasian girl backed into the corner of a luxurious room, near a lacquer chest whose lines are emphasized by bronze ornaments, all escape cut off by a man in a carefully trimmed gray goatee who is towering over her." The full syntax of splicing, blurring, stop-action, enlargement, panning, and fade-out is employed; the book lacks only camera tracks and a union member operating the dolly. The trouble is that prose does not inherently possess the luminous thereness of a projected image, and all of Robbe-Grillet's montages, visual particularization, careful distinctions between right and left, and so on do not induce the kind of participation imposed by, say, his real movie *Last Year at Marienbad*. A man sitting with a book in his lap is a creature quite different from a man sitting hypnotized in a dark theatre. The mind translates verbal imagery into familiar images innocent of a photograph's staring actuality; it seizes on a single detail and enshrouds it in vague memories from real life. An image, to have more than this hazy recollective vitality, must be weighted with a momentum beyond itself, by that movement of merged relevance that Aristotle called an "action."

For this movement, and the accumulating emotion and concern around the things described, Robbe-Grillet, in his essay "Time and Description in Fiction Today," offers to substitute "the very movement of the description." Here we have [in addition to a false analogy with the cinema,] the second false analogy—with painting. . . . A page of print can never, like a rectangle of paint, lift free of all reference to real objects; it cannot but be some kind of shadow. Further, a painting is from the painter's hand, whereas a book has passed through a mechanical process that erases all the handwriting and crossing-out that would declare the author's presence and effort. Robbe-Grillet's off-center duplications, subtle inaccuracies, and cubistic fragmentation do not convey "the very movement of the description." They instead seem mannered devices intended to give unsubstantial materials an interesting surface. (pp. 357-58)

Robbe-Grillet does have instincts, tropisms toward certain styles of experience; his first novel, *The Erasers*, a coherent detective story, shows the same surveyor's eye, the same fondness for duplication and stalled motion, as does his last. But between the two there has been a buildup of theory, a stylization of intuition. *La Maison de Rendez-Vous* is less a work of art than an objet d'art, shiny with its appliqué of progressive post-Existential thought; it has a fragile air of mere up-to-dateness, of chic. (p. 358)

John Updike, in his Picked-Up Pieces *(copyright © 1975 by John Updike; re-printed by permission of Alfred A. Knopf, Inc.), Knopf, 1975.*

Despite its title [*Topologie d'une cité fantôme*] Alain Robbe-Grillet's latest book is by no means a topographical study. Instead, the author once more explores in his own way the technique of the new novel. As in several previous works, he focuses on the process of writing fiction. Again form precedes content.

Complex and replete with variations, regressions, repetitions and intertextuality, the book emphasizes the structure. The narrator, perhaps an anthropologist, examines an ancient city, possibly situated in Greece or Sicily, with its houses, prisons, temples, brothels and harbor. At the same time, he explores techniques of the novel. He constantly modifies his point of view through a stream of consciousness in which individual words generate larger meanings. . . .

[Words] are the generative cells of the fictional body. By manipulating them, creating new words by adding or changing letters, the author creates new associations. . . . Each word becomes the center of a prose swatch that is in turn woven into a larger structural unit. The whole is a colorful collage of an ancient city, with its visible strata of successive cultures, where a catastrophic event takes place: on a peaceful day hostile soldiers invade the land, create great carnage and, in a mysterious ritual, rape a beautiful young girl. (Rape is an obsessional image of the author.) Robbe-Grillet uses the cinema technique of presenting everything in the present. The narrator moves with ease from one cultural stratum to another or, more importantly, from one fictional structure to the next.

Besides verbal structure, the narrator, much as he has in former works, uses geometrical figures such as the number eight in *Le voyeur*. Patterns in this work are more complicated, ranging from numerical and spatial forms to colors. Circular, oval and triangular shapes occur; white and red dominate as colors. Girls' white robes contrast with red materials—blood, wine, ink—all against backgrounds of dark, mysterious rooms or caves. With a painter's sensitivity to color Robbe-Grillet "paints" the white page with words.

When the narrator finds that he is again walking where he has been so often before, along the endless corridor of the book, it is clear that the structure of the novel is circular; and as in several previous works, the cyclical device destroys time, and the content comes full circle. An entirely different matter is the cultural and personal history that is hidden behind the words. As in Joyce's *Ulysses*, this level of meaning cannot be completely decoded. But this hardly matters. On the level of reading pleasure the dynamic impressions that evoke pagan cruelty and stark terror can be enjoyed as much as the impeccable prose. (p. 55)

Anna Otten, in World Literature Today *(copyright 1977 by the University of Oklahoma Press), Vol. 51, No. 1, Winter, 1977.*

Topologie d'une cité fantôme, Robbe-Grillet's most recent novel, is also his purest, purest because to a greater extent than any of his previous works it ignores the conventions of the novel (plot, character, meaning) and such external determinants as human psychology or political ideology. An archeological excavation furnishes the pretext for a series of visions, myths, anecdotes and dramas, all relating to a central terrain. However, the cohesiveness of the novel's scenes depends less on their common site than on the series of generating elements from which the scenes are constructed.

The novel's first "espace," "Construction d'un temple en ruines à la Déesse Vanadé," gradually builds up a set of elements which generate the novel's episodes. Foremost among these elements are four geometric shapes: rectangle, triangle (associated with the letter V), sphere, and line (also a short phallic stylus or iron bar). Other generating elements are naked young girls, a camera, blood, and a woman's scream.

The letter V is the most dynamic of these elements. It is born of the isosceles triangle which was the primitive form of the temple of Vanadé. In inverted form it recreates the erotic spread of two naked legs or the volcano which destroyed the city of vanadium. The letter in conjunction with the letters G and D gives rise to a series of words . . . from which the narrator constructs one of the novel's myths.

In addition to these generating elements, one of the most consistent sources of Robbe-Grillet's film and fiction is his previous work. Thus, one finds in *Topologie* the image of a mannequin tied to an iron bed which appears in *Projet pour une révolution à New York* and *Glissements progressifs du plaisir,* an allusion to the Villa Bleue at Shanghai (*La Maison de rendez-vous*) and the description of a multiroomed building which sounds sometimes like the hotel of *L'Année dernière à Marienbad* and sometimes like the chateau of *L'Homme qui ment* (also recalled in *Topologie* by a game of blind man's bluff). . . .

The novel begins with a five page "Incipit" in which the narrator as he is about to fall asleep calls forth images which will be the novel's central motifs: dripping water, ruins of an ancient city, the image of a young naked girl combing her hair before a mirror, a knife, and a pool of blood. The suggestion that the novel is the product of a dream is reinforced in the "Coda," a five page conclusion which begins as the narrator is awakened by a scream, and in which his preoccupation with butterflies (a motif of the novel) establishes an explicit comparison between the mounting of butterflies in a collection and the stabbing deaths of young girls as described throughout many of the novel's episodes.

Most of the episodes do in fact seem to relate to the murder of a young girl. Several versions of the murder stretch across historical periods from the mythological sacking of an ancient city followed by the massacre of its female inhabitants to the modern detective story version which presents the investigation of a series of knife slayings. The historical period of each episode determines the nature of the structures of the city as well as the nature of the murder which takes place in it. (p. 80)

Two names recur throughout the different episodes: Vanadé and David. The former is a mythological goddess whose temple is one of the earliest ruins on the site. David is first introduced as Vanadé's male counterpart, actually a hermaphrodite responsible for the fertilization of a race of women. In other episodes David is the "incestuous and fratricidal" twin of Vanessa (a variation on the name Vanadé). David is also the name of a biblical king, a twentieth-century photographer and the subject of two dramas described within the novel. In the Coda, Vanadé-Vanessa becomes the variety of butterfly: vanesse.

Topologie d'une cité fantôme is more difficult and less fascinating than its predecessor, *Projet pour une révolution à New York*. The many divisions of the text are a distraction and break down the cohesiveness of the novel. And the novel's descriptions never seem to attain the vividness and poetic strangeness of the earlier work. One section which strikes the reader with its freshness is the series of interior monologues of one or several young female prisoners who stare at themselves in a mirror and dream of an erotic escape with their other selves. The dedicated reader of Robbe-Grillet who has learned to expect from each new novel or film familiar images and techniques accompanied by a renewal of subject and style will not however be disappointed by *Topologie* which marks another important step in the continuing development of the *nouveau roman*. (p. 81)

Paul J. Schwartz, in The International Fiction Review (© *copyright International Fiction Association), January, 1977.*

The received idea of Robbe-Grillet is of a mechanistic, philistine writer who is hardly a literary man at all. That idea was never fair and is regularly disproved by what he has to say in *Robbe-Grillet,* where he quotes from such unexpected sources as Swift and the Bible and goes into detail over the extreme care with which he constructs his novels. He works on four versions simultaneously, each one page further advanced than its successor, and writes slowly because nothing can remain in the approved text unless the scheme justifies it. Robbe-Grillet therefore has to pick and choose between the inspirations which come as he writes, as the actually fortuitous is turned into the apparently deliberate. This is what he most enjoys about his work. . . .

This technique of *récupération* is put successfully to work in *La belle captive,* one of the two fictions which Robbe-Grillet published in 1976. . . . *La belle captive* is a text set, in some splendour, facing reproductions of works by Robbe-Grillet's favourite painter, the archetypal Surrealist, René Magritte. The writer takes elements from the pictures and turns them to uses of his own. The plot is erratic and inconsistent; fragments of it can be traced to Magritte's beautifully blank, suggestive images, though communications between the words and the pictures on the whole are poor. Just as Magritte is devoted to repetition and transformation—putting fins on a cigar, let's say, and creating a cigar-fish—so Robbe-Grillet alienates particular elements of his text by qualifying them differently at each reappearance.

The enemy . . . is "meaning". What he aims at, and more gracefully now, surely, than when he began writing, is to flood his books with meanings, to browbeat his readers with a mass of "information". Some bits of this information contradict other bits, so that meanings come and go as the plot circles on. What we do not know, and what there seems little hope of finding out (short of some massive and prolonged act of concentration), are the rules of selection and transformation to which Robbe-Grillet works; his humour and intelligence perhaps make up for that ultimate frustration.

He still has an ambition, so he says, to write a "popular" novel. Long ago he claimed that his novels *were* popular, or would be if only people read them with fewer preconceptions. No doubt he accepts by now that the taste for coherence and stable meanings is more stubborn than he had hoped. If one day Robbe-Grillet's novels are generally assimilated, it will at least be a sign that our traditional narrative forms are not inevitable or universal, and that there are more logics than one when it comes to telling tales.

John Sturrock, "The Built-In Excrescence," in The Times Literary Supplement *(© Times Newspapers Ltd., 1977; reproduced from* The Times Literary Supplement *by permission), May 6, 1977, p. 565.*

*   *   *

ROETHKE, Theodore   1908-1963

Roethke, an experimenter in forms and voices throughout his career, was one of the most important American poets of his generation. He was awarded the Pulitzer Prize in 1954 for his volume *The Waking.* **(See also** *CLC*, **Vols. 1, 3.)**

The career of Theodore Roethke remains one of the most remarkable achievements of a period whose creative vigor will surely astonish succeeding ages. Coming near the end of a great revolution in the arts and sciences . . . , his career is like a history in miniature of that artistic revolt. His work not only managed to recapitulate this culture's war against form and matter, he pushed that attack several new steps forward. Yet, coming after the futile social revolutions which rose from the same drives and so accompanied the artistic one, he also summed up our peculiar inability to capitalize on our astounding achievements—our flight from freedom, from the accesses of power we have released. I see this in his withdrawal into metaphysics, his flight from his own experimental drive, his own voice, his freedom. I must view this career, then, with an astonished awe, yet with sadness.

Roethke's struggle with form first revealed itself in his changing attitudes toward verse form and toward rhetorical and stylistic convention. (pp. 101-02)

Roethke's first book, *Open House,* seems surprisingly old-fashioned and prerevolutionary. The poems are open and easily graspable; the metric quite regular and conventional. There is even a romantic lyricism which verges on sentimentality and ladies' verse. Here is a typical example [from "To My Sister"]:

O my sister remember the stars the tears the trains
The woods in spring the leaves the scented lanes
Recall the gradual dark the snow's unmeasured fall
The naked fields the cloud's immaculate folds
Recount each childhood pleasure: the skies of azure
The pageantry of wings the eye's bright treasure.

Keep faith with present joys refuse to choose
Defer the vice of flesh the irrevocable choice
Cherish the eyes the proud incredible poise
Walk boldly my sister but do not deign to give
Remain secure from pain preserve thy hate thy heart.

This was followed, however, by *The Lost Son and Other Poems*—almost entirely in free verse. A marked prosiness, too, came into the language texture, bringing very real successes. (p. 102)

Also in that book, however, were poems which predicted the direction of Roethke's third book, *Praise to the End!*—a plunge into the wildest and most experimental poetry of the period. Though "To My Sister" is in free verse, we scarcely notice that. The verse flows easily and expressively, underlining the immediate meaning, drawing little attention to itself. It is nearly incredible that the same man could

have written [the poem "Give Way, Ye Gates"] in his next book:

Believe me, knot of gristle, I bleed like a tree;
I dream of nothing but boards;
I could love a duck.

Such music in a skin!
A bird sings in the bush of your bones.
Tufty, the water's loose.
Bring me a finger. This dirt's lonesome for grass.

Even after the wildest surrealists, that voice sounds new and astonishing; it could be no one but Roethke. It is an achieved style, carrying much meaning, and touching only tangentially other voices we have heard in poetry. (p. 103)

Roethke had opened out before himself an incredible landscape. He had regressed into areas of the psyche where the powerful thoughts and feelings of the child—the raw materials and driving power of our later lives—remain under the layers of rationale and of civilized purpose. The explorations made possible by this book alone could have engaged a lifetime. Yet Roethke never seriously entered the area again.

It is not surprising that Roethke might at this point need to step back and regather his forces. He did just that in the group of "New Poems" which first appeared in *The Waking* and which were later called "Shorter Poems, 1951-53" in *Words for the Wind.* Here Roethke returned to the more open lyricism of his earlier verse and gave us, again, several markedly successful poems—"A Light Breather," "Old Lady's Winter Words," and the beautiful "Elegy for Jane." Yet one had a feeling that he was marking time, seeking a new direction.

In *Words for the Wind,* Roethke's collected poems, the new direction appeared. It was a shock. There had been hints that Roethke was interested in Yeats's voice, hints that he might follow the general shift in twentieth-century verse by following wild experimentation with a new formalism. No one could have expected that *Words for the Wind* would contain a series of sixteen "Love Poems" and a sequence, "The Dying Man," all in a voice almost indistinguishable from Yeats's. Roethke, who had invented the most raw and original voice of all our period, was now writing in the voice of another man, and that, perhaps, the most formal and elegant voice of the period.

Yet, also in that book appeared "Meditations of an Old Woman," which suggested still another new direction, and promised, I felt, astonishing new achievements. (pp. 104-05)

[Roethke's next book] *The Far Field* opens with a poem called "The Longing" which harks back to those passages in the earlier book which had promised—both in statement and in vigor of style—further journeys, new explorations; "All journeys, I think, are the same: / The movement is forward, after a few wavers . . ." but now there is a sense of failure, or failure of desire:

On things asleep, no balm:
A kingdom of stinks and sighs,
Fetor of cockroaches, dead fish, petroleum, . . .
The great trees no longer shimmer;
Not even the soot dances.

And the spirit fails to move forward,
But shrinks into a half-life, less than itself,
Falls back, a slug, a loose worm
Ready for any crevice,
An eyeless starer.

(pp. 106-07)

These poems, recording that withdrawal, also, I think, suffer from it. The language grows imprecise with pain, or with growing numbness and half-sleep as an escape from pain. It seems less a regression to capture something and re-create it, than a regression for its own sake, to lose something and uncreate it.

Metrically, too, one has a sense of discouragement and withdrawal. (p. 107)

What had happened? To investigate that we must go back through Roethke's work and trace out something of his war against form on a different level. And this is a much more causal level—probably causal to Roethke, and certainly causal to the great war against form in our era—the revolt of the sexes against each other and themselves and, in our time, the revolt of the child against the parent. Here, we must investigate not the technical form of Roethke's poems, but rather their statements about his own human form.

Most of Roethke's best earlier poems record a desperate effort "To be something else, yet still to be!," to be "somewhere else," to "find the thing he almost was," to be "king of another condition." As he said it earliest, "I hate my epidermal dress"; as he said it last, "How body from spirit slowly does unwind / Until we are pure spirit at the end." We see his struggle against his own form, shape, and size in all these poems about regression into animal shape—the sloth, the slug, the insect. Or the continual attempt to lose his large human form in an identity with *small* forms [, as seen in "The Minimal"]:

> . . . the little
> Sleepers, numb nudgers in cold dimensions,
> Beetles in caves, newts, stone-deaf fishes,
> Lice tethered to long limp subterranean weeds,
> Squirmers in bogs,
> And bacterial creepers. . . .

This struggle against his own form reached what seemed a sort of triumph in those journey poems where he investigated the landscape as a woman, in the earlier love poems, and in the numerous poems where he spoke *as* a woman. In the earlier love poems, he did affirm a shape; not his own, but the woman's: "She came toward me in the flowing air, / A shape of change, encircled by its fire," or again: "The shapes a bright container can contain!" This containment must have seemed an answer—to lose one's shape, to *be* the woman through sexual entrance: "Is she what I become? / Is this my final Face?" and: "I . . . see and suffer myself / In another being, at last." This idea was repeated over and over. Yet ecstatic as these poems were, there were two disturbing elements. The woman was not affirmed as herself, a person in her own right, but rather as a symbol of all being, or as something the poet might become. And the affirmation was not made in Roethke's voice, but in Yeats's.

The love poems in the final book are considerably changed. Some ecstasy survives: "Who'd look when he could feel? / She'd more sides than a seal," but even ["Light Listened"] suggests a parting or failure:

The deep shade gathers night;
She changed with changing light.

We met to leave again
That time we broke from time;
A cold air brought its rain,
The singing of a stem.
She sang a final song;
Light listened when she sang.

Here and elsewhere—e.g., "The Long Waters" and "The Sequel"—there seems to be a farewell to that ecstasy, a turning away, or turning inward from the discovery that this could not satisfy the hunger. (pp. 108-09)

What appears dominant in the last book is a desire to escape *all* form and shape, to lose all awareness of otherness, not through entrance to woman as lover, but through re-entrance into eternity conceived as womb, into water as woman, into earth as goddess-mother. (p. 110)

The desire to lose one's own form has taken on a religious rationale to support itself. Where Roethke's earlier free-verse poems were nearly always pure explorations, his more ambitious free-verse poems [like "The Abyss"] now try more and more to incorporate a fixed and predetermined religious and irrational certainty:

> Do we move toward God, or merely another
> condition? . . .
>
> The shade speaks slowly:
> "Adore and draw near.
> Who know this—
> Knows all."

The poem aims to create a stasis wherein a person is one with all things; that is, where all matter is dissolved. This is related, too, to Roethke's search for pure space as an escape from time. That has been strong in the poems for some time, but now [in poems like "The Moment"] it is easier to see why he identifies space with pure being:

> Space struggled with time;
> The gong of midnight struck
> The naked absolute.
> Sound, silence sang as one.

Our only experience of identity with all space, of omnipresence, is in the womb; our first experience of time brings the mother's breast which may be withdrawn and so force one to recognize external objects, to give up the narcissistic sense of omnipresence and omnipotence, that unity with all objects which Roethke constantly seeks: ". . . the terrible hunger for objects quails me."

This, in turn, helps explain both Roethke's praise of madness (since reason forces the acceptance of external forms and objects) and the poems' increasing mysticism. For instance, in his *New World Writing* remarks on "In a Dark Time," he correctly describes the following as an androgynous act: "The mind enters itself, and God the mind, / And one is One, free in the tearing wind," but also insists that this is a search for God and, moreover, a "dictated" poem. This clarifies, also, the identification of rage with the heart, the true self. Rage is looked upon as a noble quality since it is a rage against the forms of this world, a continued allegiance to one's fantasy of life in the womb.

This intensely creative rejection of form has great destructive possibilities. On the one hand, we have a search for form; on the other (and probably causal to it), a rejection of form which may result in a rejection of all forms, including any form which one might achieve. The balance between these opposed feelings has changed in Roethke's later poems both because of the introduction of borrowed cadences and because of the religious and mystical rationale. Eliot's ideas and Yeats's cadences have rushed in to fill the vacuum of the father-model which might have suggested a shape to become, and so might have made this world bearable. Yet such a model Roethke either could not find or could not accept. (pp. 112-13)

More and more, Roethke's late poems seem to have lost their appetite, their tolerance for that anguish of concreteness.

In a sense, this combination of one man's voice and another man's ideas has given too much form—or too much comforting certainty. Roethke's formal poems had always celebrated some kind of lyrical certainty, but that was most frequently a certainty about the nature of one's feelings. Now, rejection of earthly forms has become, itself, a rationale, a convention, a form. As the ideas, the metrical shapes and cadencings all grow firmer, however, the language becomes strangely decayed—or at any rate, fixed and self-imitating. The constant terms of Roethke's earlier poems—the rose, the flame, the shadow, the light, the stalk, the wind—are almost emblems. But as all emblems of an absolute have the same ultimate meaning, so all these terms come more and more to mean the same thing. The words tend to dissolve; the poem is more of a musical rite than a linguistic or dramatic one. (pp. 113-14)

> W. D. Snodgrass, " 'That Anguish of Concreteness'—/Theodore Roethke's Career," in Essays on the Poetry—/Theodore Roethke, edited by Arnold Stein (copyright 1965 by The University of Washington Press; reprinted by permission of The University of Washington Press), University of Washington Press, 1965 (and reprinted in In Radical Pursuit, W. D. Snodgrass, Harper & Row Publishers, Inc., 1975, pp. 101-16).

Iris Murdoch has written that the greatest art "invigorates without consoling, and defeats our attempts to use it as magic." The poetry of Theodore Roethke constitutes an artistic achievement of a very high order. It is poetry suffused with magical transformations suggesting the fluidity of human experience and the metamorphic facility of the creative imagination. It is, moreover, a poetry which invigorates precisely in proportion as Roethke insistently attempts to console both himself and his readers.

Roethke's *Collected Poems* may be described by one of the poet's favorite metaphors, that of the journey. From his earliest published verse to the final posthumous volume, Roethke strove to recapture both the remembered childhood past of peace and organic security, and the archetypal past, the slime and torment of the subconscious. He grasped for these not as absolute ends in themselves but as means to accepting the inevitabilities of change, the dying of passion, and ultimate finitude. It is his triumph that his best poems permit us to embrace the principle of change as the root of stability; that his best poems, through rhythm and syntax and diction, so evoke passion that we are able actively to sympathize with his sense of loss; and that we can feel, with him, how "all finite things reveal infinitude."

Whoever wishes to write of Roethke is faced with multiple problems. It is not that Roethke is as diversified in his con-

cerns as other poets, or that his language presents obstacles to the rational intellect. Rather, it is his shifts of mood that weary us, though they never cease to fascinate and please. Just beneath the surface of the love poems lurks an almost obsessional concern with death; for every step toward the primeval sources of existence, there is a shuddering retreat toward the daylight world. Even in the middle of that magnificent "North American Sequence," published in *The Far Field* after his death, Roethke is uncertain of how far he wishes to go, how great a journey into his murky interior he is willing to undertake. In "The Long Waters," he moves confidently toward "The unsinging fields where no lungs breathe," but cries at last: "Mnetha, Mother of Har, protect me / From the worm's advance and / retreat, from the butterfly's havoc / . . . The dubious sea-change, the heaving sands, and my tentacled sea-cousins." In such poems, there is a powerful tension between Roethke's desire to explore the depths of his sensibility and his natural reticence before the specter of hideous possibilities which may be revealed. The demands of the poet's nature seem to vie with the projects of his imagination. Fortunately, the projects are not ultimately scuttled in the interests of safety, and Roethke goes as far as his imagination can take him. (pp. 131-32)

[There are] peculiar limitations of Roethke's vision, in which he especially excels. We all know that, with the possible exception of Yeats, our poetry has not for some time produced a more melodious singer than Roethke. (p. 132)

A basic approach to Roethke's work should question the direction of his consoling qualities. Roethke was profoundly conscious of impending death, but perhaps even more concerned about the ineffectuality of old age, the fragrance of life and passion lingering in the nostrils without any ability to affect or rouse a benumbed sensibility. In other poets such a fearful premonition might be construed as a nervous apprehension of the loss of imaginative daring and insight. Wordsworth and Coleridge shared this orientation with the approach of middle age. Roethke's nostalgia for youth is a complex element which somewhat resembles the longing of the nineteenth-century Romantic poets. The child's fundamental innocence is a common factor, though Roethke embraces this not as a universal principle. Rather, he sees it as unavoidably attendant upon the benevolent circumstances in which he spent his childhood. In the poem "Otto," named for his father, Roethke recaptures the sense of pride he felt in a parent who controlled a rural environment immersed in the sounds and stinks and inconsistencies of nature. (pp. 132-33)

[Roethke] covets the limited detachment that permits contemplation, and finally imaginative projection beyond the boundaries of the patently real. He strives to cultivate in a distinctly Wordsworthian sense "a wise passivity." In such a tranquil receptivity, as he reports in "The Abyss," "The Burning lake turns into a forest pool"—the violence at the heart of all creation is resolutely transformed into an acceptance of flux and perpetual restoration.

Many poets feel victimized by civilization, which is supposed to put us out of touch with what is most genuine in ourselves. Roethke's is an essentially anarchic personality, thoroughly amorphous and shifting. In his poems he associates himself most completely with water, always changing in the intensity and direction of its internal movement, always rhythmic in its perpetual ebb and flow. The aridity of conventional life, the expedient veneer called civilization, is effaced by the poet's ability to get out of himself, the self which has been erected as a mask between his nature and his awareness. (p. 133)

Roethke was not unaware of his inability to achieve union with "the other" which is the lost self, and it is his awareness which makes the perpetual longing so noble and moving. As in the philosophy of an absurdist like Camus, the absence of faith in an external power capable of ratifying the value or correctness of our actions is not sufficient motive for abandoning commitment. If there is something vacuous in commitment to commitment itself, such an orientation does enable the organism to retain its sense of vitality and purpose. For Roethke, where there is song there is life. The negative possibilities that beset us are to be at least temporarily dispelled by the singer's continuing desire to articulate them and sing them into oblivion. On occasion, the singing may resemble the chanting of a would-be conjurer, and the optimistic resolution may be unconvincing, but we are prepared to forgive the poet his lapses in gratitude for his successes. The nervous strength of Roethke's best work disposes of most notions of easy resolutions. (pp. 133-34)

The surrender implicit in the sexual act, the abandonment of what Roethke calls "the proud incredible poise," is a frightening prospect for him [in his] early period, though it is transformed into an absolutely ruthless self-revelation in the later work. This peculiar strain, peculiar especially for a passionate singer of erotic love, never quite disappears. In "Love's Progress," the warm expectation of sexual union and the eager call to action: "Love me, my violence, /Light of my spirit, light / Beyond the look of love," dwindles to the plaintive note of "Father, I'm far from home," and finally, "I fear for my own joy; / I fear myself in the field, / For I would drown in fire."

It is rather strange to find such a progression in the poems of a man who often wrote with lyrical abandon and hysterical warmth. Of course, the combination of opposites is an integral feature of Roethke's work. As M. L. Rosenthal has noted, the laughter which rings in Roethke's voice is most frequently "the pathetic hilarity of the unbearably burdened." His assertiveness is neither defiant nor forced, but a natural expression of his need for release from an introspection which often verges on the obsessive.... [It] is his ability to intoxicate with sound patterns and to make his images pirouette and dissolve without any concomitant exhaustion of clarity that first arrests our consciousness. (p. 134)

What is involved for Roethke in the surrender to sensualism, in the willingness to lower his guard, is the refusal to intellectualize his condition. (p. 135)

Roethke finally affirms the primary importance of accepting experience on its own terms, without evasion. When we are free, he says in "Journey to the Interior," we can be "Delighting in surface change, the glitter of light on waves," "Unperplexed in a place leading nowhere." There is an element of static resignation here which is somewhat unsavory. Roethke wants to stand solidly rooted in the earth he loves, gathering everything to him, all sensation, every trace of loveliness, like the rose "Rooted in stone, keeping the whole of light, / Gathering to itself sound and silence— / Mine and the sea-wind's." We must learn to be explorers of the knowable, the finite, the perishable, if we "would unlearn the lingo of exasperation." Such resignation is neither ignominious nor unpleasant in itself, but the implications are likely to seem unsatisfying to a modern audience

still smarting from the rigors of Robert Lowell's latest sequence.

It is perhaps gratuitous to refer to Robert Lowell at the conclusion of a piece which has deliberately restricted itself to Roethke, and yet I find the reference unavoidable. There are qualities in Lowell's best work that seem to me essential elements of modern poetry, and these are clearly lacking in Roethke. One is not surprised to discover this absence in the later verse, for the object of Roethke's strivings often seemed rather inane and impossibly idyllic, particularly in the early volumes. Roethke soars happily when he beholds "The cerulean, high in the elm, / Thin and insistent as a cicada, / And the far phoebe, singing, / ... A single bird calling and calling." The landscape is exotically rural. His vision is landscaped with images out of the poetic past. He refused to make himself intimately conversant with the materials of the modern world, which is, after all, an urban universe. (pp. 136-37)

The attention Lowell pays to particular varieties of the human experience enables him to bring a more comprehensive perspective to his exploration of the human heart. Roethke's speculations appear to be of the defiantly hothouse genre by comparison—they are carefully cultivated, rather lush in themselves, but somehow lacking the vitality of context. It seems to me that the surrender of the modern sensibility to things as they are, to Experience in the archetypal mode, must be preceded by a thorough acknowledgment of precisely what such acquiescence involves. Otherwise, the resignation is disappointing in its insignificance. One admires and is moved by the energy of Roethke's struggle to get beyond morbid introspection, but one is not convinced that the battle was fought along spiritually fruitful lines, at least insofar as we are concerned. There is irony in the strange spectacle of an ostensibly "universal" poetry impressing us with the basic privateness and limitation of its relevance. (pp. 137-38)

> *Robert Boyers, "A Very Separate Peace: On Roethke" (originally published in* Kenyon Review, *November, 1966), in his* Excursions: Selected Literary Essays *(copyright © 1977 by Kennikat Press Corp.; reprinted by permission of Kennikat Press Corp.), Kennikat, 1977, pp. 131-38.*

I think [Roethke] often didn't understand much of what he read. I mean he didn't understand it the way a critic or good literature teacher would understand it. I believe he so loved the music of language that his complicated emotional responses to poems interfered with his attempts to verbalize meaning.

When he read his favorites aloud, Yeats, Hopkins, Auden, Thomas, Kunitz, Bogan, poets with 'good ears,' something happened that happens all too infrequently in a classroom. If a student wasn't a complete auditory clod, he could feel himself falling in love with the sounds of words. To Roethke, that was the heart and soul of poetry. (p. 50)

> *Richard Hugo, "Stray Thoughts on Roethke and Teaching," in* The American Poetry Review *(copyright © 1974 by World Poetry, Inc.; reprinted by permission of Richard Hugo), January/February, 1974, pp. 50-1.*

[Roethke] was the first American bardic poet since Whitman who did not spill out in prolix and shapeless vulgarity, for he had cunning to match his daemonic energy and he had schooled himself so well in the formal disciplines that he could turn even his stammerings into art. If the transformations of his experience resist division into mineral, vegetable, and animal categories, it is because the levels are continually overlapped, intervolved, in the manifold tissue. Roethke's imagination is populated with shapeshifters, who turn into the protagonists of his poems. Most of these protagonists are aspects of the poet's own being, driven to know itself and yet appalled by the terrible necessity of self-knowledge; assuming every possible shape in order to find the self and to escape the finding; dreading above all the state of annihilation, the threat of nonbeing; and half-yearning at the last for the oblivion of eternity, the union of the whole spirit with the spirit of the whole universe.

Roethke's first book, *Open House* (1941), despite its technical resourcefulness in the deft probings for a style, provided only a few intimations of what was to develop into his characteristic idiom. The title poem, in its oracular end-stopping and its transparency of language, can serve as prologue to the entire work:

> My truths are all foreknown,
> This anguish self-revealed. . . .
>
> Myself is what I wear:
> I keep the spirit spare.

Some thirty years later—he seemed never to forget an experience—in the first of his *Meditations of an Old Woman,* the old woman being presumably his mother when she is not Roethke himself, he was to offer, through the medium of her voice recalling a bus ride through western country, a recapitulation of that same sensation: "taking the curves." His imagination was not conceptual, but kinesthetic, stimulated by nerve ends and muscles, and even in its wildest flights localizing the tension when the curve is taken. This is precisely what Gerard Manley Hopkins meant when, in one of his letters, he spoke of the "isolation of the hip area." The metamorphosis of the body begins in the isolation of the part. (pp. 99-101)

The confirmation that he was in full possession of his art and of his vision came seven years later, with the publication of *The Lost Son* (1948), whose opening sequence of "greenhouse poems" recaptures a significant portion of his inheritance. . . . The world of his childhood was a world of spacious commerical greenhouses, the capital of his florist father's dominion. Greenhouse: "my symbol for the whole of life, a womb, a heaven-on-earth," was Roethke's revealing later gloss. In its moist fecundity, its rank sweats and enclosure, the greenhouse certainly suggests a womb, an inexhaustible mother. If it stands as well for a heaven-on-earth, it is a strange kind of heaven, with its scums and mildews and smuts, its lewd monkey-tail roots, its snaky shoots. The boy of the poems is both fascinated and repelled by the avidity of the life-principle, by the bulbs that break out of boxes "hunting for chinks in the dark." He himself endures the agony of birth, with "this urge, wrestle, resurrection of dry sticks, cut stems struggling to put down feet." "What saint," he asks, "strained so much, rose on such lopped limbs to a new life?" This transparent womb is a place of adventures, fears, temptations, where the orchids are "so many devouring infants!" (p. 101)

Roethke's passionate and near-microscopic scrutiny of the chemistry of growth extended beyond "the lives on a leaf" to the world of what he termed "the minimal," or "the lovely diminutives," the very least of creation, including "beetles in caves, newts, stone-deaf fishes, lice tethered to long limp subterranean weeds, squirmers in bogs, and bacterial creepers." These are creatures still wet with the waters of the beginning. At or below the threshold of the visible they correspond to that darting, multitudinous life of the mind under the floor of the rational, in the wet of the subconscious.

Roethke's immersion in these waters led to his most heroic enterprise, the sequence of interior monologues which he initiated with the title poem of *The Lost Son,* which he continued in *Praise to the End* (1951), and which he persisted up to the last in returning to, through a variety of modifications and developments. "Each poem," he once wrote, "is complete in itself; yet each in a sense is a stage in a kind of struggle out of the slime; part of a slow spiritual progress; an effort to be born, and later, to become something more." The method is associational rather than logical, with frequent time shifts in and out of childhood, in and out of primitive states of consciousness and even the synesthesia of infancy. Motifs are introduced as in music, with the themes often developing contrapuntally. Rhythmically he was after "the spring and rush of the child," he said . . . "and Gammer Gurton's concision: mütterkin's wisdom." There are throwbacks to the literature of the folk, to counting rhymes and play songs, to Mother Goose, to the songs and rants of Elizabethan and Jacobean literature, to the Old Testament, the visions of Blake, and the rhapsodies of Christopher Smart. But the poems, original and incomparable, belong to the poet and not to his sources.

The protagonist, who recurrently undertakes the dark journey into his own underworld, is engaged in a quest for spiritual identity. The quest is simultaneously a flight, for he is being pursued by the man he has become, implacable, lost, soiled, confused. In order to find himself he must lose himself by reexperiencing all the stages of his growth, by reenacting all the transmutations of his being from seed-time to maturity. (pp. 102-03)

Roethke's explanation of his "cyclic" method of narration, a method that depends on periodic recessions of the movement instead of advances in a straight line, seems to me particularly noteworthy. "I believe," he wrote, "that to go forward as a spiritual man it is necessary first to go back. Any history of the psyche (or allegorical journey) is bound to be a succession of experiences, similar yet dissimilar. There is a perpetual slipping-back, then a going forward; but there is *some* 'progress.'"

This comment can be linked with several others by Roethke that I have already quoted: references to "the struggle out of the slime," the beginning "in the mire." I think also of his unforgettably defiant affirmation: "In spite of all the muck and welter, the dark, the *dreck* of these poems, I count myself among the happy poets."

In combination these passages point straight to the door of Dr. Jung or to the door of Jung's disciple Maud Bodkin, whose *Archetypal Patterns in Poetry* was familiar to Roethke. In Jung's discussions of progression and regression as fundamental concepts of the libido theory in his *Contributions to Analytical Psychology,* he describes progression as "the daily advance of the process of psychological adaptation," which at certain times fails. Then "the vital feeling" disappears; there is a damming-up of energy, of libido. At such times neurotic symptoms are observed, and repressed contents appear, of inferior and unadapted character. "Slime out of the depths," he calls such contents—

but slime that contains not only "objectionable animal tendencies, but also germs of new possibilities of life." Before "a renewal of life" can come about, there must be an acceptance of the possibilities that lie in the unconscious contents of the mind "activated through regression . . . and disfigured by the slime of the deep."

This principle is reflected in the myth of "the night journey under the sea," as in the Book of Jonah, or in the voyage of the Ancient Mariner, and is related to dozens of myths, in the rebirth archetype, that tell of the descent of the hero into the underworld and of his eventual return back to the light. The monologues of Roethke follow the pattern of progression and regression and belong unmistakably to the rebirth archetype. (pp. 103-04)

The love poems that followed early in the 1950's . . . were a distinct departure from the painful excavations of the monologues and in some respects a return to the strict stanzaic forms of the earliest work. (p. 105)

Even when he had been involved with the *dreck* of the monologues, he was able, in sudden ecstatic seizures of clarity, to proclaim "a condition of joy." Moreover, he had been delighted at the opportunity that the free and open form gave him to introduce juicy little bits of humor, mostly puns and mangled bawdry and indelicate innuendoes. . . . Now he achieved something much more difficult and marvelous: a passionate love poetry that yet included the comic, as in "I Knew a Woman," with its dazzling first stanza:

I knew a woman, lovely in her bones,
When small birds sighed, she would sigh back at them;
Ah, when she moved, she moved more ways than one.
The shapes a bright container can contain!
Of her choice virtues only gods should speak,
Or English poets who grew up on Greek
(I'd have them sing in chorus, cheek to cheek).

Inevitably the beloved is a shapeshifter, like the poet himself. "Slow, slow as a fish she came." Or again, "She came toward me in the flowing air, a shape of change." "No mineral man," he praises her as dove, as lily, as rose, as leaf, even as "the oyster's weeping foot." And he asks himself, half fearfully: "Is she what I become? Is this my final Face?"

At the human level this tendency of his to become the other is an extension of that Negative Capability, as defined by Keats, which first manifested itself in the Roethke greenhouse. A man of this nature, said Keats, "is capable of being in uncertainties, mysteries, doubt, without any irritable reaching after fact and reason . . . he has no identity— he is continually in for and filling some other body." In "The Dying Man" Roethke assumes the character of the poet Yeats; in *Meditations of an Old Woman,* he writes as though he were his mother; in several late poems he adopts the role and voice of his beloved.

The love poems gradually dissolve into the death poems. Could the flesh be transcended, as he had at first supposed, till passion burned with a spiritual light? Could the several selves perish in love's fire and be reborn as one? Could the dear and beautiful one lead him, as Dante taught, to the very footstool of God? In "The Dying Man" he proposes a dark answer: "All sensual love's but dancing on the grave." (pp. 105-06)

The five-fold *Meditations of an Old Woman* that concludes Roethke's selective volume, *Words for the Wind* (1958), is almost wholly preoccupied with thoughts of death and with the search for God. . . . Here he returns to the cyclic method of the earlier monologues. In the First Meditation the Old Woman introduces the theme of journeying. All journeys, she reflects, are the same, a movement forward after a few wavers, and then a slipping backward, "backward in time." Once more we recognize the Jungian pattern of progression and regression embodied in the work. The journeys and the five meditations as a whole are conceived in a kind of rocking motion, and indeed the verb "to rock" —consistently one of the poet's key verbs of motion—figures prominently in the text. The rocking is from the cradle toward death:

The body, delighting in thresholds,
Rocks in and out of itself. . . .

(p. 106)

Stanley Kunitz, "Roethke: Poet of Transformations," in The New Republic *(reprinted by permission of* The New Republic; © *1965 by The New Republic, Inc.), January 23, 1965 (and reprinted in* Contemporary Poetry in America: Essays and Interviews, *edited by Robert Boyers, Schocken, 1974, pp. 99-109).*

[My] chief impression [of *The Collected Poems of Theodore Roethke*] is the degree to which Roethke's first collection tells us what's coming. The end was in the beginning to an extent I hadn't realized. Previously, my impression was that one merely waited him out in *Open House,* waited for him to loosen, to enter the Kingdom of Roots and Stinks in *The Lost Son* that Kenneth Burke presciently saw as Roethke's own ("You've found it, Ted!" he's supposed to have said). But one finds the rhymes, the traditional forms, the taste for the metaphysical mode in the last poems as in the first. . . . Of course the later formal poems carry the signs of one who has developed his medium to the point where it's the perfect reciprocal of his meaning. But the fondness for epigrams and playful verses, the conspicuous absence of overtly political themes, the heavy end-stopping and verbal wit of the Donne-like lyrics, at once serious and fanciful: all of these have their parallels in the late work.

For my money, Roethke's later metrical poems don't show the same degree of advance as his looser ones. Sure, a late metrical statement such as the celebrated "In a Dark Time" is a different order of being from "The Adamant," but it's closer to its antecedent than the amazing long meditations ("Meditations of an Old Woman," "North American Sequence") are to theirs—that is, to the freest of the *Open House* poems, "The Premonition." And yet even that early memento mori anticipates "The Far Field" in its mingling of resignation and an acceptance that becomes a celebration. (p. 386)

The title of the first collection [*Open House*] proclaims its author's intentions of telling all, but either he didn't have much to tell then or he held back. In fact, the latter seems to me the more likely, since he'd already been brushed by Angst (and not so lightly) by the time of his late first book, in memory of which he used to refer to himself in Seattle as the nation's oldest living younger poet. Toward the end it's open house indeed, and both the metrical and the free poems reveal the thought of one who speaks for our collective blundering struggle from the slime of mere being into the consciousness of our divinity, of the voice that is great within us. That surely must be the most striking feature of Roethke's career. In fact, he's a test case of the writer whose interest in himself is so continuous, so relentless, that it transforms itself and becomes in the end centrifugal. With hardly a social or political bone in his body he yet touches all our Ur-selves, our fear and love of our fathers, our delight in the minimal, our sense of decrepit age tied to us as to a dog's tail when our imagination, ear, and eye never delighted more in the fantastical, our relish of the lives of plants and animals, our pleasure in women who have more sides than seals, our night fears, our apprehension of Immanence.

No more than his beloved mentor the Wild Old Wicked Man was Roethke a mystic. But I think that unlike Yeats, whose final commitment always was to the poem . . . , Roethke was a genuine ringding Godlover. . . . [He] convinces me that he's not exploiting his intimations of immortality. I guess it's the perfect finish and symmetry of Yeats' career and the ferocious act of will and dedication they imply that make me draw back a little even while they beckon irresistibly. Roethke's more human, a clumsy bear of inordinate delicacy whose dancing and risk-taking seem if not more authentic at least less guaranteed of success. By turns witty, mocking, tender, contemplative, farcical, angry, metaphysical, this charismatic and unpredictable man was above all a Fool of God and a minute observer of his presence in tendrils, elvers, salt water, shore animals, birds, streams, tin cans, flowers, rusted pipes, leaves, light. And these don't exist merely to give him metaphors for his verses; they are the Other whose presence gives unexpected, even paradoxical, dimensions to the work of this most self-centered of poets. (pp. 387-88)

> *Stanley Poss, in* Western Humanities Review *(copyright, 1975, University of Utah), Autumn, 1975.*

Roethke's free verse is end-stopped and slow [in "Orchids," and is characterized by a minimum of active verbs]. . . . The last five lines are largely a list of substantives, for example, and lines two through four are a list of modifiers.

[The] suspended, almost unpredicated syntax could be referred to static or passive attributes of the object; but it works primarily to help voice the speaker's feeling. He is obsessed, nearly overwhelmed, and more caught up by the object and its qualities than by statements he could predicate about them.

And the same emotional direction is suggested by the poem's other notable stylistic parts. The present tense, for example, works oddly with the two-part, day-then-night structure; the effect is to suggest reverie, which is a mental process, yet to maintain the natural object's dominance over the mental process. Similarly, the rhythm moves in slow, short, equal spasms, heavily defined by pronounced pauses and consonances ("soft and deceptive, / limp and damp"), a movement which suggests absorbed helplessness. A sort of enervated panic aroused by the unconscious life of the natural object becomes, by the poems's last word, so insistently suggested that we might call it explicit. The emotion of defeated hysteria emerges as an emphatic surrender of the poet's voice to the physical scene.

[In "Orchids" there is found] the general technique of description, and also an experience: wonder, the experience of fascination with a physical scene—its cruelty and its persistent unconsciousness. (pp. 125-26)

[The poem renders] the experience of being dominated by a metaphor—and by the unsuitable, unlike parts of it: orchids are like human life, but, not conscious, they have an eery persistence that is both repellently and hypnotically non-human. (p. 126)

The striking choices of word in "Orchids" tend to be affective and anthropomorphic: "deceptive," "delicate," "devouring," "ghostly." . . . Roethke embraces the pathetic fallacy easily and openly. . . . (pp. 126-27)

"Orchids" takes the fusion of emotion with the natural object as an accepted starting-point: as granted. There is no gesture toward defining a literal, personal motivation for the emotion; neither does the poet try to suggest that the emotion is irresistibly part of the orchids—this is a frankly special sensibility or mood, and the poem consists of rhetorical elaboration of the emotion by means of description. Questions of motivation are meant to be disposed of by the convention or starting-point of the poem. . . .

What does this difference in rhetorical procedure mean for the way in which [the] poem relates Romantic wonder to the sense of derangement or distress? "Orchids" emphasizes the powerful aspect of natural life which is quite alien to consciousness. . . . "Orchids" insists upon the object's predominance in a manner (or convention) which emphasizes its own voice—obsessed and neurasthenic. . . . (p. 127)

> *Robert Pinsky, "Wonder and Derangement: 'Orchids,' 'Badger,' and 'Poppies in July'," in his* The Situation of Poetry *(copyright © 1976 by Princeton University Press; reprinted by permission of Princeton University Press), Princeton University Press, 1976, pp. 118-33.*

* * *

RULFO, Juan 1918-

A Mexican novelist and short story writer, Rulfo has only two books to his credit, yet his terse, objective narratives have earned him the reputation of being, next to Carlos Fuentes, the most important living Mexican author.

[Scant] lives find a driving force. Tapping it at the source has been Rulfo's achievement. His sketches are quick probes. It is the small touches that count. He has weaknesses as a storyteller. Excessive poetization freezes some of his scenes. His characters are sometimes too sketchy to deliver their full human impact. They are creatures of primeval passion, entirely defined by their situation. Because of their lack of inner resource, ultimately they inspire little more than pity. And that is the danger. We are often on the verge of falling into pathos. But the attentive reader will go beyond that. There is a deeper grain running through the stories. To live, in Rulfo, is to bleed to death. The pulse of the days beats hard, carrying off hope, gutting life at the core, spilling forces, emptying illusions. . . . It is the ability to close in suddenly and strike home that at moments gives Rulfo the dignity of a tragedian. His style is as stark as his landscapes. Its marks are discipline and economy. Its impact is cumulative. It has the pull of irresistible impulse. (p. 246)

> *Luis Harss and Barbara Dohmann, "Juan Rulfo, or the Souls of the Departed" (originally published under a different title in* New Mexico Quarterly, *Winter, 1965-66), in their* Into the Mainstream: Conversations with

Latin-American Writers *(copyright © 1966 by Luis Harss; used by permission of Harper & Row, Publishers, Inc.), Harper, 1967, pp. 246-75.*

[Rulfo's] first collection, *El llano en llamas* (1953), details the joys and sorrows of the poor, their violence and hunger, the problems of the Mexican and his land, and talks of ghost towns, murderers and fugitives, the innocent and the guilty. He infuses these stories of the countryside and ordinary people with a primitive and magic view of life, brought to a peak of perfection in his first novel, . . . *Pedro Páramo* (1955). . . .

This novel, told in poetic and emotional language, is about an ambiguous and magical world, a kind of timeless fable of life and death, and a history of Mexico from the days of Porfirio Diaz to those of Obregón. It has been said that "nowhere in Mexican literature has the *caciquismo* theme been treated as well as in *Pedro Páramo*." But the novel completely transcends social themes in its telluric, philosophical, and metaphysical concepts of life and death. In a series of dream sequences Rulfo conveys not only the disappearance of the cacique as a political force through a re-creation of the little ghost town of Comala but also the tragic sense of life. (p. 290)

As one comes to understand the characters' intrahistory, which transcends historical misadventures, one realizes that a tragic hope for a new dawn is implied, if nowhere else than at least beyond death. *Pedro Páramo* elaborates the Mexican view of death so aptly portrayed earlier in *El luto humano.* Pedro Páramo, even though he is dead, still lives just as the good and the bad and fear and sorrow still live on in Mexican towns and in the Mexican spirit. From the days of Indian myth, the Mexican, in his solitude, accepted the notion that the dead, indeed, discourse with the living. Despite the hope of a new existence one must also recognize life's continuing anguish. Throughout the novel Rulfo maintains his double vision, uniting heaven and hell, hate and love, light and darkness and fusing Indian and Catholic myth. . . . Rulfo maintains a deliberate ambiguity in his ghost images of a hell juxtaposed with paradise through his use of fragmented and atemporal structures. Pedro represents the violent and destructive forces in the Mexican soul. He is also a hopeful and tender lover of the mad, sweet Susana, who represents unattainable love, a woman of dreams, evoked in memory as the elemental woman of the earth, the incestuous, the sweetheart, the mistress, the eternal and complete woman. (p. 291)

An obvious disciple of Faulkner in his poetic vision of "time was," Rulfo converts incredible realities into probable ones. In his short stories he had discussed the communion of man and nature, the nature of reality, and the disintegration of the human personality into its components, themes he intensifies in his novel. . . . Rulfo projects a fatalistic view of the universe and a pessimistic one about the revolution's failures as a symbol of "the futility of all history in its ineffectual consequences and its essentially barbaric nature." Rulfo exposes the inadequacy of Christianity in alleviating man's capacity to suffer and to cause pain, as he projects "doubts so deep as to question any foundations of belief in modern society." (pp. 291-92)

> *Kessel Schwartz, in his* A New History of Spanish American Fiction, *Volume II (copyright © 1971 by University of Miami Press), University of Miami Press, 1971.*

If the national elements in Rulfo's fiction (short stories in *El llano en llamas,* 1953, and the novel *Pedro Páramo,* 1955) are to be found in the use of language, the structures reveal the influence of Faulkner as well as other foreign novelists. (pp. 114-15)

Rulfo's language . . . gives his fiction a national tone; yet his style is poetic, and in *Pedro Páramo,* by means of this poetic style, Rulfo is able to give life to a dead town, a town that has been choked to death by the local *cacique,* Pedro Páramo. The transitions between the scenes are not carried out by formal linking elements, but, like the stanzas in a poem, the scenes are juxtaposed, united only by the central theme and lyrical motifs, which Rulfo can use with great effectiveness. The novel, a mixture of realism and fantasy which may be called magic realism, has been created through the use of images which, although poetic, are structured in a language that is characteristic of the countryside. (p. 115)

> *Luis Leal, in* Tradition and Renewal: Essays on Twentieth-Century Latin American Literature and Culture, *edited by Merlin H. Forster (© 1975 by the Board of Trustees of the University of Illinois; reprinted by permission of the editor and the University of Illinois Press), University of Illinois Press, 1975.*

S

SALINGER, J(erome) D(avid)   1919-

An American novelist and short story writer, Salinger is a master of contemporary dialect and idiomatic expression. A recluse of sorts, Salinger is best known for *The Catcher in the Rye,* which earned him a cult-like following among the youth of the fifties and sixties, and which, according to Stanley Hyman, illustrates Salinger's "marvelous sensitivity to the young, to the language, to the fraudulence of contemporary America." (See also *CLC,* Vols. 1, 3, and *Contemporary Authors,* Vols. 5-8, rev. ed.)

"Hapworth 16, 1924" is, for me at least, Salinger's finest work and a perfection among great short novels by 20th century Americans—as strong as "The Old Man and the Sea," "The Great Gatsby," the best of Henry James, Stephen Crane, and Faulkner. The story's idols, among others, are Cervantes and the Dostoievsky who created the 14-year-old boy genius Kolya in "The Brothers Karamazov." All this is only to say I like "Hapworth" with an even greater admiration than I have for "The Catcher in the Rye" and love it with great heart indeed.

"Hapworth's" hero is Seymour Glass, "who died, committed suicide, opted to discontinue living, back in 1948, when he was 31," as his brother Buddy tells us in a brief foreword. Seymour is also the pivot of a constellation of stories about the Glass family in which we forever wonder *why* Seymour killed himself. "Hapworth" tells why.

"Hapworth" stands alone, contains almost everything we need to know about the Glasses, and artistically is above compare with the lesser pieces. . . . I have very mixed feelings about "Franny and Zooey," "Raise High the Roof Beam, Carpenters," "Seymour, an Introduction," and "Nine Stories," but I find "Hapworth 16, 1924" a writer's ode to joy when he is in full control of his every resource.

Seymour! He's all three Karamazovs rolled into one, a Dmitry driven by sensuality, an Ivan by intellectual curiosity, an Alyosha eaten daily by the highest spiritual longings ("There is monumental work to be done in this appearance"; " . . . with maddening tears coursing down my unstable face . . . I do not in my heart hold out unlimited hope for the human tongue as we know it today"; "Also on the hearty, revitalizing side of the ledger, bear in mind, with good cheer and amusement, that we were quite firmly obliged, as well as often dubiously privileged, to bring our creative genius with us from our previous appearances"; "rely on God utterly"). And Seymour is only seven years old. Yes, seven.

Seven!

You have to suspend disbelief on the same scale as if raising Atlantis from the seabottoms by sheer mind-power. Or you simply accept seven as the number in which three (the Trinity) and four (the elements, the seasons, and so on) blend in perfect knowledge and self-realization of the Mind-Body. Seymour is fast on his way to knowing Everything, even about his brain, his bones, his phallus; wherever he looks, in any field, including Chinese materia medica, or Proust (in the original), or Eastern religions, or Russian novelists, or the Bible ("the touching, splendid Holy Bible comes in very handy, freely preserving one's precious sanity on a rainy day, the incomparable Jesus Christ freely suggesting, as follows: 'Be ye therefore perfect, even as your Father which is in heaven is perfect'"), or the obscure 19th century astronomer-mathematician Sir William Rowan Hamilton (researcher on light rays and first theorist of higher complex numbers, called quaternions), his eye lights up the subject with superhuman familiarity.

His all-knowingness is especially sharp on human nature. He also spends much time in the woods with his five-year-old brother Buddy, cooking up eatable weeds and plants with the fearlessness of Euell Gibbons. A poet with a considerable body of work behind him (with charming bravery he admits to being outwritten by Wordsworth and "the splendid William Blake"). Seymour also practices yoga and is a terrific tapdancer and gifted softshoe artist (his life, he claims, is an "unforgettable waltz"). . . .

The theme of "Hapworth," as I see it, is the redeeming power of love and that power's eternal reappearance. . . . Seymour's insight into the strengths and failings of everyone is the story's main matter. He constantly forgives each person's vices and raises their virtues to heaven. Powerfully. That's it, almost. Except that someday Seymour will run dry, finding that God has denied *him* a teacher (Hamilton was apparently his teacher in the last century); he will "opt out" of his present appearance in favor of the next.

The story takes the form of a letter Seymour writes home from a bugle-blowing Maine boys camp (Hapworth). . . . It's a superbolic letter to God, I'd say, a shining inventory, one of Holden Caulfield's telephone calls to an author, his "terrific friend."

Seymour writes—actively fighting self-deceit in every form —from an infirmary bed. He's wounded his leg on a piece of iron sticking out of a moving wagon wheel and can't walk. . . . In heaven, like a hart at the water brooks he lies sublimely abed with his vision of love, made lame by the sheer weight of the "magnificent," "elusive," "comical," "amusing," "brave," "excitable," "heartrending," "unspeakably moving" passion and rottenness of the people who burst his heart, that marvelous lump of radium and spiritual light which Salinger has given us forever. (p. 27)

> *Donald Newlove,* The Village Voice *(reprinted by permission of* The Village Voice; *copyright © 1974 by The Village Voice, Inc., 1974), August 22, 1974.*

The response of college students to the work of J. D. Salinger indicates that perhaps he, more than anyone else, has not turned his back on the times but, instead, has managed to put his finger on whatever struggle of significance is going on today between self and culture. *The Catcher in the Rye* and the recent stories in *The New Yorker* having to do with the Glass family surely take place in the immediate here and now. But what about the self, what about the hero? The question is of particular interest here, for in Salinger, more than in most of his contemporaries, the figure of the writer has lately come to be placed directly in the reader's line of vision, so that there is a connection, finally, between the attitudes of the narrator as, say, brother to Seymour Glass, and as a man who writes by profession.

And what of Salinger's heroes? Well, Holden Caulfield, we discover, winds up in an expensive sanitarium. And Seymour Glass commits suicide finally, but prior to that he is the apple of his brother's eye—and why? He has learned to live in this world—but how? By not living in it. By kissing the soles of little girls' feet and throwing rocks at the head of his sweetheart. He is a saint, clearly. But since madness is undesirable and sainthood, for most of us, out of the question, the problem of how to live *in* this world is by no means answered; unless the answer is that one cannot. The only advice we seem to get from Salinger is to be charming on the way to the loony bin. Of course, Salinger is under no obligation to supply advice of any sort to writers or readers —still, I happen to find myself growing more and more curious about this professional writer, Buddy Glass, and how *he* manages to coast through life in the arms of sanity.

There is in Salinger the suggestion that mysticism is a possible road to salvation; at least some of his characters respond well to an intensified, emotional religious belief. Now my own reading in Zen is minuscule, but as I understand it from Salinger, the deeper we go into this world, the further we can get away from it. If you contemplate a potato long enough, it stops being a potato in the usual sense; unfortunately, however, it is the usual sense that we have to deal with from day to day. For all his loving handling of the world's objects there seems to me, in Salinger's Glass family stories as in *The Catcher,* a spurning of life as it is lived in the immediate world—this place and time is viewed as unworthy of those few precious people who have been set down in it only to be maddened and destroyed. (pp. 125-27)

> *Philip Roth, in his* Reading Myself and Others *(reprinted with the permission of Farrar, Straus & Giroux, Inc.; copyright © 1961,*

1963, 1969, 1970, 1971, 1972, 1973, 1974, 1975 by Philip Roth), Farrar, Straus, 1975.

During the course of his adventures in *The Catcher in the Rye,* Holden Caulfield undergoes a startling transformation: from an existence in which his nature is dangerously divided, to a remarkably integrated state of being. (p. 432)

Although frequently referring to himself as a "madman," Holden does so without realizing the basis of the comparison: that his nature, which should be developing towards maturity, has stalled within an early state of childhood. A child, at birth, is able to perceive and to feel, but is not yet capable of thinking rationally. He remains an essentially irrational creature—like a "madman"—until he develops the capability of exerting his rational thought over his random feelings. . . . Although he is a boy of uncommonly deep sensibilities, his nature is still childishly one-sided, for his feelings, like a child's, still predominate over his inadequately developed intellect. Thus, one consistently finds Holden's thoughts being either suppressed by, or occurring as a result of, his feelings. (pp. 432-33)

Holden's feelings also predominate over his experiences of things outside himself. Each of his experiences generally arouses within him an immediate emotional response, over which he exerts no rational control. . . . Because Holden generally reacts to things outside himself . . . with no conception of the causal relationship between his experiences and his emotional responses, he views his world as a place where things usually *happen* to him *all of a sudden* as immediate occurrences—or, one might stress, they *happen* to him as though by *chance:* "Then all of a sudden, something very spooky started happening"; "Then something terrible happened just as I got in the park"; "Then, all of a sudden, I got in this big mess." It is important to realize that this sense of immediacy accompanying everything that happens to Holden divides his existence into a temporal sequence of seemingly isolated instances occurring one after the other, as is manifested on almost every page of the novel—in his thoughts: "Then, all of a sudden, I got this idea," "Then I thought of something, all of a sudden," "But all of a sudden, I changed my mind"; and in his actions: "All of a sudden I looked at the clock," "Then, all of a sudden, I yawned," "Then, all of a sudden, I started to cry."

Holden's sense of immediacy within each thing that happens to him also leads to his sense of transiency. Because he experiences his world temporally, with the present moment always becoming a segment of the past, Holden views his life as being in a state of continual change. Since a developed intellect is needed to realize immutable conceptions, and since Holden's "thinking" . . . is limited to his sense of the mutability of life, Holden remains trapped within time, unable to recognize anything permanent in human existence. (pp. 433-34)

Holden would like to keep Phoebe a child because he is troubled by the differences he sees between children and adults, both in their physical appearances and in their personalities. Holden finds children physically acceptable under any conditions, but not adults. . . . The personality of a child is also preferable to Holden. . . . (pp. 434-35)

[The] change occurring within the developing child as he experiences his world proves to be, in part, a corrupting one—as is manifested throughout the novel in a variety of ways, but most consistently, perhaps, by the change occurring in the state of one's breath as he matures. . . . The significance of [the] recurrent references to breath may at first remain elusive, for, as is often the case in this novel, a symbol introduced early in the work may not be understood until a later clarifying passage is reached. . . . [The] Biblical association of man's breath with his spirit or soul [is] established in the novel. Holden's act of blowing his own breath up into his nostrils "to see if my breath stank from so many cigarettes and the Scotch and sodas I drank" must therefore be looked upon as a more meaningful test than simply one of determining if his breath smells. In other words, the extent to which Holden's breath has been tainted, in this case by the adult acts of drinking and smoking, is, by implication, the extent to which Holden's spirit has been corrupted. (pp. 436-37)

As one's breath continues to be tainted, a loss of breath results. Holden repeatedly makes such comments as "I was sort of out of breath. I was smoking so damn much, I had hardly any wind." The older one grows, the more one experiences this loss. . . . Apparently, one finally reaches a state of existence similar to that of Holden's history teacher, old Spencer, who has the grippe, a disease of the lungs, and who must rely on Vicks Nose Drops to get breath into his nostrils.

Most of the people encountered by Holden in the novel have already experienced, to varying degrees, the corrupting influence of this world, people whose behavior Holden generally labels as *phony,* for they do not even realize that they have been corrupted. (pp. 438-39)

Holden's dilemma . . . throughout the book, is that he is unable to prevent his impending loss of that uncorrupted spirit possessed by children, such as Phoebe, before they have been immersed in the experiences of this world. (p. 440)

The solution to Holden's dilemma lies in his being able to perceive, with both sides of his nature, that everything in reality has two faces: that the ice in the lagoon in Central Park can both preserve and kill; that the "gasoline rainbows" Holden mentions are composed of "gasoline" and "rainbows"; that an old teacher can be like a child, and a child, such as Phoebe, can be "like a goddam schoolteacher sometimes"; that everyone's nature extends, at the same time, back towards childhood and forward towards adulthood. One might see Holden himself, with his hat on backwards, facing in two directions, as typifying the sense of reality established in this novel. Therefore, if something that stays the same also conveys a sense of continuous change, then something that Holden earlier saw as continuously changing, such as childhood, should also convey a sense of staying the same.

Holden gains this new awareness as a result of re-experiencing his own childhood . . . in relationship to that of Phoebe's generation. Holden is able to associate childhood, not only with the past, as something waning and ending, but also with the future, as something beginning and becoming. Holden has thus far remained trapped in time, unable to recognize anything permanent within human existence, because of his incapability of perceiving that both the past and the future may be found in the present moment. Continuing now in this new direction, he eventually reaches such a moment: as he watches Phoebe on the carrousel, his sense of the past and his sense of the future become completely integrated, and he finally experiences an immutable conception of childhood. (pp. 448-50)

[The] change within Holden's outlook is stunningly illustrated at the end of the novel when all of the movements developed symbolically throughout Holden's narrative are brought together in a manner acceptable to Holden: that is, by the movements of Phoebe on the carrousel. One must first recall, as presented earlier [in this essay], that a *forward* movement is suggestive of proceeding from one state of being to another, and that a movement *up* suggests the uncorrupting isolation of spiritual heights, and *down,* a deeper immersion into worldly experiences. As Phoebe rides upon her horse, her actions illustrate every one of these symbolic movements. . . . (p. 451)

The carrousel, . . . as a symbol composed of a complexity of opposite qualities and tenuous ambiguities, all existing together within a harmony of music and motion, typifies the sense of reality Holden finally perceives. As a result, the dilemma which he has faced throughout his narration is resolved, for he is capable now, as he sits in the rain, of accepting his world as it is. Furthermore, . . . the divisive aspects of his nature, his emotions and his intellect, are finally integrated. . . . (p. 453)

Where, then, is Holden at the end of the novel? Critics have seen him as narrating his story to an analyst in a mental institution, Holden's concluding retreat from his world. But why would Holden talk *about* "this one psychoanalyst guy they have here" if he were supposedly talking *to* the analyst? And certainly at least "one psychoanalyst" is often found on the staff of various kinds of institutions. Furthermore, why would Holden have been placed in a mental institution in the West rather than near his home? One need not surmise in this manner to determine where Holden is. There is enough information in the novel to place him exactly: within a particular state of existence. On the final page, Holden says, "I could probably tell you what I did after I went home, and how I got sick and all. . . ." The nature of Holden's sickness was clarified at the beginning of the novel, for when Holden introduced his narrative from the unidentified place he is in, he said:

> I have no wind, if you want to know the truth. I'm quite a heavy smoker, for one thing—that is, I used to be. They made me cut it out. Another thing, I *grew* six and a half inches last year. That's also how I practically got t.b. and came out here for all these goddam checkups and stuff.

Having finally attained a solution to his dilemma, Holden is now attempting to recover, at least partially, from the particular physical impairment caused by his experience of growing up within a corrupting world. He is out West—but no longer wishing to isolate himself from people—because the dry and sunny climate is beneficial to his immediate condition. . . . [Apparently] in a sanitarium for lung diseases, Holden is recovering from his loss of breath.

One might conclude by stressing that Holden is talking, not to an analyst, but to "you," the reader. . . . Holden is talking directly to anyone who might be as "troubled morally and spiritually" as Holden was about the nature of this world in which everyone exists. He offers his narration of *The Catcher in the Rye* as a record of his troubles for anyone who might wish to learn from his experiences. As Mr. Antolini says, "It's a beautiful reciprocal arrangement. And it isn't education. It's history. It's poetry." (pp. 454-55)

William Glasser, "The Catcher in the Rye," in The Michigan Quarterly Review *(copyright © The University of Michigan, 1976), Fall, 1976, pp. 432-55.*

SAROYAN, William 1908-

An American novelist, short story writer, playwright, and essayist, Saroyan is often characterized as an overly sentimental writer. A winner of the Pulitzer Prize for Drama, Saroyan refused the award in 1940. He has written under the pseudonym Sirak Goryan. (See also *CLC,* **Vol. 1, and** *Contemporary Authors,* **Vols. 5-8, rev. ed.)**

The story of William Saroyan's amazing success and rapid decline is, in microcosm, a history of American optimism. Saroyan rose in mid-Depression as a bard of the beautiful life, a restorer of faith in man's boundless capacities; he has declined as a troubled pseudo-philosopher, forced to acknowledge man's limitations, yet uncomfortable in the climate of Evil. Indeed, he has come to dwell on Evil in order to deny its reality, reasserting, blatantly and defensively now, the American Dream of Unlimited Possibilities and Inevitable Progress. As a self-styled prophet of a native resurgence—believing in the virtue of self-reliant individualism, in the innate goodness of man and the rightness of his impulses—he has followed the tradition of American transcendentalism. (One critic has quite seriously called Saroyan the creator of "the new transcendentalism.") But it need hardly be said that Saroyan is no Emerson, either by temperament or by talent. The extent to which his later work has failed reflects, in one sense, the inadequacy of his equipment for the task he set himself. Yet it is also true that Saroyan is the representative American of the mid-twentieth-century, a man baffled at the failure of the Dream but unwilling to give it up; incapable of facing his dilemma frankly or of articulating it meaningfully.

When Saroyan's stories began appearing in the early 1930's, the literature of the day was somber with gloom or protest. And though Saroyan's fiction was also born of the Depression, often telling of desperate men, of writers dying in poverty, it nevertheless managed a dreamy affirmation. Politically and economically blind, Saroyan declared himself bent on a one-man crusade in behalf of the "lost imagination in America." In an era of group-consciousness, he was "trying to restore man to his natural dignity and gentleness." "I want to restore man to himself," he said. "I want to send him from the mob to his own body and mind. I want to lift him from the nightmare of history to the calm dream of his own soul."

This concept of restored individuality governed Saroyan's principal attitudes, his impulsive iconoclasm as well as his lyrical optimism. While Saroyan joined the protestants in damning the traditional villains—war, money, the success cult, standardization—he was really attacking the depersonalization which such forces had effected. He was just as much opposed to regimentation in protest literature as in everyday life. ("Everybody in America is organized except E. E. Cummings," he complained.) Writing about foreigners and exiles, the meek and isolated, "the despised and rejected," he celebrated the "kingdom within" each man. The artists in his stories preserved a crucial part of themselves; there was spiritual survival and triumph, let economics fall where it might. And in the glowing stories about men close to the earth of their vineyards, about glad children and fertile, generous women, Saroyan was affirming what he called the "poetry of life" and exalted with capital-letter stress: Love, Humor, Art, Imagination, Hope, Integrity.

In effect, Saroyan was restoring the perspective without which the writers of the thirties had often (for obvious reasons) reduced the individual potential to a materialism of physical survival. When a character in one of his plays insisted that food, lodging, and clothes were the only realities, another responded, "What you say is true. The things you've named are all precious—if you haven't got them. But if you have, or if you can get them, they aren't." However limiting Saroyan's simplifications might prove, they none the less contained important truths which had been lost sight of amidst the earnestness of agitation-propaganda. If Saroyan is given any place in future literary histories, he should be credited with helping to relax ideologically calcified attitudes. (pp. 336-37)

Saroyan [became], for the moment, an important force in the American theatre—a symbol and an inspiration to playwrights, actors, and audiences. He had come to stand not only for personal freedom after the years of economic and emotional austerity, but also for freedom in style and form.

Whereas Saroyan's stories were often reminiscent of Mark Twain, Sherwood Anderson, or John Steinbeck, there was no recognizable literary tradition behind his playwriting. Rather, it was the showmanship and theatricality of the popular entertainers, made euphonious and articulate, that went into these early plays. . . . He had developed a decided preference for vaudeville over Ibsen, Oscar Wilde, and the other "serious dramatists" because it was "easygoing, natural, and American."

Thus, his best works for the stage gave the impression of a jamboree which was springing to life spontaneously, right before one's eyes. The inhibitions of both stage people and audience were lifted by a mood of gentle intoxication (sometimes alcoholic, sometimes not). The impulse to play and sing and dance was given free rein without concern for plot or didactic point. (pp. 337-38)

Saroyan's element, indeed, was the flexible time of childhood; he was at his best when writing about dreams fulfilled and faith justified. He was a teller of joyful tales and tales of high sentiment, making a revel of life and lyricizing death, hardship, and villainy.

But not long after the peak of his success at the beginning of the forties, Saroyan's writing began to change. Concerned about the onesidedness of his outlook, he set out to *justify* his unadulterated hopefulness. Instead of the airy, uncontested supremacy of beauty and happiness, there were now, as Saroyan began to see things, misery and ugliness to contend with, imperfection to account for. At the same time that he took cognizance of the dark side of life, he began trying to *prove* all for the best in the best of all possible worlds, with the result that his novels and plays became strange battlegrounds where belief struggled with skepticism. To retain his perfectionist version of man's life on earth, yet to get rid of the unpleasant realities he had come to acknowledge—this was Saroyan's new burden. (p. 338)

Among the earliest works to demonstrate that Saroyan was no longer able to dismiss "evil" casually or to proclaim "belief" summarily was his first novel, *The Human Comedy* (which Saroyan wrote originally as a motion picture in 1943). The protagonist was Saroyan's favorite character type—a young dreamer with untainted senses, a rich imagination, and warm sympathies. Instead of following the old blithe Saroyanesque line, however, the book became a study in doubt and faith, tracing prophetically the pattern of Saroyan's own career. The young hero . . . is nearing the age of disenchantment and is especially vulnerable because he has been nourished on inflated ideals and has never been allowed to know adversity. His trust in the benevolence of the universe is consequently threatened when his personal idol, an older brother, goes off to war and faces death.

The outcome is abrupt and arbitrary, as Saroyan contrived to dissolve the conflict with a happy ending. The brother is killed in the war, and the boy is about to plunge into despair when, before mourning can get under way, a wounded buddy of the dead soldier—fortuitously an orphan without ties—appears on the scene and quite literally takes the brother's place in the household as if nothing had happened. Saroyan explained this miracle by inflating his idea of brotherliness into a concept of universal oneness which permits live men to be substituted for dead ones. Since "none of us is separate from any other," according to the logic of the novel, and since "each man is the whole world, to make over as he will," the stranger is able to become at once the son, brother, and lover that his friend had been. It is as simple as this because Saroyan is running the show. Death and disaster are ruled out of order, and the boy's illusions are protected.

But Saroyan was paying a high price for the preservation of unlimited possibilities. This novel had lost all but a modicum of the Saroyanesque buoyancy. In the course of thwarting misfortune, the author had to let the boy abandon his pranks and dramas to face the prospect of sorrow. Meanwhile, there was a moral point that had to be reinforced by sermons on virtue. Large doses of speculative talk adulterated the dreamy atmosphere. Always inclined toward sentimentality, Saroyan now landed with both feet deep in mush. By dwelling on the love and goodness he had previously taken with a skip and a holler, Saroyan was suffocating spontaneity. (pp. 338-39)

The fact that [the] concept of the mutual exclusiveness of good and bad, right and wrong, beautiful and ugly has become an underlying assumption in Saroyan's struggle against disbelief is evidence of his "Americanism." (p. 339)

[*The Adventures of William Saroyan* and a novel (*The Adventures of Wesley Jackson*)] were weighted down with aimless vitriol about the indignities of war and the Army; and in attempting to write seriously about statesmanship, propaganda, and international affairs, Saroyan exposed to full view his lack of intellectual discipline and integrative capacity.

Saroyan has perennially boasted an aesthetics of no-effort, denouncing "intellectualism" and contending that a man should write as a hen lays eggs—instinctively, without thought or planning. Confusing laziness with casualness and spontaneity, he has continued to oversimplify. Part of Saroyan's charm had been the way he had often, in his enthusiasm about everyday things and people, blurred but intensified the lines of his picture with superlatives: "The loveliest looking mess the girl had ever seen"; "nature at its proudest, dryest, loneliest, and loveliest"; "the crazy, absurd, magnificent agreement." But when, in his later work, he applied this indiscriminate approach to questions of morality and metaphysics, the effect became one of pretentiousness. With sweeping generalizations, he now implied that he was solving man's weightiest problems, yet without evidence of any careful or systematic consideration. . . . The allegorical scheme he concocted for *Jim Dandy* was more ambitious than Thornton Wilder's in *The Skin of Our Teeth*. The assumption of Saroyan's play, as of Wilder's, was that "everybody in it had survived pesti-

lence, famine, ignorance, injustice, inhumanity, torture, crime, and madness." But instead of a cohesive drama about man's survival through history by the skin of his teeth, Saroyan wrote an incoherent hodge-podge in which everything turns out just jim dandy, as if there has never been a serious threat at all. (pp. 339-40)

Saroyan's efforts to provide clarification have often had [a] tendency to eliminate *all* distinctions, reducing meaning to some amorphous unit—if not to a cipher. In his yearning for a harmony, for an eradication of conflicts and contradictions, Saroyan is the heir of a tradition which, among Americans of a more reflective or mystical temperament, has included Jefferson's ideal of human perfectibility, Emerson's Oversoul, Whitman's multitudinous Self, Henry Adams' Lady of Chartres, and Waldo Franks's "Sense of the Whole."

In 1949, there appeared a volume of three full-length plays by William Saroyan, his major works for the theatre since the war. None of these plays—*Don't Go Away Mad; Sam Ego's House; A Decent Birth, a Happy Funeral*—has been given a Broadway production. Indeed so vaguely speculative are they that their author found it necessary to explain them in lengthy prefaces summarizing the plots and offering suggestions for deciphering the allegories. The pseudo-philosophical elements of Saroyan's writing had come more than ever to overshadow the vivid and the colorful.

Moreover, the preoccupation with death virtually excludes every other consideration, especially in *A Decent Birth, a Happy Funeral* and in *Don't Go Away Mad*. The action of the latter is set in a city hospital ward for cancer victims, and the characters are all "incurables," tortured by pain and by thoughts of their impending doom. While they clutch at prospects of the slightest delay, they brood over the crises and deaths of fellow inmates and talk endlessly about death, life, time, and the details of their physiological decadence. Yet even here, in these plays about death, Saroyan has conjured up endings of joy. . . . (p. 340)

To negate death has thus become for Saroyan the crucial test of man's free will and unlimited powers. Sometimes, instead of whisking it away by plot manipulations, he had tried to exorcise death by comic ritual, to be as airy about morbidity as he had been about little boys turning somersaults. (Many social analysts have noted the uneasy effort in America to euphemize death, glamorize it, sentimentalize it, and generally make it keep its distance.) He changed the title of his most dismal play from "The Incurables" to "Don't Go Away Mad." He tried to lighten an act-long funeral ceremony by having burlesque comedians conduct the service while they played with yo-yos and rubber balls and blew tin horns. And some years ago he hailed George Bernard Shaw as the first man "to make a complete monkey out of death and of the theory [sic!] of dying in general." But one of Saroyan's own characters declares that "Death begins with helplessness, and it's impossible to joke about." Perhaps Saroyan has begun to suspect that for him, "Death is a lousy idea from which there is no escape."

The latest novel by Saroyan is called *The Laughing Matter* (1953). Set in the California vineyards and dealing with a family of Armenian heritage, the book has on its opening pages an atmosphere of love and warmth which recalls the earliest and best Saroyan. When the boy and girl of the family are the book's concern, their enjoyment of life and their sensitivity to the world around them—the way they savor figs and grapes, drink in the warmth of the sun, won-der about the universe—are a delight. But before long, Sa-royan is trying to handle adult problems and the tale bogs down. . . . The boy, confronted by the tragic situation which is rocking the security of his beautiful family, cries to the skies, "What was the matter? What was it, always? Why couldn't anything be the way it *ought* to be? Why was everything always strange, mysterious, dangerous, delicate, likely to break to pieces suddenly?" For although his father has taught him the Armenian words, "It is right," and al-though everybody chants them over and over (one wise member of the family insists, meaning it, "Whatever you do is right. If you hate, it is. If you kill, it is."), neverthe-less, everything goes wrong and there is death and disaster, and there is futility in the face of imperfection. And after it all, at the end of the book, still crying like an echo in the wilderness, is the repeated refrain, "It is right!" (pp. 340, 385)

> *William J. Fisher, "What Ever Happened to Saroyan?" in* College English *(copyright © 1955 by the National Council of Teachers of English; reprinted by permission of the pub-lisher and the author), March, 1955, pp. 336-40, 385.*

[When "The Time of Your Life"] opened, exactly thirty years ago last month, Wolcott Gibbs summed up the occasion—and the author—in this magazine by saying, "An evening in the theatre with William Saroyan is rather like spending an evening with a drunkard—a talented, sentimen-tal, and witty man, but tight as a mink. There are times when he is very funny, with a wild, rich invention that no sober man can equal, and there are times when he is elo-quent. Unfortunately, there are also times when he gets to talking about his girl, and this is when you wish he would just put his head down on the table and go to sleep. Mr. Saroyan's girl is the human race. Speaking with the as-sorted voices of bartenders, bums, policemen, hoofers, and prostitutes, Mr. Saroyan interrupts his play again and again to explain that he and Life are sweethearts."

That opinion was sound, and it remains sound. "The Time of Your Life" is a ramshackle affair, mildly amusing when it is content to be a vaudeville; as a play, it has no center, and its surface is fatally smeared over with a sticky sweet-ness that the young Saroyan had what amounted to a patent on. He was a man who, without a blush, could speak of "little" people, meaning not leprechauns but human beings. Now, *pace* Mr. Lahr, even in the thirties there were any number of young people who, stalking their innocence like pathfinders—or maybe finding the path of their innocence like stalkers—had their doubts about Dr. Saroyan's magic cure-all; they might have been able to swallow the syrup, but they couldn't keep it down. (p. 163)

> *Brendan Gill, in* The New Yorker *(© 1969 by The New Yorker Magazine, Inc.), No-vember 15, 1969.*

[The] best of Saroyan's radically different writing keeps the real world out and thus maintains the fabulous integrity of the Saroyan world. It is the world of a child: vibrant, pow-erfully simple, with everything larger than life.

William Saroyan is a kind of Armenian Buffalo Bill. As wild and woolly as the marvelous character in "The Time of Your Life" who really and truly herds cattle on a bicycle and falls in love with a midget weighing 39 pounds. His feats and misadventures have been no less mythic—

whether it's been a matter of losing tens of thousands of hardearned dollars on the turn of a card, stubbornly marry-ing the same girl twice, or writing a Pulitzer Prize play in six days on a bet.

Admittedly Saroyan can be sentimental and silly; boastful and repetitive too. And at 64 he still astounds—discovers clichés, burnishes them, and presents them to us with a naiveté that can only be attractive in a 17-year-old virgin.

Yet books of his such as "My Name Is Aram," that glow-ing bit of radium extracted from the pitchblende of a rather grim Fresno childhood, will certainly be read a hundred years hence. . . . (pp. 13-14)

> *Peter Sourian, in* The New York Times Book Review *(© 1972 by the New York Times Company; reprinted by permission), April 2, 1972.*

Saroyan has been around so long and is so prolific that one forgets the importance of his contribution to the American short story; his first and best-known collection, *The Daring Young Man on the Flying Trapeze* (1934), brought to the short story a freshness of vision, simplicity, gaiety, and sympathetic understanding of little people at a time when the genre was becoming enmired in an angry social con-sciousness or basically meaningless slice-of-life realism. In spite of whimsy, repetitiveness, and self-imitation, Saroy-an's stories are part of the permanent literature of the American short story, and his "country"—particularly San Francisco, Fresno, and their environs—is as real in its way as Faulkner's Mississippi. Particularly effective is Saroy-an's depiction of childhood and adolescence; stories like "The Fifty-Yard Dash," "The Parsley Garden," "The Home of the Human Race" and "Winter Vineyard Work-ers" are little classics, which have about them the warmth of an August afternoon with the scent of ripening fruit in the air. (pp. 164-65)

> *William Peden, in his* The American Short Story: Continuity and Change 1940-1975 *(copyright © 1964, 1975 by William Peden; reprinted by permission of Houghton Mifflin Company), Houghton, revised edition, 1975.*

Having outlived most of the bastards and good guys of his salad time, [Saroyan] has held onto that essence of "sorrow with joy" (as he says of Chagall) that made him special in American writing. . . .

Literarily, he is sometimes considered to have been a flash-in-the-pan, but who else of that vintage, writing in the na-tion's idioms, except perhaps Robert Penn Warren in poet-ry, is still doing so well at keeping up to the mark? ["Sons Come and Go, Mothers Hang in Forever,"] Saroyan's sixth official memoir (not counting memoiristic fiction) is better, for instance, than the last one I read, which was his fourth. I don't wish to inflate its importance, but I think it's high time for a Saroyan revival. He ought again to be "dis-covered" briefly by each young writer coming along, be-cause his contribution has been to write from joy, which is in short supply lately, and sparse as a tradition in our litera-ture anyway, unless one looks back to some of the founding figures, such as Walt Whitman, Emerson, Thoreau. He predates the glut of black humor and rancorous ethnicity, the literary theater of cruelty and the absurd, though part of the point about Saroyan which is so interesting is that he has been a profoundly, innovatively "ethnic" writer—one of the very first in America, one who has been a conscious spokesman for a people who survived a genocidal holocaust —but that throughout his life he has chosen to write not of despair and dadaism and devastation, but joy. . . .

The Saroyan working method—and it can seem repetitive— is to swing way out from the trapeze, do a somersault or two, and reach out flatly for our hands, trusting partly in us, and secure in the faith that if he misses there is a God somewhere to break his fall. . . .

He has his tales of favorite cousins who burned themselves to death, as well as slower, humbler tragedies and personal regrets, yet finally, to him, almost everybody is 21 and free and white. And that is just as true a claim as we've been getting from the horde of writers who have been running about for the past 20 years discovering that everybody is in the process of dying. (p. 2)

Edward Hoagland, in The New York Times Book Review (© *1976 by The New York Times Company; reprinted by permission), August 15, 1976.*

* * *

SARRAUTE, Nathalie   1902-

A Russian-born French novelist, essayist, playwright, and critic, Sarraute is considered an exponent of the New Novel. In her rebellion against the traditional novel, Sarraute has endeavored to free herself from conventional plot and character development. Her prose is characterized by condensed images, flowing as "ripples on water," and by a repetition of prose rhythms, revealing content rather than defining it. (See also *CLC*, Vols. 1, 2, 4, and *Contemporary Authors*, Vols. 9-12, rev. ed.)

Sarraute's novels convey so stilted and meagre a sense of life that her critical judgment [as displayed in her literary criticism] could scarcely be expected to fare better. Unable vitally to respond, whatever she writes lacks vitality. Anyone suffering through *The Golden Fruits,* or even the less blatantly moribund *Portrait of a Man Unknown* for example, must know what I mean. It is next to impossible to believe that every word of them, every trail of dots, every turgid shard of banality, was written not by an over-loaded computer signaling distress but by a single human creature sequestered comfortably and alive presumably for the purpose of expressing something she felt it necessary or relieving or delightful to express. One hopes for her it was at least one of those, and for her reader to put up with it is something requiring a similar kind of delirium. Such as for instance Sartre's laudatory preface to the latter novel, which claims she made "inauthenticity . . . its subject"— whereas of course that is only its content, for there is no subject. Sartre (who has a pretty high delirium-tedium quotient himself) goes on to talk about her "protoplasmic vision of our interior universe: roll away the stone of the commonplace and we find running discharges, slobberings, mucous; hesitant, amoeba-like movements . . ." and etc. I couldn't agree with him more. That is precisely her imprecise (putting it mildly) approach to things and defines to a T her prose, which runs on like amoebic dysentery when it isn't merely suppurating. Call it action-writing if you will, the chances are it would look a lot better in paint. . . . [Sartre] and Sarraute are certainly companions in their loathing of existence. (p. 31)

Gene Ballif, in Salmagundi *(copyright © 1970 by Skidmore College), Spring, 1970.*

Nathalie Sarraute's theoretical treatise entitled *L'Ère du soupçon* announced in 1950 the beginning of a new era in French prose fiction based precisely on the role of the first-person pronoun. Ostensibly a revolt against Sartre and the politically committed or philosophically oriented novel, Mme Sarraute's view proclaimed that both the novelist and his reader distrusted the fictional character and through him each the other. The fictional character was merely presumed necessary as a viable path of communication between author and reader, and almost disappeared as an independent entity in the wake of their mutual distrust.

The modern hero had degenerated into a being without contours, indefinable, and invisible; he had become an anonymous first person primarily reflecting different attitudes of the author. Still, Mme Sarraute opted for the first-person novel as the one most legitimate for both contemporary reader and author. The first person at least had the *appearance* of having lived his experience, of exemplifying that authenticity which the reader expected. Since it was most important to Mme Sarraute to portray the coexistence of contradictory sentiments and to render the complexity of psychological life, the novelist, in all honesty, should speak exclusively of himself. Fictional "characters," in Mme Sarraute's novels, therefore, surpassed even the Sartrean point-of-view-subjectivities in becoming pure points-of-view projected from the novelist's own subjective concerns, with none of the Sartrean freedom to choose themselves.

On the other hand, Mme Sarraute was the first novelist after Sartre to enlist the reader's cooperation in interpreting the novel as the most significant development of modern fiction. . . .

To write a novel in the first person was the best way to plunge the reader into the interior of the fictional world as the author was already plunged into it. In order to effect such direct involvement, Mme Sarraute transcribed not simply the "I" of normal dialogue, or *conversation,* nor even the conscious "I" of conventional interior monologue, but also the semiconscious "I" found in *sous-conversation,* or subterranean nascent states of emotion normally kept tacit. In this way each subjectivity was tripled and at least two subjectivities were necessary to the work of fiction. Although Mme Sarraute's points of view all stemmed from the novelist's subjective concerns on the real plane, on the fictional plane they never had a single center, but continually demanded multiple centers, or several points of view.

That these points of view lost their human embodiment as physical entities and became disembodied "supports" expressing "commonplaces" in a frantic attempt to assuage their "terrible desire to establish contact" (in Mme Sarraute's own words) clearly reflected the Sartrean notion of "bad faith" carried to its dehumanized extreme. (pp. 20-2)

Betty T. Rahv, in her From Sartre to the New Novel *(copyright © 1974 by Betty T. Rahv; reprinted by permission of Kennikat Press Corp.), Kennikat, 1974.*

The clarity of [Sarraute's] observation, with its emphasis on microscopic details, creates a series of eidetic images, each imposed and superimposed upon the other, as in a series of layers. These stratifications are never static; on the contrary, they are "amoeba-like" and are in a state of perpetual flux and reflux, altering in form and content, substance and point. Sarraute's tropisms are unlike Joycean interior monologues, which "flow through one's conscious mind." They are pre-conscious incisions, pre-interior monologues clothed in a vocabulary as sensual as Proust's and as incisive as Beckett's.

Unlike conventional theatre, Sarraute's plays have no real plots. They center around a controlled or contrived situation: a conversation or a series of conversations, silences, the manner in which certain words are pronounced and thus given the power to alienate or attract people, the success or failure of a novel, the problems arising with the creation of a work of art. The tropisms or visualizations that emerge from these conversations and sub-conversations frequently unmask the participants and reveal inside relationships in the process of interacting one with the other or clashing during the short periods of a get-together. The tropism is the mechanism Sarraute uses to set her play in motion. The detail, which creates the suspense and brings forth the climax, is buried within these closely knit images and clothed in a sparse but rambling dialogue. The viewer must catch the detail and absorb it if he seeks to follow her into her labyrinthian realm.

Moreover, there are no flesh-and-blood characters in Sarraute's plays; rather, they are faceless beings without identity; so many *presences,* not in the old sense of the word, with form and substance, but *transparencies* based on an ever altering world of images. These presences are actualized feelings, concretized sensations, with the solidity and variegated transparencies of a jellyfish. Her creatures are like clusters or groups of vocal emanations, voices with heteroclite tonalities including infinite nuances in their timber and intonations. . . . Divested of personal histories, of plot, atmosphere, decors, and psychology in the conventional sense of the word, Sarraute invites us to join her in a penumbra—an inner domain of hidden and billowy movements where everything is sensed and experienced on the most instinctual of levels.

The tropism is a catalyst. In this sense Sarraute's theatre may be considered active, dramatic in scope. When the tropism comes into being, it mystifies at first, then delights; later it hurts and may attract or repel, anger or pacify. Sarraute's world of tropisms is a realm that is in a perpetual state of shifting, heaving, diminishing, and swelling sensations. This quicksand effect creates suspense and intrigue, but of a most subtle nature.

The sense of excitement or malaise aroused in the viewer in *The Silence* or *It's Beautiful* is not caused by the depth of the themes treated, nor by any *Sturm und Drang;* on the contrary, tropisms create a microcosm, a world of feeling that incises itself into the conversations, and tricks the protagonists and the viewer frequently into believing fiction rather than fact. It occasions a series of countersensations that conflict with what is considered the visible outer core. Movements are thus set up, comparable to a series of undulations, oceanic rhythms reflecting or antithetical to the atmosphere of the moment, as experienced by the participants in the dramatic ritual. (pp. 16-17)

The goal of her theatre is, as she has stated, to reveal the image or the tropism before it has been altered by the conscious mind or man's thinking principle. These sub-conversations that come to life on an undifferentiated level must be communicated to others on an instinctual plane. It is in this sense that she has opened up a new world for the theatre-goer, one in which preception is foremost: a world of appearance rather than reality, of conversation instead of

action, of intellectual travail and not diversion; therefore, concentration is required on the part of the viewer. (p. 17)

Sarraute's theatre is both realistic and unrealistic. It is microscopically precise in that she describes the state happenings in minute detail. But it is unreal in that the outside realm is virtually nonexistent. Because of the finesse of her delineations, Simone de Beauvoir has classified her as a member of the School of the Look (*L'Ecole du Regard*) along with Robbe-Grillet, Simon, and Butor. But Sarraute objects to this appelation. She claims the members of the School of the Look consider beings as they do objects. For Sarraute "the human being plays a predominant role, the object being the instrument which a man uses in order to express or to hide his anguish. The object is nothing without man who looks at it and uses it."

Affinities, nevertheless, do exist with the writers of the School of the Look. Besides being precise in their delineations, like Sarraute they are objective in their approach and their writings are impersonal. Their protagonists, if one may label them as such, are depersonalized. Yet, differences also exist. Sarraute is a poet. Her tropisms are exquisitely drawn, like fine lines juggled about, pulled together, then separated, with clashing and harmonizing color tones, frequently with kaleidoscopic effect. She captivates her viewers by the sensuality of her images. She benumbs them.

The power of Sarraute's objectivity rests on a kind of Brechtian "alienation" or distanciation technique. She believes distance must be maintained in the theatre between the event, the memory of it, and its *entree* into the conversation as well as between the protagonists themselves, each one a victim of a powerful solitude that cannot be thrust off. Distance must also exist between the protagonists and the audience. As Sarraute builds her constructs, in rhythm with a rapid or slackening pulse beat, depending upon the sensation implicit in the situation, she creates empathy between the presences on the stage and those in the audience. Feelings of annoyance, anger, pain, joy, or hatred are aroused almost spontaneously, only to be destroyed seconds later as she repels, alienates, cuts them off by altering feelings involved through changing the topic of conversation.

Interestingly enough, both the viewer and the dramatist participate in the event as it occurs. Detachment enables an understanding of the arguments, cerebrally speaking, whereas identification allows the protagonists and audience alike to undergo the anguish, disgust, joy, or hate—the inner landscape. Such detachment-identification sequences are experienced in a state of constant flux and reflux, frequently simultaneously, in a hierarchy of disturbing moods, as one eidetic sequence follows another and replaces it. (pp. 17-18)

Although the themes broached in *The Silence* are not of vital interest, the patterns the banalities make are fascinating: the harmonies and cacophanies that emanate from the voices, the perfunctory gestures that fill the stage space in web-like formation. But what has been termed by many as Sarraute's platitudes are really anything but that. In fact, her so-called banalities may be very well explained by taking the French word *lieuxcommuns* (the translation for "platitude"), which means *common places,* that is, the common places where people meet. Since tropisms only manifest themselves on the outside—in these common places—during the course of dialogues between people,

Sarraute uses them as a means of comparison to further explicate the banal. Ionesco lists a series of platitudes in his plays *The Bald Soprano, The Lesson, The Chairs,* and others, to ridicule or satirize humanity on a variety of levels and to evoke laughter. Sarraute justifies her use of "common places" in that she tries to demonstrate that these tropisms or banalities are really camouflages; that tropisms reveal rather than hide an inner architecture that enables an outsider to better scrutinize the object of his thoughts and emotions. The tropisms that come into view in her theatre reveal the workings of particular individuals and the reactions triggered off by certain thought patterns. What is born within grows and festers in an insalubrious climate. It is just this glob she concretizes. (pp. 19-20)

She sees her characters as possessed of great tenderness and understanding and, in this respect, different from those one encounters in everyday reality. (p. 20)

What Sarraute underscores in [*Isma*] is the power of suggestion: a trivial detail assumes volcanic proportions. Revealed also is the vanity, the egocentricity of man; but more important is his superficiality when it comes to questions of morality and integrity. Humanity can be aroused with such ease and over so little. Then the questions arise: What kind of people are prone to hatred? What is their way in life? their outlook? their desires, dreams, personality? We learn that anyone and everyone is capable of anger and hatred. One merely need kindle an emotion, then gather bits and pieces of information that will make the fire blaze —until it reaches the multitude. In *Isma* an all too human situation has been dramatized, and expertly so—the contagious disease called hatred. (pp. 23-4)

Sarraute offers no answers [in *It's Beautiful*] to the chasm existing within families and within the social, aesthetic, political, or psychological structure. To opt for the leftist way of alleviating problems is too simplistic for her. To offer any rightist solution would be anathema to Sarraute. Confrontation seems to be the only way in which some kind of temporary harmony may be realized. Authenticity must begin at home. Escape mechanisms are not the answer. Is there an answer?

Sarraute's plays are metapsychological. They take us directly into her protagonists' inner worlds. From this vantage point we are able to observe, sometimes identify, with the "palpitations," tensions, and emotions resuscitated. These infinitesimal reactions—tropisms—are not plotted along traditional theatrical or psychological lines. As they emerge full-blown from their insalubrious climate in words, epithets, clauses, or a series of ultra banalities, they grow and become the center of focus only to suddenly vanish, with equal rapidity, but not before triggering off new groups of sensations that again flow into focus. It is the "common place," the collective aspect of the human experience— man's dependence upon another, his need for relationships, his cruelty, vanity, hypocrisy, immorality as well as his creative instinct—that Sarraute dramatizes. . . .

The sub-conversations and sub-visions are the substance of Sarraute's plays. These protoplasmic emanations, "still brute" and undifferentiated, are built into a structure that takes on an ontological reality of its own. The impressions they create are allowed to develop in dialogue form, underscoring behavior patterns, rhythms, and ideations in the flux and reflux of nature's way. Suspense is created by an interplay between attraction-rejection, interruption-continuation, appearance-disappearance, memory-forgetfulness.

This theatrical mechanism, which has become Sarraute's convention, permits audiences to understand and react to the intricacies of the human personality: the artifices it builds up out of fear, insecurity, solitude, or pain; the masks it wears to hide what is sickly or to regress into solitary or dark realms. (p. 26)

In all of her plays Sarraute burrows into her protagonists' substructures. There she extracts the full import of an experience as human relationships coalesce or digress in clusters, waves, and sound patterns, each caught by her infallible antennae, then concretized onstage in her theatre of *tropisms*. (p. 27)

> *Bettina Knapp, "Natalie Sarraute: A Theatre of Tropisms," in* Performing Arts Journal (© *copyright 1977 Performing Arts Journal), Winter 1977, pp. 15-27.*

By emphasizing the disparate, simultaneous nature of impressions and the fluidity and interchangeability of human personalities, Virginia Woolf helped pave the way for that final dissolution of character which has become a trademark of the New French Novel—nowhere better demonstrated than in the writings of Nathalie Sarraute, one of its most vocal practitioners. To a complaint that *she* fails to create memorable characters, Sarraute would reply, "Good!" For that is what she most wants to avoid: anything that might remotely be said to have a "personality," or a life of its own. (p. 5)

Times have changed; for one thing, the moderns have shifted the primary interest in the novel from character and plot, or manners and customs, to "the revelation of a new psychological subject matter." But neither Proust nor Joyce went far enough, or probed deeply enough, says Sarraute. The people we know may *appear* to have a finished, whole personality, she argues in *Portrait of a Man Unknown,* but this is merely an illusion which we maintain as a matter of convenience, or convention. Beneath the polished surface lies one's true self, fluid and amorphous, perpetually dissolving into a series of impulses and sensations.

Wishing to get to one's *real* personality, Sarraute determined to explore the realm *beneath* the interior monologue, a region on the threshold of consciousness, where innumerable images, sentiments, and impulses jostle and collide— psychological movements which cannot be perceived directly by the conscious mind but which nevertheless affect our actions and our words. To simulate these movements (or "tropisms," as she calls them elsewhere), she developed her famous "sub-conversation," which she conceives of as taking place on the frontiers of consciousness—actual dialogue being merely the *outward* continuation of subterranean actions and sensations which cloak themselves in words. Hence, in the Sarraute novel, character is neither essential nor desirable. It is merely a prop for the psychological movements she wishes to study. Beyond that, as she freely admits, character holds no interest for her. She welcomes the depersonalization of the hero in current fiction as proof of the increased sophistication of writer and reader and considers the process of depersonalization similar to that which has already occurred in painting. . . . As she sees it, the purpose of the experimental novelist is to further that end, to make the psychological element as self-sufficient as possible. "And since what the characters gain in the way of facile vitality and plausibility is balanced by a loss of fundamental truth in the psychological states for which they serve as props, [the reader] must be kept from allowing his attention to wander or be absorbed by the characters." In fact, she criticizes Proust because, no matter how many fragments he examines from the "subsoil" of his characters, the fragments unite to form a coherent whole, a recognizable type, the moment the book is closed. (pp. 5-6)

[In] her attempt to banish character from the novel, Sarraute may have done more for its restoration than Virginia Woolf, who sought to preserve it. For, if they do nothing else, Sarraute's works show how essential character is to the novel and how impossible it is to make the psychological elements "self-sufficient."

Sarraute's first attempt to put theory into practice was *Tropisms*, originally published in 1939, a book which, according to the author, contains *in nuce* all the raw material of her later works: a series of moments in which those subterranean movements she calls "Tropisms" occur, "dramatic actions, hiding beneath the most commonplace conversations, the most everyday gestures, and constantly emerging to the surface of the appearances that both conceal and reveal them." This is what she *intended* to portray; the actual result, however, is another matter: sometimes a simple description of the inner feelings and psychological attitude of her nameless "prop."...

Many of the sketches offer psychographs of universal types.... (p. 6)

Often, her technique comes perilously close to a kind of psychological impressionism, such as she condemned in Woolf and Proust. For example, sketch X, describing the housewives, their faces "stiff with a sort of inner tension," gathering at tearooms in the afternoon: "And they talked and talked, repeating the same things, going over them, then going over them again, from one side then from the other, kneading them, continually rolling between their fingers this unsatisfactory, mean substance that they had abstracted from their lives (what they called 'life,' their domain), kneading it, pulling it, rolling it until it ceased to form anything between their fingers but a little pile, a little grey pellet"....

Tropisms not only contains the essence of Sarraute's later work, it also demonstrates vividly the limitations of her technique and the impossibility of separating the psychological element from its exterior support, or of finding equivalent images to express the inexpressible. In *Portrait of a Man Unknown, Martereau,* and *The Planetarium,* we find her using less abstract characters and at least some semblance of a plot, but, as the narrator of *Martereau* carefully explains, the attitudes and reactions he has described were actually "expressed not in so many words, of course, as I am obliged to do now for lack of other means, not with real words like the ones we articulate distinctly out loud or in our thoughts, but suggested rather by certain sorts of very rapid signs" which he has attempted to translate.

And in *The Golden Fruits* and *Between Life and Death* Sarraute returns to the goals, and the limitations, originally found in *Tropisms,* both novels presenting universalized types (the reader, the critic, the writer) which serve as props for the subterranean movements Sarraute attempts to record. One begins, says the anonymous writer in *Between Life and Death,* by setting down words, repeating them countless times until at last what emerges "is neither an image, nor a word, nor a tone, nor any sound . . . a movement rather, a brief flexing of muscles, leaps, grovelings, recoilings, gropings. . . ." One is immediately reminded of

a similar attempt by Gertrude Stein, equally futile ("Rose is a rose is a rose is a rose."), to make the word reach beyond the cognitive to precognitive levels.

In her "tropisms" and "sub-conversations" Nathalie Sarraute pushes the fragmented personality and the fragmented vision to their ultimate limits, proving how impossible it is to create a *novel* without a character of sorts. And her works remind us afresh that while universal types may be good subjects for scientific analysis, they do not make good subjects for fiction.

That Sarraute's primary interest *is* that of the scientist rather than the artist is indicated by her constant reference to her own works as "research." But, ironically, it is as research that they have the least claim to validity, relying as they do upon an extremely *subjective* interpretation of the region between conversation and subconversation. (p. 7)

> *Ethel F. Cornwell, in* The International Fiction Review, *January, 1977.*

Nathalie Sarraute's most recent venture is "*fools say*"; and I regret to say that it seems perversely to fulfill all those philistine epithets from the old days, epithets that were mainly false then, but which now have become somehow more than partly true. I cannot find "*fools say*" anything but willfully arcane, mannered, and pretentious, the product of a brilliant writer's persistence in a method that has ceased to suit her. One hesitates to judge Sarraute; several of her earlier and much better novels (*The Golden Fruits, The Planetarium, Between Life and Death*) brilliantly treat the emptiness of judgment, and of literary judgment above all. But judgment is a natural reflex (dare I say tropism?) of the thinking mind; God knows there is plenty of judgment both in and against the acid mutterings of the—well, *she* used the word first—"fools" whose disembodied voices fill the pages of her best books. On the other hand, "*fools say*" is not only stylistically more radical than the earlier books (i.e., harder to read), but it is also directed to the deeper regions of self-judgment. I, for one, am not much impressed by what Sarraute has discovered down there.

She has found a baffled, hurt child's wild insecurity, endless inner debate, and need for love; along with pride and contempt, focused sometimes on the self, sometimes on all of "them"—the "fools" out there. Fair enough: Sarraute has her finger (more or less) on the mixture of desperation and complacency that marks a typically neurotic struggle for self-esteem. But is *that* all there is? In her plunge into the depths of the self-doubting mind, she has found only the emotions one would expect. And those emotions, because they are disembodied by her prose, lack resonance; they seem almost allegorical. Something is lacking: behavior, *action*. Instead of the strictly satirical fiction that is her strength, Sarraute has tried for a genuinely psychological novel, and it turns out that the elegant manner she developed for her satirical mutterings is not appropriate to the new mode....

Sarraute's voices have been compared to those heard through a motel wall: we never see the people, never see what they are doing, never know where they have come from. It is an ideal mode for satire. We hear only the empty disconnections; the sudden petulances, the raised voices. Understanding nothing about these mutterers, we forgive nothing—Montaigne in reverse. But if one tries to carry satire to deeper levels of inner struggle, of psychology, the manner merely continues to be empty, and, what's more, we now resent the fact of still richer information withheld.

Psychology entails not only the flux of thoughts and impulses: it is behavior. And Sarraute has long since thrown away action in her effort to distill her style to its own purity. Though she now gives no signs of regretting that act of triage, it dooms an effort like "*fools say*": the book needs not only behavior, and therefore action, but also, since the muttering of impulse can be disembodied, and only a person can act, it needs characters. Sarraute used to assail the retention of characters in fiction on the grounds that they are false: they are always too statically and narrowly conceived; they are always, when compared to the polyvalence of life, flat. *A bas la psychologie!*—this standard French posture is one that Sarraute took up in new terms. But there are degrees of flatness, after all, and by refusing to enlarge her manner to include the fullness of action (whatever *its* flux, whatever *its* partial truths and confusions), she has produced a novel that is dullness itself.

> *Stephen Koch, "A Drama of Pronouns," in* Saturday Review (© *1977 by Saturday Review Magazine Corp.; reprinted with permission), April 2, 1977, p. 28.*

As someone observed, the French are enamored of profound banalities, and nothing demonstrates this so neatly as a novel like Nathalie Sarraute's "'fools say.'" Miss Sarraute is bemused by the idea that our diction sometimes betrays a striving for status and she has written a high-falutin conversational primer to prove it. Like so many avant-garde French novelists, she is a sociologist and a relentless pedagogue at heart. At regular intervals, we are given lessons in semantics: "And yet it is a word which doesn't look like much, an apparently perfectly harmless word with its 'jeal' that consolidates, and its 'ous' that unites, 'ous' like 'us'.... But you can't count on this, there's nothing trickier than these sound effects.... Remember we have 'jeal' for 'jel,' 'ous' for 'us.' It's all there, in the unpronounced letters, in the 'a' and the 'o'."

In "'fools say,'" technique overshadows character to such an extent that one wonders whether the French avant-garde may not be the Gallic equivalent of technological pollution. Miss Sarraute is a bureaucrat of fiction, less interested in the dramatization of personality than in its classification. In her chic and claustrophobic landscape, one looks in vain for the awkward and endearing grope of human contact. (pp. 14, 41)

A work like this one can be approached only through the prism of a pretentious theory of the novel. And if you should succeed in such an *engagement*, you will discover only that cleverness corrupts and that, like so many *tours de force*, this is a novel not about people, but about itself. (p. 41)

> *Anatole Broyard, in* The New York Times Book Review (© *1977 by The New York Times Company; reprinted by permission), April 3, 1977.*

* * *

SCIASCIA, Leonardo 1921-

An Italian novelist, short story writer, playwright, and essayist, to date Sciascia seems mainly intent on detailing the historical background and character of his native Sicilians. This has included both an explanation and an expose of the Mafia, which he seems to understand as well as any author writing today on the subject. Sciascia is a gifted stylist writing in the realistic tradition, and his novels can be read as thrilling en-

tertainments or as serious investigations of political intrigue and corruption.

"Sicily is still a bitter land," writes Leonardo Sciascia in the introduction to his *Le parrocchie di Regalpetra*, a volume of narrative essays.... The reasons why Sicily is still a bitter land are briefly summarized by Sciascia in a sentence, in which his moral indignation stands out from the bare facts:

> In Sicily there are laborers paid by the day who live 365 days, a long year with rain and sun, on sixty thousand lire; there are children who are employed as servants, old men who die of hunger, and persons who—as Brancati said—leave a little crease in a club's arm-chair as the only mark of their passing on the earth.

In the face of such a situation, Sciascia gives his motivation for writing:

> I have tried to say something about the life in a town I love, and I hope I have given a feeling of how distant this life is from liberty and justice, that is from reason.... Certainly I, too, have a bit of faith in writing, like the poor people at Regalpetra: this is the only justification I have for these pages.

His faith in the written word and in human reason immediately points to his engagement, which is more open and direct, in terms of neo-realism, than the objective and dispassionate representation of Verga's *verismo*. In fact Sciascia is concerned with the structure of society as the primary cause of a given situation, and therefore as a problem which is essentially political rather than humanitarian. (pp. 13-14)

Sciascia's testimony on the war of Spain is quite revealing of both a moral and a historical condition—a theme developed in a later short story, *L'antimonio*, which is imbued with the tragic sense of death and destiny, and can stand a comparison with the much longer and more famous novels *L'Espoir* by André Malraux and, obviously, *For Whom the Bell Tolls* by Hemingway....

From this point on, the inquiry into the present develops along two directions: on the one hand Sciascia gives a bare documentation of the way the poor live: on the other, he exerts his bitter satire—which at times reaches the grotesque—on the vices of the *bourgeoisie* and of the ruling classes. (p. 15)

Such is the "sociological" background of Sciascia's Sicily, to which one can apply, literally, the following sociological description by Raffaele Crovi:

> The social units of the peasant's world in the South are still the family and the town community—not the individual and the national community.... The peasant's society is still an *object*, not a subject, of political power; it judges good and evil instinctively, according to rules of utility and conservation; it tends, finally, to transform religious beliefs and popular forms of culture, traditions and customs into irrational myths.

Sciascia's stories are deeply rooted in this background. *Gli zii di Sicilia*, for instance, depicts the ideals of the poor as reflected in the popular imagination. "Uncle Sam" on one side, with the disappointment of a young boy when he meets his big and vulgar Italo-American relatives; "Uncle Joe," that is Stalin, on the other, with the gradual disappointment of the cobbler Calogero whenever international politics contradict his naive faith. . . .

The trouble is that all the expectations of the Sicilians are sooner or later frustrated. *Il giorno della civetta* is the account of a murder committed by the *mafia* and of the efforts of a young captain of the *carabinieri,* the Northerner Bellodi, to find the culprits: efforts that in the end remain utterly vain because of political support for the *mafia* bosses in Palermo and in Rome. Given the subject, the novel is not written "with the full liberty of expression which a writer should have"—as Sciascia feels obliged to point out in a note: a further proof of the terrible truth contained (and to a certain extent disguised) in this novelistic account. Nevertheless, Sciascia is very effective in unfolding his dry and nervous narration underlined by a sober compassion. . . . (p. 19)

The history of Sicily . . . fascinated Sciascia, who traces back the virtues and the vices of today in the past centuries, in search of the identity not of himself, but of his land and of his people first of all. . . . *Il Consiglio d'Egitto* especially reaches beautifully poetic and human results in this search. In XVIII century Palermo, the erudite *Abbé* Vella invents an Arab code which annuls the feudal prerogatives of the Barons, while the young Jacobin lawyer Di Blasi attempts a revolt but fails and undergoes torture and death. The events are narrated through brilliant and witty dialogues, erudite references, social and moral concern ("the right of the peasant to be a *man,*" the frightful absurdity of torture), images of serene and sensual beauty, recurrent thoughts of death, and sudden lyrical passages ("guitars like crickets in the night," for instance, as in a line by Garcia Lorca). In *Il Consiglio d'Egitto* the pragmatic power of the word becomes also a vital and aesthetic power, thus confirming what Sciascia had stated earler: "I believe in the mystery of words, I believe that words can become life, destiny—exactly as they become beauty."

But perhaps the words which summarize the poetical and moral world of Sciascia—his Sicily—are to be found in the beautiful short story *Il Quarantotto.* . . . These words are said by Ippolito Nievo to Garibaldi, but it is as if Sciascia were speaking to himself and to all of us:

> I believe in the Sicilians who speak little, in the Sicilians who don't get excited, in the Sicilians who suffer silently inside themselves: the poor who greet us with a tired gesture, almost from a distance in the centuries; and Colonel Carini, always so silent and aloof, full of melancholy and boredom but ready to act at any moment: a man who seems to have no hope, yet who is the heart itself of hope—the silent, fragile hope of the best Sicilians. . . . A hope, I would say, which fears itself, which fears words and is familiar instead with death.

Such is the Sicily of Sciascia. . . . Sicily in time, a region of the world; but above all a timeless Sicily, a region of the human soul. (pp. 20-1)

> *Gian-Paolo Biasin, in* Italian Quarterly, *Summer-Fall, 1965.*

A plot summary might hint at a Jesuitical remake of *And Then There Were None:* cassocked participants in a retreat for "spiritual gymnastics" are reduced in number as one is shot (while praying in moving squad formation), a second is bludgeoned, and a third—supervising priest-hotelier Don Gaetano—turns up a possible suicide. But, even more than in *Equal Danger* (1973), Sciascia submerges suspense and detection under dense, witty dialogues—here touching on Don Juanism, medieval Christ portraiture, poetry, Voltaire —and under the musings of the narrator, a non-participating painter-observer who has whimsically come to the monastery with "no worries, no anxieties" except for a "tiny but tenacious trinity neurosis." Guilt, political corruption, and the hovering image of the Devil-in-glasses darkly predominate as public prosecutor Scalambri ("a sphinx") investigates. There's fine Italian wine here, but for connoisseurs of slim, black-bordered belles lettres, not bodies in the library. (p. 307)

> *Kirkus Reviews (copyright © 1977 The Kirkus Service, Inc.), March 15, 1977.*

In *I pugnalatori,* Leonardo Sciascia investigates for himself the contemporary investigation of a celebrated Sicilian crime of the last century; he believes that it was, for motives as predictable as they were dishonourable, botched.

The conspiracy, a clever exercise in the now commonplace "strategia della tensione", was a political one. Its leader, locally, was the Principe Sant 'Elia, a nobleman generally thought to be a supporter of Italian unity and the House of Savoy but who seems in fact to have been in the pay of the Bourbons, currently plotting to recover the island they had lost in 1860. The hero of Sciascia's plain and bitter account of the case is the prosecutor Guido Giacosa, an honest, moderate Piedmontese who was thoroughly sickened by his exposure to the feudal values of Sicily. Sciascia accepts Sant 'Elia's guilt and has retold this upsetting story in the belief that Sicily today is every bit as bad as Sicily in 1862. The forms of corruption are the same and so are the forms of illusion: Sicilians feel an absurd nostalgia for a past of order and decency which actually the island has never known. Sciascia has assembled his narrative from the records with extreme simplicity and economy; the indignation which he allows himself he intends as a corrective to the irony of so many of his fellow-Sicilians, because irony expresses fatalism and kills all hope of improvement in the morality of Italian institutions.

> *Percival Blake, "Sicilian Capers," in* The Times Literary Supplement *(© Times Newspapers Ltd., 1977; reproduced from* The Times Literary Supplement *by permission), March 25, 1977, p. 334.*

             *   *   *

SELBY, Hubert, Jr.   1928-

Selby is an American novelist whose explicit portrayals of sex and violence in *Last Exit to Brooklyn* **catapulted him to fame, controversy, and, in several areas, censorship. (See also** *CLC,* **Vols. 1, 2, 4, and** *Contemporary Authors,* **Vols. 13-16, rev. ed.)**

It was only a few years ago that *Lady Chatterley's Lover* unexpurgated and *Tropic of Cancer* were the bold and shocking books. I can't imagine that either work would cause much of a stir today. (p. 165)

Indeed, any kind of writing that describes straight sexuality with a feeling of pleasurable excitement has begun to seem outdated and rear-guard. The new tack that the sexual revolution has taken, at least in literature, or that so-called experimental writing has taken with regard to sex, is in the direction of perversion, particularly homosexuality, whether in subject matter or in vision. Rather than banning *Fanny Hill,* the authorities should consider subsidizing it as a contribution to the maintenance of normal animal nature in difficult times.

In a recent essay in *Partisan Review,* Susan Sontag suggests that two minority groups are making the only significant contributions to contemporary culture: the Jews, who impart moral seriousness, and the homosexuals, who impart aesthetic style and playfulness. But it seems to me the homosexual imagination is having a more decisive effect in defining the moral as well as the aesthetic character of the age since its view of human nature seems much more arresting and convincing to our sensation-seeking, anxious, and cynical eyes than does the old-fashioned earnest humanism of Saul Bellow or Bernard Malamud. The darkest (deepest) truths about drug addiction come from William Burroughs, about Negro-white relations from Genet and Baldwin, about modern marriage from Albee and Tennessee Williams, about the disaffected young from Allen Ginsberg.

The latest extension of this perspective is provided by Hubert Selby, Jr., who carries it into the violent slums around the Brooklyn waterfront, where he casts a particularly lurid light upon juvenile delinquency, the homosexuality of everyday life, the degeneration of the family in public housing projects, the corruption of the unions, and, in general, upon the vicious, obscene, and cold-hearted propensities of modern man, not to mention modern woman.

Only two of the six stories in *Last Exit to Brooklyn* deal with inversion as such. . . . Selby's other vignettes of the waterfront slums, however, are no less informed by the same loving and loathing fascination with "rough trade," or by other variants of sado-masochistic fantasy. (pp. 166-67)

It takes a genuine compulsion . . . to yield up one's imagination so completely to the images and sensations of sadism, to identify so thoroughly by one's language with the mentality of the action. (p. 167)

Selby's best single piece of writing is the story of Tralala, a teen-age psychopath whose dumb and constant rage sweeps her from one gutter to another, from delinquency to prostitution and eventually into dereliction and destruction. (p. 168)

Tralala is Selby's ideal character. She has none of the normal emotions that would offer opposition, contradiction, even ambiguity to the simple, destructive point he wants to make with her. Otherwise, Selby's characters soon begin to reveal less of their lives than of the narrow, habitual grooves in which their author's sensibility runs, just as the line of action almost invariably moves toward still another explosion of violence. . . . The sentimentality of [some] passages is, of course, merely the reverse of the crude, tough tone that surrounds them and reinforces the awareness of how little range there is of thought and art in these stories, of how dependent Selby is upon the intense slant and twist of his emotions for his perspective.

The same is true of his ability to create. The world that exists apart from his own obsessions is conceived by a callow, banal, pointless loathing. (pp. 168-69)

Selby apparently sees some profound religious truth in all of this, for he prefaces each of the stories with a quotation from the Old Testament. None of them is apt: the one for "Tralala" comes from the "Song of Songs," of all things. I imagine that Selby wishes us to believe that he is describing a modern-day Sodom or Gomorrah, which of course he is, though from the point of view of a Sodomite. . . . [Still] it's a very false note. Nihilism is Selby's single true love, and one of the Grove Press crowd—Seymour Krim, LeRoi Jones, Terry Southern, John Rechy, etc.—who tell us how beautiful and true Selby is should tell him that if you're going to be like a nihilist, you can't work the religious shuck as well. (pp. 169-70)

> *Theodore Solotaroff, "Hubert Selby's Kicks" (1964), in his* The Red Hot Vacuum and Other Pieces on the Writing of the Sixties *(copyright © 1964, 1970 by Theodore Solotaroff; reprinted by permission of* The Washington Post*),* Atheneum, 1970, pp. 165-70.

I believe that [the disturbing sort of power generated by the most violent stories in *Last Exit to Brooklyn*] is deceptively intricate in nature. It results to my mind from Selby's ambivalent manner of handling retributive justice, an ambivalence of so delicate a psychological composition that its effect is deeply felt but not readily noticed, not easily transcribed into critical terminology. The language of psychology might be of some use, and I will draw on it to help me—help and nothing more, I hope. My overall intention is to appreciate Selby's novel for its special artistic merits, not to reduce it to the status of a clinical example. I wish to focus primarily on a pair of interconnected stories, "Another Day Another Dollar," and the novel's longest and most impressive story, "Strike." Both of these stories involve an important group of characters whom I refer to collectively as the "psychic avengers." My discussion of these characters and the actions they take part in will lead me to some comments about the shape of the entire novel, and this, in turn, will entail some tentative efforts to place *Last Exit* in a larger critical context. These latter efforts will be useful, I believe, in clarifying some of the problems that pertain to point of view.

Retributive justice, at its extreme, engenders a primitive satisfaction: primitive in its unabashed complacency towards violence, primitive in its sensing a serious social endangerment, and primitive in regarding the act of punishment as a manifest social necessity. Usually in literature such justice is more modest, and usually it appears in a less pure form, modified by irony, ambiguity or whatever. Modified and complicated—but not denied by any means. Narrative closures since time immemorial have been making this self-evident: the fruits of a conflict ended are resolution and repose, which allow the regenerative mechanisms to take up their work. Even in the most complex of literary works, unresolved problems and lingering uncertainties will rest upon and be "felt" against the bedrock of finality that is discovered underfoot when the central conflict ends.

When, inversely, a central conflict persists, our mental tension is sustained and we are denied the satisfactions peculiar to a so-called "just" ending. It is safe I think to say that this happens only rarely by deliberate design, even in so-called experimental fiction. But an artist may impose upon his work some resolution that we cannot accept for one reason or another: it may strike us as simple-minded, or—and this is more likely—it may rest on a scheme of values which we cannot embrace. Our repudiation might lead us to deny the work's artistry; or we might, on the other hand, have recourse to a vantage-point that allows for our disagreements (and hence our uneasiness) without in the same breath robbing us of our appreciation entirely. Most worthy narratives involve us in this process: they are tension-sustaining, exciting; they catch us between the familiar and the entirely unexpected. It can be very disturbing, however, when we cannot quite locate the source of our uneasiness, that nexus of values which we intuitively reject.

This, roughly speaking, is what happens in *Last Exit to Brooklyn*. In the triad of violent stories that culminates with "Strike," Selby gradually alters the terms in which we view his sequence of victims with the effect that by the end we find our responses divided: against the ostensible injustice of the punishment of each victim there stands a growing subliminal feeling that the punishment *has* been just. And this division in our sympathies causes us discomfort because we are forced, simultaneously, and without a clear awareness of it, to assume moral stances which contradict each other; this *in addition* to enduring the violence of the stories, which is distressing in its own right. If then, for direction, we turn to the author's viewpoint, we find ourselves further baffled: Selby seems at once obsessively involved in and ironically detached from the world which he is creating. He eschews such common forms of authorial politeness as narrative indirection and balanced characterization; he runs dialogue, action, his characters' mental workings into a harsh cacophonous pattern that is idiomatic in its typography, syntax and paragraphing. *Last Exit* is hectic with energy; it moves at eye-blearing speed, and our endurance and our powers of discrimination are taxed. Insofar as a writer's habits have any "point," Selby seems to be saying to us, Modern life does that. But this can hardly stand as an adequate summary of Selby's *Weltanschauung*, and it remains to be seen from the stories themselves just what his vision of modern man entails. (pp. 153-55)

[The] three stories, taken together, add up to more than a sum of parts. "Analogical probability" is a useful term for this effect: the likenesses which interconnect "Another Day Another Dollar," "Tralala" and "Strike" create a general coloration which somewhat dissolves the boundaries between the separate pieces, and this allows them to become at least to some extent interchangeable. "Strike," psychologically speaking, is the most disturbing of these stories. . . . It generates in us the most stressing ambivalence; Selby himself, moreover, seems unsure where he stands at a very critical moment.

The central concerns in "Strike," I believe, are also central in American culture generally—which may explain in part the tremendous power the story possesses. The terror of being one of an undifferentiated mass; the primacy of conflict and competition in human relationships; the essential fear of sex, of vulnerability and openness—these are the driving forces at work in Harry Black's life. (p. 157)

Harry's sense of deficiency derives from an unreal notion of what he ought to be instead of what he actually is. His conscience has him caught, then, in a double bind: on the one hand it condemns him as being hopelessly inadequate, and on the other hand it orders him to assume, in compensation, an identity which is beyond the power of any man to achieve. This idealized self-image . . . robs him as he pursues it of what little strength he actually does have. In analytical terminology, Harry Black has an extremely weak

ego, a pathologically amorphous and unbounded center that affords him little coherency, effectiveness or free choice, so wholly has he abdicated his real potentialities in his desperate bid to realize a Faustian superimage or ego ideal. (pp. 160-61)

Harry seeks friends, but actually gets enemies. The self, by overreaching, undermines its best interests and ironically situates itself in a position of needless jeopardy. Another way of putting it is to say that the tyrranical superego functions within the psyche as a kind of internal police force—a secret police force, even. Such police are feared and hated, but they are accepted as a necessity in that little state of man in which the citizens are unruly. Unruliness in Harry, as indeed in most psychotics, takes the form of sexual longings—longings that *prima facie* are regarded as destructive. It is also typical of such secret police that they will tempt an individual into the commission of a crime and then arrest and punish him for it. The boys from the Greeks in effect do this with Harry. They are the ones who first introduce him to homosexual pleasures; they are also the ones who spring the trap when the bait is taken. The hunt, once again, is undertaken for the sport of it, and concludes with a victory celebration which follows the kill. This is the pattern at work in "Another Day Another Dollar," and also in slightly altered form in "Tralala." Its psychological implications are worth pointing up: the punishment, it turns out, does not serve any authentic social necessity, and the ministers of punishment have engaged in a cruel ruse, a sadistic disguising; the "police" reveal themselves as being merely vicious sportsmen. Sex is not destructive to the endopsychic "society" except in perversion, and even then ruination is but a pretense to cure. (p. 161)

I would like to turn my attention now to the very end of "Strike" and to the question of the narrative perspective which governs all of *Last Exit to Brooklyn*. . . . It is certainly a relentless piece of fictional closure, and it leaves the reader sufficiently stunned not to want to go poking, at least not immediately, amid the aesthetic implications. The literary referents in the full text of this scene,—Oedipus and Gloucester, Christ on Golgotha, Ahab on his whale—are evident enough not to be difficult to utilize, and Selby manages not to let them get in his way. The reader will also notice the conjunction of the blinding and the drowning motifs, and the echoes of the nightmare: Harry addressing himself as "you"; his *hearing* his own voice loud in his head; the similarities also in the kinds of torment he endures.

But what interests me most is that sentence about the moon ["The moon neither noticed nor ignored Harry as he lay at the foot of the billboard, but continued on its unalterable journey."] I cannot quite understand what Selby intends it to do to the reader. Possibly he sees it as an aptly grim reminder that the backdrop against which all human action plays is the *néant,* the void. "All is vanity, saith the preacher." But I cannot help feeling strongly that the statement is both pointless and nonsequiturial. Its first effect, to my mind, is to diminish the power of Harry's condition by reducing it to an error, an egocentric folly. But we don't need a reminder that Harry is in error; that is plentifully self-evident, and even if we are caught up in his psychosis momentarily, our involvement won't hurt us. Does Selby himself, one wonders, feel some uneasiness at the moment, some need to establish a distance between himself here and Harry? It would seem that he does. Why else would he break stride? And why bother reminding us that the cosmos is neutral? *L'indifférence*, Proust tells us, *est la forme permanente de la cruauté*. Human cruelty, certainly, has been an issue in the story, but that the cosmos is intentionless is quite beside the point. (pp. 163-64)

Just where *does* Selby stand? I know of few novels in which the answer is so elusive. The epigraphs from the Bible seem consistent in their purpose—to establish a general tenor of moral dissatisfaction with the way people act (and more superficially to discourage the reader's inclination to see the work as pornography; Selby was doubtless clear-eyed in foreseeing this problem). Yet however dissatisfied he might be with human behavior, Selby is obviously interested in and compassionate toward man's suffering. What elicits our sympathy, if not his invention? Besides, some ironic detachment is an absolute requirement if one is to write well at all, much less give one's writing the kind of intricate formal shape which characterizes *Last Exit*.

What Selby possibly does not control are those unnervingly mixed responses which his narrative generates and the endopsychic dimensions which have been my main concern. Just why it is that for so many readers *Last Exit to Brooklyn* is an unbearable experience is a complicated matter, a matter that has to do with levels of psychic tolerance in individual readers and with some general cultural factors, and I cannot pretend to account for the phenomenon entirely. But it is my guess that Selby is more of an intuitive artist than a "deliberate" one, at least with regards to the psychological patterns implicit in his work. And this, I believe, has an intimate connection with *Last Exit*'s power, its obsessions and also its limitations. (p. 164)

[Most] novels dramatizing endopsychic conflict in the form of ostensibly different characters have the problem of being too self-conscious and hence too obvious. Selby has created one of those much rarer instances wherein there are too few forces of Good with which to identify, too little distance between the reader and the suffering he is made to witness.

This at any rate seems the case with many readers; others will feel more sufficiently insulated. Either way, *Last Exit* is a problematic book that deserves to take its place among the *Doppelgänger* literature, the literature of the "double" or the "second self." It would also be useful to compare it to the fiction of Flannery O'Connor, which at first glance looks so different from Selby's, but which on closer inspection shows more remarkable similarities. Both writers are ironic and at times satiric moralists; both are intensely preoccupied with justice; both are inclined toward violent closures, and unabashedly willing to use the same dramatic structure over as often as they wish. But between O'Connor's stubbornness and (sometimes, not always) devastating appropriateness of action to moral viewpoint and Selby's headlong plunging into retributive situations there are also telling differences. These issues, like *Last Exit*'s formal or structural elegance, so little touched on here, would be well worth exploring. (p. 165)

> *Richard A. Wertime, "Psychic Vengeance in 'Last Exit to Brooklyn'," in* Literature and Psychology *(© Morton Kaplan 1974), Vol. XXIV, No. 4, 1974, pp. 153-66.*

Hubert Selby's third novel ["The Demon"] by all odds [is] his most ludicrous to date. Ambitious young Harry White is not your ordinary cocksure hero, but possessed of a Major Sexual Urge. These things, as we know, are parceled out unfairly at birth. When Harry exchanges glances with a woman, the game is up. His every seduction is instant, hassle-free and assembly-line dull. In bed of course he outperforms all imaginable husbands. Faithful followers of "Playboy" will recognize the archetype. But there's a grand surprise in store for the thoughtful reader: Harry becomes the *victim* of his awesome urge, get it? Poor Harry must leave his baseball game, after scoring what proves to be the winning run, so that his demon can score another in bed. How's that for an original *donnée*?

Eventually it dawns on our hero, for he's not dumber than an ox, that he'd better cut out the skirt-chasing if he ever means to succeed with the Boss. Most readers will look forward to this change, if only for relief from a steady diet of such phrases as "they frolicked and cavorted until they finally went seepy seepy bye bye." Relief never comes, naturally, because (a) Harry is possessed by his demon beyond all salvation and (b) Selby's prose is equally hopeless. Such inchoate groping used to be excused as "hard-hitting" but is nowadays (on the dust jacket) "written from the gut with great compassion." Certainly none for the reader. (p. 68)

When our hero turns sadist and criminal, as we know he must—all who succumb to the demon of lust invariably do—the change again fails to surprise. He has simply reverted to type—to the snarling, suffering, sado-masochistic underground man that has always been Selby's real hero. Harry White, it turns out, is really Harry Black from the "Strike" story in "Last Exit to Brooklyn" after all the veneers of phony conventionality and sublimated impulse are stripped away.

This solemn farce comes equipped with moral gestures: two biblical epigraphs to start and no end of Christian symbolizing at the close, complete with hounds of heaven, a crucifixion (you'll never guess what Sunday) and cries to a silent God. The real moral, however, lies in the obsessive grossness of Selby's style. No wit, irony, qualification, contingency, credibility, subtlety, social or moral complexity appears to distract the monologuist from his dreary exercise. (p. 69)

> *Dean Flower, in* The New York Times Book Review *(© 1976 by The New York Times Company; reprinted by permission), November 14, 1976.*

*   *   *

SENDER, Ramón   1902-

Sender is a prolific but uneven Spanish novelist whose literary reputation is still being appraised. He has progressed through many literary styles and trends, from social realism to more experimental forms of writing. He became enmeshed early in his career with the political and social problems of pre-civil war Spain. After fighting on the side of the republicans, Sender moved to the United States, where he took up citizenship. (See also *Contemporary Authors*, Vols. 5-8, rev. ed.)

The mysterious "presence" that lurks behind commonplace existence has had a special attraction for Ramón J. Sender, who, though transplanted to American soil, remains one of the leading contemporary Spanish novelists. Years before Existentialism had become a recognized movement in France Sender was experimenting in the novel with the notion that the heart of human reality is concealed in a nonrational and phantomlike quality (*Orden público* [1931] and *Siete domingos rojos* [1932], for example) which, despite its elusiveness, is a force immediately at hand. Bolder—and less organized—than the French in his expression of ideas, and less dedicated to novelistic technique as a goal in itself, he evinces a lusty primitivism whose existentialist affinity is an aspect rather than a systematic trend of thought. His writings therefore should not be viewed with the strict interpretation of Existentialism, which is possible in Sartre's case. (p. 234)

Sender . . . often leaves us with the impression that he is trying to fathom the *mysterium tremendum* of an inscrutable Deity. Unquestionably he considers it his literary responsibility to demonstrate the "primordial vision," as Jung puts it, that leads the poet to pry into the mystery and chaos, the land of demons and gods that lies beyond the ordered world of reason. Moreover, he appears willing to fulfill his poetic mission instinctively, but his reflective self compels him at the same time to rebel at the thought of losing his "freedom" in a vicious circle that leads inevitably to the realm of death, which a person supposedly realizes himself in his own ruination. Hence the subject of mortality is one of his major preoccupations. (p. 237)

> *Sherman H. Eoff, in his* The Modern Spanish Novel *(reprinted by permission of New York University Press; copyright © 1961 by New York University), New York University Press, 1961.*

Sender is a novelist with philosophical inclinations. As such he is interested in seeking explanations behind reality—not only the reality of Spain of his day, but of human existence, as well. (pp. 168-69)

An examination of Sender's first novel reveals, under literary symbols, that he discovered in the worst of situations and people a small light shining in the midst of the surrounding darkness of chaos and cruelty. This note is his saving grace; it pervades and becomes the touchstone of all his major works; it is also the starting point for the philosophical system which he develops and continually reelaborates in succeeding editions of *La Esfera* (1947). (p. 169)

Sender, revolutionary in temperament from youth, quite naturally assimilated the anticlerical spirit of the leftist groups which he joined. There also can be no doubt that his great personal tragedies [the loss of both his brother and wife to Fascist firing squads]—in the shadow of official Catholic alliance with the insurgents—intensified his anticlericalism. (pp. 170-71)

Sender's works tend to fall into two general classifications: works before and during the [Spanish] Civil War, and works after. The earlier group evokes the fights, illusions and hardships of his fellow Spaniards before and during the Republic. *Contraataque* reflects the agonizing pain of that war. His later works reveal a continual philosophic evolution and search for values in the twentieth century world of turmoil. As would be expected, anticlericalism is found, particularly in his earlier period, although it is not entirely absent—at least by indirection—in his later work. (p. 172)

[Sender] criticizes the clergy in . . . historical and political contexts. . . . Yet, the author is clear-minded enough to distinguish between clericalism and religion. "We had the Church to face," he writes. "But that does not mean that people of religious spirit were our enemies." But Sender goes farther than Barea, who gives the impression, despite his bitterness, that the clergy's greatest fault was their failure to understand and adapt to changing times. In other passages in *Contraataque* Sender makes a closer cause-and-effect relationship between the intrinsic nature of the Church in Spanish history and the present social woe. He speaks of "the contribution of religious education to class cynicism, which is the major bulwark of fascism." He mentions the "necessity to guarantee political liberties and unwind the tentacles of the Church from the popular organs of power." (pp. 172-73)

In *El Rey y la Reina (The King and the Queen),* published in 1947, a conversation between Rómulo and the Duchess highlights the employer class in their relationships with the workers. . . . In *El Epitalamio del Prieto Trinidad (Dark Wedding)* published in 1942 there are various passages which, if taken at face value, cast the clergy in an unfavorable light. In general, however, there is not as much strict treatment of anticlericalism as can be found, for example, in Pérez Galdós, Blasco Ibáñez, or Pío Baroja. Sender, rather, accepts the anticlerical standpoint of the older authors and devotes more time to his psychological evaluation of himself or his characters and his philosophic preoccupations with the world of experience.

In the works of the Republican era, Sender's treatment of priests is very harsh. The young boy, Pepe, in *Crónica del Alba (Chronicle of Early Youth,* 1942), who largely represents Sender himself, shys away in horror from the repulsive priest who sought to proselytize him. The priest taken prisoner in *Contraataque* is a gibbering idiot. Another priest taken prisoner and released to fight with the Loyalists is commended as he begins to shed the deportment of his calling and seek secular freedom and the company of women. (pp. 173-74)

The author's distinction between anti-religion and anti-clericalism has been noted. Nevertheless, anti-religious passages of an ultimate blasphemous nature can be found in certain of his works, particularly in the important novel *Siete Domingos Rojos (Seven Red Sundays),* which was published in 1932. The book is the extreme expression of anticlericalism in its most virulent form. It is also difficult to conceive of anything more blasphemous. In creating this novel Sender draws heavily upon the Spanish revolutionary *milieu,* which he knew so well. (p. 174)

In the tumultuous pages of the novel Sender's characters run the gamut of revolutionary types: communists, socialists, syndicalists, anarchists, and their various subdivisions. Their common denominator is their anarchical drive and it is here that the author probes most deeply. Within this drive also is found the anticlericalism—if such is still the word. Here can be seen also the historical truth of the words of Leo XIII and other modern Popes who admitted that the social outcasts and certain segments of the working class had been completely, hopelessly lost to religion (and its civilizing influences). In *Siete Domingos Rojos* the Church, in the mind of the Revolutionaries, is identified completely with the worst and most ruthless elements of reaction. The book is peppered with anti-religious refrains on the folkloric level in the age-old ballad line. The priesthood and everything religious are treated with a cavalier picaresque vulgarity. But the climax is reached in a frenzied "anti-litany" of blasphemy. (pp. 175-76)

[Although] Sender's personal anticlericalism differs considerably from that of his revolutionary characters, I believe there has been some deep connection between the origin of the anti-religious spirit and Sender's own religio-philosophic searching. In the minds of the anarchists, religion and the forces of oppression, repression, and reaction are completely identified. In Sender's mind religion and the Church are continually probed and tested as vehicles of truth and answers to the deeper needs of humanity. Sender's most frequent answer is at most further doubt.

This probing can be seen, for example, in *The King and the Queen* where both Rómulo and the Duchess speak to some extent for Sender. At the beginning of the tale both accept the Church. The Duchess is hardly an ascetic; she does not object to occasional dalliance and confesses regularly. Later, however, chaos has broken loose and the supposedly Church-centered civilization is shaken to its foundation. The function of religion becomes a source of meditation to her in her long hours of seclusion. The confusion in her mind is a microcosmic reflection of the larger contemporary picture—man wandering in desperate search of values in a landscape shattered by violent clashes: "Who could make me take anything that we're seeing and hearing seriously? God? God who made the world what it is, God who tolerates all the horror we know about, and then after tolerating it exacts not only admiration for what he's made but adoration, too? How can you yield to a divinity like that?" (pp. 177-78)

Sender's religio-philosophic questionings have continued in many recent novels. Successive revisions of *La Esfera* show a pantheistic monism of a self-sufficient universe. Personal immortality is replaced by the immortality of mankind of which the individual is but a part. The woman symbolizing the light shining in the midst of darkness is Sender's conviction of humanity's ability, within this framework, to realize its own potentialities. Frankly eclectic, this philosophy offers nothing new beyond the author's enthusiastic experience of its evolution within him. (p. 179)

Mosén Millán [the priest who is a central character in the novel *Mosén Millán*] represents the clerical class and/or the classes associated with the old order—any old order, for the author in this work is not overly specific about time and place. Paco [the other central figure in the novel] represents mankind, especially the hardworking poor. Mosén had willingly devoted his long life to hard service in caring for the spiritual needs of people like Paco. Paco, for his part, had helped Mosén Millán and had been on very good terms with him. But in the end Mosén betrays Paco. He does it half unwittingly, but he does it. The betrayal stems from the weakness of the class he represents rather than from his own character. Sender implies that it was inevitable that he would betray Paco. The reason seems to lie in the fact that the priest seeks God in the abstract rather than in the hearts of his flesh and blood brother. . . .*Mosén Millán* is a modern morality piece. (pp. 180-81)

[Considering] the author's philosophical history, the [character of the lay] brother [in *Hipogrifo Violento*] can easily be interpreted as a symbol of the author's pantheistic humanity of which the individual is a passing expression. And Pepe's contact with the brother can be taken as symbolic of the boy's penetration into the core of living human reality. Furthermore, the *lego* [lay brother] fashions holy images and then prays fervently to them. His faith is indeed convincing. But, once again, given the spectrum of Sender's tendencies, the faith seems to symbolize humanity wandering in the wilderness of the universe and erecting images to a personal god who is needed but does not exist. Or, possibly, Sender simply feels God's absence more than his presence?

It is evident that Sender cannot escape from the claims that Christianity and religion make upon his whole being. They pursue him; they lurk in every corner of his superb imagination. The liturgy of the Church emerges in inverted form as blasphemy when he describes an anarchistic *milieu*. The attitudes of Christian charity and the interior life flow from his pen with the ease of long familiarity, whatever their intended symbolism. Like so many Spaniards he appears to be a God-seeker. Or again, he could be included among the thinkers whom the German Catholic critic, Karl Pfleger, called "Wrestlers with Christ" (*Geister die um Christus Ringen*). Violence and polemic in Sender's later work have mellowed into a sort of galdosian humanism. But the last lines of the surpassingly beautiful poem concluding *Hipogrifo* read ambiguously as follows:

> Oh God, great shadow of name,
> At times propitious or adverse,
> See how your absence illumines
> The cornice of the universe.
>
> (pp. 182-83)

John Devlin, "Ramón Sender," in his Spanish Anticlericalism: A Study in Modern Alienation *(copyright © 1966 by Las Americas Publishing Co.), Las Americas, 1966, 168-83.*

Iman, whose English translation is "magnet," is important not only as Sender's first novel, but also because in style and human content it accurately foreshadows the prolific Senderian novelistic production of the next four decades. Even today it remains as one of Sender's very finest novels. (p. 45)

The narrative [of *Pro Patria* (English translation of *Iman*)] falls into three major divisions: I, the Camp—The Relief; II, Annual—The Catastrophe; and III, Escape—War—Discharge—The Peace of the Dead. Part I . . . sets the tone and atmosphere for the rest of the novel; from the outset a vivid picture of the filth, rigors, privations, injustices and boredom of life in camp R., an outpost of Annual, is painted. There is an implied protest against the uselessness and senselessness of the campaign. Though the book begins with Antonio (Sender), a sergeant present at R. [the ficticious camp which is the scene of the novel], narrating in the first person, it soon introduces Viance, the Spanish private who then starts telling his own story. Later an omniscient author intervenes; most of the rest of the story is told by him in the third person, although there are occasional brief returns to first-person narrative by both Viance and Antonio. But the novel is always Viance's story. Some critics have criticized this shifting of narrative points of view, calling it confusing. In this respect it seems to have anticipated the trend during the last decade to write novels with changing points of view and perspective. (p. 47)

Viance is both an individual soldier and a symbol of the Spanish underprivileged masses, the *pueblo*. Though his inner resentment against the injustices and abuses to his dignity as a human being that he had suffered in the army made him assume an outward appearance of indifference, and even stupidity, he was, all things considered, a truly admirable human being, sound in body and mind. There is a parallel between the treatment meted out to Viance by his officers and the treatment of the Spanish lower classes by the upper classes through the centuries. It is in this implied parallel between Viance and the Spanish people that the element of social protest in the book is most clearly seen.

Pro Patria is not a pacifist book; its protest is not so much against war in general as it is against the Spanish Moroccan War in particular and its general mismanagement by the Spanish Government. (pp. 48-9)

The book's social protest is implicit from the events and action of the novel itself, and not superimposed artificially by the comments of the author except for an occasional lapse, intentional or otherwise. (p. 49)

[One] sees in *Pro Patria* the sure hand of Sender the novelist: a direct, sober, verbal style, an impersonal distancing of the author from the work, the same grim—sometimes gruesome—humor present even in his latest novels, the same interweaving of objective and subjective realities to create the novel's own private world, the harshest of realistic detail alongside lyrical and metaphysical fantasy, the flight into delirium and dreams which sometimes cast a surrealistic spell over the action, and the everpresent probing of ultimate reality, mystery. Sender does not write with what one may call elegance. . . . (pp. 49-50)

The fusion of external reality with Viance's inner, subjective world . . . is typical of the entire novel, as well as the haunting question of human guilt. (p. 50)

The novel's somber note is occasionally relieved by Sender's wry and grim humor, an ambivalent humor close to tears. . . .

In his later works, notably in *The Sphere*, . . . Sender tends to look "downward" to man's instinctive nature as the basis for the truly human rather than "upward" to what might be called a spiritual realm. In a broad sense his view is Pantheistic and he makes a great deal of what might be called the natural unity of all created objects. . . . [Viance's] musings serve as a counterweight to the demonic brutality of the novel besides impregnating it occasionally with a poetic-philosophical glow which adds interest and perspective. (pp. 51-2)

Pro Patria is not a documentary novel, but it does have documentary value; it also has dignity and true distinction as literature. It is a story of death, death to the Spanish *pueblo*, physical and moral; the sacrifice of Spain's finest resource, its common people, upon the altar of the false patriotism and the economic interests of its ruling classes. In the end Viance breaks national boundaries, becoming a universal symbol of the common man as victim of injustice and man's inhumanity to man. (p. 52)

Apart from its literary merits [*Seven Red Sundays*] is of notable importance as a serious probing of the motives of the Spanish revolutionaries, an unveiling of the mind of the Spanish anarchists, syndicalists, communists, and socialists of the early thirties. (p. 53)

Despite . . . the book's intense probing of the inner motives of the revolutionaries, a balanced probing which reveals both the sublime and the ridiculous, the true and the false, the intelligent and the stupid among the strikers and Sender's disavowal of a moral purpose for it, *Seven Red Sundays* in its totality constitutes a clear affirmation of revolutionary values. (p. 55)

The atmosphere of crisis of the uprising is to some extent reflected in the very form of the novel. There is a constant shifting of narrative points of view, especially during the first half of the book. . . . (pp. 55-6)

On balance it appears that though the novel's structure may have weakened the sharp delineation of characters, narrative thrust and other "novelistic elements," it has gained in other ways, in ways which are in consonance with the author's intention to communicate artistically "a human truth of the most generous kind". . . . Sender succeeds in capturing the atmosphere and the spirit of the revolution, imbuing it at times with a lyrical dimension. The root or the essence of the revolution seems to be what Samar calls "this longing to live which oppresses us and always will oppress us". . . . (p. 57)

Sender uses external or ordinary reality in *Seven Red Sundays* as a solid base of operations, as a kind of trampoline from which to launch his leaps to "higher" realities. The chapter in which the moon becomes a character is an example of unrestrained imagination which clearly violates the usual norms for a "realistic" work; the talking moon brings to mind the fantasies in *Paradox, Rey (Paradox, King)* by Pío Baroja. The "realism" of *Seven Red Sundays* is a strange fusion of ordinary reality with other "realities," imaginative "realities" that sometimes add an intellectual dimension, at others a lyrical or metaphysical overtone. (p. 59)

Mr. Witt, a slightly bald Victorian English gentleman of fifty-three and a consulting engineer in the naval arsenal at Cartagena, and his vivacious Spanish wife, Milagritos, thirty-five, are certainly among Sender's finest literary creations. They are characterized [in *Mr. W. H. Among the Rebels*] with consummate skill. Their story is intrinsically intermeshed with the broader scene of violent social upheaval. The contrast in character and temperament between Mr. Witt and Milagritos is sustained throughout the novel and becomes an admirable study in human psychology but never an end in itself, never divorced from the story of the revolution. (p. 60)

The narrative point of view is that of an omniscient author. The story is unified around two poles: Mr. Witt and the revolution. Scenes shift from inside the Englishman's cozy home, symbolic of Mr. Witt's isolation, to the great outside world where catastrophic events transpire, events which are at times observed by Mr. Witt from the balcony of his house. The "street" enters his home daily with the return of Milagritos from her activities as a medical aide. With an admirable economy of words Sender achieves a well-rounded impression of the revolution—its leaders, its proletarian flavor, its confusion, its weaknesses, its enthusiasms, its brutality and suffering, its heroism and greatness of spirit. Its realism is almost total. Mr. Witt the Englishman gives to the novel a note of detached objectivity which acts as a counterweight to what might otherwise have emerged as an excessively subjective portrayal of a popular uprising. (p. 62)

In its notes of retroactive social protest [*The Word Became Sex (Theresa of Jesus)*] is typical of Sender; the social climate and historical reality of the period are well recreated through the story of Theresa and her family. A heavy reliance is made on dialogue, and there are occasional passages of poetic prose of high literary quality.

O.P. (orden público) (O.P. [Public Order]), published in 1931 . . . , was the first of three Senderian novels which the author, from a post-Civil War perspective, named the *Términos del Presagio (Terms of the Presage)* trilogy. The other two books of the series are: *Viaje a la aldea del crimen (Trip to the Village of Crime)* and *La noche de las cien cabezas (The Night of One Hundred Heads)*, both published in 1934.

These novels, according to Sender, are an expression "rather direct and concrete—rather substantial, of a time that was critical for the immediate future of Spain, and form a presage "dull or clever, simple or brilliant" of events which followed their publication. (p. 64)

O.P. (Public Order), inspired by the author's experiences as a political prisoner for three months in 1927 in Madrid's Model Jail, has no plot; it merely relates in a haphazard manner—reminiscent of Baroja—of what the Journalist (Sender) observed and experienced during his imprisonment. The narrative point of view shifts from the Journalist to that of the Wind to that of an omniscient author. (pp. 64-5)

As a novel *Public Order* is second rate, its literary quality uneven. With the exception of the Journalist, none of the prisoners seems to be a living person. Real narrative drive is lacking. The author's method is more descriptive than narrative, more subjective than objective, and there is little humor. The book does, however, succeed in communicating vividly what has been felt by Sender during his imprisonment. As testimonial literature of a phase of Spanish life it is noteworthy. (p. 65)

Although noteworthy for its lucid and flowing style, *Trip to the Village of Crime* is valuable primarily as an exposé of feudalistic conditions prevailing in rural Spain in modern times. . . .

The third member of the triad of novels which Sender later baptized as the *Terms of the Presage* trilogy is *La noche de las cien cabezas (The Night of One Hundred Heads)*, 1934. Its subtitle, *Novela del tiempo en delirio (Novel of Time in Delirium)*, suggests its tendency to fantasy and allegory. (p. 66)

Although *The Night of One Hundred Heads* presents a brilliant and penetrating vision of Spanish life and contains most of Sender's favorite themes, it falls short as a novel. Except for the first two of its twenty-eight chapters it has little narrative interest. Characterization is almost exclusively fragmentary caricature. (p. 67)

Sender's deep faith in the value of man *simply because he is man* is nowhere more clearly seen than in *A Man's Place*. . . . The novel is a parable of the human condition. Sabino [the novel's central character] is representative man; the upheavals attendant upon both his absence from society and his subsequent return to that society suggest that, despite appearances, man—individual man—is of transcendental importance. To deny him his rightful "place" in life is to tempt the fates. . . . Though specific evils in the Spanish social structure are revealed in the novel, the work must be taken also as an indictment of man's inhumanity to man in general.

The style is simple; direct narration (with a minimum of description, secondary characters, and commentary) recreates vividly the scenes and flavor of the Spanish milieu in which the action occurs. (pp. 70-1)

[*Chronicle of Dawn*] is one of Sender's best novels. Its vision of life, seen through the imagination of [the character] Pepe, achieves a lyrical and very human dimension. Its sense of life is austere, yet balanced with elements of dry humor. The realistic and the romantic find a balance. (p. 75)

Requiem is a superbly written short novel, or novelette. Its tone throughout is sober and subdued. Its unity is almost absolute. Its style is straightforward narrative and lucid. Its portrayal of Spanish village life is memorable and accomplished with surprising economy. Its humor, the rough humor of the country folk it portrays, is noteworthy and contributes balance and spice. Its psychological realism in the characterization of Mosén Millán is the work of a man who deeply knows human nature. The periodic interpolation of fragments from the ballad is like a musical counterpoint to the priest's tortured memories, and together with those memories (in which past and present fuse) creates a third plane of time, an atemporal one, writes Peñuelas. Through the ballad a mythical dimension to the story becomes visible. (p. 80)

Any critical evaluation of *The Sphere* . . . runs a double risk: On the one hand it becomes easy to analyze the work too closely as though it were a philosophical treatise, forgetting, in other words, that it is a novel, not an essay, and that the author must be given an artist's license to leave loose ends and unresolved problems; on the other hand, though the author must be allowed freedom as a literary artist, we have a right to expect of him a substantial and intelligible "message," more, in other words, than the mere playing with words and concepts. We demand that he fuse content and form into a coherent artistic unity. From the first Sender obviously felt that the book's content was of vital significance; in the Prologue to its first edition he wrote that he was offering his readers "the secret mechanism of giving myself"; that he had discovered immortality (an immortality that "is neither a product of differentiation nor of individualization"), and that he wished to tell others about his discovery so that his "faith might serve as a reactive leading them to the same notions." . . . Sender's concepts [in the novel] go beyond moral and metaphysical philosophy to involve a theory of God, of Ultimate or Absolute Reality. The "mystical planes" which the work tries to suggest, as Sender says, are both poetic and religious; to him poetry and religion, in the ultimate analysis, are one and the same. (p. 84)

Sender's philosophical perspective, his persistent effort to see life calmly and to see it whole, is seen in the very title of the book, *The Sphere*, a metaphor of the author's monistic conception of total reality. (p. 87)

A preoccupation with the reconciliation of apparent opposites such as life and death, love and hate, into higher unities or syntheses here called "spheres," has been a constant in Sender's literary production. (p. 88)

An important facet of Sender's "spherical" theories is his peculiar antithesis, "man" and "person". . . .

In *The Sphere* man is viewed as a dichotomy: "man" and "person." "Man and person are antipodal," Sender writes in the passage preceding Chapter V. . . . Man "is the source of all truth, of each universal and innate truth". . . . The "person" is man's mask, the individualization of his personality which begins at birth, or soon thereafter, and grows throughout life; loosely speaking, it is man's self-consciousness. The basic question posed by Sender in *The Sphere*, according to Sherman Eoff is: "Does one's self-consciousness have meaning as a separate reflective entity, or is it significant only as identified with a vast undying and unthinking 'world spirit'?" (p. 89)

Sender has, in effect, deified what he refers to as *el hombre* ("man") or *hombría* ("manhood" or "man-ness"), a mystical essence which gives every man his true worth. (p. 90)

Since man is "an integral part of *the infinite intellect of God*," any offense to the human species, even to an individual member of that species, becomes essentially an offense to God Himself. . . . This exaltation of man for the simple fact that he is human is a constant in all of Sender's work. . . . (p. 91)

[Sender's] humanism is perhaps most distinctive in its radical reaction against the excessive individualization of people in Western European industrialized cultures in this century especially, an individualization that has isolated the individual and led to a growing depersonalization of life. Sender's attitude is seen in [the novel's main character] Saila's rejection of the "person" in favor of that part of him which is one with all other men—at the deep level of the mystically corporate man. A new morality, collectivist or corporate in nature rather than individualistic . . . can be built upon Sender's theory of "man" and "person." (pp. 92-3)

Sender's whole novelistic production has been written "against a background of eternity": death has been a constant preoccupation, almost an obsession, with [him]. He has dealt with the subject of death more extensively, more profoundly, and more artistically than have any of his Spanish contemporaries. (p. 93)

The fundamental thesis of *The Sphere*, that death does not exist, is based directly on the "man-person" dichotomy. . . . Death is the person, that growing individualization of the human being which differentiates and isolates him from all other men, which takes him farther and farther away from his eternal substance, the subterranean man. (pp. 93-4)

The dramatic tension of *The Sphere*, as it is in all of Sender's fiction, is . . . between two worlds: the one of relative appearances, of the conscious, conventional, rationalistic, unauthentic person imprisoned by the physical world and a positivist turn of mind *versus* the world of divine disorder, the unconscious and absolute world of dreams, of the passionate and natural (or authentic) man. Sender seeks ever to write in the twilight zone where these two "worlds" or "hemispheres" merge. . . . (pp. 97-8)

On almost every page of the novel one finds what might be termed a "reversal of values." The unconscious is preferred over the conscious; intuition over reason; the ganglia over the brain; abstract "man" over the concrete, individual person; death over life; potential knowledge over actual knowledge; dream over apparent reality; eternity over temporality; mystery over clarity; a state of anarchy over a state of law and order, etc. The relative devaluation of the apparent, everyday world of order and logic in which we usually live is a necessary corollary of the book's passionate exaltation of the unconscious or underlying world of disorder, dreams, and irrational forces. Indeed, the true adventure of *The Sphere* can only be understood as Saila's exploration of the underworld, his plunge to the bottom of the unknown, the unconscious, the abyss, the ganglionic world, in order to decipher the mysteries of life. . . .

A constant in Sender's total work, and a key to his *Weltanschauung*, is his belief in the almost all-powerful role of the unconscious, both individual and collective, in determining man's fate. (p. 100)

The frontier between the individual and the universal totality in Sender's novel becomes, of necessity, shrouded in impenetrable mystery. To seek to "clarify" the mechanics of the relation of the individual and the universal in this dark area would be to do so only in a verbal, rather than actual, sense. The purpose of the novel—I quote . . . from Sender's foreword to the definitive edition—"is more illuminative than constructive, and attempts to suggest mystical planes on which the reader may build his own structures". (pp. 102-03)

A secondary theme of *The Sphere* is Saila's rejection of traditional morality. On the one hand he spurns all moral absolutes as conceived by the Judeo-Christian background of Western European culture and civilization (a prescriptive morality), and on the other hand he rejects a morality which is merely the consensus of what is for the common good at different times and places, an ethics, in other words, determined by a headcount (a descriptive morality). (p. 103)

The principal philosophical objection to Saila's brand of "morality" is that it is a personal, subjective view of "right" and "wrong"; it is, therefore, entirely relative and like a mystical experience or a drug "trip," essentially incapable of being adequately communicated to others. A major difficulty lies in *how* we are to determine what the real interests of the species are in practical, concrete situations. (p. 104)

After all his rationalizations are finished, Saila still doubts. This, of course, is typical of Sender; he always evinces a questioning, ambivalent view toward reality, never dogmatizing (despite his appearance of doing so). Throughout the novel there is the dialectic of reason versus intuition: "Reason told him no, and his ganglia yes". . . . The synthesis at which Sender arrives is always a tentative "perhaps.". . . .

The Sphere is an ambitious attempt to fuse into an artistic unity the realistic, the lyrical-metaphysical, the fantastic, and the symbolic. Has Sender succeeded? Only to a limited extent. The narrative framework is inadequate to carry the excessively heavy charge of poetic, philosophical, and symbolic meaning. The narrative element can move only sluggishly in its labyrinth of levels, dimensions, and meanings. (p. 105)

> *Charles L. King, in his* Ramón J. Sender *(copyright © 1974 by Twayne Publishers, Inc.; reprinted with the permission of Twayne Publishers, A Division of G. K. Hall & Co., Boston), Twayne, 1974.*

* * *

SEXTON, Anne   1928-1974

An American poet whose work is often termed "confessional," Sexton combines in her poetry self-realization with autobiography. Her first book of verse, *To Bedlam and Part Way Back*, was highly acclaimed for its candid discussion of mental illness as well as its powerful imagery. Sexton was awarded the Pulitzer Prize in 1967 for *Live or Die*. (See also CLC, Vols. 2, 4, 6, and *Contemporary Authors*, 1-4, rev. ed.; obituary, Vols. 53-56.)

[Anne Sexton's] poems have a beleaguered and desperate honesty about them. Short on thought, long on sensation, they flog the reader into feeling. Many [in *All My Pretty Ones*] are manifestly autobiographical, and almost all sound so. If Denise Levertov's poems are obsessed with the present moment, Anne Sexton's cannot escape the vertical pronoun: the "I" is everywhere. Yet she is faithful as a poet, faithful to her own feelings, to the terrible ambiguities of imagination, to the grim joy to be taken in facts. She shows her worst habits when she goes overboard into hallucination without control; but when controlled, hallucination becomes in her hands a way of illuminating the dark recesses of existence.

Anne Sexton's first book, *To Bedlam and Part Way Back,* was a loose series of poems describing a mental breakdown and recovery. The autobiographical poems in this second book continue the story yet reveal a greater breadth of style and mood, a diversity of imagination which in the end give the second book a stronger unity. One long poem, called "The Operation," is absolutely superb. Its unflinching candor, clarity, matter-of-factness set a standard which is almost unrivaled in contemporary verse. (p. 87)

Yet no other poem in the volume approaches this height, and many suffer from sheer excess, as though the poet were straining every sense to try to identify with her subject matter.... A poem ... overshoots its mark when it slips beyond the purity of horror into the incongruity of self-consciousness. Too often, the author reaches so far for the striking simile that she makes the reader uncomfortably conscious of the "I" behind the poems—not the "I" of the sufferer but the "I" of the artificer. (p. 88)

> *Peter Davison, in* The Atlantic Monthly *(copyright © 1962 by The Atlantic Monthly Company, Boston, Mass.; reprinted with permission), November, 1962.*

There are no agreeable fantasies in Anne Sexton's *Death Notebooks* but only a remorselessly American earnestness which can all too easily set up counter-currents of exasperation in the reader. Where other members of this death-affirming Look-I-have-not-come-through school have had either the irony (Berryman) or the verbal brilliance (Plath) to make the reader want to come back and read again, Anne Sexton simply hands over her tribulations and bids for our sympathy. Sylvia Plath in her last extremity exposed herself to us without caring, but Sexton exhibits herself and her despair with a carefully judged hollow cheerfulness which reduces in the end to a kind of defiant self-pity. One feels—and experiences with her while reading—her crippling self-consciousness, her alienation from her own feelings and most of life's normalities, her inability to move beyond her own childhood, her life like a series of garments none of which fitted—and one hears the fast-talking desperation with which these deadnesses are catalogued, the only relief coming in moments of brittle and bitter wit: one feels these things, and it almost seems like knowing someone who has died; and one does sympathise. But one also feels that the story, when one finally gets to the end of it, is told, and that without some very special personal reason it would be almost unnatural to want to go back and read it again. (p. 62)

> *Colin Falck, in* The New Review *(© The New Review Ltd., 11 Greek Street, London W1V, 5LE), August, 1975.*

The irony of Sexton's poetry is often bathetically broad.... Also, as is often the case in Plath, Sexton will echo the language of children and children's games ... in an attempt to suggest the broken world of childhood myth, a land where ego differentiation and fears of separation and dissolution are pervasively threatening. Sexton wrote a book, *Transformations,* that retold the Mother Goose stories with a coarse irony, and the cyclical, almost litany-like structure of much of Sexton's and Plath's poetry mimics

the semi-hypnotic patter of children's rhymes and songs. (pp. 167-68)

But seldom is Sexton ... successful in generating a child-like playful tone, and often the histrionic, prosaic language keeps her poetry from having the artistic "rightness" of Plath or Berryman, and her reliance on a flattening irony ("that/will be that") becomes increasingly less rigorous. In a sense she was from the first the most "confessional" of the four poets discussed here [W. D. Snodgrass, Plath, John Berryman, Sexton], if by that word we mean a commitment to recording as directly as possible the shape of private pain and intimate sickness, without regard to artifice or aesthetic transcendence. If Plath seems to exhaust the verbal possibilities of the exacerbated sensibility, Sexton bears witness, perhaps unwittingly, to the same exhaustion at the level of subject matter, as one more psychotic episode, one more terminally ill relative, one more horrendous familial crisis becomes just another trauma. On a shelf of such horrors as her books present, it becomes impossible to find a title or a line that will rivet us, and finally the poetry is read more out of a duty to listen to the maimed than out of a sense of discovery or artistic energy, let alone tragedy. The public clutching of her awkward language becomes its own reproach. (pp. 174-75)

> *Charles Molesworth, in* Twentieth Century Literature *(copyright 1976, Hofstra University Press), May, 1976.*

However genuine the anguish [in "45 Mercy Street"], its rendition here raises large questions about the esthetic possibilities of raw confession in poetry. How, for instance, can one properly respond to lines as grotesquely uncontrolled as these?

> ... having ripped the cross off Jesus
> and left only the nails,
> Husband,
> Husband,
> I hold up my hand and see
> only nails.

Or, in a different vein,

> The moth, grinning like a pear,
> or is it teeth
> clamping the iron maiden shut?

Sentimentalism, by a common handbook definition, means "an overindulgence in emotion, especially the conscious effort to induce emotion in order to analyze or enjoy it; also the failure to restrain or evaluate emotion through the exercise of the judgment." In Anne Sexton's earlier books, imagery and poetic action often served to restrain and evaluate ... with a precision of observation and association that transcends simple self-pity. Some of the lyrics in ["To Bedlam and Part Way Back," 1960, her] first book remain undiminished in vigor and freshness, their material a kind of experience conventionally kept private, their technique demonstrating the author's awareness not only of such immediate and obvious precursors as Robert Lowell but of older poetic and religious traditions and of a world outside the self.... The second book too ("All My Pretty Ones," 1962) has its telling moments, particularly when the poet functions as observer ("Woman With Girdle," "Housewife") rather than self-devouring subject of the work. The title poem, accepting the discipline of rhyme and of closely-observed detail, keeps emotional extravagance in check; other pieces occasionally manage moments of epigrammatic economy.

But even these first volumes lapse frequently into bathos, betraying an apparent incapacity for self-criticism either moral or esthetic, and such lapses multiply as the career continues. In a sense, Anne Sexton can be seen as a victim of an era in which it has become easy to dramatize self-indulgence, stylish to invent unexpected imagery regardless of its relevance, fashionable to be a woman and as a woman to display one's misery. Her poetry became increasingly popular as it manifested increasing slovenliness.... Perhaps the mounting stress on self-loathing and self-punishment—also fashionable modes of grandiosity—helped to obscure the limitation of range, perception, accuracy, the effect of being trapped in a not-very-interesting mind with no capacity to see beyond its own insistent mirroring. Sentimentalism in both its definitions mars most of the lyrics in "Live or Die"; the conscious effort to induce emotion for its own sake, the failure to evaluate it by any rational standard.

This sentimentalism has increased, becoming painfully marked in the first posthumous volume, "The Awful Rowing Toward God" (1975), with its embarrassments of religious pretension.... The problem of internal division, the perception of divinity, the will to rebuild the soul: all alike register unconvincingly. The poetry through which these vast themes are rendered is simply not good enough.

Which brings us to "45 Mercy Street": definitively now, the poetry is not good enough. Inaccurate metaphors.... Vulgar imagery.... A disturbing repetitiousness of tone and technique pervades the book. Words like *little* and *tiny* recur again and again, part of the falsely deprecatory litany of self-pity.... [The] true and monotonous concern remains that self explicitly declared inadequate but nonetheless the speaker's only real interest.... [The] verse implicitly argues that anguish is self-justifying, neither permitting or demanding the further pain of balanced self-knowledge or the illuminations of controlled imagination and poetic technique. In life we forgive sufferers the necessities of their obsessions. In literature we must ask more: acknowledging the pain that produces such work as Anne Sexton's later poems, yet remembering that art requires more than emotional indulgence, requires a saving respect for disciplines and realities beyond the crying needs, the unrelenting appetites, of the self. (p. 6)

Patricia Meyer Spacks, in The New York Times Book Review (© *1976 by The New York Times Company; reprinted by permission),* May 30, 1976.

Though Anne Sexton unwittingly spawned hosts of execrable student imitators, though she was often an uneven poet, though we have certainly had too much foolish cult worship of suicide, still I think it unfair, uncharitable and untrue to lump Sexton with her untalented imitators and to see her excesses to the exclusion of her strengths....

Let's be fair about Sexton's poetry. She was uneven and excessive, but that was because she dared to be a fool and dared to explore the dark side of the unconscious. Sometimes she seemed to be imitating her own mannerisms, but this has happened to many American innovators—from Hemingway to Berryman. No one calls them "shrill" and "narcissistic" because they are men, and what is called "narcissism" in a woman writer is called "existential dread" in a man. The same charges of narcissism could be leveled at Whitman, at Neruda, at Ginsberg, at Lowell, at Berryman. Ours is a self-regarding age—for men writers as well as women. (p. 25)

Erica Jong, in The New York Times Book Review (© *1976 by The New York Times Company; reprinted by permission),* July 25, 1976.

* * *

SHANGE, Ntozake 1948-

Shange is an American playwright whose drama reflects the plight of black women in America. *For Colored Girls Who Have Considered Suicide/When the Rainbow Is Enuf* **can well be called staged poetry.**

The fuss that is being made over *For Colored Girls Who Have Considered Suicide/When the Rainbow Is Enuf*... is both ludicrous and pitiful. This is a sampling from a collection of prose and verse bits by a young black woman, Ntozake Shange....

For a long time, the Negro was, shockingly, the "invisible man" in our society. Now let him produce the slenderest work of quasi-art and the critics will carry on like disheveled maenads, vying to be first to perceive, proclaim and panegyrize the work and its maker. Out of enraptured pens pour white tributes to the supreme visibility of black art that is often no more visible than the Emperor's new clothes. Miss Shange's poetry is better than that of, say, Rod McKuen, and her prose is probably better than her verse. But look at her very title, complete with that simplified spelling; it is, I am afraid, indicative of the sensibility at work here....

What accounts for the production and inordinate praise of too many black plays is not so much black talent as white guilt. And what makes Miss Shange's work so alluring to white guilt feelings is that she is not only black but also a woman, so that a superlative flung at her is like a quarter dropped into the hat of a beggar who is blind, allowing the donor to feel doubly pious.... [Look] at the pathetic nonsense of it: Why should black girls, or anyone else, be saved from suicide by a rainbow, whatever that tired symbol is supposed to stand for? Is there anything more platitudinous than the image of looking into oneself to discover God, even if that God is a she, as has long been the case in a hoary homosexual joke?

Apparently this olio's special appeal is that it presents black suffering inflicted by blacks as well as whites, notably by black men on their women. Still, the sad thing about *For Colored Girls* is that it is no more theater than it is poetry; indeed, these random snatches of writing were not even intended for the stage. (p. 21)

Even as nontheatrical poetry this is feeble stuff, what used to be called wit-writing a couple of centuries ago.... At most, this is clever; more often it is merely Carl Sandburg and Edgar Lee Masters transposed and slightly updated, as in such outright banalities as "I will tell all of your secrets into your face" or "I was missing something promised".... Set this beside any decent young poet of today, and it becomes invisible....

Let me make myself clear: Playwrights, black or white, will not be helped by overpraise from critics, white or black. That this has happened, with unfortunate results, to several black authors should by now be obvious to all. (p. 22)

John Simon, "'Enuf Is Not Enough," in The New Leader (© *1976 by the American Labor Conference on International Affairs, Inc.),* July 5, 1976, pp. 21-2.

The subject [of "For Colored Girls Who Have Considered Suicide/When the Rainbow is Enuf"] is "colored girls"—their growing up, their coming of age, their initiation into the horrors of dreams trampled underfoot, thwarted love, abortion, rape, and the verbal sidewalk assault. Men come up only as they are relevant to the black woman's discovery of her own life. I sit back to enjoy the explosion of details considered irrelevant to the main action in black plays from "The Dutchman" to "Ain't Supposed to Die a Natural Death."

Using a patchwork of vignettes, rhythm & blues lyrics, dance steps, and memories, Shange gets at almost every cheap stereotype of black women and tells a more likely story—the seductress who cries herself to sleep, the exotic quadroon of the 19th century who dances in rags, the "evil" black woman who rolls her eyes at every man who speaks to her in the street because she's afraid. . . .

The ending immediately strikes me as abrupt and unsatisfying. Why has she followed such specific ethnic information about black women with a worn-out feminist cliche like, "I found god in myself," to the tune of what sounded like a Lutheran hymn? I feel a little like a marathon runner, moving at a good speed, plenty of wind left and halfway there, who has been grabbed by the well-intentioned driver of a Jaguar XKE and dragged bodily across the finish line at 110 mph. In other words, I got there first, but I didn't win.

I do not want to be misunderstood. There is so much about black women that needs retelling; one has to start somewhere, and Shange's exploration of this aspect of our experience, admittedly the most primitive (but we were all there at some time and, if the truth be told, most of us still are), is as good a place as any. All I'm saying is that Shange's "For Colored Girls" should not be viewed as the definitive statement on black women, but as a very good beginning.

Very few have ever written with such clarity and honesty about the black woman's vulnerability, and no one has ever brought Shange's brand of tough humor and realism to it. . . . Shange offers the black woman a religious conversion to self-love as a solution to her problems.

But can self-love so rapidly follow rejection? Can a celebration of self really wipe out the powerful forces of a profound self-hatred and a hostile environment? . . .

As for black people, the frenzied praise of the establishment critics seems to make them nervous. Many black women I know have told me that they loved "Colored Girls" but my friends, mostly feminist, may not reflect the general climate in this case. My suspicion is that some black women are angry because "For Colored Girls" exposes their fear of rejection as well as their anger at being rejected. They don't want to deal with that so they talk about how Shange is persecuting the black man. (p. 108)

Shange does not often write about her middle classness. She writes in the dialect of the black ghetto and of black women in poverty. "I found middle-class life terribly vacuous, incredibly boring. It just doesn't interest me, and I can't write about something that I'm not interested in." The language of her poetry comes from the live-in maids who cared for her as a child. . . .

Middle class signifies ordinary to the general culture. But among blacks, middle class means special, since ordinary for us is dirt poor. Most of our middle-class parents advanced in this world by doing what everybody around them had told them couldn't be done—damn right they were special and their kids were going to be special, too. . . .

Middle-class black women are slow to identify with each other's problems. We're all so special.

Shange is a very message-oriented writer. I've read the script of "Colored Girls" several times, and in every poem there is a pointed feminist message. . . .

Ntozake has managed to conquer the disease of specialness more than many of us, enough to write a "choreopoem" that has more than a little truth about *all* American black women, middle class, poor, or whatever, even if they do emphatically deny it. But she's not in deep enough yet. (p. 109)

> Michele Wallace, "For Colored Girls, the Rainbow Is Not Enough," in The Village Voice (reprinted by permission of The Village Voice; copyright © by The Village Voice, Inc., 1976), August 16, 1976, pp. 108-09.

Shange's theater-poetry is a vibrant celebration of woman's strength. A gallery of black women (a carnival queen, a waitress, a prostitute) who share tough exteriors and genuine vulnerability are presented in short sketches. The technique is far different from the novelistic *Sassafrass*. . . . Shange's poetry, like her characters, is bizarre, comical, and tingling with life. (p. 451)

> Booklist (reprinted by permission of the American Library Association; copyright 1976 by the American Library Association), November 15, 1976.

* * *

SHAPIRO, Karl   1913-

An American poet, critic, novelist, editor, and playwright, Shapiro is best known as the author of poetry which is, according to Alfred Kazin, "striking for its concrete but detached insights; it is witty and exact in the way it catches the poet's subtle and guarded impressions." Noted for his ability to write successfully in a great variety of poetic styles, Shapiro won the Pulitzer Prize for Poetry in 1945. (See also CLC, Vol. 4, and Contemporary Authors, Vols. 1-4, rev. ed.)

In essay and verse, [Shapiro] began stripping off the stucco, tearing out the walls and interior layouts and furnishings of the Poetry Institution, where he is a penthouse dweller to rebuild the establishment . . . in the name of life, of poetry, or the poet himself. Noble act of destruction; call it terrorism, if you will, anarchy. And it *must* mean something important when a learned artist goes ape. But what?

Reading him from the start, one sees it doesn't mean much. An American Auden, Shapiro was always facile with the image or epithet for a person, place, or thing: brightly using the modern categories of psychologism, sociologism, historicism, philosophasterism. Clever jargon that did, until Time-Life, etc. picked it up for a world language.

When Shapiro learned that the American society in which he was so successfully assimilated didn't really exist any longer, and had no persons in it (as Auden had known of England from his start, and made a poetry out of), he felt he had been betrayed. So he went "surrealist" in "The Bourgeois Poet," and did a Hashbury job on himself. But nothing's changed: he remains the brilliant commentator, the inverse of the Time anonymous staff, speaking still in his declarative, though now prose-jazzed sentences.

But it's still Shapiro writing ads for himself: funny, wild pages of talk, an endless late night talk show that hits everything but the bull's-eye of poetry itself.

Jascha Kessler, "Karl Shapiro Poetry," in The Los Angeles Times (copyright, 1968, Los Angeles Times; reprinted by permission), July 7, 1968, p. 35.

Karl Shapiro's slim new volume ["Adult Bookstore"] is best described as a graceful, playful stepchild of its mighty predecessor, "The Poetry Wreck: Selected Essays 1950-1970." . . .

I admit to liking his verse a good deal more than his prose, and the new book does nothing to change my opinion. I agree with Randall Jarrell about the "notable visual and satiric force," the "real precision, a memorable exactness of realization" in the poetry [see *CLC*, Vol. 4]. But the question at issue is not entirely what a reviewer may like but what the phenomenon Karl Shapiro has at 63 become in the poet's own eyes.

To treat "Adult Bookstore" as if he had suffered no metamorphosis since "Poems 1940-1953," as if he had never made those half-ecstatic, half-despairing pilgrimages to the shrine of Whitman at Camden and of Williams at Rutherford, N.J., and to Henry Miller on his mountain, would be a rank disservice all around. One reads the new title poem, for instance, and wonders why the devil this graphic but otherwise unremarkable evocation of a scruffy porn shop should rate the honor given it here. Until, that is, one remembers something Shapiro wrote in his essay "The Greatest Living Patagonian." "Morally," he said, "I regard Miller as a holy man, as most of his admirers do—Gandhi with a penis."

Now Shapiro has never unambiguously expressed much of this new Dionysian ardor in his verse. Except for his admirable "Adam and Eve" sequence, the "Selected Poems" are quite free of it. In an impressive new long poem, "The Rape of Philomel," he dwells with considerable feeling on its perversion. So one can only understand his horror at the porn shop by reading his prose. And in the essay "Is Poetry an American Art?" he will tell you that up to now the bulk of American poetry has *been* prose, that Whitman, as Eliot said, is our greatest prosateur, and finally that the highest compliment you can pay a man is to call him not a poet but a writer. "It bestows on a poet the keys to the kingdom; it takes him out of the realm of mere literature and installs him in the empyrean; it frees him from any of the normal ties to the world with which other men are bound; it makes him a kind of god."

Shapiro's exceptionally firm and elastic ties to the world are, however, what really set him apart, not his platform kit of thin neo-Nietzschean vitalist ideas. His best poems, including at least a dozen of the buoyant "surrealist" satires in "The Bourgeois Poet," are completely realized, spared by the demon of incompleteness who nags the essays—dangling leads, half-pursued arguments, careless snap judgments, surrenders to the vicious "principle of leadership" in modern criticism that he himself has justly condemned. But having said as much one still must acknowledge that since the early sixties poetry has often failed him as a vehicle for the utopian-prophetic dimension of his thought. We must continue to "destroy the religion of specialization" (cult of the well-made poem, the "poem of sensibility") by following the path of irony out to its bitter end. Hence a readiness to publish books like "Adult Bookstore" in the face of so much vehement homage to other sorts of writing.

But Shapiro would not be Shapiro if his long-practiced ironies failed to come across as a little more affectionate than bitter. Now, as always, his appeal rests not only on a nervously zestful embrace of the ordinary but in a gift for making the very act of writing poetry look sensible and businesslike. Remembering those other Southerners, James Dickey and A. R. Ammons, eminent connoisseurs of the quotidian all three, one can't but envy them their heaven-sent capacity for taking so much of our fevered life for granted. (p. 6)

R. W. Flint, in The New York Times Book Review (© 1976 by The New York Times Company; reprinted by permission), July 25, 1976.

*   *   *

SIMENON, Georges   1903-

Simenon is a Belgian-born French novelist who has written over two hundred novels under his own name and several pseudonyms. Best known for his detective stories featuring Inspector Maigret, all of Simenon's novels probe the psyche in search of human motivation. (See also *CLC*, Vols. 1, 2, 3.)

Georges Simenon is the classic French writer: neat, contained, fastidious and low-keyed. Every tyro could study with profit the first 26 pages of his new novel ["The House on Quai Notre Dame"], simply to see how effortlessly he starts the story turning and how intriguing he makes every scene and incident. And like a Gallic Ross Macdonald, he is at his best in conveying the sense of place in which his stories develop. When his characters speak, more is meant than said. . . .

Simenon never overwrites. Some of the pages in this book read like a series of epigrams on French small-town life. But sometimes he doesn't write enough either. In the new book he never quite explains the twin happenings with which the book starts. Such a shortcoming doesn't make his novella less diverting, but it does leave the reader with a vague and lingering sense of dissatisfaction. (p. 38)

Thomas Lask, in The New York Times Book Review (© 1975 by The New York Times Company; reprinted by permission), September 21, 1975.

This excellent psychological novel [*Maigret and the Black Sheep*] can only nominally be classified as a murder mystery, since it violates the fair-play deduction rule, and it is far too realistic to be called escapist entertainment. The suspense is extraordinary; I found it impossible to lay the book aside for the two hours it would have taken to watch *Deliverance* on television. However, what makes it well worth reading is not so much its plot as its mood, which, despite a gloomy reflectiveness, is surprisingly reassuring. It is a paradox that this story of kind, respectable, "good" M. Josselin's violent death—at the hands of a person he knew extremely well—should make us feel optimistic about human nature, but that is what Simenon's sympathetic insight achieves. His Superintendent Maigret is so thoroughly civilized . . . that his wholesomely masculine presence sets the sad but serene tone for the book. What makes Maigret perhaps the most believable of all famous fictional sleuths is that his qualities are realistically understated. Simenon makes us gradually aware of the character's intelligent fair-mindedness and unfailing courtesy—so obviously deriving not from social convention but from an instinct to do, always, the considerate thing. And it's easy to assume that

Maigret's humanism is Simenon's, because a subtle sense of love, all the more moving for its detached and unsentimental mode of expression, pervades his writing. We can feel his compassion even when he is at his most ironic. . . . (p. 462)

Steve Ownbey, in National Review *(© National Review, Inc., 1976; 150 East 35th St., New York, N.Y. 10016), April 30, 1976.*

How important a writer is Georges Simenon? The greatest storyteller of our day, a writer comparable with Balzac at least in the variety of his themes and characters? Or a marvel of industry and ingenuity who has given us each year six books that must be called production-line rather than custom-made? When one looks again at some of the huge output, the balance drops heavily in favor of the second view. . . .

The high claims made for Simenon are usually based on what he calls his "hard novels," which most of his admirers differentiate sharply from the Maigret stories. . . . Yet when one looks at the plots of these hard novels, it is clear that they spring from a long French sensational tradition and that purely in terms of plot they are like the detective novels of Gaboriau or du Boisgobey brought up to date. The art consists in making such sensational material plausible by a brilliant flatness of descriptive and physical detail, and by an insistent psychological analysis that succeeds in compelling our acceptance of what is often a preposterous situation.

"The Hatter's Phantoms" is a case in point. Six weeks before the story's opening, M. Labbé the hatter has killed his invalid wife Mathilde and buried her in the cellar. He conceals her death by taking up meals to the bedroom and then flushing them down the lavatory and manipulating a wooden head in an armchair. Also before the story begins he has killed six other women. Why? Because they were all at school with Mathilde and came to see her annually on Christmas Eve. Since Christmas is only a few weeks away, it is necessary to kill them.

Put the story like this, and one doesn't believe a word of it. (p. 4)

[The books of Simenon] that deal with the psychological pressures on individuals who are moved irresistibly to abandon the ordinary courses of their lives are undoubtedly [his] most ambitious works. The approach made in them is remarkable in showing the detachment, not so much of a recording angel as of a tape recorder. This detachment—from political and religious feeling, almost from any feeling about society—gives the stories their peculiar and memorable flavor, but it is also a limitation. The effect, in its bareness and its suppression of "literature," is that of reading a film script rather than a novel, and indeed one's reaction is often to feel, as in "The Hatter's Phantoms," that this would make a marvelous film rather than that it is a marvelous book.

Such a feeling is accentuated by the fact that Simenon has often been badly served by his translators. In "The Hatter's Phantoms" there are many slack and stock phrases and some really appalling repetitions and confusions of pronouns. . . . (p. 55)

In "Maigret and the Apparition" Inspector Lognon, who like some other members of the Maigret cast, strays over occasionally into the "hard novels," has been murdered immediately after leaving the apartment of a young woman whom he has visited constantly for some weeks. Was the painfully respectable Lognon a philanderer? Maigret investigates and uncovers an absorbingly interesting but outstandingly unlikely plot about art frauds.

On the whole I enjoy the Maigret stories more than the other books. They are less ambitious, and so run less risk of total failure, and the character of Maigret is also something more substantial than any individual figure the novels have to offer us. Simenon's maturing skills are seen most clearly in the development both of Maigret himself from the comparatively crass character of an early book like "Le Pendu de Saint-Pholien" (1931) to the slightly weary philosopher of recent years, and of the plots. The Maigret tales of the 1930's are often very ingenious, and they are convincing within the convention of the orthodox detective stories of that period, but the shift from these to the realistic plotting and psychology of many later books is considerable.

So far as one can generalize about the Maigret stories, they reached their peak during the 1940's and early 50's in books like "Mon Ami Maigret" (1949) and "Maigret et la Vieille Dame" (1953). One has to balance the increasing certainty in tone and plotting with Simenon's own evident decreasing interest in the whole series. "Maigret and the Apparition" . . . is 1964, not the best vintage but still very acceptable. It is marked by some of the tricks and short-cut devices conspicuous in the later Maigrets, like the one-sided telephone conversation used simply to convey information. (pp. 55-6)

This kind of thing, like the frequent use of conversations repeated to Maigret, is effective in one way, deadening in another. As compensation, there is an excellent verbal and psychological conflict between stolid bourgeois Maigret and an intelligent, arrogant Dutch art connoisseur. This is the kind of thing Simenon does best.

Or is it simply Maigret that Simenon does best? This mild bloodhound epitomizes a central figure in the classical detective story, the workaday detective who is doing a job, but he is surely something more than that. Maigret is the heir not only of all those plodding characters like Sergeant Cuff and Superintendent French but of something more formidable. He appears often to be a bourgeois Nemesis like Hugo's Javert. He is Simenon's most considerable creation, one in relation to whom he has permitted himself (in the brilliantly fanciful "Maigret's Memoirs") a little indulgence in that "literature" which elsewhere is so firmly suppressed. It is said that Simenon dislikes all kinds of lawyers but he respects the Law in the abstract, and Maigret is the most impressive embodiment of the Law in modern fiction. Simenon's achievement is more modest than that claimed for him by his fervent admirers, but it is still considerable. If he is not the greatest storyteller of our day, he has at least created the archetypal official detective of the 20th century. (p. 56)

Julian Symons, in The New York Times Book Review *(© 1976 by The New York Times Company; reprinted by permission), November 21, 1976.*

Letter to My Mother . . . is ostensibly a new kind of book for Simenon. . . . [However,] in one sense the newness is probably more important to Simenon than to the reader. For he is doing in *Letter to My Mother* essentially what he has always done, both in his *romans policiers*, where Maigret solves crimes not with Holmesian deduction from physical clues but rather by entering into the criminal's mind, and in his *romans psychologiques*, where the narrator begins from an established point of view and works backward and forward over time to correct his perceptions. The difference here is that the narrator is Georges Simenon, and the character whose motives he is trying to divine is his own loved-hated mother. There are, alas, other differences as well. Despite its smallness, the book is repetitive in a way that suggests it was indeed not typed but dictated: and perhaps also that its subject robbed the author of the ruthlessness essential to artistic control. . . . Those who do not know Simenon's work are advised to start elsewhere— *The Confessional,* or almost any Maigret book. However, dyed-in-the-wool Simenon fans will be interested, and I hope moved, by the real-life basis for the novelist's preoccupations. (p. 1367)

> *Linda Bridges, in* National Review *(© National Review, Inc., 1976; 150 East 35th St., New York, N.Y. 10016), December 10, 1976.*

In 1972 Georges Simenon announced that he would not write any more novels. For years, he stated, "I was dissatisfied. . . . As a result, I sought a world in which I would find a kindred soul. I tried to create this kindred soul two hundred and fourteen or two hundred and fifteen times without succeeding. And then suddenly I was happy, I felt at peace with myself, with the world, with a person who was not a character in a novel. And I no longer needed to write a two hundred and sixteenth novel." Instead of trying to work out his own problems through his fictional characters, Simenon decided to direct his efforts toward understanding himself directly, to draw from his own experiences lessons which could be of value to others. (pp. 59-60)

Lettre à ma mère . . . is a poignant inner monologue of the thoughts and emotions of Simenon during the week he spent watching his ninety-one-year-old mother die. *Un homme comme un autre,* composed of remembrances and veiled confessions, is an effort by an old man to recapture the images of his youth and to marvel at them once again. . . . Simenon discovered images he thought he had lost forever, images which became mixed with current ones. In this work Simenon was trying to relive certain episodes of his life, not to dictate his memoirs. As a result, he cites very few facts and gives no opinions. . . .

Des traces de pas, the remaining work, provides more intimate details about Simenon's current life. . . . By means of these [memoirs] Simenon is attempting to do what his fictional characters did—to audit his life. He wonders why, when he was able to understand them—and by extension all of humanity—and why, when his compassion for others was infinite, he is always dissatisfied with himself, "a man like any other" who, like others, does his best.

Simenon's autobiographical works, with the exception of *Lettre à ma mère,* are less successful than his novels. His genius lies in conveying emotions through fictional characters rather than in analyzing them directly. (p. 60)

> *Lucille Becker, in* World Literature Today *(copyright 1977 by the University of Oklahoma Press), Vol. 51, No. 3, Winter, 1977.*

Simenon is famous for the speed with which he has turned out several hundred novels. Perhaps he should be infamous for the impatience that has kept many of them from being more than mere entertainments, that has made him better known as a phenomenon than as an artist. . . .

[In "Monsieur Monde Vanishes"] Simenon's impatience intervenes. Instead of letting Monde evolve naturally, in-

stinctively, he pushes him around like a chess piece. . . . At the end of the novel, Monde reflects that: "He was a man who, for a long time, had endured the human condition without being conscious of it, as others endure an illness of which they are unaware." This is exactly what Simenon has needed in his books: to endure the human condition a little longer, to restrain his awareness a while and let his characters slowly suffer their way into being. (p. 14)

> *Anatole Broyard, in* The New York Times Book Review *(© 1977 by The New York Times Company; reprinted by permission), May 22, 1977.*

*   *   *

SINYAVSKY, Andrei (Also Abram Tertz)   1925-

Russian novelist, short story writer, essayist, and critic, Sinyavsky was arrested in 1965 for publishing outside of the Soviet Union under the pseudonym of Abram Tertz. His monumental *A Voice from the Chorus* is a depiction of life in the work camp to which he was assigned after his arrest. The bitter and satirical tone of his writing reveals a highly refined intelligence and wit as well as a deep compassion and understanding of his fellow man.

An astonishing book. As in "The Magic Mountain," [the] place of action [of "A Voice From the Chorus"] is set apart from the rest of the world, and, like Mann's masterpiece, it reflects upon life and death, myth and Christianity, philosophy and art. Yet this new place of seclusion, where winter also lasts seven months, is like Kafka's "Penal Colony" as well. It is not only in Kafka's world that to be born is to be guilty. In 1965 Andrei Sinyavsky, a young professor and critic at the Gorky Institute of World Literature, was sentenced to seven years of compulsory labor for having published his stories and essays in the West under the name Abram Tertz. "A Voice From the Chorus" consists of notes and letters he sent to his wife . . . from the labor camp. . . .

In 1959 the Paris journal "Esprit" published his manuscript "On Socialist Realism," smuggled out of the Soviet Union. Sinyavsky's pen name was well chosen; Abram Tertz is a hero of the thieves' ballads in Isaac Babel's stories about Jewish shoemakers in Odessa. In 1960, literary journals in the West started publishing stories by "Tertz." The first anthology in English translation appeared under the title "The Icicle and Other Stories." These tales resembled nothing published in the Soviet Union within the last 20 years. Neither did they recall Russian emigré literature. Filled with bitter and moving satire, they revived and combined in the most astonishing manner the lost tradition of Swift, E.T.A. Hoffmann and the Gogol of "The Overcoat" and "The Nose." As a genre they might be named "science antifiction." The absurd in the world can be captured only by the most grotesque of styles. Terz's fantastic tales give a "realistic" picture of everyday life in the Soviet Union. . . .

"A Voice From the Chorus" is a long and loose series of philosophical and literary meditations. The author moves easily from the myth of Oceania to Celtic legends, from the vertical structure of icons to the architecture of old Orthodox churches, from Rembrandt's "Return of the Prodigal Son" to ancient Japanese painting, from the Holy Ghost in Orthodox rites to the Soviet poets Anna Akhmatova and Osip Mandelstam. Such books are almost always written in the warm tranquility of a major university library, not in a labor camp near the town of Potma where prisoners are allowed to receive two packets of books per year. And where finding paper fit for writing is the most difficult of problems. (p. 1)

Sinyavsky's scholarly notes, which transform the labor camp into an imaginary museum and an imaginary library, constitute only the lead voice. The chorus is the voices of the camp's other inmates, the Gulag archipelago speaking in all the dialects of Russia. The most astonishing aspect of this book is that anonymous one-sentence utterances—coarse, earthy, printed in italics—continually interrupt the most sophisticated of commentaries on philosophy and literature. . . .

"A Voice From the Chorus" is like a thousand novels woven into one. Human dramas are condensed, purified of everything accidental, sketched, as in the old masterpieces of drawing, with a few unerring lines. . . . For Sinyavsky, the "craving to write gospels instead of novels" is at the core of Russian literature. He also remarks: "A Russian does nothing but tempt God with various rational proposals about the best way to run the world. Russians give a lot of trouble to God." As a matter of fact, Sinyavsky's work, like that of Solzhenitsyn, troubles everyone except God. Very few contemporary authors have this strength. (p. 27)

> *Jan Kott, in* The New York Times Book
> Review (© *1976 by The New York Times*
> *Company; reprinted by permission), June*
> *27, 1976.*

[In *A Voice From the Chorus*] Sinyavsky's achievement is to turn five years and eight months of overwork and malnourishment [in a Soviet prison] into a spiritual voyage. His equipment, as befits a senior scholar at the Gorky Institute of World Literature, consisted of an extraordinary mental armory in which Shakespeare and Homer elbow the bards of Irish sagas and Chechen religious chants. His compass is the Russian Orthodoxy sustaining the believers who share his fate. The uniqueness of the work, however, resides in the relationship of the "voice" of this Ishmael to the "chorus" of his shipmates—the common criminals whose boasts, ballads and curses counterpoint the musings of the solitary survivor. . . .

Truly, by the third year, the "chorus" has reached a pitch of annoyance that makes the "voice" snap: "The lower a man's mental or educational level, the louder, the more strident he is in most cases." To create a private space in the teeming barracks, "automatically you lower a kind of invisible veil over your eyes and, with your vision blurred in this manner, you look but do not see." But those moments of exasperation are rare.

The more usual perspective combines the objectivity of an anthropologist recording exotic data with the mysticism of a seer for whom there are secrets in faces "etched by suffering." To his amazement, Sinyavsky learns that "Here people think and philosophize more intensely than in the world of scholarship and science. Ideas are not culled from books, but grow out of a man's very bones." This unsentimental education involves descriptions of the pornographic tattoos on the genitals of prisoners, their crude tales of sexual adventures and occasional glimpses of women "sitting like condors on their bunks, displaying themselves frankly, with an air of total abstraction."

Yet, even at its most animalistic, such behavior provokes the question, "What if sex is a diabolical way of reaching the gates of paradise?" The author sublimates his own sexuality, spending nearly the entire four hours of his wife's visit merely looking at her, then composing the biweekly letters on which this book is based. But he treasures the feeling of love which, like the stirrings of art and religion, promises the bliss of transcendence. (p. 185)

As an intellectual outsider, Sinyavsky is fascinated by the earthy nature of this "chorus," though his ironic vision focuses on the warts of its members and checks the perennial Russian temptation to idealize the simple folk. In his contemplative moments, he muses, "Prophets appear among the lower classes, in out-of-the-way places and in any case not among the élite." But at night he also registers the taunts of prisoners who hear someone screaming in his sleep, "Dreaming of Yids?"—the sleeper having nightmares of the Jews, whom, as collaborator of the Nazis, he helped murder.

The "chorus" asserts, "The good thing about this place is that a man feels he is nothing but a naked soul." For Sinyavsky, stripping away unessentials leads to a Dostoevskian image of sin-ridden humanity on the brink of collective repentance: "A person in prison corresponds most closely of all to the concept of man. He is, so to speak, the most natural man—man in his pristine state." If this romantic characterization recalls us to the lost innocence of childhood, it does not deter the "snooping" observer from also recording the theft by a dying man in the camp hospital of another dying man's spectacles. The "chorus" can switch from affirmations of the communal conscience, as in a Greek tragedy, to the dampening effects of ritual chant, as in the Orthodox service where it is "a weak, murmuring accompaniment to what is being confessed and absolved."

The "voice" of the narrator shares with the "chorus" its anonymity, so that personal detail is kept to a minumum. One never learns, for example, about the physical horrors of camp life chronicled by Alexander Solzhenitsyn and Anatoly Marchenko. To some degree, this may be a function of the need to evade official censorship, though Sinyavsky, now literature professor at the University of Paris, was free to make emendations had he chosen to do so. The private quality of the "voice" reflects, rather, the compunctions that still make Sinyavsky, the literary critic, detach himself from Tertz, the novelist. (pp. 185-86)

The protean powers of Sinyavsky's art have never been more striking. They range from Zen aphorisms ("I know why the crows have been cawing so much of late: they were feeling too black on this white snow") to offbeat interpretations of literary classics and paintings. Echoing T. S. Eliot, Sinyavsky could survey his intellectual salvage with the words, "These fragments I have shored against my ruins." His readings of *Hamlet* and *Oedipus* in terms of ineluctable fate undermining the illusion of free choice parallels the tension between the "voice" obsessed by destiny and the "chorus" by a belief in luck. . . .

The regimentation of contemporary life, Marina Tsvetaeva realized in her poem "Homesickness," drives the artist into perpetual exile, out of the house "that is no more mine than a hospital or barracks." "In the toilet of the Potma transit prison," his last stop before freedom, Sinyavsky fantasizes a message from this poet, whose return to Russia in 1939 led to her suicide. His own journey ends like that of Lazarus, "a dead man appearing at life's feast." (p. 186)

> *Harvey Fireside, "The Art of Survival," in*

The Nation *(copyright 1976 by the Nation Associates, Inc.), September 4, 1976, pp. 185-86.*

A Voice from the Chorus is as surprising a book to come out of prison as could be imagined. (p. 67)

The book is made up . . . of passages from his letters to his wife, together with some brief diary entries composed after his release. The physical circumstances of his imprisonment hardly appear in it. Nothing is said about the reasons for his incarceration. Apart from the occasional description of a look or a particularly striking encounter, the other prisoners are present only through a series of italicized and unexplained quotations of remarks overheard ("The Chorus"). These anonymous quotations, for which no contexts are given, are all brief, some consisting of just a few words; but the anthologies of them which punctuate the text are in many cases several pages long. Fragments of dialogue, boasts about past misdeeds, malapropisms, idle conjectures about the future or the meaning of life—the author obviously treasured some for their bizarre power and originality, others for their excruciating banality.

At one point in his communings with his wife or with himself, the author points out that a line of verse consists "not only of the alternation of sounds, but even more the organization of pauses, the arrangement of silences and stillnesses." This remark can be extended to apply to his book as a whole. The camp, the conditions in which he is writing, the slow passage of time are all conveyed as much through the book's silences and stillnesses as through its words; that which it does not speak of is eloquently present. His extreme abstemiousness or frugality in this regard has a double effect: it puts into particularly sharp focus those sudden details of his daily existence which do appear; and it lends an extraordinary deliberateness and intensity to the reflections on other topics of which the book is largely composed. (pp. 67-8)

A Voice from the Chorus explains and entirely justifies its own form. But an interesting light is thrown on it, and on Tertz/Sinyavsky's earlier works, by a long essay, "The Literary Process in Russia." . . . In it he declares his opposition to "realism"—not the realism of the official Soviet writers, whom he regards as quite beneath notice, but precisely that of his fellow *samizdat* or underground writers. . . . "We must put a stop to our cringing and currying favor with that hectoring taskmaster—reality! After all, we *are* writers, artists in words." He pleads with his fellow writers to create instead "on this fertile, well-manured soil [of Russia] . . . something astonishing, something exotic."

In *A Voice from the Chorus* he has succeeded. To do it, he had to bear all the weight of the reality he had experienced. The last words of the book, written after his release, are: "But they will still go on and on. And while I live here, while we all live—they will still go on and on. . . ." (p. 68)

Dan Jacobson, "Sinyavsky's Art" (reprinted from Commentary *by permission; copyright © 1976 by the American Jewish Committee), in* Commentary, *November, 1976, pp. 66-8.*

While Solzhenitsyn disturbs us by his polemical revision of history, Sinyavsky deliberately avoids politics in the journals of his six years in a prison camp to leave us with a sense of wonder at an artist's ability to transmute suffering into self-knowledge. *A Voice from the Chorus* . . . lends itself to a variety of readings: a chronicle of physical mortification to test newfound faith, a brilliant critic's commentary on world literature as a survival manual, and a linguistic analysis of the banalities and deception that comfort the more common criminals.

Sinyavsky's chronicle of internal exile is, finally, a tour de force demonstrating the author's esthetic of fantasy as a more adequate response to the mindless horrors of our age than was the realism still constricting the scope of Solzhenitsyn. (p. 788)

Harvey Fireside, in Commonweal *(copyright © 1976 Commonweal Publishing Co., Inc.; reprinted by permission of Commonweal Publishing Co., Inc.), December 3, 1976.*

* * *

SISSON, C(harles) H(ubert)   1914-

A British poet, novelist, and essayist, Sisson often satirizes modern British society in his poetry. (See also *Contemporary Authors*, Vols. 1-4, rev. ed.)

[*The Trojan Ditch*] as a whole records the development of a poet whose deepest concerns have been slow to find voice.

The aspect of mind Sisson chiefly presents is that of intellect reflecting on existence. Bilious in temperament, he is given to conceptual formulations, satirical or self-critical. He writes with stringent force but his clarity can be deceptive: he uses without warning various degrees of irony, from deadpan ambiguity to open derision, his light lines skim like Marvell's deep questionings, and his latest work is both complex and obscure.

Sisson classicises. Having suppressed his juvenilia and returned to the writing of verse after submitting to the discipline of prose, he accepts at first the constraints of convention. Conditions he resists but cannot disown reflect themselves in many iambic movements and an emphatic address: diction is at times violent and the rhythms thump. There appears to remain the relic of a belief that poetry consists in the making of remarkable statements; some of his statements are odd. Fully loaded, personal utterances are liable to go off bang, others rattle along in intellectual doggerel. A stern conscience and a knack of abstracting produce however some excellent epigrams. . . . Metrically unadventurous, Sisson is very sensitive to slight variations of tone and he has made some interesting experiments in style. Strong clear statements expressing only their own insufficiency, he at length reaches out to vagueness.

The application of traditional forms to present purposes, dear to English habit, succeeds to the extent that it introduces into the model handed down some element not apparently at variance with it but actually different. Such being the process of language itself, the work of the poet is mainly conservative and selective. It is by imitation and translation that Sisson has elaborated his technique and gradually developed a loadbearing style. (pp. 45-6)

Kenneth Cox, "The Poetry of C. H. Sisson," in Agenda, *Autumn, 1974, pp. 45-9.*

C. H. Sisson resembles Larkin in one respect, that his satire clearly springs from an unresolved personal dilemma. He is his own problem. Whereas in Larkin, however, one feels that it would not be profitable, nor even possible, for him to explore this dilemma, in Sisson it is the intricate exploration of it that finally vindicates the work. I say 'finally' because part of the dumbness of which Sisson speaks is the sense that he is not always in control of his own gift. Much of the work [in *Collected Poems & Selected Translations*] seems to generate itself in rather improvisational fashion, and only slowly to move towards its real shape. (p. 114)

One wonders . . . if it was wise to print Sisson's work back to front, putting these late poems first. The early poems are very much of a piece with them, but far more accessible, compressed lyric statements that contain their tensions without needing to explain them. . . . [The] issue of plainness, first raised by Sisson in connection with his Catullus translations . . . , seems to have been a complete red herring—not least for Sisson himself. What's so plain about Catullus, anyway? (p. 115)

Plainness serves Sisson ill in his complex middle period (where, again, the reverse order of printing induces vertigo as themes unroll backwards). His absorbing theme, the relationship of soul and body, particularly the extent to which the body governs the soul, making any concept of identity dubious, is attacked time and again; other themes flow into it, the extent to which 'mind' is inherited through culture, and so whether place can be said to have 'mind': but the whole complex is finally cracked open, not by plain statement, but by the most intricate artifice, in his remarkable long poem 'The Discarnation'. . . . For the first two sections, 'The Discarnation' looks as if it is going to be a major work, a twentieth century *Essay On Man*. It is a serious loss that towards the end of section two it should adopt, without adequately countering, the terms of Freudian analysis, developing along lines Sisson himself doesn't accept: 'much and falsely simplified'. Thereafter it degenerates into Sisson the satirist, which is his lesser self.

At his best, Sisson is clearly an important poet, concerned to set the received unity of poetic thought against the disintegration of the modern mind. (pp. 115-16)

> *Roger Garfitt, in* London Magazine (© London Magazine *1974), October-November, 1974.*

*   *   *

SMITH, Florence Margaret
See SMITH, Stevie

*   *   *

SMITH, Stevie   1902-1971

A British poet and novelist, Smith wrote comic verse revealing a stunning intellectual clarity. Although death is a recurrent theme throughout her work, Smith's concern with mortality does not convey a romantic self-indulgence, but rather a clear-sighted, realistic joy in life's struggle. (See also *CLC*, Vol. 3, and *Contemporary Authors*, Vols. 17-18; obituary, Vols. 29-32, rev. ed.; *Contemporary Authors Permanent Series*, Vol. 2.)

Entrancing and sad together, over and over [in her *Collected Poems* Smith] draws up what isn't so often joy or happiness but a pure delight from her desolation. Above all, she's complete. By this I mean that we have a sense from her work of a whole and coherent world which corresponds to our own, but our own transfigured and revealed by the slightest tilting of things. She might be a female Cavafy, as her many odd anecdotes suggest, their very slightness involving and then haunting the reader. Her people are our people: they have that combination of presence and intangibility of people we meet and know.

She is like Cavafy, too, in her disdain to search for nonexistent clouds of glory. . . .

She learnt to live with the absence of a God she still pined for . . . ; and perhaps it was a sense of the vast and growing empty spaces which put such an edge to her feeling for the concrete: dogs, cats, houses, books, suburbs, hats and baronets were all taken into that sinuous style in which, however apparently garrulous, not a word is wasted. Or perhaps it was death, which possessed her work from the start. Certainty of extinction inhabits these poems, providing the impetus for her other great theme: the importance of art; sharpening and deepening a sense of the ridiculous which is inseparable from her sensuousness. What she knew she loved and what she loved she described. (p. 314)

> *Peter Washington, in* The Spectator (© *1975 by* The Spectator; *reprinted by permission of* The Spectator), *September 6, 1975.*

To read [Stevie Smith's *Collected Poems*] is to admire the consistency of her poetic enterprise over thirty-five years— a kind of poetic cartooning which amounts to a classic literary record of English cultural life. The calculated technical naiveties are symptomatic of an emotional candour and intellectual clarity which detects mystery but refuses to be mystified, a kind of comic vulnerability before experience. The tough, clear-eyed critical reasonableness is detectible from start to finish beneath the zany verbal japes. (p. 80)

> *Terry Eagleton, in* Stand (*copyright © by* Stand), *Vol. 17, No. 1 (1975-76).*

Stevie Smith's poetry gives joy as it has not been given before and will not be given again. She is, for me, among the unhoused moderns, the *eccentric* ones, in a class not with Betjeman, to whom she is sometimes compared, but with Graves and Lawrence. (p. 172)

Compassion seems too soft a word for Stevie Smith's stance toward her fellow human beings. Rather, she wants them to be better than they are, and her disappointment, unpitying as it is, takes the form of love. For relief she looks to the other creatures who do not have to be saved. This, as one sees, for instance, in *The Zoo*, is one of the many Blakean aspects of her writing. A lion is caged and waiting, a child is watching, the lion "licks his snout, the tears fall down / And water dusty London town." What shall we say to the child? . . . To each thing its purpose— but it is this that we deny to the animals. (pp. 172-73)

Her animal-portraits are of creatures great, good, obtuse, and ornery. Fafnir the dragon, the noble dog Belvoir: these have names, the indispensable panache, and prompt whole poems. But one must not forget innumerable birds, of song or ill-omen, donkeys as memorable as Peter Bell's, cats, scorpions, hybrids that are not quite themselves, and the anacondas "not looking ill-fed" who intimidate a Jungle Husband named Wilfred. The human portraits, surely exhaustive, include Monsieur Poop, "self-appointed guardian of English literature", who believes "tremendously in the significance of age"; Lord Mope; Tolly the toll of the roads; Mr. Mounsel who is "dying Egypt dying"; the Frog Prince; Helen of Troy—or rather, one who "had a dream I was Helen of Troy / In looks, age and circumstance, / But otherwise I was myself"; one Harold, who takes a risky leap; Childe Rolandine the secretary-typist, with her song "Against oppression and the rule of wrong"; Dido; Walt Whitman; and the Person from Porlock. Yet the nameless are often as distinctive as the named. (p. 173)

The ideal review of Stevie Smith would be five-hundred and seventy-one pages long and emerge as a single unbroken quotation. That one I will leave the reader to write for himself. In the meantime, it may be of some interest, from a technical point of view, to remark two curious features of her style: her music and her drawings. She writes, about half the time, from a musical not a metrical base.

> Wan
> Swan
> On the lake
> Like a cake
> Of soap
> Why is the swan
> Wan
> On the lake?
> He has abandoned hope.

This is lovely, but absurd to scan, until you realize it is a double musical phrase, which the line breaks are serving partly to conceal. *Wan* and *Swan* are quarter notes; the next line, two eighth notes followed by a quarter; *Like a cake of soap* consists of four eighth notes followed by a half. *Why is the swan*—triplets and a quarter; *Wan On the lake*—the same; *He has abandoned hope*—an eighth note, two sixteenths, two more eighths, and a half note. Many of her poems are in a similar fashion lyrics for an underheard or quietly fingered melody. Occasionally the song is a received text and its title appears below that of the poem.

I think readers will be of two minds about her drawings. There can be no doubt that the drawings, in any case, are of two minds about the poems. They are as likely to subvert a poem's tone as to enforce it, and their license is sometimes jarring, as in the following example.

> I sigh for the heavenly country,
> Where the heavenly people pass,
> And the sea is as quiet as a mirror
> Of beautiful beautiful glass.

Beneath the poem of which this forms the opening stanza, we find, seated before a table-with-vase, a woman who is the perfected essence of drabness. She seems an unfortunate development of the "speaker" theory. It is her dream, then; the poem is satiric. But we would rather have thought this up ourselves, or else—an opposite complaint which somehow does not exclude the first—she seems an unfair reduction of the poem's lyrical power. A worse offense in the same category is the leer worn by the old man, feigning blindness, who asks a "limber lad" for the time, before dragging him off "up a crooked stair". And yet the drawings are often witty or affecting, often both at the same time. They represent Stevie Smith—how she saw the poems is as important as how we see them—they are *in character* from start to finish, and we would not do without them.

Reviews are not required to have morals any more than poems are. But this review has a moral. Poetry is an activity of life. It cannot bear a steady and single diet of everything that wears away at life. The idea that there is a direct relation between the quantity of suffering a poet endures and the quality of the poetry that results—can we call it an attractive idea? It is, at least, crudely appealing. It is dramatic, it is framed in the universal language of vocational guidance, it has, to the last possible degree, the force of an imposing simplification. It will not do. The poet remains what he has always been, a person who chooses to write poems. He may be as calm about it or as desperate as he likes. But he might as well be calm.

> Ceux qui luttent ce sont ceux qui vivent
> And down here they luttent a very great deal indeed
> But if life be the desideratum, why grieve, ils vient.

Somewhere on Parnassus these lines by Stevie Smith are inscribed. (pp. 174-75)

David Bromwich, in Poetry (© *1976 by The Modern Poetry Association; reprinted by permission of the Editor of* Poetry), *December, 1976.*

If you have never read Stevie Smith, try to imagine an eccentric like Marianne Moore confronting a tragically defiant universe with Ogden Nash's love of the ridiculous and Emily Dickinson's sense of wonder. It would be a mistake to think of Stevie as a writer of limericks who illustrated her poetry with *New Yorker*-like sketches. It is true that she can toss off a couplet ("This Englishwoman is so refined / She has no bosom and no behind") and follow it with a picture of the linear lady herself. But Stevie was also an observer "standing alone on a fence in a spasm" where she could "behold all life in a microcosm."

Hers was not a simple world; on the surface it seemed incongruous, peopled by madcaps and losers. Men commit suicide when they discover the afterlife will be a reunion of relatives; lions are never given their due in the making of martyrs. Yet these incongruities grow into paradoxes which are in turn resolved into a single truth: the inevitability of death, whom the poet regards as a friend rather then a presence, "the only god / Who comes as a servant when he is called."

For all her obsession with mortality, Stevie was no puny romantic sliding into the mire of self-pity. Although she believed "all love and mankind are grass," she kept her landscape green, weeding out the melancholy that stifles art. She was the poet of strength admonishing the would-be suicide to endure, not so that he might enjoy life but that he might be deserving of death when it came. Like all great poets, Stevie Smith reminds us that dying is as much of an art as living. (p. 101)

Bernard F. Dick, in World Literature Today (*copyright 1977 by the University of Oklahoma Press*), *Vol. 51, No. 1, Winter, 1977.*

*   *   *

SPARK, Muriel   1918-

A Scottish-born novelist, poet, short story writer, playwright, essayist, and biographer, Spark now lives in Rome. Her novels are distinguished by her satirical approach and the sense of intellectual distance she puts between herself and her characters, an imaginative assortment of tyrannical nuns, languorous jet-setters, and enigmatic spinsters. (See also *CLC*, Vols. 2, 3, 5, and *Contemporary Authors*, Vols. 5-8, rev. ed.)

[Muriel Spark] seems to lack some important, or at least useful human dimensions—such as humor, compassion, generosity or tolerance.

This intrinsic compression of spirit she tries to disguise in satire, and brings it off well, as our attention is usually drawn to the glittering rapier and its victim, not the wielder. But does she satirize society, fashions in people, fads in pretension and hypocrisy? No. What Spark is after is the quick of her character's soul, and that is less satire and more hatred of life, vampirism in fact. And done in most competent if brittle prose. Tight, disciplined stories, yes;

but satisfying to think over, no. There is a taste of scorched metal. Again, why?

It is because the narrator she usually employs is too often the stereotypical convert, joyless and sexless; sometimes it's a disembodied voice, literally a spook; or it's intellectualist, bored by the drab English, or English (African) colonial, life; or it's neuter, hysterical, grim, as though suffering from menopause from the onset of puberty, and wishing only to find refuge or surcease from the life of the whole person. And that refuge is too easily found in an attitude that is self-consciously catty and complacent, spiritualistic rather than spiritual, smug about rosaries, icons, rituals, embarrassed by faith and not exalted or empowered by it, as though faith demands a show of warmth that is in poor taste. Evelyn Waugh and Greene both suffer from it too.

In consequence, death stalks through much of Spark's fiction, which is full of arbitrary violence: her stories are often spitefully ghostly, or allegoric confessions (like two long ones, ''Bang-bang You're Dead,'' and ''The Go-Away Bird''); many of her sympathetic characters are penitents, exemplifying various states of what she chooses to call sin and hell-suffering, whether or not they are aware of what she's doing to them. What saves her work from triviality, from being merely boring, is her deft touch, and a sort of queer honesty emerging from it: for, while her kind of Catholic writing suffers Protestants and deplores utilitarians and pragmatists, it also shows itself acutely aware that its true purgatory is that well-deserted one of the *other* Catholics, as in ''Come Along, Marjorie,'' and ''Alice Long's Dachshunds.''

As for her poetry—on reflection one sees that its prosaic ideas are merely tendentious, its tight and clogged syntax and vocabulary, its habitual expression in the traditional forms of ballad or blank paragraphs or misshapen quatrains, its poor and unnatural rhythms—all this mirrors a terrible split rather well-hidden by her swift light touch in fiction. It is a split suggesting a sad inability to integrate body and mind, as though in loathing the flesh and yet longing for its sensual life Miss Spark's spirit had retired to a snug apartment in the top of her head and left the building below untenanted, hollow yet dusty and full of strange thumps and knockings. Had she called her volume verses, not poems, she might have been able to claim to be in the tradition of *vers de société*: verses of social comment, and witty, metaphysical observation that survives somehow from the early part of this century and can find its audience.

> *Jascha Kessler, ''Sojourn in the Joyless World of Bitter Satire,'' in* The Los Angeles Times *(copyright, 1968, Los Angeles Times; reprinted by permission), July 14, 1968, p. 40.*

Muriel Spark converted to Catholicism in 1954, and all her novels have been ''religious'' in the sense that they have all dealt with faith or morality. But unlike ''Catholic writer'' Graham Greene, her mode is comedy: a ruthless, biting comedy which strips off the mask of hypocrisy and reveals the absurdity—and often the viciousness—of human beings. (p. 22)

Like Spark's Jean Brodie, in *The Prime of Miss Jean Brodie*, like her Dougal Douglas in *The Ballad of Peckham Rye*, the Abbess of Crewe [in *The Abbess of Crewe: A Modern Morality Tale*] has a God-complex: she believes herself to be above ordinary standards of right and wrong. Like the famous Miss Brodie, she is an autocrat, an elitist,

a tyrant, convinced that God's standards are identical to her own. Spark believes that the Catholic Church's strict hierarchy of obedience makes it particularly vulnerable to this kind of person. . . .

In all her books, Spark uses some mysterious or simply outrageous phenomenon as a catalyst to shake up our accepted notions and force a reexamination of them. In this book, the device is the electronic listening system which Abbess Alexandra has installed throughout the convent to make herself all-seeing and all-knowing, thus all-powerful. Her fondness for the wonders of modern technology contrasts ironically with her strict insistence on the ancient Benedictine Rule. But there is a double standard: one for the Abbess and her coterie, another for the plebeians. (p. 23)

Betrayal figures in all of Spark's novels. The Abbess, the Nixon-figure, has committed the greatest betrayal: that of a sacred trust. All the high comedy, the grotesqueries that are the heart of Spark's wit . . . are in the service of a deeply serious concern with the ancient moral problem of absolute power, which corrupts absolutely. Spark calls her novels ''fiction out of which a kind of truth emerges . . . I am interested in absolute truth . . . I believe things which are difficult to believe, but I believe them because they are absolute.'' In short, she believes in Christianity. . . .

The problem with all this is that Spark makes her satanic characters too attractive. Ordinary craven mortals can't help admiring the magnificent certainty of a Miss Jean Brodie or an Abbess of Crewe that God and Truth are on their side. *The Abbess of Crewe* is such a delight to read that even its real-life prototype, Watergate, emerges seeming like more of a lark than a crime. (p. 24)

The Abbess of Crewe is a little gem, a fable very much of our time, yet, like all good satire, universal. (p. 27)

> *Gail Kessler Kmetz, ''Come Let Us Mock at the Great . . . ,'' in* Ms. *(© 1976 Ms. Magazine Corp.), May, 1976, pp. 22-4, 27.*

The Takeover is certainly about the collapse of fortunes, dinner parties, Palladian retreats, civilisation as we know it, as well as our culture's less tangible appurtenances—established religion, moralities and relationships which, having likewise been turned into objects over the past few hundred years, and made spiteful and ignoble by greed, cannot reasonably complain of also finding themselves subject to the physical laws of decay.

In its sharp idiosyncratic detail, the manner in which the wit derives from the author's detached tone, the milieu of sensual conspiracy and moneyed gossip, the characters as slightly cracked decadent archetypes, vehicles for an overall attitude of mind, the book is very much akin to the disciplined farce of Ronald Firbank who was monitoring a similar collapse of civilisation as we know it fifty years ago.

As a tribe Muriel Spark's characters are highly appealing. They promise fun, sexual adventure and plenty to drink surrounded by some of the world's most beautiful architecture. Their problems are entertaining without being trivial, their passions betray a remarkable sense of proportion. It is unlikely that Jacqueline Onassis will drop in to deaden things but if she does you can always go upstairs to join somebody's son or daughter in a secret cinquecento bedroom, smoking marijuana in front of a wonderfully pagan vista of blue hills. Above all, life is not dull here, even if it is socially gracious to say you are bored now and again. . . .

People would be shocked. They want us to go back to wearing bed socks as a bulwark against the spread of anarchy. This misses the point entirely, which Miss Spark does not. The threats against our system—which in the West have gone further in Italy than anywhere else—bring a tremendous exhilaration into the lives of these characters. I daresay this book will be seen as an indictment against the new mood, a work of unguent malice, but it is not.

Maybe Maggie, a jetsy American of middle years whose riches incite all the action (plotwise), imagines that what she most wants in life is to flop down beside as many different private swimming pools as possible before dying in one. But the plain fact is that without the jewel robberies, tantrums, kidnaps, financial swindles, intrigues, and lovers, she would have no sense of significance whatsoever. She thrives on this action and at the end manages to recover her fortune in high spirits by kidnapping the quack financier who has gone off with it. . . .

[Muriel Spark's] people are not drama types to engage your pity. They are events to engage your optimism. Next time somebody suddenly deprives you of a Veronese, don't feel guilty about that uncanny sense of release. It's the opposite of being murdered.

> *Duncan Fallowell, "Campo dei fiori," in* The Spectator *(© 1976 by* The Spectator; *reprinted by permission of* The Spectator*), June 12, 1976, p. 23.*

Muriel Spark calls her latest novel, *The Abbess of Crewe*, "A Modern Morality Tale," and a superficial reading of this witty and amusing story of a scandal-ridden abbess election will suggest that the object of Spark's allegory is Watergate. Watergate and political corruption, however, form only the skeleton of this brief but biting tale; Spark's real target is the mass media and its all-pervasive influence on contemporary life. In the phenomenon of Watergate, with its obsessive examination in the mass media, its verbal and visual clichés, and its unique association with electronic surveillance, Spark has found the perfect vehicle to convey her image of media as the religion of modern man.

Spark, whose twelve novels and numerous short stories examine contemporary life in the light of her religious vision, has for some time been preoccupied with the impact of the mass media on modern consciousness. (p. 146)

In *The Abbess of Crewe* (1974), the story of the Abbess Alexandra who drinks *Le Corton* 1959, reads Machiavelli, and quotes Herrick, Marvell, and Milton, Muriel Spark shows how modern tools for recording and communicating reality have become instead instruments for its creation. She has created hilarious parallels to Watergate events and figures in this novel, and readers of course will be tempted by the game of identification, but this identification is not central to the novel. As Spark demonstrates convincingly, the media have insured that the images and phrases of Watergate have entered "the realm of mythology," and mythology, as the Abbess informs her sisters, is "history garbled". . . . Events lose accuracy in the public mind, Spark suggests, as the media create a global village and a common mythology. Words and images, once specific to an event, become a common language, their sources garbled and insignificant.

Images of Watergate have thus been cut loose from their original associations and now float free in the common consciousness of the public. Spark utilizes these images to evoke recognition and ironic laughter and to demonstrate by this very recognition the point of her modern morality tale. Recurrent motifs from the media further highlight Spark's theme: she creates a collage of communication images with her descriptions of the electronics laboratory, repeated references to buggings, television news, and photocopy machines, constant interruptions by telephone calls, and repeated calls to the roving nun Gertrude on "the green line." (pp. 148-49)

Spark puts her modern morality tale, a familiar tale of intrigue and scheming for worldly recognition and power, in the context of *"the levelling wind"*; and in her concluding lines she turns from the transcripts of the Crewe tapes . . . to a vision of eternity: "that cornfield of sublimity which never should be reaped nor was ever sown, orient and immortal wheat". (p. 153)

> *Barbara Y. Keyser, "Muriel Spark, Watergate, and the Mass Media," in* Arizona Quarterly *(copyright © 1976 by the* Arizona Quarterly*), Vol. 32, No. 2, Summer, 1976, pp. 146-53.*

Muriel Spark is an enigmatic novelist, and her forte is to imply that she knows much more than, in her short novels, she chooses to say. At times her tone is omniscient, Godlike, as when, in "The Prime of Miss Jean Brodie," she disposes of her characters not only in the past and present, but also in the future; at other times she is, more simply, knowing. She writes of the rich, the clever, the sophisticated, the experienced; the innocent and the unknowing receive hardly more than a derisory nod or an astonished salute in her collected works. She and her characters move easily from London to Paris to New York to Rome, filling in time by expensive purchases of the right shoes, the right paintings: they are the jet set of fiction. . . .

This kind of mixture has worked well before, and it works well [in "The Takeover"], at least superficially: the book presents a glittering surface. We all like gloss: we like to read of those so wealthy that they can no longer afford to insure their possessions, and we love to suffer vicariously as they attempt to foil their predators—by hiding their jewels in hot water bottles, by making false floors to false kitchens, by burying their ill-gotten gains in their mothers' well-tended graves. But, as ever, Muriel Spark raises the question: what lies beneath this dazzling game? Anything? Nothing? And, as ever, she leaves us on our own, for most of the book, to try to answer it.

At times one suspects she may not know the answer herself. It is easy to appear knowing if one says little, or if one works, as she did in "The Abbess of Crewe," on the level of tediously protracted fantasy. "The Takeover" exposes itself much more dangerously than did that last highly-praised fiction, for it can be related to everyday reality. (p. 1)

"The Takeover," despite its studied frivolity, is concerned with a very interesting subject indeed. It is true that one may read half the book, with much pleasure and some impatience, before this becomes clear, but on page 126 precisely, Muriel Spark drops her enigmatic allusions for long enough to tell us, plainly, that she is writing about money. In a couple of brilliant paragraphs, she describes the change that overtook the world in 1973, with the rise of Arab oil power and the fear of global recession. . . .

It is a wonderful subject, and one admires her for tackling

it. She is well equipped to write of the kind of colorless, odorless, tasteless, unspendable money that passes in hieroglyphics through computers from one part of the globe to another. She also raises, in a comic and orgiastic scene towards the end, the conflict of Christianity and wealth. . . .

The theme is, not surprisingly, too large for the book, but that is a welcome relief, after the thin subjects of those thin novels, "The Driver's Seat" and "Not to Disturb." It asks more questions than it can answer, but it asks them boldly. Muriel Spark does not claim to understand the new global economic situation, witty though she is about some of its effects; nor does she tell us what the future will be like, after the watershed of 1973. The omniscience that sat so easily on her in her earlier novels has been shaken. There is a future, after all. . . . It is almost as though, midway through this novel, the author recognizes that all the trappings of her former style have, in the economic sea change, lost their meaning and value too: the scenario, of Palladian mansions and expensive hotels and grand apartments with Louis XIV chairs, must change; so must the cast list of millionaires and servants and spongers; so must the wardrobe of Gucci shoes and Bulgari steel watches, the backdrop of Gauguins and Porsches. . . .

Where is glittering sophistication in this new harsh world? What will Muriel Spark do next? Will she, like her heroine Maggie, put on shabbier clothes for a shabbier future, dissimulate, learn new tricks? Will she shake off the confines of a public image and a public style that have at times looked like a *haute couture* straight jacket? It is hard to praise a plain future and a Christian ethic in jeweled prose. It will be interesting to read the speculations of post-'73 Spark. (p. 2)

> *Margaret Drabble, in* The New York Times Book Review *(© 1976 by The New York Times Company; reprinted by permission), October 3, 1976.*

The first thing one notices about [*The Takeover*] is that it is longer and fuller than Spark's brief, dry, ungenerous-seeming experiments of the past few years. In fact, this is her longest novel but for *The Mandelbaum Gate* of 1965, and for the reader this is all gain. Of the very brief novels, her last, *The Abbess of Crewe* I judge the best, since the brevity there seems just right. But now, taking myth—a Diana myth—and modern Italy, the Italy of international super-riches, of robberies, kidnappings, blackmail and the Mafia, as her material, she has given herself room in which to create several Italian scenes and situations based on witty observation—the rich at table, a couple of Italian servant women meeting in a street and talking scandalous things over (to me the finest bit of observation and writing in the book)—scenes and situations for which the extreme distillation of works like *Not to Disturb* and *The Hothouse by the East River* allowed her no scope.

What *The Takeover* is precisely about, what the authoress's precise intentions are here, I leave you to decide for yourselves. What matters most at the moment, it seems to me, is the satisfaction to be derived from seeing one of our leading post-mid-Fifties novelists giving of her impudent, stylish best in the post-mid-Seventies. If ever a civilisation needed impudence in the approach to it and style in dealing with it, ours does.

Whether the central character, American Maggie Radcliffe, . . . is supposed to symbolize the Goddess Diana from one

of the myths collected by Frazer in *The Golden Bough* . . . , I don't care a damn. Whether the authoress has succeeded in giving us a parallel of that myth in modern times and in modern Italy, which is strictly parallel all through, interests me even less. What does interest me is that in this tale, in which several of the bogus people with which our world is at present cluttered—worshippers of the Golden Calf, thieves, parasites, inept idealists, founders of phoney cults, hangers-on—Muriel Spark has written another sparkling parable. One which, while illustrating the pursuit of the Seven Deadly Sins, with covetousness and lechery in the van, is a joy to read and which, in the mere fact of its existence, is a tribute to man's intelligence. It provides the hope, if not the guarantee, that we have still mind enough to see ourselves and, seeing ourselves, to survive.

No, I'm wrong. What matters most to me is that by writing this book, Spark has demonstrated again that art and the art of satire, besides being a weapon, is a joy, if not for ever, then at least for 266 pages. (pp. 60-1)

Effective, too, is a feature which does not seem to have been present in Spark's work before, a consciousness of the beauty and peace of natural scenery, 'the kindly fruits of the earth', as compared with man's frenetic getting and spending and dashing about in all directions but the right one. . . .

Paul Bailey . . . started his review of *The Abbess of Crewe* . . . [see *CLC*, Vol. 5] with 'There was once a novelist called Muriel'. Enough said. But no, it wasn't. A few lines later, Bailey added: 'Early in her career she created a real character called Jean Brodie . . .' who had to be put down for getting the better of her author. But has Muriel Spark ever been concerned with creating character? It seems to me that that has always been beside the point to her, so that such criticism of her writing is, too. In fact, it is irrelevant. One must find authors lacking on their own grounds and not on those one would like to see them standing on. Besides, surely we have abandoned character today? Surely, today, we are left with only ideas, folly and telecommunications?

A further objection raised to Spark's work is that she always seems one up on the reader ('Muriel was a very knowing writer'—says Bailey). But surely, again, we have known *that* from the start, have always accepted that she writes sitting on God's knee—which is only a more visual way of saying *sub specie aeternitatis,* that now very tired old phrase, where her work is concerned. . . .

All I have to say further of *The Takeover* is: read it. Not only because of the author's name, but also because it is relevant to our Western society and age and, while parading man's folly, restores some faith in him, because a part of mankind, called Muriel Spark, achieved this novel. (p. 61)

> *James Brockway, "New Spark of Genius,"* in Books and Bookmen *(© copyright James Brockway 1976; reprinted with permission), November, 1976, pp. 60-1.*

"I knew," the narrator of Fitzgerald's *The Last Tycoon* says, "that since 1933 the rich could only be happy alone together." Muriel Spark, in *The Takeover,* suggests that since 1973, with the oil crisis and the onset of the new Dark Ages, the rich have lost even that insulated happiness. Sponged on, held up, ripped off, blackmailed, kidnapped, they have become an endangered species, their paintings, antiques, cash, and multiple international holdings mere invitations to swindle and looting; all their assets transfigured into liabilities. There has been "a change in the meaning of property and money," we are told. . . .

[There is a clear implication in *The Takeover*] that the rich and the crooked are birds of a feather, that the rich make the best survivors because they make the best crooks, and that the more sea-changes in the nature of reality there are, the more it's the same thing. The rich have the sufferings, to paraphrase Auden, to which they are fairly accustomed.

Spark enjoys the thought of charming larceny, and no writer of fiction, I suspect, can feel truly ill-disposed toward confidence men. . . . Spark's ironic sympathy for both victims and crooks (and especially for victims who become crooks) turns into a rather prim horror of *promiscuous* thieving and a too eagerly articulated notion that recently the world really has changed past all recognition. So she sounds, briefly, like the reactionaries in her own novel, who keep saying that things will never be the same again, and that "something is finished for always." She quickly picks herself up, though, and on the very next page remarks that if one of her characters had been able to envisage the reality to come, she "would have considered it, wrongly, to be a life not worth living."

Wrongly is marvelous, it is the voice of the writer's sanity refusing to be left out of whatever world there is. It is striking that the only other sloppy passage in this brisk and brilliant book concerns "eternal life," which remains, Spark says, "past all accounting." Accounting too ambitiously ("a complete mutation"), or accounting not at all ("the whole of eternal life carried on regardless"), Spark momentarily loses her subject, which as the title of her novel suggests is neither money nor the pulsations of everlasting nature but greed and panic and the competition for limited space and a finite number of goodies.

Whether the people in this book are rich or crooked or what Spark calls, in a graceful glance at another Seventies phenomenon, "avid for immaterialism," they are reacting to the idea of wealth, and this note is sounded throughout the novel. . . .

The point is less the omnipresence of thoughts of lucre than the quirky, obsessive behavior the unrestrained economic motive can induce: perfect material for a comic writer with a moralist's eye. . . .

The best and final refutation of Spark's notion about the sea-change in the nature of reality is the security of her own vision. She sees, she implies, just what there is to see and that is pretty much what she is used to seeing. (p. 30)

Michael Wood, in The New York Review of Books *(reprinted with permission from* The New York Review of Books; *copyright* © *1976 NYREV, Inc.), November 11, 1976.*

Muriel Spark is a disturbing writer because she refuses to offer plain sermons; she never underlines her articles of Catholic faith. She assumes that we will get her slanted messages. She is usually correct.

[*The Takeover*] is, however, especially troubling. If we merely accept the "mad" goings on—the pairing of servants and masters, the odd speech-patterns of foreigners . . . , and the shifting powerplays—we are inclined to dismiss them as an odd jumble or mistake.

But *The Takeover* surmounts most of its difficulties. Perhaps the best way to grasp its central meaning (and pattern) is by studying its title. Spark is concerned with possession —*all kinds* of possession. Superficially the plot concerns the role of money. Maggie, the heroine, is a wealthy lady who owns (or tries to own) houses, people, and antiques. She controls the money-flow; she is the materialistic queen.

But Maggie cannot completely "take over the world" because she cannot control superior, mysterious forces. The oil shortage, the computerized accounts, the "mysterious and intangible" transformations of property—the novel is filled with reproductions and fakes—are examples of unpredictable and unknown aspects of the pattern that she believes she creates.

Maggie is "stupid." She refuses, except toward the novel's end, to admit that she is simply another "servant." Thus she provokes Spark's satiric thrusts: she lives in rich darkness "hardly needing her flashlamp."

Hubert, the sometime secretary-advisor-enemy of Maggie, is also a cunning fool. . . . [He] is only another false prophet who, like Maggie, refuses to see *through* money. Hubert is perhaps more dangerous than she; he speaks in metaphors and myths, recognizing that he can clothe his materialism in striking words: "The concepts of property and material possession are the direct causes of such concepts as perjury, lying, deception and fraud. In the world of symbol, and the worlds of magic, of allegory and mysticism, deceit has no meaning, lies do not exist, fraud is impossible." He "takes over" his flock, but he is seduced by his own words.

The novel is, then, a battle for ownership—over people as well as house—but it does not stay on one comic level. Spark subtly suggests that art itself is her underlying subject. She reminds us, as she did in her first novel, that she *as writer* is on uneasy ground. She is, after all, the owner of all of her characters—she possesses them—and she has to fight the very principles of lying and deceit they practice. But Spark must *lie* in order to create truth and to instruct us about spiritual life. There is an odd—and, I must add, an ancient—battle between art and divine truth.

If we can return to Hubert's words about the falsity of language, we can see that Spark uses these not only to point her accusing finger at his ill-conceived plots but at her own artistic struggles. She implies that many readers will settle for cosy coincidence, delightful reading and forget that her novel pursues other directions.

The Takeover is, strangely enough, a fake. Although it seems made for Hollywood . . . it is underneath all the glittering and showy details, a meditation upon the relation of art and religion. It compels us to search beneath the painted surface. Once we do, we see that it deals with the passing of eras, religions (save one!), pseudo-mystical concepts, prophecies, and earthly life. . . . *The Takeover* maintains that only one kind of truth can comfort us—to play with the title of her first novel [*The Comforters*]—and that heavenly wisdom can barely be glimpsed in earth-bound texts. (p. 25)

Irving Malin, in Commonweal *(copyright* © *1977 Commonweal Publishing Co., Inc.; reprinted by permission of Commonweal Publishing Co., Inc.), January 7, 1977.*

* * *

SPICER, Jack 1925-1965

An American poet, Spicer was a literary associate of Robert Duncan and Allen Ginsberg. He used his personal experiences in his poetry, often in a surreal manner.

"sur-réal-ism, n. (F. surrealisme) Art. A modern movement in art and literature, influenced by Freudianism, purporting to express the subconscious mental activities by presenting images without order or sequence, as in a dream." The method of the surrealists can be useful, the juxtaposition of unrelated images, the discontinuity of thought and language, even if there is no real use of the subconscious. The trappings of surrealism have become almost an affectation of the New York school of poets, but in the work of these poets, as with Spicer, there is usually a conscious shaping and directing of the poem's larger movement, despite discontinuities in the poem surface. Often groups of lines, sections of Spicer's poems, seem to have this kind of unstructured form "presenting images without order or sequence," and in his juxtaposition of images without a clear interrelationship he forces the mind to consider new conceptual directions in the structure of the poem. Surrealism, as it breaks up the sense of movement within the poem, could be considered even anti-poetic, but in his questioning of poetry Spicer still moves as a poet. He uses the method—the sound—of surrealism—the limitless tying together of unlikes that is implicit in surrealist technique—but in the larger outlines of the poem he is still thinking through image to idea. The materials of the poem seem to come from the subconscious, but the structuring of the materials is done by a conscious poetic intelligence. . . . There is the overhanging sense of the surrealistic, but it is never forced. It is almost an intellectual use of the technique, with strong differences between his imagery and the imagery of a Rimbaud. Rimbaud's intensity comes from the senses, from the touch, feel, color, scene—even in his use of the discontinuous there is an opulence of the senses that Gautier would have responded to, a breathing in at the nostrils of smells, tastes, sensations. (pp. 39-40)

Spicer's surrealism is of the mind, not of the senses, the pragmatic American use of a technique, rather than giving way to its full implications. (p. 41)

> *Samuel Charters, "Jack Spicer," in his* Some Poems/Poets: Studies in American Underground Poetry since 1945, *Oyez, 1971, pp. 37-45.*

The poetry of Jack Spicer . . . is an influence on younger poets today for its seeming openness to inner and outer experiences and to the wobble between. Spicer's poetry was anti-academic, rarely boring, but occasionally verbose, and diffuse; he was not a polisher but an utterer, a maker of burlesques as well as lyrics, a drunk, a buffoon. There were rare public appearances outside of some West Coast bars during Spicer's lifetime, the most famous being a reading and lecture at the B.C. Arts Festival in Vancouver the year he died. Though he achieved little fame during his lifetime except among his friends, Spicer met and considered himself a poetic ally of the older Robert Duncan, knew Ginsberg and many others on the San Francisco scene less well. . . .

Spicer had a vocabulary problem. He was seeking to detach himself from academic language, formalist language, the poem as object, to become his own man with his own voice, that studious modernist gay poet's voice which could boast and bray in plain speech that often tipped across the divide into hallucinations. "We make up a different language for poetry," he wrote, "and for the heart—ungrammatical." His poems are full of torn shapes, abrupt laughter. . . .

It's useful to read Spicer's work in sequence, as it is ordered in ["The Collected Books of Jack Spicer"], because he came to think of his poems not as isolated, perfectly engineered machines but as occasions, explorations, "books" of experience expanding the limits of perception through "an infinitely small vocabulary." As Blaser [the editor] points out, Spicer's sense of drama and play was augmented by his seeing the books of poems in serial fashion in an ordinary language reinvested with feeling and experience until "the word's meaning tears at a sense of life, and it is the nature of such tearing that it may lead to rage and terror, as it does throughout Jack's poetry. . . ."

I also find great playfulness, humor and tenderness in some of these poems, and very little shamming, or cant. (p. 26)

Jack Spicer's poems are always poised just on the face side of language, dipping all the way over toward that sudden flip, as if an effort were being made through feeling strongly in simple words to sneak up on the event of a man ruminating about something, or celebrating something, without rhetorical formulae, in his own beautiful inept awkwardness. It's that poised ineptitude and awkwardness of the anti-academic teacher, the scholar of linguistics who can't say what he knows in formal language, and has chosen to be naive and look and hear and do. Spicer was not a very happy poet. He was obsessed with possibilities he could only occasionally realize, and too aware of contemporary life to settle for anything less in his work than what he probably could not achieve. He must have been a great spirit. He seems to have been a good teacher. Much of what he wrote sticks with me, and, according to the loving way this volume was edited, he seems to have been a good friend to poetry, and other poets. (p. 28)

> *Richard Elman, in* The New York Times Book Review (© *1975 by The New York Times Company; reprinted by permission), November 23, 1975.*

The poems [in Spicer's first book, *After Lorca*,] were "translations"—the originals of some of which you could find and tag with your Lorca alongside, while others were half or more smudged away, and the rest no Lorca at all, pure Spicer. Through it all, meanwhile, back and forth, flowed tricky perfusions, flipped coins, compromised membranes: between Spanish and English, "real objects" and "the big lie of the personal," one dead poet and one live one. The letters [addressed to Lorca] were especially arresting, thick with the roots of a plain-spoken, strong, and cumulatively elegant aesthetic. A "game"—and here not only were the rules but also the Hall of Fame (Lorca, Yeats, Blake). Had it gone no further, had we been left only with this one strange book and not finally a total of twelve, *After Lorca* would have made for a spectacular artifact rather than an opus, a reputation. A twist of the poet's beloved lemon in our national drink—and we might have been forever intrigued but ultimately hazy about whether or not we wanted to play.

But there was an opus. Spicer's poems, in fact, got firmer, not slacker, as they went, and though wetting their lips there now and again, did not sit in precious pools or clever ones. How do we take them? We must decide.

Even in a self-conscious century, the fact of which we either embrace or avoid according to our (X-rayed) lights, no contemporary poet seems more art-occupied than Jack Spicer. Or more elusive. What he giveth in self-review he taketh away in a sort of holy thundering shyness that's more

Jerome than Francis. What's more, self-consciousness leads also to sorrows, in particular loneliness—who else but me is looking?—and here also Spicer is no more fully satisfying: he's the poet's poet par excellence, no reference points except the very poem, yet he refuses to console us with homilies and buck-up, trade-union sermons. Wonderfully likable in his muscular, no-bullshit manner, and yet in a second he's gone, just as he originally intended. Is it, then, all worth it?

Yes, Spicer is something new and valuable, extremely so. He was the first poet to really *believe* the tradition that was being contemporaneously forged in American poetry in the 1950s. While others were busily crammed-mouth both with poems and announcements of the new in the making, Spicer was getting down to work, having accepted the clarion simply and at once. This is important to keep in mind. The hortatory, long-strided mode we indistinctly call the Black Mountain movement is eclipsed in subtlety by Spicer ten times over, but he is still of that widened-out mode. Clever, pithy, brilliant, daring as he may be, Spicer was set from the start upon the One Thing, larger-goaled even than Olson and his polis and culture-straddling. Spicer wanted no less than to clear the totals on poetry's machine, to introduce the proper multipliers and dividers. Poem was all; and if so, what we made it from had to be more perdurable, of more lasting and truer clay than we ordinarily contributed. Spicer asked that it only be "objects," real things that the poet, totally subordinate, could "disclose . . . to make a poem that had no sound in it but the pointing of a finger." . . . Arguing for collage in poetry, in *After Lorca,* he says:

> But things decay, reason argues. Real things become garbage. . . . Yes, but the garbage of the real still reaches out into the current world making *its* objects, in turn, visible— lemon calls to lemon, newspaper to newspaper, boy to boy. As things decay, they bring their equivalents into being.

A luminous, bracing, finally naïve incantation. The equivalents, of course, never really do show; they knock on the door perhaps, but when the poem comes to answer they hide, and he has to fashion them himself in order not to stand dumb at the jamb. Spicer may always have known this—I would surely think he did—but not until the last works did he really give up hoping that the original garbage, set into the poem consciously, *dead-seriously,* would call up a metaphysical rhyme: an anti-poem, the "thing language" he wanted so hugely being neither an imagism or concretism but an anti-poetry. Spicer, finally, is an anti-poet. (pp. 5-7)

Spicer, by certain lamps, may look more trendily *meta-* than *anti-,* which may explain some of whatever audience he has, but not for long. The gradual, opus-long defeat of his own First Principle shows us this, and conversely shores up his triumph. . . . [For] a poet who embraced a Yeatsian sort of "dictation" that directed him at times to purposely misspell, duplicate poems exactly, shackle not only the literary will but also the emotive one ("you're trying to write a poem on Vietnam and you write a poem about skating in Vermont"), Spicer maintains a balance that's astoundingly sure. . . . Yet in the end he must hand himself over to a tremendous irony: that a poet who tried so hard to write personality-less poems brings forth one of the language's strongest personalities. That if his poems could never quite point the finger in that "infinitely small vocabulary" he hoped they could lead the way with, he himself

did. The world is, alas, perfect, and the poet moves further away from it with each effort. To read these collected books is to watch a fine poet get finer but lose every gain. But the direction remains. It is a moving, exhilarating, and expanding journey. (pp. 7-8)

When personal contacts of the poet's life intrude into the poem, they will be, he declares, "encysted" by the poet— "and the encysted emotion will itself become an object, to be transformed at last into poetry like the waves and the birds." Fancy footwork—but it's crucial: the tension and contradiction of this very point go a long way in highlighting both Spicer's attractiveness as a poet and also one of his major flaws. The personal is made out to be not much better than a germ, yet its appearance is relished for the sake of Spicer's controlling idea, which is leukocytic and wants the workout. The poet's homosexuality is unconcealed, and his poems have drawn a certain cultural nourishment—they cruise, so to speak, ready to "encyst" friends, lovers, and personal contact, at the same time chuting them into a world of objects. . . . [From] the start it's apparent that Spicer required, to make his poetry work, a gathering: real friends in a bar, real lovers, real gulls on a pier or lemons on a tree. His poems are all "serial," they all are in "books" that are as insulated and close, raucous and definable as a crowd in a North Beach bar. The "I— never seen" is tacitly replaced with a "we"; the poems echo off each other, never lacking for a comforter, illuminator, extricator, foil. They speak best tribally and to the sentimentality of cognoscenti—be they homosexuals, baseball fans, or, best of all poets. Spicer the poet becomes a "character" who makes his point and then fades into the ensuing din. (pp. 10-11)

A Book of Music ("with words by Jack Spicer," 1958) is much better [than the preceding books], less communally narcissistic than the "admonitions" and more direct. It is the first application of the aesthetic only through poems. . . . But, though striking, it's too sketchy a book. Almost in haste, the poems all take a dying fall—what the reader soon recognizes as a very Spicerian fall, an ironic thump—that here is yet to be completely convincing and seems more willy-nilly than eventual. This eagerness of their aggregate "points" makes the poems slightly too attention-directing to work effectively.

Billy the Kid (also 1958) has Spicer forsaking an investigation of the large for the small: his work will continually jump back and forth between verities we see clearly enough to either accept or try to civilize away (the world, the poem, God, language) and those that are incompletely revealed (mythology). (pp. 12-13)

The Heads of the Town Up to the Aether, dated 1960-61, borrows its title from a Gnostic text, and Robin Blaser, in his afterword, tells us that Spicer thought of this triune work in terms of the classical division: Hell, Purgatory, Paradise—but this, like the title, is concealed and crepuscular, the erudition isn't plaited before our eyes. I can think of no book of American poetry quite like this one. It's Spicer's best work, I'd say, the most rigorous, most dilating, undeterred by any thought of the reader's meekness and caution. Its self-attention is so manifest and unflagging that the superficial sour tastes—the weak jokes, camp silliness, overly with-it lordliness—lie close to the surface, covered only by daring. Yet what he began with, that scorn of the "big lie of the personal" has by this time been thaumaturged and become sublimely beside the point. If there's any triunity about this book, it is in the stripped-down annexing of poetry, poetry, and poetry—divined, discovered, and defined—and nothing else. (pp. 16-17)

The prose paragraphs [in *Homage to Creeley*] are not only a wizardly half-light image of the Hell motif ("Hell is where we place ourselves when we wish to look upward"), but also a running meditation on the very reality of the consciously recalcitrant poems. They are their ghosts, and own a second, eerie sight; sometimes trivial, always compensatory for corners and impossible fits. When the poems act up anticly, changed dictationally in composition, the ghost-answers are cool and unflustered; when the poems speak in the terrifyingly final rhythms of children's verse (and a pleasure it is to watch Spicer's brilliant perception of the nursery rhyme, that most supremely closed of all poetic forms, used as a wedge to open up his own), the "explanations" aerate them. What comes through so strongly here is a sense of the poet having calibrated his entire intellectual and sensible voice; then coming away so gracefully with its pattern. Assurance, a poet's most deadly affliction, is Spicer's pair of shears—with it he snips, pins, trims, refuses to make the poem a cenotaph. Preferring balsa to granite, he puts together mock-ups, and mock-ups are investigatory. Is this what a poem is? Statements made? Questions? Or perhaps questions-that are answers-that are questions again? Where should the poet step in? Assuming the ghost persona, Spicer might brazen out "Not anywhere," yet his written answer is more like: In the flow, helpless, the poet as turnstile, listening for echoes. Spicer has finally succeeded here in making his poetic a poetry. (p. 19)

Of all the books, it is perhaps *Language* (1964) that has received the widest recognition. A linguist by training . . ., Spicer came to the focus with lumbering ease, the abdicated, passed-beyond expert. Which may possibly account for the book's more than usual acceptance: poets often exhibit a continuing, tinkerer's fascination with formal linguistics; and Spicer, lopping off technical corners as he goes in order to make the thing fly, was articulating—most of the time brilliantly—a well-historied grounding for poetry that no other 1965 ideology (or ideolect) was providing. Poetry, said Williams, was "a small (or large) machine made out of words," and this book is a Spicerian assent, parsed down to the cogs. In sections titled Transformations, Morpheics, Phonemics, and Graphemics, each building-block is subjected to manifold tossings before being dropped into the poem's capacious bag. (p. 23)

[One] suspects [in *Language*] that the serial poem has failed, that its parameters are abused in weariness, that Spicer cleaves it out of loyalty and nothing else. The "idea" of the book constricts more than frees. The "big lie of the personal" is flogged weakly by weary reportage, some of the poems play to the grandstand, there's a nervousness, stuffiness, and brilliance that never melds.

But *Book of Magazine Verse* (published, next, in 1966) recoups. It is a posthumous volume, Spicer exiting in glory. In seven sequences of extraordinary poems, the social edginess has become an almost fearsome clarity. Real objects, the lemon of lemonness he began with, have turned, in these last powerful works, into skin: all and only what we can see—

> It's the shape of the lemon, I guess that causes
> trouble. It's
> ovalness, it's rind. This is where my love,
> somehow, stops.

The garbage Spicer proposed be set into the poem minus all

personalization ("As things decay they bring their equivalents into being") hasn't obliged. Strong hides have resisted the pinnings. It was no more than the sentimentality that bruised the earlier poems to think they could be, no more than a terrified dream. . . . The love is patently Christian, though undeclared. Desperate and futile love—a crowning correspondence to the poem's. In this last book, Spicer has become as careful with the two as a man transporting beakers of acid. The erotic poems here are his best: hard, smooth, ungassy, the loved ones honored by not simultaneously being made objects—that's *a priori*. (pp. 26-7)

The last ten poems were meant for *Downbeat*, the jazz magazine. . . . [The] poems have wonderful things to say about California and our romantic sixties fetishism for guerillas. But more than anything they are about Spicer himself, much as the final *Cantos* are a totting-up of Pound. . . . The towel seems thrown in, thrown to those who from beginning to end have been closest at hand: other poets. In the very final poem, [to Allen Ginsberg, the] . . . tone tells all. It didn't work, the collage didn't stick, things remained stubbornly, goldenly discrete, and there was an absence of answers. The moon, at the end of his life, comes to Spicer not directed to by the poem but on television, watching the astronauts. . . . (pp. 29-30)

> *Rose Feld, "Lowghost to Lowghost," in* Parnassus: Poetry in Review *(copyright © by* Parnassus: Poetry in Review), *Spring/ Summer, 1976, pp. 5-30.*

* * *

STEAD, Christina   1902-

An Australian novelist and short story writer, Stead has successfully relied on personal experiences and travels for much of the material of her fiction. (See also *CLC*, Vols. 2, 5, and *Contemporary Authors*, Vols. 13-16, rev. ed.)

[In *The Little Hotel*, Christina Stead's] small hotel in Switzerland holds, embraces, madmen and predators, snobs and sentimentalists. Her laconic brittle style, with transitions that look blind in their curtness but nevertheless allow us to glimpse some haunting insights, finds its dramatic correlative in the narrative voice of the woman who runs the limping hotel. "My English is not very good," the woman may say, but such words take their place within the way in which Miss Stead's English is very good. . . .

[Miss Stead depicts] a tragicomic shabby-genteel world, in which the upper lip is stiff and the lower one is trembling, and [she] has a great gift for sensing the words that escape from just such a divided mouth. . . . The desiccation of such a life, its fear of sexuality, its embittered clutch upon its ancestors and its descendants—all this makes *The Little Hotel* at once painfully impressive and yet painedly narrow, like a wince. The allied ironies which coursed through what is still Miss Stead's best book were more ample, for *The Man Who Loved Children* was open to larger failures of imagination in its terrifying family than those which fret and lacerate the denizens of the little hotel. (p. 14)

> *Christopher Ricks, in* The New York Review of Books *(reprinted with permission from* The New York Review of Books; *copyright © 1975 NYREV, Inc.), June 26, 1975.*

["The Little Hotel"] takes place in Lausanne, and has for a narrator Mme. Selda Bonnard, the proprietress of a small

Swiss *pension* patronized for its moderate rates and tolerant management. Beginning in the breathless, flustered voice of a stage monologuist, Mme. Bonnard tells us of her guests, concentrating upon the Mayor of B., a Belgian official boisterously suffering from a nervous breakdown; the subtle portrait of his derangement is too real to be funny. A globe deranged seems implied in the sketches of the other guests. . . . [A] "Magic Mountain"-like microcosm of Europe appears intended, though on a less Alpine scale. Yet the book never quite takes hold as that; its locus in time seems vaguely scattered, as if it had been composed over a long stretch of years. Wilson's Labour Government appears to rule England, but a more immediately postwar atmosphere colors the financial manipulations and political anxieties of the characters. Rather indistinguishably aged and reactionary, they all agree that the Russians are about to invade Switzerland. Thus immersed in the Cold War, the book is slow to thaw, though chips of icy vividness fly when Miss Stead gives a character more than a passing glance. . . . A deep experience of life speaks in such phrases as "the unmistakable trotting and nodding of the long-married" and "the fresh beauty of blood newly mixed." Yet for much of the book the reader feels about these glimpsable guests as Mrs. Trollope [one of the guests] does: "I can see everything that everyone does; and it all has nothing to do with me."

This compact novel, full of anecdotes, seems to lack a story; we only slowly realize that, by a remarkable technical sleight of hand, the story has become Mrs. Trollope's. The narrator, Mme. Bonnard, begins to tell us of conversations at which she was not present, and in the end enters very intimately into the private emotions and history of this Mrs. Trollope. . . . Though the other characters continue to pose, to flaunt their individual terrors and cruelties with increasing shamelessness, our interest remains caught up in this middle-aged, kindhearted half-caste's brave, hopeless, and salutary effort to end a liaison prolonged to the point of degradation. (pp. 79-80)

Throughout, money or its lack is crucial, and it is the women, rich and poor, who are exploited, Mrs. Trollope's decisive, revolutionary gesture is to give money meant to buy her lover a car to the dying Miss Abbey-Chillard, for her medical expenses. Miss Stead, an outspoken left-winger, enriches her perceptions of emotional dependence with a tactile sense of money as a pervasive, unpleasant glue that hold her heroines fast, in their little hotels of circumstance. (p. 80)

> *John Updike, in* The New Yorker (© 1975 *by The New Yorker Magazine, Inc.), August 18, 1975.*

Readers of Christina Stead will find her ninth novel, *The Little Hotel,* a refinement of the riches that delighted them in her *House of All Nations* and *The Man Who Loved Children.* They have come to expect abundance, even to put up with the "mechanical superabundance" which Randall Jarrell, one of her most perceptive critics, acknowledged while celebrating her gift for concentration and swift conclusiveness. They will not be disappointed now, for in spite of this book's much smaller frame she does not stint. Yet neither is there excess, although not until we finish *The Little Hotel* do we realize the significance of the information so casually given—almost thrown away—in the course of a brief, crowded narrative. (p. 21)

It is difficult to convey Christina Stead's special style with-

out quoting her, and difficult to quote without . . . suggesting that she is compiling a postwar bestiary of the lunatic Right. She is caricaturing, in a way, but the constant crisscrossing of relations, influenced less by ideology than by small social snubs, stinginess and generosity, boredom and amusement, affection and hatred, cuts across political lines, and keeps these grotesques from being the mere cartoons they might have become in other hands. . . .

Stead's direction is clear, her vision all of a piece. She is too subtle . . . to stress the obvious continuity between *House of All Nations* and *The Little Hotel,* and too original to exploit the foregone, sententious "ship-of-fools" convention. (p. 22)

> *Ruth Middleton Mathewson, "A Bestiary of the Lunatic Right," in* The New Leader (© *1975 by the American Labor Conference on International Affairs, Inc.), September 29, 1975, pp. 21-2.*

If [*Miss Herbert*] came from an unknown author, it would be described as parts of three separate novels, shakily dovetailed by the presence of a single heroine who is necessarily (since she must operate in widely different areas) of vaporous character and indeterminate abilities. Eleanor begins as a liberated Bohemian type, a would-be writer supported more by her lovers than by her talentless pen. She next appears as the wife of a dismal twerp, dedicating her time to children, house repairs, and bad cooking. Ultimately, she is a middle-aged divorcée scratching along on fringe literary jobs. Her literary activities, incidentally, do not hold the episodes of the novel together because they are unbelievable; she simply has no ability whatsoever and even her modest success as an agent and manuscript reader is incredible. Each of Eleanor's incarnations trails loose ends—a mysterious religious sect, an experimental farm, a man who is either a blackmailer or a spy; one learns no details and nothing ever comes of these intriguing items.

The action of the novel runs from some time after World War II to the present, but much of the conversation, particularly the sexual opinions, suggests the 1920s, while such descriptions of costume as occur are vaguely out of period. Eleanor always wears silk stockings, for example, in this age of nylon. Throughout her adventures, Eleanor remains invincibly self-centered and boneheaded, her mind functioning in a string of clichés whether the topic is a woman's right to erotic experiment, the noble duties of a wife and mother, or the merits of hard work and independence. These clichés, which eventually become quite amusing, account for the structure of the book. Miss Stead puts her heroine through three cliché feminine roles—trollop, housewife, and worker—and demonstrates that a girl is bound to lose at all of them. (p. 87)

> *Phoebe-Lou Adams, in* The Atlantic Monthly (copyright © 1976 by The Atlantic Monthly Company, Boston, Mass.; reprinted with permission), August, 1976.*

Christina Stead is a caustically keen observer of a wide spectrum of human scenes; she writes a direct prose that can rise to all but the largest occasions of poetry; she is politically thoughtful without being propagandistic, giving her characters a sufficient but not crushing burden of ideological significance; and she has travelled well in the human interior and can be devastatingly clear about some of its uglier turns. The portrait, for instance, in ["Miss Herbert"] of Eleanor's husband, Heinz (he rechristens himself Henry), gives us the very anatomy of a pill, of a prissy, snobbish, rigid, parentally babied Swiss petit bourgeois who turns vicious and hysterical in divorce without surrendering his self-righteousness and cunning. Though he is absent from most of the novel's pages, he remains the best and the worst thing in it, and the female antagonist sheds her air of inert, trivial enchantment whenever he touches her. It is an odd, and possibly unintended, comment on the state of women that this woman, drifting through squads of dream men, comes to life chiefly in connection with her horrid little husband; this may be the point of "Miss Herbert's" uneasy subtitle, "(The Suburban Wife)."

Among the gifts Miss Stead does not conspicuously possess is that of joy, which translates, in the narrative art, into the gift of lubrication. Her plots move chunkily, by jerks of hasty summary and epistolary excerpt; her dialogues are abrasive, full of dry, twittery self-exposition and clichés that may or may not be deliberate.... The historical background is vague. Eleanor sows her wild oats in what must be the thirties, appears to sleep soundly through the Second World War, and awakens to middle age in a postwar world soured by discontented allusions to America and its dollars. This softness of periphery would not matter if Eleanor were herself firmly in focus, but she is not.... How much—the novel's central uncertainty—are we meant to like her? Is she a woman embodying a universal femininity, or is she seen throughout as a hopeless English woman—pink, hearty, energetic, romantic, tame, futile, essentially stupid? (pp. 75-6)

If some heroines seduce their own creators into liking them, some heroes, such as the narrator of Camus's "The Stranger," are meant to challenge our notions of what likability is. What we like, in the end, is life, and Eleanor Brent lives too little in what she does. We are pleased that she is handsome, and appreciate her capacity for hard work; but good looks and daily works are not defining actions in the Aristotelian sense: "Life consists in action, and its end is a mode of action, not a quality." The "Poetics" continues, "Now, character determines men's qualities, but it is by their actions that they are happy or the reverse." Eleanor's actions are chiefly acts of avoidance.... The sad, and clearly intended, irony is that we have been made to feel, after three hundred pages, that not much of a life has been lived.... Well, what actions *has* society made available to women? Not every woman can be Clytemnestra, as Aristotle should have realized. Nor an empire builder, as even Ayn Rand might admit. The moral stature that Jane Austen gave to the search for a husband can no longer be assumed; and even the decision to betray the marriage bed—the nineteenth-century wife's revolutionary alternative—no longer seems momentous. If there is such a thing as a "woman's novel," it finds itself bound, at least in the honest hands of [Miss Stead] to the figurative description not of an action but of a quality—the quality of femininity, static and wary, hugging to itself the bleak dignity of solitude. (pp. 76-7)

> *John Updike, in* The New Yorker (© *1976 by The New Yorker Magazine, Inc.), August 9, 1976.*

*   *   *

STOPPARD, Tom   1937-

A Czech-born British playwright and novelist, Stoppard is noted for his humorous and innovative dramas. Best known for his popular play *Rosencrantz and Guildenstern Are Dead*,

Stoppard is the recipient of a Tony Award and a New York Drama Critics Circle Award. (See also *CLC*, Vols 1, 3, 4, 5.)

The external brilliances in *Travesties,* its manic virtuosity of language, its diabolical manipulation of time and notion, cannot elude any visitor to Tom Stoppard's verbal prank....

Stoppard's collage is ... a jostling of dissimilar elements, personages related only in that they all happened to be in Zurich in 1917: James Joyce, Vladimir Lenin, Tristan Tzara (a founder of Dada), and a British consular flunky named Henry Carr. As [Luciano] Berio uses Mahler as his *objet trouvé,* Stoppard uses [*The Importance of Being Earnest*]. That is because [his protagonist] Carr's one moment of relative glory, in a life otherwise uncrowded with incident, was his appearance as Algernon in a production of the play put together by Joyce. That event, and the petty squabble that arose from it, were of no importance to anyone except Carr but, as his senile memory struggles to construct a portentous memoir of that time and that place, his thoughts take shape as scenes from *Earnest.* ...

Under the sheen of its immense daring, the play reveals a touching center, a study of a useless but endearing chap frantically beating off the onrush of obscurity. His struggle is inept, but ineptitude has been his life companion....

Multilayered, complex, intellectually astringent, Stoppard's play bats about a remarkable number of important ideas.... Stoppard involves his historical characters in a web of fictions: Joyce (who made words dance) bickering with Tzara (because he loathes the way the Dadaists make words dance); Lenin, the spirit of a progressive age, whose idea of a good evening at the theater is a performance of *Camille....* The very disorganization of Carr's memory becomes the play's organizing force. As the old man gabbles along, his thoughts go off in opposing directions and take on clashing tone-colors. This Stoppard translates into a broad spectrum of theater techniques: a music-hall number here, a dance there, a spy-behind-the-arras routine worthy of the Keystone Kops....

"Great days ... Zurich during the War," says Carr at the start of his last monologue. That much we know from history, and that chapter might serve for an excellent historical play. The ultimate, mind-tickling travesty in *Travesties* is the way history becomes vivid as anti-history. It is thinking-man's theater that makes it a privilege to think. (p. 102)

> *Alan Rich, in* New York Magazine (© *1975 by NYM Corp.; reprinted by permission of* New York Magazine *and Alan Rich), November 17, 1975.*

About *Travesties* [in an earlier review] ... I had written that [Tom Stoppard] is "brilliantly adept as well as highly cultivated. He is certainly entertaining. Besides his shrewd theatrical sportiveness there is in him an itch to communicate matters of philosophical import." I failed however to grasp exactly what the import of *Travesties* might be. I supposed it to be contained in the play's concluding lines—"You're either a revolutionary or you're not, and if you're not you might as well be an artist as anything else.... If you can't be an artist, you might as well be a revolutionary...."

I realize now that this aphorism sums up an attitude that informs Stoppard's other plays: *Rosencrantz and Guildenstern Are Dead* and *Jumpers*. This attitude—in its context it cannot be called a "philosophy"—is one of almost total skepticism: we can be sure of nothing. Humankind is tossed about in a storm of experience with no certainty as to its origin, direction or outcome. The thought may cause us to shed tears or arouse laughter. Stoppard laughs.

The joke in *Travesties* is that the memory of our own past is as unreliable as everything else. . . . [The] individual person can't alter the course of history. It's a rationalization for social passivity—or for becoming an artist! . . .

[In] this play Stoppard is neither a revolutionary nor, except in a most limited sense, an artist. The play is a charade, full of antic capers, educated allusions and bright writing in high-grade English. As such it is a superior show not entirely without significance. Its amused skepticism suggests flaccidity of will, the weakening of moral sinew characteristic of our time. It gratifies those for whom a jocular literacy and a modicum of theatrical and intellectual glitter are sufficient. (p. 540)

Harold Clurman, in The Nation *(copyright 1975 by the Nation Associates, Inc.), November 22, 1975.*

Since I tend to think that *Rosencrantz and Guildenstern* has a genuine point to make about the relation of role to identity and that *Jumpers* is a serious statement about the failures of traditional humanism, I expected to find substance under the glitter of *Travesties*. The word *travesty* is used just once in the play, when Henry Carr, recalling the legal decision which went against him, labels it "a travesty of justice." This usage suggests to me that the travesties of the play are not simply those of the ideas and words of Joyce, Lenin and Tzara, but that—in his usual pessimistic way—Stoppard is viewing all of art and politics as travesty, and certainly, through Carr's reminiscence, the remembered life becomes burlesque. The Russian revolution, the writing of *Ulysses,* the anarchic implications of Dada have the same validity and the same importance as the cucumber sandwiches in *The Importance of Being Earnest.* Stoppard has been doing a soft-shoe around existential chaos ever since he turned up in the English theater, and *Travesties* is either his blackest statement to date or his assumption that the surface joke is what counts. I tend toward the second reading, classing *Travesties* with *After Magritte* rather than *Jumpers.* (p. 114)

Gerald Weales, in Commonweal *(copyright © 1976 Commonweal Publishing Co., Inc.; reprinted by permission of Commonweal Publishing Co., Inc.), February 13, 1976.*

In the beginning was *Rosencrantz and Guildenstern,* a puzzling and therefore profound comedy; then came the Fall: from *Jumpers,* a witty satire on linguistic philosophy, to *Travesties,* a clever farce about nothing in particular. Such seems to be the commonest current view. It should be scotched before it hardens into critical orthodoxy; for Stoppard's wild Wilde is greater than his domesticated Shakespeare.

Admittedly, *Rosencrantz and Guildenstern* is profound comedy, in spite of some unclarity, but *Jumpers* offers a good deal more than satire on philosophy, while *Travesties* is Stoppard's greatest and most superficial play—as Wilde's *Importance of Being Earnest* is his. There is more, however, to *Travesties'* travesty of Wilde than there is to Wilde's travesty of Scribean melodrama. Like Wilde, it is everywhere paradoxical, but its paradoxes far more often open

up the nature of reality. Though blatantly artificial it resembles reality by being ambiguous and multi-layered. In fact, Stoppard's latest play is an onion; superficial at every level: *profoundly* superficial. Like the world of appearances it is heartless; no inner truth or more real reality is to be found by stripping off layers of appearance. An idea anticipated by the striptease that opens *Jumpers:* the secretary swinging by her legs from a trapeze 'between darkness and darkness . . . into the spotlight and out' discarding layers of clothing (but not her knickers). A brilliant *coup de théâtre,* but in retrospect, surely, a symbol of the Naked Truth, seen only in glimpses, flashes of illumination, and never quite whole. Throughout the play she never speaks (the truth is not self-explanatory). She is the mistress of McFee the rationalist 'acrobat' and the secretary of George Moore the metaphysician; she 'takes down' for both, but in different senses. Theatrically speaking, both sides are seen to possess her in some way, but neither knows the Whole Truth. In *Travesties* the idea is given an extra twist when Cecily strips (again, only to her knickers) while incongruously purveying at length the Marxist 'truth' about the economic nature of reality.

If some truths, as distinct from mere facts, involve values then such values, not being given, must be constructed (as Joyce put it) 'upon the incertitude of the void'. Or so it would seem. To say so definitely would not only be undramatic but also unStoppardian. . . . For Stoppard the problem of knowledge has no solution; we must just learn to live with it—and laugh about the absurdities it generates.

Fundamentally, all three of his plays deal with the problem of knowledge (how do we know we really *know* what we think we know?); and all three are travesties. . . . Moreover, something of each is to be found in all. In *Jumpers* philosophical debate, not quite travestied, but satirical in so far as it concerns Archie, dandy leader of the scientific rationalists, humorous in connection with George Moore, outgunned but undefeated metaphysician. *Rosencrantz and Guildenstern,* texturally, often travesties philosophical debates on reality and illusion while structurally calling in question the nature of reality through its triple perspective: of the worlds of *Hamlet,* the Players, and Rosencrantz and Guildenstern. And *Travesties* travesties not only Wilde (and Joyce) but also Shakespeare. . . . (pp. 66, 68)

All three plays, by evoking literature as often as life, merge questions of art with those of nature and reality—and also, almost inevitably . . . raise questions of identity. Is 'the truest poetry the most feigning' as Shakespeare said? Is the truest person the most posing, as Wilde maintained? After all, characters are not being 'themselves' when travestying some other author (or even travestying the travesty . . .). (p. 68)

All are remarkable comedies combining brilliant surfaces with deep themes. The difference is that in *Travesties* Stoppard has so mastered his medium that with deceptive ease he provides more of everything, as if it were nothing.

So much more, that this play requires a new concept. Where most, including *Rosencrantz and Guildenstern* and *Jumpers,* have a theme or themes, *Travesties* is constructed as a thematic network: some twenty interrelated aspects of the problem of knowledge, areas of uncertainty, working in varied permutation. All, of course, are dramatized either in the Library, repository of fiction and faction (mirrored in the characters of Joyce and Lenin), of illusions and truths, or they are set in the Room, where Carr's often unreliable memories are cultivated.

That life is layered is most obviously, but by no means only, suggested by the underlying Wilde play and the fact that *Travesties* is a play about doing a play, in the middle of a war. The problem of layered personal identity is constantly posed.... (p. 69)

Design and Chance, Appearance and Reality, Art and Delusion, all ... are reflected throughout in innumerable touches, for the thematic network is built up, insinuated almost, by a verbal *pointillisme*. In that way contextual density is triumphantly married with textural lightness, gravity with levity.

Occasional touches, it is true, simply serve to maintain the sunlit atmosphere.... Mostly, though, what might appear to be only textural playwit turns out to be also relevant to theme and structural form. So, for instance, 'My art belongs to Dada' recalls Joyce's repeated Yes to life (something echoed elsewhere in *Travesties*), and it prompts subliminal reflections as to whether a mercenary 'heart' represents a falsity or a true (or realistic?) attachment as compared with romantic illusion. Similarly the two Joyce chapters travestied are relevant to theme as well as character. For the Oxen of the Sun chapter, itself made up of chronological parodies, suggests that men in every age stylize basic realities—but leaves open the question whether they thereby falsify a true identity or, through the pose, create one. (pp. 70-1)

The general flippancy over the great and bloody issues of the First World War and the Russian Revolution, too, avoids censure by being always relevant to such highly abstract concerns. (This is a play of ideas, not characters; that is why the characters have no characteristic diction.) Joyce's rejoinder to Carr is a miniscule example: '"And what did you do in the Great War?" "I wrote *Ulysses*," he said. "What did you do?".' In retrospect, which *was* the better thing to do? (p. 71)

In brief, the mode of *Travesties* is metaphoric, parodic, and semifactual—constantly, therefore raising the question: What is literal truth? What is authentic? What is fact? The mood, appropriately paradoxical, is hilarious and nostalgic: gradually Carr's youth is revealed as the youth of our world and of modernism in art (and this hints—no more—that these, like Carr himself, may have turned to seediness and disillusion now). The form is almost a contradiction in terms—again appropriately, for we are not to be allowed to settle into assumptions of certainty. Wild Wilde, it mingles the well-made play and its elegance of dialogue with the dislocations of Brechtian expressionism and its shock tactics (imagine *Wilde's* Gwendolen musing: 'Gomorrahist ... Silly bugger!') The texture is shot-silk, always shifting and shining—and, like life, paradoxical. Patches of rhyme and dance demonstrably turn life into art and, some might argue (depending on their views of modernist art), *vice versa*.

Travesties travesties both the literature and the lives it is based on, in the cause of something other than 'the facts'. Concerned *with* the problem of knowledge, however, it is unconcerned *about* it; like most of the best comedies it encourages us to enjoy what we must endure. (pp. 71-2)

[Stoppard's] is the kind of comedy nearest to farce; and much of his work ... *is* farce—but neither pure nor simple. Indeed, [the] farces are curiously complementary to the comedies. His is the kind of farce nearest to comedy—'divertissement' might identify it better.

After Magritte is a sort [of] *Jumpers* in rompers, *Dirty*

(New-Found-Land) Linen a bourgeois *Travesties* in black bowlers.... Appealing, respectively, to the infant anarchist and the feet-of-clay fetichist in all of us, they are not consciously problematical. Though they concern inquiries, the problem of knowledge is no part of their meaning; merely a significance that could be extrapolated from them for the sake of metacritical argument. Appearance and reality, identity and hypocrisy occur as matter for amusement only. Moreover, their latent problems of knowledge, if wilfully actualized, would seem to be shown as unreal or easily soluble. The scenes of apparent polymorphous perversity, the weird interpretations of identity, in *After Magritte* turn out to have rational, even humdrum, explanations, while the Freudian slips (and knickers) exposed at the opening of *Dirty Linen* leave us in no doubt of the underlying truth.

However, these pieces are complementary to the major works in two ways. Firstly, they obviously spring from the same source, but the laughter is less that of conscious recognition than of a defensive and escapist reaction to some subconscious awareness of nightmare uncertainties that are in fact neither unreal nor easily soluble. Secondly, the assured structures here operate as reassuring frameworks of order rather than demonstrations of absurdity.

Taken as a whole, then, Stoppard's work to date is all of a piece, but three-dimensionally so, the divertissements only expressing what the comedies also consider—and, by considering, conquer. (pp. 72-3)

Allan Rodway, "Stripping Off," in London Magazine (© London Magazine *1976), August-September, 1976, pp. 66-73.*

Having demonstrated (to anyone's satisfaction, I should think) an awesome mastery over the English language in the service of elegant and witty game-playing, Tom Stoppard has now moved gloriously onward. *Dirty Linen*, Mr. Stoppard's latest verbal sally ... represents the author's conquest of something new for him, and very old for anyone else. On the surface, his work is pure, old-fashioned knockabout farce. Beneath that surface, however, there is a great deal more.

The premise is farcical enough, no less so for being as timely as tomorrow's headlines. A parliamentary committee is in session to investigate press accusations of moral whoop-de-do within legislative ranks. The setting is London but, as any fool can see, that choice of venue is purely arbitrary; Washington, Rome, or perhaps even Katmandu would do as well. The committee members are, we are soon to learn, up to their own quivering necks in the same stuff they're out to explore....

Mr. Stoppard's manner of treating this material is, as I suggested above, the most elemental kind of comic theater.... But there is also a circularity to the joke-writing, an underlying web of comic leitmotiv, a complex texture of cross-references that keep the mind—and, even more, the memory—constantly and congenially at work as the play winds its brief course. This is Mr. Stoppard's peculiar, individual skill. He has taken the easiest of theatrical forms, and infused it with a structure, an ability to challenge the intellect, that raises the level of farce to something approaching sophistication....

There is also something else. The committee recesses, and into the same room come two more governmental flunkies.... Basically this insert (called *New-Found-Land*) is a pair of monologues. The older man delivers a dithering memoir of Lloyd George; the younger, a weird and wonderful flood of blather about romantic America, a coast-to-coast travelogue so full of overblown hyperbole and misinformation as to make a Fitzpatrick blush. The whole diversion is a wonderful knockabout of language at its most useless; its insertion into a wholly different context is, like everything else in this wild and dazzling flight of theatrical fancy, the work of a cockeyed, original theatrical genius.

> *Alan Rich, "'Dirty Linen' Is Pure Silk," in* New York Magazine *(© 1977 by NYM Corp.; reprinted by permission of* New York Magazine *and Alan Rich), January 24, 1977, p. 89.*

Mr. Stoppard is a particular hero of mine, and it is an ineradicable defect in our relationship with heroes that we assume they can do no wrong; on occasions that prove the contrary, we feel indignation along with disappointment, as if we were in the presence not of a momentary failure of talent but of an act of personal malice directed by the hero against his worshippers. In my awareness of the perils of such pitfalls, I must take care not to be *too* angry with Mr. Stoppard for being fallible; it was I who invented and praised the inhumanly perfect playwright he isn't. The glee with which I listened to the opening volley of badinage in "Dirty Linen" was, I perceive now, an emotion more appropriate to the play than the irritation with which I responded to the operatic exclamation—"*Finita la commedia!*"—that arbitrarily concludes it. Mr. Stoppard has written a trifle, better suited to summer camp than to Broadway; in his grand Collected Works, to be brought out in twenty folio volumes in the year 2000, it is likely to survive as little more than an asterisk. (p. 63)

> *Brendan Gill, in* The New Yorker *(© 1977 by The New Yorker Magazine, Inc.), January 24, 1977.*

Dirty Linen displays the unencumbered Stoppard of *The Real Inspector Hound* and the first act of *Travesties*, rather than the weightier and duller one of the existential implications in *Rosencrantz and Guildenstern Are Dead* and *Jumpers*, and the political ponderosities of the second act of *Travesties*. Here Stoppard has actually created two larger-than-farce-size characters: Maddie Gotobed, whose simple and unpremeditated copulations, coupled with shrewd observations on human nature, make her a splendid comic archetype; and Malcolm Whitenshaw, the committee chairman, a lowly Lancastrian with brazen aspirations to a peerage, the peerless paradigm of inept opportunism that will eventually make it on sheer dumb persistence. (p. 24)

> *John Simon, in* The New Leader *(© 1977 by the American Labor Conference on International Affairs, Inc.), January 31, 1977.*

In a certain sense, Mr. _____ is to me our only thorough playwright. He plays with everything: with wit, with philosophy, with drama, with actors and audience, with the whole theatre.

Bernard Shaw wrote that in 1895 about Oscar Wilde, thus neatly anticipating what I want to say about the most brilliantly playful of living playwrights, Tom Stoppard. Of course, Shaw's formulation is far from being the whole truth about Wilde, beneath whose levity can generally be discerned a desperate seriousness—not surprising in one who labored under the crushing burden of inventing and

exemplifying a whole outcast subculture (now, of course, arduously casting itself back in).

Since Wilde, the frivolity of many gay writers (from Coward to Ortun, not to mention Tavel and Ludlam) has tended to have an edge, an animus, a driven quality about it; wit for them, as for Wilde, is their main armament in a guerilla war against respectable society. Mr. Stoppard is more nearly purely playful than they; being evidently not gay, he can afford to be less sad. As a literary dandy he can go plume on plume with anyone, but his plumes, on the whole, are not weapons in disguise. (Which does not in itself make him better or worse—just different.)

He can, however, in his own way, be serious in the midst of his playfulness; he does not even try to hide it, as Wilde did. *Rosencrantz and Guildenstern Are Dead* and *Jumpers* are about real predicaments, real states of feeling; we can get into a personal relationship with their protagonists, and be touched by them. As for *Travesties*, I have maintained that there is something serious in Mr. Stoppard's *refusal* to be serious about the serious matters he deals with in that play: a paradox that Wilde would have found congenial. In *Travesties*, as in so much of Wilde's own work, playfulness becomes a kind of assertion of freedom.

But Mr. Stoppard's *Dirty Linen* . . . is *merely* playful. . . .

[As] satire, *Dirty Linen* doesn't get very far. Mr. Stoppard is not primarily interested in satire; he's interested in playing word games. They are unbelievably brilliant word games—parodies, allusions, running gags, puns, puns, puns in mind-boggling profusion—but there is nothing much in *Dirty Linen* to become involved with. In the very best comedy, from Aristophanes to Groucho and beyond, there is usually someone whose fate, in however odd a way, we come to care about; not here. Like *The Real Inspector Hound*, *Dirty Linen* is one of Mr. Stoppard's minor works, a *jeu d'esprit*, and somewhat . . . insubstantial.

But the show is saved by Mr. Stoppard's most playful stroke of all. Inside *Dirty Linen* he has ingeniously contrived to place an entirely different play, a tiny interlude entitled *New-Found-Land*. (p. 69)

The high point of *New-Found-Land* [is] . . . what [Mr. Stoppard] mocks: the yearning for a new land, the vision that America has created, and that has in turn created America. Here is the moment of feeling that the evening had needed to raise it from mechanical laughter and dispassionate admission to real delight. (pp. 69-70)

> *Julius Novick, "Going Plume on Plume," in* The Village Voice *(reprinted by permission of* The Village Voice; *copyright © by The Village Voice, Inc., 1977), January 31, 1977, pp. 69-70.*

*   *   *

STOREY, David   1933-

A British playwright and novelist, Storey often uses athletic situations as his literary settings. Concerned with the effect the past has on an individual's ability to live life to its fullest, Storey depicts persons alienated from their families, friends, teams, class, and themselves. Storey is a recipient of, among other awards, the New York Drama Critics Circle Award. (See also *CLC*, **Vols, 2, 4, 5.)**

[Storey] has refused to stand still. He has gone from vigorous naturalism to the most florid, turbulent romanticism;

has experimented with cool, dry humour, adapting his expertise in the theatre to evolve a lean and bony style, strong and self-effacing and depending mainly on dialogue; and has achieved in his latest book, *Saville,* a highly individual way of treating, with honesty and sympathy, the conventional theme of poor boy's flight from family ties and oppressive home environment. (p. 80)

David Storey has not rested on the laurels of *This Sporting Life.* You can never predict what his next book will be like. What could have been more different from the account of machinations in scrum and boardroom of a Rugby League club than the sultry, sombre romanticism of *Radcliffe,* with its heavy sexual symbolism, its frequent use of the pathetic fallacy, and its larger-than-life characters who all seem to want either to destroy or to save someone else? The atmosphere is of *Wuthering Heights* re-written by Lawrence. *Radcliffe* was a clumsy, blundering, groping and yet oddly impressive book. And it gave only false clues to the direction in which Storey would develop.

It was almost impossible to believe that Storey's next two novels were by the author of *Radcliffe.* Where *Radcliffe* sprawled, *Pasmore* was compressed as tight as a nut. Where *Radcliffe* was completely humourless, *A Temporary Life* was cool, witty, elegant; and in the Head of the Art School, 'Skip' Wilcox, potato-soup addict and simple-life fanatic, Storey created a comic character who would have been unthinkable under the lowering skies and crumbling crenellations of *Radcliff.* (pp. 82-3)

Saville . . . is no ordinary novel about growing up and away. Nor is it like any of Storey's earlier novels. He avoids both the extravagances of *Radcliffe* and the somewhat 'flip', cool humour of *A Temporary Life.* He has achieved a more honest and true-to-life account of childhood and school days than any I have read. He is the master, equally, of description and of dialogue. He has looked and listened closely, and remembered accurately. (p. 83)

One reason why Storey is all the time developing and improving . . . is that he takes art seriously. There are quite specific indications of Storey's attitude in several of his books. In *Radcliffe,* Leonard says, 'The only real politics is art. The rest is just sentiment.' Storey, like Colin in *Saville,* has the artist's receptivity to experience, a 'faith in impossibility'. 'Everything is allowable; everything is permissible; anything can happen. It's arrogance to assume it can't.' . . . Storey finds it 'touching . . . that if everything is meaningless, nevertheless we still ascribe some meaning to it'. It is a fertile philosophy for a writer. (p. 84)

John Mellors, in London Magazine (© London Magazine *1976), October-November, 1975.*

I am not quite sure what David Storey was trying to do in writing "Life Class," but whatever it was, I doubt if he has done it. . . .

"Life Class" (double-edged title?) is full of pronouncements by Alott [the protagonist] and others concerning Art, Life, Revolution, and other topics of general interest, which are supposed, I think, to function in counterpoint to the goings-on, first desultory and then violent, in the classroom, with talk and action fusing into an ironic commentary on the place of art in modern society. But the counterpoint never gets working properly, leaving the pronouncements out on their own as empty gassing, and the action, also out on its own, amorphous in the first act, gratuitous in the second, and frequently, in both acts, not quite convincing.

The play is like some of the students' drawings: smudgy.

Julius Novick, "When Does Art Turn into Rape?" in The Village Voice *(reprinted by permission of* The Village Voice; *copyright © by The Village Voice, Inc., 1975), December 22, 1975, p. 115.*

David Storey is one of the most interesting of present-day English playwrights. Though *Life Class* is not as finished an accomplishment as *The Contractor* or *Home,* it is nonetheless an arresting piece. It strikes me as a fragment of a larger design. It is an expression of an inner disquiet related to a persistent preoccupation. "Don't you get the feeling at times," the play's central figure says, "that [art is] a substitute for living?" . . .

The play is densely written with dashes of nervous and jagged wit. The various types, laconically and sardonically sketched, ring true. The tone is just: compassionate without sentimentality, objective without cruelty. The play disturbs, but it is not unhealthy or sadistic. (p. 27)

Harold Clurman, in The Nation *(copyright 1976 by the Nation Associates, Inc.), January 10, 1976.*

David Storey's [*Saville*] is a period piece. It begins in about 1926—the indefiniteness of the overture has an almost Victorian feel—and proceeds to follow the fortunes of collier Harry Saville's family up to the early fifties. . . . The story, absorbing, often painful, culminates in Colin's bleak realisation that he is alienated from all the relationships by which he has defined himself since childhood—family, neighbours, friends, lovers, enemies, employers, colleagues alike, the whole social process in fact, of which he is, in his final vision of himself, both scourge and victim. This revelation leads to a brutal rejection of the past, and the inevitable train journey from the 'blackish smoke' of Saxton, his now disintegrating pit-village in South Yorkshire, to London. By the time Colin leaves, he is (literally and chronologically) an Angry Young Man. . . .

[The] book is not merely a piece of richly-observed naturalism. The intention is much further-reaching than to chronicle. In fact, the observation of social detail takes place within relatively narrow limits: the polarities of otherness and intimacy. Storey advances his narrative in a steady pulse of contrasts. Some of the most effective moments in the book come from their reversal: the intimate, for example, can suddenly become oppressively strange. His mother, mechanically scrubbing the floor, absorbed in her grief for her dying parents, becomes 'like some other person'. Much later on, the familiarity of her habits seems inexplicable and faintly obscene to Colin. . . . By contrast, the 'otherness' of his friend Stafford's upper-class detachment is a source of intimacy. In this sense, the focus of the whole book is not ultimately naturalistic or historical, despite its obvious weight of detail. Observation cuts a narrow swathe, returning again and again to obsessive reference points.

The key to what amounts to a restraint of scope and method lies partly in the character of Colin himself. The narrative is cast in an intimate/other third-person and the reader is made progressively aware of the knot of repression implicit in the apparently dead centre of Colin's responses to his environment. At school, he is nicknamed the Brooder, because of his melancholic self-absorption. On the lists read out in class, his name is last—a piece of patterning which conveys the self-centredness of the boy's growing consciousness, but also symbolises the obscure threat that he is not really there for other people.... [When] Colin gets a job as a teacher, having no class of his own he is listed on the rota as 'supernumerary'. The prophecy of his non-existence for others has symbolically come to pass.

In the early part of the novel, this emptiness at the centre of the narrative point of view serves as a device to remove explicit commentary. There are several enjoyable set-pieces, written, tongue-in-cheek, in a ponderous, euphemistic style that is almost Dickensian.... But if some of these early vignettes float free, there is a dialectical relationship between Colin's responses and his environment. Most of the time, we find ourselves staring out at the world through the grotesque angle of his stubborn eyes; we overhear, as if at a distance, the monologues of his mentors; and later, his friends. A lot of the comedy in the book comes from the observed regression of various individuals to a state resembling childhood. (p. 60)

Colin seems to see his fellow-humans in a distinctly lobster-ish light: the invariable symptom of their self-absorption is the appearance of the red face. This obsessive image is not ultimately consistent; but it has a number of symbolic meanings ranging from the flush of abashed sensitivity to the beacon of self-regarding authority. Each, equally, seems to involve a loss of self.... One by one, sooner or later, the people round Colin join the gallery of selves reduced to roles: caught in the act, red-faced.

But the negative element in Colin, the apparent passivity that causes him to be talked *at* rather than *to,* is not simply a device. It is at the centre of the book's main opposition between character and circumstances. Throughout his childhood, Colin's dogged acquiescence to the pieties of his family's life is besieged by its opposite: the effortless freedom, glimpsed usually in physical action, he seems to see in others. (p. 61)

Colin's distressing recognition of his own conditioning depends ultimately, it seems, on the shaky proposition that the inner reaches of the self are inarticulable, and perhaps because of that, inaccessible, finally, to social process. The idea, for example, quite feasible from the narrative, that Colin's notion of not-self (his real self) might also be a product of his background is never seriously entertained....

The narrative abounds in 'insights' (more like revenges).... The attempts of various characters to offer their explanations of the social process to Colin are almost invariably undermined in some way by what they *are* (what, that is, they have been made to be). Behind them, stands the image of the mother.

It seems to me that the naturalistic format finally has a compromising effect. The restraint, the craft, the implicitness, is more often than not admirable; but it is a restraint of the impulse towards myth that seems to me such a unique part of David Storey's talent. Occasionally it peeps through in images: Colin sees the armchairs at Elisabeth's as boulders; or his parents' house appears to him at the end of the novel like 'some cave they'd lived inside, worn, eroded, hollowed out by the vehemence of their use'.

Saville is a psychological drama, despite its impressive detail, not a social novel. Colin's negative awareness has very little conscious political content. His judgment on 'commu-

nity' is impressively anti-pastoral ('It exists . ... of its own volition. When the volition goes, the community goes with it.'); but one feels it has finally more to do with his own internal development than the disintegrating village of Saxton. Elisabeth sums up Colin's situation in what look like social terms:

> 'You don't really belong to anything,' she said. 'You're not really a teacher. You're not really anything. You don't belong to any class, since you live with one class, respond like another, and feel attachments to none.'

But there's no real connection offered between the disintegration of the community, strongly felt at the end of the novel, and Colin's alienation. The former seems to be an objective correlative for the latter. If this novel really were a form of social history, we should have to ask for more than that. (p. 62)

Victor Sage, "Out of Class," in The New Review *(© The New Review Ltd., 11 Greek Street, London W1V 5LE), October, 1976, pp. 60-2.*

[*Saville*] makes a thorough investigation of the Arnoldian theme of the divided self. Painful enough to read, some of it must have been agony to write. And brave, too, because it goes over all the old, black, literary ground surrounding the coalpit. Yet what a forcing-bed for the pen this remains.

Here we have the familiar drama of a man whose culture sprouted because of the pit and the society it created, but who, because of education, is severed from his roots. Only no one has written of this classic dilemma with such detail and penetration as we find in *Saville*, nor has any previous novel so totally described a working-class family in spiritual transition during the drab, though real, revolution of the Forties and Fifties.

One of the telling things about this book is that it shows how hard it was for people like the Savilles, massively ritualised and made inert by the conditions of existence before the changes came, to make any forward movement at all. The writing manages to suggest this listless waiting time without ever being quiescent itself. On the contrary, Storey's imagination seethes just below the surface of the decrepitude he portrays. What he hates about it is tangled with what he respects and, bad as things were, he is far from welcoming what was to replace them. 'We advance at a price' is his warning. . . .

Gradually, one sees—and the slow realisation is dramatically very powerful—that Storey has invented [three] brothers both to personify the main strands of his own individuality—the writer, the painter, the sportsman, the exile and the indigenous man who stays put—and to examine the brother relationship. . . .

It is a melancholy tale. A passionate chronicle of an aversion. It gives little away in the outright affectionate sense, and, as for such releases as the erotic, they don't get so much as a look in.

Ronald Blythe, "Saville Rows," in The Listener *(© British Broadcasting Corp. 1976; reprinted by permission of Ronald Blythe), October 14, 1976, p. 486.*

*   *   *

STUART, Jesse   1907-

An American novelist, short story writer, and poet, Stuart,

who was born in the mountains of eastern Kentucky, writes about the poor Appalachian hillfolk of his native region. While his name is rarely mentioned in surveys of American literature, there are many admirers of Stuart's novels who feel that his work has not been duly appreciated, but that belated recognition is certain to come to him. Stuart's strengths as a writer are his skilled use of dialect and his compassionate understanding of the people of his native region. (See also *CLC*, Vol. 1, and *Contemporary Authors*, Vols. 5-8, rev. ed.)

In *Harvest of Youth* (1930), [Jesse Stuart] went through a period of exploration, and *Man with a Bull-Tongue Plow* (1934) marked a period characterized by a spontaneous outpouring of literally thousands of lines. The period of spontaneity was followed by a concentrated effort to become a craftsman. *Album of Destiny* (1944) is unique because of Stuart's sustained effort, the only one like it in modern American poetry, to impose free-verse prosodic techniques upon a very traditional and conservative verse form. Paralleling the progression or genesis of craftsmanship, there is the working out of an ontological view—an attempt to make mankind and the universe at large mutually meaningful. Also paralleling the development of Stuart's craft is his evolving concept of the image, a concept which in *Album of Destiny* results in a pictorial method remarkably similar to the one worked out by Walt Whitman.

Stuart's primary problem has always been (and continues to be) that of how to be a natural poet in a world that demands of its poets that they be craftsmen—artificers. (p. 251)

One comes away from such books as *The Year of My Rebirth* with a realization of Stuart's distaste for contriving, for being an artificer. He also comes away with a realization that for Stuart the poet is "nature's child," a medium and a bridge between a natural world and a populace that has lost contact with the world. He sees about him, symbolized in the sterotype of the effeminate artist, a world that he cannot accept, and this has done much to keep him adding to his chronicle. Using an isolated community as a vehicle for expression, he exalts the "old verities" . . . love, honor, pity, pride, compassion, sacrifice, endurance, courage, and hope [that] according to Faulkner, are things of the heart. (pp. 251-52)

The "old verities" are the same for Stuart as they are for Faulkner, and like Faulkner, Stuart sees that the times are "out of joint," that the human heart is in conflict with itself. Also like Faulkner, Stuart believes that mankind can and will prevail. . . .

Stuart's attempt to chronicle his Appalachian area has been successful. He has published voluminously. He has written in haste, and all that he has written is one writing. His prose has received much greater acclaim than has his poetry, but that may make little difference since one is necessarily an adjunct to the other. Stuart sees no clear point of cleavage between the poem and the story. (p. 252)

He says that he has memorized, not that he has remembered. The distinction is important to Stuart's pictorial method. To remember a rosebush may be a very general thing. To memorize a rosebush is a matter of specific detail —of line, of space, of proportion, of color, and of balance. Stuart says that he has memorized his valley "down to the smallest details." Paths, trees, and waterholes, he says in "Memory Albums," often change and play "havoc with that memory of mine that once photographed them to perfection." (p. 253)

Bulk in itself is at the present time a deterrent to a wide appreciation of his poetry. The poetry has often been hurriedly written, as in the case of *Man with a Bull-Tongue Plow*. (p. 255)

One can only hope that his poetry will endure, and that through enduring it will gain the kind of recognition that it deserves. There are several reasons why it should endure. In the first place, it is part of one of the most elaborate chronicles ever written in America about a single place. Second, as part of the chronicle, it likely contains more information about a fairly isolated community than any other single source. Third, it contains a record of Stuart's own life—a fascinating life by anyone's standards. And finally, Stuart's poetry should endure because some of it is good poetry, is well-written, and can therefore be a great source of pleasure to future generations of American readers. The story of W-Hollow has not ended, and Stuart himself will never let it die. (pp. 255-56)

> *J. R. LeMaster, "The Poetry of Jesse Stuart: An Estimate for the Seventies," in* Southwest Review, *Summer, 1971, pp. 251-56.*

Jesse Stuart finds sermons in snakes as well as stones. Blacksnakes, copperheads and water moccasins, slithering about in the undergrowth of the author's native Kentucky, are arranged into a reptilian nosegay of stories—plus 11 poems that close the volume. Why this fascination with the snake? Its primal nature, perhaps, in the scale of being. Its ubiquity in legend. Its patient rhythms. And its circular propensity, symbolic of the cyclical nature of life, which Jesse Stuart has always celebrated.

The short stories, a delightful assortment, treat of snakes in love, snakes and moonshine, snakes and motorcycles, snakes and minnows, snakes and dogs. Also present are frogs, wrens, ground squirrels, mountain people and a home-grown humanism that enables the author to see some good even in scorpions. A timely whiff of spring. (p. 44)

> *Martin Levin, in* The New York Times Book Review *(© 1972 by The New York Times Company; reprinted by permission), March 26, 1972.*

Stuart is a good storyteller whose tales have the quality of oral narrative at its best—quick moving, vibrantly alive—and his humor, sincerity, and affectionate understanding of the Kentucky hill country and its people are a refreshing antidote to the groanings and lamentations of so many of the metropolitan Jeremiahs. (p. 162)

> *William Peden, in his* The American Short Story: Continuity and Change 1940-1975 *(copyright © 1964, 1975 by William Peden; reprinted by permission of Houghton Mifflin Company), Houghton, revised edition, 1975.*

Stuart writes most, and best, of nature. The majority of [the] nearly 300 poems [in *The World of Jesse Stuart: Selected Poems*] are lyrics of sonnet or near sonnet-length and traditional in form. The reader who knows only Stuart's prose will be surprised at the excellence of many of these poems, but he will find very familiar Stuart themes: his basic belief in the land and the work ethic, his love affair with nature, and his total devotion to God. The quality of some of the more recent poems shows a decline; when he writes of Hiroshima and Vietnam his voice is too strident and hysterical and loses poetic strength. (p. 48)

T

TANIZAKI, Jun'ichirō   1886-1965

A Japanese novelist, short story writer, and dramatist, Tanizaki wrote in a detached, analytical style about sexual obsession and perversion. While often morbid, Tanizaki never descended to the sordid or the sensational, for it was not his intention to exploit his sexual themes but to reveal the compelling and mysterious nature of sexuality and its relation to cruelty and violence. (See also *Contemporary Authors*, obituary, Vols. 25-28, rev. ed.)

Tanizaki Junichirō represents an extreme emphasis on art as opposed to naturalism. He chose to use the favorite materials of the naturalists but gave them altogether different treatment. He has been variously described as a Satanist, a decadent, an esthete, a lover of the grotesque, a poet in prose, and a number of other things, all of which stem from the intensity of his sensual themes and vivid imagery. His favorite reading was in Poe, Baudelaire, and Oscar Wilde, a combination which influenced practically every paragraph he wrote. His appetite for sensuous stimuli was insatiable. Like Poe he constructed complete plots around a character with hypersensitive hearing or touch, with overtones of mystery and horror (though never of occultism). Like Baudelaire he dwelt on sexual themes, giving due attention to the perverted and orgiastic. He was especially fascinated by group fornication and by masochism in the male. But again like Baudelaire he rises above pornography because he deals with the pathetic searching of sensitive personalities in the midst of grossness. Tanizaki seems to possess a full understanding of sexual symbolism; eroticism as such is inadequate as subject matter unless it provides scope for psychological analysis. Although Tanizaki's interest leans toward the abnormal and the exotic, his characters are given personality and motivation as well as glands.

One of his earliest works, and one which indicated the trend of future stories, was a tale of sexual symbolism entitled *Shisei* (Tattoo), 1909. (pp. 69-70)

Akuma (Satan), 1912, develops the theme of male masochism in less symbolic fashion, as does *Fumiko no Ashi* (Fumiko's Feet), 1919. In the latter the apparently common fetish suggested in the title receives full treatment. *Otsuyagoroshi* (The Murder of Otsuya), 1913, is a tale of murder and amorality set in the *apache* area of the capital. The Japanese variety of gangsterism, the carnality of old Yedo, and the general depravity of urban outcasts is dealt

with here, although Tanizaki seems interested in depiction only, not in social criticism. In back alleys and smoky rooms lovers are passed around like a platter of olives, and jaded passions are stimulated by devices which remind one of the notorious *tableaux* of the Marquis de Sade. *Osai to Minosuke*, 1915, and *Chijin no Ai* (A Fool's Love), 1924, are novels similar in kind. The latter is an exposition of Tanizaki's theory that the female is the real sexual aggressor. His male protagonist in the story, a young rake named Kawai, suffers keenly from the discovery that his lady is insatiable. She cannot be content with one lover, not even with one at a time. In spite of his mortification Kawai accompanies her on her plural adventures, as a member of the team. One of her orgies takes place in a large mosquito net, chosen apparently for its symbolism of captivity rather than as a protection against the distraction of insects.

In later years Tanizaki became less concerned with erotic descriptions and much more with introspective analysis. *Tade Ku Mushi* (A Matter of Taste), 1919, is the story of the failure of a marriage. The hero is unable to hold his wife's affection, although it is clear that with a little effort he could do so. The woman's emotional needs remind one of Tanizaki's earlier heroines, but the emphasis is different. The story is tempered and restrained, and although the dramatic conflicts stem from sexual maladjustment, their resolution is less spectacularly and progressively depraved than was the case in the author's earlier work. (p. 71)

> *John W. Morrison, in his* Modern Japanese Fiction (*copyright 1955 University of Utah Press*), *University of Utah Press, 1955 (reprinted by Greenwood Press, 1975*).

The conflict between the claims of East and West is particularly apparent in the works of Tanizaki Junichiro. His early productions dealt mainly with themes which might have been suggested by the writings of Edgar Allan Poe, and are marked by strong overtones of sadism and masochism. This period reached its height with *A Fool's Love* (1924), the story of a man who is so fascinated by a coarse, European-looking waitress that he tolerates her repeated cruelties. Even in this work, however, there is implied a condemnation of the excessive worship paid to Western things. In the next major novel, *Some Prefer Nettles* (1928), the hero is drawn both to an Eurasian prostitute and to a Kyoto beauty. Each stands for a world, and we sense that it is Japan which will win. The later novels of Tanizaki expand this conservative aspect of his work. Many of them deal with events of Japanese history of the recent or distant past. *The Thin Snow* (1944-1947), perhaps Tanizaki's masterpiece, tells of the Japan of the years immediately before the Pacific War, but contains many suggestions of *The Tale of Genji,* a work which Tanizaki has translated into modern Japanese. (pp. 25-6)

> *Donald Keene, in his introduction to* Modern Japanese Literature, *edited by Donald Keene (reprinted by permission of Grove Press, Inc.; copyright © 1956 by Grove Press), Grove Press, 1956.*

Tanizaki's theme is not really devotion, but devotion curdled into neurotic fixation. In the fashion of Japanese culture, he is very matter-of-fact about the body. What is quite remarkable is the way Tanizaki combines this with a sense of the body's mystery. There is no matter-of-factness, but a burning sensuality, in the professor's photographing his wife naked in *The Key,* published when the author was 70, or in Tadasu at his stepmother's breasts in "The Bridge of Dreams," published when the author was 73.

In this respect, as in many others, Tanizaki reminds me of the Leskov of "Lady Macbeth of the Mtensk District." If one cannot be Tolstoi or Dostoevsky, it is not too bad to be Leskov. (p. 183)

> *Stanley Edgar Hyman, "A Japanese Master," in his* Standards: A Chronicle of Books for Our Time *(© 1966; reprinted by permission of the publisher, Horizon Press, New York), Horizon, 1966, pp. 179-83.*

Tanizaki is the greatest Japanese writer of our time. Like other Japanese contemporary writers, Tanizaki began his career under the spell of the West: Poe, Baudelaire, Wilde. The Western influence is manifest in the condensed form of his short stories. But in both substance and imagination, the influence of the Japanese novelists of the seventeenth and eighteenth centuries is much stronger. In his early period the stories were imbued with the satanic powers of the spirit and the flesh, the mysterious forces of fatal love and exacerbated eroticism. Tanizaki created female characters with strong, fiendish powers for love that are unique in Japanese literature. (p. 153)

[*Tatoo*] is the perfect work of a great master. The Western technique of exposition and condensation is cleverly combined with the traditional Japanese ability for exploring the dark world of the instincts, the satanic forces of man.

In his long career, Tanizaki always drew his strength and inspiration from genuine Japanese soil. From the West he took only the technique, which he mastered splendidly. It is comforting to find a man so true to himself.

In 1932 he wrote *Ashikari* (Reed Pickers), a short story impregnated with melancholy and an evocative love for old Japan. In it Tanizaki shows a rare gift for expressing the feelings inspired by nature:

> Readers, you all have, perhaps, some old memories charged with deep emotion. As for me, a man nearly fifty years of age, I find myself strongly affected by the melancholy of autumn, with a force unknown to me when I was young. Even the sigh of the wind, rustling through the leaves of *kuzu,* can make me unbearably sad.

Shunkin-sho (The Story of Shunkin), published in 1933, is an impressive work. It is not that it attracts so much by its striking Japanese details—like the explanation of the ingenious way of teaching nightingales to sing still more beautifully than they usually do, nor by showing how to appreciate the true excellence of the lark's song. The exceptional attraction of this story lies in the impassive cruelty and irresistible power of the blind teacher of samisen, and in the boundless devotion of her servant, Sasuke. . . . The narration has a rare intensity, gradually deepening the torments of the heart into an intolerable cruelty.

In 1928 Tanizaki treated the contradiction of both Eastern and Western attractions for the modern Japanese in *Tade kuu Mushi* (Some Prefer Nettles). It is considered by some critics to be his best work. It is beautifully written and its construction is perfect. There is an impressive contrast between the young couple drifting aimlessly towards gratuitous adventure—the wife to a lover with her husband's consent and the husband to the casual love of a pretty Eurasian—and the steadiness of the wife's father, who is firmly rooted in old Japanese habits and culture. The old gentleman tries to bring stability to the emotional life of the couple by leading them to the spiritual sources of old Japanese art and enjoyment, to the puppet theatre, which is described with enticing penetration. The clever construction of the novel is not balanced by a strong characterization. The young man and his wife never become very real to us. The old man and his mistress Ohisa seem more like caricatures of an old traditional Japanese gentleman who is a connoisseur of the delicate refinements of yore, and a pretty feminine type who is kept and trimmed exclusively for man's pleasure. Where Tanizaki was an incomparable master is in the refinement and delicacy of combining or just sketching the subtlest nuances, "pushing back into the shadows the things that come forward too clearly," in giving us, as he says, "the pattern of shadows, the light and the darkness which things produce."

Tanizaki's power came, no doubt, from the sources of the past, from the strange beauty and spiritual strength of old Japan. This rich soil on which the greatness and inspiration of his work was built enabled him to reach a true universalism. It is a universalism that springs from the turbid sources of life.

Nostalgia for the past inspired Tanizaki to write a *roman-fleuve* in the period 1943-48, *Sasameyuki* (translated as The Makioka Sisters). It is a novel about a merchant family of Osaka which is decaying from past grandeur. It is concerned with a vanishing world to which the last war has dealt a mortal blow. The plot is thin, nearly nonexistent. The pace is slow, and flooded with minute, exhaustive description. But the human milieu is real. The complex atmosphere of a family, its complicated affairs, prejudices, proud traditions, and secret shames, and the character of its members—especially the four sisters—are drawn in a masterly way. It is achieved through a long narration animated by an extremely detailed realism and by the poetic vein, the breadth and force of a great writer. (pp. 154-55)

[Tanizaki's] erotic books, absorbed in the world of flesh and carnal desires, have been accused of decadence and of nearly falling into the category of pornographic literature. In his last novels he combined the Japanese tradition of the erotic with the Western trend of psychoanalytical fiction. Perhaps it was this Western bent for the analysis, the overemphasis of the erotic together with the clear consciousness of its moral implications, that gives Tanizaki's novels more

CONTEMPORARY LITERARY CRITICISM TANIZAKI

complexity. At the same time it makes them weaker in carnal force.

Compared to Saikaku, Tanizaki evinces the decadent moral dissolution of a society contaminated by de Sade and his successors, the weakness of a man divided between a certain longing for moral integrity and a licentious thirst for pleasures. Tanizaki was far from the wholesome, natural eroticism of Saikaku. Saikaku's pagan desire is naked and brutal, but it still keeps all the innocence of nature.

Tanizaki has a sense of power and depth rarely found in Japanese writers. He is . . . a Japanese writer who, with artistic taste and harmony, combined the old Japanese tradition—on which he based his strength—with Western values, through which he attained modernity, wide vision, and true greatness. (pp. 155-56)

Armando Martins Janiera, in his Japanese and Western Literature *(© 1970 by Charles E. Tuttle Co., Inc.), Tuttle, 1970.*

Tanizaki's novel cannot be considered pornographic, though it is rather erotic, and the merely sexual aspect of the novel which plays such an important role, as well as the various interpretations of the novel previously offered, should not confuse us.

The Key describes the sexual life of a fifty-five-year-old Professor and his forty-four-year-old wife, Ikuko, through their diaries covering a period just short of six months. (p. 216)

At first glance, it seems quite easy to establish *The Key* as a novel. The classification "novel" covers many diverse works, and the *The Key* is "a special form of narrative" by Michel Butor's approximation of a definition of a novel.

We then become aware of the complexity of this novel. In the first place, it is composed of two private diaries, written not only to preserve the intimate thoughts of their authors but written to be read by each other. They are diaries with a specific addressee, thus they lose the character of impressions of a soul, of a mirror or portrait of the spirit, and instead become an extrovert expression of self in intimate confidences. They are both partial autobiographies and messages, born of the tacit agreement between the Professor and his wife that they will read each other's diaries without mentioning the fact to each other. To utilize a distinction made by Tzvetan Todorov, they are letters on the "being level" and diaries on the "seeming level".

On a deeper level, they are drama, for a dialogue structure develops between the two writers, a result of the similarity between epistolary and dramatic styles. As such, they can be considered a tragicomedy, for both characters are masked by common consent. Thus they both know how much one knows about the other, but continue to appear ignorant. The play is a farce as well as a tragedy, caused by love, hate, taboos, repression and daring. When one of the actors dies, his wife throws off her mask.

From a different point of view, *The Key* can be considered a chronicle. (pp. 216-17)

Finally, *The Key* is undoubtedly a detective story. Tanizaki enjoyed this type of novel during his early period, and its influence can be seen throughout his works. *The Key* keeps the reader in suspense till the end, not through desire to discover the author of the crime, but to know the motives which led him to it, coupled with a perhaps futile desire to know the extent of sincerity in the diaries. . . .

The complexity of literary genre is reflected in the equally complex structure of the novel, and, given his aesthetic ideas, Tanizaki was obviously aware of this. . . .

Structure is the form in which the various parts of a narration are organized. It becomes clear the structure of *The Key* does not follow a straight and static line. It can more aptly be defined as a spiral with non-uniform radius and great elasticity, subjected to constant force so that parts of the spiral are in contact at times. Each curve deviates sufficiently from its point of origin to open the possibility of a further curve without doubling back upon itself. The narrative forms the spiral, and the turns are the various entries in the diaries, forming an uninterrupted continuity but separated from previous curves by no uniform distance. Movement in the narrative comes from pressure imposed on the turns, such that they coincide with and touch each other. Progress and withdrawal are followed by another advance, rather like a dynamic illusion or, more precisely, a dialectic fantasy. (p. 217)

But this structure is even more complex. The wealth of Tanizaki's technique offers us a surprise in the final sections of Ikuko's diary. Here we see a multiple elasticity, such that it not only represents curves or turns under pressure, but of variable diameter in continual flux. The final turns coincide, in hallucinating movement, with all previous turns, and acquire "real meaning". The illusion of dynamism is at its peak. (p. 218)

[Tanizaki's technique] provides for the representation of one event not only by two different people, but even by the same person at different times. We are thus offered, in a plurality of perceptions, a stereoscopic view more complex than the described phenomenon. This draws our attention to the character who describes and perceives the phenomenon, if we know or think we know the phenomenon. At the same time, different views of a single event by the same individual reveal his complexity, hypocrisy, and ability to disguise himself. (pp. 218-19)

The traditional role of all-knowing narrator is discarded. The novelist reduces perspective, the style is in the first person (in this case he can offer us only what is plausibly happening). At the same time, the authors of the diaries, acting as narrators writing a letter, are not so well informed as the reader, as they cannot communicate about what they write with one another. The reader has an advantage over the characters, who are like chessmen on a board of intrigue. At the same time, there are moments when the reader is surrounded by mystery while the characters seem to have clear knowledge, since the reader cannot know anything not expressed in the diaries. . . . Mysteries, irresolutions, uncertainties, changing impressions, call into question a balance of awareness: who is more completely aware of what happened, the reader or the characters?

Tanizaki limits himself to outlining the chaos which defines life itself. Chaos in *The Key* adopts ambiguity as its most characteristic expression. The characters are perplexed by the coils of ambiguity such that even they cannot understand what is happening. The reader is trapped in this game and suffers the illusion that he is a puppet, manipulated by threads of certainty and doubt, truth and falsehood, knowledge and ignorance, until he finally feels identified with the characters. (p. 219)

Sex, which may be considered as a fundamental theme, is at the same time an abstract omnipresent character, acting as a common denominator in the entire novel. . . .

In *The Key,* sex is a giant which manipulates puppets on a stage. The other characters are hung from invisible threads, and movements, gestures and distorted notions are provoked by the giant giving them life. (p. 220)

The structure of the novel itself is sex-inspired. It is sex which puts dynamic pressure on the spiral forming the various sections or curves of the diaries, as the writers are inspired by sex: the diaries, written to be read, are, depending on the occasion, a means of communicating tacit desire, an incentive to awaken desire, a means of mocking, a strategy to produce the other's destruction. (pp. 220-21)

It may seem that Tanizaki presents his characters with a degree of determinism. They may appear to be puppets, but Tanizaki wanted his characters to remain at this level and has not described them further. He perhaps wished to caricaturize. Let us not forget that it has been said that the caricature is the quintessence of the personality. (p. 228)

> *Jaime Fernandez, "A Study of Tanizaki's 'The Key'," in* Approaches to the Modern Japanese Novel, *edited by Kinya Tsuruta and Thomas E. Swann (copyright, 1976, by Monumenta Nipponica), Sophia University, 1976, pp. 215-28.*

*   *   *

TERTZ, Abram
See SINYAVSKY, Andrei
*   *   *

THEROUX, Paul   1941-

Theroux is an American novelist, poet, short story writer, critic, and travel writer. His work is wonderfully evocative of place, a quality no doubt enhanced by his observations during his many and frequent travels. (See also *CLC,* Vol. 5, and *Contemporary Authors,* Vols. 33-36.)

One of the most interesting of younger American writers is Paul Theroux, whose novels *Girls at Play* and *Saint Jack* were well-received by critics in both the United States and England. If he is not so well-known among general readers as he is among critics, and his fellow-writers, it may be partly because his fiction is located outside the territorial boundaries of the United States—in the Far East, in Russia, in Africa, and in England. *The Black House* is a mysterious work: it is ostensibly set in a small English village in the Dorset countryside, and at the same time it is set—psychologically—in Uganda, in an isolated Bwamba village, where the novel's protagonist, an anthropologist named Alfred Munday, lived for a long period of time, researching the Bwamba people. . . . The novel does not yield its meanings easily; its "plot" is at times rather baffling. But Theroux's ability to contrast cultures and to focus upon the bizarre similarities between them is as powerful in this novel as it was in his earlier, more realistic works. (p. 102)

> *Joyce Carol Oates, in* The Ontario Review *(copyright © 1974 by The Ontario Review), Fall, 1974.*

Though it is a travel book and not a novel, ["The Great Railway Bazaar"] incorporates many of the qualities of Theroux's fiction: it is funny, sardonic, wonderfully sensuous and evocative in its descriptions, casually horrifying in its impact. . . .

Though he is a certified American, born in Medford, Mass., . . . Paul Theroux has . . . staked out for himself a fictional terrain that is generally thought of as British. He writes about the anomalies of post-imperial life in central Africa ("Jungle Lovers"—1971), where he spent five years, in Singapore ("Saint Jack"—1973), where he spent another three, and in England itself, where he presently lives. Unafraid of ethnic generalizations, he spares no one—African, Englishman, Chinaman, Indian, American—in his wildly absurd confrontations between the old and the new exploiters and the poor bastards caught in the middle; recklessly he juxtaposes the crumbling institutions of colonialism with some of the more bizarre outgrowths of the Third World. . . . If Theroux sees mainly decay, sloganism and impoverishment in the present, he is also mercilessly aware of the racial blindness, the stupidity, the arrogance and cruelty of the colonial past.

Another element in Theroux's work that is more typically British than American is his comic celebration of seediness. The suits his characters wear tend to be ill-fitting, stained with gravy or curry or beer. As Calvin Mullet, the former insurance agent from Hudson, Mass., muses in "Jungle Lovers," "there was something cozy and familiar in an undershirt that had been worn for a week or two." Jack Flowers, the tattooed American pimp-protagonist of "Saint Jack," dressed for a special occasion in his best black suit and a white shirt, discovers, in the lounge of an expensive Singapore hotel, that he has forgotten to put on socks. The characters eat revolting meals. They booze away their days in sordid bars, sleep with whores or native girls in unmade beds in dirty rooms. Although this seediness proliferates most luxuriantly in the steamy tropics, "The Black House" (1974) reveals its existence (no longer comic) in England too. In "The Black House," his most impressive novel yet, Theroux seems almost defiantly to be claiming his authorial right to an especially British genre: the macabre tale of a haunted house, of witchcraft in a remote village in Dorset. The break with his earlier work is not as complete as this sounds, for the chief character of the book is an anthropologist who for 10 years has studied the inhabitants of a Ugandan village which turns out, in surprising ways, to be the counterpart of the one in Dorset. There is not a single American character in the novel. . . .

"The Great Railway Bazaar" also belongs to an English tradition, that of the eccentric travel book whose origins go back two centuries to Sterne's "A Sentimental Journey." For no better reason than to counter a sneering question as to whether he has been to France, Sterne's Mr. Yorick hastily packs a half-dozen shirts and a pair of black silk breeches and sets off for the Dover-Calais packet-boat; just as whimsically Paul Theroux kisses his wife good-by and sets off on a three-month parabolic trip around Asia because he likes trains. (p. 1)

The traveling persona adopted by Theroux is acerbic, bookish, deadpan, observant, bibulous and rather passive. . . .

There is a lot of . . . pleasant fooling-around, but as it does in Theroux's novels, horror has a way of suddenly ripping the comic mask. . . .

The author's deadpan narrative manner can usually be counted on to keep his indignation under control, but the rape of Vietnam—visited during the eerie period between the "Cease-fire" and this spring's capitulation—is too much for him. . . .

Paul Theroux is such a well-read and extravagantly well-informed writer that it is fun to catch him out on small [factual errors].... But these very lapses indicate the quality of Theroux's sensibility. ''The Great Railway Bazaar'' is the most consistently entertaining and the least boring book I have encountered in a long time. (p. 2)

> *Robert Towers, in* The New York Times Book Review *(© 1975 by The New York Times Company; reprinted by permission), August 24, 1975.*

Paul Theroux is a train-lover, though not one of those who dote only on puff-puffs on the branch line to Little Gidding. He wanted to suffer on those long bazaars or ramshackle supermarkets that snake along from one desperate frontier to another, eastward across Europe into the smells of Asia, hauling alleged sleeping cars and imaginary diners. (p. 474)

[In] its dereliction, the railway offers what up-to-date forms of travel cut us off from: passengers. There is an instant meeting with the desperate, anxious, boasting, confessional, jabbering hopefuls and casualties of the modern world. We are not palmed off with national customs and crafts, public problems: we see private life as it screams at this very hour, sweating out the universal anxiety, the conglomerate Absurd. This is what Paul Theroux, with the eyes and ears of the novelist and the avidity of the responsive traveller, brings home to us [in *The Great Railway Bazaar*], awaking us to horror, laughter, compassion at the sight of the shameless private will to live. His book is the most vigorous piece of travel among people I have read for years. (pp. 474-75)

He has Dickens's gift for getting the character of a man or woman in a flash, of discovering the fantasies and language of the food-stained bores who settled upon him. We understand why poor old Mr Duffill, who treads on the cuffs of his trousers at Victoria, smells of bread crusts and travels with paper parcels, will get left behind at the Italian frontier —not so much from incompetence but because he is fated to have fits of sensibility when a train moves off as he gesticulates with his sandwiches.

The Victorian enemies of railway travel used to warn us that we would find ourselves close to the breath and bodies of people we had not met socially: Mr Theroux leaned eagerly and philosophically towards them....

Mr Theroux is brief and vivid on the view from the window. He is especially fine on the mixture of magnificence and abandoned ironmongery in Laos. His generalised grasp of cities is always to the contemporary point. (p. 475)

The whole book is more than a rich and original entertainment. His people, places and asides will stay a long time jostling in the mind of the reader. (p. 476)

> *V. S. Pritchett, "On the Tracks," in* New Statesman *(© 1975 The Statesman & Nation Publishing Co. Ltd.), October 17, 1975, pp. 474-76.*

While exile is undeniably a ticket to miseries it does carry advantages. Not only does it give home a sharper perspective than the stick-theres possess but—bigger boon still—it frequently helps you focus the new place clearer than the locals. That's why so many good novels about London are written by foreigners ... [like] Paul Theroux. And, as all these novelists prove, it's frequently the sleazier undersides of London life that the newcomer is drawn to, perhaps because, as Orwell suggested of Henry Miller in Paris, he lacks a steady milieu and family roots, and so is driven to

haunt the fringes of settled respectability—bars and dives, crummy rented accommodation, areas like Deptford.

The thickly textured prose of Paul Theroux's *The Family Arsenal* marvellously gives us this seedy world of the transient—where the ageing accountant Gawber, who's stuck it out in Catford, is engulfed in tides of less-than-colourful coloured *immigrés,* and an American consul on the run is holing up in a Deptford pad with a nursery of Provo kiddies and their bomb-kits, and gun-runners, nickers of tellies, middle-class stealers of paintings for ransom, radical actresses and anarchist aristocrats are tumbled together in a richly criminal brew.... Theroux also knows that exiles ... and hoodlums, and for that matter novels, run to surrogates for families....

[Everyone] turns out to be related to everyone else, including their enemies. All one big unhappy urban family. Even the ordinary inhabitant of the fated urbs is netted into the catch of relationships, if only through the crossed telephone connections Gawber keeps getting. And the whole uneasy shebang, so resourcefully ravelled and unravelled, ends with a suitable doomy bang. The remnants of Hood's 'family' split to Brighton (there no doubt to rewrite Graham Greene)....

Fong and the Indians isn't only valuable as a nice reminder that a prose style and structuring capacities can improve in just the merest while; it does have its own mild attractions.... Unheavy-handedly, the novel satirises the idiocies of African politics, the lunacies of the foreign interferers, the mendacities of the commercially uppity Indians. Things do move a mite woodenly at times, but Paul Theroux can also organise some tellingly bizarre and funny, if in the end quite frightening, international misunderstandings. You laugh, as does the novel, to stop yourself crying: for even the last-minute arrival of Fong's dreamed-of-gravy— well, *milk*—train seems little compensation for all he's been forced through. (p. 410)

> *Valentine Cunningham, in* New Statesman *(© 1976 The Statesman & Nation Publishing Co. Ltd.), March 26, 1976.*

Narrative verve, the brightly sketched collection of urban desperadoes, and the extraordinary vividness of physical London will make ''The Family Arsenal'' a deservedly popular novel. For an American, Theroux has a remarkable ear for the rhythms and elisions of English underworld slang, and he even manages at this late date to make obscenity expressive. No foreign writer I've read has so skillfully caught the blend of coarseness, provincialism and bigotry that is one distinctive (and usually unexportable) brand of popular British humor.

In all these respects, ''The Family Arsenal'' is an assured success, like Theroux's fine travel book of last year, ''The Great Railway Bazaar''; but Theroux has ambitions that go beyond the expert construction of a timely thriller. Opening with an epigraph from ''The Princess Casamassima'' and alluding a dozen times to ''The Secret Agent,'' he wants much of what happens in ''The Family Arsenal'' to play off against the two famous novels by James and Conrad that have shaped the way many people think about the anarchist impulse. (p. 1)

The allusiveness and direct imitation create some fine incidental comedy, and taken together they also gradually reinforce several of Theroux's larger themes. In London of the 1970's, terrorism seems more inevitable, degenerate and futile than it did even in the 1880's and 90's. The establishment enemy is vague, seen mainly through the crazed egotism or drug-sodden fantasies of the conspirators. Protest itself often takes the form of sporadic, vaguely motivated bursts of violence—desperate play divorced from any clear principle or belief.

One of Theroux's best scenes is a shivery demonstration of terrorism as mindless pleasure, when goofy adolescents giggle about the dynamite needed to bring down Nelson's column or the Admiralty Arch: "It was the only way they could possess the city, by reducing it to shattered pieces. Exploded, in motion, it was theirs." Santayana's warning that those who cannot remember the past are condemned to repeat it has a particularly sharp ring. Never having heard of James or Conrad [the bomb-makers] cannot know they are actors in a failed plot written decades before they were born. (pp. 1-2)

These ironies work well for Theroux, but they also have the effect of continually diminishing his characters and the significance of their actions. In "The Princess Casamassima" and "The Secret Agent" terrorism is futile too, but its impulses and targets are more fully communicated, the implications and emotional effects of its failure more resonant. James and Conrad create worlds elsewhere: what used to be, what may now still exist or what could possibly occur in the future. Theroux obviously knows all this well enough—diminishment is a vital theme of his novel—but it does create problems that he can only partially solve. Most of his characters are so thoroughly reduced—isolated, aimless, inarticulate, mindlessly desperate—that it is hard to see them as more than grimly (often comically) exposed. For all of his craft and intelligence, Theroux is better at documenting destruction than at convincing us that things of significance and value have been lost. . . .

Theroux's efforts to provide by implication an analysis of a historical situation and an ample sense of personal motivation are finally less successful than his handling of narrative excitement, satiric portraiture and the evocation of urban violence and distress. To ask for more power and analysis from an intelligent, absorbing thriller is not to debunk Theroux's achievement (or to grumble that he doesn't stack up against Conrad and James), but to suggest some of the critical issues raised by his work and the promises it holds out. (p. 2)

Lawrence Graver, in The New York Times Book Review *(© 1976 by The New York Times Company; reprinted by permission), July 11, 1976.*

[In *The Family Arsenal*], Theroux is writing . . . about terrorists, would-be terrorists and all sorts of mock revolutionists against the background of England in decay. He has worked up his material like a documentary journalist with more knowledge than empathy. The book is full of wild goings-on and hideously empty people who seem straight out of Graham Greene rather than Theroux's professed desire to carry on (a bit) with James' *The Princess Casamassima* and Conrad's *The Secret Agent*. . . .

I didn't believe any of it; Theroux's style is so self-conscious and the English scene is worked up with such labor. But the book is certainly complicated, dense, ominous. *Why* is American fiction this complicated now, *why* does the style come on so portentously? My guess is that the human figure that dominates us is still that old American problem, the self-enclosed psyche. (p. 23)

Alfred Kazin, in The New Republic *(reprinted by permission of The New Republic; © 1976 by The New Republic, Inc.) November 27, 1976.*

[In *The Family Arsenal* Theroux] communicates the significance of his London setting not by anxious directives but by feeling, through Lawrence's "spirit of place." On the one hand, we are overwhelmed by the grimy facticity of South London—terraces of houses, slogans chalked on walls, slashed railway seats, pubs, cemeteries, fog, docks—but the physical details become transparent, recreating through the reader's apprehension of emotional nuance or concentration a vision of London, seemingly venerable, cultured, a guardian of trust and order, as a focus of the anarchy and contingency of the contemporary psyche. London imperceptibly is transformed into Vietnam and experiencing Vietnam—as Americans, including Valentine Hood, know—is a condition of being contemporary. Violence—murder, hot-wiring, theft, mugging, explosions—are as easy, alluring and arbitrary as in Vietnam and in both, men are escapees, exiles, conspirators, actors, and barbarians. The atmosphere of the novel is thus surely but subtly established. Its ongoing structure is equally firmly rooted in the reader's responses by a series of interconnected symbols: a stolen picture which seems to reflect the viewer's moods, amusingly crossed telephone conversations about *The Times* crosswords which underline the confused clues of the mystery in the wider world, and the theater people who intertwine confusingly with radical political groups and revolutionaries. Theater, disguise, symbolic actions, link actors and conspirators alike; acting, like violence, is a gesture of defiant liberation.

Overhanging the novel's action is a London not only frighteningly collaged with Vietnam but an image of the decay and unpredictable destructiveness of the past. The city is "great" and "fantastic" to the young Provos simply and fearfully because it is such a tempting target: "it was the only way they could possess the city, by reducing it to shattered pieces," just as Hood's compatriots have ravaged Vietnam. The "arsenal" of the title is at once the name of a football team and of Hood's small group of variously "displaced" revolutionaries in South London where he is "continuing the journey he had started abruptly in Vietnam." The only hope in such a world where history and external order have failed the resources and desires of the individual is Hood's reluctantly growing love for a woman whose husband he has himself pursued and killed. At the book's conclusion the "family" has been shattered and the survivors—Hood, the woman and her child, and one of Hood's young protégés—escape to Brighton, still a family of sorts, their arsenal replaed by a grim hope of escape, to "smoke and tell lies."

Theroux's London demonstrates how—as in the Detroit of Joyce Carol Oates's *Do With Me What You Will* or the McCarthy era of E. L. Doctorow's *The Book of Daniel*, to take two recent instances—the world of public history and observable place, the world, in other words, of facticity—may become emblematic of the inner recesses of the struggling human personality. (pp. 95-6)

G. F. Waller, in The Ontario Review *(copyright © 1976 by The Ontario Review), Fall-Winter, 1976-77.*

TOLKIEN, J(ohn) R(onald) R(euel)   1892-1973

A South African-born British novelist, poet, and Anglo-Saxon scholar, Tolkien is best known for his trilogy, *The Lord of the Rings*. Along with C. S. Lewis and Charles Williams, Tolkien has been credited with reviving the romance. Certainly his fantasy is many-faceted: history and fairy story, realistic and magical, pessimistic about society and hopeful for the individual. (See also *CLC*, Vols. 1, 2, 3, and *Contemporary Authors*, Vols. 17-18; obituary, Vols. 45-48; *Contemporary Authors Permanent Series*, Vol. 2.)

[J.R.R. Tolkien's children] received a letter from Father Christmas every year. The first arrived in 1920 when Tolkien's oldest son was 3, and they continued to arrive for 20 years thereafter. In "The Father Christmas Letters" Tolkien's daughter-in-law, Baillie Tolkien, collects and edits them for our enjoyment.

The facsimiles included show a handwriting that is shaky but elegant.... Fortunately age does not prevent the writer from sending richly detailed paintings of his house, his sleigh gliding over Oxford ("Your house is just about where the three little black points stick up out of the shadows at the right"), and the misadventures that make these letters such lively reading....

Nobody, I think, knows more about elves than Tolkien, who never confuses Father Christmas with that old moralist, Santa Claus....

By 1939, even Father Christmas finds the world a chilly home for magic. The Tolkien children are growing up. "The number of children who keep up with me seems to be getting smaller. I expect it is because of this horrible war...." But wars between nations pass. The war between Father Christmas and the Goblins is as old as Good and Evil, and his magic survives our technology. "You need not believe any pictures you see of me in aeroplanes or motors. I cannot drive one, and I don't want to."

Father Christmas lives. And never more merrily than in these pages. (p. 90)

> *Nancy Willard, in* The New York Times Book Review (© *1976 by The New York Times Company; reprinted by permission), December 5, 1976.*

The sequel to *The Lord of the Rings* [*The Silmarillion*] is actually its prologue, both in narrative time and in the mind of the creator. Spanning vast landscapes and thousands of years, the stories in this book tell us what happened in Tolkien's universe from the beginning of time until that eventful period, late in the Third Age of the world, when Frodo Baggins obtained the fateful ring and (with a little help from his friends) finally carried it through numerous perils to its destruction in the Crack of Doom.

There is an enormous Tolkien readership, including some who devour his books and read practically no others.... Unbelievers will scoff because this not-quite-digested mass of material is Tolkien and fantasy; hobbit-fanciers may find their loyalties divided because it is Tolkien but contains not a single hobbit, until the very end when the name of "Frodo the Halfling" appears once and the whole *Lord of the Rings* cycle is compressed into two pages.

From the viewpoint of the Ring trilogy, what we have in this new volume is a substantial part (one hopes that more can be edited and published from the remaining Tolkien manuscripts) of the *Translations from the Elvish* to which

Bilbo Baggins devoted himself for long years after celebrating his eleventy-first birthday and slipping quietly out of hobbit society. Its central and longest part, from which the entire volume takes its name, is the epic tale of the theft and quest of the silmarils, three jewels of extraordinary powers which were made by the hot-tempered elven king and craftsman Feanor and were stolen by Morgoth, a demigod devoted to darkness and chaos, who wished to make himself master of all Middle-earth.

The slow unfolding of this story covers centuries and all sections of the old creation before the earth was changed (one of the things that happen in the various wars chronicled here is that it becomes round). Titanic forces struggle after building up their strength for centuries to prepare for a gigantic encounter. The central myth, of earthlings banded together under a rash oath to do hopeless battle against a demigod, is one of great power and considerable nobility, with splendidly varied episodes of idyllic love and unearthly joy, wanton destruction and high heroism.

Vast landscapes and towering strongholds are evoked, only to perish in smoke or tidal waves; twisted creatures—orcs and balrogs and firedrakes—lurch blood-maddened through the flames; crabbed dwarves plot small-minded revenge for fancied hurts, and the whole centuries-long, panoramic action works out in massive and intricate variations a single, simple theme: "Love not too well the work of thy hands and the devices of thy heart."

The Silmarillion is the chief book of the collection, but only one; the volume opens with a creation myth of singular beauty, and continues with a rather scholarly discussion of the varied demigods who are known as "the Valar, the Powers of the Earth." (pp. E1-E2)

To devotees of the more familiar Tolkien (though not so much to those superfans who pore over the appendices) all of this may come as a bit of a shock. *The Lord of the Rings* is a special kind of fiction, midway between medieval romance and modern novel; *The Simarillion* and those works which accompany it in this volume are altogether a different kind of writing—primitive in some places, rather dry and scholarly in others, primarily epic in style and vision, dealing with the fate of whole peoples and focusing only momentarily on an occasional key individual. If the Ring trilogy competes for attention mainly with almost-forgotten medieval romances, *The Silmarillion* demands comparison with Hesiod and *The Iliad, Paradise Lost* and the *Book of Genesis*. And although it is unevenly written (the author would surely have revised it before publication had he lived), its best parts stand up well under such comparisons....

Tolkien found an enthusiastic audience for one small corner of his massive vision and no market at all for the greater part of his imaginings. And like a true professional (and a hobbit-fancier himself), he adapted—shrank—his vision to suit the available market. One is reminded of Shakespeare, whose magnificent series of historical plays produced, offhand and almost by accident, a minor character named Falstaff....

The vision of the First and Second Ages was already fully formed (it had been accumulating in notebooks since 1917, 20 years before *The Hobbit* was published), and although he could not publish it as such—never, in fact, put it into final, publishable form—Tolkien continued to tinker with its details through the rest of his life and crammed much of it into the various appendices to *The Lord of the Rings*. So the contents of this posthumous volume will not come as a complete surprise to Tolkien-lovers, though its tone, content and style have only a tenuous connection with his more familiar work. . . .

As to its importance in the Tolkien canon, even those (misguided, I believe) who prefer the hobbit books to this newly published material must recognize that the myths of the Elder Days are what make their favorite author unique. These early fantasy writings . . . are fundamental Tolkien, the underpinning without which he would not have been able to produce his later works in the form that we know. For though the matter of the Ring trilogy is peripheral to what is given here—almost an afterthought—the matter of *The Silmarillion* pervades Tolkien's other fantasies and gives them a flavor unique in that field of writing.

Looked at objectively, Tolkien is not, in fact, a great writer of pure adventure; others are his equal or better at conveying the concrete detail, the breathless excitement of steel clashing with steel, muscles straining in combat, dangers encountered and overcome—and yet his books are literature while theirs are pastimes, entertainment, something to be read quickly and thrown away. The reason, or at least part of it, is that other writers convey adventure and little else (and after a while, one sword cleaving a helmet begins to look like all the others), while Tolkien's stories take place against a background of measureless depth. Frodo moves in a landscape where others have moved before him through long, busy millennia; he comes at the end of a process that began before the sun and moon were sent aloft; he is a part, small but essential, in a timeless war between the forces of order and disorder, and whether he understands it or not—whether the reader understands it or not—that background is ever-present in the creator's mind and it gives Frodo and company a three-dimensional reality that is seldom found in this kind of writing.

Compared to this historic depth, and the thematic and philosophical unity which it underlies, the other distinctions of the Ring trilogy are relatively insignificant—the richness and variety of invented languages, the intricate geography of Middle-earth, the array of creatures familiar and exotic (orcs and dwarves and elves and hobbits, as well as men and dogs and horses) that enliven its landscapes—though these alone would make Tolkien unique.

In a commercial sense, those who declined to publish this part of his work in the '30s were surely correct. Our time has not been hospitable to cosmogonies and epics unless they are cleverly disguised as something else. . . .

Artistically, we have been deprived by the forces that postponed publication of *The Silmarillion* until now and decreed that it would be a posthumous work with no final revisions by the author. What we have is imperfect but magnificent in its best moments. Until this volume appeared, I had felt that Tolkien's greatest service to English letters was his translation of the splendid medieval romance, *Sir Gawain and the Green Knight*. He has surpassed that work, and that is no small achievement. (p. E2)

> *Joseph McLellan, "Frodo and the Cosmos," in* Book World—The Washington Post *(© The Washington Post), September 4, 1977, pp. E1-E2.*

As background material for much of his published work, *The Silmarillion*, J.R.R. Tolkien's history of the world's creation and its First Age, may be of scholarly interest to those readers who approach him in all seriousness. For many of his admirers, however, this posthumous epic will prove a disappointment: it had neither the charm of *The Hobbit* nor the magic of *The Lord of the Rings*. . . .

Some sixty years in the making, *The Silmarillion* is probably a faithful indication of the scope of Tolkien's imagination. But his attention to detail makes the book rather dull going in the end. What bits of enchantment exist—Morgoth's confederate Ungoliant, a memorably grotesque she-spider, or the love story of Beren and Lúthien—are imprisoned in a morass of battles, characters, and places, often with multiple names, so that one rapidly loses track of—and interest in—who has gone where and why. Most people prefer their fantasy a bit frothier than this. (p. 105)

> *Martha Spaulding, in* The Atlantic Monthly *(copyright © 1977 by The Atlantic Monthly Company, Boston, Mass.; reprinted with permission), October, 1977.*

It comes as an enormous letdown to discover that Tolkien spent all those decades laboring over something very much akin to the *Book of Mormon* [in *The Silmarillion*]. (p. 39)

[When] you try to play in the same league with Milton and the King James Version, you have to own a hardball or you don't qualify. The book, moreover, is narrated in an elevated style that has the effect of making the action appear to take place at the bottom of an enormous teacup. There is no immediacy about it and still less mystery; all the characters are 37 feet tall and live for a million years and you can rest assured that if things really get out of hand, Daddy in the form of Eru-Iluvatar will put down his pipe and lend an omnipotent hand. I realize that the editor has been forced to choose between many different versions, both in prose and poetry, and difficult compromises have doubtless been made. Nevertheless, the book is little more than a weak gloss on Tolkien's infinitely more mature later work, and so it should be read, if at all; indeed, much of the material is included in the appendices of *Lord of the Rings* in condensed and more intriguing form. Its publication now, especially when accompanied by such unbridled enthusiasm on the part of the industry, is not only questionable but is bound to lead many of Tolkien's admirers to grave disappointment. Noble intentions do not necessarily produce a noble work. Perhaps the opposite is more often true than otherwise. (pp. 39-40)

> *L. J. Davis, in* The New Republic *(reprinted by permission of* The New Republic; *© 1977 by The New Republic, Inc.), October 1, 1977.*

*   *   *

TRAVEN, B.   1890-1969

An American-born short story writer, novelist, and screenwriter, Traven wrote in both German and English. Interest in Traven has been piqued by the deliberate screen of mystery that he set up about his background. However, in recent years the facts of Traven's identity have begun to emerge. According to his will, Traven was born in Chicago, but spent his youth in Germany. For his revolutionary activities in Bavaria, Traven was sentenced to death but managed a last minute escape. Signing on as a seaman, he jumped ship at Tampico, Mexico. He died in Mexico City. Traven was a trenchant critic of modern bureaucracy and a compelling storyteller. His *Death Ship* will certainly endure, as will his well-known classic, *The Treasure of Sierre Madre*. (See also Con-

temporary Authors, **Vols. 19-20;** obituary, **Vols. 25-28,** rev. ed.; *Contemporary Authors Permanent Series,* **Vol. 2.**)

The Death Ship (1926) depicts a voyage which takes the protagonist, Gerard Gales, away from civilization and leaves him on a raft in the middle of the ocean. He is alienated from a society which first denies him an identity because he has neither job nor papers, and then threatens to destory him by condemning him to work on an illicit tramp steamer. The climactic wreck of this death ship represents the severing of the protagonist's last bonds with society and, ironically, with reality. Alone on a raft in a mounting storm, the sole survivor of the shipwreck, Gales, has hallucinations of a haven for his drowned comrade. Thus the basic theme of Traven's works appears: a romantic journey of escape from corrupt, modern industrial civilization, and paradoxically, the disintegration of the ego in the absence of civilization.

The three books that comprise the novel deal with the shore civilization, the death ship itself, and the escape.... Perhaps the first book is a wild comedy rather than a "humorous satire." It deals with the adventures of Gales, who is stranded in Antwerp without documents or money by the premature departure of his ship, the *Tuscaloosa.* (p. 16)

Gales uses humor against the bureaucracy which is denying his existence. The nightmarish situation may recall Kafka, but the treatment is wildly comic, suggesting the silent film comedians, particularly Chaplin as the "little tramp." Gales is the little man at whom the policeman pokes his thumb, evicting him from hotel room, park bench, and train compartment. His involuntary hobo's tour of Europe, with its constant and purposeless movement, recalls Chaplin's journeys. Both men confront a world of mechanism and bureaucracy with stoicism and small gestures of defiance. (p. 17)

[The] impasse remains: with neither documentary proof of identity nor a job, Gales's sense of identity as American or sailor does not suffice. The indispensable recognition of identity by society is lacking, and Gales, beneath his comic exuberance, feels the lack. (p. 18)

The ultimate cause of [Gales's] predicament ... is his illegitimacy. Behind the agressiveness of Gales's retorts and possibly behind all his humor lies uneasiness and shame at having his illegitimacy revealed. (p. 19)

Gales finds himself [aboard the deathship *Yorikke*] in a Dantean inferno, whose motto is, "He who enters here will no longer have existence!" ... Tormented by memories of their former lives and by the knowledge that they can never return to them, the men of the death ship have "vanished from the living".... The "inscription over the crew's quarters" that forms the epigraph to the second books reads, in part:

> He
> Who enters here
> Will no longer have existence;
> His name and soul have vanished
> And are gone for ever.
> Of him there is not left a breath
> In all the vast world.
> He can never return ...

Dante's characters are tortured for the evil deeds they committed on earth, but Traven's outcasts are innocent victims. As members of the "black gang," Gales and his fellow stoker, Stanislav, must create their own hell by feeding the nine fires of the *Yorikke's* furnaces. They are in the inner ring of Traven's inferno, the ninth circle reserved not for traitors to their countries, but for men who have been betrayed by their countries. (pp. 22-3)

The grotesque journey ends abruptly when Gales and Stanislav are shanghaied to serve as stokers aboard the *Empress.* From a nightmare of living death on the *Yorikke* the men are transported into a dreamlike state as rulers of the wrecked *Empress.* (p. 25)

The Death Ship shows Gales's continuous retreat from society. He escapes from the shore society of the first book as a member of the crew of the *Yorikke* and the "black gang" of the stokehold. Gales achieves semi-solitude with Stanislav on the *Empress* but he must become completely isolated from men to be fully reborn as Pippip, the orphaned castaway. (p. 26)

The novel has become a pure fantasy in [the] last book of dreamlike wrecks and hallucinations. The only alternative to the mazes of bureaucracy and the tortures of the death ship is regression to an infantile state. Gales's final vision suggests that only in death is escape possible. In a hallucination prompted by weariness, Gales imagines that the drowned Stanislav has signed on for a long voyage without papers.... *The Death Ship* ends with [a] glimpse of a sailor's Paradise that balances the infernal image of the death ships. But rest has come only for Stanislav who, in death, is reunited with the Great Skipper, or father. Gales ... must continue to search for the answer to his paternity. As the names "Gales" and "Pippip" imply, he is destined to survive the stormy seas only to remain an orphan. (pp. 27-8)

On the level of social criticism the death ship itself, rather than the shore bureaucracy, is the central symbol. It stands as a powerful, radical symbol of the betrayal and exploitation of anonymous workers, as well as representing a cross section of society. (p. 29)

Traven's social and political analysis is simplistic in its exaggeration and failure to draw distinctions; his ideas are secondary to the power of his symbols and narrative. (p. 30)

Traven is class-conscious, but he is hardly a Marxist.... Traven is a romantic yearning for preindustrial times, a kind of anarchist. The essence of his radicalism is expressed in the powerful central image of the book: nameless workers stroking the engines of the modern industrial economy. His power derives from his vision of life at the bottom of the stokehold....

A comparison between Traven's sea story and Conrad's work is inevitable. Although both are writing in the same nebulous genre, their viewpoints are directly opposed: Traven sees life from the bottom of the stokehold; Conrad's point of view is generally from the bridge. There is an explicit allusion to Conrad as "that heavenly, that highly praised, that greatest sea-story writer of all time [who] knew how to write well only about brave skippers, dishonored lords, unearthly gentlemen of the sea, and of the ports, the islands, and the sea-coasts; but the crew is always cowardly, always near mutiny, lazy, rotten, stinking, without any higher ideals or fine ambitions".... Traven's distortion of Conrad nearly cancels out his praise of him; Traven suggests that his own narrative is somehow more balanced and realistic. (p. 31)

Traven's use of expressionism to heighten the story of a stoker's exploitation and betrayal shows his indebtedness to O'Neill's *Hairy Ape*. The extent of the debt may be reflected in the violence of his attack on a work in which expressionist distortion plays such a vital part. A basic problem in the critical treatment of expressionism is to determine whether the distortion is induced by the author for expressive purposes, or whether it is supposed to be a reflection of the protagonist's disturbed mind. Neither alternative precludes the other, of course, but in *The Death Ship* most of the distortion originates in the mind of the narrator. The progression from expressionism lightened by wild comedy, through the grim inferno of the stokehold, to the final apocalyptic fantasy reflects the changing emotions of Gales. The very distortion stems from Gales's projection of his feelings as an illegitimate child onto society and the death ships. (p. 34)

Traven's self-consciousness may be reflected in the abundance of his literary allusions. In addition to his debt to Conrad and O'Neill, there are allusions to Dante, Melville, and Shakespeare, and there are echoes of Kafka. Melville's influence pervades this "*Moby-Dick* of the stokehold" in which the narrator alone has escaped to tell the story. Both the *Pequod* and the *Yorikke* are microcosms of society; their voyages are romances of the sea filled with naturalistic details. A primary parallel is the first-person narrative of Gales, who, like Ishmael, boasts in rich colloquial tones of never going to sea as an officer. Gales: "I second mate? No, sir. I was not mate on this can, not even bos'n. I was just a plain sailor. Deckhand you may say. You see, sir, to tell you the truth, full-fledged sailors aren't needed now" . . . ; and Ishmael: "No, when I go to sea, I go as a simple sailor, right before the mast, plumb down into the forecastle, aloft there to the royal mast-head." Both men engage the reader in a kind of dialogue. Gales's colloquial American English echoes that of his equally direct Yankee predecessor. Gales, like Ishmael, insists upon his rank, which separates him from much of the crew. (pp. 34-5)

Both Gales and Ishmael narrate stories which begin with a wild farce that contrasts sharply with the ensuing journey into blackness. In both, the comic beginnings may be a cover-up for the narrators' anxieties over their uncertain identities and roles. "Gales" may not have been the narrator's legal name, and Ishmael's real name is never revealed. Disguises are prominent in *The Death Ship* in which the entire crew signs on with aliases. On Traven's ship, as on Melville's *Fidèle* in *The Confidence-Man*, "rarely if ever did anybody reveal his real name". . . . Disguises are a necessary defense against a society that shows its lack of charity in refusing to recognize its orphaned underdogs. Ishmael tells nothing of his family background except for an episode involving a punishing stepmother, and Gales seems strangely uncertain about his own mother. . . . (p. 35)

Wit, particularly phallic wit, serve both Ishmael and Gales as defenses and gestures of defiance. . . . [Gales] and Ishmael intend their hyperbole, gibes, and puns as rejections of the values of civilization. The ultimate defenses of these two orphans might be the very stories they tell in which the entire civilization is condemned to annihilation. Traven may have seen *Moby-Dick* as a fantasy of the type he himself was to write: a fantasy of a rejected outcast who avenges himself on society first by loosening his bonds to it, then by symbolically destroying it. (pp. 36-7)

That *The Death Ship* has a fresh and unique quality, despite its wealth of literary allusions, is due in large part to the original language Traven creates for Gales. . . . Just as

the *Yorikke* has its own *lingua franca*, so Gales has his own idiom. (p. 38)

Gales's language is a weapon. The verbs "swallow," "plunge," "kick," "sock," and "spit" show him to be nearly choking with hostility. . . . Gales's personification of the death ship as "pest *Yorikke*" and his own suicidal impulses as the "beast" . . . reduces vague terrors to the level of the familiar. Gales's language is Traven's substitute for the active self that in Melville controls the direction of the voyage, if not its outcome. Like Ahab, Gales is "up again" after being knocked down. But while the captain can say "Naught's an angle to the iron way!"', Gales can only tell himself: "Now back into your bunk." (p. 39)

Ultimately, the *Yorikke* is a symbol of the grim joke that death has become in Western civilization. In *The Death Ship* the greatest "Joke is on Death itself."

Although the novel deals with betrayal and flight, its tone is one of triumph. Gales survives against all odds; the coal-drag, having seen life from the bottom of the stokehold, is still undefeated: "I won't give up and I won't give in. Not yet. Not to the ground port" . . . Although Gales, despite his resolve, almost yields to his death wishes, the story itself, told in the "barbaric yawp of an underdog," expresses defiance and a will to live. A major theme of the novel is the disintegration of the ego, but the technique, with its fusing of literary allusions and colloquial narrative and its carefully modulated change from satire to expressionistic nightmare to sea fantasy, represents integration and control. (pp. 40-1)

In *The Treasure of the Sierra Madre* (1927) Traven deals directly with the disintegrative effects of greed and fear on the individual psyche. For this modern exemplum on the text *Radix Malorum*, he employs the ancient theme of the three companions whose search for gold ends in death. The novel is also an exciting adventure narrative of the quest for fabled treasure in the wilderness of the Mexican Sierra Madre, as well as an acute psychological study of the paranoid breakdown of a personality. (p. 42)

The center of interest is in the psychological element, not . . . in the social commentary of a proletarian author. (p. 45)

In this sardonic tale, the three companions [Dobbs, Curtin, and Howard], in their differing attitudes toward gold, represent three aspects of personality. All are motivated by a desire for gold, for it represents freedom from constant need and an escape from their low status. But it is Howard who makes the crucial decisions of the search, and only he knows how to recognize the gold. . . . Howard represents a strong sense of self. Curtin, whose name suggests a shadowy presence, is less individually characterized than the other two men. . . . [He] is opposed to depriving another of the results of his labor. A spokesman for the dignity of labor and the rights of the worker, he speaks for the moral conscience; he tries to prevent Dobbs from stealing Howard's gold and is unable to murder Dobbs even when it is clear that if he does not, Dobbs will murder him. Dobbs lacks both Curtin's moral sense and Howard's sense of self. If Howard is the character we wish to emulate, Dobbs is the one we fear we might become. Dobbs represents more than the unrestrained lust for gold; he represents the forbidden wishes and impulses that we cannot think of without experiencing guilt and fearing punishment. (p. 49)

Traven may have written a modern exemplum analogous to Chaucer's "Pardoner's Tale," but Traven's tale has another moral that is found in the epigraph:

The treasure which you think not worth taking trouble and pains to find, this one alone
is the real treasure you are longing for all
your life. The glittering treasure you are
hunting for day and night lies buried on the
other side of that hill yonder. . . .

The "real treasure" is the self, to be found in a real goal
such as healing the Indians. Perhaps Howard's adopting
the profession of "medicine man" is an implausible ending,
but it is a symbolic alternative to the perpetual hunt for illusory treasure. (p. 50)

The severe penalty paid by Dobbs is the loss of self. His
beheading by the thieves is a punishment that fits the offense: he literally loses his head after having lost it from
fear. Like Gales at the end of *The Death Ship*, Dobbs loses
control over his actions and loses contact with reality; he
becomes the victim of his fears. . . . The fear of disappearance or loss of self lies behind both the paranoid breakdown
described in this book and the strange state of living death
described in *The Death Ship*. (p. 51)

The Treasure of the Sierra Madre may be characterized as
an adventure narrative whose psychological depth distinguishes it from other books of the genre. The voice of the
author is cool and sardonic, his narrative ironic and controlled. Although the unstable Dobbs is the focus of narration, there is none of the distortion of *The Death Ship*.
Traven eschews the expressionism and literary allusions of
that novel to suit the genre of pulp fiction which he is using
quite consciously. (p. 59)

The first page of the novel illustrates Traven's method of
narration, which alternates between glimpses into Dobbs's
mind, comments by the author, and, later, extensive dialogue. Traven begins by commenting that "the bench on
which Dobbs was sitting was not so good. One of the slats
was broken; the one next to it was bent so that to have to
sit on it was a sort of punishment". . . . Dobbs, however,
does not notice the condition of the bench, for he "was too
much occupied with other thoughts to take any account of
how he was sitting". . . . The terse, ironic tone that pervades the author's comments and the protagonist's mind is
suited perfectly to the action of the novel. (pp. 59-60)

Dobbs's disintegration, at least in the dramatic moments
leading up the shooting of Curtin, is described for the most
part in dialogue. The reader deduces Dobbs's paranoia
from his words and his laughter, comparing his distorted
interpretation of the events with Curtin's and Traven's relatively objective viewpoints. (p. 60)

In the absence of Curtin, the glimpses into Dobbs's mind
necessarily become more frequent; his fears and continuing
projections are now central to the book. These insights are
deeper and more frequent in the short period of time elaps-
ing between his encounter with the three thieves and his
murder. Traven is building up the identification with the
protagonist to intensify the shock of his death. (p. 61)

The . . . chapter [after Dobbs's murder] begins with a witty
speculation of the minds of burros, again in Traven's terse,
ironic tone: "Dogs often show a real interest in what men
do, even when the men in question are not their masters.
Dogs even like to meddle in the affairs of men. Burros are
less interested in men's personal doings; they mind their
own business. That's the reason why donkeys are thought
to have a definite leaning toward philosophy". . . . The tension arising from Dobbs's murder is thus reduced; the nar-

rative voice directs attention to the murderer, the burros,
the capture and execution of the thieves, and finally to
Curtin and Howard. The narrative becomes objective again
and the point of view is that of a detached and omniscient
author. (p. 62)

When Howard says "gold is always very expensive, no
matter how you get it or where you get it" . . ., he means
that the price is paid not only in hard work but also in fear
and possibly in death. Howard, having previously made
and lost fortunes in gold, has always known that the goal is
unattainable, that the "glittering treasure . . . lies buried on
the other side of that hill yonder". . . . Traven suggests that
no amount of work can make gold valuable, any more than
the alchemists could make precious metals out of dross.
Only an irrational civilization values what is, paradoxically,
false or fool's gold, and work aimed at amassing wealth is
doomed to result in self-alienation. *The Treasure of the
Sierra Madre* suggests that the lust for gold is a disguised
death instinct, an archetypal theme that gives Traven's
adventure story its universality. (p. 63)

The Bridge in the Jungle (1929), in which Gales [of *The
Death Ship*] becomes involved with a primitive settlement
of Mexican Indians, can be seen as another chapter in
Traven's continuing fantasy of escape from Western civilization. . . .

As in *The Death Ship*, Gales is the narrator, but he is observer rather than protagonist; that role falls to "inexorable
fate" and to Señora Garcia, the bereaved mother of the
little boy [drowned in a tropical river]. (p. 64)

The mother, conspicuously absent in the other novels, is
here the central focus of the narrative. Yet through her
symbolic presence Señora Garcia becomes more than a
mere human being. *The Bridge in the Jungle* is the culmination of the major works of the motif of descent into the
womb. The death ship *Yorikke* and the Mexican wilderness
of the Sierra Madre, the womb symbols of the other works,
are replaced by a more direct symbol—the mother herself.
Since Carlos makes the journey rather than Gales himself,
the latter's role is largely passive. Half of the book consists
of Gales's close observation of the mother's fears and sorrows, and her reactions to the child's death. But Gales is
more than an observer; he shares the intuitions and feelings
of the primitive woman. (p. 66)

Gales's sense of isolation and susceptibility to "hallucinations" foreshadow the nearly uncontrollable fear he suffers
during the climatic recovery of the body. . . . Traven emphasizes not the superstitiousness of the Indians, which
Gales uses to justify his fears, but rather the fears themselves. Death by drowning, anonymous death, and betrayal
are the obsessions of all of Traven's protagonists. The
rising action of the book, leading to the discovery of the
body, is directly related to the intensification of Gales's
feelings about the boy. As the discovery of the body draws
nearer, Gales's sense of guilt and fear of retribution are increasing. His reactions to it will determine whether he, like
Dobbs, will yield to his paranoia and fall victim to "terror
almost to madness." (p. 68)

Although Traven thought of *The Bridge in the Jungle* as his
best novel, it is inferior to *The Death Ship* and *The
Treasure of the Sierra Madre*. Since Gales plays a passive
role in this drama, the psychological impact is lessened.
Traven is at his best when the potential victim of his compulsive fears is his persona, Gales, or an alter ego such as
Dobbs. The interest in the novel declines sharply after the

body is found, because Gales has little left to do but comment on the natural grace, honesty, and decency of the Indian community. Traven himself may have thought of his novel primarily as a study of primitivism. (p. 74)

Traven makes it appear that Gales's catharsis comes at the same time as that of the community. If the novel were primarily a study of primitivism, the climax would be the funeral scene in which the sympathetic Westerner becomes a member of the community by mourning the death of one of its members. But *The Bridge in the Jungle* is of particular interest only when viewed in the context of Traven's obsession with identity and fear of disintegration. The true climax, then, comes halfway through the book with the recovery of the body and the reunion of the child with his mother. After that, Gales is a superfluous character; Traven may have found that he could best describe Indian life without a narrator, as he did later in the series of Jungle Novels. (pp. 77-8)

Government is a comic masterpiece which echoes the first book of *The Death Ship*. The bureaucratic society is moved to Mexico; expressionism with comic overtones is replaced by comic fantasy. The later novel is a satire on government in which all the laws are for the benefit of the Ladinos and to the detriment of the Indians. (pp. 94-5)

[*Government*] breaks all the accepted canons of novel writing: there is no focus on a central character, no sustained narrative line. It is a book without a protagonist, since Don Gabriel, far from determining the action, is only an agent of the system. The Indians here, unlike the protagonists of the other novels in the series, are anonymous; the people of Pebvil are the heroes. It is perhaps the absence of a sympathetic central character that creates the comic lack of affect which enables this book to succeed where the others in the series of Jungle Novels fail. In the other novels, Traven is outraged at the treatment of Andrés, Candido, Celso, and the other Indians uprooted from land and family. Yet he does not seem to feel close enough to his Indian protagonists to project himself and the reader into their psyches. When they have their revenge, the bloodshed and brutality become the focus of his interest. Without a character through whose mind the experiences can be filtered, that is, without a Gales or a Dobbs representing Traven himself, the brutal action fails to become psychological terror. Traven succeeds as a writer when the central character is his persona, as in *The Death Ship;* when that character represents some aspect of his personality, as in *The Treasure of the Sierra Madre;* or when, on the other hand, he is writing a comic fantasy in which there is no question of identification with the characters. (p. 95)

From *The Death Ship* to [the short story] "Macario," Traven's works display a fear of death and a pervasive anxiety which originate in this fear. They also reveal a deep-seated fear of betrayal, connected with paranoia and loss of identity. (p. 107)

Traven never quite solved the problem of form. The structures of his best books are adaptations from other writers. *The Treasure of the Sierra Madre* is an updating of Chaucer's "The Pardoner's Tale" combined with an adventure narrative. "Macario" also has an archetypal motif; the Grimm tale "Godfather Death," which is its source, has many analogues in folklore and myth. *The Death Ship* borrows theme and structure from *Moby-Dick* and the *Inferno*. *Government* is the one completely successful work in which Traven relies on his own invention to supply the

structure; but since *Government* is a short novel centering around one important incident, the revolt of the Indians of Pebvil, the problem of form is not crucial. The rest of the Jungle Novels fail largely because they lack the form that would act as a restraint on Traven's political digressions and gratuitous violence. (p. 115)

> *Donald O. Chankin, in his* Anonymity and Death: The Fiction of B. Traven *(copyright © 1975 by The Pennsylvania State University), The Pennsylvania State University Press, University Park, 1975.*

The Death Ship is . . . an attack on two institutions: nationalism and capitalism. Nationalism creates boundary lines and confers citizenship on lucky middle-class people; but woe to the workingman who finds himself abroad in the early 1920s without the papers that establish his right to walk through foreign streets. If, like Gales, he should commit the additional crime of being penniless (because his ship has sailed away not only with his seaman's papers, but with the money due him), he will forfeit his very right to live—he will become a nameless being, a creature "without existence". . . . As such, he is shunted across one European border after another, in the dark of night, by the minions of law and order, until he winds up, quite inevitably and as if by a law of mutual attraction, in the only refuge of stateless, homeless, and nameless men: in the limbo of a death ship. Here he finds a home at last among outcasts like himself; they are members of a crew that does not legally exist. The death ship itself is the embodiment of predatory capitalism, of the Moloch that feeds on helpless humans, that enslaves men, uses them up, and lets them die—with no one the wiser, nor anyone the sadder. (pp. 38-9)

The Death Ship's open, urgent, and still pertinent attack on nationalism and capitalism does not, however, make it a proletarian novel, if we use this term arbitrarily—there being no critical agreement on its meaning—to designate a novel that protests against the conditions that a capitalist society imposes on its workingmen. If Traven were a socialist or a communist there would be no question as to his position in the class struggle, but . . . he is neither, and he does not regard the worker's struggle as a class struggle. . . . Superficially at least, Traven's political orientation in *The Death Ship* is obvious and needs no exegesis. The author's continual and personal sense of outrage at justice betrayed is the impulse behind *The Death Ship*'s attack on capitalism and nationalism, as it is the impulse behind all of Traven's writings. But there are aspects of the novel that are less obvious. . . . For beneath Traven's fury at institutions like nationalism and capitalism lies a tolerant attitude toward human weaknesses, a sympathy for erring man. There is an undercurrent in the book of acceptance of human beings as they are that runs counter to its protest against the conditions human beings have created. Things ought to be better, the book asserts accusingly; they won't be, it appears to reply, until human beings are better. And so its Promethean author continues to beat his heels against the rocks while the disparity between his desire for the betterment of the human lot—particularly the workingman's, the homeless stray's, the exploited underdog's—and his unconfessed recognition of that lot's very fixity vibrates inside the story and vitalizes its narrative drive. (pp. 39-40)

The author's sense of the human condition is manifested, first of all, in the seemingly inconsequential act that becomes fateful—and whose consequences are stoically accepted by the hero. (With Traven's Indians in later novels, this stoicism is a way of life.) Twice in the course of the novel Gales does something he need not do; twice he takes the initiative, becomes active instead of remaining passive; twice he makes a decision—really against his better judgment—and both times it turns out to have been the wrong decision, a decision that has totally unforeseen and terrible consequences. But after his initial disappointment, Gales wastes no more time regretting the actions that landed him in his predicament. (p. 40)

The irony is that both acts, leaving the *Tuscaloosa* and boarding the *Yorikke,* though unnecessary, are perfectly normal acts and would be, outside of a Traven novel, perfectly inconsequential. No ethical gravity attaches to them; they involve no one but Gales himself. . . . [In] a Traven novel, any act, even a morally neutral one, may lead to unforeseen events, because the world of Traven's novels is one of accidents that follow essentially innocent acts. In the end, of course, it may come to the same thing, namely, that the gods plague and even kill us for their sport, no matter how innocent we are. . . . [In] Traven the characters accept accidents as a matter of course, even if accidents mean the expulsion from Eden—with death imminent. (Gales has been in Eden on the *Tuscaloosa,* and he knows it. "What a ship the *Tuscaloosa* was!" he tells us on the first page. . . . [Gales's] impulse to leave the *Tuscaloosa,* at least for a stroll, is perfectly normal. Gales is, after all, only one of us. An ordinary person who happens to be an able-bodied seaman, with no particular ambitions and no unusual traits, he is not a man of extraordinary abilities or perceptions, and, though an articulate observer, no hero—not an Odysseus after all, *Odyssey* motifs in *The Death Ship* notwithstanding. (pp. 40-1)

The Death Ship, insofar as it is an exposé of two evils—the cynical practice of sending ships to the bottom of the sea for their insurance money and the unbelievably bad conditions that existed on some merchant ships in the early part of the twentieth century—may have been written with the intention of bringing about changes in the law. . . . But . . . *The Death Ship* is more than a protest novel, and although Gerard Gales is not a tragic hero, a tragic attitude is implicit in the book. Gales is not exclusively the victim of capitalist inhumanity; he is also . . . the victim of his own acts and of the impulses behind those acts. . . . What happens to Gales as a result of his being human is outside his control. If the world were a better place to live in than it is, his adventures would be more pleasant. . . . It is unjust, however, regardless of the economic system operating in it. An innocent act in a Traven novel would have unforeseen and terrible consequences under communism as well as under capitalism. For Traven, communism is as bad as capitalism, and it may be even worse. But if capitalism is bad for the workingman, Traven would appear to be asking in *The Death Ship* whether the workingman deserves a more beneficent system. For Traven is perfectly realistic about the workingman, and *The Death Ship* is filled with observations on his baseness and perfidy. (pp. 44-5)

Brotherly love and charity are what Traven misses in all white men; this is a theme that runs through the entire Traven canon. It is not stated as such in this novel, though one can hardly overlook it. Another unstated theme in Traven's works is one that forms part of his tragic view, for it explains why men will probably never be better off than they are now. It is the recognition of man's ability to get used to almost anything. Not only will human beings get used to almost any kind of hell, so long as they do not ac-

tually die there, but they will often come to like it. (pp. 46-7)

So far, then, two very diverse elements undermine the classification of *The Death Ship* as a proletarian novel of protest. They are, first, the fatefulness of innocent acts and, second, the fact that men become used to bad situations. Neither is caused by nationalism or capitalism, even if the fate of Gerard Gales is shaped by those two institutions, since Gales happens to be living in a world where nationalism and capitalism operate. A third item must be added to the list as well. Traven mentions it explicitly in *The Death Ship,* and it may be considered part of Traven's tragic outlook. It too is an aspect of human nature, which, for Traven, remains constant: it is the fact that men hope. (p. 50)

Traven is saying that the sailors of the *Yorikke* and, by logical extension, oppressed workers everywhere can always be their own masters, can always take their fate into their own hands by jumping overboard and committing suicide, if such a "fate" seems preferable to being "used" as slaves. If the sailors of the *Yorikke* hadn't "abandoned their souls," Traven further implies, they would have jumped overboard. It is an indictment of most of mankind, since most men prefer living on almost any terms to dying. . . . (p. 51)

What Traven is saying is that once the workingman sees that the odds are overwhelmingly against him and that he would probably lose his life in a struggle for his own rights (for that is what it boils down to), he would do better to take his own life instead, not only for his soul's sake, for his self's sake, for his dignity's sake, but in order to defeat the oppressor and exploiter, the imperator Capitalism. For if the worker did away with himself and thus removed himself from the scene, who would do the work? It would obviously never get done. Where, then, would capitalism be?

But since Traven evidently feels that the worker will do the work (and suffer), that he will neither do away with himself nor take up arms against the capitalist oppressor because he hopes—and because he gets used to his wretched lot and sometimes even comes to like it—Traven's protest against institutions is somewhat self-defeating. Or, to put it another way, Traven is protesting not merely institutions but immutable conditions, those that blind human beings and induce them to endure. Traven's protest is thus less against social injustice than against a higher form of injustice: it is a protest against the gods for making man what he is, a protest against man's own nature. And as such, it lifts *The Death Ship* out of the category of proletarian fiction. (pp. 51-2)

The Death Ship . . . while it does protest against institutions, protests more vehemently—and impotently—against the human condition itself. If the book protests against institutions with political passion, which, for Traven, is always personal, it protests against man's fate with what might be called humanist passion, which, for Traven, is equally personal. The distinction is not significant, but it should allow me to emphasize that, for Traven, the human being quite clearly comes before the political being. (pp. 56-7)

It is the state which anarchist Traven cannot accept because it stands in the way of freedom—because it stamps out freedom with it bureaucracy. Traven does not see the state as protecting the freedom of the individual to develop his own personality, his freedom to do the things he wants to do, to move about like an insect. For Traven, the state signifies the end of all such freedoms. Significantly, the protagonists of his early novels never see the state do anything for *them*. Nor does the state, or its embodiment, government, do anything for the enslaved, disenfranchised Mexican Indians of Traven's later novels. (p. 58)

Traven's anarchism, so far, is still fairly "classical": opposition to the state and disbelief in institutions and authority. Implicit in Traven's attack on the state is the conviction that in nature man is free. (p. 60)

Traven's white protagonists do tend to stay away from civilization (the question is hardly posed for his Mexican Indians) in order to remain outside society; they are loners either by choice (disgust with bourgeois society) of because society has cast them out—as it has cast Gales out. (p. 61)

There may be inconsistencies . . . in Traven's *Land des Frühlings*. This fascinating oddity of a book, bristling with opinions and ideas, presents a number of theses. One has to do with man's nature. Traven actually posits *two* natures: the white man's and the Indian's. The white man, according to Traven's thesis, is driven by ambition, greed, and lust for power, while the Indian is driven by a communal sense of feeling—Traven admits being unable to define this trait with enough precision for the white man to understand. The implication, however, is clear: the white man is bad, the Indian good. Rapprochement between the two is difficult, though their union may be desirable. In *Land,* Traven also rants against the individualism of the white man—it is individual ambition that drives him. But Traven seems to mean the individualism of free enterprise, the individualism that says I must *have*—and I shall *take* at the cost of the poor! (pp. 77-8)

In his fiction . . . Traven is astonishingly consistent, if not always in the logic of his philosophic position, at least in his emotional attitude. Toward the end of his life, Hal Croves expressed that sense of consistency. "See," he said to Judy Stone in 1966, "how, among all of Traven's books, there goes one thought like a red thread from the first line of his book to the last line of his last book." . . .

Traven's "one thought" might be formulated as follows: "No man should be *coerced* into being or doing anything against his will." For the fear of coercion, we know, is the primal instinct of the anarchist. . . . Traven's concern for the happiness of all and his wish to hurt no one is the red thread that runs through all of his books from first line to last. (pp. 78-9)

Traven habitually employed English and American expressions in his German prose. Yet Traven's Anglicisms do not necessarily violate the German language, not even when he introduces American idioms or uses words that do not exist in German. (p. 84)

Traven did not . . . have sufficient command of American English to write in that language. This is so obvious that one wonders how he could have deluded himself into trying. He tried . . . in several novels: *The Death Ship* (1934), *The Treasure of the Sierra Madre* (1935), *The Bridge in the Jungle* (1938), and *March to the Monteria* (1964). (p. 85)

Traven's malapropisms in English are of three kinds: (1) those that miss being full-fledged idioms, (2) those that miss being genuine colloquialisms, slang expressions, or curses, and (3) metaphrases, or literal translations. The third kind predominates. (p. 86)

Traven, finally, is guilty of a fourth kind of malapropism in English: he structures sentences according to German syntax. One example should be enough to show what I mean: "Here nobody pushes down your throat your nationality." (p. 87)

Yet for all of Traven's incorrect use of American English, it seems fair to say that this linguistic weakness does not detract from the vitality of a novel like *The Death Ship,* from its narrative drive, or from its emotional impact. (p. 88)

We know today that Traven was not at all "unlettered"; as the author of *Der Ziegelbrenner* he was perfectly literate. As for his "expert literary technique," we must not forget that, as Ret Marut, he had already written a number of effective short stories and novellas. . . . [Traven] exhibits an easy, professional erudition, the kind of erudition we would expect a European journalist or intellectual to have. (p. 91)

Readers of *The Death Ship* must be struck by a singular dichotomy: the narrator Gerard Gales claims to be an uneducated American sailor, yet his prose is full of allusions to other writers, and he even quotes in Latin. . . . [Traven] attempts to confound author and narrator in the reader's mind. Since author and narrator are not one and the same, the attempt fails and Traven, at least in this respect, sounds false.

A novelist's education, particularly when his protagonist-narrator is supposedly uneducated, need not show. But Traven's education, however hard he may try to conceal it or pretend it doesn't exist, does show in *The Death Ship,* in allusions to other writers, in echoes of famous lines, even in Latin quotations. Yet the pretense itself is of interest, and it reveals itself best, I think, whenever Traven-Gales, in his pose as antihighbrow sailor, feels he must make a comment on the falsity of the culture produced for "opera-audiences, movie-goers, and magazine readers" who want "a happy ending". . . . "The true story of the sea is anything but pleasant or romantic," Gales informs his readers, because he thinks—because Traven pretends to think with the mind of the uneducated sailor—that the reader has the wrong notion of what is "romantic." "All the romance of the sea . . . died long, long ago. . . . The life of the real heroes has always been cruel, made up of hard work. . . . Even the hairy apes are opera-singers looking for a piece of lingerie". . . . This last is, of course, a reference to Yank, the "hairy ape" of O'Neill's play. It is, I think, an unfair attack on the action of that play, or on its supposedly fake "romance." . . . To call the "hairy ape" an opera singer looking for a piece of lingerie is doing the grossest kind of injustice to O'Neill. In giving this line to an uneducated sailor, Traven is not speaking for himself, of course, but I think he misunderstands the sailor for whom he is speaking. (pp. 92-3)

Unless Traven wants to show an illiterate man reacts to a specific item of culture, the function of Gales's implicit attack on O'Neill's play in *The Death Ship* is not quite clear. For it reveals that Gales is not illiterate at all; he obviously reads serious literature. The attack on O'Neill also demonstrates Traven's continued interest in American writers, even if Traven can also put them down rather hard.

He puts a non-American writer down rather hard, too. "There is a chance, one in a hundred, maybe," Gales says at the beginning of the novel, "that at some time romance and adventure did exist for skippers, for mates, for engineers''. . . . This innuendo is surely aimed at Joseph Conrad—at his having written sea stories only about the elite. (pp. 93-4)

If Traven's pose as an ''unlettered stoker and forecastle hand,'' to use Colcord's phrase, seems suspect on the face of it, it breaks down altogether when Traven-Gales makes explicit allusions to other authors. It is as if Traven himself felt guilty for making these allusions, for letting his erudition show, for allowing Gales to refer to writers that Traven suddenly remembers an illiterate worker surely has not read, so that he twists what Gales says before the words are out of Gales's mouth. Hence Gales says petty, negative things about O'Neill . . . such as an unlettered worker *might* say if he had accidentally read these authors —and if he happened also to be a little stupid. But the ruse itself, as I hope I have shown, doesn't work.

It doesn't work, needless to say, with the implicit allusions found in *The Death Ship* either. Authors explicitly referred to may demonstrate Traven's need to keep up—or catch up, if prolonged periods of travel or residence in the jungle outposts of Chiapas, for example, have kept him out of touch. O'Neill may have been a contemporary author Traven caught up with and subsequently introduced into the American version of *The Death Ship* in 1934, though *The Hairy Ape* had been published in 1922—four years before *Das Totenschiff* appeared in Germany. Authors explicitly referred to, at any rate, are less likely to have ''influenced'' Traven's own style or Traven's ideas than authors implicitly referred to or echoed in some of his lines, if only because Traven seems almost too conscious of the O'Neills and the Conrads when he refers to them. Explicit references, finally sound awkward even when they do not criticize. At one point Gales talks about ''old man Faust'' who knew ''devils'' ''personally'' and who therefore knew that they would need more ''culture and civilization'' than the *Yorikke* could provide. . . . The one ''devil'' who might need more culture and whom Faust knew ''personally'' is, of course, Mephistopheles. But to hear Mephistopheles referred to as ''devils'' and Faust as ''old man Faust,'' as if both of these figures were comic strip characters a sailor might casually, banteringly mention to a buddy, sounds absurd.

But if the explicit allusions force us to take note of Traven's pose as an illiterate American sailor-workingman, the implicit allusions at least allow us to go along with that pose. The explicit allusions, particularly those meant to show the falsity of the ''romance'' associated with the sea in literature, make us conscious of Traven's pose, while the implicit allusions do not impel us to ask whether or not the author is also the narrator. We don't care *whose* the erudition is so long as it doesn't call attention to itself. . . .

We don't worry about where he got his Latin—or how Dante or Blake can have slipped into this or that line—as long as the narrator doesn't awkwardly step out of his role by appearing to flaunt his learning. (pp. 95-6)

''When the last glimpse of Spain had been veiled from my eyes,'' says Gales in the American version of *The Death Ship,* after the *Yorikke* has left the harbor of Cadiz, ''I felt that I had entered that big gate over which are written the solemn words: he who enters here will no longer have existence.''. . . . Apparently this gate is in every reader's cultural domain. Is it the gate to Dante's hell? No, the gate turns out to be one we cannot really know, for it leads to the crew's quarters of the death ship *Yorikke.* The words above it are the beginning of a long inscription, but they do remind us of the words above the gate to Dante's hell. (pp. 96-7)

Perhaps it does not . . . matter whether we call Traven an American writer or a writer who exhibits certain American characteristics. The evidence is not yet conclusive: the similarities between his works and the works of . . . American writers . . . do not prove beyond a shadow of a doubt that those writers ''influenced'' Traven. (p. 113)

[Traven] was a man possessed. One feels in Traven's *Empörung,* in his indignation, a ''calling.'' And his calling seems once again to be peculiarly American, for it is really the fundamentalist's, the revivalist's calling. . . .

Driven by the inner compulsion of the American fundamentalist to cry out the word, but refusing to be preacher or prophet—here lies the explanation of Traven's vocation as novelist. Perhaps the language question is related to the sense of a fundamentalist's calling: if the attraction to the word is deeply American in nature, how better to hide that Americanness (and hence deny the calling's religious quality) than by writing in a second language, German? (p. 114)

Michael L. Baumann, in his B. Traven: An Introduction (© *1976 by the University of New Mexico Press), University of New Mexico Press, 1976.*

V

VASSILIKOS, Vassilis 1933-

One of the leading Greek novelists, Vassilikos is best known in this country for Z, a novel of political intrigue set in modern day Greece. Several other of his novels and stories have been translated into English, but in his native country it was _The Plant, The Well, The Angel,_ three parables of love and alienation, that established his reputation and earned him the most prestigious literary award in Greece, _The Award of the Group of the 12._ He is also a poet and a playwright. (See also _CLC,_ Vol. 4.)

It may give you some idea of the profound symbolic depths plumbed in [_The Photographs_] by the author of _Z_ when you realize that it is set in the Greek city of Necropolis and the hero's name—are you ready?—is Lazarus. The book is just chockfull of heavy stuff like that, some of it almost as good.

The plot is easily summarized. Lazarus is in love with a girl. Then he turns into a cat. Then he turns back into a person. Then he goes away. Then he comes back. Then he goes away again. . . .

I wish Lazarus had remained a cat. Some interesting things happened to him when he was a cat. After he turns back into a person, the novel is all downhill. It is like a hangover, unpleasant but not very interesting, and one can scarcely wait for it to get itself over with. Fans of Hermann Hesse will probably love it. Everyone else will have a hard time staying awake.

> _L. J. Davis, "Better a Cat than a Man," in_ Book World (© The Washington Post), _May 9, 1971, p. 2._

Vassílis Vassilikós is one of the most prolific writers of post-World War II Greece. From the corpus of works he has published—thirty-three volumes of prose, poetry and comedy—the trilogy _Ghláfkos Thrassákis_ stands out as the best example of his style of prose writing. . . .

The trilogy has no beginning, no sequential middle and no closing. Vassilikós's technique rises and falls, ebbs and flows like a tide expanding in time and place. . . .

[No] concrete and well-rounded characters or reconstructions of dramatic events exist. Names and events pop up wherever and whenever they are to serve in knitting together the author's narrative. Scatological expressions, pornographic scenes, declarations of international political outcasts fill in the canvas of the trilogy. The work is loaded with poems (in fragments or in whole), citations from other writers such as Sartre, news items, TV commercials, ads in neon lights, newspaper headlines, hotel bills, radio broadcasts, songs, et cetera, all of which constitute what can be called today's pop culture. Journalistic, cinematographic and linguistic devices are all in full force. With the latter, however, Vassilikós is original: he breaks words down into their original meaning, and through the etymologies and anagrammatisms he injects a dose of humor which contributes to a pleasant reading of the "printed" word.

It is hard to say whether such a style will either survive the times or influence other writers, or whether one can accept the novelty that today's journalism may become tomorrow's literature. Vassilikós's narrative is difficult to follow; but if the reader is able to do so, he will enjoy the black humor and the manner in which the human condition is ridiculed, as in Jarry and Joyce. (pp. 698-99)

> _George Giannaris, in_ Books Abroad _(copyright 1976 by the University of Oklahoma Press), Vol. 50, No. 3, Summer, 1976._

The Monarch by Vassilis Vassilikos . . . aspires to literature and ends up hitting the ground with an awful thump. Nor can the curious writing be blamed on the translation from the Greek by Mary Keeley, for no mere translator could invent the forced and unnatural imagery of "The Monarch."

Thus: "When I started smoking again, she hung over the balcony of insomnia like wet laundry that cannot dry because of the humidity. I was anxious." As well he might be, with a girlfriend made of wet laundry. . . .

You will need plenty of patience for this one. On the other hand, you will come up with some writing that will make the long winter nights go much faster, especially if selected excerpts are read aloud to connoisseurs. (p. 25)

> _Newgate Callendar, in_ The New York Times Book Review (© _1976 by The New York Times Company; reprinted by permission), August 15, 1976._

[_The Monarch_] is rich in both socio-political implications and in probings into human psychology and motivation. [Vassilikos] has rarely written better or more objectively where both personal and political factors are inextricably intermingled, and yet an individual integrity is insisted on as blossoming apart from the inroads of historical necessity. There is an acceptance of a new order of life wherein the masses may be freed of exploitation but where the individual also may retain his unique freedom, a planned economy that establishes a give and take between these two equal forces. . . .

Those who have seen the film *Z* or have read the book in one of the forty languages into which it has been translated may now be assured that Vassilikos has a range that extends beyond the last letter of any alphabet. (p. 933)

> *Kimon Friar, in* Books Abroad *(copyright 1976 by the University of Oklahoma Press), Vol. 50, No. 4, Autumn, 1976.*

*   *   *

VIDAL, Gore   1925-

An American novelist, playwright, screenwriter, and essayist, Vidal is equally celebrated for his historical fiction, which reinterprets events to comply with his social and political theories and convictions; his brilliant essays; and his frequent and lively appearances on television talk shows. Vidal has written detective stories under the pseudonym Edgar Box. (See also *CLC*, Vols. 2, 4, 6, and *Contemporary Authors*, Vols. 5-8, rev. ed.)

"Words, after all, define us," writes Gore Vidal. The reader's mind then staggers about as it is exposed to Vidal's dazzling sentences. How do you envision this person whose words turn each page into a tray of jewelry? As a bullfighter, perhaps. Arrogant body drawn like a bow, eyes disdainful. The clumsy stupid bull so easy to handle that the great danger is boredom. Or maybe he should be seen, Gore Vidal, as a prizefighter born with hands that think. . . .

How, then, do the words of *1876* define the writer? . . .

[They leave] you with the notion of Vidal as a man sitting in Italy for six months while this magnificent gift with which he was born pours out the words in arrangements which please the mind, please the ear, please the palate. Somewhere, somebody may be able to write sentences as well as Vidal, but I wonder who there is who can write as easily. Vidal's is a smashing gift, allowing him to write with so much less effort than is usually associated with the trade. Which is a very good thing. A common laborer he is not. This *1876* is a glorious piece of writing, and it should and will be bought and read and kept and reread by anybody with a taste for words. But do not come to this book looking for a new, interesting character: Vidal is too busy concentrating on words to provide us with that. . . .

Vidal uses Schuyler as the narrator of this book, and while Schuyler fails to couple himself to you, his words always do. As for daughter Emma, her I cannot even see. Murky murk. This ends Vidal's notions of character creation. Past these two, the people in his book—Samuel J. Tilden, William Cullen Bryant, James G. Blaine, U. S. Grant—are familiar to anybody who has attended high school. So many of these characters displease Vidal—only Grant, and Tilden, whom Vidal elevates to the priesthood, dissolve his scorn—that the effect is nearly wearying. And I know Vidal deliberately twists characters to make the bad into the good. Therefore, I trust none of these judgments. But again, what does it matter? The sentence is supreme.

> *Jimmy Breslin, "The Rules of Sentence," in* Harper's *(copyright 1976 by Jimmy Breslin; reprinted by permission of The Sterling Lord Agency, Inc.), March, 1976, p. 106.*

1876, the latest of Gore Vidal's historical novels, is the book everyone expected Mr Vidal to write. The voice with all those plummy vowels, enunciated with a Miss Jean Brodie twang, and that fruity exterior—in the sense that a lemon, however sharp, is still a fruit—have been perfectly transposed in this new novel and *1876* represents all that Mr Vidal thinks that politics ought to be: gossip, corruption, money, dinner parties, more corruption, and all the tacky panoply of power. Mr Vidal has now become the great chronicler of power, and in the course of [his three books, *Washington, D.C.*, *Burr*, and *1876*] he has pinned himself so successfully to the wall that he is now all but indistinguishable from the surroundings. . . .

Washington, D.C. . . . takes a lounge-lizard look at American politics in the period of the late 'thirties to the early 'fifties. This gives Mr Vidal plenty of opportunity to dish the dirt on a world he knew and, despite his protestations, loved. . . . Gore Vidal . . . is something of a teenage fantasist. And far from being the sharp-eyed observer of human weaknesses, he is a writer who insists upon sentimentalising politics and politicians; his books are melodramas, and his characters are really only mouthpieces.

Burr is the second of Vidal's political novels, and veers backward to the time of the American Revolution and the early years of the Republic. . . . Mr Vidal quite rightly refuses to accept, and works actively to undermine, those social myths which bind human communities together but, in the process, he has created a much more dangerous myth of his own: that politics is interesting, and that politicians make interesting characters. So Aaron Burr, the murderer of Alexander Hamilton, the wild man of American folklore, becomes everything that Vidal would like a politician to be: devious but spontaneous, clever but with a clever man's cunning. . . .

And so to the new novel, *1876*, perhaps the last of Vidal's historical fictions, and in many ways the most accomplished. . . . [Gone] are those moments of inexplicable passion which peep fitfully through *Washington, D.C.* and *Burr*; what we have instead is a novel perfectly contrived, a solid bourgeois entertainment which avoids seriousness as remorselessly as Vidal had once pursued it. . . . The book has pace, the narrative has wit and the prose has a sort of campy authenticity which we normally associate with revivals of 'forties pop and 'thirties clothing. But there is very little else to be said for it which could not be said about a hundred other 'good reads'.

> *Peter Ackroyd, "Blood, Thunder and Gore," in* The Spectator *(© 1976 by The Spectator; reprinted by permission of The Spectator), March 27, 1976, p. 20.*

[*1876*, supposedly the notebook of Charles Schuyler,] keeps behaving like a novel. This is not surprising, since it is a novel, but it is disquieting to find a man writing so novelistically in his notebook, and even at one point prematurely addressing his future readers, only to banish them as promptly as he can. . . . The difficulty here, I think, is Vidal's not Schuyler's. He has committed himself to a verisimilitude which creaks every time the writer moves. The same is true of *Burr* and *Two Sisters* (but not of *Myra*

Breckinridge); only in *Burr* the pace is so fast we don't stop to listen to the creaking.

Vidal is scrupulous about historical detail, and tactful in his allusions to famous events and people and inventions. . . .

But neither here nor in *Burr* is there a real flavor of the nineteenth century in the writing. There is no attempt at sustained pastiche, which is probably wise. But it does mean that the verisimilitude which dominates the book . . . places it in a rather strange literary corner. *Burr* and *1876* are new novels about the old century written in a manner that goes back about halfway toward the time of the action; the manner of Galsworthy or Arnold Bennett, say. Clearly technical experiment for its own sake is pointless, and writers of course should write exactly as they want to. But I do find it odd that America's most intelligent novelist should linger so long among old styles. Perhaps this is Vidal's way of hanging on to the large audience that he says a novelist needs. . . .

1876 is a slow book—we don't reach the year of its title until page 121—and its real virtue is not its meticulous reconstruction of old New York and old Washington, or even its scrutiny of the motives of historical figures. "Why a historical novel and not a history?" Vidal asked in an afterword to *Burr*, and one of his answers was that the historical novelist can "attribute motive—something the conscientious historian or biographer ought never to do." But Vidal really seems less interested in motive than he is in power, in political destinies found and missed. The central subject of both *Burr* and *1876* is what might have been, measured by a steady investigation of what actually was. Both books perform a recurring double take. We see the great man—Washington, Jefferson, Irving, Garfield—in unattractive close-up, a map of moral warts. Then we see how the warts enter into the composition of his greatness, which is not denied by this inspection, but rather reinforced. Only it is a greatness ratified by historical success, and Vidal's gift is to be able to view such success in the light of other options—historical failure, for example—without falling into sentimentality. (p. 30)

1876 seems to carry a double message. There is the broadly cynical view . . . , which is what the book seems to *say*. And then there is a more diffuse, faintly promising argument communicated by the sheer energy and passion with which, here and in other novels, Vidal explores American politics. An arena that can command such loyal attention can't simply be a bath of corruption, and Vidal's writing itself assumes a constituency which hopes for something better than to be governed by more or less cautious crooks forever. This constituency may be entirely wishful, but the wish seems to me a necessary one.

Vidal is discreet but firm about historical parallels. *1876* had its recent war, its recent assassination, its break-in, and its seedy administration, and Vidal touches on all these subjects, not so much to suggest that history repeats itself or that *plus ça change, plus c'est les mêmes shows,* as to remind us that we are not a historical island. *1876* is less vivid than *Burr* because there is less mischief in it, because it affords Vidal less of a chance to romp among famous American names, scattering suspicions as he goes. But it is in one sense a more serious book. It asks us to believe . . . in politics itself, that grimy and intricate activity we can't afford to give up. (p. 31)

Michael Wood, "Passions in Politics," in
The New York Review of Books (*reprinted*

with permission from The New York Review of Books; *copyright © 1976 NYREV, Inc.), April 29, 1976, pp. 30-1.*

Gore Vidal has not done it again. The year 1876 witnessed the popularity of a cocktail called the "razzle-dazzle," but much of Vidal's customary dazzle is missing from [*1876*]. Characterization and plot are thin while even Vidal's celebrated cynicisms fail to raise Charles Schuyler's voice above a monotone. Schuyler, who narrated *Burr* (where we learned he was Aaron Burr's illegitimate son), rarely displays any of his father's brilliant wit in *1876*. (p. 273)

The bulk of *1876* is occupied with colorful descriptions of American life in 1876 (the most satisfying aspect of the book), superficial dinner-party gossip in the rarefied atmosphere of the Astors and other society figures, and tediously drawn-out political reporting of the ins and outs, ups and downs of the 1876 election. Unfortunately, the sum of the parts, in this case, does not make a unified and aesthetically pleasing whole. While it is fun to relive the introduction of popped corn, "speaking tubes," and "perpendicular railways" (elevators), the protracted attempt to create suspense over a historical election whose outcome is known becomes mere boring cuteness. With the exception of [Schuyler's daughter] Emma's escapades, a faint shadow in the background, almost everything in *1876* receives undiscriminating treatment. The journalistic approach is all too pervasive, giving the impression of a book dashed off in a hurry—to be in time for the Bicentennial?

With respect to my recent conjecture (*Prairie Schooner,* Spring 1976) that Gore Vidal actually wrote the Gothic parody *Clara Reeve* (ostensibly by Leonie Hargrave), *1876* offers more proof, sharing with its predecessor verbal parallels peculiar to Vidal such as *mephitic* and *cicerone*. Vidal continues to share with Hargrave a fondness for obscure Sicilian relatives, laudanum addiction, a certain prostitute named Polly, and the murders of assorted husbands, wives, and mistresses. Curiously, in both *Burr* and *1876* someone mentions that "no one knows the name Achilles took when he hid himself among the ladies." I would venture to suggest that the name was Leonie Hargrave: with the Bicentennial hoopla mercifully passing, I look forward to another of *her* novels in the coming year. (p. 274)

A. Joan Bowers, "Vidal's Centennial," in
Prairie Schooner (© 1976 by University of Nebraska Press; reprinted by permission from Prairie Schooner), Fall, 1976, pp. 273-74.

[In *1876: A Novel*], Gore Vidal provides a fairly accurate portrayal of one stratum of American social and political life during this outrageous year. But he is only concerned with the wealthy and influential. He has no skill in understanding or communicating the problems of the lower classes. Besides, he is rather naive as to what history is all about. He wants truth. Gore Vidal! Thus, he has one character say, "We cannot know any history, truly. I suppose somewhere, in Heaven perhaps, there is a Platonic history of the world, a precise true record. But what we think to be history is nothing but fiction." Obviously, Vidal is a spoiled historian as well as a failed politician (at least he tried) and a successful writer. In his attempts at reconstructing the past for his novels he goes to a great deal of trouble to get it right.

1876: A Novel is not nearly as successful as *Burr: A Novel* probably because Vidal was more passionately involved in the latter work on account of his anti-Jefferson bias. Also he was determined to peddle that old chestnut about Martin Van Buren being the illegitimate son of Aaron Burr. Poor Matty. The things he has suffered even after death. (p. 26)

Robert V. Remini, in Commonweal *(copyright © 1977 Commonweal Publishing Co., Inc.; reprinted by permission of Commonweal Publishing Co., Inc.), January 7, 1977.*

Interest in himself as a character is one of the elements that make up an essayist. Gore Vidal has all these elements, but they are not always in play. Of course, he does not want them to be. He is often more concerned with saying something—conveying a mass of information or expressing a strongly held point of view—than with the manner of saying it. However, the penalty of occasional portentousness is that when he is being most serious he can look frivolous; whereas when he is being funny he is always himself, and therefore serious. . . .

There is one essay in ["Matters of Fact and of Fiction: Essays 1973-1976"] which I shall go on reading till I die, and that is about Tennessee Williams, titled "Some Memories of the Glorious Bird and an Earlier Self." All the elements are here in play and in balance. The machinery is alive and moving, and it has the fascination of some object one cannot take one's eye off. (p. 1)

It would be exaggeration to say that Gore Vidal is serious only when he writes the kind of criticism which his targets in political and academic life repudiate by calling "irresponsible." In several of these essays he reveals himself to be a critic of a very exceptional kind today—one who can bring to bear on novels considerations about other forms of art and about society which are not purely literary.

The first essay here is a brilliant examination of ten best-selling novels, which he relates to the dialogue and attitudes in movies from which they are partly derived. This is an extremely original and rewarding approach. Vidal also has the virtue, rare among critics, of going out of his way to defend a writer whom he thinks unduly neglected, as in his perceptive essay on Louis Auchincloss. . . .

As a critic of manners as well as literature, Vidal is in the tradition of Matthew Arnold and Edmund Wilson. This is excellent in itself, but being the boy who saw the Emperor walk naked doesn't always go with being an intellectual powerhouse. He can stingingly attack academia and America, but when it comes to his trying to impress on us his own erudition we are left with the feeling that he has mugged up a subject—the *nouveau roman*—for example, and then written an article about it. This anti-academic paradoxically puts his readers in the position of being examiners who have had a thesis submitted to them and have to mark it. I suspect that his essay "French Letters: Theories of the New Novel" would get only an A minus from a benighted academic who knew modern French literary theory. . . .

He is excellent and serious as a polemical critic attacking the behavior of institutions of the academy and the Presidency; he is less certain when he adopts the role of academic critic or Presidential speechwriter. (p. 46)

Stephen Spender, "Gore Vidal, Essayist," in The New York Times Book Review *(© 1977 by the New York Times Company; reprinted by permission), April 17, 1977, pp. 1, 46.*

Gore Vidal as an essayist accomplishes what so many Victorian novelists set out to do—to entertain and to edify. He is always funny and often witty. His paradoxes at their best rival Oscar Wilde's best. . . .

[In *Matters of Fact and of Fiction: Essays 1973-1976* Vidal] is willing to discuss first principles clearly—a rare treat in the United States, where, as Vidal points out, our spokesmen prefer to uncover scandals rather than to question basic premises. (p. 97)

Bracing (and hygienic) as Vidal's opinions are, they sometimes are too clever to be true, too hasty to take time for real complexities. For instance, Vidal assumes entertainingly enough that the "United States has always been a corrupt society" and that the corruption originates with the Founding Father (or the "Inventors," as he calls them), men who "believed profoundly in the sacredness of property and the necessary dignity of those who owned it." The virtue (from a journalistic point of view) of positing vice (as the basis of American politics) is that the notion can be presented with brevity and éclat and is cynical enough to be readily believed. But the notion ignores the intellectual side of the Federalist era. Edmund S. Morgan, for example, argues persuasively that for the Federalists politics had replaced theology as "the most challenging area of human thought," and that these men "addressed themselves to the rescue, not of souls, but of governments, from the perils of human nature." In short, the Federalists feared human nature but believed in the possiblity of guarding against it though a science of politics. The same fear of inherent human evil was characteristic, moreover, of the Antifederalists as well, and what divided the two groups was not a disagreement over the primacy of property but over the question of how large government could grow before succumbing to the malign temptations of power.

Since this pessimistic preoccupation with political corruption as a version of sin sounds so remarkably like Vidal's own approach to national affairs, I'm struck by his lack of sensitivity to the Inventors' moral concerns. If I am dwelling on the founding of the Republic, I do so only to isolate an unexamined determinism that seems to run throughout Vidal's politics. America was founded to protect property, and it is still in the grip of ITT and the Rockefellers, Vidal tells us. True enough, but even a partial understanding of how this state of affairs came about requires a look at the conscious values of the Americans of different epochs. Let me hasten to add that when Vidal does write about particular individuals in history, whether they are U. S. Grant or E. Howard Hunt, he is extraordinarily alert to their ideas, values, foibles, and quirks of vanity. . . .

When he turns to contemporary fiction, Vidal is too dogmatic for my taste. "American Plastic: The Matter of Fiction," his survey of several living American writers, is as exhilarating as Mailer's look at the "competition" many years ago in *Advertisements for Myself* and twice as funny, though Vidal is less candid about his own competitiveness. Granted, Vidal, unlike the "hacks of academe," as he likes to call them, does recognize that technique is more important than "themes" and plot more interesting than "influences." . . . Throughout his examination of American fiction Vidal appears to be uneasy about experimentation. . . . Traditional fiction is dull. Attacks on the avant-garde are philistine. The avant-garde is in disarray and infected with self-doubt. Occasionally a new masterpiece surfaces in one of the arts, and it has usually been created by someone who considers himself to be avant-garde. What can be made of these contradictions eludes me, but Vidal has not approached a serious question seriously.

These quibbles aside, I should say that I have not enjoyed a book of essays so much since Susan Sontag's *Against Interpretation.* (p. 98)

> *Edmund White, "Aristocratic Rebel," in* Harper's *(copyright © 1977 by* Harper's *Magazine; all rights reserved; reprinted from the May, 1977 issue by special permission), May, 1977, pp. 97-8.*

In Vidal's fourth and latest offering of essays, collected under the camel-humped title of *Matters of Fact and of Fiction,* the problem of the writer's relationship with a dwindling audience persistently bobs up, sinks, resurfaces. "The Top Ten Best Sellers" is about the Hollywoodization of popular literature. "The Great World and Louis Auchincloss" examines the predicament of a writer out of fashion with both bestsellerdom and Academe because he writes about Wall Street intrigue. Other essays discuss how novels have been kidnapped by the semiological killer-elite and whisked off to university laboratories where professors and students conduct fiendish experiments, creating plastic-membraned monsters.

As Vidal sees it, the University novel (as practiced by John Barth and others) is a hulking mutation, barely able to draw breath, while the Public novel (as practiced by Bellow, Mailer, Vidal) is losing its readership to mass-culture mind-benders. In between is the "book-chat" establishment, which decrees that "U-novels must always be predictably experimental . . . while the respectable P-novel is always naturalistic, usually urban, often Jewish, always middle-class, and, of course, deeply, sincerely heterosexual."

Often Vidal squanders his scorn on scribblers high and low. Of one P-novelist, Herman Wouk, V. writes, "In his low-brow way he reflects what one has come to think of as the *Commentary* syndrome or all's right with America if you're not in a gas chamber, and making money," a remark which will please highbrow anti-Semites everywhere. And in the Auchincloss essay he flogs critic Granville Hicks so relentlessly that one begins to pity Hicks, as if he were the lashed horse in Raskolnikov's dream.

However, when writing of those he considers equals (Calvino, Nabokov), Vidal spins prose that is lucid and elegant, magisterially Shavian. Vidal recently said that memoirs are what one writes when "the waters of the mind have gone dry." Not true: of the later essays published in his previous collection, *Homage to Daniel Shays* (1973), two of the best are recollections of Eleanor Roosevelt and Anais Nin, in which anecdotes, mimicry, sly asides, and critical observations are beautifully interwoven. In *Matters,* the finest essay is a review of Tennessee Williams's *Memoirs,* entitled "Some Memories of the Glorious Bird and an Earlier Self." Vidal brilliantly [discusses] Williams's con-man stratagems, from his Judy Garland theatrics ("it has always been the Bird's tactic to appear in public flapping what looks to be a pathetically broken wing") to his fake candor about writing for money ("the sniffy tone is very much that of St. Theresa scrubbing floors"). Not since Thomas de Quincey's chronicles of halcyon days with Wordsworth and Coleridge has there been such a hilarious wedding of criticism and remembrance; "Some Memories" is a masterpiece of tender malice.

Malice surges more hotly through "American Plastic," an assault on University avant-gardist fiction as represented in the works of John Barth, Donald Barthelme, William Gass, and Thomas Pynchon—works which he considers anemic offspring of the French New Novel. Since the author of *Burr* and *Julian* is held in low esteem by such writers (in *The New Fiction,* a collection of interviews with Barth, Barthelme, & Co., Vidal is only mentioned once, by Tom Wolfe), "American Plastic" is at one level a St. Valentine's Day massacre of the competition; only Gass escapes, with flesh wounds. Wilfrid Sheed wrote that Vidal's essay on the French New Novel (reprinted in *Matters*) made for a "negative aesthetic worth arguing with," and "American Plastic" is even more aesthetically arguable.

Unfortunately, the argument will have to be made elsewhere, for I find Vidal's judgments lethally just. Like Vidal, I find the decibel level of Pynchon's prose excruciating (louder than the Ramones revving up). I also agree that the reputation of *The Sot-Weed Factor* is a dragon deservedly slain, that Gass is more stimulating in his essays than in his fiction, and that Barthelme's entertainments have a sickly mandarin cuteness. Vidal's attack is much too narrow and neat—he doesn't, for example, discuss Vonnegut, Gaddis, Ishmael Reed—but the exuberance carries one along, and at his most wickedly ironic, he reminds one of Edgar Allan Poe routing the provincials. Yet, as always, Vidal's polemical elation is tempered by pessimism. "[The] academic bureaucracy, unlike the novel, will not wither away, and the future is dark for literature. Certainly the young in general are not going to take up reading when they have such easy alternatives as television, movies, rock."

I don't believe any of this. And I don't believe Vidal believes it either—it's just another Decline of the West flourish. Leaving aside the John Simonized notion that a passion for rock precludes a passion for literature, what emerges here is an actorish sigh of despondency, and there are many such sighs in *Matters. Reflections Upon A Sinking Ship* is the title of yet another of Vidal's previous collections, and he always seems in a rather curious hurry for the Republic to go glub-glub into the deep.

Similarly, throughout *Matters* he too quickly ushers literature into the intensive-care ward, and with a gleam in his eye, like an overeager mortician. At the conclusion of the best-seller-list essay, Vidal writes of Isherwood, Huxley, and himself: "By preferring perversely to write books that reflected not the movies we had seen but life itself, not as observed by that sterile machine the camera, but as it is netted by the protean fact of a beautiful if diminishing and polluted language, we were, all in all, kind of dumb." A lovely rippling sentence, but cant, sheer cant. As a machine, the camera is no more "sterile" than the typewriter or the ball-point pen, and Vidal's best novel, *Myra Breckenridge* (1968), owes its steamy funhouse vitality not to "life itself" but to movie kitsch.

Again, the problem of audience. The essays that shimmer in *Matters* are those originally written for *The New York Review of Books,* where beauty is truth, truth beauty, and a classified ad only 75 cents a word. When Vidal has written directly for the anti-literature "alternatives," his work has never been better than second-rate. Even his most successful screenplay, *The Best Man,* is glib and brittle, an Allen Drury drama with a locker-room smirk. Writers like Vidal and Mailer want the acclaim that comes from reaching a movie audience but they don't give the best of themselves when writing for the medium. . . . At the risk of making cinema sound like a Victorian maiden, I don't think they *respect* the medium; worse, they don't respect the medium's audience.

In *Matters,* Vidal repeatedly slams the coarsening influence of television, but only a few weeks ago he turned up on another talk show, sitting between McLean Stevenson and Merv Griffin, which is really the Zabriskie Point of mindlessness. Gore Vidal is now living in Los Angeles, which means that he may turn up more often on TV, lecturing his countrymen on the folly of their ways. *Matters of Fact and of Fiction* is so bracingly intelligent that one hopes he will restrain himself. On television, addressing an audience he regards disdainfully, Vidal's intelligence curdles: He becomes a stiff, a nag, the Anita Bryant of bisexuality.

> *James Wolcott, "Gore Bulls Through Again," in* The Village Voice *(reprinted by permission of* The Village Voice; *copyright © by The Village Voice, Inc., 1977), May 9, 1977, p. 77.*

The title of Gore Vidal's latest collection [*Matters of Fact and of Fiction: Essays 1973-1976*] has a dark inner meaning. Half of the pieces deal with the shrinking hopes of our novelists, half with American political history; but the politics and politicians have become fictions and the novelists have been either taken over or driven out by the public appetite—natural under the circumstances—for fact. The politicians have grabbed even love—in the form of self-love—from the novelists. . . .

Gore Vidal is a glancing wit who has the good essayist's art of saying serious things personally and lightly. Where others lumber along earnestly in professional prose, he rides gaily in and quickly unhorses his man. He is not one of those brutal wits, bloodied but unbowed, who destroy themselves when they destroy others. He is a moralist whose subject is hypocrisy and the clichés which provide the public with short cuts to self-congratulation. (A political example: Socialism-Sweden-suicide: no facts encourage one to take this drug.) Underneath his rapid mockery and laughter there is a passion for social justice and truth-telling, and his command of a nonchalant prose and care for the English language give his sarcasms their edge. His frivolity is on the surface; beneath it, both as a reviewer and a writer on American history, he has a well-grounded intelligence. There is nothing light-minded about his study of the Adams family or his portrait of Grant, or in his wrestlings with the theorists of the *nouveau roman.* (p. 8)

One can agree or disagree with [Vidal's] views on this or that American novelist very profitably, for he is a professional, but he is on richer ground when he is writing about the supreme American fiction: political history and the political families. Here he has festive powers of candor and detection, in his studies of the ruling class and the rich, and done from the insider's alcove. He loves family history—especially its dubieties. His "West Point" with its theme of America as a garrison is caustic, and he has some vanity in going romantically into action with one socialite arm tied behind his back. His accounts of the continuing story of E. Howard Hunt, the Bay of Pigs, and Watergate, and on what Robert Moses did for and to New York City leave a foreigner like myself wondering why anyone should worry about the fate of the novel when politicians can, every time, outpace the art novel in fantasy or the best seller in its deep faith in the spurious emotion. (p. 9)

> *V. S. Pritchett, "How to Say Serious Things," in* The New York Review of Books *(reprinted with permission from* The New York Review of Books; *copyright © 1977 NYREV, Inc.), May 26, 1977, pp. 8-9.*

* * *

VONNEGUT, Kurt, Jr.   1922-

An American novelist, short story writer, and playwright, Vonnegut satirizes American contemporary life through the use of fantasy, black humor, and the absurd. Although many of his books have been best sellers, Vonnegut is probably best known for *Slaughterhouse-Five.* (See also *CLC*, Vols. 1, 2, 3, 4, 5, and *Contemporary Authors*, Vol. 1-4, rev. ed.)

Today, many of the best writers are . . . writing about art, primarily. *Slaughterhouse-Five,* Vonnegut's major achievement, is essentially different from Nabokov's *Pale Fire* or Borges's *ficciones,* however, because it insists on both the world of fiction or fantasy (Tralfamadore) and the world of brutal fact (Dresden). Vonnegut's novel urges the primacy of the imagination in the very act of facing one of history's most infamous "massacres," the fire-bombing of Dresden in World War II, the source of its great originality.

The poignancy and force of *Slaughterhouse-Five* derive largely from an attitude about art and life that Vonnegut apparently shares with Louis-Ferdinand Celine, whom he quotes in the first chapter as saying two things: "No art is possible without a dance with death" and "the truth is death." Taking his cue from Celine, Vonnegut calls his novel A DUTY-DANCE WITH DEATH on the title page. Ultimately, however, *Slaughterhouse-Five* goes beyond the fatalism implied in Celine's statements by stressing survival through the use of the imagination. . . . The ability to go on, to escape fixity by motion in time is precisely what *Slaughterhouse-Five* is about, and its success comes from being able to effect a regeneration in reader as well as writer.

In keeping with the theme of regeneration, the form of the novel avoids the climax and denouement typical of linear narration, as indicated by Vonnegut's rejection of the grid-like outline of the story he proposes in the first chapter. . . . Essentially, Vonnegut avoids *framing* his story in linear narration, choosing a circular structure. Such a view of the art of the novel has much to do with the protagonist of *Slaughterhouse-Five,* the author's alter ego, Billy Pilgrim, an optometrist who provides corrective lenses for Earthlings. For Pilgrim, who learns of a new view of life as he becomes "unstuck in time," the lenses are corrective metaphorically as well as physically. Quite early in the exploration of Billy's life the reader learns that "frames are where the money is" . . . , a statement which has its metaphorical equivalent, too, and helps to explain why Vonnegut chose a non-linear structure for his novel. Historical events like the bombing of Dresden are usually "read" in the framework of moral and historical interpretation. (pp. 55-6)

The cyclical nature is inextricably bound up with the large themes of *Slaughterhouse-Five,* time, death, and renewal. . . . The most important function of "so it goes" [the recurrent phrase in the novel] . . . , is its imparting a cyclical quality to the novel, both in form and content. Paradoxically, the expression of fatalism serves as a source of renewal, a situation typical of Vonnegut's works, for it enables the novel to *go on* despite—even because of—the proliferation of deaths. Once again we come upon a paradox: death keeps life in motion, even the life of the novel, but the movement is essentially unaided in Vonnegut's silent universe. As he emphasizes in *The Sirens of Titan*, beyond man's interior universe is only the emptiness of space eternal. In a world where life must renew itself arbitrarily, the mental construct becomes tremendously important. The phrase "so it goes" is a sign of the human will to survive, and it recurs throughout the novel as an important aid to *going on*.

Vonnegut's fiction deals heavily with survival by the arbitrary imposition of meaning on meaningless reality, as demonstrated most forcefully in *Cat's Cradle*. Tralfamadore is another mental construct, like Bokononism, that goes beyond the question of true of false. As Eliot Rosewater says in *Slaughterhouse-Five* to the psychiatrists: "I think you guys are going to have to come up with a lot of wonderful *new* lies, or people just aren't going to want to go on living".... The statement is certainly a clue to the meaning of Tralfamadore, since it comes right after the statement that Rosewater and Billy had found life meaningless, partly because of what they had seen in the war: "So they were trying to re-invent themselves and their universe. Science fiction was a big help." Vonnegut lets us know that an act of re-invention is going on within the novel, just as the novel is Vonnegut's own re-creation of his past and even of his other novels. Mental constructs like Bokononism and Tralfamadore, both re-inventive fictions, are models of Vonnegut's own fiction, throughout which one can see the pattern of meaninglessness/re-invention.

That Tralfamadore is ultimately a "supreme fiction," a product of the imagination, and that Vonnegut emphasizes using the imagination as a method of survival are obvious from his preoccupation with the value of works of art, especially in the novels from *Cat's Cradle* on. (pp. 58-60)

What makes self-renewal possible in *Slaughterhouse-Five* is the human imagination, which is what the novel finally celebrates.... The imagination ... beholds the immaterial core of every living thing, the "unwavering band of light" that the minimalist artist in [*Breakfast of Champions*] paints. (p. 66)

In using the idea of regeneration to integrate both theme and form, Vonnegut has written in *Slaughterhouse-Five* his best and even most hopeful novel to date. (p. 67)

> Wayne D. McGinnis, "The Arbitrary Cycle of 'Slaughterhouse-Five': A Relation of Form to Theme," in Critique: Studies in Modern Fiction (copyright © by James Dean Young 1975), Vol. XVII, No. 1, 1975, pp. 55-68.

In *Happy Birthday, Wanda June*, Kurt Vonnegut, Jr. satirizes Ernest Hemingway in the character of Harold Ryan, a big-game hunter and professional soldier who returns after being lost in the Amazon rain forest for eight years. The interesting thing—apart from Vonnegut's doing to Hemingway what Hemingway did to Sherwood Anderson—is that Vonnegut attacks not Hemingway the writer or what he has to say in his writing, but rather Hemingway the *machismo*-man, "the slayer of nearly extinct animals which meant him no harm." Harold Ryan is a rather silly, swaggering bully; but beneath these qualities his real importance is dual: he seems out-dated and irrelevant; and he is very dangerous.

In one sense, of course, Vonnegut's attack on the older man is subtly unfair: he satirizes Hemingway from a sensitivity to the ecological crisis dimly felt in Hemingway's youth and young manhood and from a distaste for the mas-culine *ethos* largely foreign to Hemingway's background; nor is Hemingway the only or necessarily the best reflector of the behavior and qualities Vonnegut derides. Still, it is not the behavior and qualities in themselves that primarily disturb Vonnegut so much as their anachronistic irrelevancy and contemporary danger; and it would be difficult to imagine anyone—with the possible exception of John Wayne—more dramatically effective than Hemingway the man to embody these echoes of a younger age.

But Harold Ryan also establishes a connection between Hemingway and Vonnegut as writers which becomes increasingly revealing the further it is pursued. (pp. 173-74)

Hemingway and Vonnegut are middle-Western Americans taken by events in their youth into the wider world. Both undergo in a world war a profoundly traumatic experience which becomes the center of their thought and art. Both reflect the new sense of reality which came to dominance in human consciousness in the middle and end of the nineteenth century. Both have similar views of the human condition and explore in their writing the problems of living in it. Both are centrally concerned with the problems of illusion and truth and with the relationship between them. And both stress love and human relationship as meaningful answers to the human condition.

Despite these extensive similarities—and often, indeed, within them—vast and far more significant differences separate Hemingway and Vonnegut, both as men and as writers.... Hemingway's vision of man shines from afar and above the collapsing structures of a dying age; it serves as a reminder—perhaps even a faintly embarrassing reminder—of still another lost, lamented Eden. Vonnegut, whatever the value he may ultimately be accorded, stands outside the Garden, among the ruins, beside us all. Of Hemingway, it once was said that he shows us the truth of our world and teaches us how to live in it; of Vonnegut, it can be said that he shows us a world absurd and frightful beyond knowing and teaches us how nearly impossible it is to live in it; and it is Vonnegut's, not Hemingway's, vision which is characteristic of our time. (pp. 174-75)

For Vonnegut, as for Hemingway, reality has no supernatural or divine or metaphysical or transcendent or absolute dimension; but, unlike Hemingway, he satirizes man's efforts to find one in religions and philosophies. The universe, Vonnegut believes, is "composed of one-trillionth part matter to one decillion parts black velvet futility," and Vonnegut considers it silly and arrogant for man to feel that "something up there likes me." In *The Sirens of Titan*, Winston Niles Rumfoord creates a new religion—The Church of God the Utterly Indifferent—precisely so that man will no longer be able to praise or blame "something up there" for what happens to him down here.... Referring to "'a parable about people who do things that they think God Almighty wants done,'" Rumfoord says that "'you would do well, for background on this parable, to read everything that you can lay your hands on about the Spanish Inquisition'." ... In *Cat's Cradle*, Vonnegut creates another new religion, Bokononism, which derides the notion of purpose in the universe and which helps men by providing "harmless untruths" to make them "brave and kind and healthy and happy." ...

In an empty universe, a universe with no correspondence whatever to man's mind or emotions, reality for Vonnegut as it is for Hemingway is entirely secular, human, and internal. But there is in Vonnegut nothing of Hemingway's rich awareness of the external world as objective reality including man and shaping his consciousness: for Vonnegut, reality is entirely within man, in the mysterious processes of belief and behavior.... Moreover, Vonnegut argues in *Mother Night* that the reality within man is no essential self, no independent soul unconditioned and untouched by his behavior. "We are what we pretend to be," says Vonnegut, "so we must be careful about what we pretend to be." We are, that is, what we do, not what we say; what we do at any particular time establishes the reality of what we are. For Vonnegut, existence does not precede essence as it largely does for Hemingway; for Vonnegut, existence denies essence. In *Cat's Cradle,* Bokononists who are about to commit suicide always say, "'Now I will destroy the whole world'." ... [Vonnegut] erases the distinction between fact and fiction and implies that "real" people are as much a product of their own imaginations as fictional characters are the product of the writer's imagination. (pp. 178-79)

No less than Hemingway, Vonnegut sees the human condition in terms of the basic realities of suffering, violence, and death. Revolution and war, suicide and death are everywhere in Vonnegut's writing, not only as general subjects and allusions but also in particular and graphic scenes. Revolution and war are central in all but one of his novels, and the destruction of Dresden appears in *Mother Night* and in *God Bless You, Mr. Rosewater* and is the motivating event in *Slaughterhouse-Five.* (p. 180)

Still, for all these similarities in their views of the human condition, Hemingway and Vonnegut differ drastically and in significant ways. If he sees man trapped in the void of nada, the older writer nevertheless retains a sturdy and essentially nineteenth-century conviction that man can find or create patterns of meaning and order and value. Not so with Vonnegut: for him the empty and meaningless universe is both source and measure of the repetitive, vaguely fatalistic, and utterly futile state of man. (p. 181)

For Vonnegut, man can do little to improve or change his condition; he can neither find nor create meaning or purpose, order or beauty. He has no capacity for knowing either himself or his world, and he succeeds best at making himself ridiculous and at making life unliveable. One of Vonnegut's major themes is his continuing indictment of man for serving "evil too openly and good too secretly," for doing evil in the name of good. In Vonnegut's view, man is insane and impossible; and man's only remedy is to seek illusions and relationships which can help him endure a human condition he can neither change nor bear.

Hemingway's essentially nineteenth-century positivism, his conviction that man can find meaning and value in his experience of life, turns to mockery in Vonnegut. "'History!'" writes Bokonon. "'Read it and weep!'" ... *The Fourteenth Book of Bokonon* has a long title: "What Can a Thoughtful Man Hope for Mankind on Earth, Given the Experience of the Past Million Years?"; and it contains but one word: "Nothing." ... Similarly, Vonnegut ridicules experience throughout his works in highlighting the absurdity and failure of man's traditional ways of coping with the problems of life. Traditional religion, science and technology, wealth and philanthropy—none has really improved man's lot; and most have simply made it worse. (p. 185)

[If] Hemingway would strip away all illusion to confront directly the unsparing truth, Vonnegut turns away from that truth in horror and disgust and tries to mask it in new illusion. But such illusions contain their own irresolvable tensions: the real key to Vonnegut's thought and art is "the cruel paradox of Bokononist thought, the heartbreaking necessity of lying about reality, and the heartbreaking impossibility of lying about it." ... Throughout Vonnegut's writing, the necessity of lying about reality in new illusions also underscores the reality they seek to mask. (pp. 186-87)

Cat's Cradle has two epigraphs: "Nothing in this book is true" and a quotation from *The Books of Bokonon:* "Live by the *foma* (harmless untruths) that make you brave and kind and healthy and happy." Bokononism is, of course, itself a system of such *foma* created by Bokonon to help the people of San Lorenzo endure in their miserable conditions. (p. 187)

Superficially, [Vonnegut] seems to see in love and sex and in warm human relationships ways for man to endure the human condition with some meaning....

Still, Vonnegut writes of sex with some curious ambivalences. He never describes lovemaking directly, and there is rarely in Vonnegut and then only by way of generalized statement any view of sex as the intense and meaningful experience it is for Hemingway....

Vonnegut seems to value love most when it is non-exclusive and uncritical. (p. 188)

Except for Howard Campbell's memories of his wife [in *Mother Night*] there are simply no mutual and passionate loves and marriages in all of Vonnegut and almost no real friendships. In *The Sirens of Titan,* Unk and Beatrice fall in love—but only after a lifetime of wandering around the solar system and ending up alone on a moon of Saturn. "'It took us that long,'" Unk explains, "'to realize that a purpose of human life, no matter who is controlling it, is to love whoever is around to be loved'." ... But no one else in Vonnegut's world, especially on earth, seems able to find and keep such love.

So too with friendship. ... For Vonnegut, life on earth is a ridiculous ordeal men must struggle through blind, a little crazy, and mostly alone. (p. 189)

[The] despairing humor of Vonnegut's writing evokes an essentially comic vision of man. To Vonnegut, the human condition has become absurd and terrifying beyond anything in Hemingway; for man himself has become the most absurd and terrifying thing in it. "'All people are insane,'" Vonnegut believes. "'They will do anything at any time, and God help anybody who looks for reasons.'" Man is locked into a condition he can neither tolerate nor change, a condition in which he is not only both destroyed and defeated but in which he destroys and defeats himself for childish reasons and to silly ends. Only with the irony, wit, and detachment of a comic vision and with the escape into new fairy-tales can man endure the world and himself in our time. Vonnegut owes much to the existentialists in all this, and his vision is clearly late twentieth-century; but for all its relevance and effectiveness, it is a diminished vision of man and of his possibilities and a lesser art. (p. 191)

> *Clinton S. Burhans, Jr., in* Modern Fiction Studies *(copyright © 1975, by Purdue Research Foundation, West Lafayette, Indiana, U.S.A.), Summer, 1975.*

Middle-class moonscape is an apt description of the America evoked in the fiction of Kurt Vonnegut, where outraged social criticism, sentimental moralism and science-fiction fantasy form a piquant if not altogether credible *ménage à trois*. The case of Vonnegut is an instructive one because the comic-strip clarity of his novels lucidly illustrates a conception of history largely shared by Pynchon and Barth, though perhaps partly camouflaged through the complicated elaboration of design in their more ambitious work. Vonnegut has obviously been the most widely read of the new novelists because his stylistic, structural, and psychological simplicity, coupled with a genuine verve of narrative inventiveness, makes him the most easily accessible of these writers. I would attribute at least some of his popularity, however, to the need of many readers over the past decade for a novelist who could write away history while seeming to write about it. . . .

[Vonnegut's conclusions] are worth summarizing because they embody, at the lower limits of complexity, attitudes of a whole literary generation.

Most pressingly, the novels articulate an uncompromising cynicism about politics, about all forms of nationalism, all collective endeavor, about the potential for destructive evil in even the most seemingly innocent and private of men. As a character in *Cat's Cradle* (1963) is made to say, "Man is vile, and makes nothing worth making, knows nothing worth knowing." The individual, especially if he is in any way an artist, is bound to be misrepresented, violated, viciously exploited, by the sinister powers that govern collective existence. (One might recall that Pynchon's *Gravity's Rainbow* makes paranoia a central formal theme, repeatedly invoking a ubiquitous Them—the capital T is the author's—out to get the hapless individual.) Characteristically, . . . the novelist can only adopt a series of strategies of self-protective flippancy and cheerfully apocalyptic pessimism, converting the novel into an extended evasive action taken against Them, the powers that would rape—or as we unfortunately say in America these days, "co-opt"—the artist or any individual trying to guard his own fragile and private truth.

It will be observed that there is a Manichean split here between the unalterable forces of boundless evil and the residual nostalgia for goodness, truth, and love in some individuals (hence the sentimentality beneath the cynicism in Vonnegut). Such dualism in itself implies an avoidance of real history, which presents itself as a highly variegated set of mixed moral phenomena, not as a simple split between good individuals and evil collectivities. What is still more revealing, however, in regard to the dehistoricization of history in Vonnegut is the absolute equality he requires of horrors perpetrated on all sides. Man, at least in his political guise, is equally vile everywhere, whether he is a Nazi, an American, or a Soviet Russian, and so Dresden and Hiroshima are, quite without qualification, the exact equivalent of Auschwitz and Dachau. Taking the symmetricization of history even one step further, Vonnegut implies that all these loci of horror mean no more or less on the moral scale than the thoughtlessness with which an absent-minded scientist (in *Cat's Cradle*) idly invents a doomsday weapon that subsequently destroys all life on earth. (p. 46)

> *Robert Alter (reprinted from* Commentary *by permission; copyright © 1975 by the American Jewish Committee), in* Commentary, *November, 1975.*

"Slapstick" opens with a typical Vonnegut cynicism about America having become a place of interchangeable parts,

so that Indianapolis, which "once had a way of speaking all its own," now is "just another someplace where automobiles live." I can't speak about Indianapolis, but one thing I resist in Vonnegut's books is that they seem formulaic, made of interchangeable parts, though this is one quality which may endear him to others. Once Vonnegut finds what he takes to be a successful character, motif or phrase he can't bear to give it up, and so he carries it around from novel to novel. Thus Eliot Rosewater, Kilgore Trout, and Vonnegut's fellow Hoosier humorist Kim Hubbard, having done a stint in "God Bless You, Mr. Rosewater," all unblushingly reappear to fill up a few pages of "Slaughterhouse-Five" and Trout then takes over "Breakfast of Champions." "Slapstick" picks up a clever lawyer from "God Bless You, Mr. Rosewater." Vonnegut had so much fun sprinkling "So it goes" all over "Slaughterhouse-Five" and "And so on" throughout "Breakfast of Champions" that he couldn't bear to leave "Slapstick" innocent of such confetti. Well, as Eliot Rosewater once said in an idle moment, "Hippety Hop." But Vonnegut, older now, and more wan, contracts that to "Hi ho" for "Slapstick" and leaves very few pages uncluttered by the phrase. . . .

The story in "Slapstick" is part "Cat's Cradle," part "God Bless You, Mr. Rosewater," part Kilgore Trout, part Thomas Pynchon. . . . (p. 3)

[Vonnegut] bears about the same relation to the great imperialist, Pynchon, as Mrs. Henry Wood bears to Dickens. Where Pynchon's mania leads him into huge soaring flights of paranoic fantasy he calls the history of our century, Vonnegut's easy, sentimental cynicism leads him into endless parading of the dumb notion that life isn't much good in America because we're all stupid, unloving or both. It takes stamina, determination and crazy intelligence to read Pynchon's two enormous novels; it takes nothing more than a few idle hours to turn the pages of "Slapstick" or any of the others. Pynchon is responsible to the integrity of his terrible paranoia; Vonnegut is responsible to nothing except the ease of his cynicism. . . .

"Hi Ho," thus, is not just a bored grunt that disclaims all responsibility for having to look at something; it is a gesture of contempt for all writers who are willing to be responsible for their creations; for all readers who long to read real books; for anyone whose idea of America is more complicated than Vonnegut's country of interchangeable parts full of poor people with uninteresting lives. (p. 20)

If my sense of Vonnegut is at all accurate, how can one explain the serious attention he has been given? My hunch is that the mistake is a generic one; people like him because they enjoy the *kind* of novel he writes. When "God Bless You, Mr. Rosewater" was published a little more than ten years ago, the imperial novel was just beginning: "Crazy in Berlin," "V.," "Catch-22," Vonnegut's own "Cat's Cradle." It may have seemed then that Vonnegut was as good, or might become as good as any of the others, but where Thomas Berger went on to finish his interesting trilogy, where Pynchon and Joseph Heller took seven and twelve years trying to get "Gravity's Rainbow" and "Something Happened" right, Vonnegut just became formulaic. . . . Books that are self-confessed verbal constructions simply need more earnest and witty inventing than Vonnegut has shown himself capable of. (p. 22)

> *Roger Sale, in* The New York Times Book Review *(© 1976 by The New York Times Company; reprinted by permission), October 3, 1976.*

Much has been written about the reasons for Vonnegut's appeal to the first television generation. The time-tripping, the McLuhanite non-"linearity," the pacifism, the jokes, the sci-fi inventiveness, the quick sympathy for life's losers and has-beens—these have all been repeatedly cited and have evoked little disagreement. But there is a more interesting question. Why has Vonnegut encountered such strong and continued resistance from so many literate members of his own generation, which may be extended to include serious readers from thirty to seventy? . . . After all, the elements that endear Vonnegut to his cult are not in themselves antipathetic to older readers who cherish *Catch 22,* love the Beatles, and feel themselves magnetized by the phallic hardware of *Gravity's Rainbow.*

An examination of *Slapstick* cannot by itself provide a satisfactory answer, for the novel is too obviously vulnerable. A few things may be said in its favor. I found the autobiographical opening interesting and even touching in its account of Vonnegut's relationship to his scientist brother, his dead sister, and his roots in Indianapolis. . . .

Vonnegut can always be counted on to empathize with the plight of the rejected child confronted by unapprehending or frightening parents. In this case the twins are repulsively ugly neanderthaloid monsters, while the parents are sweet, well-meaning multi-millionaires who—shamed by their hideous offspring—allow themselves to be convinced that the babies are idiots destined to die before they reach fourteen. The parents' solution is to isolate the twins on a vast gothic estate in Vermont, where their animal needs are supplied by a staff of servants and supervised by the daily visits of a doctor. Far from being idiots, the twins, especially when they put their heads together, are brilliant. Undetected, they lead a rhapsodically happy life until, on the eve of their fifteenth birthday, they decide to throw off the disguise of their idiocy—only to encounter not merely their parents' guilt over the past but their terror at the prospect of trying to force themselves to love such monsters—now *intelligent* monsters—in the future. In his zany allegory of the twins' symbiotic passion (more intellectual than physical) and the shattering of their idyll by parental forces, Vonnegut has been able to suggest—however briefly and incompletely—the unconsolable suffering of gifted but unloved children.

But the rest of the novel—most of it—is a sorry performance, full of the kind of bored doodling that made its predecessor, *Breakfast of Champions,* so annoying and self-defeating a work. Most of Vonnegut's conceits are mere throwaways, hardly mentioned before discarded. Except in the story of the twins, Vonnegut's often voiced concern for the freakish and the lonely seems, as it so often does in his work, merely perfunctory—as if he had decided to doodle a weeping rather than a smiling face. Running on the slogan "Lonesome No More," [one of the twins, Wilbur] Swain wins the presidency at a time when the United States is falling to pieces. He succeeds, however, in implementing his program for ending loneliness, which involves the division of the American population into ten thousand artificial extended families, each with a distinctive middle name: Daffodil, Razorclam, Muskellunge, Helium, etc., etc. . . . There is more of this sappiness, lots more. Vonnegut seems to be saying, "Here's a bright idea. Maybe you'll think it's cute. Maybe you'll think it has something in it. But if you don't—hi ho." It is this persistent refusal to take responsibility for either his inventions or his feelings that finally renders this book so inconsequential.

But if *Slapstick* is mostly a throwaway and *Breakfast of Champions* a dispirited failure ("I feel lousy about it," Vonnegut writes in the preface, adding with disarming intent, "but I always feel lousy about my books"), what do these works share with the novels that brought Vonnegut to superstardom in the late 1960s? Do they represent a radical falling-off? Or are they essentially more of the same but in a depleted vein? I believe the latter to be the case and suggest that Vonnegut's clownish irresponsibility toward his own creations—while it may ingratiate him to his fans—is a major source of that resistance mentioned at the beginning of this review.

The phrase "bright idea" points to a constant in Vonnegut's work since its beginnings—his remarkable inventiveness. He is the Henry Ford or Thomas A. Edison among recent novelists. . . .

At his best, Vonnegut is inventive in ways that extend beyond gadgetry. *Mother Night* is an imaginative variation on the Eichmann case in which the narrator, Howard J. Campbell, Jr., is an American who has contributed to the Holocaust by broadcasting vicious anti-Semitic propaganda from Germany during the war while at the same time transmitting secret information to the Allies. The idea is original and "bright," rich with paradox and fictional possibilities, and the zigzag of events leading to Campbell's voluntary surrender to the Israelis is full of surprises. You never know who—or what—is going to pop up next. The rapid succession of short chapters, short paragraphs, and short simple sentences that increasingly characterize the novels beginning with *Mother Night* is the stylistic equivalent to Vonnegut's restless improvisation.

But a consequence of all this invention is to defuse the potential impact of the novel. I am not speaking of the juxtaposition of the funny and the horrible—"black" humorists from Waugh to Heller have shown what can be achieved in that mode—but rather of an adolescent fooling-around, a compulsive trivialization of emotionally appropriate responses. (p. 29)

Vonnegut's novels contain a gallery of boosters, inventors, organization men, grotesques, and failures who are the direct—though caricatured—descendants of the inhabitants of Zenith, Gopher Prairie, and Winesburg, Ohio. . . . Vonnegut draws his characters with a thick black outline and colors them crudely. Too often the cartoons are hardly more than clichés of the American scene, as is the case with H. Lowe Crosby, the right-wing manufacturer of bicycles in *Cat's Cradle,* or with the Pontiac dealer Dwayne Hoover in *Breakfast of Champions.* The problem is not with two-dimensional characters as such—a novelist is perfectly within his rights to eschew psychological depth or rounding—but with the fact that Vonnegut is too restless or uncaring to endow even a protagonist-victim like Billy Pilgrim or a recurrent figure like the science-fiction writer Kilgore Trout with that loving particularity that might make them as memorable as Mr. Pecksniff or even George F. Babbitt. Most of Vonnegut's characters are as forgettable as last Sunday's funny papers.

Vonnegut's admirers find him funny, sad, and ironic. I suspect that most of the unconverted—among whom I obviously include myself—find him prankish, often silly, sentimental, and (as is often the case with bleeding hearts) more than a little cruel. They find him too thin, too lacking in depth to merit much consideration as a serious or comic literary artist. His humor too often calls attention to itself with an excess of elbow-nudging and guffaws. His most poignant feelings seem to center upon the traumas of parent-child relationships, but the situations derived from them are seldom developed, with the result that his work is full of gobbets of raw, unassimilated pain; a fairly extended treatment like the story of the twins in *Slapstick* is exceptional. Usually Vonnegut is content to exclaim over the plight of the dumb, the downtrodden, the berserk, and the deformed, the plight of all the lonely people—the myriad Eleanor Rigbys—who populate the books. Or else he is culling choice examples of man's fiendishness to man, such as Heliogabalus's Bull, the Iron Maiden, the torturing of aged women accused of witchcraft or the victims of the Inquisition—all recounted with exquisite detail.

I find it hard to resist the impression that Vonnegut's work is permeated by a sense of futility and self-contempt. The incessant fooling around, the half-baked quality of his extraterrestial fantasies, the dismissive attitude toward his characters and his own best ideas, the bratty-child repetition of tags like "Hi ho" and "So it goes" and of such analisms as "doodley-squat," the references within his novels to his boozing and heavy smoking, the description of himself as an old fart—these suggest to me an underlying depression so pervasive that the very feat of writing is like a soft-shoe dance upon the lid of his own coffin. (pp. 29-30)

> *Robert Towers, "So It Went," in* The New York Review of Books *(reprinted with permission from* The New York Review of Books; *copyright © 1976 NYREV, Inc.), November 25, 1976, pp. 29-30.*

"So it goes" used to be Vonnegut's standard response to the world, a patented Kurt dismissal of painful absurdities. It had some ironic resonance. But his new all-purpose comment, "Hi ho," is simply deadpan idiocy:

> It is a thing I often say these days:
> "Hi ho." It is a kind of senile hiccup.
> I have lived too long.
>
> Hi ho.

That's what *Slapstick*'s hundred-year-old narrator says, but Vonnegut continually mumbles "Hi ho" in his proper person in a long Prologue. (p. 1300)

We find out in the Prologue that Vonnegut has daydreamed the whole novel while flying to Indianapolis for his uncle's funeral, and that it is all meaningful. Unfortunately, the meaning is personal rather than universal; Vonnegut's first sentence is, "This is the closest I will ever come to writing an autobiography." And we are then supposed to extrapolate from a few family reminiscences to the action of the novel and marvel at something or other. Vonnegut's sister Alice had been embarrassingly tall, and had died of cancer at 41; she had described her impending death as "soap opera" and "slapstick"—obviously a Vonnegut through and through. So *Slapstick* is "really" about Kurt and Alice; "it depicts myself and my beautiful sister as monsters, and so on." Alice's husband died in a grotesque accident two days before she did; he was a passenger on "the only train in American railroading history to hurl itself off an open drawbridge." Consequently *Slapstick* is "grotesque, situational poetry"; it is supposedly about "what life *feels* like" to Vonnegut. But Hi ho? . . .

Kurt Vonnegut is proud of his extensive family. Too proud. Apparently the notion of giving everyone an extended family was supposed to be earthshakingly delightful, the hope-

ful vision of *Slapstick,* but it doesn't work. . . . [It] is so silly that Vonnegut had already ridiculed it in a much better novel, *Cat's Cradle.* There, Hazel Crosby wanted all Hoosiers to call her Mom. She wanted an arbitrary extended family. Vonnegut ridiculed the notion. He called it a *granfalloon.* I'm afraid Slapstick is a great *granfalloon,* and as Bokonon said, "If you wish to study a *granfalloon,* / Just remove the skin of a toy balloon."

What's gone wrong? Simply, as Vonnegut rather circumspectly admits, he has lost the inspiration of the Muse. His sister "was the person I had always written for." He felt her "presence" for a number of years after she died, "but then she began to fade away, perhaps because she had more important business elsewhere." Now Vonnegut is without his own "audience of one," and it shows. This grotesque tribute to their growing up together hasn't brought back his sister's presence, and *Slapstick* is dedicated not to her, but to Laurel and Hardy. It doesn't live up to their memory, or Vonnegut's either. (p. 1302)

> *Charles Nicol, "Kiss Me, I'm Senile," in* National Review *(© National Review, Inc., 1976; 150 East 35th St., New York, N.Y. 10016), November 26, 1976, pp. 1300, 1302.*

Breakfast of Champions can only be understood as a novel *about* "facile fatalism." Like *Slaughterhouse-Five* (1969), it is a novel in which Kurt Vonnegut is his own protagonist, but the "Vonnegut" of this book is rather less appealing than in the earlier novel—so much so that his facile fatalism and banal social criticisms have tended to alienate his readers altogether. The effect is largely deliberate: *Breakfast of Champions* is "a moving, tortured, and honest book," because in it Vonnegut turns an extremely cold eye on his own artistic practices and philosophical assumptions. In a rather zany way, it is a *Bildungsroman* about a fifty-year-old artless artist and facile philosopher. It is also a novel about the regeneration of this sorry figure. Far from being the dispirited effort its reviewers have taken it to be, *Breakfast of Champions* is an artistic act of faith. (p. 99)

Most crucially, *Breakfast of Champions* is not a traditional novel of character. Vonnegut remarks in *Slaughterhouse-Five* that "There are almost no characters in this story, and almost no dramatic confrontations, because most of the people in it are so sick and so much the listless playthings of enormous forces." The characters in *Breakfast of Champions* are "stick figures" for much the same reason, since the novel also examines the apparent "sickness" and "listlessness" of contemporary man. The novel's thematic structure requires that Vonnegut's characters seem wooden or mechanical, for they are exemplary figures in a moral fable. As a number of critics have suggested, all of Vonnegut's novels are fables. . . .

Still, the novelist of ideas must somehow interest us in the fictional debate which informs the work. In *Slaughterhouse-Five* and *Breakfast of Champions,* Vonnegut focuses on his own attempt to comprehend the problems of his characters. Vonnegut has said that these two novels were once "one book," and nothing points up the family resemblance so well as Vonnegut's use of himself as a persona in each novel. (p. 100)

[*Breakfast of Champions*] involves two characters who embody different aspects of [Vonnegut's] own personality. Dwayne Hoover represents his Midwestern, middle-class background, while Kilgore Trout is a somewhat comic embodiment of his artistic and philosophical career. Like his creator, Trout has become a devout pessimist in his old age: "But his head no longer sheltered ideas of how things could be and should be on the planet, as opposed to how things really were. There was only one way for the Earth to be, he thought: the way it was".... Vonnegut contrives to bring Trout to Midland City, Hoover's home town, to confront the folk with this bracing "truth" and contrives to have Dwayne Hoover suffer the experience of receiving this "truth." Vonnegut seems to want to rub middle America's nose in the sheer ugliness of life. (p. 103)

The Kurt Vonnegut we meet early in *Breakfast of Champions* may be a pessimist, but even he must concede that it will take more than chemicals to unhinge his "hero," Dwayne Hoover: "Dwayne, like all novice lunatics, needed some bad ideas, too, so that his craziness could have shape and direction".... Kilgore Trout, of course, will provide the bad ideas through one of his own books. Trout's attitude toward ideas is contradicted by his misanthropy. As a young man Trout has understood that if bad ideas can destroy us, humane ideas can give us health. He has known that "the purpose of life" is to be "the eyes and ears and conscience of the Creator of the Universe".... Implicit here is the notion that we *can* exercise conscience. At the time of the novel, Trout has turned away from such implications, yet he will return to them, for in 1981 he will say that we are healthy only to the extent that our ideas are humane. What happens to cure Trout of his misanthropy?

What happens is that both Trout and Vonnegut encounter a *wrang-wrang*. According to Bokonon, the prophet of *Cat's Cradle* (1963), a *wrang-wrang* is "a person who steers people away from a line of speculation by reducing that line, with the example of the *wrang-wrang's* own life, to an absurdity." The narrator of *Cat's Cradle* meets such a figure in Sherman Krebbs, a nihilistic poet. The narrator lends his apartment to Krebbs for a brief period of time. He returns to find the apartment "wrecked by a nihilistic debauch".... The narrator comments: "Somebody or something did not wish me to be a nihilist. It was Krebb's mission, whether he knew it or not, to disenchant me with that philosophy".... In *Breakfast of Champions,* Dwayne Hoover is Trout's and Vonnegut's *wrang-wrang.* (pp. 104-05)

Hoover is in the same position as Billy Pilgrim and Eliot Rosewater in *Slaughterhouse-Five.* In the aftermath of Dresden, Pilgrim and Rosewater find themselves dealing with "similar crises in similar ways. They had both found life meaningless.... So they were trying to re-invent themselves".... (p. 105)

Hoover reasons that if all other men are "unfeeling machines" ..., he can do whatever he wants to them. At the end of the novel he acts on his belief, beating up everyone around him until he has sent eleven people to the hospital, Trout among them. He acts with no sense of shame, for he has been "liberated" from such feelings: "I used to think the electric chair was a shame, ... I used to think war was a shame—and automobile accidents and cancer." But now

he does not think *anything* is a shame: "Why should I care what happens to machines?"....

Dwayne Hoover's thematic function is to point up the disastrous consequences of adopting a deterministic view of man. Dramatically, his function is to reveal these consequences to Trout and Vonnegut. Following his trip to Midland City, Trout rejects his belief that "there was only one way for the Earth to be." He returns to his former task of alerting mankind to its inhumane practices in the belief that man's capacity to believe anything can be his salvation as well as his cross.... Trout has become a true "doctor"— one who would restore us to health through good ideas. (p. 106)

Vonnegut's dark "suspicion" about man's nature, expressed at the beginning of the novel, must be identified with the "bad ideas" Dwayne Hoover learns from Kilgore Trout. At the end of *Breakfast of Champions,* Vonnegut rejects both the suspicion and the ideas, just as Trout will do in the last years of his life.

In the novel's final pages, the newly-rescued Vonnegut bestows a final gift upon his most famous creation. Vonnegut arranges a final meeting where he tells Trout that he is going to follow Jefferson's and Tolstoi's example and set all his literary characters at liberty. From now on, Trout is *free....* Earlier, Trout has offered freedom to his parakeet, but the bird has flown back into his cage.... That man will reject the possibilities inherent in his freedom is always a danger. What Vonnegut is telling us on every page is that man has been doing just that from the beginning of time. He is also telling us, in the fable he contrives, that only by asserting our freedom can we possibly adapt to the requirements of chaos. (pp. 107-08)

Vonnegut *contrives* this fable because throughout *Breakfast of Champions* he insists on his role as master puppeteer.... Vonnegut allows no pretense about the status of his fictional creations; toward the end, Vonnegut even seats himself at the same bar with his characters. While sipping his favorite drink, he proceeds to explain why he has decided to have these characters act as they do—such a Nabokovian device is, of course, anticipated in *Slaughterhouse-Five.* The insistence on the artificiality of his dramatis personae emphasizes that *Breakfast of Champions* really has only one "character." ... *Breakfast of Champions* is about its author's triumph over a great temptation. Saint Anthony's temptation was of the flesh, and Vonnegut's is of the spirit; we should know by now that the spirit both kills and dies. At the end of the novel, Vonnegut's spirit refuses to die: "I am better now. Word of honor: I am better now".... His hope is that we might all become "better"; his message is that to become so we must resist the seductions of fatalism. (p. 108)

Robert Merrill, "Vonnegut's 'Breakfast of Champions': The Conversion of Heliogabalus," in Critique: Studies in Modern Fiction *(copyright © James Dean Young 1977), Vol. XVIII, No. 3, 1977, pp. 99-108.*

W

WARREN, Robert Penn   1905-

American novelist, poet, short story writer, playwright, and essayist, Warren is an influential figure in twentieth-century American letters. One of the original members of the "Fugitive Group" of poets, the founding editor of *The Southern Review*, and one of the earliest innovators in the New Criticism, Warren has been awarded the Pulitzer Prize for both fiction and poetry and the National Book Award for poetry. A central theme in his work is the moral imperative to exercise personal responsibility and the difficulty of this stance in a world of random justice. Although Warren is best known for his novels, he is generally better respected for his poetry. (See also *CLC*, Vols. 1, 4, 6, and *Contemporary Authors*, Vols. 13-16, rev. ed.)

It was a pity that the reviewers regarded *All the King's Men* as primarily another life of Huey Long to be compared with the other lives of Long and not with the other works of Warren. It must be obvious by now, if my account of the book is halfway accurate, that it is not a political treatise about Long or anything else. Like *Proud Flesh,* it is another study of Warren's constant theme: self-knowledge. Nevertheless, it has political implications—and we may understand them correctly if we see them within the broader frame. Indeed to say that we must see politics within a broader frame—the frame being morality and human life in general—is precisely Warren's thesis. Willie Stark, Adam Stanton, and Tiny Duffy are wrong politically because they are wrong humanly. (p. 265)

When Robert Penn Warren fails, as he sometimes does, it is not . . . because he is too naturalistic, but because he is not naturalistic enough. His symbolism is too often something superimposed. The vehicle which Warren devises to carry his meaning is not always as "natural," as "real," as it should be. (p. 270)

If the symbolist in Warren seems not to submerge himself in the naturalist, the thinker in him seems not to submerge himself in the artist. Trite as it is nowadays to stigmatize an author as a dual personality, I cannot help pointing to a duality in Warren that may well constitute his major problem: it is his combination of critical and creative power. I am far from suggesting that the critical and the creative are of their nature antithetic and I am fully ready to grant that what makes Warren remarkable among American writers is his double endowment. The problem lies precisely in his

being so two-sidedly gifted; he evidently finds it endlessly difficult to combine his two sorts of awareness. (p. 271)

Warren is a faulty writer; but he is worth a dozen petty perfectionists. Though commonly associated with "formalists" and "classicists" in criticism, he is close to the type of romantic genius: robust, fluent, versatile, at his worst clever and clumsy, at his best brilliant and profound. On the other hand, he is remarkable for self-discipline. . . . [It] is very refreshing to find a good writer whom one may meaningfully call deeply American and genuinely regionalist. This means, paradoxically enough, that Warren is not *too* American and not *too* regionalist. (pp. 271-72)

> *Eric Bentley, "The Meaning of Robert Penn Warren's Novels," in* The Kenyon Review *(copyright 1948 by Kenyon College; reprinted by permission of the author), Summer, 1948 (and reprinted in* Forms of Modern Fiction, *edited by William Van O'Connor, Indiana University Press, 1959, pp. 255-72).*

What is new here [in *Or Else*] . . . is the arrangement of the volume as sequence, forming a kind of trajectory like a comet seen at evening, the old poet singing vespers in a time of general drought. Warren suggests both the image of evensong and of parched wilderness in his epigraph to the entire collection, a passage taken from *Psalms:* "He clave the rocks in the wilderness, and gave them drink as out of the great depths." There are wasteland images everywhere in this book: landscapes . . . the poet remembers or through which he is now passing. (p. 179)

One of the most powerfully realized of these landscapes is the image of a black sharecropper's hovel remembered from the Depression. Here Warren slows down the image, freezing it, rendering it immovable, implacable, one of those secret images we carry with us into death, an image stripped of sociological significance, even of philosophical "meaning," and presented instead as the hard thing itself. . . . ["Forever O'Clock"] reads like a zen study in composition, and in fact many such visual meditations are scattered throughout the volume, as though the poet were composing (in both senses of that word) his world as parts of an extended indwelling on the mystery of being. . . . (pp. 180-81)

It is this paradox, of a reality so much in flux that what is is always becoming was, that constitutes one of Penn Warren's most characteristic concerns, and which, for me at any rate, is both a strength and a weakness in the poetry, at least when I measure it up against the sense of immediacy, of present-action, that I find in long sections of Pound's *Cantos* or something like Williams' *Desert Music* or some of the younger poets working in that tradition (and even in some of the old Objectivists). You do not have to read very much of Warren's work in whatever genre to see that he has been preoccupied for most of his life with the nature of time and with one of its principal corollaries: history. (p. 181)

Warren's ability to reconstruct our past, to flesh it out into a meaning, is for him, as he says at the end of "Rattlesnake Country," "The compulsion to try to convert what now is *was* / Back into what was *is*." (p. 182)

Time is an obsession with Warren, here as in his other work: the sense of time running out, with its attempts, usually fumbled, to order one's priorities, to somehow grasp the mystery of its passing. Approaching his own end, though in no hurry to do so, Warren keeps swinging back to his own beginnings. Many of these poems are about his own youth, half a century and more gone.... [For example,] there is ... the recollection of his father's terrible virtue, an old man with "blanket / Over knees, woolly gray bathrobe over shoulders, handkerchief / On great bald skull spread, glasses / Low on big nose" reading Hume's *History of England*, or Roosevelt's *Winning of the West*, or Freud on dreams, or Coke or Blackstone. How to explain his father's going, his disappearance into the past, that "unnameable and de-timed beast" which lifts its brachycephalic head with its dumb, "magisterial gaze" looking into the distance?

[How] to redeem the time, to understand the fact of being, to learn to live well so that one can at least die well? These are very old questions, shared by all, or at least most, of us.... One thing the poet can try to do is to keep the past —which annihilates but also preserves—from slipping away. And this Warren does by blooding that past with his words. The other thing, tied to this evocation, is to celebrate the redemptive presence of love. (pp. 185-87)

I could quarrel with certain things in Warren I find alien to my own sense of poetics: a sometimes loose, rambling line, a nostalgia verging on obsession, a veering towards philosophical attitudinizing, the mask of the redneck that out-rednecks the redneck. But I would rather leave such critical caveats for others. There is enough here in the space of a short review to praise, and I am thankful to have been given to drink, if not out of those too rare "great depths," then at least from a spring sufficiently deep, sufficiently clear. (p. 188)

> Paul Mariani, "Vespers: Robert Penn Warren at Seventy," in *Parnassus: Poetry in Review* (*copyright © 1976 by* Parnassus: Poetry in Review), *Fall/Winter, 1975, pp. 176-88.*

Sometimes it is the way the tone changes and sometimes the way the syntax explicates itself and often the way the figures follow—but throughout [*Or Else-Poem/Poems 1968-1974*] Robert Penn Warren keeps the reader just off balance.... [In the first poem, *The Nature of a Mirror*,] Warren slips from graphic image through what looks like surrealism to didactic abstraction. Yet it all happens as

effortlessly as the light changes, so that one finds the incongruities growing superficial. (p. 349)

[In] *Vision Under the October Mountain: A Love Poem*, ... overripe, Hopkinesque images give way to a dryasdust, professorial language.... *Interjection #2: Caveat* ... begins in philosophical savvy and ends in mystical delight.

In *News Photo*, a poem about a Southerner who has killed a minister "Reported to Be Working Up the Niggers", Warren modulates his point of view continually and with a marvelous delicacy. The protagonist gets one long unmediated speech (a *tour de force* as irritatingly comic in its malicious prejudice as anything in Faulkner), and throughout the rest of the poem we move from an ironic detachment into the killer's confused self-righteousness and back again by passages as uncanny as those in Escher. The poem ends with a section in which Warren first imagines the acquitted killer fantasizing a congratulatory appearance by Robert E. Lee and then converts this benevolent revenant into the skeleton in the closet of the South.... [A] wry, even anti-sentimental tone is characteristic, as are the liking for the *frisson* and the line break that fragments the syntactical unit. Such recurrent factors notwithstanding, this sequence of poems, like many in it, is protean. *Natural History*, a small parable of the unbearable strangeness of pure understanding and love, is so different, not only from the other poems touched on above but from most poems, that it embarrasses the terms one would praise it in. If it were a sculpture, it would be made of some radiant otherworldly metal, seamless, obeying conventions clearly strict but obscure.... Then there is the perversely entitled *I Am Dreaming of a White Christmas: The Natural History of a Vision*, the first seven sections of which read weirdly like a scenario of a silent underground film, the camera never panning but instead closing first on one object and then another in the house, as it turns out, of the poet's youth.... That odd and moving poem is followed by *Interjection #3: I Know a Place Where All Is Real*, a tame, hedging allegory that might have been written by—why, almost anyone.... *Ballad of Mister Dutcher and the Last Lynching in Gupton*, on the other hand, is a narrative that almost anyone would like to have written—or at least would like to have the skill to have written. Whatever made Warren think that he could adapt its idiomatic gait to a syllabic line is a mystery, but the result—the line breaks punctuating the narrative with the deliberateness of the shifting of a chaw or the stroke of the whittling knife—is a small triumph.

Warren also includes the fine *Homage to Theodore Dreiser*, several love poems drawn from two earlier works, a poem about Flaubert, and many others just as apparently diverse—and yet, we are told in a curiously phrased prefatory note *à la* Lowell, "This book is conceived as a single long poem composed of a number of shorter poems as sections or chapters". Indeed, what must be considered the central poems are numbered I through XXIV, while interspersed among them are "interjections", numbered 1 through 8. The latter term cannot but suggest the tentativeness of whatever unity exists here, but by the same token it is clear that one is meant to discern a main current. Well, one does, and its source is "The compulsion to try to convert what now is *was* / Back into what was *is*". Those lines come from *Rattlesnake Country*, which in spite of distracting echoes of Faulkner is one of the most powerful poems here. It consists of memories of time spent on a desert ranch in the company, among others, of a half Indian hand called Laughing Boy, whose early morning duty and pleasure it is to keep the ranch house lawn free of the rattlers that sleep there each night. Laughing Boy executes his charge with ingenuity, first dousing a snake with gasoline and then snapping a match alight:

> The flame,
> If timing is good, should, just as he makes his rock-hole,
> Hit him. . . .
>
> Once I get one myself. I see, actually, the stub-buttoned
>   tail
> Whip through pale flame down into earth-darkness.
>
> "The son-of-a-bitch," I am yelling, "did you see me, I
>   got him!"
>
> I have gotten that stub-tailed son-of-a-bitch.

Magnificently told, this incident brings together an initiation into the temporal world (for what else can that youthful crime on that "One little patch of cool lawn" in that "long-lost summer" suggest?) and the transcendence of it. In the next section, Warren will say "What was *is* is now *was*" and then ask "But / Is *was* but a word for wisdom, its price?" That *was* is at least that, and *a fortiori* that *was* is, are propositions underwritten by the synthesis, as it were, of the two verbs in the noun's first syllable. But the snake has ogygian associations with time as well as with wisdom, and here the snake seems to be destroyed. In other words, the raconteur's sense of "timing" is only one reason that this passage is in the present tense; another is that in it *was* becomes *is*. The flaming rattler embodies that conversion, just as its disappearance down the hole (a fine touch) insists on what we might call the immortality of time.

Implicit in many of these poems, the world of "no-Time" figures explicitly in *Small White House, Sunset Walk in Thaw-Time in Vermont,* and *There's a Grandfather's Clock in the Hall.* The latter opens with a miniature Whitmanesque catalogue of meticulously jumbled events:

> There's a grandfather's clock in the hall, watch it closely. The
>   minute hand stands still, then it jumps, and
>   in between jumps there is no-Time,
> And you are a child again watching the reflection of early
>   morning sunlight on the ceiling above your bed. . . .

That "no-Time" is not simply an ironic term is guaranteed by the nature of the catenated incidents, which are as remarkable for their metaphorical relationships among themselves as for their relationship to the movement of the minute hand. Here Warren has hit upon the perfect device for establishing simultaneously the discreteness and continuity of events in the world and for representing in a linear, schematic fashion the weave of temporal and eternal that has its inevitably flawed analogue in the texture of this volume.

There are more burls than necessary in the fabric. Neither *Flaubert in Egypt,* which incidentally owes a lot to Francis Steegmuller's book of the same title, nor *Interjection #4: Bad Year, Bad War: a New Year's Card, 1969,* nor *Little Boy and Lost Shoe* contributes much to this "single long poem". But for the most part these poems do seed and ramify one another, so that although much of "the evidence / Is lost" . . . , we have a sense, as from mosaic bits still in place, of a whole, which is at once "the original dream which / I am now trying to discover the logic of" . . . and the book that Warren might have written had he already discovered that logic. (pp. 350-53)

The various relationships among the parts of Warren's

world are not always clearly formulated, and for that we can be thankful, since we can rest assured that he will continue to be engaged in "the process whereby pain of the past in its pastness / May be converted into the future tense / Of joy". . . . (p. 354)

Stephen Yenser, "Timepiece," in Poetry (© *1976 by The Modern Poetry Association; reprinted by permission of the Editor of* Poetry), *September, 1976, pp. 349-54.*

In a literary culture like ours, . . . in which commercial success is often felt to be at odds with academic scruples, Mr. Warren has enjoyed the best of both worlds. . . .

As a critic . . . he has exhibited a . . . versatility of interests. . . . In politics, also, he has traveled a long, hard road from the reactionary Southern orthodoxy of "I'll Take My Stand" (1930) to the liberalism of "Segregation: The Inner Conflict in the South" (1956) and "Who Speaks for the Negro?" (1965). Few other writers in our history have labored with such consistent distinction and such unflagging energy in so many separate branches of the literary profession. He is a man-of-letters on the old-fashioned, outsize scale, and everything he writes is stamped with the passion and the embattled intelligence of a man for whom the art of literature is inseparable from the most fundamental imperatives of life.

Yet it is no idle paradox to suggest that this writer, so heaped with honors and awards, remains in some sense an obscure figure. Certainly as a poet he has not been accorded the readership he deserves. We are not used to finding our greatest poets among the authors of best-selling novels or best-selling textbooks. We prefer them to be a little more specialized in their vocation, a little more remote from the hurly-burly where we live our lives and pursue our worldly interests. For a poet to succeed in the marketplace of letters is—well, unexpected. It diverts attention from his seriousness, and generates suspicion about his quality.

For this reason, it will come as a surprise, perhaps, at least to readers who have not kept up with the large quantity of poetry Mr. Warren has written in recent years, to be told that he is one of our greatest living poets. His poetry is so unlike that of most other poets now claiming our attention, however, that it requires a certain adjustment of the eye and the ear, and of that other faculty—call it the moral imagination—to which Mr. Warren's verse speaks with so much urgency and that of so many other poets nowadays does not. We are a long way, in this poetry, from the verse snapshot and the campy valentine—a long way, too, from the verse diaries, raw confessions and dirty laundry lists that have come to occupy such a large place in our poetic literature.

Mr. Warren's language, reaching in long-breathed lines across the page or building to its revelations and climaxes in verse paragraphs as highly charged with emotions and events as any of his stories, is at once grave and earthy, an instrument of metaphysical discourse that lives on easy terms with the folklore of the past. This is a poetry haunted by the lusts and loves of the flesh, filled with dramatic incident, vivid landscapes and philosophical reflection—a poetry of passion recollected in the tragic mode. It teems with experience, and with the lessons and losses of experience. One would be tempted to call it elegiac if that did not suggest something too settled and too distant from the urgencies of appetite and aspiration that inform its every line.

In all of this poetry there are forceful reminders of the author's gifts as a novelist, for no matter how compressed or telescoped the fable may be, these are poems that often tell a story, or evoke the setting and characters for one. The language, too, with its flow of "regional" Southern speech tempered to the economies and elisions of the verse medium, is alive with narrative continuities and the atmosphere of fictional episode. (pp. 1, 26)

The impulse to narrative retrospection was there in the early poems—in the "Ballad of Billie Potts," based on a folk tale of his native Kentucky, and in the more metaphysical poems, "Bearded Oaks" and "Original Sin: A Short Story," which decades of anthologizing have done nothing to diminish—and it is there in the new poems, "Can I See Arcturus From Where I Stand?," which open the ["Selected Poems 1923-1975"]. The voice, the themes, the obsession with evil, with the transience and glitter and dreamlike quality of experience, are there too, strong and forthright, both in the early and in the late verse.... [It] is the actions of "mere men," in all their atavism and primitive ambition, that occupy the landscapes and dreamscapes of these poems, with their expert shifts of narrative detail and moral reflection....

[Its] power is cumulative, building on a shrewd structure of story, metaphor and outright statement, with each element in the sequence orchestrated to enlarge and amplify what precedes it....

[No] single poem can adequately "represent" this volume, either, which is a collection of many kinds of verse—but all of it so fluent, so vivid with experience and reflections on experience, that it does indeed grip us like a "novel" of the poet's innermost life.

If there is, even so, some fault to be found in Mr. Warren's poetry, it may be in this very fluency, in the very ease and flow of a verse style that threatens at times to slacken the tension and blur our perception. Or is it that our taste for this natural flow of speech in poetry—for a poetry that goes on and on, and says all that it has to say—has been spoiled by the short-breathed artifice we are used to? Criticism, in any case, has not yet caught up with Mr. Warren's poetry —which is pretty odd, when we consider the role that he once played in developing the criticism of poetry in this country. When it does, we shall no doubt understand his virtues as well as his failings better than we now do. But it will confirm his place, I think, among the finest poets of our time, and one who speaks to us with a moral intensity few others have even attempted. (p. 26)

> *Hilton Kramer, in* The New York Times Book Review *(© 1977 by The New York Times Company; reprinted by permission), January 9, 1977.*

In the vision of Robert Penn Warren, a vision overtly anti-Emersonian, something sublimely repressed in and by the poet longs to be what Wallace Stevens once termed "a hawk of life." Stevens said he wanted his poems "To meet that hawk's eye and to flinch / Not at the eye but at the joy of it"—still a Whitmanian ambition. Warren is as embedded in what he takes to be a hawk's Nature as he is in time and history, and his poems merge part of their joy *with* the hawk's state of being. To trace that merging is to start to appreciate Warren's supreme achievement in a lifetime's poetry.

Warren always was a strikingly good poet, as a reading of his *Selected Poems: New And Old 1923-1966* revealed to many critics and lovers of American verse. Yet his indisputable greatness, his canonical strength, is demonstrated only by the work of the last decade—*Incarnations, Audubon: A Vision, Or Else,* and the 10 poems written in 1975 that open this new volume [*Selected Poems: 1923-1975*]. As he turned 60, Warren turned also into his true power as a poet, so that now, at 71, he alone among living writers ranks with the foremost American poets of the century: Frost, Stevens, Hart Crane, Williams, Pound, Eliot. Reading through this collection, arranged in reverse chronology, one discovers Warren is that rarest kind of major poet: He has never stopped developing from his origins up to his work-in-progress. (p. 19)

[The] sunset hawk, first seen in boyhood, keeps returning in Warren's poems. In the still relatively early "To A Friend Parting," the inadequacy of "the said, the unsaid" is juxtaposed to seeing: "The hawk tower, his wings the light take," an emblem of certainty in pride and honor. Perhaps it was the absence of such emblems in his confrontation of reality that stopped Warren's poetry in the decade 1943-1953, when he wrote his most ambitious novels, *All the King's Men* and *World Enough and Time.*

Whatever the cause of his silence in verse, it seems significant that *Promises: Poems 1954-1956* opens with an address to the poet's infant daughter that culminates in a return of the hawk image.... In *Tale of Time: Poems 1960-1966,* he explicitly compares "hawk shadow" with "that fugitive thought which I can find no word for," the consummate poetry upon whose threshold he stands at last.

That threshold is crossed in *Incarnations: Poems 1966-1968,* where Warren consciously takes on his full power over language and the world of the senses. The strongest poem in an extraordinary book, "The Leaf" stations its poet "near the nesting place of the hawk," and then grants him an absolute vision: "I saw / The hawk shudder in the high sky, he shudders / To hold position in the blazing wind, / in relation to / The firmament, he shudders and the world is a metaphor . . ." Warren's equal shudder is into a language finally his own, rather than Eliot's—away from ". . . my tongue / Was like a dry leaf in my mouth" and toward a precursor-overcoming sense that: "The world / Is fruitful, and I, too, / In that I am the father / Of my father's father's father. I, / Of my father, have set the teeth on edge."

Henceforward, in a great decade of poetry, Warren celebrates his being blessed by a new voice "for the only / Gift I have given: *teeth set on edge.*" This prophetic trope governs the long poem *Audubon: A Vision,* where the painter who wrote ". . . in my sleep I continually dream of birds" becomes the surrogate for the boy, Warren, whose poetic incarnation came about as he stood in the dark, and heard "the great geese hoot northward."

The last poem in Warren's best volume, *Or Else—Poem/Poems 1968-1974,* ends with a different kind of hawk's vision, as a figuration for the poet's new style: "The hawk, / . . . glides, / In the pellucid ease of thought and at / His breathless angle, / Down." As the hawk breaks speed and hovers, he "makes contact," giving us a trope that stands, part for whole, for the tense power of Warren's mature art....

Emerson, says Warren's poem ["Homage to Emerson"], "had forgiven God everything," which is merely to say that Emerson had begun a truly American vision sensibly, by forgiving himself everything (something Nietzsche could not quite do). Warren goes on forgiving God, and himself, nothing, and implies that this is the only way to love either God or the self. I read Warren's poetry with a shudder that is at once spiritual revulsion and total esthetic satisfaction, for he has done for the School of Eliot what Eliot could not do: He has invented a poetry that fights free even of its own ideological ferocity by way of a sublime energy of language.

The second poem in these *Selected Poems* is "Evening Hawk," written in 1975. After 40 years, it completes "Watershed's" image of the "sunset hawk." With preternatural persistence and unsurpassed energy of invention, Warren has made himself one with his own astonishing vision of the bird. . . . (pp. 19-20)

> *Harold Bloom, "The Sunset Hawk," in* The New Leader *(© 1977 by the American Labor Conference on International Affairs, Inc.), January 31, 1977, pp. 19-21.*

Robert Penn Warren is a vigorous and rather inspiring exception to the rule that American writers burn themselves out early. Now in his seventy-second year, and close to completing a full half century as a published writer, Warren is as good a poet as he has ever been, and a novelist still trying to bring his fierce energies under control. *A Place to Come To* is Warren's tenth novel, his first since the disastrous *Meet Me in the Green Glen;* it is not going to satisfy those many readers who keep hoping that he will write another *All the King's Men,* but it is a work of considerable power, narrative drive and intellectual integrity.

Warren's problem as a novelist has always been that his strength of vision and theme is greater than his self-discipline. All of his novels sprawl. They are filled with ideas, arguments, questions, challenges—all of them thrown at the reader in a maelstrom of characters, incidents, explosions and digressions. Of late, in fact, it has become fashionable in some circles to say that Warren is a better poet than novelist, which may at least be true to the extent that he accepts the disciplines of poetry while granting himself full artistic license in the novel.

A Place to Come To, in both its strengths and its weaknesses, is quintessential Warren. It is concerned, as so much of his writing is, with the search for the meaning of the past and for an identity with a place. It moves right along with a forceful, interesting plot and a cast of reasonably believable, lively characters. It grabs onto ideas and wrestles handsomely with them. But on the negative side, it turns in a few places upon twists of invention that strain credulity; it wanders this way and that while Warren picks over an idea or a nuance that particularly pleases him; and it really does go on too long. . . .

[The story of Tewksbury, the narrator,] is told with a knowledge and awareness of the South that have not faded in the many years since Warren moved North. His portrait of upper-class life in Nashville is especially acute, and he presents a delightful definition of what he calls "the art of the mystic promise," an art peculiar to Southern womanhood. . . .

Warren is preoccupied as usual with the clash between free will and predestination, the search for self-knowledge, the implacable demands of old roots and loyalties, the persistent existence of the past. Warren may slip and slide around, and from time to time make a terrible mess of his plots, but

he is always serious. He is always straining to answer the big questions, to take on the great concerns of human existence. If *A Place to Come To* is imperfect, its flaws are the grand ones made by a writer who has yet to flag in his quest for the words that contain the answers.

> *Jonathan Yardley, "A Writer to Come To," in* Book World—The Washington Post *(© The Washington Post), March 6, 1977, p. 1.*

For all the vivid sensuous detail in his work, Warren has a synthesizing, almost allegorizing imagination; it is not so much that he deliberately imposes mythic patterns upon his work as that his characters struggle against the modern condition of alienation that their habit of relentless self-analysis creates. For that reason Warren's fiction works best when it has comic overtones—nobody ever talks about how funny "All the King's Men" is. Jack Burden's sardonic self-deprecation makes the book a triumph of tone. When Warren's books lack that saving humor, as many since then have, many critics and ordinary readers have found them somewhat tedious and preachy; an all-too-visible intellectual scaffolding lends an air of contrivance to long sections of "Band of Angels" (1955), "Wilderness" (1961), "Flood" (1964), and "Meet Me at the Green Glen" (1971), and renders the amplitude and the digressive nature of Warren's prose style more an annoyance than a glory.

Such harsh judgments, of course, are only relative. Were it not for the very high order of Warren's gifts and his achievements in other forms—especially poetry—no one would ever have been disappointed with his novels. But the brilliance and the power of "All the King's Men" have tended to diminish its successors by comparison, and readers who have kept up with Warren's more recent novels have savored their fine moments while hoping that he would find it within himself to write another almost perfect book. "A Place To Come To," Warren's tenth novel since 1939, is not that book. (p. 4)

Warren's many admirers will find isolated passages and striking images scattered throughout that are the equal of anybody now writing in English. But taken separately they cannot overcome the contrivance of the whole. (p. 24)

> *Gene Lyons, in* The New York Times Book Review *(© 1977 by The New York Times Company; reprinted by permission), March 13, 1977.*

As poet, novelist, critic, and teacher, Robert Penn Warren has been for 40 years a powerful presence in American letters. And his characters—Billy Potts, Jerry Beaumont, Perse Munn, Jack Burden, and perhaps most memorably Willie Stark—share a quality Warren found in Thomas Wolfe's portraits of the Gant family: They are "permanent properties of the reader's imagination." All the more disappointing, then, that in his latest novel, *A Place to Come To* . . . , we are given a series of absences, a gallery of missing persons.

This is true in an almost literal way throughout most of the adult adventure of the hero and narrator, Jed Tewksbury—by birth a poor-white Alabaman, by profession a distinguished Dante scholar at the University of Chicago. (p. 15)

Many of the novel's episodes, be it said, are dramatic and moving—after all, the writer is Robert Penn Warren—and even at its worst the plot has a lively soap-opera appeal. Indeed, those who like narratives crowded with sex, conversation, changes of scene, and coincidence will enjoy the part of *A Place to Come To* (more than two thirds of it) that describes Jed Tewksbury's 40-year absence from Dugton, Alabama.

It is Jed's status as a Southerner away from home, however, that accounts for some of the novel's most troublesome technical problems and, possibly, for the odd insubstantiality of the characters. On the one hand, Jed carries the region with him all his life. . . . On the other hand, there is nothing particularly Southern about his experiences outside Alabama; they could be those of any "alienated" American.

Warren has, I think, made this doubleness a part of his point. In an interview given just before the book came out, he said he was writing about "a Southerner who hates (or is ashamed of) the South . . . and it is my observation that such a Southerner, even if a great success in the world, is always a 'placeless' man." Unfortunately, having this kind of figure narrate the novel makes Warren's task a more difficult one. He must contrive to provide the memories that Jed, in his hatred and shame, has blocked or blotted out. Moreover, if Jed is to be kept wandering for 40 years, his horror at his past must be satisfactorily established; if he is to be brought back at the very end, reconciled and forgiving, his change of heart must be convincingly accounted for. Had Warren achieved this design, *A Place to Come To* would have been a tour de force; I do not believe he has.

He could have followed a different, more gradual course, showing in Jed's mind the slow unfolding of real memories behind the screen he has constructed. That Warren lets the screen stand is evidence that the novel is not really "about" the South. The region has become an abstraction for Jed and hence for the reader: Individuals become types, myths become clichés. This process is not unrelated to the South's homogenization with the rest of the country, but Warren has not summoned up from his great resources the patience to make this connection effectively.

Still, the novel begins with a brilliant promise of experience closely rendered. The opening sentence states Warren's theme—Jed's patrimony, real and symbolic—with a poet's economy and force, and conveys immediately Jed's combination of classical locution and the vernacular. . . .

Jed has certainly come back to the mythologized South, lost cause and all. Yet he never makes it back to [his home]. Looking at a little church where the people "used to sweat and moan and anguish for their salvation," which has been abandoned to wind and weather, he says the scene "was the same as that of one of the more famous photographs by Walker Evans, but a generation of damage later." Jed's association, even now, is not with an actual place, but with a picture of it. We remain, with the hero, at a second remove from his home. (pp. 15-16)

Ruth Mathewson, "A Placeless Southerner," in The New Leader *(© 1977 by the American Labor Conference on International Affairs, Inc.), April 11, 1977, pp. 15-16.*

Warren's novels read like essays about themselves. His fictions continually resolve into apologues. It is scarcely possible while reading them to have the experience but miss the meaning. Where commentary does not preempt drama, it quickly intrudes to explicate it. While in "Pure and Impure Poetry" he argues that ideas "participate more fully, intensely, and immediately" in poetry by being implicit, his

own work typically incorporates ideas "in an explicit and argued form." Such a habit of mind stations Warren on the border between two modes of imagination, between the artist who works from experience and the critic who works toward meaning.

Warren's double career in the creative and critical establishments seems to be the central fact here. There is nothing remarkable about a divided allegiance in a man who set out to devote himself to both worlds. But had Warren never written his major articles on Frost, Faulkner, Conrad, and Coleridge, or his textbooks on *understanding* poetry and fiction, we would still need some term for a writer so concerned to usurp, within the body of his own fictions, the critic's task. Warren has revived interest in Wilde's claim that "it is very much more difficult to talk about a thing than to do it." His works constantly "talk about" themselves. In the midst of overwhelming adolescent arousal, a Warren narrator can suddenly step out of himself to tell us: "I was lost in the flood of sensations." How can one both feel and say this? Through the curious doubleness of this sentence, at once both in and out of time, Warren tries to convert self-consciousness into ecstasy. His characters are placed out of themselves, the bemused or obsessive spectators of their own wayward acts. . . . We abstract; we embody. Warren has dedicated his career to proving the indivisibility of the critical and the creative imaginations. He thus joins that central American tradition of speakers—Emerson, Thoreau, Henry Adams, Norman Mailer—who are not only the builders but the interpreters of their own designs.

The stance of a critic is the stance of a son. Both are fundamentally indebted as both take up their positions in response to prior achievement which surrounds and defines them. . . . Warren's central character is a son (or daughter) whose only hope lies in *not* rebelling against father, tradition, home. In 1960 Leonard Casper nominated "exploration of unbroken years of homesickness" as Warren's central theme. Warren has not been coy about proving him right. *A Place To Come To* depends upon a place one has come *from*. Warren's most recent novel explores once again the psychology of exile and return.

Adam's first word to Eve in *Paradise Lost* is "Return," and it is upon her reluctant but ultimately obedient response to this command that Warren models his plots. . . . Warren the critic always shepherds us toward the destination the artist knowingly withholds. The best way out is always back.

In the character of Jed Tewksbury, Warren has found his perfect hero. As if in passing a last judgment upon himself, Warren writes a novel about a critic writing a novel. . . . Warren goes far beyond his earlier judgment in *World Enough and Time* that the world must redeem the idea. It is no longer a question of working from the concrete toward the abstract; there seems little hope here that the two can be brought into any relationship whatsoever. The author of this novel seems to have rejected Wilde's boast and embraced Faulkner's dismissal: "those who can do, those who cannot and suffer enough because they can't, write about it." All writing comes under indictment here as an evasive sublimation, a criticism of rather than a participation in life. . . . Jed suffers an alienation of word from world which he is never fully allowed to resolve. (pp. 475-78)

The best writing in the book is reserved for the return to Rozelle, Jed's rejected high school prom date who becomes his middle-aged adulteress. . . . Sex proves, however, less a way to redeem time than to stay it. The critic who would return gives way to the artist who will escape. Sex becomes an anti-metaphysic. Making love leads to "the death in life-beyond-Time without which life-in-Time might not be endurable, or even possible." (p. 478)

A Place To Come To is Warren's most ambitious attempt to study "the relation of the concept of Love to that of Time." Love finally proves subordinate to time; the only abiding love is a repetition, not a revolution. (p. 479)

A reviewer of this novel may well feel cheated in having nothing climactic to give away. Surprise endings are impossible in a book which knows from the beginning that there is finally only one place to come to. Home hovers over Warren's novels like the threat of death—it will get you in the end. What one may come to resent about Warren's work is not its end but its means. The necessity for return no one will question, but where it emerges as inevitability rather than option, we are deprived of the very chance to wander and even lose our way, which makes arrival seem an achievement rather than a gift.

The end of Warren's *Selected Poems: 1923-1975* entirely defies prediction. One usually reads such a volume with a gathering sense of a poet's hard-earned maturity. But this selection begins with the poems of 1975 and ends with those of 1923-1943. As one reads into the book, the past looms up as if it were the future.

>   This
> Is the process whereby pain of the past in its pastness
>   May be converted into the future tense
> Of joy.

This inverted presentation of his poetic development is Warren's most profound act of criticism. It is also his biggest lie against time.

The most obvious motive for such reversal is to present the best work first. Warren has had the luck to live a long life. It took 60 years for his poetic voice to mature into his great volume, *Or Else*. Naturally he might wish to begin with his triumph. More compelling, however, must have been the impulse to revolt against a career dedicated to the awful responsibility of Time. This is a book in which poem after poem defines man as a creature caught up in irreversible history. Yet all these propositions inhabit a structure which belies chronology. The arrangement of the *Selected Poems* constitutes a rebellion against the priority of an earlier self, and, by extension, earlier selves. Through an illusion of presentation, early Warren becomes indebted to late Warren. In throwing off the yoke of time, the critic/son finally becomes the artist/father. (pp. 479-80)

Not until *Promises* [written 1954-56] does Warren achieve a fully personal voice over the length of an entire book. The birth of his son and daughter suddenly converts the abstractions of Time and History into a continuity of blood in which he has chosen to participate. In the moment of watching his son asleep, we can begin to hear all the voices of his past absorbed into the poet's own. . . . [In *Or Else*] Warren heals the past by blessing the future. He realizes the great possibility of reversal, and in so doing recovers a sense of rhythm more sure than anything he has previously known. *Or Else* is a triumph of rhythm, in the line, and in the self. . . . In "Birth of Love" Warren develops into what is perhaps most difficult, because least determined: a faithful lover. (pp. 480-82)

["Birth of Love"] is . . . poetry of the verb rather than the noun. Warren rediscovers the power of words which enact over those which abstract. Our fate in the poem depends upon its verbs. Stationed at the beginnings and ends of lines, granted a full and measured breath of their own, these carefully positioned action words reach forward to create an anticipation which carries us through the poem. They draw us, like enduring love, into time. (pp. 482-83)

What then shall we further be able to see?

An abstraction:

> This moment is non-sequentila and absolute, and admits
> Of no definition, for it
> Subsumes all other, and sequential, moments, by which
> Definition might be possible.

"This" closes the growing gap between the man and his vision, the reader and the poem. "This" testifies to the presence of a thing and our familiarity with it. We have had our moment; now we savor it through commentary. An immediacy becomes an example. Yet the poet speaks of this moment as still happening. It "is." We again question whether one can speak of a moment and still experience it. The poet's way of saying contradicts the force of his statement. He advances a definition about the inadmissibility of definition. He denies sequence in a poem dependent on it. The moment, we are told, subsumes and dissolves history. And yet the poem, as we have seen, involves us in a necessary sequence of seeings. Our movement through it is as much like walking as stationary looking. In its own words, it is "stair-steep." It is torn between asserting its moment as "non-sequential and absolute," and the necessity of entrusting any such experience to the mediation of language and emotion working in time.

The genius of Warren's poem is to locate this lapse from unconscious grace not after but *within* the swelling present moment. The abstraction interrupts rather than completes the poem's movement. So it is with relief that the reader returns to the unfolding of the actual sense. (pp. 484-85)

"Birth of Love" confirms the love between men and women which makes generation possible. Any enduring love is profoundly historical, growing through change, confirmed through repetition. Yet poetry represents love less in its confirmation through repetition than in its freshness through transformation. Warren's poem is a repetition *experienced as* a beginning. It fuses, as fully as one might ever wish, the imagination which conserves and the imagination which creates. This birth is really a re-birth. The man has again fallen in love with this woman, as he will, with grace, again. He falls in love again, however, *as if* for the first time, *as if* he were free to choose, apart from all the historical obligations determining such a choice. The whole poem is structured to be experienced as "the non-sequential" moment of which it speaks. It is given greater force than a poem of actual beginning by virtue of the very history it excludes, and yet which surrounds this moment to define and give value to it. We know that the body has been marked by time's use; we know that the day is late. Yet we are left with another image of beginning:

>   Above
> Height of the spruce-night and heave of the far mountain,
>   he sees
> The first star pulse into being. It gleams there.

Of course the star of Venus: of course the poem is a repetition in modern time of the myth of her birth. But Warren's mode of indirect allusion frees us from a mere rehearsal of the archetypical—the poem was originally titled "The Birth of Love"—and preserves the illusion of an original event. What is lost for mythic inevitability is gained for imaginative freeplay. (p. 486)

[The] star's pulsing forth every night, not what it might symbolically promise, *is* the promise. It too marks a pattern of repetition, yet it, too, in its nightly pulsing forth, is always ready to be seen and felt as if for the first time. In this quiet refusal to interpret his own imagery, Warren acknowledges the critic's desire to know while protecting the poet's will to present, a resolution worthy of his most mature and beautiful poem. (p. 487)

> *David M. Wyatt, "Robert Penn Warren: The Critic As Artist," in* Virginia Quarterly Review *(copyright, 1977, by the* Virginia Quarterly Review, *The University of Virginia), Vol. 53, No. 3 (Summer, 1977), pp. 475-87.*

Like so many Southern writers, [Warren] is obsessed by the shortcomings of the South; but he writes about them with an eloquence and an elemental rage worlds apart from the sordid bitterness of some of his literary colleagues. The subject matter of his principal books is the moral significance of particular political and social behavior.

And to their composition he has applied uncommon talents: a headlong narrative pace which makes his novels intensely readable, a fierce emotion which charges his pages with contagious tension and an exuberant delight in poetic imagery. (pp. 24-5)

The faults of Mr. Warren's novels seem complementary to their virtues. Often one feels that their author has become so fascinated with verbal effects that he overdoes them; that he is so interested in some of his characters, often minor ones, that he neglects to make the others as convincingly motivated and persuasive as they should be; that he spends too much time in irrelevant digressions. And in his best and most important novel, *All the King's Men*, there is a disturbing refusal to face the most important political significance of the central character. (p. 25)

> *Orville Prescott, in his* In My Opinion: An Inquiry into the Contemporary Novel *(copyright © 1942, 1943, 1944, 1945, 1946, 1947, 1948, 1949, 1950, 1951, by* The New York Times; *copyright, © 1952 by Orville Prescott; reprinted by permission of the publisher, The Bobbs-Merrill Co., Inc.), Bobbs-Merrill, 1977.*

*   *   *

WAUGH, Evelyn   1903-1966

Waugh is a British novelist whose writing can best be divided into pre- and post-Catholicism. Before his conversion in 1945, Waugh's works were humorous social satires. His later works continued to use satire, but in an increasingly cynical and pessimistic vein. (See also *CLC*, Vols. 1, 3, and *Contemporary Authors*, obituary, Vols. 25-28, rev. ed.)

Traditionalism—that past elegantly embodied in aristocratic pastoral of great houses, chestnut-tree drives, craftsmanship, hierarchy, culture—establishes the ideal of civilization, order, and permanence; but Waugh's comic act is to violate it with modernity. The novelist of instability, be-

yond such humanism, he depends on the *memento mori*, the macabre intrusion, the bleak reminder of the folly of seeking fulfilment inside time or history; the posture consorts elegantly with a modernizing history which, to his comic eye, is devoted to the same riotous and brutal reminder. The tradition of social comedy he belongs to is not Fielding's but Gogol's: society is an unstable, extraordinary fiction in a wilderness of space; and we embody it as caricature, strangely, absurdly—as his own surrogate, Gilbert Pinfold, does in acting the part of 'eccentric don and testy colonel' until that is all his friends and critics see. Waugh's version of history is of a disintegrating proceeding, a movement from greater to lesser, civilization to chaos; but that releases Dionysian comedy and a self-ironizing but poised narrative posture.

Indeed one reason why he seems so pure a comic writer is that—like his hero in *Decline and Fall*, Paul Pennyfeather, who accepts all outrage as it comes and is inert—he takes a disingenuous stance. . . . He is not a dialectical comedian of ideas in Huxley's way; his work yields ideas only dramatically. Instead the narrator stands at the centre of his comedy, omniscient yet evasively neutral, surrounded by outrage and absurdity; the world around is conveyed as an impression, a moving collage without psychological depth, flickering, quickly rendered, given largely through dialogue, short scenes, rapid transitions of place, and a wide range of characters whose inner lives rarely detain us. This economical technique Waugh seems to have got partly from the cinema and partly from Ronald Firbank, another important figure in this stylistic phase. (pp. 154-55)

His books are very much comic *fictions*, each making a coherent absurd world with its own laws; but each of these worlds makes reference to the prevailing one, and exposes it, by means of an entirely comprehensible vision of barbarism and disintegration. The realization of comic wholeness has its distinct historical location; it belongs to the times and has its roots in them. (p. 156)

The comic throughout is the form for treating a world in which Waugh takes enormous, delighted curiosity but no moral pleasure whatsoever; that is why the notion of him as pre-eminently a traditional writer is false, since it suggests only the basis of how he arrives at his contrasts and vision, not the basis of his invention or, above all, its form. (p. 157)

> *Malcolm Bradbury, in his* Possibilities: Essays on the State of the Novel *(copyright © 1973 by Malcolm Bradbury; reprinted by permission of Oxford University Press, Inc.), Oxford University Press, 1973.*

[Waugh's] constant target is fraudulence: heretical beliefs, sentimental behavior, derivative or picturesque art and architecture, impostors of every kind—all these bear the brunt of Waugh's fierce satire. What accounts for Waugh's obsessive hatred of the pseudo, so much more virulent than the usual satiric dislike of pretence? The answer lies, at one level, in the convert's conviction that the world he has repudiated as valueless is now a grossly-blurred caricature of the genuine. Thus it is that the major action in most of Waugh's novels consists of his persona's quest to escape from the condition of a cartoon. In *Men at Arms* Guy Crouchback feels "diminished and caricatured by duplication" and in *Brideshead Revisited* Charles Ryder observes, "We are seldom single or unique; we keep company in this world with a hoard of abstractions and reflexions and counterfeits of ourselves . . . all in our own image, indistinguishable from ourselves to the outward eye. We get borne along, out of sight in the press, unresisting, till we get the chance to . . . outdistance our shadows." "Outdistance our shadows": one thinks of Paul Pennyfeather, Tony Last, and Guy Crouchback attempting to elude Potts, Mr. Todd, and Apthorpe—attempts which are really outward expressions of the artist's need to exorcise a dimly-intuited fraudulence from within his own soul.

We may never learn just how consciously Waugh resorted to autobiography in describing his personae's repeated struggles to escape from their shadows. It is sufficient to say that when Waugh "outdistanced" Angel in *The Ordeal of Gilbert Pinfold* he re-enacted the basic movement of all his novels. In defeating Angel he ritually exorcised an incubus which had begun to drive the very critic of the counterfeit into a state of self-caricature. No wonder that Waugh felt "there was a triumph to be celebrated". . . . (p. 331)

[As] the result of Gilbert Pinfold's ordeal Evelyn Waugh triumphed over fraudulence by finally acknowledging its possible inward origin. In closer touch with reality, which he no longer viewed "with insufficient charity," Waugh went on to complete *Officers and Gentlemen* and the even more compassionate *Unconditional Surrender*. (p. 336)

> *Jeffrey M. Heath, "Waugh and the 'Pinfold' Manuscript," in* Journal of Modern Literature (© *Temple University 1976), April, 1976, pp. 331-36.*

Evelyn Waugh's early novels are often thought to express the view that a traditional, stable, and dignified social order in England is quickly being replaced by a state of near chaos in which dishonesty and ruthless hedonism reign supreme. (p. 119)

But *A Handful of Dust* does not really support the view that Waugh believes the modern era to be marked by a decline in the quality of life. The Myth of Decline, the belief that beauty, order, and significance existed at some point in the past, but exist no longer, is certainly present in the novel, but it seems to be certain of the novel's characters, rather than its author, who cling to this belief. For Waugh undercuts these characters in a variety of subtle and not so subtle ways. If Waugh's earlier novels, *Decline and Fall* and *Vile Bodies*, did indeed embody a simple version of this Myth of Decline, then in *A Handful of Dust* Waugh is carrying his satire a step further by attacking one of his earlier positives. But probably it would be more accurate to say that although Waugh's early novels of English life all play with the idea of decline, it is only in much later novels, like the notorious *Brideshead Revisited*, that Waugh uses the Myth of Decline uncritically, as an organizing principle which gives meaning to his book.

The main technique that Waugh uses in *A Handful of Dust* to undercut those characters who believe in one or another version of the Myth of Decline is that of playing off their beliefs against each other through ironic juxtaposition. Various characters choose to locate the lost "golden age" at various periods of the past, but no character is able to give very compelling reasons for his choice. Tony's vision of the golden age is at once the most interesting and the most confused in the novel. For Tony, the golden era is that of the immediate Edwardian and late-Victorian past—the age when owners of country houses like Hetton had the resources with which to maintain them, when the country house and the county family were still important elements in English society. Tony's dream is to restore Hetton in all

its details to its late-Victorian state. . . . Of course, it isn't really possible for Tony to restore prelapsarian purity to Hetton. As Tony himself tacitly admits . . . , there is a contradiction at the heart of a dream that tries to preserve a social institution that was once vital but now has no significant function to perform. The country house, once a center of English social and economic life, is so no longer. People will not even come to such a house for the weekend unless they are offered all the amenities of modern city living. (pp. 119-21)

The antique Hetton Abbey was entirely rebuilt in 1864 in the Gothic style, and this extravagant gesture suggests that Tony's Victorian forbears, like Tony himself, found beauty and significance in the past rather than in the present. Yet, . . . the Middle Ages was hardly the era of beauty, order, spirituality, and elevated ideals that certain Victorians, in full retreat from materialism and modernity, imagined it to be. Apparently the Victorian era was not so satisfying to Tony's forbears as Tony feels it would be to himself, so they in their turn idealized the Middle Ages in a manner notorious for its disregard of historical fact. And . . . their confused Gothicism has become an element in Tony's essentially Victorian dream world. (p. 121)

Tony's unsatisfactory, obsolete life style is . . . idealized by his impoverished successors, just as Tony himself idealized the lives of his Victorian forbears, who in turn idealized . . . and so on. The golden era exists not in the past but in the mind. (p. 123)

Reggie's absorption in a supposedly significant past distracts him from truly significant present responsibilities. . . . It's no accident that Reggie is going to search for meaning in a desert. His rejection of the present in favor of the past makes him a worse man, just as the well-meaning Tony's sterile preoccupation with the restoration of Hetton blinds him to such important present problems as his wife's unhappiness.

Tony and Reggie are not the only characters in *A Handful of Dust* who satisfy their longings for order and significance by retreating into dream worlds located in the past, while remaining selfish and insensitive to others' sufferings in their handling of everyday life. The syndrome takes its most extreme form in the case of Mr. Todd. Todd's golden era is located in the fictionalized Victorian world of Dickens' novels—where kindness and charity have the power to alter reality, where human suffering has meaning and arouses pity and indignation. Superficially, Todd is Dickens' ideal reader: "at the description of the sufferings of the outcasts in 'Tom-all-alone's' tears ran down his cheeks into his beard". . . . But Dickens intended his readers to be moved to moral action by his novels, and for Mr. Todd, the retreat into the imaginary, significant past which Dickens' work provides is an end in itself, giving his altruistic emotions a good workout which apparently incapacitates them for further action. . . . Todd has located all moral significance in an imaginary past totally severed from the ugly and hedonistic present which he accepts quite matter-of-factly. This is the danger inherent in using a Myth of Decline to satisfy one's longings for a more beautiful life. Both Tony and Todd's emotional lives take place in a past world which never really existed as they imagine it—both neglect the present. (pp. 124-25)

Tony actually encounters two people—Thérèse de Vitré, daughter of an old, Catholic family in Trinidad, and Mr. Todd—who unmistakably suggest or represent the two past periods that are blended in Tony's English Gothic dream, the Victorian era and the Middle Ages. (p. 126)

Given Waugh's Catholicism, we might expect him to idealize the conservative Catholic society of Trinidad. Here, if anywhere, Waugh would be likely to employ a straightforward version of the Myth of Decline by portraying traditional Trinidadian life as more satisfying than English modernity. But in fact what is most striking about Thérèse's response to the stable, ordered life of Trinidad is her unavowed, yet obviously violent, desire to escape from it. (p. 127)

In addition, Waugh's description of Thérèse's father as "the complete slave owner" reminds the reader that Trinidad's aristocrats did not gain their social pre-eminence in a morally irreproachable manner. So the encounter with Thérèse vaguely and suggestively, yet unmistakably, undercuts Tony's belief that the orderly Victorian past was a satisfying and edifying time to live.

The Gothic element in Tony's English Gothic Myth of Decline is at least as deeply undercut by his dealings with Mr. Todd as its Victorian element is by Thérèse. (p. 128)

Critics of *A Handful of Dust* often describe Todd as crazy, but Todd's sanity isn't really at issue here. Whether he is sane or not, it is clear that Todd's behavior closely resembles the behavior of all the aristocratic English characters in the novel. Like them he uses the social power circumstances have placed in his hands ruthlessly and selfishly (Tony . . . is at best a partial exception to this generalization); like them, he demonstrates a schism between moral ideals and practical conduct. If Todd is extreme, he is also typical, and the ruthlessness with which he uses his power demonstrates something about the nature of power which undermines the Gothic element in Tony's Myth of Decline. Those whose society gives them great and unquestioned authority over other human beings (the sort of authority Todd has inherited, with the gun, from his missionary father; the sort of authority feudal aristocrats inherited from their fathers) are likely to accept that authority as their right and to use it with little human sensitivity. The extremely powerful feudal aristocrats who use their monopoly of physical force chivalrically, in the interests of the whole community, are a figment of Tennyson's and Tony's imaginations. The real aristocrats are Reggie, Brenda, Mr. Todd, and, alas, Tony himself, who all unquestioningly accept the social arrangements which give them rank and power and use their power in a basically selfish manner. And Todd's cruelty is the greatest at least in part because his powers are the most absolute. Thus Tony's "journey into the past," like so much else in this novel, suggests, not decline, but rather the essential similarity between past and present. (pp. 129-30)

> *Jane Nardin, "The Myth of Decline in 'A Handful of Dust'," in* The Midwest Quarterly *(copyright, 1977, by* The Midwest Quarterly, *Kansas State College of Pittsburgh), Winter, 1977, pp. 119-30.*

* * *

WEISS, Theodore 1916-

An American poet and critic, Weiss has taken the position that poetry has surrendered "immense sectors of the world to prose." He has tried to regain some of this lost ground by incorporating elements of the epic, Homeric poetry that he admires into his own poems. In this respect his poetry has run counter to the personal, confessional poetry that has been lately in vogue in America and England. (See also *CLC*, Vol. 3, and *Contemporary Authors*, Vols. 9-12, rev. ed.)

When I opened [*The World Before Us*], . . . I found myself on the first page, as it were, eating Proust's madeleine: I was cast back on waves of sensuous language to the exact feeling of literature in our youth a quarter-century ago. In Weiss's early poems I seemed to hear at once every bell of a distant peal. Not just Valéry or Pound or Joyce or Rilke or Ford or Stevens but the entire tintinnabulation, our epoch's first literary renaissance, jumbled timbres both great and obscure, the linguistic intoxication of an age. Not that we young ones merely imitated our seniors, though imitation in some sense was important to us. We were poor scholars, by and large, lazy readers, and half the time didn't know what our predecessors had been talking about; besides, we wanted to be ourselves. But how we reveled in their reputations, their power won through words! It was the triumph of language, or so we thought. We set out to equal them, and what we wrote, the good or the bad, could not have been in greater contrast to the studiously plain, careless, unambitious writing of young poets today. It had its dangers, that old wild dream of style. . . . But it had its pleasures too; *raptures, ecstasies,* as we kept calling them, only half in irony; and I can think of no better poet than Weiss with whom to celebrate our nostalgia. . . .

War-battered, we needed love. Denatured, we needed ways to restore a pre-Freudian mystery to sex. Don't think we did not write in urgency simply because we chose set themes. But notice the language [of the early poetry]. Imitative, of course. . . . But there is plenty of Weiss in it too, especially the way he uses language, uses it with purpose and for all it is worth, every craftsmanly element, every device, vocabulary, grammar, rhythm, tone, all the nuances of association and echo, with the result that his poem has a quality of tension which rises through its imitativeness and nearly through its substantial meaning. And this quality of language, this tension and tensility, is to my mind what characterizes the best poetry by young poets of that period, whatever our writing may have lacked in perceptual directness and experiential relevance, just as it is the quality I find so evidently and regrettably absent from the poetry of today's young writers, who may have ample other merits and whose unfortunate disdain for the craft of poetic articulation has a certain historical justice. (p. 25)

His book, *The World Before Us,* naturally places the emphasis . . . not on origins but on destinations, and is a splendid selection for this purpose, though Weiss's longest poem, *Gunsight,* which is one of his best, is not included. Other shorter narrative and dramatic poems, like "Wunschzettel" and "Caliban Remembers," show his storytelling skills equally well perhaps, and the rest of the poems, lyrical, reflective, erotic, show a remarkable diversity of themes within a remarkable consistency of texture. The inner part of this consistency comes from the poet's characteristic turn of mind, which is dialectical, the simplest questions being posed in terms of conflict, so that often quotation marks are used to distinguish abstract points of view even where no speaking persons are present. The outer part of the consistency comes, of course, from language. Weiss has evolved in a straight line from his early poems. . . . He soon sloughed off the imitative elements . . . and turned from set themes to more personal frames of reference and firmer concepts of expressiveness; yet still with the same winding syntax, precise diction and rhythmic tension. A poem by Weiss is indelibly his own. Indeed I often cannot understand the separate components of his idiosyncratic prosody, such as his hyphenated line endings or absolutely capricious interior line breaks; yet where I question such matters in the work of other poets, here I cannot, because they are so firmly and unalterably fixed in their totally individualized parent structures. They are the essential parts of a poem by Weiss, whose prosodic reasoning, even intuition, may be obscure, but whose end product, the poem in its wholeness, is not.

The shape of Weiss's poetry on the page, its coiling, spiraling movement up and down, corresponds to the way his language winds ever back on itself in the search for more precise discriminations of feeling, moral and aesthetic judgment and descriptive rightness. It is civilized poetry, in both the ordinary meaning of polish and refinement and in the higher meaning of eagerness to discover, reaffirm, and transfigure its own primitivism. It does not appeal to everyone. Impatient readers, who are willing to overlook the moral consequence of the moment when a feeling passes from one state to another, find it finicky or pedantic. But it is nothing of the kind, and I am sure its appeal is not limited to the poet's contemporaries. On the contrary, young people will prize this work, perhaps more than we do, because like all poetry which is both intrinsically sound and somewhat at variance with the immediate cultural and social needs of the day, this poetry is prophetic. It cannot help being prophetic. It bears one required phase of the cycle of human sensibility, from whose turning civilization is generated. If it is on the downturn now, it will come up again. (pp. 25-6)

Thus a fine and modest book may have a role greater than its appearance across a cultural gap. (p. 26)

> *Hayden Carruth, "The Cycle of Sensibility," in* The Nation *(copyright 1971 by the Nation Associates, Inc.), January 4, 1971, pp. 25-6.*

The poetry of Theodore Weiss achieves its effect by not reaching for an effect: it offers relief from heightened language, and reassurance by not straining credulity. The sensation is that of entering a world freed from sensationalism. Readers who explore this world often develop a taste for its flavor, its shady tang.

"Fireweeds," listed as the seventh of Weiss's poetry volumes, from a beginning in the early 1950's, gathers his quiet poems from a range of recent literary magazines—his Acknowledgments page is a chart of the scene. . . . (p. 8)

I say "quiet poems." Theodore Weiss does not depart just a bit from high-impact wording. He consistently departs a lot. He lounges into a poem, often with phrases like "Imagine that time . . ." or "And so there are. . . ." He is steadfastly relaxed in wording. The reader lives on a taste for casualness and accuracy rather than for intensity.

"The Storeroom" exemplifies this style. It is a long poem —17 pages—and it gathers itself slowly and openly. The reader follows Penelope as she goes over objects and thoughts, waiting for Odysseus's return. Reinforcing the reader's gradual involvement, the parts of the poem—the sentences themselves—unwind, act out the message, while mentioning it: "At first the shapes seem satisfied / to keep the dark. But glimmers of them gather- / ing in huddled companies, next one / by one they press toward her. . . ."

And these things, these elements of the poem, these accumulating touches that become the total experience, unfold by unspectacular constructions. Often, and typically, the sentences link forward by appositives, by gradual refining of the assertions that the poems consist of. It is as if Theodore Weiss picks up some topic and then examines it deftly and relentlessly till he has brought out more aspects than other people would have noticed. Then at the end of the poem he is satisfied just to wait: the journey of discovery is enough; the reader is to abide and know, but not to be nudged by the author. (pp. 8, 10)

Weiss's poems stretch the attention through their multiple appositives and successive adjustments, and through interruptions that delay the expected closure. These suspenseful entries leading into calm new experiences often give a poem a surreal effect, a holding off of the ordinary world. But suspense resolves itself, and by close reading one discovers clear resolutions. The upshot is that the poem satisfies even the matter-of-fact reader, but only after flights over some dreamlike terrain.

But the audience otherwise natural for these poems encounters a complexity. Despite their low-key language and ultimate consistency—their straightforward quality—the poems homogenize into themselves a host of literary allusions. This literary aura complicates the appeal of the plain style: a reader must like accuracy and directness, but also be ready for myths and legends, and even for references to the vocabulary of literary criticism. (p. 10)

> *William Stafford, in* The New York Times Book Review *(© 1977 by The New York Times Company; reprinted by permission), January 2, 1977.*

The miniaturist . . . finds its counterpart in Theodore Weiss, or at least in an attitude echoed throughout *Fireweeds*. . . . His St. Atomy is its spokesman, in a poem called *A Slow Burn:*

> Although I am a very little
> known and even less respected saint,
> I have my uses. Unlike those who pant
> for the instant bliss, consummate
> glory, of an all-consuming blaze, I am
> content with less, a steady smolder.
> Let the godly say who lasts longer,
> who's the one grows soonest cold.

Elsewhere Weiss celebrates the poetry tuned to the minor scale: "not a mad beeline / to the honey but laying out the slow, / pedestrian cobbles block by block, / then footing it uphill." Such insistent modesty risks turning coy or, worse, pharisaical. But more to the point, in Weiss's case the caution is unnecessary—and therefore annoying—since he is a fine, substantial poet. The reader familiar with Weiss's previous work will find nothing unexpected here. The tone is familiar, with its slightly professorial, gently self-deprecating accents of a man who meets "the monster deep / inside with a paper shield, a vision / that's bifocal, and a year's supply / of ballpoint ink." Weiss composes these poems as if they were letters to acquaintances who share his values and culture, but whom he does not know well enough to write with any urgent intimacy. Poems like *The Library Revisited, News from Avignon,* or *A Charm Against the Toothache* are warmly humorous and intelligent, but do tend to grow discursive. Even as several poems could have been pruned from this long book, so too any single poem could have been sharpened or braced—say, by Hollander's flair for wit and paradox, or Wilbur's elegant schemes and grids.

In his critical study of Shakespeare, *The Breath of Clowns and Kings* (1971), Weiss admires that poet's prodigious learning and canny economy. Not surprisingly, these are prominent qualities of Weiss's own nostalgic and domestic poems, which ring changes on a few themes and situations, especially the ways in which marriage completes its couple, and the relationship memory establishes with the past. . . . And this book's jewel and its touchstone is its longest poem, *The Storeroom*, a sixteen-part lyric retelling of *The Odyssey*'s last books. The figure of Odysseus, with his frank curiosity and ironic heroism, has always attracted Weiss, but the speaker in this poem is Penelope, at the moment she visits the cool, dark room in which her absent husband's gear is stored. And that storeroom is, of course, memory's own. The poem employs a kind of stylized archaism, not of diction (as Pound might have done it) but of a syntax which diffuses its accounts and suspends its resolutions, resulting in a language half-dream, half-chant, appropriate to the woman's projective invocation of her husband. . . . But the poem is no conventional romance; or else it is precisely that. In its generic perspective, the poem poses time as a story in which we read our parts, accomplish our plots. The final section is an eloquent summary of that confidence:

> But still she takes her time as he knows how
> to do, for time is what they have together,
> have apart, proved most accomplished in.
> Both understand like stars tales of such deeds—
> the lightning and its thunder, laggarding—
> require time, time to be heard, be felt.
>
> Had they not learned it at the first
> from one another, earth's own seasoned dance,
> the measured pace of things completing
> themselves,
>   from their good time together,
> the great tide washing over them, yet lovely-
> slow, as honey, pouring from a vase?
>
> (pp. 45-7)

J. D. McClatchy, in Poetry (© *1977 by The Modern Poetry Association; reprinted by permission of the Editor of* Poetry), *April, 1977.*

*   *   *

WILLIAMS, Tennessee   1914-

An American playwright, novelist, and short story writer who once was hailed as the most important playwright in America, Williams has been unsuccessful in recent years in meeting the standards set by such earlier works as *A Streetcar Named Desire* **and** *The Glass Menagerie*. **His works chronicle man's ambitions and his eventual, inevitable ruin. Williams was awarded the Pulitzer Prize in 1948 and 1955. (See also** *CLC*, **Vols. 1, 2, 5, 7, and** *Contemporary Authors*, **Vols. 5-8, rev. ed.)**

Whatever your feelings about him, there is no denying that Tennessee Williams is one of America's authentic bards. And when such a person attempts to "tell all," it is perhaps our cultural duty to pay close attention to what he has to say about his life, about the material and spiritual conditions under which his songs of neurotic desperation and misery were written.

The most arresting aspect of [*Tennessee Williams: A Memoir*] is its patent honesty; only someone talking from the heart could be so corny. The style, moreover, is off-

hand, slipshod, hardly the work one would expect from the creator of *A Streetcar Named Desire* and *The Glass Menagerie*. Yet it is precisely the author of those plays who is addressing us, using a social and literary manner derived almost solely from the faded, tacky elegance, the wistful falls of Blanche DuBois' characteristic rhetoric. . . .

In putting together this book, Williams clearly hoped to reach the roots of the hell he has suffered during the last 15 years. He manages a bare, albeit moving recital of the terrible events that landed him in the psychiatric ward, but neither he nor we learn what caused his breakdown. It would be easy to suggest that Blanche, or her spirit, got in the way; more likely, the playwright instinctively realized he had better leave the sources of his art unexamined if he hoped to go on writing.

Williams suffers from an intense narcissism that prevents him from standing back to look at himself. It is a measure of his honesty, though, that faced by pages uncovering so much a cautious person would want to hide, and surely aware that he was not achieving his original objective, he did not burn the manuscript. Instead, he kept right on with his undigested confessions. . . .

He is a bard who speaks for some part of every man yet is utterly incapable of speaking for himself—although, as he repeatedly declares, his life depends on it. (p. 18)

The social goad is more accurately described than any other—sexual, philosophical or artistic—because it is the one Williams reacts to with his whole being. And his personal inflection of the social problem—all those ladies fallen from former grandeur, itself shoddy and rather squalid but nevertheless believed in—would seem to account for his public status much more than his concern for what Jean Cocteau called "the malady of love."

Remarkably, throughout the '60s when Williams was so bound up by neurosis and guilt and paranoia that he literally could not speak, he continued to write play after play—a fact attributable, I suspect from his tongue-tied memoirs, to his violent need for success, his devouring ambition, and not to some vague esthetic predilection. Indeed, looking back on his plays, it is the social content that looms ever larger, making Williams into a kind of sensitive John O'Hara or, in his best moments, a grotesque F. Scott Fitzgerald. (pp. 18-19)

Raymond Rosenthal, "Inhibited Introspection," in The New Leader (© *1976 by the American Labor Conference on International Affairs, Inc.), March 29, 1976, pp. 18-19.*

[Tennessee Williams] is a great ventriloquist, in both the literal and the metaphoric meanings of the word. [In his Memoirs he] speaks from the belly and also casts his voice onto those around him, especially those who shared his early years. The sections on his childhood and adolescence —a period not entirely over, as he is the first to suggest— confirm my long-held view as a critic of his work in performance that it is sometimes too personal, too intimate, too incestuous, to be acceptable to outsiders without embarrassment. In a sense, we have already had his Memoirs in his work, especially in *The Glass Menagerie* and *Cat on a Hot Tin Roof*. This is not to say, on the evidence of his own report, that he is simply a transcriber from life. The skeletons in his cupboards are the real ones all right but he fleshes them with imaginary curves and muscles the way we all do with our past when we make the dead or dying dance to entertain our coevals. But where our audience is numbered on one hand, his are numberless.

Though he appears in *Memoirs* to be saying only one thing at a time in a clumsily truthful way about his family and his friends, he is actually saying several things at once on different levels. For this reason, he is often, and this is the best definition I know, writing poetry.

> *Alan Brien, "Tennessee in Pyjamas," in* The Spectator *(© 1976 by* The Spectator; *reprinted by permission of* The Spectator), *November 20, 1976, p. 19.*

Williams' plays—the comedies as well as the tragedies—are chronicles of incest, whether the characters involved are aware of it or not. (Often, it is a character's subliminal awareness of the desire to commit incest that Williams embodies onstage, to great effect, as a scarcely treadable knife-edge of hysteria.) Williams' ideal hero is the incestuous homosexual, who, however guilty he may feel at being tempted to break the gravest of our taboos, runs no risk of leaving behind a proof of his misconduct. This lack of risk becomes, in Williams' writing, a kind of schoolboy glee, otherwise inexplicable.

"The Eccentricities of a Nightingale" . . . is Williams' ingenious reworking of an earlier, failed play of his, "Summer and Smoke." "Eccentricities" is certain to find a place for itself in the Williams canon as a pleasing small play of the second rank. . . . (pp. 134-35)

> *Brendan Gill, in* The New Yorker *(© 1976 by* The New Yorker Magazine, Inc.), *December 6, 1976.*

There was an unexpected prologue to last Friday night's performance of *The Night of the Iguana.* At about the time the performance was scheduled to begin, a woman in the audience—a stout, middle-aged woman in a blue print dress —suddenly began shouting, "Start the show! Start the show! I want to see Dorothy McGuire! I love Dorothy McGuire!" The people sitting next to her were quickly evacuated to other seats; usherettes, and someone who must have been the house manager came to reason with her, but she continued to shout. . . .

After a moment of shock, the audience began to get ugly, applauding and laughing derisively. The woman applauded back, moving her hands stiffly as if they were flippers. "Listen, you old bag, get out!" somebody shouted at her. "Throw her out and start the show!" shouted somebody else. Some people began to boo the shouters. "All I want to see," said the woman in the blue dress firmly, "is Dorothy McGuire, and then I will leave."

Finally Miss McGuire herself appeared, crossed the stage to where the woman was sitting, spoke to her soothingly and hugged her. And the woman, who had pulled back when anyone had touched her, quietly allowed Miss McGuire to lead her away—as if, like Blanche DuBois, she had always depended on the kindness of strangers. As they crossed the stage toward the exit, Miss McGuire—who had met the situation with remarkable poise and grace and kindness—paused and said to the audience. "I'd just like to introduce another fellow human being." It was a deserved rebuke to those who had shouted abuse at the madwoman —and it was also everything Tennessee Williams has ever written, in a nutshell. . . .

Sometimes, especially in his more recent plays, [Mr. Williams] begins to get tiresome, endlessly manhandling our pity: Brother, can you spare a tear? He has always been inclined to sentimentality. But in his best plays he *earns* for his characters the pity he demands, and what becomes astonishing is the lush richness and variety that he finds within the nutshell of his obsession. *Night of the Iguana* (1961) is the last of these best plays—or, rather, the last so far; is there anyone who does not hope that Mr. Williams, like Nonno, will fulfill himself as a writer at least once more before the end of his career . . .?

There are only two basic character types in Williams. One is the subject of his obsession, the lady in the blue dress— call her Blanche—unable to operate on the realistic level; the other is the one who shouts, "Throw her out and start the show!"—call him Stanley. In *Night of the Iguana,* there are three Blanches; two of them are men. Analogously, Stanley is a woman: a raucous, sexy widow named Maxine who is entirely at ease on the realistic level—it is doubtful whether she really understands that any other level exists. In an early scene of *A Streetcar Named Desire,* Stanley Kowalski takes off his shirt. "Be comfortable is my motto," he explains to Blanche. In *Night of the Iguana,* Maxine walks in with her shirt on, but her boobs practically hanging out of it. "I never dress in September," she explains to Shannon, who replies, "Well, just, just—button your shirt up." Shannon, like Blanche, is both promiscuous and puritanical. Mr. Williams's concerns are always the same, but their contexts and configurations change in fascinating ways. . . .

Mr. Williams loves his unlikely waifs and strays, his yearning, idealistic derelicts, his end-of-the-rope brigade—as well he might, since they are all clearly aspects of himself. He wants us to love and honor them as he does: if we do, he has succeeded; if not, not. In this play, he treats them, as they treat each other, with a touching delicacy and tenderness. As usual, he is scrupulous in not offering his damaged idealists as examples of moral perfection. Shannon is as big a phony as Blanche herself and has the additional unpleasant habit of seducing young girls and then devastating them with his disgust in the morning. Miss Jelkes and Nonno are also hustlers in their way. But, like Blanche, none of them ever lied in their hearts, whatever that means (and I can't tell you, but I know). They are among "The last cavaliers, the ones with the rusty armor and soiled white plumes," on whom he invokes a blessing in Camino Real—and in every other play.

But how attractive they are, these "cavaliers," how exotic, how gallant! How *easy* it is to pity them! The stout woman in the blue dress . . .—she was not attractive, nor exotic, nor noticeably gallant, lacking a sentimental playwright to romanticize her. Where were her plumes, her armor? Was *she* a cavalier? For Mr. Williams, perhaps, she would be. Perhaps the fraud is not in the colorful romanticism of the playwright but in the apparent drabness of real life, which prevents us from seeing that the shapeless crazy lady with her awkward gestures and her slurred speech is really a cavalier and taking her to our hearts.

And yet, should it really take all those trappings, those plumes, those fascinatingly exotic histories, to introduce us to those at the ends of their ropes as fellow human beings? Isn't it often precisely for their drabness that those at rope's end must deserve to be pitied? I was not only touched by stirred by *The Night of the Iguana;* it opened things in me. I respect the respect for discipline and understatement that appears in the midst of its lushness. But I do not entirely trust it. Mr. Williams lavishes sympathy on all his con persons, but he has little or none for the women in Shannon's party, the "football squad of old maids" from Baptist Female College in Blowing Rock, Texas, whom Shannon has failed and cheated and misused in so many ways. They are not to be forgiven for being who they are. (p. 73)

> *Julius Novick, "Mr. Williams and the Crazy Lady," in* The Village Voice *(reprinted by permission of* The Village Voice; *copyright © by The Village Voice, Inc., 1976), December 27, 1976, pp. 73-4.*

What gives *The Night of the Iguana* a special position in Tennessee Williams' *oeuvre* is that it is his last decent play. Not great, surely; not even very good, I dare say; but decent. It is still cut from the good old cloth even if the tailoring has become sloppy. After that comes a depressing sequence of ever-worse works in which a glimmer of the former great talent can only occasionally be detected amid the debris. . . .

The subject of *Iguana* is really loneliness and what, if anything, can be done about it.

One can find the theme of fleeting, generally sexual associations as a compromise between the demands of commitment and the fear of loneliness throughout Williams' works, the best known example being Blanche DuBois' famous line about having always depended on the kindness of strangers. Though typical of many homosexual lives, this casual promiscuity is by no means limited to them. And, at the other end of the scale, there often appears in Williams the pure and virginal young woman—sometimes sweetly resigned, sometimes neurotic and hysterical—the resigned archetype being Laura Wingfield in *The Glass Menagerie*. (p. 25)

[When] Williams now tries to expunge [a torrid steaminess], by rewriting his plays, [he] only leaves them diminished. But there remains as evident as ever [in *The Night of the Iguana*] that unfortunate, heavy-handed symbolism of the iguana, representing both the tied-up Shannon and humanity in general at the end of its rope. If only the symbolism could be cut loose from Williams' plays! This one is altogether overlong anyway, having (like other Williams dramas) grown from a short story into a one-acter, and thence into three acts. There are, accordingly, painful longueurs here along with sparks of genius. . . .

This sad fact was confirmed by the first Broadway production of *Eccentricities of a Nightingale*, Williams' 1964 reworking of his 1948 *Summer and Smoke*. In a prefatory note to the published text, he declares it "a better work than the play from which it derives." Not so; the original had much more texture, variety, intensity and, yes, steaminess. On however melodramatic a level, a great deal more was going on in *Summer and Smoke;* the hero and heroine had flesh-and-blood complexities rather than being stripped down to single characteristics, and those insufficiently analyzed. As in *Iguana*, Williams provides far too simplistic explanations for his creatures' neuroses—a schematic overinvolvement with the parent of the opposite sex complicated, not very subtly or interestingly, by an aborted relationship to God.

Nightingale comes across as a pale outline of a play. . . . (p. 26)

John Simon, "Two from Williams' Menagerie," in The New Leader *(© by the American Labor Conference on International Affairs, Inc.), January 3, 1977, pp. 25-6.*

Poor Tennessee Williams! He is, or was, our greatest living playwright, second only to Eugene O'Neill at his best, and it is infinitely sad to see him deteriorate before our eyes. It is even worse than watching a woman we love grow old, because that happens gradually and symmetrically with our own aging. But here we are, still as alert as ever, and Williams, for a long time now, has been giving us stones for bread—really merely watered-down reworkings of his old situations, characters, ideas, and dialogue, exactly as in all the recent plays bearing his signature, itself most likely merely stenciled on.

A man who would steal and resteal from himself is the saddest of failures. Reprehensible as it may be to steal from others, it is at least enterprising: a sign of awareness that the outside world exists. . . . Whatever fund he had for attending to the life of people and ideas around him, he has long since dissipated. When he does write a play, it is perforce a rehash, or at the utmost a replay of youthful memories that have been getting thinner and dimmer. And when he tries to write about his later experiences—as in *Small Craft Warnings* and *In the Bar of a Tokyo Hotel*—it comes out lifeless and third-hand, as if seen through the double screen of his former writings and a mind grown soft from self-indulgence.

Vieux Carré, his disaster this season, is a depressing example. For the umpteenth time—if you count Williams' long plays, short plays, long and short fictions, poems and memoirs—we are back in a boarding house in, naturally, New Orleans. Or perhaps unnaturally: Now that Williams has confessed his homosexuality, the plays are allowed to assume a more flagrant deviancy. . . . (p. 21)

As if [the plot] weren't ghastly enough—decked out with every kind of pseudopoeticism, painful attempt at humor and even more painful stabs at pathos—[the play] is further undercut with frequent interlardings of recitative. Writer [the protagonist] either sentimentally reminisces about the house and its inmates from the point of view of the future, or, right in the present, summarizes bits of the play that Playwright was too lazy to dramatize.

The writing is consistently pastiche-Williams: "Now they enter into the lighted area of my memory—which is not realistic, as you may know by now." A dramatist who has to explain his play is in sorry shape indeed. (pp. 21-2)

Consider, finally, the truly insufferable would-be lyrical closing line: "All that remains is echoes, echoes of echoes —of no voices. This house is empty now." Note the flat, anticlimactic last sentence meant to provide a dying fall, but actually dropping dead. It worked so much better in that incomparably finer memory play, *The Glass Menagerie*, where the autobiographical narrator hero concluded with, "Blow out your candles, Laura—and so goodbye . . ." Nothing so pretentious as echoes of echoes, only a simple good-bye—not a spelling out of the obvious: We can see for ourselves that Williams' house is empty now. (p. 22)

John Simon, in The New Leader *(© 1977 by the American Labor Conference on International Affairs, Inc.), June 20, 1977.*

WILSON, Edmund   1895-1972

Essayist, critic, novelist, short story writer, poet, and playwright, Wilson, whose writing spans nearly a half century, was one of the foremost American men of letters of the twentieth century. Most of his later works, for which he will probably be best remembered, are discussions and histories of literature. (See also *CLC*, Vols. 1, 2, 3, and *Contemporary Authors*, Vols. 1-4, rev. ed., obituary, Vols. 37-40, rev. ed.)

Young Wilson [once said, "What] I want to do is to try to get to know something about all the main departments of human thought." This ambition remained his for a lifetime, and in it he succeeded to a degree that makes nearly all other contemporary intellectuals seem parochial. (p. 386)

Wilson was explicit both about the values of literature and about his own designs on it. He wrote, in *The Shores of Light,* of gaining from his Princeton mentor Christian Gauss "the vision of language and literature as something representing the continuous and never-ending flow of man's struggle to think the thoughts which, when put into action, constitute in the aggregate the advance of civilization." In *The Triple Thinkers* he told us that "my purpose [in discussing literature] has always been to try to contribute something new. . . ." And in *The Bit Between My Teeth* he wrote that, as a critic, "My function . . . has been to make an effort to concentrate synoptically, as they say of the Gospels, to bring into one system, the literatures of several cultures which have not always been in close communication, which in some cases have hardly been aware of one another."

In executing this function Wilson was always able to move among languages, literatures and disciplines with an authority that is rare enough for anyone these days, and nearly unheard of for an American. He learned Greek, Latin, French, Italian, and German early in life; Russian, when he was in his forties; Hebrew, when he was nearly sixty; and Hungarian, when he was past sixty. . . . [His] remarks on English and American novels and poems arose from an uncommonly catholic sensibility. Furthermore, his evaluations of literature were sharpened by his wide reading in such other disciplines as history, politics and psychology.

He wrote, I believe, three first-rate works of literary criticism and one of an order still higher. In *The Wound and the Bow* and *The Triple Thinkers,* . . . Wilson discusses—always thoughtfully and sometimes dazzlingly—writers as diverse as Hemingway, Casanova and Housman. A third book, *Patriotic Gore* (a study of the literature of the American Civil War) was initially planned as a single volume and is an exemplary literary history. It is with a fourth book alone, however, *Axel's Castle,* his study of the French Symbolist poets and their influence on Yeats, Joyce and Eliot, that Wilson can be said to have made a seminal contribution to the study of literature. As much as later critics may have extended and refined Wilson's ideas in *Axel's Castle,* it is that rare work that can never really be dated or superseded. Despite its narrower chronological scope, it belongs on the shelf near Erich Auerbach's *Mimesis.*

Edmund Wilson did so much so well that it may be ungracious or perverse to wish for more. But looking over his books . . . , I noticed how seldom he took on the real giants of literature, other than those of this century. There are exceptions to his neglect of these figures: he wrote brilliantly on Sophocles' *Philoctetes* and on Dickens; he helped to give Pushkin to the English-speaking world; and he discussed Ben Jonson, though badly, I think. That is

nearly all. Intelligent and germane references to Dante, Shakespeare and Goethe pervade his judgment of infinitely lesser writers, but there is no substantial comment on these men. There is, in *Classics and Commercials,* a review of J. Dover Wilson's book on Falstaff, in which Edmund Wilson makes a few brief and unconvincing remarks on the nature of Shakespeare's art. There is even less on Homer, Virgil, Milton, Dostoevski, Tolstoi.

C. S. Lewis once observed that no poet is under contract to write every poem that we think suitable for him, and the same independence surely must be allowed to literary critics. The proposition, moreover, that a critic of great talents *should,* for some abstract reason, focus on older rather than newer writers is quite unsupportable. But at the same time one naturally wonders what is down the road not taken. Edmund Wilson had those gifts of erudition, critical acumen and linguistic ease, together with a blessed distance from jejune academic quarrels, that, on the evidence of *Axel's Castle,* just might have allowed him full membership in the tiny community of great modern philologists—along with Auerbach, E. R. Curtius, Leo Spitzer, a few more Europeans, and perhaps a single American, Kenneth Burke. (pp. 386-87)

> *Mark Taylor, "Edmund Wilson and Literature," in* Commonweal *(copyright © 1972 Commonweal Publishing Co., Inc.; reprinted by permission of Commonweal Publishing Co., Inc.), July 14, 1972, pp. 386-87.*

[After] World War II a change can be seen in Wilson's work, that he becomes more aloof and misanthropic, that his writing moves toward fragmentation as if suffering from the loss of meaningful direction, and that the tone of some of this writing is one of weariness. Wilson's remoteness can be seen in *Europe Without Baedeker* (1947), his collection of pieces on England and Europe immediately after the war, in which he tends to regard Europe as a sordid piece of real estate and, oddly enough, to make no distinction between the Allied and the Nazi powers. In some respects, his mind seems already closed and unreceptive. He gives no sense of sympathy with people in their suffering during the war or after, and sometimes describes them with biological images. In *Upstate* (1971) he describes people who seem to him very common, and wonders why they should wish "to reproduce their kind." A deep disillusionment runs through all of the latter half of Wilson's career.

The crisis of Wilson's later years would seem to involve not only the political disillusionment he felt at the end of the thirties, but even the rational life itself. War is a recurring subject in some of the later books, and in *A Piece of My Mind* (1956), attempting to account for it, Wilson rejects Marx's economic exploitation as an adequate explanation. Its causes are irrational. Having lived through two World Wars in which he did not believe and which produced only an accelerated cheapening and depersonalization of society, as well as the nuclear age that threatens our survival, he can no longer believe in the power of rationality to create a humane and meaningful world. He withdraws into his "pocket of the past," into the period of the early republic in which rationality and individual integrity were important. *Patriotic Gore,* apparently about the Civil War and its consequences, is Wilson's disillusioned testament of the 20th century experience he has known. In this, Wilson comes to resemble his friend John Dos Passos who returned to a Jeffersonian vision, and even to resemble his college friend F. Scott Fitzgerald, whose *Tender Is the Night* uses the tragedy of the American Civil War to express his sense of the betrayal of life. (p. 286)

> *Robert Emmet Long, "The Decade of 'Axel's Castle'," in* The Nation *(copyright 1972 by The Nation Associates, Inc.), October 2, 1972, pp. 285-86.*

Wilson was the foremost American man of letters of the twentieth century. He was also, I think, a great American sage. He embodied that rare combination of stubborn scepticism, inveterate innocence and sturdy, clarifying common sense which we used to consider peculiarly American—almost an American invention—but whose exponents are now sunk under the horizon, as deep as Atlantis. Wilson's sort, if it has not quite vanished from America, is in the fast-dwindling, minuscle minority: although once dominant in the Republic's affairs, this old American type is now almost completely disfranchised and disregarded. . . .

His place in the hall of literary immortals is secure; in fact, he is there already, looking unimpressed by the company, and seated between Sainte-Beuve and Dr Johnson. (p. 210)

> *T. S. Matthews, "Edmund Wilson Revisited," in* The Spectator *(© 1974 by The Spectator; reprinted by permission of The Spectator), August 17, 1974, pp. 208-10.*

"The more kinds of character a man has," Edmund Wilson wrote in an early entry in his journals, "the more kinds of characters he can create." The remark was made about literary artists generally but it applies handsomely to Wilson in particular. Wilson's character was unitary, of a piece, stamped in brass. It explains why he never turned out first-class fiction. He had not the artist's ventriloqual gift; his own voice too easily drowned out all others. Fiction for Wilson was criticism by other means. A character too bold in outline, too firm in impress is a defect for a novelist, but for any other prose writing a marvelous asset. Yet to criticism, to history, to social reportage Edmund Wilson nonetheless brought the sensibility of the artist. (p. 1)

> *Joseph Epstein, in* The New York Times Book Review *(© 1975 by The New York Times Company; reprinted by permission), June 15, 1975.*

The publication of Wilson's notebooks of the '20s . . . show his sexual scorecards mingled as if naively with landscape descriptions and intellectual ruminations and the anecdotes of his rather silly upper-class friends. The lonely bookish child is staring with a frown from the shadows of the Red Bank mansion, where the mother was deaf and the father nervously fragile; the America he perceives seems grim and claustrophobic, though hectic. There is a true whiff of Hell in Hecate County, less in the specific touches of supernatural diabolism with which this utter rationalist rather quaintly adorned his tales, but in the low ceilings and cheap underwear of the sex idyll, the clothes and neuroses of the copulators. America has always tolerated sex as a joke, as a night's prank in the burlesque theater or fairground tent; but not as a solemn item in the work of life. It was Wilson's deadly earnest, his unwinking naturalistic refusal to release us into farce, that made *Hecate County* in all its dignity and high intent the target of a (successful!) prosecution for obscenity.

Rereading, now, in this liberated age, and in the light of the notebooks, one expects to find the sex tame. And so, in a sense, it is. . . . In the fiction, Wilson sets down no sexual

detail in simple celebration, to please and excite himself, but always to illuminate the social or psychological condition of the two women. The Anna of "Princess," compared to the confusing love-object of the journals, is admirably coherent, as the product of certain cultural and economic conditions, in Brooklyn; how telling, for instance, is her reluctance to be seen naked, as if nudity—to the upper classes an esthetic proclamation, a refutation of shame—evokes inhibitions having nothing to do with sexual acts, which she performs freely. And how plausibly, if ploddingly, are the clothes of the two women described and made to symbolize their social presences. Such details—seized, we sometimes feel, by a sensibility that doubts its own grasp on the "real"—lend the factual sexual descriptions a weight, a heat, far from tame. It is Imogen . . . who occasions Wilson's subtlest, harshest instances of sexual realism. . . . Gently enough, the failure of an overprepared, ideal love to connect is masterfully anatomized, and movingly contrasted with his tawdry, harried affair with Anna. . . . (pp. 40-1)

"The Princess with the Golden Hair" is a love-poem to [Anna] and one of the best of his writing generation's obligatory love-poems to the lower classes. . . . It is, like Thornton Wilder's *Heaven's My Destination,* a generous aberration, a visit to the underworld by a member of the last predominantly Wasp generation of writers, the last that conceived of itself as an aristocracy. Wilson's portrait of this one slum-child lives by her light, the "something so strong and instinctive that it could outlive the hurts and infections, the defilements, among which we lived." The fiction she inhabits, as its true princess, overtops the flanking Gothic vignettes (though "Ellen Terhune" has its authenticity, and the last story a wrenched pain). . . . His fiction, generally cluttered, savoring of the worked-up, of collected details moved by *force majeure* of the writer's mind, here finds a theme that moves *him.* Sex was his one way in, into the America to which his response, however much he wished it otherwise, was to reach for anaesthesia, whether found in books or bottles. Imogen, in this respect, is a better metaphor for America than Anna; her flamboyant costumes and greedy orgasms serve the same narcissism, reflect the same blank passion to succeed; in her richly, ironically particularized and overfurnished setting, she ends as a comic vision, empty but not unlovable, a gaudy suburban witch, in a land of Hecate Counties. No longer shocking, and never meant to be, this "memoir" remains, I think, a work of exemplary merit, still the most intelligent attempt by an American male to dramatize sexual behavior as a function of, rather than a suspension of, personality. (p. 41)

> *John Updike, in* The New Republic *(reprinted by permission of* The New Republic; *© 1976 by The New Republic Inc.), January 17, 1976.*

*   *   *

WILSON, John Anthony Burgess
See BURGESS, Anthony

*   *   *

WINTERS, Yvor   1900-1968

Winters was an American poet, essayist, and critic whose strict adherence to what some considered a rigid concept of poetry made him extremely controversial. (See also *CLC,* Vol. 4, and *Contemporary Authors,* Vols. 11-12; obituary,

Vols. 25-28, rev. ed.; *Contemporary Authors Permanent Series*, Vol. 1.)

When D. H. Lawrence died, E. M. Forster, in his famous letter to the *Nation and Athenaeum,* observed that "no one who alienates both Mrs. Grundy and Aspasia can hope for a good obituary press." Where criticism rather than sex is concerned, the cases of F. R. Leavis and Yvor Winters are somewhat analogous. I have spoken elsewhere . . . of some of the ways in which their work can offend academics. This offensiveness would not by itself, however, have been enough to account for the boycotting that for a number of years their works endured in the academic world. For even academics, faced with disturbing critical innovators, can be intimidated or impressed if it is known that those innovators are in good standing in intellectual circles outside the academy. (p. 963)

Well, obviously enough, [this] could not be said of Leavis or, after the early thirties, of Winters. Leavis on Auden, Woolf, Joyce, the Pound of the *Cantos,* Marianne Moore, Wyndham Lewis, Lawrence Durrell, the Sitwells and so on; Winters on Yeats, Pound, Joyce, Eliot, Hart Crane, *et al.*—the record is horrendous, or at least has generally been judged to have been so. Actually the record is a trifle more complex than that. I mean, if there is a book that takes one more illuminatingly than *In Defense of Reason* into the dynamics of modern American poetry, I have still to come across it. (p. 964)

[It] seems to me that something more is involved than simply the nature of specific judgments—something involving the whole notion of the "modern" in relation to the "traditional." The real offense of Leavis and Winters consisted—and still consists—in their having presumed to attack a sizable number of avant-garde writers at all. And to admire either or both of the two men strongly is to feel ineluctably, at least if one is an academic oneself, that one is liable to be considered guilty of opting for an inhibitingly academic kind of traditionalism, as against the stir and flow of all that is vital today. (pp. 964-65)

[One must note] the intensely individual quality of both Leavis and Winters, their obvious striving to see as precisely as possible, to record as precisely as possible, and to act upon as full a range of their perceptions as possible. And both men are in fact intensely "modern" in the sense in which such figures as Kierkegaard, Camus, and Eliot are "modern." This is most apparent, perhaps, once one gets past his alleged and much misrepresented classicism, in Winters' case, especially in his poetry and in that very distinguished short story "Brink of Darkness." "Every poem of Winters'," Alvin B. Kernan observes in the course of an excellent brief discussion of Winters' verse . . . , "is a dramatization of the conflict between the moral perceiver and a spiritually empty world which is nevertheless so solid and real that the confrontation cannot be avoided. . . . In this war the struggle is a deadly one, and it is always intensified by the attraction that the object exerts over the poet, threatening to pull him into its chaos, its emptiness, its darkness. . . ." But this same metaphysical dread seems to me to pervade his critical prose too, not in the sense that a thesis is being argued but in the sense that to admire the works that he celebrates, in the contexts that he furnishes for them, is to feel oneself being edged toward a perception of the world that is at times almost overpowering in its absence of reassuring solidities and unquestionable "natural" *données.* And when, apropos of Hopkins' "No worst, there is none," he says impatiently, "But what are these

mountains of the mind? One does not enquire because one holds them cheap, but because one has hung on so many oneself, so various in their respective terrors, that one is perplexed to assign a particular motive," one believes him as one would believe virtually no other critic. . . . [In] general, if what we are talking about are the intense, and often intensely painful or disturbing, experiences of very sensitive, intelligent, passionate and complex minds, then both Leavis and Winters, in the revealed quality and scope of their awareness of their times, are modern in a way that our professional propagandists on behalf of The New—promoters, that is, of a reassuring collective sense of what stratagems we should be using to avoid being annoyed or puzzled or overly agitated by the unfamiliar—never come within streets of.

But of course with both men we are also about as far as one can intelligently get—outside of an orthodox religious system at least—from any notion of discrete selves, creative or otherwise, flourishing by virtue of an inner light or faltering because that light mysteriously dims or because there is an insufficient confidence in it. Both of them have again and again emphasized the fact that, in poetry especially, the preponderant tradition at any time (which is not to say the *only* tradition) helps to nurture or to starve a writer's native talents. (pp. 967-68)

[What] we see in Winters, I believe, is a heroic endeavor . . . to give back to ideas their existential weight by looking intently at the quality of individual minds engaged in certain kinds of dealing with them (Henry Adams, Emerson, Melville, Poe, Eliot, Hart Crane, and so on). He has brought out brilliantly the key positions that certain figures occupy in relation to twentieth-century American thought, either as enthusiastic participants in it, or as the makers of certain moves in the past that are logical prerequisites for some of the moves made now, or, obliquely, as exemplars of major qualities that are now significantly undervalued. (His dealings with the formal aspects of poetry in terms of the implicit revelations in specific works of possibilities inhering in certain forms, conventions, and procedures are similarly existential.) And among the more memorable of his tracings of the existential histories of ideas . . . are his eight pages in *The Anatomy of Nonsense* about Deism and Romanticism, his discussion in the same book of New England theology from Calvinism to Unitarianism, and the masterly long paragraph in *Maule's Curse,* apropos of Henry James, about New England intellectual history. Furthermore, when he says, "I do not believe . . . that the history of literature can be grasped unless one has a critical understanding of it; but it seems to me equally obvious that a critical understanding is frequently quite impossible unless one knows a good deal of history. The critical and the historical understanding are merely aspects of a single process"—he is clearly not speaking only of the history of literature and ideas. Though one would not immediately adduce his work as evidence of what Leavis calls "the inevitable way in which serious literary interest develops towards the sociological," one carries away from a reading of it as a whole a considerably stronger sense of the density and intractability of past phases of society than one does from, say, such critics as ostensibly preoccupied with the past and "tradition" as Eliot, Pound, and Tate. . . . [The] actual number of pages or passages [in *Maule's Curse*] touching on [historical] topics may be relatively few. But I can only say they *tell* and that when, for instance, apropos of the history of frontier America, Winters casually lets fall a remark like, "Anyone who will take the trouble to acquaint himself with the works of Parkman—and anyone who will not is to be commiserated in general and distrusted in particular as a commentator on certain aspects of American literature and history . . . ,'' one believes him.

In sum, then, I think that one can see Winters as having been engaged in a lifelong struggle with the sort of conditions that Leavis points to when, apropos of a particular kind of "mistaken preoccupation with being American," he comments that "it rejects something profoundly and essentially American that held the promise of a rich future, and rejects it for what is American in an excluding and impoverishing way. . . ." . . . [It] is, one feels, with a peculiarly insidious kind of temporal provinciality that Winters has been concerned in his animadversions on a particular kind of modernity. It is the kind that involves an attempt to shake free of "forms," an excessive confidence in the goodness of the untutored human heart (as located in the bosom of the untutored or self-tutored artist), and a general conviction—fostered, ironically, by a good many "traditional" academics—that in any particular period the distinguished artist not only does but ought to surrender himself gratefully to the procreative embraces of whatever is assumed to be the *Zeitgeist*. I have in mind here such things as his reference to "Dr. W. C. Williams, . . . who more perhaps than any writer living encourages in his juniors a profound conviction of their natural rightness, a sentimental debauchery of self-indulgence . . ."; or his judgment that "It does not occur to Frost that he might learn from his betters and improve himself; he can see only two possibilities in his relationship with them—he can be silenced by them or he can ignore them and proceed as before". . . . And one very important consequence of Winters' steady concern with the kind of tradition constituted and the kinds of standards provided by the works, American and European, in which one finds the highest concentration of ordered energy and intelligence is that he can successfully bring off moves that are difficult in the normal American Studies approach to American literature. In the latter, however strong the revealed desire to display the depths and cultural richness in American masterworks, one is all too often, in the absence both of effective comparisons with other works and of firm discriminations between the works of individual authors, faced with what seems to be merely a more sophisticated form of the kind of America First approach of Van Wyck Brooks. But when Winters, in contrast, points to individual works by Americans, whether James or Cunningham, Hawthorne, Stevens, or Bowers, as being quite simply among the greatest in the language, or when, apropos of English poetry from Wyatt to Dryden and American—or largely American—poetry from Jones Very to the present, he declares that "as a result of almost endless reconsideration of the materials of both periods, I have come to the conclusion that the second is certainly the greater"—the judgments, I can only say, invite a good deal of very respectful pondering.

I would like to glance, finally, at [his] handling of the quasi-philosophical position underlying a good deal of modernist thinking. I am speaking of the assumptions that at bottom all is a flux and that the only options are to assume that all perceptions and values are equally unreal and "subjective" or to believe that one can somehow break through to a different and superior kind of reality if one can only get free of enough mind-forged manacles. Certain related moves seem to me involved in [Winters'] dealings with this position.

One—the simplest—is a flat insistence on experiential psy-

chological realities that require no traditional metaphysical underpinning to make them real. I am thinking here of such things as . . . Winters' assertion that: "The realm which we perceive with our unaided senses, the realm which our ancestors took to be real, may be an illusion; but in that illusion we pass our daily lives, including our moral lives; the illusion is quite obviously governed by principles which it is dangerous, often fatal, to violate; this illusion is our reality. I will hereafter refer to it as reality. . . . [It is] the situation in which we live, from which there is no escape save self-destruction, and which we would do well to endeavor to understand." (pp. 976-80)

The second move, which is in no way in conflict with this sort of insistence on the ineluctably *given* in each person's reality, is not simply an acceptance of but an insistence on the *made* aspect of reality and on the centrality, in that making, of all that we mean by "language." . . . This is Winters: "It would be false to say that the occidental mind created the languages of metaphysics, scholasticism, and modern science in order to express what it knows; it created these languages slowly, as ways of living and discovering. The languages were modes of being which were slowly enlarged to discover and embody an increasing extent of reality; they were forms of being and forms of discovery." Here he is again: "But to say that the scholastics made Latin a tool for thought is imprecise: they made it rather a way of thinking, the life of the mind. . . ." (pp. 980-81)

> *John Fraser, "Leavis, Winters and 'Tradition','' in* The Southern Review *(copyright, 1971, by John Fraser), Vol. 7, No. 4, Autumn, 1971, pp. 963-85.*

The Yvor Winters collection [*Uncollected Essays and Reviews*] could only be called distinguished by those who think him a distinguished critic (and he is usually thought a distinguished critic only by those who think him a distinguished poet), but it should prove very useful as an extended demonstration of how he arrived at his hopelessly limited view of poetry, despite a bitter rearguard action fought by his natural intelligence—his crankiness had thoughtful beginnings. . . .

Winters was always a theoretician, yet his early theories were so complicated that anything good could gain acceptance. Lyric poetry was the only kind of poetry you could have. There were, however, five different kinds of lyric, and each kind could have an 'essential unit' composed of either an 'image' or an 'anti-image', which really made, by my calculations, at least ten kinds altogether. There was no hope of applying this scheme with any rigour, and responsiveness was unfettered as a result—everything he admired could be accommodated in it somewhere. He admired extravagantly, but there are worse faults in a young critic, and anyway his heroes and heroines included Marianne Moore and Hart Crane, about both of whom he said some acute things. (p. 243)

It was a considerable gymnastic feat on Winters's part to transform this impressionable but energetic flexibility into the dogmatic torpor he evinced in the Thirties, when Robert Bridges became 'the most valuable model of poetic style to appear since Dryden', and the drear T. Sturge Moore was presented as outsoaring Yeats. Formal versatility and purity of diction: those were the new watchwords. That Bridges's diction abounded with nays, thro's, 'neaths, 'tises and yeas, and that Moore's diction was choc-a-bloc with fains, quaffings, e'ens and dosts, and that the 'formal versatility' of either bard was the most abject pattern-making, Winters didn't mind or even mention. (pp. 243, 46)

Clive James, in New Statesman *(© 1975 The Statesman & Nation Publishing Co. Ltd.), February 21, 1975.*

Y

YATES, Richard 1926-

Yates is an American novelist and short story writer. His novels deal with loneliness and the inability of people to deal with the demands of everyday life in contemporary America. He is probably best known for his novel *Revolutionary Road.* (See also *CLC,* Vol. 7, and *Contemporary Authors,* Vols. 5-8, rev. ed.)

The journey from innocence to experience, from illusion to reality, has long been a traditional undertaking of the novel. "Easter Parade," the fifth novel of Richard Yates, plays with this tradition as he describes a journey from innocence to renewed innocence, from illusion to fresh illusion.

"Easter Parade" explores the lives of a woman and her two daughters; it is a sad tale of marriage and divorce, and a still sadder one of sexual liberation. . . .

"Easter Parade" is a spare, yet wrenching tale. Yates enters completely and effortlessly into the lives of his characters. There are no calligraphic embellishments of any kind, no stunts, nothing flashy. The author is wholly absorbed in his story; his prose is very close to the rhythms of actual speech.

Yates is capable of speaking eloquently on the death of the family with a casual, deft question. When Emily visits her sister in the state hospital where both Sarah and Pookie are confined, she asks Sarah how to reach her mother's building. "And Emily instantly realized what a foolish question that was. How could Sarah know the location of any other building when she was locked into this one?"

The image of mother and daughter locked into separate stone buildings in some vast impersonal construction is never underlined by the author; it is nothing spectacular, but its strength is considerable and cumulative, and, when compounded with others like it, takes on the solidity of brick upon brick. . . .

Taking upon himself a seemingly thankless task, Yates writes powerfully of exasperating people, of people who refuse to shape up, of experience that never ripens into wisdom, of reality persistently shunned, but never evaded for long. (p. 4)

> *A. G. Mojtabai, in* The New York Times Book Review (© *1976 by The New York Times Company; reprinted by permission), September 19, 1976.*

[For many years it] appeared self-evident that [Richard] Yates, who is now fifty, was not, and would not become, a prolific writer, and then, suddenly, two . . . novels in two years, *Disturbing the Peace* last fall and *The Easter Parade* now. The fact is all the more remarkable when one considers the kind of writer Yates is: careful, scrupulous, exact, faultless, every inch a purveyor of *le mot juste,* the antithesis of someone like, say, Thomas Wolfe. His pages must have been reworked many times, but it is impossible, seeing them in print, to imagine them in any other, earlier state.

And the creative outburst is more remarkable still when one considers the consuming desolation of Yates's world, perfectly uniform in its misery throughout the five books. Loneliness is part of it, what Yates has himself called "the spectre of personal isolation that haunts everyone." His characters need, as Forster wrote in *Howards End,* "only connect," and yet they almost never can. . . . Profound human inadequacy is part of Yates's world, and so, more superficially, are alcohol and hospitals. . . . For all Yates's supreme mastery over his materials, it sometimes seems a wonder he can go on. It may be, however, that now he has arrived somewhere we had every reason to hope for and no reason to expect. (p. 632)

Most of Yates's fiction "works" [because] . . . the incidents that constitute the plot seem always to grow out of the characters and never to be arbitrary. . . . Yates can tell us in advance [the future of his characters] because he knows that the character he has drawn can behave no other way, and we know it, too. It is in the inevitability with which his characters' lives proceed that Yates shows that tragic art is still possible.

A recent essay by Gore Vidal in the *New York Review of Books* got a friend and me to talking about some of the limitations of contemporary fiction. Generally agreeing with Vidal's severe critique of several of our most prominent writers, my friend said that the problem with our fiction— he meant American novels since World War II— was its dearth of characters who were convincing and, more, memorable as characters, who led the reader to be genuinely concerned with them as with complicated, sympathetic, real, and yet individualized human beings. We tried to name exceptions to this generalization, characters who inspired the happy fallacy of having one regard them as people independent of the books where they live (as one can regard Jake Barnes and Jay Gatsby), and didn't get very far: Holden Caulfield, Sebastian Dangerfield, a few of Bellow's creations. This list can surely be extended, though I doubt very far, but it will imperatively include a dozen or more characters in the work of Richard Yates, not only his protagonists but also slighter figures like John Givings in *Revolutionary Road* and Charlie and Dr. Spivack in *Disturbing the Peace*. There is no more certain sign of Yates's importance among our writers. (p. 634)

> *Mark Taylor, "Modern Tragedies," in* Commonweal *(copyright © 1976 Commonweal Publishing Co., Inc.; reprinted by permission of Commonweal Publishing Co., Inc.), September 24, 1976, pp. 631-34.*

[The] real magic of Yates's art [is] the ability to command our interest in . . . submissive characters, lost navigators who refuse to rechart the doomed course of their lives. (p. 285)

The prose of *The Easter Parade* is remarkably spare. Story is never sacrificed to metaphor and the characters are always seen through their actions, or *lack* of action, rather than through the linguistic manipulation of their author. . . .

The Easter Parade is about [a] denial of feeling. It is about the tragedy of failed family life and the repeatedly self-defeating choices of its member-victims. In this, his most powerfully affecting novel since *Revolutionary Road,* Yates insists upon, and earns, our intense attention to people who move like dreamwalkers toward their sad destinies, who try to compensate through careers or sexual encounters for the absence of real human involvement. It is relentless in its despair until a thin note of hope is sounded at the very end as Emily speaks, taking an apparent leap into consciousness:

"And do you know a funny thing? I'm almost fifty years old and I've never understood anything in my whole life." (p. 287)

> *Hilma Wolitzer, in* Ploughshares *(© 1977 by Ploughshares, Inc.), Vol. 3, Nos. 3 + 4.*

Cumulative Index to Critics

Cumulative Index to Authors